D0906609

Society and Religion in Elizabethan England

Society
and Religion
in
Elizabethan England

Richard L. Greaves

Department of History
The Florida State University

UNIVERSITY OF MINNESOTA PRESS □ MINNEAPOLIS

Publication of this book was assisted by a grant
from the publications program of the National Endowment
for the Humanities, an independent federal agency.

Publication assistance was also provided by
The Florida State University

Library of Congress Cataloging in Publication Data

Greaves, Richard L.
   Society and religion in Elizabethan England.

   Bibliography: p.
   Includes index.
   1. Great Britain—Moral conditions—Sources.
2. Sociology, Christian—Great Britain—History—
Sources. 3. Great Britain—History—Elizabeth,
1558-1603—Sources. I. Title.
HN460.M6G7   942.05'5   81-2530
ISBN 0-8166-1030-4   AACR2

To
Sherry Elizabeth
and
Stephany Lynn

Preface and Acknowledgments

Fascination with the Elizabethan age has led to a mountain of books and journal articles, many of which deal with society and religion. No one, however, has fully analyzed Anglican, Puritan, Catholic, and Separatist social thought and practice. This study attempts to examine the views of the clergy and the laity as revealed in such varied sources as manuscript letters and reports, diaries, printed tracts and treatises, visitation articles and ecclesiastical injunctions, quarter session and court leet records, the acts of the Privy Council and the Parliament, medical texts, parish registers, the marginalia in Tudor Bibles and Testaments, and memorial brasses.

I am indebted to many scholarly works, in particular the epic studies of Lawrence Stone, whose contributions to social history are remarkable.

Yet like Keith Thomas in his magisterial study, *Religion and the Decline of Magic*, I have had to rely primarily on traditional historical methodology, for much of my material was not quantifiable. Happily there is still scope for the human element beside the graphs, charts, and percentages that are prominent in recent social history.

The limitation of this study to the period 1558 to 1603 was motivated partly by the extraordinary amount of pertinent material for the Elizabethan period alone. In religious history, the chronological boundaries are readily defensible, and parallel the classic studies by M. M. Knappen and Patrick Collinson. From the social standpoint, an excellent case can be made to carry the period forward to 1640, as Stone and others do. Given the scope of this study, however, extending it to 1640 would have required another massive volume and considerably more financial support than was available. This work of necessity cites only a portion of the evidence I amassed, but I have endeavored to select representative examples, keeping in mind the stringent maxims of J. H. Hexter. It has not, however, been possible to provide all the contextual information for the more than five hundred Elizabethan printed tracts and treatises; that would have required another book.

I have analyzed the thought of Elizabethan clergy and laity on nearly every topic of social significance to ascertain to what extent there was agreement among Anglicans, Puritans, Catholics, and Separatists, and I have related this thought to social practice as much as possible. Because of the lack of systematic or comprehensive studies in this area, and because it is important to examine the works of all the prominent Elizabethan authors, the scope and detail of this work is unusually full. Past studies often have been marked by sampling and not enough analysis in depth, with inevitable distortion. I trust that the book will be a useful guide and that the endeavor to relate social thought to practice will encourage other historians to undertake more detailed studies in this area.

In quotations the original orthography has been retained, except for typographical peculiarities (e.g. "comon" is rendered "common"). The Elizabethan spelling conveys some of the flavor of the period, and it is no more difficult to read than much of the spelling one finds in today's undergraduate essays. With respect to dating, the year has been taken to commence on 1 January.

This work could not have been done without a fellowship from the American Council of Learned Societies that enabled me to work at a hectic pace for half a year in England, especially at the British Library, the Public Record Office, Lambeth Palace, the Bodleian, and Sion College Library. (Regrettably, the lack of additional funding prevented me from examining the manuscripts in other public and private collections throughout Britain. In particular, it was impossible to find monetary support to fund research in local archives, where there is so much critical material on social practice.)

The staffs of the manuscript room of the British Library and the Public Record Office were very helpful. In the United States, the staffs of the Henry E. Huntington Library and the William Andrews Clark Memorial Library, where I worked as an Andrew W. Mellon Fellow in 1977, were particularly gracious. Miss Carolyn Taylor and Mr. Joseph Pettigrew of the Strozier Library at Florida State University worked heroically to provide me with essential research materials.

My debt is particularly great to three outstanding scholars: Dr. Paul Seaver of Stanford University meticulously criticized much of this work and provided countless insights, without which this book would be much the poorer. Dr. Leo Solt of Indiana University and Dr. Robert Zaller of the University of Miami read many of the chapters and graciously shared their expertise with me. The following scholars also provided encouragement and academic assistance: Dr. Virginia Beauchamp, Dr. John Bossy, Dr. Kenneth Charlton, Dr. Patrick Collinson, Dr. Michael Galgano, Dr. Sheldon Hanft, Dr. Michael McDonald, Dr. Sears McGee, Dr. Geoffrey Nuttall, Dr. Laura O'Connell, Dr. Richard Schlatter, Dr. Robert Schnucker, and Dr. John Somerville. Publication of this work was made possible by grants from the National Endowment for the Humanities and from Dr. Werner Baum, Dean of the College of Arts and Sciences, Florida State University. Dr. Richard Abel of the University of Minnesota Press has been an enthusiastic and helpful supporter of this work, and my thanks go to him and to the University of Minnesota for their commitment to scholarship and historical research. Mrs. Carol Masters provided expert editing.

Words are inadequate to express my gratitude to my wife and daughters for their sacrifices and understanding during the course of this study. Dedicating it to Sherry Elizabeth and Stephany Lynn is a token of my appreciation for their love and encouragement. In their own youthful way, they too love the age of Elizabeth.

Richard L. Greaves
March 1980

Contents

Introduction   3

Part I: Society and Religion

Chapter 1: Social Pressures and Christian Leadership   33

Chapter 2: The Social Behavior of the Clergy and the
           Anticlerical Reaction   71

Part II: Marriage and Sex

Chapter 3: The Marital Quest   115

Chapter 4: The Marital Quest Consummated   155

Chapter 5: Sexual Mores and Social Behavior   203

Part III: The Family and Education

Chapter 6: Married Life and Parenthood   251

Chapter 7: The Household   291

Chapter 8: The Role of Education   327

Part IV: The Christian in Society

Chapter 9: Work and Worship   377

Chapter 10: Social Entertainment and Recreation   431

Chapter 11: Food and Fasting   471

Chapter 12: Social Conduct and Social Order   501

Part V: The Christian and Social Problems
Chapter 13: Wealth and Poverty   547
Chapter 14: Economic Problems   595
Chapter 15: Legal Problems   649

Part VI: The Social Order and Death
Chapter 16: Last Rites and Monuments   695

Conclusion   737

Appendix   771

Notes   775

Bibliographic Essay   873

Index   881

Society and Religion in Elizabethan England

Introduction

Elizabethans perceived society substantially in religious terms, though their perspective was not monolithic, even within the Church of England. Despite the difficulties of elucidating the differences between Anglicans (or Conformists) and Puritans, who made up the Church of England, the historical evidence clearly indicates that such differences existed, and that they influenced social ideology, as suggested in the magisterial but controversial studies of Lawrence Stone and Christopher Hill. This study analyzes Anglican and Puritan social thought, relates it to social practice, and demonstrates that in numerous areas there are dissimilarities, sometimes substantial; there are also major areas of agreement where scholars have suspected discrepancies. Although English Catholic and Separatist authors in the Elizabethan period did not explore social views as fully as their Anglican and Puritan counterparts, their positions are examined. A necessary background to this study is a working concept of "Anglican" and "Puritan," and their general perception of society, particularly their commitment to the principle of social moderation.

(1) Anglicans, Puritans, and the Religious Continuum

Religion is become nothing lesse then Religion, to wit, a matter of meere talke: such politizing is there on all parts, as a man cannot tell, who is who.

Christopher Sutton[1]

3

A puritan is a curious corrector of thinges indifferent.

John Manningham[2]

A consensus of judgment on the nature of Puritanism has been notoriously difficult to achieve. Elizabethans themselves disagreed about
the meaning of the term even while acknowledging, as the age matured,
the existence of Puritans. In 1603, one Anglican sourly depicted the
capital as "that great city of the contrarie faction."[3] More than a decade earlier, a Puritan clergyman estimated that there were 100,000
Puritans in England, with the number increasing daily among people
of all estates. In a country of about five million people, Puritans were
a small minority, but their influence was greater than the numbers suggest. There are three reasons: first, the discontent with traditional
forms of religion and the Puritan ability to spark enthusiasm among
those who desired changes; second, the quality of most Puritan clergy and the social position of Puritan lay leaders, providing the movement with effective leadership and potential for growth. In Yorkshire,
for example, only 25 of 567 gentry families were Puritan in 1570, but
by 1642 the number was 138 of 679 families, an increase of 15.9%.[4]
Finally, the appeal of Puritanism was enhanced by its piety.

Because modern misunderstandings of Puritanism are often rooted
in Elizabethan accounts, an overview of Elizabethan conceptions of
Puritanism is requisite. The term "Puritan" was coined by the Catholic
author Thomas Stapleton at Louvain in *A Fortresse of the Faith* (Antwerp, 1565) as an epithet for English Protestants opposed to the use
of traditional vestments. Another Catholic, John Martial, an Oxford
don exiled in Brussels, used the word in the same context in 1566. By
1568 Catholics applied the word to the early Separatists as well. The
first Protestant usage of "Puritan" was apparently in 1572, when
Matthew Parker, archbishop of Canterbury, used it as an appellation
for Protestant critics within the Church of England.[5]

From an early period, people realized that the term threatened the
unity of the church, especially because of the opprobrium it conveyed. Thomas Sampson, who refused the sees of Hereford and Norwich and became a prebendary of St. Paul's, London, in 1570, warned
Edmund Grindal, archbishop of York, on 9 November 1574, that "unjustly to impose this name [Puritan] on brethren, with whose doctrin and life no man can justly find fault, is to rend the seamless coat
of Christ, and to make a schism incurable in the Church." Like the
Puritan Sampson, Edwin Sandys, a bishop who minimized controversy over ritual conformity, considered that religious dissent rendered
"consent in love" impossible.

One God, one king, one faith, one profession, is fit for one monarchy and commonwealth. Divison weakeneth: concord strengtheneth. . . . Let conformity and unity in religion be provided for; and it shall be as a wall of defence unto this realm.

Such unity could not be attained by uniformity or by harrying dissenters out of the land. A number of Anglicans and Puritans determined to play down their differences, to present a solid front against their common foes. Thomas Sparke, the Puritan minister at Bletchley, Bucks., dedicated a book to John Whitgift, archbishop of Canterbury, in 1597, asking that the controversies dividing the Church of England be reserved for friendly conferences of godly learned. The religious ignorance of the English populace mandated, in his judgment, a unified front. The proponents of harmony thus recognized the division within the church between Anglicans and Puritans.[6]

Elizabethans judged that the difference between the groups was not essentially doctrinal. Although William Haller and Everett Emerson find the essence of Puritanism in Calvinist dogma, the Puritan mathematician Thomas Digges correctly asserted that "this word *Caluinists* comprehendeth *Protestants* as well as *Puritans.*" Edward Bulkeley, an unlicensed Presbyterian preacher in Northamptonshire, retorted to a Catholic in 1602 that "you might well enough haue forborne this distinction of protestants & puritanes; for although some haue differed in some outward matters concerning ceremonies & externall orders in the Church; yet these all greatly agree and consent in all points of the doctrine of faith." The same year, Josias Nichols, the deprived Presbyterian rector of Eastwell, Kent, asserted that Anglicans and Puritans were one in all substantial theological points. "The renowned Fathers and other Prelates of the Church of England, standing for conformitie (such as vnfainedlie doe fauour the present estate of the Church, and doe faithfullie hold and beleeue the true religion and faith of Christ, maintained by publike authoritie among vs) are one and the same, with the godlie Ministers & people, who desire reformation of some things in the Ecclesiasticall state." Yet affirmations of doctrinal unity must be seen particularly in reference to Catholics, against whom English Protestants strove to present a united front.[7]

Most commentators analyze Puritanism as a movement to purify the Elizabethan church, with roots among the Marian exiles.[8] Leonard Trinterud illustrates the growth of Puritanism from an anti-vestment party, represented by such men as Laurence Humphrey and John Foxe, to a passive-resistance party that embraced most Elizabethan Puritans, to the aggressive Presbyterians of the 1570s and 1580s.[9]

This approach is historical, based on similar analyses by Elizabethan writers, the fullest being that of Josias Nichols.

Early in Elizabeth's reign, according to Nichols, many people began to feel "some taste of the heauenlye comfort" and to rejoice in hearing sermons, singing Psalms, reading Scripture, and joining in godly conversation. They determined to refrain from profane customs and admonished neighbors to attend sermons. "The greater sort of the people, beeing olde barrels which coulde holde no newe wine, addicted partlie to Poperie & partlie to licentiousnesse, hauing many of them no other God, but their bellie, woulde deride and scoffe at them, and called them holye brethren and holy sisterne: saying, *Here is one of the pure and vnspotted brethren.*" Some clergy began to voice doubts about the prescribed liturgy, though these ministers were treated sympathetically by the bishops. When subscription to the *Book of Common Prayer* was enforced, the admonition controversy ensued, characterized by a mutual lack of moderation. Grindal's tenure as archbishop of Canterbury restored tranquillity, but his death brought a return to subscription and controversy. Now "it was a verye common name to all these Ministers to be called Puritanes: As men which made conscience of many things, which the reuerend Fathers, and many learned men affirmed to be lawfull." The offense of Puritans, Nichols argued, was fourfold: their scruple in the use of certain ceremonies, their scruple "in subscribing beyond the state," their attempts to reform ceremonial and discipline, and their hearing sermons, discussing Scripture, and singing Psalms in private homes.[10]

As a movement within the Church of England, Puritanism was concerned with the reform of ceremony and discipline. Yet Nichols shows that Puritans existed before there was any movement for reform and that what made them Puritans was the nature and manifestation of their religious experience. This is a key reason that they offended the Anglicans, who were suspicious of Puritan gatherings in private homes. The moderate Grindal, as bishop of London, extracted a written promise from the Puritan William Bonham not to frequent private assemblies or illegal religious meetings. This fear was not always shared by lay Anglicans in the government. In 1584 Sir Julius Caesar reported to Sir Francis Walsingham that he had examined Essex conventiclers who attended evening meetings involving reading from John Foxe's *Acts and Monuments,* Psalm singing, and praying, but he believed them to be persons to be emulated rather than punished. The religious experience characteristic of a Puritan gathering is witnessed by Lady Anne Bacon, who told Lord Burghley that by attending Puritan exercises for seven or eight years she learned more about God than in nearly twenty years of hearing "odd sermons at [St.] Powlis [London]."[11]

A Puritan was characterized by a particular kind of religious experience, which was more than a simple state of mind or a transient event. It amounted to a spiritual reorientation of his person and typically induced a conviction of predestination and the need to reform the church. This experience is the foundation on which all other characteristics of Puritanism rest. Something of what the experience entails is explicated by John Deacon, minister at Nottingham and Ridlington, Rutland:

Without this proper experience & feeling of some power thereof in themselues, their [ministers'] speeche is nothing so gratious: neither are the hearers any thing so well affected to their vsual preachings. For euen as one log of tymber cannot possibly kindle another vnlesse the same be first kindled it selfe: no more may those keye colde preachers inflame the hearts of their hearers, which are not firste inflamed themselues with the loue of Religion and godlinesse.

This infectious warmth (as perceived by the Puritans) accompanies a sense of purity of heart and its manifestation in a good conscience. The experience involved Puritans in an "endeuour to followe the same Ghospell, with all their soules, and in simplicitie and humblenes of minde . . . [to] drawe nearer and nearer vnto God . . . ," and to desire that the Church of England "might more & more growe forward vnto such perfection, as in this fraile life might bee attained." The experience is characterized by an acknowledgment that one is a grievous sinner whose righteousness is as a "stayned cloth," and whose purity is imputed only by divine grace. This experiential element prompted Basil Hall to regard Puritanism as a kindred spirit to Continental Pietism.[12]

The emphasis in the Puritan experience on purity of heart, mind, and worship led to their identification with ancient heretics. Whitgift charged that "this name Puritan is very aptly given to these men; not because they be pure, no more than were the heretics called Cathari; but because they think themselves to be *mundiores ceteris,* 'more pure than others,' as Cathari did, and separate themselves from all other churches and congregations, as spotted and defiled." Although he knew better, Whitgift implied that Puritans were Separatists. In response, Thomas Cartwright, the Presbyterian leader, denied the imputation of Catharism, asserting that the only purity that concerned Christians was the innocence of Christ and the sanctification that came through him. Likewise, Sampson informed Grindal in 1574 that "if Puritans now be noted to be such as do revive the old rotten heresy of Novatus, from whom the old Καθαροὶ [Cathari] did spring, I do not know any in England which do hold that desperate doctrin." Others, such as Nichols, castigated the Catholics as the true followers of the Cathari, Pelagians, Ebionites, and Donatists.[13]

The combination of self-perceived warmth and conviction of internal spiritual purity manifested in a godly life provided a target for satirists and those impatient with the struggles of the spirit. To the satirist Thomas Nash, Puritanism was a manifestation of hypocrisy. Similarly, "an hypocrite or puritan," according to the son of a retainer of Sir Robert Cecil, "is like a globe, that hath all in *conuexo, nihil in concauo*, all without painted, nothing within included." "A puritane is such a one as loves God with all his soule, but hates his neighbour with all his heart." Anglican invective accused Puritans of robbing clergy of their livings and not resting until "their mothers bowels be pulled out."[14]

William Barlow, one of Whitgift's chaplains and rector of St. Dunstan's in the East, London, depicted Puritans as rebellious members of the church and noxious humors in a sound body. To their enemies, Puritan zeal for reform was rebellion or greed, and their quest for a godly life was hypocrisy. The name "Puritan" in some circles was an epithet: "the world will note thee to be a Puritan, and so thou shalt become odious vnto thy friends."[15] The important point is that Puritans were essentially recognizable to Anglicans *as Puritans*, people whose religious experience manifested in personal behavior and reforming zeal gave them an identity.

At the root of the Puritan religious experience there appears to have been—at least initially—a deep-rooted anxiety. Such anxiety gave birth to the casuistry of William Perkins as well as the self-discipline that Michael Walzer elucidates: "Sainthood," he writes, "offered a way out of [the] anxiety" born of a deep sense of sinfulness, the instability of the mid-Tudor period, the decline of stable social relationships, the uprooting experience of exile, and a religious world of contradictory claims and counterclaims. In Puritanism was the assurance of a religious experience that instilled in the saints the confidence of zealots who knew their role in the cosmic struggles and who could find comfort among comrades in arms. In their congregations, they claimed to feel the binding, comforting presence of Christ, and, said Henry Ainsworth, "for this cause did his people love the habitation of his house." There they found identity, meaning, edification, and a sense of direction as well as assurance of the rightness of their cause.[16]

From this experience grew an outlook that came to be differentiated from that of the Anglicans,[17] at its root a subtle but significant difference of opinion about spiritual authority. Puritans repudiated both the Anabaptist and Lollard view that only those things can be accepted in the church that have express biblical warrant, and the Anglican position that those things not expressly prohibited in the Bible are permissible as *adiaphora*, that is, as long as they are not repugnant to Scripture and their use is in positive accord with the Bible. In contrast, Puritans insisted that on matters for which there is no express biblical direction, only those *in positive accord* with the general Pauline rules qualify as adiaphora. In effect, Puritans restricted the scope of adiaphora to those matters that could meet these tests: They must not be offensive to any, especially in the church; they must be orderly and comely; they must be edifying; and they must glorify God.[18]

The Puritan outlook also differed from the Anglican with respect to Christian liberty. To the Puritan liberty is essentially the obligation to do only those things that God has commanded, so that "whatsoever is not done by the word of God is sin." In contrast the Anglican position was more concerned with permission than obligation, with freedom than command. To Whitgift the Puritan view so bound the conscience that it created a servitude that destroyed "that part of Christian liberty which consisteth in the free use of indifferent things, neither commanded nor forbidden in the word of God, and throw[s] man headlong into desperation." This difference in outlook was manifested in social matters and does much to account for the concern of Puritans with such issues as sexual behavior. Although sometimes little difference appeared in social theory the frequent difference in emphasis stemmed from the notion of Christian liberty as obligation, or freedom. In the Elizabethan period, in apparent contrast to the Stuart era, it is not a difference in emphasis on the two tables of the Mosaic commandments that distinguishes Anglicans and Puritans but a difference in treatment. Puritans are no less concerned than Anglicans with second-table duties, but they approach them in a different spirit, based on their more restrictive perception of Christian liberty.[19]

The Puritan outlook is further distinguished from the Anglican by its aniconic emphasis. More than Anglicans, Puritans were determined to make the liturgy strictly conformable to their theology. The heart of the aniconic mode was the spoken word, hence the stress given to sermons and prophesyings. Whereas Anglicans periodically recognized their value, they were less willing to do away with the traditional iconic liturgy. Aniconic worship provided Puritans with greater opportunity to inculcate social values in their adherents than Anglicans had, particularly those Anglicans who rarely preached and relied on official homilies.[20]

Perhaps the most accurate way of understanding Elizabethan religious groups is to use a continuum of varying religious outlooks. The Elizabethan continuum runs from the Jesuits and militant Catholics on the far right, such as Robert Persons and Anthony Babington, to more quiescent Catholics such as William Lord Vaux,[21] to crypto-Catholics,[22] to conservative Anglicans of the Whitgift-Hooker-Hatton variety, to moderate Anglicans such as James Pilkington, John Parkhurst, and William Cecil, Lord Burghley (who are closely akin to Puritans spiritually), to conservative Puritans such as Laurence Humphrey, Robert Crowley, and Robert Dudley, earl of Leicester, to a moderate Puritan group including Richard Greenham, William Perkins, and Henry Hastings, earl of Huntingdon, to Presbyterians such as Thomas Cartwright, Anthony Cope, and Edward Lewkenor, to the various Separatists,[23] and ultimately to fringe sects such as the Family of Love. This delineation of the continuum shows two Anglican and three Puritan sub-groups, but such delineations are arbitrary, given the almost limitless possibilities of subcategorization. It is, of course, true that Puritans in particular thought more in terms of opposites than of a continuum, especially as they engaged in spiritual warfare against Catholics. Yet historically they were part of the same Christian tradition, and a continuum has the merit of reflecting historical development, if not contemporary perception.

A continuum is helpful in discussing the laity, whose interests are not precisely the same as the clergy's but whose religious inclinations can sometimes be ascertained from letters, wills, diaries, and ministerial associations. Even so, there are lay figures whose religious views are difficult to label, as Sir William Cecil.

The enigma of Cecil's religious views has produced conflicting comment. An early writer argued that in religious matters Cecil dissented from both Puritans and Catholics, disliking the singularity of the former and the superstition of the latter. Yet he shared the mood of the Puritans during the first dozen years of the era; he thought highly of John Calvin; he patronized the Puritan leaders Peter Wentworth, James Morice, and Robert Beale; he appointed the Presbyterian Walter Travers to a lectureship at the Temple and possibly as tutor to his son Robert; and he sought to mitigate Whitgift's hostility to the Puritans. Significantly, however, neither his advice to his son nor his will (the overseer of which was Whitgift) reveals Puritanism. Edward Dering, Puritan rector of Pluckley, Kent regarded him as a friend of the Puritans, yet chided him in 1570 that "you have Dealt hardly with God's children and your brethren." In 1590, Francis Merburn expected Cecil to sympathize with his view that "we stand before a people partly impatient of all reprehension, and partly nourishing in themselves idolatrous affections, making insurrection against the truth, but coming in at the postern of supposed Puritanism." Perhaps, as Joel Hurstfield suggests, Cecil sympathized with Puritan ideals but was generally critical of the Puritan movement, certainly in its more radical forms. A clue to his position is found in a 1590 letter to Whitgift, asking that Cartwright be favorably treated as one who in recent years had given no cause to be charged with disorders in religion. Cecil noted that he was not moved by respect for Cartwright or support for religious disorder, but desired to persuade Puritans by learning or courtesy. He was motivated by a political goal of English unification, in the pursuit of which he positioned himself in the religious continuum as events demanded.[24]

Caution is necessary in studying religious perceptions in relation to social views and actions. As defenders of the established church, Anglicans must have had numerous hangers-on whose social views and practices would not necessarily correspond with those of committed Anglicans. The problem is compounded by the impossibility of determining the religious outlook of many of those, from the gentry down, whose social actions and expressions are recorded in ecclesiastical documents, quarter session records, and kindred materials. One is especially frustrated by "the iron curtain which hides the religious opinion of the really humble laity." For gentry, merchants, yeomen, and even a few husbandmen, wills are sometimes useful, but the pitfalls in their use are numerous.[25] We are more fortunate for laity who expressed close religious ties to known figures, though the numbers are relatively small. The effect of these difficulties is to reduce severely the use and value of statistical analyses in this study. Rarely can the religious views of significant numbers of people be verifiable enough to make statistics and graphs reliable. A careful scrutiny of religious writings, social documents, diaries, letters, and other records provides a good indication of what the various groups believed on social issues and gives a reasonable impression of how they acted. Beyond this the nature of the surviving evidence does not permit us to go.

The bulk of the religious writings comes from the clergy, and it is therefore to them that we must look for the fullest elucidation of social ideals. The Elizabethan clergy, particularly the Puritans, were striving to develop a uniform value system, based on scriptural prin-

ciples and embracing the premise that society is hierarchically ordained. Thus in the case of moderation, every class was exhorted to
apply this standard to such things as dress and diet, with the understanding that what was moderate for the upper echelons was excessive for the middle or lower orders. As a rule, however, clerical moralists were unwilling to develop a dual ethical code with one standard
for the aristocracy and another for the rest of society. Although
some parish clergy or chaplains may have been inclined to accept a
double standard, the religious literature reveals a single ethical standard for social issues. Moralists did not, for example, use the printed
word to justify the double standard in sexual relations for the aristocracy, nor did they justify acts of violence by the aristocracy to
defend their honor. Consequently, there was tension between what
the clerical reformers sought to inculcate and what the aristocracy
in particular tended to accept on the basis of tradition. At the bot-
tom of the social order there could hardly have been much concern
about most facets of socio-ethical conduct, because the sheer task
of staying alive consumed nearly all energy.

The clerical moralists made headway in the Elizabethan period in
gaining some lay acceptance of their ideals. In the process, the aristocratic code of values was gradually modified by Christian ethical
principles, though never completely and always on the understanding that the Christian code of values supported the social hierarchy.

The literature that developed a socio-ethical code was religious.
Excluding the writings of the Separatists and works on health, medicine, and food, of the remaining 503 Elizabethan printed books or
tracts examined for this study, 101 (20.1%) were single sermons
and another 33 (6.6%) were collections of two or more sermons. An
additional 34 (6.8%) works were expositions of Scripture, 20 (4.0%)
were catechisms, 55 (10.9%) were works of religious controversy,
and 103 (20.5%) were general religious and doctrinal writings. Ten
(2.0%) are best identified as casuistry, 7 (2.6%) are Marprelate tracts,
13 (2.6%) are epitaphs, 31 (6.2%) are writings in verse, and 5 (1.0%)
are compilations. Only 54 (10.7%) dealt principally with a social
theme. The remaining 37 (7.4%) are a miscellany. The controversial
writings and probably the expository pieces were primarily intended
for the clergy, but the bulk of the material was directed to the laity
as well. The catechisms, devotional writings, and simple verse were
appropriate for literate laity to read to the unlettered. Little social
theory per se was written in this period. Most of the writing about
social problems came from the clergy, much of it a consequence of
their reflecting on current social problems as they prepared sermons

and undertook biblical exegesis. Little of it was generated by casuistry, though near the end of the age, Perkins, England's first great casuist, addressed social issues in this fashion.

Generally these writings are not directed to any one social group, though the intended audience was essentially restricted to the literate, broadened in some instances to those in their care, such as children, servants, and apprentices. The emphasis on the word—printed as well as spoken—caused Puritanism to have its principal appeal to the literate and their immediate dependents, that is, to the yeomen, the gentry, and some of the upper aristocracy, and through them to servants and apprentices. Otherwise Puritans probably attracted few adherents among the lower orders. Michael Walzer argues that the gentry were particularly attracted to Puritanism as a cure for their anxiety, a defensible thesis if it is extended to include spiritual as well as social anxiety. The urban middling sort were apparently attracted to Puritanism by its ability to salve their spiritual turmoil, its zealousness, its emphasis on the family, and its clear code of ethical conduct and deep sense of Christian responsibility. Elizabethan Catholicism too held many of its adherents for some of the same reasons, including the ability of the Old Faith to resolve doubts through the confessional and the psychological strength and authority of centuries of tradition. Catholicism retained popularity in many rural areas because it upheld traditional ties and social customs, merging religious observances with the recurring events of agricultural life. Yet the religious and social thought of this age is not fundamentally a reflection of "class" interests or a rationalization of existing social and economic practices (perhaps with the exception of the fundamental notion of social hierarchy). The reformers instead assayed to propound a socio-ethical code in harmony with scriptural principles. Although reformers were not divorced from their social surroundings or unaware of the need for the support of the influential classes—as the epistles dedicatory show—they began with Scripture as the guide to social behavior. But especially for the laity, the acceptability of the ideals cannot be understood purely in religious terms. Many Puritans in the Commons, for example, were willing to condemn pluralism but could not support Presbyterian polity, with its negative effect on their advowson rights.

As in ecclesiastical matters such as polity, vestments, and liturgy, so in social matters the reformers did not produce a uniform program based on their biblical studies. Differences in social outlook existed between Anglicans and Puritans, though not in all areas. Such differences were not due to attempts to appeal to disparate socioeconomic groups or to varying emphases on the two tables of the Mosaic commandments, but to divergent experiences and outlooks. It is not surprising that a faith appealing to anxious souls should evoke zeal from those who found assurance, or that the zeal is in some sense a means to such assurance. The Puritan quest for reform in the church carried over into society, where the same conviction and zeal are evident; millenarian expectations drove Puritans to sèek further purity in the church,[26] and it is probable that they were similarly driven to reform society. Puritan soteriology, with its stress on good works as a sign of election, inculcated an ardor for improved morality in the social sphere. Numerous Anglicans shared the Calvinist theology of the Puritans as well as the endeavor to find in biblical principles a pattern for social conduct, which helps explain why Anglicans and Puritans sometimes shared social views. The Christian tradition fostered commonly held social ideals by people as diverse as Catholics and Separatists, but there were divergences, and these stemmed fundamentally from religious rather than socioeconomic factors.

(2) Reflections on the Social Order

Order is ye mother and preseruer of things: for sure it is that the societie of men consisteth in ruling and obeying, obedience is the vertue that teacheth all their duty to God & man.

Christopher Sutton[27]

Take away authority, and the people will rush headlong into every thing that is bad.

Edwin Sandys, bishop of London[28]

The prevailing view of society in Elizabethan England was that society was divinely determined, hierarchic, organic, orderly, and amalgamated by an insistence on obedience to authority. The principal advocate of this conception was the queen herself, who was "solemne and ceremonious, & requiring decent & disparent order to be kept convenient in ech degree." Support for her position came unstintingly from the Anglican clergy. The bishop of Durham, James Pilkington, set forth Nehemiah as one to be emulated for placing every man in an appropriate order to fulfill his appointed task without loitering and without troubling his fellows. Where order was maintained, the bishop insisted, a state was strongly built and divinely blessed. "Men must," a colleague said, "be studious, faithfull, and diligent in their places," else society lacks requisite order.[29]

With this view Puritans firmly agreed. "Order is in all other things, and should be in christian life most of all," hence a Christian's charge is to uphold order and maintain "his standing, his raunge, and his rancke." God is a God of order whose assistance must be sought to terminate confusion, and within orderly society private interests must be subordinated to the demands of church and commonwealth.[30]

Of all the Tudor Bibles and Testaments, it is the Puritan oriented Geneva version whose marginalia emphasize an orderly society. A note to Ecclesiastes 4:9 reveals the purpose of this society: "Forasmuche as when man is alone, he can nether helpe him self nor others, he sheweth that men oght to liue in mutual societie, to ye intent thei may be profitable one to another, & that their things may encrease." Readers are exhorted to preserve the divinely established order and to be cognizant that each estate and degree has its charge. In fulfilling this obligation, divine assistance is crucial, for "his secret working in all creatures is as a commandment to kepe them in ordre, & to giue them mouing & force." Moreover, "there is an horrible disordre among that people, where the true preaching of Gods worde wanteth." If clergy are corrupt, disorder ensues. Judah's rulers are accused of inverting right religion and political order, and under Saul, laws were broken and order disrupted as dissolution reigned. "All things are out of ordre, but onely where God reigneth." According to these principles, clerical immorality and social vices threaten social order, and efforts for their eradication must be redoubled. The conviction that God demands an ordered society is the basis of Puritan activism in social and political affairs. Such activism, however, is not intended to disrupt the social hierarchy, for "no man oght to vsurpe anie thing further then God giueth him." In Puritan thinking, social stability is grounded on the advance of true religion and the abolition of idolatry by God-fearing magistrates. Like the Anglicans, the Puritans were cognizant of the psychological climate created by the Peasants' Rebellion in Germany, the Münster fiasco, and the revolts of 1549 in England. Their historical experience as well as their theology convinced them of the need for a healthy degree of social conservatism.[31]

The belief that the social hierarchy is divinely instituted and maintained was shared by Anglicans and Puritans. Social status is, according to the Anglican Robert Abbot, minister at Bingham, Notts., assigned by God, who, as Parker told Cecil, "is the true nobleman indeed." The diversity of estates and degrees, explained the Puritan Edward Dering, is divinely instituted in accord with the requirements of each commonwealth—a clever explanation for the divergencies in social hierarchy from one country to another. Another Puritan, Thomas Becon, rector of St. Dionis Backchurch, London, contended that social inequality was a necessary fact of earthly life, though equality would exist in the kingdom of Christ. "He that in the king-dome of the world wold go aboute to make the lowest equal with ye highest, shold bring ye comminalty to confusion." At least one Puri-tan, however, looked back to pristine life in Edenic times and found that social hierarchy and the inequality of estates were not divinely instituted:

> Yet in this age was euery man a king,
> All freely wearing royall diadems,
> Content was held the chiefe and worthi'st thing,
> Exceeding riches, glory, gold, or iems.
>   All men were peace-embracers and content,
>   In euery minde sate Prince and President.

It was a vision worthy of Sir Thomas More, but of little significance as long as no one sought a return to pristine society.[32]

To prevent such thoughts, Anglicans and many Puritans repeated-ly exhorted people to be content with their social estate. Bishop Sandys, urging contentment, asked his followers to be quiescent like sheep rather than contentious like dogs. A colleague thought that God framed people's hearts to be satisfied with their estates.

> Be lowly-minded, and of humble cheare,
> Thinke glory vnmeet for men of base degree.

Thus John Woolton, the canon and future bishop of Exeter, asked everyone to live according to his calling, remembering "that all men are fed and sustained of God, not to riot, but to live; and to learn with the Apostle, to 'be content with that they have, &c.' [Phil. 4:11]." Some of the laity acquiesced in this view: Lady Lumley's epitaph in-dicates that she was "not desirous to channge her estate and condi-tion with any other." A Devonshire yeoman, whose family was as-cending and who was probably as wealthy as many West Country gentlemen, praised his forebears in 1593 because they "always kepte themselves wytheyn ther o[w]n boundes."[33]

Puritans likewise urged contentment with one's place in the social hierarchy. No person must strive to equal another of a higher degree, but must maintain his state at least "vntyll that God shall open hym the way to a better." Some scope is allotted for social mobility, though contentment is stressed and the instigation of change is, at least theoretically, left in divine hands. Further to the left on the religious continuum, the acceptability of social mobility appears to increase. John Penry, who moved leftward in religion, linked social mobility to the spread of spiritual reformation: "Our Saviour Christ Iesus doth vouchesafe vnto nations and kingdomes, the fruition & vse of his holy worde and gospell vpon no other condition, then that all men of all degrees and callings, as well high as low, will be content to have their states altered . . . at the pleasure, appointment, and determination of his wil & worde." Penry specifically had in mind the expulsion from the church of nonresidents, clergy who could not preach, bishops, archbishops, and other ecclesiastical officials.[34]

Regardless of what most clergy sought, some degree of social mobility existed in Tudor England, and had done so since at least the turbulent period of the Hundred Years' War. The fluidity between landed, professional, and merchant groups is well-known. There was also mobility in the lower orders, where change was effected by rapid population growth, a decline in real wages, and the progress of commercial farming, which required increased supplies of wage-laborers. Middle and lower ranks of cottagers were sinking to the level of a landless proletariat. Even sons of the upper peasantry left the farms to seek careers in London. Of 1,088 freemen admitted by apprenticeship or patrimony in London between December 1551 and September 1553, only 244 were from London and an additional 30 from Middlesex and Southwark. More than half had come from an agricultural background, especially the upper peasantry.[35]

Many of the laity as well as clergymen were displeased with social mobility. Lawrence Stone has argued that those achieving upward mobility, such as prosperous merchants and successful lawyers, resented their lack of sufficient social prestige and their exclusion from the inner circles of political power. The less fortunate, such as many wage-earners, became increasingly dissatisfied with their declining status and sometimes resorted to mob violence, though such action more often was caused by people in a community who believed themselves threatened by economic variables and who demonstrated in favor of the traditional hierarchy (as occurred in Kent in the late Elizabethan period). Often the clergy, especially at the parish level, suffered loss of income and sometimes decreased respect. Yet university-trained clergy continued to be regarded as gentlemen, and their numbers increased in the Elizabethan period. On balance the latter part of the age seems to have brought a general rise in their status if not their income.[36]

Manifestation of discontent against social mobility took varying forms, including a stress on marrying within one's social class. Burghley was unhappy with the marriage in 1592 of Frances, daughter of Lord Howard of Bindon, to Henry Pranel, son of a London alderman and vintner, whom he regarded as socially incompatible. The emphasis on vocational stability was another instance of the reaction against social mobility. The government in 1575-76 sought to circumscribe social mobility among the clothiers of Wiltshire, Somersetshire, and Gloucestershire by restricting their purchase of land.[37] The emphasis on degree and hierarchy suggests a psychological reaction to social mobility, but that such accentuation continued after several centuries of fluidity shows that other factors are present. One is a conservative bent in the minds of those who formulated social theories, and another may have been a desire to confine mobility to the contemporary hierarchical structure rather than risk the evolution of new orders. Finally it appears that even those on the rise in society, such as the Furse family of Devonshire yeomen, accepted the ideals of order and contentment.

To persuade people to accept their places in the social schema, analogies were developed, each implicitly based on the notion that England as a commonwealth with an hierarchical social structure was "a society or common doing of a multitude of free men collected together and vnited by common accord & couenauntes among themselues, for the conservation of themselues aswell in peace as in warre." Sandys developed the military analogy in which some are generals, others captains, some trumpeters, and the rest common soldiers. "Every one must keep his standing, answer his calling, fight, and manfully strive for the victory." Common soldiers were exhorted to be ready, obey, and withstand warlike miseries in the expectation of a future reward. Sandys also used the biblical analogy of the human body in which the head is the monarch, the shoulders and arms are the nobility who defend and bear the burden of the commonwealth, the ears are the judges who hear the complaints of the people, and the inferior parts of the anatomy are the lower orders who painfully work for the sustenance of themselves and others. Music provided a third analogy; "for as good Musike consisteth not of one, but of diuers soundes proportionablie answering together: so doth a Commonweale of sundrie kinds of men keping themselues within the limits of their owne callings." A fourth analogy was used, especially in literature, in which earthly order was seen to be animated by cosmic order.[38]

These analogies were intended to reinforce a sense of permanency with respect to the social order. So too was the emphasis on coats of arms and social pageantry, particularly in christenings, weddings, and funerals. What stained glass and statuary were to medieval Christian pedagogy, coats of arms and related paraphernalia were to Elizabethan social indoctrination. The pedigree of Lord Ogle was emblazoned in red letters on the wall of the church of St. Andrew, Bothal, Northumberland. Three pyramids decorated with the arms of English peers and Northamptonshire gentry greeted visitors to Sir Christopher Hatton's hall at Holdenby, while the Fairfax family painted the dining room of their home at Gilling, Yorks., "with trees for each Wapentake, bearing the arms of the gentry listed in the 1584 Heraldic Visitation." The parlor of Tamworth Castle in Staffordshire was adorned with a frieze of shields tracing the ancestry of Sir John Ferrers to the Norman invasion in 1066.[39] A visitor to England in 1592 reported that in the hall of Burghley's mansion at Theobalds "is depicted the kingdom of England, with all its cities, towns and villages, mountains and rivers; as also the armorial bearings and domains of every esquire, lord, knight, and noble who possess lands and retainers."[40] Commemorative brasses provided another way to display coats of arms; the unusual 1593 brass to Thomas Beale at the church of All Saints, Maidstone, Kent, depicts five generations of his ancestors, extending from 1399 to 1534.

All this reminded the Elizabethan of the gulf between those who did, and those who did not, possess a coat of arms. That coveted symbol bound together peers and gentry in a common aristocracy and set them apart from the lower strata of society.[41] This was recognized by William Vaughan, a Puritan poet of Jesus College, Oxford, when he delineated three degrees of gentlemen: first, the prince; secondly, dukes, marquesses, earls, viscounts, barons, and knights of honor; thirdly, graduates in law, esquires, masters of arts, captains, and those who bear the countenance and port of gentlemen. A possible fourth category embraced those who paid heralds to find (perhaps ficticiously) a title in old registers, entitling them to a coat of arms.[42]

The quest for gentility provoked comment regarding its essence. The highly regarded teacher Richard Mulcaster thought of a gentleman as one who bore a cognizance of virtue and honor, not one who merely amassed wealth through "the vilest diuises." The essence of gentility was found, according to another author, in one who is affable and courteous, adventurous to battle in just controversies, merciful in forgiving trespasses, and liberal to soldiers and others in need.

> Ye *Gentlemen*, right vertues hold,
> let land, and auncient rent
> Mainteine your port, and families,
> liue well, and be content.

Gentility was supposed to consist in virtue and birth together, which then served to justify inequalities in wealth and power, but some writers in Elizabethan times gave a more pronounced emphasis to virtue. This viewpoint underlay Pilkington's maxim that nobility before God is the only true nobility. The point is well illustrated in a story recounted by the Puritan gentleman and author Philip Stubbes, who tells of a gentleman of birth disdainfully reproaching the son of a poor man who had attained a position of authority by his virtue. "What? saith the Gentleman by birth, arte thou so lustie? Thou arte but a coblers sonne, and wilt thou compare with me, being a Gentleman by byrth, and calling? To whome the other answeared, thou arte no Gentleman, for thy gentilitie endeth in thee and I am a Gentleman, in that my gentilitie beginnith in me." The goal of the moralists was to persuade the aristocracy of the importance of a virtuous life.[43]

Several Puritans criticized what they considered to be false forms of gentility. On one side, Dering condemned the nobleman who bragged of his parentage without recognizing his mortality. On the other Stubbes lashed out at the *nouveaux riche*: "He who hath moni enough shal be *rabbied* & maistered at euery word, and withal saluted with the vaine title of worshipfull, and right worshipfull, though notwithstanding he be a dunghill Gentleman, or a Gentleman of the first head, as they vse to terme them."[44] Another author, perhaps of Anglican persuasion, condemned the man of mean estate who brags of gentility and keeps company with men of substance, not wanting to be counted their inferior.[45] Like it or not, such writers were faced with the fact that some Elizabethans felt social pressure to acquire or assume the status of gentility.

Anglicans and Puritans shared a concern about the dangers of the pressures of lower on higher orders. Sandys was unhappy at the quest to climb ever higher, "to sit aloft," and Nash acridly commented on those "obscure vpstart gallants" who "without desert or seruice are raised from the plough to be checkmate with Princes." They are created

Barons of the beanes, and Marquesses of the mary-boanes: some by corrupt water, . . . to which we may liken Brewers, that by retayling filthie *Thames* water, come in few yeres to be worth fortie or fiftie thousand pound: . . . Others [seek upward advancement] from the putrified flesh of dead beasts, as . . . Butchers by fly-blowne beefe, . . . and Hackney-men by selling their lame iades to hunts-men for carrion.

At the Middle Temple, the barrister John Manningham likened the attempts of persons of mean worth to advance beyond their condition and ability to the appearance of rough mortar and pebbles in an elegant room of squared stones. At no point in the social hierarchy was the upward pressure of the lower orders more resented than in attempts to achieve gentility. "That *Iacke* maye be a gentleman" was believed to be the reason that many paupers were oppressed by ambitious men amassing wealth. Since he likely taught the sons of such persons at the Merchant Taylors' School and at St. Paul's School, London, Mulcaster must have known whereof he wrote: "As they came from the common, so they might with more commendacion, continue their children in that kinde, which brought vp the parentes and made them so wealthy, and not to impatronise themselues vnto a degree to[o] farre beyond the dounghill." In a funeral for an esquire in Llandaff in 1595, Bishop Gervase Babington expressed pity for those who struggled to achieve gentility while neglecting their eternal destiny. As another writer put it, there are "many vpstarte gentlemen now in these dayes."[46]

The upward pressure of the lower orders was likewise a Puritan concern. Francis Trigge, rector of Welbourn, Lincs., criticized clergy who accumulated land so that their children might become gentlemen. Stubbes regretted that the dissolution of the monasteries had not led to widespread provision for schools, poor relief, national defense, and clerical livings, for then there would have been fewer upstart gentlemen. A gentleman himself, he grimaced when butchers, cobblers, tailors, and husbandmen were accorded the title of worshipful or master, names proper to the "Godly wyse" for inherent virtue, in respect of their birth or calling.

> So long the righteous gods will surely frowne,
> And we shall finde the world turn'd vpside downe.

To reduce the pressure of the lower orders on the upper, religious leaders taught proper behavior toward superiors and inferiors. Robert Shelford, a Catholic, suggested that civil behavior required rising, uncovering one's head, and obeying one's betters, acting courteously toward one's equals, and treating inferiors gently and "lowly." Whitgift insisted that everyone must have the honor to which he is entitled by social status, office, and person. In humbleness he may remit such honor, but it is contemptuous for inferiors to expect equal treatment. Following the execution of Robert Devereaux, earl of Essex, William Barlow observed that those who flattered great persons or sought popularity with the masses were guilty of *"Parasiticall Simony."* In the spirit of early Christian teaching, the future bishop of Exeter condemned courtiers and noblemen whose haughtiness and personal ambition made them hold themselves aloof from the lowly. Anglican teaching required respect for superiors and gentleness toward inferiors as the means of preserving social tranquility.[47]

The Puritan Richard Rogers, lecturer at Wethersfield, Essex, echoed Anglican teaching when he required superiors to treat inferiors courteously as brothers and to provide exemplary lives to emulate. Inferiors must acknowledge their subjection and submit to their betters, recognizing that contempt violated the divinely bestowed authority of the higher orders. William Perkins, fellow of Christ's College, Cambridge, reinforced traditional social behavior with Scripture when he stipulated that inferiors must rise before superiors, go forth to meet them, bow, grant them the best seats, allow them to speak first, and address them with titles of reverence. Superiors must treat inferiors as brothers and yet "keepe their state and place; yet so, as they haue respect also to such as are inferiour to them, without scorne or contempt." Every one, in effect, must be honored in his place, whether high or low—a view which did not foster equality but recognized that all orders were necessary and divinely ordained for the good of mankind. To these requirements were added individual responsibility, for John Knewstub, rector of Cockfield, Suff., insisted that to live righteously one must so order his life that every man "may haue his owne at our handes," that is, one must give each person the honor due his social position. Yet men's actions are not well ordered unless they are tempered in accordance with the degree *and worthiness* of others, so that the Puritan is required also to assess the *moral* stature of his fellows.[48]

To what degree such exhortations were followed is impossible to assess. One adherent was the Nottinghamshire gentleman Sir William Holles, who was reputed to have a general kindness not only towards the gentry of his county but also towards his lesser neighbors, hence he was accorded similar treatment by them. The advice that William Wentworth of Wentworth Woodham left to his son, the future Sir Thomas, provides a concrete example of the idealized social behavior of the lower landed classes. Wentworth has been labeled a Puritan, but his sympathy for Catholics suggests Anglican leanings. His son was urged to beware of familiarity with or dependency on nobles, whose thoughts were occupied with weighty matters and whose estates and actions were governed by policy. "Againe albeitt they be the most courtlie in wordes, yet they could be contented that riche gentlemen weare less able to liue without depending on them, even as the gentleman lookes with a discontented eye upon the stoute riche yeoman." Just as the gentry prefer a dependent yeomanry, so the peerage prefers a dependent gentry. To avoid the dangers inherent in this dependence, Wentworth urged his heirs to pursue an apolitical course. The company of equals should be sought out, as long as they are not declining socially and have a good conscience and well-governed tongue. Otherwise, the company of social inferiors is acceptable if they have ample wealth and are humble and discreet in their actions and words.[49]

With the exception of a greater tolerance for social mobility among the more thoroughgoing Puritans and a slightly increased emphasis on individual judgment and action, the Puritan view of social order is virtually akin to that of the Anglicans. Yet Anglicans considered Puritans a threat to the social order. When Parker complained to Burghley in 1573 that "if this fond faction [of Puritans] be applauded to, or borne with, it will fall out to a popularity, and . . . it will be the overthrow of all the nobility," he was implying that the Puritan attack on the clerical hierarchy might become an assault on the lay hierarchy as well. Parker was associating Puritans with Anabaptists. Two months earlier, the bishop of Peterborough had complained to Burghley of the unruliness of Puritans in his diocese, contending that their practices were contrary to public order. The complaints appear to have originated in the context of the controversy over vestments in the 1560s. Richard Cheyney, bishop of Gloucester, complained to the Privy Council that for Puritans, "lawe semeth to be no lawe & ordre no ordre." Parker thereafter complained in that context that Puritans were a threat to order. An exasperated Cartwright protested to Sir Christopher Hatton in 1582 that he was wrongly accused of teaching a "mislike of Magistrates, and especially of Monarchs; to like of equality of all Estates, and of a headless ruling of the unruly multitude." True or not, the charge of fostering disorder was good propaganda, and Separatists hurled it against the Church of England.[50]

The principal case against Puritans as a threat to social order was made by Richard Hooker and Richard Bancroft. Hooker warned against any reform which would bring "equally high and low unto parish churches" as repugnant to the nobility. Privileges in accord with their high estate must be granted to important persons, in ecclesiastical as well as civil affairs, "to the end they may love that religion the more which no way seeketh to make them vulgar, no way diminisheth their dignity and greatness."[51] Presbyterians as well as Separatists were a threat to Hooker's postulate that social hierarchy hinged on the preservation of ecclesiastical hierarchy—no bishop, no noble.

The most sustained attack on Puritans as a threat to social order came from Bancroft, a chaplain of Whitgift's, in 1593. His remarks were directed against Presbyterians, but he noted with sarcasm that Puritan preachers courted popularity by decrying the sins of social superiors in the pulpit. He blamed the Genevan system of discipline, so highly touted by English Puritans, for the declining state of the Swiss aristocracy, suggesting that its English advocates threatened social hierarchy. Presbyterian polity was likened to the republican governments of Venice and the Swiss cantons, where tendencies toward social leveling existed. Moreover, the Puritan cry for a return to *"the firste institution"* could easily be misconstrued, as in the days of Jack Cade's rebellion: "When Adam digged, and Eue spanne, who was then the Gentleman?" Now, argued Bancroft, some contend that nobles and gentlemen usurp the honor that the common people originally bestowed upon their ancestors for defending them. He believed Presbyterian polity would lead to an Anabaptist-like society in which every person was equal. "Shomakers, Peuterers, Barbers, Pinners, Pointers, & Painters, (being chosen to be of this synagogue) . . . become presently therby, our pastors, leaders, watchmen of our souls, Christs vicars, Gods prelats, Bishops, & Archbishops, continuing their occupations, & hauing nothing to doe with the word & sacraments." Presbyterians, he argued, advocate equality and detest superiority, except for the domination that they endeavor to impose on others,[52] in effect replacing one system of social hierarchy with another. Bancroft overlooked the fact that French Calvinism and Scottish Presbyterianism were not incompatible with the aristocratic social order in those countries.

Lawrence Stone has reasserted the Elizabethan Anglican thesis that Puritanism was a prominent factor in social mobility. The Puritan ethic, he contends, by stressing a moralistic approach to economic affairs, increased the likelihood of social mobility. The Puritan maximized profits while adhering to the just price concept, and was a self-disciplined striver whose efforts increasingly bore financial fruits. Yet Stone acknowledges that this ethic was not fully operative until the 1630s. He also points to the Puritan emphasis on Bible reading as a causative factor in the spread of elementary education, which affected social mobility. Moreover the Puritan's self-consciousness and sense of righteousness prompted him to aspire to high achievements and challenge his social superiors. Finally, Stone sees the oligarchic or democratic tendencies in Puritan (i.e., Presbyterian) ecclesiastical polity as a factor conducive to social mobility.[53] Stone does not discuss the general emphasis in Elizabethan Puritanism on social stability, the similar nature of Anglican and Puritan economic teaching in the Elizabethan era, or the emphasis placed by the more forward Anglicans on Bible reading and elementary education; his concern is with Puritanism as a destabilizing factor in the century before 1640. He does acknowledge, however, that these destabilizing effects of Puritanism were late and unintended. He is closest to his Elizabethan Anglican predecessors in his use of the potentially revolutionary principles in Presbyterian polity.

The government beat back the Presbyterian challenge, and the social order was able to withstand the internal pressures, passing into another century in ideal if less so in fact. Manifestations of this social order are found throughout Elizabethan society. In the parish churches, churchwardens seated men and women accordingly to degree; in marriages, some equality of social rank was generally a desideratum; in education, stratification was sought (but not always achieved) more by social class than age. The social order was reflected in the homes; Pilkington pronounced his blessing on building costly houses as long as one did not exceed one's estate or oppress the poor. Within the houses, the order was reflected, down to the details of where people sat at meals and how guests were received. One of the household rules of Lady Jane, second wife of Lord Berkeley, was that the gentleman usher must see that each guest is entertained "according to his calling [,] liking and estimation that is to be made of him." Even in the making and enforcement of laws, social degree was an omnipresent fact. In Parliament there was strong opposition to a 1593 proposal to empower justices of the peace to whip, place in stocks, or imprison the parents of bastards, for fear that such punishment might be applied to the upper orders. A sheriff who whipped a woman of degree in the Tower was censured by the Privy Council and imprisoned in the Counter, while rumors circulated that he would have to pay her £1,000. In clothing, diet, recreation, and the pageantry of death, considerations of social order were ideally maintained, though within each degree moderation was expected. Over all hung the specter of disorder, which stemmed, one preacher warned, from people who "know not truelye their gyftes and callinges. . . . They haue broken out of their standing places, and burst a sunder the listes of their callings, and cannot neither will [not] be bounde to order and obedience."[54]

(3) The Ideal of Moderation

Temperaunce, is the fountayne of Nobilitie: It is a vertue wherby a man obserueth a moderacion, and a reasonable meane in the vse of all thinges pertayning to bodie and minde: It is the mother of all other vertues.

Richard Davies, bishop of St. David's[55]

Too much of one thing, is good for nothing.

Thomas Rogers[56]

To judge from the literary evidence alone, the Elizabethan age was dominated by the ideal of moderation, but in the interpretation and application of the ideal, there was considerable latitude. The goal was not questioned; the Geneva annotators enunciated what became the Elizabethan standard when they asserted that material goods can be used in moderation and with sobriety. "We must live in suche sobrietie as God doeth call vs vnto, seing he wil make it more profitable vnto vs, then all deuteis: for his blessing onely sufficeth."[57]

Clerical intellectuals, as good Protestants, did not ground the appeal for moderation in Aristotle, the obvious source, but in the Ten Commandments, despite the intellectual difficulties this created. Hebrew morality is based on absolutes, which are antithetical to the Aristotelian notion of balance. At least some differences between Anglicans and Puritans on social issues result from the tendency of Puritans to lean toward absolutes and Anglicans to moderation. Yet according to the Puritan Dudley Fenner, the suspended curate of Cranbrook, Kent, the Ten Commandments are suffused with the ideal of moderation: "There is commanded in the whole, Sobrietie or temperance, which is the moderate and sparing vse of all bodilie benefites, as of foode, apparell, rest & recreation, the which temperance is a means to maintaine and increase both the other," namely, godliness and righteousness. Even the seventh commandment, prohibiting adultery as an apparently absolute maxim, was regarded by one author as a demand for temperance. The last commandment prohibiting covetousness was interpreted to mean that everyone must be content with his estate, "and so consequently requyreth so notable a moderation to be grounded in vs, as may very well, both helpe forwarde our Common Societie; and also prepare a man the better to walke the harde and painefull way of these Commaundementes." The problem with Elizabethan society, according to the Anglican poet Abraham Fleming, was that no one, from the prince to the clergy to the masses, was willing to accept his estate but was determined to attain sumptuous superfluity.[58]

Anglican writers uniformly urged moderation, for, as Nash remarked, hell is a place for intemperate men and evildoers. One who immoderately loves the world hates God. Sir Thomas Bromley's servant instructed his master's children that temperance is "a preserving prudence, or a kinde of wisedome that keepeth & conserueth the health of the body, the soundnesse of our naturall powers, and the puritie of lyfe and conuersation, without shame or any vndecencie." A temperate man, said Thomas Rogers, eschews superfluity but embraces modesty, continency, honesty, moderation, sobriety, and *pudicitia* (chaste purity). "Obserue a meane, and then shall you be that Temperate man." Leonard Wright pondered that he who has little and spends much is a prodigal fool; he who has much and spends little is a miserable "carle" or niggard; but he who moderates his expenses according to his means is wise. In an age where the higher orders were often wracked by debt, this ideal appears in retrospect to have been honored mostly in the breach. Presumably with this in mind, Sir William Segar, Norroy King of Arms, made it the duty of every knight and gentleman to detest intemperancy. In practice the ideal of moderation was made subordinate to social hierarchy, so that what was temperate for a peer was lavishly extravagant for a gentleman. Honor and social rank had to be preserved, even when this entailed what is now perceived as extravagant patterns of consumption. Thus the aristocracy found it possible to embrace the clerical and humanist ideal of moderation without substantially altering their traditional pattern of living.[59]

The Puritans shared the ideal of moderation in social affairs. Because extremism is satanic, divine blessings must be used moderately. Becon advised his readers to spend moderately as need required and to beware of superfluous expenses. The auditors of a 1584 sermon by John Stockwood, headmaster of the grammar school at Tunbridge, Kent, were told that a major reason for Jerusalem's destruction was that "incontinencie gotte the vpper hande of temperancie, verletry troade downe honestie in the duste, lecherie was too good for chastitie, drunkennesse, subtiltie, riot and al vices, banished sobrietie, vpright dealing, frugalitie and all vertues." There would be more justice in England, thundered John Knewstub, if people adhered to temperance and sobriety in their dealings. Social order would be strengthened by moderation, Edward Vaughan argued, for "Temperance alone is the sustayner of ciuill quietnesse, for it taketh care that the realme bee not corrupted with riot and wanton delights, whereby diuerse states haue been cast away." Moderation hinders dishonesty, restrains pleasures within tolerable bounds, and distinguishes men from beasts.

Vaughan blamed the nobility for the widespread deviation from this ideal, for they provided the masses with evil examples.[60]

Moderation was considered socially utilitarian. If the opulence of the higher orders could be decreased, many felt poverty and dearth could be sharply reduced. In August 1596, Whitgift recommended to the Privy Council that persons of means should be more moderate in their diet to aid victims of crop shortages facing malnutrition and starvation. Early in the era, the physician William Bullein made a similar plea:

Oh that moderacion wer vsed in a common wealth, then should not the riche die in glotonie . . . nor the poore perishe for lacke of bread. Extremes are euill, to[o] moche fastyng, or to[o] moche hunger.

The jurist William Lambarde urged moderation in his charges. Although some in the upper orders apparently adhered to such admonitions (as will be shown), it was more common for these people simply to donate table scraps to the poor at their gates. Burghley, however, had a reputation (apparently exaggerated) for governing his household with moderation and being temperate in his diet. Appeals for moderation on religious or utilitarian grounds were tempered by the recognition that some sumptuousness was regarded as essential to distinguish social estate and thus uphold social order. Concern for the visual preservation of social hierarchy as well as personal comfort appears to have been behind the Lords' refusal of a bill to restrain the use of coaches in November 1601. Certainly the quest for moderation was qualified to take into account the needs of each estate: "I woulde wishe therfore eche state to consider his callinge, and to remember the inconuenience of superfluitie." What was immoderate for one degree was not so for another.[61]

The socially utilitarian concept of moderation that Anglicans and Puritans espoused was fundamental to the Elizabethan attempt to maintain a hierarchic, organic, and orderly society. Obedience and authority in matters political, ecclesiastical, and familial were essential themes of the age. The political and religious ideals to which obedience was urged have been studied often, but no comprehensive examination has been undertaken of the social ideals. This study intends to fill this gap by a full analysis of Elizabethan social teaching, with its underlying themes of order and moderation. An attempt will be made to suggest the extent to which Elizabethans adhered to these teachings and the means that authorities used to enforce acceptance of the social dicta. Because leadership in the promulgation of social principles was primarily in the hands of the clergy, their role in society must be analyzed, particularly since they were under attack for factors ranging from antiprelatical hostility to clerical immorality to dereliction of duty. Their involvement with the systems of patronage, pluralism, and tithes bound them inextricably to the laity, who must have been conscious of ministerial activities and demands. Undoubtedly the hostility that some clergymen encountered because of tithes, pluralism, or basic anticlericalism hindered the inculcation of their social ideals, and such hostility was probably a factor in the periodic divergences between the ministers' exhortations and the laity's actions. This is not to imply that the only barrier to increased lay spirituality was ministerial misbehavior, but corrupt shepherds do not usually make effective religious leaders.

In this analysis of social thought and practice, Elizabethan religious groups are viewed in the context of a religious continuum extending from Catholics on the right to Separatists on the left; sometimes, therefore, we encounter degrees of emphasis rather than sharply differentiated positions. Despite the difficulties that this poses in the case of someone like William Whittingham or Thomas Becon, the categories of Anglican (or Conformist) and Puritan are justified. Although periodically it has been fashionable to gloss over the differences, it is historically irresponsible to deny the substantial dissimilarity between, say, Bancroft and Cartwright, or Whitgift and Greenham. Puritans are ultimately and necessarily distinguishable from Anglicans not principally by their doctrine, with the exception of their interpretation of *adiaphora*, but by the nature of their religious experience, the thrust of which was the quest for an inner purity of heart and mind, manifesting itself in spiritual warmth, aniconic worship, and a frank acknowledgment of personal sinfulness and dependence on the divine imputation of grace. The result was a confident healing of the original state of anxiety that many shared. According to surviving literary evidence, Puritanism was particularly a Spirit-oriented faith that brought its adherents the conviction of internal spiritual purity. That those who had such an experience deviated in some of their social teachings from Anglicans is demonstrable. The motivation for such deviation was not bourgeois interests, political considerations, material acquisitiveness, or social ambition, but the outworking of this religious experience in lives intended to conform to biblical standards of conduct (elucidated in marginalia, sermons, and tracts) and moral purity.

Part I: Society and Religion

CHAPTER *1*

Social Pressures
and Christian Leadership

In turning back the Donatist challenge, the Catholic church maintained the principle that the efficacy of the priestly functions was not dependent on the moral worth of the priest who performed them. In the Reformation, however, the nature and function of the ministry were redefined, so that the emphasis was on the clergy as teachers and exemplars of God's will for man, rather than as agents of the miracle in the mass or the dispensation of grace in the sacraments. The moral quality of the Protestant minister had an impact on his capacity as a spiritual teacher and adviser in a way that had not been true for a Catholic priest, whose immoral activities would have no effect on the efficacy of the mass. Yet English reformers failed to change the structure and nature of the clerical order to make it more compatible with the new ministry. Prelatical pomp, patronage, pluralism, and nonresidency were problems carried over from the Catholic church and never effectively solved in Tudor England, and all of them detracted from the ability of the Protestant ministry to function as it should with respect to religious and social leadership.

(1) Godly Bishops and Prelatical Pomp

Onely this I require, that gnats, bee not turned into Elephantes, and moulehilles be made Mountaynes, that is, small blemishes, no faultes in other, horrible and great crymes in vs, onely of affection to deface our calling.

Thomas Cooper, bishop of Lincoln[1]

What is more contemptible among the best, and basest of our people, then to be a Priest, yea a priestly Lord-Bishop?

John Penry[2]

As early as 1530, prelates were subjected to withering attack in biblical marginalia; Tyndale accused them of failing to fear God because they preached improperly, and of being as covetous as Judas for receiving from the devil the wealth and pomp Christ refused. Drunken with the desire of honor, they pursued material possessions to satisfy their lusts and failed to live soberly and teach what Jesus had commanded. These comments (reprinted in 1534) were dropped in 1551, but by that time they had become one of the fountains of antiprelatical hostility.

Tyndale used the prologue to Titus in his 1534 New Testament to set forth the qualities that bishops and lower clergy ought to possess, namely, virtue, learning, a willingness to preach and defend the gospel, and a determination to confute the Catholic doctrine of salvation and the authoritative place accorded human tradition.[3]

When the Matthew Bible appeared in 1537, John Rogers' note to 1 Timothy 3 defined the bishop's role as feeding Christ's flock with his word, not seeking honor, wealth, increased rents, pomp, and dominion. The covetousness of prelates and priests was condemned.[4] Edmund Becke did not delete these comments in his editions of 1549 and 1551. In the meantime Rogers, in his 1538 edition of Tyndale's New Testament, averred that bishops whose doctrine was pure could be tolerated, despite unholy lives.

But who can soffer them agaynste Christs doctryne for theyr awne profytes to make & vnmake lawes exercisynge vpon ye people playne tyrannye, & measuringe all thyngs for their awne aduantage & aucthorite? They that with tradycions ymagyned for theyr awne lucre and tyrannye to hamper the people, do not syt in the chere of the Gospel, but in ye chayre of Symon Magus & Cayphas.

This was heady stuff, and did not reappear in the 1549 edition. The Tyndale-Erasmus New Testament of that year instead lauded prelates as servants who preached Christ's doctrine.[5]

Relatively little attention was devoted to bishops by the Geneva annotators, whose key principle in this regard was that ministry and service rather than lordship and dominion are the highest dignity in the church. In Revelation the fallen angels in the bottomless pit were identified as bishops and ministers who had forsaken the word of God, whereas the locusts that plagued the earth were false teachers, heretics, and "wordlie subtil Prelates, with Monkes, Freres, Cardinals,

Patriarkes, Archebishops, Bishops, Doctors, Baschelers & masters which forsake Christ to mainteine false doctrine."[6]

The notes in the Rheims New Testament do not specifically criticize prelates, concentrating on their needed qualities. Bishops must perform good works, manifest patience in tribulation, zealously discipline offenders and diligently try false apostles and teachers, be wise and simple, and "commaund in Gods cause." Like other clergy they must not leave their flocks in times of persecution unless they alone are threatened. They exercise sovereignty in matters of faith and manners, but tyrannical dominion is prohibited. Directly responding to criticism from English Protestants, the annotaters point out that there are many worthy bishops who lack the gifts of preaching and teaching, but who render service in administering the sacraments and governing the church. Pride prompted Protestants to condemn Catholics, "pretending that they can not preach as they do, with meretricious and painted eloquence." A nonpreaching episcopate was an abomination to Puritans, hence the Rheims note provoked a retort from Fulke that Paul requires bishops to teach.[7] Thus the marginal notes to the Tudor Scriptures placed the conduct and qualities of the bishops squarely in the minds of the Bible-reading laity, implicitly encouraging them to judge their spiritual leaders.

It is beyond the scope of this work to reexamine the controversy over episcopacy though it should be noted that the serious challenge to episcopal polity developed only when disillusionment with the episcopal bench became intense. Because bishops were part of the hierarchical structure of society, it was more natural to consider them as instruments of reform than as obstacles to be excised. The preoccupation of most Elizabethan reformers was with the sins of prelates rather than the unlawfulness of episcopacy, but the tendency to berate the bishops' evils gave way in some minds to a demand to remove the episcopal bench altogether. Thus John Penry remarked of Edward Dering: "There was one Deering, that by our [Anglican] neglygence preached [before Elizabeth at Lent]: if he and such as hee, hadde but continued the whole Lent, I am afraide, there would haue bene neuer a Lord Byshop left in England before the Next Lent had come againe." Anthony Gilby, minister at Ashby de la Zouch, Leics., accepted godly bishops, but regarded "archbishop" and "bishop" as popish names and objected to prelatical domination over the clergy.[8] Dering and Gilby represent the Puritans who came close to calling for the abolition of episcopacy but retained some hope of reforming existing polity.

In self defense, the embattled bishops and their allies sought ways to protect themselves, such as Bancroft's *jure divino* arguments. One effort to shore up episcopal prestige was reported by Dering to the Privy Council in November 1573:

I hard of late one in the wide churche of [St.] Polls [London] preache mutche for authoritie of bishops, and what a thinge it weare to have them honourable; and sayde thus, "I would five or six of the counsell weare Aarons; I would the Lord Keeper weare a bishop (not that I think justice ill ministered, but I would have the cleargie in honor); I would a bishop were Master of the Rolls; I would all the vj. clarkes of Chauncerie weare priestes; this would make the order in estimation. In times past a good justice of peace durst not offende a parishe or hedge priest; now everie brave man in Kent Streete will controll bishops." These words [Dering concluded] do not edify the conscience of man.

Whitgift took a different tack, declaring that disorder would reign if the radical challenge to episcopacy prevailed. If bishops lost their lands and authority, and each church were to elect its own minister, there would be no law to prescribe order, and every minister would pursue his wishes as king and pope in his parish. There would be as many kinds of religion as there were parishes, as many sects as ministers. The earl of Hertford in 1589 was convinced the nobility should defend the bishops out of self-interest, for "as they shoot at bishops now, so will they do at the nobility also, if they be suffered."[9]

What provoked these defensive measures were unremitting attacks culminating, but not ceasing, in the invectives of the Marprelate tracts. The chorus of abuse began early and mushroomed in the late 1580s. A sampling of the attacks and retorts is necessary to appreciate the socio-religious atmosphere in which bishops struggled to preserve their position in the social hierarchy. One of the earlier attacks began with the outspoken Puritan Dr. William Turner. In March 1564 the bishop of Bath and Wells complained to Cecil that Turner, dean of Wells, was behaving indiscreetly in the pulpit, calling bishops "white-coates, [and] typpett gentlemen." Turner was reprimanded by a temporary suspension for nonconformity the same year. From the Catholic writer Lewis Evans, a student at Louvain, came the unjust accusation the following year that the new bishops were selected from the basest element in the clergy.[10]

The failure of the crown and ecclesiastical hierarchy to implement reforms, particularly in the Convocation of 1563, provoked Puritans to step up their attacks on bishops. In 1566 Becon charged that the most spiteful enemies of the Gospel were the pope, the bishops, the Catholic priests and monks, and the doctors in the universities. The following year, Robert Crowley, deprived vicar of St. Giles without Cripplegate, London, castigated the prelates:

Then may we gesse,
In what distresse:
Such leude bishops shall stand:
When Christ shal come,
At the last dome
By fire to iudge the land.

That some of this antiprelatical hostility affected the laity is apparent from an incident that occurred in Bristol in 1568. Richard Cheyney, bishop of Gloucester and Bristol, preached a series of three sermons in August and September, urging the people not to follow Calvin on every matter but to accept the teachings of the patristics. Nor did he approve of their insistence on *sola scriptura*, which doctrine he regarded as the tool of heretics, preferring that the Bible be understood in the light of patristic thought. A local Puritan preacher (Norbrook), whom Cheyney regarded as "more earnest then skilfull," led the outcry against the bishop's sermons. Although Cheyney complained to Cecil, the citizens of Bristol, including their schoolmaster Thomas Turner, countered with a remonstrance accusing the bishop of uttering "very strange, perilous & corrupt doctrines" that hindered the Gospel and disrupted the people's tranquility.[11]

Feelings against the prelates were strong in other areas as well. In June 1571 the Privy Council discussed the fact that the officers and servants of John Scory, bishop of Hereford, had been physically assaulted at Bromyard, Herefs., and that the bishop could not travel without a heavy guard. As Puritan agitation mounted, Edwin Sandys, bishop of London, complained to Burghley that "these are dangerous days, full of itching ears, mislying minds, and ready to forget all obedience and duty." An example of what troubled Sandys occurred in 1579 at Cookham, Berks., where Puritan feelings were strong. A man of local influence, opposed to the new Anglican clergyman, asserted "that though the Bishop [of London, John Aylmer] himself should come and sit with Keltridg [the Anglican cleric] in Cookham church, he should have a very warm seat, and he would make them both weary of their places." Although Burghley did not condone such attitudes, he warned Whitgift in 1584 that many of the men elevated to the episcopal bench were adversely affected by their new prominence and were adopting secular ways. Resentment against the bishops was exemplified in 1586 when Aylmer was at Malden, Essex, on an episcopal visitation. A plot was discovered in which some young tradesmen hired a man to dress like a fool and seize the bishop's cap while he was preaching, twirl it on his finger, and toss it back and forth among the congregation.[12]

All hell broke loose in 1588 and 1589—or so it must have seemed to the bishops who bore the brunt of the satirical invective in the Marprelate tracts. The author's key assertion was that "our church-gouernement in England by lord archbishops, and bishops, is a gouernement of maimed, vnnaturall, and deformed, members, seruing for no vse in the church of God."[13] John Udall, the curate of Kingston upon Thames, Surrey, who is sometimes suspected to be the author, declared in 1588 that archbishops, bishops, and archdeacons were in league with hell and had made a covenant with death. John Penry, also associated with the Marprelate agitation, observed that antiprelatical hostility was so pronounced that some persons considered the detestation of bishops to be the essence of religious faith, and in 1589 he castigated bishops, archdeacons, dumb ministers, and nonresidents as spiritual sons of idolatrous monks and friars. The basis of his fervor appears to have been his conviction that in the first three decades of Elizabeth's reign the Welsh people were starved of the Gospel because of these men. Continually frustrated by the lack of reforms, he called in 1590 for the abolition of episcopacy and accused the bishops of a threefold corruption: They usurped the authority of the civil magistrate, claimed titles that belonged to secular dignitaries, and manifested lordly preeminence over the church. They are "nothing els, but a troup of bloody soule murtherers, sacriligious church robbers, and suche as haue made them selues fatte with the bloude of mens soules, and the vtter ruine of the Church."[14]

The defenders of episcopacy counterattacked, retaining the upper hand for the rest of the reign, partly because moderate Puritans backed away from antiprelatical statements for fear of being associated with the Marprelate pamphlets. Thomas Cooper, bishop of Winchester, wrote a serious theological defense, which provoked the satirical response, *Hay Any Worke for Cooper*. Among those joining Cooper in the counterattack was Leonard Wright, who set forth reverence for prelates as a Christian obligation. Richard Turnbull, fellow of Corpus Christi College, Oxford, asserted that if Marprelate and his cohorts had dealt with the bishops face to face, their zeal for reform might have been taken more seriously. In a kindred spirit, Robert Temple, prebendary of St. Paul's and canon of Bristol, regarded the derogatory assaults as a plague on the church and their bitterness, a reflection of insanity.[15] Although one may sympathize with the frustrations of men such as Penry, the inclusive, uncritical censure of the episcopal bench hardened the attitude of bishops and made them reluctant to undertake reforms.

The Marprelate controversy had an adverse effect on those who sought moderate reform. Perhaps the most important of these because of his kinship with the queen and his position in the government was Sir Francis Knollys, treasurer of the household and member of the Privy Council. In November 1583, prior to the Marprelate tracts, he asserted that bishops and archdeacons, in maintaining the order and ceremonial of the *Book of Common Prayer*, usurped the authority of judges and justices of the peace. They do not take into account "whether wylfully, or vppon resonable cause, any order or ceremonye be omytted or broken, as by the Archedecons inquysytyon amongste churche wardens, and yngnorant redying mynysters may easelye appere." They also were accused of reaping personal profits from visitations. The following June, Knollys reported to Burghley of his attempts to persuade Whitgift to allow zealous ministers to preach even if they refused to subscribe. "The reasons that moved me to make this reqwest alleaged to be, that the safetye and preservation of hir majesties parson, crowne, and dygnytye, be not ympayred, nor layde wyde open (for lacke of zealous preachers) to the vndermynyng Jesvytes, and theyr dylygent trayterous skollers and folowers." Whitgift, however, was convinced that Elizabeth's position would be more secure if her laws were obeyed and not "vppon so frivolous and vayne Reasons condemned." But the real condemners of her majesty's laws, complained Knollys, were not those who refused to subscribe to human traditions but were those bishops who imposed subscription without proper legal authority. Their "absolvte" authority has no foundation in Scripture, and Knollys was convinced that it was dangerous for the queen "that the poletyke government of matters of state, as well concernyng formes and accidentes of and to Religion as otherwyse, should be taken from all cownsayllors of hir majesties estate, and onely to be gyven over to the Rvle of Bysshoppes that are not alwayes indyfferent in theyre owne cases off svfferentye." Even then he feared to respond directly to Whitgift's arguments without Burghley's encouragement.[16]

Knollys continued to support the Puritans, and was still asserting his antiprelatical views to Burghley on the eve of the publication of the first Marprelate tract in October 1588. In August he drew a contrast between a grave, learned minister who spoke according to the Spirit, and the courtly divine animated by the spirit of the Antichrist. The superiority claimed by bishops, he warned Burghley, was the foundation of popery. A September epistle reiterated his thesis that the bishops' claimed superiority and unlawful imposition of subscription revealed their true ambition.[17]

As the Marprelate controversy unfolded, Knollys continued his antiprelatical campaign. He was incensed by Whitgift's claims for episcopal authority in his dispute with Cartwright. The queen, Knollys believed, was endangered unless prelatical ambition and covetousness were restrained; the bishops must be forced to acknowledge that they have no authority over lower clergy except that granted by the sovereign. A few months later, he returned to the same theme, proposing also that Burghley persuade Elizabeth to have the universities discuss episcopal authority; at the same time, he disassociated himself from the Marprelate tracts. In the fall of 1590 he sought Burghley's judgment of his writing on episcopal authority, promising to compose nothing further unless Burghley approved, and again denouncing Martin Marprelate. The conservative backlash made continued attacks on prelacy dangerous and probably fruitless, but Knollys continued to support the Puritan cause.[18]

Although the more radical Puritans failed to shake the bishops from their lofty perch in the social hierarchy, a legacy of religious and social hatred remained. In part this attitude seems to have been due to the inability of the bishops to live up to high expectations. As reflected in Bishop Cooper's synopsis, the duties of prelates are formidable: They are to teach biblical doctrine, confute error, superstition and idolatry, exhort to virtue, reprove vice, and comfort those with afflicted consciences. When the archbishopric of York was vacant in 1568, Matthew Hutton, dean of York, wrote to Cecil recommending Edmund Grindal, bishop of London, setting forth the desired qualifications: He must first be a teacher "because the countrie ys ignorant: a vertuouse and godly man, because the countrie ys geven to sifte a mans life: a stout and coragious man in gods cause, because the countrie otherwise will abvse him: and yet a sober and discret man, least to muche vigorousnes harden the harte of some, that by fayre meanes might be mollyfyed." He must be educated and a lover of learning, "that this rude and blynde countrie maye be furnished with learned preachers." The government's appointment of men with such qualifications was not a foregone conclusion, as witnessed, for example, by the appeal of Francis Russell, earl of Bedford, to Burghley in 1578, asking that a diligent preacher rather than a dumb dog be appointed to the bishopric of Exeter.[19]

A major social factor accounting for antiprelatical hostility was disgust with the pomp of bishops. Patrick Collinson suggests that such ostentatious display intimated their pretension to additional authority, whether inherent in themselves or in the pope. Certainly, Anglicans assailed Catholic prelates for excessive spendor. John Jewel, bishop of Salisbury, accused them of being worldly princes gaily arrayed and accompanied with bands of men. Strip them of such accouterments as crosses, hats, mitres, and palls, and what, he asked, do they teach and how do they live? George Wither, the Puritan dean of Colchester, censured Catholic prelates for heaping up treasures for voluptuous living and warfare.[20]

It required no ingenuity for Puritans to apply these castigations to Anglican bishops. Gilby deplored their princely parks and palaces, their wealth and dress, and their "pompous trayne of proud idle swingebreeches, in the steede of Preachers & Schollers." Dudley Fenner blasted their ostentatious pomp, dainty fare, superfluous expenses, great retinues (more befitting aristocrats than ministers of Christ), disorderly households, bribes, and other abuses. The ministers of Ashby de la Zouch, Leics., where Puritanism was strong, protested to the bishop of Lincoln in 1576 that "you yourselves that be great bishops would not joigne with Christ's poore mynisters, either for your great affaires which you commonly alleadge, or for your great travaile or great chardges, that cannot come without some great troupe of horses." They urged him to lay aside his popish lordliness and come in Christian humility to exercise his gifts.[21] In preserving the visual trappings and comforts of their social station, the bishops offended Puritans who held to an ideal of New Testament simplicity. Moreover such offense exposed the bishops as lordly prelates to an assualt on their lifestyle by any group—Puritan or not—hostile to them or their actions.

It was galling to the Puritans to observe the households of prelates, replete with coveys of chaplains, at a time when the kingdom was short of qualified ministers and many parishes went without sermons. The problem was compounded in that chaplains normally held benefices on a nonresident basis. Such chaplains might be used for worthy purposes, as were Whitgift's, who instructed young gentlemen in his care in the arts and sciences. Apart from chaplains, the number of servants in episcopal households was a further source of irritation, prompting Thomas Sampson, who had refused the bishoprics of Hereford and Norwich, to complain to Grindal in 1574 of the idle men in his household.

Christ his patrimony ought not to be bestowed and employed on a sort and company of idle serving men, which do only serve the pomp of one person. I knowe that *necessarii famuli* are to be had; but this number and multitude of idle serving men is unprofitable and unmeet for a minister of Christ to feed and maintain with the patrimony of Christ.

Parker laid out £448 *p.a.* on servants' wages in addition to their maintenance. Parkhurst had thirty-two servants, Downham forty, and Aylmer eighty. When Whitgift visited Kent the first time he was accompanied by one hundred servants, of whom forty were gentlemen wearing gold chains. Jewel defended the bishops by contending that their Catholic predecessors had enjoyed greater worldly benefits.[22]

Another major reason for hostility to bishops was the extent of their lands and wealth. Given the size of the household they deemed necessary, their responsibility for hospitality, the support required for their families, and episcopal expenses, their income had to be fairly substantial. Inflation required them to make the best use of their possessions, though this left them vulnerable to charges like those leveled by Roger Lord North against Richard Cox, bishop of Ely, in 1575:

My Lord, it wilbe no plesure for yowe to have hir Majestye & the Councell knowe howe wretchedlye yowe live within & without your house, how extremly covetouse, howe greate a grazier, how marvelous a dayrye man how ritche a farmer, how grete an owner. It will not lyke yowe that the world knowe of your decayed howses, of the lead & brick that yow sell from them, of the leases that yowe lawlesslye enter into, of the fre land which you wrongfullye posese, of the toles & impostes which yowe rayse, of Goddes good minesters which yowe causeleslye displase.

Bishops often depended on the men who managed their affairs to keep them financially solvent, but the actions of these men were bound to reflect on the bishops. One unsavory character was George Thymelthorp, an appointee of John Parkhurst, bishop of Norwich. Thymelthorp was assigned the task of collecting the tenths in the diocese of Norwich, but instead of giving the proceeds to Parkhurst, he pocketed the funds, leaving the bishop two or three years in arrears to the Exchequer and presumably facing a strain on his revenues.[23] The fortunate bishop was one whose agents kept him fiscally solvent without alienating the people of his diocese.

Charges of financial mismanagement and personal gain were made against the bishops, sometimes deservingly. The Puritan Eusebius Pagit, rector of Kilkhampton, Corn., was upset about bishops who confirmed leases of benefices to kinfolk, noting that one (unnamed) bishop had confirmed twenty of the best benefices in his diocese to his children, relatives, officials and general purchasers. When Aylmer died in 1594, his sons were provided with episcopal lands worth

£16,000, though St. Paul's Cathedral lacked £4,000 for repairs. Other bishops did not fare as well. When Nicholas Bullingham, bishop of Worcester, died in April 1576, his liabilities totalled £1,224 6s. 8d. against assets of £1,052 11s. 6d. His indebtedness was largely due to expenses for the militia, his move from Lincoln to Worcester, repairs to former houses, funds still due (£205) as first fruits for his Worcester see, entertainment of the queen, and ordinary hospitality. On top of this were his funeral expenses, which were considerable for persons of this rank. His assets, including goods and chattels worth £486 and plate valued at £300, were respectable but hardly adequate in view of his social and financial responsibilities. The case of Richard Fletcher, bishop of London, who died in June 1596 is similar. He had assets of £1,412 19s. 4d. including £263 in cash, £414 17s. 2d. in plate, and £453 2s. 2d. in household goods, but liabilities of £1,464 12s. 6d., including debts of £600 to Elizabeth, £200 to Aylmer's heirs, and £100 to the dean and chapter. The first fruits charged by the crown were onerous for the prelates, prompting Richard Vaughan, bishop of Bangor, to complain to Sir Robert Cecil in 1596 that after he had paid them he would have less than £50 *p.a.* on which to live. Other expenses, however, were less justified, such as the marriage portions bestowed by Bishop Robert Horne on his five daughters, which moved the Puritan Thomas Wood to protest to the earl of Leicester in 1576: "Looke upon Winchester, what large sommes of mony he hath given with his daughters, and how he hath matcht them." Still, short of a drastic reduction of the social obligations expected of bishops and the remission of such fees as first fruits, the proposal of the Separatist Henry Barrow, that the state should convert episcopal lands to civil use, was unrealistic.[24]

The crown had a vested interest in the episcopacy, and helped the bishops fend off attacks and demands for a redistribution of episcopal wealth, partly by supporting High Commission. The bishops felt compelled to justify their position. James Pilkington, bishop of Durham, faced with accusations that bishops provided insufficient hospitality, given the extent of their lands, retorted that their accusers "consider not how barely they [Protestant bishops] came to their livings, what pensions they pay, and annuities, which their predecessors granted; how all commodities be leased away from them; what charges they bear for first-fruits, subsidies and tenths; how they lack all household stuff and furniture at their entering; so that for three years' space they be not able to live out of debt, and get them necessaries." In response to Cartwright's proposal to use episcopal lands to provide poor relief, Whitgift argued that such lands were beneficial to the church and commonwealth, and to take them away would require the bishops to live by "pilling and polling." The great houses and lands that the bishops possessed, he argued, were inherited, not obtained by making spoils of the church's goods, as Cartwright had charged. According to Whitgift, all the clergy, including prelates, would benefit by riches and fair houses properly used, for poverty and simplicity were guises for hypocrisy and pride. If the masses were to honor the bishops, asserted Leonard Wright, an apologist for episcopacy, they must have wealth meet for their social position.[25] The Puritans, however, preferred that bishops command respect by godly lives and fervent preaching.

The personal lives of the bishops drew less attention. One celebrated case, however, involved Edwin Sandys, archbishop of York, who allegedly made love to the wife of a Doncaster innkeeper named Sysson. Sandys tried to hush up the affair by paying Sysson £500 and Sir Robert Stapleton, who, with Sysson, discovered the couple, £200 plus a £1500 lease and a loan. Stapleton claimed he was not involved, though Sandys accused him of plotting the affair.[26] Whatever the truth, the gossip did the archbishop's reputation no good.

More concern was expressed about the quality of ministers appointed to benefices. In a sermon before Elizabeth in 1570, Dering urged her to forbid bishops from privately ordaining ministers as a means to keep ignorant persons out of the pulpit. Udall blamed prelates as "the causers of that damnable ignoraunce, wherein the people are so generally wrapped, for that you haue from time to time stopped the streams of knowledge . . . and in stead of able and painefull ministers, haue pestered the Churche, eyther with presumptuous proude persons, that are esteemed learned and take no paines to bring the people vnto the knowledge of Iesus Christe, or (which is the greatest nomber) such ignorant asses . . . as are not worthy to liue in a well ordered common-wealth." In Wales, charged Penry, bishops admitted rogues and vagabonds into the ministry, to say nothing of adulterers, drunkards, thieves, swearers, and roisterers. Robert Crowley placed some of the blame on patrons who presented unqualified nominees, though the bishops did accept them.

Knollys made the same point to Burghley in 1589, attributing the bishops' willingness to their quest for uniformity; what mattered was not the quality of the nominee but his acknowledgment of episcopal authority.[27]

Some concern was expressed in Anglican circles about this problem.

In the province of York around 1585, as in Canterbury a decade earlier, it was recognized that ordaining unworthy ministers created scandal. Orders were issued prohibiting any bishop from ordaining ministers without first giving public notice and requiring that potential ordinands come from the bishop's diocese or from one of the universities. Ordinands must provide testimony of their character and be examined by the bishop and other learned clergy, demonstrating an ability to explain Scripture from a Latin text. The ordination ceremony must be public and conducted according to the *Book of Common Prayer*. Moreover, no one was to be ordained unless a vacancy existed.[28] Had such efforts been made earlier and carried out with thoroughness, the bishops might have reaped a harvest of good will instead of a common suspicion that their primary concern was the preservation of their social perquisites.

In fairness to the bishops, it is essential to remember the tension inherent in their dual role in Elizabethan society. They were expected to be exemplars of the evangelical ideal — men of high character, able preachers or at least administrators, and paragons of virtue. Yet the queen expected them to be lordly prelates, loyal supporters of the crown in the Lords, and dutiful servants of the government in their dioceses. Even in their latter role, the queen impeded their efforts, by allowing her courtiers to obtain beneficial leases of ecclesiastical lands, thus depriving the prelates of income essential to their aristocratic function. Moreover, she furthered the fiscal problems of the bishops by forcing nominees to sees to surrender episcopal lands in exchange for impropriated tithes and livings. Consequently a number of prelates spent undue time stewing over their financial circumstances. On the whole, the Elizabethan bishops were superior to their predecessors in frequency of preaching and visitation and regularity of residence. But they reaped the consequences of centuries of episcopal irresponsibility.[29]

(2) Patrons and Parsons

The state of Asses, was better then the state of Horses: for the Horses runne to patrons for benefices: but many ignoraunt Asses doe obtaine them.

R. Lewes[30]

Captaine Cuffe of the bouncing band of all Surebies, the olde sheepe biter . . . will haue their [the clergy's] Manors and landes to make his brats Gentlemen.

John Chardon[31]

As a social concern, patronage affected property rights, episcopal control, the quality and number of clergy, and the capability of reform. In the nontheological area no act, apart from the change from papal to royal sovereignty and the dissolution of the monasteries, had such a profound impact on English religion and society as the rapid extension of lay patronage, already extensive before the 1530s. To raise funds and secure support for their religious policies, Henry VIII and the dukes of Somerset and Northumberland had sold to laymen ecclesiastical lands with patronage rights, but the price was high. Their actions had jeopardized the crown's ability to control the appointment of qualified, loyal men in the future. In the Elizabethan era the ecclesiastical patronage of the laity increased, in part to bind recipients more effectively to the regime, as in the case of nonecclesiastical patronage. The necessity of episcopal approval notwithstanding, practical control over the selection of many ministers became vested in a landed class, whose primary interests were often at variance with the spiritual concerns and religious policies of the episcopal bench and even the crown. This was particularly so in the case of donative cures, unendowed vicarages served by stipendiary curates whose tenure was at the discretion of lay impropriators. Such curates required only a license from the bishop, which might be dispensed with, and were not at first subject to episcopal visitation, though by 1583 Aylmer was visiting donative curacies in London. Donative cures, often found in urban parishes, were susceptible to Puritan influence, depending on the religious persuasions of impropriators, as in the case of Denham, Suffolk, where Edward Lewkenor's minister was Robert Pricke. A parish might also hold its tithes in trust, administered by feoffees, who, as in the parish of St. Andrew's, Norwich, or St. Anne's, Blackfriars, London, selected Puritan clergy. More problematical were patrons who selected unqualified men or left livings vacant to reap the profits themselves, though bishops could present a minister to any living vacant more than six months. Bishops could reject patrons' nominees if the nominees were ignorant or immoral, but they risked a common-law writ of *Quare impedit* if they did. Many bishops probably accepted dubious nominees rather than risk legal entanglements.[32]

Given a system of lay (as well as ecclesiastical) patronage, the character of the patron was crucial. One preacher distinguished five types of patrons: (1) Catholics; (2) materialists who for monetary gain selected unfit men; (3) irreligious patrons who bestowed benefices on kindred, friends, or suitors; (4) religious men determined to profit from their benefices; and (5) patrons who provided clerics with ample funds for pastoral work. The evidence supports such a classification. One extreme is represented by William Webbe, patron of Marnhull, Dorset, whose forcible dispossession of his parson, Giles Thorneborow, involved the commission of "outrages and insolences," including the murder of Thorneborow's servant by one of Webbe's men. Near the other extreme was a patron such as Thomas Legh of High Leigh, Lancs., whose 1589 will left his grandson a lease of certain lands "so that he doe keepe yearlie some honest learned man that cann saye divine service . . . at my chappell at High Leghe for the ease of my tenante frendes and wellwillers."[33]

Most factions along the religious continuum expressed concern for the character of patrons. Lawrence Vaux, an Augustinian canon, condemned patrons who bestowed benefices for profit, and Anglicans used the open air pulpit at Paul's Cross, London, to castigate unsatisfactory patrons. In 1581, Anthony Anderson, rector of Medbourne, Leics., expostulated that "the poore Minister muste crouch to such patrons, his knee to the grounde, his steeple to theyr stealth, his tythe to their granary, and his due portion to their vnsatiable prouision." Another Anglican protested in 1594 that patrons were divinely instituted as instruments for the behoof of Jacob but instead bestowed Jacob's living on Esau. Too many, Dr. John Spenser warned in 1602, tried to remove ministers to obtain financial benefits themselves. In the same year, Dr. Dawson of Trinity College, Cambridge, compared the lean kine devouring the fat but remaining thin to those patrons who swallowed church livings. Puritans were no less concerned with immoral patrons. John Rainolds, fellow of Corpus Christi College, Cambridge, preached at Oxford against patrons who "deale with the matter as *Polymestor* did with *Polydore,* that is, as euill gardians doo with their wardes, and turne their patronage into pillage." For the Separatists, Barrow and Robert Harrison extended disapprobation of lay patrons to the institution itself. Barrow was irate that some patrons had no contact with the churches for which they selected clergy, while other patrons were women and children.[34] Anglicans and Puritans, however, were willing to settle for the reform rather than the abolition of lay patronage.

The character of the patron normally was reflected in the quality of the clergy he appointed. The outcry was widespread that unqualified and immoral men were a blot on the reputation of all clergy. In a courageous sermon before Elizabeth in 1570, Dering accused her of sitting by while patrons bestowed benefices on children, other youth, servants, and men of such disreputable character as "shake bucklers," ruffians, hawkers, hunters, gamblers, and dumb dogs who could not

preach. When the livings were small, Stockwood charged, they sometimes went to "their Faukener, their Huntesman, their Horsekeeper,
or any other such like, so as he can reasonablie read englishe." This
complaint became almost a litany, with much of the same language
used repeatedly. The future bishop of Exeter, John Woolton, condemned the appointment of "faukenners, horsekeepers, . . . dogge-
dryuers," and simple Sir Johns; Christopher Shutte, vicar of Giggleswick, Yorks., spoke against hiring Sir John Lacklatins, and Jewel
criticized the "blind sir Johns, not only lack-Latin, but lack-honesty,
and lack-conscience, and lack-religion." Pilkington warned that those
who appointed such men consented to the evil they did, a caveat repeated by the Puritan Robert Some, rector of Girton, Cambs. "Liuinges [said James Bisse] are not geuen, they are solde as common as
oysters at Byllingesgate. . . . Doltes, ignorant Asses, idle, & idole
Shepheardes haue the liuinges."

Exasperated by patrons who selected men for financial gain regardless of education, Leonard Wright sarcastically remarked that
whoever sought an ecclesiastical living "must needs bring this learning with him, to know who was Melchizedecks Father and Mother,
or else a dish of maister Latimers apples, or he may cough for any
benefice."[35]

Apart from the quality of the clergy, lay patronage had a negative
influence on clerical income, placing ministers at a disadvantage in
the fulfillment of hospitality and poor relief as well as in their maintenance of the trappings appropriate to their standing in the social
hierarchy. Of the approximately 8,800 benefices in England, Dr.
John King, rector of St. Andrew's, Holborn, reckoned in 1602 that
in excess of 3,000 provided poor stipends for ministers: "Their
bread is broken amongst strangers, the foxes and their cubbes liue in
their ruines, . . . the Church liuings are seised vpon and possessed
by the secular." In a Commons' debate the preceding year, Dr. Francis James, a civilian lawyer and ecclesiastical official estimated that
only 600 livings were adequate. Insufficient livings, he judged, were
responsible for clerical corruption and excessive competition for
deaneries and prebendaries.[36]

William Harrison, rector of Radwinter, Essex, calculated that the
minimum stipend necessary to support a minister was £30 *p.a.* In
south Lancashire c. 1590, vicars averaged only £23 9s. 3d., though
rectors averaged eight times that much. Fluctuations from one living
to another were considerable, with the curate of Blackley, for example, receiving a mere £2 3s. 4d. Only four parochial benefices in the
diocese of Chichester were worth £30 *p.a.* or more, and these ranged

from £30 to £60. An examination of the 1579 figures for the archdeaconry of Chichester shows that of the 86 rectors whose incomes are known, 59.3% had annual incomes of £10 or less, and 80.2% of £15 or less; of the 57 vicars whose incomes are known, 78.9% had incomes of £10 or less, and 98.2% of £15 or less; of the 40 curates and readers whose incomes are known, 72.5% had incomes of £10 or less, and 92.5% of £15 or less. Livings in Lincoln were also poor: the vicar of St. Mary le Wigford received £5 3s. 9d., the rector of St. Peter at Arches, £5 2s. 8½d., and the vicar of St. Martin, £3 13s. 4d. *p.a.* In many Welsh parishes tithes were worth £100 *p.a.*, but a curate might receive as little as £6 6s. 8d. The extent to which the livings were impropriate provides a rough indication of the sort of income a minister received in a given area: 40% of the livings in the province of Canterbury were impropriate (including 62% in the diocese of Ely), over 50% in the diocese of Llandaff, and 62.6% in the province of York. One effect of impropriated livings and the resulting inadequate incomes was a shortage of qualified clergy. In the diocese of Llandaff there were five preachers in the beginning of Elizabeth's reign, while St. Asaph had five and Bangor two. Conditions improved, so that there were fifty in Llandaff by 1603, yet there were 192 cures. Sir William Bowes estimated that there were only three able ministers in the Middle Marches as late as 1595. Under these circumstances, the inculcation of social ethics in the people was severely hindered. Another effect of inadequate livings was clerical activity detrimental to the social conduct that concerned Anglicans and Puritans advocated. In Lancashire, for example, to supplement their incomes the vicar of Huyton (1578), the curate of Singleton (1578), the curate of Stretford (1581), and the curate of Ormskirk (1601) ran alehouses, and an enterprising fellow of Manchester (1571) conducted illegal secret marriages. Poor incomes, of course, did not necessitate such questionable activities, for other clergy in similar plights turned to agriculture, mining, weaving, teaching, and similar occupations.[37]

The financial plight of many ministers and its relation to lay patronage provoked a chorus of dissent from Elizabethan clergy, especially Anglicans, who realized that the concomitant problems of inept or immoral parsons provided ammunition for the Puritans. John Howson, prebendary of Hereford and Exeter, posited that an industrious man could live decently in any calling in England except —unless he could afford to buy a benefice—the ministry; ministers had to depend on their parishioners for alms. The clergy, grumbled Leonard Wright, suffered inadequate maintenance, poor diet, simple clothing, and debt, with nothing to sustain their families after their deaths. For £10 a year, said Anthony Anderson, a cleric must "carry a dyshe to his maysters Table, or else stande at the dresser, orderly to set out the messes of meate, and supply the Clarke of the kytchyns place, his Seruice and Homilyes he must cut short, and measure them by the Cookes readynesse, and dynner dressing, the roste neare ready, the kitchin boye is sente to master Parson, to bydde hym make hast." A preacher at St. Peter's, Paul's Wharf, London—perhaps the Separatist Henoch Clapham—suggested that patrons kept ministers poor to prevent ministers from criticizing them by the well-timed gift of a coat or dinner.[38]

Some patrons used devious practices to mulct benefices and potential incumbents of funds. Stephen Bateman, rector of Merstham, Surrey, with a benefice worth £40 *p.a.* (but officially valued at £20 in the 1535 *Valor Ecclesiasticus*), suggested that patrons might require a candidate to pay three years' value but receive only £8 *p.a.*, out of which he had to support his family, purchase books, and maintain hospitality. The buying and selling of advowsons increased the tendency to regard patronage as an investment that ought to provide a reasonable return. Grindal disliked advowsons both before and after his appointment to the episcopal bench, and Pilkington considered impropriations that deprived ministers of an acceptable living contrary to the biblical principle that a laborer is worthy of his hire, and detrimental to the poor, who might otherwise be relieved by tithes.[39]

The social ramifications of lay patronage also are seen in education. Frequent assertions were made that the market in advowsons was responsible for an uneducated ministry since it encouraged the allotment of positions for economic considerations. Charges of simony were commonplace when questions of religious qualifications were entangled with the dealing in benefices as forms of financial investment. This situation prompted the Anglican John Howson to apply an investment analogy to the inability of the Church of England to supply its pulpits with educated men. In his estimate, a university education in divinity required an outlay of approximately £500 to 1,000 marks; to expect the father of a divinity student to pay a patron for a life lease on a parsonage, especially one with an income commensurate with the social status of a man possessing a university education, was unreasonable. William Vaughan's estimate of the cost of higher education was somewhat lower—£300 minimum—but to this, he said, a parent would have to add £200 for a benefice or £400 for a chancellorship. "Learning now adaies," grumbled Thomas Nash, "gets no liuing if it come empty handed. Promotion which was wont to be ye free propounded palme of paines, is by many mens lamen-

table practise, become a purchase." Blatantly to charge for the bestowal of a benefice could bring a patron into court on a complaint
of simony, but there were ways around this, one of them being to
have friends of a potential incumbent assure his payment for the
receipt of a benefice.[40]

Quite apart from the question of patron-imposed amercements for
entry to a benefice, lay appropriation of a share of the tithes discouraged educated candidates. Jewel anticipated Mark Curtis' thesis on
the alienation of intellectuals when he maintained that "the vicarages
in many places, and in the properest [sic] market towns, are so simple, that no man can live upon them, and therefore no man will take
them." The bishop of Winchester complained that in one impoverished shire there existed in excess of eight chapels with small stipends
served by poorly trained men, for educated clergy refused to serve
for such meager incomes. Pilkington was disturbed that parents encouraged their sons to study law and medicine rather than divinity
because of the low financial returns for clerics. Rainolds echoed
these complaints, warning that inadequate livings forced educated
persons to seek employment elsewhere or distracted them, because
of financial worries, from their duties. The long-term result, said
Robert Temple, would be the decay of the universities as good students sought education and careers on the Continent. Parker thought
he saw evidence of this displacement as early as 1570, when he informed Elizabeth that at Cambridge there were "not two men in the
whole able or willing to read the lady Margaret's lecture, although
preachers they have many, but I fear divers of small consideration."[41]
In reality, the Elizabethan period did not experience a serious "brain
drain" to the Continent, except for Catholic students, for those who
studied abroad regularly returned, and few of these studied divinity.

Perhaps over no other issue were proposals for reform so complex,
because of the entanglement of political, religious, social, and economic factors. In visitations, bishops manifested concern over the financial abuses inherent in lay patronage. The prime example comes
from Grindal's 1576 visitation articles for the province of Canterbury,
for it illustrates the complexity of the problem facing the bishops:

Whether any minister or priest presented to any benefice in this diocese have
covenanted, promised, or practised to or with the patron thereof, or any other
person or persons that had the advowson or gift of the same benefice, or with
any person or persons on his or their behalf, to give to him or his friend any
sum of ready money for presenting him to the same; or have offered by promise or bond any lease, either of the whole benefice, limiting the rent far under
the just value, or of the mansion-house, glebe-lands, or any portion of the tithes

and fruits of the same benefice, receiving little or nothing therefor; or suffering the patron, or any other person that presented him, to have his own tithes within the benefice free unto himself; or else have granted some yearly pension, or other yearly commodity to him, his child, servant or friend, for preferring him to the same benefice; or otherwise have suffered him to make a gain by any colour, deceit, simoniacal pact in bestowing the said benefice?

The clarity and scope of this article imply considerable experience with patrons whose ingenuity to reap profits from an investment prompted increased judicial scrutiny from the episcopal bench. Visitation articles attempted to eliminate related abuses, including vacant livings. The most progressive attempt to reform patronage abuses was launched by William Overton, bishop of Coventry and Lichfield. After laying the decay of sufficient maintenance for ministers at the feet of corrupt patrons, he stipulated that in his diocese every patron and nominee for a benefice must appear before the bishop, the chancellor, or the chancellor's deputy, and at least four other preachers, who would examine the candidate's learning. The boldness in his plan was the new requirement that each nominee serve the parish for one month before returning to the bishop for institution to the living, if the parishioners were satisfied.[42] In part this plan was a response to Presbyterian and Separatist calls for a congregational role in the selection of ministers, but it is also evidence of the episcopal conviction that reforms in the patronage system were needed if the churches were to be served by qualified men.

Additional reforms were proposed. Sandys advocated that bishops who admitted candidates to livings in return for the financial gain of patrons be removed from office and the patrons stripped of their patronage rights. The Glamorgan preacher Lewis Thomas implied that such patrons should be excommunicated. More controversial was the suggestion that smaller livings be combined to provide an income sufficient to attract qualified clergy. This was proposed in the 1563 Parliament; it was also advocated by Josias Nichols in 1602, who coupled the proposal with the idea of redeeming impropriations (thus ironically foreshadowing Archbishop William Laud's plan). But combining smaller benefices directly affected the property rights of lay patrons, and Bishop Cooper felt this could not be done: "Nowe to attempt the matter, by making a law for that purpose, woulde be occasion of so great troubles and alterations, as would draw with them more inconueniences, then would stand with the safe state of this common weale." Rather than risk revolution by tampering with property, he preferred to tolerate unqualified ministers as long as they were godly and capable of catechizing. In the diocese of Chi-

chester, Bishop Curteys amalgamated several benefices, but the resulting incomes still were hardly adequate. He proposed to the Privy
Council that "the help whearof consisteth in the Bishop & his Chaun-
cellour who assisted by your honours may very muche mend it partly
by vniting partly by making vp stipends for these my parishes & allowing soom large portions owt of ye benefices whear vnlearned men
or non residensaries bee."[43]

In Parliament, proposals to reform the patronage system fared
poorly. The Commons in March 1563 gave two readings to a Lords'
bill empowering bishops to unite parish churches in cities and corporate towns with incomes less than £24 *p.a.* On 9 April, a new bill
to unite churches in boroughs or towns with incomes under twenty
marks *p.a.* received a first reading, but the following day was Easter
eve and the first session ended. The second session did not commence
until 1566, by which time reformers (perhaps Puritans) were ready
to introduce six bills in the Commons, five of which dealt directly
or indirectly with patronage. As a matter of strategy the bills' proponents decided initially to seek passage only of the first bill (involving statutory confirmation of the Articles of Religion). The queen's
opposition finally led to the dissolution of Parliament, leaving the
patronage quagmire unchanged. Efforts resumed in 1571, but only
one bill concerned with patronage was passed, the bill against simony
known as "An Acte touching Leasses of Benefices and other Ecclesiasticall Lyvynges with Cure." After its first reading in the Commons,
Thomas Snagge spoke directly to the patronage problem, noting that
Catholics slandered Church of England ministers because of their
humble origins:

The Livings are detained by the Patrons from the Spiritual, in their own hands,
to their own private uses; whereas the first original of the creation of Patronages,
being considered, it appeareth that nothing is left to the Patron of right. The
manner of their original he shewed at large, and that the same was granted *Deo
& Ecclesiae*, and concluded that the Patron had nothing of worth or value, but a
bare nomination, if it be truly vsed; since that dealing sincerely, he is neither to
respect Commodity, Blood, Affection, Friendship, nor any thing else, but the
worth and sufficiency of the Man, *&c.*

The bill Snagge and his supporters got could not have satisfied them,
given the extent of their reforming desires, but it was a step in the
right direction. Because its key principles involve pluralism and nonresidency, it will be discussed in the next section.[44]

In the 1576 Parliament, a bill to provide relief for poor vicars and
curates was not completed before the session ended. The same bill
apparently was revived without success in 1581. Before the Christmas

recess in 1584, a new bill was introduced in the Commons to require that impropriate parsonages be used for godly and charitable
purposes, but it met a kindred fate. Patronage was raised again in the
1586-87 Parliament in the discussion of the sweeping bill for religious reform proposed by Sir Anthony Cope, the heart of which espoused Presbyterian polity. The discussion that surrounded this bill
included recognition of the importance of preaching and a learned
ministry, as well as the dangers of nonresidency and corrupt patrons.
The crown's counterattack came in speeches by Sir Christopher
Hatton, Sir Thomas Egerton, and the Puritan Sir Walter Mildmay.
Hatton objected that Cope's bill would transfer patronage from laymen to the presbyteries; "it toucheth us all in our inheritances," and
intends deliberately "to draw from us, maugre our heads, our impropriations." The expenses of Presbyterian pastors, doctors, deacons,
and elders, he continued, would require the return of church lands
that had been secularized. Hatton's conservatism made these views,
which he apparently borrowed from Bancroft, palatable enough, but
it was harder for Mildmay. Admitting that there were many "evill
disposed Patrons" who placed unworthy men in benefices and ought
to be punished, he reminded reformers of the work of conscientious
patrons, without whom, he might have added, the Puritan cause
would not prosper. Elizabeth's resolute opposition overcame all, and
the abuses of patronage remained unreformed. A bill to support
a learned ministry never received a first reading in the 1589 Parliament.[45]

Royal resistance, coupled with members' fears of the financial repercussions, blunted the thrust for the reform of patronage through
Parliament. Other interest groups had a stake in the system and opposed significant changes. The universities relied partly on impropriations to maintain colleges and scholars. Considering the necessity
of such support for ministerial students, Rainolds proposed that the
rents from impropriate parishes be reserved for the universities, with
the remainder used for pastors in those parishes. "I speake not so
much for those that publikely our Uniuersitie hath, to be let by
Conuocation, whereof the greater part hath shewed well already
them selues to bee of this minde: as for those that priuately belong
to our Colledges, to be lett by the heades thereof and the fellowes."
The towns too controlled a share of the impropriations, sometimes
using them to finance the salaries of officials or the activities of the
councils and guilds. Such practices incensed Woolton, who claimed
that in many corporate towns, out of a living worth 200 marks *p.a.,*

a preacher received £20, a curate £10, and a schoolmaster £10, with the remainder going to secular uses.[46]

The bishops too had a heavy stake in impropriations. Elizabeth's first Parliament gave her statutory authority (1 Eliz. I, c. 19) to appropriate bishops' lands in exchange for impropriate tithes or other property of a nominally equivalent amount, thus committing bishops to patronage and impropriations. In St. David's diocese, nearly all revenues derived from impropriate tithes. Reliance on such income placed bishops at a double disadvantage, for impropriations were difficult to increase to keep pace with inflation, and they provided funds to prelates at the expense of adequate incomes for some parochial clergy. In practice, the bishops could have used the patronage power associated with these tithes to appoint qualified men to benefices, but such was not always the case. Howson plausibly suggested that corrupt appointments by bishops were due to debts, stemming from the fees imposed by the state for their own appointments.[47]

Neither the crown nor its principal servants wished to see the patronage system terminated, in part because it was a major financial undergirding for episcopacy, and because they found it advantageous to harness episcopal involvement for their own purposes. Cecil in 1570 sought to persuade Nicholas Bullingham, bishop of Lincoln, to bestow the advowson of the prebend of Faringdon on his own nominee, an Oxford scholar. He wrote (and then scratched out): "I know my L[ord] that you haue kinsmen and Chaplaines of your own who you wold provide for/ and yet it may please you to think that a frend som time may be as worthie to be well considered." Cecil and his son Robert diverted episcopal revenues into private pockets, including their own, and knew the importance of maintaining bishops' patronage rights for the latters' fiscal solvency. Retaining control of the benefices also was important to the crown and its servants if Puritanism was not to get out of hand. The situation is illustrated in Sussex, where control of patronage was a factor in keeping West Sussex under Anglican control. In the diocese of Chichester in 1579, of 81 advowsons, 42 were in the possession of the queen and ecclesiastical persons or corporations. (The queen held 11, the bishop of Chichester 14, the dean and chapter 12, and other ecclesiastical corporations and persons 5.) In the archdeaconry of Lewes, where Puritanism was stronger, 63 of 79 patrons in 1603 were laymen.[48]

Puritans, too, profited from the patronage, though the *significant* benefits were less financial than political. The Dudley brothers, earls of Leicester and Warwick, did much for the Puritan cause by the patronage of such men as John Field and Thomas Cartwright, though Anglicans also were among their beneficiaries. Sir Francis Walsingham was another noteworthy Puritan patron. Burghley even extended his support to Walter Travers. At least six of the approximately two dozen clerics Sir Nicholas Bacon appointed to livings in Suffolk and Norfolk were Puritans. Francis Russell, earl of Bedford, was praised by Thomas Sparke for being a worthy patron of the clergy; his support was especially important in the West Country, and Woolton owed his elevation to the see of Exeter to him. Bedford's funeral sermon was dedicated by Sparke to another Puritan patron, Arthur Lord Grey of Wilton, whom he described in 1593 as "the honorablest & most louing and faithfull patrone, that euer poore minister of my condition lost." One of those aided by Lord Grey was James Stile, rector of St. Margaret Lothbury, London. Many Puritan patrons were lesser figures, such as the Bristol draper William Prewett, who in 1594 left an advowson purchased for approximately £150 to the parishioners of St. Nicholas' church, Bristol, to enable them to continue having Puritan preachers. Another was Thomas Aldersey, a Cheshire-born London haberdasher who purchased the tithes of Banbury in 1594 and used them to endow a preachership and curacy in the town. The Haberdashers' Company administered the benefaction after he died and maintained a succession of Puritan clergy.[49]

Three other peers should be mentioned whose aid to Puritans strenghtened their cause. Robert third Lord Rich, was commended by Thomas Stoughton, a preacher at Billericay, Essex, and East Bergholt, Suffolk, for his "singular care [in Essex] for the placing of godly and sufficient ministers in all places, where the patronage of benefices by the auncient lawes of this realme hath beene your right." His activities typify the contribution of the more enthusiastic Puritan patrons. His grandfather had amassed thirty-two advowsons in Essex. About 1581 Rich invited a former Cambridge classmate, Robert Wright, to be the chaplain at Rochford Hall. With Rich's help, Wright, who had been ordained by Cartwright, established a Puritan congregation there, to which the tolling of a bell summoned the local people from the (rival) parish church. In response to complaints of disorder, the queen commanded Aylmer to stop Wright and Rich. Aylmer was already incensed at the Riches because he had suffered physical abuse from Lord Rich's uncle for refusing to license Wright to preach in the diocese of London. At Aylmer's orders, Wright and Rich were imprisoned until September 1582, when Aylmer recommended their release after they subscribed to the *Book of Common Prayer*. Rich also was engaged in a controversy with William Rust,

Anglican vicar of Felstead, who was deprived that year of his simulta-
neous appointment as rector of Rayleigh, allegedly through Rich's
influence. Rust slandered Rich and was summoned to the quarter
sessions at Chelmsford in February 1583 for saying "that if the Lord
Riche might have his will to putte men out of their benefices he
wolde kepe their livings and have some serve the cure for little or
nothinge." Rust accused Rich of supporting Henry Greenwood, a
schoolmaster, and Mr. Rogers, probably the noted preacher Richard
Rogers, whom he cited as misliking the *Book of Common Prayer*.
Moreover, he charged, "there were none of the Lord Riche his neighbours but wolde be gladd if he were further from them, and that the
Lord Riche was in the Commission of the peace, but as a cypher in
agriment for he coulde doe nothinge."[50]

The zeal of Henry Hastings, earl of Huntingdon, was important to
the spread of Puritanism in the northern areas, especially Lancashire.
His chaplains included the Puritans Robert Monk, Robert Sparke,
and Richard Holdsworth, as well as the Anglicans Lancelot Andrewes
and John Favour. In 1560, he owned seven advowsons in Leicestershire, and subsequently added an eighth (at Loughborough). He had
ten additional livings in Devon and Somerset, but his mother had
granted away their presentation rights. He bought a Dorset living in
1572, and may have owned four livings in Hertfordshire, Wiltshire,
and Derbyshire. During his life he placed or maintained no less than
forty-four clergy, at least twenty-four of whom had studied at the
universities. Among them were the Puritans John Philpot, Richard
Spicer, Robert Sibthorpe, and William Saunderson. Huntingdon's
younger brother, Sir Francis Hastings, used his patronage power to
strenghten Puritanism by assisting such men as Sibthorpe, Robert
Dike, and Thomas Crane. The eminent Puritan John Stockwood aptly referred to Huntingdon as "my verie singular good Lord and maister." Some support for the Puritan cause came from Anglican patrons, such as Henry Stanley, early of Derby, who agreed with some
Anglican divines (such as Aylmer) that Puritan preachers could profitably be used to convert northerners from Catholicism. Derby patronized various Puritan ministers in the diocese of Chester, including John Caldwell, rector of Winwick, Oliver Carter, preacher at Manchester collegiate church, William Leigh, rector of Standish, Richard
Midgley, vicar of Rochdale, and Robert Eaton, vicar of Leigh.[51]

Although lay patronage was a supportive factor in the spread of
Puritanism, its patrons sometimes abused their power by appointing
unfit candidates to benefices. Sir Anthony Cooke, usually regarded as
a Puritan, named a man to the church at Chadwell (near Havering)

who failed to maintain (or perhaps repair) it and was in trouble for this on four separate occasions in the archdeacon's court in Essex. Moreover, he failed to hold the required Wednesday services and was finally excommunicated. Another case involved Jonas Wheler, curate of Hanwell and schoolmaster at Banbury, a town under the influence of the Presbyterian Sir Anthony Cope; Wheler was cited in 1584 for failure to perform required services on Wednesdays and Fridays, though his actions may have stemmed from principle, not dereliction. A notorious case involved Sir Nicholas Bacon, who appointed two lay servants as prebendaries of Norwich, one of whom served in his household and the other "in the face of the whole city." It incensed Parker enough to complain to Sir Nicholas' wife, Lady Anne Bacon. Such examples notwithstanding, the importance of Puritan patrons was unintentionally acknowledged by the Anglican Richard Turnbull. Failing to grasp the fervency of conviction that motivated most Puritan clergy, he attributed their zeal to a willingness to please their patrons: "Let them live of their lawfull vocations; let not them like beggerly Friers, crouch and creepe for a peece of money vnto men; let them keep the liberty of their tongues, without feare of their benefactours, to vtter the truth indifferently: . . . let them leaue off the pleasing of penny fathers, for a morsell of bread, or a good meales meate, to slaunder their brethren." [52]

Lay patronage thus produced a host of abuses in the Elizabethan church, yet was harnessed by men of conflicting persuasions to support their causes. All parties recognized the need for reform, but only Separatists favored total abolition, which opinion marked them as social revolutionaries. When Barrow averred that "Christ's servantes are now no longer wardes, neither are in this maner to be bought and sold, as . . . sheep in a faire or market," men must have wondered if an attack on wardship would follow. [53] Certainly the right of congregations to choose their ministers—the Separatist alternative to patron selection—was feared as a prelude to political democracy, which usually conjured up the specter of a concomitant social revolution. Even the Presbyterian plan to transfer patronage to the presbyteries met a storm of criticism from the landed classes. For social reasons, patronage had to stay.

(3) Pluralism and Nonresidency

These non-residents and plurality-men teach not, they know not, nor care for the people of their charge.

John Jewel, bishop of Salisbury[54]

[Many clergy] are hirelings, non residents, dumbe dogges, going a whooring (not after many women, which the world would detest) but after manie benefices.

Edward Dering[55]

The economic plight of many Elizabethan clerics was manifested not only by the flourishing market in impropriated tithes and advowsons but also by the prevalency of pluralism and nonresidency. The social consequences of these practices were unqualified clergy or, in many parishes, the absence of an effective guide to social conduct and religious belief. Although concerned Anglican ministers condemned these abuses as vigorously as did Puritans, the latter reaped the most from the propaganda campaign against the abuses.

Despite abundant legislation against both practices, abuses were prevalent. At the visitation of Exeter in 1561, it was discovered that there were six vacant parishes, ten resident incumbents, and one nonresident; all eleven were pluralists, but none preached. In the archdeaconry of Chichester in 1579, of the rectors whose status is known, 38 were resident, 6 partially resident (having amalgamated parishes where their churches were within half a day's journey), 18 nonresident, and 28 pluralists. Of the vicars, 38 were resident, 3 partially resident, 6 nonresident, and 9 pluralists; of the curates and readers, 36 were resident, 3 partially resident, 1 nonresident and 4 pluralists. The sizeable percentage of resident vicars, curates, and readers looks promising until one recalls that some were unqualified. Looking elsewhere, 46% of the London clergy were pluralists in 1586, while in the diocese of York the visitation of 1590 resulted in 15 convicted pluralists and 9 convicted nonresidents. Approximately one-third of all Lancashire benefices were held by men who were not resident in 1590. Of the 484 clergy in the diocese of Norwich in 1593, 23.1% were pluralists, all but two with two benefices each. A survey of nine counties in 1586 indicated that 565 parsons in 1,933 livings were nonresident. In the diocese of Lincoln, 77 of the 466 parish clergy were officially recognized as pluralists in 1576. The situation in this diocese worsened, as there were 140 pluralists in 1585, though this number dropped to 90 in 1603. In the diocese of Canterbury, 58 of the 153 parochial incumbents were pluralists in 1569.[56]

Helpful as the statistics are, they do not convey a complete picture of what pluralism and nonresidency meant to parishioners. In 1568, Dr. William Turner, dean of Wells, had been absent from the cathedral for the past three years. At Thorp-Arch, Yorks., in 1567

there had been no sermons for the preceding twenty years. In Lancashire where the best benefices allegedly were held by nonresidents,
William Whitlock, possessing a dispensation for pluralism, was absent
almost continuously from 1559 to 1583 without providing for sermons. The rector of Eccleston, who was also a chaplain to the earl of
Derby, was not resident from his institution in 1563 throughout the
Elizabethan era. In a similar case, the rector of Winwick, a pluralist,
was not resident from 1576 on, and a parish clerk held sway from
1593 to 1596. An unsavory character, the clerk conducted burials
illegally, had a bastard by a cousin, lived with another woman, piped
and danced during services, and ridiculed a curate who tried to read
the liturgy.[57]

In the Midlands John Holme, vicar of North Clifton, Notts., was
presented in 1567 for nonresidency; he had failed to preach in three
years. The pluralist Christopher Parker, vicar of Mansfield, Notts.,
and Tattershall, Lincs., had not preached his quarterly sermons for
two years when he was presented in 1567. The vicar of Longstanton,
Cambs., had in 1564 been absent from his cure for twenty years
while serving as a canon of St. Paul's, London; his church was in
ruins. In East Anglia as late as 1597, 8 churches in Norfolk had no
quarterly sermons, 88 lacked monthly sermons, and 17 had no homilies. At the same time, 6 in Suffolk had no homilies and 42 were
without monthly or quarterly sermons. In Sussex the parson of
Barnham enjoyed an income of £40 *p.a.* but was not resident and allowed his curate only £6 *p.a.* (increased to £8 in 1585); the church
wardens did not know his name. The vicar of Eastbourne and Burwash in 1585 was a vicar choral at Chichester Cathedral and had not
seen his parishioners more than once in two years, and his curate at
Burwash was an uneducated man who pursued a base occupation.
The parson at Herstmonceux was present so seldom that few parishioners recognized him, while the vicar at Rye had been gone so many
years that few could recall his name.[58]

Some Puritan clergymen, too, were guilty of nonresidency and
pluralism. Among Puritans cited for nonresidence were Adam Rose,
vicar of Gargrave, Yorks. (1578), John Frewen, rector of Northam,
Sussex, Thomas Hunt, rector of Cotgrave, Notts. (1596), and Henry
Ducket, also rector of Cotgrave, Notts. (1596).[59] In 1590, Peter
White, the Puritan vicar of Poulton, Lancs., was away from his parish
but made no provision for services at his chapel at Bispham, and
John Caldwell, the Puritan rector of Winwick, Lancs., preferred to
preach to the household of the earl of Derby and the church at Mob-
berley, Ches. The Puritan pluralists included William Alred, vicar of

Ruddington (1572-73) and rector of Colwick, Notts. (1569-1627), Thomas Beckingham, vicar of Barnby by Newark (1566-76), rector of Winthorpe (1569-73), and rector of Bilsthorpe, Notts. (1573-99), Robert Blackwood, vicar of Walesby (1576-91), vicar of Rotherham (1577), and rector of Kirkton, Notts. (1585-1603), and John Savage, whose positions included rector of St. Michael, Sutton Bonington, Notts. (1581-1620), and rector of South Sheepy, Leics. (1586-1604). Even in Lancashire, where the struggle against conservative forces was intense, Puritan ministers sometimes were lax in performing their duties. Of the twenty-four Puritan vicars and rectors in Elizabethan Lancashire, ten were pluralists, and no fewer than twenty-three of the forty Puritan clergy in this diocese were accused of pastoral neglect of some kind. The Puritan incumbents of Bolton, Poulton, Standish, and Winwick were normally absent in the 1590s. The vicar of Eccles held three posts in the deanery of Manchester, and the curate of Oldham had a benefice in Nottinghamshire that he visited. Edward Fleetwood, rector of Wigan, was not resident in 1578, did not provide curates for his chapels, and was remiss in catechetical responsibilities. In 1601, only one of the seven clerics at Manchester College preached.[60] No attempt has been made, however, to examine every English parish throughout the Elizabethan period to determine the extent to which Puritans were guilty of nonresidency and pluralism.

The Puritan attack on pluralism was multifaceted. Dering condemned pluralities as "drunken dregs of Popish abhominations" and called for their abolition in his 1570 sermon before the queen. Edward Bush called for their abrogation in a sermon at Paul's Cross in 1571. If one excluded dumb dogs and nonresidents, Digges believed, England would have ten Puritan ministers for every formalist, and he argued (erroneously) that one characteristic of a Puritan was an aversion to multiplying benefices. Nichols stressed that each minister was bound to one charge, to teach and serve his congregation, and not to "lie in a cathedrall Church or in the Vniuersitie, or dwell in some towne like a Gentilman, and ioyne benefice to benefice, and liuing to liuing, passing his time in wealth and pleasure and his flocke 20. 30. 40. or 100. miles of[f]." Thomas Wood asked the earl of Warwick in 1576 not to defend pluralists, who were responsible for "pore sellie sheep" perishing from want of spiritual care. It was a common complaint.[61]

Anglicans tended to defend limited pluralism, though Stephen Bateman condemned it outright. Archbishop Parker generally disliked pluralities but, given the bleak economic picture facing the clergy, he preferred them to having ministers lose social esteem or be unable to

provide hospitality. Responding to the Presbyterians, Matthew Sutcliffe placed beyond criticism the prerogative of the queen to bestow
multiple benefices on her own chaplains, but others he restricted to
a maximum of two benefices. Richard Hooker elaborated this point,
which was the official Anglican position:

The household chaplains of men of honour or in great office [and] the brethren and sons of lords temporal or of knights if God shall move the hearts of such
to enter at any time into holy orders, may obtain to themselves a faculty or license to hold two ecclesiastical livings though having cure, any spiritual person
of the Queen's council three such livings, her chaplains what number of promotions herself in her own princely wisdom thinketh good to bestow upon them.

In effect Anglicans argued that pluralist rights were directly associated with the maintenance of the social hierarchy.[62]

Additional arguments Anglicans used to defend pluralities included the need to bestow multiple benefices to lure learned men. When
the bishop of Chichester sought Henry Blackstone (Blaxton), D.D.,
formerly of Clare Hall, Cambridge, and the schoolmaster at Higham
Ferrers, Northants., he offered to make him prebendary of Highleigh,
rector of West Thorney, and vicar of Cocking, Sussex, and allowed
him to serve as master of the school at Chichester Cathedral, vicar-
general, and commissary. (Blackstone did have to provide for nine
children.) Adam Hill, prebendary of Salisbury, in a sermon at Paul's
Cross in 1593, justified pluralities against the attacks of Martin Marprelate by pointing to the right of a noble or gentleman to accumu-
late benefices. The most substantial reasons in defense of pluralism
were provided by Whitgift, in response to an attempt in the Commons in 1584 to establish reforms. The bill, he said would strike at
the royal prerogative; reduce crown revenues; lead to an uneducated
ministry by depriving learned men of a due reward; lead to the abolition of divinity degrees (which the radicals desired); fail to recognize that England had less than 600 educated men for its more than
8,800 benefices; deprive governors of colleges of the benefices with
which they supported themselves; and render members of cathedral
chapters unable to provide hospitality in cathedral towns. The primary thrust of the Anglican defense of pluralism was contained in
Whitgift's letter to the bishop of Ely in 1575, noting that unless
men could be pluralists there would be a beggarly clergy and the decay of learning and religion.[63] Short of a substantial infusion of funds
into ministerial livings by the state, pluralists had to be tolerated if
the clergy were to fulfill their social and religious responsibilities.

Whitgift's observation about the shortage of trained clergy was true, but the reaction to the shortfall was varied. Whitgift believed that if the income from benefices was properly used, there would be more livings than could be supplied with able ministers. Yet Puritans claimed that nearly 200 graduates at Oxford and 140 at Cambridge lacked livings. From the standpoint of simple vacancies, there were always openings to fill, and in this sense the Puritans were wrong. But the crucial point is that the income from benefices was not being directed in sufficient amounts to attract educated clergy, even when their expectations were not great. Puritans pointed to the benefices and called for reforms aimed at the reduction of pluralities and the abuse of impropriations, whereas Anglicans argued that the financial condition of the benefices was so poor that pluralism was a fiscal necessity *and* that a reform of pluralism would be rendered ineffectual by a shortage of trained men. The crux of the argument was the Puritan contention that "there be . . . ynough worthie men, if they were sought after, both in the vniuersities & other where: but while men are suffered to runne and ride, and ketch before they fall, manye worthie men are passed ouer and not knowne; some are faine to be scholemaisters, & some (because of these troubles) change their studies."[64] Since in the Elizabethan period, the number of educated clergy did increase (to be discussed in the next chapter), Puritans had the better of the argument, but the availability of livings with decent incomes did not keep pace with the rise in qualified men, producing an alienated intelligentsia in the early Stuart era.

In Wales, the shortage of adequate ministers would have been acute if pluralism had been abolished and unfit men driven from the pulpit. This situation did not daunt Penry, who looked on most clergy in Welsh parishes as "vnsauerye salte." Although he wanted them ousted, he proposed that the magistracy provide for them and their families to see that they were neither in want nor idle. To deal with the clerical shortage, he recommended that people within a reasonable distance of a parish with a qualified minister go there for services. Others were to attend their parish churches, each of which would be provided with a discreet man to read Scripture and say prayers prepared with the advice of the godly learned. Preachers alone would be allowed to minister the sacraments. [65] This plan was similar to the solution advocated in 1560 for Scotland in somewhat similar circumstances. Penry had faith in the availability of godly clergy once the need became known and places were made available.

Pluralism often led to nonresidency, the subject of a torrent of Puritan criticism. Dering masterfully linked nonresidency to loathsome vagrancy, asserting that Satan has "giuen liberty to all that will to be *Non residens*, to forsake their charge, to goe where they will, like maisterles hounds, to fill the common wealth with worse then any idle or vagabond persons." Dering's campaign sometimes got him in trouble, as in 1573 when the Privy Council investigated, though witnesses in his behalf testified that he had become concerned with a Mr. Blogge, who was not serving his cure. When Dering inquired why he was derelict in his responsibilities, Blogge retorted that he was too busy writing a book for the archbishop of Canterbury. Kindred frustration led the Puritan Robert Cawdry—who had been presented to the living of South Luffenham, Rutland, through Burghley's influence and who was deprived sixteen years later for criticizing the *Book of Common Prayer*—to blast bishops for tolerating nonresidency despite their criticism of it. Penry wholeheartedly agreed. Henry Smith, lecturer at St. Clement Danes, London, thought nonresidence, bribery, and usury were odious sins because they were harmful and because their capacity for financial gain caused them to be regarded as occupations rather than sins. In 1579 an audience at Paul's Cross heard John Stockwood deplore "all Strawberie Preachers, as the good old Father *Latimer* somewhere termeth them, for that like vnto strawberries, they come in the Pulpit but once a yere." Nichols accused such preachers of being "a companie of idle men in their silkes and veluetts . . . [who] fare delitiouslie." The truth of such indictments was widely believed among Puritans.[66]

Anglicans were seemingly caught in a bind by the problem of nonresidency. As an abuse it hindered their program of religious and social work, yet to criticize it too vehemently might encourage Puritan and Separatist reformers. On 19 June 1582, Edmund Scambler, bishop of Peterborough, petitioned the queen to enforce the ecclesiastical statutes since he found himself unable to compel his prebendaries to remain resident. Bishop Jewel condemned nonresident clerics, whether educated or not, for failing to instruct the people, and Hooker spoke of a threefold blot on the clergy, consisting of ignorance, the insatiable quest for spiritual preferments, and the "unconscionable" absence from cures. The critical term is "unconscionable," for although Hooker recognized the dangers in nonresidency, he considered it reasonable to support men attending the universities and serving in bishops' households. The latter "schools of gravity, discretion and wisdom, preparing men against the time that they come to reside abroad, are in my poor opinion even the fittest places that any ingenuous mind can wish to enter into between departure from private study and access to a more public charge of souls, yea no less expedient for men of the best sufficiency and most maturity in knowledge, than the universities themselves are for the ripening of such as be raw." For Sutcliffe the storm over nonresidency was much ado about nothing. No one, he said, defends it, and there are abundant laws condemning the practice. Let violators be punished, but if men are absent for lawful causes, do not blame them but the "skittish puritanes, that . . . are like malecontent and mutinous persons still wandring vp and downe to places where they haue nought to doe."[67]

Although dispensations for nonresidency were issued in numbers too large for the well being of the church and the fulfillment of its social obligations, the bishops tried to reform abuses. The 1571 canons prohibited ministers from having more than two benefices, and these had to be within twenty-six miles of each other. As archbishop of York, Grindal revealed his concern in stipulations attached to grants for nonresidency. Richard Jaques, for instance, was allowed to hold two benefices if he would preach thirteen sermons a year in each and provided hospitality in each at least two months a year. In the case of Richard Laing, also in the diocese of Lincoln, sixteen sermons a year were required. Shortly after Grindal became archbishop of Canterbury he submitted a proposal to the Privy Council to reform the Court of Faculties. The proposal included the reform of pluralities, which he wanted only for bachelors of divinity or approved preachers, on condition that the distance between benefices not exceed twenty miles, and that at the benefice at which the minister did not dwell, he provide at least thirteen sermons and eight weeks of hospitality a year. Otherwise, nonresidence would be tolerated for only short periods, such as to recover health. His recommendations were approved by the Privy Council on 20 June 1576, but his fall from royal favor ended his program of projected reforms.[68]

Visitation articles regularly inquired about clerical residency as well as pluralism,[69] and the episcopal injunctions manifest a determination to reform. Whitgift's injunctions for Worcester Cathedral (1577) fine a prebendary 20s. for each assigned Sunday on which he fails to preach or to provide a licensed deputy to preach for him. In 1583 the injunctions of the bishop of St. David's required that each minister be resident in his benefice or, if he had a dispensation for nonresidency, provide a substitute approved by the ordinary. The advertisements for the diocese of Coventry and Lichfield (1584) include Overton's provision that pluralists (who must possess dispensations) are to provide curates who can pass an examination by the bishop or his officers. The 1591 episcopal orders for the province of York include a proviso exempting some nonresidents from providing curates for fiscal reasons: "*Item*, all non-residents to be called home and constrained to residence upon their charge, so far as the law will warrant. And all those who be lawfully absent from their benefices, to maintain . . . a godly preacher there during the time of their absence, at the discretion of their ordinary, if the living be able to bear it." Despite such actions, Puritans remained dissatisfied with the slowness and limited extent of the reform program. In any case the bishops were prevented from a total reform because as holders of impropriated tithes and livings *in commendam*, they were prime practitioners of pluralism and nonresidence. William Hughes, bishop of St. Asaph, for example, held an archdeaconry and sixteen benefices *in commendam*, and John Scory, bishop of Hereford, presented three sinecure prebends to his wife and another to his son.[70]

In Parliament discontent with pluralism and nonresidency periodically erupted in demands for reform. In the 1566 Parliament, the Commons gave two readings to a bill proposing to avoid pluralities, but the bill apparently was sidetracked by the introduction of a code of reforming bills on 5 and 6 December, one of which ("Bill C") dealt with pluralism and nonresidency. Consideration of the latter was postponed to the 1571 Parliament, where it did not proceed further than a first reading in the Lords. Nonresidency also was raised in this Parliament in connection with a bill introduced in the Commons by the Puritan George Carleton to ban dispensations contrary to the word of God. Francis Alford, a civil lawyer, spoke against the bill, partly because dispensations for nonresidency sometimes were essential, as in the case of ministers dispatched in ambassadorial work. William Fleetwood, the recorder of London, expressed doubts about nonresidency on the grounds "that Livings are given to Ministers for the instructing the King and his People, and for the keeping of House, and other deeds of Charity: all [of] which, if they were absent by dispensation, he inferred must of necessity be neglected." A redrafted version of the bill was passed but did not proceed beyond a second reading in the Lords. The reformers did succeed in passing "An Acte touching Leasses of Benefices and other Ecclesiasticall Lyvynges with Cure" (13 Eliz. I, c. 20), which specified that leases of unimpropriated benefices with cure would lapse unless the incumbent were resident and serving the cure, apart from allowable absences not in excess of eighty days a year. Each person holding two benefices was required to reside in one and provide a curate for the other, with the curate allowed a maximum absence of forty days a year.[71]

Pressure for reform continued in Parliament, with the Commons in 1581 demonstrating an interest to join the bishops in seeking royal action. The Commons delegated a committee consisting of Mildmay,

Walsingham, Hatton, and Dr. Thomas Wilson to treat with the prelates regarding the shortage of qualified clergy, the excessive use of
excommunication, the commutation of penance, and the prevalency
of dispensations and pluralities. The committee reported that they
found the bishops ready to join them in beseeching Elizabeth to
intervene. The queen, however, acquiesced only to commit the problems of her clergy for resolution, and in fact submitted the matter to
Archbishop Sandys, who consulted Whitgift and four other bishops.
Their response did not satisfy advocates of major reform, who returned to the problems of nonresidency and pluralism in the 1584-85
Parliament.[72]

Various Puritan members came to the new Parliament with petitions from their counties demanding reforms in the church. On 16
December Mildmay moved that a committee be appointed in the
Commons to examine the petitions and reduce them to articles that
could be sent to the Lords as the basis for joint action. Of the sixteen
grievances agreed upon by the House committee, two were directly
involved with nonresidence and pluralism: (1) Because licenses for
nonresidency and pluralities caused many laity to be deprived of religious instruction, their use should cease; and (2) no one currently
in possession of a license for nonresidency should be permitted to
use it unless he provides a suitable preacher—not merely a reader—to
serve in his stead. Burghley and Whitgift gave the Lords' response to
the reforming articles in February 1585. Whitgift was responsive to
those dealing with nonresidency and pluralism, promising with regard
to the former that "it should be holpen and redressed as soon as
might be." He claimed that he personally granted dispensations for
nonresidency only to those eighty or more years of age. Life pluralities would no longer be allowed, and temporary dispensations would
insist on the service of competent curates in benefices where the incumbent was absent. In conclusion, Whitgift, perhaps sensing the dissatisfaction in the Commons with his total response, urged members
to think well of the bishops, "if not in respect of their places, yet for
Charity sake, and for that some of them were Preachers when many
of the House of Commons had been in their Cradles." Numerous
bills were introduced to end the grievances, including a bill promoted
by Sir Francis Knollys against pluralities and nonresidence. The clergy
was opposed, hence Convocation submitted a petition to the queen,
opposing its passage, Among the reasons advanced were that the
crown's prerogative would be breached and its revenue impaired; the
study of divinity in the universities would be adversely affected;
ministers would be deprived of livings they lawfully possessed; the

clergy would be beggared; and an unlearned ministry would result. The bill, in the face of this hostility, did not pass.[73]

A bill proposed by Sir Anthony Cope in the 1586-87 Parliament would have ended pluralism and nonresidency, but the queen blocked its passage. Undaunted, the reformers resumed the struggle in the 1589 Parliament when Henry Apsley, Puritan member for Hastings, attacked pluralities and nonresidence, and offered a bill for their reformation. After being rewritten in committee, it was passed and sent to the Lords. The bill allowed the holding of two benefices if the distance between them was no more than three miles and if their value did not exceed £8 *p.a.* each. Existing pluralists were barred from accepting new benefices without first resigning their original ones. Except for those serving the crown, residence was mandatory, and a fine of £10 a month was imposed on those who were absent for a total of three months a year. Pluralists were to be fined £5 per month if they failed to provide preachers where they did not personally reside. No dispensations from these provisions would be allowed. In the Lords, a full debate over these proposals ensued, but the bill received only one reading, meeting heavy opposition from Whitgift and his supporters, especially on grounds of a shortage of qualified men. They also objected to the £8 per parish, with a £16 maximum, arguing that such a sum could not maintain a learned divine, and the number of educated men entering the ministry would decrease.[74]

A final Elizabethan assault on pluralism was mounted in the 1601 Parliament as an amendment to 21 Henry VIII, c. 13. The crux of the amending bill was a prohibition of pluralism for all benefices worth at least £8 *p.a.*, and the cessation of all pluralities in violation of this principle. Dr. Daniel Dunne, a Whitgift man, civilian lawyer, and dean of Arches, assailed the bill because of its equalitarian principles. There was "no reason that men of unequal desert should be equally Beneficed or equalized with the best." His argument was specious, for the abolition of pluralism would not alter the fact that individual livings had vastly disparate incomes, ranging from less than £5 *p.a.* to more than £100 *p.a.* Another Whitgift man and civilian lawyer, Dr. Thomas Crompton, demanded that the laity first be stripped of their plurality of offices and impropriations returned to the clergy. Without the pluralities *or* the impropriations, Crompton argued, the clergy could not maintain hospitality or support their families—a realistic argument. In retaliation, supporters of the bill blamed pluralism for the damnation of many souls and urged the clergy to provide leadership for its abolition. Dr. Francis James, another Whitgift supporter, retorted that the cessation of adequate livings for the clergy by the abolition of pluralities would lead to the refusal of able men to study divinity. Resuming the equality thesis, he contended that "to give the best Scholar but as great proportion as the meanest Artisan, or to give all alike, there is no equality." Speaking for the bill, David Waterhouse, an official in the Queen's Bench, favored applying a common law principle to the clergy, noting that secular officers forfeited their positions for absences in excess of eighteen days a year. Although the Whitgift people stressed the negative impact this bill would have on education, he observed that the most ignorant divines were pluralists. Perhaps the most telling point, which Thomas Harris made during the debates and Whitgift reiterated to Elizabeth, was that the bill impinged on the royal prerogative. By striking at her ability to regulate pluralities through the Court of Faculties, the bill reduced her authority. In committee, the bill was replaced by another whose provisions would have increased pluralities. Given a first reading, it disappeared, presumably because of intervention by the queen, who abhorred legislation affecting her prerogative.[75]

As in the case of lay patronage, Puritan reformers failed to achieve changes through Parliamentary legislation. Partly this failure was due to Elizabeth, who jealously guarded her authority, and partly to Whitgift, whose adamant opposition to the Puritans prevented a compromise and prompted opponents to advocate more extreme proposals to alter the church. Whitgift demonstrated his power in crushing the Presbyterian movement and suppressing reform endeavors such as the 1601 bill to abolish pluralities. In his judgment, pluralism was necessary to reward both educated clergy and those loyal to the ecclesiastic hierarchy. Yet he and the Puritans were one in desiring an educated clergy, adequately financed and devoted to spiritual and social responsibilities.[76] The crucial differences between them were not theological but regarded the means required for the church to fulfill its spiritual and social task. As Whitgift and his episcopal colleagues failed to achieve substantial redress of grievances, Puritan hostility mounted, manifesting itself in legislative campaigns and outbursts against prelatical pomp.

Faced with the need for an enlarged number of trained ministers, but unable to finance them without either a major infusion of state funds, which Elizabeth did not have, or a drastic redistribution of patronage, which the landed class would not accept, the only alternative left to the Anglican hierarchy was a radical reduction in their own incomes coupled with a crackdown on pluralities, nonresidence, the appointment of unfit clergy, simony, and the leaving of benefices vacant. The latter reforms met with resistance from many lay patrons and would have necessitated a unified campaign on the church's part with firm encouragement from the crown. But the church was not united, the queen was wary of impingement on her prerogative, and the crown's domestic and foreign problems prevented a reform effort that would have alienated the landed class. The Anglican hierarchy was left with the possibility of radically reducing their own incomes and thus their social perquisites. To do this would bring them closer to the equality they feared and despised. Moreover, it would reduce their ability to command respect, especially from the landed aristocracy. Whitgift thus kept a steady hand on the helm as he steered a course of gradualism in the troubled waters of Elizabethan society.

CHAPTER 2

The Social Behavior of the Clergy and the Anticlerical Reaction

To a considerable degree, educational qualifications and social behavior determined the effectiveness of the Elizabethan clergy. Apart from a few uncouth louts who would welcome a minister devoid of learning and morality as a good fellow and drinking companion, parishioners sought knowledge, ethical behavior, and spiritual qualities in their clergy. Ministers lacking such qualifications intensified a heritage of anticlericalism that extended back to Chaucer and beyond. Resentment against tithes sometimes contributed to this anticlericalism. Others reacted to ill-trained or overeducated clerics by asserting claims of spiritual inspiration as the sole qualification for the propagation of religious truth. Anticlericalism, the attack on tithes, and the spiritual challenge to formal education in divinity are themes normally associated with the 1640s and 1650s, but they were manifested in Elizabethan society as well.

(1) The Problem of Clerical Ignorance

There neither is, nor ever was, a more learned ministry in any nation under heaven.

Edwin Sandys, archbishop of York[1]

A greate many of oure ministers are so ignorant, that they hadde need to learn Catechismes themselues.

John Stockwood[2]

71

On the importance of an educated ministry, there was agreement. One Anglican regarded knowledge, eloquence, and holiness of life as necessities for a clergyman. Learning, Bishop Curteys asserted, was not merely desirable but was a necessary handmaid to the word of God; his episcopal colleague, Bishop Sandys, however, warned not to be overly impressed with learning, but to respect the message instead of the messenger. Pilkington charged that clergy ignorant of Scripture were dumb dogs who could not rebuke sin and blind guides who could not rule their flocks. "But if ye want one to keep a cur rather than a cure, to be a hunter or a falconer, to be an overseer of your workmen, to be your steward, or look to your sheep and cattle, to be your gardener, keep your orchard, or write your business, who is meeter for any of these businesses than Sir John Lacklatin?" Implicitly, Pilkington shifted the blame for uneducated clergy to lay patrons, where much of it undoubtedly belonged, and Jewel agreed.[3]

Repeatedly Puritans argued for an educated ministry. Laurence Chaderton, master of Christ's College, Cambridge, was upset that men entered the clerical vocation devoid of Latin, Hebrew, Greek, logic, rhetoric, and other pertinent disciplines. The Cambridge Puritan Robert Some, an advocate of Cartwright's views, likened learning without godliness to a gold ring in a swine's snout, whereas godliness without learning in a minister was "as a faire colour without light to shew it by, and as a goodly bell without a clapper." Digges saw utilitarian reasons for a learned clergy, who could increase the number of loyal Protestants in England, thus reducing the Catholic threat. Concerned for Wales, Penry urged Parliament to replace "dumbe" ministers with godly learned men.[4]

Given this recognition of learning's significance, the outcry against ignorant clergymen is hardly unexpected. In April 1581 Anthony Anderson, an Anglican, preached at Paul's Cross that the clergy in the countryside were mostly ignorant and idle or poor and needy. "Olde wilie Foxes," remonstrated J. Baxter, "such as whose loue to religion may be iustly suspected, are admitted into this great calling . . . : blinde guides are made ministers, such as haue no more knowledge then idolles of woode and stone." Cooper's response to Marprelate included an admission that there were numerous uneducated clergy in the Church of England: "That some lewde and vnlearned ministers haue bene made, it is manifest: I will not seeme to defend it," and urged all bishops to exercise care in ordaining ministers. Puritans were the most vociferous in their condemnation of uneducated clerics. Stockwood complained of great numbers of ignorant ministers, idle shepherds, and dumb dogs, who, Udall added, draw their parishioners to hell after them. "Yea, I woulde to God," grumbled Edward Hake, soon to become recorder of New Windsor, Berks., "that the number were not great of suche Godlesse Hipocrites, suche vnlearned loyterers, and verye pieuishe pelting Parasites, which for liuing sake haue intruded and thrust themselues into the Church." Edward Bush agreed with the Anglican Anthony Anderson that this problem was acute in the countryside, although the capital had a more able clergy. Penry sarcastically observed that by a learned ministry Anglicans meant only men who had memorized part of Alexander Nowell's catechism or Heinrich Bullinger's *Decades*. Puritans favored a university-trained clergy, but their attacks brought from their Anglican opponents charges that they lacked discretion, charity, and modesty.[5]

Catholics too used the accusation of an uneducated ministry in their polemics against the Church of England. From Louvain, Lewis Evans characterized Elizabethan clerics as rude and unlearned, "and for the most parte but poore labourers of handie craftes." If a parish had "any pastthrifte and rashe mate which colde but reade, such an vnrulie runneagate is nowe, not onlye, in the churche a reader, but also . . . a preacher and a pulpitte possessor." The annotations to the Rheims New Testament insist that bishops should exercise care not to ordain ministers without a thorough examination of their faith, learning, and behavior.[6]

The Catholic charge that Anglican clergy commonly were recruited from the laboring groups had substance; this indeed had been true of the pre-Reformation church (in contrast to the Elizabethan Catholic missionaries, who generally came from aristocratic backgrounds). Yet it was not unusual for Protestant ministers to come from business or professional families, and some were of gentle background who entered the pastoral vocation out of religious conviction or because their families used benefices to support younger sons. This happened, for example, in the case of John Culpepper of Wakehurst, rector of his family's parish church at Ardingly, Sussex. Despite recruits from these areas, many clerics came from baser backgrounds. An examination of ordination lists at Lincoln from 1555 to 1585 and the *Liber Cleri* of 1585 reveals that many nongraduate clergy came from such vocations as day laborers, servingmen, husbandmen, carpenters, glovers, shoemakers, fishermen, and tallow-chandlers. The situation in Essex in the 1580s was comparable. In his autobiography, Dr. Simon Forman, a physician and astrologer with anticlerical leanings, provides an example: "Ther was a certain minister named William

Ryddonte, *alias* Ridear, that by his trade and occupation was a cobler, but after Quen Maries dayes, when the lawe did turne, he was made a minister, and soe withalle became a scolmaster and teacher of children." Although he could read English well, he knew only a token amount of Latin that he picked up from his two sons who attended a free school.[7]

Archbishop Parker admitted that such practices existed in the first two years of Elizabeth's reign, but on 15 August 1560 he informed Grindal, bishop of London, that the uneducated men of base occupations whom they had been ordaining offended the laity because of their previous occupations and light behavior. Because such men were doing more harm than good, the archbishop admonished Grindal and the other bishops in the province of Canterbury to exercise discretion in admitting men of base occupations into the ministry. Henceforth such candidates must possess character references and some education, or at least have experience teaching children. Jewel subsequently defended such ordination practices against the Catholic apologist Thomas Harding, who castigated the Church of England for using cobblers as ministers, asserting that lowborn Protestants were better able to serve God than many Catholic priests and cardinals. "And what great wonder were it, if a good simple godly man were made a priest," seeing that Julius II, "a man utterly void both of learning and virtue, from a wherry-slave not long sithence became a pope?" John Walsall, rector of Eastling, Kent, and tutor to Francis Bacon, agreed with Jewel in a sermon at Paul's Cross in 1578, but cautioned men to remain content with their vocations "and not to leape of[f] from their stalles, and out of their shoppes and trades into the ministerie, to the offence of the godlie." The Puritan Laurence Chaderton demanded that all ignorant and ungodly ministers and readers leave the clerical vocation and enter occupations that they could in good conscience fulfill. Nevertheless, insufficient numbers of the landed, professional, and business groups were willing to enter the ministerial vocation because of the inadequate pecuniary rewards and perhaps declining social prestige. A decline in prestige, however, was not a universal phenomenon in the Elizabethan period, for some clergy enjoyed considerable status and popularity. Status was more important for Protestants because they married and had children for whom spouses had to be found, and because their role was to provide spiritual leadership, not serve as divine agents to perform the miracle of the mass.[8]

A related problem involved ministers from base occupations who continued to practice their trades because of insufficient income from their ecclesiastical positions. For practical reasons, the bishops were less concerned with this problem than with clergymen who left the ministry (as Puritans advocated) and assumed secular occupations. In Sussex, for example, no attempt seems to have been made to prohibit artisans and servingmen from plying their trades while they held benefices. One curate of Preston was a fisherman, and the vicar of Lynminster and curate of Warningcamp Chapel was a servingman. Other clerics were merchants, clothiers, drapers, tailors, mercers, glaziers, and husbandmen. William Overton, bishop of Lichfield and Coventry, ordained seventy ministers in one day, including shoemakers, tailors, and other artisans, who probably continued to practice their crafts as clergy. In the 1580s the parson of South Hanningfield, Essex, who had been a fishmonger, was a button maker, but he was also notorious as a careless minister and an alehouse haunter. Husbandry was popular as a supplementary vocation for clerics. The records of the episcopal visitation in the diocese of Norwich in 1597 show that Thomas Cheshier, rector of Nacton, Suffolk, "useth all kinde of husbandrye, as plowe, harrowe and Carte;" Edward Ketle, rector of Semer, Suffolk, "stamped crabbs" to make apple cider and labored at harvest time "in byndinge of oats without anie hatt on his head, or dublett on his back, but onelie in his hose and shirte;" and Robert Wattkinson, curate of Dunwich, Suffolk, practiced medicine. Such burdens made it more difficult to fulfill pastoral obligations and acquire theological learning, but those fortunate enough to possess a glebe had to exploit it themselves or lease it. These practices were not new to the Elizabethan church; the note to Leviticus 21 in the 1551 edition of Tyndale's Pentateuch specifies that priests tend to their vocation. The Rheims annotators, aware of what was happening in the Church of England, asserted that the practice of medicine, business, "or any other profane facultie and trade of life to gather riches" is forbidden. However, in cases where the honor of God, the growth of religion, the peace of the people, or the spiritual benefits of Christians necessitate, involvement in "worldly busines" is permissible.[9]

The Anglicans recognized the problem but reacted defensively to criticism. Bishop Cooper was emphatic that he did not oppose a godly, learned ministry, but to fill pulpits, he had to accept those with insufficient education. Cooper ordained Thomas Morley in 1573, though he was unacquainted with the Scriptures, on condition that he study the Bible; three years later, Morley was still so ignorant that Cooper refused to approve his presentation to a living. At Paul's Cross Gervase Babington, bishop of Llandaff, recognized that lack of clerical learning was due to financially inadequate livings, and Jewel admitted that superior remuneration led educated men to enter the legal and medical professions, forcing bishops to appoint inadequately trained ministers. Even where livings were sufficient to attract learned men, lay patrons sometimes bestowed them on unqualified candidates. An irate Stubbes deplored men who could "speake but little congrue latine, much lesse preach the word of God (nay would God they could read english well)" and who enjoyed plural livings while competent clergy lacked adequate maintenance.[10]

Anglicans felt that the general thrust of Puritan criticism regarding an uneducated clergy was unfair. Richard Turnbull attacked Puritan preachers, especially in London, who were "content to sell their brethren, their fellow Ministers; by condemning them of ignorance, by accusing them vppon falsely surmised suspition, by defaming their persons, and slaundering their names at their pleasures." In Wright's judgment, Puritans and Separatists would be better idle than using their learning to wreak dissension among the populace. Puritan criticism was misunderstood by Thomas Jackson, rector of Wye, Kent, who felt that many clerics were being accused of ignorance because their sermons were not replete with quotations in exotic languages. Faced with the proposal of lay advocates of reform, who called for a reduction in ecclesiastical lands to restore the clergy to apostolic simplicity and responsibility, Bishop Curteys insisted that there were many godly, learned ministers. One congregation, ironically, thought that its pastor was too educated: The parisioners of Eakring, Notts., accused their Puritan rector, George Higgin, of frequently omitting services because he was busy studying divinity![11]

The soundest defense of the Anglican position was made by Hooker. After stating the case for an educated clergy, he turned to what he conceived to be the real question, namely, the dilemma of a church confronted with an insufficient supply of learned men to fill every pulpit. To wait until enough candidates were available would mean letting thousands of souls "grow savage," depriving people of church services, letting children die unbaptized, withholding the Lord's supper from prospective communicants, and burying without Christian rites. As it was, there were places in England where people were ignorant of the Gospel. One woman first heard the account of Christ's sufferings with considerable distress, but

after some pause and recollection of her spirits, she asked where this was done, and when: it was answered, many thousand miles hence at Ierusalem, and a great while ago, about fifteene hundred yeares. Then (quoth she) if it was so farre off, and so long ago, by the grace of God it might proue a lye, and therein she comforted her selfe.

To prevent the spread of such ignorance, Hooker and his Anglican colleagues tolerated inadequately trained clergy.[12]

Various remedies were used to alleviate the situation. Efforts were made to require all parsons, vicars, curates, and stipendiary priests with less than an M.A. degree to study (in Latin and English or Welsh) a chapter a day in the New Testament. They also had to study a sermon a week in Bullinger's *Decades*. William Chaderton, bishop of Chester, allied with Puritans in his diocese to develop a scheme of exercises for the improvement of the theology, morals, and learning of the clergy, but three synods a year did not satisfy the Puritans, who favored a monthly exercise in each deanery. Archbishop Sandys supported similar synods, directed by archdeacons, on a quarterly basis throughout the province of York. Once again, however, too little was done and too slowly to satisfy Puritan demands.[13]

As the period progressed, the shared interest in an educated clergy helped to produce more university-trained men. On the eve of the Tudor period (1454-86), only 20% of the clergy in the diocese of Canterbury were university graduates, but by 1603 some 41% of the clergy in the province of Canterbury and 42.6% in the province of York had university degrees. The greatest improvement came in the middle and later years of the Elizabethan era. When Exeter was visited in 1561, none of the 11 incumbents had a degree. Of the 58 institutions to Exeter parishes between 1552 and 1602, 47 were listed as *clericus*, 8 were M.A.s, and 3 B.A.s, but 9 of the 11 degree holders appear after 1585, a period during which only 14 appointments were made. In the archdeaconry of Chichester in 1585, of the 118 clerics, 34 had university degrees, 21 others had attended a university, and 5 had been to a grammar school, but nearly half presumably could do little more than read and write English. Nearby in the archdeaconry of Lewes, the situation was better by 1603, when 43.3% of the incumbents and curates about whom there is information had university degrees. Yet as late as the early 1580s, there was only one university graduate in Chichester itself, and he was not licensed to preach.[14]

Conditions in the Midlands and East Anglia likewise improved. Between 1570 and 1580, 71% of the men instituted to Ely livings were university graduates or had attended a university. In the diocese of Lincoln, only 9.9% of those instituted to benefices had university degrees in the period 1540-1570, but this figure rose to 50.8% in the period 1578-1584. In this diocese 31.1% of the clergy had university degrees in 1585, contrasted with 54.6% in 1603. The diocese of Norwich was roughly comparable, with 40.9% of its clergy holding university degrees in 1592-93. Although these figures show progress, in many places the clergy remained ignorant. In the visitation of the archdeaconries of Leicester, and Lincoln and Stowe by Bishop Cooper in 1576, at a time when growth in the number of educated clergy had started, of the 906 clergy, 24.9% were ignorant of Latin and 22.7% were ignorant of virtually all book learning.[15]

Further north, there was improvement in some areas, though as late as 1599 the majority of the clergy in the diocese of Carlisle were unable to read English distinctly. The educational level of the clergy in the diocese of Durham began to improve in the 1570s, thanks especially to the work of Bishop Richard Barnes. A report to the Privy Council c. 1591 on Lancashire and Cheshire asserted that few preachers served there, and that most of the parsons were uneducated. During the tenure of William Downham as bishop of Chester, little was done to improve clerical learning. Between 1562 and 1569, he ordained 176 clergy from the diocese itself and not one had a university degree. From the diocese an average of 22 men a year were ordained by Downham for 17 years, but only 4 were university graduates. Piecemeal attempts were made to reform the situation, such as requiring a Manchester curate to attend grammar school and to learn a chapter of the New Testament each month. In another case, the Ecclesiastical Commission in 1565 ordered the rector of Ashton to study at Oxford for three years. William Chaderton launched a drive for more educated clergy when he succeeded Downham in 1579. Of the 80 men he and his successors ordained from the diocese of Chester between 1580 and 1603, 29 had university degrees. Still, as late as 1592 the sprawling diocese had only 103 clergy who had graduated from a university, which was less than a third of the total. The same situation prevailed in the diocese of York.[16]

The striking improvement in clerical education that began in the 1570s substantially paralleled the growth of Puritanism, with its cries for an educated ministry, suggesting that the bishops may have been partly motivated by these demands. Yet Anglicans were aware of the need for reform, and improvement was bound to come. The Puritans probably hastened the process.

(2) Education and the Ministerial Task

What be many Ministers of our time and Country, other then dumb dogs?

Edward Dering[17]

Dumbe dog is a great word in their mouths: that sermon where dumbe dog is
left out is not worth a pinne.

Leonard Wright[18]

The concern in Puritan circles for an educated, resident ministry was
a consequence of the conviction that the main responsibility of the
clergy was preaching. Emphasis on a liturgical service made it feasible
to use clerics who could do little more than read the service, including the homilies, so that "the drone of the homilies replaced the mut-
ter of the mass."[19] Preaching, however, required greater education
and talents, with the prospect of a more substantial pecuniary reward. Curates with meager stipends could hardly be expected to possess qualifications to preach, hence the demand for a preaching ministry called into question the practices of pluralism and nonresidency.
In addition to the social implications of the attack on pluralism and
nonresidency, the positive effect on education of this quest for
preachers underscores the social significance of the Puritan emphasis
on preaching.

Puritans were not alone in stressing preaching, which to some extent was part of the Protestant tradition. The 1538 edition of the
Tyndale-Coverdale New Testament warned, in a note to Matthew 5,
that "when the mynysters of Gods worde ceasse from teachyng of it/
then must they neades be troden downe with mens lawes and inuen-
cyons." It was not dislike of sermons but recognition of the state of
the clergy that prompted Henrician Anglicans to institute homilies as
a temporary expedient in the Convocation of 1542. Twelve model
sermons were prepared the following year but were not issued until
31 July 1547. These were supplemented with an additional twenty-
one homilies, mostly by Jewel but with one by Grindal and perhaps
another by Parker, in 1571, though they had been prepared some
eight years earlier. Grindal believed that sermons were superior to
homilies, particularly since the former can be varied according to
the diversity of hearers, times, and places. In 1560, Pilkington, before becoming bishop of Durham, lamented that in uprooting popery, English Protestants were interested in enriching themselves
rather than in fostering learning and replacing "dumb dogs" with
preaching ministers. Apparently dismayed at the ease with which
unlettered parish clergy altered religious persuasions to suit changes
in government, he insisted that "priests, which have not the salt of
God's word to season man's soul withal, are meet for nothing in
that kind of life, but to be put to some occupation which they can

do, and get their living with the sweat of their face, and not occupy a place among God's shepherds, seeing they be rather dumb and devouring dogs than good preachers." Sandys, who also was near the Puritans on the religious continuum, condemned nonpreaching ministers as "dumb dogs," a phrase that by 1589 had become a hallmark of Puritan propaganda. In Sandys' judgment such silent ministers made their belly their God, and their preferment their religion. [20]

Despite the intentions of such reform-minded Anglicans as Pilkington and Sandys, the conditions responsible for uneducated clergy (especially inadequate livings, patronage abuses, pluralism, and nonresidence) continued to be widespread. An account of Lancashire deaneries made c. 1563 surveyed 56 churches, serving perhaps 122,500 people, and found 34 dumb dogs, 6 inadequate ministers, and 6 Catholic clergy. Of the remainder only 7 were deemed able preachers. In London, 62 of the 107 clergy early in the reign were unable to preach, while in the diocese of Rochester 5 of the 8 members of the cathedral chapter could preach, but only 13 of the 64 parochial clergy. Of 129 clergy in the archdeaconry of Leicester, only 15 could preach, and the archdeaconry of Coventry was worse, with 3 of 67. In North Wales 90% of the clergy were unable to preach in 1567. As late as 1584 it was estimated (probably with exaggeration) that in the archdeaconry of Staffordshire only one of 150 clergy could preach. In the early 1590s the diocese of Gloucester had 84 preachers and 169 nonpreachers, whereas the figures for Chester were 172 and 213, for Ely 79 and 38, and for York 207 and 372. In 1603 the archdeaconry of Lincoln and Stowe had 228 preachers and 292 "dumb dogs." There are numerous examples of clerical offenders, such as the vicar of Midhurst, Sussex, who had neither preached the monthly and quarterly sermons for three years nor catechized, but contented himself with reading the homilies four times in this period. Other parishes fared worse. In Lancashire the episcopal visitations discerned that the books of homilies were not found in four churches in 1578, three in 1581, seven in 1601, and eighteen in 1604. The absence of preaching was a factor that enabled Catholicism to maintain or regain its strength. Almost 60% of the students registered at St. Alban's College, Valladolid, between 1589 and 1603 were from Yorkshire, Staffordshire, Herefordshire, and Wales, areas where the shortage of preaching ministers was acute. The situation led Nichols to warn that lack of preaching encouraged the growth of Catholicism and atheism. [21]

The serious deficit of preachers provoked Puritan outcries against

You idle Drones, that fleece and cannot feede,
You speechless ones, than can not barke nor bay.

For Puritans the sermon was the climax of the worship service, and no other religious group seemed so to elevate the proclamation of the word. Puritans had a reputation in Norwich, according to Bishop Freke, as "Godly Preachers." The institution of lectureships, though some lecturers were Anglicans, is a manifest example of the Puritan concern with preaching. Paul Seaver has shown that the impetus behind the lectureships was Puritan, and that most lecturers were Puritan preachers. A fundamental indictment of Catholicism was that the priests—90% said George Wither—could not preach. The predominantly sacramental role of the Catholic priest as a mediator of divine grace sharply contrasts with the Puritan subordination of the sacraments to the sermon—in practice if not always in theory, for Puritans regarded the preaching of the word and the proper administration of the sacraments as indispensable marks of the true church. The Anglican attempt to maintain a balance between word and sacraments made them suspect in Puritan minds for not withdrawing from Catholic sacramentalism. [22]

Fear of sacramentalism as well as the conviction of the primacy of the word motivated the Puritan unwillingness to be satisfied with clergy who could only read. Homilies seemed to the Puritans to sanction a nonpreaching ministry unable to provide spiritual food for hungry souls. George Gifford, appointed to the living of All Saints' with St. Peter's at Maldon, Essex, in 1582, caustically remarked that a boy of ten could read prayers and homilies, and Penry charged that in the Church of England an unlettered plowman could be a minister after only a month's study because no more than a reading knowledge of English was required. Whitgift was branded as a seducer of the people because he allegedly equated reading with preaching. To the Anglican objection that England lacked sufficient preachers, Gilby retorted that he sought only what Jesus demanded: "I require nothing, but that Christ . . . requireth. . . . It is not enough to be a priest of cloutes, or a dumbe dogge that can not barke."

"Dumb dog" became the battle cry of Puritans and Separatists in their war against nonpreaching clergy. Becon believed, probably correctly, that a majority of beneficed clergy in England could not preach, and Dering wanted them ousted from their livings. To Nichols, a nonpreaching ministry was contrary to Pauline admonitions (1 Timothy 3:2, 6; Titus 1:9) and consequently a sin in the church and a source of trouble in the state. John Northbrooke, minister at St.

Mary de Redcliffe, Bristol, cited Augustine, Ambrose, Jerome, and Chrysostom to prove that nonpreaching clergy cannot be tolerated.[23]

A counterattack was mounted by Anglicans against these charges, beginning in the mid-1580s. Thomas Rogers reverted to the Catholic view that the bestowal of grace through the word and sacraments was not affected by the qualifications or personal character of the clergy. It was better, said Wright, for younger ministers to forbear preaching in favor of reading homilies and Scripture, and using catechisms until maturity brought discretion. He accused Puritans and Separatists of despising clergy who were

more pleasant and sociable of nature, or more delighted in mirth and honest pastime for their health and recreation than agreeth with their own Stoicall disposition: or if his [an Anglican's] gifts in preaching doe not altogether satisfie their fantasticall humors, . . . though the man be neuer so honest in life and conuersation, nor so carefull and diligent in discharging his duetie according to his talent: yet in the eies of these vehement accusers, he is but a dumbe dogge.

Wright mentioned the Separatist Robert Browne as one such accuser, but Wright wrote in the context of the Marprelate controversy where such inculpations were commonplace.[24]

A few years later, Sutcliffe attacked those radicals who claimed the necessity and right to preach based on the inner revelation of the Spirit rather than formal education. The bishops were thereby defended for restricting licenses to preach and allowing those without adequate education to read the homilies and liturgy and privately admonish parishioners. Sutcliffe declared that to permit the uneducated to preach—which the Puritans did *not* advocate—would cause Scripture to be marred and novelties espoused. A more sophisticated analysis of the disagreement between Puritans and Anglicans over the role of preaching was rendered by Hooker, who acknowledged that sermons were keys to the kingdom of heaven, but judged Puritans excessive in their praise of sermons and their derogation of the plain reading of Scripture. Puritans, he (erroneously) complained, insisted that the divine word was mediated only through sermons—and not even read sermons—"but sermons without book, sermons which spend their life in their birth and may have public audience but once." For Hooker, the gospel could be equally conveyed through sermons, homilies, Scripture lessons, and sacraments; there was no justification in the attribution of primacy to preaching. "As medicines provided of nature and applied by art for the benefit of bodily health, take effect sometimes under and sometimes above the natural proportion of their virtue, according as the mind and fancy of the patient doth more or less concur with them," so reading homilies, Scripture, or religious books (in private) can be as effectual as sermons. William Covel, vicar of Sittingbourne, Kent, went a step further by asserting that the variety of those in the pews is best served by allowing men to preach or read according to their abilities. In effect, Anglicans believed that preaching was of the *bene esse* rather than the *esse* of the ministerial vocation.[25]

In various ways, Anglicans attempted to improve preaching. Convocation in 1586 stipulated that a bishop, archdeacon, or ordinary (with the bishop's advice and consent) should appoint six or seven preachers to provide Sunday sermons in parishes near their residences where no licensed preachers were present. The goal was to arrange at least a sermon each quarter. Those responsible for such parishes were to pay for a dinner "and horsemeate" for the visiting preacher, and procure someone to serve his benefice while he was away. Visitation articles inquired if quarterly sermons were preached and if, in the absence of sermons, homilies were read distinctly. In 1586 Herbert Westfaling, bishop of Hereford, asked if ministers were diligent in the study of Scripture and whether, if they lacked the M.A. degree, they owned and studied the New Testament in Latin and English. Concern was expressed whether the cathedral clergy preached personally or at least provided learned substitutes. Around 1580, every unlicensed minister had to obtain a copy of the Bible and Bullinger's *Decades*, and every licensed preacher was expected to preach at least twelve sermons a year. In the diocese of Norwich, Edmund Scambler stipulated that every cleric unable to preach must read a book from the Old or New Testament appointed by the commissioners each quarter, make notes on each chapter, and be examined by the commissioners. Abundant kindred examples from visitation records indicate episcopal hope that regular study in the Bible and the *Decades* would eventually enable these men to preach. Nevertheless, the continued shortage in the last years of the era necessitated the appointment in 1599 of four Queen's Preachers to spread the gospel in Lancashire. The irony of the Anglican failure is highlighted in that these preachers were so unpopular that they had to be protected by the High Commission.[26]

Despite the hostility in Lancashire, evidence shows that in much of the country sermons were popular. The growth of lectureships indicates as much, as does the increase in the market for published sermons. About 1,200 different Elizabethan sermons still exist in print. An examination of publication dates for these sermons (some of which were included in published collections, and have therefore not been separately counted) shows that 9 were published in the 1560s, 69 in the 1570s, 113 in the 1580s, and 140 in the 1590s. The growing popularity of published sermons weakens Hooker's argument that sermons were liked because their content was novel each time. Yet those faced with a steady diet of repetitious homilies must have found even a printed sermon at least a temporary novelty.[27]

Another indication of the popularity of sermons is provided by the crowds drawn to Paul's Cross, normally the preserve of Anglicans, though some Puritans preached there. Among the latter were Thomas Sampson, Laurence Humphrey, John Knewstub, John Stockwood, Laurence Chaderton, George Gifford, and Henry Smith. William Fisher, master of Ilford Hospital, Essex, believed so fervently in these sermons that he called for an annual outlay of £52 to support them, and in his will Aylmer provided £400 toward this end. The sermons included numerous social comments. According to their historian, the Paul's Cross sermons were particularly concerned with unity (or security) and the power and happiness that accompany it. Their effectiveness must have been diminished by the difficulties inherent in the physical setting; John Manningham observed: "I thinke many of those which are fayne to stand without dores at the sermon of a preacher whom the multitude throng after may come with as greate deuotion as some that are nearer, yet I beleeve the most come away as I did from this [a sermon by Francis Marbury], scarse one word the wiser." The same would have been true of some sermons preached in large cathedrals.[28]

So much has been made of the stylistic differences between Anglican and Puritan sermons that a word of caution is necessary, for a correct understanding of sermon styles is necessary for a study of the principles behind the radical challenge to the educated clergy (which will be discussed in the ensuing section). J. W. Blench has provided a sophisticated analysis of sermon styles, giving "the most definite and illuminating grouping which the material makes possible," and repudiating the notion of a dichotomy between Puritan and Anglican styles.

There were three styles, the first of which was the plain type commonly associated with Puritans. The first form of this style was characterized by austerity. Although exemplified by numerous Puritans (e.g., Stockwood, Perkins, Chaderton, Pagit, Udall, and Gifford), it was also used by Anglicans (e.g., Whitgift, Simon Harward, and William Cupper). The second form of the plain style, characterized by tropes but not schemata (artificial word patterns), was adopted by Puritans (Cartwright, Thomas Gibson) and Anglicans (Richard

Maddoxe). The use of tropes and some schemata, which typifies the third form of the plain style, is again found in the sermons of both Puritans (Greenham, Dent, Gosson) and Anglicans (Jewel, Pilkington, Sandys, Grindal). The second style, which was colloquial and used a racy idiom, apparently was shunned by Puritans. The third, ornate, style had a classical form (Hooker) and an euphuistic form, the latter used by Anglicans (Drant, Carpenter, Thomas Playfere) and Puritans (Trigge, Bush).[29] Although Anglicans and Puritans differed over the necessity of a minister preaching and the value of homilies and unexplicated scriptural lessons, the style used in the pulpit was a matter of individual preference or conviction and cannot be categorized in religious or social terms. Stylistic differences notwithstanding, there is no evidence that Elizabethan preachers regarded the message as subordinate to the medium. Some disagreements, however, were voiced over the use of traditional learning in the expression of that message, which led to the repudiation by radicals of the necessity for formal education in the preparation of ministers.

(3) Education and the Radical Challenge

Let us not make of the pulpet a schoole of philosophie, nor of the Churche the deske of an Oratour.

John Stockwood[30]

A blow giuen in the pulpit against learning (a fault too common) leaueth a scarre in the face of knowledge, which cannot easily be cured.

William Covel[31]

For Puritans, the centrality of preaching required appropriate education, and although most Anglicans placed less emphasis on homiletics in the pastoral function, they too acknowledged the necessity of learning for those who preached. Both groups supported the educational instututions. Catholics in the post-Tridentine age emphasized higher education for their clergy, particularly missionaries dispatched to England from seminaries on the Continent. But the left wing of the religious continuum questioned the necessity of formal academic training for the ministry, for a variety of reasons—an extension of Puritan ideas on the role of learning in the pulpit and the relationship of natural and revealed knowledge, a dissatisfaction with the divinity taught at Oxford and Cambridge, and, possibly, a recognition that the solution to the shortage of adequate ministers was reliance on men moved by the Spirit.

Although Puritans were adamant on formal learning as a prerequisite for preaching, once in the pulpit, they minimized learning (except for those who developed a more ornate style). Chaderton urged ministers to dispense with a show of human learning in favor of rejoicing solely in the knowledge of Christ.

Many doe stuffe their sermons with newe deuised words, and affected speaches of vanitie, not being content with the words which the holy Ghost teacheth. Many with vnnecessary sentences, prouerbes, similitudes, and stories collected out of the wrytings of prophane men: many with curious affected figures, with Latine, Greeke, and Hebrewe sentences, without any just occasion offered by their teste, with multitudes of humane authorities, and diuers opinions of men.

Human wisdom, argued Udall, was unfit for proclaiming the gospel, and Gifford declared the yearning for Latin phrases and learned quotations in sermons was the hallmark of an atheist. Arthur Dent, rector of South Shoebury, Essex, had no intention "to flie an high pitch, to some out the froth of mans wisedome, & to make a great shew of learning, by blowing the bladder of vanitie, til it burst with swelling." Even Henry Smith, whose sermon style was somewhat ornate, advocated preaching plainly and perspicuously to enable the simplest persons to understand, though he cautioned against preaching unlearnedly or confusingly.[32]

The Separatist Henry Barrow took a position nearly akin to that of Puritans on the place of education in the pulpit. He claimed he had no objection to the use of works in addition to the Bible in the study of divinity, but he repudiated the utilization of such writings in homiletics. Anglicans were castigated for reliance on theological tomes, without which they were as blind as moles and as mute as fish. "He that can most learnedly fetch out his sermon from them, and preach their notes in manner of discourse, he is the only man, he hitteth the point aright, though the text be never touched or broken up." Barrow also used an economic argument, referring to the unnecessary expenditure of funds to acquire theological education in the universities, correctly noting that the money bestowed by one man to achieve this learning exceeded what many a householder had to support his family and relieve his neighbors. Here, then, was the crucial break. Theological study was acceptable (if it did not intrude in the pulpit) but not mandatory. The door had been opened for unlettered men inspired by the Spirit to expound the biblical text: "I with my whole heart wish, that al the Lord's people were prophets."[33]

The Anglican position on learning in homiletics differed from Puritan and Separatist views. Wright believed that sound doctrine alone was insufficient to hold the attention of parishioners, hence he favored canonical authorities, similes, historical references, and pithy sayings in sermons. Because pagan authors had written persuasively about virtues and vices, John King, archdeacon of Nottingham and chaplain to John Piers, archbishop of York, was convinced of their worth in sermons, on the principle that "good is good wheresoever I finde it." Moreover he wondered why "we traine vp our children, in poets, orators, histories, Greeke & Latine, old & new, & not presently set them to the testaments, & everlastingly keepe them in the reading & conning of only catechismes, if all that elementary learning . . . must be wholly forgotten and laide aside in the exercising of an higher calling?" Sectaries wondered about that too, but came to a different conclusion. King did not believe such learning could be omitted from the pulpit, if for no other reason than that Catholics required classical and historical proof of Protestant interpretations. Sandys, however, warned ministers not to become so puffed up with learning that they took pride in their sermons.[34]

Whatever the merits of the Anglican case, the Separatist approach to learning in preaching appears to have met with popular appeal.

Tell them [the laity] where they may heare an Honourable Bishop preach, a reuerend Prelate, or an auncient graue diuine, tush, they know what these are, temporising formalists, a sort of silken Doctours, such as when a man heares their text, hee may gesse himselfe what will be al their Sermon: but if yee can tell them of a trimme yong man, that will not quote the Fathers (and good reason, for his horse neuer eate a bottle of hay in eyther of the vniuersities): that neuer yet tooke orders, but had his calling approued by the plaine lay-elders (for he was too irregular to be ordred by a Bishop): that will not confounde the congregation with latine sentences, (for he is not guiltie of the Romane language): that will not sticke to reuile them that are in authoritie, that his sectaries may crie he is persecuted, when hee is iustly silenced: if yee can giue them intelligence of such a man, Oh for Gods sake where teacheth hee, to him they will runne for haste without their dinners, sit waiting by his church till the doore be open, if the place bee full, clyme vp at the windowes, pull downe the glasse to heare him, and fill the Church-yard full, sende him home euerything: one man plate, another hangings, this Gentlewoman naperie, that goodwife money.

This remarkable passage indicates that the simplicity and comprehensibility of Separatist sermons were a key factor in the growing popularity of this movement. Hooker himself testified to this.[35] A century later John Bunyan, a practitioner of this approach, drew large crowds to his London sermons for this reason. The Anglican tendency to display theological erudition in the pulpit cost them some popular support in Elizabethan society.

Anglican acceptance of the necessity for human learning in homiletics presupposes a belief in the compatibility of natural and revealed knowledge. That which is revealed by the Spirit must be essentially harmonious with that which is discovered by rational processes, a thesis Hooker defended. There was no attempt to make natural and revealed knowledge coequals, for the former was subordinate to the latter and must be tested by it. King claimed that the study of divinity, "the science of sciences," could not be undertaken without the use of grammar to determine the propriety of words, logic to disclose ambiguities, rhetoric to determine rules of speech, philosophy to analyze causes and effects, and history to calculate chronology. Jewel compared the liberal arts to "that part of the carpenter's wimble [or boring tool] which turneth about, goeth round, and by little and little draweth in the iron or steel bit. The wooden handle entereth not into the wood, but wreatheth in the piercer: so do these arts, if they be rightly used, further the understanding of the word of God." Without learning, Jewel judged religion defenseless. Formal education became a *sine qua non* for an Anglican who determined to preach and not merely read.[36]

But there were limits to human knowledge, and Jewel typifies many Anglicans who maintained the value of traditional learning in divinity without allowing it to be exalted. On the one hand, the gospel, the fountain of knowledge, could not be maintained by ignorance, and those who presumed to rely excessively on the Spirit without concomitant studious endeavor tempted God. On the other hand, the mysteries of the Christian faith could not be ascertained by natural wisdom but only by spiritual revelation. Because of the uncertainty of human knowledge, "the professors thereof oftentimes run a masket [lose their way]: they leese themselves, and wander they know not whither." When Thomas Harding, writing from Louvain, berated the ignorance of many Anglican clergy, Jewel retorted that God had the ability to make even poor asses speak.[37] The danger, however, was that the delicate tension in Jewel's position (which Puritans shared) might be disrupted and lead to rationalism or radical sectarianism.

The threat of rationalism was effectively countered in the Elizabethan age by a conviction of the necessity for divine revelation. In the Geneva Bible, the note to Daniel 2:22 stipulates that because of man's natural ignorance he knows nothing apart from God. A companion note to Ecclesiastes 12:12 explains that "these things can not be comprehended in bokes, or learned by studie, but God must instruct the heart that you maiest onely knowe that wisdome is the true felicitie, & the way thereunto is to feare God." The theme was reiterated in the Beza-Tomson Bible, where the note to Colossians 2:3 affirms that without Christ there is no true wisdom. Not even the most extreme sectary could have quarrelled with the note to 1 Corinthians 2:10: "If it surmount the capacitie of men, how can it be vnderstoode of any man, or howe can you declare and preach it? by a peculiar lightning by Gods Spirite, wherewith whosoeuer is inspired, he can enter euen to the verie secretes of God." Anglicans and Puritans alike accepted this need for divine revelation, thus precluding a fully rationalistic epistemology.[38]

The preservation of the tension between natural and revealed knowledge was endangered by emphases within Anglicanism and Puritanism on spiritual infusion. Four common themes threatened the balance, and with it the need for preachers to attain a traditional education. The first was the tendency to treat human and spiritual reason antithetically rather than compatibly. Biblical precedent supports this view, which received some attention in the notes to the Tyndale-Coverdale New Testament as early as 1538. The wisdom of God is portrayed as foolishness to human reasoning, hence man's wisdom is vanity. The Rheims annotators cleverly adapted this to contrast human wisdom, especially that of heretics, with the teaching of the Catholic church. For the Anglicans, Pilkington labeled human learning deceitful, and Cooper deprecated natural reason. Puritans too sometimes sharply contrasted human and divine knowledge, the former attainable by reason, the latter by the teaching of the Spirit through Scripture. Without caution, the pursuit of such conclusions could lead to the extremism expressed by Lewis Thomas: "Let the foolish Philosophers henceforth burne their bookes, as the Ephesians did their vaine bookes [Acts 19]: they build al vpon reason, & vpon the causes of things."[39]

A second theme that menaced the relationship between natural and revealed knowledge was the emphasis on God or Christ as the only schoolmaster of Christian scholars. This is found in the explanatory material of the 1549 and 1551 Matthew-Becke Bibles, the 1551 Matthew Bible, the Geneva Bible, and the Beza-Tomson Bible. As early as 1538 the Tyndale-Coverdale New Testament asserted that the knowledge of Christ must be taught by God. Thirty years later the Bishops' Bible spoke of "usyng that wisdome whiche God gaue me from heauen." Sandys and Pilkington often referred to God or Christ as the Christians' schoolmaster, and Sandys argued that no man could discover wisdom unless God were his teacher. Yet Sandys recognized the inherent pitfalls in these remarks and distinguished between his position and that of the sectaries: "Now, although Christ only openeth the book of knowledge, giveth understanding, and revealeth unto us the will of his Father; although the Spirit only be the schoolmaster that inwardly guideth the heart in the way of truth; yet may we not gape for revelations, as the anabaptists do, or think that God hath revealed unto us whatsoever we do vainly imagine and conceive in our brains." Puritans too acknowledged a divine schoolmaster. Dering used such phraseology several times, and Gifford observed that the person to whom God reveals the heavenly mysteries is truly learned. John Norden, an attorney and probably a Puritan, admitted that in divinity he was unlearned, "a greene head, & of no iudgement," but he was convinced that God was an instructor in arts, sciences, and vocations, who gave men of base degree an understanding of his will while often hiding it from the learned. The implications of these conceptions for traditional learning as a prerequisite for preachers are obvious.[40]

The tension also was challenged by a third theme that cited New Testament precedents for formally uneducated preachers. One was Acts 18:24-26, where Apollos, a knowledgeable Alexandrian, agreed to be taught in religion by Aquila, "a base and abiect handicraftes man" and his wife, Priscilla. The Bishops' Bible, the Geneva Bible, and the Beza-Tomson Bible call this passage to the readers' attention. The story was used by Charles Gibbon, a former Cambridge student, as evidence that God did not always restrict the revelation of his truth to such traditional means as educational study. Another precedent was the apostles' lack of formal education in divinity. According to Robert Some, this was because Christ did not want early conversions attributed to eloquence and learning, hence he bestowed special knowledge upon the apostles. The crucial question was whether special revelation continued to be infused in the formally uneducated to enable them to preach. Pilkington asserted that no longer could men expect divine assistance without prior study (and prayer), and Whitgift likened the argument that religious truth was manifested in the simple and ignorant to the Franciscan assertion that *Apostoli nesciebant literas; ergo Franciscanis non est opus literis.* The Rheims annotators would not accept the divine infusion of knowledge in the formally uneducated either, for there is no longer spiritual endowment of knowledge without previous study. Advocates of preaching without formal education would have been more attuned to Sandys' comments on the centurion Cornelius as he perceived a fisherman approaching: "What is Peter? Some odd sectary fled from Jerusalem. . . . What learning, what piety can I look for to come out of such a school, and from such a school-master?"[41]

The final theme that potentially threatened the tension between natural and revealed knowledge was the oft-repeated observation that divine truth often was manifested to the ignorant. The marginal notes to John 3:1 and Acts 17:16 in the Beza-Tomson Bible explain that because the learned are sometimes the most ignorant God utilizes "the curiositie of fooles, to gather together his elect." Jewel believed that the obscure places in Scripture were oftener grasped by the unlearned than the educated. Gifford used the opening verses of Revelation to contend that a few despised persons can see the truth when the dignitaries of the church do not. Simple people are instructed by divine wisdom, according to Norden, who claimed that simplicity. Because Matthew 11:25 seemed to support these contentions, the Rheims annotators expostulated that the little ones to whom Jesus refers were not unlearned cobblers, weavers, and housewives, but the humble, including doctors of theology. Cartwright retorted that Christ was indeed referring to the ignorant, though the learned were not therefore barred from the truth.[42]

If divine and human reasoning are antithetical, if God or Christ is the only schoolmaster for Christian scholars, if the New Testament precedents for formally uneducated preachers are still relevant, and if divine truths are often revealed to the ignorant rather than the wise, then the logical conclusion for Separatists and other sectaries was that traditional training at Oxford and Cambridge is not required for men with a calling to proclaim the gospel. Unlike the 1640s and 1650s, in the Elizabethan age there are relatively few written statements by those who felt this way. The lawyer Norden, though no sectary, asserted that many "sillie men" inspired by the Spirit but lacking the usual education had successfully repudiated Catholic doctors. A dialogue by the Puritan Anthony Gilby includes this rather startling exchange:

Mil. [a soldier] That is madde seruice, to serue two or three maisters, for the gayne of proling proctors. . . .

Bern. [a priest] What then? shall they call forth Coblers and Taylours, that euerie parishe may haue one? . . .

Mil. Yea a great deale better were it so to doe, than to place popishe Priestes, the deuourers of Christes Lambes.

Better to use uneducated Protestants in the pulpit than Catholics. Barrow, a learned man who believed the Church of England erroneously used erudition to suppress divine truth and conceal ecclesiastical corruption, thought its clergy should cast aside human authors and rely solely on Scripture. It was then but a short step to assert, as he did, that all men who are spiritually able have the right to preach and do not require ordination. In effect, the argument concerning the place of learning in public preaching evolved into an argument on ordination. A group of Separatists at Hatfield Peverell, Essex, so antagonized Aylmer that he complained to Burghley in 1586 that their leader was unable to speak three words of Latin and taught that the word rather than water was important in baptism. The Separatists were, the bishop fulminated, detrimental to good order. So was the widely detested, extremist sect known as the Familists, whose members tended to be drawn from the ignorant in society, but found affinity and purpose in their understanding of the Spirit.[43]

Anglican and Puritan attacks on the sectaries focused on their challenge to a traditionally educated ministry. Gifford accused them of opposing conventional education because logic disproved their contentions. To William Wilkinson, a Cambridge schoolmaster, they were libertines for insisting that the learned cannot preach the word truly, in light of Christ's affirmation that the truth is revealed to babes. Their tendency to boast of never having been to a university to study profane sciences and the "dark" languages of Hebrew, Greek, and Latin, as well as their claimed dependency on divine visions, were adversely received by Lawrence Barker, lecturer at St. James Clerkenwell, London. Nash acridly suggested that such advocates belonged in Bridewell because of their condemnation of the liberal arts as unprofitable, "contenting themselues with a little Countrey Grammer knowledge god wote, thanking God with that abscedarie Priest in Lincolneshire, that he neuer knewe what that Romish popish Latine meant." Bancroft extended such charges to the Presbyterians, whom he accused of allowing private men, under the pretended guidance of the Spirit, to amend, restrain, and punish at their pleasure anyone they desired. Finally, Wright spoke particularly for the governing classes when he castigated "euery hairebrainde foole" who pretended to know as much as doctors of divinity for taking upon himself, as an inferior subject, the task of controlling the state and prescribing laws to prince and prelate. "That presumptuous Asse, which dares turne his heeles and kicke agaynst the noble Lion: is worthie of punishment."[44]

The ultimate danger, then, was that proponents of an unlettered clergy allegedly moved by the Spirit could overturn the established order in favor of a spiritual democracy or an oligarchy of saints. The ferocity of the counterattack against these forces is understood only in the light of the revolutionary implications of the sectarian position. Ironically, the sectaries, who gave primacy to preaching in the worship service, developed principles kindred to those of the Anglicans and Puritans with respect to the role of the Spirit in understanding the gospel. By destroying the tension between natural and revealed knowledge, they bypassed traditional education as the proper pathway to the preaching vocation and challenged the control that defenders of the existing order maintained through education and ordination. In effect, the sectaries threatened the educational system, the church and its legal agencies, and the social order itself.

(4) The Problem of Clerical Immorality

There be many as it seemeth, whiche are entred into the ministery for none other purpose, but to liue an idle life, to haue leysure to play at Cardes, or Tables, and bowles all the Weeke.

George Gifford[45]

The maners of ministers are not to be folowed as an example.

Beza-Tomson Bible[46]

In addition to ignorance, nothing brought the clergy into disrepute quicker than immoral living, the extent of which was considerable in Elizabethan society. Uneducated, dissolute clerics were a source of dismay among the godly of all religious persuasions. Profligacy was an easy charge to hurl against those of different religious views, but it was especially telling used by Puritans against Anglicans, whose cause was hampered by men of ill morals and loose convictions who found harbor in the ecclesiastical establishment. In terms of morality, ministers of the Church of England were a microcosm of society.

The alarm this provoked was reflected many times over in the Elizabethan pulpit and press, though it was hardly a new situation. A few months after his consecration as bishop of Carlisle, John Best complained to Cecil that his clergy were ignorant and "wicked impes of Antichrist." Robert Horne, bishop of Winchester, found that many clerics were haunters of taverns, common brawlers, drunkards, sodomites, and whoremongers. The Anglican apologist, Thomas Rogers, who was worried that parishioners were imitating their pastors, urged that evil clerics be convicted and deposed. The Rheims annotators lamented that the clergy were guilty of those sins they condemned in others.[47]

The real storm of protest against clerical turpitude came from the Puritans. Because

> the cleargy,
> Liueth fleshly,
> And myndeth no godlinesse,

Stockwood pressed magistrates to require that idle clerics undertake the church's work or to expel them. Curates and readers were singled out by Chaderton as ungodly, idle men who lacked integrity. Becon, on the other hand, found the real offenders—the hunters, the "layse lubbers," and other—at court, in the universities, and in the houses of bishops and noblemen. One of the sources of clerical debauchery in Gifford's judgment was the practice of befriending parishioners by playing cards or bowls, or drinking at the alehouse. Some Puritans were concerned enough in 1586 to survey the ministry in the Church of England, subsequently terming the clergy "miserable." Numerous clergy were depicted as lewd, unlearned, nonresident, and indifferent. Although the survey was undertaken by Puritans, ample evidence supports the substance of its allegations. It is hardly surprising (though unfair) that one Puritan concluded that an Anglican minister was often "either vnlearned, or els wicked and lewd of conuersation, and consequently vnfit" to handle cases of conscience. Eusebius Pagit was troubled that some people regarded all ministers as drunkards, ruffians, whoremongers, and blasphemers. The seriousness of the situation is made clearer by a letter of recommendation written for Robert Dobbes, vicar of Runcorn, Ches., to his bishop, in which the author found it necessary to point out that Dobbes had not resorted to alehouses or played unlawful games during his tenure.[48]

One of the most flagrant profligate acts in which some clergy indulged was sexual incontinency. The 1586 survey by the Puritans shows that clerics accused of such activity totaled 3.2% in Essex, 6.5% in Norfolk, approximately 4.5% in Cornwall, and 2.4% in Warwickshire. These figures may be too low, for the principal intent of the survey was to ascertain the extent of pluralism, nonresidency, and the absence of preaching, not immorality. Visitation records provide further evidence of sexual offences. Between 1571 and 1601, eight clerics in Lancashire were presented for adultery or fornication, and a ninth, George Hesketh, rector of Halsall, was accused of corrupting "all the women in the country." The 1590 visitation in the diocese of York resulted in accusations against three clergy for immorality, and in the same diocese, the High Commission in the period 1590-95 convicted one cleric of keeping suspicious female company, a second of adultery, a third of immorality, and two others of incontinency. Evidence of illicit sex is given in wills, such as that of George Wilmslow, the illegitimate son of George Savage, rector of Davenham, Ches. In some offenders, the lapses may have been momentary, but others were notoriously profligate. One of the latter was John Wainhouse, rector of Kirk Smeaton, Yorks., who "haithe been suspected to lyve incontinently with one Perkins wif . . . and with certeyne other light women comers and goers thyther. And moreover kepeth in his howse one Francis Lancaster a woman of evill Conversacion and an incontinent lyver." Mr. Barton, parson of St. Mary Abchurch, London, tried in 1563 to persuade a woman to have sexual intercourse with him; she informed her friends, who hid at the appointed time, waited until the parson had removed some of his clothes, and then broke in on the couple. The minister, a married man, was taken to Bridewell in the company of approximately a hundred people—an object lesson to other clergy and grist for the mill of anticlericalism.[49]

Sexual improprieties provided propaganda for the Catholic Lewis Evans, who charged that in Protestant England "incontinencie is . . . mayntayned in maried Moonkes, Priestes, and Ministers howses." As an example, he referred to a married minister in a town near London who had been caught in bed with another man's wife, but whose punishment by Grindal was limited to transferal to a church near Windsor. In a similar case, the archdeacon of Westminster was not forced to do penance in a public cart "for vent[u]ring lyke a *Hardyeman* so farre with *Venus*," but was transferred to a rural parish. The punishment meted out to offending clerics was not consistent. Samuel Beck had been deprived of his benefice at Lambeth for incontinency with nine women, yet because of his claimed descent from the duke of Lancaster, the queen recommended him for another ecclesiastical position. Parkhurst, bishop of Norwich, had to defend himself in the Court of Arches for refusing to accept the clergyman Sir John Norton, who had been presented to the living of Morley, Norfolk, c. 1571, although Norton already had been publicly punished (by riding in a cart) for his associations with a harlot and for forgery. Other clergy did not fare as well for their indiscretions. When John Hall, minister at Wereham, Norfolk, was accused (perhaps wrongly) of having sired a bastard, he was whipped. William Rae, vicar of Oundle, Northants., was excommunicated for fornication in 1591, but

Edward Binder, minister of Blackmore, Essex, was only suspended for adultery in 1586.[50]

A second dissolute act in which some ministers engaged was inebriety. In the 1586 survey, the figures show this was a problem for 9.5% of the clergy in Warwickshire, 8.5% in Essex, 6.2% in Norfolk, and approximately 5.3% in Cornwall. In these four counties, sixty-five clerics were accused of drunkenness and alehouse haunting. In Lancashire only ten clergymen were in trouble for intoxication in the Elizabethan age, but one of these, George Dobson, vicar of Whalley, was accused in 1575 of being "a common drunkard and such an ale-knight as the like is not in our parish; and in the night when most men be in bed at their rest then is he in the ale-house with a company like to himself, but not one of them can match him in ale-house tricks, for he will, when he cannot discern black from blue, dance with a full cup on his head, far passing all the rest—a comely sight for his profession." Another was the vicar of Dean, a drunkard who sired a bastard.

The 1590 visitation of the diocese of York resulted in a number of clergy being presented for inebriation, alehouse haunting, or maintaining an alehouse in the vicarage. In the same diocese the High Commission convicted one cleric of alehouse haunting and another of intoxication between 1590 and 1595. John Birkbie, rector of Moor-Monkton, Yorks., was reputedly a drunkard and a fornicator who danced "verie offensivelie at alehouses and marriages in the presence of common people." A chronic offender might be excommunicated or deprived, as was George Acworth, rector of Wroughton, Wilts., c. 1575.[51]

Gambling was a third form of dissipate behavior. In the 1586 survey the number of clergy accused of this offense was 8.2% in Norfolk, 7% in Essex, approximately 8.3% in Cornwall, and 4.2% in Warwickshire. The vicar of High Easter, Essex, spent so much time at cards, tables (backgammon), and bowls that his family suffered. William Wilson, the minister at Fulmodeston, Norfolk, played cards and backgammon so often that his parishioners were offended, a situation conducive to anticlerical sentiment. Another case involved Thomas Young, who had been collated to the prebendary of Barnby, Yorks., at the age of eleven, apparently with an archepiscopal dispensation. Although nearly twenty in 1563, he was neither deacon nor priest, but spent his time gambling, hunting, hawking, and fishing. One Whitsuntide he appeared in York Minster wearing a colored rather than a black coat, leather britches, and yellow stockings. Nicholas Jackson, vicar of Mappleton, Yorks., was presented in 1567 for gambling and drunkenness.[52]

Additional immoral actions brought disrepute upon ministers. One of these was swearing and blasphemy, though the numbers involved were relatively slight: 4 of the 284 clergy in Essex in 1586, 1 of 168 in Warwickshire, and 2 of 292 in Norfolk. This offense was part of a broader pattern of misconduct. In 1580, for example, the parson of Leaden Roothing, Essex, was charged with swearing, gambling, hawking, and hunting, while in 1597 Thomas Cheshier, rector of Nacton, Suffolk, was accused of swearing and brawling. One of the worst offenders was Matthew Odell, rector of Bulwick, Northants., who was "a grievous blasphemer of God's holy name and useth to swear both by God's blood, body and God's wounds for every trifle, both with his servants and others, and bringeth up his children in the same order." To compound matters, he sold lead from his church and replaced it with slate. [53]

Some clergy displayed a proclivity for brawling, as did the minister at Sheepy (Sheppeys), Leics., who was charged by his parishioners in 1586 "with tumultes and broyles in the time of Divine Service and bludshed in the churche"; the Privy Council ordered the bishop of Lincoln to investigate. In 1592 a female parishioner informed the consistory court at Chichester about the vicar of Rudgwick, Sussex: "I woulde wishe to god that wee had a minister that had some honestye and not a common drunkerde a lier a swearer & a quarreller." Brawling turned to violence in a controversy involving two Wiltshire clerics, who were finally summoned to Star Chamber. Thomas Haytour had been presented to the living of East Knoyle, allegedly with episcopal approval and a dispensation for nonage from the archbishop of Canterbury. He was, however, ousted from the living by an armed band (possibly a sheriff's posse) that included John Mervyn, a rival cleric. The latter claimed to possess a grant to the living on the next vacancy (an expectative), and to have been instituted as incumbent by the bishop of Salisbury, which grant he claimed was vindicated in an ecclesiastical court. The ugly scene did not benefit the reputation of clergy in western Wiltshire. [54]

Other clergy were accused of lewd speech, acting in interludes, theft, gluttony, and bigamy. The curate of Kirkby, Lancs., was a sorcerer, hawker, and hunter. The bishop of London was ordered by the Privy Council in 1580 to remove a Northampton minister from his living for his "very unquiet and indiscreat" behavior and to dispatch him to a benefice in Devon. One of the most colorful offenders was John Birkbie, rector of Moor-Monkton, Yorks., who in 1567 was alleged to be "of verie dissolute lieffe and lewde conversacion and usethe veine undecent apparell namelie great britches cut and drawen oute with sarcenet and taffitie, and great ruffes laid on with laceis of gold and silk."[55]

That the bishops were concerned by such dissolute behavior is shown in visitation articles, which regularly inquired about clergy who engaged in sexual misconduct, gambling, drinking, swearing, brawling, hawking, and hunting. Although the marginal notes to various English Bibles attributed evil living to ignorance, in the case of the clergy, economic inadequacies (which encouraged some to turn parsonages into alehouses) and the appointment of unfit men through the patronage system also were important factors. Early in the period it is also feasible that the demoralizing effect of the recent changes of official religion caused some to drift into drinking (to compensate for insecurity) or illicit sex, gambling, and swearing (from loss of conviction). Others drank or swore to develop a closer relationship with their parishioners. The Puritans attributed much of the problem to the absence of a rigorous, public examination of ministerial candidates, for which they blamed the prelates. Such a system might have brought substantial improvement. In any case, clerical immorality, which sometimes caused enough concern to be reported to the Privy Council, certainly contributed to anticlerical hostility and weakened the effectiveness of ministers as moral and social leaders.[56]

(5) The Swelling Tide of Anticlericalism

What is more houted at, scoffed and scorned in Englande now then a religious man in his wede?

Thomas Stapleton[57]

How darke, and vnsauerye are they? for some are *idols*, some are *strangers*, some are *theeues and robbers*, some are *hirelinges*.

Adam Hill[58]

Besides dissipative activity on the part of ministers, the factors responsible for anitclericalism were numerous. One was ignorant, nonpreaching, or absentee clerics, whom Dering regarded as causing more clerical discredit than inebriate ministers. "There hath not beene among vs any Popish Priest so drunke, nor any Alehouse Chaplin, at such a perpetuall truce with his drinking Pots, that hath possibly purchased so much discredite to his belly god, and kitchin faith, as our dumbe dogges and guides." Similarly, Gifford damned careless clerics as ravenous wolves and unskillful guides. This was not a concern limited to Puritans, for an Anglican like Anthony Anderson

worried about idle clergymen who could not or would not preach
and thus left their flocks starving for spiritual food. The anger that
this caused led to another factor conducive to anticlericalism, the
tendency of reforming ministers to use language for clerical offenders
that the undiscriminating could apply to the clergy as a whole. Two
lines of verse originally written in reference to Cardinal Wolsey suddenly were used in a context applicable to Elizabethan clerics:

> O cursed priestes, that prate for profits sake,
> And follow floud, and tyde, where ere it floes,

and were found in Elizabethan parishes. Pilkington lashed out at
clergy who reaped the profits of ecclesiastical livings without undertaking the pains of pastoral responsibility, comparing them to corrupt lawyers, greedy physicians, engrossers, leasemongers, and cruel
oppressors. Social gadflies in clerical garb are collectively described in
Puritan doggerel as

> A yong princockes,
> Sir John smelsmockes,
> A piece of flesh alone:
> To sing and daunce,
> And make pastaunce,
> With Tib, Cisly, and Jone.

None of these writers castigated all clergy in derogatory terms, but
the widespread usage of language depicting incompetent ministers as
mass men, idle shepherds, dumb dogs, sleepy watchmen, ignorant
shepherds, "wine-prophets," loiterers, "slowbellies," time servers,
and "scraping fleecers" made such phrases common coinage, ready
for use by those who disliked all clergy.[59]
    Anticlericalism also was fostered by disillusion, the belief that
ministers were devoid of spiritual light. Dering's feeling that some
clerics were more fit for the plow than the parsonage must have been
echoed in private homes throughout the land, perhaps especially in
the case of ministers who for economic reasons spent weekdays in
the fields. Anticlericalism was also fostered by ecclesiastical courts,
which some offenders regarded as oppressive. Nor did mandatory
attendance at services (though never fully achieved) increase clerical
prestige. Spitting, rude remarks, obscene stories, shuffling, gossipping,
improper singing, and other uncouth behavior were hazards confronting the cleric who mounted the pulpit. This prompted Henry Smith
to ask, "Hath not this despising of the preachers, made the Preachers
almost despise preaching?" Sandys attributed such behavior to pa-

rishioners who resented parsons for criticizing their social ills, pride, insolency, and covetousness. Other lay people had disgust for the clergy because some were turncoats whenever it was expedient to change, an acute problem in the middle decades of the century. Clergy who retained Catholic beliefs or practices came in for some withering criticism, such as that of Dering: "But our Vicars and Curates, we haue some of them yet of the old Morrowmasse Priests, whose salt is so vnsauory with such Popish leuen, that there is no tast in them of the gospell of Christ."[60]

Another source of anticlericalism was biblical marginalia. The real damage was done by the Matthew Bibles of 1537 and 1551, and the Matthew-Becke versions of 1549 and 1551. The synopsis to Jeremiah 23 in these Bibles explained that the prophet was declaiming against "euell Curates that make hauock of the flock of the Lorde." The note to Isaiah 3 complained against clerical exactions, including those for christenings, marriages, burials, and visiting the infirm. The clergy were blasted for being "effemynate & womanly: because they moast fylthely & ydely spende & waste that / which they haue scraped with iuggeling / violence / & most naughtie facions." In the note appended to Ezekiel 18, ministers who "pycke mennes pursses / thorow Masse pence / Dirige grotes / Trentalles / yeare myndes / moneth myndes &c." are damned for the harm they do to the poor. Some of this hostility was reflected in the Geneva marginalia, such as in the attacks against false pastors and hirelings in the notes to Jeremiah 23. On the whole, however, the thrust of the Geneva notes relating to ministers is positive, reflecting responsibilities more than failings.

The Rheims annotators vigorously asserted the necessity of respect for the clergy and denounced those who detracted from it. According to the comment on Luke 10:16, to despise Catholic priests was to denigrate Christ. Pastors and prelates have the authority to command and parishioners the duty to obey.[61] The proper attitude of the laity to the clergy is exemplified in Acts 5:11, where the people manifest reverence and fear toward the apostles. The note to Galatians 6:6 requires that the laity respect the clergy and "do good to such, or (as the Apostle speaketh) communicate with them in al our temporal goods, that we may be partakers of their spiritual." The strength of these affirmations suggests both a direct appeal to English Catholics to honor the missionary clerics and a reaction against the spread of anticlericalism in English society.

Greed for ecclesiastical lands generally has been considered a motive for Tudor anticlericalism, though written expressions of this feeling are not abundant. In the Elizabethan era the most outspoken critic of Anglican clerics for economic reasons was the fiery Welshman John Penry, who urged Elizabeth to abolish clerical offices in the church of England, for attached to them is "an infinit mass of wealth[,] even the very greenes of the land, which these locustes now unprofitablie devour, and therby ar made fatt and strong to warr agaynst Jesus Christ and his church." Glebe land should go to the crown unless the heirs of those who bestowed it on the church could demonstrate that it would have been their patrimony had their ancestors not been "seduced" by the clergy. "The interest that such heyres can have notwithstanding is grounded no otherwise then hir maiestie by consulting with the word of the Lord shall fynd hir self in conscienc bound to grant unto them of the free liberality of hir roiall heart." Cathedral churches should be destroyed as relics of Rome and their lands appropriated to royal use. These ideas appear in the draft of a letter intended for Robert Devereux, earl of Essex. Penry detested Anglican clergy on other grounds as well, particularly the persecution they inflicted on left-wing reformers, reviling and imprisoning them and rifling their homes. "You drive us from our familyes trades wifes children, especially from the society of the church and sayntes of god wherby though you gett us not, wee our wives children and poor Orphanes live in outward misery."[62]

Separatists directed a torrent of abusive language at the established clergy for religious reasons. Robert Harrison mocked Anglican ministers for receiving honor only from their household servants, and claimed most Englishmen held them in reproach; "they are become a Byworde and a common talke." Barrow and Greenwood castigated them as cursed merchants and relics of Rome who originated in the bottomless pit. Such ministers made merchandize of the word and auctioned the gospel, "compounding for their bellies before hand with the gluttons and profane people to whome they administer." Their selling and exchanging of livings was compared to the horse-trading at a fair, and Barrow objected that they assumed or vacated benefices without the consent and goodwill of the people. They were criticized for charging fees for christening and burial, and their apparel was denounced as too nice, too curious, or too affected. When he was taken to Lambeth Palace on 27 November 1587, Barrow sarcastically observed that he "found a very great traine without, but within a goodlie synode of bishops, deanes, civilians, etc., beside such an apparance of wel-fedde silken preistes, as I suppose might wel have beseemed the Vaticane." Such feelings spread rapidly in the underground world of Separatism.[63]

A good deal of Elizabethan anticlericalism is manifested in manuscripts and court records, and what we see is probably only the tip of the iceberg. For criticizing the London minister John Veron, rector of St. Martin, Ludgate, and vicar of St. Sepulchre, a young man had to stand in a sheet during a sermon at Paul's Cross in November 1561. In 1572, three or four boys, egged on by others, entered the parish church of St. Simon, Norwich, while Bishop Parkhurst was reading the service. When he read the words, "My soul doth magnify the Lord," they began singing and refused to desist despite his orders. On other occasions, some clergy were physically dragged from the pulpit, stripped of their gowns, and beaten for what they preached. William Hutchinson, curate of Langford, Wilts., complained to the Privy Council in May 1579 that he and his wife had been beaten. In July of the same year the Council ordered justices of the peace to investigate charges that the vicar of East Wellow, Hants., had been treated in a disorderly manner by one of the local gentry. The following year the Council learned that a schoolmaster of Andover, Hants., had used "lewde" language against the local minister and church officials and had assaulted a churchwarden.[64]

Anticlericalism increased in the late 1570s and continued at a more intense level through the Marprelate years. An Oxfordshire man found himself in the archdeacon's court for an impetuous reply to clerical criticism of him: "On Sundaye the third of Maye 1584 [in the] afternone Mr. Phippes ye Vicar of Burceter and Mr. Saule a preacher passed bye the howse of this respondent whoe then sate on his blocke at the churche wall in Burceter, and Mr. Phippes and Mr. Saule passing bye weare talking of a plague of God in soe much as Mr. Saule sayd when they came neare this respondent, call you this the plague of God; wheareunto this respondent sayde a plague on a knave." There was substantial anticlericalism in Yorkshire and Lancashire, where there were numerous complaints about poor attendance at church and sabbath violations. A man from Aysgarth, Yorks., resented church discipline so much that he vowed "he would make my lord archbishop spend £100 and call him up to London, and that if his friends knew that he were here in trouble by means of the vicar some of them would meet him in a water and turn him off his horse, and hang his foot in the stirrup and see how he could swim." Another man in the same area sneered that "the preaching of the Gospel is but bibble-bubble, and I care not a fart of my tail for any black coat in Wensleydale, and I had rather hear a cuckoo sing." Two Rochdale, Lancs., men spoke contemptuously of their Puritan vicar in 1585, asserting the supremacy of the old religion and belittling him as the plague of Yorkshire who had brought "Mr. Greaves and other strange prattling preachers of no good report, who clog with their tongues and only for much wages."[65]

In another dark corner of the land, anticlericalism was pronounced. The educator Adrian à Saravia, who later became Whitgift's chaplain, complained to Cecil of Guernsey:

As to religion there are only three or four people in the island who attend service, and if an ecclesiastic goes into the country, he is greeted with jeers and laughter, and often has dirt thrown at him. They are worse than Turks, and the jurats connive all at this.

Even in less backward areas hostility was generated by clerical exactions. When a widow was taken into an ecclesiastical court for refusing to pay a mortuary fee to the minister at Combe Florey, Som., popular resentment against the clergy and their fees ran in her favor, forcing the Privy Council to transfer the case to the Court of Arches. Some anticlerical sentiment was directed against wives of ecclesiastics, as in the case of a woman from Beddingham, Sussex, who accused her minister's wife in 1593 of being "the mistriss of a Redyng prists trull [concubine] ," adding "that all prists wyvs were counted trulls." Anticlerical hostility exasperated the clergy. At Paul's Cross in October 1602 Dr. John King complained that no matter how qualified a cleric was and how good his family background, he was derided "like a bird of diuers strange colours" because he was a minister.[66]

Anglicans and to a lesser extent Puritans defended themselves from these anticlerical outbursts. Visitation articles sometimes inquired if there were parishioners who abused ministers or defamed them as "dumb dogs." Concern was widespread that anticlericalism prompted able young men to avoid the ministry. Turnbull sagely observed that untrue accusations against the clergy were easily believed, but the guilt of some clergy made it easier for critics to smear the innocent. "The sily asse because he is simple, fyt by nature to beare heauy burdens, beaten, kicked, and spurned at by euerie one," preached John Dove, rector of Tidworth, Wilts., and St. Mary Aldermary, London, at Paul's Cross in 1596, "doth represent the Cleargie, which are sore loaded with slaunders, and manifeste wrongs, being strucken on the righte cheek turne the left, being robbed of their cote, give also their cloke, being cursed, they blesse, reviled, reuile not againe." Sutcliffe, who attributed most anticlericalism to licentious youths, was incensed that those uneducated in divinity presumed to teach divines.[67]

Other Anglicans tried to stem the tide of anticlericalism, including Bishop Cooper, who in the Marprelate controversy warned that contempt for bishops and ministers would result in religious and social confusion. To Sandys, standing before a preacher was standing in the presence of God, hence fear and reverence were due. Similarly, Edward Vaughan contended that the majesty of the message necessitated that a cleric not demean himself, and that the greatness of his calling rendered him unmeet for mean men. This point of view was a psychological reaction against the debasing attacks of anticlerics, whom he portrayed as pariahs in a Christian society. "Euerie base and beggerly fellow, euerie lewd and wanton mistres, euerie prophane and ruffianly gentleman, euerie swearing swashbuckler, and many such as make shew of honesty, and conscience of religion, in their feasting, in their gaming, in their riding, in their going, yea, in all their affaires, they will be medling and sensuring of ministers." Wright attributed the spreading anticlericalism—with some justification—to the attacks of Puritans and Separatists; better, he said, for them to be concerned with the evil conduct of the mighty than to be "cockes nipped with kites clawes . . . [who] cackle, but . . . crow not." Wright also blamed anticlericalism on the lesser magistrates, whom he accused of discrediting the clergy with bitter invectives and teaching the masses that ministers were ignorant asses.[68]

The picture that emerges is one of an embattled clergy striving desperately to preserve its hereditary position of social and religious leadership, in the face of encroaching secularism and religious sectarianism. The incursions were largely withstood in the Elizabethan era, but the portents of a future onslaught against clerical supremacy are evident. The urgency with which Puritans sought reforms may have been motivated in part by recognition of these warnings, and educated Anglicans regarded the portents as a threat to the social order.

(6) Tithes and Popular Hostility toward the Clergy

They ought to be maintained nether by mercenarye wadges, nor Jewishe tithes, to support them in idlenes, or worldye pompe.

Henry Barrow[69]

> Foure times a yere,
> You shall him heare,
> Full clarkely teach his flocke:
> What sinne it is,
> To tithe amisse,
> And with Gods part to mocke.

Robert Crowley[70]

The controversy over tithes in the mid-seventeenth century has roots in the fourteenth century, where anticlericalism, social unrest, heresy, the popularity of friars, and poverty were principal factors in provoking resentment. In the sixteenth century, economic developments in such areas as mining, mercantile activities, and agriculture, coupled with the rise in prices, prompted the clergy to look more closely into ways to tap this wealth and to hinder attempts by the laity to evade the payment of tithes. Simultaneously, there was an outburst of opposition to tithes from left-wing reformers, who resented compulsory exactions to support an ecclesiastical establishment they repudiated. Their attack coincided with popular indignation, fostered partly by litigation over tithes. Tithe collectors were sources of popular pique; their activities moved the Privy Council in July 1578 to ask the lord president of the North, the archbishop of York, and the bishop of Durham to consider complaints against tithe collectors who spoiled corn and hindered tillers. The Council became involved in other tithe disputes. When, for example, the parishioners of Greystock, Cumb., complained to the queen in 1582 that their parson was trying to increase tithes, the Council ordered Lord Scrope to resolve the controversy.[71]

Such attempts by the clergy were common enough to prompt the Puritan Francis Trigge to recommend that ministers accept a loss in tithes as the price of maintaining the love of their people. One clergyman who did this was the minister at Danby Wisk, Yorks., whose congregation lost its crops in the 1569 rebellion. Their parson commuted the tithes to cash and required less than the tithes would have been worth. Such cases, however, are difficult to find, and the average ecclesiastic probably garnered as much as he could in tithes. Greenham testified that the clergy's greater diligence in collecting tithes than in providing hospitality led to anticlericalism.[72]

Part of the problem was that some clergy looked on a benefice primarily as freehold property that entitled the incumbent to an income from tithes. Legally, of course, an incumbent did have freehold rights, which provided him some security of tenure and was supposed to guarantee him an income. This view of tithes as essentially personal property ran counter to a medieval tradition that viewed tithes as communal property held in trust by the cleric and administered on behalf of the local society. The death blow to this tradition, except in mind only, was delivered by the wholesale redistribution of ecclesiastical lands beginning with Henry VIII. Lay owners of tithes did not buy church property to become communal stewards, and their treatment of tithes as personal income appears to have been widely followed by ministers. Elizabeth contributed significantly to this phenomenon by selling or granting titles to tithes in 2,216 parishes.[73]

As tithes increasingly became matters of property transactions and legal payments to owners, the spiritual foundations of the tithing principle crumbled. As in other economic transactions, men paid the bare minimum, thus Babington grumbled that those who pay tithes in kind "choose out the broken and blinde, the halte and lame, the scabbed and scuruie." Such clerical disenchantment was matched by lay disgust with the commercial aura that surrounded the paying of tithes. The result was increased litigation, often between clergy and laity, but sometimes between rival ministers, as in the case of the tithe dispute between Robert Wesley, parson of Wetherden, and William Cooke, parson of Woolpit, Suffolk. Dering neatly summarizes the display of litigiousness: "The Parson against the Vicar, the Vicar against the Parson, the Parish against both, and one against another, and all for the belly." It was not, however, only clergy who sued for tithes, but lay owners as well. In the diocese of York, suits by the latter were as frequent as those by the former. In the first three terms of 1591, forty-two tithe cases were instigated in York courts, of which twenty were by laymen.[74]

Both sides were blamed for the litigious mess. George Abbot berated those who claimed to be too poor to aid the destitute but had funds to force a minister to sue at law for tithes. An opposite picture emerges in the case of the parson of Whitchurch, Ches., who sued tenants at Temple Newsom, Yorks., over disputed properties for three years until they could no longer afford the legal struggle; the parson was judged victorious because 'the spiritual Court favours the case of tithe." The multiplicity of courts in which tithing cases could be heard compounded the problem. Cases could and sometimes did go as high as the Court of Requests, Chancery, the Exchequer of Pleas, and the Star Chamber. Legal confrontations contributed nothing toward clerical prestige and exacerbated relations with the laity.[75]

One of the most outspoken critics of the tithing system was Penry, whose attacks embraced religious and economic considerations. Tithes, he argued, should be abolished as relics of the old religion. A new method of maintaining ministers was appointed by Christ to replace the Judaic institution of tithing. Elizabeth should remit tithes to her subjects, "reserving notwithstanding such a portion therof unto hir maiestie[s] prerogative hir maiestie unto hir self, as shee may tak out of the same for the use of hir publick affayres, what may bee thought needfull for hir state, as in stead of tenthes to have the 40th, 30th, 20th or 15th part of hir subjectes goodes returned yearly unto hir treasures, wheras now the tenth part is devoured by the preisthood and prelacy of the kingdom of Antichrist and such as depend upon them."[76] In fact, however, the presence of numerous tithes in lay hands rendered such reform impossible. The virtue of increasing crown revenue was more than offset by the attack on property rights that such a plan would entail, to say nothing of the social revolution that would ensue.

No person was more vehement and voluminous in his attack on tithes than Barrow. Because they belonged to the Levitical priesthood, tithes — "Balaam's wages" — must be abolished. They were idolatrous inventions, more appropriate for idle hirelings than true ministers. The fixed system of tithes in the Church of England resulted in "miserable rapine and extortion," with the clergy "thrusting their fleshhook into everie poore bodie's kettle, and (as it were) plucking the bread from them and their children's mouthes." Moreover, the clergy had nothing to do with the lowly until their tithes were due. Barrow's assault, with its appeal to the socially down-trodden, was motivated by his belief in ecclesiastical voluntarism. Allotting lands and tithes to sustain the ministry in each parish was unsupportable because not every parish had a gathered church. Demanding a contribution to support a believers' church was contrary to the principles set forth in Romans 15:26-27 and Philippians 4:18. The clergy of the Church of England, he charged, were intruded into their livings and cannot be supported by popish tithing, hence he advocated the revolutionary plan of refusal to pay tithes even when commanded by a magistrate.[77]

Barrow's advocacy of the abolition of tithes required him to consider the questions of ministerial support and the proper disposition of the tithes. True to his principle of ecclesiastical voluntarism, he called for voluntary maintenance of ministers. A pastor must live *"ex pura eleemosyna,* of clere almes (cleane almes-deedes) as Christ in his Testament hath ordeyned, and as he and his apostles." Proper provision for the clergy cannot be bought and sold like tithes, which destroy the spiritual relationship between pastor and flock. The amount of the gifts was not restricted to 10% but was determined by the ability of the giver and the need of the minister, with the proviso that his living must be adequate. For the disposition of tithes, Barrow proposed virtually the same solution as Penry. The crown should remit tithes to its subjects, retaining only those deemed necessary by the queen. Barrow recommended that tithes be restored to the people as the true owners, and the glebe lands deeded to the crown. Because glebes, like tithes, had an idolatrous origin and history, and lacked

New Testament warrant, he wanted them devoted to civil purposes. Ultimately even Barrow's economic arguments rest on a theological rather than a social foundation, the doctrinal principle that tithes and glebe lands, because they are rooted in Old Testament law, are no longer valid by virtue of the replacement of that law by the gospel.[78]

The spread of these ideas in Separatist congregations is evidenced in the testimony of two men in the early 1590s who were examined by ecclesiastical officials. The first of these was Thomas Hale of Welwyn, Herts., who testified that tithes ceased with the coming of Christ, and that ministers now depended on the support of their flocks. The testimony of Robert Abraham, a servant from the parish of St. Olave, Southwark, was more substantive. Their ministers, he claimed, were supported by weekly collections from members according to ability to pay, with deacons using some funds to aid the needy of the congregation.[79] These men believed that voluntary maintenance was not only biblical but feasible, and the tithing system of the Church of England and those who enforced it were resented as unscriptural and financially oppressive.

The attack on tithes ran counter to the views in the marginalia of Elizabethan Bibles. Tyndale's Pentateuch of 1530 had adopted a critical posture in the note to Numbers 18, which chided that the English clergy sought "tithes & landes & rentes & emperies and all," but this comment was dropped in the less provocative 1551 edition. In the Geneva Bible, tithes were viewed as appropriate for the maintenance of ministers and relief of the needy, with a promise that liberal donation would be divinely rewarded. The annotators were, however, concerned that tithes be used only to support right religion, godly clergy, and deserving poor. The Bishops' Bible, in the note to Deuteronomy 14:29, called attention to the proper employment of tithes to support the clergy and the destitute. A note to 2 Chronicles 31:10 reminded readers that Hebrew ministers had been liberally maintained. Tithes were not questioned in the Rheims New Testament, but were viewed as the means through which the clergy received their legitimate living.[80]

The principles on tithes in the marginalia of the Geneva and Bishops' Bibles were defended by Anglican and Puritan alike, for both had a stake in the system. No less than three Paul's Cross sermons in October and November 1602 defended tithes against sectarian and popular reaction. On 10 October, the president of Corpus Christi College, Oxford, Dr. John Spencer, spoke on the theme, "there is a synn amongst us which hath not bin heard of amongst the Gentiles, that wee should robb God, and that is in tithing." Two weeks later Dr. John King suggested that refusal to pay tithes would deprive a person of spiritual reward and perhaps material prosperity. Dr. Thomas Holland, fellow of Balliol College and Regius Professor of Divinity at Oxford, returned to the tithing theme, arguing that as God made miraculous provision for his disciples, so Christians must make ordinary provision for the ministry. One of the ablest Anglican apologists for tithes was Bancroft, who refuted Barrow's views. Troubled by a perceived decline in church giving, especially through attempts to conceal wealth to reduce tithes, Bancroft acknowledged that clerical attempts to obtain tithes, by legal suit if necessary, produced anticlericalism, with some clergy being "indited for common Barators." He agreed to consider a plan similar to those advocated by Penry and Barrow, that is, tithes could be abolished if the laity undertook an alternate system of provision "as preachers were dealt withall in the Apostles times." By this plan the laity would be sworn to support the clergy, but Bancroft felt that payments should not be exacted from believers only. Because of the extensive involvement of the laity in the ownership of tithes, however, the proposal was unworkable.[81]

Among Puritans, Fulke stipulated that payment of tithes was abrogated by Christ's death to the extent that tithes had been required under Hebrew ceremonial law. Yet he defended their retention, for the maintenance of the clergy, or an adequate alternative system. Richard Allison, lecturer at St. Nicholas Acon, London, was convinced that sufficient clerical maintenance was impossible if left to individual discretion. The principle behind tithing—the provision of a set maintenance for the ministry—must be retained, though tithes as part of the ceremonial law are no longer required. Eusebius Pagit came to essentially the same conclusion by arguing that Levitical tithes supported both ministerial work and sacrifices. Because the coming of Christ did not abolish the need for ministerial work, tithes were still valid and must be enforced by magistrates. The absence of adequate tithes, he argued, led to abuses in the church, by forcing clergy "eyther to make marchandize of the word, or for gaine to flater the welthy, or with shame for want to beg, or for need to starue." Too many of the wealthy received rather than bestowed tithes, so that ministers relied for support on the poorest, who ought to be receiving alms instead of rendering tithes. To the objection that tithes were relics of popery, Robert Some retorted that on the basis of this argument churches and universities would have to be abolished, leaving atheism "in steade of Gods religion, and Macciauell in the place of the new Testament." Stubbes pointedly observed that if ministers were reduced to voluntary maintenance, they would reach a state of virtual poverty as in Scotland. An indication of Puritan support for tithes was the *Decimarvm et oblationvm tabvla,* prepared in 1591 by William Crashaw, sizar of St. John's College, Cambridge, which set forth canon and statutory laws governing tithing.[82]

Tithes, then, placed Church of England clergymen in an awkward position. They were faced on the one hand with the Separatist challenge to relinquish them, and live on voluntary gifts, as the Separatists managed to do. Yet they doubted this practice would suffice for a national ministry. Moreover, the involvement of tithes in a system of freehold property rights that included powerful laymen rendered any substantive reform potentially revolutionary. Parliament enacted legislation (18 Eliz. I, c. 11) allowing parishioners to withhold tithes from nonresident ministers if the bishop refused to punish the nonresidents, but beyond this it dared not go without striking at property rights. The clergy were not helped by a system in which some of the most rapacious collectors were laity, who siphoned funds intended for the church and whose rapacity reflected adversely on the clergy. Nor was the clergy's standing enhanced by the litigiousness that characterized the tithing system. If the ministry was to be distinguished by learning, residency, and high moral standards, adequate funding was essential. Weaknesses in those areas fed sectarianism and anticlericalism. Yet the attempt to increase clerical funding to develop an educated, resident, moral clergy involved improving the efficiency of the tithing system, which itself was a source of anticlericalism. Such was the paradox that confronted the clergy and had a direct bearing on their capacity for social leadership.

The chronic underfunding of the Elizabethan church frustrated Anglican and Puritan alike, and undoubtedly intensified the differences between them. Although both groups agreed on the value of an educated clergy, Anglicans found little sympathy among Puritans when they bestowed ecclesiastical appointments on inadequately trained men in the belief that such clergy were better than none. The aniconic orientation of Puritanism, with its stress on the sermon, necessitated educated ministers, whereas the greater liturgical focus in Anglican worship could better accommodate men able to do little more than read homilies. Moderate Anglicans such as Sandys and Pilkington were, however, determined to improve preaching in the church. The number of university-educated clergy began to increase substantially in the 1570s, and in 1586 Convocation launched its program to provide periodic sermons in parishes normally devoid of them. Once in the pulpit, Puritans were customarily more chary than Anglicans in the employment of erudition, preferring to make their sermons models of simplicity and comprehensibility, whereas educated Anglicans were more prone to draw on classical, historical, and theological authorities to buttress their arguments.

Underfunding of the church hampered the employment of sufficient numbers of suitably qualified spiritual leaders, particularly as inadequate remuneration encouraged pluralism and probably demoralized ministers. With numerous advowsons in lay hands, the patronage system complicated the quest for a godly, educated clergy, even though some patrons exercised care in the appointment of fit men. Puritans were incensed with clergy who were sexually incontinent, excessive consumers of alcohol, gamblers, or blasphemers, though bishops too were troubled by such behavior, especially since such behavior was a factor in motivating anticlericalism. Anglicans were sensitive to anticlerical attacks, viewing them as a threat to the religious and social order. In this context the Puritan condemnation of clerics who were dissipate, ignorant, or derelict in duty struck at the roots of anticlericalism, though to embattled Anglicans such criticism was too close to the wholesale castigation of ministers by Separatists. Anticlericalism also was fostered by the ecclesiastical courts, which played a crucial role in enforcing social behavior. Although Puritans did not favor mitigating the punishments meted out in these courts for social offenses (but demanded harsher penalties), their emphasis on sermons in worship, predicated on a godly, educated ministry, provided a counterpart to church courts as a means of inculcating proper social conduct. The sermon, like the Bible and its marginal notes, was a vehicle to mold social as well as religious attitudes, a fact most clearly appreciated by Puritans and moderate Anglicans.

These matters directly affected the ability of the clergy to serve as moral leaders and exemplars. A good deal of tension was generated by their relationship to society, ranging from the conflicting demands on bishops to be both spiritual shepherds and lordly prelates, to the involvement of the clergy in a system of lay patronage. Caught in a political and economc web of secular ties and obligations, the church was never free to establish the spiritually dedicated ministry that might have made a more effective assault on social problems. Instead the presence of unlettered and immoral clerics, and the friction inherent in the economic plight of the clergy, provided grist for the mill of anticlericalism.

Part II: Marriage and Sex

CHAPTER *3*

The Marital Quest

In their role as religious and moral leaders, the clergy sought to influence all significant aspects of matrimony. Much effort was expended to develop the proper ends of marriage and refute the Catholic exaltation of the celibate life. These efforts contributed to a more dignified role of the family and especially the married woman in English society. When ministers endeavored to influence the qualities to be sought in a mate they were less successful, particularly in their attempt to play down financial considerations. Some of the clergy, particularly Puritans, expressed concern about the marriage of children, but Anglican reaction was mixed. In considering these questions, Anglicans and Puritans often expressed divergent views.

(1) The Nature and Purpose of Marriage

Were it not for that holy Institution, what would the world be but a brood of haplesse bastards, like to the cursed seed of *Cain*, men fit for all manner of villany, and such as would leaue behind them a race of runnagates, persons that would liue as badly as they are lewdly begotten.

Thomas Deloney[1]

I say the world had more need of weeding than wedding.

Thomas Lodge[2]

115

Traditional concepts of marriage were challenged in Elizabethan society. At the dawn of the sixteenth century, near unanimity existed
concerning the sacramental nature of matrimony, but well before
the end of the century competing views began to supplant traditional conceptions. Catholics retained their sacramental understanding of marriage, as manifested, for example, in the explication
of its mediatory role in the transmission of grace by Nicholas Sanders, regius professor of theology at Louvain. Marriage, he explained
in 1567, is "a Sacrament, which by the outward and visible signe of
mutuall consent in faithfull persons signifieth the gratious vnity of
Christ and of his Churche, and whiles it signifieth such a singular
grace, it partaketh of the grace whereof it is the signe." Similarly,
the note to Ephesians 5:32 in the Rheims New Testament asserted
that marriage is a sacrament of Christ and his church prefigured in
Adam and Eve. Despite this adherence to the sacramental interpretation of matrimony, subtle but meaningful changes occurred in
Catholic thought in the last half of the century. Perhaps the most
significant was the recognition for the first time by an ecumenical
council of the role of love in marriage. This came in 1563 when
the Council of Trent, in affirming the indissolubility of marriage,
proclaimed that "Christ himself has promised the grace which per-
fects that natural love" between man and wife, as indicated by the
Pauline admonition for husbands to love their spouses as Christ
loved his church.[3]

By the Elizabethan era, English Protestants had ceased to regard
matrimony as a sacrament, though Anglican theologians attributed
to it near sacramental quality, and continued the custom of concluding weddings with the celebration of the Eucharist. Puritans
were uncomfortable with this proclivity towards sacramental marriage and objected to the depiction of matrimony in the *Book of
Common Prayer* as a signification of the mystical union between
Christ and his church. To them this made marriage an effectual
sign of grace. Instead, the Puritans, reflecting the covenantal theme
in their theology, viewed wedlock as the "ioyning of one man and
one woman togither by the couenaunt of God," thereby creating a
"communion of life" between the marital partners. In Puritan
writings, a fourfold analogy was used to represent the covenantal
nature of marriage, that is, marriage as friendship, as government
(with the husband and wife being fellow citizens and governors of
the household), as a church (with the husband as pastor and the
family and servants as the congregation), and as a business partnership (with the husband and wife sharing a contractual relationship).[4]

Against this background of the nature of marriage, there was general agreement that it served a tripartite purpose, which was procreation, avoidance of fornication, and companionship. An examination of seventeenth-century English works about marriage led James Johnson to conclude that Puritans rearranged the ends of marriage to assert the primacy of mutual help rather than procreation, largely because they listed companionship first. As adherents of Ramist logic, he argued, primacy went to the end first mentioned. Johnson asserted that the origins of this shift in importance were in the writings of Perkins, particularly his *Christian Oeconomie*, initially published in Latin in 1590.[5] An examination of the Elizabethan background reveals that the question of the ends of marriage was undergoing study in Catholic and Protestant circles alike.

The traditional Catholic view appeared in 1565 in the *Summa of Christian Doctrine* by the Dutch Jesuit Peter Canisius, who taught that the ends of marriage were propagation, companionship, and avoidance of fornication. A year later, however, there was a stunning change in the Roman Catechism, which was an outgrowth of the Council of Trent:

The causes for which a man and woman ought to marry should be explained. The first of these, then, is this very partnership of diverse sexes—sought by natural instinct, and compacted in the hope of mutual help so that one aided by the other may more easily bear the discomforts of life and sustain the weakness of old age. Another is the appetite of procreation, not so much indeed that heirs of property and riches be left, but that worshippers of the true faith and religion be educated. . . .

The third is one which after the Fall of the first parent was added to the other causes, when, because of the loss of justice in which man had been established, his appetite began to fight with right reason; so indeed he who is conscious of his weakness and does not wish to bear the battle of the flesh may use the remedy of marriage to avoid the sins of lust.

Presumably the Roman Catechism became known to some English Catholics after 1566, but the available evidence indicates that the older emphasis on marriage for procreative purposes prevailed among English Catholics throughout the Elizabethan period. The 1574 catechism of Lawrence Vaux viewed procreation as the special cause of matrimony. In the Rheims New Testament the note to Matthew 1:20 spoke of a triple perfection being accomplished in Joseph and Mary, namely, reproduction, fidelity, and sacrament. As late as the publication of the Douai Bible in 1609-10, the note to Genesis 1 stressed the institution of marriage for propagation. Yet on this occasion, the battle with Protestants over the role of the celibate life was more consequential than the ends of marriage, hence the annotators argued that man had so abundantly reproduced that the obligation to marry for procreation had ceased. The conclusion might seem to be that men could not wed primarily for procreation, but the intention of the annotators was to defend the superiority of celibacy.[6]

In Elizabethan Protestant views, the emphasis in the Geneva marginalia is on matrimony as a means to avoid fornication and propagate mankind, not as a covenant for mutual society. Genesis 2:18, which Johnson regards as a definitive passage for Puritan marriage doctrine, did not receive comment by the Geneva annotators. Bullinger's popular tract on marriage, however, reiterated the threefold purpose of procreation, sexual remedy, and mutual comfort, the same order used in the Edwardian *Books of Common Prayer,* Bishop Cooper's exposition of Old Testament passages commonly read in church services, and Thomas Cogan's popular medical handbook. Sandys, however, anticipated Perkins and later Puritans by according primacy of place to mutual society, assistance, and comfort, which helped lay the foundation for the idea of the companionate marriage.[7]

Elizabethan Puritans tended to accept the traditional order for the ends of marriage, with emphasis on procreation. Some (John Gardiner, Thomas Becon, and Robert Allen) concentrated only on dual ends, attributing a subordinate role to the very companionship that emerges in the seventeenth century as the focus of Puritan marriage doctrine. Perkins and Robert Cleaver, rector of Drayton, Oxon., however, sometimes stressed mutual society, with the latter professing that wedlock was instituted "to the end, that they may dwell togither in friendship and honestie, one helping and comforting the other, eschewing whoredome, and all vncleanenesse, bringing vp theyr children in the feare of God." While most Puritans emphasized matrimony for procreation, a strong minority focused on its role as a remedy for incontinency. Pagit nevertheless reminded people that because matrimony had been instituted (as was commonly accepted) in Eden, it could not have been intended initially as a means to avoid lust, but this reason was added after the fall of Adam and Eve. The tendency of some Puritans to stress marriage as a remedy for incontinency led Louis Wright mistakenly to conclude that the Puritan "began to concentrate his interest upon preserving the purity of the married state rather than the physiological purity of the individual." In fact, most Puritans, like Anglicans, emphasized the positive aspects of marriage (procreation, mutual society) as a holy institution. At least two Puritans (Stubbes and Vaughan) attributed a fourth end to matrimony, a variation of the sacramental theme in Anglican thought. To them marriage was intended also to be a figure or type of the spiritual marriage between Christ and his church, not as a means of grace but in order "that aduersaries might be reconciled by meanes of it, and made perpetuall friends."[8]

In marital theory, then, the Elizabethan period was one of flux. Whereas English Catholics adhered to the orthodox view of marriage as a sacrament, Anglicans no longer accepted this view but still attributed an essentially sacramental quality to matrimony. The Puritans deviated by stressing the covenantal nature of wedlock, and Separatists radicalized marriage as a civil rather than a religious institution. With respect to the ends of marriage, English Catholics do not seem to have acquiesced to the novel emphasis in the 1566 Roman Catechism on marriage as fellowship, though in Protestant circles its importance was manifested in the writings of Sandys, Perkins, and Cleaver. Most Anglicans and Puritans agreed with the Catholics that the primary end of marriage was procreation, though some Puritans focused on wedlock as a remedy for incontinency. Perkins, after asserting the primacy of fellowship in 1590, changed seven years later to emphasize matrimony as a means to prohibit sexual immorality.[9] These views had practical effects in terms of birth control and family size, marital fidelity, and husband-wife relationships; but first the question of celibacy must be examined.

(2) Marriage or Celibacy?

Single life, for many causes, is the best, I grant. Yet is it not best for every body, but only for him that hath the gift of chastity, and can with quiet mind and upright conscience live single.

John Jewel, bishop of Salisbury[10]

Hee that shuneth marriage, and auoydeth societie, is to be esteemed a wicked wretch (as the Pope is) or more then a man, as he whom Homer reprehendeth, saying: that he was triblesse, lawlesse, and houselesse.

William Vaughan[11]

From the social perspective, an obvious change resulting from the adoption of Protestantism was the cessation of mandatory celibacy for clerics, with a concomitant rise in the status of marriage. For wives, the abandonment of virginity as the highest goal opened the door for the gradual attainment of a new dignity, while simultaneously, humanist and Protestant educational views resulted in increased numbers of learned women. That these phenomena were more than casually associated is likely in that the virtual closing of the celibate life as a vocation probably prompted some women to turn their energies toward learned achievements. Although Catholics never fully denigrated matrimony, which was a sacrament, their high regard for the celibate life denuded marriage, sex, and the family of the social dignity that the Protestants accorded them.

As developed by English Catholics in the Elizabethan age, the supremacy of the celibate life was founded on the dichotomy in human nature between the rational and the sensual. Because the former was believed to be harmonious with the angelic sphere and the latter with the animal realm, abstinence from corporal pleasures to pursue the rational and spiritual was considered the superior course. Nevertheless, both states were honorable, as Christ made evident by being born of a virgin but married mother, indicating, according to the Rheims note to Matthew 1:23, the superiority of the continent life. Thus the Catholic apologist Thomas Stapleton advised fathers of daughters:

He that ioyneth his virgin in mariage, doth well, and he that ioyneth not his virgin in mariage, doeth better. Thus in holy scripture [1 Cor. 7] we see holy virginite commended before the state of wedlocke.

The Rheims annotators commented at length on the crucial seventh chapter in Paul's epistle to the Corinthians. The apostle, they explained, did not counsel the single life simply because of the problems inherent in marriage but also because of the greater rewards in heaven for unwed, chaste Christians. Virginity is a quieter life and more conducive to divine service, and it has "a grateful puritie and sanctitie both of body & soule, which mariage hath not." Virginity and innocency, asserted an apologist, were companions in paradise, preceding matrimony which (contrary to Protestant teaching) "began with miserie." [12]

Catholics contended that despite their attribution of primacy to celibacy they held wedlock in higher esteem than did Protestants, because they deemed it a sacrament. If all men were celibate it would be prejudicial to mankind, consequently they developed three states of chastity, the highest of which was virginity, which preceded a widow's chastity and the moderate use of sex in marriage. Even so, in the Catholic conception, sexual relations were far from noble, as Matthew Kellison, regius professor of divinity at Rheims, candidly admitted: "We are ashamed of all carnall copulation, even of that which by mariage is made lawfull, . . . [for] Chastitie is more beseeming the nature of man." Although Catholics acknowledged matrimony was a remedy for illicit sex, they urged as the superior remedy the vow of chastity upheld by prayer, fasting, and the chastisement of concupiscence. Although chastity was a divine gift, it was available to any who requested it, contrary to Protestant teaching.

> Whensoeuer a man is bound to abstaine, either by vow or any other necessarie occasion (as if one of the parties be in prison, warre, banishment, siknes, or absent perpetually by lawful diuorce) the other must needes in pain of damnation abstaine, and can not excuse the want of the gift of chastitie. For he is bound to aske it and to seeke for it of God by fasting, praying, and chastising his body. . . . Therfore detest the doctrine of the Protestants in this point, that when they list not fast nor pray for it, say they haue not the gift.

The vow of chastity was regarded (despite papal dispensations) as perpetual, and in the context of the Catholic doctrine of soteriology, vows of chastity were more meritorious than marital vows.[13]

On this theological foundation, English Catholics asserted the necessity of the celibate life for clergy. The twin disadvantages of married clerics were involvement in marital concerns rather than total dedication to spiritual endeavors, and the taint of carnal copulation. The thrust of Matthew 19:21 was that following Christ meant "to be without wife and care of children, to lacke propriety, and to liue in common." The Rheims annotators argued that the apostles left their wives to follow Jesus, and that all notable bishops and priests in the church had been single or (if married before they became clerics) continent from their wives. Because Protestants approved clerical matrimony they were linked to ancient heretics; Protestants made much of the Pauline admonition (1 Cor. 7:9) that it was better to marry than burn, but Catholics retorted that Protestants used this as an excuse to wed. Paul was not referring to simple temptation but to surrender to concupiscence in mind or deed, which Catholics felt could be prevented by prayer and fasting. The admission of Protestant writers that some ministers married to avoid fornication became a weapon in the arsenal of Catholic propaganda. Protestant clergy, according to Lewis Evans, "doe no sooner attayne this one newe onelye order, but then busylie seeke they for some bassing gyrle to make vpp theyr newe godlynes: . . . this is the ende of theyr studie, . . . theyr *summum bonum*."[14]

Elizabethan Protestants retaliated with their own invective, aided by the infamous reputation of Rome as a city of prostitution. In 1527 the city of some 55,000 people had approximately 1,500 prostitutes, or something on the order of one harlot for every ten adult males. Pius V and Sixtus V tried to repress whoredom, so that by 1600 the number of professional prostitutes had declined to about 800 in a city then in excess of 100,000 people. Nevertheless the notoriety was such that Protestants found it a convenient argument against clerical celibacy. Jewel referred directly to the prevalence of prostitution in Rome, and others made similar, broader accusations. Stoughton heard that prices for a courtesan ranged from the equivalent of 6d. to 10s. Jewel charged that since England had become Protestant, there were fewer brothels, concubines, and matrimonial breaches, but currently no statistics are available to determine the validity of his statement. The accusations linking whoredom and marital infidelity to clerical celibacy were hardly novel in Elizabethan England, for they had appeared, for example, in Tyndale's prologue to Numbers in the Matthew-Becke Bibles of 1549 and 1551 and the Matthew Bible of 1551. Abuses in the issuing of licenses and dispensations for sexual matters lent further credence to Protestant charges. Nichols worried that clerical celibacy led not only to sexual offenses but also to diminution of the population and the exemption of clergy from civil service. Exactly the opposite argument was used by the rector of Wickersley, Yorks., Michael Sherbrook, who contended that the procreative efforts of married clergy caused a rise in population, expanding the labor supply and depressing wages. [15]

Whereas Catholics relegated chastity within wedlock to a status inferior to that of celibacy and even a widow's abstinence from sexual relations, Protestant writers treated the manifestations of chastity as equal. Their position was succinctly enunciated in the Matthew-Becke Bibles of 1549 and 1551 and the Matthew Bible of 1551, where the note to 1 Corinthians 7 states:

Chastitye is a gifte of God, and is . . . an honeste habite of the mynde wherby the outragiouse lustes of the fleshe be repressed and kepte vnder, so that they cause vs not to vse or desyre the vnlaufull companie of the contrarie secte [sex]. . . . This chastitie ought to be in euery Christian man and woman, be they maried or vnmaried. Thys chastitye haue we not of longe tyme compted worthy the name of chastitye, but thought them onely to be c[h]aste: whiche haue refrayned mariage.

This conception of chastity made it insignificant whether a person was married or not. Sexual intercourse did not diminish chastity so long as it was properly used among marital partners. Because the essence of chastity was purity of soul and body, the mind and body were chaste when free from fleshly concupiscence in thought and deed. Chastity was not associated with sexual abstinence but the suppression of sexual lust, unnatural sexual desires (e.g. homosexuality, sodomy, and incest), and sexual affections for someone other than one's spouse. To be chaste, a single person must not burn with sexual desires, engage in sexual relations, or sexually abuse his mind or body. Chastity for a married person involved the use of wedlock as God ordained.[16]

Having asserted the equality of chastity in celibate and wedded life, Protestants were still faced with the apparent Pauline preference for continency. To this their response was to acknowledge continency as a divine gift (as did Catholics) but not one bestowed on any who desired it (contrary to Catholic teaching). The note to Matthew 19:12 in the Geneva Bible indicated its rarity and warned men not to abstain from marriage rashly. Marriage, according to the note to 1 Corinthians 7:6 in the Beza-Tomson Bible, "is not simplie necessarie for all men, but for them which haue not the gift of continencie, & this gift is by a peculiar grace of God." Cartwright and Perkins repudiated the Catholic contention that this gift was available to those who sought it by prayer and fasting, but two other Puritans adopted a mediatory stance. Fulke thought God might bestow the gift in response to prayer if, as Origen said, it was expedient for his glory and man's salvation, and William Hergest, the tutor of Sir Thomas Bromley's children, affirmed it was granted to those who sought it by continual prayer. Greenham was concerned that too many people married without first praying, fasting, and avoiding occasions provoking concupiscence to determine whether they possessed the gift of celibacy. Those who exercised such means and found themselves unfit for the single life were expected to avail themselves of the gift of procreation and marry. Protestants did not deprecate the celibate life so long as one possessed the gift requisite for it. They were quick to affirm that the gift of celibacy was not automatically bestowed on clergy, who had to determine which type of chaste life they were by God and nature intended to pursue. Those with the gift of celibacy, whether clergy or laity, were expected to refrain from marriage. Sutcliffe observed that he knew none so forward in marrying as Puritans, of whom he knew none who possessed this gift of continency. In the early decades of the age, substantial numbers of Anglican clerics were unwed, but by the time Sutcliffe wrote in 1592, an overview of Anglican clergy turns up relatively few celibate ministers. Among Puritan clerics celibacy never caught on as an ideal.[17]

Sharp disagreement also existed between Catholics and Protestants over the necessity of perpetual adherence to vows of celibacy. No unanimity existed among English Protestants over whether such vows could even be properly made. Perkins, referring to 1 Corinthians 7:9, found them prohibited by divine command, and the note to Matthew 19:11 in the Beza-Tomson Bible reproved them. Fulke, on the other hand, accepted celibate vows for those who possessed the necessary gift. George Estey, a preacher at Bury St. Edmunds, Suffolk, had no objection to vows by those with this gift, but cautioned that the gift was not perpetual. A continuing resolution to lead a single life was acceptable to Perkins, but not a vow of continency. The Geneva annotators and Christopher Shutte could not accept a celibate vow because they judged it a rash act conducive to sin. General agreement was reached that no one could impose celibate vows on other persons or require celibacy in particular vocations. [18]

For those who had taken such vows in Marian England, Protestant marriage was allowable. In the latter decades of the century the question again arose, particularly in anti-Catholic literature. Perkins, who opposed the vows, nevertheless argued that once taken, they had to be fulfilled as long as the gift lasted. If one who had taken the vow possessed the gift but determined to marry, the sin was in the breach of the vow rather than in matrimony. In his refutation of the notes to the Rheims New Testament, Fulke built on a principle he had enunciated in 1583:

Such as be assured they haue the gift of continencie, may professe to keepe it, and after such profession or promise, made to God, they sinne if they breake it. But if any haue rashly vowed that which they are not able to keepe, they haue sinned in vowing, and can not keepe their vowe by abstinence from mariage, except they abstaine also from all filthines out of mariage: . . . it is better to marye, than out of mariage to liue incontinently.

The basic principle required keeping vows already made, but for those unable to meet celibate standards, the sin of breaking the vow was preferable to illicit sex. [19]

For a Protestant who seriously sought to determine whether he or she possessed the celibate gift, the process must have been hard enough, but Cleaver—apparently alone—imposed an additional burden on persons of authority, making it their responsibility to prohibit persons with the gift of celibacy from marrying. [20] Apart from the limited authority vested in parents and guardians, it is inconceivable that this could have been done. For those making their own decisions, evidence is insufficient to determine how seriously Elizabethans considered celibacy for religious reasons when the question of marriage arose. Some documented cases exist of widows declining further marriages and wedded couples abstaining from sex, hence it is conceivable that some single persons did remain unwed in Protestant England for religious reasons.

Of the various ends of marriage, the only one regarded as important enough to overcome a vow of celibacy was the use of wedlock as a remedy for sexual incontinency. Neither fellowship nor procreation was deemed a sufficient reason to break that promise. Marriage was not an option for those devoid of the celibate gift, but a mandatory responsibility. It was the parents' duty to counsel children to find a fit spouse. It was equally the responsibility of the ministers unable to lead a celibate life to marry, though Cartwright cautioned that every temptation to lust was not the burning of which Paul spoke, and did not justify the marital remedy. Yet to restrict the clergy from marriage was viewed as an invitation to prostitution, incest, and buggery. One clergyman who married because he could not withstand sexual temptations was Richard Cox, bishop of Ely. He explained to Cecil on 29 December 1568 that he married in good conscience, reminded Cecil of the Pauline admonition to marry rather than burn, and asked him to intercede with Elizabeth on his behalf. (Cox was in trouble with the queen not only for marrying, at the age of sixty-nine, a young widow, but also for urging Elizabeth to marry.) Among the laity perhaps the most famous case is that of Edward, son of Edward Seymour, earl of Hertford, who informed his father on 16 November 1582 that he had wed to stop offending people by his dissolute life and would try to bridle his sexual drives.[21]

It was one thing for Protestants to assert the validity of clerical marriage, but it was another to determine its advisability, especially considering Paul's deprecatory remarks on wedlock. There was also the question of biblical precedent. The Old Testament posed no serious problem, for Abraham, Moses, and Aaron were married men, and Mosaic law allowed priests to wed. Among the prophets, Hosea provided an obvious example of matrimony with divine sanction. The New Testament was more problematical, in part because Jesus and Paul never married. Yet some disciples had wives, forcing the Rheims annotators to claim that the disciples sexually abstained from their wives after their calling. The Protestants rejected this as unproved and comforted themselves that if Jesus had disapproved of married ministers he would not have chosen so many husbands as his disciples.[22]

The 1562 Articles of Religion allowed the clergy to marry or abstain at their discretion, "as they shall iudge the same to serue better to godlynesse," though Elizabeth preferred that they remain single. The queen insisted in August 1561 that families of women and children be removed from the colleges because their presence was contrary to the "comely order of the same." In theory, if not often in practice, a number of Protestant writers agreed with the queen that unmarried clerics were preferable. They had, said Sandys, fewer cares and thus were better suited to labor in the church. This view was presented in the note to 1 Corinthians 7 in the Matthew-Becke Bibles of 1549 and 1551 and the Matthew Bible of 1551: If celibate clergy "refraine the busines of the worlde, [they] are moste apte to preach the word an[d] minister. . . . But otherwise the quiete maried man is more apte for that office." Various writers agreed, but a medical treatise translated by Thomas Newton, the future rector of Little Ilford, Essex, cautioned that sexual drives might offset the advantages of a celibate life for the study of divinity. Fulke concurred, noting that a man without the gift of continency could more effectively perform his pastoral function if he were married, adding that a prudent wife might enable her husband to be less entangled with earthly matters than a single person—exactly the opposite of the Pauline view. Another Puritan, Francis Trigge, resorted to Chrysostom to support the view that marriage was no hindrance to the ministerial task. "One maie be maried, and be a prophet, maie talke with God, euen as *Moses* did; . . . mariage hinders not godlinesse or virtuous liuing." Puritans, though not repudiating the value of the celibate life for clergymen, elevated the status of married ministers in a manner that altered the Pauline outlook that had prevailed in the church for centuries. In so doing, they enhanced the status of matrimony and women by providing parishioners with concrete examples of married pastors who proclaimed the importance of the role their wives played.[23]

One further subject requires examination, that is, the relative advantages and disadvantages of marriage or celibacy for the laity. Popular lore is filled, as one would expect, with deprecatory comments on married life. The ballad "What way is best for man to chuse" judged that

> if thou have noe wyfe at all,
> full simply thou shalt fare.

On the other hand, a writer of doggerel disliked both alternatives:

> In marryage is unquietnesse;
> In lacking of a wife

> All sollitary we remaine,
> And leade a loathsome lyfe.

A brass in the church of St. John the Baptist, Norwich, praises the virtuous life of an Elizabethan virgin:

> Winifred Browne the davghter of Phillip and Ann his wife
> Vnder this stone incloesed is devoide of breathed life
> A virgin pvre she livde and dide, God garnisht hir with grace
> And lke a christian in his feare she ran hir pilgrims race.

But Winifred may have been unable to find a husband and made the best of imposed virginity, while cracks such as "wedlock is padlock" may have been used only in jest. In practice, the frequency of marriage among Elizabethans was very high—over 90%, for example, among the squirarchy and upper aristocracy. Probably most who were inclined to marry did so.[24]

A serious case for matrimony is found in biblical marginalia and prologues. The note to 1 Corinthians 7 in the Matthew Bible of 1537, the Tyndale-Rogers New Testament of 1538, and the Tyndale New Testament of 1549 praises the celibate life for those with the requisite gift, because such a life provides more quietness to serve God. Yet the annotators acknowledge that a single person distracted by sexual drives is better off married, for neither state is better than the other. Tyndale's prologue to Numbers in the Matthew-Becke Bibles of 1549 and 1551 and the Matthew Bible of 1551 counsels celibacy if one anticipates that the burdens of marriage are excessive or that governing and providing for a household are too disquieting, or if one determines he can better serve his neighbor if he is single. In the Geneva Bible, the preference is for the celibate life, due to the incommodities inherent in family living, which are attributed to human corruption rather than divine institution. A virgin, the annotators affirm, can attain to holiness more swiftly than married folk because of the absence of such cares. Ultimately, the decision must be made with respect to the time, place, and persons involved. The notes in the Beza-Tomson Bible adapt this Pauline position, warning of the distraction of married life, especially for women.[25]

Judging from the views expressed by Anglicans, advice to young people contemplating marriage varied widely. Edmund Tilney, who became master of the revels in the royal household in 1579, regarded celibacy as the purest estate, but recognized that wedlock was holy and essential; it "containeth the felicity of mans life, the *Flower of Friendship,* the preservation of Realmes, the glorie of Princes, & that which is most of all, it causeth immortalitie.'' Nicholas Gibbens, who was incorporated at Oxford in 1592, thought marriage was preferable to virginity before the fall but not afterwards, though like all Protestants he rejected the notion that virginity was meritorious. Those without the gift of celibacy should marry, and for them such an act is honorable, particularly because it increases the church by nurturing children in the faith. Despite his preference for virginity, Gibbens advised that "it is not good for man to be alone: not good in respect of sanctified loue and godlie delectation in the societie of marriage: not good in respect of profit, either increase of children, or houshold gouernment: not good in respect of iustice, honestie, or continencie, since the fall of man: not good for *Adam* nor the greatest part of his posteritie." The last phrases provide the key to the paradox, for virginity is superior only for the few accorded the talents to pursue the celibate life.[26]

Other Anglicans balanced the worth of the married and celibate estates, and one or two even exalted the former. For Jewel, marriage was neither good nor evil in itself, but became so in accord with its use. Impediments were associated with matrimony, but the same was true of wealth. Babington regarded the single life as no more worthy than marriage, for both were divine gifts. Paul's preference for celibacy was not determined by its special godliness or merit, but by such temporal concerns as the persecution he confronted and the scarcity of single Christian women. Marriage was not such a pernicious thing, remarked John Terry, minister at Stockton, Wilts., that abstinence could be regarded as a precious act. "Is it a worthier worke to abstaine from mariage, then to bring vp children in the information of the Lord?" This tendency to give primacy of place to marriage was more pronounced in the writings of George Whetstone, a former military officer serving in the Low Countries, who lauded matrimony as more precious than virginity because it was a sacred institution to which men attributed higher honor. That observation, coming in 1582, probably accurately reflected the elevated status that matrimony was coming to have in a Protestant society. Whetstone also stressed the origins of marriage in natural law, with the wedding ceremonies perfecting what nature had determined. Moreover, a chaste married life honors God by presenting the world with his image and profits man by providing posterity who "preserueth him alyue." Finally, for Whetstone the superiority of marriage is revealed in his belief that the administration of justice in a commonwealth should be the province of married men, "for that the care of wife, & children, presupposeth them to be setled: when the vnmarried, though their wittes be good, rayseth a suspition in the wise, that their thoughtes, are vagrant."[27]

When Puritan writers considered marriage for the laity, they balanced its advantages with celibacy or accorded it superior status. Richard Rogers considered marriage a preferable state because of the worthwhile duties involved in governing and supporting a family, though he experienced some longing for the lack of distraction he had enjoyed as a bachelor, which had given him more time for spiritual contemplation. Cleaver repeated the adage that it was better to bury a wife than to marry one, but he intended this only as a warning against ill-advised marriages. Although Perkins saw advantages in the celibate life, including greater liberty in times of persecution, freedom from family responsibilities, and more ease to worship, he regarded the marital state as preferable because it was a remedy for incontinency and a means to increase the commonwealth and church. Likewise for Becon matrimony was the best life because it replentished the population, profited the commonwealth, and lightened the burdens of others.[28]

Nowhere were Puritans more adamant in praising the married estate than in their repudiation of the Rheims marginalia. That Catholics regarded matrimony as a sacrament made it inconceivable to Puritans that it could be relegated to a status below that of virginity, which was not a sacrament. Fulke acknowledged the Pauline view on celibacy, but insisted that attention be paid to what each person was enabled to do by divine grace and what was conducive to the glory of God. Cartwright's basic principle was that marriage and celibacy were divine gifts and would be rewarded if properly used. Yet "he that hath the gift of continencie, is in that poynt better then he which hath it not: so farre as he hath receiued a heauenly gift aboue the other." Preference for one state or the other depends on circumstances and ends. If parents of a maiden with the gift of continency enjoin her to wed, she will possess greater peace of conscience by parental obedience, and will be following the example of Adam and Eve, who were married in a state of innocency, not to avoid fornication but for companionship (and reproduction). If "the virgins estate be in some case, person, or time to be preferred before the married, the same ariseth not of the nature of virginity, but in regard of the disorder that sin hath brought into the world." Because the sober use of marriage is, like virginity, a gift of God, there can be no pollution in it. No more virtue consists in abstaining from marriage than from meat, but circumstances in both cases determine the proper course. Those with the gift of celibacy, said Cartwright, sin if they marry, for the single estate offers greater ease to serve God; to compensate for

this, married persons must be beneficiaries of special grace to overcome these obstacles.[29]

It is impossible to distinguish between Anglicans and Puritans on
the advisability of matrimony for the laity, except that a few Anglicans exalt celibacy more than any Puritan. Both groups find the Pauline position almost embarrassing, hence they give it lip service while
according a wholesome role to wedded life. Puritans in particular
found advantages in matrimony for the clergy. These Protestant views
were significant for the future, for greater acceptance of sexual drives
as wholesome (within the married state) was predicated upon Protestant attempts to accord a higher status to marriage. In addition, Protestant writers praised celibacy not for its sexual restraint but for its
freedom from familial responsibilites. To be sure, marriage continued
to be in part a remedy against fornication, but this viewpoint was an
objection to the misuse of sex rather than to its proper role in wedded life.

(3) Qualities of Prospective Mates

If thou be learned, chuse one that loueth knowledge: if thou be Martiall, chuse
one that loueth prowesse: if thou must liue by thy labour, chuse one that loueth
husbandrie: for vnlesse her minde stande with thy vocation, thou shalt neither
inioye thy wife, nor thy calling.

Henry Smith[30]

My councell is, the rather you encline to *Pallas* for some rewarde of wit, then
either to *Iuno* for her honor, or *Venus* for pleasure.

Andrew Kingsmill[31]

Much was written with respect to appropriate qualities in a spouse,
though in practice those that counted most, at least among the landed
and propertied classes, were wealth and good birth. There was nothing particularly English about this, for the Roman Catechism of 1566
acknowledged the legitimate motivation to wed according to such
factors as wealth, genealogical considerations, physical attraction, a
desire for heirs, and similarity in manners.[32]

The most generally accepted qualification for matrimony was religious agreement, which was asserted in the marginalia of the principal Elizabethan versions of Scripture. The key biblical principle was
the Deuteronomic admonition not to yoke an ox and an ass together
and make an unequal match. There was a warning from Paul that
marriages between believers and unbelievers were subject to disrup-

tions and desertions. The Rheims annotators contended that it was not lawful for Catholics to wed heretics or infidels, and Protestants adamantly prohibited the marriage of their people to Catholics, an act regarded by John Dod, Puritan minister at Hanwell, Oxon., as rendering wedded life unclean in God's sight. To marry an infidel infringed the second commandment. Other reasons were advanced by Dod for prescribing marriage to one of like faith, including the inability of husbands and wives in mixed (Protestant - Catholic) marriages to fulfill their responsibility to raise children in the Protestant faith. Cleaver suggested that in a marriage of believers the husband and wife could use their relationship as a mirror to perceive the love of Christ. The results were the opposite in mixed marriages, according to Andrew Kingsmill, fellow of All Souls College, Oxford, "for it is commonly seene that the vnbeleeuyng wife ouerruleth the beleeuying husbande, and causeth hym either to make a plaine shipwracke of faith, or so cooleth his godly zeale, that hee maie hardely bee discerned from an Infidell." Babington urged that religion be given consideration before all other factors in determining whom to marry, particularly since divine consent—as essential as parental consent—would be withheld from a mixed marriage. Most mixed marriages occurred, Sandys plausibly suggested, because of the excessive regard accorded physical attraction and wealth. On the wrongfulness of mixed marriages, there was no disagreement between Anglicans and Puritans, nor is there any indication that Puritans opposed marrying Anglicans or vice versa.[33]

Evidence shows that religion was in practice an important qualification in considering wedlock. Particularly after 1570 but even in the 1560s prominent Catholic families sought intramarriage when feasible, though among the landed classes, Anglicans continued to wed Catholics to the end of the reign. Sir Everard Digby, one of the queen's gentleman pensioners, wanted to marry his sister to a Catholic because "they were good and honourable people." Rising Protestant families in Durham and especially Newcastle whose fortunes came from commerce, coal, or offices intermarried with established landed houses with Catholic backgrounds in the northeast. However, Lady Elizabeth, wife of Sir Francis Willoughby, successfully opposed the marriage of her third daughter Margaret to Griffin Markham of Ollerton, Notts., because the young man was a Catholic. Henry Hastings, earl of Huntingdon, was pleased that Edward Manners, earl of Rutland, wed a Protestant, and informed him on 27 July 1573: "I am glad of your coming shortly to Belvoir with your lady. I trust you have chosen well, and I am sure of it if the report be true that she fears God, loves the Gospel, and hates Popery." Parkhurst was concerned that a Protestant bride be found for Rudolph, son of the Protestant theologian Rudolph Gualter, and suggested to Josiah Simler that a good candidate was Dorothea, daughter of Heinrich Bullinger. R. C. Richardson has shown that among Puritans a good deal of intramarriage took place. Probably the prayer of the young Grace Sherrington was echoed in many Puritan homes: "O Lord, if ever I marry, send me a man after Thine owne hearte."[34]

A second qualification widely sought in a prospective mate, especially among the landed, business, and professional classes, was good birth. Edmund Tilney, an Anglican layman, urged men to seek brides who possessed good lineage and virtue rather than wealth, but most authors were primarily concerned that the bride and groom be of approximately the same social standing. "Where parties be matched equally according to their birth and abilities there is euer best agreement." Those who seek to wed above their social station manifest disrespect for matrimony as a divine ordinance. In Wright's judgment, contentious relationships between husbands and wives were likely in socially unequal marriages. Cleaver cautioned that a man who wed below his estate must bear in mind "that Matrimonie maketh equal many differences: & further, yt he hath not taken her for a slaue or seruant, but for a fellow & companion." A woman who marries beneath her social degree must remember that the marital bond requires subjection to her husband. Whetstone regarded a woman who wed beneath her as foolish and in danger of marital instability. A courtier who weds a "kitchynstuffe" will find the better sort disdaining his wife for presuming to share her husband's estate; "in Pryde, she wyll pearch with the hyest: whiche Soueraigntie, in the one, & saucines in the other, separats pleasantnesse from their Husbandes, and quietnesse, both from themselues and their Houshouldes." Marriages with servants were taboo, but if a servant wed his mistress, Whetstone thought he should allow his wife to govern. Wilcox banned masters from marrying their maid-servants because of the pride that the servants would display. Anglicans and Puritans agreed on the importance of marrying within one's social class.[35]

The views of Anglican and Puritan writers notwithstanding, marriages between persons of differing social degrees were not infrequent. Marriage was an important avenue of social mobility; one of the most striking examples was the Finch family of Kent, members of which wed thirteen heiresses in successive generations, until in the seventeenth century the senior branch became earls of Winchelsea. The extent to which peers married below their status has been documented by Lawrence Stone, whose figures for the marriage of peers (after creation) show that 46% wed below the peerage in the period 1540 to 1569, and this figure increased to 67% in the period 1570 to 1599. The majority of these marriages outside the peerage were to women of gentry status, largely because of their better financial prospects. The peers had limits to what they would do for money, however, for between 1561 and 1590 only one peer married the daughter of a London merchant. Financial pressures began to change this situation in 1591, when Edward Lord Stafford asked Burghley to persuade "a riche citizen for his only dowghter and heire to be maryed unto my sonne." The merchant community was not always enthusiastic about proposals from peers or their heirs. A classic example is the hostility of the wealthy financier and former mayor of London, Sir John Spencer, to William Lord Compton, who finally eloped with Sir John's daughter Elizabeth by disguising himself as a baker's man and bearing her away in a bread basket. Sir John refused to acknowledge the validity of the marriage and locked up Elizabeth when she came to seek his pardon. Only after Lord Compton had Sir John committed to the Tower for mistreating his daughter, and the queen interceded following the birth of a son, was Sir John reconciled.[36]

Other examples of unequal marriages throw light on the relationship of the ideal to actual practice. The government tended to agree with ministers in preferring marriages within respective social classes, but not so much for religious reasons as to maintain social order and decorum. When Sir Thomas Perrot wed Lady Dorothy Devereux, daughter of the earl of Essex, in July 1583, the Privy Council investigated, though in this case the principal offense may have been the marriage of one of the queen's maids of honor without permission. In 1592 Henry Pranel, son of a London alderman, who married Frances Howard, Lord Bindon's daughter, apologized to Burghley, asserting he expected little or nothing from her and would grant her a large jointure. On numerous occasions, those of peerage status held conditions other than social preeminence in the highest regard. Alice Stanley, countess of Derby, informed Sir Robert Cecil that his niece, Lady Vere, had not gotten a worthy match when she married William, earl of Derby, in 1594. Some gentry did not want their children marrying into the peerage. Sir Walter Mildmay advised his son Anthony to wed a virtuous girl not above his social status, and Sir William Wentworth's counsel to his son Thomas was similar, for "maryinge a superior bringes ever charg and after danger." Social status was more important than religion to Robert Pole, a Catholic gentleman from Radbourn, Derby, who instructed the executors of his will to see that his nephew and heir married a girl of "a worshipfull stocke." When George Clifford, earl of Cumberland, fell in love with Gertrude, daughter of Sir William Holles of Houghton, Notts., and asked her father for her hand, Sir William declined on the grounds that he would "not like to stand with my cap in my hand to my son-in-law. I will see her married to an honest gentleman with whom I may have friendship and conversation." The gentry also had the opportunity to intermarry with the business and professional communities as well as with the yeomanry; among the latter there often was interest in gentry alliances. [37]

A third factor often judged significant in selecting a spouse was wealth. From the religious standpoint, there was a consensus of opinion (contrary to Stone) that wealth should not be a factor in choosing a marital partner. One reason was fear that good relations would continue only as long as the money lasted. Nash and Babington were unhappy with young men who sought rich brides, for the brides tended to dominate and be intolerable. Puritan writers were equally displeased; Henry Smith complained that dowries exceeded goodness and upbringing in importance. The parental quest to find husbands for their daughters by providing substantial dowries was likened to ranchers selling horses and sheep. Charles Gibbon hoped Christians recognized that true wealth consisted of contentment, and the best gentility of piety, though he acknowledged that one should not marry before assuring sufficient wealth for daily maintenance. [38]

In practice the admonition not to marry for wealth often was ignored. Between 1570 and 1599, as Lawrence Stone has shown, 20% of the marriages of holders of peerages or their heirs were with heiresses, but in the early seventeenth century wealth and birth became even more important considerations (presumably reducing the importance of religion). The figure for marriages with heiresses jumped to 34% for the next period of thirty years, while the percentage of peers who married peers' daughters increased from 33% (1570-99) to 35% (1600-29), or 56% if new peers are taken into account. The families that led the way reflect a spectrum of religious views: the Howards, dukes of Norfolk and earls of Arundel; the Howards, earls of Suffolk; and the Norths and the Russells. Wealth triumphed over social equality as peers sought to wed their daughters to lawyers or London merchants. The latter were advantageous marriages, for a merchant's widow received half her husband's estate if there were no children, or one-third where there were offspring, and most of this was usually in personal property such as cash, bonds, and shares. William Lord Compton reportedly sought £10,000 and the redemption of an £18,000 mortgage on his land from Sir John Spencer, which may explain why Sir John opposed Lord Compton's marriage to his daughter Elizabeth.[39]

Wealth was frequently a factor in arranging marriages among the propertied classes, including the yeomanry, but there is no way to categorize cases along religious lines. When Edward Parker, Lord Morley, sought to arrange a marriage between his son and the daughter of Roger Manners in 1586, it was not money but the wishes of his deceased wife that motivated him. Richard Bourke, earl of Clanricarde and governor of Connaught, turned down an opportunity for a good marriage to Anne Stanley, daughter of the earl of Derby, because he placed courtly ambitions ahead of personal profit. Examples to the contrary are numerous, with businesslike negotiations typified by those between Thomas Lord Wentworth and Burghley in 1581, over the former's attempt to have his son wed Burghley's daughter. When Elizabeth Lady Russell sought in 1597 to have her daughter Elizabeth marry Lord Herbert's eldest son, she informed Sir Robert Cecil that the girl was not only virtuous and of good birth, but also had an inheritance of £200, plus an additional £200 *p.a.* for ten years when Lady Russell died. Such attempts to provide for daughters were behind much of the anger displayed by Protestant writers against considerations of wealth in matrimony.[40]

Wealth apparently figured even more prominently in marriages between the peerage and the gentry. In 1594 Henry Percy, earl of Northumberland, married Dorothy, widow of Sir Thomas Perrot, who had a pension from the crown of £400 *p.a.*, the lease of Sion House and other income. Her estate was worth some £3,000, and brought £800 *p.a.* to the earl in the early years of their marriage. He gave her a pension of £360 *p.a.* in 1594, £500 in 1596, and £600 in 1602. He admitted that he had sought a wife who could "bring with her meat in her mouth to maintain her expense," and she did exactly that. Such satisfactory results were not without exception. When Sir Arthur Gorges took as his bride Douglas, the only child of Henry Howard, Viscount Bindon, in 1584, he was supposed to receive £10,000, but when she died in 1590 the lands she had brought reverted to her father. Normally it was the peerage who sought financial gains in these mixed marriages. Sir Henry Sidney paid dearly to consolidate the position of his prestigious family by arranging the wedding between his daughter Mary and Henry Herbert, earl of Pembroke, in 1576. What this entailed he explained to the earl of Leicester, his brother-in-law: "Twoo thousand £. I confes I haue bequethed her, whych your lordshyp knowyth I myght better spare her whan I wear dead than one thousand lyuyng; and in troth my lord I haue yt not, but borro yt I must and so I wyll." Fear of the financial repercussions prompted a friend of Sir Francis Willoughby to try to prevent him from marrying his daughter Dorothy to Henry Hastings, nephew of the earl of Huntingdon, for the latter was £20,000 in debt. As the financial factor increased in marriage negotiations, some sensitivity about it was expressed, perhaps because the preachers denounced it so vehemently. When Robert Carey, son of Henry Lord Hunsdon, married Elizabeth, daughter of Sir Hugh Trevannion and widow of Sir Henry Widdrington, in 1593, he explained that he desired her more for her worth than her wealth, since her estate was worth only £500 *p.a.* and her ready cash amounted to £500 or £600. Yet Carey's own income was only a £100 *p.a.* pension from the Exchequer, plus 500 marks *p.a.* for serving as the deputy of Henry Lord Scrope, warden of the West Marches and keeper of Carlisle; and he was nearly £1,000 in debt. He might have desired a wealthier match, but Elizabeth was no financial burden.[41]

In marriages among the gentry, legal, and business groups, instances are numerous that money was a factor, but again no pattern along religious lines is apparent. Sir Thomas Tresham, a Catholic who was £4,000 in debt, partly because of recusancy fines, found it almost impossible to arrange satisfactory marriages for his children. Sir Henry Cholmley, a Catholic sympathizer, was so indebted that he married his son Richard, a Cambridge student, to Suzanne, daughter of John Legard, a Yorkshire gentleman capable of paying a portion of £2,000. The spendthrift, John Kingston, son of a merchant and gentleman of the horse to Edward Manners, earl of Rutland, ran into extensive debt for such items as apparel, and consequently jumped at the opportunity to wed a wealthy widow some seventeen years his senior.

When he heard that hir husband [Henry Needham of Kirklington, Notts.] was dead he swore (his usuall oath when he spoke earnestly) "Body of our Lord I will go marry this olde widdow [Catherine, nearly 40] and pay my debts; then when I have buried hir will I marry a young wench and get children." This it seems was his designe, but shee deceaved him in part for shee held him tug above 38 yeares and lived neare 12 yeares after him.

Sir Nicholas Poyntz was equally businesslike in his approach to marriage, claiming he would never marry a woman for her favor or personality.

Now for Mistress Deny, her portion is to defray sumthing moer then her charge she wyll bring me, for except I be falsely informed she hathe the park she dwellithe in and a 116*l.* rent bysydes her parck, and sum wods in the forest. . . . She hayth no chyld in her care. This shall satisfy me iff she be a good woman and wylbe an obedient wyff. Butt iff Mr. Deny with this litle living hath given her his prodigall hart, then ys she nott for me, for so wold hitt be the spoyle off my children, and the beggeri off such as I myght have by her.

The lavish use of money to buy a husband for his daughter and heir was not enough for Mr. Androes of Sandy, Beds., who gave £1,000 to Mr. Mayne of Gray's Inn for that purpose, and then offered him that much again if his daughter gave birth to a child.[42]

Financial considerations loomed large in the marital plans of both the Wentworth and the Sidney families. William Wentworth of Wentworth Woodham, Yorks., went to London about a year after his father died and there met his bride, Anne Atkinson, whom he depicted as a virtuous woman with £2,000. To his son Thomas he later recommended a woman with a good portion, but only after Thomas sought the advice of his friends and an attorney. "For hir frends woll laie plotts and worke upon yow and corrupt your seruants and frends all they can to procure such a riche matche for their daughter or kinswoman." Financial considerations were present in Puritan circles as well, though examples are harder to find, which suggests that Puritans gave less emphasis to wealth in matrimonial arrangements. One who did was Sir Henry Sidney, who asserted to Walsingham in 1583 that he was £5,000 in debt and some £30,000 poorer than in 1553. He hoped to recover his position by a grant from the queen when his son Philip wed Sir Francis' daughter, Frances, but this did not happen.[43]

A fourth factor in selecting marital partners was personal qualities. At the popular level, this criterion appears in poetry, doggerel, and balladry. The Catholic student Lewis Evans penned "A New Balet Entituled how to Wyve Well," in which he set forth "the extreme uncomfortableness of having a froward wife, as so many women turn out to be." The advice of the noted Protestant author of ballads, Thomas Deloney, to women was to

> Receive such Suitors friendly,
>   as do resort to thee;
> Respect not thee outward person,
>   but the inward gravity.

From the Shropshire poet Richard Barnfield came complementary counsel for men:

> Take not a flattring woman to thy wife,
> A shameles creature, full of wanton words,
>
> ·
>
> Cast not thy minde on her whose looks allure,
> But she that shines in Truth and Vertue pure.

In prose, it was the Puritans who stressed the importance of inner qualities. The basic maxim was expressed in the note to Proverbs 18:22 in the Geneva Bible: A man with a virtuous wife is divinely blessed. In Cleaver's estimation the most desirable qualification in a maiden is chastity and modesty. (Legally, the absence of chastity in a maid could provide an impediment to her marriage.) Before marriage an examination must be made—"to make an Anotamie" was Kingsmill's phrase—to determine if a prospective spouse possessed godly virtues by observing personal reputation, appearance, speech, apparel, companions, education, and upbringing. Virtue was more valuable to Puritan authors than a substantial dowry or physical attractiveness, hence parents must counsel children to have more respect for inward graces than external appearances.[44]

Evidence to determine how much personal qualities mattered is not plentiful. The Puritan Sir Walter Mildmay advised his son in 1570 to choose a wife for virtue only. Robert Furse, a substantial yeoman of Dean Prior, Devon, and probably an Anglican, gave comparable counsel to his son in 1593: "But whate so ever she be inquyre dylygentlye of what nature quallytes or condysyones her mother ys of for comenly the dofter do lerne the quallytes and maners of ther mother and marke also howe and yn what companye she hathe bynne brofte uppe from her yuthe." The Puritan John Rainolds congratulated young Rudolph Gualter in 1576 on his marriage, hoping his bride would be a helpmate and a guide and mistress in godliness. When Henry Parker, Lord Morley, wrote to his wife in 1570 concerning the marriage of their daughter, virtue and good birth were major considerations:

The greatest care is of my daughter, weighing how now-a-days without great sums of money few come to preferment. . . . Above all things I pray you have regard with whom and with what race she doth match, for if the stock be not virtuous, the fruit can never prove well.

The letters of Sir Michael Hicks, Burghley's secretary, to two widows, one of whom he hoped would marry him, claimed he sought them primarily for their virtuous reputation. Nevertheless, in December 1594, he married Elizabeth Parvish, widow of a London merchant, whose share of her husband's estate was in excess of £5,000 plus a life interest in lands in Surrey and a country house at Ruck-holt, Essex. A virtuous reputation was uppermost in Dering's mind when he proposed to Anne Locke, the widow and friend of John Knox: "I write unto you as before, sekinge you alone, whome the grac of God in myne opinion hathe made a good possecion." They were married in 1572. William Wentworth's maternal grandmother approved her daughter's marriage to Wentworth's father because "she perceiued truth in his face." Thus there is some evidence that Puritans in particular heeded inner qualities in matchmaking, though it is impossible to ascertain how common this was.[45]

An even more difficult factor to assess is mutual liking or love. Again, this criterion was a matter of greater concern to Puritan commentators than to Anglicans, although Tilney argued that wedlock should be based in part on a love (not infatuation) that grows and endures. The note to Proverbs 5:21 in the Geneva Bible set the tone for Puritans by affirming that God requires a husband and wife to be joined "in heart." Henry Smith emphasized the necessity of compatibility, and Richard Greenham, preacher at Christ Church, Newgate, London, explained that a man could know his wife was brought to him by God if there was "any agreeing or proportionable liking" between them, especially "in the gifts of ye mind, concerning their generall calling as zeale, faith, godlines; and also concerning particular calling."[46]

Some Elizabethan marriages for love took place, such as that of William Oglander of Nunwell on the Isle of Wight. When he returned from Oxford in 1574 at the age of twenty, he fell in love with Anne Dillington, daughter of a family unable to provide a marriage portion. Oglander's mother and uncle urged him to marry the heiress Dorothy Hamond, but he wed Miss Dillington when he was twenty-one, "and had not with her above £50." Love matches occurred in the peerage, usually made possible by an heiress being over twenty-one and unwed at her father's death or a maiden of honor at court. Peregrine Bertie, the future Lord Willoughby, met Lady Mary de Vere at court and wed her against the wishes of his mother, the duchess of Suffolk, and her brother, Edward de Vere, earl of Oxford. Edward Seymour, earl of Hertford, was involved in love matches with Lady Catherine Grey in 1560 and Frances Howard in the early 1580s, though he had his son and heir imprisoned in the Fleet for following his example. Love matches may have been fairly common among the lower classes where considerations of property and birth were minimal, though Lawrence Stone may be correct in asserting that many were more concerned to find "an efficient economic assistant rather than an affectionate companion." Yet Elizabethan ballads, as Christopher Hill observes, suggest that companionate marital relations existed among the lower social orders. There must have been many throughout Elizabethan society who would have agreed with Sir Michael Hicks' conviction that mutual liking was the principal point in determining marriage. A flagrant exception was Sir Nicholas Poyntz, whose letter to his sister, Lady Elizabeth, candidly states:

If you procide for me, lett me not wyn her love like a foole, nor spend long tyme like a boy. As God shall help, I am moch trobled to think I must speake to any woman won loving word.

Lu Emily Pearson suggests that the increased education of girls resulted in a greater capacity for emotional experience, including love, but there is no way of verifying this impression. To the extent that marital love existed, it was a factor in psychologically detaching the husband and wife from parents and kin, thus contributing to the rise of the nuclear family.[47]

Puritan writers commonly agreed that physical attraction was inconsequential in determining matrimony. Physical beauty was viewed as frail and a vain temptation, though Pagit acknowledged a subordinate role for appearance because "a man must chuse him such a one as with whom alone, he can holde himselfe contente." William Wentworth urged his son not to accord excessive value to beauty in a woman, since the fairest in appearance were often the foulest within. Speaking from experience, he claimed, "their nature is so fraile and variable and temptations so ryfe as nether for anie worde nor othes will a wise man trust them for constancy." It is impossible to determine how much importance was placed on physical appearance in practice, though Sir Michael Hicks begged Mrs. Woodcock not to judge him on that basis. One man to whom beauty meant little was Nicholas Trott of Quixott, Herts., who in 1602 wed Anne Perient, "a lusty tall wench able to beat two of him."[48]

Other factors were accorded some attention, including age, with Anglicans and Puritans agreed that a close approximation in age was important. "Equalitie," according to Tilney, "is principally to be considered in this matrimoniall amitie, as well of yeares, as of the giftes of nature, and fortune. For equalnesse herein, maketh friendlynesse." The English, Tilney believed, should not follow the Aristotelian admonition to have a twenty-year gap between husband and wife, or even the sixteen years proposed by Hesiod and Xenophon, who felt the age differential facilitated the husband's rule of the household. At most Tilney favored a difference of four or five years, based on what he considered to be decreasing longevity in the sixteenth century. His fellow Anglican, Whetstone, also argued against significant age differentials. Elderly men must not marry young women, in part due to their inability to satisfy the latter sexually: "Withered Flowers, are more fit for a Dunghill, then meete to deck a house." Moreover, people tend to blame the husband's death on a young wife for causing him worry about her sexual behavior. Neither should a young man marry an older women; to do it for wealth is wrong and leads to female domination, and jealousy and unfavorable comparisons with a former husband create unpleasant relationships. Puritans condemned such marriages on the grounds that covetousness and lechery were more likely. Greenham and Henry Smith criticized wedlock between persons significantly disparate in age because of their possible inability to procreate.[49]

Yet in a society where wealth and birth were valued, and wardship was a reality, marriages of spouses substantially different in age occurred, often because of the desire for family alliances or property considerations. The rate of mortality in childbirth forced some men to marry several times in the hope of producing a male heir; for such a purpose they tended to select young wives. An age discrepancy might appeal to some, as John Carey hoped in the case of the heirless widower Thomas Sutton, an elderly financier. Carey offered Sutton the hand of his unwed daughter "to put the cares out of youer hed of youer owld Bess; withe summe younger sportes she wold feyne to make you merrie; and yet this much I will saye faythefulley to you of her: albeit she be younge she is respective, discret, wise, and dutyfull, and canne fitte herselfe as well to be an old mane's wife as aney yonge mayd in Ingland." Mary Sidney was sixteen when she wed Henry Herbert, earl of Pembroke, who was nearly forty. For financial reasons, Dudley Lord North married Frances, daughter of Sir John Brockett, when he was twenty and she was "not yong nor well fauoured," prompting the diarist John Manning to observe, "noe maruaile yf he loue hir not." In another case, an elderly doctor of law delayed marriage to a young girl so long that he died before the wedding occurred, inspiring Chamberlain to observe that she became "a widow before she was a wife." The question of unequal marriages came before the Dedham Classis in January 1585, when a query was raised about a man aged twenty-four who sought to marry a woman over fifty; the Puritan ministers urged a clergyman to dissuade the couple and assess the legality of the marriage contract. Opposite advice allegedly was given by Mr. Cliberye, vicar of Halstead,

142   The Marital Quest

Essex, in a marriage sermon urging young men to marry older, wealthy women: "Take an old woman, thoughe she haue never a tothe in her head, it is no matter if she haue a bushell of money. Thou mayest haue a whore where thow wilt, yea two or thre for a nede." In an infamous case in Northampton, a young man aged twenty-two married a ninety-two year old woman on her deathbed at 6 P.M., and the bride was dead by 2 A.M. The norm, however, was for modest differences in age. Among the peerage in the first quarter of the seventeenth century, the mean age of bridegrooms was 24.28 while that of brides was 19.39. Corresponding figures for the gentry in the diocese of Canterbury were 26.54 and 21.66, respectively, between 1619 and 1660. Moreover, the respective mean ages for all applicants in this diocese were 26.87 and 23.95.[50]

Another consideration was health; Cleaver urged his readers not to wed someone with a contagious disease or a mental illness. William Wentworth advised his son to choose a woman with a healthy body and a good complexion, and William Vaughan regarded the likelihood of a woman's fertility as important—an opinion widely shared, especially among the landed classes. Other factors occasionally were mentioned: Robert Allen believed vocational preparation had to be undertaken prior to marriage, hence a girl should refuse a young man not duly prepared. Political advantage sometimes was considered in the upper social levels, as when Walter Devereux, earl of Essex, and Thomas Sackville, Lord Buckhurst, offered their sons in 1573 as a husband for Burghley's daughter. Similarly, Roger Lord North, the death of whose eldest son had "frustrated all my resolutions formerly established" and forced him "to begine ye world againe," proposed to Burghley in 1597 that his next son, Dudley, age fifteen, marry into the lord treasurer's family. Henry Herbert, earl of Pembroke, sought political advantage by the marriage of his eldest son William to Burghley's granddaughter Bridget, age thirteen. Burghley was dubious, especially because of her age, but Pembroke suggested the couple be separated after the marriage until such a time as Burghley thought fit. "I seek not by this match," Pembroke wrote in 1597, "to enrich myself or advance my younger children, for whatsoever you give I am content that the young couple presently have, and will increase the same with as great a yearly allowance as my estate and course of life can spare."[51]

Thus, Anglican and Puritan writers agreed concerning the significance of religious harmony, good birth, and age approximation, but Puritans placed more emphasis than Anglicans on inner qualities and mutual liking, and insisted more strongly that physical attraction was of little or no consequence. Both groups deplored marriage for financial considerations. In practice, however, variations from these ideals were common with respect to financial conditions, and more deviation from social equality occurred in marriage than the clergy approved.

(4) Age at Marriage

Litle infants, in swadling clowt, are often maried by their ambicious Parents and frends, when they know neither good nor euill, and this is the origene of much wickednesse, & directlie against the word of God.

Philip Stubbes[52]

Crabbed Age and Youth
cannot live together.

Thomas Deloney[53]

Closely related to the recommendation of approximate equality of age as a desideratum for successful marriage was the question of the appropriate age at which to wed. The medical author Thomas Cogan, following Aristotle, recommended that a couple wed at ages that would enable them to cease procreating simultaneously. Because a man was believed to remain fertile until around seventy and a woman fifty, the optimum ages for marriage were thirty-eight and eighteen, respectively, but this prescription conflicted with the ideal of age affinity. Legally, boys could marry at fourteen and girls at twelve, with espousals as early as seven. Espousals could be broken by either party at the ages of fourteen (for boys) and twelve, but Lawrence Stone observes that children at this age rarely had the strength of character or will to reject a marriage arranged by their parents or guardians. Bullinger's handbook on marriage urged parents not to allow children to marry who had not reached "theyr laufull & iuste yeares," with preference given to perhaps nineteen or twenty. From the medical standpoint, Bullinger doubted a very young wife had the physical strength to nourish her children, potentially resulting in deaths in childbirth or feeble children. "But herin may euery man behaue himselfe after the best and most honest maner/ accordinge as the kynde complexion and cause requyreth." [54]

Anglicans had little to say on the abuses of child marriage. In 1580 John Chardon at St. Peter's, Exeter, expressed concern in a sermon that the end of the world was near, owing partly to the prevalency of early marriages, for never did men "faster marry wyues in the [pre-flood] days of *Noe*." Babington complained twelve years later that children of the wealthy were marrying before they knew how to keep house. The poet James Yates placed the onus on young people for allowing their emotions to govern their actions:

> But *Amorous* toyes of *Youthfull* youth
>   respecteth not with care:
> The truethlesse troth, and friendlesse fraud
>   that some full closely bare.

Puritans lashed out most vigorously against marriages of the very young. Stubbes, who wed Katherine Emmes in 1586 when she was fifteen, proposed that none be allowed (except for urgent reasons) to marry until they were in their early twenties, or at least their mid-teens, in part because this would reduce the number of beggars. A counter argument, which he rejected, opposed raising minimum ages for marriage on the grounds that this would increase bastardy. Henry Smith supported a minimum age of nineteen.[55]

Although it was once believed that fourteen was a popular age for girls to marry, in the period 1560 to 1646 the mean age of females at their first marriage was between twenty-six and twenty-seven. Teenage marriages of Elizabethan girls were relatively rare, particularly at the minimum statutory age of twelve. In the parish of Colyton, Devon, in the period 1560-99, the mean ages at first marriage were 28.1 for men and 27.0 for women; this altered slightly in the period 1600-29 to 27.4 and 27.3 respectively. In the entire period 1560 to 1646, only 6.5% of the girls at Colyton married at age nineteen or younger, whereas 25.6% wed in their thirties and 4.9% in their forties. These figures do not reveal the mean age of espousals, which in some cases undoubtedly occurred when the parties were considerably younger.[56]

Various reasons may be advanced for delayed marriages in Elizabethan society. In rural areas, a young man had to wait until he had land or a cottage with a loom or other means to support a family before he could marry. The tendency of rural young people to begin laboring as live-in servants doing agricultural or domestic work delayed wedlock. If a young man were an eldest son he might have to wait until his father, if a freeholder or tenant farmer, died. In times of economic expansion or high mortality, earlier marriage was feasible. In urban areas, the seven-year apprenticeships, to the extent that they were enforced, discouraged marriage until about the age of twenty-four or twenty-five. Personal factors also accounted for later marriages. William Wentworth was still unmarried at the age of twenty-seven, but not by choice. Only after his father's death was he able to travel to London, the major matrimonial market for nobility and gentry, where he met and married a suitable woman. The physician and astrologer Simon Forman avoided marriage until he was forty-seven, when he wed a girl of sixteen. A decade earlier, in 1590, he reported in his diary that he "was offred a wife mani tymes this yere betwen Ester or Whitsontyd, and had the sight and choise of 4 or 5 maides and wydowes." Others would have preferred to delay marriage but were pressured to make an early trip to the altar. Anthony Mildmay, though "more willinge to travile to get experience of the world than to marry so soone," took fifteen-year old Grace Sherrington as his wife c. 1567, when he was approximately nineteen.[57]

The average mean age for first marriages was higher for the population as a whole than for the peerage. In the late sixteenth century (1540-99), the average marital age for eldest sons of peers was twenty-one, but for all children and grandchildren of peers the age was between twenty-five and twenty-six. Between 1550 and 1625, daughters of the upper classes married between twenty and twenty-one, whereas the average age for girls of the lower classes, according to Lawrence Stone's figures, was approximately four years older. In the peerage, only 6% wed at fifteen or younger in the late sixteenth century (1540-99), but 21% were married by the age of seventeen, and 78% by the age of twenty-five. Only 2% failed to marry at all. One young marriage involved Elizabeth Manners, daughter of the earl of Rutland, who wed Burghley's grandson, William Cecil, in January 1589 at the age of thirteen, and bore her first child when only fourteen years and five months.[58]

Early marriages were attractive to the landed classes because of property settlements, family alliances, the need for male heirs, and—especially for the peerage—the limited number of potential mates. Simultaneously, the system of wardship was conducive to early marriages. Joel Hurstfield cautions that many child marriages had nothing to do with feudal tenures, but he overemphasizes child marriages among the nonlanded classes (an opinion fostered by the research of Frederick Furnivall, discussed below).[59] Reliable statistical analyzes are needed, though the historical evidence suggests that wardship was a major contributing factor to young (principally teenage) marriages.

Unless a marriage had been publicly contracted before wardship, a ward could not wed without the approval of his or her guardian or, in the case of wards of the crown, the queen. Only a father had to die to make a child subject to wardship, and mothers did not automatically become guardians of their children, though some tried and succeeded. A guardian with marriage rights for his ward normally intended to make a profit from the transaction, though any marriage he arranged had to be *absque disparagatione,* that is, a ward could not be wed below his social rank or to someone of unsound religion (though there is no evidence of lawsuits for disparagement). If a male heir was under twenty-one at his father's death, his land went to the crown until he sued livery, but if he was over fourteen and was either married or fully contracted he could not be offered an alternative marriage. If not, he was obliged to accept a marriage proposal put forth by the crown or his guardian. If he refused, he was required to reimburse the crown or guardian when he came of age for the amount the guardian would have received for his marriage. If he wed without his guardian's consent the latter was entitled to hold his land until double the value of the marriage was received. If there was no male heir, the estate was divided equally among the surviving daughters. If they were over fourteen, they were not liable to wardship, but those under fourteen became wards until the age of sixteen. Female wards could not enter a binding contract of marriage before the age of fourteen, even if proposed by the guardian. Between the ages of fourteen and sixteen she had the right to refuse a proposed marriage, but the guardian then had the right to retain her lands until he recovered the sum he would have received for her marriage. If a female ward had been precontracted before her fourteenth birthday, she could marry that person or the guardian's choice. If the guardian refused to propose a marriage for her before her sixteenth birthday, he lost his right to the profits a marriage would bring. Legally and financially, therefore, guardians had ample reason to arrange marriages for their wards. This would mean marriages for boys between their fourteenth and twenty-first birthdays, and for girls between their fourteenth and sixteenth birthdays.[60]

In analyzing the relationship of wardship and young marriages, one sees that a financial motivation dominates. In June 1572, for example, George Talbot, earl of Shrewsbury, wrote to Burghley regarding the recent death of Thomas Lord Wharton. Because of the proximity of the lands of the ward (Philip) to his own, and because he had a daughter Philip's age, he favored a marriage between them and offered to pay as much for the wardship as any other bidder. Burghley himself was at the hub of Elizabethan wardship activity, so it was natural that his daughter Anne married his ward, Edward de Vere, earl of Oxford, but the match was not a happy one. Neither was that of George Clifford, earl of Cumberland, whose guardian, the earl of Bedford, arranged Clifford's marriage to his daughter Margaret. After nearly thirty years of married life Cumberland wrote: "God . . . matched us in lawful manner in one, though our minds met not, but in contrarys and thoughts of discontentment." George Luttrell of Dunster Castle fared no better when his guardian, Hugh Stewkley, offered him either of his daughters when the boy was fifteen. The marriage occurred five years later, in 1580, and proved to be so unhappy that Luttrell took a mistress and sired two children by her. When his wife died in the 1620s, he married his paramour.[61]

The complications involved in calculating the effects of wardship and marriage are revealed in a letter Burghley received in September 1578 from his son Thomas. The latter acknowledged that the earl of Leicester had given his approval for Thomas to purchase the wardship of Edmund Lord Sheffield, aged twelve, with a view to his marriage to one of Thomas' daughters.

Wherein, as I am to thank his Lordship, so, for lack of ability, and the rather being disappointed, against my expectation, of the selling of Sawley at this present, I must be driven to pass it over unless your Lordship could obtain some deferment of it for a time; for I have already heard by Mr. Roger Manners that my Lady holdeth the wardship at two thousand pounds, which money, I hope, when I shall be better able hereafter, will procure my daughter, though perhaps not so noble a marriage, yet it may be in living more present and in match more assured, for that my daughter being young, the adventure of the money [by Thomas Cecil] will be great, and a hazard whether the match shall take place, or no, to both their likings. And yet . . . the house being noble and in that country which I count a neighbour to your Lordships living and mine, I would be loth to overship a match that might be hereafter a strengthening to your posterity. And, therefore, I beseech your Lordship the matter may be entertained from conclusion as long as may be.

Financial considerations were paramount for Thomas Cecil, yet he had to consider family alliances, the location of the Sheffield lands, and the possibility that either his daughter or Lord Sheffield could veto the proposed marriage on coming of age.[62]

The stakes involved in wardship called for intense maneuvering by interested parties. Sir Edward Fitton complained to Sir Robert Cecil in 1600 that he had been cheated out of the wardship of the son of Mr. Brereton because Brereton, facing death, had moved quickly to find a bride for his son. A similar concern was shared by Cuthbert Fleming, a gentleman of Sharlston, Yorks., who stipulated in his 1585 will that after his demise his wife should inquire if his daughter had been made a ward. If so, Mrs. Fleming was "to gett her brother Thorney to make speede in her busines, consideringe howe the case standethe, and that all my lyveinge is in statute marchaunte for sixe hundred poundes." Her brother, in other words, was to seek the wardship himself or for the widow. Fleming stopped short of contracting a young marriage to avoid wardship, but the wealthy Devon yeoman Robert Furse did not. In 1593 Furse became worried that his son and heir, then aged nine years, might be encumbered with an unequal match or one leading to his financial ruin, so he arranged for his son to wed Susanna Alford, daughter and ward of a woman whose second husband was his relative Edmund Furse. Susanna was almost ten, but the wedding would be delayed until both were fifteen, and only if both consented at that time would the match be consummated. In this case the marriage, for unknown reasons, never transpired. Although mothers did not usually obtain guardianship of their sons, there were numerous instances where this occurred, as in the Alford-Furse case. William Whittingham, dean of Durham, had not made special provision for the wardship of his elder son, but his widow Katherine requested and received the right of his custody and marriage from the crown.[63]

Children were often pawns in the wardship process. Edward Saville, ward of George Talbot, earl of Shrewsbury, was spirited away in 1562 by his base brother Robert Saville and married to a "simple poore woman" so that Robert could gain control of the inheritance, but the queen directed that custody of Edward be delegated to the master of the rolls. In another case, when allegations were made concerning "sundrie abuses committed about the contracting and keeping of Elizabeth Hill, a yong maiden, daughter of Gilbert Hill, deceased," the Privy Council awarded custodial rights and ordered that she not be contracted to anyone without the sanction of the archbishop of Canterbury. Thomas Howard, fourth duke of Norfolk, was adamant about an alliance with the Dacres of Gilsland, and wed the widow of Thomas Lord Dacre to become guardian of her son George, whom he intended to marry to his daughter Margaret. When the boy died in an accident at about age eight, Norfolk gained control of his wife's three daughters and had two of them marry his sons Philip and William. The third daughter was saved from a ducally imposed marriage by an early death.

Sometimes young wards married without their guardians' approval despite the consequences. When Elizabeth Hooke, a ward of the queen, contracted a marriage to a kinsman of Francis Alford in 1586 without royal approval, one of the gentlemen in Burghley's employ advocated that Alford be fined and committed to the Fleet. Whether the young couple subsequently achieved happiness is not known. In another case Walter Aston, son and heir of Sir Edward Aston, secretly wed Anne Barnes in 1600 without the sanction of his guardian, Sir Edward Coke, the attorney general. The marriage was dissolved in High Commission and the girl was imprisoned in the Fleet for a year, but young Aston subsequently married a woman Coke did not approve. This time Aston, whose wardship had cost Coke £1,400, had to pay the attorney general £4,000.[64]

One of the most bizarre cases was that of Walter Calverley of Haysthorpe, Yorks. After his father's death, he became a ward and arranged on his own an espousal to a girl of humble birth. The guardian, however, had the espousal terminated and then pressured him to marry Philippa, daughter of Sir John Brooke. Calverley, despising his wife, turned to drinking and gambling until he had squandered his inheritance, mortgaged his lands, and dissipated his wife's dowry. In 1605, while inebriated he killed two of his children, stabbed his wife, and attempted to murder a third child; he was pressed to death in October 1605.[65]

The impact of guardianship on early marriages was not confined to gentry and nobility, though most of the extant evidence relates to these groups. In May 1562 Thomas Radcliffe, earl of Sussex, requested the wardship of the daughters of a deceased yeoman to marry them to two of his men. Several cases in the ecclesiastical court of Chester in 1562 involved child marriages arranged by guardians. One of these occurred c. 1544 in the parish of Blackburn, Lancs., when by "the advise and Compulsion" of those responsible for Margery Heydocke, age eight, she was wed to Peter Haworth, age seven. The evidence suggests that the couple lived together until she reached the age of twelve and repudiated the marriage, never having copulated. In a similar case, Constance Entwisell, age eleven, had been orphaned, so the father of Andrew Haworth, age nine, "did obteyne the Landlordes goodwill of the Tenement wherein the father of the said Custance did dwell, and so maried the said Andrewe his sonne, & the said Custance, together" in the parish church of Bolton, Lancs., c. 1550. They lived in the house of the groom's father and then in their own home for several years, but alleged that no copulation had taken place during this time.[66]

The stipulations of the absence of sexual intercourse in these cases were customary for child marriages. Three arguments for abstinence from early consummation were made: first, stunted offspring could result; secondly, immoderate emission of sperm in adolescence hindered physical and intellectual growth; and thirdly, parturition by a girl under sixteen rendered permanent physical damage. Nevertheless, consummation normally made a marriage binding, so that some parents and guardians pressed for early cohabitation. One such was the duke of Norfolk, whose son Philip had married Ann Dacre when he was twelve, but the boy refrained from copulation until he was seventeen. More common was the physical separation of youthful brides and grooms, perhaps by dispatching the boys to travel, study, or serve an apprenticeship in another locality. After Sir Robert Cecil had his nine-year-old son and heir William married to Catherine, daughter of Thomas Lord Howard of Walden, in 1600, William was returned to Paris to complete his education and Catherine remained at home. Anne, daughter of Sir Edward Fitton, was married to John Newdigate in 1587 when she was twelve, but she continued to stay at her father's home until 1595 or 1596 when she began to live with her husband. William Stanley, wed in 1560 to ten-year-old Anne Dutton at Hatton Hall, Cheshire, when he was twelve, spent the next five years at school in the service of the earl of Derby. The bride remained with her father, but the marriage ended in divorce proceedings in the ecclesiastical court at Chester in 1565. In another Cheshire case, George Hulse, age seven, married a four-year-old girl named Elizabeth because "her frendes thought she shuld have a lyvinge bie hym," but when the inheritance did not materialize, he bound himself as an apprentice to a shoemaker at Congleton. When he returned to claim his bride ten years later she refused him as a "poore wastes man." The results were hardly better in the case of Elizabeth Tanfield, who was married at the age of fifteen to Sir Henry Cary, master of the queen's jewel house. An older man interested primarily in his bride's dowry, Cary left her with her parents for the first fifteen months of their marriage. He was then dispatched to the Netherlands on a diplomatic mission, which gave his mother the opportunity to assert control over Elizabeth, whom she virtually imprisoned and deprived of her library.[67]

Cases of early copulation by those wed young are difficult to locate. A. L. Rowse found two cases of early Tudor child marriages in which the brides, aged twelve and eleven, refused sexual relations with their husbands. One husband in desperation raped another girl and the second accepted 13s. 4d. from his father-in-law in return for yielding back the girl. Thomas Dampart, who had taken a wife at Warrington, Lancs., c. 1554, admitted to having sexual relations with her when he was twelve. In a later case involving the marriage of John Bridge, age eleven or twelve, and Elizabeth Ramsbotham, age thirteen or fourteen, at Bury, Lancs., the groom was so distraught on his wedding night that he refused to eat and wept to return home. His father and a clergyman persuaded him to go to bed with his bride, but he refused to engage in sexual relations. One may suspect that the frequent denial of copulation in divorce cases involving child marriages may not always have been true, for the admission of a sexual act would normally have rendered divorce impossible.[68]

A crucial question is the extent to which child marriages were practiced. Hurstfield judged they were fairly common but refrained from estimating percentages. Laslett, on the other hand, used the evidence adduced by Furnivall to assert that less than half of one percent of those marrying in the diocese of Chester between 1561 and 1566 were children. Furnivall, however, was concerned only with cases in the ecclesiastical court of Chester involving ratification and divorce. Normally these cases entailed property settlements, so that legal action was essential. Presumably in many instances formal ratification was not sought, especially if property was not a problem. Moreover, these cases do not reveal how many child marriages terminated because of the early death of a spouse, such as the mother in childbirth. The evidence indicates a laxity to ratify marriages, as a close reading of the divorce cases reveals; sometimes legal action was deferred for years. Laslett's estimate is too low, but it would be hazardous to assert any other figure until more data have been compiled. For Tudor Cornwall, Rowse concludes that child marriages were exceptional and not generally approved. Child marriages did not receive much attention in the writings of Anglicans and Puritans, suggesting that the practice was limited.[69]

One of the most striking facets of the extant evidence for child marriages is the involvement of very young people. William Lord Eure was ten when he wed Marcy Darcy, approximately four; she had to be held by her nurse and was barely able to repeat her matrimonial vow. John Somerford was only three when he married two-year-old Jane Brereton at the parish church of Brereton, Ches., c. 1552, and the marriage ended in divorce proceedings in 1564. In other marriages, the children were as young as four, five, and six. Usually such marriages were performed in parish churches, but sometimes they were held in private chapels, such as Hatton Hall, Ches. Elizabeth Tilston, aged approximately eight, was married to William Pole, age eleven, at Marbury, Ches., before sunrise, despite the fact that "they were bothe so ignoraunt, they knewe not what the matter meanid." A license had been procured, but the curate did not ask the customary banns. In several instances, children were wed without consent from their guardians, as in the cases of Grace Boyes, age nine, c. 1558 at Blackburn, Lancs., and James Ballard, age eleven, in 1560 at Colne, Lancs. The latter informed his uncle the morning following the wedding that his bride "had intised hym with two Apples, to go with him to Colne, and to marry her." Robert Mason, age nine, and Margaret Dugdale, age ten, were married at Preston, Lancs., because their parents were paramours.[70]

Numerous attempts were made to stop such abuses. Marriages of children under age could not be made without ecclesiastical license, though these were sometimes obtained under false pretences or by bribery. There were efforts, especially by Whitgift, to tighten up the issuing of licenses, and there were endeavors to ferret out child marriages by visitation articles. A Marian law (4 & 5 Phil. and Mary, c. 8) made it possible to imprison someone simply for being in the presence of a person who wed a girl under sixteen without the consent of a parent or guardian. This happened to Richard Lane in 1580, when he was found with Thomas Morgan, husband of a child-bride. The ecclesiastical courts punished numerous offenders, including clergy who performed such marriages without approval. William Fleetwood, recorder of London, informed Burghley in 1575 that "a man of my Lady Meutes, for that he stolle an Orphant of the Citie of 11 yeres olde, and maried her in Leicester, he being 30 yeres old, dothe publique penauns for the same by the Judgement of the Ecclesiasticall Commission." Eight years later, Fleetwood complained to Burghley about a fencer and his wife who forced a young maiden to be married by an elderly priest. The city of Exeter tried to curtail child marriage abuses by imposing a fine of 12d. for every pound held in recognizance if a female orphan under the age of twenty-one wed a free man without the consent of the mayor and court of orphans. If she wed someone from outside the city or an unfree person, 3s. in every pound was forfeited. Male orphans marrying under age without a license from the court of orphans lost 12d. of every pound of recognizance money.[71]

The Privy Council also acted to curtail child marriages. When a suitor of Katherine, heiress of the deceased John Whitelocke of Goldhanger, Essex, tried "by all forcible and indirecte meanes . . . to possesse himselfe of her," the Council ruled in 1588 that she must remain in the custody of her guardian until age eighteen, as the will of her father stipulated. The following year, in response to a complaint that a fifteen-year-old boy had married a woman ten years his senior, the Council ordered that the boy be sequestered and educated during his minority, and the adults responsible punished. The Council's action was less straightforward in another 1589 case. Thomas Brakin, a gentleman, sought to arrange a marriage between his son and young Elizabeth Hill, but the dean of St. Paul's intervened and held the girl in custody. At Brakin's request the Council placed her in the care of a matron until the case was decided. Nearly fifteen months later, however, the Council learned that Thomas Caverley (or Calvert) had seized and married the girl. The sheriffs of London were ordered to place her in protective custody until the archbishop of Canterbury determined the validity of the marriage. The Council dealt with only a small percentage of child marriages, and could redress only the grossest abuses.[72]

For child marriages in Elizabethan society, the Church of England bears the major responsibility, for without a license, such marriages were illegal for girls under twelve and boys under fourteen. Where clerics performing child marriages have been identified and their religious persuasions are known, they are Catholics or Anglicans, never Puritans. The bishops and their officials issued the licenses and could have stopped or reduced the practice at any time. Yet even Bishop William Chaderton married his daughter, age nine, to an eleven-year-old boy.[73] Several Anglicans condemned child marriages, revealing a division among Anglicans on this practice. Fortunately, the parents or guardians of those who married early normally kept young couples separated to avoid sexual intercourse. Child marriages were never common; perhaps no more than 2 or 3% married below the legally minimum ages, and the Colyton figures show that only 6.5% of the girls married as teenagers. Wardship and property settlements were the major factors behind early marriages, but these endeavors to head off legal controversies did not have an enviable record of success.

To recapitulate, in a number of areas the views of Anglicans and Puritans on marriage differ. Marriage was still regarded as almost sacramental in conservative Anglican circles, whereas Puritans treated it primarily as a covenant, using analogies of friendship, government, the church, and business partnerships. Protestants and Catholics accepted the tripartite purpose of marriage, with primacy allotted to procreation over companionship or avoidance of fornication. Nevertheless, some Puritans placed more emphasis on marriage as a sexual remedy than as the means of reproduction. In contrast to the Catholic exaltation of celibacy, Elizabethan Protestants regarded married life as equally virtuous and interpreted chastity as the repression of lust and unnatural sexual desires rather than as sexual abstinence. Although Protestants gave lip service to the Pauline preference for sexual asceticism, the positive Protestant attitude to marriage laid the foundation for the recognition of sexual drives as wholesome. The advantages of a celibate life for the clergy were acknowledged but not exalted. With respect to the laity, Puritans demonstrated a greater enthusiasm than Anglicans for the married as opposed to the celibate life, particularly since procreation increased the church and commonwealth.

Differences between Anglicans and Puritans existed with respect to the qualities sought in prospective mates. Both groups insisted on the importance of religious agreement. Greater deviation occurred between ideal and practice in the attitude of ministers and government toward marriage within one's social degree. Likewise, although Anglican and Puritan clergy urged that wealth not be a consideration in selecting a mate, in practice, laity of both persuasions regularly made it so. Puritans, in word and deed, placed more stress on personal qualities such as virtue and modesty, and on mutual liking or even love, than did Anglicans. Puritans warned as well that physical attractiveness was not important. Ministers of both persuasions agreed that prospective mates should be close in age, though in practice exceptions were relatively common. Thus, apart from strictly religious considerations, the endeavor of the clergy to influence the laity in evaluating potential spouses was not particularly successful.

Elizabethan clergymen were not outspoken about child marriages, though Puritans were more concerned than Anglicans. The absence of marked concern was partially because youthful marriages were not commonplace: Between 1560 and 1646, the mean age of females at first marriage was between twenty-six and twenty-seven. Among the landed classes, however, young marriages were more frequent owing to property settlements, the need for male heirs, family alliances, and the limited number of suitable mates. Wardship, with its financial considerations, was also a factor. Attempts to restrict child marriages were undertaken in both secular and spiritual spheres, with leadership from the bishops and Privy Council. With respect to age at marriage, ministers exercised a wholesome influence, and their success probably explains the relatively small amount of written material on this issue.

CHAPTER 4

The Marital Quest Consummated

One of the most divisive issues on marriage was the role of parental consent and individual choice. At stake was the institution of the arranged marriage and ultimately the question of familial *versus* personal rights. Weddings in the upper classes were social pageants, mainly intended to reinforce the social hierarchy. Yet pressures were brought within the Protestant tradition to simplify the celebrations, particularly the allied festivities rooted in social custom. The person whose spouse died faced the question of remarriage, often acute for widows. Pauline teaching advocated continued widowhood, in keeping with the apostle's views on a celibate life. Elizabethan widows, however, were subjected to intense pressure that made the question of remarriage more complex than the ability to withstand sexual drives. In all three areas—parental consent, weddings, and remarriage —the Anglicans and Puritans came into conflict with the practices of a property-oriented society.

(1) Parental Consent and the Arranged Marriage

If a man may giue his goods to whome hee will, hee may as well bestow his Children where hee thinketh best, for Children are the goods of the Parents.

Charles Gibbon[1]

The fathers auctoritie ought not to take away the consent of the chylde in mariage.

The Bishops' Bible [2]

The norm in Elizabethan society, at least among the landed classes, was for a young couple to marry in accord with the decision of their parents, particularly because of the financial implications. The bride's father was expected to provide a portion and wedding expenses whereas the groom's father was responsible for a jointure in the event of the groom's death, usually 20 to 25% of the value of the portion; an allowance suitable for his son's social status; perhaps room and board in his home for several years; and the settlement of part of his estate on his son. Reliance on parental choice was greater for elder sons, whose fathers sought relatively early marriages to obviate wardship complications. Younger sons were in a poorer financial position, hence their fathers would be less likely to gain monetary advantage in seeking early marriages for them. A younger brother was often financially dependent on his father or older brother, which rendered him amenable to pressure in the choice of a spouse. Girls of the upper classes were particularly dependent on parental discretion in view of the necessity of dowries, but Lawrence Stone argues that the emancipation of women in the selection of a spouse occurred between 1560 and 1640, with most of the development coming in the Stuart era. Daughters of the nobility and gentry also tended to be reliant on arranged marriages, because they had little opportunity to meet eligible men in most country houses. The greater freedom enjoyed by young men increased their chances of finding a compatible mate. Opportunities were greater for young people of lesser status in rural areas and for virtually all in the towns, presumably increasing the pressure for individual choice as opposed to parental arrangement. Children of the propertyless were probably much freer with respect to choosing mates, for their parents had no hold over them in the form of significant bequests and they had often left home by their early teens to become apprentices, servants, or laborers.[3]

An argument some modern scholars use to support the prevalency of arranged marriages is the age at which people wed. Pearl Hogrefe believes that parental choice was necessitated because the usual age for girls of royal or aristocratic blood to wed was fourteen or fifteen, and other girls sixteen. Yet the mean age for females at their first marriage was between twenty-six and twenty-seven, long past the minimum age of twelve. Hogrefe correctly asserts that young girls under parental control had little opportunity to marry according to emotional desires,[4] but this is true of only a small minority of Elizabethan marriages—something on the order of 6.5% if the Colyton figures are representative, but in any case hardly more than 10%. With most Elizabethans marrying in their twenties, parental domina-

tion in the choice of marital partners is easily overstated, except for
the nobility and gentry, especially eldest sons and their brides.

Written admonitions on parental involvement in the selection of
a spouse abound. One of the most influential works was Bullinger's
Christen State of Matrimonye, translated by Miles Coverdale, which
asserts that children must have the consent of parents to wed in accord with natural, divine, and civil law, or the marriage will be annulled. Simultaneously, Bullinger warned parents not to constrain
children to marry or allow them to wed too early. Parents and children alike must acquiesce to a proposed marriage. A father must not
contract his daughter in marriage until he knows she can be a good
housewife and govern the home, "for it becometh hir better to haue
a payer of roughe and harde handes/ then to be fayer & softe glister-
ing with ringes or kovered continually with smothe gloues." Once
children come of age they can wed with discretion and parents must
not break up the marriage. In effect, Bullinger balanced parental
rights and the wishes of young people by insisting on the approval
of all concerned unless the children were of age, when they could
marry as they wished.[5]

The marginalia of Elizabethan Bibles express disparate views. The
Geneva annotators reiterated Bullinger's position, calling for parental
consent but denying parents the authority to marry their offspring
without the latter's agreement. Neither do parents possess the right
to enforce celibacy on children, "for the fathers wil dependeth on his
childrens in this point: in so muche as he is bounde to haue respect
to their infirmitie, nether can he iustly require of them singlenes, if
they haue not that gift of God so to liue." The Bishops' Bible empha-
sizes parental consent, though parents must not be motivated primarily by personal gain in arranging marriages. The Beza-Tomson
Bible restored a balance and infused a new condition requiring that a
couple "must with singular affection, entirely loue one the other."
Parents must consider what is best for children and direct them to
marriage or celibacy.[6]

Both positions on the parental role are reflected among Anglican
authors. Men such as Cooper, Parker, and Thomas Rogers stressed
consent by parents or guardians, without a companion emphasis on
the agreement of the young couple. William Wentworth embodied
this position in his advice to his son: "Nether in your mariadge conclude, naie attempt nothing, withoutt their privitye." Other Anglicans defended the balanced view. Nicholas Gibbens found evidence
for this in Genesis 2, where God's bringing Eve to Adam indicated
parental consent, and Eve's coming and Adam's rejoicing showed

their acquiescence. No children are to be compelled to wed, an admonition also asserted by Edmund Bunny, rector of Bolton Percy
and sub-dean of York Cathedral, who was critical of parents devoted
to their own profit and pleasure. Babington too condemned parents
who forced children to wed against their desires. He advised parents
to consider that where love is lacking the marriage is not of divine
making; however, they must not give children liberty "directly without cause" to select mates or deviate from the parents' choice. Young
people must strive to like those chosen by their parents. Babington
disapproved of both the "licentious rage of children" to choose without parental advice and parents who arranged matches that caused
marital grief. [7]

The two most substantive Anglican advocates of the balanced view
were Sandys and Whetstone. To demonstrate that parental consent
was requisite, Sandys marshaled natural, civil and canon law, patristic
precedent, reason, and Scripture. Marriages without such consent
were unrighteous and harmful to the commonwealth. Sandys even
questioned the legitimacy of children born to such marriages, and
called for more laws to restrain "unlawful" contracting. "If youthful
children have so little reverence both of God and men, that such admonition will not make them leave such disordered marriages, it be-
hoveth magistrates, who are the common parents of the weal public,
to bridle their lusts with severe laws for the redress of this evil and
the mischiefs ensuing of it. " But Sandys also insisted that there could
be no lawful wedlock without the couple's full consent. Convinced
that marrying young people against their wills for financial motives
was a common disease, he warned that such marriages seldom proved
successful. [8]

Whetstone, the ex-soldier who wrote professionally, expressed
views generally harmonious with those of other Anglicans. Some of
his work consisted of verses on "the discommodities of forst marriages," with a particular view to those who wed their progeny for
wealth. His major work on this subject, completed in the early 1580s,
was *An Heptameron of Ciuill Discourses*, with an epistle dedicatory
to Sir Christopher Hatton. Parental consent was necessary, with parents selecting spouses for their children based on experience and
virtue, but not excluding financial considerations. Children must not
be allowed to heed only the appearance of their lovers, or to marry
in the expectation that good behavior would win parental approval
and monetary support, "for necessitie wyll accustome the Husband
with dishonest shyftes, and keepes his fayre Wife from being ydle:
for want muste be supplyed, what shame so euer ensue." Although

financial realities rendered marriages without parental sanction unworkable, Whetstone was impatient with parents who married their
children for financial gain:

The coueitous Marchaunt, with no more delight heereth the passing bell of his
ritch neyghbour, which promyseth hym the first loppe [lopping] of his sonnes
liuyng, then the poore gentleman eyeth the able heyre, with desyre to match
him . . . with his fayre proude Daughter. . . . In most of these matches, the
sorowe begynneth, before the solemnitye of the Marriage endeth.

Forced marriages were no more acceptable to Whetstone than matrimony without parental acquiescence. The foundation of wedlock is
free choice, for without the satisfaction of personal fancy nothing
can produce love, with its power to tolerate defects. In any arranged
marriage, he urged parents to consider physical attraction and personal behavior; children who abhor their prospective mates but dissemble
to please their parents have disastrous marriages in store. Instead of
financial improvement, forced marriages, he argued, lead to riotous
living and economic ruin.

It is the office of the [one to be] married, to be aduised ere he loue, and louing
to be reposed in his choise: It is the office of the married to prouide for an Household, before he take possession of his hearts delight: and it is the office of the
marryed, to examine the conditions of his Mistresse, before he enter into any
couenaunt of Mariage. And how can he be aduised, that marrieth without the
priuitie of his Parents? and how can he supporte an household, that marryeth
with his Parents displeasure, vpon whose deuotion he liueth? and how can he
iudge of his Mistresse conditions, that wanteth discretion to consider of his owne
estate?

Parental consent and individual approval are equally requisite in
Whetstone's judgment. [9]
    Puritans, like Anglicans, were not of one mind on parental consent.
A number of Puritans asserted the right of parents to determine marital partners for their offspring without insisting on the right of some
choice for the young people. Dod required parents to consider the
natural inclination of children to celibacy or matrimony, and then
make a fit selection of mates for godliness rather than financial considerations. Children were expected to honor their elders by recognizing their wisdom in these matters. If they wed without approval,
Dod, contrary to Sandys, accepted the marriage as lawful, though unclean until the couple was reconciled to God by repentance and to
their parents by submission. Perkins, on the other hand, finding support for parental consent in the fifth commandment, denied the legality of marriages of children who had wed without consent, as long as

they were under parental government. Richard Rogers made it the parents' responsibility to provide partners for their progeny and insisted upon parental consent. As children grew older he, like Fenner, was willing to allow them some freedom, but never without final parental acquiescence. Puritans stressed acceptance of parental guidance as part of the honor and obedience owed to elders. Greenham used the seventh commandment to buttress parental rights in matrimony, which rights were based, he believed, on the proposition that children were their parents' goods. Puritans insisted that parental authority not be abused, and writers such as Gifford asserted the duty of children to refuse a proposed spouse who was evil or of another faith. [10]

Other Puritans balanced parental rights and individual choice. Pagit, who regarded marriages without parental approval as breeches of divine commandment, nevertheless insisted that elders lack authority to force children to wed or to hinder godly matches because of preference for a union based on wealth. William Vaughan prohibited parents from arranging marriages while their youngsters were minors or against their wills. A common objection to an arranged match was that it was akin to one who "fitteth his foote by anothers last," and then discovers that the shoe does not fit. Whereas Charles Gibbon believed rejection of parental authority in matrimony was both rebellion and contrary to divine commandments, he cautioned parents against forced marriages, denying them the right to insist on a match in which the couple has no disposition toward each other. If, however, parents insist in their selection of marriage partners, children cannot rebel, hence for Gibbon, the attempt to strike a balance was unsuccessful. [11]

The two principal Puritan advocates of a balanced view were Cleaver and Stockwood. For Cleaver, parental consent in matrimony is mandated by Scripture (particularly the fifth commandment), natural law, and the concept that children are goods of their fathers. In determining matrimony, parental sanction "ought to beare the chiefest sway, and strike likewise the greatest stroke, in this most holy and heauenly action." For an eldest son under twenty-five to reject a suitable marriage proposed to him by his father and to engage instead in illicit sex was judged grounds by Cleaver for disinheritance. It is not clear if Cleaver intended this punishment for eldest sons who repudiated such a match but remained chaste. In any case, the stipulated age is notable, for these authors intended parental consent to extend well beyond the minimum age for marriage and in some cases beyond the age of majority. Cleaver's attempt for balance is evident in his discussion of espousals. If parents agree to a contract of espousal between unmeet persons, the latter must break the agreement. At the espousal stage, the couple must be willing to marry, though it is not essential at this stage that they love each other, for love grows gradually. A couple must not be constrained to espouse by parental fear, threatened loss of preferment, or physical punishment. If betrothed persons loath each other, parents must break the contract or postpone the wedding in the hope of a change in attitude. Parents must allow their children to wed those they like—as long as they are not of a higher social degree. If a child selects someone honest and godly, regardless of wealth, parents must acquiesce. There "ought to bee a knitting of hearts, before striking of hands," for "how can such two become one flesh lawfully, when as ther wanteth the vnion and coniunction of the heart, the true naturall mother of all marriage duties?"[12]

Stockwood's views on parental consent and individual choice are enunciated in *A Bartholmew Fairing for Parentes, to Bestow vpon Their Sonnes and Daughters* (1589). This work seems to have been an outgrowth of an event that occurred a decade earlier when he was accused (erroneously, he claims) of marrying a girl without her parents' acquiescence. At that time he preached at Paul's Cross, defending himself and the proposition that parental authority to bestow children in wedlock was divinely bestowed, which many parents no longer accepted. He returned to this theme in *Bartholmew Fairing*, citing Scripture, natural law, common custom, and proper order. Continental Protestants, including Luther, Calvin, Beza, Musculus, Peter Martyr, and Rudolph Gualter, were also cited. The treatment of children as property, which was popular with some Puritans, appears in Stockwood; those who entice children to wed without parental consent in effect steal another's goods and deserve capital punishment. Vows of children without parental consent are neither valid in human and divine law nor matters of conscience and need not be fulfilled.

To make a vow vnto the Lord, being in it selfe and of it[s] owne nature an holy and acceptable action vnto God, . . . is notwithstanding in children vnlawfull, because it is such an action as they onlie may performe which are free and at their owne disposition, the which they are not: so in like maner to consent in matrimonie, although in it selfe it be both honest & lawfull, yet is it not an action of force in children, without the consent and allowance of their parentes.

Those who wed without parental sanction could, in Stockwood's judgment, make the marriage acceptable by procuring such approval. In its absence he called for punishment at the magistrate's discretion as an example for others.[13]

Stockwood vested the choice of spouses in parents, particularly fathers. Children must accept these selections as long as the proposed mates are not infidels, infamous persons, or "in shape or fauour so blemished, as it may worthelie bee supposed that the same may be an occasion of the withdrawing of loue." Parents must discuss with a child of marriageable age whether he or she intends to wed or remain celibate; if the former, there must not be unnecessary delay that would cause them

either to be derided, or laughed to scorne as stale bachelers, or otherwise to bee suspected of bad husbandrie, or huswifrie, or of pride and disdaining all others, . . . or that there is in them some secrete & hidden vice or infirmitie the which maketh them vnfit for mariage, or otherwise of couetousnesse, because they are loth to depart with mony towards their maintenance.

Stockwood advised a young man of marriageable age to inform his parents if he was in love, and they should accept his choice if she is worthy, regardless of the dowry. Fathers were prohibited from imposing matches that children did not like. In cases of dispute, Stockwood favored intervention by a godly magistrate.[14]

The range of views expressed by Anglicans and Puritans on this subject is thus coextensive. The only difference is the treatment by some Puritans of children as property. To the extent, however, that Puritans sought love as a foundation of wedlock, the arranged match was more difficult to bring about, since it tied the arrangements to the personal outlook of the prospective couple.

Relatively little was written by Elizabethan Separatists and Catholics on this subject. Barrow made it the responsibility of parents to provide marriages for children as long as the children remained in their care, and he wanted affiancing to occur in private homes without the involvement of Church of England clergy. The *Catechisme* of the Augustinian canon Lawrence Vaux emphasized the necessity of mutual consent by the couple, warning that those who married only because of parental pressure were not husband and wife in the sight of God. Any sexual relations that ensued rendered the couple guilty of fornication.[15]

The evidence indicates a considerable discrepancy in practice regarding the role of parental consent. In numerous arranged marriages, little if any consideration appears to have been given to the wishes of the young persons. At the hub of these arrangements one often finds Cecil, who was concerned with members of his own family and others from the landed classes. Some of this interest was connected with the desire of ambitious men to improve their political station by marriage with a Cecil. One such person was Sir

Henry Percy, who proposed to Cecil in January 1562 that his second daughter, age fifteen, should marry one of Cecil's sons. He admitted he wanted to be linked to Cecil by such a marriage, and dangled as his bait a daughter "not muche vnredie for mariage," with virtues of godliness, wisdom, sobriety, temperance, maturity, and beauty. Apparently no consideration was given to the feelings of the couple. In 1569 Cecil was involved in attempts to arrange a match between his daughter Anne, age thirteen, and Philip Sidney, age fifteen, but this fell through, and Cecil accepted a proposal from Edward de Vere, earl of Oxford, for his daughter's hand in 1571. Yet only in August of that year he had written to Edward Manners, earl of Rutland, that when the Sidney match failed "I was fully determined to have of myself moved no marriage for my daughter until she should have been near sixteen, that with moving I might also conclude." Cecil was also active in arranging marriages for his other children.[16]

Even his grandchildren were involved. In the winter of 1589-90, he sought a husband for his eldest granddaughter, fourteen-year-old Elizabeth de Vere, and selected the royal ward, seventeen-year-old Henry Wriothesley, earl of Southampton, with the approval of the dowager countess of Southampton. The boy, however, pleaded he was too young and sought a year to make up his mind. His grandfather, Anthony Viscount Montagu, proved unable to dissuade him, and the match was never consummated. In 1592 Burghley tried to arrange a marriage for Elizabeth with Henry Percy, thirteenth earl of Northumberland, only to have her reject the idea, presumably because she was in love with William, second son of Henry Stanley, earl of Derby. Not until William succeeded to the title on the death of his brother (without posterity) in 1594 could he wed Elizabeth, which occurred in the presence of the queen at Greenwich in January 1595. Less than three years later Burghley sought a match for Elizabeth's younger sister Bridget, now thirteen. Henry Herbert, earl of Pembroke, and the countess Mary had proposed a marriage between their eldest son William and Bridget, with early agreement necessary because of the earl's failing health. Although Burghley's son-in-law, the earl of Oxford, approved, the match never materialized, and in 1599, after the lord treasurer's death, Bridget wed Francis Norris, grandson of Henry Lord Norris of Rycote.[17]

Burghley, whose example must have been considerable, was also instrumental in negotiated marriages apart from his family; this involvement is not surprising, in view of his role as master of the Court of Wards.[18] In September 1575 he was asked by Sir Arthur Champernoun to persuade Lord Edward Seymour to approve a

match between the latter's son and Sir Arthur's daughter. The couple
had been betrothed without the knowledge of either father. Burghley
sought in 1582 to arrange a match for the youngest daughter of Sir
Thomas Ryvett, brother of Thomas Lord Paget, with the latter's assistance. Two years later Burghley was approached by the gentleman
Roger Cave, who had two unwed daughters, the youngest of whom
was in her early twenties; concerned about this, he sought the lord
treasurer's advice. In 1590 Sir Thomas Stanhope assured Burghley
that he did not favor a marriage between his daughter and Henry
Wriothesley, fourth earl of Southampton, whom the lord treasurer
sought as a husband for his granddaughter.

Many marriages were arranged without apparent consideration for
the feelings of couples, especially when wardship was involved. When
the wealthy John Gamage died in 1584, the guardian of his daughter
Barbara swiftly arranged a marriage to Robert Sidney, the future earl
of Leicester, and the couple apparently never saw each other before
the wedding day. When such couples found themselves alone in bed
for the first time, it must have been awkward. Lawrence Stone suggests that the most advanced parents in allowing individual choice
were Puritans, such as Sir Walter Mildmay, yet some Puritan families
arranged matches, oblivious to the emotions of the young people.
Mildmay himself did so. Grace Sherrington's parents had arranged a
marriage for her when she was fourteen with Mildmay's son Anthony,
but the young man,

being then more willinge to travile to get experience of the world, than to marry
so soone, was unwillinge to give eare thereunto. But his father told him, yf he
did not marry me, he should never bring any other woman into his house. Upon
which importunitie of his father he was content and entered into communication what joynter he would make me, and what allowance he would give for our
maintenance in his owne tyme.

There was no free choice for Anthony Mildmay.[19]

A classic case of Puritan arranged marriages is the saga of Margaret
Dakins. At age eighteen she married Walter, second son of the deceased Walter Devereux, earl of Essex, in 1589, with the match arranged by Robert Devereux, earl of Essex, and Henry Hastings, the
Puritan earl of Huntingdon. When her husband was killed in the Low
Countries in 1591, two men sought her hand—Thomas, younger son
of Sir Henry Sidney, and Thomas Posthumous Hoby, whose uncle
(by marriage) was Burghley. The lord treasurer urged Margaret's
father to accept Hoby, promising a good jointure and urging speed to
give young Thomas time to court her and win her love. Yet by the

time Arthur Dakins received this letter Margaret had left for London
bearing letters authorizing Huntingdon and his wife, in whose home
she had been trained, to select a husband for her. Their choice was
their nephew, Thomas Sidney, and the wedding occurred no later
than July 1592. Three years later Sidney died and Hoby resumed his
courtship, with the support of Sir Robert Cecil and Edward Stanhope, a member of the Council of the North. Although first reluctant,
she wed Hoby in August 1596, probably because she needed his assistance in a lawsuit pending against her in the court of Chancery. After
(or because of) all this, Lady Hoby continued to believe that parents
should choose spouses for their children.[20]

The balanced view between parental rights and individual consent
that some Anglicans and Puritans advocated was practiced in Elizabethan society. One case involved Barnaby Googe, a kinsman and
servant of Cecil's who was trying to win the hand of Mary, daughter
of Thomas Darrell of Kent, who was precontracted to Sampson
Leonard. The girl's father accepted the balanced view, for in a letter
to Leonard's father in 1563 he explained that before he broached the
subject of this marriage he "knewe ryght well yt was my daughters
goodwyll and desire to haue it to come to passe: and so [I] moued
it by her consent and desire." Googe, however, wanted Mary for his
wife, and persuaded Cecil to intervene on his behalf, but without
success. Googe finally wrote to the Darrells, sarcastically commenting that he had been "certyfied of a pretye laffynge toye as touch-
ynge a pre contracte declarynge at full ye sharp inuencyon of mr
lennardes graue hedd." Mary finally asked him to cease his suit, for
"nether presentlye I haue nor I am well assured neuer shall haue, ye
good wyll or consent of father nor mother to whome I am both by
ye lawe of god and nature bound to geue honoure and obedyence.
. . . And do well consider yt my chefe obedience and dutye towardes them, is to be bestowed in maryage by there consentes."
Taken with her father's statement, this illustrates the balanced view,
even to the point of using some of the same arguments as in its defense.[21]

There are other instances of the balanced view. In August 1578
John Stanhope, a gentleman of Harrington, Northants., reported to
Hatton that he had gone to Carlisle to discuss with Henry Lord
Scrope of Bolton a match between their children. Both fathers agreed
that the couple should meet and resolve whether negotiations should
be culminated. Matters went even further for Sir Richard Cholmley,
who arranged for his duaghter to wed John Lord Lumley and paid
£1,000 as part of her portion. On her wedding day she begged her

father to cancel the marriage, asserting she preferred death to this husband, whom she could never love. He allegedly responded, "Rather than marry thee against thy liking, I will lose my money," and broke the match. She had fallen in love with her music teacher, a servant of her father, whom she subsequently wed with her father's acquiescence. An indenture dated 1 July 1562 between John de Vere, earl of Oxford, and Henry Hastings, earl of Huntingdon, provided for the marriage of Oxford's son, Lord Bolebec, to one of Huntingdon's sisters when Bolebec reached the age of eighteen if the couple consented (though the marriage never transpired). A further example is found in an indenture dated 22 August 1601 between two yeomen, John Parker of Little Norton, Derby, and Thomas Bright of Carbrooke, Sheffield, Yorks. Parker covenanted that his eldest son John would marry Dyonise, Bright's daughter, "if she will thereunto consent; and the said Thomas Bright covenants for his said daughter in like manner." In 1593-94 a father who practiced the balanced view became involved in litigation in the Court of Requests because of questionable judgment on his daughter's part. Ellen, daughter of Thomas Nixon of Flint, had contracted to wed John Cartwright, a yeoman of Aston, Ches., if she gave her consent, but not until the eve of the wedding did she exercise her discretion and marry another suitor.[22]

The majority of Elizabethan marriages for which evidence is sufficient to judge, apart from those involving mature persons free to make their own decisions, were of the arranged and balanced variety. For most of the population, however, evidence is insufficient to ascertain their practices. In the arranged match, the couple normally expressed a minimal degree of acquiescence, though there are cases where, contrary to the views of Anglican and Puritan writers, a couple was forced to the altar. Katherine, dowager countess of Northumberland, complained to Burghley in December 1587 that her son, Henry Percy, the thirteenth earl, was endeavoring by fraudulent means to accomplish a marriage between her eldest daughter and John Wotton, a man of ill repute who had threatened the lives of the countess' servants. Presumably, the threats were part of a campaign to force the match. In a more celebrated case, the beautiful Penelope Devereux was forced by her guardian, the Puritan earl of Huntingdon, Lord Burghley, and her friends to marry Robert third Lord Rich in 1581. By 1589 or 1590 she had become involved in adulterous relations with Sir Charles Blount. In the later 1560s, after Elizabeth St. Loe had lost her third husband, she was involved in negotiations with George Talbot, earl of Shrewsbury. Before she would marry him, she determined that her eldest son Henry must wed Grace, the earl's eldest daughter, and her youngest daughter Mary, age eleven, must wed the earl's second son Gilbert, age fifteen. Such arrangements were probably forced unions.[23]

The more independent sort rebelled against arranged and forced matches, sometimes marrying without parental consent, contrary to the socio-religious views of the age. Sir Richard Cholmley, who did not force his daughter to wed Lord Lumley, disapproved of the marriage of his son Francis to Jane Boulmer, a woman of "no good fame," though he had no objections to his son having her as a mistress. When his son persisted, Sir Richard placed the boy's share of the estate in entail to prevent his daughter-in-law from gaining it should his son predecease her (as happened). In another case, John Danvers, sheriff of Oxford in 1588 and an enemy of the Puritans, had married without parental consent and was subsequently separated from his wife; both were suspected adulterers. In May 1592 Lady Fitton pled with Burghley to aid her son Ned, who had wed without his father's approval; without such assistance her son would "fall into some desperate action for his father will not yett do anythinge for him," and would not allow her to see the boy. Sir Michael Hicks, who had been Burghley's secretary, received a letter in 1601 from an irate Richard Neile, indicating Neile's brother had wed "without eyther my consent or priuity," and now had the temerity to bring his bride to Neile's home. In another instance, when Hicks courted Miss Loftus, he urged her to accept his proposal if she liked him, regardless of what those advising her said, for "in cases of mariage, the principall poynt is the mutuall lyking of the parties them selues, and the consent of the freindes in respect of it/ but an accessarye." A 1592 letter of courtship from Francis, son of Sir Thomas Tresham, to Anne, daughter of Sir John Tufton, stressed his determination to defy his father if necessary to marry her (as he later did):

When children are in their swathe cloutes, then they are subject to the whip, and ought to be careful of the rigour of their parents; as for me, because I am of riper age, I am not to be led by their persuasions, and for my own part, so religiously do I esteem of the vow which here I have protested before you, that my father shall sooner disherit [sic] me of my patrimony than dishonour me for breaking my promise.

Rebellion in asserting individual choice could also be directed against one's superiors, as in the case of the poet John Donne, who married the niece of the lord keeper's wife despite the fact the the lord keeper, to whom he was secretary, objected.[24]

Parental authority in matrimony was often exercised for sound reasons, apart from the ideals professed by religious leaders. In the Grindal family, the bishop's brother Robert, of St. Bees, Cumb., had died in 1568, and his wife and only son were also deceased by 1569. Of the four surviving daughters, Anne, the second, was made sole executrix and was to follow, according to her father's will, the advice of her uncle, the bishop. Contrary to the latter's wishes she wed William, son of Richard Dacre, a gentleman of Carlisle. William was a participant with Leonard Dacre in the abortive 1569 rebellion, and in 1570 was expected to have to forfeit his goods to the crown. Grindal, now archbishop of York, intervened with Cecil to see if the portions of the other daughters might be reserved for them or redeemed by Grindal on their behalf, thereby averting the disastrous consequences of their sister's marriage. In another case, Richard Dudley was angered when his widowed daughter, Lady Stephenson, wed Thomas Vaux, "a man of no great stay neyther of any good opynion in the countrye," without his approval. The groom appropriated to himself a patronage office in Penrith, Cumb., which Dudley had given his daughter to support her son by her first marriage, and Dudley had to seek Burghley's assistance to regain it for his grandson.[25]

Matrimonial stakes were sometimes high enough to provoke parents or guardians to block undesired matches. This interference might involve nothing more than temporarily sending a young person away, as in the case of Edmund Haylles of Somersetshire, who dispatched his daughter Anne to Southampton out of dislike for her suitors. It could extend as far as trying to break up a marriage that had already occurred, such as that between William, son of Sir Edward More of Odiham, Hants., and the daughter of Arthur Milles. Sir Edward believed his son had "been verie leawdly inticed to intangle himselfe with [her] . . . , by whom he hath noe other portion but of suspected fame, her breedinge . . . beeinge far from any good disciplyne." He therefore persuaded Sir Robert Cecil to intervene with Sir George Carew to place the boy in an Irish garrison while his father tried to have the marriage declared unlawful.

The widow Mrs. Frances Cook had the opposite problem with her son, for whom she was offered either £2,000 cash or £200 *p.a.* after the mother of her proposed daughter-in-law died and £30 *p.a.* before then. She intended to keep half of this money for herself (as her son's guardian), but the boy refused the marriage and Mrs. Cook appealed to Burghley to require her son to pay her £1,000. Thus monetary and familial concerns often took precedence over individual wishes. Among the propertied, the family had a principal obligation to future heirs to preserve the integrity of the estate, hence the subordination of the individual to the corporate interest.[26]

Examining the role of consent and individual choice in the history of three families reveals considerable deviation from the socio-religious ideals. Two of the families—Holles and Willoughby—were Protestant, and one—Vaux—was Catholic. Sir William Holles' refusal to allow his daughter Gertrude to marry George Clifford, earl of Cumberland, because of the discrepancy in their social station has been noted. Subsequently, Sir William arranged a match between his grandson John, eldest son of Denzil Holles of Irby, Lincs., and a relative of George Talbot, earl of Shrewsbury. The match was not consummated before the deaths of Sir William and Shrewsbury, hence John, age twenty-six, defied their arrangement and wed Anne, daughter of Sir Thomas Stanhope of Shelford, Notts., in 1591. The new earl of Shrewsbury, Gilbert Talbot, was irate, and fighting ensued, with the death of at least one servant resulting. Controversy also surrounded the marriage of Gervas, younger brother of Denzil Holles, who was in love with Frances, daughter of Peter Frescheville of Staveley, Derby, and co-heir apparent of her father. The latter would not agree to the marriage, owing to Gervas' wild character and younger-son status, though the couple secretly "engaged their faythes one to another." When the fathers discovered the state of affairs and determined to separate the couple, Gervas and Frances eloped to London. Her father remarried, had further children, and cut her off from any inheritance; Sir William was not reconciled for years. The eldest son of this marriage, Frescheville Holles, became enamored with Elizabeth, heir apparent of John Kingston, esquire, but her father received several offers of marriage from men more financially endowed than Frescheville and refused him permission to wed. Elizabeth, however, declined these offers. After seven years, the couple was allowed to marry in 1600, but "without any provision of joynture settled by . . . [Gervas] Holles upon her or any assurance of inheritance from . . . [John] Kingston to the issue he [Frescheville] should have by hir, that they might appear to have rather his permission than consent." The history of this family illustrates the tension between parental rights and individual choice, and shows a reluctance to adhere to the prescriptions of the preachers.[27]

The case of the Willoughby family is similar. Edward Sutton, fourth

Lord Dudley, suggested that Sir Francis Willoughby marry Elizabeth, daughter of Sir John Lyttleton, a match favored by her father. "After good deliberation it . . . pleased God to give him [Sir Francis] a liking to the young gentlewoman, who had . . . a good education and was descended from a house of great antiquity, well friended and alyed." Financially Sir Francis had a good match, for the bride's father offered £1,500, apparel for Elizabeth, wedding expenses, three years' board, six attendants, and provision for six geldings. Yet the marriage did not prove to be happy. Sir Francis had ambitious plans for his daughters. In August 1581 Henry Hastings, earl of Huntingdon, tried to persuade him to agree to a match between his second daughter Dorothy and Henry Willoughby, a kinsman of Sir Francis and the earl's retainer. "The liking between them is great, ' wrote the earl, "but without your liking to proceed to a match would be thought hard." Sir Francis did not like the match and nothing came of it, though three years later he stated that he would never require his daughters to marry without mutual affection. Dorothy married the earl's nephew in 1587; her younger sister Winifred hoped to wed Edward Willoughby, but her mother was so opposed that she kept her daughter locked up and required her to serve as a maid. Lady Willoughby at this time was estranged from Sir Francis, but managed to make him think ill of Winifred. To rescue her, Edward eloped with Winifred, despite the lack of approval from either father. For years afterward Sir Francis refused to see his daughter, and the couple suffered financial hardships.[28]

An historian of Elizabethan Catholicism has posited that Catholic landowners usually pursued the same marital policies as their Protestant counterparts, with an emphasis on arranged marriages and the absence of romance, and sometimes with the same difficulties with strong-minded young people. In 1583 William Lord Vaux sought to wed his eldest son Henry to someone who could restore the family's fortunes, depleted by losses during Vaux's imprisonment and recusancy fines. Money was also essential to provide a dowry for his daughter. A suitable match was offered but Henry refused, having determined to enter the priesthood. Lord Vaux urged him to resign his interests as heir to his half-brother, George, which occurred two years later. The settlement was to be void if George married without the consent of his father and either his mother or his half-brother. George, however, was in love with Elizabeth Roper, great niece of Sir Thomas More's daughter Margaret, and wed her without consent in July 1585 while his father was confined at Hackney. George's uncle, Sir Thomas Tresham, later wrote:

I withstood her marriage to my nephew, first in respect of the relief Lord Vaux should have had by his son's marriage, being offered £3,500, and divers other great matches; next that his lordship's eldest son should not be frustrated, who relinquished his birthright to relieve his father by his brother's marriage, when he himself professed a single life, and lastly that in regard of her creditless carriage when she went for a maiden, I thought her an unfit wife for my nephew.

George was disinherited. The family was not yet free of matrimonial difficulties, for in 1597 Sir Thomas arranged a match for Muriel, Lord Vaux's youngest daughter, now twenty-seven, but she secretly married Sir Thomas' servant in his own house and eloped. Although her uncle was furious, he gave them over £1,200 of her marriage money. In 1599 they sued for the remaining £750, and his refusal to pay resulted in his imprisonment in the Fleet. Again the deviation from the socio-religious ideals of the age is clear, though the Vaux children at least fulfilled the prescription of mutual agreement found in the catechism of Lawrence Vaux (who was no relation).[29]

There is an interesting case in the records of the Court of Requests in the 1590s involving both a forced union and a marriage without parental consent. The parents of Elizabeth Jerningham had arranged the marriage of their daughter to Charles Forth without the consent of his parents, convinced that it was an advantageous match for their daughter and that his father would accept it. The wedding occurred in the bride's house, against her will, and the couple subsequently lived with his parents at Butley, Suffolk. She was older than her sixteen-year-old husband, and soon had an adulterous liaison with a young gentleman before leaving her husband. In despair, he defied his parents' wishes and went to sea, but not before asking his father to ensure that neither she nor her children received any of the Forth lands. When he died shortly thereafter, his father, Robert Forth, went to law to seek the remainder of the marriage money.[30]

From the extant evidence, it appears that marriages without parental or guardians' consent were more common than is usually recognized, indicating that the religious writers were substantially correct in claiming that this practice was widespread. It was even a problem at court, where Elizabeth proved unable to control the marriages of some of her peers and maids of honor. She was angry with the widower Henry Neville, earl of Westmorland, early in her reign for taking a third wife, Margaret, daughter of Sir Roger Cholmley, because she was the sister of his deceased wife Jane; the marriage was within prohibited degrees. She was also wrothful about matches between persons of unequal social degree, such as those between John Wingfield, nephew of Elizabeth Talbot, countess of Shrewsbury, and Susan Grey, countess of Kent, and between Robert Devereux, earl of Essex, and Walsingham's daughter Frances, the widow of Sir Philip Sidney. The queen tried to prevent marriages between her maids of honor and courtiers, presumably because of suspicions of intrigue, decreased loyalties, and a concern for discipline and order. She was "liberal both with blows and evil words" when she discovered Mary Shelton intended to wed, and when Elizabeth Throckmorton became pregnant by Sir Walter Raleigh and plans to marry were revealed, she imprisoned them in the Tower. Similarly, when Dorothy Devereux, a maid of honor, became the wife of Sir Thomas Perrot, Elizabeth imprisoned the groom and the offending chaplain in the Fleet. Although the queen's record was far from uniformly successful, her court was important enough to merit appeals from persons who wanted matches prevented, such as Lady Lucy Harrington's entreaty to Cecil in 1566 asking that he stop the proposed marriage between her son and a Miss Wynser, and see that Elizabeth and the earl of Leicester were not offended.[31]

Because of its dynastic implications, the most serious case in which the queen's consent was not sought involved the marriage of Lady Catherine Grey and Edward Seymour, earl of Hertford. Seymour's mother Anne, duchess of Somerset, sought to extricate herself from the ramifications of this match by insisting to Cecil in August 1561 that her unruly son had "moch over shotte hys bounden dutye," and that she had no prior knowledge of the wedding and had not consented to it. She wanted the queen to know "that nether for chyld nor frynd shall [I] wyllyngly neglect the dutye of a faythfull subject." The following May, Archbishop Parker, following a commission of inquiry, pronounced that their carnal copulation was illegitimate and unlawful, and censured them for fornication. Nevertheless Lady Catherine bore Hertford two sons, Edward and Thomas, in the Tower, and Edward's son William succeeded to the peerage when his grandfather died in 1621.[32]

In later life the earl who had thus defied his queen was inconsistent in his matrimonial dealings. In October 1579, Sir John Thynne wrote to Hertford proposing a match between Thynne's daughter and John Seymour, the earl's cousin. Sir John favored the match if he could agree with Hertford and if the couple liked each other, but the earl blocked the marriage. Early in 1582 he also sought to prevent the marriage of his son Edward Viscount Beauchamp to the latter's cousin, Honor, daughter of Sir Richard Rogers. He failed, but after the wedding he disputed its validity, forcing his son to seek assistance from the queen and Walsingham. Although Beauchamp insisted to his father that he married Honor to halt rumors about his dissolute life, Hertford had him confined and separated from his bride. As late as August 1585, Beauchamp, now released, threatened suicide rather than return to his father's domination. The queen sympathized with Beauchamp and (unsuccessfully) used "many persuasions" to keep Lady Frances Howard from marrying Hertford, though she did not absolutely prohibit it. Thus Hertford himself enjoyed personal choice, but for his family, he insisted on parental authority.[33]

Besides royal pressure and statutory regulations, various other means were used to enforce parental or guardian consent. In the private sector, one of the most common was the use of wills to impose matrimonial restrictions on children, particularly daughters. Some wills, mostly from the gentry, stipulated whom a child or guardian was expected to wed. The 1568 will of William Swift, esquire, of Rotherham, Yorks., required the marriage of his ward, Ralph Byston, esquire, to whomever of his daughters the ward preferred. Furthermore,

in case either of my daughters shall use them selves wantonlie or lightelie withoute gyveinge due obedyence to theire mother, and followinge the wyse counsell of my freindes in theire choyce of marriage, most especially that then it shall be lawfull to my wyfe and frieindes to staye in theire handes suche porcon and to bestowe suche parte to my other daughter usinge her selfe soberlie, for surelye it wolde me greve to knowe that anye of my goodes shoulde be wasted with youthefull and dissolute parsonns.

The 1573 will of John Atherton, a knight with lands in Lancashire and Yorkshire, stipulated that his son and heir marry a daughter of John Byron of Newstead, Notts. In his 1587 will Sandys set forth heavy financial penalties for his ward, Elizabeth Norton, and his son George if either refused to wed the other. The gentleman John Legh hoped in 1593 that his base-born daugher Ellen would marry Ralph, son of his cousin Godfrey Hyde; if not, she had to wed with Hyde's consent. Six years later, the will of the squire William Shaftoe of Northumberland included this clause: "To my daughter Margerie, LX sheep, and I bestow her in marriage upon Edward, son of Reynold Shaftoe." I have not found such matrimonial prescriptions in the Puritan wills I have examined.[34]

More commonly, makers of wills required parental or guardian consent only while their daughers were minors (though sometimes up to age twenty-one), and did not stipulate a marital partner. The usual penalty for refusal was loss of all or part of bequests or marriage portions. Such wills come from a variety of classes, particularly the landed (for which wills are most common). Examples for the peerage include the testaments of Richard Lord Rich (1567), Edmund Brydges, Lord Chandos of Sudeley (1573), John Lord Darcy of Chiche (1580), Henry Wriothesley, earl of Southhampton (1581), and Henry Herbert, earl of Pembroke (1596). Gentry examples include Dame Jane Gerard (for a female relative, 1575), George Trafford, a Catholic gentleman of Lancashire (1576), Originall Babington, esquire, of Rampton, Notts. (1577), Roger Mainwaring, a gentleman of Nantwich, Ches. (1589), Thomas Crompton, esquire, of Bishop Burton, Yorks. (1592), and Robert Jopson, a gentleman of Old Hutton, Westmor. (1597). Wills of yeomen often included such provisions, and scattered examples come from the nonlanded classes, such as that of Cartwright, the Puitan preacher (1603). The 1568 will of John Holmes, a London weaver, left a legacy to a yeoman and his wife to bestow on their daughter if she wed as they wished.[35]

In addition to parental consent or a preferred mate, other factors sometimes appear in wills as conditions for potential legatees. In his will (1598), Burghley left his granddaughters, Bridget and Susan de Vere, £4,000 if they married earls or heir apparents to earldoms, £3,000 if they wed barons or heir apparents to baronies, or £2,000 for lesser marriages. The 1583 will of Edward Manners, earl of Rutland, bequeathed numerous manors to his daughter Elizabeth "on condicion if my daughter marye any parson other then a Baron, or heire apparaunt of a Baron, or one above the degree of a Baron, or other then a gentilman having landes of the yearlie value of 1,000^{li}, that then the landes shall remayne unto my nephewes." Denzil Holles' legacy to his three daughters was conditional on their marriages according to the advice of the executors or on their obtaining good matches. Religion was sometimes a factor, as in the case of the Cambridge printer and Puritan, Thomas Thomas (1588), whose niece would not receive her bequest of £50 if she wed a Catholic. Richard Pole, a Catholic esquire of Radbourn, Derby (1560), left his four nieces ten marks each at their weddings "if they find god and use themselves honestlie & do marry by the advice of their friends & myn executors." Age was a factor in the 1575 will of Sir Thomas Gresham, whose niece Catherine would receive £300 if she did not enter wedlock before age fifteen. The will (1596) of Richard Dilke, a gentleman of Kirkby Mallory, Leics., left each of his daughters two hundred marks if they wed according to the direction of his executor; if not, they would receive the bequests when they reached the age of twenty-six. Elizabeth, daughter of John Robinson, a merchant of the Staple, married without her father's sanction, hence his 1599 will left her only £10:

And as for my daughter, Elizabeth Robinson, who of a wilfull minde, contrary as well to her dutie as to the laudable customes of the honorable cittie of London, hathe bestowed herself in marriege withoute my consent and privitie, my full minde is that in regard of her disobedience she shall enioy neither parte nor portion of anie parte of my goodes.

There are even wills in which the makers (such as Burghley) sought to influence the matrimonial ties of their grandchildren. Sir John Holcroft (1559) left bequests to the daughters of his sons-in-law on the condition that they married according to the advice of his executors. The daughter of his son, however, received £20 on her wedding day with no conditions attached.[36]

Not all parents sought to control the marriages of their offspring by threatening legacies. Among the peers, the will of John Lord Sheffield (1568) included no such stipulations for his daughter Elizabeth, nor did the wills of such gentlemen as Robert Holte of Stubley, Lancs. (1561), Thomas Radclyff of Foxdenton, Lancs. (1567), Sir Thomas Gresham (for his niece Margaret and a female cousin, 1575), and Thomas Wilson, the queen's principal secretary (1581). Nor did the will of Robert Nowell (1563) make gifts to his nieces contingent on parental approval of their marriages. In the case of the sons, the eldest usually were contracted or married before their fathers' deaths; if not they became wards if under age. Younger sons normally were not encumbered with restrictions regarding matrimony in the testaments of their fathers, though there are exceptions, such as the will of Henry Stanley, earl of Derby (1592). Richard Lord Rich even provided for the marriage of his bastard Richard in his 1567 will: The executors were instructed to "provide or buy one woman warde or summe other woman having mannors, londes, and tenements in possession of the cler yerely value of two hundreth pounde by yere over all chardges at the leaste for a mariage to be had and solempnised to the said Richard." If he refused to take her, the wardship was to be sold.[37]

Officially, there were numerous ways to reinforce parental consent. Enforcement in the secular courts could be brought under 4 & 5 Philip and Mary, c. 8 and 39 Elizabeth I, c. 9. In Exeter an orphan who married without his or her father's consent while he was still living could not receive a bequest from his estate until the age of majority. Ecclesiastical courts could be used through litigation involving such matters as precontracts and espousals. Couples could procure ecclesiastical licenses to wed without parental consent, but a minister at the Tower of London required one such couple to delay their marriage six months. A cleric who married persons lacking both parental consent and an ecclesiastical license could be cited by his superiors, as was Thomas Hancock, Puritan vicar of Elksley, Notts., in 1602. Visitation articles inquired about persons marrying without parental sanction. The injunctions issued by Richard Barnes, bishop of Durham, in 1577 required clerics to warn young people each quarter during Sunday services that there could be no marriages without the approval of parents or guardians. This rule was in keeping with the 1571 canons, and was reflected in other episcopal injunctions, such as those of the bishop of Lincoln in 1577. In the 1580s there were crackdowns on the abuses of licenses to wed without consent, so the church was cognizant of the problem and sought to restrict it.[38]

Disputes arising from matrimonial consent could be taken to the Privy Council. In 1570, the Council heard an appeal from George Lawrence, gentleman, against his father Edward, who had disowned him for not fulfilling a marriage with Frances Kellewey contracted by the father. In an unusual case in 1574, the Council examined a yeoman who attempted to marry his master to a girl he provided, and in 1579 the Council discussed the elopement of Sir Henry Lee's daughter. The Council upheld the validity of contracts made without parental consent in a 1587 case involving John Stafforde, esquire, whose son Humphrey had contracted to wed Amy, daughter of Robert Drake, esquire, without his father's sanction. On learning of this, the latter secretly went to London, "where entringe into great mislike with his said sonne, he founde the meanes to take him awaie with him," and endeavored to match him with another girl. The Council's finding that the original contract was valid in human and divine law was contrary to the views propounded by preachers such as Stockwood. The same year, the Council learned that the youngest daughter of Elizabeth Ratcliffe had been "stollen" by Elizabeth's brother-in-law, who then married her although the girl was already contracted to someone else and had consented to marry him. The case was turned over to the archbishop of Canterbury, who presumably resolved it in favor of the girl's mother. One of the longest cases in which the Council was involved began in 1580 when it learned that Jane, daughter of the late archbishop of York, Thomas Young, "was without the consent of her mother conveyed out of her house by one William Stanley, his sonne, and is yet detained upon pretence that she is since married to him." Young Stanley agreed to bring proof of the validity of the marriage to Archbishop Sandys, but when he failed to do so, he was excommunicated. The case dragged on until 1589 when the Council had had enough, and a compromise decision was reached in the archbishop's court at York. Stanley's cause was aided because his bride had apparently consented to the marriage.[39]

In conclusion, as an ideal the Elizabethan writers could agree with the poet Thomas Churchyard that two social evils must be avoided: There could be no countenancing of the fact that

> . . . wilfull men, (that wealth may wrest awry)
> Will force poore babes, to marry or to morne.

But it was equally unacceptable that

> . . . childrens choise, should breake the fathers hart
> Or breede debate, as wilfull marriage proues.[40]

Anglican and Puritan authors agreed that consent of parents or guardians was requisite in matrimony, but some representatives of both camps balanced this opinion by an insistence on mutual affection between the prospective bride and groom. In practice, there were adherents of both positions, with Burghley providing the country with a prime example of a father and grandfather arranging matches with little regard for the feelings of those involved. Anglicans and Puritans alike emulated him; perhaps the leading Puritan to do so was Henry Hastings, earl of Huntingdon. Although Lawrence Stone believes the Puritans stressed individual choice, some Anglicans practiced the balanced view. Some young people resented all attempts to direct their matrimonial plans and wed in defiance of their elders, probably more often than is recognized. Parents or elders frequently had good reasons for determining matches, though commonly financial motives prevailed. Pressure to obtain consent was exerted in various ways: the court, secular and ecclesiastical tribunals, the use of wills, and the Privy Council. The battles were not along religious lines, nor apparently even social (or "class") ones; rather, a society dominated by familial priorities was challenged by emergent individualism.

(2) Weddings and Social Pageantry

One that would needes be married in all the hast, though he were soe verry a beggar that the preist told him he would not marry him because he had not money sufficient to pay him his duty for that service, 'Why then,' said he, 'I pray you, Sir, marry me as far as that will goe. Nowe I am here I must needes have something ere I goe.'

John Manningham[41]

Of all the dyseases, that euer wore Weddynge is nexte, vnto the gowte.

Anonymous[42]

Weddings were one of three great social spectacles used by the monied and landed classes to reinforce social order through pageantry. Weddings, christenings, and funerals reflected status in the divinely ordained hierarchy. For some, other ceremonies focused, for example, on court, the legal and academic institutions, or the investiture of ecclesiastical dignitaries, but weddings, christenings, and funerals lacked such exclusiveness. It was natural therefore that some Elizabethans imitated their betters by engaging in pageantry not befitting their social status. Such activities prompted complaints, like that of William Burton, the Puritan vicar of St. Giles, Reading, that it was not appropriate for "euery obscure Gentleman" to solemnize a marriage with the sound of trumpets, as if he were a prince or person of high calling.[43]

Bullinger's handbook on marriage prescribed a simple Protestant service. Once the contract was made he thought a wedding should not be deferred excessively. The social customs of the engagement banquet and laying the engaged couple together were unsuitable. Weddings must be performed in churches, with prayer and a sermon. Bullinger expected relatives and neighbors to proceed to the service soberly and discreetly, in comely apparel and without pomp or drumming and piping. After the wedding he approved a simple dinner, but sumptuous banquets and wasted food were not tolerated. Social responsibility should be manifested through gifts to the poor. Customary wedding dances, with the "lyftinge vp and discoueringe of the damesels clothes and of other wemens apparell," were denounced. In effect, Bullinger wanted a simpler celebration of weddings; writing largely for a bourgeois audience in an essentially republican state, he showed no interest in weddings as pageantry to reinforce social order.[44]

The church regulated the weddings and some of the accompanying social rites. The prescribed form for solemnizing matrimony in the *Book of Common Prayer* manifested continuity with the ancient Sarum rite. There were some changes, including replacement of the mass by a sermon, but the married couple was still required to partake of the Eucharist. Protestant reformers preferred that the wedding takc place in the church proper, but the older custom of performing the ceremony at the church door or on the church porch never died out during Elizabeth's reign. The bishops sought to enforce the official ceremony, but Catholics and Separatists repudiated it. The radical Puritans William Bonham and Nicholas Crane, and probably others, married their followers according to the simpler Geneva ceremony found in *A Booke of the Forme of Common Prayers*. Henry Ainsworth, a teacher in Francis Johnson's congregation in Amsterdam, reflected the Separatist view when hc denounced the Anglican ceremony as unscriptural and unfit for Christian use.[45]

The Separatists advocated civil marriage, challenging canon law, civil law, and the monopoly of the established church. Marriage was an ordinance associated with the second table of the Mosaic law and thus a civil matter, so that performing weddings in churches was akin to conducting economic transactions there. Ruth and Boaz's civil wedding was cited as precedent for Elizabethans to follow. Barrow found no scriptural evidence that matrimony was "an ecclesiastical action, belonging to the worship of God in his church, to be done by the minister as part of his office and function, and that in the church, but especially upon the Lorde's day with such a set leitourgie of collectes, exhortations, psalmes, anthemes and blessings framed to the purpose." He agreed with Greenwood that weddings could be performed by lay persons anywhere and at any time, as long as there was parental consent when appropriate and witnesses. Weddings were not restricted to churches. The less radical Penry acknowledged that for convenience, marriages were best performed by clergy, but he insisted that this function was not part of their ecclesiastical work nor did it bar laity from marrying couples when authorized by a magistrate. The goldsmith Christopher Bowman of Smithfield testified in 1593 that he had been married in Penry's house. A day later Francis Johnson attested that hc did not regard matrimony as an ecclesiastical matter or ministerial duty.[46]

Separatist weddings were not according to the established rites. Although Robert Harrison, one of their leaders, was wed in a church by a parson, he insisted that the latter, Lancelot Thexton, vicar of Aylsham, Norfolk, eliminate objectionable portions of the established ceremony. When Christopher Bowman was married in the Fleet prison in 1588 or 1589, Greenwood offered a prayer, but did not read a service. Rather the couple "did publickly acknowledge their consent before the assemblie." After his release, Bowman became a deacon in a Separatist church in London, and when his first wife died he remarried in Penry's home. The scrivener Daniel Bucke of

Southwark testified in 1593 that Separatists were marrying in their "congregacion." An entry in the minute book of the Dedham Classis notes that John Tilney raised the matter of a parishioner who had been denied a wedding for his vile speech against the church, and consequently had been married by Greenwood in a private home. Familists married by a simple declaration before the congregation. Anglicans and Puritans agreed with Richard Allison that these Separatist weddings were "vngodlie and disordered."[47]

Some civil marriages did not involve Separatists, but these were probably performed for expediency rather than religious conviction. Around 1557, Goerge Johnson married Anne Yate, a victualer, at Davenham, Ches., before witnesses but not in a church or by a clergyman. In 1564, Roger Bybbye, about to sail for Ireland and desirous of a speedy solemnization, persuaded the lord mayor of Liverpool to marry him in the mayor's home. Sometimes the customary "handfasting" or betrothal rites may have substituted for a formal wedding, for although they were not performed in church, they had the force of a contract according to canon law and spared the poor the expense of a church wedding. For example, sometime before 1566, John Brotherton and Alice Ince pledged to be husband and wife on a village green in the diocese of Chester. No minister was present, but the pledge was made on a book they thought was a psalter.[48]

To prohibit such abuses the Church of England imposed regulations, beginning with one requiring a couple to recite the catechism prior to marriage. A second regulation stipulated that banns must be published three times on Sundays or holy days before a wedding. The bishops sought to enforce this injunction in visitations, and Whitgift inquired in 1577 if ministers in the diocese of Worcester were improperly asking banns twice in one day. It was possible to wed without banns by procuring an ecclesiastical license, but this was more expensive. A parish received a fee ranging from 1s. to 4s. for a wedding with banns, but from 3s. to 6s. for a licensed one without banns. Licensing abuses were debated in the House of Commons in 1597, and Grindal urged the Privy Council to support a reform of the Court of Faculties, including terminating licenses for marriages without banns. Ultimately, however, men such as Whitgift and Sutcliffe won the battle to retain licensing privileges, which Puritans like Robert Cawdry opposed.[49]

Some ministers, such as Mr. Palmer, parson of Widford, Essex, regularly married couples without the required banns, as did such Puritans as Robert Southworth, curate of Headon, Notts., and John Nayler, vicar of North Clifton, Notts. The Lancashire Puritans Robert

Barber, curate of Manchester, and Leonard Rowe, curate of Winwick, performed clandestine marriages to augment inadequate stipends. Clerics found guilty of this offense could be suspended or excommunicated, and the High Commission considered violations serious enough to warrant its attention. Between 1590 and 1595, the Commission convicted five clergy in the diocese of York of performing clandestine marriages. When Edward Seymour, earl of Hertford, took as his third wife Frances, daughter of Thomas Howard, Viscount Bindon, they were married by Thomas Mountford, prebendary of Westminster, in the earl's house without banns or license. Mountford was suspended for three years but appealed to Whitgift and was absolved in 1601 on grounds of ignorance. In 1600 George Bibson, curate of Deighton, Yorks., was cited in the Court of Officialty for marrying a couple without banns, license, or parental consent. Although he was excommunicated, he repeated the offence.

Couples who wed without banns or license were subject to excommunication. Whitgift forgave an Oxfordshire couple c. 1600 who claimed ignorance, on condition that they render public penance in the parish church and pay a fine to be bestowed on the poor. Such penalties could be imposed on the mighty, as in the case of Sir Thomas Egerton, the lord keeper, and his wife, who had been illegally married in a private house without banns or license. Bishop Bancroft absolved the couple of the sentence of excommunication in 1597. Clandestine marriages could involve serious abuses; Sir Edward Coke, the attorney general, informed Burghley in 1596 of a midnight wedding between a drunken gentleman and a horsekeeper's daughter. Another man used a secret wedding to avoid marriage to a woman with whom he had a trothplight.[50]

A third regulation to control marriages required that a wedding be performed in the parish church of one or both persons being married. In visitation articles and injunctions the bishops tried to enforce this, and the canons of 1597 and 1603 curtailed licensing abuses. Licenses were issued to Anglicans and Puritans alike. In the diocese of York there were five licenses in 1590, six in 1591, fifteen in 1592, and seventeen in 1597. Metropolitan injunctions required churchwardens and sworn-men to present to the ordinary twice each year the names of those who married outside their parish churches or without banns. Yet throughout the age, the gentry and nobility preferred to be married in private chapels rather than parish churches, especially in the north. Sometimes there were legitimate reasons for this. The dowager Lady Elizabeth Russell, Sir Robert Cecil's aunt, wanted her son married in her house at Blackfriars, London, in 1596, preferring a private occasion with a few friends rather than a magnificent affair. Sometimes a private home was more appropriate for second marriages, as in the cases of Sir Nicholas Fairfax and Lady Alice Sutton in 1563, and the elder Bassingbourne Gawdy, a widower, and Margaret, widow of Thomas Darcy, in 1588.[51]

The authorities feared that private places might be used for marriages that otherwise might not be approved. Robert Sidney wed Barbara Gamage in 1584 at the home of her cousin and guardian, Sir Edward Stradling, in St. Donat's, Glam.; the queen's approval had not been sought, and her prohibition of the match arrived after the ceremony was concluded. A private home was used by Robert Bradshaw, Anglican curate of the chapel at Newton in the parish of Manchester, to marry two children without banns in 1587. In 1602 Manningham recorded in his diary that "Mr Cokayne of Hertfordshire gott his brother H. Norton by a wile to his house, and their married him upon a pushe to a kinswoman of his, and made a serveingman serve the purpose insted of a preist." The visitation books for the diocese of York in 1578 record that seven couples married without banns, some in chapels but others "in prophane places[,] yea it is doubted whether they be maryed at all." In the diocese of Chester a presentment book for 1595-96 cites Robert Drake of Siddington chapelry for being "maryd under a hedge by John Warde a straunger without any knowne lycence." Abuses such as these, and not merely a desire for an ecclesiastical monopoly, motivated church officials to restrict the locations of weddings.[52]

A fourth regulation controlled the times of weddings. Although the church preserved medieval prohibitions on inappropriate times, such rules were not included in the canons or *Book of Common Prayer*, though the bishops reiterated them in visitation articles. No marriages were to take place from Advent Sunday until eight days after Epiphany, from Septuagesima Sunday until eight days after Easter, and from the Sunday prior to Ascension Day until eight days after Pentecost. John Terry explained: "The purpose of the church of Christ, in forbidding Marriages about the times of the three great solemnities of Christians was, lest by the more free vse of these earthly pleasures and delightes which abound most commonly at marriage feastes, the peoples mindes should bee somewhat hindered from the carefull preparation to receaue the holy sacrament." Puritans and Separatists regarded such prohibitions as superstitious, but most Elizabethans avoided these periods, particularly Lent. April and November were popular wedding months, falling after the Easter season and before the beginning of Advent. Clergy who violated the prohibitions were subject to ecclesiastical punishment. During the accepted periods, weddings were preferably to be held during daylight hours, since marriage was judged a work of light. Whitgift informed the bishops in his province in 1598 that those with valid licenses could marry only between 8 A.M. and 12 P.M. Weddings periodically occurred, however, at night. In 1601 Alexander Emott, Puritan rector of Bolton by Bowland, Yorks., was cited before the High Commission for performing a wedding at night, but because he had been at a conference that day and was delayed, the case was dismissed. When Elizabeth Kingston wed Frescheville Holles at St. James', Great Grimsby, Lincs., in 1600, the ceremony was conducted by torchlight before dawn. Sometimes night hours were used to cover an illegal marriage, as at Balderstone, Lancs., where a young couple went to a cleric's house about midnight, and the Anglican minister, "sittinge vp in his bed, apon his pillowe, (beinge a very old and a sicklie man,) did marry them together." [53]

Weddings performed clandestinely, perhaps at private homes or at unusual times, often were the work of Catholic priests. On 11 November 1563, the Council of Trent approved a decree (*Tametsi*) governing Catholic weddings, but it was to come into force only where promulgated, and this never occurred in Elizabethan England. The decree stipulated that a valid marriage had to be performed by a priest or his deputy with two witnesses present, which appears to have been normal with Elizabethan Catholics who married according to Catholic rites. Although most Catholic ceremonies probably were conducted in the northern counties, there were Catholic weddings even in London. In May 1559, for instance, Matthew Draper wed the daughter of William Blakewell, a town clerk, in the parish of St. Andrew-in-the-Wardrobe. In was a morning service, using the Latin mass and followed by a bridal cup, wafers, "epocras" (spicy wine), and muscatel. A wedding breakfast and dinner were celebrated at the bride's home, so the wedding was hardly secret. The London minister John Veron in 1561 told of a Catholic priest who,

when any of his parishioners should be maryed, would take his backe-pyppe and go fetche theym to the church, playnge sweetelye afore them, and then would he laye his instrument handsomely upon the aultare tyll he had maryed them and sayd masse. Which thing being done, he would gentillye bringe them home agayne with backe-pyppe.

As Grindal and his colleagues established control in London, open Catholic weddings ceased, but clandestine ones continued. Ralph Cresswell of Nunkeeling, Yorks., confessed he had been secretly married by a priest in a chamber at the Inner Temple, and Robert Poley was wed by a seminary priest at the home of a tailor in Bow Lane. There were probably numerous cases that the authorities never discovered.[54]

In the north, Catholic weddings were more prevalent. A report to the Privy Council in 1591 on Lancashire and Cheshire complained of clandestine weddings celebrated by priests. Between 1590 and 1603, more than fifty cases in Yorkshire courts involved secret marriages in which at least one of the persons was a Catholic. Such weddings were not confined to the nobility and gentry, for in the same period at least a score of clandestine Catholic marriages took place in the Ripon, Craven, and Cleveland areas where the parties were of the farmer or laboring classes and were consistently contumacious. Some of these Catholic ceremonies were held at night: Richard Cholmeley of Bransby, Yorks., was wed at 10 P.M.; Thomas Fleetwood married Mary Sherburne at 3 A.M.; and Hugh Claypham of Giggleswick, Yorks., was married in a night service. Private homes and open-air places also were used: Cholmeley was married in a close; Edmund Lord Sheffield (a Protestant who wed a Catholic), Hugh Claypham, and Thomas Fleetwood in private homes; Christopher Thorp in a field at Billingham, Durham; and Henry Warwick of Ripon, Yorks., under a tree. Richard Conyers of Layton, Yorks., was, however, wed in a remote Cumberland church. When the government learned of such marriages, the couples usually were summoned before the High Commission and ordered to conform and produce witnesses. Those who refused were deemed fornicators and required to do the customary public penance in white sheets and to marry in a parish church with an Anglican minister and witnesses. Stopping clandestine unions was thus a factor in controlling Catholicism.[55]

Within the Elizabethan Protestant tradition, one of the most controversial aspects of the wedding ceremony was the use of the ring. If a ring had been used during the espousal period, it was transferred during the wedding ceremony from the right to the left hand, where it was popularly regarded as a remedy against unkindness and discord. Anglicans defended its use and attributed a fuller meaning to it. Hooker and Pilkington made it a pledge of the groom's love and fidelity to his spouse. "The close Joyning of the ringe," said Whetstone, "is a figure of true vnitie of the married: betweene whom, there should be no diuision in desire, nor difference in behauiour." Gold rings were preferred because the precious metal signified the preeminence of marital love.[56]

That all Puritans opposed wedding rings is a myth that circulated as early as the Elizabethan era. The wedding ring was acceptable to Andrew Kingsmill and Henry Smith. For the latter, the ring, being neither too tight nor too loose, reflected the evenness and compatibility of the marital partners. Other Puritans, however, condemned wedding rings. For Gilby, their use was a Catholic practice unworthy of continuation, particularly since, as Fenner asserted, Catholics used the ring as a symbol of the matrimonial sacrament. Cartwright, though not opposed to the use of rings *per se*, repudiated wedding rings because they caused husbands to make idols of their wives, referring specifically to the passage, "with this ring I thee wed, with my body I thee worship." He rejected Whitgift's interpretation of "worship" in this passage as "honor" (as Whitgift believed it was used in 1 Peter 3). Thomas Sampson protested to Burghley in 1574 about the mandatory utilization of the ring in marriage ceremonies. Nor would the Separatists accept its use, with Barrow castigating it as "an idolatrous relique." The opposition of the more radical Puritans and Separatists to wedding rings reflected their hostility to relics of Catholicism and the quest for simplicity in religious services, as exemplified in Bullinger's marital tract.[57]

Any simplification of weddings tended to reduce their influence as pageants reflective of the social order. Such pageantry was important enough to prompt resistance to simplification, though some instances of plainer ceremonies are due to the application of religious principles. Weddings of the peerage were traditionally gala affairs, sometimes involving two couples, as in the case of Francis Lord Talbot and Lady Anne Herbert, and Henry Lord Herbert and Lady Katherine Talbot in 1563; and of George Clifford, earl of Cumberland, and Lady Margaret Russell, and Philip Lord Wharton and Lady Frances Clifford in 1577. The Talbot-Herbert weddings in 1563 occurred at the ancestral home of the earls of Pembroke, Baynard Castle, "and after was a[s] grett denner as [has] bene sene, for iiij days, and evere nyght gret mummeres and m[asques]." Such entertainment was expensive; it cost Burghley £629 to entertain guests for three days at the wedding of his daughter to Thomas Lord Wentworth's son and heir in 1581. In a 1586 wedding at the home of Anthony Browne, Viscount Montagu, the number of nobility and gentry present was so great "as it was thought there were not ten gentlemen of Sussex, which might dispend two hundred pounds lands [*sic*] by yeare, that were absent." At the wedding supper, approximately 1,500 were served; "the beere tap neuer left running, during the space of foure daies; a time wherein a great part of the good prouision was spent, to the founders praise and the feeders releefe."[58]

One of the grandest weddings of the age was a Puritan affair in which Lady Anne Russell, eldest daughter of the earl of Bedford, married Ambrose Dudley, earl of Warwick, in November 1565. On the morning of the wedding, the bride left her chamber in Westminster Palace and was conducted by Edward de Vere, earl of Oxford, and Edward Manners, earl of Rutland, to the queen's great closet, preceded by various lords and gentlemen, and followed by young gentlemen and royal maids of honor, dressed in yellow satin trimmed with green velvet and silver lace. The bride wore "a kirtle of cloth of silver mixed with blue, a gown of purple velvet embroidered about with silver, and a caul of gold upon her head." Her train was borne by Katherine, daughter of Sir Francis Knollys. When the bride was in the closet, the lords escorted the groom, wearing a gown of purple velvet "furred with sables, and embroidered with gold." Robert Dudley, earl of Leicester, followed him, robed in a gown of purple satin embroidered with gold. The peers then escorted the queen to the ceremony. When it was concluded, the bridal party dined in the council chamber, which was decorated with rich tapestries for the occasion. In the afternoon "a goodlie chalenge was made and observed at Westminster at the tilt, each one six courses: at the tournie twelue strokes with the sword, three pushes with the punchion staffe: and twelue blowes with the sword at barriers, or twentie if anie were so disposed." Because the groom was general of the ordnance, that night a master gunner commemorated the marriage by making "three great traines of chambers, which terriblie yeelded foorth the nature of their voice, to the great astonishment of diuerse." The master gunner was killed when he set off the second round of fireworks. The celebrations continued another two days, which was modest by Elizabethan standards, for revelries sometimes lasted ten days.[59]

The Russell family was involved in a magnificent wedding in June 1600 between Lady Anne Russell, daughter of John Lord Russell, and Henry Somerset, Lord Herbert. The splendor was signified five days before the ceremony, when Lady Anne, a maid of honor, left court in a train of eighteen coaches; "the like hath not bene seen amongest the maydes." The queen attended the wedding at Blackfriars on the sixteenth. That night there was a masque after the wedding supper, featuring eight ladies, "each clad in a skirt of cloth of silver, a rich waistcoat wrought with silks and gold and silver, a mantle of carnation taffeta cast under the arm, and their hair loose about their shoulders, curiously knotted and interlaced." Subsequently "a fine speech was made of a *ninth* muse, much to her praise and honour." Others then danced, including the queen. The gifts bestowed on the couple included over £1,000 worth of plate and jewels. Those who saw or heard about the elegance of such weddings were reminded of the dignity and social status of the peerage, so that grandiose trappings were visual symbols of the divinely ordained social order that both Anglicans and Puritans embraced.[60]

Gentry weddings tended to be scaled down versions of their noble counterparts. That between Edmund Cooke, a Kentish gentleman, and Elizabeth, daughter of the London gentleman John Nicolls, in July 1562, reflected peers' ceremonies and included anti-Catholic amusement. The ceremony featured a sermon by Becon and was attended by the lord mayor and aldermen of London. Dinner followed at the Bridgehouse, the afternoon was taken up with music and dancing, and after a late supper a midnight masque was performed. "No maner mettes nor drynges [drinks] that cold be had for m[oney]" were wanting. The celebrations continued the following day, with three masques that night: "on[e] was in cloth of gold, and the next maske was frers, and the iij was nunes; and after they dansyd be-tymes, and after frers and nunes dansyd to-gether." When John Zouch, esquire, wed Mary, daughter of Henry Lord Berkeley at Coventry in 1584, religious convictions were responsible for the excision of some traditional pagan songs; this was "a marriage whereat no singing was of I-opean, nor epithalamians to Juno the goddesse of marriage." Puritan ideals were probably responsible for a simpler celebration at the marriage of Thomas Posthumous Hoby to Margaret Dakins Sidney in 1596. As Hoby explained to Anthony Bacon:

Good Cosyne, althogh yt have been one of my artycles with my mother, yt ther be noe musyke at my tyme of maryage, yett upon Condytione yf you were in time to grace the place with a gallyarde, ther shoulde be owlde revelynge: but synce th[e] one is as farr from my humor, as th[e] other from your ability; I will have all lett alone, & seeke only to please the beholders with a sermon & a dynner: & my selfe with behouldynge my mis[tress].

Nevertheless, some gentry weddings were sumptuous, such as that of Ralph Sadler of Standon, Herts., and Anne, daughter of Edward Coke of Stoke Poges, Bucks., when the bride's father "furnished the feast with all magnificence" and friends gave plate worth more than £800. In 1580 Sir Francis Willoughby spent £156 18s. 9d. on wedding apparel for his daughter Brigit and £500 on goods for the wedding. In 1561 Sir William Petre had been able to get wedding clothes for his daughter Catherine and her groom, John Talbot, for £170. Where possible, the gentry included a wedding feast and a masque as part of the festivities, further straining the financial obligations of the bride's father.[61]

In London, the merchant community emulated the weddings of the landed classes. When the daughter of the alderman Sir Thomas Rowe was married to a merchant in a Protestant service in October 1559, Sir Thomas provided the customary dinner, two masques, and two hundred pair of gloves as gifts. The following summer, a triple wedding of the daughters of a scrivener took place, with a sumptuous banquet afterwards. When William Drury married Lady Williams, widow of Lord Williams of Thame, in October 1560, trumpeters escorted the wedding party from the church, accompanied by flutists and drummers, who continued to play during the wedding dinner. Music was prominent at the wedding of a vintner and an alderman's daughter in 1561, where the guests included the aldermen of London garbed in scarlet. A wedding dinner and a supper were followed by mummeries and masques. When Nicholas Bacon's niece, the daughter of the London salter James Bacon, married Valentine Brown, the auditor of Berwick, in April 1562, the lord keeper, most of the Privy Council, and many of the queen's maids of honor, "gorgyowsly aparrell[ed]," were in attendance. The Guildhall was a popular site for marriage festivities, and rented in the early 1590s for fees ranging from 20d. to 3s. 4d. It is hardly surprising that merchants emulated the landed aristocracy, in view of the intermarriages. Blurring the visual symbols of social hierarchy perhaps enhanced the prestige of the merchants and planted seeds of resentment in some landed aristocrats.[62]

Evidence is scarcer for wedding ceremonies of other groups. Yeomen celebrated with a wedding dinner at the bride's house, sometimes with both families sharing expenses. Guests might be required to give donations for their drinks, hence the term "bridale." A classic example of wedding pageantry as a reinforcement of the social hierarchy appears in a 1563 marriage covenant for the children of two Yorkshire yeoman families. The bride's father was required to provide her "with all maner of wedding apparel, as shall be seemly and comely for his and her calling." In 1579 the material and trimmings for the bridal dress of a yeoman's daughter cost 31s. 6d., but in 1601 a Staffordshire yeoman had to pay 31s. for the cloth to make the wedding gown, 7s. 6d. for bones to line it, 16s. for trimming, and 8s. 6d. for a hat. A 1589 case in the Court of Requests provides details of a wedding between Jane Colby, a yeoman's daughter, and Robert Dunckon, a tanner's son of Suffolk. The bride's father paid for most of the wedding dinner, except for a bullock and cornbread that the groom's father supplied; the rest of the meat for the feast consisted of seven sheep.

Husbandmen had relatively simple weddings, but not without the customary dinner. Music might be provided, but hollow bones, cleavers, tongs, shovels, saucepan lids, and tin kettles full of pebbles were the musical instruments. When present or former servants married, their masters normally attended or sent representatives. When a servant of Nicholas Garness was to be wed at Bungay, Suffolk, in 1602, his master invited a friend: "I hartely intreat your favor to send your men with your benevolence what you shall please." Garness promised to reciprocate in the future.[63]

Weddings were social occasions of merriment and often community fellowship. In a village, it was a social duty to invite neighbors to weddings as well as christenings, funerals, sheep-shearings, and harvest celebrations. Not to do so might incite retribution, particularly if the offended person were a witch. Celebrations had a way of getting out of hand, as the groom's friends might commence feasting and drinking before the wedding and continue afterwards for perhaps as long as ten days. The celebrations were often filled with profane songs, dancing, games (often involving kissing), outdoor sports, and, for the well-to-do, masques. A principal rite took place in the newlyweds' bed-chamber, where guests saw the bride and groom, in nightwear, placed in their nuptial bed and sometimes sewn between the sheets. Witnesses might remain to ensure the consummation of the marriage.[64]

A number of traditional customs associated with weddings demonstrate the communal interest in fecund marriages, the importance of fidelity, and the concern about omens for the future. A bride was customarily led to the church between two boys dressed in bride-lace with sprigs of rosemary (the symbol of constancy) tied to their sleeves. Preceding her came a silver cup filled with wine and a branch of rosemary, decorated with colored ribbons, which served as a love *(agape)* cup. Before drinking from it the bride and groom had to dip rosemary in it as a pledge of fidelity. Bridal lace was dyed blue to symbolize chastity, and gloves symbolized innocence. The bridal veil was a derivation of the Anglo-Saxon custom of the care-cloth, originally held over the bride and groom by four men to symbolize conjugal rights. In Elizabethan England, bridesmaids carried cakes and garlands of gilded wheat, which were symbols of fertility. Likewise, throwing rice and cakes at the newlyweds was a fertility charm. The ancient practice of marriage by capture was commemorated by the groom's carriage of the bride over the threshold and by the custom of requiring the groom's friends to tilt at a quintain, a post on the village green, before they could approach the bride. In a variation, the groom was given a white spear bedecked with flowers by the master of the quintain that he had to break on the first tilt, symbolizing his piercing or breaking of the bride's hymen.[65]

Among other customs was the utilitarian practice of a poor couple sending a cart, or bridal-wain, through the community to collect grain and other offerings in kind. Another way of helping a poor couple was to place a large basin in the church as a receptacle for presents to be deposited "at the very instant of the marriage." In the ceremony itself, while a groom of some means repeated, "With all my worldly goods," he took gold or coins to pay the cleric and placed the remainder in a handkerchief which a bridesmaid retained for the bride. At Jarrow, Northumberland, brides sat in the chair of the Venerable Bede as an omen of offspring, while at Great Yarmouth brides avoided the devil's seat, a cause of ill fortune. At Belford, Northumberland, the bride, groom, and attendants had to leap over a stone at the church door; to trip was a bad omen. The church at Bamburgh, Lincs., had a three-legged "parting stool" at the door that the bride and groom had to jump. Good omens also were sought by young men and women who flung the stockings of the bride and groom over their heads in an attempt to hit the newlyweds, thereby signifying early marriage.[66]

To keep the celebrations under control, limitations were imposed, such as restricting the number of guests to thirty-two or limiting the quantity of malt brewed for wedding festivities. An example is found in the court rolls of Halesowen, Wors., for 1573-74:

No Person or Persons that shall brewe any Weddyn Ale to sell, shall not brewe aboue twelve Strike of Mault at the most, and . . . the said Persons so married shall not keep nor have aboue Eight Messe of Persons at his Dinner within ye Burrowe: and before his Brydal daye He shall keep no unlawfull games in hys House nor out of hys House on pain of 20 Shillings.

In 1583 one of Bishop Middleton's articles for the diocese of St. David's inquired if parishioners had celebrated a wedding dinner in a church, chapel, or churchyard, particularly because of the drinking associated with such celebrations. So weddings were not only social pageants intended to reflect and reinforce the social order, but also community gatherings replete with feasts, games, music, and dancing. Whereas clerics tended to be amenable to the former, the abuses of the latter caused concern, and presumably reinforced the desire of reformers for simpler celebrations. Yet too much movement in this direction would have weakened the wedding as a buttress (through its pageantry) of the social hierarchy.[67]

(3) Widowhood and Remarriage

What better husbands may she haue, then her owne Children, whom shee may bothe commaund and controule, whose dutyes are to labour in her causes, and to vnburden her heart of cares?

George Whetstone[68]

But widdowes state exceedes excesse,
So fickle and so fraught with feare.

Peter Colse[69]

The question of remarriage after the death of a spouse was discussed in Elizabethan society usually regarding widows rather than widowers. The prospect of remarriage was common enough, for nearly 30% of all marriages were terminated by death (with death in childbirth being a serious factor) in the first fifteen years. Approximately 25% of all marriages were remarriages for the bride or groom. Widowers were widely accorded the right to remarry if they desired, though some urged restraint in the case of advanced age or potential ruptured relations with children by a previous marriage. Elizabeth was angered in 1595 by the marriage of the widowed and elderly bishop of London, Richard Fletcher, to the widowed sister of George Gifford, a gentleman pensioner.[70] Remarriage of widows was hotly contested by religious writers and noted in the marginalia of Elizabethan Bibles and Testaments. Supporting widows of the lower classes was a serious social concern, for unlike widows with lands or wealth, there was no great demand for their hands in marriage. Some widows, particularly in towns, supported themselves by continuing the vocations of their deceased husbands, thus contributing to the country's economy.

The notes to the Rheims New Testament reiterate the Catholic position that widowhood is a state next to virginity and more blessed than matrimony. Its superiority to married life was due to the greater time for service to the church and to the "continencie, chastitie, and puritie" of a widow's life. Professed widows must be honored for devoting their time to prayer and fasting, which they could not do if they remarried and engaged in carnal acts. Catholics, unlike Protestants, allowed widows who had been wed only once to qualify as deaconesses, responsible to perform "some necessarie seruices about women that were to be professed or baptized, for their instruction and addressing to that and other Sacraments, and also about the sicke and impotent: and withal sometimes they had charge of the Church goods or the disposition of them vnder the Deacons." The Pauline prescription that widows be at least sixty before making vows of perpetual widowhood was judged applicable only for the early period of Christianity.[71]

The Catholic ideal was alive in Elizabethan England, but it is difficult to ascertain how widely it was practiced. When Sir Everard Digby was dangerously ill, his wife, Lady Mary (née Mulshaw), purposed that if he died she would take a vow of perpetual chastity and obedience. Sir Everard lived, and Lady Digby subsequently bore children, including her famous son Kenelm. The Jesuit John Gerard tells of a Catholic widow who had perhaps taken the vows, for while she was imprisoned for recusancy she refused to hire servants to do her cooking and laundry, and used the money she saved doing her own work to support poor Catholics.[72]

The Geneva marginalia exhorted the faithful to honor widows by caring for them, though church assistance was limited to those without other succor. Family and relatives were obligated to provide for their own widows. Widows who pursued pleasure were reckoned unprofitable, and the church was urged to refuse aid to those who did not follow the vocation of widowhood. A woman who had been widowed more than once was not discriminated against, as in Catholicism, unless a second or subsequent marriage had been scandalous. Nor did the Geneva annotators regard widowhood as a superior state to matrimony; Paul's preference for the former in 1 Corinthians 7:40 was passed over in silence. In the Beza-Tomson Bible, those who condemned second marriages were denounced on the basis of 1 Corinthians 7:8. Widows without the gift of continency were urged to remarry for peace of conscience, and younger widows were advised to find other husbands and have godly homes. As in the Geneva Bible, families and relatives were responsible to assist their own widows rather than depend on the church, but godly widows destitute of aid must be helped.[73]

In his refutation of the Rheims New Testament, the Puritan William Fulke followed Paul to the extent that he declared widowhood, when characterized by a continent life of prayer and fasting, was honorable and in some respects more conducive to serving God than was wedlock. A young widow, as Paul suggested, must remarry unless she possessed the gift of continency. She must not take vows of perpetual widowhood until at least age sixty "when the heate of lust is past." As long as her marriages had been godly, it was immaterial whether she had been widowed several times. "For although the naturall infirmitie of incontinencie, is declared by often repeating of mariage, yet seeing mariage is an holy medicine for yt disease, it hindreth no more once vsed then often.'' Abstinence from marriage was advocated only for widowers who had no need to marry. For widowers, Fulke found nothing unchaste about remarriage. Fulke's outlook was compatible with that of his fellow Puritan, George Wither, who believed widowhood was not absolutely superior to marriage, but had relative advantages because of its freedom from the encumberances of wedded life.[74]

Cartwright's repudiation of the Rheims New Testament adopted a rather different outlook on widowhood. Young widows, including those who were poverty-stricken and dependent on the church for relief, were urged to marry again and bear children; the admonition to remarry was extended to all below age sixty. Cartwright found nothing more holy about widowhood, though he acknowledged it was preferable for those suited to a solitary life. He considered it acceptable for widows to remarry not only to avoid incontinency but also to have children or advance and educate progeny from a previous marriage. He also sanctioned remarriage out of "a loue and liking of some singular vertue and pietie that they see in him with whom they ioyne in a second marriage." Cartwright was thus more encouraging for widows considering remarriage, particularly by broadening the legitimate desires for remarriage.[75]

No major differences existed between Elizabethan Protestants on remarriage, and where minor discrepancies were present, no division can be made along Anglican-Puritan lines. Puritans did devote more attention than Anglicans to widowhood from a religious perspective. They agreed on the right of widows and widowers to remarry, though some discongruity existed on the attitude of children towards another marriage by their parents. John Newnham, whose 1590 tract *Newnams Nightcrowe* was an invective against rapacious step-mothers, took the extreme position that a widower with children who remarried introduced discord into his family. The Puritan poet Nicholas Breton, who was patronized by Mary Herbert, countess of Pembroke, argued that a widower must consider the welfare of his children before taking another wife. On the contrary, Samuel Bird, minister at St. Peter's, Ipswich, warned that love for one's children should not keep a person from obeying God if remarriage was necessary to prevent incontinency. "True it is, that a man should choose rather to liue single, if he may with a good conscience: but if he can not no naturall loue to our children must hinder duty."[76]

Although remarriage was acceptable, a number of authors were reluctant to recommend it. Becon thought widows could remarry if they found godly men who were their equals in age and social degree, but he denounced those who lustfully sought younger husbands, and preferred widows who regarded God as their husband and defender. When the Puritan diarist Richard Rogers reflected on a second marriage he was fearful, for he deemed such marriages dangerous. After Bullinger's wife died, Richard Hilles, a merchant tailor and former religious exile, urged him in 1566 to follow Paul's advice and not remarry.[77]

Some persons—probably a small minority—gave religious considerations a prominent place in considering remarriage. The clearest example is Anne Locke, a woman of deep devotion who left her husband in England to follow her spiritual advisor, John Knox, into exile in the Marian era. After the death of her husband, Henry Locke, in 1571 she was courted by Edward Dering, who was perhaps ten years younger than she. In a letter of proposal he wrote with religious sensitivity:

Thoughe I atempte nothyng but that which ys verye laufull and becomethe any Christian in plac and condition agreeable to every mane's estate, yet our nature is so full of nedeles shamfastnes that bothe nowe it makythe me almoste afearde to write unto you, and sync my last letters it hathe made me carefull to shunne your good companye.

The couple married—a classic Puritan union—but Dering died of tuberculosis in 1576 at the age of thiry-six. His widow was not ready to accept the Pauline exhortation to remain unmarried, but took as her third husband Richard Prowse, an Exeter draper and a probable Puritan.[78]

Helen Nicholson provides another interesting case of a widow's religious considerations. Her first husband was the wealthy draper John Minors, to whom she was married forty years. After his death she was in her late fifties, but found another pecunious citizen of London, Sir John Branch, the former lord mayor; her marriage to him "much increast hir stile, her state, and store." When he died, Dame Branch was primarily motivated by spiritual considerations, if we may believe the author of her elegy:

But now become hir self, hir selfes commander,
To shield hir life safe from al shot of slander,
(As 'twere) sequestred from much conuersation,
She past hir time in holy meditation,
In thanks and praier vnto Christ our Lord,
And often hearing of his sacred word;
In godlie almes, and liberal pensions rife,
And al the duties of a christian life.

Although Elizabethan elegists and preachers tended to exalt the spiritual qualities of the deceased for the benefit of their audiences, it is plausible to accept religious motivations for Dame Branch's not re-marrying again.[79]

In a society where financial matters often loomed large in marriages, religious admonitions must have been commonly shunted aside in considering remarriage. In an era generally characterized by rising population and land shortages, a widow with lands was an attractive match, and could drive a hard bargain, enabling her to retain some control over the lands or wealth she brought to the new marriage. If her late husband had held land by knight-service in chief, however, she came under the jurisdiction of the Court of Wards. She was entitled to her dower, a life interest in one-third of her husband's estate. When she died, this went to his heir unless the original marriage settlement or his will had made it absolutely hers. If her husband had not held land by knight-service, she was free to marry as she wished, though if she did she might lose her share in her deceased husband's estate, depending on his will. A widow who held all or part in knight-service could not be forced to marry by the crown or the superior lord, but she had to promise not to marry without the crown's or the lord's consent. Usually in these circumstances, a widow could purchase the right to marry for one-third of the annual value of her dower. If, however, she wed without approval she faced a fine equal to the dower's value, and her new husband was subject to a fine for contempt of court. Other widows usually were allowed control of their husband's estates if their children were minors, in order to rear them. When the eldest son came of age, a widow in these circumstances could expect a room and maintenance, with such provisions ceasing on remarriage. Peter Laslett has found that the senior generation lived with mature sons and daughters in 5.8% of the houses, but since widows comprised only 6.2% of the population, a large majority must have lived with their grown children.[80]

In the period immediately following the death of her husband, a widow might face extraordinary pressure. Etiquette dictated that no one court her until her spouse was buried, but the prospect of an advantageous match sometimes overcame etiquette. Thomas Posthumous Hoby waited only one week after the demise of Thomas Sidney in 1595 before he began his pursuit of Sidney's widow, Margaret (née Dakins). In 1599, the widow of William Paulet, marquess of Winchester, married a youth under eighteen before her husband's burial. News of the death of a man with a substantial estate could trigger a chain reaction in quest of a marriage contract with his widow. This happened in 1588 when John Piers, bishop of Salisbury, was asked by the brother of his former servant to seek Leicester's approval for the petitioner to be a suitor to a new widow with a large estate; Piers dutifully wrote to Leicester in this regard. In 1597, the temptation to marry such a widow prompted a Kentish yeoman to break off a planned wedding with a maiden, though he still wanted her father to pay him the promised dowry of £20![81]

Other pressures could beset the new widow, including fear of an unsatisfactory union. Most probably knew stories of disastrous remarriages. Thomas Price, third husband of the mother of James Whitelocke, "proved a notable unthrift, and a verye unkinde and insolent husband." To safeguard the portion left by her second husband to her children, this resourceful woman "preserved in the handes of the city [of London] as orphans' goods 600*l*., for her fower suns . . . , and by meanes underhand bought out the interest of her husband in certeyne leases he had by her, helde of the parishe of St. Dunstan's in the Est" worth £50 *p.a.* She was able thus to provide her children with an education that included classical languages, French, music, and writing. The widowed mother of Richard Creswel, gentleman, was less fortunate, for he complained to the Privy Council in 1590 that a vagrant had enticed her to marry him and had then wandered the country until most of her wealth was depleted.[82]

Widows were not helpless in the face of these pressures, nor were they easy game for the relentless pursuers of their estates. They could decline all offers, as some did, though I have found no cases of widows doing so to follow Paul's advice, of such concern to the religious writers. Maria, widow of Otwell Johnson, received a marriage proposal from a wealthy suitor, but declined because she did not love him as she had her first husband. Instead, she lived with her children until, in 1561, she married an old friend, the draper Matthew Colclough. A Devon widow accepted gifts from a yeoman suitor, fixed a date for their wedding, then changed her mind and wed another man; the resulting quarrel over the gifts had to be settled in the Court of Chancery. In another Chancery case, a widow in need of funds allegedly encouraged a suitor until her bills were paid, then married another man. Although the queen favored the marriage of Richard Neville to the widowed Lady Elizabeth Frescheville in 1574, the latter declined on the grounds that she was physically unfit. Abraham Campion used a similar argument on behalf of his widowed sister after she lost her second husband at age thirty-nine. Lady Essex informed her suitor, Sir Thomas Benger, in 1562 that she was "past mariage and yf I wolde

have married I myght have bin married Longe ago but I have re-
fewsed honorable men."[83]

Finances often proved problematical to widows and pressured
them to marry. Sometimes their husbands had left substantial debts
and meager incomes, as in the case of Susan Grey, dowager countess of Kent, whose income was £70 *p.a.* In other instances, the
pressures were due to recalcitrant children or in-laws, as in the case
of Susan Rowland of Worcester, whose son-in-law withheld most of
the legacy bequeathed to her by her husband. Women who inherited
wealth sometimes managed it unwisely. William Wentworth's "mother,
being aged and givinge too much care to those that flattered hir for
their own gaine, did in hir wydowhead by fine make a lease of the
manor of Arthorp in Linconshir to my sister Darcie and hir husband
for threscore yeares, if my said sister so long lyved." With considerable difficulty, Wentworth regained control of this property, on
which his father had built a home. A deed to her brother made by
the widowed Lady Bowes fomented trouble with her new husband
after she remarried. The financial pitfalls of widowhood and remarriage were many.[84]

Other widows demonstrated enough business acumen to assume
their husbands' vocations, though religious writers are silent on the
advisability of such action. These women could remain unmarried
if they desired. Of the forty smiths in Chester in 1574, five were
widows. In Elizabethan London, 17 of the 383 publishers and patentees were widows. Joan Butter ran her deceased husband's business from 1590 to 1594, and Thomas Orwin's widow from 1593 to
1597. Some of the widows were in the printing business a long time:
Joan Broome for ten years, Elizabeth Oliffe for fourteen, Alice Gosson for sixteen, and Mrs. John Alldee for twenty-one years. Widows
of the yeomanry and gentry, if their children were under age, were
normally responsible for running the affairs of their estates until
they remarried or the eldest son came of age. Thereafter, they might
continue to manage the lands that formed their dowers. Women such
as Lady Margaret Hoby who were given active roles in running the
family estates while their husbands were alive should have been competent to assume such responsibilities. One of the more powerful Elizabethan widows was the wife of the deceased George Mills on the Isle
of Wight.

Mistress Milles . . . lived longe a widdowe, kept a braue howse, soiurned Sir
Edward Horsey [d. 1583], browght up moste of ye yonge gentlewomen in ye Island, and had ye swaye of ye Island for many yeres. She and Sir Edward lived

together at Hazely; not without soome taxe of incontinency; for nothinge stoped theyre maryadge but that he had a wyfe alive in ffrance.

Among the lower classes, widows sometimes supported themselves as alewives who sold their own brew.[85]

Husbands, particularly among the gentry, sometimes desired to rule widows from the grave through their wills. Becon objected to husbands prohibiting widows from remarrying through property restrictions, but the practice continued throughout the age. A typical restriction is found in the 1578 will of Robert Tatton of Withenshaw, Lancs.: " . . . provided alwaies that if my seid wieff happen to marrie . . . that then all the demyses geiftes &c. bequeathed to my seid wieff to sease and be utterlye voyde." The principal motivation for such clauses was not jealousy but concern for the welfare of the testator's children, including their education and inheritance. A representative example appears in the will of Richard Lee of Leigh, Lancs., who instructed his wife

to brynge uppe my sayd chyldren in godly and honest order[.] And also kepynge her selfe sole and unmaryed[.] And yf she do marry ageyne and take an nother husbande then I wyll that my other executors shall have and entmeddell with the orderynge and settynge forthe of my sayd chyldren and they[r] good[s.]

Similar restrictions appear in the wills of other social groups. Robert Entwysle of the Foxholes, Yorks., a yeoman or husbandman, left his wife a feather bed, two sheets, two blankets, one coverlet, one bolster, and two pillows in 1574, conditional on her remaining unmarried. The 1591 will of John Barlow, rector of Warmingham, Ches., gave his wife rule over two of his sons and their lands as long as she remained a widow. When such women considered remarriage, financial concerns must have weighed more heavily on their minds than religious injunctions regarding the benefits of a chaste widowhood. Other men made no restrictions of this type or adopted a more moderate stance. William Glaseor, vice chamberlain of Chester, provides an instance of the latter. His 1588 will specified that if his widow remarried she was to "demise the said howse lands &c. in Lea aforesaid unto my said sonne John Glaseor for a reasonable rent so as he doe kepe howse in the same and also to sell unto my said sonne the said oxon and kyne for a reasonable price[,] he payeinge the same price and to live in dutie and obedience to her his said mother[.]"[86]

The widow who decided to remarry had to determine a respectful interval. The Puritan Richard Greenham recommended temporary abstention to demonstrate humility to God and love for the deceased.

"For besides that, it is almost vnnaturall, to get another bodie in bed, before the former be rotten in the graue." Greenham suggested waiting a year before remarriage.

There are cases of some very short periods between a spouse's decease and remarriage: Hooker's widow Joan married an alderman of Canterbury within five months of Hooker's death. Grace Calderot of Orwell, Cambs., wed Roger Davies, the local vicar, within five months of her first husband's death, and when Davies died the following year she took another husband within three months. Margaret Dakins, a Puritan girl, lost her first husband, Walter Devereux, on 8 September 1591, but by 22 December of the same year she was licensed to wed Thomas Sidney. Within two weeks of Devereux's demise, Burghley fostered the candidacy of Thomas Posthumous Hoby. After Sidney died on 26 July 1595, Hoby was actively in pursuit of her in a week, and visited her before Sidney was buried. Lady Sidney finally yielded to Hoby's proposals, but this time there was a decent interval, for the wedding did not occur until 9 August 1596. Hoby's mother, however, had waited eight years after the death of his father before marrying John Lord Russell.[87]

In summary, the principal concern of religious writers was the virtue of the state of widowhood and the legitimacy of marrying again, particularly for sexual reasons. In reality widows were subjected to various pressures such as financial considerations, the desire of eligible males for any land or wealth they might possess, fear of an unsatisfactory remarriage, and the activity of suitors soon after the demise of their husbands. Some widows, such as Anne Locke, remained firm in their religious convictions, but Protestants generally favored remarriage for young widows who would otherwise be dependent on the church for financial aid. This consideration too increased the pressure on them. Those widows who were fortunate had sufficient means and talent to support themselves financially, supervising landed estates, running businesses such as printing shops or smithys, or even eking out a living as an alewife. Anglicans and Puritans were fundamentally agreed in their outlook on widowhood and remarriage, though it was a subject to which Puritans devoted more attention than Anglicans. An Elizabethan widow presumably would have found the most comfort in Cartwright, who recognized the legitimacy of remarriage for a broader range of reasons than other religious leaders.

The agreement among Anglican and Puritan authors on widowhood and remarriage parallels the essential unanimity they expressed on parental choice in marriage. In both areas, the real discrepancies came between the ideals and the practices, not between Anglicans and Puritans, and in both areas financial considerations were important in persuading some laity to diverge from the religious ideals.

Anglican and Puritan authors developed two views on determining marital matches. Some emphasized the decision of parents, whereas others sought a balance by insisting on a place for individual preferences. Although Lawrence Stone attributes this change to the Puritans, in theory and practice some Anglicans also embraced the balanced view. Curiously, Puritans were moving in contrary directions when some advocated the importance of affection or love in selecting a mate, whereas others spoke of children as property to be disposed of in matrimony by their parents. Most Elizabethan marriages (where we have sufficient evidence to judge) either allowed some acquiescence by the children or were of the balanced variety. Nevertheless, instances are numerous of parents (even of Puritan persuasion) arranging marriages with no regard for the feelings of children. Simultaneously, there is evidence—more than commonly recognized—of young people rebelling against parents and marrying whomever they preferred, as religious authors charged. The Elizabethan age had various means to restrict such individualism to buttress family and property by preserving parental authority. Pressure could be exerted from the court and Privy Council, though not always successfully, in episcopal visitations, through statutory regulations, and by provisions in wills threatening the withholding of legacies. In these matters, it was not Anglican versus Puritan, but developing individualism versus traditional patterns of authority.

Pageantry in weddings enhanced the maintenance of the traditional order. Aristocratic weddings, whether Anglican or Puritan, were often gala affairs that reflected social rank and provided ostentatious hospitality. Some Puritans reacted against the pageantry, preferring simpler celebrations. This quest for simplicity, as well as a dislike of popish relics, was behind the hostility of more radical Puritans and the Separatists toward wedding rings. Separatists advocated civil marriage, which Anglicans and Puritans found unacceptable. The established church sought to maintain control over weddings by restricting their times and places, requiring banns, and insisting on recitation of the catechism by the prospective bride and groom. Further regulations were enforced by ecclesiastical and civil authorities to control the drinking and rowdiness that often accompanied lower-class weddings, which were occasions for community fellowship. To the extent that religious differences over wedding services were expressed, they involved the Separatists and more radical Puritans with their objections to traditional rites accepted by

Anglicans and moderate Puritans. On the whole, however, in the areas of parental consent, weddings, and widowhood and remarriage, there was broad agreement among Anglican and Puritan writers, though their record of success in persuading the laity to follow their ideals was checkered.

CHAPTER 5

Sexual Mores and Social Behavior

In Elizabethan society, sexual questions were viewed from the social as well as the moral perspective. Fornication, adultery, bastardy, and prostitution were dangerous because of their potential disruption of inheritance rights, family unity, social order, and care of the poor. Fine lines were sometimes drawn between fornication and prenuptial sex by affianced persons, or between adultery and tolerance of the double standard. Punishment of violators never seemed harsh enough for Puritans and Separatists. Married folk also had to consider the legitimate use of sex, with respect to purpose and frequency, including the question of temporary or perpetual abstinence. A related question was the use of the contraceptive measures discussed in medical works and herbals. In these areas, there is considerably more literary evidence from Puritans than Anglicans. Apart from the visitation articles, Anglican writers were not very concerned with most of these sexual issues, not because they condoned immorality, but because they lacked the fervent religious zeal borne of the Puritan religious experience. Conceiving of religious liberty more as freedom than obligation, Anglicans felt less constrained than Puritans to inculcate strict sexual morality. Moreover, the marked interest of Puritans in sexual morality is part of their broader concern with the integrity of the family as a microcosm of the church. The evidence for sexual practices points to some differences along religious lines.

(1) Premarital Sex and Fornication

Now some will say, that I haue a Woman to [be] my Mistresse, I will not denie it,
for Saints are none vpon the earth, and Diuels I would be loath to doo seruice too.
A Woman of honour, may well be Mistresse to a Man of worship.

Nicholas Breton[1]

As amongst many dishes it is hard to bee temperat,
so amongst many women to bee well minded.

Gervase Babington[2]

In Elizabethan society sex between single persons normally took three
forms: obvious fornication, intercourse between espoused couples,
and, between these extremes, a third form in which a couple with
some mutual attraction copulated and subsequently determined to
wed, perhaps because of pregnancy. Social and religious attitudes
toward these forms of prenuptial intercourse varied, especially if
Peter Laslett is correct that an affianced couple was not expected to
remain chaste until the wedding. However, most of the literary evidence setting forth sexual ideals does not bear out this opinion, and
Laslett himself believes that the men and women of preindustrial England generally obeyed the code of sexual morality espoused by their
religious leaders.[3]

Turning first to the official Catholic position as enunciated in a
papal bull confirming a decree of the Council of Trent in 1564, we
see that sexual relations subsequent to espousal but prior to wedlock
are prohibited. But if copulation does transpire in this period, according to Vaux's catechism, it is fornication only if that is the couple's intent. "If carnall copulation followe the spousage or trothplight,
with this minde to be one to the other, as man and wife, it maketh
Matrimonie." Anglican condemnations of fornication are common
enough, but specific discussion of prenuptial intercourse by espoused
couples is rare. In the visitation articles for the diocese of London in
1586, Aylmer disapproved such copulation when he queried if any
had been wed who were pregnant or had had sexual relations without
first making public acknowledgment of their sins and being reconciled
to the parish. Thomas Bentley, a student at Gray's Inn, London, and
perhaps an Anglican, prepared a devotional manual that included
prayers to enable virgins to remain chaste before marriage.[4]

Puritans disapproved of all sexual relations before matrimony, including copulation between espoused couples. The Puritans at Dedham, Essex, ordered that

if anie be knowen to haue knowne one another carnally before the celebratinge of their mariage, that none accompanie them to the Church, nor from the Church, nor dine with them yt day, and that the pastor at the baptisinge of the children of any such as be knowne to haue committed such filthines before the celebratinge of their mariage do publikely note and declare out the fault to all the congregation to the humblinge of the parties and terrifyinge of others from the like filthie profaninge of mariage.

Becon, Greenham, Cleaver, and Allen explicitly prohibited premarital sexual relationships.[5] I have, in fact, found no religious leader of any persuasion who sanctioned copulation between espoused couples. At best, one can argue that the silence of most Anglican religious leaders amounted to implicit approval.

Prenuptial sex does not seem to have been the ordinary practice in Elizabethan society, but neither was it rare. An examination of the parish register of Braithwell, Yorks., shows that of the fifty-six couples who wed between 1559 and 1602 and had one or more children baptized in this parish, at least ten had had sexual relations prior to marriage, as indicated by the birth of the first child seven and a half months or less after the wedding. An eleventh couple had their first child eight months and one day afterwards, barely meeting the minimum period Laslett uses as the basis for judging post-nuptial copulation. The figures for this parish indicate that at least 17.9% of the couples with children had sexual relations prior to marriage but probably after espousal or at least serious consideration of wedlock. This figure should be increased to about 22% to take into account prenuptial pregnancies which terminated in stillbirths, abortions, and miscarriages, and perhaps to 27% to compensate for late baptisms.[6]

An analysis of selected parish registers by P. E. H. Hair shows an interesting but uneven record of prenuptial sex in the Elizabethan era. His figures for the percentage of traced maternities occurring within eight and a half months of marriage range from 0% for Sidestrand, Norfolk (1570-97) and 13% for Chesham, Bucks. (1575-78), to 30% for Rushton, Northants. (1580-88) and 44% for Kildwick-in-Craven, Yorks. (1577-78). The parish of Standish, Lancs. (1565-67) had a middling figure of 23%. If these figures are increased by 9%, as Hair suggests, to account for pregnancies terminated early and for late baptisms, over half of the marriages in Kildwick-in-Craven involved pregnant brides, but in other cases, such young ladies were in a minority, ranging from 9% to 39%. Hair believes 6 to 8% of the brides never became pregnant, and presumably a portion of these girls also engaged in premarital sex (e.g., about 3% at Kildwick). Based on studies extending throughout the sixteenth and seventeenth centuries, Hair concludes that some 20% of English girls were pregnant at marriage, and that the rate in the north was approximately twice that in the south.[7]

In Leicestershire, certain regions followed a custom of sexual relations by affianced persons, as explained in a 1598 entry from the registry of the archdeaconry of Leicester:

The common use and custom within the county of Leicester, specifically in and about the town before mentioned (Hoby and Waltham) and in other places thereunto adjoining for the space of 10, 20, 30, or 40 years past hath been and is that any man being a suiter to a woman in the way of marriage is upon that day appointed to make a final conclusion of the marriage before treated of. If the said marriage be concluded and contracted then the man doth abide the night the next following after such contract, otherwise he doth depart without staying the night.

Brides in Leicester, according to Laslett, normally went to their weddings pregnant. The prevalence of this practice in the Leicester region coupled with the general silence of the Anglican clergy points to the latter's acquiescence to this form of prenuptial conjugation.[8]

In other areas, however, a stricter view of early sex prevailed, and violators were subject to punishment in ecclesiastical courts. In Oxfordshire, the archdeacon's court heard a case in 1584 involving an Oxford couple who had plighted their troth and then engaged in carnal relations, with a resulting pregnancy. In this instance, the girl was cited for incontinency. The same year, a Sandford-on-Thames man was accused of incontinency in a comparable situation, but the court dismissed the case in the absence of evidence; the girl obviously was not pregnant. One further case in the same court is worth noting, for this time a Charlbury man and the girl to whom he was espoused were cited for living together though unwed. He intended "to marie her as sone as he [was] owte of service." The court was primarily interested in their cohabitation rather than the sexual liaison, though the latter was sufficient grounds for appearance in this court.[9]

Cases in the ecclesiastical court of Chester early in the period show that prenuptial sex was practiced, though various aspects of matrimony account for the cases being heard, not any intention to reduce early sexual relations. In a 1561 case, a couple had copulated and then exchanged tokens (money and a handkerchief), leading the girl to expect marriage. When the young man refused, the court heard the case, with the principal issue being breach of contract. Another case at the same time involved an affianced couple who had had intercourse leading to the birth of a child. Marriage did not occur because the girl's friends failed to provide the agreed dowry, which he felt was necessary for their support. He subsequently wed another girl, but when the latter discovered his previous relationship, she had the marriage annulled. In 1562, the court heard another case in which a girl cited premarital sex to claim pregnancy (falsely) and force a marriage, though the man later committed adultery and was suing for an annulment. These cases illustrate the complications to which premarital sex could lead, but they do not support the idea that the clergy in the diocese of Chester sought to reduce early intercourse. Elsewhere, not until the 1590s did the clergy in the deanery of Doncaster, Yorks., seriously begin to make presentments for prenuptial intercourse. To what extent clerics themselves were involved in sexual relations while espoused is difficult to determine, though in 1571-72 Chancery heard a case involving breach of promise by a beneficed clergyman of York who had been intimate with a woman he later refused to marry.[10]

Some writers offered explanations of the causes of premarital sex. The medical author Thomas Moulton, a Dominican whose work was republished in 1565, considered such acts a matter of astrology, so that a man born under the sign of Pisces, for example, was ordained to be a lecher. The balladeer Leonard Gibson advised abstinence from carnal affairs, and the Puritan poet Edward Hake was suspicious of women, warning his readers to be wary of wanton maids. Of more substance was the verse of the Oxford student Henry Willoby in his 1594 work *Willobie His Avisa,* published "for the incouraging and helping of maides and wiues to holde an honest and constant course against all vnhonest and lewd temptations."[11]

Among Catholics, Matthew Kellison thought sexual incontinency was fostered by the Protestant doctrine of justification by faith. Vaux was more helpful, explaining that the sixth commandment prohibits "all consent in delectation, and voluptuous pleasure of carnal concupiscence and leachery: as vnhonest handlyng or touching themselues or others, for lust or vnlauful appetite, whereby nature is stirred, or concupiscence kindled." Therefore he urged that physical contact be discreet, and that inordinate kissing, provocative songs, suggestive speech, dissolute behavior, unchaste sights, and sexually stimulating dancing be eschewed.[12]

Among Protestants, the Puritans provided most of the advice on how to avoid premarital sex. The problem is rooted in human nature, for as the note to Ecclesiastes 11:10 in the Geneva Bible explains, young people are prone to lust. The solution, according to Richard Rogers, is to order the heart so that it does not allow affections to stray or evil desires to be harbored. Robert Allen proposed that children receive sex education, but beyond this, his recommendations parallel those of Vaux. Immodest pictures, amorous books, "the vnshamefast representation of the lewd and filt[h]y behauiour of naughtie-packes, by enterlude vpon the stage, or by dauncing," lascivious speech, suggestive songs, wanton kissing, and unseemly dalliance are condemned as conducive to improper sexual relations.[13]

One of the fullest discussions of the means to avoid prenuptial sex is found in a work by the tutor of Sir Thomas Bromley's children, William Hergest, entitled *The Right Rvle of Christian Chastitie*. Control of the flesh is achieved through prayer, Bible study, moderation in diet, apparel, and games, avoidance of idleness, recollection of divine promises and threats, godly companions, and remembrance of final judgment. He also warned of the dangers of physical contact. Whether or not Hergest was a Puritan, his recommendations are compatible with those of Puritan authors. No writer of any religious persuasion recommended that parents use wills to govern premarital sexual behavior. There is, however, at least one instance of this in practice, for the 1558 will of Edward Osbaldeston of Blackburn, Lancs., left twenty marks to a niece on condition "that shee doe behave and use her self well and honestly at the discrecon of my executors if in the meane time shee bee not preferred in mariage." This statement must have been intended to discourage sex at least prior to espousal.[14]

Writers of all persuasions condemned fornication. Vaux, the Augustinian canon, believed that such lechery would disrupt order, undermine social degree, weaken the body, destroy one's reputation, and offend neighbors. For the Anglicans, Jewel castigated fornication as an offense against the body and a hinderance to holiness, and Alexander Nowell, dean of St. Paul's, London, condemned it as a violation of the seventh commandment. To the woman who yielded to the persuasions of a male fornicator, Whetstone asked:

> What meanst thou wretch, from ioy exilde,
> To yeald vnto his fained teares?
> With carelesse vowes why wert begilde,
> And fearelesse othes, the traytor sweares,
> Ere nuptial rites, whie didst thou trust,
> His faith, and yeelde vnto his lust?

Fornication was condemned in the marginal notes to the Geneva and Beza-Tomson Bibles, the latter asserting that this vice was sacrilegious because bodies were consecrated to Christ. Among the Puritans, Allen lashed out at fornication because it disrupted inheritance, especially among princes and nobles, and Greenham, like Nowell, judged it a violation of the seventh commandment. Northbrooke was incensed because social standards tolerated fornication among the landed aristocracy: "If he [a gentleman] be a whooremaister, they say he is an amorous louer and a *Venus* bride, it is the course of youth." Whatever differences existed between Anglicans and Puritans over the propriety of sexual intercourse by affianced couples, they united in condemning fornication.[15]

The force of sermons and writings of religious leaders against fornication probably was weakened by fornicating clerics. William Downham, bishop of Chester, ordered a Staffordshire rector to pay £20 towards the marriage of a girl with whom the rector had illicit sex, yet the bishop wanted the affair kept quiet "forasmuch as Mr [Thomas] Elcocke [rector of Barthomley] was an honest gentleman and a preacher, lest it should redound to the reproach of the ministry." Other cases could not be handled so discreetly, especially if improper behavior had occurred in public, as in the case of the notorious minister William Underne, who was involved with "canvasinge a yonge mayde of xiiij. or xv. yeares olde in a blankett and wyndowe [winnowing] clothe at mydnyght" in an alehouse. David Ireland, vicar of Offchurch, Warws., Mr. Levit, parson of Leaden Roothing, Essex, and Mr. Mason, parson of Rawreth, Essex, had sexual relations with their maids, and the latter two had bastards by them. Other clergy were involved in lewd and incontinent activity; they included Mr. Goldringe, parson of Laindon, Essex, Mr. Warcoppe, minister at Colney, Norf., Mr. Robart, minister at Sprowston and Beeston, Norf., and Mr. Polewhele, vicar of North Petherwyn, Devon. Some of this behavior may be traced to the universities, for the Puritan diarist Samuel Ward recorded that on a winter night in 1596 a woman was carried from chamber to chamber in Trinity College, Cambridge. Although Ward avoided the sexual temptations, he confessed in his diary to have had an "adulterous dream that night."[16]

In addition to the bad example that some of the clergy provided, the court developed a reputation for sexual licentiousness, especially on gala occasions. Nash wittily noted that "the Court I dare not touch, but surely there . . . bee many falling starres and but one true *Diana.*" On the whole, Elizabethans proved more reluctant than they were in ensuing reigns to criticize (at least openly) the abuses of the court. Early in the period, the government charged fornication in its attempt to annul the marriage of Edward Scymour, earl of Hertford, to Lady Catherine Grey. Parker, Grindal, and others were deputed in January 1562 to examine the circumstances of his intercourse with Lady Catherine who was then pregnant. One of the most spicy scandals involved Mary Fitton, a maid of honor to the queen, and the object of considerable attention by the married Sir William Knollys; she became pregnant by the earl of Pembroke, who refused to marry her. The flirtations of the queen herself with Dudley and Alençon caused hostile minds to suspect fornication, though Elizabeth normally took a rather strict view of the moral tone of her court. Dudley had illicit sex with Lady Douglas Sheffield and Lettice Knollys, whom he wed when she became pregnant a third time. In 1603 Lady Anne Clifford claimed that ladies of the court had ill names because of their scandalous sexual activities.[17]

Most cases of fornication in Elizabethan society probably involved young people exploring the mysteries of sex, but one of the more troublesome areas had to do with masters taking sexual liberties with their maids, who were in a difficult position to resist. Such behavior undermined the master-servant relationship envisioned by religious leaders and diminished the effectiveness of the master's role as the spiritual bishop of the household. Men who acted in this fashion might answer for their behavior in the ecclesiastical courts, but the temptation was more than some masters could handle. Yet the idea of marrying a pregnant maid was repulsive to most of them. Anthony Bacon was informed by William Dell in 1596 of a man whose servant became pregnant by a kinsman of the master, who was offended at the suggestion that he wed the girl. Sir Thomas Gresham probably enjoyed sexual intimacy with his servant Anne Hurst, who became pregnant. He had her wed another of his servants, John Markham, and granted the couple £30 *p.a.* for ninety-nine years, plus £600 for the child when the marriage settlement was concluded. Sir Thomas continued to visit Anne after her marriage until his death three years later.[18]

Church courts actively punished fornicators. With respect to all types of sexual offenses, cases in ecclesiastical courts more than doubled between 1595 and 1635. In Essex, with an adult population of 40,000, some 15,000 persons were summoned to answer charges of sexual offenses between 1558 and 1603, an average of approximately 330 persons *p.a.*, or nearly 1% of the sexually mature population. Between 1559 and 1590, a substantial number of cases involved fornication in the Yorkshire courts, especially in the clothing areas of the West Riding, such as Halifax. Visitation records for Yorkshire in 1595-96 show frequent citations for fornication. In the Yorkshire deanery of Doncaster in 1590, 141 of the 286 presentments were for sexual immorality. This figure compares with 55 of 97 presentments in the Cheshire deanery of Frodsham (1590) and 33 of 154 presentments in the Suffolk deanery of Sudbury (1593). Yet to a surprising degree, offenders ignored the church courts. Of the sexual offenders, the figures for contumacious persons in these deaneries was 75% (104 persons), 27% (15 persons), and 67% (22 persons) respectively. In every deanery the percentage of contumacious persons for sexual offenses exceeded the percentage of contumacious persons for all offenses (66%, 21.5% and 34% respectively). Church authorities could sue out a writ *de excommunicato capiendo* for a contumacious person, enabling a sheriff to arrest and imprison the offender until his or her submission, but time and expense made this impractical in the face of widespread contumacy. Therefore, "the average contumacious person lived and died excommunicate. If he was poor, the legal disabilities would weigh lightly on him, and the only pressures which would induce him to seek absolution were the persuasions of the minister or of his employers." Excommunication was harder on women, in depriving them of the assistance of midwives. But the efforts of church courts to punish fornicators were marginally successful at best.[19]

Ecclesiastical and civic officials were interested in prosecuting fornicators and, usually, imposing public penance as a deterrent for others. In the diocese of Ely, Bishop Cox was more concerned with the morals of the laity than with Puritanism; fornication and related sexual problems were the focus of his interest. In Exeter, magistrates vigorously enforced sexual morality, partly for religious reasons and partly because sexual offenses threatened civil order. Women were punished more often than men, and tended to come from the lower social classes. Fornication was often coupled with vagrancy. The punishments imposed on fornicators throughout the kingdom varied. Carting and whipping were common, sometimes in conjunction with the stocks. In 1563 a physician who fornicated with two wenches had to ride around London on a market day, and though he wore a damask gown lined with velvet, a velvet coat, and a velvet cap, pinned to the latter was a blue hood to indicate his offense. In Exeter a man who got a maid pregnant was imprisoned in the pit of the guildhall for forty days, and fed bread and water every Wednesday and Friday night. Other fornicators were banished from Exeter. Lancashire justices stripped male and female fornicators to the waist, whipped them, and put them in the stocks. Somerset justices usually restricted whipping to women, but proceeded until their backs were bloody. In the West Riding and Nottinghamshire justices combined whipping and stocks with penance in the church. Men usually received lesser punishment because evidence against them was normally limited to the testimony of the women involved.[20]

In religious circles, reaction toward such punishments varied. A note to Deuteronomy 7:16 in the Geneva Bible warned that "we oght not to be merciful where God commandeth seueritie." Yet one of the lightest penalities imposed on a fornicator was proposed by the Dedham classis in 1588 when it learned of a young man who copulated with a maid while her master was away; the classis recommended that the church suspend him from communion until he repented. Bishops such as Jewel and Cox favored excommunication. Between 1571 and 1584 in the diocese of Ely, most excommunications were for moral matters; only 37 of 346 cases involved doctrine, or failure to commune or attend services. Thomas Cogan, the physician and Manchester educator, was not satisfied that some offenders only stood in a sheet during church services; he favored mandatory dowries and marriage for fornicators. Robert Allen wanted any who had sexual relations with a girl under ten executed, and Stubbes accused magistrates of laxity and demanded harsher punishments. "For what great thing is it, to go ii. or three dayes in a white sheete before the congregation, and that somtymes not past an howre or two in a day, hauing their vsuall garments vnderneth, as commonly they haue?" Light punishment encouraged illicit sex: "I have heard some miscreants impudently say, that he is but a beast, that for such white lyuered punishment would abstaine from suche gallant pastyme." He proposed that fornicators be branded on the cheek, forehead, or other visible area. Puritan proposals for harsh punishment contrast sharply with the recommendation of the Dedham classis in a fornication case.[21]

Medical advice tended to work in two ways with regard to premarital sex and fornication. On the one hand, unwed couples had access to medical prescriptions intended to enable couples to enjoy intercourse with diminished risk of pregnancy (as discussed below). Detailed information also was available for girls who found it useful to restore the physical appearance of virginity. Christopher Wirtzung's *Praxis medicinae vniuersalis,* translated by Jacob Mosan (1598), recommended that "to make a woman to be as narrow as a Mayden" she must anoint her vulva with a compound of *consolida saracenica,* plantain, red roses, and shepherd's purse (a wild plant) in melted May butter. Conrad Gesner's *The Newe Iewell of Health,* translated by George Baker (1576), prescribed the distilled water of *alchimilla* drunk and injected daily into the uterus, or used as a concentrated solution in which a girl sits, so that "the priuie place [is] made so straight, that hardly she can be knowne from the chaste Mayden."[22]

Nevertheless any inducements that such advice might have given for single persons to copulate were somewhat countered by warnings of venereal disease. Syphilis was believed to have been brought by the Spanish from America to Naples c. 1495. The French subsequently contracted the disease, it was believed, by infected women banned from Naples, and from the French it came to the English. Four sweat wards at St. Thomas' Hospital, London, were needed to treat venereal disease in 1561, and in 1579 William Clowes, the first English venereologist, asserted that three-fourths of the patients at St. Bartholomew's Hospital were victims of syphilis. Serious works on the disease were written in the Elizabethan era by Clowes, John Banister, John Read of Gloucester, and Peter Lowe of Ayr. John Hester's *The Pearle of Practise* (1594) was one of the medical texts that prescribed cures, and the author urged every diseased man to seek early assistance. Surprisingly, however, the religious authors rarely used venereal disease as a warning not to commit fornication. The only writer to do so substantively was Stubbes, who vividly depicted the physical horrors of gonorrhea: "It dimmeth the sight, it impaireth the hearing, it infirmeth ye sinewes, it weakneth the ioynts, it exhausteth the marrow, consumeth the moisture and supplement of the body, it riueleth the face, appalleth the countenance, it dulleth ye spirits, it hurteth the memorie, it weakneth ye whole body, it bringeth it into a consumption, it bringeth ulcerations, scab, scurf, blain, botch, pocks & biles, it maketh hoare haires, & bald pates: it induceth olde age, & . . . bringeth death before nature vrge it, malady enforce it, or age require it." One suspects, however, that particularly in rural areas the relative rarity of the disease mitigated fear of it.[23]

Anglicans and Puritans agreed on the immorality and social dangers of fornication, but their attempts to reduce it were frustrated by the inability of ecclesiastical courts to punish contumacious offenders in sufficient numbers. Puritans in any case apparently preferred that fornicators be punished by local congregations and especially magistrates. Prenuptial intercourse by affianced persons was not condemned to the same degree, though Puritans refused to sanction it. The absence of strong criticism of this practice in areas where it was fairly common, as in Leicestershire, suggests acquiescence by Anglican clerics. The medical advice available to young couples to avoid pregnancy and restore the appearance of virginity in the female presumably helped foster prenuptial sex. The immoral behavior of some ministers, coupled with reports of licentious activity at the royal court, must have compounded the difficulties of reformers intent on reserving sex to married persons. The endeavors of the moralists also were frustrated by the late age of first marriage and the presence of male and female servants and apprentices in many households.

(2) Bastardy, Prostitution, and Other Sexual Problems

We store the realme with basterd borne,
to help our natyve soyle.

Anonymous ballad[24]

O, oh, how many brothell Bawdes
within the towne doe dwell?

Edward Hake[25]

One of the principal social evils of illicit sex was bastardy. In the Elizabethan age, the causes of bastardy cannot be tied to the movement of military forces in England or to psychological conditions associated with political crises. Some bastardy may be due to economic conditions, as an increase in the number of bastards occurred in the latter decades of the century when inflation, periodic dearths, and increased government expenses due to military activities created financial hardships. Yet bastardy also appears to have been influenced by the relatively late age of marriage, imperfect methods of birth control, and the loose sexual atmosphere common during festive and sporting occasions. In the quarter sessions at Devon in July 1595, there was a complaint that parish ales, revels, May games, and plays drew people from surrounding parishes on the sabbath, increasing disorder and bastardy. Stubbes suggests a further reason by attributing bastardy to those who regarded illegitimate offspring as a sign of masculinity. Bastardy "is so little feared in *Ailgna* [Anglia, England], that vntill euery one hath two or three Bastardes a peece, they esteeme him no man, (for that, they call a mans deede) insomuch as euery scuruie boy of twelue, sixteen or twenty yeeres of age wil make no conscience of it, to haue two or three, peraduenture half a dosen seuerall women with childe at once, and this exploite beeing doon, he showes them a faire pair of heeles, and away goeth he." The willingness to acknowledge bastards in wills lends support to Stubbes' view.[26]

Known illegitimacy rates were highest in England in the Elizabethan era and the mid-eighteenth century. Despite the attempt by Protestant leaders to tighten up morality, there was more bastardy in Elizabethan England than Catholic France, which suffered the psychological and physical effects of civil and religious warfare. Generally speaking, bastardy rates in England increased sharply from c. 1561 to the 1590s before decreasing in the first decade of the seventeenth century. The rates continued to fall until 1660, though caution is necessary because records were poorly kept in the 1640s and 1650s. The figures for registered baptisms of illegitimate children at Prestbury,

Ches., are 3.7 to 4.5% in the 1560s, 13.8 to 16% in the 1570s, 6.2 to 15.9% in the 1580s, 1.7 to 15.9% in the 1590s, and 6.4 to 10.7% in the 1600s. (The percentage variables are due to uncertainty regarding the illegitimacy of some infants.) Illegitimacy ratios were high in some parishes of Lancashire and Cheshire, running around 9 or 10%, sometimes higher. At Ashton under Lyne, Lancs., the mean percentage for the years 1594 to 1640 is 6.82%, with the maximum being 16.6% in 1594. In Ludlow, Shrops., the mean for the period 1590 to 1640 was only 3.8%, with a maximum of 9% in 1593. In the London area, at St. Margaret's, Westminster, the percentage of illegitimate births did not exceed 2.5% between 1539 and 1648, whereas in the period from 1612 to 1621, the parish of St. Botolph without Aldgate had an even lower illegitimacy ratio of 1.61%. At Dedham, Essex, where Puritan influence was strong, the bastardy ratio in the period 1581 to 1640 was a mere 0.5%, though Puritan clergy were not uniformly successful in reducing illegitimacy. On a broader scale, a more representative picture is made possible by the bastardy ratios of 23 parishes in the 1580s and 1590s, and 24 parishes in the 1600s; the figures are 3.7%, 4.6%, and 4.4%, respectively. A larger sampling of 98 parishes produced lower figures of 2.84%, 3.08%, and 3.20%. In the period 1581 to 1640, bastardy ratios were highest in the conservative West and Northwest (3.6%) and the North (2.9%), lowest in the East (1.2%) and Midlands (1.6%), and moderate in the South (2.1%). The regional figures suggest less of a bastard problem in the more Protestant and economically progressive areas before 1640. All recorded levels of illegitimacy are, however, underestimates, for illegitimate offspring of married women are not recorded, nor were all bastards baptized, and there is the additional factor of abortion and infanticide. Some mothers went to London and had their babies secretly, which may account to some degree for the lower recorded illegitimacy ratios in the southeast.[27]

As in the case of premarital sex, most substantive literary comment on bastardy came from Puritans. Concern commonly was expressed because of the taint attached to bastard children; in Henry Smith's judgment they were not divinely blessed nor did they enjoy an earthly or heavenly inheritance, a view Perkins echoed. The balladeer and London silk weaver Thomas Deloney has a light but pointed reflection on the origins of bastards in adulterous affairs: When the married man

> hath in a little time a daughter or a sonne,
> hey downe downe adowne, God grant they be his owne.

Allen fretted about the abandonment of bastard children, who were taken by vagabonds and assimilated into their lifestyle. Many, he claimed, were disfigured by vagabond masters or died early, though he saw improvement by 1603.[28]

Anglican concern about bastardy was expressed in visitation articles and injunctions, despite the relative absence of discussion among Anglican authors. The articles regularly inquired about mothers of bastards who had been churched without first acknowledging their fault and rendering penance before the congregation, and persons who harbored such women or allowed them to leave the parish without penance. The bishops also expressed concern in a note to Exodus 6:20 in the Bishops' Bible, explaining that "Moyses glorieth not in his kin[d]rede, who was borne of vnlawfull maryage." Sometimes their work was hampered by the loose morals of their own clergy. Mr. Cliberye, vicar of Halstead, Essex, allegedly preached that girls who intended to copulate should procure a pledge from the boys to have proof of paternity. Siring bastards was a favorite charge to hurl at Catholic priests, especially since an occasional instance of the practice still was made public in Elizabethan England, such as that involving Nicholas Arscot, vicar of Cubert, Cum., who was accused of keeping a whore and fathering five or six bastards.[29]

Because religious sanctions alone were insufficient, legislative action was considered in 1576 and again in the 1590s. Parliament recognized in 1576, in 18 Eliz. I, c. 3, that when bastards were kept at the charge of the parishes in which they were born, financial hardship resulted, particularly in terms of reduced funds for deserving poor. This, Parliament felt, provided a bad example, hence justices were instructed to punish parents and require them to maintain their children or be jailed. In 1593 an unsuccessful attempt was made to add a proviso on bastardy to the bill for the continuation and repeal of statutes. Four years later, under the apparent leadership of a Puritan group in the Commons, fifteen bills dealing with poverty and vagrancy were introduced and given at least two readings, but the bill against bastardy never became law. Not until 1610 were further provisions dealing with bastardy enacted, though Puritans in Parliament desired additional reforms.[30]

Even without further legal penalties for bastardy, conditions often were difficult for parents, especially mothers, of illegitimate children. Shelter was a problem, for those harboring an unwed mother were liable for prosecution in ecclesiastical courts. Parents of bastards sometimes gave them to vagrants, who used the children to excite pity from donors. In towns such as London and Norwich a special problem was created by the abandonment of illegitimate children in the streets. In 1571, the city authorities in Norwich determined to provide guardians for illegitimate children and force the mother or reputed father to reimburse them for maintenance costs. Throughout the country local authorities boarded illegitimate and abandoned children in foster homes rather than face fines imposed by the justices of the peace on the parishes.[31] Thus when religious leaders, particularly Puritans, condemned illicit sex, they struck at the roots of a problem that had far-reaching social consequences. Puritan concern with sexual morality was a part of a broader endeavor to eliminate such social ills as bastardy and vagrancy.

The usual punishments imposed on parents of bastards, apart from penance in church in a white sheet, were whipping and mandatory child maintenance. At the Devon quarter sessions in Easter 1598, any woman giving birth to a bastard was ordered whipped, and the reputed father could be lashed at the judge's discretion. One unfortunate woman was ordered flogged until she named the father, though she escaped before divulging her secret. The penalties imposed on perpetrators of bastardy had a twofold purpose, to provide a public warning and financial support for the children that would not tax local funds for poor relief. This intention is evident in a case handled in the quarter sessions at Preston, Lancs., on 14 January 1601:

Henry Horneby of Woodplumpton, husbandman, reputed father of the bastard child of Elizabeth Atkinson, is to be whipped at Garstange on his naked body next market day, and he and Elizabeth shall then be put in the stocks during all the market time, naked from the middle upward and having papers on their heads inscribed: 'These persons are punished for fornication.'

Horneby was also required to pay 26s. 8d. a year to the mother for child maintenance, but he refused to provide sureties and was imprisoned. Similar punishments were regularly imposed on Kentish offenders by William Lambarde.[32]

The period of time for which fathers were required to support their bastards varied widely. In some instances, financial payments had to continue until a child was ten or twelve, old enough to be apprenticed, but in Cheshire and Lancashire the justices sometimes held a father financially responsible only for periods ranging from one month to two years. At Wigan, Lancs., in 1602 the justices ordered a father to pay the mother 10s. to maintain their daughter for one year, after which he was required to keep the girl until she was twelve. In the early 1590s at Chester, local authorities encouraged parents of bastards to wed, and in one case ordered a man to marry the mother of his bastard child if she was willing and the church approved. I. Pinchbeck claims that the growth of Puritan influence led to ecclesiastical demands for penance enforceable by civil authorities, but there is no clear evidence. Of at least equal importance in the crackdown on parents of bastards was the campaign of the bishops through visitations and the financial realities of supporting bastards or facing a further growth in vagrancy.[33]

The related problem of prostitution was condemned by Anglicans and Puritans, but the latter were more zealous in denouncing it. Among the Anglicans, Jewel was disturbed that maintainers of brothels defended them on the grounds that men would face a greater peril in their absence, though no explicit claim was made of higher health standards in supervised bordellos. If Nash is correct, prostitutes were common in London and the suburbs, and were particularly frequented by students from the Inns of Court. "As dailie gheasts at ordinarie Tabls," observed Whetstone, "a man shal fynde neate Bawdes, that onely lyve vppon the brocage of loue, fellowes that wyl procure acquaintaunce for a dumbe man." It was not so much the morality as the wasted money that troubled Henry Bedel, vicar of Christ's Hospital, London, in 1571, for he longed to have the funds that were lavished on prostitutes donated to the poor instead. Perhaps Samuel Gardiner agreed, for he argued that poverty was the reason maidens became prostitutes and elderly women bawds. Generally, Anglican concern about prostitution was directed more to the social than the moral aspects of the problem.[34]

In contrast, the Puritans were at least as concerned with the spiritual as the social ramifications of prostitution. The tone was set in the Geneva marginalia, which assert that human nature is inclined to whoredom. Those who consent to idolatry and false doctrine commit spiritual prostitution, the forerunner of its corporal counterpart. The proposed remedy was capital punishment, which was justified by the law written in men's hearts. Prostitution is, according to Dent, a sign of damnation, but Norden believed it was possible for a prostitute to be chastised by perpetual continency. Mark Wiersdale, the Puritan rector of Costock, Notts., was accused in 1600 of preaching of nothing but whores and thieves. On the social side, Wilcox blamed prostitution as a cause of poverty and beggary, and Henry Smith agreed with Bedel that money spent on whores ought to be donated to the poor. In Trigge's judgment, stews were supported by Catholics as a way for poor men and servants to engage in sex without fear of producing children they could not support.[35]

Other Puritans were alarmed about the practices of prostitutes and pimps. Stephen Gosson, a reformed playwright and later a lecturer at Stepney, complained that on Sundays prostitutes who had been watched closely throughout the week by magistrates went to the theater, where they kept "a generall Market of Bawdrie." Others, he said, had rooms in inns and taverns at their disposal, while pimps ran their businesses under the guise of music instructors whose students went to their homes. Baser prostitutes were found in alleys and blind lanes, whereas others "liue a mile from the Cittie like *Venus* Nunnes in a Cloyster at *Newington, Ratliffe, Islington, Hogsdon* or some such place." Edward Hake, reflecting on his years at the Inns of Court, blamed pimps who enticed maidens and wives, particularly from the country, so that the men could pander for them.[36]

One of the most thorough treatments of prostitution came from Stubbes, who depicted courtesans garbed in the dress of gentlewomen and undertaking sexual rendezvous without their husbands' knowledge. He also claimed wives of peasants sold their bodies with their spouses' awareness because of financial need. The cold disapproval of such conduct in Puritan circles is reflected in a story repeated by Stubbes that probably circulated widely in religious homes, and is worth repeating because of its tone of pious indignation:

There was a man whose name was *W. Ratsurb* [Brustar], being certenly knowen to be a notorious vserer (and yet pretending alway a singular zeale to religion, so that he wold seldom tymes go without a byble about him . . .) who vppon occasion of busines visiting *Lewedirb* [Bridewell] . . . saw there a famous whore, . . . whom . . . he procured her delyuery from thence, bayled her, & hauing put away his own wife before, kept her in his chamber, vsing her at his pleasure. . . . Hauing a litle pan of coles before them . . . it pleased GOD . . . to strike these two persons dead. . . . The Woman falling ouer the pan of coles, was burned that all her bowels gushed out, the man was founde lying by. . . . But which is most wonderfull, his arme was burned to the uery boone, his shirte sleeue, and dublet, not once perished, nor tutched with the fire.

Divine vengeance was not frequent enough for Stubbes, who lamented that gentlemen maintained prostitutes and escaped legal penalties through bribes.[37]

Stubbes' views influenced the Oxford student, William Vaughan, who deplored bawds who procured young women and taught them their trade, enabling them to charge fees ranging from 20s. a week to £10 a month. Pimps were castigated for providing courtesans with drugs to improve their color and "disguise their first naturall shape, onely sophistically to seeme fayre vnto the outwarde viewe of tame and vndiscreete woodcocks." One female procuress, Long Meg of

Westminster, reportedly kept twenty cocottes in her house and used their pictures to lure customers. Vaughan reiterated the popular view that the spread of syphilis was divine retribution for the increase in brothels. [38]

If the Puritan survey of the clergy in Cornwall is accurate and indicative of other counties, the battle against prostitution was retarded by ministers who frequented prostitutes. John Cornish, rector of Whitstone, Thomas More, rector of Lanteglos and Advent, and Mr. Fletcher, rector of Martin, were suspected of illegitimate relations with courtesans, and Richard Mainard, vicar of Talland, was allegedly a panderer and drunkard. Another accused clerical pimp was Mr. Dewe, rector of Redruth, believed to be a Catholic. [39]

When local authorities apprehended panderers and courtesans, public penance was imposed. The diary of the London undertaker Henry Machyn records a number of cases from 1559 to 1562, in which offenders rode about the city on horseback or in a cart, with a sign proclaiming their offense and a tingling basin announcing their presence. One offender was the goldsmith Harry Glyn, who had solicited for his daughter, and another was Mrs. Warner, widow of a serjeant of the admiralty, who was a procuress for her daughter and her maid. The problem of prostitution may not have been serious in Southhampton until 1576, when court leet records call for a cucking-stool, which could also be used for scolding wives and other malefactors. It had still not been erected in 1577, but by 1601 it had been used enough to require repair. In Oxford the archdeacon's court dealt with two guardians (churchwardens) of the parish of Caversham accused of tolerating a brothel. Attempts to eliminate prostitution were also made by striking at those who housed them, as happened in the quarter sessions at Lancashire and on the Isle of Wight. In Essex, authorities concentrated on punishing brothel-keepers, not prostitutes or their customers. In episcopal visitations, the bishops sought to discover persons who housed prostitutes, as well as pimps. Had reformers succeeded in enacting the *Reformatio Legum Ecclesiasticarum*, prostitutes would have been subject to excommunication and perpetual exile. [40]

Carol Wiener argues that most Elizabethan prostitutes did not operate in a fixed place or normally have formal arrangements and price structures. Evidence in Puritan tracts and court records suggests her judgment requires modification, particularly in view of known operations of pimps, who normally used modest business procedures in soliciting clients, setting fees, and paying cocottes. Fixed places of prostitution can be identified, such as the bawdry house at

Caversham, Oxon., and Long Meg's brother at Westminster. Brothels were common in Southward, West Ham, Barking, and Walthamstow. Fees are hard to discover, but generally ranged from £4 to £10 a month in London for the provision of regular services. Occasional rendezvous with lower class prostitutes were probably much less expensive, as were the sexual favors of rural housewives. Outside the larger towns, Wiener's assessment is probably accurate. A woman at Hitchin, Herts., represents a more casual approach; the man with whom she slept gave her money, but when she became pregnant, he paid her to accuse another man of siring the child. A similar case was brought to Burghley's attention in 1579, when a harlot accused Sir John Smyth of fathering her child. Generally, however, village prostitutes operated secretly but casually, in search of funds with which to pursue a better life, sometimes with the acquiescence of their husbands or, on occasion in Cornwall, their ministers. The ranks of prostitutes were fed by poverty, sexual promiscuity, the plight of unwed mothers, and the bleak prospects of unwed girls from poor families, who often faced a choice of becoming a seamstress or a harlot.[41]

Other forms of sexual behavior deemed undesirable in Elizabethan society rarely appear in extant evidence. Homosexuality was denounced by the Puritans Allen and Perkins and the Anglican Turnbull, with the principal biblical evidence against it being Genesis 19:4-5, Leviticus 18:22 and 20:13, and Romans 1:24-27. Turnbull labeled homosexuality "the Sodomicall sin" and "the sin of the Romish Clergie" who relied on it to fulfil their lusts rather than use the approved remedy of matrimony. Allen also condemned masturbation. Sexual relations with animals were denounced by Turnbull and Allen, the former referring to Leviticus 18:23 and 20:15-16. In at least one instance a clergyman — Thomas More, rector of Lanteglos and Advent, Corn. — was alleged to be a bugger, but it is unclear whether this indicated homosexuality or sodomy with animals. Henry Wriothesley (d. 1624), earl of Southhampton, Edward de Vere, earl of Oxford, Sir Humphrey Gilbert, and Francis Bacon were thought to be homosexuals.[42]

In 1563, Parliament revived the Henrician statute (25 Henry VIII, c. 6) against sodomy and bestiality on the grounds that "dyvers evyll disposed persons have been the more bolde to committ the said most horrible and detestable vice of Buggerie." The Henrician act, which made buggery a felonious vice, rendered it punishable by death or loss of goods and lands. No convicted person could receive benefit of clergy. The Henrician statute removed buggery from the jurisdiction of the church courts and made offenders subject to civil magistrates.

In the Edwardian period, Parliament (in 2 and 3 Edward VI, c. 29) kept buggery as a capital offense, but removed the penalties of loss of goods and lands. At the outset of Mary's reign this statute was repealed (1 Mary I, c. 1), restoring the prosecution of buggery to ecclesiastical courts. The 1563 Parliament not only placed the problem in the hands of the secular courts but revived the harsher Henrician statute. [43]

Cases of incest were likely more common, given the relatively late ages of marriage and the proximity of family members in small houses, though apprenticing male children and placing female offspring as servants helped keep incest in check. Regular inquiries about incest in visitation articles suggest it was not rare. A 1573 case was taken to the Privy Council, which referred it to the archbishop of York and the bishop of Carlisle. In June 1560 Machyn reported that a brother and sister found naked together were required to ride around London in a cart. The daughter of John Danvers, sheriff of Oxfordshire, allegedly engaged in incest, as her illegitimate child was secretly baptized by her lay brother; her parents, who had separated, were suspected of adultery. Manningham tells in his diary for 1602 how a Northamptonshire gentleman married his bastard daughter, who was pregnant after his death but refused to name the father. At least one minister—Mr. Ampleforth, vicar of Much Baddow, Essex, who had a child by his sister—was guilty of incest. Barrow criticized the High Commission's handling of incest cases on the grounds that divine law prescribed capital punishment, not ecclesiastical penance. Church courts in the Elizabethan period were in fact lenient in treating incest. [44]

Rape in Elizabethan society has not been systematically studied. No preacher condoned it, but neither are denunciations common, perhaps because it was normally a secular offense. Parliament passed a bill in 1576 to take away benefit of clergy from rapists, who were liable to capital punishment. Middlesex records for the Elizabethan period include fourteen cases of rape, ten of which involved girls from three to twelve years of age, one involved one male raping another, and one involved rape by a yeoman in the earl of Lincoln's cellar. Various rape cases appeared before the Privy Council, and these suggest the difficulty of proving the crime. In a 1570 case an alleged rapist took legal action against his accusers in the Court of Exchequer. Ten years later, the Council ordered the lord mayor of London to proceed against a man who reputedly raped and wed a twelve-year-old orphan girl. In 1590 a man imprisoned in Newgate for two rapes persuaded the Council to require his accusers to prove his guilt. Selected types of rape, particularly that of children under the guise of child marriages, were possible through improper use of ecclesiastical licenses. A west country case illustrates *de facto* rape by use of a license:

One Bernard of Upton in Gloucestershire woed a widow, as she and her friends thought, for himself. Yet afterwards conveying her among her own friends, by a wile brought the man to her bed; and through his threatning to kill her, forced her to lie with him. And within two days after was married to his man by a licence. Her friends sued him for a rape. And had not the licence been, the law was thought to have gone against him.

The violence of rape led to murder in the case of girls aged six and thirteen (1587, 1594) in the parish of St. Botolph without Aldgate, London, but the fate of the rapist-killers is unknown. In view of the seriousness of this offense, it is surprising that Anglican and Puritan authors were largely silent, though some cases, such as that of an Oxfordshire maid raped by two men in her master's home, were tried in ecclesiastical courts. [45]

Anglicans and Puritans could not accept bastardy, prostitution, sodomy, incest, and rape, yet Puritans made a greater effort in their writings to censure these ills than did Anglicans. Nevertheless the bishops demonstrated concern in visitation articles.

The social as well as the moral consequences of these actions disturbed religious leaders, particularly the ramifications of bastardy for vagrancy and poor relief. Even in the case of prostitution at least one Anglican and one Puritan wanted the money lavished on courtesans diverted to victims of poverty. With regard to prostitution, Anglicans were largely concerned with its social rather than spiritual ramifications, whereas Puritans had a more balanced view. Little was said about sodomy, incest, and rape.

(3) Sex in Marriage

So that marriage is not a madde and dissolute estate, neyther are husbandes to turne their wiues into whoores, or wiues their husbandes into whore-maisters, by immoderate, intemperate, or excessiue lust.

Robert Cleaver[46]

Moderate venerie is very expedient for preseruation of health.

William Vaughan[47]

Elizabethans seeking guidance for sexual conduct in marriage found it in various places, including scriptural marginalia and commentary. In the Matthew Bibles of 1537, 1549, and 1551, attention is directed to two areas, the first of which, in a note to Exodus 19, advocates that husbands periodically abstain from sexual relations to pray. The second admonition, in a note to Deuteronomy 25, warns a wife to be more modest than to touch his penis. The Geneva annotators treated the latter passage as a declaration of female modesty, and the Exodus passage as applicable to the Hebrews in Sinai. The significant comment on sex in marriage in the Geneva marginalia is the note to Malachi 2:15, where moderate sexual intercourse between husband and wife is advised. The Bishops' Bible implicitly reflects the older view that the purpose of marital sex is procreation. The Beza-Tomson Bible returned to the idea of sexual abstinence for prayer, but advised that this must be done only with mutual consent and not for excessive periods, lest it lead to incontinency.[48]

In Catholic circles, the Roman catechism of 1566 approved occasional abstinence for prayer, but also taught that sexual intercourse should not be undertaken for pleasure or lust. Yet the catechism did not insist that intercourse be used solely for procreation, for unlike Augustine, it implicitly allowed partners to have marital sex to avoid adultery. Neither the catechism nor the theologian Peter Canisius linked love and intercourse. The Rheims annotators found that in the apostolic church the early Christians practiced sexual abstinence to make their prayers and fasts more acceptable to God, and they chided Protestant clergy for failing to follow this example. With respect to "the bond and obligation that is betwene the maried couple for rendring of the dette of carnal copulation one to an other . . . the maried persons haue yelded their bodies so one to an other, that they can not without mutual consent, neither perpetually, nor for a time, defraude one the other." Nevertheless, the Rheims scholars insisted that even for married persons perpetual continency was preferable to copulation, though Paul gave no precepts requiring it. Those who found it necessary to copulate were warned to keep the marital bed undefiled by avoiding the "many filthy abuses" that could be committed there. The Catholic position on marital sex is negative in tone, limiting it to a procreative act and a remedy for incontinency.[49]

The refutations of the Rheims New Testament by Fulke and Cartwright emphasize sexual abstinence for fasting and prayer. Temporary abstinence by mutual consent is approved, but the period must not be overextended and lead to incontinency. "They should prevent the distemperance, and haue company together before they be over-

taken with any disorder of their affections that way." Cartwright referred to 1 Corinthians 7:10, 14, and 1 Peter 3:7 as proof that Paul
and Peter accepted normal marital intercourse. Fulke warned that
the ability to abstain was not possible for all but was a divine gift,
which also was bestowed on all persons temporarily separated from
their mates by imprisonment, war, or exile. The basic position enunciated by Fulke and Cartwright is reflected in the writings of the Puritan preachers Cleaver, Pagit, and Henry Holland, vicar of St. Bride's,
Fleet Street, London, and of the Anglican Samuel Gardiner. [50]

The Georges suggest that the Puritan view of marital sex is essentially positive, but this is not often so. Perkins, for example, argued
that marital intercourse must suppress rather than satisfy "that corrupt concupiscence of the flesh, " though its fundamental purpose
is to enlarge the church through procreation. Similarly, Richard
Rogers asserted that the marriage bed is to increase posterity and
subdue concupiscence; George Estey summed it up as "necessitie,
and child-procreation." Pagit edged away from the "somewhat to[o]
narrow" view that marital sex is intended to satisfy lust, but he
failed to develop a positive view of sexual intercourse. Essentially
Catholics in the sixteenth century said the same things about marital sex. [51]

Elizabethan Protestants, particularly Puritans, began to take a
more wholesome attitude toward marital sex by applying the principle of moderation. Intemperancy in marital intercourse was labeled fornication by Cleaver, and Dod cautioned that "in mariage one
may deale vncleanly by excesse for want of moderation," hence,
offspring are malformed, mentally retarded, or stubborn and ungodly.
Spouses were urged by Rogers to do nothing sexually to wound their
consciences or disrupt the peaceful bond between them. Gravity and
modesty, not lust, are the watchwords used by Estey. Among Anglicans, Sandys urged due regard for nature so that marriage is not
dishonored by "unseemly copulation." Anglicans and Puritans generally failed to follow the lead of Cope, whose exposition of Proverbs
(first published in French in 1557 and English in 1580) expressed a
positive view of marital sex. God, he explained, "hath not onely or-
deined marriage for necessitie: but also for ioy and comfort of the
parties ioyned together in this holy estate, so that it is lawfull vnto
the married folkes to receiue themselues together [i.e. copulate]
with temperance and modestie." Elizabethan religious leaders generally used the theme of moderation but not enjoyment. [52]

Among Elizabethan lay writers, excluding the playwrights and poets,
two views toward marital sex are evident. Tilney's positive outlook

is manifested in his advice to the husband gently to "steale away hir priuate will, and appetite, so that of two bodies there may be made one onelye hart, which she will soone doe, if loue raigne in hir, and without this agreeable concord matrimonie hath but small pleasure, or none at all." In contrast, Hergest inculcated in Sir Thomas Bromley's children the idea that sexual intercourse is intended solely for procreation; his emphasis was placed not on sex but a wife's chastity, which was attained by keeping the covenant of matrimony, having intercourse only with her husband, and keeping her mind and body pure.[53]

Moderation in copulation was reinforced and perhaps influenced by medical thought. Cogan's *Haven of Health* followed Galen in developing the importance, particularly for men, of moderate intercourse. Because semen, like milk from mammary glands, was thought to be produced by the body from blood, periodic diminution was necessary. Moderate evacuation of semen was said to increase the appetite, make the body lighter and nimbler, open pores, purge phlegm, quicken the mind, revive the senses, dispel sadness, anger, and melancholy, and liberate one from lecherous thoughts. On the other hand, excessive copulation weakened the senses. William Vaughan's *Natvrall and Artificial Directions for Health* reiterated Cogan's advice on moderate intercourse, but expanded on the dangers of excess. Too much copulation would reduce strength, impair the brain, extinguish "radicall moisture," and hasten old age and death. Masturbation also was prohibited on medical grounds: "Sperme or seed of generation is the one[l] y comforter of nature: which wilfully shed or lost, harmeth a man more, then if he should bleed fortie times so much."[54]

Thomas Newton's translation of Lemnie's *Touchstone of Complexions* similarly urged moderate intercourse, for excess exhausted vital joices, caused lameness, depleted physical strength, and dulled mental powers. Moreover, it engendered inflammation and gout, and exhausted "that power of the body which serueth to concoct the meate and to couert the same into Blood;" superfluous humors and excrement are produced, which cause disease. Moderate coitus, on the other hand, diminishes excess phlegm and humors. The work of Lemnie and Newton is particularly interesting in their treatment of medical problems associated with sexual abstinence. Women deprived of coitus suffer not only from "vnruly motions of tickling lust," but also from poor complexions and unsteady minds caused by the ascent of a "naughty vapoure" to the brain. Nightly emission derives from sexual abstinence or, in the case of males, earlier lust involving erections but not seminal ejection. Sexual dreams are responsible for the "quaking of the hart, by reason of grosse fumes, which inuade the pannicle or coffin of the hart, . . . and lye heauely vppon the Body pressing it down as though they were night Hegges, or hobgoblins." Clearly, then, the call for moderation in sexual intercourse was supported by contemporary medical opinion.[55]

Cogan and Vaughan also provided recommendations to married couples on the best times to copulate. Following Galen, Cogan suggested that the optimum time was after a period of sleep, and he posited that the best ages for sex were between twenty-five and thirty-five. Vaughan favored intercourse during the winter and spring, when physical desires were strongest, and at night, with a full stomach and a "somewhat" warm body. Unlike Cogan, he recommended that sleep follow copulation, when "it may lenifie the lassitude caused through the action thereof." Religious writers refrained from giving such advice, but Perkins warned that it was contrary to the seventh commandment to engage in sexual relations when a woman was in menstruation.[56]

Evidence of sexual practices among married couples is not plentiful for Elizabethan England, though records of adultery are fairly common. Two pertinent cases are in the records of the archdeacon's court at Oxford for 1584, in which the unwillingness of spouses to engage in sexual intercourse led to legal action. In the first, Meriam Marshe of Steeple Barton, Oxon., testified that she refused to cohabit with her husband because he had "abused her dyvers tymes and did (abowte three yeres agoe) send one John then his man to her bed for to haue lyne with her and dothe continuewallie ever synce abuse her in wordes and calleth her whore and other raylinge wordes so that she cannot lyve in quiet by him." Faced with excommunication, he acknowledged that he and his wife no longer had sexual relations, but the case was dismissed. In a second case, Thomas Paulinge of Standlake, Oxon., was excommunicated for refusing conjugal rights to his wife. An interesting but undated letter in the Lansdowne collection, from a Richard Jacob to his estranged wife, responds to her charges that he refused intercouuse with her and put her away. He retorted that "yt ys an evell byrde that will defile her owne nest," and argued that "yf yowre husbande had mysused you, or were an evell man, yt were yowre honesty & part . . . ferve[n]tly to admonyshe and persuade him to amend & reforme his doinges," not slander him. A different problem was posed by the husband who imposed himself too forcefully on his wife for sexual gratification, although such reports are not common. In 1573 an Essex man was charged with living "so ungodly with his wife that the neighbours are greatly offended." [57]

In widows and widowers who remarried rather late in life, absence of sexual relations may not have been unusual, but in at least one instance it provoked comment. After the death of his first wife in 1596, Henry Lord Berkeley, age c. sixty-two, married Jane, widow of Sir Roger Townshend, age c. sixty-four. "They never bedded togeather that any of their attendants could observe, whereby they might have become one flesh; soe were themselves and their families for most part as farre asunder as Barbican in London, and Callowdon by Coventry: neither medled hee more with her lands or goods, or ought else that was hers, then with her." [58] On the whole, however, the sexual practices of husbands and wives who remained faithful are largely unknown.

Anglicans, Puritans, and Catholics substantially agreed that marital sex was intended for procreation and as a preventive for incontinency, but Protestants were not as extreme as Catholics, who asserted the superiority of perpetual abstinence from sex even for married persons. Elizabethan Protestants, particularly Puritans, developed the idea of moderation in cohabitation, laying a foundation for a more positive view of marital sex, but they failed to pursue Cope's concept of sex for enjoyment. The importance of moderation in copulation was reflected in medical works. Hard evidence of sexual practices in marriage is rare, but a spouse who refused conjugal rights could be cited in ecclesiastical court and excommunicated. Writers of varying religious persuasion favored temporary abstinence from intercourse by mutual consent to pray and fast.

(4) Extra-Marital Sex

> I am a wife,
> Not free, but bound by plighted oath,
> Can loue remaine, where filthy life
> Hath staind the soile, where vertue gro'th?

Henry Willoby[59]

[Adultery] never abounded more in Sodome (so that almost there is not one amongst them [Anglicans] that hath his wife chast or their bed private).

Henry Barrow[60]

Adulterous affairs occurred in two guises, the first of which was a continuation, predominantly among the landed classes, of the double standard, which allowed husbands tacit freedom to enjoy sexual rendezvous with mistresses. The other type of adultery, involving husbands and wives in illicit affairs with lovers, was never accorded tacit social sanction. In theory, religious leaders made no distinction in their attack on adultery, and even in practice the double standard became less acceptable as the age progressed, perhaps partly owing to Puritan influence. Yet the double standard aided the success of the arranged marriage in allowing the husband to find sexual gratification outside the marital bonds. Perhaps the increasing interest of Puritans in matching persons drawn by mutual attraction was part of their campaign against adultery. If the double standard was to be suppressed, greater place had to be accorded to individual choice in marriage.

Signs of the waning of the double standard exist in wills, for peers left bequests to their bastard children until c. 1560, after which instances are rarer. Yet landed persons in Lancashire and Cheshire left legacies to illegitimate offspring throughout the era. Lawrence Stone has determined that between 1560 and 1610 bastards were fathered by the mistresses of one marquis, eight earls, one viscount, and six barons, though the use of mistresses appears to have been more frequent in the early sixteenth century. In his earlier years, Henry VIII provided the cardinal example with Elizabeth Blount and Mary and Anne Boleyn. Elizabeth I sought a refined moral tone for her court, but in the 1590s a more promiscuous atmosphere prevailed, apparently favoring adulterous affairs. Among those involved were Henry Herbert, earl of Pembroke, Robert Devereux, earl of Essex, and Sir Charles Blount. The decline of the double standard created an atmosphere conducive to the more flamboyant adulterous relationship, which elicited a torrent of Puritan criticism of court morality in the years prior to the civil war.[61]

Criticism of the double standard was voiced in Bullinger's tract on marriage, but only indirectly. Despite her spouse's infidelity, a wife was expected by Bullinger to remain faithful and chaste in the face of his "prouocacions." Generally, however, Elizabethan Anglicans did not build on this criticism. Visitation articles regularly inquired about the commission of adultery, but these can hardly be construed as an episcopal attack on the double standard. Grindal appears to have had the double standard in mind when he preached a funeral sermon for the Emperor Ferdinand on 3 October 1564:

For in these days it is to be feared that not only princes, but others of far meaner estate, think unchaste life and the breach of matrimony a thing not only in themselves worthy of no reprehension, but also account others, of like state in power and authority, very fools and dastards, if they of conscience forbear to do the same.

Other Anglican comment on adultery is too general to link to the double standard. John Dios, in a sermon at Paul's Cross in July 1579, likened adulterers to American cannibals, and Babington warned that committing adultery even in ignorance was a grave sin. Turnbull associated adultery with the Anabaptists, depicting them as social libertines. He erroneously accused English Anabaptists of teaching "that a woman may take another man then her husband, her husband being a sleepe: for he is then as dead: and a man may take another woman, and vse her as his owne, his wife being a sleepe, for then and so long, she is dead." Surviving Anglican commentary on adultery is shallow and generalized, and probably had little impact on social behavior.[62]

The general tone of the Puritan attack on adultery is set in the note to Proverbs 6:30 in the Geneva Bible, where adultery is compared to theft, but is found more serious because it is "a perpetual infamie, and death by the Law of God." A companion note to the thirty-fourth verse warned that a man who abused his wife by an adulterous affair sought his own death under natural and divine law. Adultery, as prohibited by the seventh commandment, was believed by Cleaver and Dering to include all provocations, indecent gestures and looks, filthy speech, and idle pastimes. It also condemned those who secretly lusted after neighbors' wives, even though their outward conduct was respectable. Field used the charge of adultery in the propaganda war against Catholics, claiming that "al their Cloisters, Abbeys, and Nunneries, [were] very stewes and brothelhouses."[63]

A common Puritan theme was the adverse influence of adultery on property as well as on spiritual welfare. This idea was expressed in Bullinger's marriage tract; because of adultery, inheritances are altered and heirs disinherited. Among Puritans, Wilcox, Dod, Dent, and Thomas Timme, rector of St. Antholin's Budge Row, London, used variations of this theme against adultery. Wilcox depicted adultery as a form of theft as well as a consumer of goods, a waster of bodies, and a destroyer of reputations. Dod accused an adulterer of being "a theefe for foisting in his child into an other mans lands or goods, that, that which one hath laboured for, and taken paines for, and hoped to leaue to his own seed and his posteritie after him, he should bestow vpon his most mortall foe." Women were castigated by Timme because their adultery altered inheritance rights, shamed husbands, and forced the latter to expend labor and goods to raise another man's children. To warn a woman against such behavior, the governess of Grace Sherrington, future wife of Sir Walter Mildmay's son, Anthony, called her attention to an adulterous couple and composed verses condemning licentious behavior.[64]

A social and moral offense that threatened the sanctity of property provoked an examination of its causes: these were described as idleness, evil company, gluttony, excess in apparel, lewd speech, jealousy, ribald songs, dancing, and unchaste looks, all of which were judged violations of the seventh commandment. Dent asserted that wanton apparel led to adultery because it was "a minstrelsie that pipes vp a daunce vnto whoredome." Idleness and gluttony were conducive to the lust at the root of adultery. In *Thomas of Reading* the London balladeer Thomas Deloney laid some blame on the opportunistic occasions provided by absentee husbands; a wife tells her lover:

> If long he keepe him out of sight,
>   Trang dilly do, trang dilly.
> Be sure thou shalt haue thy delight.

On a more serious note, the anonymous author of *The Interlude of Johan the Evangelist*, which had been popular in England since 1520, pointed an accusing finger at gentlemen who whispered "of maters partaynyng to Uenus actes" in the ears of susceptible young wives, enticing them to adulterous relationships. In contrast to the prevailing explanations of adultery, this attempt to fix the blame on the gentry is unusual.[65]

Some of the surviving records of adultery cases reveal other causative factors. Child marriges may have led to more adultery than later marriages. Depositions in the ecclesiastical court at Chester in 1562 show that the child marriage of Reginald and Jane Downes was unhappy, motivating the husband to contract an adulterous liaison. In the case of Ralph and Katherine Fishe several years later, the wife rejected her childhood husband for a lover. Thomas Bentam, age twelve, had wed Ellen Bolton, age ten, at Ingleton, Yorks., but "she, not fansienge hym, fell to lightnes," and had three illegitimate children by two lovers. Another adultress had an excuse reflecting the religious climate of the age, for she explained that "her grace was no better." In a bizarre adultery case, the High Commission learned of a wife who was unfaithful while her husband, William Nelson, was a prisoner in York castle. In the meantime Nelson sold his wife to a fellow prisoner, the Catholic gentleman Charles Barnby, for £20. Desirous of a divorce, Nelson arranged with the keeper's wife to have Mrs. Nelson closeted with Barnby where the two could have sexual relations while the keeper's wife spied. In Sussex, a husband who wanted to be rid of his wife admitted to adultery so she could marry someone else, though his admission was contrived. Adultery, then, whether real or pretended, might be occasioned by the desire to be rid of an incompatible spouse.[66]

A small number of Elizabethan clergy were adulterers, including Mr. Jurdan, minister at Old Buckenham, Norfolk, and Richard Wood, a royal chaplain and prebendary of St. Paul's (1585-1609) and Westminster (1587-1609). Mr. Hailes, vicar of Witham, Essex, allegedly bribed two men to conceal his adulterous affair and "promised that he would never inveigh against adulterie while he lived, which vow he hath hitherto kept." Geoffrey Heath, the Catholic parson of Oldberrow, Warks., "maried first another mans wife, got a maide with childe, [and] married a third." Some clergy were victims of undeserved slander; George Higgin, the Puritan rector of Eakring, Notts., was accused of adultery in 1599 but defended himself and got his case dismissed. In the case of William Whittingham, dean of Durham, accusations of adultery were "partly proved." The dissolute behavior of adulterous clergy adversely contributed to the credibility of Elizabethan ministers as moral leaders of society.[67]

The most celebrated case of adultery among the laity involved Penelope, wife of Robert, third Lord Rich, and sister of Robert Devereux, earl of Essex. Their marriage had been arranged by Burghley in 1581. Although she had been trained in the Puritan household of Henry Hastings, earl of Huntingdon, by 1589 she had become the mistress of Sir Charles Blount, the future Lord Mountjoy. In October 1589, she bore the first of Sir Charles' six bastard children, all of whom were subsequently acknowledged in his will. Lord Rich tolerated the situation in return for the good will of the earl of Essex. Blount justified his conduct thusly:

A Lady of great Birth and virtue being in the power of her frends, was by them married against her Will unto one against whom she did protest at the very solemnity, and ever after: between whom from the first day there ensued continuall Discord, although the same ffears that forced her to marry constrained her to live with him. Instead of a Comforter he did study in all things to torment Her, and by fear and fraud did practise to deceive her of her Dowry . . . yet as he had not in long time before in the chiefest duty of a Husband used her as his wife, so presently after his [Essex's] death he did put her to a stipend, and abandoned her.

A divorce was finally granted on 14 November 1605, and William Laud married Lady Penelope to Mountjoy on 26 December.[68]

The church apparently was powerless to stop such flagrant examples among the landed classes. Robert Radcliffe, earl of Sussex and earl marshal, kept a gentlewoman attendant of his wife as his mistress and called her his countess, finally forcing the real countess to ask for (and receive) £1700 *p.a.* to live separately with her children. The gentleman Denzil Holles of Irby, Lincs., built a farmhouse for his mistresses. Possessed of "an immoderate love to weomen . . . from which neither the virtues nor fertility of a noble wife could at all reclayme him," he was the subject of a contemporary pasquil:

> Hollys hits in every hole
> And Denzell drives through all their dintes.
> He gets his neighbours wives with fole
> And yet they say the man but mintes [feigns].

Sir Edward Horsey, captain of the Isle of Wight, lived openly with a widow while his wife stayed in France, and the Anglican gentleman Sir Richard Cholmley was "extraordinarily given to the love of women," which diminished his estate. George Clifford, earl of Cumberland, maintained an adulterous relationship for years that finally resulted in a separation from his wife around 1603. Both John Danvers, sheriff of Oxfordshire, and his wife were believed to be adulterers. The physician Simon Forman had numerous adulterous affairs with his patients, including the wife of the royal chaplain, Thomas Blague, though he shied away from prostitutes. The church was not vigorous in its pursuit of influential offenders.[69]

Occasionally, the church acted against adultery in the landed classes. One case involved John Stawell, who cohabited with a gentlewoman while his wife was alive, but the latter took her case to the Court of Arches. When Stawell refused to respond, as he had before the High Commission, Parker committed him to prison, though Burghley and Leicester had intervened on his behalf. Edmund Freke, bishop of Norwich, was once directed by the Privy Council to deal with the wife of a Suffolk gentleman who had had an affair with her husband's servant. The Council was involved in other adultery cases, including one in which a gentleman's wife ran away with another man.[70]

Puritans and Separatists were troubled by the feeble enforcement of provisions against adultery and the inadequate punishments. The Geneva annotators asserted that Jesus had not abrogated the Old Testament law against adultery, and that perpetrators of this offense would be divinely destroyed. Bullinger called for capital punishment for adulterers, a view subsequently adopted by Stubbes, Stockwood, Gifford, and Timme. Dent believed adultery was partly caused by insufficient fear of punishment, and Gilby criticized commissary courts for punishing adulterers lightly. Among the Anglicans, Alexander Nowell called for sharper laws against adultery, but not capital punishment. Sandys thought such punishment was probably necessary, but Dove contended death was too extreme and contrary to the law of Christ, though every kingdom had "Christian libertie" to decide as it pleased.[71]

Among the Separatists, Greenwood and Barrow called for the execution of adulterers, both male and female. Without this penalty, Greenwood argued, adultery flourished, for guilty parties could return to their spouses or divorce and remarry, despite legal provisions to the contrary, if they had ecclesiastical licenses. Greenwood insisted that capital punishment be imposed only by civil magistrates, but he also wanted "a new covenant before the lawes can be executed least all were cut of[f]." Barrow believed that the High Commission was remiss in punishing adulterers, settling for penance in white sheets or mulcting rather than death. His solution was an end to ecclesiastical courts and the punishment of adulterers by civil magistrates.[72]

Penalties for adultery in Elizabethan England were not harsh. Bishops were concerned that offenders be subject to open penance, and they queried how many were winked at or allowed to escape by paying a church official. The usual punishment inflicted in church courts required an offender to appear before the congregation in a white sheet on two or three occasions. At Graveley, Cambs., in 1570, a male offender was forced to "stand iij severall Sundays or holye dayes in the church porch . . . from the second peal to morning prayre untill the readinge of the second lesson, be clothed in a white shete downe to the ground, a white wand in his hand and ij papers with great letters of abhomynable Adultrye, thone uppon his backe and thother uppon his brest." An unbeneficed cleric who committed adultery was fined £3 by an ecclesiastical court at Nottingham in June 1592. Excommunication was imposed in some instances, as in the case of an adulteress at Durham in 1579 who broke her oath not to cease meeting her lover and refused to appear before church authorities.[73]

In fairness to the ecclesiastical courts, adultery was not always provable. A case in point involved John Johnson of Shincliffe, Durham, who was rumored to have been involved in an adulterous affair and was presented by a churchwarden in June 1600. The case dragged out nearly a year, and was handled in nine different court sessions at

Durham. At first Johnson refused to appear and was threatened with excommunication. In court he denied the accusations, but the prosecution got nine persons to swear to the general belief in his adultery. The accused repudiated the charges on his oath *ex officio* and produced four neighbors who attested to his innocence. This compurgation resulted in acquittal, but he paid court costs of £1 3s. 4d. [74]

Difficulty of proof also figured prominently in a notorious London case in 1586, in which an irate minister was dissatisfied with previous legal action. The offending adulterer had to stand before the preacher at St. Paul's in the customary white sheet, holding a rod approximately eighteen inches long, and wearing a paper on his head inscribed with his offense. For five years, he had engaged in adultery with his maid, who bore him several children, each of whom she murdered. She was executed, but her master and lover was acquitted. He nevertheless was required to confess publicly by the minister, repeating a written confession after the clergyman. The preacher then commended the harsher treatment of adulterers in other states, noting such punishments as requiring a man to be stripped naked in public and given a thousand lashes, cutting off an adulteress' nose, allowing a victimized husband to strip his wife in public and whip her through the streets, and stoning the guilty to death. The preacher's identity is not recorded, but his views reflect Puritan concerns. [75]

Punishment also varied among secular authorities. A convicted adulterer on Guernsey appealed to the Privy Council for remission of corporal punishment on grounds of age in return for public acknowledgment in church. When two gentlewomen were imprisoned in the Fleet for adultery and prostitution and then whipped, Elizabeth was so incensed at the aldermen responsible that they were incarcerated and fined £2,000.

The gentry had to do more than commit adultery before secular authorities sanctioned more than token punishment. A case in point occurred in 1600 involving Mrs. Fowler, wife of a gentleman and "as infamous allmost as Mall Neubery" for her dissolute behavior. She was sexually involved with Captain William Haynes, an ex-servant, who "insinuated [himself] so far into her famyliarytye as at euery inn and alehouse they grewe bed fellowes." The couple unsuccessfully accused her husband of treason, and Star Chamber finally sent her to Bridewell and sentenced Haynes to be "nayled on the pylory," fined £200, and perpetually imprisoned. In this instance, it was not adultery that resulted in stiff punishment but perjury in connection with charges of treason. [76]

The controversy over proper punishment for adulterers was evident in the House of Commons in 1601, when a bill to suppress adultery received a first reading. The bill stipulated that a convicted male would lose his "Tenancy by Courtesie, and she her Tenancy in Dower." Serjeant Thomas Harris, an experienced defender of Anglican and royal conservatism, led the opposition to the bill, partly on the grounds that the determination of adultery rested on "two or three blind Witnesses" in an ecclesiastical court. He wanted no ecclesiastical judges exercising a voice in matters of lay inheritances; he pointed out that such punishment would not affect the poor, who possessed only personal goods. "But if the Woman be taken she is to lose the third of the Goods, or if it be in the City by Custom she loseth the half, which is *jus inaequale*, and not to be admitted by this House." The majority agreed, and this poorly conceived bill, probably Puritan-inspired, never received a second reading.[77] The episode reflects the unwillingness of the propertied classes to sanction severe punishment for a moral offense that was enmeshed in ecclesiastical jurisdiction. White sheets, public acknowledgments, and even excommunication were safe enough to trust to church courts; life and property were not.

In sum, no religious leaders approved of adultery, but Puritans and Separatists were more forceful in attacking it than were Anglicans. This difference is evident in their calls for the imposition of capital punishment for adultery, a penalty some Anglicans opposed. To attack adultery was to undermine the arranged marriage, which was bolstered by the double standard. To condemn adulterers to death or to impose stringent penalties, as proposed in the Commons in 1601, was too severe for a society that tolerated mistresses; such penalties would vest too much power in ecclesiastical authorities, even if they were carried out by civil magistrates. Thus the landed aristocracy in particular could continue, if they wished, adulterous relationships with relatively little to fear from temporal punishment.

(5) Birth Control and Family Size

Sir Thomas Norris lady was lately brought abed there [Ireland] of three daughters, which the Lord Norris imputes to the fertilitie of the soyle, and exemplifies yt by a mare he sent two yeares ago to his sonne Thomas that brought two foales.

John Chamberlain[78]

There is some fertile planet abrode that layes downe our Ladies so fast.

John Chamberlain[79]

In Elizabethan society, birth control was discussed primarily in medical works, a number of which were intended for lay readers. Guidance on birth control from religious leaders, at least in print, was rare. Robert Schnucker argues that five fundamental beliefs of the Puritans led them to reject methods of birth control. These beliefs were the biblical command to be fruitful and multiply, for this injunction referred to those born in the divine image; the acceptance of children as a blessing from God; the need to increase the elect through procreation; the maintenance of legitimate succession within the commonwealth and body of Christ; and the recovery of a woman's honor through childbirth. [80] With the possible exception of the third principle, however, Anglicans subscribed to the same ideas. Empirical evidence is therefore necessary to determine whether either group was reluctant to use birth control techniques.

Catholics made a greater effort to state the church's teaching on this subject. Before the sixteenth century, some Catholics accepted *amplexus reservatus* (or *coitus reservatus*)—withdrawal of the penis prior to ejaculation in the vagina, followed by the inhibition of ejaculation—by mutual agreement of husband and wife in cases of poverty. In the sixteenth century, economic pressures were considered justification for a unilateral decision to practice this form of birth control. *Coitus interruptus*, involving ejaculation outside the vagina, was considered an unnatural act. Before and during the sixteenth century, Catholics allowed the use of anaphrodisiacs to reduce sexual drives; this too was a form of birth control. The Roman Catechism of 1566, however, regarded the use of medicines to impede conception or abort birth as homicide, but *coitus interruptus* was not so categorized. The papal bull of Sixtus V, *Effraenatam* (29 October 1588), amplified this position:

Who does not abhor the lustful cruelty or cruel lust of impious men, a lust which goes so far that they procure poisons to extinguish and destroy the conceived fetus within the womb, even attempting by a wicked crime to destroy their own offspring before it lives, or if it lives to kill it before it is born? Who, then, would not condemn with the most severe punishments the crimes of those who by poisons, potions, and *maleficia* induce sterility in women, or impede by cursed medicines their conceiving or bearing?

The prevailing theological view among Catholics in the sixteenth century was that the sexual act was generative by nature, and attempts to frustrate semination were mortal sin, as asserted, for example, by Thomas de Vio, Cardinal Cajetan. Yet neither in public preaching nor in catechetical works was much said about contraception, leaving the possibility that the principal vehicle for the dissemination of the church's views on birth control was the confessional. This silence makes it a distinct possibility that English Catholics, often deprived of regular confession, took advantage of birth control techniques set forth in medical works. Yet from 1574 on, at least some Catholics possessed Vaux's catechism, in which any who made themselves or others barren were condemned.[81]

Generally, Protestants in search of nonmedical advice had to be content with recommendations to reduce sexual desire by moderate diet, the avoidance of wine and strong drink, good company, moderate sleep, respectful speech, the eschewal of provocative books and pictures, the reading of Scripture, prayer, and fasting. Calvin had opposed *coitus interruptus* on the grounds that this killed a child before birth, but this view was not developed by Elizabethan Protestants. Late in the period, the Puritan William Vaughan, who was studying civil law at Oxford, combined practical, spiritual, and medical advice for the diminution of sexual drives. Ostensibly for the unwed, his recommendations could be adapted by married persons. He advised refraining from wine, sexual fantasies, and down beds; reading the Bible and moral philosophy; exercising; and using "the seede of *Agnus castus*, in English Park seede," which produced "a straunge effect."[82]

To avoid procreation, Elizabethans had a choice of abstinence (especially through spiritual and dietary aids), *coitus interruptus*, magical charms to prevent conception, or potions and other preventives discussed in medical works. Publication of such works were frequent in the Elizabethan age, averaging three or four each year. Yet some authors, such as Leonard Mascall and Andrew Boorde, believed medicine pertained only to specialists, hence they opposed the publication of medical works in English for the layman. Moreover, not all books for the layman provided advice on birth control; Moulton's *This Is the Myrrour or Glass of Healthe* [c. 1565], for example, did not. Herbals, including the famous one by John Gerard, were another source of information on contraception. Two Puritan women who presumably had such information were Lady Grace Mildmay, who left books of medical prescriptions at her death in 1617, and Lady Margaret Hoby, who read an herbal. Lady Grace had only one child and Lady Margaret none.[83]

In the area of reproduction, medical works addressed two and sometimes three concerns: the prevention of unwanted pregnancies, sometimes discussing abortion for those who failed; methods to increase the possibility of conception and the causes of sterility; and sometimes explanations, based loosely on Aristotle, of the relation of sexual functions to physical properties. In the last-named area, the 1561 edition of Sir Thomas Eliot's *The Castel of Health* provides a typical example. Those with hot, distempered genitals were said to have strong sexual appetites and a propensity to procreate male children; cold, distempered genitals meant little sexual appetite and the likelihood of female offspring; moist, distempered genitals indicated ample but watery sperm; dry, distempered genitals were a sign of scarce but thick sperm, and so forth. Elaboration of such theories is found in the works of Levine Lemnie (translated by Newton) and Philip Barrough. [84]

Explanations for infertility were based on theories concerning the relation of physical properties to sexual functions. Lemnie and Newton contended that female infertility was caused by an absence of heat and a "slippery" womb. In men they attributed the cause to physical immaturity due to early marriages, leaving the sperm too cold and thin. Barrough attributed male sterility to sperm which was excessively hot, cold, watery, or thick, "or because the men be halfe geldings, and haue a very short yard, so that they can not caste their seede into the innermost place of the matrice, which also sometime chaunceth through much fatnesse." Obesity was judged a cause of female sterility, as was a matrix that was excessively hot, or cold and moist, or dry and filthy. Barrough thought women who were too lean could not conceive or were prone to miscarriages. The shape of the womb also was believed to be an influence in conception, with women who had straight, short, blocked, or scarred wombs unlikely to conceive. Barrough also suggested that unwilling coitis, particularly in the absence of love, was unlikely to result in conception. Age too was a factor, with the preferred minimum being thirty for the male and twenty for the female. A woman's physical shape was significant for successful conception, "for a woman that is fertile, ought to haue a moderate stature and height of the bodie, breadth of the loynes & the share, buttockes sticking out, a handsome and conuenient greatnesse of the belly, a straight breast and large pappes." [85]

Various remedies are suggested in the medical works to induce conception. Most of these were intended for the male, though females were counseled to use mandrake, a narcotic sometimes utilized in witchcraft, or drink three ounces of the water of the "garden claree" three times daily, which removes "the payne of womens places, and prepareth them apt to conceiue." Another option was to anoint the male genitals with distilled resin or gum before intercourse, which was supposed to render the female more fit for conception and end sterility.[86]

For men, a variety of oral remedies was suggested to increase sperm. Among these were such potions as powdered nettle seed drunk in wine or broth; mercury or asparagus syrup; the stalk of the "Clote Burre," peeled and eaten raw with salt and pepper or boiled in meat broth; the root of the plant *Callamus odoratus* mixed with sage and wine; and the powdered seed of the ash tree mixed with nutmeg and drunk in a liquid. A host of plants, oils, and spices was believed to increase sperm; they included almond oil, anise seed, rocket, mustard seed, garden cress, cotton seed, asparagus, pine nuts, chich (chick-pea), sesamum oil, sea or prickwillow, and "kitkeies" (the fruit of the ash tree). Men experiencing difficulty producing erections were to try bastard parsley or the dried and powdered testicles of a fox drunk in liquid. Barrough suggested that they "exercise the neather partes, and . . . vse meates that do heate and engender good humours," such as hens, capons, partriches, pheasants, young doves, and sparrows, or other foods similar in value, including beans, leeks, parsnips, almonds, and scallions. Behind these dietary suggestions was the thesis that flatulence-inducing foods provoke sexual desires. Besides remedies proposed specifically to increase sperm or induce erection, suggestions were made for the more general problem of moving "a man to haue great deuocion, to praie in Uenus temple, or to be Uenerus." It was recommended that his sexual desires be increased by pistachio nuts, parsnips, pineapple seeds, cloves, ginger, anise seed, cinnamon, garlic, rocket, leeks, cress, partrich eggs, artichokes, saffron, wild carrot roots, nettle seed, buttered sunflower buds (with pepper and vinegar), and numerous other plants. Genital ointments to increase heat were advised, as were soft beds and sexually stimulating books and pictures. Thus, besides the Elizabethan interest in contraceptives was the concomitant existence of, and presumably the demand for, medical recommendations to induce erection and conception.[87]

To prevent conception, Elizabethans could select pessaries, genital baths, bloodletting, or oral contraceptives (including vomits and laxatives). Pessaries for insertion into the vagina were composed of a blend of castoreum, rue, and the ground roots of lilies and nenuphar, or alternatively of bitter almonds blanched and ground. Uterine clysters or douches also were used. Genital baths were believed effective to diminish sexual desires and desensitize the genitals to avoid erection or orgasm. The physician William Bullein proposed anointing the penis and testicles with a compound of camphor, vinegar, water lilies, and nightshade. Humphrey Lloyd's translation of John XXI's *The Treasvry of Health,* first published in English c. 1550, suggested several genital baths: the juice of water lentils; a mixture of opium, mandrake, and henbane seed in a solution of wax and oil; vinegar and the juice of nightshade and sengreen; camphor oil; henbane juice; or bean flower in the form of a plaster. Bloodletting was based on the theory that sperm was produced from blood made white by the heat humor. Decreasing the quality or quantity of blood would thus adversely affect the production of sperm.[88]

Oral contraceptives, including vomits and laxatives, were intended to reduce sexual desire or the quantity of sperm. Caution was necessary because the same ingredient might work differently on men and women. "Thyme, Rue, & many others that be very hoat & dry, quench and take away in men all desire of carnall lust, because they waste the generatiue humour, whereas women therby are much prouoked, & stirred to venery, by enforcing heat into theyr secret parts & priuities." Other oral contraceptives thought to suppress sexual desires were the broth or conserves of lentils and water lilies, coriander seeds, purslane, endive, chicory, lettuce seed (in large quantities), flowers of willow and poplar trees, angelica, camphor, and muskmelon. Lightly washed lettuce served with salad oil, vinegar, and sugar was also thought to reduce physical desire. For pregnant women, Gerard's *Herball* advised harsh, unripe wine for the same purpose. Women could quench lust by a potion of chicory and betony in vinegar, or by eating wild or unripe grapes, or the branches of a grape vine; applying the grape leaves externally was deemed useful. To reduce sperm in the male, the prescriptions included lettuce or hemp seed, the root or seed of water lilies, rue, pepper, castor oil, and calamint. Barrough recommended water in which smiths had cooled hot iron. There were warnings, however, that continued use of certain contraceptives could produce premanent sterility. Among these were spleenwort, honeysuckle water, calamint, and the seed of white violets.[89]

Advice on abortion was provided in some medical works. Abortifacients came in the form of pessaries to induce vaginal bleeding and flush out the foetus, or oral medicines to cause violent vomiting or bowel movements. Such advice was regularly in the form of cures for removing a dead foetus. Bullein discussed the herb savine as an abortifacient, but he opposed aborting a live foetus and cautioned that this herb could kill the mother. Among the recommended abortifacients were pessaries made of nettle leaves or camomile in water;

kernels of sour pomegranates could also be used. *The Treasvry of Health* urged that abortions be limited to the period from the fourth to the seventh month, and suggested bloodletting to kill a foetus. Although such advice came in a work attributed to John XXI, Vaux's catechism warned English Catholics against abortion. The use of medicines or other means to kill a foetus was condemned as a violation of the fifth commandment. Elizabethan Protestant leaders, however, generally avoided the question of abortion. The most extreme alternative was infanticide, but this left the guilty party confronting legal penalties. The jurist William Lambarde imprisoned a mother who killed her child on the day of its birth in 1586.[90]

Childbearing was dangerous and painful, and surely not all Elizabethan women found solace in regarding the experience as retribution for Eve's sin. Yet the preachers continued to use this explanation. In 1590, the gentlewoman Elizabeth Savile was informed by the Puritan minister Christopher Hooke that "the multiplying of your paines in the conception & bringing foorth [of a child], it proceeded of the curse of God [in Genesis 3:16], the deliuerance from those paines, that therein you perish not, it is of the great mercie of God." R. C. Richardson plausibly suggests that the dangers of childbearing prompted some women to take a serious interest in religious matters. In one Northumberland region, childbearing was important enough to be the subject of local legislation: In 1592 the manorial court of Seaton Delaval ordered that "every mann's wife within this lordship shall, within half ane howre after warning, presentlie repaire and go to every woman laboring of child, if they be thereto called and invited, *sub pena* xij^d." Childbirth was so dangerous in this era that Lawrence Stone calculates that the chance of a wife's dying in the first fifteen years of marriage was more than twice that of her spouse; nearly one in four childbirths ended in the mother's death. Some women who defied these odds ultimately became victims: Anne, wife of the London alderman Richard Malory, died in childbed in 1560 with her seventeenth child, and Joan, wife of the London poulterer and alderman William Allen died in childbed the same year with her ninth child. Multiple births increased the peril, as in the case of a London poulterer's wife who died in 1575 after giving birth to quadruplets.[91]

Women who survived childbirth were confronted with the strong possibility that the baby would die. In the rural parishes of North Shropshire in the period 1561 to 1610, 6.2% of the infants died within one month of christening, and 10.9% within the first year. If Wallace Notestein is correct, two-thirds of the children (counting stillbirths) were lost before they reached four years of age. This figure probably errs on the high side, but it is not difficult to discover women such as Mary, wife of Sir Thomas Ro, lord mayor of London, who lost five of her eleven children. Information on contraceptives was desirable for women who did not wish to continue bearing offspring until their early forties. In the parish of Colyton, Devon, in the period 1560 to 1646 the mean ages at which women bore their last child was 39.8 (for women marrying before the age of thirty) and 40.5 (for those marrying from age thirty on). During this period a woman typically gave birth approximately every twenty-eight months. The mean birth interval for Colyton (1560-1646) is 27.5 months, and for Sheldon, Solihull, and Yardley in the Forest of Arden (1575-1624), 28.6 months. Some women had birth intervals far smaller than this. John Donne's wife bore twelve children in sixteen years (and died at the age of thirty-three); the wife of the London turner John Wallington, Sr., had twelve in eighteen years; Justice Bramston's wife had ten in twelve years; and Sir Peter Young's twelve in twelve years (including three sets of twins). Mary Honeywood of Charing, Kent, a correspondent of Dering, reputedly amassed a total of 367 children and grandchildren before she died at the age of ninety-three.[92]

There was thus motive and opportunity for birth control techniques. Determining whether or not they were used is difficult, and requires data on family size. In the parish of Colyton, Devon, the mean completed family size (based on family reconstitution) for the period 1560 to 1629 was 7.3 for brides married by the age of twenty-four, 5.7 for those wed between ages twenty-five and twenty-nine, and 2.7 for those married in their thirties. These figures are only for women still living at age 45 whose husbands were alive. Figures for (unreconstituted) average family sizes indicate significant class variations, though partly owing to inferior nutrition and living conditions among the lower orders. An Elizabethan census of some 450 poor families with children in Norwich showed only 2.2 children per household, yet substantial merchants in Norwich and Exeter averaged 4.25 and 4.7 children per household. In 1599 the average family size in Ealing was 4.75. Stone's figures for peers between 1540 and 1659 indicate an average family size per fertile marriage of 5.08, and this figure would be larger if it included children who died in infancy. Moreover, Stone, following Hollingsworth, has found that between 1580 and 1630, children of peers produced 50% more children per generation than the lower social orders. Watts' study of Northumberland gentry c. 1615 resulted in a corrected figure of 5.66 children per fertile marriage, further underscoring the fact that the peerage and gentry tended to have the largest families. Several factors account for this finding, including differences in infant mortality; and the adverse effect of lactation on fertility. The tendency of the upper classes to use wet nurses increased their capability for larger families, but poorer mothers tended to breast feed their infants for up to two years.[93]

These figures make no attempt to discriminate along religious lines. It is, however, possible to compare average family sizes of selected religious groups to judge whether or not birth control techniques were used. Schnucker's study of forty Puritan clergy between 1560 and 1640 determined that they fathered 272 children. Omitting the five who were childless, the average number of children per family was 7.8 (or 6.8 if childless marriages are included). On this evidence, Schnucker suggests that Puritans tended not to use birth control techniques.[94] A smaller sample, restricted to Elizabethan Puritans, results in a figure of 5.8 children per fertile marriage. If Andrew Willett, father of eighteen children, is added to the group (as Schnucker did), the mean size is 6.6, though Willett's religious persuasions are a matter of dispute. A sampling of forty Anglican clergy in the Elizabethan period with fertile first marriages shows a total of 229 children, or a mean size of 5.7 (omitting children by second marriages). As in the case of Stone's figures for the peerage, these statistics (and presumably Schnucker's) omit most children who died in infancy, and therefore err on the low side. Included in the sample of Anglican clergy is one minister, Adam Loftus, who sired twenty children, eight of whom died in infancy. Removing him from the sample leaves a mean figure of 5.4. Although the difference of 5.8 for Puritans and 5.4 for Anglicans is minimal, particularly with such a small base, it suggests that Puritan clergy in the Elizabethan era had families slightly larger than their Anglican counterparts, which may be due to a greater unwillingness by Puritans to use contraceptive measures. Certainly the Puritan Thomas Becon argued that the ideal situation was for parents to have many children.[95]

Whether or not religious reticence toward contraceptives influenced the laity can be tentatively determined by comparing the number of children born to Catholic, Anglican, and Puritan gentry families. A sample of forty-two gentlemen from ten counties (especially Sussex and Northumberland) who were Catholics or suspected Catholics produced a total of 222 children in fertile first marriages, or an average of 5.3. A comparable sample of 37 Anglican gentry from at least fourteen counties showed a total of 202 children in fertile first marriages, or an average of 5.5. For Puritans, a sample of 21 gentlemen from at least half a dozen counties showed a total of 113 children, or an average of 5.4 per fertile first marriage. There is no meaningful difference by religious grouping. Watts' research for Northumberland gentry c. 1615 reveals 379 children born to 76 fertile first marriages, for an average of 4.99. (His corrected figure of 5.66 takes into account girls whose births he suspects were not recorded.)[96] In the case of the gentry, the similarity of family sizes does not suggest that the laity were influenced by differences in religious teaching on birth control.

Because of the effect of lactation on fertility, some attention is necessary to attitudes toward breast-feeding. Few Anglicans comment on the subject, but a note to Genesis 21:7 in the Bishops' Bible makes it the mother's duty, if she is physically able, to nurse her child. Babington's commentary on this passage agrees on the grounds that breast-feeding is a natural act, and that using a wet nurse endangers a child through disease, "ill qualitie," and unsatisfactory growth. Puritan writers similarly urged breast-feeding. Not to do so was, according to Smith and Cleaver, a violation of natural and divine law. Perkins made refusal an infringement of the fifth commandment and deriliction of duty to one's inferior. Puritans used Genesis 21:7 to support their position, but Dod buttressed this interpretation with the example of the early church. "For in the primitiue Church, when widows were to be chosen that should haue the sicke and weake seruants committed to their charge and tending, none were to be admitted to this office, but those that had nourced their children themselues." Those who use wet nurses unnecessarily are warned that their children are subject to infirmities in the bodies or minds of the nurses, and the mothers become ill for failing to use their milk properly. Recourse to a wet nurse is likened to hatching a cuckoo in a sparrow's nest. Smith, in a passage repeated by Cleaver, found it odd that dry breasts primarily afflicted the wealthy: "Forsooth it is like the Gowte, no beggers may haue it, but Citizens or Gentlewomen." Although they realized that some women lacked the ability to breast-feed, following Hosea 9 they judged this a divine curse and urged fasting and prayer to remove it.[97]

Generally the landed classes preferred wet nurses, despite the views of religious leaders and earlier humanists such as Erasmus and Sir Thomas More. There were exceptions, including Henry Percy, earl of Northumberland, who advocated breast-feeding in 1596 on grounds of the infant's health. Simonds D'Ewes' mother Cecilia, decided against a wet nurse in 1602 after the midwife injured his eye at birth, but she breast-fed him only twenty weeks.

In practice, the principal objections to breast-feeding were sore nipples, inability to produce milk, underdeveloped breasts, insufficient knowledge of the technique, hinderance to employment, inconvenience and messiness, and increased aging and sagging breasts. Those who did breast-feed were cautioned to avoid sexual relations on the grounds that they would spoil a mother's milk and in fear that a new pregnancy would cut off the milk and starve the infant. When wetnurses were used, fathers endeavored to prohibit the nurses' husbands from copulating with their wives.[98]

It is likely that the Puritans and some Anglican clergy had their wives breast-feed their children. If so, this lactation reduced fertility. It is therefore striking that the average number of children in fertile first marriages involving Anglican and Puritan ministers is relatively high—5.8 for Puritans and 5.4 for Anglicans. Peerage and gentry families averaged five to six children per fertile first marriage, but here the greater fertility could have been due to the use of wet nurses. Moreover, the landed classes tended to marry earlier than the clergy, who normally completed their schooling first, so the former had a longer period in which to procreate. Presumably, therefore, Anglican and especially Puritan clergy often chose not to use contraceptive measures, yet their views in this regard, like those on breast-feeding, were not widely accepted among the landed classes, regardless of religious persuasion.

In the area of sexual concerns, then, certain differences between Anglicans and Puritans are apparent. Both groups agreed on the spiritual and social dangers of fornication, but Anglicans were less inclined to condemn prenuptial sex by affianced persons.[99] Again, both groups found bastardy, prostitution, sodomy, incest, and rape unacceptable, socially as well as morally, though Puritans devoted more attention to these social ills in their writings than did Anglicans. As for prostitution, Anglicans were concerned primarily with social ramifications, whereas Puritans were equally concerned with the moral aspects. For married persons, neither Anglicans nor Puritans agreed with Catholics that perpetual abstinence from sexual relations was the preferred estate. Puritans, in fact, led the way in advocating moderate intercourse—a view supported in contemporary medical works. Sex outside marriage was not acceptable, but Puritans and Separatists distinguished themselves by demanding capital punishment for adulterers, which Anglicans generally opposed. Puritan attempts to impose such a penalty or harsh property exactions were defeated in the Elizabethan era. Birth control techniques apparently were largely unused by Puritan clergy and probably Anglican clergy as well, though the latter appear to have had slightly smaller families. Although Anglican and Puritan clergy favored breast-feeding, which curtailed fertility, their mean family sizes per fertile first marriages were comparable to the size of peerage and gentry families, where the use of wet nurses was normal and earlier ages of marriage resulted in longer periods of potential procreation. Use of birth control techniques therefore appears to have been more common among the gentry and peerage than among the clergy.[100] Among the gentry alone, no appreciable difference has been found in mean family size per fertile first marriages between Anglicans, Catholics, and Puritans, suggesting that in the area of birth control the laity deviated from the ideals of their religious leaders.

Part III: The Family and Education

CHAPTER *6*

Married Life and Parenthood

Elizabethan authors wrote prolifically about the relations of husbands and wives, their parental responsibilities, and the duties of children to elders. Their opinions were significant not only for the domestic scene but also for the political and social order, for the role of the husband and father often was cited as parallel with that of the prince. This ideological comparison, coupled with the reliance of the Tudor sovereigns on the head of the family to maintain order in the absence of a traditional police force, underscored the importance of marital and parental relations. These considerations weighed as well in the questions of annulment and separation. When Catholic dogma and authority were being challenged on a wide scale, it was perhaps inevitable that medieval views on the indissolubility of marriage would be queried as well, as the Puritans did in theory and various Elizabethans did in practice. A related issue is the parental obligation of christening, another of the principal pageants that reinforced the social order.

(1) Marital Responsibilities

They must think that they are like two birds, the one is a Cock, and the other is a Dam: the Cocke flieth abroad to bring in, the Dam sitteth vpon the nest to keepe al at home.

Henry Smith [1]

A merry fellow hearing a Preacher say in his sermon: and whosouer would be saued, must take vp, and beare his crosse: ran straight to his wife, & cast her vpon his back.

Leonard Wright[2]

The appropriate relationship between spouses, particularly their mutual responsibilities and the husband's authority, received considerable attention in Elizabethan writings, reflecting not only interest in this topic but also the clergy's desire to regain the control over family relations lost when Protestantism ended the resort to the confessional. Interest is manifested in the biblical marginalia as early as Tyndale's 1534 Pentateuch and New Testament. Genesis 3 was used to underscore male governance as due to the curse laid on women for Eve's disobedience. For Tyndale, wives must obey their husbands even if the latter are unbelievers, and dress in a manner compatible with godliness. Husbands must patiently bear their wives' weaknesses "and lyue accordinge to knowledge with them," that is, govern them in accordance with biblical precepts. This patronizing tone was softened by Tyndale's exhortation to both sexes to treat each other with courtesy, patience, and friendship. The Tyndale-Coverdale New Testament published four years later reiterated the wife's obedience to her husband, and dealt with the problem of mixed marriages by allowing a Christian (Protestant) husband to live normally with his wife and bear children. The general tone of female subjection expressed in these early Scriptures (including the 1538 Tyndale-Rogers New Testament, the 1539 Taverner Bible, and the 1549 Tyndale New Testament) remained dominant the rest of the Tudor age. It received classic expression in the note to 1 Peter 3 in the 1540 Matthew Bible, which admonished the husband of a disobedient woman "to beate the feare of God into her heade" until she performed her duty.[3]

No Tudor Bible devoted as much attention to the husband-wife relationship as the Geneva Bible, which foreshadowed the keen Puritan interest in this subject. The tension in Puritanism on the nature of the marital relationship is initially expressed in the Geneva marginalia. On the one hand, marriage is a covenantal relationship in which the spouses are companions and virtual equals, for a spouse is "the one halfe of thy selfe." It is a relationship properly characterized by mutual love and benevolence, and though the wife is the weaker vessel, both are fellow heirs of eternal life. The use of Pauline and Petrine imagery in this manner enabled the annotators to depict marriage as a partnership. On the other hand, greater emphasis was given to the biblical theme that the wife must be subordinate to the husband. The male is seen as the image of divine majesty and power, but the female receives her glory only in subjection to him. Covering her head is a sign of such subjugation. The disobedience of the Persian queen Vashti to her husband was condemned, and wives were exhorted to obey and do nothing without their husbands' consent. "Willingly do your duetie: for your condicion is not ye worse for your obedience."[4]

The Geneva annotators elucidated the duties of wives and husbands. In addition to obedience, the wife must profit her family and perform her household duties. She must love her husband and children, be discreet and chaste, not allow the Bible to be mentioned in evil terms, remain at home, and speak in an edifying, scriptural manner. The husband was expected to teach his wife the fear of God, and to nourish, govern, and defend her. She must not be governed too strictly, but neither is she to receive excessive liberty, for the husband is accountable to God for her actions. The man must stay within proper bounds, be sober in mind, bridle his affections, and realize that his first obligation is to his wife rather than his parents. Marital dissension must be avoided as an impediment to prayer. These obligations were widely accepted in Elizabethan society, at least in the more devout families.[5]

In comparison with the Geneva Bible, the Bishops' Bible had little to say on marital responsibility. The husband was depicted as the wife's schoolmaster, and she was placed in subjection to him. His principal responsibility was to love her, and he was cautioned not to desire other women.[6]

The Beza-Tomson marginalia point up the Pauline analogy of the married couple to Christ and the church. In the order of creation, the woman was viewed as one degree lower than the man, with the latter being subject to Christ in such a manner that "the glory of God ought to appear in him for the preeminence of the sexe." Ironically, spiritual equality was undermined by the attribution to the husband of a special relationship with Christ in their respective headships over wife and church. Man was created so that divine glory could appear in this marital governorship, whereas woman—spiritually inferior by implication—was made to honor her husband through her obedience. The Beza-Tomson Bible explicitly stated that a woman who defied her husband disobeyed God, the author of her subjugation. The justice of this inferior status was explained by reference to the woman's economic dependence as well as her "fearefull" nature. Female subjection was deemed especially necessary if the husband was not a

Christian, for a chaste and obedient wife might persuade him to convert.[7]

Having laid a foundation of male supremacy, bolstered by the Pauline analogy of spiritual kinship between Christ and the husband, the Beza-Tomson notes give special attention to the husband's responsibilities. Lest he misappropriate his authority, he must treat his spouse in such a manner that "mutuall coniunction may be cherished," though this is no union of equals. He must love her as Christ loves his church and treat her gently as the weaker creature, though her "vses" are more excellent than her husband's. Presumably this statement is an implicit reference to her role as a mother. The husband must be patient with his spouse and handle her with circumspection. As in the Geneva Bible, there is an admonition not to brawl and chide because of the negative influence of such behavior on prayer and religious service. Unlike the Geneva Bible, neither the Beza-Tomson Bible nor the Bishops' Bible moderates male supremacy in the direction of a mutual partnership.[8]

In the Rheims New Testament, the annotators took a similarly conservative position, characterized by insistence that the wife's proper role is one of silence and subjection. Women are deemed especially susceptible, owing to their frailty, to heretics, hence women must refrain from teaching or religious disputation. In refuting this note, the Puritan William Fulke advocated the right of wives to instruct their families privately, and recalled that women had been effective in the past in achieving the divine purpose. The Rheims annotators, reflecting their view of the inferiority of the marital to the celibate state, exhorted husbands to live moderately and if possible refrain from sexual relations to be better prepared for meditation. The Catholic position on marital relationships was thus firmly Pauline and conservative.[9]

The strong interest shown by biblical annotators in the roles of husbands and wives was equalled in the religious literature of Elizabethan England. Female inferiority was explained as punitive, purposive, or natural. Punitive explanations focused on Eve's transgression in Eden, where she was accused (by Cooper) of having "lightly giuen place to the lying allurement of the Serpent, thereby to Satisfie hir owne lust and affection." Babington emphasized that she had done this without her husband's knowledge, hence all wives must be ruled by their spouses. Eve, however, found some defenders among Elizabethans who sought to elevate the status of women. Edward More, Sir Thomas' grandson, made his point in doggerel:

And yf that he [the serpent] to Adam fyrst, had cum, no
   dowt he myght
Haue tempted hym as well as Eue.

In kindred manner, the Puritan poet Nicholas Breton, whose patroness was Mary Herbert, countess of Pembroke, blamed the serpent for the deceit usually attributed to Eve, and judged that Adam deceived himself.[10]

Purposive explanations for female subordination pointed to Eve's derivative creation and her role as a helper. Hooker, commenting on this role in propagation, observed that it could not transpire "unless there were subalternation between them, which subalternation is naturally grounded upon inequality, because things equal in every respect are never willingly directed one by another." Despite the prevalence of this view, a few writers mitigated the significance of derivative creation. Gibbens, for one, noted that Eve was created of a nobler substance (flesh) than Adam (dust) so that she should not be despised. Eve's creation from Adam's rib did not therefore justify authority over her. Cleaver theorized that Eve had not been created out of Adam's head, and thus was not equal in authority with him, nor had she been formed out of his foot, fit to be despised and downtrodden. Rather she had been made from his rib in order to walk jointly with him even while obeying his government. A manuscript in the Lansdowne collection by Henry Howard, earl of Northampton, refuting John Knox's *First Blast of the Trumpet*, insisted that Eve had not been subordinate to Adam when she was created, for God had not required her to render homage to Adam.[11]

Natural explanations for female inferiority were based on a differentiation in the respective natures of the sexes. Charles and Katherine George sought but failed to find the quality of this female weakness, though it is concisely expressed in Sir Thomas Smith's *De repvblica Anglorvm*:

So nature hath forged ech parte to his office, the man sterne, strong, bould, aduenterous, negligent of his bewtie, & spending. The woman weake, fearefull, faire, curious of her bewtie, and sauing.

Male superiority was thought by Tilney to rest on divine and human laws, and the natural factors of the man's skill, experience, comprehension, wisdom, strength, solicitude, patience, means to sustain, and courage. Hooker pointed to the delivery of the bride to the groom by her father in the wedding ceremony as a reminder of the "imbecility" of her sex, which required her to be perpetually governed by others. An attempt was made in Newton's translation of Lemnie's *Touchstone* to find anatomical evidence of male superiority: "That heate . . . pricketh forward & emboldneth to take in hand worthy attempts . . . : for this cause, are men quicker witted, deeper searchers out of matters, and more diligent and rype of iudgemente then women: for a woman compasseth and doth al things after a worse sort, and in going aboue affayres and making bargeins, hath not the like dexterity and seemelynesse that a man hath." In these discussions of the punitive, purposive, and natural bases for female subordination, Anglicans and Puritans substantially agree.[12]

To reinforce these theories of sexual discrimination, spiritual analogies were used, especially by Puritans. The husband's sovereignty reflects divine glory and wisdom so the wife owes honor to her husband because he bears within himself the *imago Dei*. Moreover, the wife's obedience is a reflection of the church's subjection to Christ. These analogies were offered primarily to spiritualize female subjection rather than explain the origins of that subordination.[13]

Exhortations to wives to submit to their husbands' authority are common. Even if a woman had qualities superior to those of her husband, she was expected to honor his office, rendering obeisance. The same was true if her husband were not a Christian. Because wives were expected to obey, in 1588 the Privy Council released the recusant Ann Houlet of Norwich from prison, for her conforming husband agreed to persuade her to accept the Anglican way. Obedience was no less essential if a husband were cruel, froward, or irrational. Not even discrepancies in social status exempted a wife from this duty, as Sir Michael Hicks explained to Lady Elizabeth Willoughby. Moreover, this dutifulness must be performed meekly and reverently. Greenham regarded obedience as a wife's most important gift and a special grace. A contemporary ditty warned husbands of the consequences of not enforcing submissiveness:

> Concerning wives, take this an certaine rule
> That if at first, you let them have the rule
> Your self with them at last shall bear no rule
> Except you let them evermore to rule.[14]

Nevertheless, on occasion a wife was expected to disobey her husband, for obedience was required only insofar as a spouse's directives did not contravene Scripture. Although this was a proviso most often espoused by Puritans, it was also enunciated by Whitgift and Sandys. The husband's will, Henry Smith explained, was to be regarded as the divine will only to the extent that it conformed to the latter. Cleaver, who explored this question fully, extended the woman's rights of disobedience to matters that adversely affected her honor and credit. In other instances, she was admonished not to provoke her husband by disobeying in a matter that could be performed without offending God. She was particularly not to refuse his wishes in matters that would disrupt household peace. "Shee may in modest sort shew her mind, and a wise husband will not disdaine to heare her aduise, and follow it also, if it bee good." If he refused, Cleaver expected her to acquiesce. The wife as a truly equal partner was not conceived by either Anglican or Puritan. Even Cleaver, with his relatively liberal attitude toward female disobedience, felt a man had more authority over his family than a king over his kingdom.[15]

The extent to which wives heeded these exhortations is difficult to ascertain. There are indications that women were less subservient than their religious leaders wished. John Carpenter, the Anglican rector of Northleigh, Devon, complained that too many English women were like Lot's wife in refusing to accept overlordship. In 1602, John Chamberlain, the future commissioner for the repair of St. Paul's Cathedral, grumbled that "yf wenches have not theyre will, and . . . husbands come not at call we shall have them [wives] all discontented and turne Turke." Babington admitted that unruly men were unfit to govern their wives, and thus were subservient to them. In 1592, the foreign visitor Jakob Rathgeb observed that "the females have great liberty and are almost like masters." This impression was corroborated eight years later by William Vaughan, who thought English wives had more freedom than their Italian and Spanish counterparts, and almost as much as women in France and Germany. It was commonly remarked that the wife of Gilbert Talbot, earl of Shrewsbury, had an unusual amount of authority in their marriage. In fact, Shrewsbury wrote to Burghley in May 1591: "For the power that my wife hath with me, I confess . . . it is very great," though he was not ruled by her "more than were fit for any man to be by his wife." Lady Anne, the Catholic wife of Thomas Lord Berkeley, was noted for the power she wielded over her husband. A final example is in a letter of Walsingham to William More in 1574: "Bear, Sir, with my earnestness in recommending my wife's causes. You are yourself a married man. You know therefore of what force Mrs. More's commandments are to you."[16]

Some indications of quiescent female subordination are documented, especially in letters from wives to husbands. Lady Grace Mildmay commended her mother-in-law, Sir Walter Mildmay's wife, for obedience to and fear of her husband, and noted that she had urged Lady Grace to behave similarly towards her own spouse. Lady Grace later wrote of her own subservient relationship with Sir Anthony, noting that she was unable to challenge the actions or words of her husband that she disapproved. One suspects that normally women who were this passive rarely wrote about their marital relationships. Sir Francis Hastings noted approvingly that his wife, Lady Magdalen, "yeelded herself to doe whatsoever I perswaded, and not to doe whatsoever I mislyked."[17]

Elizabethan authors devoted much attention to a wife's duties to her husband, with Anglicans and Puritans in general agreement. Wives must emulate Sarah in calling their spouses "Lord," accept their instruction and supervision, give no offense, display godly manners and speech, dress moderately, exercise frugality, care for and instruct the children (especially daughters), govern the household with special attention to domestic servants, and provide companionship and assistance. She must refrain from jealousy, immoderate company, and public criticism of her husband. Chaste behavior and faithfulness were mandatory. The ideal was reflected in Lady Lumley's epitaph:

> A wyfe with out all spott, carefull
>   tender, and louing
> Whose vsuall behauioure in
>   ioyning all modestie with that whiche was
>   due to her birthe and calling was verie rare.

Comportment was as necessary as obedience, perhaps because her behavior reflected on her husband. Comportment included religious behavior, which was especially relevant when sectarian activity had a greater appeal to women than men. Bishop Cooper cited the case of Dame Lawson, a married woman condemned for "her vnwomanly and skittish gadding vp & down to Lambehith" without her husband to frequent conventicles, and Whitgift threatened to send her to Bridewell unless she ceased. One of the charges against Brownists was that they lured wives from their husbands in defiance of their marital contracts. In this context, exhortations of wifely obedience had clear socio-religious implications.[18]

Generally, a wife was expected to remain at home, the proper sphere for her obligations. Gadding about damaged reputations, encouraged immorality, and wasted time. Henry Smith, however, cautioned that a wife should not be so closely confined to the home that it became a prison. Lady Grace Mildmay was not worried about this when her husband frequently traveled on business during the early years of their marriage. When her friends urged her to go to court and frequent feasts, plays, and weddings for fellowship, she demurred in preference to fulfilling her domestic responsibilities.[19]

Anglicans and Puritans show a difference of emphasis concerning a woman's physical labor. This question primarily centered on wives in the landed classes and among the urban wealthy, for wives of lesser status traditionally toiled beside their husbands to survive economically. Although Anglicans admonished wives to be frugal, Puritans went further by insisting that profitable labor is virtuous. Wilcox stressed the necessity for wives to eschew idleness in favor of productive labor that would contribute to family maintenance. Social overtones are expressed in his caustic observation that "a good woman is not so fine fingred as many daintie dames are at this day, but will lay her hands to any worke that may either saue or get." He praised wives who made and sold linen as well as those who created their own apparel. Productive labor included activity with domestic servants, both to assist them and to provide them with a worthy example.[20]

As with the wife's responsibilites, Puritans and Anglicans essentially agreed about a husband's duties. He must instruct and reform his spouse, protect and provide for her, treat her with honor and patience as a weaker creature, speak courteously to her, avoid criticizing her before others, and provide for her after his death. The Puritans also stressed sexual cohabitation and fidelity, the responsibility to keep the wife profitably at work, and the protection from physical harm. For William Vaughan, sexual intercourse is a marital duty because it reconciles disputing spouses. Sexual infidelity was recognized as a serious impediment to a stable marriage, especially by Puritans. The expected norm was expressed in an epitaph for Henry Wriothesley, earl of Southampton, in 1581:

> In wedlock hee obserued, the vow that he had made:
> In breach of troth through lewd lust, he ne would seeme to wade.

The double standard undermined this ideal conduct, hence it is consistent with Puritan standards that sexual fidelity was stressed as a husband's duty. Although Anglican clergy did not oppose this duty, it was the Puritans who emphasized it.[21]

These precepts on the behavior of husbands are reflected in the advice of William Wentworth to his son Thomas. His wife must be instructed in the governance of her tongue and appropriate company, and cautioned not to hear tenants' complaints. "For flatteringe tenants will sone seduce a woman, who neither is lyke to haue a true intelligence of the matter, nor so sound a iudgementt as the wyser sortt of men haue." Thomas was advised to give her a small jointure, perhaps with an increase after the birth of several children, but with provisions contingent upon her remaining a widow. It was preferable to make a son the executor of the will, and to deal with the wife through a separate legacy. This advice was based on his experience with his mother, who had held approximately half of his father's estate as a tenant entail, and additionally possessed a jointure amounting to one-third of the remainder. She had been the sole executor of his father's estate, and had "removed much mony . . . and all the best goods" to her property prior to his death.[22]

Despite Wentworth's caution, the trend in the Elizabethan age was towards the appointment of wives as sole or joint executors (executrixes), though most wills still had male executors. Sir Thomas Smith and William Vaughan commented on this trend, and Smith thought many women outside London (where the civil law tradition prevailed for testaments) were named executors. In Becon's tract for the dying, the sick man made his wife the sole executor, with four male overseers, providing an example for others. No evidence exists that this practice was preferred by one religious group more than another. Among the Anglican clergy who designated their wives as sole or joint executors were Alexander Nowell, Lawrence Nowell, Edwin Sandys, Leonard Pilkington, Arthur Yeldart, and Richard Hooker. Others, including William Tod of Bedford and Roland and William Blenkinsopp of Durham, named female relatives. Among the Puritans, Perkins appointed his wife sole executor; Thomas Thomas named his wife and daughter; but Cartwright selected his sons as executors. Wives were joint or sole executors for such Puritan laymen as Sir Philip Sidney, Sir Francis Walsingham, Arthur Dakins of Hackness, Yorks., and the merchant Henry Locke. Comparable Anglican examples are found in the wills of the musician William Tallis, the lawyer Robert Forth, the gentlemen William Garforthe of London, and Richard Corbet. The women affected came from a wide range of socio-economic categories; their husbands included clergy, gentry, lawyers, yeomen, husbandmen, Merchant Adventurers, drapers, merchants, blacksmiths, and goldsmiths. They embraced such men of power as Edward Saxby, a baron of the Exchequer, as well as those of lower orders, like the Scarborough apprentice Leonard Appleby (whose executor was his sister). Most female executors had male supervisors or overseers.[23]

Given the number of women named as sole or joint executors, the results usually must have been satisfactory. Some indications of difficulty crop up, though hardly more than one would find with male executors. A Star Chamber case involving the will of Thomas

Hollinshedd, a member of the Vintners' Company, includes testimony that his widow initially refused to be the executrix, in hope of gaining greater control over the estate. In June 1588, the Privy Council handled the case of a widow who had defrauded her deceased husband's creditors by secretly conveying his goods and bonds to her friends; restitution was ordered. In a 1589 case, the Council was confronted with a widow and her new husband who forged a will to exclude her son, with whom she was a co-executor, from his share of the estate. In 1581 the Council intervened on behalf of a widow who could not perform her executor's function because her son had seized the estate. A 1588 case involved a widow whose minor son had come under the influence of overseers who defrauded her of some £5,000. In 1590 the widow of George Carleton, a Northamptonshire gentleman, was a prisoner of the crown and unable to function as sole executor, hence the bulk of the estate was embezzled. Despite these and kindred cases, women normally must have handled the executor's task successfully. One such woman was the widow of the Merchant Adventurer, Richard Whitelocke, who "did prove it [the will] and execute it most faythefully and lovingly toward her children."[24]

That many men entrusted estates to their wives after their deaths may indicate that they were more generous in sharing property with them during their lifetimes than English law required. Legally the husband controlled the disposition of her real property, including the right (with certain restrictions) of alienation. Her personal property, including clothing and jewelry, was owned by the husband outright, and he exercised the power of alienation over her chattels real, such as wardships or leases. Cleaver approved of this system: goods in marriage were held in common, yet the husband's headship empowered him to discharge the goods as he deemed best. The Privy Council periodically ensured some semblance of justice for wives. In 1576 it ordered Thomas Cheynye, who apparently traveled frequently, to provide his wife with sufficient means to maintain herself and her servants, and guarantee an appropriate jointure. In a case involving an insane husband in 1578, the Council ordered that a portion of the estate be set aside for his wife to maintain herself and her children. A Northumberland widow received a sympathetic hearing from the Council when she petitioned for recovery of a tenement given to her by her father and alienated by her late husband without her consent. In 1590 the Council intervened on behalf of the wife of John Tamworth of Tamworth, Warks.; he had "by threates and other uncivill and unnaturall compulcions enforced his . . . wife . . . to acknowledge a fine . . . for the continuance of the lande of inheritaunce by his fraudulente devises to him and his heires, and to retorne her joynture backe to him againe." The laws were not adequately structured to prevent serious abuses of the few property rights women possessed, but the Council revealed a sense of justice for their plight.[25]

Elizabethan wills reveal the awkward position of the wife with respect to property, especially that of a personal nature. When a husband died testate, a widow normally had a right to her personal clothes and jewels, but not her bedding, plate, and related items. A thoughtful husband might deed them to her, as did Sir Thomas Smith in 1576. His wife received all the apparel, jewelry, bedsteads and bedding, plate, and so forth which she had brought with her to the marriage, plus the use of 700 ounces of his plate during the remainder of her lifetime. Jane, widow of Peter Stanley of Moore Hall, Lancs., received half of her husband's goods and chattels, as well as her own apparel and jewelry. The 1596 will of Henry Herbert, earl of Pembroke, bequeathed to his wife the use of plate, jewels, and household goods worth 3,000 marks for the duration of her life or until she remarried, yet when he died in 1601 he left her "as bare as he could . . . bestowing all on the young Lord [William] even to her jewells."[26]

Under these conditions, wives were in an enigmatic position regarding charitable obligations. Cope, the Geneva pastor, recommended (in a work published in England in 1580) that husbands urge their spouses to aid the poor. Since wives were normally deprived of their own means under the law, how could this be done short of a *de facto* partnership in which a woman exercised some control over family wealth? Perkins sanctioned her donation of "gifts" which were "excepted from marriage," but legally she had no personal property and her real property was under her husband's control, requiring his consent before she could alienate it. With respect to goods held in common (i.e., legally the husband's) Perkins insisted that the husband consent to charitable gifts his wife proposed to make. Fenner thought it was a wife's duty to bestow alms on the poor while her husband was away; this recommendation presumably involved continuation of a practice already established. Another Puritan, Thomas Wilcox, curate of Bovingdon, Herts., thought a wife must be liberal to the needy. An excellent example was Dame Mary Ramsey, wife of a lord mayor of London, who bestowed £243 *p.a.* to relieve poor children at Christ's Hospital (with her husband's consent) beginning c. 1577. Yet for legal and social reasons (familial domination by husbands) the percentage of female donors, including widows and single persons, remained small. In Bristol, where a larger proportion of women donated to charity than in other areas, including London, the percentage hovered between 9.62% and 12.50% between 1571 and 1600, but rose to 30.77% in the first decade of the seventeenth century.[27]

Puritan interest in a wife's responsibility to be a charitable donor was related to the trend to regard marriage as a partnership, albeit between two unequal persons. Although this trend is particularly noticeable in Puritan writings, it is also reflected in some late Elizabethan Anglican literature. Babington, for example, cautioned husbands not to make decisions without consulting their spouses, and Hooker asserted that married persons no longer exercised full sovereignty over themselves but shared that authority with their mates. Puritans insisted that the wife was a fellow helper, though the husband retained the governorship. Henry Smith depicted the wife as a yokefellow who shared her husband's burdens and in turn the husband was to regard everything as common between them and treat his wife as "an vnder officer in his Common weale." Proper treatment of this junior partner entailed gentleness and patience, and demanded on both sides an understanding of one another's nature. A wife was likened to a vineyard that required sowing, dressing, watering, and fencing to make it bear. The husband's dominant status was not questioned, even as the wife shared the responsibilities and decision-making.[28]

The Puritan ideal was manifested in the marriages of Richard and Barbara Rogers, Henry Hastings, earl of Huntingdon, and Lady Katherine, and Sir Thomas and Lady Margaret Hoby. When Barbara Rogers narrowly escaped death in the fall of 1588, her husband wrote: "I saw then more cleerly what benef[it] it was to have her. Purpos[e] to be more profit[able] togither." Three weeks later he "convenaunted, to inioy more heavenly communion with ba[rbara], so thereupon we prayed to that ende, and came in the morneinge with much cheerefulnes to study and med[itation]." Huntingdon discussed the purchase of property with his wife, and she sought to enhance his financial condition and political career. Lady Margaret Hoby discussed business affairs and matters of religion with her husband. On one occasion, they walked about the village of Hackness, determining the best sites to build cottages, which surely exemplifies a spirit of partnership. Of the relationship enjoyed by the Hobys, Francis Bacon told Sir Thomas: "No man may better conceive the joys of a good wife than yourself, with whom I dare not compare." However, too much must not be made of the partnership concept. In a sense, it had existed for centuries, as wives ran the family estates while their husbands were away. When Cleaver stressed this responsibility for wives, he reiterated what had long been standard practice. If husbands expected wives to function adequately in this respect, Lady Margaret Hoby was not unique in surveying the family estate with her husband. Artisans, husbandmen, and rural laborers, by virtue of the need for cooperation in those vocations, had to treat their spouses as partners. The concern of religious writers with male governorship may partly be a reaction to the pragmatic partnerships that already existed.[29]

Ruptures between spouses created concern. Whetstone likened domestic disputes to hell, whereas Deloney felt such disharmony was inevitable without divine blessing. Cleaver placed the blame for marital disputes on the husband, for failing to purge his wife of the vice that engendered discord. Dissension between spouses troubled religious commentators because it threatened family stability and impeded worship.[30]

Marital dissension was not rare in the Elizabethan period. Manuscripts in the Lansdowne collection often refer to divisive relationships. William Turner, dean of Wells, and Nicholas Poyntz complained to Cecil in 1564 about Sir Thomas Dyer's ill treatment of his wife. Poyntz, her son, attributed her death to Dyer but found no illegal behavior. The second marriage of Thomas Randolph in 1572 prompted George Buchanan to complain of "the tem[p]est and stormes . . . of mariage." One of the stormiest was that of Sir Francis Willoughby and Elizabeth, daughter of Sir John Lyttleton. Lady Willoughby was convinced her husband treated her like a fool, and the marriage was not aided by servants who fomented dissension between them. Lady Willoughby also detested her sister-in-law so much that she kept her away for years. When she finally visited her brother, Lady Willoughby, after staying overnight at the vicarage, addressed her nemesis with vile language. Sir John Lyttleton intervened on several occasions in the hope of establishing harmony. The couple separated in 1579 after sixteen years of marriage and twelve children, but Lady Willoughby did not find the separation acceptable. When their son died in 1580, she sought reconciliation by promising to try to become pregnant again, though she was over forty. In 1581 she threatened to complain to the queen, and the following year Elizabeth directed Sir Francis to pay her £200 *p.a.* for separate maintenance. Lady Willoughby continued to seek a reconciliation, and even accused her father in 1585 of treating her unfairly in this matter. For his part, Sir Francis charged her with failing to confess her errors and submit to him. Sir Francis remarried, but after his death in 1596 rumors spread that he had been poisoned by his second wife, Dorothy Tamworth.[31]

On various occasions, the queen intervened in the marital disputes of her nobility. In November 1563, for instance, she summoned William Somerset, earl of Worcester, to court after he had sent his wife to her father, Edward Lord North; Elizabeth wanted "no furt[he]r inconvenience to follow without very great and necessary cause." In 1568, she asked Edward Stanley, earl of Derby, to take back his wife after a quarrel due to "some mislykyng conceaved ageynst hir by your children." The bitterest dispute in which the queen became involved was probably that between George Talbot, earl of Shrewsbury, and his wife Elizabeth ("Bess of Hardwick"), whom he regarded as a wicked enemy. A servant aptly commented that "that howse is a hell." The countess accused the earl of intimacy with Mary Stuart while he was her guardian, but the queen refused to sanction a legal separation and repeatedly intervened to seek a reconciliation. Ultimately the queen and Burghley achieved a year's trial reunion, but the earl remained hostile because the countess refused to kneel before him and confess her faults as well as repay a loan. The dispute also involved actions undertaken by the countess, while the earl was gravely ill, to transfer some of his lands to her friends, using her powers as sole executrix. Thomas Overton, bishop of Coventry and Lichfield, also sought to reconcile the feuding pair, writing to Shrewsbury in October 1590:

Some will say in your Lordship's behalf that the Countess is a sharp and bitter shrew and therefore like enough to shorten your life if she should keep you company. Indeed, my good Lord, I have heard some say so, but if shrewdness or sharpness may be a just cause of separation betwixt man and wife, I think few men in England would keep their wives long.

A month later Shrewsbury died, still unreconciled to the indomitable Bess.[32]

The marriages of Sir Francis and Lady Elizabeth Willoughby and the earl and countess of Shrewsbury faltered mainly because of bitter dissension over the wife's role. Both husbands found their spouses insufficiently submissive. The same problem afflicted the marriage of Edward Seymour, earl of Hertford, and Frances Howard. Attempts to make wives submissive may be reflected in the numerous complaints about the cruelty of Elizabethan husbands. Husbands accused of such conduct included William Bourchier, earl of Bath, Henry Hastings, nephew of the earl of Huntingdon, Henry Percy, thirteenth earl of Northumberland, and Edward de Vere, earl of Oxford. Some cases are mentioned from lower levels of society, including a Warwickshire sheriff named Marrow who "useth his wife verry hardly, would not allow hir mony nor clothes fit for hir, not trust hir with any thing." Some Puritan marriages were similarly troubled: Margaret Dakins and Walter Devereux experienced difficulty because of his tempermental behavior, and the Puritan minister Laurence Humphrey lived unhappily with his wife, though perhaps she was at fault. The husband of Manningham's Puritan cousin treated her so poorly that when she fell from a horse he never bothered to return for her. Such conduct was far removed from that of a husband who apologized to the archdeacon's court at St. Albans for refusing to receive communion on the grounds that he had a guilty conscience after a dispute with his wife. The evidence suggests that a common cause of marital dissension was the nature of the wife's subordinate role, which likely accounts for the attention that religious writers devoted to this subject.[33]

The same writers were concerned about the beating of wives. Puritans were the most outspoken in condemning this practice, perhaps owing to the inspiration of Geneva, where the consistories actively opposed it, but certainly to the negative effect beatings had on the home as a microcosm of the church and on the husband as a spiritual leader. At least one clergyman, the vicar of Stickford, Lincs., beat his wife—and in the churchyard! When a Staffordshire man beat a woman in an alehouse at Bosley, Ches., he defended himself by saying he intended to wed her. After Sir Francis Willoughby's daughter Frances married Montague Wood of Lambley, Notts., she was beaten and expelled from her home. Such violations were punishable in the quarter sessions, but the Privy Council intervened on behalf of the queen to prevent one gentleman, Thomas Clinton, from assaulting his wife. When a woman beat her husband, social custom provided for a public display of disapprobation. In February 1563 at Charing Cross, London, a man was carried about by four other men, preceded by a bagpiper, a drummer, and other musicians, because his "next neybor['s] wyff ded bett here hosband; ther-for yt [is] ordered that ys next naybor shall ryd a-bowtt the plase." This double standard is also reflected in the legal provision that a wife who killed her husband was guilty of treason, not just homicide. Two Kentish women who poisoned their spouses in the 1570s were executed by burning and hanging respectively.[34]

In summation, Anglicans and Puritans agreed with respect to the punitive, purposive, and natural bases for the subordination of wives. Anglicans and especially Puritans asserted, however, that wives must obey spouses only when their commands are not contrary to Scripture. The evidence suggests that Elizabethan wives were less obedient to their husbands than the preachers desired; a common cause of marital dissension was a husband's cruelty to his wife when she was not subordinate. Although Anglicans and Puritans essentially agreed on the duties of husbands and wives, Puritans emphasized productive labor for all wives, and sexual fidelity for husbands. Elizabethan men increasingly appointed their wives as sole or joint executrixes, despite the fact that during their lifetime wives had virtually no legal control over their own property. The Puritans, however, believed a wife had charitable obligations, and this belief seems to have been a factor in the gradual acceptance by some religious writers of marriage as a partnership, though the two parties were not considered equal. In practice, many Elizabethan husbands had to treat their wives as partners if they expected them to supervise their estates in their absence or cooperate in the shops and on the farms. Marital dissension concerned the religious authors, but it was the Puritans who spoke out strongly against wife-beating.

(2) Separation and Annulment

Seriant [Christopher] Yelverton said a pore bachelor to be maried had no money to pay the prist, only 8d: the prist in congregation refused to mary him without full pay: he desired he might be maried as farre as his money wold go & promised to pay the rest: & so was: the priest after asking the dett: nay said he, I will geve 10 tymes as much to unmarie us.

Roger Wilbraham[35]

For this bande can not be broken at mans pleasure.

Geneva Bible[36]

Canon law did not permit divorce in the modern sense, but provided two means of separation. One was a divorce or *separatio a mensa et thoro*, that is, a separation in which neither party was allowed to remarry. The other was a divorce *a vinculo matrimonii*, annulling the marriage from the beginning because of one or more impediments, and bastardizing children born to the couple. This form allowed both parties to remarry, and for that reason encouraged debate over impediments. A more fundamental question was raised by a number of writers, mostly Puritans, who favored divorces with a right to remarry for those whose spouses committed adultery and sometimes for other reasons.

As early as 1537 the Matthew Bible accepted divorce for persons whose spouses committed adultery, but in the context of canon law this presumably meant only divorce *a mensa et thoro*. The Geneva Bible proclaimed that divine vengeance would be wreaked on marriage breakers and that wedlock involved the inseparable conjunction of husband and wife. The annotators, however, allowed divorce for adultery, with the innocent wife having the right to remarry, but nothing was said about a husband's right to marry again if his wife committed adultery. If she deserted him "for hatred, dissension, angre, &c." he was not allowed to take another wife. A note to Esther 1:19 must have suggested to some Elizabethans the annulments of Henry VIII's marriages to Anne Boleyn and Catherine Howard. The Beza-Tomson Bible asserted that marital bonds could be broken only for adultery; a man whose spouse was unfaithful had the right to divorce and marry again. The crucial passage in Luke 16:18 was not interpreted as a denial of this right, for the Jews executed adulterers, hence Christ's prohibition on remarriage applied only to Jewish divorces on nonadulterous grounds. Such divorces were no longer allowable, nor was divorce acceptable for religious incompatibility.[37]

The Rheims annotators asserted the traditional Catholic position forbidding remarriage to persons divorced for adultery. If both parties were guilty of adultery, no divorce was possible. The indissolubility of marriage was based on its character as a sacrament, hence even adultery was grounds only for divorce a mensa et thoro. Only the death of a spouse made remarriage possible. In refuting the Rheims notes, Fulke and Cartwright reasserted the right of a person whose mate committed adultery to divorce and marry again. To forbid remarriage Cartwright judged unjust, for it deprived the guiltless party of the benefits of matrimony, including children and the remedy against incontinency. Fulke accused the Catholic church of propagating the narrower position for financial reasons: "The Popes Canon lawe restreineth the libertie of mariage and diuorcing, because he may take more monie for bulles of licence and dispensation to marie."[38]

Attempts to liberalize the Catholic conception of divorce as embodied in canon law were made in the *Reformatio legum ecclesiasticarum*, specifically in the section *De adulteriis et divortiis*. Here the Edwardian reformers proposed to allow the innocent party divorced for adultery or desertion the right to remarry while the spouse was alive. Moreover marital partners shown to be hostile or guilty of illtreatment could be divorced by their spouses, who were free to remarry, and the former were to be punished by exile or life imprisonment. The *Reformatio* did not allow divorce when both parties committed adultery. Divorce a mensa et thoro was to be abolished as contrary to Scripture and conducive to evil and confusion. The *Reformatio* was never enacted, and there is no compelling evidence that its principles were followed in the Elizabethan era, though it influenced some thinkers, especially Puritans.[39]

Elizabethan Anglicans substantially agreed that remarriage after divorce for adultery was not permissible, as stated by Edmund Bunny in his work on divorce, first published in 1610 but written a decade and a half earlier, though he allowed remarriage after desertion by an unchristian spouse. In 1602 John Howson defended the thesis *Uxore dimissa propter fornicationem aliam non licet superinducere* for the D.D. degree. The same year a preacher at Paul's Cross spoke on the theme "that a man could not be divorced from his wife, though she should commit adultery." Lancelot Andrewes, minister of St. Giles', Cripplegate, opposed remarriage after divorce for adultery in his *Discourse against Second Marriage*.[40]

A prime example of the conservative Anglican position appeared in a sermon by John Dove at Paul's Cross on 10 May 1601. His theme was that remarriage of the innocent party was acceptable if a divorce were lawful. Yet because Christ condemned all who remarried as adulterers, all divorce was wrong, and to remarry amounted to adultery and bigamy. Dove condemned an interpretation that allowed divorce but not remarriage, which practice would cause persons to burn in lust. Divorce rendered asunder that which was divinely joined. Even divorce a mensa et thoro was acceptable only as a temporary separation followed by reconciliation. If a wife committed adultery, Dove approved a temporary separation under a magistrate's supervision. Even this action was not acceptable if her sexual relations had occurred because of rape, deceit, an erroneous assumption of her husband's demise, the husband's consent to her adultery, his failure to prevent an adulterous situation, his temporary acceptance of her sin, or his own adultery. A person who could not be reconciled to an adulterous mate lacked Christian faith and charity, and disobeyed the precept in 1 Peter 3:7. Dove was concerned that if persons could remarry because of adultery, some would confess to or commit adultery simply to be rid of spouses. A Sussex sheriff revealed that he knew a man who was bribed to admit (falsely) that he was an adulterer in order to allow his wife to marry another man.[41]

The Puritan position was differentiated from the Anglican by the willingness of Puritans to approve remarriage for persons who divorced adulterous spouses. Cleaver, Pagit, Kingsmill, and Henry Smith allowed divorce and remarriage only for adultery, but Becon included idolatry (especially if a spouse tried to force a mate to become an idolater), and Estey and Perkins allowed it for desertion. Cleaver insisted that a woman whose husband deserted her must live as a widow without the right to remarry. Apparently no Puritan except Perkins accepted divorce for incompatibility; the unharmonious couple was normally expected, in Henry Smith's words, to keep "their noses together, till wearines make them leaue strugling." It was not acceptable for a husband and wife to separate because they regarded the single life as holier than marriage. Divorce a mensa et thoro, for whatever reason, was denounced by Cleaver and Pagit as a violation of the ends of marriage. In 1596, Thomas Meade, the Puritan vicar of Prescot, Lancs., practiced the Puritan position by suing his wife for divorce on grounds of adultery.[42]

A few individuals held views on divorce that differed from those of their religious colleagues. William Vaughan, the Puritan lay poet, disagreed with other Puritans that a guiltless party should be allowed to remarry if the spouse was an adulterer, for this would lead to numerous divorces. "Wheras otherwise, men knowing, that eyther they must liue singly, or be reconciled, seldome or neuer should we see diuorcements." The Norwich cleric Robert Hill, apparently a Puritan, also held to the strict indissolubility of marriage, resting his belief on 1 Corinthians 7. Andrew Willett, prebendary of Ely and usually identified as an Anglican, viewed divorce in the usual Puritan manner, that is, as acceptable for adultery and desertion, provided that the deserted spouse seek to restore the marriage and, failing that, procure judgment from a magistrate. He allowed remarriage in cases of divorce for adultery, even for the guilty party—an unusual position—but only after rebuke and punishment.[43]

The Separatists took a distinctive stand by insisting on divorce in cases of adultery, when divine law breached wedlock. If however, the offense was not known to outside parties, the adulterer could cohabit with his or her spouse following repentance. "It is the open conviction and the knowledge of the partie to who[m] the wronge is done or the magistrate that must disanull this outward covenant." If the church had evidence of adultery, the adulterer could no longer dwell with his or her mate even if the offended party forgave and the guilty person repented. A subsequent marriage was not to be disrupted by the discovery that adultery had been committed in an earlier match. These views were developed in the early 1590s by John Greenwood, and are reflected in the ensuing decade by Francis Johnson and his fellow Separatists.[44]

A more extreme attitude was held by Familists. In May 1561 two adherents of this sect confessed that when a member died, the survivor had to wed another person in the sect, even if the couple had never met and the woman had to be brought a great distance. This happened when Thomas Chandler of Surrey married a stranger from the Isle of Ely. If such matches were incompatible, divorce was allowed, which happened to Chandler after a year of marriage. This practice of sectaries may have been the basis for the complaint of George Talbot, earl of Shrewsbury, to the Privy Council in 1565, that "diverse in the counties of Yorke and Derbye forsake their lawfull wyves and openly take other in mariage as they terme it."[45]

Such perceived abuses, coupled with attempts by persons to remarry after divorce a mensa et thoro, led the bishops to include pertinent queries in visitation articles. They sought persons who had separated and remarried, persons who were divorced but still living together, and husbands who had unlawfully forsaken their spouses. Sandys' articles for Minster Cathedral in 1578 inquired about clergy and ecclesiastical officers separated from their wives. Such questions suggest that violations respecting divorce and separation were not rare. Further proof is found in the canons of 1597, which were intended in part to check "divorces lightly passed" and require that separations a mensa et thoro be permitted only when security was provided that no remarriage would occur. The canons, the first concerning divorce since the Reformation, allowed only annulments and separation, not divorce for adultery or desertion.[46]

Whitgift defended this position, especially in a 1602 Star Chamber case. Hercules Fuljambe, who had been divorced twice for adultery, married the daughter of Edward Rye, who subsequently sued for the return of a lease given to Fuljambe on the grounds that this marriage was invalid. After consulting the divines at Lambeth, Whitgift persuaded Star Chamber to void the marriage, on the understanding that divorces granted in ecclesiastical courts were only a mensa et thoro. The Puritans, however, may have flouted ecclesiastical law, for in March 1583 the Dedham Classis decided that "the worde of god alloweth that a man iustlie diuorced from his first wieff might mary a second, so his proceedinge to the second mariage be orderly and in the lorde." Perhaps this was a reference only to divorce *a vinculo matrimonii*, but given Puritan approval for the legitimacy of divorce for adultery and sometimes other causes, some Puritan ministers may have been willing to perform second marriages in such cases.[47]

The Anglican position was conducive to the abuse of annulments. For a marriage to be annulled, ecclesiastical law required proof of the inability to marry or lack of consent. Lack of consent could be shown by insufficient age (twelve for girls, fourteen for boys were the legal minimums), mental incompetence, or duress. Incapacity to marry involved precontract, affinity, consanguinity, and impotence at the time of marriage. A physically impotent person could not remarry, but one who was frigid in relations with a mate could be divorced and remarried. In the ecclesiastical court at Chester in 1562, Margaret Pierson claimed her husband Richard was impotent, but he retorted that he had sired a bastard. He did acknowledge he had never copulated with Margaret because on their wedding night she "bie chaunce hurt hym before he could have his pleasure; and therapon, thinkinge he shuld have mendid, he absteynid from her Companye." Another indication of the difficulties of an annulment for reasons of impotency is found in a 1594 Chancery case. A woman whose marriage had been annulled in an ecclesiastical court because her husband was *frigidus natura*, and who was now suing him with respect to an annuity and jointure, heard medical testimony from five physicians that medicine could correct her husband's difficulty and enable the marriage to be consummated.[48]

Of course, some legitimate cases did exist in which the provisions for annulment were used honestly and for beneficial ends. In 1581 William Bourchier, earl of Bath, who was in his early twenties, became inebriated at his grandfather's home and was married at 2 A.M. by a felonious priest to a woman who had designs on him; the marriage was annulled. In 1586-87, Star Chamber had to determine the status of a woman who had wed one man, then left him when informed the marriage was not lawful because the minister was defrocked, and finally married a second man. In neither of these cases would Anglican or Puritan thought on divorce have provided an alternative other than annulment or separation.[49]

The Puritan position on divorce (with remarriage) for adultery would have provided a satisfactory means to resolve cases of the kind in which Sir John Stawell of Cothelston, Som., was involved. After his wife Mary committed adultery with a servant, he obtained a divorce a mensa et thoro in the Court of Delegates in 1565. Seven years later he wanted to wed Frances, sister of the courtier and poet Edward Dyer. Because Mary was still alive, Stawell petitioned Gilbert Berkeley, bishop of Bath and Wells, for permission to remarry. The case was referred to Archbishop Parker, who dispensed with the canon law prohibition in April 1572. Mary Stawell, however, sued for restitution of conjugal rights in the Court of Arches the following November, and Sir John was charged in the Court of Audience with a public offense for living with Frances while his wife was alive. Despite protestations from Burghley and Leicester, apparently influenced by the Puritan position on divorce, Stawell was prosecuted and temporarily imprisoned for his obstinate behavior towards the courts, but both cases were ultimately deferred *sine die*. Stawell prevented further action by paying Mary's family £600. A simple divorce with the right to remarry would have been more satisfactory.[50]

Anglicans feared that granting divorces *a vinculo* for adultery would increase illicit sexual relations as a means of dissolving marriages. A case in point was the 1598 affair described in the preceding chapter, in which William Nelson, the prisoner in York Castle, intended to procure a divorce by arranging for his wife and a fellow prisoner to be seen making love. Adultery appears to have been used as well to expedite annulment cases involving child marriages. Cases in the ecclesiastical court at Chester cite evidence of adultery in addition to ages at marriage, as if this would ensure annulment. Sometimes inability to procure an annulment or a divorce a vincolo created manifest hardships for the spouse of an adulterer. In the case of Katherine and Kenelm Willoughby of Kent, the husband's adultery with various maids led to separation, but Katherine had to sue in the Court of Requests to receive her annuity of £20 *p.a.* Getting husbands who were separated to pay such annuities was a common difficulty, sometimes requiring intervention by the Privy Council.[51]

Canon law notwithstanding, some Elizabethans sought divorces for reasons other than adultery and impediments. In 1560 the marriage of Edward Seymour, earl of Hertford, to Lady Catherine Grey was annulled for political reasons, despite its legality. Similar problems were posed by the marriage of Thomas Keys to Lady Mary Grey in 1566. Thomas Lord Paget separated from his wife because of their incompatibility. In September 1569 Lady Stanhope complained to Cecil that her son-in-law sought a divorce because of jealousy and love for another woman; he was given "over to his owne will, a[n]d he forgetteth God, [and] abuseth his owne body with evill company," and he mistreated her daughter. Henry Percy, earl of Northumberland, reconciled with his wife, Dorothy, daughter of Walter Devereux, earl of Essex, long enough to get an heir and then left her, keeping the child with him at Sion House on the Thames. In 1599 Percy allegedly offered her £1,000 *p.a.* to live separately, though she insisted on £1,500, the worth of her dowry. Lady Dorothy was generally blamed for their faulty relationship, which may have been the lot of most estranged wives. Sir Michael Hicks told Lady Willoughby, for example, that "according to ye ordinance of god, and the covenante of your mariage, yow [must] endeuor to subdue and submytt your will to ye plesure of your hedd, in all honest and lawfull thinge[s] seking rather to wynne his goodwill with covering his faultes and bearing with his commandemente."[52]

If remarriage was considered, especially to obtain an heir, an impediment had to be found to justify divorce a vinculo. Walsingham cautioned Hertford in 1582 not to let his son, Lord Beauchamp, separate from his wife in an unlawful manner and thereby lose the right to remarry and have an heir.[53] Elizabethan divorces appear to have been determined in strict accordance with canon law when questions of remarriage and heirs were involved, but otherwise such factors as incompatibility and political expediency were accepted for divorce, at least a mensa et thoro. The Puritan position on divorce was probably more compatible with lay desires than the Anglican view.

(3) Parental Responsibilities

The louing and tender gouernement of naturall parents, is the principall patterne and example whereunto all other gouernement is to be framed.

Robert Allen[54]

Fathers and mothers are to their children in Gods stead.

Robert Cleaver[55]

Prior to the publication of William Whittingham's New Testament and the Geneva Bible, little attention was given in marginalia to parental responsibilities. The thrust of earlier marginal notes was the duty of parents to instruct children. In his 1530 edition of the Pentateuch, Tyndale complained that fathers were so religiously ignorant that they could not fulfill this obligation, but his comment was dropped in the 1551 edition. The Geneva annotators underscored the educational responsibilities of parents and displayed interest in parental attitudes and treatment of children. The latter must not be provoked by excessive rigor or austerity, or treated cruelly. Adequate provision must be made for the family, for "the couetous men yt spare their riches to the hinderance of their families, shal be depriued thereof miserably." Yet parents must not become so involved with household concerns that spiritual duties are neglected. The ideal is to have well-nurtured children sheltered from worrisome cares. In family relations, honor to God has precedence over natural affections. The Geneva annotators showed unusual interest in the effects of godly or ungodly actions by parents on successive generations, concluding that God could reward or punish offspring for their ancestors' conduct, but others must not.[56]

The educational duty of parents was reiterated in the marginalia of the Bishops' Bible, which also urged fathers to serve as examples in obeying divine commands. Fathers were admonished to place a high priority on correcting their sons. Whereas the bishops accused Adam of not raising his children ideally, given the unacceptable offerings of Cain, the Geneva annotators blamed Cain for hypocrisy and praised Adam's religious instruction. This difference in interpretation indicates a greater emphasis on individual responsibility in the Geneva Bible. In the Beza-Tomson edition, the tone of the remarks on parental responsibility shifted; parents were urged to treat children with gentleness, and fathers were cautioned to use their authority with moderation *ad gloriam Dei.*[57]

Although parental responsibilities were not extensively discussed in the biblical marginalia, they were important in a society that relied on family discipline as a fundamental preserver of public order and private morality. The absence of a genuine police force made the role of parents — especially fathers — crucial to the maintenance of stability. Many writers drew analogies between parents (or fathers) and magistrates and princes. Hooker depicted fathers as lords and kings of their families, evoking a patriarchal concept fundamentally Hebrew in origin. William Vaughan similarly wrote:

The image of a Monarchic is found in priuate families. For the authority of a father ouer his children, may bee resembled to a royall gouernment, because the children are the fathers charge: hee alone must prouide for them, and their offences are by him chastised. . . . Euery man is a King in his owne house.

Perkins went further, arguing that the father should be honored because he bears the image of God's paternity. Reversing the analogy, Thomas Rogers portrayed princes as parents of their subjects, and Alexander Nowell argued that superiors must govern subordinates as parents do children. The interdependence of family, church, and state was stressed by Greenham, who warned that legislation in church and state was ineffective unless doctrine and discipline were practiced in the home. Patriarchal authority could, in fact, be harnessed by the state as a tool to govern. In 1588, for example, the Privy Council ordered Richard Lee, a gentleman of Langley, to use paternal authority to see that his son made restitution to another gentleman for losses he sustained.[58]

Generally, Anglicans and Puritans agreed on the basic responsibilities of parents. Provision was an obvious obligation, though both groups insisted on moderation. There were frequent warnings to avoid excess, especially in apparel; clothing must be clean, frugal, and in keeping with one's estate. John Woolton was angered by parents who dressed children "with sumptuous and gorgeous apparel of divers colours, sometime like routers, sometime like ruffians, but seldom like honest folks." Vaughan saw no reason for children to be garbed in new fashions. Robert Allen denounced parents who excused inadequate charity by pleading the necessity of providing sumptuous apparel for their children. Food provided for the family also must be in moderation.[59]

Puritans stressed the necessity of keeping children from idleness, a point also made by the Catholic Robert Shelford. Udall believed that failure to keep children profitably occupied would end in their inability to provide for themselves. Anglican and Puritan concurred that children must be taught an appropriate vocation. "He that hath no wealth to leaue them," wrote Charles Gibbon, "may do little if he teach them not some trade to liue on." William Wentworth advised Thomas to urge his younger sons to study law, and perhaps apprentice one to a merchant.[60]

Other obligations on which religious writers agreed were education and religious instruction; youngsters must learn to fear God, pray, and know the creed and Ten Commandments. Catechizing was not a duty reserved for the clergy but a family responsibility. Several Puritans, including Henry Smith, Estey, and Wilcox, included mothers in the pedagogical function. Jewel placed instruction in godliness above the provision of material benefits as a parental duty. Failure to provide this instruction, for servants as well as children, warned Udall, caused domestic disobedience. Pilkington, however, wondered how fathers could teach religious matters when they were dependent for their knowledge on "Sir John Mumble-matins;" Puritans shared his concern.[61]

The educational responsibilities of parents ranged from instruction in the home to the provision of qualified, godly tutors. In a work dedicated to the mayor and masters of Plymouth, William Kempe, master of the Plymouth Grammar School, admonished parents to see that children, from the moment they began learning to speak, were in the company of honest, civil persons. Children must be sheltered from "barbarous nurses, clownish playing mates, and all rusticall persons," as well as wanton, rude behavior and indecent speech. Bullinger too was concerned about the effect of speech on young minds. Parental responsibility in education was so important that Shelford insisted parents acquire knowledge to teach their offspring.

Edward Hake warned of parents who were overly gentle with young sons, "euen in those yeeres when as they shoulde chieflye bee framed vnto suche constitucion of bodye as the importaunce of Studye doeth . . . requyre, and as throughe wante whereof, they become vnfit in after Age bothe for learning and all other good exercises tending to the succour of a common Wealth, as falling through theyr sayde yll Education into feminine delightes and vaine Curiosityes."[62]

With respect to professional instruction, Greenham was concerned that some parents delayed formal education until children were ten or twelve, because they believed that any learning acquired before this age would be apish imitation. He saw no harm in emulating the good, and he feared that children whose education was delayed would be too headstrong to instruct. Burghley, however, warned that trying to make sons into men "seven yeres too soone" caused depravity. Once sons began formal education, Kempe made it a parental obligation to see that free time was used to further knowledge. This responsibility included reviewing sons in their schoolwork and providing further training in deportment. A major parental responsibility was teaching children to respect and obey superiors. The emphasis on male education moved Hake to complain about neglecting the education of daughters, which he considered a major reason for the prevalency of lewdness and vanity among mature women. In a kindred spirit, Cleaver urged parents to teach girls as well as boys to read and write because of the utilitarian and religious value.[63]

In practice, parental attitudes toward educational responsibilities varied. Lady Anne Bacon was praised for educating her children, but Anne, the Catholic wife of Thomas Lord Berkeley, was not. The latter was "noted to bee most tender hearted to her children; And to them soe over and above reason indulgent, as not contentedly shee admitted them out of her sight, whereby they after complayned of that want of Learning which a juster education should have afforded their estates and parentage." An indication of parental responsibility for education appears in the wills of those who left instructions for their offspring's schooling. John Barlow, rector of Warmingham, Ches., had four sons, two of whom were bound as apprentices. When he made his will in 1591, another son was at Cambridge, and the executors were instructed to see that the fourth son had a choice of being apprenticed or going to Cambridge. Robert Newall, a yeoman of Rochdale, Lancs., provided for the education of his daughter as well as his son in his testament. A Yorkshire gentleman, Francis Rodes, set aside £50 *p.a.* in the hope that a younger son would study common law. Financial provisions for education are found in wills of

social groups ranging from aristocracy to yeomen as well as professionals, and from religious beliefs from Catholic to Puritan. Another
indication of educational responsibility appeared in the written instructions of fathers to sons, such as those of William Wentworth to
Thomas, and Richard Senhouse to Simon (on the occasion of his entering Anthony Bacon's service).[64]

It was generally agreed that parents were responsible for helping
progeny find suitable spouses, but the question of legacies was more
enigmatical. Essentially, the obligation to provide a moderate inheritance was accepted, and Perkins recommended using a will to avoid
contention. Dod deplored the practice of bestowing the most on the
eldest child, preferring that legacies be determined according to virtue, and that each child receive something. Cleaver, however, favored
equal legacies. Dod also urged parents not to scrimp to provide inheritances. A number of Puritans, especially Robert Allen, demanded
that parents bestow a fair share of their goods on the poor and not
hoard everything for legacies. Allen was troubled by parents who
channeled all available funds into legacies designed to upgrade the
social status of their children: "Many, though they be not Gentlemen themselves, yet do they put forth so farre, to make their children, or at the least their eldest sonne a Gentleman; that they make
themselues beggers before they die, and make their eldest so mightie
aboue the rest, that he spoileth and impouerisheth all his brethren."
Jewel made the same complaint, and there were numerous warnings
that excessive legacies were a spiritual threat to children. Conceivably
this concern with unequal and excessive legacies was engendered in
part because so many clerics were younger sons, but the subject must
also have been of interest to younger sons who did not enter the
ministry.[65]

Disinheritance was particularly touchy. Cleaver found nine reasons
for it: violence to the father, attempted fratricide, sexual intercourse
with one's mother, prohibiting a father from making a will, heresy,
refusal to be a surety for one's father, an unsavory vocation, insanity,
and refusal of a proposed match to pursue an immoral life. In other
cases, the disinheritance of an eldest son in particular was condemned
as unlawful and unnatural—the exact charges used by Sir William
Heydon to Burghley when the former's son tried to wrest control
of his estate from him. Religious differences were sometimes grounds
for disinheritance. John Gerard reports that William Heigham's father
sold the estates that comprised his patrimony to keep his son, who
converted to Catholicism, from inheriting them. Thomas Chaderton
of Oldham, Lancs., cut off his third son, Laurence, from his legacies

because the latter repudiated Catholicism. The elder Chaderton informed him, "If you will renounce a new sect which you have joined you may expect all the happiness which the care of an indulgent father can secure you; otherwise I enclose a shilling to buy a wallet with. Go and beg for your living. Farewell!" When the esquire William Button disinherited his eldest son for less substantial reasons, he fell afoul of the queen and Privy Council, for his son was reputedly "of verie good behaviour and wel affected in Religion." The Council became involved in other cases of this nature. Apart from such disputes, landed men and persons of substance generally agreed with William Wentworth that fathers were obligated to provide reasonable legacies for their sons.[66]

The emotional relationship between parents and children was in a state of flux in the Elizabethan era. Available evidence does not bear out the customary view that Elizabethan families were based on a cold, formal relationship, with parents determined to make strangers out of their children as they grew older. There was more to Elizabethan family life than (as Lawrence Stone argues) an institution grounded on custom, convenience, and law rather than affection. Examples can be found of families matching this description, but the statements of some Puritans and empirical evidence do not bear out this stereotype.[67]

Elizabethan authors were divided over the proper role of affection, and the division does not strictly follow religious lines. In 1602, Lancelot Andrewes preached that children who grew fond of their parents should be weaned, and Greenham thought God intervened to alter the immoderate affections of parents, especially when children manifested inappropriate behavior. Thus divine intervention was required in the cases of Abraham's love for Ishmael, Isaac's love for Esau, and David's affection for Absalom. Greenham approved parental love "in the spirit" but not "in the flesh," and Norden blamed "fond foolish" love for the failure of parents to provide sufficient correction. Although Norden did not sanction such affection, his criticism indicates it existed, and the Catholic Robert Shelford claimed it was too common. Yet Dering encouraged fatherly love as the best way to prompt a son to obey. Similarly Nicholas Bownde thought children, recognizing parental affection, preferred correction by their fathers rather than servants. With respect to mothers, Bownde asked, "how many grieuous things doth the mother put vp [with] at the hands of her froward child, whome shee tenderly loueth?" John Newnham argued that the most essential parental attribute was natural love for children.[68]

Some Elizabethan parents favored an affectionate relationship with their offspring. The Nottinghamshire gentleman Sir William Holles was commended for exemplary love to his children and grandchildren, whose presence he enjoyed. When Cecil's son, Thomas was on the Continent in 1562, his "fond father" became concerned that he was being influenced in wanton ways by his servant. The elder Cecil also worried that his son might travel to Louvain and fall under Catholic influence. Some of the concern, no doubt, was for Sir William's own reputation, for he urged Thomas not to "disclose his lewdnes to my discomfort and shame." Thomas' response reveals a respectful, affectionate relationship. Sir Nicholas Bacon enjoyed a warm relationship with his family, which his biographer attributes to humanist and Puritan influences. In one case where this relationship was lacking, outside intervention became necessary: When Frances, wife of Sir John Berkeley of Beverston Castle, Glos., died in 1576, Sir John lacked "the grace to show himself a natural father" to his children, hence Sir Nicholas Poyntz and his sister, Lady Elizabeth Heneage, intervened; the absence of parental affection on Sir John's part was regarded as abnormal.[69]

Another parental responsibility was providing a suitable example, "for commonly such egge such chickin, such syer such childe." On this point, writers of varying religious persuasions concurred, though Pilkington cautioned that good or evil in a father did not automatically produce like qualities in his child. Henry Holland concluded that it was more common for good parents to have evil children than vice versa. The significance of setting a good example rested on the belief that children learned more by observing behavior than by precept or instruction. Education, contended Greenham, was rendered ineffective by profane parental action. An Elizabethan ballad blamed the disruption of family relations through deceit on unsuitable parental examples:

> The father wyll deceyue the chylde,
> the chylde the father likewise agayne,
> thus one another dothe begylde,
> By false deceyt, that now doth raigne.

The proper example of parents entailed correction of the child for misbehavior.[70]

There was agreement on the need for physical punishment to correct errant offspring. Among the Catholics, Vaux used the fifth commandment to justify the rod to prevent harm to a child's soul by unreproved misbehavior, as long as chastisement was governed by reason. Shelford thought physical punishment should continue until a child was fifteen or sixteen, and not be restricted by inordinate love. Among the Anglicans Babington and John Bridges, a prebendary of Winchester Cathedral, shared Shelford's concern about doting parents, with the former complaining that "many of vs had rather shake off, all Gods commandements, then once make our children smart a day." Nevertheless moderation must govern chastisement. Like Vaux, John Rogers treated physical punishment as a means to preserve the souls of children from eternal damnation.[71]

Puritans shared Anglican and Catholic concerns with doting parents, the necessity of moderate chastisement, and the threat of laxity to children's souls. Using the rod to chastise corruptions of the soul was likened by William Vaughan to calling physicians to heal physical diseases. For Fenner, discipline was beneficial in inculcating religion, manners, and conscience. Puritans stressed moderation in punishment, with attention to the nature and circumstances of the fault. A wise parent must "weigh circumstances of ages, discretion, and occasions, that moued the partie [to offend], and whether it bee customarie, or a slippe; by ouersight." Suitable chastisement proceeded by degree, increasing in severity as appropriate, to benefit the child. Greenham was rather unusual in insisting on the mildest means of correction, and he called for cessation of punishment when the child submitted, though it could be extended for stubbornness. Mild correction when a child first erred was more beneficial than major chastisement later, but never was punishment to be followed by a merry countenance by parents. There must be compassion and affection but no lenity. Cleaver recognized that correcting a child before his awareness of errant behavior was doomed to fail, hence it was sometimes necessary to overlook faults. Young people inclined to live virtuously, suggested Vaughan, should be encouraged by praise rather than threatened by the rod. Behind such admonitions was the awareness that in the family the father was a minister, whose treatment of his children must be rendered accordingly.[72]

The moderate use of physical chastisement that religious writers advocated was harmonious with the views of leading educators. Mulcaster found that gentleness and courtesy were more effective than beating in dealing with children, though in the classroom "the rod must needes rule." William Kempe judged that the threat of sharp punishment was less effective than moderate penalties actually inflicted. Fathers must correct offspring as often as necessary and not expect a schoolmaster to impose all the physical chastisement.[73]

Exhortations to punish moderately were in part a reaction to excessive physical punishment by some parents. In July 1563, for example, a man was placed in the pillory in London for beating his son with a leather girdle with buckles until the boy's skin was peeled off. The lord mayor had the father whipped until he bled. The boy had to stand beside the pillory with his clothing removed so observers could see how hideously he had been beaten; it was, said Machyn in his diary, "the petest [most piteous sight to] se at any tyme." In the 1520s, Peter Carew ran away from Exeter Grammar School, climbed a turret on the city wall, and threatened to leap if his master pursued him. As punishment Carew's father tied him to a hound, led him home, and kept him chained in a dog kennel until the boy escaped. In the colleges, where younger students were subjected to corporal punishment (while older ones were fined), the Puritan diarist Samuel Ward had a guilty conscience when he showed little pity for a boy whipped in 1595.[74]

Generally, leaders of differing religious persuasions viewed parental responsibilities in similar ways. Some differences in emphasis are seen, as in the greater concern of some Puritans with the education of girls. Most striking is the stress such Puritans as Dering and Bownde placed on parental affection, which runs counter to the stereotypical picture of the Elizabethan family in modern scholarship. Such affection was more common in practice than is normally recognized. With respect to the punishment of errant children, Puritan authors dwelt on the necessity of matching penalties to offenses. Yet in matters such as the basic responsibilities of parents and the need for moderate corporal chastisement, there was widespread concurrence.

(4) Children's Responsibilities

The dueties of younger persons to the ancient is to shewe a reuerent opinion of them, and to shew all reuerent and submissiue behauiour vnto them, in respect that they carry vpon them as it were a print of Gods eternitie.

John Dod[75]

It is the duty of children to frame their life according to the will of their fathers.

Alexander Nowell[76]

The focal point of discussion of the responsibilities of children was the fifth commandment. In 1537, the Matthew Bible extended this principle of obedience to the provision of essentials for parents, and this was commonly reiterated in later biblical marginalia. In 1538, the Tyndale-Coverdale New Testament explained that obedience was required in all matters except those contrary to the word of God, that is, the same principle that applied to commands by political authorities. The Geneva annotators renewed the emphasis on limited obedience, and insisted that it be rendered with reverence. Disobedience to parents was so serious an offense that the Mosaic code appointed the punishment used for idolaters and blasphemers. Those who disobeyed were divinely cursed. If, however, parents blasphemed God or committed idolatry, their authority was to be disregarded. The Geneva annotators encouraged children to imitate parents in maintaining the true faith, but warned them not to use obedience as an excuse to emulate parents in pursuing false religion. A child's final duty was to provide a suitable burial for his parents.[77]

The Bishops' Bible was mostly concerned with extending obedience due parents to other superiors, though it asserted the importance of fulfilling one's duty to parents. Apart from the responsibility to "procure . . . long lyfe" for them, what this duty entailed was not discussed. The Beza-Tomson marginalia hammered at the theme that obedience to God takes precedence over obedience to parents. As in the Bishops' Bible, honor to parents was defined as all duties owed them. One aspect of this duty was care of needy parents according to one's ability. The Rheims annotators reiterated the responsibility of dutifulness to parents in all respects except those contrary to divine precepts. Like many Protestant annotators, Catholics asserted the importance of providing for parents in need: "The forsaking of a mans parents in their necessitie, pretending or excusing the matter vpon his giuing that which should relieue them, to God or to the Altar, that is impious and vnnatural." Thus Tudor annotators were unified on a child's responsibility to his parents: obedience in all matters not contrary to divine precepts; reverence; and care for needy elders.[78]

Anglican authors commenting on the fifth commandment stressed reverence and obedience to parents and others in authority. Babington alone discussed reverence in the context of social mobility, stipulating that respect was due even if parents belonged to a lower social status. Virtually all Anglicans dealing with obedience included the standard caveat that obedience was not required if godly commands were contravened. Anglicans continued to assert the duty to support parents in adverse circumstances. Pilkington added a special task that entailed admonishing parents who departed from biblical precepts, and parents were expected to listen. The best summation of Anglican comment on children's responsibilities is found in Nowell's catechism: "The honour of parents containeth love, fear, and reverence, and consisteth as in the proper work and duty of it, in obeying them, in saving, helping, and defending them, and also finding and relieving them if ever they be in need." William Wentworth adhered to this formula in advising Thomas to be humble, dutiful, and patient towards his parents, and to follow their example when they were good but otherwise to ignore it. Obedience, to Wentworth, meant an authoritarian relationship, for his son was to "attempt nothing" without parental sanction.[79]

Puritan exegesis of the fifth commandment was in fundamental agreement with Anglican thought, and is capsulized in Dering's catechism: "We should honour (that is to say) loue, feare, obey, and relieue our Parents, or any other that are vnto vs in their steede." A standard restriction was that obedience was limited to matters not opposed to divine precepts. Puritans upheld the traditional role of the authoritarian father, insisting that children obey parents even when the latter failed to fulfill their responsibilities. This included suffering unjust punishments. Daughters, according to Becon, must do nothing without their mothers' counsel. This authoritarian attitude was partially justified on the grounds that children were "part of their parents goods." Puritans regularly enjoined reverence for parents and support for them when they were in need. Greenham, like Pilkington, made it a child's responsibility to admonish parents, but discreetly, more in the manner of advice than correction. Some Puritans set forth other responsibilities, including the provision of funerals and restraint from instigating law suits against fathers. Children must be dutiful to parents even after coming of age. "Their reuerence and obedience," explained Richard Rogers, must "continue . . . euen vnto their end, although with more libertie, when they shall be of more ripe yeeres, their parents themselues consenting thereto."[80]

The Catholic attitude toward children's responsibilities was substantially one with that of the Protestants. Vaux's catechism required children to honor elders through reverence, obedience, and succor. Obedience must be rendered in all honest and legal matters, and parents in economic or physical distress must be relieved. The Jesuit spirit of obedience is reflected in Shelford's admonition that a child must give "vnfayned obedience without any semblance of disliking in all things that . . . [the father] shall commaunde him, not being contrarie to the word of GOD, yea though hee seeth no reason of the thing commaunded (as Isaack went obedientlie . . .) nay though his owne reason goeth against it." Such obedience was important for

Elizabethan Catholics in maintaining their children's fidelity to the old church.[81]

Separatist writings have little to say on children's duties. Barrow blamed the prevalence of disobedience and contempt for elders on ineffective teaching of the fifth commandment, and Penry likened the willingness of Separatists to suffer under harsh magistrates to the tolerance showed by children to severe parents. These glimpses into the Separatist family suggest an attitude toward children's responsibilities akin to those of other Christians, perhaps more stringently enforced. Separatists, however, encouraged their adherents to defy parents if the latter opposed their activities in the Separatist community.[82]

In practice, children usually fulfilled the prescribed obligations to their parents. At least formal deference to parents was expressed in letters, which typically began something like this: "Most humbly remembring my duty vnto you and to my very good mother," and ended: "Your most humble and obedient sonne." Parents encouraged reverence and obedience, which were reinforced by the spiritual shepherds. Edmund Campion, the noted Jesuit, advised Edmund, son of William Lord Vaux, to honor his parents. Respect for parents was manifested in various ways, as when Lionel Cranfield, the London merchant, went to the Continent in 1600, leaving his widowed mother in charge of his household. The previous year he had arranged for his family to live with her if he paid the household expenses. When he was gone, his mother, not his wife, reigned over the household and commanded reverence. Failure to render respect could weigh on a person's conscience, as in the case of a Cheshire gentleman whose 1575 will sorrowfully recorded how as a young man he had gambled and disobeyed his father. In numerous ways, then, Elizabethans heeded the responsibilities delegated to them as children.[83]

Violations of expected behavioral patterns obviously occurred, and of these the most troublesome probably involved failure to support needy parents and the subjection of parents to physical violence. The Privy Council heard cases of sons who ousted mothers from their homes and livings, and even threatened their lives. Sir Cotton Gargrave, the brother-in-law of William Wentworth, and his three and four-year-old daughters allegedly were poisoned by his son Thomas. Burghley received complaints citing misconduct of children, including one from the gentleman Gilbert Lyttelton in 1597. His case, pending in Star Chamber, accused his sons and their companions of attacking his house and threatening him with weapons. The sons had been provoked by their father's dissolute behavior following the demise of their grandfather. Lyttelton's wife and children reportedly were left without adequate maintenance while he spent £20,000 on pleasures, evil companions, and women of loose morals. Burghley also received complaints involving the dowager countess of Huntingdon and her son, George Hastings, earl of Huntingdon, and Lady Drury's accusation of her "unkind sons dealinge" with her. The disinheritance of the gentleman Thomas Dowryche led to retaliation against his widowed mother and family; he was accused of threatening to beat his sisters in his mother's presence, frequenting her house with lewd persons while she was away, threatening to burn her home, forcibly seizing her house, molesting her tenants and servants, threatening to rustle her cattle, and generally ignoring his duty to her.[84]

The Dowryche case required legal action, in this instance in the quarter sessions, as well as an appeal to Burghley. When outside action was necessary it could be obtained from various sources, including Burghley, the Privy Council, the quarter sessions, town governments, and ecclesiastical courts. Punishments varied considerably, but the courts appear to have been more interested in restoring proper parent-child relationships than in punishing offenses per se. When an elderly Chester tanner petitioned for financial assistance in 1598, the quarter sessions ordered his son and heir, also a tanner, to provide him with a gown and 20s. per quarter. Similarly, in 1589 the Privy Council settled a quarrel between Edward Parker, Lord Morley, and his brother Thomas regarding support of their mother, who was imprisoned in the Netherlands. The Council did not wish Lord Morley to be considered "unnaturall towardes his mother in not yeilding unto her suche due for her daylie maintenaunce as she maie justly demaund." Firmer penalties sometimes were imposed. The archdeacon's court at Oxford excommunicated Richard Walter of Chipping Norton in 1584 "for schoulding with his ffather & beating of him extremelie;" he was also admonished to seek his father's forgiveness and submit to him as a dutiful child. Harsher punishment was imposed on an Exeter girl, who was whipped and banished for calling her mother a whore and her father a thief.[85]

In the Elizabethan period, no major differences existed between religious groups concerning the obligations of children. But on the Continent, Jean Bodin revived the ancient Roman concept of *pater familias*, with the father (like a king) possessing the power of life and death over his child, and refusing him the right to resist unjust commands. This view was embraced in England by Convocation in 1606, and was enshrined in Robert Filmer's *Patriarcha*. Yet such a view, according to Lawrence Stone, was never foreign to Tudor England, but was manifested "in the quasi-absolute authority of a despot" which fathers in patriarchal aristocratic families possessed. Although this seems an overstatement for the Elizabethan era, a father was expected to manifest substantial authority in view of the analogy between princes and fathers. Because the parallel was frequently used, disobedience to fathers must have been feared as a dangerous example that could incite political disobedience. The authoritarian interpretation of the fifth commandment was applied to all forms of authority, especially civil and familial. In England, however, the interpretation of this authority in absolute terms was largely a product of Stuart, not Elizabethan, times.[86]

(5) Christenings and Social Pageantry

Ceremonies have more in weight than in sight, they work by commonness of use much, although in the several acts of their usage we scarcely discern any good they do.

Richard Hooker[87]

Yt was butt a seremony.

Mr. Harold[88]

A long-standing duty of parents was to provide Christian baptism. The monied and landed classes took this occasion to engage in another display of pageantry intended to bolster the social order. The ritual was so much a part of social custom, as well as religious tradition, that even Yorkshire recusants regularly had their infants baptized in parish churches until the religious divisions became seriously pronounced in the early 1580s. Christenings normally occurred in the first week of an infant's life. An examination of eighty baptisms in the parish of St. Peter's Cornhill, London, in the period 1574-78 reveals that 25% of the infants were christened within two days of birth, 50% within three days, and 75% within five days. Nearly two-thirds of the christenings were on Sunday. A family normally paid a parish fee ranging from 4d. to 11½d. for the ceremony, but less (1d. to 2d.) if the infant died. Fees probably were waived or collected on a voluntary basis for the poor.[89]

Those who could afford it could turn a simple religious ceremony into a lavish social spectacle. The christening ceremonies for the eldest son of Henry Herbert, earl of Pembroke, in 1580 lasted ten days and must have cost a substantial sum. Christening clothes for the infant, and perhaps new apparel for the parents, could be expensive. In 1562 Sir Henry Williams provided his daughter with a white satin gown and a mantle of crimson satin trimmed with a four-inch gold braid. Further expense could be incurred by lavishly decorating the church, perhaps with rich tapestries (cloth of arras) for the walls, as in the christening of Sir Thomas Chamberlain's son in 1559. When Robert, son of Sir Gilbert Dethick, a Knight of the Garter, was baptized in 1561, tapestries and a cloth of state were used, and the parish church of St. Giles without Cripplegate was strewn with green rushes and herbs.

After the ceremony, the well-to-do hosted elaborate banquets. When the daughter of the French ambassador was christened in 1602, the banquet reportedly featured a thousand different dishes. The greater the banquets, the more varied the wine lists, which sometimes included French, Rhenish, and Gascon wines as well as hippocras, muscatel, and wassail.[90] I have found no specific complaints by Anglicans or Puritans directed against such social pomp.

A sense of what such displays entailed is conveyed in the christening of Elizabeth, eldest daughter of John Lord Russell, and the granddaughter of Francis Russell, earl of Bedford, at Westminster Abbey on 27 October 1575 at 10 A.M. Elaborate preparations for the family were made in the dean's house, replete with a cloth of state for an earl and other rich furnishings. At the appointed time, the christening party processed from the dean's lodging to the church, with gentlemen leading the way, followed by knights, barons, earls, the earl of Leicester as godfather, the baby garbed in crimson velvet trimmed with gold lace, her face covered with fine linen decorated with white and gold flowers, and carried by the midwife, followed by the countess of Sussex as godmother, a gentleman usher, the countess of Warwick (as the queen's deputy), with her train borne by Lady Burghley and Lady Bacon, and other ladies. The service began with a collation by the dean. "Now assoone as the Deane had made an ende the Lady Bacon tooke the child & brought it to the font, where the Deane attended in his Surplice, then the E. of Leicester & the Countess of Sussex aproched neare to the Trauers and there taried vntill the deputie came forth[,] from whence they leasurely proceeded to the font[,] the deputies traine still borne[,] where they christened the child." After the midwife had dressed the infant, basins, ewers, and towels were brought for the queen's deputy, the countess of Sussex, and the earl of Leicester to wash. The traditional hippocras and wafers were served, followed by the recessional in formal order, with Lady Bacon carrying the baby.

The formal banquet that ensued continued the pomp of the occasion. Three tables were prepared, one for the thirteen principal dignitaries, another for the gentlemen, and a third for the ladies. A two-course meal was served, following which the tables were cleared. "Then came in a costly and delicate banquet at the vper table only," after which Lord Russell's chaplain said grace, and the lords washed, paid their respects to the infant, and departed. Among the presents were a great standing cup from the queen, another from the countess of Essex, and a great bowl from Leicester. The queen also bestowed 3s. on the midwife and 40s. on the nurse. Unlike weddings and funerals, such pageants normally did not involve participation or viewing by the lower orders. Gifts might, however, be bestowed on the infant by persons not present at the ceremony.[91]

Apparently Puritans did not object to such pomp for christenings; indeed, most of the principals in the Russell ceremony were Puritans. Some disagreements occurred in other areas, such as the use of the sign of the cross in baptism, which have been thoroughly explored by modern historians. Some controversy existed concerning the use of godparents. Normally there were three at a christening, two of whom were of the same sex as the infant. Parker learned in 1564 that some parochial clergy advocated as many as seven godparents, while others preferred that a child's natural father be his principal godfather. (Some clergy allegedly preferred that a father christen his own child.) Instances are recorded of no godfathers being used, as when a Southwark minister baptized a child without godparents in 1560 because christening "was butt a seremony." Sir William Locke, the grandfather of a child christened in 1561, "had nodur godfather nor godmother hym-seylff," so the absence of godparents cannot be tied strictly to Puritans or Separatists. In fact, the Separatist Robert Harrison served as a godfather in 1574, but was ousted from his post as schoolmaster at Aylsham, Norfolk, for asking the deacon who performed the ceremony "to change the word of the book, viz. *thou* into *you*; and to leave out the sign of the cross." Godparents undertook to teach a child the principles of religion, but there was considerable debate about the validity of godparents' answering baptismal queries for the infant. Gilby, for example, deemed it a popish practice for godparents to promise that a baby believed in Christ and forsook the devil.[92]

Other concerns were expressed by religious leaders, including the name given to a child. Pilkington urged that Christian names be used to remind children of their duty to God; heathen names and the names of "feigned foolish saints" were eschewed. Cleaver and Fenner agreed; the latter advocated names in the vernacular "which may haue a godly signification, fit for that work," but not profane or foreign names. In May 1599 the Puritan schoolmaster John Symons sought to name his child "Doe well," but the vicar refused and named the boy John, causing "a great murmuring among the Brethren, who said it came from the Hebrew word Abdeel." Another matter was raised by the Puritan Christopher Hooke, who was called by Lady Paget and her daughter, Elizabeth Savile, to conduct a thanksgiving service, featuring the singing of Psalms, at the birth of Elizabeth's sons. Hooke favored this practice by all parents.[93]

Visitation articles reveal numerous deviations from accepted baptismal practices that troubled the prelates. Queries concerned christenings not performed according to the *Book of Common Prayer*, which omitted the sign of the cross or failed to include godparents. There was concern that some godparents were ignorant of the catechism, Lord's prayer, and Ten Commandments, or had not partaken of communion. Aylmer's articles for the diocese of London in 1586 inquired if any delayed baptism past the Sunday following birth, except for illness or other urgent reasons. From the 1580s, it was common to inquire about children taken outside their parishes for Catholic baptism. No prelatical concern, however, was expressed about the pageantry used in christenings.[94]

Thus in the area of married life and parenthood, areas of broad agreement existed among Anglicans and Puritans. Despite dissension regarding the theology of baptism and such related matters as the sign of the cross and vows by godparents for infants, the social pageantry of christening was not in dispute. Nor was there substantial disagreement concerning the duties of children to parents, viz. reverence, obedience, and support for needy elders. Differences of emphasis are apparent with respect to parental responsibilities, notably the interest of some Puritans in parental affection, and the Puritan insistence that punishment of erring offspring suit the offense. There were also broad areas of concurrence between Anglicans and Puritans concerning duties of marital partners, but Puritans stressed sexual fidelity for husbands and the necessity for wives to engage in productive labor at home. Puritans emphasized the charitable obligations of wives, and moved more rapidly toward marriage as a partnership, though no Puritan or Anglican writer regarded the partners as equal. In practice, some Elizabethan men found it necessary or desirable to accord an important share of responsibility to their spouses. On divorce, the Anglican and Puritan positions are not identical, with Puritans differing sharply in their advocacy of divorce with the right to remarry for those whose spouses committed adultery.

CHAPTER 7

The Household

For Elizabethans, the household was the basic social unit in which the head exercised a responsibility analagous to the prince. The discipline, order, and godliness believed necessary for a healthy state were rooted in the household, which included servants as well as family members. The extent to which religion was emphasized in the household could make each a mini-parish, with the master and mistress vested with pastoral and pedagogical functions. In Puritan households especially, the task of the wife was broadened to embrace greater spiritual duties, thus enhancing her status. Religious instruction of children and servants tended to devolve on her shoulders, giving her an important role in shaping their minds. In Catholic circles too, women were active in the household, helping to shelter the family chaplain or supporting the work of Jesuits and seminary priests. The household was the nucleus of the state, and for this reason the state could not tolerate its subversion by religious forces foreign to its outlook.

(1) The Household as a Religious Unit

A Familie is a communion and fellowship of life betweene the husband & the wife, the parents & children, and betweene the master and the seruant.

William Vaughan[1]

The Churches spring out of instructed families.

Josias Nichols[2]

291

To the extent that Elizabethans viewed the relationship of husbands and fathers to their families as analagous to that of princes to states, households were microcosms of the state. Puritan leaders, though, were more interested in developing the conception of the household as a microcosm of the church. Heads of households in effect exercised a role similar to that of a minister in his congregation. "A good and carefull housholder," wrote Cleaver, "so ordereth and frameth his houshold, so as it may manifestly appear, that it is indeed the house of a faithfull christian, and that hee himselfe is as a Pastour ouer his familie, that hee instructeth it in good and godly discipline, by continuall exercise in godlinesse." Becon and Knox depicted each man as a bishop in his own house. The Puritan ideal was for every man to make of his household a church, and to govern it accordingly. Udall reversed the analogy, making the church the house of God, and God the great householder. Puritans believed that a family rightly governed was a principal stay for church and commonwealth. Anglicans apparently did not adopt this analogy, though the Catholic Robert Shelford urged his readers to make their houses sanctuaries for divine worship. Something of the contrast between Anglican and Puritan concepts of the household can be seen in the analogy of the schoolhouse: For Pilkington the church is God's school, but for Perkins, the family serves this function. The difference reflects Puritan disenchantment with conditions in the church and a heightened concern for spiritual edification, which could not be sufficiently developed in regular church services. By itself the institutional church was not adequate to educate and train the godly, so the family was exalted and given added responsibility.[3]

The biblical marginalia do not depict the household as a church or school of God, but focus on the religious obligations of the head of the household. The Geneva annotators urged householders to be preachers to their families, instruct members to worship, and teach the law of God. Mothers too were encouraged to teach children. In the Geneva and Bishops' Bibles, the annotators gave the example of the exiled Joseph in instructing his family in the ways of God. The note to Genesis 17:13 in the Bishops' Bible summarized the masters' duty by asserting that they must "trauayle to bring al their householde to true religion." In the Beza-Tomson Bible, Cornelius was praised for doing exactly that.[4]

In the Elizabethan age, four basic responsibilities were attributed to householders, primarily by Puritans: oversight of religious duties, attendance at church, catechetical instruction, and family worship. Puritans stressed the necessity for the head of the household to supervise the spiritual obligations of each member. "For the familie," said Fenner, "the dutie which regardeth them is, to keepe them in subjection, for the performance of al duties of holines and religion, and for the diligent performance of those woorks and labors, which are fit for everie one." This responsibility was commonly asserted by other Puritans, who made it a principal duty of the householder to provide godly instruction. Stockwood averred that this responsibility applied regardless of degree or vocation, and Chaderton and others insisted that wives share this responsibility. Francis Johnson appealed to the Privy Council and other magistrates in April and May 1593 to release the Separatists from prison for fear of their "families' distruccion through lacke of guiding."[5]

A householder's second responsibility was to see that his charges attended church. Apart from official pronouncements, such as visitation articles, Anglicans did not emphasize this duty nearly as much as Puritans. The latter were adamant that whole households frequent services to worship and learn their responsibilities. When available, lectures must be attended insofar as possible. The Puritan congregation at Dedham, Essex, enacted "yt all the housholders frequent the two lectures read euery weeke with some of their servantes, at the leaste as many as may be spared in regard to their trades and callinges." On Sundays householders were expected to attend services with their families and servants, "as many as may be spared at home for necessary uses of children etc." Puritans did not want householders to assign responsibilities to servants or allow them to miss religious services to rest or play on the sabbath. Stockwood complained that most householders let servants do as they wished on the sabbath and "runne at random to all kinde of licentiousnes, vanitie and lewde excercises." Attendance at church was not enough for the Puritans, who insisted that householders require those in their care to spend the rest of the sabbath in private devotions.[6]

Numerous attempts were made in Elizabethan England to require householders to bring their families and servants to church. From 1577 on the bishops inquired if this was done. In 1564, however, Sandys, as bishop of Worcester, had been content to ask the Privy Council to see only that gentlemen and others in authority attended church and received communion once a quarter as an example for others. The attempt to impose stricter requirements on householders was probably due to Puritan influence. In the borough of Leicester, the Puritan Henry Hastings, earl of Huntingdon, appears to have been largely responsible. In February 1562 at least one person from every household had to attend the Wednesday and Friday sermons, or the offending householder was fined 4d. The fine was increased subsequently to 12d., then reduced to a scale of 1d. to 4d. in 1580. In November 1587 it was "ordered and agreed that euerye Alderman in his warde, or his Deputye or Constable, shall from henceforth take order and compell all suche persone and persons whatsoeuer inhabitinge, cowchinge [lying] or beinge within this warde, to cum to the Sermondes with ther wyse [wives], [who] wolde not." Although the earl died in 1595, his influence lingered as the ordinance was reenacted in October 1600.[7]

At best, attempts to force the householder to bring his subordinates to church met with limited success. Extant regulations for the households of gentry and nobility sometimes include this duty. When William Chub preached at Tidworth, Hants., in 1587, he saw William Paulet, marquess of Winchester, attending with his family and servants. In 1584 the archdeacon's court at Oxford had trouble getting just one member of some households to attend church. If the head of the household refused to attend, it was often difficult for servants to go to services. Householders sometimes had difficulty persuading their charges to go to church. Sir Robert Tirwight, for instance, could not get his sons to attend church with him. Catholic householders sometimes found it advantageous to attend services alone, while providing Catholic ceremonies in their homes for their household. The testimony scattered throughout the State Papers points to a sizeable number of Englishmen who would not or could not bring their households to Sunday services.[8]

Catechizing, the third responsibility for the head of a household, was generally recognized by religious commentators. Among the Anglicans, Sandys urged that catechizing be done by householders, but the more conservative Hooker thought schoolmasters were equally acceptable. Curteys exhorted the householders to read enough of the Bible to teach themselves, their family, and their servants to fear God, obey their prince, love their neighbors, and render duty to their superiors. As archbishop of York and then Canterbury, Grindal instructed his clergy to catechize every Sunday and holy day; during the instruction they were to note which children between the ages of six and twenty were ignorant of the catechism, thereby learning which parents and masters were negligent in sending the young for instruction. Anglicans wanted their youth catechized, but there was no unanimity that householders be involved in this, other than sending young people to church or school. Elizabethan Catholics, however, found family catechism essential to preserve their faith. Lawrence Vaux wrote a catechism, and Shelford urged that Catholic homes be made sanctuaries for worship and that householders instruct their families and servants.[9]

The Puritans strongly emphasized catechetical instruction by householders, though not always successfully. Nichols complained that "many times when we take great paines, the backwardnes of the masters doth pull downe all that wee build." Preferably catechizing or religious instruction was to be done in the household on a daily basis, or even twice a day, as Edward Vaughan urged. Nichols provided a detailed outline for household catechizers, beginning with the Lord's prayer, the creed, and the Ten Commandments. After this came instruction in the creation, Christ's redemption, the sanctifying work of the Holy Spirit, the Trinity, and death and resurrection. The Ten Commandments, a short catechism, biblical stories and verses, and a scriptural example of the breaking of each commandment had to be memorized. Psalms also were to be memorized and sung in English meter. As the child progressed, more difficult catechisms had to be mastered but not memorized. In all Nichols suggested that nine levels of catechisms be learned. "By that time . . . [the householder] hath beaten the former Catechismes into his peoples heads, [he] shal perceiue them better able to receiue stronger meate." Nichols thought two hours each weekday was sufficient for this, plus extra time on the sabbath. The work was to be performed primarily by nobles, gentlemen, university tutors, schoolmasters, and women. Religious instruction included rehearsing the household in the principal points of sermons. Puritans were in earnest with respect to religious instruction in each household, especially by parents.[10]

An indication of success in domestic religious instruction is provided by the number of catechisms printed in the Elizabethan era, often for the use of parents and masters. Approximately one hundred catechisms were published for household use between 1550 and 1600. Allen compiled a special collection of Proverbs for this purpose, with most alphabetized and some with short expository comments. Some catechisms were simple, such as Christopher Watson's *Briefe Principles of Religion, for the Exercise of Youth*, which was only seven pages. Others were more substantial, but these posed a financial problem for families of limited means. Stockwood revised Dering's catechism to reduce the cost. Apparently even the poor tried to purchase catechisms, for Stockwood reports that "a penie or two pence, is a great deale of monie" for them, hence they "did repine and grudge at the charges." John Thaxter, a minister at Bridgeham, Norfolk, proposed in 1585 to publish two catechisms for his parishioners: "My peoples iournye must not be over long &

tedious; for then will they sit downe in the entrance, & stirre not a foote further: neyther must it want any necessarye foode & viand; for then I may be accounted to them an ill stewarde."[11]

Puritans took their catechetical responsibility seriously. The borough of Leicester in 1580 stipulated that each child aged eight and over be taught the Lord's prayer and creed; failure to do so could result in a fine or three days' imprisonment for the offending parent or master. The Dedham classis enacted that householders "cause their youth to present themselues at the times appointed to be examyned in the pointes of their Catechisme." Lady Margaret Hoby's Yorkshire household provided catechetical instruction for servants as well as "the poore and Ignorant" each evening, with Lady Hoby assisting her chaplain. Samuel Ward catechized his brother Henry on Sunday afternoons while the former was a student at Christ's College, Cambridge; in September 1595 he reports guilt for neglecting this duty.[12]

The fourth obligation of householders, the provision of family worship, was emphasized by Puritans. Generally this included collective prayers at the morning and evening meals, daily Bible reading, religious exhortations or instruction, thanksgiving, and Psalm singing. The ideal was to worship twice daily, and this practice could include neighbors. Perkins cautioned that conducting this worship did not make the householder a minister, for the former "teacheth onely by the authoritie of a father or master: whereas ministers of the word teach & exhort by the authoritie and name of God." No householders could provide sacraments or marry couples, and in theological matters the authority of the minister prevailed.[13]

Household worship was practiced in many Elizabethan homes. In landed families, such worship was a natural consequence of having residential chaplains. A plan for the regulation of a nobleman's household, formulated c. 1597, required every person, regardless of status, to attend the services. In 1580 Robert Openshaw, author of a short catechism, described a gentleman's household characterized by daily worship services in the parlor using the *Book of Common Prayer*. Robert third Lord Rich held Puritan exercises at his Essex home in the early 1580s, which got him into trouble with the queen and Bishop Aylmer; his father had done the same. Walsingham was praised because of the chaplains who preached daily in his household. Henry Stanley, earl of Derby, who was not a Puritan, brought the best preachers in the county to his home on Sundays to lead services, "and he giveth favourable countennance to all the professors of religion." Nicholas Bownde, rector of Norton, Suffolk, and Greenham's son-in-law, praised the household of Robert Foorth, a gentleman of Butley, Suffolk, for its "most excellent orders . . . for daily praier, for reading the Scriptures, and for singing of Psalmes." A comparable gentry household was that of John and Jane Walrond. In his household, Eusebius Pagit read a chapter from the Old Testament at breakfast and one from the New at supper, following which he commented on the passages and questioned his household. Sir Robert Tirwight tried to provide household worship, but his sons, daughters, and servants refused to participate. The Catholic Edmund Lord Sheffield used the *Book of Common Prayer* for his household on Wednesdays, Fridays, and Sundays, and in return was allowed to use his own prayers in the mornings and evenings on the assumption that "it will we[a]ry him to vse so muche to praye."[14]

A natural way to provide religious services and catechizing was to hire a residential chaplain, but this practice sparked debate. Whitgift defended domestic chaplains for the nobility and gentry, especially those hindered from attending parish services by infirmity, distance, and urgent business. In such cases, preaching and the administration of the sacraments in the household were commendable. William Barlow, bishop of Chichester, informed the Privy Council in 1564 of the advantages of domestic chaplains for the landed classes on their estates: "It is to be wished that men of honour, whyles they be resiante in the sheire, to haue learned preachers of their own or others, shewinge themselves wyllinge to heare the worde of god, whose example draweth a nombre of people after them." The Puritan George Gifford approved chaplains if they admonished the aristocracy in godly matters and refused undue deference. Puritan peers such as Francis Russell, earl of Bedford, had domestic chaplains, as did many Anglican nobility. Yet Henry Percy, earl of Northumberland, had no household chaplain until 1626, when he was in his early sixties.[15]

Critics of household chaplains sought to end or restrict their use. The Puritan Thomas Wood complained to Leicester in 1576 that chaplains in episcopal households lived on income from beneficcs they did not serve. He had no objection to chaplains in aristocratic households if they were privately maintained and were not supported by plural livings or funds diverted from poor relief. Others, such as the Puritan Robert Crowley, thought domestic chaplains objectionable because of their excessive deference. In the same vein, Barrow blasted domestic chaplains as sycophants and trencher priests who insinuated themselves into the homes of the powerful and were fattened by fine foods and pleasant company, avoiding their duties. The Puritan Simon Harward, preaching at Manchester in 1582, condemned those who worshipped privately, as nobles with chaplains often did, rather than in parish churches. This exclusiveness was "to rob God of his honour, and commit Sacriledge, in keeping back their tongues from the publique confessing, & their bodies from the open glorifying of the name of the Lord Jesus." Even Bancroft worried about the growing reliance of the gentry on household chaplains rather than parish churches.[16]

A significant reason for concern over private chaplains was the presence of Catholic priests. As early as 1564 the bishops of Worcester (Sandys), Hereford (Scory), Peterborough (Scambler), and Ely (Cox) complained to the Privy Council of the role of Catholic priests as household chaplains and tutors. Sandys accused these priests of perverting the simple and blaspheming the truth, and urged the Council to restrict their liberty and require subscription to the Oath of Supremacy. To Scory, aristocrats who allowed Catholic chaplains to perform masses and catechize in their households were "a marvelous stombling block to the Quenes majestes loving subiectes." Scambler and Cox wanted to allow the landed classes to retain private tutors only if they were examined and licensed by a bishop. The Puritans Stockwood and Field were concerned with private instructors—"the sweepings of the Uniuersities"—because of their evil effects on youth. They could serve as chaplains and doubly offend by saying mass, as happened in Lancashire.[17]

The government took this threat less seriously than the Commons and prelates. In the stormy 1571 Parliament, a bill aimed at Catholic chaplains masquerading as servants went through three readings in the Commons in two days, but did not become law. The prelates manifested concern in injunctions and visitation articles. In 1571, for instance, Grindal required that all schoolmasters, including those in domestic service, be licensed. Visitation articles inquired if priests or Jesuits were active in households as chaplains or tutors, or if persons were preaching in aristocratic homes without episcopal license. Offenders were apprehended whenever possible, as in the case of the Jesuit John Moone, who was taken in April 1594 by Sir Walter Raleigh at the house of Lady Stourton, formerly the wife of the deceased Sir John Arundel.[18]

Striking at chaplains and tutors was not enough; the government also removed Catholic children from their homes and placed them in Protestant households for instruction. Wardship rights provided an ideal vehicle for this purpose, and were used to take the young George Clifford, earl of Cumberland, from his Catholic uncle, Anthony Browne, Viscount Montagu, and place him in the care of Francis Russell, earl of Bedford. Similar means were adopted for Philip Lord Wharton and others. It was not always the government who initiated the action. In 1575, for example, Henry Guildford petitioned Burghley that his sister-in-law, Lady Guildford, not be allowed to educate her son lest he be raised a Catholic. The previous year twenty-three people, including Lady Guildford, had been apprehended at her home when mass was being said. Guildford wanted wardship rights of his nephew granted to a Protestant. As members of the Council of the North, William Chaderton, bishop of Chester, and Henry Stanley, earl of Derby, took Catholic children from their homes and placed them in Chaderton's care for religious instruction. Some of these youngsters went to Manchester Grammar School and then to Oriel College, Oxford or to Cambridge. Stockwood sanctioned such action, arguing that the English must emulate the Turks in this regard, and that natural parents must pay the costs of such instruction. If such children lived with their parents while undergoing Protestant catechizing, the parents must not teach them. Nevertheless such action was not always effective. Despite Chaderton's efforts, some Manchester boys ended up at Douai instead of Oriel. The Jesuit John Gerard tells how at the age of five he, along with his brother Thomas, was placed in a Protestant household. The boys were later sent to Exeter College, Oxford, but left with John's Latin tutor, Edmund Lewknor, after less than a year. They were subsequently tutored by the priest William Sutton under the guise of a Greek tutor. [19]

Elizabethan Catholicism survived in large measure, as John Bossy has shown, owing to its social organization. Before 1569, bastard feudalism was important in the border regions as a means of continuing Catholic ways, but after the Northern Rebellion, this type of social organization declined. For the remainder of the era, independent seigneurial households in areas weakly controlled by the government and larger households in other areas carried on the Catholic tradition. The great houses merged occasions of substantial hospitality with the liturgical cycle of the old church, especially at Christmas and Easter. The seigneurial households normally could not do this, but they sustained their faith through Catholic chaplains and tutors. Gerard converted Grace, wife of Sir Francis Fortescue, to Catholicism and persuaded her to keep a Catholic chaplain, Anthony Hoskins. The extent to which the larger households maintained some independence vis-à-vis the established church was apparent in 1581 when

William Lord Vaux was presented for not coming to church with "his household and familiars and divers servants," for which his defense was that his household was a parish by itself. Catholic households were jeopardized by the latent threat of recalcitrant servants or disgruntled tenants informing the state, as happened to Sir Thomas Tresham, a rack-renter and encloser. A greater threat to the household religion of Catholics was the dynamism and militancy of missionary priests, who from their principal base at Douai endeavored to topple the Elizabethan settlement. Catholic households were altered as servants whose loyalty was questionable were dismissed, priests' holes were built, and the household was integrated into a network of routes leading to the Continent.[20]

Thus Puritans and Catholics, who differed so sharply in theology, shared a realization of the importance of household religion. Puritans differed from Anglicans in their emphasis on the householders' obligations to supervise the spiritual life of the household, to see that each member attended church services, to catechize personally, and to provide household worship. This conception of household religion required unity as its prerequisite, but simultaneously it reinforced familial solidarity. Household religion also was important in enhancing the role of the wife, particularly through catechizing servants and young people. For Puritans especially, catechetical instruction was a parental task, not something reserved for a parish priest, family chaplain, or schoolmaster. The family orientation of Puritanism suggests that its appeal was strongest in those social groups and geographical areas that fostered close family relations. Puritanism has been associated primarily with the merchants, professionals, and artisans (for example, by Christopher Hill) and the gentry (by Michael Walzer), and to these groups must be added the yeomanry and some higher aristocracy, and servants and apprentices associated with these groups. Catholicism too appealed to some of the same social elements, though not precisely for the same reasons; the household element in Catholicism essentially evolved because of the threat of persecution, on the one hand, and the associations of the Old Faith with traditional customs for the maintenance of the extended family, on the other. A sampling of 128 recusants in 1586, of whom 110 were men, includes 1 peer (Lord Vaux), 7 knights, 94 esquires and gentlemen, 3 lawyers, 2 physicians, and 3 of undesignated status. Of the 20 women, 2 were from noble families, 5 were wives or widows of knights, 1 was a servant, and 11 were probably from gentry or wealthy urban families. Geographical studies (for example, by R. C. Richardson) generally show a predominance of Puritans in areas of pastoral farming, where the farmhouse was the focal point, rather than in highly manorialized regions where the focus was on village life. [21]

(2) The Household, Uniformity, and Order

Euery kingdome or houshold, must be gouerned onely by the lawes of the king, or orders of the housholder.

John Udall [22]

Families are the fountains of all common-weals, purge the fountaines and the streames shall be clean.

Henry Holland [23]

In a society where the government depended on householders to maintain order in their establishments, firm control was necessary. The religious writers saw order and uniformity as means to maintain a godly household and ultimately a thriving church and Christian commonwealth. "How needfull houshold gouernment is towards our children," reflected Greenham, "it may appeare by the slender thriuing and small profiting of religion or vertue, either in the Church or Common-wealth." Like an orderly commonwealth, the family, as a little commonwealth, requires governance and rules of order. In the household, according to Greenham, the husband must formulate rules for the petty commonwealth and the wife must see that they are executed for the welfare of all. Failure to enforce such order was deemed as ruinous to a household as civil and criminal disobedience in a state; thus Sir Walter Mildmay advised his son Anthony to govern his home in an orderly fashion, for no household can exist in disorder. Good government in families is conducive not only to godly behavior and socio-political stability, but also to thrift and good husbandry. [24]

On the importance of maintaining an orderly household there was no disagreement among religious writers. Abraham's family, well taught and effectively governed, was an ideal to emulate. Parents and masters must govern themselves and their subordinates, "restraining their children and seruants from all loosenesse and lewd behauiour, and training them vp with all care to vertuous and godly life." Orderly government entails correction of misbehavior, appropriate instruction, restraint from idleness, and enforcement of the sabbath. This must be done decently and moderately to benefit the governors and the governed. "Lordlinesse is vnmeete in a housholde gouernment, and yet familiaritie with such as are vnder gouernment, breedeth contempt." Achieving this mean was a goal of Lady Margaret Hoby, who taught and worked alongside her servants. As in the state, authority in the household must be exercised firmly but moderately to avoid rebellion.[25]

Some Elizabethans took these prescriptions very seriously. Burghley was praised for governing his household with moderation and maintaining standards of decency, as was Bishop Jewel. Among the peerage and gentry, regulations were formulated to ensure an orderly household. A set of rules prepared by Lady Jane, second wife of Henry Lord Berkeley, stipulated that the gentlemen of the household "should endeavour themselves to the uttermost they may to live orderly" by following her regulations. The wives who formulated such ordinances, or played, as Lady Hoby did, a major role in enforcing household behavior, often enhanced their position vis-à-vis their husbands, more closely approximating marriage as a partnership. Another indication of the seriousness with which some Elizabethans regarded household order is found in instructions left by fathers to sons. A prime example is the 1593 admonitions of the West Country yeoman Robert Furse, which advise his son to delight in good housekeeping as a means of religious blessing, and to "be carefull for your householde[,] use mesure yn all thynges."[26]

To obtain and preserve order in a household sometimes required expelling unsuitable persons, a course approved by Anglicans and Puritans alike. Sandys, Fenner, and Stockwood called for the removal of ungodly members of the household, but Openshaw limited expulsion to evil servants who showed no signs of reformation. Ungodliness could be displayed in errant behavior or false doctrine, hence Fenner urged householders to "suffer none in their house vnrefourmed: which either in judgment is known to erre from the truth of the worde of God, or in maners, from the practise of the same." Sandys found support in Psalm 101 to excise ungodly members, whom he likened to serpents. Ungodly children and faithless servants were subject to expulsion in Sandys' judgment, and such admonitions were sometimes put into practice. When the unwed servant of John Woolton, bishop of Exeter, became pregnant, she was permanently expelled from his household, and the male servant who got her pregnant had to leave for two years. Parker reproved and fined members of his household who missed the worship services he conducted twice a day, but apparently no one was expelled. When William Wiseman of Braddocks, Essex, converted to Catholicism, he dismissed his Protestant servants, but with kindness and generosity.

When, however, Sir Francis Hastings' cousin Anne converted to Protestantism in a Catholic household, he exhorted her to remain steadfast regardless of pressures against her. For religious and moral reasons, householders were exhorted to maintain order and uniformity, but members of a household were expected to stand by their faith if the head of the household was of a contrary religious view.[27]

The structure of the Elizabethan household enhanced the ability to maintain order. The decline of kinship as the major organizing principle of society resulted in greater control being placed in the head of the household, though it is erroneous to see this as "one obvious cause" (as Stone does) for the "decline in the status and rights of wives in the sixteenth and early seventeenth centuries." Stone cites deprecatory remarks about females in this era to support his view, yet the evidence points to an improving position for wives because of—not in spite of—the development of the nuclear family. Decreased familial horizons made it more necessary than ever for the husband to rely on his wife as a partner in running the household, raising children, catechizing servants and young people, and (among some landed families) managing the estate. Husbands absent for long periods on state business left the running of their households and other affairs to their wives, not their kin. Barbara, wife of Sir Robert Sidney, and Anne, wife of Henry Carey, Lord Hunsdon, provide notable examples.[28]

Although the nuclear family was in the ascendant in Elizabethan England, households were still large among the more well-to-do elements, making the question of order essential. Available statistics are somewhat misleading, for they tend to obscure the relatively few very large households among the aristocracy and closely related groups. In 1574 the mean household size in Poole, Dorset, was 6.05 (with a population of 1,357), and in 1599 Ealing, Middlesex, had a mean household size of only 4.75 (with a population of 427). Nobles nevertheless had substantial households: Burghley had 80 servants in London, 26 to 30 at Theobalds, and others at court. Thomas Percy, earl of Northumberland, had 145 in his household in October 1568, but his brother left his nephew a smaller household of 57 in 1586. Roger Lord North's household included 24 gentlemen and 70 yeomen in 1578, and Henry Stanley, earl of Derby, had 145 on his household roll in 1590. Richard Bertie and his wife, the duchess of Suffolk, had a household of 80, in addition to gardeners, dairymaids, laborers, and retainers in the early 1560s. The domestic staff of Robert Lord Spencer numbered 38 in 1599 at his principal residence. When the family fortunes of Henry Lord Berkeley waned after the execution of his brother-in-law, Thomas Howard, duke of Norfolk, he dismissed some 20 household servants but retained at least 70. Gentry households were typically smaller. Sir Thomas Tresham, a Catholic, had 52 servants, at least 40 of whom his wife thought unnecessary. The Puritan Sir William Fitzwilliam of Dogsthorpe, Northants., had only 14 resident servants in his household in the 1590s, the same number as in the Puritan household of Sir Thomas Hoby in 1600. Lady Grace Mildmay had only 10 in her household. Generally gentry households seem to have had between 10 and 60 domestic servants, making the problem of order and uniformity important. A well-to-do yeoman normally had from one to three household servants. Prelatical households tended to be sizeable as well, and included Aylmer's 80 servants, Parkhurst's 32, and Downham's 40.[29]

The regulation of households through holding heads responsible for members' actions was manifested in numerous ways. Church courts were involved, as exemplified in the records of the arch-deacon's court at Oxford. An Elsfield ("Elsford") man was cited in 1584 for "kepinge an evell rule in his howse." The same court summoned the vicar of Lewknor on an identical charge, but found him not guilty because he had expelled a male and a female servant "who plaide the naughtie packes together" in his house. Sir Thomas Hesketh of Lancashire was imprisoned when his kinsman complained that he did not keep strict rule in his household. Hesketh admitted negligence in seeking reform and promised Leicester, whose favor he sought, that his household would conduct itself dutifully or be punished. The House of Commons tried to make heads of households responsible for disciplining families and servants, even to the point of having heads be answerable for penalties incurred by household members. This situation occurred in 1601 in connection with a bill mandating attendance at church, but when a new bill was drafted, there was enough opposition to omit such provisions. One of the arguments that carried the day reveals a problem faced by house-holders who imposed order and religious uniformity: "Every man," argued Anthony Dyott, member for Tamworth, Warks., "can tame a shrew but he that hath her: perhaps she [his wife] will not come [to church]; and for her willfulness no reason the husband should be punished."[30]

On household order and religious uniformity there was, then, no disagreement among religious leaders. The nature of the belief imposed in a household of course differed, and there was the stand-ard proviso that no superior could require belief or actions contrary to scriptural principles. Thus Catholics and Protestants had a ready defense for those of like persuasion who defied the head of a household for reasons of faith. Some disagreement was expressed over how far a householder could be held responsible for his subordinates. One suspects those who opposed the extended responsibility were not Puritans. Sir John Neale argued as much when he found Puritan support for the 1601 bill on church attendance, which attempted to increase the authority of justices of the peace, at the expense of ecclesiastical courts, by having them fine guilty householders. That this bill lost by only three votes, 140 to 137, underscores how far many leaders of the "political nation" were willing to go in enforcing household order.[31] Anglicans agreed in principle with the idea of an ordered household, but Puritans sought tough means of enforcement through statutory legislation.

(3) Women and the Household

[The wife must] be able to gouerne and direct her houshold, to looke to her house and familie, to prouide and keepe necessaries, though the goodman pay, to know the force of her kitchin, for sicknes and health, in her self and her charge.

Richard Mulcaster[32]

It is the parte of a shamefast and chast woman not bee gadding abrode but to keepe themselues at home.

William Hergest[33]

In theory Anglicans and Puritans substantially agreed on what they expected of a wife in the household. Her responsibilities included governance and conservation of goods, and to this Puritans added religious instruction and industry. A dominant concern was that wives remain in the household and refrain from frequent visiting. A good wife was supposed to act like a queen bee, remaining at home and keeping the household in order. She must stay home to avoid gossip, reduce the need for fine apparel, and use time profitably. Becon worried about women frequenting taverns, and Cope warned that women who traveled were often suspected of whoredom. A woman who did not have a "setled gouernment of her selfe in [the] house" was prone to "a misdeeming minde and a pratling tong." According to Cleaver, only four reasons to leave the household were valid, viz. to attend religious services, visit the needy, obtain provisions, and accompany her husband at his request. Tilney thought moderation was the key, for a wife must not be "continually lockt vp, as a cloystred Nonne."[34]

Women who stayed at home were praised. Stubbes lauded his deceased wife not only for her household governance, gentleness, obedience, and affability, but also because she remained at home and refrained from gossip, feasting, and merry making. Katherine Brettergh was commended because "she vsed not to gad abroad with wandring *Dinah*, to dancing, greenes, markets, or publike assemblies." Anne Herbert, countess of Pembroke, thought Anne Clifford, countess of Cumberland, was remarkable because she had never been to London, but instead "applyed herself in domestick & home affairs, while she was maid, wife & widow." That such women were singled out suggests that wives, especially of the middle and upper levels of English society, were not prone to remain at home as much as Anglican and Puritan authors desired. This possibility is also borne out by the Antwerp merchant Emmanuel van Meteren, who commented in 1575 that English wives spent much time visiting and attending such social functions as christenings and funerals.[35]

Concern about women's involvement in activities outside the household must have been due partly to their religious pursuits. The orthodox view prohibited women from preaching, except in extraordinary circumstances (as in infidel lands without male ministers). Yet because women had a major role in family worship and household religious instruction, it was perhaps inevitable that their spiritual concerns spilled outside the household. Sir Christopher Hatton, referring especially to Lady Egerton of Ridley, Ches., commented on the "certain preciseness of conscience incident to divers of her sex." There are clear manifestations of this in the Elizabethan period. In 1566 Grindal tried to silence the Puritan John Bartlett, a lecturer at St. Giles Cripplegate in London, who continued to preach after his suspension. When Grindal confined him to his house, some sixty women demonstrated at the bishop's residence, but Grindal "would not in such case deal with such numbers of women, as much misliking such kind of assembling; but willed them to send me half-a-dozen of their husbands, and with them I would talk." It took another suspended Puritan, John Philpot, to persuade the women to disperse. Contemporary evidence also shows that a preponderance of London Separatists were women. In 1593 a group of them carried a supplication on behalf of Penry and other Separatists to Sir Thomas Puckering, the lord keeper, and Sir Edward Coke, speaker of the House of Commons. When they presented their petition they were "entertayned in such sort, as it is smally for the credit of the upper house by whome they wear so heardly delt with" and imprisoned. Such instances must have reinforced the determination to keep wives in the household.[36]

Other women actively supported religious dissidents in less dramatic ways. In February 1585 Lady Anne Bacon asked Burghley to permit Puritans to plead their case before the queen and Privy Council. She condemned the 1584 Lambeth conference because it was designed to discredit the Puritans, who labored for "right Reformation in the ministery of the gospell" but feared to meet lest they be accused of holding conventicles. Lady Bacon claimed she attended their public exercises and learned more from them in seven or eight years than in nearly twenty years of "odd" sermons at St. Paul's. In 1591 Anne's sister, Lady Elizabeth Russell, intervened with Burghley on behalf of Cartwright, imprisoned in the Fleet, requesting him to "do what good yow can to ye poore man."[37]

Women actively intervened on the Catholic side as well. The countess of Arundel assisted priests and found a printer named Charlewood to issue Catholic material. Aristocratic wives, such as Lady Margaret Neville and Lady Constable, harbored priests and found themselves in jeopardy with an unsympathetic government. Margaret Clitherow, wife of an Anglican tradesman in York, was convicted at the York assizes of hearing mass and harboring seminary priests and Jesuits. In March 1586 she was executed in accordance with the sentence pronounced against her:

You must return whence you came, and there, in the lowest part of the prison, be stripped naked, laid down, your back upon the ground, and as much weight laid upon you as you are able to bear, and so to continue three days without meat or drink except a little barley bread and puddle water, and the third day to be pressed to death, your hands and feet tied to posts, and a sharp stone under your back.

Although her husband was a conformist, Sir Ralph Gray's wife harbored priests at their House at Chillingham, Northumberland. Walsingham complained in 1580 that on his travels in the diocese of Winchester he had not persuaded many wives to convert from Catholicism, though their husbands were willing to change. The Privy Council consequently ordered that husbands of such women give bonds to ensure that their wives stayed home and did not see any Catholics. Husbands who refused were jailed. No attempts were made to have Protestant wives control Catholic husbands, for there were no useful sanctions to enable the government to control their husbands' behavior through them. The government could, however, manipulate wives through husbands because the latter, with their control of family property, were susceptible to actions threatening that property. Some doubt was expressed as to the wisdom of imprisoning Catholic wives, because this would undercut the services to which their husbands were entitled. Acting on his prerogative as president of the Council of the North, Henry Hastings, earl of Huntingdon, temporarily imprisoned some wives and separated others from their husbands to facilitate catechizing by Protestant ministers.[38]

A number of wives established close relations with ministers, particularly Puritans, or seminary priests. Lady Margaret Hoby and Margaret Clitherow are cases in point. Lady Hoby's diary gives the impression that she spent more time with her chaplain than her husband. Patrick Collinson suggests that many wives had leisure to develop spiritual neuroses and opportunity to cultivate intimate friendships with physicians of the soul. These friendships might be particularly comforting for a wife with poor marital relations. Dering advised Mrs. Mary Honeywood: "Hath your husband beene unkind to you? Beare it and you shal winne him at the last; if not, thank God that you can continue loving and obedient even unto an unkind husband." Dering had spiritually intimate relationships with Lady Mary Mildmay, Lady Elizabeth Golding, Mrs. Catherine Killigrew (one of Sir Anthony Cooke's daughters), and Mrs. Barrett of Bray, Berks. Wilcox's spiritual correspondents included Bridget Russell, countess of Bedford, Frances Radcliffe, countess of Sussex, Lady Anne Bacon, Lady Elizabeth Walsingham, Lady Mary Grey, Lady Fielding, and Lady Rogers. Lest too much be made of this as a pastoral foible, the Puritan peer, Edward Lord Zouche, corresponded extensively with women, sometimes on spiritual topics. His correspondents included Ann Dudley, countess of Warwick, the countesses of Cumberland and Kent, Lady North, Lady Laighton, Lady Bowes, Lady Willoughby, Lady Ridgeway, Mrs. Anne Shorland, and Mrs. Yelverton.[39]

Psychologically, women appear to have been attracted to movements where religious convictions demanded the greatest commitments, namely, Catholicism, Puritanism, and Separatism. In a male-dominated society, religion was one of the relatively few outlets for their energy and creativity, and Anglicanism did little to assuage these needs. Women's ability to respond to these movements, especially as champions and patrons of ministers, was enhanced by their relative freedom from government sanctions. Legally, conditions were conducive for spiritually motivated women, perhaps with an inclination toward real or induced spiritual neuroses, to develop intimate relationships with physicians of the soul and encourage their work. In Catholicism, there was the added inducement of performing the traditional ritual functions associated with fasting and holy days.[40]

Some women took advantage of their social position to patronize religious authors, and others had spiritual works dedicated to them. William Fulke published a sermon on faith (preached at St. Botolph's, London, in February 1574) at the request of the widow Mary Harris. Lady Catherine, wife of John second Lord St. John of Bletso, persuaded the Puritan Edward Bulkeley to publish a sermon on the Lord's supper. Henry Peacham dedicated a sermon on Job to Lady Margaret Russell and Anne Dudley, countess of Warwick, two prominent Puritan women. The countess of Warwick also had a collection of eight sermons by Gifford and lectures on Exodus 20 by Knewstub dedicated to her by Perkins in 1595. Although the countess is remembered primarily as a patroness of poets, she financed Thomas Tymme's translation of Fenner's *Sacred Divinity* from Latin. Estey dedicated biblical expositions to Lady Anne Drurie. Anglicans too dedicated works to women. Babington dedicated a popular work on faith to the countess of Pembroke in 1583, and Thomas Lant dedicated a devotional manual to Thomas Cheyney's wife; a treatise on the state of man by Thomas Morton honored Lady Elizabeth Cary. Nevertheless, more works were devoted to Puritan than Anglican women. Too much must not be made of epistles dedicatory, but as a group they indicate the spiritual interests and often personal relationships of the honorees.[41]

Lady Knyvett, wife of Sir Thomas Knyvett of Norfolk, was a moderate Puritan whose religious activities reached beyond the household. She disputed the Norfolk Puritan Samuel Greenaway's contention that communicants in the Lord's supper must first hear a sermon, and she was involved in the search for a family chaplain, preferring a man who was "nether over precise, nor yet dissolute." She sought a suitable living for William Middelton, and looked to John More, the "apostle of Norwich," for advice in the selection of a minister.[42]

Within the household, religious study could be a major daily undertaking for a wife. Thomas Bentley's three-volume work, *The Monvment of Matrones* (1582), was a collection of prayers and meditations for women in the household. Every day Katherine Brettergh read eight chapters in the Bible and sometimes biblical expositions,

Foxe's *Acts and Monuments*, or other religious works. Lady Margaret Hoby had daily religious exercises, wrote notes in her Bible, and kept a common-place book with sermon notes and extracts. She applied her spiritual knowledge by counseling a woman about to have an incestuous marriage annulled. The wife of Richard Hilles, a Protestant merchant and twice a religious exile, was another religious devotee, as her husband told Bullinger in 1566: "I am anxious to explain to my wife some portion of the confession of the Helvetic churches. She occasionally reads in the book, and sometimes makes it the subject of her meditation, as she is tolerably conversant with your language." Lady Margaret Clifford, countess of Cumberland, knew only English but read translated works. Lady Grace Mildmay daily read a chapter each from the Torah, the prophets, the gospels, the rest of the New Testament, and the Psalms.[43]

Religious devotion and scholarship motivated some women to translate spiritual works. Lady Elizabeth Russell translated John Ponet's work on the Lord's supper from French, and Lady Anne Bacon translated Bernardino Ochino's sermons from Italian and Jewel's *Apologie* from Latin. Her sister, Lady Mildred Cecil (Lady Burghley), studied the Greek fathers Basil the Great, Chrysostom, and Gregory Nazianzen; c. 1550 she translated a sermon of Basil's on Deuteronomy 15:9 from Greek. In 1560, Anne Locke published a translation of Calvin's sermons, and in 1590 (as Anne Prowse) published a translation of Jean Taffin, *Of the Markes of the Children of God, and of Their Comfort in Afflictions*. In the epistle to the latter she wrote: "Euerie one in his calling is bound to doo somewhat to the furtherance of the holie building; but because great things by reason of my sex, I may not doo, and that which I may, I ought to doo, I haue according to my duetie, brought my poore basket of stones to the strengthning of the walles of that Ierusalem, whereof (by grace) wee are all both Citizens and members." Mary Herbert, countess of Pembroke, turned Psalms into English lyrics, made translations from French and Italian, and edited and published the works of her deceased brother, Sir Philip Sidney. Translations were not the only approved vehicle for women with literary talents. Among other works were Lady Katherine Knollys' *A Heavenly Recreation* (1569), Lady Elizabeth Tyrwhitt's *Morning and Euening Prayer* (1574), Lady Frances Abergavenny's *Precious Perles of Perfecte Godlines* (1577), Anne Wheathill's *A Handfull of Holesome . . . Hearbs* (1584), Anne Dowirche's *The French Historie* (1589) and *A Frenche Mans Songe* (1589), and Elizabeth Melville's *Ane Godlie Dreame* (1603).[44]

Much of the scholarly interest of women was religious, yet some was directed, as in the case of the countess of Pembroke, to secular subjects. Apart from editing her brother's works, the countess wrote poetry, including an elegy and a pastoral dialogue honoring the queen ("Astrea", 1602). Lady Katherine, wife of Henry Lord Berkeley, studied natural philosophy and astronomy. About 1595 she was given a globe, "Blagraves' mathematicall Jewell, a quadrate, Compass, Rule, and other instruments, wherein shee much delighted her self till her death." Mulcaster thought some English women were comparable to "the *Italian* ladies who dare write themselues, and deserue fame for so doing, whose excellencie is so geason [*sic*], as they be rather wonders to gaze at, then presidentes to follow." Mulcaster approved housewives reading Scripture, history, and works to serve as guides for daily living. Among essentially nonreligious writings by women were Isabella Whitney's *The Copy of a Letter, Lately Written in Meeter* [1567] and *A Sweet Nosgay, or Pleasant Posye* (1573); four epitaphs on her son by Anne de Vere, countess of Oxford (1584); Jane Anger's *Her Protection for Women* (1589); and verses by Catherine Killigrew and Lady Elizabeth Russell.[45]

Few women achieved such intellectual prominence, but most would have been expected to help with the instruction of children or catechizing. Lady Hoby helped catechize her servants and apparently a neighbor woman. The 1598 will of Sir William Fitzwilliam of Milton, Ches., indicates that his wife Anne, daughter of Sir William Sidney, "took the most care of the educatyon" of their two sons and three daughters while he applied himself "wholie to the chardges and services . . . [he] was employed unto." These pedagogical tasks of women were important in shaping the religious and cultural outlook of the family.[46]

Perhaps to a greater degree than is commonly recognized, women were involved in the supervision of the household and sometimes the estate. Lady Elizabeth, wife of John Lord Russell, had a knowledge of law and estate management, and Lady Grace Mildmay kept the household books for the Mildmay estate. While Anthony Bacon was in France in 1582, his wife satisfactorily managed their estate. Lady Margaret Hoby kept a household book, paid servants' wages, workmen's bills, and household bills, collected rents, supervised the granary, and arranged at least one lease. Lady Anne, the Catholic wife of Thomas Lord Berkeley, made "country huswifery" a major part of her life, and undertook regular morning visitations to her stables, barns, poultry pens, and swine troughs. Katherine, wife of Henry Lord Berkeley, for a time managed their funds as his receiver general, "to whom all officers forraine and domestick made their Accompts,"

but she proved a poor manager and was instead given an allowance of
£300 *p.a.* for apparel and chamber expenses. Nevertheless she "much
coveted to rule her husbands affaires at home and abroad, And to
bee informed of the particular passages of each of them," to the
point that "few fines or Incombes from his tenants were raised, and
never any land sold, but shee had a sixt, 8th., or tenth thereout, unknown to him." In another case, Lady Anne, wife of Henry Carey,
Lord Hunsdon, was deputed by her husband to pay domestic accounts while he was away in state service. With a household of forty
persons, plus another hundred (including captains, lieutenants, and
pensioners) who sought food each day, she could not manage and
asked Cecil in 1568 to intervene with the queen on her behalf.
Whether successful managers or not, women apparently exercised a
fair degree of responsibility in the management of households and
sometimes estates.[47]

Women also provided for the household in more expected ways.
Lady Hoby was undoubtedly typical of many wives, especially those
of lesser gentry, yeomen, and husbandmen, when she baked pastry
and gingerbread, preserved quinces and damson plums, distilled brew,
made wax lights, and spun and dyed cloth. She also fished, assisted
midwives, sowed seeds, and distributed food to the poor. She was a
far cry from those London wives depicted by Emmanuel van Meteren
who sat "before their doors, decked out in fine clothes, in order to
see and been seen by the passers-by." According to his limited observations, English wives seldom worked, but left household matters
to servants.[48]

A woman could perform special duties to benefit the community,
though these were not part of her household obligations. Women
served as churchwardens in the parish of Kilmington, Devon. Other
women provided medical care: Lady Grace Mildmay read medical
books and an herbal, and cared for the sick and injured. Mrs. Elizabeth Bedell practiced chirurgery without payment, and Lady Margaret Clifford, countess of Cumberland, was intrigued by alchemy,
"by which she found out excellent medicines, that did much good to
many. She delighted in distilling of waters, and other chymical ex-
tractions, for she had some knowledge in most kind of minerals,
herbs, flowers, and plants." Lady Hoby provided medical treatment,
including surgery, for friends and neighbors. In August 1601 a baby
boy was brought to her "who had no fundement, and had no passage
for excrementes but att the Mouth: I was ernestly intreated to Cutt
the place to se if any passhage Could be made, but, althought I Cutt
deepe and seearched, there was none to be found."[49]

Some women were forced by necessity or enabled by opportunity to engage in business or political affairs. Of the approximately 383 publishers and patentees in Elizabethan England, 17 were women. All were widows, but they must have learned the occupation working with their husbands, thus making business activities an extension of their household responsibilities. London silkwomen, some of whom were probably married, had their own apprentices, some of whom were male, yet in the Elizabethan age silkshops were increasingly taken over by men. Other women invested funds. In 1576, before she married, Mary Sidney invested £25 in the expedition of Martin Frobisher. At least 83 women invested in joint-stock companies between 1575 and 1630, of a total of 8,683 investors. Of the 62 whose social status is known, 54.8% were of merchant background, 25.8% nobility, and 19.4% gentry. Of the 83 women, 41% invested in the East India Company and 30.1% in the Virginia Company. Social status apparently had some bearing on where women invested, for 8 noble-women and 6 gentry women invested in the Virginia Company, but only 2 and 3 respectively in the East India Company. On the other hand 23 women of merchant status invested in the East India Company and only 4 in the Virginia Company. Interest and involvement in political affairs were confined mostly to the high-born, such as Lady Penelope Rich, Anne Dudley, countess of Warwick, and others close to the court. In 1596, for example, while Lady Rich was away from court, she wrote to Anthony Bacon requesting news of political and military affairs in France, and received it. The countess of Warwick procured a company of soldiers in 1586 to send to Leicester in the Netherlands.[50]

Investment and political involvement were restricted to a small number of Elizabethan women. Most spent their lives in household activities that focused on religious concerns, teaching and catechizing, household supervision, and the provision of household goods. The educated might read, translate, or write. Stubbes' Puritan wife Katherine was continuously "poaring vppon a [godly] booke, and studying." Music was popular, at least among women with sufficient domestic help to have time to practice. Lady Katherine, wife of Henry Lord Berkeley, played the lute and sang, and Lady Margaret Hoby sang and played the alpherion. Elizabeth Lucas, a Merchant Taylor's wife, could play the lute, viol, and virginal. Lady Grace Mildmay not only played the lute but also set five-part songs to music. Needlework and related crafts were popular: Lady Mildmay made carpets and cushions, and drew pictures of flowers and fruit. Household routines could be broken by recreational activities; Lady Hoby enjoyed bowling, fishing, and boating. According to the the Antwerp merchant van Meteren, English wives devoted much time to playing cards.[51]

To the extent that household routines differed for wives, social status was the primary reason. Beyond this difference, it was a matter of personal taste and religious conviction. Puritan and Catholic wives probably devoted more time to religious matters, including devotions, study, family worship, and catechizing. Particularly in the latter half of the age, the character of Catholicism was largely determined in the aristocratic household, which might have a domestic chaplain or be involved in the network of seminary priests and Jesuits. The household orientation of Elizabethan Catholicism originated because of government persecution and the major role women assumed as protectors of priests. In Puritanism, the emphasis on household worship grew out of the wife's instructional responsibilities and close association with the Puritan clergy.

(4) Masters in the Household

Thou art bounde to thy servant as thy sonne, and so is he bound to thee.

Francis Trigge[52]

The servants and attendants are the shaddowes of their master; they moue at his motion.

Mr. Fenton[53]

An important aspect of the household involved the relationship of masters to servants. The Geneva marginalia outline the conduct expected of Christian masters, who were exhorted to love servants as their children and not treat them disdainfully. Masters have dominion over servants' bodies but not souls, hence they cannot expect wicked commands to be obeyed. Moreover masters must heed the godly counsel of their servants, treat them liberally, even generously bestowing goods on them. Job was praised for pitying his servants and recognizing them as creatures of God. In the Bishops' Bible, the tone of the marginalia is more practical. Masters must not withhold servants' wages, or motivate them to rebel by treating them austerely. Masters who cannot govern servants moderately must release them. The theme of moderation was reiterated in the Beza-Tomson Bible: "It is the dutie of masters, to vse the authoritie that they haue ouer their seruants, modestly and holily, seeing that they in an other respect haue a common master which is in heauen." Masters must deal with servants in an equitable manner. Thus the Geneva Bible took a more spiritual view of the role of masters in the household than did the Bishops' Bible, with the Beza-Tomson version adopting a middle road.[54]

Puritans exhorted masters to be cautious in selecting servants, who must be godly or children will be corrupted and masters treated unjustly. Servants should not be accepted unless they are governable, and servants who prove disreputable by such acts as swearing, gambling, drinking, and illicit sex must be dismissed. In keeping with such exhortations, Sir Walter Mildmay advised his son to choose his servants wisely. There is no indication that Anglicans disapproved of such care, but they made no equivalent attempt to insist on such a selection process.[55]

Once in the household, the servants, the Puritans stressed, must be provided with religious instruction by the masters. "Maisters of families ought in a second degree [after children] to extend their parent-like affection, euen toward their seruants also, in a tender care and desire of their euerlasting saluation." This care entailed catechizing and general religious oversight. Lady Margaret Hoby assisted in catechizing her servants, and Walter Devereux, earl of Essex, gave "heauenly lessons and exhortacions" to his servants—but on his deathbed. Likewise when William Whittingham was dying, he summoned his servants individually, admonished their faults, and exhorted them to fear God. Presumably both men had endeavored to provide their servants with counsel on previous occasions, and in any case the Puritans insisted that regular religious instruction was mandatory—a view shared by the Catholic Robert Shelford. Thanks especially to the role of the wife in Elizabethan Catholicism, excellent progress was made converting servants to the Old Faith. In the gentry home of Roger Lawson of Brough, Yorks., his wife Dorothy gradually filled her household with Catholic servants and guided them in the faith by reading religious books to them and telling stories about the saints. The significance of religion in Puritan and Catholic households was again manifested in the importance assigned to the instruction of servants. A few Anglicans, including Edmund Bunny, encouraged such training, but the prevailing attitude apparently was to leave this instruction to local clergy.[56]

Puritans insisted on the masters' taking servants to church. Masters who assigned tasks to retainers or who allowed them to participate in recreational activities on the sabbath were accused of profanation. According to Perkins, "it is the libertie that Gods lawe giues to seruants, yea and to beasts, that they shall not be oppressed with labour by working on the Lords day; & this liberty is grounded vpon the law of nature, & common equity." Merely bringing servants to church did not satisfy Dod, who expected masters to ensure that they remained throughout the service, sat in a place conducive to hearing and learning, and refrained from "prating or scoffing or sleeping or such like." In a Norfolk case, the Privy Council, having learned that servants of the recusant Sir Henry Bedingfeld refused to attend church, ordered them dismissed, prohibited them from being hired by Bedingfeld's friends, and refused to allow him to retain new Catholic servants. It is an apt illustration of the importance the government attached to household discipline as a means to preserve state security.[57]

Although most religious responsibility rested with the masters, Anthony Anderson, an Anglican cleric, and Greenham, a Puritan, expected servants to reprove ungodly masters, thereby placing service to God before service to man. Greenham suggested, however, that reproof of superiors should be in the form of advice rather than admonition. This responsibility of inferiors, however, was not widely suggested. Babington, for instance, judged that the admonition of inferiors by superiors was a beneficial thing, but he was careful not to reverse his phrasing.[58]

An obligation of masters to servants that attracted extensive comment was prompt payment of wages. Delaying payment or unfairly altering wages was condemned as covetous. In this spirit, the West Country yeoman Robert Furse advised his heir to "lette always thye hyrede sarvante have hys penye for his payne." Wages must be paid according to the tasks and on time. Knewstub urged improved compensation for servants, including an assurance that they would not leave empty-handed when their service terminated. Parker emulated kindred ideals by increasing the stipends of his servants, aiding those in need, and leaving them a decent legacy at his death. On the other hand, when Henry Hastings, earl of Huntingdon, died in 1595, his servants had not been paid, though about 75 nevertheless attended his corpse. Anglican and Puritan agreed on the importance of prompt payment, probably because servants' wages were low at best; honesty was important in fulfilling agreements, and masters were obliged to treat subordinates justly. The annual wages paid by Henry Lord Berkeley were five marks for a gentleman, four marks for a yeoman, forty shillings for a groom, and "a tawny coate for summer and a white frize coat for winter lyned with crimson tafaty."[59]

Provision of livery for servants was a commonly accepted obligation, and was expected by retainers. When Elizabeth Bourchier, countess of Bath, recommended a former maid to a Devon friend in 1594, she indicated the maid would be loath to serve without appropriate livery each year; the countess thought a "cast [used] garment" of her friend would suffice. Livery, particularly for male retainers, was often a uniform. A visitor to England in 1592 remarked on the retainers of courtiers, who wore jerkins in their master's color, "bearing his arms rolled up and buckled behind," and with his arms on their sleeves for identification, but without cloaks. Some servants rebelled against designated apparel, for Gabriel Powel, sinecure rector of Llansaintffraid-yn-Mechan, Mont., castigated malapert servants who refused to wear their master's livery.[60]

Despite the earlier Tudor legislation and attempts to reduce disorder stemming from liveried retainers, the problem continued in Elizabethan society. Incidents of violence involving such persons were frequent, and Babington warned that those who dispensed livery had to curtail the unjust actions of retainers. The strongest complaint came from Pilkington, who suspected aggressive persons deliberately became liveried retainers to engage in violence without fear of suppression. "Men do commonly sue to be servants unto noblemen, and wear their liveries, that whosoever seeth their coat may fear them, and under their master's name they may rule in their country . . . ; and though they were slaves afore, yet now they shall be every gentleman's fellow." Retinues were sometimes sizeable, with a real potential for disorder. Whitgift had 60 armed retainers, and Thomas Cheyney, Lord Warden of the Cinque Ports, had 205 liveried servants. As sheriff of Nottinghamshire, Sir William Holles never appeard at the quarter sessions without 30 in his retinue. Excluding servants, Edward Seymour, earl of Hertford, had 59 retainers of modest social standing from London and six counties in 1583.[61]

Attempts were made to control liveried servants and other retainers. Henry Lord Berkeley and his wife Katherine, granddaughter of the third duke of Norfolk, took special care to maintain an orderly household. Because they traveled frequently between Norfolk and London, usually with 150 or more dependents, they issued regulations to ensure an orderly progression. A gentleman usher was responsible to see that gentlemen retainers in the entourage rode before the lord in pairs and without lewd speech or rude behavior. Servants were expected to proceed in orderly fashion "in their tawny cloth coats in summer, with the badge of the white Lyon rampant imbroidered on the left sleeve; And in coats of white frize lined with crimsen taffety in the winter, This lord allowing only cloth, buttons, and badge." In the household, Lady Berkeley required the gentleman usher and gentelman retainers to wear livery coats in the dining chamber when guests were present, and when riding with the lord or lady. William Somerset, earl of Worcester, had sufficient control over his retainers to see that most enrolled in the trained bands in 1588.[62]

The importance of correcting errant servants was impressed on masters, especially by Puritans. Correction had to be done moderately and be the same type as that imposed on children. Discreet lashing was acceptable, but Henry Smith insisted masters must not lay their hands on servants, nor was cruel treatment acceptable. Correction must motivate servants to obey rather than rebel. Guidelines were laid down by Dod:

> First, that it [correction] be not in passion to ease ones selfe by the servants paine, but with compassion to helpe him out of his sinne. Secondly, that it be ioyned with prayer, or else it is not instruction but reuenge. Thirdly, that for ordinarie, and lesser infirmities one take not notice of them, but let them slip.

Generally male servants should be corrected by the master and female servants by the mistress of the household, though Bullinger thought husbands could intervene if wives mistreated female servants. In 1600 Sir Robert Sidney questioned the usefulness of a female servant of his wife, which caused the servant to be malicious and Lady Sidney distraught. In contrast, Sir Francis Hastings was pleased with his wife, Lady Magdalen, for treating her servants with kindness if they were deserving but firmness if they neglected their responsibilities. Several authors recognized the dangers in excessive correction, with Bownde warning that this encouraged servants to leave their positions. Dering was convinced that trustworthy servants were bred by gentle treatment. In the Puritan household of Sir Henry Sherrington of Laycock Abbey, Wilts., however, the master scourged the bare back of a male servant with rods "for making but a showe and countenance of a saucie and unreverent behaviour towards us his children, and put him from his service."[63]

Elizabethan masters had various additional obligations. Servants must be taught a suitable trade, restrained from idleness, instructed in deportment, cared for when ill, and given adequate food and lodging. Masters must not impose excessive duties, as did Nash's "Mistris Minx, a Marchants wife, . . . what toyle she puts her poore seruants vnto, to make her looking glasses in the pauement." Work must be distributed equitably, avoiding night labor. William Vaughan warned masters not to allow servants to be away from the household overnight. Several writers felt masters should avoid becoming too familiar with servants or trusting them too much, but Becon cautioned that servants who perceived they were not trusted would neglect their duties. It was important to exercise discretion in speaking before servants, as William Wentworth advised his son.[64]

Care for the general welfare of servants was expected, and might be manifested in various ways. Dod expected masters to reward servants in relation to the length and value of their service when it terminated. Sir Thomas Barrington, a Puritan, used his social position to help one of his servants recover a debt from the beneficiary of a deceased debtor. Sir William Holles was so bountiful to his servants that several improved their social positions dramatically; Sir Thomas Williamson of Marcham, Berks., the descendant of one, was created a baronet in 1642. Dod, however, was convinced that many masters ignored servants' welfare, particularly when the servants aged, and insisted that masters provide relief for retired servants.[65]

Evidence of the concern of masters for servants appears in bequests. A sampling of wills of the nobility shows a tendency toward legacies amounting to a value of six months to a year's wages. Burghley, however, bestowed gifts of two to four years' wages and personal items. Life annuities and outright grants were also popular legacies. Some servants of George Talbot, earl of Shrewsbury, received farms, while Lady Anne Cobham bequeathed yarn, hemp, and wool to her servants. Some gentry left bequests amounting to twelve to eighteen months' wages; generally gentry gifts were outright grants of money. Sir Francis Drake left as much as £100, but the commonest amounts in gentry wills range from a few shillings to £10. Sir Walter Mildmay granted his servants £685 out of total bequests worth £7,532. Material gifts, including silver spoons, geldings, clothing, and tenements, were often bestowed on servants. An Essex husbandman bequeathed a calf to a female servant if she learned the Ten Commandments and the principles of Christianity, and behaved well toward her master and mistress. Annuities apparently were used less commonly by gentleman masters. Legacies to servants by prelates are comparable to those of the lesser nobility, with sums often amounting to three or six months' wages. Lower clergy provided as they could in view of their limited incomes. No pattern emerges for differences in legacies to servants by Catholic, Anglican, and Puritan clergy. The servant of the Catholic priest Thomas Paynell received £40 plus clothing and household goods, whereas Cartwright left only 5s. each to his servants. Most gifts from lesser clergy amounted to a few pounds.[66]

The finest Elizabethan overview of a master's role is Wentworth's advice to his son. He urged the boy to use retainers who were diligent, honest, and humble — and to avoid trusting them. "For allmost

all trecheries haue bene wrought by seruants and the finale end of
their service is gaine and advancementt, which, offred by anie to them
that wants itt and longes for itt, bringes a dangerouse temptation."
Servants must not be allowed to wed without consent of friends and
means to provide for themselves. It is "not good to kepe those that
will marie longe, for they wilbe confederate &c." The wisest course is
to marry a servant to a widowed tenant, if she acquiesces. Menial servants should receive monetary gifts in return for special diligence,
but caution must be used in bestowing preferments. Annuities should
be avoided in preference for tenements at will. In selecting key servants, special qualities must be sought: the household steward
should be at least forty years old and of plain wit; the chamber servant about fifty and able to keep secrets; the eldest son's servant
about forty, "nott simple, but of a sad witt, both able to giue advice
and good example," and the bailiff must be a man of steady character, showing diligence and humility. The general tenor of Wentworth's advice would have been acceptable to most English masters.[67]

The proper role of masters was not viewed in substantially different terms by Anglicans and Puritans, but there were differences in
emphasis. Puritans, not Anglicans, stressed the cautious selection of
godly and governable servants, and Puritans and Catholics agreed on
the significance of religious instruction in the household for servants.
Puritans emphasized that masters must take servants to church; Anglicans generally would have acquiesced in this. In other areas, such
as the prompt payment of servants and other basic obligations, Anglicans and Puritans concurred. Puritans stressed the maintenance of
discipline by moderate correction. Concerning legacies to servants,
religious differences did not lead to disparate gifts or amounts.

(5) Servants in the Household

Many prophane seruing men also, do falsely suppose, that they were borne, onely to game, riot, sweare, whoore, ruffle it, and roist it out, & to spend their time
in meere Idlenesse.

Arthur Dent[68]

If to serue others thow be bent,
serue with goodwill, and be content
To do thy lordes commandement.

Master Thorne[69]

Servants, hired hands, and apprentices were supposed to be treated
as members of the household, though subordinate in position to

children. Henry Smith depicted them as inferior children or sons-in-law, though subject to the authority of the *pater familias.* Masters were expected to treat servants as children rather than beasts of burden, and servants were urged to look on superiors as fathers. The familial relationship between masters and servants was intended primarily to ensure the obedience of servants rather than to show a concern for their welfare. Order in the state was predicated on order in the household, the achievement of which required, at least in theory, this familial relationship.[70]

In the biblical marginalia the earliest concern, as in Tyndale's 1534 New Testament, was the servant's obedience to his master, whether good or evil, and righteous suffering at the hands of an immoral master. The Tyndale-Rogers New Testament of 1538 continued this emphasis, explaining that servants are commanded in Scripture "to be obedyent with loue & diligence and all things aggreable to Godds holy worde." The Geneva annotators reiterated the admonition to obey, but added the qualifier that obedience must not be rendered to commands that contravene Scripture. Servants should be faithful, placing their masters' interests before their own, and stewards must be diligent overseers of their masters' lands to make them profitable. Servants are warned not to abuse their state by usurping authority or conspiring against the dominion of their masters. Contentment with one's estate is encouraged: "Although God hathe called thee to serue in this life, yet thinke not thy condition vnworthie for a Christian: but reioyce, that thou art diliuered by Christ from the miserable sclauerie of sinne and death."[71]

The Bishops' Bible deals with servants' obedience in a familial context. They are admonished to comply with the orders of masters as they would with those of fathers. The Beza-Tomson Bible repeatedly demands obedience even to pagan or cruel masters, but with the proviso that prior obedience is owed to God, whose dictates must not be violated to please a master. Faithful subordination to superiors is important because the actions of servants must not give the impression that the gospel encourages rebellion. Nevertheless the corporal service owed by servants does not cancel their spiritual freedom, and such service must be rendered so as to maintain a "safe conscience." Like the Geneva Bible, this version reinforces contentment with one's lot by explaining to servants "that it is Gods will that some are either borne or made seruants, and therefore they must respect Gods will, although their seruice be neuer so hard."[72]

With respect to servants, the obedience issue was the most commonly discussed subject by Elizabethan religious writers. A key biblical passage was the fifth commandment, in which the dictum to honor parents was interpreted to include masters and other superiors. Babington asserted that a servant who obeyed his master was serving God, and Dod argued that a master "stands in the place of Christ in his family, and is to be obeyed, as if hee were the most honourable and wise in the world." To these familial and religious analogies were added parallels between obedience to masters and subordination to magistrates. At root was the concern that without the subservience of subordinates, well-ordered households, churches, and states were impossible. The ideal was expressed by Becon: "The duty of a good seruant is to serue his maister and mistres willingly & with a fre courage euen for conscience sake, not with the eie, but with ye heart, to obey them, to honor them, gently to aunswere them, not to picke or steale away their goods, but to be faithfull vnto them in all thinges."[73]

Religious commentators agreed that the duty of servants to obey did not extend to matters that violated divine precepts. Acts of disobedience in such instances might bring punishment, which servants must bear passively, but rebellion is not justifiable. Thus Anthony Bacon's servant, Richard Senhouse, advised his son, who entered Bacon's service:

First, serve God effectually at all times. Secondly. Honor ye Prince. Ite. serve your Master iustly, truely, faithfullie, dutifully, willingly with all humilitie & lowlinesse, And what he commaundes you so doe it accordingely as afore, exerfitly with all expedition.

The right of disobedience did not extend to matters that did not violate divine precepts, no matter how base or distasteful. Becon thought performing such works was more pleasing to God than other service. Servants' obedience was mandatory even if masters reneged on their obligations. Obedience included passive reception of correction and instruction, even if undeserved, but servants were warned not to imitate or acquiesce in the improper behavior of masters. Puritans urged servants to rebuke sin in their superiors, and masters were expected to listen. The Anglican homily on matrimony, however, frowned on this: "When we reforme our seruants, and tell them that they should obey their masters, . . . If they should tell vs againe our dueties, we should not thinke it well done."[74]

The tone of Anglican authors concerning servants' duties was one of quiescence. Servants were expected to fulfill their master's bidding and depend on him for external things. "It is required in a good seruant, to haue the backe of an Asse, to beare all things patiently: the tongue of a sheepe, to keepe silence gently: and the snout of a swyne, to feede on all things heartily." The Puritan outlook on servants' duties was oriented toward a reverential obedience aiming at the master's welfare. The key obligations were the cheerful performance of required tasks, preservation of the master's goods, moral behavior, avoidance of flattery, appropriate secrecy concerning the master's affairs, defense of the master, and general faithfulness and diligence. Servants must refrain from idleness, gossiping, evil company, improper speech, sexual offenses, and negligence. Dod criticized servants who acted disdainfully toward poorer masters or presumed to be their social equals. In advising his son, Richard Senhouse urged that in Bacon's service he keep secrets, refrain from gambling, drinking, idleness, sexual misconduct, and brawling, and rise early to fulfill his responsibilities.[75]

A servant was expected to worship properly, regardless of his master. In Lancashire Simon Harward believed numerous servants and tenants were prohibited from worshipping in Protestant services by Catholic masters and landlords. Another problem occurred in large households, where some servants, such as cooks and butlers, were required to remain on duty and miss church services. Others were allowed to do as they saw fit and sometimes did not attend church. For such reasons the Glamorgan preacher Lewis Thomas suggested that servants with godly masters should be grateful, for they shared the master's divine blessing. With the emphasis on godliness in the servants, perhaps some masters had trouble with retainers who devoted excessive time to prayer and Bible reading.[76]

Servants could legally contract marriages themselves, but Stockwood thought it preferable for them to seek their masters' consent, especially if the parents were deceased. An unscrupulous servant could cause embarrassment by an inappropriate match, or, as occurred with the servant of William Cornwallis, a match made unethically. In 1595 the attorney general, Sir Edward Coke, accused Thomas Swift in Star Chamber of having Cornwallis' daughter sign a contract of marriage to him on the pretence that is was a bill of debt. In order to cancel the contract, Swift demanded £30 *p.a.* plus substantial cash from his master.[77]

Complaints about errant servants who failed to measure up to the ideal are numerous. Dent asserted that servants made an occupation of dissembling, while Cooper was troubled by negligent and untruthful retainers. In Pilkington's judgment, English servants were becoming wealthy through excessive wages. Careless servants, Turnbull lamented, deceived their masters to acquire wealth. There are ample instances. In 1602 and 1603, the gentleman Paul d'Ewes of Milden, Suffolk, sustained business losses because his servants were untrustworthy. In 1589 the Privy Council intervened in the case of a former servant of a London merchant who had made contracts on his master's behalf without the latter knowing, leaving substantial debts. Men as diverse as Henry Lord Cheney and the physician Simon Forman complained of dishonest, negligent servants, and Sir William St. Loe had a housekeeper "very well learned in loitering." Young Grace Sherrington's governess counseled her to avoid serving-men because of their ribald talk, idleness, and evil desires. Some complaints against servants probably resulted from personality conflicts. Godfrey Allen served Antonio Perez with great success in 1595, but by 1597 he had so offended Robert Devereux, earl of Essex, in whose service he was then employed, that he was imprisoned.[78]

One of the most difficult situations involved the embezzlement of goods. Pilkington lambasted offending retainers as thieves, urging good servants to seek their master's profit. To deal with this problem, Parliament, in 1563, revived the Henrician act (21 Henry VIII, c. 7) against servants who embezzled goods worth 40s. or more, which was punishable as a felony (5 Eliz. I, c. 10). As the age progressed, inflation brought increasing numbers of items under the provisions of this act. More serious cases were placed before the Privy Council. In 1581, for instance, the Council dealt with the fraudulent conveyance of goods by a servant of the London citizen Robert Lee. A decade later, a more substantial case involved three London servants who embezzled goods worth £35. News of such cases must have reinforced the opinions of masters and religious authors who were chary of servants' trustworthiness.[79]

The worst servant misbehavior was violence toward masters. No evidence indicates this was widespread, but cases did occur. Machyn recorded several cases of London maids poisoning households early in the age. In April 1559, the family of a royal poulterer was saved by taking salad oil as a remedy. In May 1560 two maids were punished for poisoning the households of their masters; both were placed in the pillory and had their eyebrows burned, and one had her ears cut off. In 1570 a London apprentice who had stabbed his master to death "was hanged on a gibet . . . (to the example of others)."[80]

Termination of service by retainers caused some difficulties. The rapid alteration of masters was frowned on as unconducive to good service, but the note to Deuteronomy 23:15 in the Geneva Bible wanted servants to flee cruel masters to serve Protestant superiors. Concern was expressed about servants quitting to marry without sufficient maintenance and thus being forced into beggary. The problem of frequent terminations was brought to the attention of Parliament in 1559 by those who wanted no one received into service without a testimonial from his former master. The proposed legislation intended to increase obedience not only to masters but also to the government and church. The sort of thing masters feared occurred in 1576, when a Cambridgeshire servant fled his master's service "lewdelye, not givinge up certaine accomptes wherewith he was trusted by his said master." From the servant's standpoint, a serious problem was involuntary termination, which affected maintenance and the prospects of future employment. Apart from admonitions of religious writers for masters to deal responsibly and equitably with retainers, nothing was done to protect the servant.[81]

Anglicans and Puritans generally agreed on the proper behavior of retainers, especially the necessity of obedience in all matters not contradictory to Christian precepts. The one marked difference involved servants admonishing errant superiors, which Puritans considered a necessary duty. Both groups were concerned about untrustworthy and idle servants, the irresponsible termination of service, embezzlement of goods, and kindred matters. The essential concurrence on servants was compatible with the views of Anglicans and Puritans on masters, though Puritans stressed the hiring of godly servants, religious instruction for subordinates, and the maintenance of discipline by moderate correction. Proper governance of servants was essential in a society without a standing army or police force. Household discipline and order, buttressed with religious instruction, were crucial to maintain a secure state. Puritans were more vigorous than Anglicans in asserting the householder's duty to oversee the religious life of those in his care, including church attendance, catechism, and household worship. The increased attention to religion in the household also enhanced the role of the wife and mother, on whom many of the spiritual responsibilities devolved, particularly in Catholic and Puritan homes.

CHAPTER 8

The Role of Education

The battle to secure Protestantism in England gave education a significant role. Religious considerations continued to dominate much educational thinking, and giving to schools was presented as a spiritual duty. The growth of literacy was due partly to the desire to increase people's ability to read Scripture and partly to vocational needs. The educational curriculum was assessed by many in religious terms, and the indiscriminate use of classical sources was condemned by Elizabethans who feared the material world would corrupt youth. In some respects, the government was slow to recognize the significance of education—as modern governments often are—but by the 1580s the influx of Jesuits and seminary priests shocked it into action in an attempt to stem the exodus of young people to the Continent for Catholic schooling. It was a matter of recognizing that education involves not only vocational preparation but ideological maturation, and in the Elizabethan world, ideologies were still religious in nature.

(1) The Purpose of Education

For noble youth, there is nothing so meete
As learning is, to knowe the good from yll:
To knowe the toungs and perfectly endyte,
And of the lawes to haue a perfect skill.

John Higgins[1]

327

The Childe were better to be dead borne, then barren of good Letters, for that Ignoraunce is a graue which buryeth life.

George Whetstone[2]

The purpose of Elizabethan education reflected changing intellectual and social conditions. Though the primary goals of education were religious, simultaneously there was a growing interest in using education to increase literacy, promote civilizing influences, serve the commonwealth, inculcate good manners and discipline, obtain socio-political preferment, enhance social status, and provide vocational training. Humanism and Protestant piety combined to encourage a literate, godly laity, conversant in the fundamentals of the faith and good citizenship. It was an age characterized by "the evolution of a system of schools administered locally by lay governing bodies under the general supervision of the state." Lay involvement in education paralleled the increasing laicization of religion, particularly the growing emphasis on household religion and family worship. The increased responsibility of the householder to catechize and conduct worship required education, and it was as important to obtain schooling for this duty as to serve the commonwealth or manage an estate. It was an age that could subscribe to the dictum, "better vnborne, then vntaught," as long as "vaine idle Curiositie" was avoided.[3]

A striking characteristic of Elizabethan education is the degree to which laity became involved in what had, in the medieval era, been substantially a clerical monopoly. As they increasingly recognized "the Vtilitie of Schooling," laymen founded schools, provided for the training of their sons, even at the university level, and sometimes became teachers themselves. The Tudors encouraged this by creating a demand for lay administrators and diplomats, as symbolized by the fall of Thomas Cardinal Wolsey and the roles accorded to Sir Thomas More and Thomas Cromwell. The demand was reinforced by the growth of internal trade, which led to an increased need for vocational literacy. The underlying belief that education aided a godly society received practical reinforcement from the needs of the state and the economy.[4]

The Elizabethan age witnessed a continuation of the old along with the new in education. The expansion of lay-controlled schools, endowed by laymen, did not bring a cessation of traditional educational patterns, but an opportunity for more students to learn. Alternatives to clerical-oriented schools and education in the household or at court became more common. Although the household attained greater significance in religious matters, educationally its importance declined relative to the new schools. "As the nuclear family of parents, children, and close relatives withdrew into the privacy of their apartments, a decline took place in the socializing function of the household, the school becoming the latter's natural complement in this respect." This was a gradual development and was not complete when the queen died in 1603. The great households, including those of prelates as well as nobles, continued to serve as schools. Those of Burghley, Parker, and Whitgift are prime examples. At the end of the age a young student such as Francis Cottington of Godminster Manor, Somerset, could still be sent to an important household (in this instance that of the diplomat Sir Edward Stafford) to learn riding, field sports, the duties of a courtier, and gentlemanly conduct. The royal court inculcated in the young and ambitious a code of honor and loyalty to one's patron, whereas grammar schools and universities encouraged religious and academic values. Where and what one learned was determined partly by social status and partly by educational goals. Cecil did not want his eldest son Thomas to be "scholarly learned but civilly trained," hence he sent him to the French court to acquire a linguistic and courtly education.[5]

Extant evidence reveals a marked concern with education for religious purposes. Puritans, who expected so much of the laity in the household, valued education for the godly society. With the exception of the Presbyterians, Puritans evidenced more interest in educational questions than issues of ecclesiastical polity. Education was intended to enable Christians to live godly lives as well as to attain traditional learning. The principal goal, particularly of university students according to Dering's catechism, was the advancement of the church and the maintenance of the commonwealth. The religious benefits of education gave it a universal relevance, hence Puritans called for more schools. "Hee that hath learning," wrote Cleaver, "although it bee but small, shall much better vnderstand the Preachers, and take more profit by hearing of them, to his great and endlesse comfort, then hee that hath no learning." Dering thought his brother would be richer (spiritually) if he studied Scripture, read books, and learned to reason about his faith. A more direct theological purpose for education was suggested by such Puritans as Greenham and Perkins, who thought religious education might help people discover their "hidden" election. Education was also intended to help children live a virtuous life, hence masters were expected "alwaies to be dropping in true godlinesse." Finally, Puritans stressed schools as seminaries for future ministers, or "nurseries of *Prophets*."[6]

Anglicans shared this zeal for the religious value of education. According to Nowell's catechism, children must receive more education in godliness than in liberal arts. A conviction prevailed that ignorance fostered superstition, not devotion. Consequently, averred Bishop Woolton, "the mind of man is to be garnished and informed with the science and knowledge of many excellent matters; but especially with those which are available to a blessed life, to correct and frame manners to true religion and sincere worshipping of God: for unto this end ought we to refer all our studies and endeavours." Education, as several Anglicans argued, would not only correct manners but make warped natures godly. Schools are nurses in a Christian commonwealth to raise children in the knowledge of God and prepare some for the ministry. Control of the universities should remain in ecclesiastical hands and not be treated, as Cartwright advocated, as civil institutions. Anglicans and Puritans thus recognized the value of education to advance their spiritual views, and no Elizabethan was more aware than Whitgift that whoever controlled the schools would dominate the pulpit and polity of the Church of England. [7]

Evidence of the seriousness with which many Elizabethans took these religious admonitions is plentiful. It appears as a principal reason for founding schools, including the famed Merchant Taylors' School in London. Richard Lord Rich's deed for the founding of a school at Felsted, Essex, stipulated that it teach eighty Essex boys "in the lernyng of Grammer and other Vertues and godly lernyng according to Christes religion." School statutes underscore the substantial role accorded to religion. Those for St. Bees School, Cumberland, call for masters to train pupils in the fear of God, sound learning, and good manners. In addition to basic skills in English and Latin, students were instructed in the Psalter, the *Book of Common Prayer*, and English and Latin catechisms. Such a religiously oriented curriculum was standard fare, and was commonly accompanied by regulations calling for attendance at church, note-taking during sermons, and reiteration of the principal points at school. When Sir Walter Mildmay formulated statutes for Emmanuel College, Cambridge, the spiritual ideal was so paramount that no fellowships were provided in law and medicine. The religious emphasis was not without effect, as was apparent at St. John's, Cambridge, about 1573, where "there is almoste never a Boye in the College which hathe not in his heade a platforme of a churche." [8]

The seriousness with which many Elizabethans viewed the religious function of education is also manifested in their lives. When Rudolph, the son of Rudolph Gualter and grandson of Bullinger, came to England to be educated, Sandys sent the boy to Cambridge with twenty crowns and promised Bullinger he would help him "engage with greater freedom in those studies which may some time or other be of advantage to the church of Christ." Burghley encouraged Roger Manners, earl of Rutland, to increase his learning and see that it was governed by Christian considerations lest it become vain. The tutor of Sir Thomas Bromley's children viewed his role as that of a spiritual parent whose task was to raise his charges in godliness, virtue, and honesty, as well as reading and writing. In the judgment of Lady Grace Mildmay, however, too many English aristocrats neglected the spiritual content of their children's education in the quest for their social and political advancement. [9]

Henry Hastings, earl of Huntingdon, reflected a deep devotion to the religious aims of education. To ensure that young people were reared in the faith, he established a school at Ashby de la Zouch, Leics., in 1567, and granted lands for the perpetual maintenance of a schoolmaster. As a result of his efforts, the free school at Leicester was reorganized because it had been a center of Catholic instruction. The statutes of this school, signed by the earl, stipulated that students attend their parish churches on Sundays and "all sermons as well on the woorkinge daye as on the hollie day . . . and the twoe chiefest foormes [of the six] shall come to the dyvynytie exercyse called the prophecyinge, the schoolemaster comynge with them." In 1574, the earl increased the endowment to raise the headmaster's salary, support poor scholars, and locate "certain scholars who should set their minds and apply themselves to the earnest study of divinity, and to become preachers of the Gospel." [10]

A major reason for Elizabethan concern with education was fear of a general reversion to Catholicism, either through the spread of ignorance or through direct Catholic instruction. The latter was a serious problem, especially in the north. Forty-two schoolmasters in Elizabethan Lancashire reportedly ran Catholic schools or were presented as recusants, and in at least nine more Catholic schools, the masters have not been identified. Some Lancashire schools fell into Catholic hands during the age. When the Puritan vicar of Prescot attempted to get the local school to teach Protestant precepts, some parents withheld their children and local gentry tried to place the school beyond the vicar's influence. Another type of concern is found in Yorkshire, where commissioners of the London stationers visited in the 1560s to examine the ABC books and manuals for the instruction of Latin grammar, which were being used for Catholic instruction. York had four Catholic booksellers in the

1560s. Frequent presentments were made for unlicensed dame schools, a number of which were probably Catholic. Although the two grammar schools in York should have been easier to control, four of the later Gunpowder Plot conspirators were educated at St. Peter's School under John Pullen, perhaps a Catholic sympathizer. [11]

The religious potential of education was the reason the government was so interested in schooling. Forcibly requiring Catholic children to receive a Protestant education was not permitted by statute except for those sent overseas without license, yet the royal prerogative achieved this end. Burghley originated the plan for the seizure of Catholic children in a memorandum of the early 1580s entitled *Advice in Matters of Religion and State*. The means involved action by a bishop and lord lieutenant, a decision of the Privy Council, the device of wardship, or the action of the Northern Commission. On occasion the last-named stipulated how children of a Catholic gentleman ought to be educated, as in October 1592 when Leonard Calvert of Kiplin, Yorks., was forced to place his two sons in the care of a Protestant schoolmaster, subject to quarterly checking by the commissioners. In 1584 the earl of Derby and the bishop of Chester decreed that the four sons of the Catholic Worthington family of Blainsborough, Lancs., would not be returned to their parents but educated as Protestants. In 1583 the Privy Council procured Protestant training for the children of the York draper William Hutton. [12]

In 1593 the government sought statutory sanction for its policy but failed. The Privy Council worried that gentlemen were sending their sons to the Continent for Catholic education under the pretext of learning foreign languages. In 1590, when the son of George Brettam was caught trying to leave Dover for Calais, the Council accused the elder Brettam of having "small regarde . . . of the good and godly educacion of your childe." The boy was remitted to the custody of an Essex schoolmaster and the father required to pay £15 *p.a.* for his education and maintenance. Such actions did not stop these attempts, so the government's parliamentary defeat in 1593 increased alarm. Elizabeth ordered an inquiry to determine who was or had been abroad in the last seven years. The Council sought a list of the parents, tutors, patrons, and sons involved, and those found to be recusants had to post bond to assure their appearance before the Council, and to have their homes searched for Jesuits and seminary priests. [13]

The struggle to control the minds of young people through pedagogy was keenly waged on both sides. The second son of the gentle-man William Grey was placed in the care of a tutor to receive Protes-tant training, but he was kidnapped by Catholics. Catholics acted shrewdly to preserve their religious ideals in their children. Although the wardship of Edward Lord Vaux, grandson and heir of the Catho-lic peer, William Lord Vaux, was purchased by Richard Frampton, a servant of Sir Thomas Cecil, it was subsequently sold to the boy's mother, who desired that he receive Catholic schooling. The state sometimes achieved its aim in turning children against the religion of their parents through education, as in the case of John Fitzherbert, whose son denounced him as a recusant, causing his imprisonment and the placement of his daughters under Protestant tutelage. [14]

Elizabethans manifested some interest in harnessing education to extend functional literacy. Grindal's 1571 injunctions for the pro-vince of York called on able parish clerks to teach children to read. In 1577 in the diocese of Durham, Bishop Barnes asked all unlicensed preachers to teach children to read and write without charge. Nearly two decades later, the Puritan Josias Nichols urged householders to see that those in their care could read English, and he made it a holy duty of the wealthy to provide funds to train poor children and ser-vants to read. Those lacking such aid were encouraged to find some-one to devote fifteen minutes a day to teach them. The classis at Dedham, Essex, required "that all yonge children of the towne be taught to reade Englishe, and that the moity of that [money which] is giuen at the Communion be employed for the teaching of such poore mens children as shalbe iudged unable to beare yt themselues, and a convenient place to be appointed for the teacher of them." [15]

The extension of literacy had obvious religious applications, but it was socially, economically, and politically useful as well. It might be dangerous, for the literate could obtain ideas from the printed page as well as their parsons, who were often spokesmen for patrons. Literacy improved in the Elizabethan age, but social and regional factors were important determinants. In the consistory court at Durham between 1565 and 1573, nearly 80% of the deponents could only make a mark. Some 70% of the gentry were literate, compared with less than half of the yeomen, and in both groups most of the illiterates were of the older generation. Under 20% of those in craft occupations were literate, and the figures were worse for husband-men (7.6%) and common laborers (5.2%). At the beginning of the seventeenth century, a select group of adult male householders in Worcester was subscriptionally literate, but at Chester the rate for adult male householders as late as 1642 was 58%. Literacy probably was more common in towns than in rural areas because it was a prerequisite for admission to a guild. [16]

Recent studies of David Cressy demonstrate that literacy was affected by social stratification. An examination of more than 5,000 depositions in ecclesiastical courts in the diocese of Norwich in the later Elizabethan and early Stuart years (1580-1700) reveals subscriptional literacy rates of 100% for the clergy and professional classes, 98% for the nobility and gentry, 88 to 94% for merchants and superior shopkeepers, 65% for yeomen, 56% for tradesmen and craftsmen, 21% for husbandmen and lesser peasants, 15% for laborers, 12% for common artisans and craft workers, and 11% for women. The Elizabethan period witnessed dramatic improvement in literacy by the 1570s, only to have this advance followed by a regressive period into the 1610s. Yeomen went from 45% in the 1550s to 70% in the 1570s, but regressed to 62% in the 1610s. Husbandmen improved their literacy from 10% in the 1550s to 30% in the 1570s, only to retreat to 12% in the 1610s. [17] The regressive era was probably due to the worsening economy in the latter part of Elizabeth's reign.

One significant but not universally accepted aim of education was preparation for service to the commonwealth. Because of this utilitarian value education was necessary, according to William Kempe, master of the Plymouth Grammar School, for all degrees of men. Since responsibilities to the commonwealth increased with higher social status, Cleaver wanted children of high birth and inheritance to be adequately schooled. There was mounting concern that this was not happening, even in the universities, where, according to William Covel, a fellow of Queens' College, Cambridge, many graduates were "vnmeet for the common wealth." The Catholic critic Robert Shelford protested that children of the gentry in particular were not learning trades useful to society and conducive to obedience, but instead were pampered in leisure. Although not all young people had to learn a trade, he insisted that each must be educated to serve the commonwealth. These critics reflected a principle enunciated early in the age by Valentine Leigh: All Christians "muste addicte thy mynde to the studye and learnynge of some serious and lawdable science, or knowledge, whiche maye eyther presently be a lanterne to thy lyfe and behauiour, or nowe and hereafter profitable to the mayntenance and lawfull honeste augmentation of thy lyuynge and substaunce." Means of achieving this end were proposed, such as Bishop Barnes' plan to have unlicensed preachers direct young people to schools for traditional academic programs or to apprenticeships in crafts or husbandry. Perkins believed parents should expose children to varied stimuli in public places, to determine the service for which they were best suited. Idleness was denounced by men of all religious persuasions; education must enable persons to serve the commonwealth either in the direct employ of the state or in a worthy vocation.[18]

The growing laicization of government in the Tudor years, coupled with land redistribution and expanding mercantile and legal classes, created enticing possibilities for social and economic advancement, particularly for those possessing the necessary educational skills. Advancement within fields was increasingly more dependent on education. For those who acquired land or extended holdings and thus aspired to gentry status, education at a university or an Inn of Court was a desideratum, partly to acquire the cultural accomplishments of a humanistic experience and partly to develop skills of estate management and legal knowledge. The Tudor years saw the life style of the gentry become associated with an appropriate educational background, though not without some opposition.

> What needeth lawe or logicque ought,
>   (sayth shee) or else such like?
> My sonne hath landes whereon to liue:
>   he needth no learning seeke.
> And hath he so in deede good wife?
>   what, shall he haue such staye?
> So much the more he learning needth,
>   to shield him from decaye.

The Essex rector Thomas Newton thought "education[,] institution and discipline" were the distinguishing factors between the landed aristocracy and the commoners. Walter Devereux, earl of Essex, was lauded because in his youth he attained those "sciences, properties & vertues" that enhanced his nobility. Likewise, Sir Robert Sidney's wife was praised because she saw that her children were educated in preparation for their social position. For those who lacked this status by birth, education was one means to achieve it, for, as the courtier William Lamb remarked, "learning bringeth preferment, yea euen to them which are but baselie borne." With this possibility in mind, he founded a grammar school at Sutton Valence, Kent, and provided funds to the Maidstone Grammar School.[19]

Another important purpose of Elizabethan education was the inculcation of good manners and discipline, rendering persons fit members of society. A basic premise of many Elizabethans was that an educated man was disposed towards godly and civil duties, whereas the uneducated followed evil whims. Those who despised knowledge were enemies of the commonwealth, "most currish and rude of condition, barbarous and sauage, as . . . vntamed beast[s]." Appropriate social manners were a necessary subject of education. Dame Helen Branch, widow of a London mayor, was praised in 1594 because her "vertuous manners, by good education, Brought to hir youth the greatest commendation." The civilizing role of education was stipulated when some Elizabethan schools were founded. The Merchant Taylors' School in London was established in 1561 "for the better educacon and bringing vp of Children in good manners and Li[te]rature." The school founded at Abingdon, Berks., two years later by the London mercer John Royse was to teach nurture and good manners, virtuous living, and literature (mostly Christian). [20]

The element of discipline in education was closely related to its civilizing influence. This entailed obedience to the established social and political order, including such superiors as fathers, masters, and magistrates. The child most likely to be the best subject in a monarchy, according to Mulcaster, "in his tender age sheweth himselfe obedient to scholeorders." Education, as William Kempe said referring to Socrates, must discipline youth to produce good men just as colts must be broken to render them tractable as horses. Youngsters unbroken by discipline would be intolerable adults. Thus education, as the balladeer Elderton wrote, was

> for the derection of life by correction
> from lyberties that lust desireth.

In practice, obedience was fostered in various ways. At the universities, the independence of younger fellows and undergraduates was decreased and the authority of college heads augmented. When Sir Henry Sidney's son Philip entered Shrewsbury school in 1564 at the age of ten, his father advised him to "be humble and obedient to your master; for, unless you frame yourself to obey, yea, and to feel in yourself what obedience is, you shall never be able to teach others to obey you hereafter." School statutes also reinforced discipline. Students at Rivington School could be punished or expelled for being dullards, gamesters, negligent students, alehouse haunters, dalliers with girls, and so forth. Those who did not attend church services or spend ample time in prayer were liable to the same penalties, so that the disciplinary and religious aims of education were

clearly related. At the Stafford Grammar School the same relationship was evident in the disciplining of such offenses as improper
speech, gambling, fighting, and lying and the enforcement of proper
behavior on the sabbath.[21]

With respect, then, to the aims of education, the basic emphasis
was on the inculcation of religious values. Other motives often were
present, the most common being a desire to increase literacy (partly
for spiritual reasons), preparation for serving the commonwealth,
the quest for higher social status or preferment, and the improvement of manners and discipline. Among the landed classes, the acquisition of management skills and legal knowledge, which was useful
for justices of the peace, was also a fundamental education goal. Normally several motives were operative simultaneously, and schools
reflected this. To take just one example, the royal charter of Ipswich
Grammar School noted the queen's desire "that the children and
youth of our Kingdom of England should be instructed as well in
probity of manners, and the study of virtue, as in good letters and all
kind of erudition, especially in Grammar, which is the beginning and
foundation of all other learning." The statutes consequently called
for the master and usher to teach not only the usual academic subjects but also Nowell's Latin catechism, the New Testament in Greek
and Latin, good manners, and suitable behavior toward superiors.
Attendance at sermons was required of faculty and students on Sundays and at least once during the week, and students had to report
the contents of the sermon to their master.[22]

In the elucidation of the purposes of education, no difference between Anglicans and Puritans is manifest. Both stressed the religious
orientation of education, though Anglicans were more interested in
developing loyalty to the established church and polity than were
Puritans. The differences that did exist do not follow religious lines.
In some instances, social status was a factor, as with the aristocracy's
pursuit of education for estate management, cultured accomplishments, and legal knowledge. In other cases some men were suspicious
of education, especially in its secular manifestations or bookish treatment of religion. Robert Dobbes, vicar of Runcorn, Ches., believed
immoderate study was a rock that hindered Christian religion and
led to barren knowledge. The Puritan John Bartlett (Barthlet), lecturer at St. Giles, London, depicted Simon Magus as overtly ambitious for knowledge and puffed up with science; he "is the example
or forme of such, as chalenge to themselues muche learning: ambi-
ciously coueting to be aduaunced vnto godly honour, [and] arrogate
the authoritie of yoking religion and superstition togither." Sir

Henry Sidney was afraid his son Philip would spend too much time in study, "and yet I have hard of few wyse fathers dout that in thear chyldern." Such fear was also present in Catholic circles, particularly for spiritual reasons: Immoderate study without devotion leads to vanity; study must not be focused on "impertinent" subjects but on heavenly matters effective in serving God. In short, these warnings reflect concern that Elizabethans were neglecting the religious orientation of education through a growing—but not yet dominant— process of secularization. [23]

(2) The Extent of Education

In times past, ignorance in eache sexe was so odious, that women as well as men, were well seene in all liberall Sciences.

Thomas Nash [24]

Naturally the *male* is more worthy, and politikely he is more employed. . . .

Richard Mulcaster [25]

Elizabethans disagreed on two principal issues concerning the extent of education, the first involving social status, and the second, schooling for females. The strongest case against universal education was made by Richard Mulcaster, who taught at St. Paul's School, London, before moving to Merchant Taylors'. An excessive number of educated persons, in his judgment, would burden the state and threaten stability by creating unemployed, seditious individuals. Scholarship is conducive to the quiet life, hence the educated are "disdainefull to deale with labour, vnlesse neede make them trot, or the *Turkish captiuitie* catch them, the greatest foe that can fall vpon idle people, where labour is looked for, and they not vsed to it." Only those who demonstrate aptitude are to be educated, with the others assigned vocations for the welfare of the state. Even if private funds were adequate to endow schools to educate all children, Mulcaster would object. Although he acknowledged that all children needed the rudiments of reading and writing for religious understanding and daily affairs, he expected such skills to be learned in leisure time, perhaps from the local minister. [26]

Mulcaster based his case for restricted education on the primary obligation of the citizen to the commonwealth. Parents must recognize that their first obligation is to the state, not their children. Young people with an aptitude for learning are to be maintained in their studies "till the common weale minding to vse their seruice, appoint their prouision, not in hast for *neede*, but at leasure with *choice*." Although he favored public assistance for talented children of the poor, he recommended that parents with inadequate means find their children trades rather than place them in school. Mulcaster thought such children would be content with their lot when they realized the state's needs were paramount, especially if they had never been given a taste of formal education. The informal acquisition of reading and writing skills would create no problem, but he cautioned against letting such persons acquire a foreign language unless their trade demanded it; otherwise "they will not be content with the state which is for them, but bycause they haue some petie smak of their booke, they will thinke any state be it neuer so high to be low ynough for them." Mulcaster believed access to education should be restricted in a Protestant state. Catholic states had many persons superficially educated, but Protestant England should educate only a few, but in depth. Unlike Catholic England, with an "infinite" supply of livings for the superficially educated, the new state had only limited possibilities for preferment, hence the number of educated persons had to be curtailed.[27]

In the Elizabethan era the *idea* of restricting education according to social degree gradually fell into disfavor. A conservative Anglican such as Leonard Wright looked with nostalgia on the (mythical) time when education was the province of the nobility and gentry. That children of the meaner sort could now obtain schooling he attributed to the gentry's neglect of their responsibilities through preference for an idle, sensual life. Wright acknowledged that some children of inferior birth were disposed to learn, but others lacked "the right nature & condition, of a courteous ciuill Gentleman." Puritans, with their conviction of the importance of Scripture reading, favored at least rudimentary education for all youth. The Catholic Shelford urged that each child be educated in the liberal arts or trained in a craft, and since the guilds insisted on literacy, his position was tantamount to calling for basic education for virtually all males.[28]

In practice, economic conditions imposed a practical barrier to the schooling of numerous children at the lower reaches of the social spectrum, particularly children of the indigent and unskilled. The usual inability of laborers and small farmers to spare children prevented their education, even when schools were available. At the yeoman level and above, this was not a problem, and education therefore depended on the accessibility of a school or tutor. The government, however, looked with disfavor on the retention of schoolmasters in private homes by persons below the degree of baron on the grounds that this practice led to the decay of educational institutions. The government probably was concerned as well about priests that might be supported as household tutors. The governmental disapproval, and the expense, of tutors in homes of the non-nobility encouraged Elizabethans to found many new schools. The inhabitants of Willingham, Camb., endowed a school by public subscription in 1593, perhaps at the instigation of the local rector, Dr. William Smyth (who became master of Clare College eight years later). A total of £102 7s. 8d. was raised by 102 people to educate the children of Willingham residents who had contributed or who were impoverished. Most who benefitted from the school were sons of yeomen. John Hart endowed a school at Great Chesterford, Essex, in 1592 for children of parents too poor to be assessed in the subsidy book, but this case was unusual. [29]

The founding of new schools, coupled with more scholarships for poor students and better educated clergy, brought educational basics within reach of more families. Margaret Spufford's examination of the Ely diocesan records from 1574 to c. 1628 shows that education was readily available in southern Cambridgeshire; in twenty-three places, usually the larger villages, a school existed with essential continuity in this period. In the diocese of Lichfield in the period 1584 to 1642, at least 200 of the 388 parishes at some point had a schoolmaster, and of these 93 had a continuing tradition of education. During the Elizabethan period schoolmasters taught in at least 44 towns or villages in Cheshire and 60 in the diocese of Hereford. The interest shown by such prelates as Grindal, Cox, and Barnes in teaching children to read, as well as the placement of godly literature in parish churches, also contributed to the spread of education. The Elizabethan interest in founding "free" grammar schools, where often only minimal payments for miscellaneous items were charged, made it possible for a broader range of social groups to advance their sons educationally. The list of students at the Rivington Grammar School in Lancashire in 1575-76, for instance, records 114 names of children from families ranging from knights to husbandmen. Some of these local schools established such sound reputations that sons of squires, knights, and peers began to attend, diminishing social distinctions in education. [30]

Admission requirements in grammar schools provided places for financially poor students, and sometimes for intellectually unprepared youth. The grammar school at Rivington admitted — reluctantly — boys who could not read and write, and the usher and the advanced students taught them. The statutes of the Manchester Grammar School made a similar provision, but most schools insisted on a knowledge of basic skills, and the Tunbridge School required that an incoming student read English and Latin "perfectly." Of the 250 students admitted to the Merchant Taylors' school, 100 were to be poor men's sons and receive instruction without charge, providing only that they were "meete & apt to learne." Another 50 were to be children of poor men, but parents or friends had to pay 2s. 2d. per quarter for each of them. Wealth was not a consideration in the admission of 100 other students, whose fees were 5s. per quarter. Apart from a charge of 1d., admission to Manchester Grammar School was free, and "no scholar nor infant, of what country or shire soever he be, being man-child, [shall] be refused except he have some horrible or contagious infirmity infective." Some schools, however, placed geographical restrictions on potential students.[31]

At the university level, social distinctions also were becoming less important, though the government had hoped in 1559 to restrict legal study to the immediate descendants of the nobility and gentry on the grounds that such study was the entry to political power, "and generation is the chiefest foundation of inclination." Whetstone urged the gentry to send their sons to the Inns of Court, England's third university, partly to enable them to instruct ignorant neighbors. William Wentworth encouraged Thomas to see that his sons spent two or three years at a university and additional time at an Inn of Court. Increasing numbers sent their sons to the Inns of Court or universities in the early Elizabethan period, but in the mid-1580s a modest decline set in, perhaps because as Lawrence Stone suggests, Puritans feared that Whitgift would punish the godly sort in the universities, or because of economic pressures or a declining number of suitable positions for persons with higher education. The average number of university entrants per year went from 654 in the 1560s to 780 in the 1570s, 770 in the 1580s, 652 in the 1590s, and 706 in the 1600s. The pattern at the Inns of Court was slightly different, with an estimated average of 80 a year in the 1560s, 79 in the 1570s, 103 in the 1580s, 106 in the 1590s, and 119 in the 1600s. The results of the increased attendance are striking when seen in terms of the men who governed England at the county level. Of the 143 members of the working commission of the justices of the peace in Kent, Norfolk, Northamptonshire, Somerset, Worcestershire, and the North Riding of Yorkshire in 1562, 7 had been to a university and 44 to an Inn of Court. By 1584, of the 246 justices in these counties, 57 had been to a university and 114 to an Inn.[32]

Stone argues that Tudor education sought stratification by social class rather than age, but even the universities were becoming more socially integrated in the Elizabethan era. Mulcaster favored admitting sons of the poor to colleges if they demonstrated ability. At Caius College, Cambridge, the matriculation figures indicate modest gains for sons of clergymen and professionals in the 1580s and 1590s.

	Gentlemen	Clergy, Professionals	Merchants, Tradesmen	Yeomen, Husbandmen	Mediocris fortunae, Unclassified
1580-89	34%	6%	7%	11%	42%
1590-99	33%	10%	8%	10%	38%
1600-09	38%	19%	6%	17%	20%

Matriculation statistics at Oxford, however, indicate a growing proportion of sons of nobility, gentry, and clergy in the late Elizabethan years. The percentage of sons of nobility and gentry increases from 39% in the period 1575-79 to 52% in the 1600s, and the respective figures for sons of the clergy are 1% and 9%. Between 1560 and 1580, commoners had not increased significantly at Oxford, but the records of Corpus Christi College indicate that sons of the rural and urban well-to-do had been coming to pursue humane studies and manners from early in the century. At the Inns of Court the social mixture remained relatively stable from the 1570s to the 1600s, with a heavy percentage (82-86% of admissions to the Middle Temple) coming from the gentry and clergy. The gentry, in fact, preferred the Inns to the universities. Although the numbers were relatively small, sons of freeholders, copyholders, and urban artisans attended the institutions of higher education, but in general they were still beyond the reach of the unskilled and propertyless laboring families. [33]

Concerning the education of girls, probably most Elizabethan families would have agreed with Bullinger that females learn at home. Bullinger, however, insisted that they receive a puritanical training, which many Englishmen would have found too severe. Girls must be barred from inappropriate games, speech, gestures, and company, and must not be idle. They must learn to read, but only godly books, and to spin, sew, and weave. Singing Psalms and spiritual songs also was acceptable. This ideal was reflected in verse compiled by Richard Robinson, a household servant to George Talbot, earl of Shrewsbury, while he watched Mary Queen of Scots:

Keepe in your daughters strayght, best counsell I can geue:
Least that perhaps shee catch a bayte, that both your harts may greue.
And bring them vp in feare, and godlie bookes to reede:
And then be sure that thou shalt heare, that wel thy chi[l]de shall speede
And banish wilie will, from out thy daughters place.

Whitgift was less severe, tolerating the education of girls in dames'
schools, but he was adamant that no girls be taught in the Queen's
School or the choral school at Canterbury.[34]

Other writers, including Nash, Hake, and Mulcaster, supported
female education. Hake cited historical examples, mostly classical
and early Christian, to support his position, and asked at the minimum that girls be taught honest trades if traditional learning were
not possible. Curiously, he was critical of Elizabethan females who
were educated, for they "doe so greatlye abuse it, that much better
were it they shoulde vnlearne that againe which they haue alreadie
learned." He blamed parents for educating daughters "to make them
companions of carpet knightes, & giglots, for amorous louers;" better
to keep them home and instruct them in virtue.[35]

Mulcaster's advocacy of female education was predicated on the
assumption that girls were inferior to boys, and should not be allowed to matriculate at grammar schools or universities. "I allow
them learning with distinction in degrees, with difference of their
calling, with respect to their endes, wherefore they learne." He favored their admission to elementary schools, which he said was the
English custom, to learn reading and writing, and he acknowledged
their propensity for music and foreign languages. The education of
girls must keep them from idleness, provide for mothers "well furnished in minde" and physically fit, teach obedience to husbands,
provide suitable cultural awareness for women of birth, and enable
them to read religious literature. Common opinion, according to Mulcaster, dictated that girls be educated until they were thirteen or
fourteen, but he thought additional schooling was sometimes essential, especially for girls of higher birth. Mindful of the social order, he
recommended against excessive education, which led to undue social
ambition. A girl should learn what is necessary, whether in an elementary school or from a private tutor. Yet girls from inferior social
backgrounds might, with Mulcaster's blessing, manifest singular
ability in their education and thereby achieve higher-than-expected
matches. Daughters of princes and peers or girls likely to marry into

the peerage must be exposed to geometry, law, physics, divinity, philosophy, speech, and foreign languages. In short, Mulcaster favored female education as long as it was religiously and socially utilitarian, and conformed with the Elizabethan social structure.[36]

Elementary and dames' schools were responsible for educating most Elizabethan girls who received instruction outside the home, but grammar schools normally were closed to them. In some instances, girls attended a grammar school with the petties, but probably never to study Latin. The 1594 statutes of the Banbury Grammar School allowed girls to matriculate to learn English, as long as they left by the age of nine. Norwich provided free elementary education for children of the poor, apparently girls as well as boys, and other cities probably did the same. Generally, education for females was oriented toward domestic or vocational activities. When Elizabeth visited Sandwich, Kent, in 1573 she observed 100 to 120 English and Dutch girls spinning yarn, and when she saw a pageant at Norwich in 1578 it included 16 girls spinning and knitting. The London area had a number of schools that accepted girls and were run by immigrants from France and the Netherlands. Christ's Hospital, founded in the early 1550s, provided schooling for girls as well as boys; according to Machyn, four hundred of them appeared in a funerary procession early in the reign.[37]

For families of means, a private tutor was an alternative to an elementary or dames' school. Such tutors ranged from professional scholars to clerics and governesses. Sir Henry Sidney hired Johan Tassel to teach his daughter French, and Sir Robert Sidney provided for his daughter to study writing, dancing, and the virginals. Lady Katherine, wife of Henry Lord Berkeley, wanted her girls to study Italian, and Jane, daughter of Henry Howard, earl of Surrey, received a classical education under John Foxe. Lady Anne Clifford's tutor, the poet Samuel Daniel, was allowed to teach her only English because her father disapproved of the study of foreign languages by females. Like many other gentry girls, Margaret Dakins was placed in a noble household, in this instance that of Henry Hastings, earl of Huntingdon, where she was educated with the children of Walter Devereux, earl of Essex, viz. Walter, Penelope, and Dorothy. Sir Anthony Cooke, who was something of a classical scholar, personally taught his five daughters, and Henry Fitzalan, earl of Arundel, acquired additional books for his library to benefit the education of his girls. John Kingston, a friend of the Holles family, gave his daughter Elizabeth "the best and choysest education, which render'd hir, who had judgment beyond most of hir sex, aequally accomplisht with the best of them," especially in music and orthography. [38]

Other fathers were less interested in the intellectual abilities of their daughters. William Wentworth advised Thomas to leave the education of his girls "to the advice of some aged discrete Matron's direction." Sir Robert Cecil, referring to his orphaned daughter, would undertake "no office necessary for her Education, being a Man, and wholly dedicated to ye publick seruices." How this duty kept him from training her is not clear, but she was deformed and he cared deeply for her, wanting to keep her from becoming a spectacle at court. Denzil Holles of Irby, Lincs., wanted his children to be raised in learning and virtue, but his will showed that his primary concern for his daughters was suitable matches, not education.

The Northamptonshire yeoman Robert Furneis was more interested in his daughter's learning, for his will stipulated that her guardian provide her with "such further education for books and needle and other qualitys fitt for her degree and calling" until she was eighteen. In Essex, those below the level of the gentry gave almost no attention to the education of girls in their wills. Some governesses may have been effective tutors. When Grace Sherrington's cousin and governess found her idle "she would sett me to cypher with my pen, and to cast up and prove great sums and accompts, and sometimes set me to wryte a supposed letter to this or that body concerning such and such things, and other tymes let me read in Dr [William] Turner's Herball & Bartholomew Vigoe [on chirurgery], and other times sett me to sing psalmes, and othertimes sett me to some curious [needle] work." [39]

That some strides were made for the intellectual improvement of females is evident in the accomplishment of some women. Sir Anthony Cooke's daughters knew Latin, Greek, and possibly Hebrew, as well as the works of early Christian writers and contemporary Protestant scholars, and perhaps secular classics. Sir Anthony's will (1576) left each daughter, including Burghley's wife Mildred, volumes in Latin and Greek. Anne and Elizabeth made scholarly translations, and Mildred studied the Greek fathers. Elizabeth also composed epitaphs in Greek and Latin on the family tombs at Bisham, Berks., and Westminster Abbey. Cartwright told her in 1591 that "the mark of learning in yourself [is] rare in your sex." Lady Lumley was praised for her knowledge of Greek and Latin, and Elizabeth Tanfield, the future Lady Falkland, instructed herself in those subjects as well as French, Spanish, Italian, and Hebrew. She also studied

Transylvanian from a native. As an only child, she had easy access to her father's library, and he gave her a copy of Calvin's *Institutes* before she was twelve, in which she discovered contradictions. Mary Sidney knew French, Italian, and possibly Latin; Jane Howard knew Greek and Latin; Katherine, wife of Henry Lord Berkeley, was knowledgeable in Latin, Italian, and French, and could play the lute and sing; Catherine Tishem, whose son became a professor at Heidelberg, knew French, Italian, Latin, and Greek; Elizabeth, wife of the Merchant Taylor Emanuel Lucas, could speak, write, and read Latin, Spanish, and Italian, as well as play the lute, viol, and virginals. Other women were adept translators, including Mary (Sidney) Herbert (from French and Italian), Margaret Tyler (from Spanish), Mary Fitzalan (from Greek and Latin), and Jane Fitzalan (from Greek). Lady Margaret Russell and Lady Margaret Hoby were avid readers. Overall, such accomplishments were true only of a small percentage of Elizabethan women, who came from the landed or mercantile classes.[40]

On the extent of education, then, social barriers were gradually falling in Elizabethan England, and interest in educating girls was growing. Puritan names are prominent among the educated women—Sidney, Hoby, Cooke, and Sherrington, but Anglicans and Catholics are represented too—Tanfield, Howard, Fitzalan, and Berkeley. A mixture of humanistic and Protestant (especially Puritan) influences encouraged learning for a fuller life and for religious purposes. The Protestant interest in schooling for spiritual and vocational purposes helped lower the social barriers to education, but there is no clear demarcation of opinion among Anglicans and Puritans on this matter. To the extent that lower social barriers enabled more persons to be better educated for the ministry, Puritans in particular would have been pleased. The degree to which Elizabethans endowed schools testifies to a heightened concern to extend education to greater numbers of children for religious, civic, and vocational ends.

(3) Masters and Tutors

The perverse obstinate untowardness of divers young gentlemen in religion doth argue a manifest and most intolerable corruption in their bringing up, and in schoolmasters.

William Overton[41]

The master ought to be to his scholars a second parent and father, not of their bodies, but of their minds.

Alexander Nowell[42]

Because of the religious content of Elizabethan education, spiritual leaders impressed on parents the importance of carefully selecting a private tutor or schoolmaster. For the Catholics Shelford urged parents to choose godly, "wise hearted" masters and dames, and to check with them periodically regarding their children. The Puritan Edward Hake recommended a careful inquiry into the qualifications of a teacher, and reliance on a few instructors rather than many. Several Puritans, especially Robert Cleaver and William Vaughan, were troubled by the unwillingness of many parents to exercise care in selecting teachers. In Vaughan's estimation, parents were concerned primarily with the instructor's genteel ways, his charges, and his willingness to be lenient in discipline. These, he complained, were the same parents who sent their sons to the universities before they were intellectually prepared, removed them before they attained a degree, and placed them in the Inns of Court with "shriuers, Caualeers, and mad-cappes." These charges had some substance, but many parents did exercise due care in selecting teachers. When Robert Cecil went to Cambridge, Burghley insisted that his son have an honest and good scholar as his intellectual guide; the master of St. John's dispatched a fellow of the college to Theobalds for Burghley to examine. Lady Harrington, troubled by a froward son, sought and received outside assistance in locating a suitable tutor rather than giving up on the boy's education. Edmund Campion was hired by William Lord Vaux to tutor his son Henry, and Catholics in general sought teachers of the same faith for their children. Sir Robert Sidney demanded a French tutor for his eldest son, because "our Oxford yong men have seen nothing but the schooles, and need for most thinges them selves to be taught." [43]

One reason alleged for the inferior quality of some masters and tutors was inadequate income. Mulcaster called for greater remuneration for masters in grammar schools, and warned that good scholars would never teach elementary school, because of the insufficient monetary rewards. Vaughan likewise believed schoolmasters received insufficient stipends, forcing parents to pay large amounts to send children to such schools as Eton, Westminster, and Winchester, perhaps depleting funds that might ultimately have sent their sons to the universities for degrees. Nash wittily remarked that "the seauen Liberall Sciences and a good legge, wil scarse get a Scholler bread and cheese," and that "a Scriuener [is] better paid for an obligation, than a Scholler for the best Poeme he can make." Roger Ascham bitterly alleged that a horseman was chosen with more care than a teacher, the former receiving two hundred crowns a year while the latter got only two hundred shillings. Thus parents "finde more pleasure in their horse, than comforte in their children."[44]

The salaries of masters and ushers in the grammar schools underscore the validity of these complaints. A master received about £10 *p.a.* at the beginning of the century, £15 at the middle, and approximately £20 near the end, with ushers receiving around half these amounts. Lodging was occasionally provided without charge, and special fees sometimes were imposed on students to increase earnings, but overall the income of masters and ushers did not keep pace with inflation. In 1569 the master of the Southampton Grammar School received £20 *p.a.*, supplemented with £6 13s. 8d. *p.a.* for reading a weekly divinity lecture at Holy Rood Church. The master of the grammar school at Berkeley, Yorks., received £21 *p.a.* in the late 1570s, whereas the local minister got £30 *p.a.* (in 1585) and his assistant £16. The 1602 statutes of the school founded by Whitgift at Croydon, Surrey, called for the master to receive £20 *p.a.* and miscellaneous necessities. One of the most prominent masters in England, Richard Mulcaster, got £10 *p.a.* plus lodging, and another £10 privately, whereas the headmaster at St. Paul's School received £34 13s. 4d., a gown, lodging at the school, and a country house at Stepney. At Eton the master received £16 *p.a.*, whereas Westminster provided total compensation worth £27 11s. 8d. A scholar might do better working for the nobility; in 1572 Edward Seymour, earl of Hertford, paid £30 to the tutor of his children. In 1597 Sir Robert Sidney was willing to pay £20 *p.a.* for an able schoolmaster, but by 1600 the sufficiency of this amount to retain his tutor was in doubt. At Tiverton, Devon, the master of the grammar school received £50 *p.a.* in 1599, substantial as compared with normal stipends for masters, even that late in the century. A teacher's situation was compounded by the absence of the patronage rights that many other professionals enjoyed. In fact, teachers often had to rely on patronage for employment. Sir Anthony Bacon, for example, enjoyed virtual patronage powers over the school at St. Albans, Herts., in the 1590s.[45]

Guidelines for the selection of a suitable master commonly stipulated godliness, learning, and honesty. William Wentworth recommended that his son select a master who was a sober, godly man over the age of forty. When Thomas Wotton was ready to appoint a master for the school at Sandwich, he wrote to Lawrence Humphrey, Regius Professor of Divinity at Oxford, seeking a Puritan who would "rather sufficiently instructe a fewe, then slightly instructe a manye." The most comprehensive statement of desired qualifications was enunciated by William Vaughan. The nine qualities he sought in a master were skill in grammar, rhetoric, and poetry; discretion to judge a student's nature; ability to motivate problem students; perseverence; an exemplary life; moderate discipline; a strong, majestic countenance; abstinence from lechery and excessive drinking and apparel; and an awareness of the appropriate amount of schoolwork to assign. At the university level he expected tutors to have such qualities as godliness, thorough education, sober speech, and an age between 27 and 40.[46]

The high standards advocated for teachers are reflected in the statutes of some grammar schools. The master of the Rivington Grammar School, with which Pilkington was closely involved, had to be learned, honest, at least 24 years old, a Protestant, and one who had been at Oxford or Cambridge for at least four years. The usher had to be honest, learned, a good teacher, a Protestant, and not a curate unless his teaching load was small. Above all, the master and usher at Rivington must encourage students to godly living as well as learning, hence prayers and Scripture were used regularly. Other schools had comparable requirements. The Puritan standards of Henry Hastings, earl of Huntingdon, are reflected in his statutes for the school at Leicester:

> The schoolemaster shalbe of sounde religeon, he shalbe noe papist nor heretique, he shalbe of honest conversacion[,] he shalbe neyther adulterer, fornicator, dronkard, neyther game player, noe swearer or blasphemer, neyther faultie in any grevous cryme, he shal aswell by lyfe as by good exhortacion labor to trayne up his schollers in true religeon and in godly lyfe, he shalbe learned, and apte to teache the greeke and lattyn tongues, and he shalbe A good versyfier.

The statutes of some schools were less demanding. The Manchester Grammar School wanted a man who was honest, physically fit, and suitably educated, though not a cleric. Whitgift's school at Croydon was interested primarily in the ability of a master to write and versify, and in his knowledge of Greek and Latin. The statutes of the Ipswich School and Queen Mary's Grammar School, Clitheroe, Lancs., treat the qualifications of a master by implication. The evidence suggests that where committed Puritans or moderate Anglicans played a major role in drafting statutes, more care was taken to specify the qualifications of masters and ushers.[47]

Because masters stood *in loco parentis*, a necessary qualification was the ability to exercise appropriate discipline. Robert Allen advised teachers to avoid excessive levity and severity, especially unreasonable correction by the rod or fists, and Mulcaster warned that beating young children implanted hatred rather than love of learning. Moderation was preferred; Stockwood proposed that the normal behavior of a teacher be gentle, using reasonable correction as a last remedy.

Even the best students, according to Pilkington, occasionally required the rod, but he favored expelling those who regularly required physical chastisement rather than harm good students. Thus the statutes of the Rivington Grammar School required the master and usher to appoint monitors at least each week "to spy who offendeth, and . . . have both rods, ferula, and palmer to correct them withall, whom the Monitors shall present to have offended."[48]

Flogging was a common punishment in Elizabethan schools for all children, regardless of age or rank. William Denman, the master at Braintree, Essex, was reputedly an excellent instructor but a harsh punisher. As a result of austere treatment one of his students, John Bedell, "grew so out of love with learning, that his parents were forc'd to take him home." His brother William, a future bishop, was once beaten by Denman "off a pair of stairs, and had one side of his head so bruis'd, that the bloud gush'd out of his ear, and his hearing was in consequence so impair'd, that he became in process of time wholly deaf on that side." When the future physician Simon Forman was in school, his master, William Ryddonte, beat him for his inability to spell, and regularly required him to sleep nude during the winter, "which kepte him in greet feare." There was good reason for the pleas of moderation from religious and educational authors.[49]

Teachers whose behavior was errant or whose qualifications were inadequate were subject to dismissal. Sometimes school statutes provided for this, as at Rivington, where a master or an usher could be dismissed for frequenting alehouses, gambling, swearing, associating with prostitutes, quarreling, failing to attend church services, failing to discipline students in moderation, or teaching students views contrary to Scripture. In 1571 the school master at Gisburn, Yorks., avoided dismissal by promising to attend church with his pupils on Sundays and holy days, and there "to knele about the minister when he shal be singing or reding the Litany and awnswere the Curate himself together with his Schollers." In the 1560s John Rokeby, vicar general for the archbishop of York, conducted hearings on the qualifications of masters: John Ireland of Halifax and John Lacy of Bradford were judged inadequately educated and deprived of their positions. Edward Sandall, a York cleric, was dismissed as a teacher because he was "a corrupter of yowthe": "Whereas he ought to reade the bokes of the Scriptures and therin to be exercised, he dothe most commonlie use to reade the vaine bokes of the iiijor sonnes of Amon, Reynard the Foxe and suche like." In a more serious case, a master and his thirteen-year-old pupil were imprisoned at Ipswich for conjuring.[50]

For political and ecclesiastical authorities, the principal problem with teachers involved Catholicism. In 1564 John Scory, bishop of Hereford, complained to the Privy Council that some landed gentlemen allowed masses to be said and Catholic schools to operate in their homes. In the same year, Edmund Scambler, bishop of Peterborough, addressed the Council on the same problem, and asked that no masters be allowed to teach in private houses except by episcopal license. The prelates continued to see this rule as necessary throughout the reign. In 1571, for example, Grindal issued an injunction for the province of York that forbade anyone to teach in the houses of gentlemen or other places without a license from the bishop's ordinary, and called for masters to use Nowell's Latin catechism and "profane chaste authors." Visitation articles repeatedly queried whether schoolmasters were licensed and were Protestant, as well as whether they attended church services. Grindal's 1576 articles for the province of Canterbury also inquired if masters used William Lily's grammar and Nowell's catechism. The bishops sought Catholics who served as tutors in private homes, perhaps in the guise of servants. One enterprising Catholic priest was discovered going from house to house on the pretext of teaching the virginals.[51]

The campaign against Catholic masters was largely in the hands of bishops until the 1580s, when the specter of treason prompted more active involvement by the rest of the government. Masters who dutifully switched to Protestantism at the outset of the reign, as did Edward Pendleton of the Manchester Grammar School, probably never relinquished Catholic sympathies. John Fletcher, master of St. Peter's, York, reconverted to Catholicism and was deprived and imprisoned by Grindal in 1574. Catholic tutors in aristocratic homes were seen as a serious threat, particularly in counties such as Lancashire, and the government periodically responded with harsh penalties. Thomas Woodhouse and R. Crockett, who served as Catholic tutors, were executed in 1580, and Swithen Wells, who ran a school for local boys in the household of Henry Wriothesley, earl of Southampton, met the same fate in 1591. Yet the government never eradicated Catholic education. Sometimes, as in Leicester, Puritans took a direct hand in ousting Catholics from educational positions. In 1568 Thomas Sampson, newly appointed master of St. Ursala's Hospital, took the lead in driving out John Pott as master of the Leicester Grammar School. In 1594 Henry Hastings, earl of Huntingdon, was responsible for the ouster of the school's usher, Thomas Jesson, possibly for religious reasons. The government was perhaps more concerned with tutors of the high-born. In 1575 Burghley received a report on the methods and books used to educate the earl of Surrey, and in 1601 the Privy Council inquired "what masters, mistresses or dames do retain or keep in their houses or service any schoolmasters or servants or other persons that forebear to come to the parish church or chapel." It was a clear indication that the bishops had failed to stop the use of Catholic teachers.[52]

The selection of proper masters was thus significant from a religious standpoint. Catholic theology, not inadequate knowledge, concerned the government. Spiritual considerations figured high on the list of desired qualities, whether or not parents seriously inquired into the religious outlook of a prospective master or tutor. Certainly some did, but the frequency of complaints that many parents were lax in this duty suggests another effect of creeping secularization, as well as a difference of perspective between parents and clerics with regard to religious qualifications for tutors.

The inability of masters to maintain their standard of living in an inflationary age is odd, in light of broad interest in educational endowments, and may be owing to the inability or unwillingness of parents of school-age youth to invest sufficient sums in education. Endowments, however, were relatively painless, since they usually came from deceased donors. The problem was compounded by the 1580s by the rise in the number of university-trained men seeking teaching positions or ecclesiastical preferment. Yet despite the unwillingness to provide reasonable stipends and the sometimes callous manner in which teachers were selected by parents, religious motives remained strong enough to arouse concern about the presence of Catholic teachers. Stockwood was not alone in believing conspiratorial activities were associated with Catholic tutors in private homes. To him, these men were "the sweepings of the Uniuersities, I meane, suche rotten Papistes, as by the broome of godly discipline, as vnprofitable duste, haue bin sweeped out thence," only to be admitted into the homes of the landed classes to corrupt young people. Elizabethans saw education as a battleground for the minds of youth, waged in large measure on spiritual grounds. On this point Anglican, Puritan, and Catholic leaders agreed.[53]

(4) Thoughts on the Curricula

For what trade and science is there so meane and base, which is not much amended and brought to further perfection sithence the late time of our religion, then it had before in the depth of poperie?

Thomas Stoughton[54]

To destroy noble sciences, is a mischiefe intollerable.

George Gifford[55]

Elizabethan Protestants were not in full agreement on the academic curriculum. Within the Puritan tradition, views differed on the propriety of several subjects and the authors appropriate for study. Stricter Puritans, typified by such men as Dering, Stockwood, and Francis Marbury, lecturer at St. Saviour, Southwark, demanded a biblically oriented program of study, devoid of vain topics, meaningless eloquence, and inappropriate literature. Appropriate subjects were those capable of producing profitable, godly members in the church and commonwealth, and did not encourage students, in Marbury's words, to "delight in shewes of learning, eloquence, pleasant phrases and wordes which haue no substance in them." Stockwood expected masters and tutors to teach from the Bible, but allowed some secular authors if they were subordinated to Scripture. The use of "moste vile and filthy bookes, full of al most filthy speach and beastlines, in such excesse of vncleannesse" was intolerable. Authors to whom he specifically objected included Aulus Gellius, Martial, most of Ovid, Tibullus, Catullus, and Propertius, as well as the obscene poems (the Priapea) addressed to the god of fertility, Priapus.[56]

Stephen Gosson was another Puritan with a relatively narrow view of the curriculum. A onetime playwright who underwent a conversion c. 1579 and subsequently became a lecturer at Stepney, Gosson was critical of introducing students to poetry and music (especially piping and fiddling), for these arts encouraged leisure. Referring to Pythagoras, he advocated that students study only the music of the spheres; right music consisted of politic laws in a well-governed commonwealth. As for poetry, "Poets are the whetstones of wit, notwithstanding that wit is dearly bought." Gifford may have favored this stricter approach, for he proposed that arts and sciences should be studied only if they enabled man to perform "higher and better things."[57]

A more moderate Puritan approach to the curriculum is found in John Rainolds, who believed such subjects as rhetoric and logic were essential for preachers. Reading and disputing such authors as Aristotle and Tully were effective in preparing young men to confute error and confirm truth. Nevertheless, he was willing to lay aside "so fine a Poet" as Terence to procure knowledge from "purer fountaines." Terence was not in favor, however, with other Protestant reformers.[58]

One of the fullest expositions of the moderate Puritan position came from William Vaughan. Logic was judged the most praiseworthy of the arts, with value for intellectual exercise, disputation, and philosophy; it was divinely revealed. Philosophy was lauded because it revealed knowledge of the natural world and promoted ethical living. Grammar, properly studied, had to embrace philosophical knowledge as well as an understanding of foreign languages. Unlike Rainolds, Vaughan did not find rhetoric profitable, especially for preachers.

For although Rhetorical speeches do delight their auditory; yet notwithstanding, they make not much for ye soules health. Simple & material speeches are best among friends. Preachers therefore must labour to speake & vtter that, which the hearers vnderstand.

Vaughan defended poetry, and referred approvingly to Philip Sidney's apology for it: Those who objected to Ovid, Catallus, and Propertius because of their alleged lasciviousness, he felt, did not distinguish between a subject and the abuse of it. He was willing to exile many English poets and balladeers for composing bawdy sonnets and amorous poems, but he was unwilling to condemn all poetry. Those who castigated poetry also abused godly ministers by calling them bookish fellows and Puritans. Moreover, "Poetry is more philosophicall and serious then historie, because poetry meddleth with the generall consideration of all things: whereas Historie treateth onely of the particular." In contrast, stricter Puritans preferred history to poetry. In addition to these subjects, Vaughan insisted that students be taught to fear and love God and to act with good manners.[59]

The moderate Puritan approach is reflected in Huntingdon's statutes for the grammar school at Leicester. The authors to be studied included Ovid, Tully, Virgil, Terence, Caesar, and Horace, as well as Erasmus and Calvin. Greek would be learned from Calvin's catechism, the New Testament, *Aesop's Fables,* Isocrates, and the *Verbal Figures* of Petrus Mosellanus. The classical and biblical curriculum was kept in spiritual perspective by regular religious observances. Children in all forms had to attend church services on sabbaths and holy days, those in the upper six forms had to attend week-day sermons as well, and the upper two forms had to go to prophesyings with the master.[60]

Generally the moderate Puritan position on curricula was harmonious with Anglican views. There is no serious criticism by Anglicans of classical authors or rhetoric. Pilkington's curriculum for the Rivington Grammar School included rhetoric as well as classics and music. The statutes required younger students to know the catechism of Calvin or Nowell, and the senior students preparing for the ministry had to "be diligently practised and perfect in Calvin's Catechism and Institutions, and the New Testament." Regulations for attendance at church services were firm, but not as comprehensive as those at

Leicester. Pilkington criticized the subtleties of schoolmen for defacing truth; similar spiritual concern is evident in Edmund Bunny, who urged schoolmasters to abolish authors who might infect students with heathen or Catholic ideas. Several Anglicans, including Wright and Covel, defended the teaching of astronomy, which Wright defined as "the secret knowledge of nature and course of the heauens." Covel found the proper use of astronomy acceptable, but ruled out astrology as an attempt to govern by superstition rather than divine precepts.[61]

Further evidence of Anglican views of the curricula is found in the recommendations of leading laymen. For the twelve-year-old earl of Oxford, Burghley recommended French, Latin, writing, drawing, and cosmography. In 1578 he advised Sir John Harrington at Cambridge to read Cicero for a knowledge of Latin, Livy and Caesar for Roman history, and Plato and Aristotle for logic and philosophy. To his son, William Wentworth recommended logic, philosophy, cosmography, law, and especially history. Among the clerics, Tobias Matthew, dean of Durham, was pleased that his nephew Timothy was fond of history. Under the tutelage of Whitgift at Oxford, George Clifford, earl of Cumberland, did not learn much Latin, but he acquired "a general knowldge and an insight into all the arts, and especially into the mathematicks," which motivated his subsequent interest in sea voyages and navigation.[62] Not so much the subjects with the exception of rhetoric, but the emphasis on Scriptures rather than the classics distinguishes stricter Puritans from Anglicans. The latter did not obliterate religion from the curriculum, but neither did they give it the pronounced centrality in all areas as did stricter Puritans. Moderate Puritans strove for a balance, but generally agreed with the Anglicans.

The views of Thomas Nash, the Anglican poet, continued the humanistic ideas espoused earlier by Eliot. For Nash, education must inculcate virtue, hence he supported historical studies to enable students to emulate worthy men. "Students [must] wisely prefer renowned antiquitie before newe found toyes, one line of *Alexanders* Maister [Aristotle], before the large inuectiue *Scolia* of the *Parisian* Kings Professor." Rhetoric was esteemed for its ability to enhance other subjects. Poetry was defended as a hidden, divine philosophy containing moral precepts and basic truths, but he cautioned against excessive reading that might lead to paganism. Nash's basic rule was that studies must be wholesome and conducive to morality: "There is no extremitie either in actiue or contemplatiue life, more outragious then the excessiue studies of delight, wherwith young Students are so besotted, that they forsake sounder Artes, to followe smoother eloquence." Although Nash was concerned with virtue in education, he did not press for the development of morality through intensive biblical study.[63]

The Separatists condemned the standard curricula as "heathen and vaine artes," though they had no objection to foreign languages or "lawful" Christian subjects. Such liberal arts as logic and rhetoric were acceptable if taught without pagan, Catholic, or profane authors. The focus of the Separatist attack was the grammar schools and universities, where classical literature or Aristotelian studies formed the core of the curriculum. Around 1589 Robert Browne proposed to Burghley that all subjects in the universities be taught in accord with the general rules of Scripture. Then students would "by divine wisdom and prudence . . . confute their [traditional] *logic*: by right speech and language, disprove their *grammar*: by right use of proverbs and proverbial speeches, or by words, disprove their *rhetoric*: also their *arithmetic*, by the right rules of numbring. Their *geometry*, by better mesuring: their *music*, by better melody: their *metaphysics*, by the laws of creation, covenant, and sanctification: their *ethics, oeconomies, politics*, by true religion and righteousnes." Unlike Puritans, Separatists thought the most objectionable subject was divinity as taught in the universities, especially in conjunction with logic and rhetoric, and through commentaries of the Scholastic variety. Disputations on Scripture in Latin and sustained with multiple philosophical glosses were ridiculed. The Separatists also were opposed to the study of divinity as the basis for an occupation. Although Puritans repudiated the Separatist position, the latter was derived from an intensification of the biblically oriented curriculum they favored.[64]

Elizabethan students were confronted with a blend of Christian and classical literature that allowed masters and tutors considerable leeway in assigning emphasis. The 1573 statutes of Wolverhampton School sanctioned Terence, Ovid, Horace, Virgil, Tully, Isocrates, and Xenophon on the one hand, and Juan Vives and Nowell's catechism on the other. A comparable curriculum was established in the statutes of the Leicester Grammar School. Some laity accepted such a blend, at least to the point of wanting their sons to acquire a knowledge of Latin and perhaps Greek as well as Christian doctrine. A relative of Burghley's secretary, Sir Michael Hicks, proudly described his son as one educated in Latin, French, writing, ciphering, music, dancing, riding, and sword-fighting, but above all one who had been "specially bred . . . to know and feare God. Sir Robert Sidney searched carefully in the Netherlands before he found an impoverished gentleman skilled in Latin, Greek, Dutch, and French to tutor his son.[65]

Other Elizabethans were chary of classical languages and literature, and almost certainly were influenced by the stricter Puritan views. In April 1582 the Privy Council commended to the High Commission a book by Christopher Ocland, master of St. Olave's School, Southwark, entitled *Anglorum prelia*; dedicated to Lady Burghley, it was a history of England in Latin verse, and the Council thought it should be used especially in the common schools "where divers heathen poetes are ordinarily read and taught, from the which the youthe of the Realme receyve rather infectyon in manners and educatyon then advauncement in vertue." The Council wanted such classical works excised from the curricula and ordered the commissioners to inform the bishops of this. Ovid's *De arte amandi* was mentioned for such censorship. The seven councillors who made this decision included the Puritans Ambrose Dudley, earl of Warwick, Sir Francis Knollys, and Sir Francis Walsingham. At a humbler level, the Devonshire yeoman Robert Furse advised his heirs to "geve yourselves to the redynge and herynge of the holy scryptures and churche like good docteren[,] be lerned in the laws of the realme and have to rede the old crownenekeles and shuch like awnshyente hystoryes." There was no mention of classics, which was also the case with Richard Senhouse's recommendation to his son Simon. The latter was first to serve God and then use his leisure hours to study French or Italian, and to learn to dance and play the lute or the virginals.[66] Thus in theory and in practice, some Puritans found an educational curriculum dominated by classical instruction contrary to their ideals of a biblically oriented program of study. Although not as extreme as the Separatists, stricter Puritans advocated a position distinguishable from that of the Anglicans.

(5) Demands for Educational Reform

Surely, surely, so many adulterers, robbers, stealers, cutpurses, coggers, carders, dicers, sellers of lands, and bankrupts, issue out of that lake and filthy puddle of negligent and perverse education.

John Woolton[67]

Manie there bee, that wish our Colledges to bee vtterly suppressed, and our schooles of learning to bee made barnes or wooll-houses; which were euen to wish vs peasaunts and witals like themselues.

William Vaughan[68]

Calls for educational reform focused primarily on the universities and largely stemmed from religious considerations. The complaints increased during the age but were hardly original to it. In 1552 Bernard Gilpin, rector of Houghton-le-Spring, Durham, bemoaned

the decaying state of the universities, warning—with exaggeration—
that 90% of the students had left, and that Oxford and Cambridge
might cease to exist by 1559. As Parker surveyed the impact of Catholicism on the universities in Mary's reign, he lamented that the
schools were in a miserable state, but he still preferred to go to Cambridge rather than become dean of Lincoln. The government was concerned about the universities, and in 1559 urged the nobility to send
their sons to Oxford, Cambridge, or a foreign university, and recommended that one-third of the scholarships be bestowed on sons of the
lesser gentry. "The wanton bringing up and ignorance of the nobility
forces the Prince to advance new men that can serve," but these, the
queen and her advisers feared, were too ambitious to serve the commonwealth faithfully and respect the social order.[69]

Complaints of the decaying state of education failed to die down
despite increasing enrollments (in the universities into the early 1580s)
and new educational foundations. The speaker of the Commons in
1563, Thomas Williams, calculated that the Tudor years had seen the
disappearance of a hundred schools due to the dissolution of the
monasteries, chantries, and guilds. "The universities are decayed, and
great market towns and others without either school or preacher."
Jewel's letters are filled with complaints of the decay of learning in
the universities at the commencement of Elizabeth's reign. As late as
1590 William James, dean of Christ Church, Oxford, told his audience
at Paul's Cross that the number of paying students at Oxford colleges
had declined by 50 to 80% from the Marian era, and that fewer students were studying divinity, partly owing to the adverse financial
impact of patronage on ecclesiastical positions.[70]

Overdrawn as these laments are, they do signal a concern regarding
educational conditions, particularly at Oxford and Cambridge. Complaints were lodged against the universities and Inns of Court for being
lax in the discipline of students. Separatists castigated founders' days
and religious holidays, academic degrees, and other "idolatrous profane usages, mysteries, othes, vowes, [and] ceremonies." Even Cartwright repudiated divinity degrees, a position Whitgift feared would
open the door to confusion and overthrow of the universities. "It
should seem that they would have a confusion of degrees (which they
call equality) as well in universities as in parishes." Bancroft likened
the Separatist attack on degrees to the Continental Anabaptists, but
stooped low when he suggested Cartwright's criticism stemmed from
being denied a D.D. degree. The Separatists condemned academic garb
because of its Catholic associations and lack of biblical warrant. The
authorities were concerned, especially at Cambridge, that Puritan

criticism led to the wearing of "vnscholerlike apparell," and in 1580 Aylmer requested that Burghley enjoin heads of Cambridge colleges to see that traditional academic garb was worn.[71]

Separatist criticism of academic degrees and dress was symptomatic of their fundamental concern with divinity in the universities. Barrow deplored those "instructed in the schole of heathen vanitie, brought up in the colledges of more than monkish idlenes and disorder, exercised in vaine and curious artes, whose divinitie is by tradition." Debating, glossing, and applying logic and rhetoric to theology was repulsive to the Separatists. Although Puritans were not opposed to theological study in the universities, they created a stir by extending such study to include demands for reforms in the church. It was important to control academic appointments, as Burghley recognized when he responded to Dering's request in 1572 to appoint Cartwright to a chair at Cambridge: "It is my duty to further all good learning and quietness in that university, that indecent contentions be excluded from thence." The following year Matthew Hutton, dean of York, pressed Burghley to govern the universities more closely to prevent Puritans from creating contention. In Nash's judgment, these reformers were men who merely wanted to perpetuate their names by founding new sects.[72]

Puritans and Anglicans viewed university reform primarily in terms of improvements in the quality of faculty and tutors. Early in the age Parker was troubled by Cambridge masters who planned to resign with substantial profits after ensuring that friends would succeed them. In May 1559, Parkhurst advised Bullinger not to send his son to Oxford as long as it remained "a den of thieves" populated largely with Catholics. Pilkington found few "ancient learned men" of either faith in the universities and worried about replacements when they died. A Cambridge preacher echoed this concern, for "manie in their universitie had long beards and short wittes, [and] were of greate standing and small vnderstandinge." In his view, the basic problem involved the preferment of inferior students, an assessment with which Mulcaster later agreed. In 1576, the Commons considered a bill to prohibit buying and selling places in colleges and schools, and in 1589 Parliament approved "An Act against Abuses in Election of Scholars and Presentation to Benefices" to end bribery in the universities. Nevertheless as late as 1600, William Vaughan berated "counterfeit and vnsufficient teachers" in the universities. Some of these complaints reflect the underlying religious struggle in the country. In 1586, for instance, Mr. Willis, the master of St. John's College, Oxford, was described by the Puritans Leicester and Walsingham as a godly, learned man, but by Whitgift as an unlearned man skilled primarily in husbandry with a wife and two female relatives with immoral reputations. From St. John's, Whitgift contended, came "almost all the evle bishops and denes now living in England, and yet where is greater zeal pretended." Other complaints reflect serious problems, such as John Davies' accusation in the House of Commons in 1597 that masters enriched themselves from college endowments.[73]

One means to improve the universities was reform of the college statutes. Recognizing this, in 1574 Walsingham pressed Burghley to reform the statutes of Magdalene College, Cambridge. Yet when the university statutes were revised, the impetus was not educational reform but a determination to increase the powers of masters to check the reforming zeal of the more radical fellows. After Cox and Grindal urged Burghley to do something about the statutes of St. John's College, Cambridge, which were blamed for breeding contention, an official visitation occurred in 1576 and new statutes, increasing the authority of the master, came into force in 1580. The difficulties inherent in the existing statutes, especially those involving the curriculum, are manifest in that they were sometimes unenforceable.[74]

The Separatists saw little hope to reform Oxford and Cambridge, hence Barrow proposed that they be abolished like the monasteries and chantries. He faulted their Catholic origins, incurable abuses, lack of a foundation on biblical principles, and the quality of graduates they produced. They are "the verie hyves and nurseries of these armed poisoned locusts and venemous scorpions," especially the prelates, as well as "cages full of uncleane birds, of foule and hateful spirites," which poison youth. Those at the universities lived in "munkish dennes" in pride and idleness, engaging in unnatural sexual acts. Instead of Oxford and Cambridge being successors of the Hebrew schools to train prophets, they were "Sodomitical colledges." Greenwood hoped that the universities could be reformed to teach foreign languages and "other honest christian and lawful artes," but not Anglican divinity. If such schools existed, Barrow agreed to support them.[75]

Anglicans and Puritans defended the universities and other schools as necessary institutions to prepare men to teach in and govern the church. The "giddy heads" who opposed them failed to recognize that they were the foundation of humanity and Christianity. John Madoxe, fellow of All Souls College, Oxford, eulogized the universities by comparing them to Mount Ephraim, "where the Children of the Prophets be reared, . . . [and] Mount *Syon*, where the Lord is truely worshipped." The Puritan Stephen Gosson argued that abuses in the universities and lower schools were not the province of all to discuss or even understand. That, of course, was precisely what the Separatists could not accept, for every believer, enlightened by the Spirit, was responsible to condemn evil wherever it existed. The attempt to make Christianity mysterious through academic divinity was at the heart of the Separatists' attack on the universities.[76]

One of the most comprehensive programs for educational reform originated with Mulcaster. At the university level he proposed to reorganize colleges according to professions or faculties, so that each university would have seven colleges: foreign languages, mathematics, philosophy, medicine, law, divinity, and education. He favored the vernacular for all instruction. Instead of training young men in common, civil, or ecclesiastical law, he wanted them taught simply "English" law. To improve the quality at the universities Mulcaster wanted the number of livings reduced but their value increased, and pensions provided to enable the most learned scholars to end their days in the colleges. At the lower levels, Mulcaster advocated uniformity in teaching and texts to reduce expenses and increase learning efficiency. The publication of school regulations was supported as a means of establishing closer relations between parents and teachers, and informing parents of the punishment to be used for their children. He criticized parents who placed children in grammar schools before they were intellectually prepared. These reforms were based on pedagogy, not religion, and in this respect differed from the reforms discussed earlier.[77]

Some Elizabethans thought educational reform required new schools. In 1597 Giles Wigginton, a Puritan ejected from the living of Sedbergh, Yorks., urged Burghley to establish a "cownter-semynary colledge" to train scholars to refute the views enunciated at Rheims and Rome. Early in the age Sir Nicholas Bacon proposed a special academy to educate wards of the crown, with a curriculum that included Latin, Greek, French and other modern languages, physical education, and Christian devotion. Advanced wards would be trained in common law, martial arts, and horsemanship.[78]

Along the same lines, Sir Humphrey Gilbert called for the creation of an academy in London to educate wards of the crown and other landed youth. His curriculum embraced Greek, Latin, Hebrew, logic, rhetoric, moral and natural philosophy, mathematics, horsemanship, cosmography, astronomy, navigation, cartography, history, medicine, law, divinity, French, Italian, Spanish, Dutch, dancing, music, and heraldry. Without such an academy, he feared that the aristocracy would continue sending their sons to the universities, where "they vtterly lose their tymes yf they doe not follow learning onely. ffor there is no other *gentlemanlike qualitie* to be attained" at Oxford and Cambridge. Moreover the university curriculum was oriented solely to intellectual endeavors and not balanced with active subjects. Gilbert thought universities should devote attention to more scholars from lower social backgrounds, who would not be diverted by well-born youth who had been enticed to idleness by the overly academic curriculum. Gilbert's scheme was motivated by considerations that were fundamentally humanistic, oriented toward the welfare of the commonwealth, not religion.[79]

The more substantive proposals for the reform of Elizabethan education originated from pedagogical, humanistic, and secular motives, but the greatest chorus of complaints came from those with spiritual motivations. The universities were the principal object of the religious reformers, particularly the Separatists, who were incensed with the divinity being taught, the academic degrees and dress, and the ceremonies. The Puritans refused to join in such extreme attacks, but Cartwright and his followers did find the D.D. and B.D. degrees objectionable, and Puritans balked at wearing the full academic regalia. From their positions within the universities, Puritans adapted the content of the curriculum to further their cause, which created consternation among Anglicans such as Whitgift. Essentially the debate over educational reform in the Elizabethan age previewed that which occurred in the 1640s and 1650s, as later radicals knew. In 1642, a digest of Barrow's views was published under the title, *The Pollution of Vniversitie-Learning*.

(6) Educational Support

Founders and benefactors be very rare at these days.

Matthew Parker[80]

He built vp no Pallace, nor purchaste no Towne,
But gaue it to Schollers to get him renowne.

Anonymous[81]

One of the most practical affirmations of faith, in the eyes of religious leaders, was financial support for education. Although educational giving was virtually unprecedented in the sixteenth century, Protestant leaders sounded notes of gloom and pled for increased giving. Jewel was typical when he argued that learning in England had decayed since the commencement of the Reformation, and he warned that a decline in education would lead to the decay of the gospel. Stubbes, arguing essentially the same point, subjected his readers to a litany of historical examples of educational donors going back to the mythical founding of Cambridge University in 375 B.C. by the Spaniard Cantabar. Blame for the alleged decline in giving was cast on the clergy (by Adam Hill, prebendary of Salisbury), or on the rapacious spirit that prevailed in the aftermath of the dissolution of the monasteries and chantries (by Jewel and Pilkington).[82]

Complaints of religious leaders about declining educational donations were in error, as W. K. Jordan has demonstrated. Mulcaster perhaps realized this when, in 1581, he asserted that more schools had been erected in Elizabeth's reign than in all other reigns together. We now know that in Elizabethan England the proportion of charitable giving (31.4%) devoted to education was higher than at any other time in the period 1480 to 1660. In the period 1561 to 1600 Bristol donors gave more to education (£12,651 7s.) than any other charitable cause, with the closest recipient being poor relief (£8,299 6s.). In Somerset, however, aid to the poor in the same period totaled £5,565 15s., whereas education got only £1,030 14s., the second largest sum. Lancashire donors gave more to education in the Elizabethan years than all other sources combined—a total of £7,054 9s., or 58.92% of charitable gifts. In London the favorite charity of the clergy and lawyers was higher education, but merchants gave the most to poor relief. Bristol merchants, on the other hand, gave nearly half of their charitable gifts to education. In Kent, £11,465 1s. went to education, but more than double that—£24,048 10s.—went to poor relief.[83]

Jordan refers often to the secularization of charitable giving, though he recognizes that most of the important benefactors of education were Puritans and that religion was a factor in philanthropy. Given the religious orientation of educational motives in this period, it is proper to speak of educational gifts as secular only to distinguish them (as Jordan does) from direct donations to ecclesiastical institutions. Giving to education was exhorted as a religious duty, in effect the bestowal of manna not required for one's family on schools, hospitals, and other charitable sources. The recognition accorded donors to such "secular" endeavors underscores the fact that aiding education could be as much a spiritual duty for an Elizabethan Protestant as giving to the church. A brass in the parish church of St. Mary, Harrow on the Hill, Middlesex, exhorts worshippers to emulate the example of a locally noteworthy "secular" donor:

Heare lyeth . . . Iohn Lyon . . . yeoman deceased the iii[th] daye of October
. . . 1592 who hath Fovnded a free Grammer Schoole in this Parish to have
continvance forever and for maintenavnce thereof and for releyfe of the poore
and of some poore schollers in the vniversityes, repayringe of high wayes, and
other good and charitable vses hath made convayavnce of lands of good valve
to a corporacion gravnted for that Pvrpose. prayse be to the avthor of al goodnes
who make vs myndefvll to followe his good example.

Not all giving, of course, was piously motivated, and even William
Vaughan urged financial support for education in part to "eternize
our names and magnificence."[84]

Because of the difficulty of determining the religious persuasions
of many laity and some clergy, Jordan's assertion that most major
benefactors of education were Puritans is difficult to substantiate. A
sampling of 65 Elizabethan wills of persons known to have been
Anglicans produced 30 donors (46.2%) to education. In contrast,
a smaller sample of Puritan wills indicates a donor rate of 92.9%, but
this figure likely errs on the high side. Among Anglican clerics a
sampling of 33 wills of the lower clergy shows that only 24.2% donated to education, which partly reflects their unsatisfactory remuneration.

The range of gifts was wide. John Crawfurthe, a prebendary of
Durham Cathedral, left 8d. each to the grammar schools "belonging
to o[u]r churche"; Robert Dallison, precentor of Lincoln Cathedral,
left an annuity of £4 for St. Peter's Grammar School, York; and Edward Michell, a pluralist rector in Northumberland and Cumberland,
bequeathed 3s. 4d. to two schoolmasters. Other gifts from lower
clergy were more substantive, and included John Stokys' gift of his
estate at Oakley, Beds., and £90 to Queens' College, Cambridge; and
William Bill's legacies of 100 marks to Trinity College, Cambridge,
for a new chapel, £10 to the same college for poor students, £20 to
St. John's College, Cambridge, for poor students, plate and bedding
to Westminster College, and coverlets to Eton College. Inadequate
finances cannot explain the relative lack of interest in educational
legacies in some cases. The lawyer Robert Nowell, for instance,
whose brother Alexander was a leader among moderate Anglicans,
left £60 for his funeral and various smaller legacies to the poor, but
only his books to the library at Gray's Inn. Generally, Anglican
clergy were more interested in donating to the poor than to education. A sampling of 24 wills of lesser Anglican clergy who did not
give anything to education shows 66.7% of them donated to the
poor, usually in small amounts indicative of their financial status.
Yet Sir Francis Trollope, vicar of Sockburn, Durham, who left

nothing to education or the poor, insisted on a funeral dinner for his friends and last rites according to "my birthe and calling." [85]

Some Anglican prelates and deans made excellent educational donations, even though in 1563 Parker informed Cecil that bishops were too poor to endow schools. Parker himself gave extensively to education during his career. He established scholarships and fellowships at Corpus Christi College, Cambridge, for students from Canterbury, Norfolk, Suffolk, and Lincoln, and left substantial legacies (worth £4,000) to Corpus Christi and Caius Colleges and Trinity Hall, Cambridge, and books and manuscripts to the Cambridge Library. He also helped found a school at Rochdale, Lancs., in 1565. Grindal manifested similar interests, including founding and endowing a free school at St. Bees, Cumb., and land and a chapel for a free school at Highgate, Middlesex. He gave to Pembroke, Magdalene, Christ's, and Corpus Christi Colleges, Cambridge, and Queen's College, Oxford. Whitgift led a drive to establish a grammar school at Hereford in 1583 and founded a grammar school at Croydon, Surrey, to which many of his household donated, as did Thomas Neville, dean of Canterbury and master of Trinity College, Cambridge. Sandys joined with William Chaderton, bishop of Chester, and Henry Hastings, earl of Huntingdon, to found a free school at Kendal, Westmorland; and Sandys was largely responsible for founding a grammar school at Hawkshead, Lancs. As archbishop of York, Matthew Hutton founded a free school at Warton, Lancs., in 1594. [86]

The archbishops were rather unusual in the extent of their donations to education. The bishops tended to support it financially, but to a lesser degree. Pilkington founded a school at Rivington, Lancs., in 1566, and with Charles Neville, earl of Westmorland, supported the refounding of the grammar school at Darlington, Durham, in 1567. Pilkington's successor at Durham, Richard Barnes, left £20 to Brasenose College, Oxford, and Richard Cox, bishop of Ely, left legacies worth the same amount to poor scholars at Cambridge. Yet neither Robert Horne nor William Day, bishops of Winchester, left anything to education in their wills. At a slightly lower level in the church, Alexander Nowell, dean of St. Paul's, founded a school at Middleton, Lancs., in 1572, and established scholarships at Brasenose College, Oxford, for Lancashire students. Gabriel Goodman, dean of Westminster, founded a grammar school at Denbigh in 1598, and Robert Johnston, archdeacon of Leicester, founded another at Uppingham, Rutland. The dean of Lincoln, Francis Mallett, provided no legacies for education, but gave £10 to the poor and £6 13s. 8d. to poor prisoners. [87]

Educational bequests of Puritan clergy were normally moderate. Hugh Gray left £13 5s. 8d. to Trinity College, Cambridge, and plate valued at £5 to Gresham College. The 1575 will of William Birche, Puritan pastor of Stanhope, Durham, left 50s. to twenty poor scholars in the grammar schools at Durham and Houghton, 40s. to those of the Manchester Grammar School, £4 10s. to eight scholars at St. John's or Clare College, Cambridge, £4 to scholars at Oxford, and £6 to another scholar. Cartwright provided a legacy of twenty marks to poor ministerial students at Cambridge, but £20 to enable his son Samuel to study for the ministry. The will of Robert Beaumont, Lady Margaret Professor of Divinity, master of Trinity College, Cambridge, and probably a conservative Puritan, left £40 to his college and £10 for poor students at Trinity.[88]

A number of Puritan lay leaders distinguished themselves by their financial support for education. Lady Frances Radcliffe, dowager countess of Sussex, and the sister of Sir Henry Sidney, desiring to provide "some good & godly monument for ye maintenance of good learning," bequeathed £5,000 to found Sidney Sussex College, Cambridge. Lady Burghley donated numerous books to Cambridge and Oxford colleges, including a copy of the Great Bible to the University Library at Cambridge, and also books to Westminster College. Among her many anonymous donations to charity was land to provide two scholarships at Cambridge. Francis Russell, earl of Bedford, left a bequest of £20 *p.a.* to University College, Oxford, to educate two poor divinity students. One of the greatest Elizabethan benefactors of education, "as *Oxford* and *Cambridge* can rightly declare," was the earl of Huntingdon. Apart from his activities on behalf of the Leicester Grammar School, he supported scholarships for its deserving students at Oxford and Cambridge, and established a library in St. Martin's church, Leicester, for the use of Leicestershire clergy, especially those who had not attended a university. Walsingham established a divinity lecture at Oxford in 1586, donated books to the library of King's College, Cambridge, and gave an advowson to Emmanuel College, Cambridge. Another staunch Puritan supporter of education was Sir Walter Mildmay. In 1569 he gave Christ's College, Cambridge, an endowment of £20 *p.a.* to provide for a lectureship in Greek, six scholarships, and a stipend for a preacher of the college. The college received books from him, including a Latin Bible, a Greek Testament, works of Plato, Aristotle, Cicero, Demosthenes, and Plutarch, and Averroes' commentary on Aristotle. His greatest monument was founding Emmanuel College, Cambridge, which

Huntingdon and Walsingham also supported. Sir Anthony Cooke advocated education but did not support it financially in his will.[89]

In this upper aristocratic stratum were various Anglican laity equally zealous in providing educational support. Anne Seymour, dowager duchess of Somerset, bequeathed £20 to poor students at Oxford and Cambridge, and Sir Christopher Wray, Lord Chief Justice of the Queen's Bench, was a principal benefactor of Magdalene College, Cambridge. In 1594 Burghley, having "had good experience of the good virtuous bringing up and education of scholars in the Queen's free Grammar School at Westminster," donated twenty marks *p.a.* to buy books for students elected to go to the universities. Anglican aristocrats founded a number of schools. Sir Roger Manwood, Lord Chief Baron of the Exchequer, joined with Parker to found a free school at Sandwich, Kent, in 1563, and Thomas Lord Wharton founded the grammar school at Kirkby Stephen, Westmorland, in 1566. Henry Neville, earl of Westmorland, joined with Pilkington to support the refounding of the grammar school at Darlington, Durham, in 1567, while Edward Lord Clinton (created earl of Lincoln in 1572) founded a grammar school at Horncastle, Lincs., in 1571. There were, however, peers who gave nothing to education, among them Edward and John Manners, successive earls of Rutland, and George Talbot, earl of Shrewsbury.[90]

A useful way to determine religious motivations in educational benefactions is to analyze the religious preferences of the founders of Elizabethan schools, particularly those at the grammar level. In the Elizabethan age only two colleges were established at Cambridge, Emmanuel and Sidney Sussex, both by Puritans, and one at Oxford, Jesus College, founded by the queen with funds from the Welshman Hugh Price, probably an Anglican. At the grammar school level, approximately 130 institutions were founded during Elizabeth's reign; there were some 360 grammar schools in England in 1600, of which about 100 were in Yorkshire. A number of schools were founded by community initiative, making it virtually impossible to assess religious motives. In this category were such grammar schools as those at Southwark, Surrey, and Gainsborough, Lincs.; Richmond, Halifax, and Wakefield, Yorks.; Ashbourn, Derby, and Daresbury, Ches.; and Blackburn, Lancs. Local initiative also was responsible for refounding grammar schools at Wymondham, Norf., and Faversham, Kent. An interesting example of local initiative occurred in 1575 when the inhabitants of Guildford, Surrey, petitioned the Privy Council to require the executors of the will of John Parkhurst, bishop of Norwich, to pay various legacies, including his Latin books, to the library of their free school.[91]

Of the approximately 130 Elizabethan grammar schools, I have identified the religious persuasions of the founders of 46, or between one-third and one-half of the schools not founded by community initiative. Puritans were responsible for 11 of these 46 foundations and refoundations, or 23.9%, a percentage perhaps larger than that of Puritans in society as a whole. Six schools, counting those at Tadcaster, Yorks., and Bangor, for which permission had been granted in Mary's reign, were founded by Catholics. The remaining 29 schools — 63% — were Anglican foundations. The fact that Anglicans apparently founded two and a half grammar schools to every one by Puritans does not support the thesis that Puritans were the major benefactors of education, though it suggests that given their smaller numbers Puritans probably supported education at least as much as Anglicans. Still, the Anglican achievement is impressive.

Anglican and Puritan leaders shared concern about education, and it would be misleading to see their interests in this area simply as manifestations of a rivalry for control of the Church of England. An example of their cooperation was the proposed "Ecclesiasticall Seminarie and College General of Learning and Religion" at Ripon, Yorks. Sandys proposed that the revenues of the hospitals of St. John the Baptist and St. Mary Magdalen (confiscated in 1544) be used to found a college with an emphasis on divinity and staffed by two ministers and two assistants. Support came from a group of Anglicans and Puritans including Huntingdon, Walsingham, John Harn, mayor of London, Alexander Nowell, dean of St. Paul's, and William Day, dean of Windsor. Archbishop Hutton subsequently pursued the idea, calling for nine senior divines, six junior divines, and six assistants, with lectures on a broad curriculum that included Oriental languages, music, astronomy, law, and divinity. Hutton's expanded plan received the encouragement of Burghley, Edmund Lord Sheffield, and Hooker.[92] Such cooperation over the establishment of a seminary overcame any religious rivalry.

Another example of shared interests involved proposals for schools in Ireland. The bishop of Meath wrote to Burghley from Dublin in October 1583 proposing the erection of a grammar school in the Pale, for "within the whole Inglyshe pale, there is not so much as *one* free schoole wher a child may learne the principles of grammar." Earlier he had proposed founding an Irish university, but nothing came of the plan. Sir Henry Sidney favored establishing schools in Ireland that might one day become universities. His goal was "the better reformation of the barbarisme of that countrie," but his plan failed. [93]

Educational giving was thus a religious duty in the minds of Protestant leaders, who pled that insufficient amounts were donated to prevent the decay of the gospel; education donations were high in the Elizabethan age, perhaps in large measure owing to the success of pleas from the divines. The percentage of gifts to education appears to be considerably higher in Puritan than in Anglican wills, but the degree of giving by educational donors shows no clear pattern along religious lines. There is insufficient evidence to assert that most of the substantial donors were Puritans. The apparent Anglican achievement of establishing two and a half grammar schools for every one by the Puritans reflects an Anglican commitment to education essentially parallel to that of Puritans. Anglican support for education was weakest among the lower clergy, where probably only one of every four men left legacies to education.

(7) Travel as Education

It is growen to that, that *Dauids* sonne can not be nourtered aright, vnlesse he be sent to *Pharaohs* Court.

John Udall [94]

The Sequell of his Brothers travell, and example of Anthony Bacon, doth make me resolute in no wise to Consent to his going over the sea.

Lady Elizabeth Russell [95]

In Elizabethan aristocratic circles some families regarded travel abroad as a desirable or even an essential part of the education of young men. The intention was fundamentally utilitarian: to acquire linguistic skills and knowledge of Continental states. The young traveler could observe social and legal institutions, schools, military strength, ideals, and customs of foreign peoples preparatory to a career of public service. When the youthful Edward Manners, earl of Rutland, was about to travel in 1571, Burghley advised him to observe "how noble men do kepe ther estates, ther wyves, ther children, ther servantes, and the rest of ther expences . . . how they provyde for ther yonger children, how they order ther landes, by what officers and ministers, how they kepe ther howsholdes for dyett." The motivation for travel was a quest for useful experience rather than a broadening of culture. [96]

Another impetus to foreign travel was a conviction that English education was less than satisfactory. Robert, the youngest son of Henry Carey, Lord Hunsdon, who did not think much of the education provided by his tutors and governors, was taken by his father to Brussels, Luxemburg, Mons, and Dunkirk when he was approximately seventeen. He subsequently accompanied his father to Antwerp and Paris, and Walsingham took him to Scotland. After studying under Mulcaster at the Merchant Taylors' School in London, Edmund Whitelocke went to Christ's College, Cambridge, and Lincoln's Inn, after which he traveled abroad "by studye and experience to redeem his mispent time." For twelve years he remained in Europe, visiting the universities at Rostock, Wittenberg, Prague, Rome, Paris, and other French towns, and serving the governor of Provence. At the age of sixteen his brother Richard went to Denmark and ultimately wed a Danish girl. Sir Thomas Smith took his son on embassies to France in 1565 and 1567 to train him to serve his commonwealth, and the young man subsequently visited Spain. After a period as University Orator at Oxford, Thomas Bodley "waxed desirous to travell beyond the Seas, for attaining to the knowledge of some speciall moderne tongues, and for the encrease of my experience in the managing of affaires, being wholly then addicted to employ my selfe . . . in the publique service of the State."[97]

Puritan clergy were critical of this practice. Thomas White, vicar of St. Dunstan in the West, London, and the founder of Sion College, objected because of the influence of Catholicism on young travelers, a complaint reflected in Udall's caustic reference to David's son being educated at Pharaoh's court. Udall was critical of young men bringing home "the practises of *Machiuel*," or un-English ways in matters of state. Stockwood was incensed at the sons of Catholic gentlemen, who avoided the High Commission by going to France, allegedly to study language, but in reality to worship as Catholics. There were, however, defenders of foreign travel for educational purposes, including "a plaine plodding fellowe, sometimes of Queenes Colledge in Cambridge," who preached at St. Clement Danes, London, in 1602, on this theme: "Abraham went into a straunge country; therefore trauailing lawefull, soe it be either specially warranted by Gods call, or to profitt the country, not to see and bring home ill fashions, and worse consciences." Bullinger defended educational travel in foreign lands as long as it was done with modesty and sobriety. Anglican clergy left no written objections to foreign travel as part of a young man's education.[98]

Leading educational theorists were nearly as displeased with educational travel as the Puritans. Because of the availability of books,

Mulcaster saw no need to send youngsters to the Continent, especially since the study of foreign laws and customs had sometimes "misfashioned our owne home." He also cited the dangers of foreign travel and urged as an alternative that a foreign tutor be brought to England. Elizabeth herself was cited as an example of learning "by domesticall discipline." Moderate travel in England was acceptable to Mulcaster, as it was to Stubbes, who spent more than three months traversing the country to study local customs and visit monuments. To those youth who insisted on foreign travel, Mulcaster urged study to profit the commonwealth rather than pleasure. Ascham too warned of the perils of travel on the Continent, particularly in Italy, for in Rome "vice now maketh that contrie slaue to them, that before, were glad to serue it." Fathers determined to send their sons to Italy were admonished to do so only in the care of an experienced guardian lest the boys return with intolerable manners and less learning, or with predilections for Catholicism.[99]

The government and the church were concerned that children of Catholic parents were sent abroad for schooling. Catholics had begun emigrating in the aftermath of the passage of the Acts of Supremacy and Uniformity in 1559, but laity enjoyed the liberty to leave England without losing their property as long as they stayed away from Rome. Under the leadership of Nicholas Sanders, Louvain was quickly established as a center of Catholic education for English students. Following the passage of an act in 1563 to impose a religious oath on all schoolmasters and tutors, the government began to show concern about travel to the Continent. In 1565 the Privy Council demanded to know why Lady Waldegrave of Borley, Essex, intended to send two daughters abroad. After the Northern Rebellion, an act was passed in 1571 to keep Englishmen from leaving the country without license, on pain of forfeiting their property, and to require those abroad to return home. Although licenses were required, the government was not strict in restraining Catholic youth from leaving England. At the age of fourteen, Gerard received a license to visit France to study the language, and he stayed at Douai and then Rheims (where the Catholic college moved in March 1578), before going to the Jesuit school at Claremont in Paris. Security was tightened in the late 1570s. In August 1578 the Privy Council was concerned with Mr. Thomson, parson at Winwick, Lancs., who was "suspected of some lewde practises by reson of his passing to and fro ouer the seas," as reported by Henry Stanley, earl of Derby. In 1580 the government attempted to learn who had children in the seminaries in Flanders and Rome, and a royal proclamation in January 1581 ordered that all persons with children or young people in their care who were abroad should give the government their names and procure their return (unless licensed) within four months. Beginning with the diocese of London in January 1582, visitation articles sought the same information. As part of its campaign against Jesuits and seminary priests, in 1585 Parliament made it illegal to send a child or ward out of the realm without a license (except for merchants engaging in normal commerce).[100]

Most of those who went to Continental seminaries came from Catholic homes, such as that of Richard Rookwood of Coldham, Essex, who sent his three sons to a Catholic school at St. Omer and his daughter to the Augustinian convent at Louvain. The imprisonment of William Lord Vaux in the 1580s did not prevent his four sons from illegally emigrating to the Continent. The sort of situation that Puritan ministers feared took place when George, son of Ambrose Gilbert of Beaconsfield, Bucks., studied under Dering and then went to the Continent to complete his education; at Paris he met and apparently was converted by Father Thomas Darbishire, and from there he went to Rome and was influenced by Robert Persons.[101]

The government and the church (apart from the Puritans) were not really opposed to foreign travel *per se* but to its abuse by Catholics seeking to undermine the religious settlement. In some instances, travel was undertaken for innocent reasons, as when the wife of William Parr, marquess of Northampton, went to Antwerp to see physicians about a breast ailment. Young men such as Edward de Vere, earl of Oxford, and Philip Sidney traveled uneventfully on the Continent, with apparent benefit to their subsequent careers. Walsingham tried to keep a nephew doctrinally safe on the Continent by having him pray and read the Bible daily and converse only with honest, godly men. At the same time he was to concentrate on matters important to a state servant and record his experiences in a diary. Yet Cecil was not satisfied with his son's educational progress at Paris, and Lady Elizabeth Russell was opposed to sending her son abroad:

The proffitt vncertayne, frivolows; the languages to be learned, with th Seite of Cuntryes here at home by bookes, with less dawnger then in theis dayes by iorney. The Certayne fructes dayly fownd of yong mens travell now a dayes nothing but pryde, Charge, and Vayitie in deming better of theyr owne Conceyts, then wisdom woold.

Such an expression from Puritan laity is rare, for Puritan clergy do not appear to have effectively persuaded their adherents of the peril of Continental journeys.[102]

In education the clearest difference between Anglicans and Puritans was the latter's disapprobation of educational travel on the Continent, though Puritan laity were less strict in this respect. Both groups agreed that the principal goal of education was the development of spiritual ideals in young people, but other aims included preparation to serve the commonwealth, increased literacy, the enhancement of discipline and manners, and the improvement of opportunities for socio-political preferment. Some religious leaders were uneasy about the incipient secularization in learning, but a combination of humanistic and Protestant ideals kept educational interest growing. Social barriers to education were slowly lowered, but the lowest reaches of the social spectrum continued illiterate. It is impossible to distinguish clearly between Anglicans and Puritans on social barriers to education and female education. Nor did Anglicans, Puritans, and Catholics disagree on the importance of selecting tutors and schoolmasters with appropriate spiritual qualifications, though the laity were sometimes lax. Religious differences are evident with regard to the curricula, with stricter Puritans manifesting hostility to rhetoric and programs of study in which classical examples outweighed the Bible. Separatists were more extreme, particularly in their willingness to abolish the universities if necessary to end their unsatisfactory curricula, particularly Anglican divinity with its Scholastic pedagogy. Most calls for educational reform came from those with religious motivation, though some were persuaded by pedagogical, secular, and humanistic concerns. Support for education through donations reveals a stronger interest among Anglicans than has hitherto been recognized. Anglicans apparently founded or refounded two and a half grammar schools to every one by Puritans, though donations to education by lesser Anglican clergy were relatively low, and were exceeded by concern for poor relief. Religious considerations remained strong in the Elizabethan age and were revealed in the educational sphere. In education more than in most other social areas, Anglicans and Puritans often agreed.

Part IV: The Christian in Society

CHAPTER 9

Work and Worship

In the Elizabethan period, much discussion was devoted to vocational and religious duties. The concept of vocation (or calling) was useful to limit social mobility and inculcate industry and responsibility, especially since vocation was not simply a matter of one's place in the economic schema, but was also a religious duty. Men of all religious persuasions praised industry, as they abhorred idleness and ambition. Diligent toil was advocated to meet religious, familial, and social obligations, not out of ambition for social advancement. Calls for productive labor were coupled with demands for spiritual observance of the sabbath—demands voiced by Protestants of all shades. Six days of honest toil followed by a sabbath of rest made economic sense, but it was not primarily for this reason that religious leaders advanced their case for regular work weeks and the devotion of Sundays to religious purposes. The principles of work and worship in the Elizabethan period illustrate the depth of religious motivation, though other factors were operative as well.

(1) Vocation

We are placed in this worlde to followe the vocation wherevnto wee are called.

Abraham Fleming[1]

Whensoeuer we are out of our place and calling, Sathan hath a fit occasion of temptation.

Richard Greenham[2]

For a society concerned with hierarchy and preoccupied with order, vocational stability was inherently attractive. The Statute of Artificers reinforced it legally and provided a means, as the records of quarter sessions reveal, to punish those who threatened the social order. Against this background, Elizabethan preachers as part of their task addressed vocational responsibility in sermons and biblical marginalia.

The first important attempt to use biblical marginalia to influence vocational responsibility occurred in the Geneva Bible, with its antecedents in Whittingham's New Testament. A distinction is made between the vocation or calling that each believer has with respect to the Christian life and the vocation that is the basis of his livelihood. These cannot be distinguished as sacred and secular, for even the latter is divinely ordained and infused with spiritual significance. The principal end of any vocation is service to God and living an upright life, "teaching euerie man to walke in soundenes of conscience in his vocation, with all patience and humblenes, reuerencing, and obeying the magistrate, exercising charitie, putting of[f] the olde man, and putting on Christ, bearing with the weake, and louing one another according to Christs example." The Christian's responsibility is to be constant in the pursuit of his vocation. A righteous life requires a lawful and just occupation, a premise that is the basis for repudiating illegal or immoral occupations and idleness. Even if a vocation is not necessary to procure a living, it is essential as a means of doing good to others.[3]

The Geneva marginalia do not directly discuss vocational mobility, but the principle that there is to be no upward movement is stated. Men are not to pass the limits of their vocation or presume above their place. The penalty is social disorder and personal confusion: "When man forgetteth him self, and thinketh to be exalted aboue his vocation, then God bringeth him to confusion." Readers were not encouraged to improve their social status but to be constant in their vocations, and thus be divinely preserved from peril.[4]

The other Elizabethan Scriptures had less to say about vocation. The annotators of the Bishops' Bible exhort each man to take pains in his vocation to be humble and fear God, and not to be ashamed of the baseness of any legal occupation. In the Beza-Tomson Bible most comments on vocation refer to theological calling, but there is an admonition that each person must quietly and carefully perform his duty in the vocation in which God has placed him. As a corollary to this affirmation of divine vocational placement, the annotator warns against zeal that carries one beyond the bounds of vocation, thereby constraining any impetus to vocational mobility.[5]

Anglicans generally concurred on the fundamental aspects of vocation. Individual callings were, for the most part, regarded as divinely determined. Sandys typically wrote that "we are not called to stand or sit still, but to walk every one in that vocation wherewith he is called."[6] There was broad agreement that individuals must remain in their vocations, though Whitgift recognized that not everyone had the ability for his occupation. Nevertheless he did not suggest that one alter his vocation or "aspire to greter dignitie, and . . . take those things in hande which commonly turne to . . . ruine and destruction." Aspirations for social mobility frustrated Anglicans, who saw this as a threat to the social order: "Jacke must be a Gentleman, say nay who shall." A less familiar but no more acceptable form of mobility was manifested by the man who left his vocation to become a sectarian preacher. To prevent mobility Anglicans reiterated the importance of contentment with allotted callings and conditions.[7]

To some extent, this emphasis was moderated by Edmund Bunny. Rather than emphasize divine assignment to callings, he concentrated on the choice of occupations with a view to making life profitable to God and productive. "We offend, when as eyther we chuse our Trade amisse; not regarding therin the calling of God, but our owne corrupt affections: or els hauing rightly chosen, do otherwise vnder the name of our calling, then our calling alloweth, or will beare vs out." The latitude Bunny allowed is implicitly restricted to horizontal movement, for each person must be content with his estate. The principle of horizontal social mobility is also found in Mulcaster, except that he stresses occupational choice as something that rests in the hands of those who know where young people, considering their abilities, are most needed. The decision in essence must be made for the benefit of the state. All Anglicans insisted that unlawful vocations, such as harlotry, conjuring, and fortune telling, were unacceptable. Vocations must glorify God by serving the church or commonwealth, and be pursued with diligence and industry. Undertaking an occupation in this manner was in effect a manifestation of the doctrine of sanctification, for one must "work his own salvation as far as an instrument may."[8]

In most respects, Puritans agreed with Anglicans on vocation, though some differences of emphasis show up. A number of Puritans agreed with the Anglican idea that men are divinely appointed to their vocations, and Robert Allen argued that each person receives the skills required for his position from God. "Where God doth place anye man," said Udall, "there his continuall trauaile is needfull, for God is most wise in disposing euery thing."[9] Working with this premise, various Puritans drew the Anglican conclusion that was critical of vocational mobility. The ideal was to remain in the occupation to which one had been called, thus maintaining a commonwealth free of confusion. Wilcox held out some possibility of altering vocations, but only in the light of divine approval: "Hee that rashly changeth his dwelling place, and stayeth not in the state wherein God hath set him, but enterpriseth new things, and that not being well assured of Gods will, and his owne calling, is no wiser or better stayed then a bird, that fluttereth hither and thither." Several attempts were made to encourage men to continue in their callings and not leave them for an ascetic life or out of a mistaken notion that such callings were unlawful. Those engaged in illegal trades were warned by Trigge that they were violating the divine order.[10]

Other Puritans accorded a role to choice. Usually this did not go beyond what Mulcaster advocated, namely the right of parents to select the vocation for which the child seemed suited. This was the position of Cleaver, Estey, Allen, Perkins, and Fenner. Perkins, in fact, denied children a vocational choice, leaving the decision to the parents. Fenner and Estey stressed the responsibility of parents to make the choice in accord with the dispositions and gifts of their children, whose duty it was under the fifth commandment to acquiesce.[11] Udall went further toward individualism by bestowing on each person the right to select an occupation: "Religion is so far from hindering or exempting a man from his calling, that it is the onelie direction for man, both to choose vnto himselfe such a calling as is lawfull: and also . . . to employ him selfe in the same aright, and to vse it lawfully." Similarly Richard Rogers allowed each Christian liberty to alter his vocation for weighty reasons, such as the decay of his trade, and Vaughan permitted idle persons to select a master to instruct them in a trade. English divines did not consistently favor a nonindividualistic society devoid of vocational mobility: some Puritans and the Anglican Edmund Bunny contributed to individualism by allowing some personal choice in vocation. [12]

Puritans differed from Anglicans in their pronounced emphasis on diligence in vocations and the slight attention paid to contentment with one's calling. Puritan authors seem fixed on the idea of vocational diligence as a preventive for idleness and disorder. "Euery man," wrote Bownde, "hath or ought to haue some speciall businesse to attend vpon in the sixe dayes, and being in an honest calling hee should labour in it diligently, that he might not eate the breade of idlenes." Diligent pursuit of one's calling maintained chastity, brought prosperity and discouraged evil thoughts and actions. Dent made faithfulness in one's calling an infallible sign of salvation. The eighth commandment reinforced the importance of diligent labor, and the punishment accorded Jonah was a warning to those tempted to neglect their callings. Samuel Ward's diary reveals the seriousness with which such admonitions could be taken by a Puritan: "Thou hadst bene so negligent in looking to thy puples, and therfor God had layd this heavy crosse upon the[e], which did hang upon the[e] continually all the week, so that thou couldst do nothing cherfully." Whereas Anglicans commented on the diligent pursuit of one's calling, they did not accord it comparable emphasis.[13]

Like Anglicans, Puritans insisted that a vocation be lawful, excluding such activities as acting, peddling, jesting, bear baiting, witchcraft, divining, and gambling. Stubbes condemned the government for permitting men to live by piping, which he deemed an unlawful vocation. Becoming a monk, friar, or chantry priest was not acceptable, for such callings were not profitable to church or commonwealth. An acceptable vocation enabled one to fulfill his obligations to family and neighbors, glorify God, and preserve the church and state, but it must not require continual breach of the sabbath. "The end of a mans calling, is not to gather riches for himselfe, for his familie, for the poore; but to serue God in seruing of man, and in seeking the good of all men."[14]

The Separatist position was based on the premise that since men are placed in their callings by God, they must remain in them. Separatists prided themselves on staying "within the bounds of our owne callings, christianly refrayning [from] such things as God hath forbidden us to doo." A disapproval of vocational mobility was inherent in their charge that Anglican clergy ignored the social ambition of the rich, powerful, and noble. Those who aspired to higher estate, Barrow asserted, were wrongfully lauded for their virtue. Separatists deftly used the vocational theme to condemn the Anglican hierarchy, demanding that secular authorities compel the Church of England's ministry to pursue lawful callings, "as God shall make them fit and call them thereunto." Those who assumed the ministerial vocation without divine calling were castigated as usurpers. The Separatists thus were more concerned with the vocation of Anglican clergy than vocational mobility among their own adherents.[15]

Preserving social stability was aided by an insistence, particularly from the pulpit, on the equality of callings. The Georges assert that there is no distinction in the Protestant tradition of kinds of calling, whereas "the Thomistic estimation of the worth of labor is inextricably intertwined with considerations of differing levels of social or institutional status and differing degrees of occupational dignity." Unfortunately no such clear distinction can be made. The Rheims marginalia continued the long-standing belief that the comtemplative life is better than the active, though both are recognized as essential. Yet Shelford stresses that no occupation is divinely despised and berates sons of the gentry for refusing to learn trades. Among Protestants, on the other hand, there are affirmations of differing worths among callings. The clearest of these was enunciated by Dr. Thomas Holland, fellow of Balliol College, Oxford, and Regius Professor of Divinity, in a sermon at Paul's Cross in November 1602: The hierarchy of professions is the clergy, husbandry, trade, and the military. Deacon, with a different set of values, argued that princes, nobles, clergy, and soldiers bring contempt on themselves if they become involved in business. Many peers did exactly this, for of the seventy-three families in the Elizabethan peerage, fifty-seven (78%) were involved in business activities, especially joint-stock investment, mining and industry, and shipping and privateering. When, in the early 1560s James Blount, Lord Mountjoy, was managing his alum mine at Canford, Dorset, he remarked that "som saie that I varrye fromm my vocacion farr to becom a myner," Vocational distinctions were recognized by Vaughan, who regarded the occupations of butchers, cooks, fishmongers, toll-collectors, and usurers as odious, and those callings requiring the most physical strength as servile. Protestants were a long way from uniformly equating occupations.[16]

Some occupations were singled out, particularly by Puritans, as especially meritorious; these were principally agriculture and craftsmanship. The Geneva annotators referred to the excellency of tillage and noted that "the reuenues of ye earth are to be preferred aboue all things, which apperteine to this life," while the Bishops' Bible warned that the decay of husbandry would lead to the decline of the prince. For Vaughan there could be no better life than that of a yeoman, and Gibbon praised the husbandman and the shepherd. Commentators found grounds to acclaim husbandry in Gen. 4:2 and Prov. 14:4. The Geneva and Bishops' Bibles remarked that the products of an artisan were divine gifts; and Trigge was bothered by craftsmen who wanted to relinquish their trades to become farmers. He warned that those who meddled with more than one occupation violated the divine order. King disagreed with Chrysostom in approving a mercantile vocation (as did Vaughan), but Greenham was less than enthusiastic about the seafaring life, because so many sailors were irreligious. Henry Smith reminded the servile occupations that their vocation was not vile since Jesus had been called a servant.[17]

The emphasis on husbandry and vocational stability interested the government in 1559. The "Considerations" sent to Parliament that year reveal a determination to restrict apprenticeships and prevent a decay of husbandry that might result from a flight to the towns. The government got what it wanted in the 1563 Statute of Artificers (5 Eliz. I, c. 4), though the historian of that law rightly concludes that efforts to "crystallize a changing social stratification" proved futile. Still, W. G. Hoskins estimates that 75% of the sons followed their fathers' occupations in the period 1580 to 1600. Fathers sometimes contributed to vocational stability by using their wills to entice sons to continue in their steps. Simon Ponder of Lavenham, Suffolk, bequeathed his son Henry a house, money, and tools if he became a pewterer, and Robert Allen of Ridgewell, Essex, left his house to his son Edward if he became a chandler. Other parents allowed some vocational mobility. John Torner of Stansted Mount Fitchet, Essex, left his youngest son a set of looms and provisions to learn their use if he entered that vocation. In 1599 Francis Coke recognized the futility of forcing his brother Robert to pursue a rural calling, and allowed him to go to London to follow a career of his choice. Those Puritans who allowed some choice in vocation thus echoed a practice already existing to some degree, though they were out of step with the government's desires. Although the distinction between Anglicans and Puritans on this subject was not great,[18] the difference of emphasis found Anglicans more in tune with state policy.

(2) Idleness

It is idlenesse my sonne, that seduceth thee, for the minde that is well occupyed, neuer sinneth.

Thomas Lodge[19]

Idelness is ye chief mistresse of vices all.

Thomas Becon[20]

A sea of ink has been spilled in support, modification or refutation of the thesis that Protestantism and in particular Puritanism fostered the growth of an entrepreneurial spirit in stressing vocation, the eschewing of idleness, and the dignity of labor. Yet the clergy who urged the fulfillment of vocational responsibilities appear to have been less concerned with the structure of the economy than with such considerations as the maintenance of socio-political stability (through attention to vocation), the achievement of moderate economic gains (to support a family, tithe, and donate to charity), and the development of a style of living in marked contrast to that popularly associated with monasteries.

The concept of monastic idleness in the propaganda of Thomas Cromwell and his associates in the 1530s made a lasting impression in English Protestant circles, though the concept was hardly original with Cromwell. In 1537 the note to 1 Thessalonians 4 in the Matthew Bible remarked that this passage was "a good lesson for monkes and ydle freers." Although reiterated in 1549, this comment was dropped in 1551. The Matthew-Becke Bible of that year explained that 1 Thessalonians 4 was "a good lesson for them that wold liue ydle."

Curiously the Geneva annotators, though confronted by reviving Catholicism, focused on labor as part of a Christian's duty and worship, not on the associations of idleness with the monastic life. Even in the Garden of Eden, they remarked, God ordained labor despite the abundance of material provisions, hence the ideal is "to serue God vnfainedly, and not to seke ease." Divine blessings were predicated on the rejection of idleness and the performance of duty as a means to glorify God. Readers were asked to observe Ezekiel's singling out of four vices—idleness, pride, excess, and contempt of the poor—as causes of divine retribution. Rather than linking idleness to the monastic life, the Geneva annotators tied it to those whose wealth enabled them to live without toil, thus injecting a note of "class" criticism into their remarks: "The worlde estemeth them happie, which liue in welth, and ydlenes: but ye holie Gost approueth them best, yt liue of the meane profit of their labours." Paul, the readers were informed, detested idleness so much that he made it grounds for excommunication.[21]

The annotators of the Bishops' Bible paid scant attention to idleness, though they cautioned that God expected his servants to use the graces they had received. In the Beza-Tomson Bible, however, the older attempt to associate idleness with monasticism reappeared, buttressed with a citation from Socrates:

What shall we doe then with those idle bellied Monkes, and sacrificing Priests? A Monke (sayth Socrates, booke 8. of his Tripartite historie) which worketh not with hands, is like a theefe.

Any life of contemplation was ruled out as an acceptable vocation. All persons are divinely assigned "a certaine standing and roome," partly to avoid idleness.[22]

Idleness came under strong attack from Anglican and Puritan clergy alike. Adam's toil in the Garden of Eden was the precedent to condemn the inactive life, a point also made by the jurist William Lambarde to a Maidstone jury about to inquire into rogues in June 1582. Idle persons were likened by the clergy to thieves and spendthrifts who ruined themselves and their possessions by their inactivity. The Puritan John Northbrooke made it clear that the idleness that concerned the clergy was no mere refraining from physical labor:

Idlenesse is a wicked will geuen to rest and slouthfulnesse, from all right, necessarie, godly, and profitable works, &c. Also idlenesse is not only of the bodie or minde to cease from labour, but especially an omission or letting passe negligently all honest exercises.

He urged that every waking hour be spent in good exercises. Little attention was given to the causes of idleness, though Dent regarded them as evil examples, poor education, and the absence of a vocation.[23]

Anglicans and Puritans alike associated idleness with monasticism. Idleness was a popular charge to hurl against "the idle Abbots, the foggie and fat Monkes . . . who fare deliciouslie euery day; who at feastes and banquets pamper vp themselues like Mules and Horses without reason or reuerence, stuffing and stretching out their bellies through banquetting and drunkenness." Richard Lewes, rector of Kilmarsh, Northants., told an audience at Paul's Cross about 1594 that though the English abbies had been dissolved, "Abbey-lubbers" remained in the church who refused to work. Lewes freely borrowed from Pilkington, who had attacked lazy servants in private houses as "abbey-lubbers" and thieves. Nevertheless it was the "swarm of idle monks and friars" that drew the brunt of Anglican ire. It incensed Pilkington that the church's wealth supported idle regular clergy instead of godly ministers and the poor. Monks and eremites were censured by John Terry for violating the sabbath commandment by not engaging in a profitable calling during the six days allotted to labor. Monkish idleness also was condemned by Jewel and Babington, the latter portraying them as cloistered parasites.[24]

Puritans fully agreed with the Anglican endeavor to associate idleness with monasticism, though they distinguished between the earliest monks who engaged in physical toil and the "Popish Monkes and Nunnes" who lived idly and devoured the fruits of others' labor. "The fatnesse and haughtinesse, and idlenesse of Monkes," asserted

Trigge, "came into a Prouerbe amongest all men: In so much, that idle persons were called Abbey lubbers: fatt men were saide to haue Abbots faces." The monastic life was repudiated as an unlawful vocation and because persons pursued it to live idly, like thieves and Epicureans. Stockwood extended the accusation of idle and riotous living to the pope and his court, while Becon surmised that Catholics invented the sacrifice of the mass, pilgrimages, trentals, and dirges to preserve idle ways.[25] In the Elizabethan world, masterless men became in effect secularized monks, for neither pursued lawful vocations or eschewed idle living.

The concern over idleness was due not only to its monastic associations but also to the catastrophic effects it was believed to have. Anglicans considered it a causative factor in adultery, theft, vain ballads, wanton books, sedition and civil dissension, idolatry, and many physical diseases. "It causeth," according to Babington, "contention and strife by pratling speeches, it nurceth and nourisheth whoredome and filth, it pulleth on pouertie, and looseth honour, it hindereth vertue, and mayntayneth vice." Idleness is the mother of all mischief, vice and crime, for inactivity increases susceptibility to temptation. Idleness causes poverty; if men worked more, they would have greater resources to relieve the needy. There was resentment that men who were idle by choice forced others to bestow aid to keep them alive. At Paul's Cross in September 1593 Adam Hill argued with some justification that if gentlemen and their servants were prevented from being idle, homicides, especially in London, would decrease. The references to violence and disorder of this nature scattered through the records of the Privy Council bear out Hill's concern.[26]

Puritans too were convinced that idleness was a primary cause of many ills, including adultery, theft, lust, drunkenness, gluttony, blasphemy, irreligion, and contempt of magistrates. "Concerning Idlenesse," wrote Dent, "this I say briefely, that it is the mother of all vice, and the step-dame of all vertue: yea it is the great Bedlame of all enormities," What especially concerned Dent about this sin of Sodom were the economic implications, for he feared that idleness led to poverty and rendered one incapable of providing for the indigent. Anticipating Dickens, he lamented that artisans and laborers sat idly in taverns, gambling and blaspheming, "while their poore wiues and children sit crying at home for bread, being ready to starue, to beg, or to steale."[27]

Medical authors shared fears for the effects of idleness, agreeing that it was contrary to nature, harmful to the body, and dulling to the mind, "Idlenesse and plentie of victualles, is fitte for soche citezeins, as wer in Sodom and Gomorha, which perished in their lust, idlenesse and fatnesse." The medical argument was incorporated by John Dios in a sermon at Paul's Cross in July 1579, when he warned that idleness diminished strength and caused such infirmities as indigestion.[28]

The attack on idleness included concern for the appropriate amount of sleep, based on the idea that

> Muche slepe ingendereth
> diseases and payne
> It dulles the wyt
> and hurteth the brayne.

Excessive sleep was regarded as idleness and thus a vice with serious ramifications. Moderation must prevail. According to Dr. Andrew Boorde, moderate sleep improves digestion, nourishes the blood, refreshes the memory, moderates the liver's heat, quiets humors, and animates natural powers. Immoderate sleep, on the other hand (quoting William Vaughan), "maketh the braine giddie, ingendreth rheume and impostumes, causeth the palsey, bringeth obliuion, and troubleth the spirits." The medical case for moderate sleep was used by the Puritan minister John Northbrooke: "When we sleepe too much, all the moystures and humors of the bodie, with the naturall heate, retire to the extreme parts thereof, no where purging or euacuating whatsoeuer is redundant." The result is slothfulness, weakness, and effeminacy. Religious and medical arguments were thus meshed to wean the Elizabethan from idleness in the form of excessive sleep.[29]

There were various attempts to combat idleness. Some Puritans were concerned with idleness in their own lives, but most persons directed their attention to inactivity in others. Richard Rogers reproached himself in 1587 because "the most part of my lif hath been veary hoverly [lightly] and idlely passed over," and in 1590 he prayed for "fredome from sottish idlenes." At Cambridge Samuel Ward succumbed to "myne idlenes in not rising to prayers" and "my idlenes att the repitition of the sermons, as also in prayer that night." While her husband was away, Lady Margaret Hoby busied herself with essential tasks to prevent temptation. Norden confessed that he had enjoyed "too much liberty in the seruice of the right worshipfull, Lady *Ann Knyuet*, . . . spending many dayes in idlenes and voyd of good . . . exercises," so that some considered him sullen or proud.[30] I have found no comparable examples in Anglican writings, suggesting that Puritans were more willing to reproach themselves for idleness than were Anglicans.

Warnings against idleness were given by Elizabethan fathers to their sons. Sir Henry Sidney urged Philip to study and be virtuously occupied, making a habit of well-doing. In 1583 Thomas Wotton warned his son-in-law, George Morton, under penalty of disinheritance not to "spende so precious a thing as tyme ys idellye (whiche ys yll), or in lewde playe (which ys woorse) and that playe manye tymes accompanyed with wicked othes (which ys woorst of all)." Despite the advice, Morton offended Wotton and was cut off in his will (proved in 1587). When Simon Senhouse entered Anthony Bacon's service, his father cautioned him to rise early, work and study hard, and avoid idleness. The inactivity of Thomas Windebank's son in 1561 concerned Cecil, who held the elder Windebank accountable but received the latter's gratitude for his concern.[31]

Some contemporary observers believed Elizabethans were prone to idleness. In 1575 the Antwerp merchant Emmanuel van Meteren observed that the English were less industrious than the Dutch or French and for the most part pursued the indolent life characteristic of the Spaniards. Moreover, "the most toilsome, difficult, and skilful works are chiefly performed by foreigners, as among the idle Spaniards." Adrian à Saravia depicted the inhabitants of Guernsey as "so inert that they had rather live poor and idle than rich by labour." The poet James Yates was so impressed that his patron, Henry Reynolles, Esq., bore good will toward the industrious, that he wrote a book of verse on the virtuous life. William Fulwood, a Merchant Taylor in London, prepared a manual teaching people how to write letters to avoid idleness, "the capital enimie to all exercise and vertue." An exception from the general laments was Becon's observation that in Sandwich, Kent, all persons were occupied in their vocations and there was no idleness.[32]

Civil authorities intervened to suppress idleness. In 1560 the Privy Council ordered Thomas Lord Wentworth to watch recently discharged soldiers and other idle persons in Suffolk. The queen was concerned in 1575 with robberies committed in the North Riding "by some young gentlemen and others riding and travelling abroad as masterless men, not having whereupon to live, nor using any lawful art, science or mystery," but living idly in market towns and gentry homes. When Elizabeth ordered Grindal on 8 May 1577 to suppress prophesyings, she justified her decision by an unwarranted accusation that these exercises fostered idleness and disrupted the common order. Idleness was visible in the cities, particularly London, hence in 1602 Sir William Periam, Lord Chief Baron of the Exchequer, ordered monthly searches in the City to uncover and punish idle and masterless men, of whom there were believed to be 30,000. The court leet records of Southampton reveal a concern with idle persons, such as the pimp Thomas Fawen, "a very Loytering person . . . [who] Lyveth very ydelly to the most evill exsample of others;" he faced banishment unless he entered an honest vocation. Twice in 1579 the court leet was asked to expel loiterers from the town because they "breede evell acts."[33]

The problem of idleness sparked calls for reform, undoubtedly more because of the threat of inactivity to social order than concern for the spiritual welfare of the slothful. In a sermon to Parliament in January 1563 Alexander Nowell urged martial law or something comparable to suppress vagabonds, "for he that liveth idly, having not any ways whereon to live, is a thief, and robbeth the poor of their duty and living." When Lambarde charged the justices of the quarter sessions in Kent in April 1586, he insisted that they "hew in sunder the master roots" of idleness and other deceitful practices that sapped the nourishment of honest folk. The Bacon Papers in the Lambeth Palace Library contain a 1597 proposal to reform cake bakers, a disparaging reference to the idle lingering in alehouses as "the most vnnecessarie members, that liue in the Comon wealth; for them selues liue ydelie, and doe no labor, but what their poore wiefes and seruants can gitt, that consume they in ale and cakes." This proposal wanted to suppress alehouses and allow only victualing houses for wayfarers and the sale of bread, beer, and ale to the poor. On a smaller scale, individuals acted, such as the establishment of a house of correction for the idle at Canterbury in 1578 by Sir Roger Manwood, Lord Chief Baron of the Exchequer.[34]

Although the clergy and landed classes loudly demanded the suppression of the idle, questions were raised about the inactivity of these groups. The Separatist Henry Barrow called for the expulsion from the church of all clergy who were "thieves, intruders, and idlebellies." The Puritan Arthur Dent was equally harsh towards ministers who spent their time idly in taverns with lewd company. Among those castigated in the Puritan survey of the clergy in 1586 were John Raulph, vicar of Wendron and Helston, Cornwall, "an idle Ruffian," and Matthew Braoke, the Catholic vicar of Miller and Hanappe [Lavappe], who "liveth idlely, and cometh seldome to church." Three years before he became bishop of Exeter, John Woolton admitted that an idle bishop was no Christian, and Pilkington insisted that even the "solemn prelate" had to labor diligently. Generally, however, Anglicans, especially those of the conservative wing, were reluctant to comment about idle clergy. Jewel, in fact, came to the defense of clerics castigated because they performed no physical labor. With kings and counsellors, they were likened to the master of a ship whose direction and vigilance were essential for a safe voyage. The toil of ministers, Jewel argued, was greater than manual labor.[35]

The landed aristocracy was strongly criticized for idle living, particularly by Separatists and Puritans. Barrow lashed out at Church of England clerics for refusing to rebuke aristocrats:

If they keep . . . troupes of idle servingmen and followers, this . . . belongeth to their degree: if they and their whole household spend al their life time in fleshly and vaine sportes and gaming, so that numbers of men have no other trade, and be wholy employed to the keeping of hawkes and doggs to serve the lust of these men: al this is covered under christian recreation and pastime, and is tollerable inough so he will heare a sermon, and cal his familie to a lecture.

Since Separatists had little aristocratic support, such criticism is not surprising, yet it has close parallels in Puritan writings, though Puritans did enjoy some support from nobles and gentry. Dent, asserting that many aristocrats believed they were born to live in idleness, attacked their devotion to hunting, hawking, gambling, and reveling. Dent expected them to work for the benefit of church or commonwealth, or at least provide good government for their households and relief for the poor. Dorcas (Acts 9) was held forth as an example of how aristocrats could use their time to make clothing for the poor. Burton and Richard Rogers also stressed the aristocracy's responsibility to govern their families and communities, aid the needy, and punish the evil. The aristocracy, warned Stubbes, had no more liberty from God to waste time than did the poor. Idle gentry bothered Gifford, "for many haue a glory to bring vp their children in idlenesse and vaine pleasures, this is gentrie among a number." The prevailing tendency, as he saw it, was simple: To be gentle was to be idle. "If he be a gentleman, though he haue not two groates by the yeare to spend, yet he may not labour."[36]

Among Anglicans criticism of the aristocracy for idleness normally was muted. Perhaps the most outspoken was Pilkington, a moderate Anglican:

Gentlemen . . . and men of the world are not born to live in pastime and pleasure, as they list, and many do, no more than poor men; but first to serve the Lord, promote his word and religion earnestly, minister justice severely, maintain peace quietly, defend the commonwealth stoutly, relieve the oppressed mightily, follow learning and study diligently; . . . and after all these great travails refresh themselves with honest pastimes measurably.

Anglicans and Puritans did not judge aristocratic responsibilities differently, though the former were more reluctant to condemn offenders. Even Pilkington focused on the limited area of active work for the church, with Nehemiah as the prime example of how an aristocrat should behave. Pilkington's major interest was the common Christian vocation, in which lords and ladies were duty bound to share. Something of the Separatist's anti-aristocratic attitude was still evident in a comment of Henoch Clapham after he returned to the Church of England c. 1596: "Christ was not published to lazie idle Nobles and Churles of the World; not yet to the presumpteous Priest, or glavering Prophet, but to well exercised shepherds, feeding their flocks."[37]

Thus the idle came under fire from all elements of the religious continuum, but only the Puritans were especially self-conscious about predilections to idleness within themselves. Anglicans and Puritans repeatedly associated idleness with the monastic life, particularly as it evolved in the High and Late Middle Ages; they attributed numerous social and moral evils to inactivity. Medical writers concurred, citing the ill effects of idleness, particularly on physical and mental health. Elizabethan fathers advised their sons to eschew idleness, particularly on physical and mental health. Elizabethan fathers advised their sons to eschew idleness. Idleness also concerned reformers and necessitated civil action. The clergy and aristocracy were attacked for idle living, particularly by Separatists and Puritans, but most Anglicans refrained from such potentially disruptive criticism.

(3) Industry and Ambition

The word of God hath parted the whole worlde into a vineyarde of worke, and a market place of Idlenes, and God hath aswell forbid loytering as commanded labouring: therefore he taketh men from Idlenes, and sendeth them to their occupation.

George Phillips[38]

Ambitious men are like little children which take great paynes in runninge vp and downe to catch butterflyes, which are nothing but painted winges, and either perishe in takinge or fly away from them.

Andrew Downes[39]

Recognition of the importance of labor was neither uniquely Puritan nor distinctively Protestant in Elizabethan England, despite Protestant attempts to associate idleness and monasticism. Yet Elizabethan

Catholics did not emphasize labor as did the Protestants, at least partly because of more pressing problems, including apologetics, propaganda, and survival. From Rheims, Matthew Kellison praised Adam's toil in Eden, which he thought was a pleasure to Adam. For the present, Kellison believed that "all creatures are created to worke & labour, and so they must attaine vnto their ende and perfection, because God and nature hathe so ordained it."[40]

The only English Bible in the sixteenth century to emphasize labor was the Geneva version (and its forerunner, Whittingham's New Testament). In 1538 the Tyndale-Coverdale New Testament had commented only that a workman who toiled faithfully received sufficient sustenance from God. This concept reappeared in the Geneva Bible, but with the warning that the goods of the negligent would be divinely consumed. It was not the dignity but the necessity of labor that the annotators stressed. Men must live by their own toil and provide for others from their earnings. "If the word of God cannot instruct thee, yet learne at the littel pismire to labour for thy self and not to burden others." Those who worked diligently and obeyed the Ten Commandments were promised some success, at least daily provision. Readers were cautioned to be frugal with their time and to sacrifice temporal pleasures for worthy pursuits. Nothing in the Geneva notes is distinctively capitalist, though the stress on diligent labor is, as Weber and Tawney stressed, a compatible characteristic.[41]

Among Elizabethan Anglicans, three points were made with respect to labor; the first is that labor is dignified. "Certainly," wrote Christopher Sutton,

the labouring mans life is commendable, his estate is a remembrance of *Adam* created to worke, his body is refreshed with rest, his health is maintained by trauaile, his hungry morsels make him more thankfull to God, then the greatest delicates of the rich, his course bread, and small drinke bring healthfull nourishments.

Similarly Pilkington referred to the great honor of toiling because such labor (which made possible aid to the poor) involved building "God's city." The second theme was the necessity of honest labor to support one's family and fulfill vocational responsibilities. Work was conceived as glorifying God and in keeping with the world's abhorrence of idleness. A third theme in Anglican writings is anger toward those who refuse to work or who perform their tasks unsatisfactorily. The balladeer William Fulwood reflected this concern in 1562:

lasie loiterers will not work:
and honestly their liuings get:
But had rather in corners lurk,
then that they wold with labor swet.[42]

The three themes on labor in Anglican literature are paralleled in Puritan writings, which stress the necessity of labor to provide family sustenance and assist the needy. The ideal is beneficent self-sufficiency, fortified with the idea that work is divinely required and indicates one's election. The harnessing of religion to labor, creating a work ethic of self-reliance and charitable assistance, is summarized in a model prayer of the attorney John Norden:

Graunt mee so to flye ydlenes, the mother and Nurce of all euill, that both this day and all my life, I may, be godlie care and trauaile, get me a sufficient, & competent liuing heere, that I be no burden and charge to such as are rich and welthie, nor depend vpon the succor, helpe, and furtheraunce of others, whose helpe is moste slippery and deceitfull Least that in hope thereof, I giuing my selfe to ydlenes, and loytering . . . I be driuen . . . to goe in a ragged coate, & to want my foode. But contrary wise . . . graunt that I may so imploy my selfe, to laboure, and diligent execution of thy busines . . . that, I may . . . luckelie prosper therein, and shew my selfe . . . helpefull to the poore impotent and needy.

In addition to this emphasis on the necessity and dignity of work, Puritans echoed Anglican complaints about the indolent.[43]

Although labor was extolled in pulpit and print, economic life in Elizabethan England made diligent toil the only means of survival for many, regardless of religious views. Paul Seaver's examination of the papers of Nehemiah Wallington, a London Puritan and turner, reveals a man diligent in his calling and concerned above all with preserving a good conscience, not with seeking approval from his faith for entrepreneurial energy and profits. This must have been the case with countless Elizabethans who took their religion seriously and were conscientious in their callings. It was the point of several lines of James Yates' verse:

The labouring man, with breade and drinke,
Liues merrier in mind I thinke,
Then some which feede on dayntie fare.

The Puritan Samuel Ward echoed a common belief among the godly that those who serve God prosper, implying essentially spiritual prosperity. As tutor to Sir Thomas Bromley's children, William Hergest inculcated this gospel of work in his pupils, for "*diligent,* honest and painful labour, is a vertue, wherby wee do execute and dispatch the

proper and needefull labours of our owne function or speciall vocation, and that diligently, faithfully, and constantly, for conscience
sake, because it is our dutie and pleaseth God, for the good example
of others, and the ornament of the common wealth."[44]

This gospel of work was enforced by a general social insistence on
the necessity of labor, for Elizabethans viewed the indolent as threats
to the material well-being of honest folk. Not only were many of the
idle prone to theft and other crimes, but they were burdens on the
poor rolls, taking funds from deserving poor and increasing the levies.
The popular resentment this caused is amply evident; to take but one
example, the inhabitants of Little Onn, Staffs., complained in the
1590 quarter sessions about William Alcocke, who "ys vehementlie
suspected for the manner of his lyffe[,] for his lyveing and maynten-
aunce beyng verye smale, yet he never worketh or endevereth hym-
selfe in honest, seemelie or lawfull manner about his busines in suche
husbandlie sort as other poore men are gladde to do. " If the Cambridge schoolmaster William Wilkinson was correct, some libertines in
Elizabethan society excused their reluctance to toil on the grounds
that the Holy Spirit did not tarry in a weary body.[45] Such a view
was diametrically opposed to the social as well as the religious acceptability of a work ethic.

Any encouragement an entrepreneurial spirit received from the
emphasis on hard work was tempered by hostility to ambition. In the
Geneva Bible, which devoted more attention to ambition than other
Tudor Scriptures, the onus is on the attainment of worldly pomp,
though ambition for material acquisitions was likewise unacceptable.
"To be content with that which God hathe giuen, is better then to
followe the desires that neuer can be satisfied." Ambition, pride, and
pomp must be eschewed and modesty embraced. In the Beza-Tomson
Bible ambition is linked to hypocrisy, and readers are warned that
"the ende of ambition is ignominie; but the ende of modest obedience is glory." One must not work hard to advance socially, but to
fulfill vocational responsibility, support the family, and give to
charity.[46]

Anglican and Puritan alike condemned ambition. For Thomas
Rogers it entailed the immoderate pursuit of wealth, the condemnation of which did not encourage capitalist activity. Anglicans deemed
ambition, to quote Bishop Cooper, "very wicked, & . . . a perillous
instrument of the deuil to make mischief." About the time he converted to Catholicism, the author Thomas Lodge castigated ambition
as a subtle evil that sired hypocrisy, hate, and sin; it is "the bait of
offence, the rust of vertue, the moth of holinesse, the blinder of

hearts." One could be either ambitious or obedient to Christ, a choice designed to encourage the godly to remain content with their estates. Among William Wentworth's papers is a poem counseling against ambition:

> The ambitiouse man that fryes in honor's fyre
> and hath his thoughts lyft up aboue the clouds,
> they vanishe thear as smoke in open ayre,
> whilst burning hopes do reach at soueraign sway.

Whether or not Wentworth was the author of this verse, he was convinced of the evil of ambition and warned his son that the three most powerful passions were ambition, love, and anger.[47]

To Puritans, ambition was an evil to be eschewed, originating as it did with original sin. Ambition was damned as a disease borne of excessive desire for honor and conducive to pride. The ambitious person was castigated because he could not abide equals or superiors, attributed honor to himself that was due to God, and pursued false glory. "Of riches, [come] wicked thinges; and of ambition, foolish thinges." Cardinal Wolsey was set forth as an example of what could happen to an ambitious person. When someone sought to smear Huntingdon in 1585, he accused the earl of being ambitious, prompting Sir Francis, the earl's brother, to write: "Some late libeller hathe laboured to lay the blot of ambition upon you, (a faulte most vile and servile bothe before God and man); and I am out of doubt I shal never live to see you infected with that disease."[48] There were, of course, ambitious men, but in view of the disopprobrium attached to ambition, relatively few must have been willing to acknowledge it. The general abhorrence of ambition dampened any tendency to make the work ethic a support for capitalism.

Thus Anglicans and Puritans developed a work ethic in keeping with Elizabethan economic realities. Hard work was not only virtuous, but economically necessary for survival, particularly to support a family and assist the needy. The emphasis was on familial and social responsibility, not the acquisition of wealth or the ambitious desire to improve one's social state. Puritans did not develop a work ethic distinctive from that of Anglicans.

(4) The Doctrine of the Sabbath

The spending of the afternoones on Sundayes either idly or about temporall affayres, is like clipping the Q. coyne; this treason to the Prince, that prophanacion, and robbing God of his owne.

The Rev. Mr. Archdall[49]

. . . men as beasts
Would break the Sabboth day.

William Elderton[50]

The importance of diligent labor was closely associated with sabbath observance and holy days. In the Elizabethan age there was a growing concern to curtail Sunday labor and recreation, and to terminate most of the traditional holy days. Initially, basic agreement existed in the religious community with respect to sabbath observance, but in the 1570s and 1580s an attempt was made, principally by some Puritans, to achieve stricter adherence to spiritual duties on Sundays. This movement culminated in the 1580s and especially the 1590s in the development of full-blown sabbatarian views that exacerbated the differences between Anglicans and most Puritans. The essence of sabbatarianism was a conviction that the fourth commandment is a perpetual, moral law originating with the creation and antedating the Mosaic law. Recognition of Sunday as the Christian sabbath was conceived to be of divine and apostolic appointment, not ecclesiastical tradition. Sabbatarianism required that the entire day must be devoted to the public and private exercise of religion, with no time for labor, idleness, or recreation.[51]

Concern for sabbath observance was expressed in most Tudor scriptural marginalia. A note to Exodus 31 in Tyndale's Pentateuch stipulates that the sabbath is a day of worship and spiritual reconciliation, and "a signe vnto them also [which] . . . did put them in remembraunce that it was god that sanctified them with his holye sprete and not thei them selues with their holy werkes." This anti-Catholic emphasis does not recur in the Matthew Bible (1537), which advocates observance of the sabbath by performing works of faith and charity to neighbors. The Tyndale-Rogers New Testament is concerned that no "commen merchaundise" be engaged in on the sabbath. To counter an excessively rigorous (or pharisaic) interpretation of the sabbath, the Matthew-Becke Bibles of 1549 and 1551 and the Matthew Bible of 1551 insist that "man is not so bound to the outwarde obseruacyon of the Saboth, that he maye in no case breake it, but that vpon necessarye consideracions, he may do thynges forboden to be done as then." In Sir John Checke's manuscript of Matthew, the note to the twelfth chapter assigns to the state the responsibility to determine sabbath duties. Thus the earlier Tudor Scriptures reveal a changing concern, ranging from anti-Catholic polemics to appropriate sabbath activity (works of faith and charity) and the state's authority, but show no rigid sabbatarianism.[52]

On this matter, there is more of substance in the Geneva Bible, which was intended for use in the home and pastoral study as well as the church, than other Tudor Scriptures. The focal point is the total dedication of Sunday to praise God, that is, "the whole seruice of God & true religion." Mere cessation from labor was insufficient and toil for financial gain was reprehensible, though sabbath observance must not be so strict as to cause one "incommoditie". The Geneva annotators also insisted that the Christian Sunday replaced the Jewish sabbath and its ceremonies.[53]

The thrust of the Geneva comments was reiterated in later Tudor marginalia. The one comment of substance on the sabbath in the Bishops' Bible reiterated the principle that the sabbath must be wholly reserved for God's service. The Beza-Tomson Bible cautioned against excessive rigidity and asserted, unlike other Tudor Scriptures, that the most important part of the sabbath is love of one's neighbor. The Tudor Bible directly related to the development of mature sabbatarianisn was that of Emmanuel Tremellius and Franciscus Junius of Heidelberg, who had an edition published in London by Henry Middleton in 1580. Their notes stress that the sabbath is perpetual and moral, not figurative. Copies were bequeathed by Frances Jermyn, a gentlewoman, to some Suffolk preachers in 1581, and two years later the note on Exodus 31 was cited by a Puritan minister from Suffolk in a debate. Tht Tremellius-Junius edition was used by Bownde in his treatise on the sabbath. Catholic marginalia reveal little interest in the sabbath, though a note to Genesis 2 in the Douai Bible defends the observance of Sunday to commemorate Christ's resurrection.[54]

The impact of the Tremellius-Junius version on English sabbatarianism underscores, as Patrick Collinson demonstrates, the influence of the second-generation Continental reformers. This influence is apparent in the debate on the sabbath at the Dedham Conference in 1584, when there were references to Bullinger, Beza, Peter Martyr, Tremellius, and Danaeus.[55] Yet interest in persuading the English people to observe the sabbath more reverently existed long before the 1580s.

In the first decade and a half of the Elizabethan era, there was relatively little comment on the doctrine of the sabbath, and most of it was Anglican. In 1560 Pilkington complained about people who missed church services to frequent alehouses, and about the same time John Rogers urged the sanctification of the sabbath by the forsaking of vocational labor and such harmful pastimes as plays and gambling in favor of religious exercises with families. Nowell's catechism, first published in 1570, called for "the godly" to lay aside worldly business and devote their time to spiritual pursuits, and insisted that masters leave servants free from labor on the sabbath. A sermon by John Bridges at Paul's Cross the following year reiterated the latter theme. At Christ's Hospital, London, in November 1571, Henry Bedel asked that the sabbath be used to collect funds for the poor rather than "consume all that the weeke hath before gotten." When Whitgift refuted Cartwright's attack on holy days the following year, he acknowledged that rest on the sabbath was divinely commanded, though he argued that necessity or a magistrate's decree permitted exceptions. None of these men provided a thorough exposition of what sabbath observance entailed and why it was necessary.[56]

The fullest statement on the sabbath in the early Elizabethan years came in the 1563 "Homilie of the Place and Time of Prayer," which exhorted the people to cease from regular labor on the sabbath and "giue themselues wholly to heauenly exercises of GODS true religion and seruice." To commemorate the resurrection, the sabbath must be observed on Sunday. Two types of sabbath violators were condemned, the worst offenders being those who dressed or ate excessively, or engaged in brawling, railing, "toyish talking," and "filthie fleshlinesse." Lesser offenders violated the sabbath by unnecessary travel or business. In other words, hypocrisy was a more serious sabbath offense than failure to use the entire day for religious exercises.[57]

Little Puritan comment on the sabbath was published in this period, though in 1566 Becon provided a synopsis of sabbath responsibilities. As far as hearing and obeying the Word and aiding others, every day, he argued, is the sabbath, yet Sunday is set aside for these things, with no ordinary labor allowed. A neighbor in peril can be assisted, even if physical toil is involved, for this is a godly work that sanctifies the sabbath. In any case, the sabbath is not a day of idleness, for works of mercy and charity are required. Another Puritan, William Kethe, pressed in the early 1570s for stricter observance of the sabbath in Dorset, and preached at the quarter sessions at Blandford Forum in January 1571 to persuade the justices to suppress irreligious assemblies. Dering's catechism, first published in 1572, says only that the sabbath requires rest from one's calling, and public worship embodying preaching, prayer, repentance, and the sacraments.[58] As of 1574 Anglicans and Puritans did not disagree on the doctrine of the sabbath.

In contrast to the first decade and a half of the reign, the next ten years (1575-1584) witnessed a substantial increase in Puritan concern with sabbath observance. In his lectures on Hebrews (1576), Dering called for total abstinence from work on the sabbath and dedication of the day to meditation. Becon reiterated the call for total abstinence, insisting that the godly "haue our minde set on his lawe, after what manner true Christians euer keepe the lawe." Knewstub's lectures on Exodus 20, published in 1577, rejected physical ease and recreation on the sabbath in preference for religious exercises. A turning point in the doctrine of the sabbath came when he made the day not simply an occasion for religious exercises but a special spiritual experience: "Our spirituall Sabbaoth . . . consisteth in becomming newe men concerning our dooinges, from that wee haue beene, before wee knewe the Gospell."[59]

The Puritans made no immediate attempt to build on Knewstub's principle of the sabbath as a spiritual experience, but showed instead a growing outrage with sabbath violators. In an attempt to explain the latest outbreak of the plague in London, Thomas White preached at Paul's Cross in November 1577, condemning those who engaged in games, plays, and banquets on the sabbath. Again at Paul's Cross, Stockwood deplored gambling, plays, fairs, dancing, drinking, and bear-baiting on the sabbath. "In some places, they shame not in ye time of diuine seruice, to come & daunce aboute the Church, and without to haue men naked dauncing in nettes." In 1579 he called on the High Commission and other authorities to expel fiddlers and minstrels from London to improve sabbath observance, and on the governors of the Inns of Court to enforce church attendance for those in their care. In Stockwood's judgment the entire sabbath must be spent in divine service, as Lancelot Andrewes demanded in a lecture on the fourth commandment at Cambridge. In contrast, Northbrooke sought a moderate position, using the principle that the sabbath was made for man to argue that the usual religious and charitable duties could be dispensed with when necessary. He accepted Augustine's judgment that it was better to work on the sabbath than to be idle or drunk; but he also asserted an idea that subsequently became a key tenet of sabbatarianism, namely that "the whole keeping of the lawe standeth in the trve vse of the Sabboth." It was thus in the late 1570s that a cleavage of opinion on sabbath observance began to develop within the Puritan tradition itself.[60]

Puritan concern in the early 1580s continued to focus on the condemnation of activities that violated the sabbath. In 1581 Anthony Gilby and Christopher Shutte blasted fairs, markets, plays, games, and banquets on Sundays. The intensification of the Catholic threat prompted John Field, radical Puritan lecturer at St. Mary's Aldermary, London, to associate sabbath violators with Catholicism: "Nothing was vnlawfull if once they heard their abhominable masse." Yet he admitted two years later that preachers had effected little or no progress in stopping the profanation of the sabbath. Still, he called for the devotion of the day to spiritual duties and for masters to see that servants spent the day in this fashion. Catechisms of Gifford and Richard Jones, a Cardiff schoolmaster, published the same year reiterated the importance of abstaining from activities that hindered religious exercises. In one of the fullest statements on the sabbath to this date (1583), Stubbes reaffirmed Puritan concern with sabbath infractions and insisted on an end to holding courts and leets on Sundays, for these fostered malice, perjury, railing, oppression of the poor, bribery, and deceit. In the next two years Udall, Alexander Gee, and Norden added their voices to the Puritan chorus of discontent over lax sabbath observance, with a call to devote the day to godly service. Norden remarked that "the true obseruation and hallowing of the Saboth day is, ceassing from sinnes."[61]

In the same decade (1575-84) that saw Puritans become increasingly concerned with sabbath observance, Anglicans shared their disquietude, though one—Edmund Bunny—repudiated the attempt of some Puritans to make the sabbath binding as part of the moral law. The idea of keeping the sabbath as a spiritual rest appertained, he argued, only to the Isrealites before the coming of Christ, but he urged Christians to spend the sabbath in public worship, private meditation, and works of charity. "We may very well imploy that day also to our vsuall labour, yf at any tyme the rule of charitie or Christian dutie shall so requyer, vppon some extraordinarie occasion." Stephen Bateman complained, however, that too many persons took advantage of this exception to justify working on Sundays. Complaints about people engaging in sabbath sports, vain pastimes, recreation, and idleness were made by such Anglicans as Woolton, Babington, and Abraham Fleming, shortly to become chaplain to the countess of Nottingham (1582). A year before Stockwood pressed the High Commission to suppress fiddlers and minstrels, Walsall grumbled that "euery vaine fidler, and vagabound Piper in the country doth carrie away the vnthankefull people, euen vppon the Lorde his holy Saboth dayes." In his judgment it was better to toil than dance on the sabbath. Similarly, Babington was concerned primarily with such sabbath abuses as idleness, gambling, "tossing the alepot," plays, bull and bear-baiting, and feasting, not with vocational labor. The latter had to be abandoned only in "so farre as they are hinderances to that sanctifying of the Sabaoth, that is required of vs," namely, communal worship, godly conversation, meditation, and provision for the poor. Babington underscored the value of sabbath observance to inculcate ecclesiastical discipline and a sense of commonwealth. Despite much shared concern over sabbath offenders, however, a split between some Puritans and Anglicans developed in this decade over the association of the sabbath with the moral law.[62]

In the remaining years of the age, this split deepened. One of the earliest direct confrontations over the sabbath occurred during Lent, 1586, when John Smith, an M.A. of Christ's College, Cambridge, was examined by the vice-chancellor, Dr. Andrew Perne, for preaching the Jewish doctrine that the sabbath was, *jure divino,* twenty-four hours in duration, and that it was violated by anything not religious or necessary. Most Puritans insisted on strict sabbath observance, characterized by total cessation from physical labor and devotion to spiritual service, even (said Robert Some) by the prince. One must sanctify the sabbath, preached Edward Bulkeley before John St. John, Baron Bletso, in 1586, by "not doing his own wayes, nor seeking his owne will, nor speaking a vaine word." That the sabbath was perpetually ordained by the apostles and beyond the ability of the church to alter was a thesis reiterated by Cartwright in refuting the Rheims New Testament. At least one Puritan, Dr. Richard Crick, preacher at East Bergholt, Suffolk, rejected this thesis, insisting that the observance of Sunday was an ecclesiastical convention. Generally, however, Puritans regarded sabbath observance with a seriousness that many could not appreciate. Richard Fletcher, future bishop of London, was not sympathetic to the assertion of John Stroud, a schoolmaster and printer of Cranbrook, Kent, "that it is no greater a sinne to steal a horse on Munday then to sell him in a fayre on the Sunday; that it is as ill to play at games [such] as shoutinge, [or] bowlinge on Sundaye as to lye with your neyghbor's wiffe on Munday."[63]

The Puritan doctrine of the sabbath received its fullest exposition in the writings of Perkins and especially Greenham and Bownde. Perkins, who regarded the sabbath day as a duty under the moral law, was chiefly concerned with the practical question of legitimate activities on Sundays. Normally he expected people to rise early for prayer, attend public worship, and spend the remaining time in meditation and works of charity, such as visiting the sick, giving alms, admonishing the wayward, and reconciling the discordant. Fairs, sports, and banquets were prohibited, and household servants were not allowed to cook for masters. People were admonished not to undertake "any ordinary worke of your callings, and such as may be done the day before, or left well vndone till the day after." In cases of charity and necessity labor was acceptable, providing four caveats were observed: The labor could not (1) be scandalous to anyone, (2) distract from sanctifying the sabbath, (3) be a work of gain, or (4) be other than for the immediate preservation of life, health, or goods. Physicians could aid the sick or injured, mariners could sail, shepherds could tend flocks, and midwives could assist with childbirth. Such recreation as shooting, bowling, hunting, hawking, and wrestling was ruled out, for "if the duties of the ordinary vocation, otherwise lawfull and commendable, be . . . forbidden, because they destroy the rest commanded, and take vp the mind, that it cannot be freely emploied in the affaires of God, then much more are workes of pleasures forbidden, because they doe the same things much more, though otherwise in themselues they be not vnlawfull." In effect the fourth commandment requires cessation from physical labor and recreation, with a "holy dedication" of the day to the worship and service of God. Perkins showed no concern with the economic benefits of the sabbath.[64]

Greenham's treatise on the sabbath was published posthumously in 1599, but it circulated in manuscript while he was alive and was read by his step-son, Bownde.[65] Greenham's work is significant in that he was the first writer to develop the argument that sabbath observance makes good business sense. All that had been written in Elizabethan England previously on the doctrine of the sabbath built on religious, not economic, principles. Thus the doctrine of the sabbath developed primarily in a spiritual rather than a social context, and it was only in the early 1590s that an appeal was made to the godly to observe the sabbath on economic as well as religious grounds.[66]

With a congregation that almost certainly included numerous London artisans, shopkeepers, and businessmen, Greenham periodically couched his doctrine of the sabbath in commerical terms. The sabbath was not only a day of harvest for gathering spiritual blessings but also "the market day for the soule;" "the Sabboth day is the schoole day, the faire day, the market day, the feeding day of the soule." Just as good businessmen cast their accounts daily or weekly to ascertain gains and losses, so the bodly must devote the sabbath to an examination of their spiritual estates. Keeping the sabbath, Greenham argues, is good business, for those who observe the sabbath "are in their iournies in one day better prospered, in their affaires in one houre more furthered, then many others contemning the ordinance of God are in many houres, and in many daies." For six days people fulfill their callings, subordinating religious exercises to complete vocational tasks, but on Sunday vocational labor is set aside in favor of spiritual duties. Greenham's strict division of labor and worship was suited to most industrial and commercial situations.[67]

Greenham's discussion of sabbath activities was more comprehensive than anything previously published in English. Fairs and markets were ruled out and the Catholics held up for emulation for "no necessitie, profit, nor pleasure could cause the Papists to haue their Faires on their Christmas day, Easter day, holy Thursday, and Corpus Christi day." Ordinary traveling was prohibited, though in cases of necessity lawyers and physicians could journey. "Playing and pleasures," including sports, drinking and similar "vanities" were unacceptable, as were shooting, military training, planting, and harvesting. Works of mercy, such as visiting the sick or imprisoned, aiding the needy, and admonishing the unruly, were acceptable in accord with the principle that the godly were helping others, not themselves. Approval was given to postmen in government service to work on Sundays if delay harmed the commonwealth. Bakers, brewers, herdsmen, and others unable to perform their duties in the usual six-day week could work on Sundays if they did it either very early or very late in the day and did not let the work interfere with church attendance. Mariners had to observe one day in seven, even if it were not Sunday, for religious duties, and wealthy shipowners were urged to provide chaplains on ships. Above all, Greenham was concerned with the actions of the *spirit* on the sabbath, for "we must be circumspect not to rest in any drowsie or sleepie securitie in the flesh."[68]

Greenham's concern with the unbroken rhythm of the six-day work week followed by a sabbath of spiritual duties led him to consider the question of Sunday marriages. The sabbath was suitable for marriage "because on that day as it is a day of reioycing, there is a more lawfull libertie of speech, and a more liberall vse of cheerfull behauiour." Marriage feasts, however, were deferred to weekdays, with only modest love feasts permitted on Sunday. Thus religious rather than economic concerns were paramount with Greenham, for a purely business standpoint dictated holding marriage feasts on Sundays to avoid disruption of labor, but to Greenham the frivolity of such feasts would be an intolerable distraction to the sanctification of the sabbath.[69]

Although Bownde's 1595 treatise is sometimes regarded as the commencement of the Anglican-Puritan controversy on this subject, debate had already begun in earnest, and Bownde himself testifies that "this argument of the Sabbath is full of controuersie, aboue many other points of diuinitie." Despite Bownde's belief in the importance of the sabbath as a spiritual experience, with its use "referred to our sanctification and the deniall of our selues," his treatment was conducive to the inculcation of sabbatarian legalism. All buying, selling, or carrying of food on Sundays was condemned, and buyers of almost any goods were judged sabbath violators. Like other religious leaders, Bownde allowed works of necessity, but these had to be performed without pay. A physician could not charge for services rendered on Sundays, nor could an apothecary, though the latter could charge for the goods he dispensed. Lawyers required to work on Sundays could not charge, and if fees were paid, they had to be donated to the indigent. Schoolmasters could not teach on the sabbath and students could not study liberal arts and sciences. Nor was the sabbath a day on which judges could examine evidence or try cases, or magistrates conduct public affairs. Setting someone else, even servants, to work on the sabbath was forbidden, and masters had to require servants to fulfill their religious obligations.[70]

Bownde favored using the powers of the state to enforce sabbath regulations and called on magistrates to restrain the people by law from working on Sundays. He also asked them to ban fairs, unessential travel, marriage feasts, loitering in taverns, and so on. Working in the fields, even at harvest time, should be terminated. Bownde pinned his hope on the disciplinary powers of the state, not the church, to enforce sabbath observance.[71]

Bownde emphasized that the sabbath was no mere day of rest but a time for total occupation with "those workes of God which hee hath prescribed." Yet the very act of resting from traditional labor was part of obedience to God. Bownde was less interested in the economic aspects of sabbatarianism than Greenham, but he acknowledged that rest on Sunday was beneficial by its restoration of physical strength. The second book of Bownde's treatise was devoted to the theme that the sabbath must be kept holy by spending it in worship, including private meditation, Bible reading, public services, godly conversation, Psalm singing, visitation of the sick, and relief of the poor. The ministers must have achieved some success in persuading congregations to donate funds to the poor on Sundays, for Bownde describes, with disgust,

the disordered gathering for the poore that is in many places [on Sundays], where in the time of diuine seruice, you shall see men go vp and down asking, receiuing, changing, and bestowing of money, wherein many times you shall haue them so disagree, that they are louder then the minister: and the rest stand looking, and listning vnto them, leauing the worship of God . . . and thus all is confused.

Despite such problems, provision for poor relief was such a fundamental sabbath obligation that Bownde suggested that funds be collected before services and dispensed after them, implying that the destitute must sit through the services to receive assistance.[72]

No subsequent work by an Elizabethan Puritan treated the sabbath as legalistically as Bownde's, but the proper observance of Sunday remained a prominent Puritan concern to the end of the age (and much beyond). Much attention was directed to censure of Sunday gambling, plays, recreation, idleness, and frequenting taverns, though some Puritans, such as William Burton, continued the deeper spiritual emphasis, urging a "reforme [of] the heart." Proper spiritual orientation was so important to Allen that he sanctioned absence from church services to preserve goods or physical well-being as long as one's spiritual outlook was proper. Like other Puritans, Allen expected people normally to spend Sundays at church and "in and about the holy things of God," with even "harmlesse sporting and delighting of the mind" unacceptable on this "market or fayer day of our soules." Allen did not, however, argue that sabbath observance was good for business (as had Greenham), not did such other late Elizabethan writers as Dod, Richard Rogers, and Estey.[73]

Puritans approached the sabbath through the pages of Scripture rather than the account books of business and industry; even Greenham's concern was fundamentally religious. Christopher Hill's association of sabbatarianism with the economic conditions of Tudor England is intriguing,[74] but Elizabethan Puritans did not (apart from Greenham) derive their position from, or base their appeal for sabbath observance on, economic factors. Their hearers may have deduced the economic advantages of a six-day work week followed by a day of rest, but Puritan ministers stressed spiritual duties and the fourth commandment.

Anglican thought in the period 1585 to 1603 continued to evince concern about sabbath abuses while shying away from the strictness Puritans sought. The deepening rift was symbolized in the Marprelate tracts when Whitgift was accused of bowling on the sabbath. Cooper came to his defense on the grounds that the sabbath was intended for man, whose health was improved by physical exercise. Puritans, however, would have agreed with Wright's complaint that "our Sabboth

in many places, is so vilely abused, as though it had bene rather ordained to serue Bacchus and Uenus." Late Elizabethan Anglicans
such as Goerge Abbot, vice-chancellor of Oxford and dean of Winchester, Adam Hill, John King, and Richard Turnbull were as unhappy with sabbath violations as the Puritans. Anglicans remained in
fundamental agreement with Puritans about the religious uses to
which Sundays should be put. Christopher Sutton, rector of Caston
and incumbent of Wood Rising, Norfolk, and John Howson stipulated
that the obligation to keep the sabbath was part of the moral law, as
did most Puritans. Yet in a sermon at Oxford in 1602, Howson made
the curious distinction that the moral law only required worship on
the sabbath, not abstention from labor, which came under the ceremonial law. Still, he argued that labor was improper.[75]

Until the publication of Bownde's treatise, differences between
Anglicans and Puritans on the sabbath were not substantial. To the
end of the age, preachers from both groups were concerned about
inappropriate activities on Sundays. Nor was there clear-cut disagreement on the relationship of the sabbath to the moral law—a
relationship denied by at least one Puritan but affirmed as late as
1602 by the Anglicans Sutton and Howson. Bownde's legalistic treatise with its stringent interpretation of what could be done on Sundays made the sabbath into a potentially explosive issue. On 10 September 1599, Thomas Rogers preached at Bury against the doctrine
that Christians were required to keep the sabbath, a view he deemed
anti-Christian and unsound. Sundays were "the Queen's dayes" and
his opponents were Sabbatarians and Dominicans. Whitgift called in
the remaining copies of Bownde's book and Lord Chief Justice
Popham forbade the publication of additional copies in 1600 at the
Bury assizes, though censorship only increased its popularity. Patrick
Collinson has aptly remarked that "initially the identification of
Sabbatarianism with presbyterian Puritanism was effected in an attack from the opposite camp."[76]

What concerned Anglican authorities and provoked them to make
their ill-fated attempt to suppress Bownde's views was the length to
which some clergy went to condemn sabbath abuses. A Norfolk minister claimed that a feast or wedding-dinner on Sunday was as great a
sin as infanticide, while a Suffolk cleric contended that ringing
church bells on the sabbath was as serious a sin as murder. Likewise,
an Oxfordshire minister argued that working on the sabbath was as
heinous an offense as adultery, and a Somerset preacher equated
Sunday bowling with murder. Technically, these clergymen had a
point, for observance of the sabbath was one of the Ten Command-

ments, yet the crux of the issue was the type of behavior allowed on Sundays, particularly if sabbath observance was part of the moral law.[77]

The Separatists had little to say about the sabbath. Like other Protestants, they wanted Sundays devoted to public worship and prayer, but their published remarks mostly attacked the Church of England for treating the day in a heathen manner by tolerating idleness, games, and gluttony, and by naming the day in pagan fashion after the sun. Barrow criticized Anglican worship—"a stagelike fleshly pompe"—and Anglican sermons, which he claimed approved superstition and loose living. "The Sabbothe is sanctifyed, where God is rightlye worshipped, and our lives framed according to Godde's worde." On the sectarian fringe, two Familists reportedly confessed in 1561 that the Family of Love repudiated the notion of a sabbath, preferring to treat all days alike.[78]

The principal Elizabethan Catholic statement on the sabbath is in Vaux's catechism, which applied the fourth commandment to Sundays and holy days alike. To sanctify the sabbath entailed worshipping God by attending public services and saying "our diuine seruice that we be bound vnto." The sabbath can be broken by hearing mass irreverently, spending the day idly, misusing the church or churchyard, working or causing others to work (except in cases of necessity), traveling unnecessarily, and attending wanton plays. The sabbath is also violated "if we myspende the holy daye in vnthrifty games, as cardes and dyse for couetousnes, or when we should be at diuine seruice: or if we vse daunsing for wantonnes, or if we idlely stray about, when we should be at diuine seruice: or yf we frequent tauernes or bowlyng alleis, or if we vse any vnhonest place or cumpany."[79] Less strictness is seen here than in the Puritan view, for recreation, plays, and dancing on the sabbath are tolerable if they do not interfere with church attendance or involve wanton behavior or gambling.

The Puritan view of the sabbath was objectionable to some Elizabethans because of the rigorous limitation placed on activities that for generations had been accepted. When such behavior was viewed by some zealots as the moral equivalent of infanticide, murder, and adultery, the Anglican hierarchy repressed the apparent source of this reforming endeavor, Bownde's treatise on the sabbath. Consequently sabbatarianism came to be associated with Puritanism.

In sum, whereas the Geneva marginalia stressed the total dedication of the sabbath to the priase of God, the real inspiration for sabbatarianism was the Tremellius-Junius version. Before 1574, relatively little comment on the sabbath was published and much of it was Anglican. In this period Anglicans and Puritans agreed about the sabbath, though there was no substantive exposition of sabbath observance. In the next decade, Puritans became troubled by sabbath violations, probably largely because of their increasing prevalency. Anglicans shared this worry, though there were signs of a rift over the attempt of some Puritans to associate sabbath observance with the perpetual moral law, probably to underscore the importance of its observance. Yet to the end of the age, disagreement existed among Anglicans and even Puritans over this association, with Anglicans like Sutton and Howson agreeing with most Puritans that the sabbath was part of the moral law. Although Christopher Hill believes the emphasis on sabbath observance was tied to the recognition of the economic value of a six-day week followed by a day of rest, Greenham was the only Elizabethan author who used this argument. On the contrary, overwhelming evidence indicates that the rationale for sabbath observance was rooted in Scripture, not economics.

Debate over the sabbath was a divisive issue among Anglicans and Puritans before the publication of Bownde's treatise, often taken as the commencement of the controversy. The emphasis given to sabbath observance in the earlier works of Perkins and Greenham contributed to the growth of the debate. Another factor in making the sabbath a divisive issue was the endeavor of Puritan clergy, especially in the southeast, to equate the violation of the sabbath with heinous crimes. Thomas Rogers' attack on sabbatarians in September 1599, probably motivated in part by such equations, made the sabbath a major area of contention that increasingly distinguished Anglicans and Puritans. This division was intensified by Anglican repression of Bownde's treatise.

An area in which Anglicans and Puritans initially held common beliefs was a hotly disputed sphere of contention by 1603. Partly this stemmed from exegesis that made sabbath observance part of the perpetual moral law. This in turn increased the frustration of ministers who sought effective civil enforcement of the sabbath, and motivated them to equate sabbath violators with murderers and adulterers. The hostile reaction of the Anglican hierarchy to such an extreme interpretation was perhaps inevitable, but the issue remained to plague the first two Stuart monarchs, whose declarations on Sunday sports were issued against a background inflamed by religious convictions over the proper interpretation of the fourth commandment.

(5) The Sabbath in Practice

Custome and sufferaunce hath brough it to passe that the multitude do most shamefully prophane the Sabboth day, . . . [calling it] there reuelyng day, whiche day is spent in bulbeatings, bearebeatings, bowlings, dicyng, cardyng, daunsynges, drunkennes, and whoredome.

William Kethe[80]

Search Tauernes through, and typling bowres,
    eche Saboth day at morne:

. . . .

What else but gaine and Money gote
    maintaines each Saboth day
The bayting of the Beare and Bull?

Edward Hake[81]

Sabbath violations were commonplace in Elizabethan England and provoked attempts at stricter enforcement by civil and ecclesiastical authorities. Although it has been argued that this was an endeavor to impose an urban ethos on the dark corners of the realm,[82] the struggle was carried on in the towns as much as the countryside and entailed far more than an attempt to extend urban values. It was a religious struggle, for violations were particularly common in Catholic areas; a socio-economic struggle that enforced a measure of stability by imposing a common pattern of work; a cultural struggle because of the threat to traditional observances and practices on Sundays; and a political struggle focused on the ability of secular and ecclesiastical authorities to reduce a disorderly populace to obedience. Further complicating matters was the growing disagreement in this period between Anglicans and Puritans over sabbath activity.

As Greenham and some other religious leaders recognized, economic or vocational considerations were prominent reasons for violating the sabbath. John Deacon's irreligious peddler asked if it was "not then . . . the best time of all to sell our wares when the Cuntry may be at most leasure to buye the same?" An Oxford man admitted as much in 1584 before the archdeacon's court, and in his defense maintained that it was onerous for rural folk to come to town on weekdays to make purchases. The same court admonished a Witney man who moved a pile of wood into his yard lest it be stolen. Some ranchers had to shear sheep on Sundays, which got them in trouble. Despite attending morning and evening services a Stanton, Oxon., man was cited for mowing hay for his sheep on a Sunday when "he could not hire anie other to cutt yt nor coulde have ennie other convenient tyme because his is a servant & did not the same but onlie vpon necessitie." Housewives who washed clothes on Sundays were likewise in trouble. Fullers found it advantageous to set their racks on Sunday mornings "because otherwyse they cannot kepe promise with theire custmers for that there is somtymes scarce one fayre daye in a whole weeke."[83] Such people were not necessarily irreligious.

Apart from business of necessity, people had frequent temptations to violate the sabbath by attending plays, engaging in recreation, dancing, piping, hunting, or frequenting bear and bull-baitings and taverns. Numerous complaints were made that these activities were frequent, particularly in a county like Lancashire, where the citizens often were hostile to government attempts to enforce church attendance. Such attempts ran counter to conservative religious convictions and centuries of traditional Sunday activities. As late as c. 1600, the masses in northern Wales gathered on Sundays and holy days to hear "harpers and crowthers" sing of their ancestors' exploits. Visitations in Lancashire resulted in numerous presentments for selling and drinking ale in service time, though in 1601 presentments began to decline, possibly owing to the reduced danger of recusancy. Yet it was not so much Catholicism as traditional mores that prompted people to engage in these forbidden activities, for counties as disparate as Cheshire, Dorset, and Devon were frequent scenes of such Sunday activity.[84]

To the consternation of Puritans, enforcement of the sabbath was sometimes directed more at those who violated it for vocational reasons than for recreation and amusement. Of the thirty-six persons cited in the archdeacon's court at Oxford in 1584 for breaking the sabbath, twenty-one were for physical labor, eleven for traveling, two for hunting, one for frequenting an alehouse, and one for bowling. In the last four cases, the defendants were in trouble only because they undertook these activities during service time. All thirty-eight persons accused in the court at Hitchin, Herts., of breaking the sabbath in the late Elizabethan period gave economic reasons for their behavior. Thomas Fletcher of Aldenham, for instance, claimed he ordered his servant to rake hay on Sunday lest dampness ruin it. In York, parishioners of All Hallows-upon-the-Pavement were cited in 1575 for regularly opening their shops on Sundays and holy days if fairs or markets fell on those days.[85]

In contrast, at the Lancashire quarter sessions, concern was focused on persons who violated the sabbath by frequenting alehouses, playing games, and so forth. In April 1588, for example, the gentleman William Radclyffe and nine other men were presented for bearbaiting at Manchester on the sabbath. When Richard Worsley, a gentleman of Pendleton, Lancs., was licensed by the justices in July 1592 to keep an alehouse, he was warned not to entertain those who broke the sabbath by wakes, fairs, markets, hunting, bowling, cockfighting, bear-baiting, May games, and ale-drinking. Similar warnings were regularly given to alehouse licensees, and the justices tried to enforce these regulations in their sessions. Although the justices devoted considerably less attention to economic violations, the session at Preston in July 1590 noted that a market was kept at Garstang on Sundays. In Leicester, where a good deal of Puritan influence was present, concern was equally expressed for sabbath violations of an economic and pleasure-seeking nature.[86]

Attempts to enforce the sabbath were made at various levels by lay and ecclesiastical officials, with local authorities evidencing most concern. Justices of the peace were sometimes in the forefront of the battle, though one Dorset justice licensed Sunday gatherings, which the masses interpreted to mean approval for dance, bear and bullbaiting, and free drinking. An incensed William Kethe complained to the justices at Blandford Forum in January 1571 about the resulting revelry. In 1595, Devon justices, alarmed because church ales, revels, May games, and plays on Sundays attracted people from various parishes and caused disorder, contempt for law, and increased bastardy, ordered a cessation of such assemblies on the sabbath. Even the Sunday market at East Budleigh was suppressed. At Bodmin, Cornwall, in April 1598, justices of the peace ordered each householder to see that his children and servants refrained from illegal games and frequenting taverns. Staffordshire justices of the peace apparently had few cases of sabbath violations, in contrast with Lancashire justices. In Salford hundred, justices of the peace joined with ecclesiastical commissioners in 1580 to stop Sunday games, and in January 1603 the constables of Cheshire were ordered to present those who sold wares on the sabbath (except butchers selling victuals) to the quarter sessions. Norfolk, Middlesex, Worcestershire, Warwickshire, Somersetshire, and Yorkshire JPs also were active in the late Elizabethan period in enforcing Sunday observance.[87]

Town records show attempts to enforce the sabbath. At Ipswich in 1563 it was decided that no inhabitant could sell wares on Sunday except for butchers, and they were prohibited from selling during church services. In 1599 another regulation stopped carriers from working on the sabbath, "forasmuch as the waggoners and comen carriets of this town haue and doe vsuallie begynne to travell to-wardes London euerie weeke on the tuesdaie with there wagons and carriages and doe come out of London on the Frydaye att after-noone and by most parte of the Sabothe daie to the greate offence of Allmightie God."[88]

In Lincoln, regulations for closing shops on Sunday were normally enforced rigidly, though tradesmen were allowed to accept wares from London, Stourbridge, and Stamford on the sabbath. Except in Lent, butchers could sell between 5 A.M. and the market bell, and between 1 P.M. and 3 P.M. as long as no sermons were being given. Although butchers were closed in Lent, fishmongers could be open during these hours. On any Sunday, strangers passing through the town could buy goods. In the 1580s, the sabbath became the focal point of two competing political factions in Lincoln. The lenient fac-tion tolerated maypoles (and was opposed to the clothiers brought to Lincoln to put the poor to work), but their puritanical opponents urged strict enforcement of the sabbath and imposed tighter controls on alehouses, reducing some seven or eight score of them.[89]

Leicester was a borough concerned throughout the period with sabbath enforcement, owing to Puritan influence. In February 1562, inhabitants were warned that anyone except common innkeepers who traded during service time were subject to a fine of 3s. 4d. Nine months later butchers were prohibited from selling between 7 A.M. and the cessation of services on pain of a 12d. fine, and millers and carriers faced a similar fine if they transported goods to or from the mills on Sundays before the end of evening prayers. In 1578 a law was enacted that no one could enter an alehouse to drink or tarry un-lawfully on Sundays, Wednesdays, Fridays, or holy and festival days while services (including catechizings) were in progress. The 12d. fine for such offenders was not sufficient to curb such practices, so in November 1580 the mayor was empowered to levy appropriate fines or commit "to warde" persons found in alehouses during sermons. In October 1600 the fine an alehousekeepers who allowed such vio-lations was increased from 12d. to 3s. 4d., though they were permit-ted to serve travelers. The following September every alderman was instructed to have the alehouses in his ward searched during sermons, indicating that not even four decades of effort could persuade the en-tire town to sabbath observance.[90]

At Southampton the court leet records show comparable difficul-ties in enforcing the sabbath. The court requested that one or two persons be appointed each Sunday "to seeke wheare ye place of vnlawfull games are most vssid & to apprehend ye players" and fine them. Unlawful games were a problem in the later 1570s and 1580s, despite fines as high as 40s. In 1594 and 1596 complaints were common that inns and alehouses sold victuals during Sunday services, and in 1601 two shopkeepers were fined 12d. each, to warn others to stop selling before morning services and in the afternoons. Southampton allowed a Sunday fair during harvest time, but in 1602 the traditional Trinity fair was commenced on Tuesday instead of Sunday.[91]

Visitation articles and injunctions invariably were concerned with sabbath observance. As early as 1560, when sabbath violations were problematical, Parker's articles inquired if innkeepers or alewives admitted persons to their houses during church services, or if people profaned the sabbath. An ordinance for the province of Canterbury stipulated that

> on Sundaies there be no shoppes open, nor artificers goinge aboute theire affairs worldlie. And that in all faires and common markettes, fallinge upon the Sundaie, there be no shewinge of anye wares before the service be done.

As archbishop of York, Grindal ordered in 1571 that churchwardens prohibit peddlers from setting out wares during services on Sundays and holy days. Nor could innkeepers and their sort allow persons to eat, drink, or play games at such times. Shops had to close during services, and churchwardens were required to ensure that no one sat idly, played games, or behaved irreverently. The essence of Parker's ordinance on Sunday fairs was reiterated. When Grindal became archbishop of Canterbury in 1576, he issued similar injunctions for his new province. Comparable injunctions and articles were issued by other bishops and some archdeacons. In 1583 Bishop Middleton issued an injunction "that the Lord's day and other lawful Holy-days be spent in the Divine Service of Almighty God."[92]

To a degree the visitation articles were perfunctory, as indicated by the tendency for bishops to borrow articles from earlier visitations. Yet it is misleading to overemphasize this perfunctoriness. The 1597 visitation of the diocese of Norwich, for instance, led to frequent accusations of sabbath violations. Around 1590 William Chaderton, bishop of Chester, ordered his secretary to report to the High Commission on conditions in Lancashire, in which concern was expressed that "the lords daie is generallie prophaned with vnlawefull trade & marketts, with heathenish and popishe pastymes, some tendinge to the norrishinge of Idolatrous Supersticon, others to the increas of horedome & dronkenness, all purposelie maynteyned &

countenanced by ye Gentrye and better sortt, for the hinderance & defacying of the Religious & holie excercyses of the Sabaoth." Chaderton's concern is another indication that sabbath enforcement in Lancashire was linked to the program of the government and church to convert the county to Protestantism and reduce it to total obedience to the crown.[93]

Records of ecclesiastical courts also reveal concern with sabbath enforcement. The chief responsibility lay with the churchwardens, and the courts could punish by admonition, penance, fines, or excommunication. In the parish of Nantwich, Cheshire, twenty-four of the thirty-five persons presented to the court in 1595 were accused of breaking the sabbath. In archdeacons' courts, numerous presentments were made for violating the sabbath, but the emphasis was normally on prosecuting those who worked on Sundays, not those engaging in recreation, as long as it was not during services. Yet between 1590 and 1596 the archdeacon of Huntingdon's court dealt with nineteen cases of working on holy days, but only one of working on Sunday. As Christopher Hill suggests, this may be because of an attempt to crack down on Puritans. Puritans were clearly the object of presentments in the archdeacon's court at Colchester from the 1580s because they traveled on the sabbath to hear sermons. Punishments imposed in these courts varied—when the accused appeared. Fourteen of the twenty-four alleged sabbath violators in Nantwich failed to appear in 1595 and were found in contempt of court. Of the remainder, five were admonished, three were required to perform penance, and two were fined 12d. each. At Norwich the archdeacon excommunicated a woman from Sloley for washing clothes on Sunday, but similar cases at Oxford in 1584 were dismissed. The usual punishments in church courts for sabbath violators involved admonition, and sometimes a fine or penance. A worthy excuse sometimes brought dismissal, as in the case of a man at Oxford who on the sabbath had "vpon vrgent occasion . . . [been] constrayned to take a fewe faggotes out of ye waye wheare they might easelie have beene lost." Generally sabbath violators had little to fear from church courts.[94]

Ironically, sabbath violations normally brought stiffer sentences in secular than in ecclesiastical courts, with fines normally going to aid the poor. The admiralty court at Rochester fined a man 3s. 4d. "for working with his lyter" on Sunday. On the Isle of Wight a craftsman who had his shop open "after the second peal to morning prayer" on the sabbath was fined 6d. Violations in Leicester and Southampton could result in fines as high as 3s. 4d. Reformers therefore sought tougher measures in Parliament and favorable action at court, though some Puritans also acted at the local level. Because clothiers prepared some dyes on Sunday, the Dedham classis recommended in November 1585 that conversations be undertaken with the godliest clothiers to find an alternative. The Dedham congregation determined that "for the right use of the lordes daie, [this was] to be spent in holie exercises publikely and at home, in readinge and examyninge of their seruantes, all travaylinge to ffayres, marketts[,] mariage dyners and dyners abroade or in the towne lefte of[f]." Such local endeavors, however, could not stop many sabbath violations.[95]

In 1563, Alexander Nowell, in a sermon to Parliament, complained about poor attendance in the churches wheras "unruly places" were full. Referring to this offense as a hitherto capital crime, he called for a law to redress it. In the reforming zeal of the 1566 Parliament, a bill to avoid markets and fairs on Sundays got a second reading on 21 December, only to become a victim of the battle between the queen and Parliament over the bill to give statutory confirmation to the Articles of Religion. In 1571 a bill to prohibit fairs on Sundays got no further than a first reading in the Commons.[96]

Before the next Parliament met in 1584, two events provided additional ammunition to those battling for better sabbath ovservance. An earthquake on the evening of 6 April 1580 prompted many to speak of divine retribution for breaking the sabbath. More dramatic was the tragedy at Bear Garden on the Bankside, where perhaps a thousand persons had gathered as usual on a Sunday afternoon in January 1583 to watch bear-baiting. When the jammed scaffolds collapsed, two to three hundred were injured and seven or eight were killed. The dead were from the lower and middling sort: a tanner, a baker, a clerk of St. Mary Woolnoth, three servants, and the daughter of a waterbearer. Anglican and Puritan ministers were quick to cite the accident as evidence of divine displeasure.[97]

When Parliament met in 1584 the first bill of the session was for a more reverent observance of the sabbath; it quickly received two readings and was sent to a committee chaired by Sir Walter Mildmay, a Puritan. In committee this bill was scrapped and a new one formulated to ban unlawful games, hunting, hawking, bear-baiting, and wakes during church services, and to prohibit fairs, markets, and setting up stalls on Sundays. Burghley was on the committee that steered the new bill through the Lords, but the queen, who guarded her religious prerogative jealously and who had no personal taste for a strict sabbath, vetoed the bill.[98] Her action probably stimulated the development of the stricter views subsequently propounded by such Puritans as Greenham and Bownde.

Parliament returned to the question of sabbath observance in 1601. A bill "for better keeping of the Sabbath day," which included a provision voiding contracts made on Sundays in markets and fairs, was recommitted on the third reading, probably to draw up separate bills dealing with church attendance and Sunday fairs and markets. On 11 December Commons passed a bill banning all fairs and markets on the sabbath, except the annual fair at Great Yarmouth, but in the Lords it was never brought to a third reading, perhaps because of royal opposition.[99] No Elizabethan Parliament drafted legislation acceptable to Elizabeth for improved sabbath observance, whether by banning commercial activities or by prohibiting recreation and amusements.

In the absence of effective legislation, appeals were made to Walsingham and Burghley, usually seeking assistance to gain stricter sabbath observance. In December 1583, for instance, the lord mayor of London, Edward Osborne, sought Walsingham's assistance in extending the order restricting carriers on the sabbath from the City to the suburbs. Burghley received an appeal in June 1585 from Leonard Chambers, vicar of Enfield, Middlesex, and probably a Puritan, asking that the Sunday market be moved to Saturday because the sabbath was for fasting and prayer. When an irate Chambers went to the market stalls in the summer of 1586 and threw meat on the ground, the local folk complained to Burghley, seeking his approval to continue selling meat before the commencement of services. In 1592 the lord mayor of London reported to Burghley about a riot at Southwark on 11 June when a crowd tried to free a man committed to the Marshalsea. Such disorder arose, the mayor contended, because crowds were allowed to attend plays on the sabbath.[100]

Some appeals to Burghley called for more substantive action. In 1589 John Crompton not only sought Burghley's signature on a warrant to suppress disorders in alehouses on the sabbath, but also proposed fining offenders 12d. for the first offense (with half going to assist poor prisoners) and punishment at the discretion of a justice of the peace for the second. Crompton fretted that children and servants were drinking and swearing in taverns instead of attending church. In another case, Walter Stephens, a preacher at Bishops Castle, Shrops., urged Burghley in 1595 to ban the Sunday fair in his town and persuade the Council to do the same for all of Wales and the Marches. The Council in the Marches had already been given authority (in 1582) to execute the statute against unlawful games on the sabbath.[101]

Although such appeals were directed to some of Elizabeth's chief ministers, the court as a whole provided a poor example of sabbath observance. On Sundays the Privy Council often met, the queen sometimes gave audience to foreign ambassadors, and government ministers composed dispatches. Although Elizabeth expected people to attend church services, she had no objection to her subjects enjoying Sunday sports or working on the sabbath at harvest time. She even issued licenses for Sunday games. In 1569 she licensed a poor London poulterer with four small children to arrange Sunday games and plays in Middlesex as a means of obtaining financial relief. When Convocation debated a bill in 1562 to postpone fairs that fell on Sunday to the following day, Elizabeth intervened to squelch it.[102]

Throughout the reign, Elizabeth manifested a personal preference for Sunday entertainment, such as banquets and plays. On the afternoon of Sunday, 28 April 1560, jousts at court featured the participation of the earls of Sussex and Northumberland, Ambrose and Robert Dudley, and Lord Hunsdon. The judges included the marquess of Northampton, the earls of Rutland and Pembroke, and William Howard, Lord Effingham. When Elizabeth visited Killingworth Castle on her progress in the summer of 1575, the first Sunday morning was spent in the parish church, but in the afternoon there was music and dancing, and at night a fireworks display that lasted until after midnight. The following Sunday would have raised Puritan eyebrows:

After diuine seruis in the parish church for the sabot day, and a frutefull sermon thear in the forenoon: at after noon in woorship of this kenelwoorth Castl, and of God & saint kenelm, whooz day forsooth by the calendar, this waz: a solem brydeale of a proper coopl waz appointed: set in order in ye tyltyard, too cum and make chear sheaw before the Castl in the great coourt, whear az waz pight a cumly quintine for featz at armz which when they had don, too march oout.

A Morris dance, tilting, plays, a banquet, and a masque ensued. The queen had a penchant for plays on Sundays and holy days, and leading figures at court had their players entertain her. Many pious folk probably felt as the Puritan William Fuller, who in 1586 lamented that the queen had "to[o] litle used so to sanctifie the Lords Sabaothes; for if you had, things could never have gone as now thei doe."

Anthony Bridgeman's proposal to Elizabeth in 1589 to suppress bear-baiting and minstrelsy on the sabbath fell on deaf ears.[103]

Diaries and letters of the period reveal the concern the devout felt about sabbath observance. Arthur Lord Grey of Wilton was "a religious and deuout keeper of the Saboth, consecrating it wholly to publicke and priuate holy exercises." Katherine Brettergh was praised by William Harrison for having a special care to observe the sabbath, particularly by hearing sermons. When Lady Margaret Hoby, who had read Bownde's treatise, spent time with her husband on a sabbath in 1599, she felt guilty for having thought about "many Idle mattres" instead of meditating on the sermon. This Puritan propensity for the troubled conscience is also apparent in Samuel Ward's diary. An entry for Saturday, 31 May 1595, describes his remorse for not having prepared for the next day, and on 1 June he wrote:

My late rising in the morning to sanctify the Sabaoth. My negligence all that day, and idleness in perfourming the dewtyes of the Sabaoth. My want in not meditating sufficiently on the creatures, as also in prayer. My by talk in the bed, of other matters then are meet to be talked of on the Sabaoth. My ill dream.

Two years later he lamented his negligence in not sanctifying the sabbath "all that night after 9 aclock." Bassingbourne Gawdy and a friend refused to travel to the quarter sessions on Sunday, and Philip Wyot of Banstaple, Devon, reported approvingly that the fair in 1588 was held on Monday "because there should be no buying and selling [on] Sunday." Thus calls for proper observance of the sabbath did have some effect, not only on individuals but also on a town such as Barnstaple.[104]

Some of those one might expect to observe the sabbath strictly did the contrary. Whitgift enjoyed bowls on Sunday afternoons, a practice defended by the moderate Bishop Cooper. Sir Thomas Mildmay won 30s. playing maw (a card game) on a Sunday afternoon in 1576 with that habitual gambler Roger Lord North. The curate of Rufford, Lancs., was cited for dancing on Sundays and holy days. Presumably it was not an offense for Anthony Bacon to write to the earl of Essex on the sabbath to recommend a minister seeking preferment.[105]

The quest by some Anglicans and Puritans for better observance of the sabbath was frustrated by various factors, including the queen's hostility, the popular love of traditional Sunday recreation, the economic necessity for some to toil on the sabbath, and the lack of a centralized system of sabbath enforcement. With lay and ecclesiastical tribunals both involved, the objectives of enforcement varied. In

Lancashire the JPs concentrated on punishing those who spent the sabbath in alehouses or playing unlawful games, for their ultimate concern was the reduction of recusancy. In Oxford, however, the archdeacon was primarily concerned with those who worked on the sabbath. Offenders normally received harsher penalties in secular than in church courts, especially since towns such as Leicester and Southampton imposed fines up to 40s. Efforts to improve sabbath observance must have been undermined in part by the example of the royal court, for in this matter the queen was at odds with her Puritan subjects.

(6) Holy Days or Holidays?

Wee haue our feasts and new Holidaies, to put vs in minde of those blessings we haue receiued of the bounty of God.

John Howson[106]

Wherefore as we now denie Church-feasts as imitations of the Heathen: so doe we deny holie day playes, as remnants of ancient prophanenes.

Richard Greenham[107]

The question of holy days was volatile in Protestantism, involving a clash between religious zeal and traditional customs. Edwardian Protestants had reduced holy days from about 165 to 79 a year, but Puritans were dissatisfied with even this number. Economic considerations were involved as well, particularly as Puritans claimed the right to work six days, though their concerns remained fundamentally religious. The Lollards had sanctioned Sunday as the only holy day, and in 1530, Tyndale's Pentateuch included critical asides about religious feasts. "Talke of robynhod," not God, "saye oure prelates," read the marginal note to Deuteronomy 11. The prelates were concerned with holy days as means to preserve the unity of the parish, or at least to achieve whatever unity was possible. The rituals and festivities of holy days were vehicles to relieve social tensions and calm quarreling parishioners, as well as times to focus the attention of parishioners on the church. To abolish them was a matter of social and religious concern.[108]

Anglican justification of holy days was based on scriptural precedent, particularly Joel 2 and Esther 9. In view of human frailty, holy days served, through reading and hearing Scripture, as reminders of the principal points of religion and godly examples of saints. Through the administration of the sacraments, preaching, and homilies the special days supposedly withdrew persons from the superstitions associated with medieval holy days. Moreover "by our Feastes (say-eth *Tertullian*) . . . we sanctifie vnto God the memorie of his bene-fites." Holy days characterized by orderly solemnities were occasions to take the minds of parishioners from worldly pleasure and provide opportunities to assist others. They also enabled householders to in-struct their families.[109]

With respect to the fourth commandment, Anglicans argued that it allowed but did not command six days of labor, hence it did not ban holy days. It was a violation of the commandment to forbid rest on the seventh day, but not to restrain men from labor on the other six, particularly if ordered by a magistrate, who "hath power and author-ity over his subjects in all external matters, and bodily affairs; where-fore he may call them from bodily labour or compel them unto it, as shall be thought to him most convenient." Abstaining from physical labor to toil spiritually in hearing the word of God and performing works of charity was compatible with the fourth commandment. Otherwise, asked Whitgift pointedly, "how might the people lawfully come to our sermons and lectures in any of the six days?"[110]

The association of holy days with Catholicism caused the Angli-cans some difficulty. In August 1561, John Scory, bishop of Here-ford, complained to Cecil about the observation of Catholic holy days and fasts in his diocese, prompted particularly by exiled Cath-olic priests from Exeter who were received and feasted in the streets by torch light. Whitgift subsequently distinguished between Catholic and Anglican observance of holy days: Catholics used Latin that did not edify, wheras Anglicans used English; and Catholics sought, un-like Anglicans, to earn merit by their religious rites. Whitgift careful-ly stated that holy days were named after saints not because Angli-cans held a doctrine or purgatory, but because "the scriptures which that day are read in the church be concerning that saint." Sutton ad-ded that celebrating the saints and martyrs provided examples of re-pentance, faith and piety.[111]

Some Anglicans worried about the abuse of holy days. Richard Cox, bishop of Ely, expressed concern to Burghley in July 1580 about the sins on holy days "whereby godlie seruice is lett, and hindered, whiche wee in our tyme ought withe all diligence to staye." The Wiltshire minister John Terry condemned the custom of celebra-ting a lord of misrule at Christmas, "as if our Saviour had come in the flesh to deliver vs from obedience to all good lawes, and to pro-cure a dispensation for all disorder." Equally unaccaptable were celebrations at Whitsuntide that resulted in "a freer vse of all such exercises, as kindle the coales of vncleane lustes." Profaning holy days and minor religious feasts was judged by John Howson, the future vice-chancellor of Oxford, a breach of the sabbath.[112] Anglicans had cause to be concerned about the profanation of holy days, for this a-buse provided Puritans and sectaries with ammunition against them.

The essence of the Puritan position is that specific days set aside for religious observances are not objectionable, so long as they are not made "matters of faith and religion." Puritan motivation was not, as Christopher Hill has argued, economic concern for the rhythmic six-day work week, but opposition on theological grounds to re-quired holy-day observances. For Puritans the question of days or times to commemorate Christ's nativity, resurrection, and ascension, or the pentecost, or simply fasting, prayer, and thanksgiving, was a matter of indifference, in the sense that any time would suffice. "That any [days] are necessary more then be of the holy ghostes appoynting in the Scriptures, we deny," wrote Fulke. Holy days may be observed if free of superstition, idolatry, and Jewish and heathen customs, and the church has the liberty to appoint or abrogate ob-servances with a view to edification. Aware of the stringent Separa-tist criticism of holy days, Gifford underscored the Puritan thesis "that the whole matter lieth in the diuers endes of obseruation."[113]

The fourth commandment was normally interpreted by Puritans to mean that the only day apostolically recognized as a mandatory time of worship on a perpetual basis is Sunday. Other days can be or-dained by the church or civil authority on occasion, but such days were not perpetual or binding on the conscience. Perkins insisted that "God alone hath this priuiledge, to haue a Sabboth consecrated vnto him: and therefore all holy dayes dedicated to whatsoeuer ey-ther Angell or Saint, are vnlawfull." Fulke had no objection to recol-lecting pious deeds of saints, but denied biblical institution of special days for this purpose. The Elizabethan Puritan most attuned to econ-omic considerations, Richard Greenham, argued that during week-days, worship had to be planned so as not to interfere with the obli-gations of one's vocation. "Our Easter day, our Ascension day, our Whitsontide is euery Lordes day: and therefore wee ought to make a speciall care of sanctifying of this day." The attempt to avoid all holy days is, nevertheless, rare in Elizabethan Puritan literature.[114]

In contrast to the Anglicans, Puritans generally associated holy days with Catholicism. Although Cartwright did not object to occa-sional special days for religious purposes, he urged the abolition of traditional holy days, not because they interfered with the rhythm of the work week, but because of their Catholic associations. Their con-tinuance, he argued, encouraged superstition at a time when there were insufficient preachers to counter it. With propagandistic intent, Northbrooke accused the pope of instituting holy days to "traine vp" the people to be idle and ignorant. Working with the same theme, Fulke contended that festivals for the martyrs failed to teach people the essence of martyrdom and suffering for Christ, but showed them instead how to be epicureans. Moreover "the blessed virgine Marie, is neuer more dishonored, then in your festiuall dayes, with those blasphemous Antemes, *Salue regina, Aue Maria stella*, [and] *O regina mundi*. Once again, Puritans put a substantial distance between themselves and the Catholics.[115]

The severe criticism of the Separatists focused on holy days as idolatrous, with the rationale for this belief the first commandment. Barrow and Greenwood lashed out against "the double idols of your [Anglican] solempne and double feasts," and the "devised worshipp" on saints' days. Holy days lacked express scriptural sanction and led to gluttony, prodigality, idle games, superfluity, and vanity. Parishioners of the Church of England were accused of celebrating holy days "with gay clothes, cleane houses, good cheare, the viole in the feast to stir up lust in stead of devotion, eating and drinking and rising up to play and daunce, after the maner of Bacchus in his feastes, with their lords of misrule, commonly called Christmas lordes, games, enterludes, mummeries, Sodomitish maskes, wassal cuppes, with thowsandes of abhominations." Such criticism was not without some justification, and marked a Separatist repudiation of much traditional custom.[116]

Elizabethan Catholics were defensive about such an onslaught; annotations to the Rheims New Testament argued their position. Vaux's catechism asserted that the sabbath commandment applied to holy days. For the Rheims annotators, the authority bestowed on the church to move the sabbath from Saturday to Sunday also gave it the right to prescribe additional holy days, a warrant they claimed had been exercised in the apostolic period. Therefore "Christian Festivities be holy, auncient, and to be obserued on prescript daies and times, and . . . this is not Iudaical obseruation of daies." In the next century, the Douai annotators reaffirmed that the distinction of days is a matter pertaining to religion, not merely human invention or custom. In a treatise by Richard Bristow, a key assistant of William Allen at Douai and Rheims, published posthumously at Antwerp in 1599, a country observing traditional holy days was a *regnum sacerdotale*, a veritable heaven on earth in which Christ and the saints were "by such meanes continually seene here by representation & remembrance, as there in face and fruition." This is a clear reminder of the iconic preferences of Catholicism in contrast to the aniconic character of Puritanism that Bristow criticized.[117]

The holy day most prone to abuse in the Elizabethan age was Christmas. Many devout persons would have agreed with Sutton's insistence tht passing Christmas without a solemn religious observation encouraged Christians to wax cold in their love and spiritual duties. Stubbes agreed that the feast of Christmas ought to be an occasion to meditate on the incarnation and birth of Jesus, but he was an outspoken critic of Christmas abuses, castigating those who celebrated the season with masques, games, gambling, sexual promiscuity, and banqueting. "Who is ignorant, that more mischiefe is [at] that time committed than in all the yeere besides?" In his Christmas sermons at Worcester Cathedral in 1596, Dr. Robert Abbot was not offended that people observed the holiday with "daintie fare" and fine attire, but he condemned, particularly in the great houses, the excessive vanity and unbridled behavior, which he likened to bacchanalias.[118]

One of the most offensive customs of the Christmas season, particularly to Puritans, was honoring a lord of misrule. Chosen by either his parishioners or his classmates, the lord selected a group, distinguished by special livery, to serve and guard him. Bedecked with scarfs, ribbons, lace, jewelry, and bells on their legs, and carrying dragons and hobby horses, the lord and his court danced to the church to the accompaniment of pipes and drums. "Then the foolish people, they looke, they stare, they laugh, they fleer [sneer] & mount vpon fourmes and pewes to see these goodly pageants." In the churchyard, arbors and banqueting tables were erected, and revelers feasted and danced, sometimes throughout the night. Badges festooned with images were sold and worn in caps, and villagers provided the lord of misrule and his court with bread, ale, cheese, custard, and cake. The lord of misrule propagated his own laws, and offenders could be fined, "stocket or pumpt, which they call beheadding." For the villages it was an occasion for community spirit, amusement, and the temporary release of social tensions, but to the godly it was strikingly out of keeping with the spiritual meaning of Christmas.[119]

Lords of misrule were not confined to rural villages; even London enjoyed them. Early in January 1562, after the lord mayor, aldermen, and livery companies had attended a service in St. Paul's, a lord of misrule came from Whitechapel into Cheapside with a company armed with guns and halberds, marching to the sound of trumpets. Passing through Newgate and Ludgate, they paraded around St. Paul's before returning to Cheapside and Aldgate. In his diary the physician Dr. Simon Forman records that at Christmas 1583 he was chosen "lord

of the revells, and had privy enemies, [and] friendshipe of women."
At Westminster School Christmas was celebrated by selecting Paedon-
omus, a type of lord of misrule, who was outfitted in black silk trimmed with gold lace and silver buttons, topped off with a cloak of rich
carnation taffeta. Surrounded with guards armed with halberds, the
honored student presided over revels (including fireworks) and a
play. [120]

Although some clergy opposed lords of misrule, the custom was
rooted in tradition and caused popular resentment when attempts
were made to suppress it. In 1590 a tailor of Little Wyrley, Staffs.,
"mayntayned a lorde of myssrules foole in a pyde coote to make an
unsemelye occacion." When the local curate reproved the fool, the
tailor came to the latter's defense on the basis of custom but had to
answer for his actions at the quarter sessions. [121]

Surviving records depict Elizabethans celebrating Christmas with
more merriment than meditation. For some it was an occasion to provide hospitality. At Yate, Glos., in 1559, Henry Lord Berkeley observed Christmas "with great port and solemnity, as the extraordinary guilded dishes, the vanities of Cookes arts (having none other
guests but the gentlemen and ruralty of the Country), served to the
table in Twelvth day, will declare; whereof one was a whole bore inclosed in a pale workmanly guilt by a Cooke hired from Brisol." In
Nottinghamshire, Sir William Holles provided hospitality to all comers
during the twelve days of Christmas, and each day served a fat ox and
mutton. Alexander Dence of Cranbrook, Kent, left funds in his 1573
will to provide a Christmas dinner for all householders and farmers
in his village. Christmas was an expensive occasion for those of substance. William Carnsew, a Cornish gentleman, gambled with his guests
on the Twelfth Night c. 1576 and lost heavily. The Christmas of 1575
cost Sir Thomas Smith some £130. Cornish gentlemen sometimes
went to Exeter to celebrate the holiday, as did Sir William Courtenay,
Sir Arthur Basset, Sir John Gilbert, and Sir Gawen Carew in 1576.
Joining them were William Bradbridge, bishop of Exeter, and the canons. [122]

Christmas caused some consternation for the authorities. John
Danvers, the unsavory sheriff of Oxfordshire, entertained his household with dancing on Christmas day, 1588, keeping them from
common prayer and catechizing. The Privy Council was afraid that
under the guise of Christmas hospitality, recusants gathered for illegal activities. In December 1581 the Council ordered that William
Shelley of Sutton, Herefs., who had earlier been imprisoned for recusancy, and his family be prohibited from making "great preparation

for the keeping of a solemne and extraordinary Christmas, a thinge very inconvenient for him."[123]

Compared with Christmas, Easter was a relatively quiet holy day, though some Puritans nevertheless opposed it. Cartwright insisted that Easter be celebrated every day, while Percival Wyborne, a Puritan minister at Whiston, Northants.,

> sought by all the meanes he could
> The Easter to plucke downe.

Yet Anglicans stood firm, viewing Easter as a special time to consider the benefits of the death and resurrection of Christ. "The especial celebrating of the memory of Christ's resurrection once in the year is no more a fettering of our meditation thereof to that day only, than the receiving of the communion once in the month is a straiting of our consideration of the death and passion of Christ to that time only wherein we receive the holy sacrament." Puritans probably were offended most by the tradition in some communities of challenging rival villages to football matches on Easter Monday. Mercers and peddlers sold wares, and spectators probably imbibed a good deal of ale. Traveling companies performed plays to celebrate Easter, and the populace enjoyed cockfights, morris dances, and rustic games.[124]

Other holy days were the occasion for community activities. St. Bartholomew's Day provided an opportunity for athletic contests. On 24 August 1559, the lord mayor and aldermen of London attended a wrestling match at Clerkenwell, and the day was also celebrated—to the undoubted delight of pious Protestants—with bonfires of roods and icons of Mary, John, and other saints. Three days later ambassadors joined the mayor and aldermen for an archery contest and wrestling match, with similar events on the three ensuing Sundays. Shrove Tuesday was celebrated with banquets, cockfights, football games, masques, and pancake tossing. In Coventry, Reading, and some other places Hock Monday, when the men captured and ransomed the women, and Hock Tuesday, when the females had their turn, were celebrated. Ransoms went to the churchwardens for charity. Whitsuntide was celebrated with church ales, athletic contests, and dancing, while on All Saints' eve people played games and ducked for apples. These were clearly holidays, not holy days.[125]

May Day was the holiday (though not holy day) that troubled the godly the most, though it was supposed to be an occasion to thank God. The quest for a maypole, according to Stubbes, provided an excuse for people to spend the night in the woods and hills in promiscuous activities. In the morning they returned, their oxen adorned with nosegays as they pulled the maypole covered with flowers and herbs and sometimes painted. When erected, this ancient phallic symbol, with flags and handkerchiefs fastened to the top, had the ground around it strewn with boughs. "And then fall they to daunce about it like as the heathen people did at the dedication of the Idols." Trigge associated the custom with Catholicism, and Puritans such as Richard Rogers and Samuel Bird called for an end to such celebrations. In Scotland those who took part in May Day games could be excommunicated, but Anglicans refused to go to this extreme.[126]

The May Day celebrations were prone to accidents, disorder, and controversy. On 1 May 1559, with the queen watching from her palace at Westminster, the people celebrated on two pinnaces by throwing eggs and oranges at each other and setting off small fireworks known as squibs. When one of these detonated a bag of gunpowder and set some people aflame, others pushed to the opposite side of the vessel until it capsized and one person drowned. When the curate of Deighton, Yorks., tried to stop a man from bowling in the churchyard on 1 May 1575, he was stabbed and beaten. A Lincolnshire celebration in 1602 degenerated into violence and resulted in Star Chamber proceedings. A yeoman's daughters hosted a dance in their home, though the house was already the object of a disputed possession; when a female claimant refused to leave, the girls physically attacked her. Constables and allegedly "lewd and evell disposed persons" arrived, forced their entry, wounded the girls and their mother, evicted them, and ransacked the house. Tempers probably were inflamed by the drinking that accompanied May Day dances.[127]

Secular authorities made scattered attempts to keep celebrations under control, particularly in areas where Puritans exercised influence. In Lincoln in 1584-85 those seeking political power in opposition to the puritanical faction that controlled the city apparently expected to gain support by their approval of maypoles and festivities. In Shrewsbury in 1588, the maypole was banned and members of the shearmen's guild were jailed for opposing the order. At Banbury, Oxon., a Puritan center whose M.P. was Anthony Cope, the high constable ordered the parish constables to take down all maypoles and prohibit festivities in May 1589. The sheriff, John Danvers, appealed to Whitgift and Hatton, taking the occasion to charge Cope with maintaining deprived Puritans in his house and sponsoring Puritan conferences. On 24 May the Privy Council informed Lord Norris, lord lieutenant of Oxfordshire, that it saw "noe cause that those pastymes of recreacion, being not used at unlawfull tymes as one the Sabboth Day in tyme of Dyvyne Service, and in disordered and riotous sorte, should be forbidden the people." The Council warned, however, that such festivities must not be used as a pretense for unlawful assemblies or to commit unlawful acts. When a ban on a maypole at Tetbury, Glos., occasioned by the plague, was defied, violators had to appear in Star Chamber, though in this case religious considerations were not an issue. Beyond dispute, however, the disorders of May Day celebrations were a factor in Puritan opposition to them.[128]

Ecclesiastical courts were concerned with abuses of holy days, particularly as regarded those who labored on such occasions and those Puritan clergy who opposed the holidays' observation. Grindal's injunctions for the provinces of York (1571) and Canterbury (1576) endeavored to stop the profanation of churches and churchyards by lords of misrule, morris dancers, May Day celebrations, and the like. Visitation articles inquired about lords of misrule, morris dancers, and other disorderly celebrants of holy days. Middleton's injunctions for the diocese of St. David's in 1583 included the provision "that the Lord's day and other lawful Holy-days be spent in the Divine Service of Almighty God; and that old superstitious Holy-days be justly abrogated and put down, yet bidden to be observed by the minister in the churches." In the diocese of Durham, Richard Barnes ordered in 1577 that no Catholic holy days be observed or superfluous fasts honored, including those for St. Trinyon (Ninian) and St. Margaret, and the Black fast and Lady fast. He also prohibited clerics from engaging in May games. Aylmer worried about similar observances in his London diocese the same year. In the diocese of Hereford in 1586 Herbert Westfaling, newly consecrated to the see, inquired if ministers were urging the observation of abrogated holy days or fast days or if persons were observing them. Numerous other examples could be cited from articles and injunctions. Visitations did turn up clerical violators, such as Richard Hackney, rector of Cranoe, Leics., who was reprimanded by his bishop for allowing morris dancers and Catholic plays in his church. Puritans also were cited, but for failing to encourage parishioners to observe holy and fast days. Among those cited were Robert Kennion, rector of Harpley, Norfolk, and John Trendle, Presbyterian rector of Ovington.[129]

Puritans, for reasons of conscience, and lazy clerics seemed particularly to fall afoul of the ecclesiastical authorities for failing to go on the required perambulation during Rogation week. The practice was to have a clergyman walk the bounds of his parish to know it better, improve the fertility of the ground, and obtain good weather. Undertaken on Monday, Tuesday, or Wednesday of Ascension week, the cleric was accompanied by churchwardens, one or more important men of the parish, and sometimes younger folk. At various places the assemblage stopped, sang or recited Psalms 103 and 104 and the litany, and a homily was read and prayers offered. Parishioners were admonished to give thanks for the fruits of the earth and were warned not to remove neighbors' landmarks. No surplice was to be worn and no banners carried. Although this was supposed to be another occasion to manifest village solidarity, Puritans saw it as a superstitious carryover from Catholicism and an excuse for drinking and other unacceptable behavior.[130]

That the church hierarchy had difficulties in enforcing Rogation perambulations is evident in that firty-two parishes of the archdeaconries of Norfolk and Suffolk in 1597 had not held perambulations. Some parishes had not done so for five to seven years. Some of this failure was undoubtedly due to negligent clerics, but there is no mistaking the hostility of Puritans to this duty. Among Yorkshire Puritans who omitted Rogation perambulations were Stephen Street, rector of Emley (1586), Christopher Taylor, vicar of Bradford (1590), Richard Skipton, vicar of Skipton (1590), Christopher Shutte, vicar of Giggleswick (1594), Edward Horsman, vicar of Skipton (1594), Walter Jones, vicar of Easington(1596), George Kay, rector of Huggate, who claimed his parishioners refused to accompany him (1596), and Adam Rose, vicar or Gargrave (1599-1600). Although the Puritan vicar of Headon, Notts., Robert Southworth, refused to go on perambulations in 1591 and 1592, ecclesiastical pressure prompted him to agree to do it in the future "with all his heart." After similar refusals in 1592 and 1593, George Turvin, vicar of East Redford, Notts., excused himself by saying "that they have no felds nor cause of perambulacion nor can have companie for that purpose." In the 1597 visitation of the diocese of Norwich, twelve clergymen were cited for omitting perambulations, compared with only six for not bidding holy and fast days. In the city of Norwich with its thirty-three churches (some served by pluralists), five clergy men were cited for not going on perambulations. The authorities had trouble enforcing this obligation, though only partly because of Puritan convictions.[131]

As for the laity, officials in some church courts were concerned primarily with persons who violated holy days by working rather than recreation. This focus may indicate, as Christopher Hill suggests, an attempt to repress Puritans, but it may also be a tacit recognition by ecclesiastical authorities of the use of holy days to release social tensions. In the archdeacon's court at Oxford in 1584, at least a dozen cases came up of men (but no women) accused of working on a holy day (five on St. Peter's day alone), but only one involving inappropriate conduct. In the latter case, two alemen of Blackthorn were cited "for kepinge of evel rule in the tyme of service at there ale howse" on Whitsun Monday, for which they were admonished and dismissed. Between 1590 and 1596, the archdeacon of Huntingdon's court dealt with nineteen cases of persons working on holy days, but only one concerning labor on the sabbath.[132]

Any attempt to improve the religious observance of holy days presumably was hindered, as in the case of the sabbath, by the example of Elizabeth's court. On 25 June 1559 the queen and her Council were entertained at Greenwich with May games involving "sant John Sacerys [Zachary], with a gyant, and drumes and gunes [and the] ix wordes [worthies], with spcchys, and a goodly pagent with a quen . . . and dyvers odur, with spcchys; and then sant Gorge and the dragon, the mores dansse, and after Robyn Hode and lytyll John, and M[aid Marian] and frere Tuke." The following year, the court was entertained with morris dancing, bears, and the music of trumpets, flutes, and drums. The court's Christmas festivities at the Temple in 1561 included banquets, minstrels, dancing, and a lord of misrule. Christmas at Hampton Court in 1572 was celebrated with backgammon and dancing. Age did not stop the queen from enjoying holy days, for on 1 May 1602 she "went a mayenge" to Sir Richard Buckley's home at Lewisham, Kent. Although John Chamberlain anticipated a dull Christmas at court that year, with many aristocrats celebrating elsewhere, it turned out to be lively, with dancing, bearbaiting, plays, and gambling (Sir Robert Cecil lost £800 in one night). To the end, Elizabeth used holy days more for amusement than spiritual pursuits, an example that must have disappointed Puritans.[133]

Attempts to improve the observance of holy days by legislation were few. In 1559 the Commons approved a bill to revive the statute for keeping holy days, but it did not become law. By one vote, Convocation in 1563 defeated a proposal with Puritan support to abolish all holy days except Sundays and the "principal feasts of Christ," such as Christmas and Easter. In the face, however, of a moderately conservative religious hierarchy, deep-rooted popular traditions, and a sovereign who enjoyed the traditional gala of holy days, the godly had to be content with encouraging parishioners to observe such days with greater devotion and less gaiety.[134]

It is, in conclusion, worth noting that the principal concern of Puritans with holy days and the sabbath was religious rather than economic. Although Puritan hostility to holy days was strong, throughout most of the era Anglicans and Puritans fundamentally agreed on the sabbath. The publication of Bownde's treatise, Thomas Rogers' attack on it in 1599, and the extremes to which some Puritans went in comparing sabbath violators to murderers and the like made the sabbath a divisive issue at the end of the age, though the origins of the controversy preceded Bownde's work. The court failed to provide the kind of moral leadership with respect to the sabbath and holy days that the godly preferred, and the queen effectively foreclosed Parliament as a vehicle to achieve reform in these areas. For the most part, the ecclesiastical courts were more interested in prosecuting persons who worked on the sabbath and holy days than those who played, suggesting that the ecclesiastical hierarchy was aware of the depth of attachment to games and other amusement on Sundays and holy days.

Although there was a clear division between Anglicans and Puritans over holy days, and a growing one over the sabbath, there was no distinctive work ethic that can be labeled Anglican or Puritan. Both groups abhorred idleness and praised industry, not for the accumulation of wealth but to support the family and aid the needy. Puritans showed a greater sensitivity in their consciences about idleness, as they did about sabbath observance, and they were more willing to castigate the aristocracy and clergy for idle living. Some Puritans were more inclined to allow vocational mobility, though Anglicans such as Bunny and Mulcaster agreed with Puritans such as Cleaver and Perkins that parents should choose vocations for their children; the clearest case for freedom of occupational choice was made by Udall, a radical Puritan. Puritans stressed diligence in one's vocation while Anglicans emphasized contentment, but the positions were not mutually exclusive. Thus differences in these areas between Anglicans and Puritans are apparent, though there is no distinctive Puritan work ethic as has so often been argued.

CHAPTER *10*

Social Entertainment
and Recreation

When James I issued the Declaration of Sports in 1618 and Charles I renewed it in 1633, they inflamed religious opinion by sanctioning recreation on the sabbath. A long-standing controversy had existed over the appropriate forms of recreation and social entertainment. An effective compromise had to be found to permit mental and physical relaxation and yet avoid idleness and licentiousness. The state provided some guidelines by the imposition of statutory limitations on such games as bowls, but considerable leeway remained for debate about the suitability of various games, gambling, bull and bear-baiting, cockfighting, dancing, and music. In general the restrictions that the religious reformers sought to impose ran contrary to traditional practices, and for that reason met with widespread antipathy. Dancing, music, and recreation were regularly harnessed by the church at ales and wakes to raise money and improve relations between parishes and parishioners, and as the reformers stepped up their attacks on various types of dancing, music, and recreation, ales and wakes were viewed with increasing opprobrium. Religious reformers, notably the Puritans, were not attacking merely the old religion but the old way of life. The New Jerusalem was not a new theological edifice but a society stripped of many traditional amusements and games, including mixed dancing, ribald songs, animal-baiting, football, and gambling. Yet not even the most zealous Elizabethan reformer was so

431

extreme as to ban all games or dancing or music; the emphasis was on purging society of abuses to enhance holiness and physical well-being.

(1) Games Lawful and Unlawful

Now in pleasures and play what is there followinge, but extreme folye, waste and losse of that previous trasure Tyme, and in the ende (for the moste parte) myserye, pouertye, and dispayre?

Valentine Leigh[1]

Deep play [gambling] is no pastime, but a lost time misspent.

Sir Matthew Carew, Master of the Rolls[2]

Diligent use of time was a duty, with most time devoted to vocational responsibilities and religious obligations; the remaining hours were the subject of a dispute involving religious principles and the regulatory abilities of the government. Anglican clerics adopted a moderate stance, recognizing the value of physical exercise for the maintenance of health and of games in general for mental relaxation. Recreation had to be moderate and confined to suitable times and places. In a sermon at Paul's Cross in October 1578, John Walsall restricted recreation to activities that "seeke the glorie of god, by endeuouring to put of[f] the olde man of sinne, and to shewe foorth liuely fruites of true regeneration." Games conducive to quickness of body and mind, providing they were neither illegal nor ungodly, were acceptable.[3]

Deciding which forms of recreation met these criteria created disagreement. Wright recommended chess—"a princely exercise: hauing in it a certaine Maiestie, wherein is shewed a warlike order, and politike gouernement"—archery, and tennis, but Pilkington warned that tennis was unprofitable except to refresh the mind after great study or "travail in weighty affairs." The dean of Winchester, George Abbot, worried about dangerous sports, notably the riskier forms of tumbling and tight-rope walking, both of which he condemned as suicidal. Because swimming was potentially useful for fishermen and soldiers, he sanctioned it as a form of recreation, but not for younger children, or in deep water, or on the sabbath. Anglicans did not object to bowls, except among classes for whom it was illegal.[4]

More problematical were cards, backgammon, and dicing. Wright prohibited all games involving chance, but Babington approved cards and backgammon if no gambling was involved. Dice-play, however, he repudiated because it involved no wit, art, or exercise. Cooper regarded dicing as an impious practice, even for the aristocracy, but

John King approved cards and dice-play for discreet persons, though not dicing and card parlors. Cards and dicing, Sandys admitted, were not sinful *per se,* but because they were occasions for evil it was better for people to be idle.[5]

Several Anglicans, particularly Whetstone, vehemently opposed gambling. He called on magistrates, especially in London, to suppress gambling houses as a threat to the landed classes. Some gentry at the Inns of Court were vulnerable to London gamblers with loaded dice and sleights of hand. Gambling lured masterless men to London, who found stakes by stealing, pawning, or borrowing at usurious rates. "Close in a chamber a cogging knaue getteth more money in an houre, than many an honest man spendeth in a yere." Whetstone was scandalized that more gambling tables than churches could be found in London, and he noted gambling led to other vices, especially prostitution and profanity. Because of these associations, Edmund Tilney, another layman, thought it best to avoid gambling, though he saw no harm in wagering for small sums if one could afford the potential loss. Pilkington, to the contrary, argued that even gentlemen had no business wasting money gambling, and Henry Bedel recommended that such funds be donated to the poor.[6]

Referring to Puritan hostility to the moderate Anglican position on recreation, Sutcliffe contended that the "honest" games played by Anglican clerics were more commendable than the sabbath exercises of Puritans. Wright was convinced that Puritans and Separatists despised clergy who were "more pleasant and sociable of nature, or more delighted in mirth and honest pastime for their health and recreation than agreeth with their [the Puritans'] Stoicall disposition." Sutcliffe and Wright, both conservatives, reflect the significance Anglican clergy attached to social behavior, as distinct from the stricter Puritan and Separatist concern with what might be called godly exclusiveness.[7]

Among the Anglican laity, William Wentworth advised his son to forbear violent or dangerous exercises, such as football, vaulting, and jumping. Games must be played only with honest companions for recreation, and gambling avoided if it involved more than small amounts. "Noble men and knights and esquyers of great lyving that use to plaie great game, knowe all or most of the secrett deceipts and advantages in gaming." For Wentworth, the possibility of excessive loss, not immorality, made gambling dangerous. His views suggest that Anglican gentry were inclined to follow the recommendations of their religious leaders, with perhaps more leniency toward very modest gambling.[8]

A key point in the voluminous Puritan diatribes against inappropriate games was confining recreation to activities conducive to physical and mental refreshment. Such activities must be pursued in moderation and cannot impinge on spiritual duties. The general rule was aptly phrased by Stubbes: "One Christian may play with another, at any kind of Godly, honest, ciuile game, or exercise, for the mutuall recreation one of the other, so that they be not inflamed with coueitousnes, or desire of vnlawfull gaine." A common caveat in Puritan writings warned readers not to devote excessive time to recreation.

> Nor do I trifle out the time in play,
> Yet stil vse honest recreations.

Overly strict abridgment of recreation was unacceptable, and those who sought by immoderate austerity to make a show of godliness were rebuked.[9]

Several Puritans explicitly connected their faith and recreation. Perkins insisted that recreational activities be conducive to the glory of God and profitable to oneself and others. In a kindred spirit, Fenner thought it offensive to play games that were unedifying or troubled those who were godly but weak. All recreation must be sanctified by prayer and thanksgiving. At Ipswich, Samuel Bird approved only activities that edified and increased faith, and these had to "agree in euerie point with Christian doctrine." Bird specifically objected to games that made participants objects of laughter (e.g., "hinch, pinch, and laugh not") or involved promiscuous conduct.[10]

Puritans expressed concern about the tendency of games to undermine the social hierarchy and foster inappropriate associations. Fenner cautioned people to keep within the bounds of their callings, which partly entailed avoiding recreation with persons of higher social standing. Age and occupation also were factors in selecting recreational companions. We must, he said, "square our selues according to the most sober of our age, degre, condition and sort of life." Burton castigated the higher born who became "haile fellow with euery base companion at cards, at tables, at dice, and quaffing, and so liue amongst men not like rulers, but like *Aesops* blocke, drowned in the bottome of carnall and base delights."[11] Curiously, Anglican authors showed no similar concern with the leveling potential in games, though class privileges are evident (as will be seen) in the relevant statutes.

Abhorrence of idleness played a major role in creating Puritan discontent with recreational practices, particularly among the gentry, whom Puritans were not loath to criticize. Moderate recreation was one thing, but to devote excessive time to amusing pursuits when there were households to instruct, needy to assist, and other obligations to perform was unconscionable. Greenham stretched the seventh commandment to include a prohibition of idleness and vain sports. "A man," said Bird, "doth redeeme the time sufficientlie, when hee maketh anie lawefull delight, an occasion to lift vp a thankfull minde vnto God for it," but when excessive time is devoted to play, this spiritual end is ignored and evil associations result.[12]

With respect to specific games, there was diagreement among Puritans. Chess was commended for its enhancement of critical powers, as was draughts. Most physical activity was approved, including running, wrestling, archery, fencing, weight-lifting, and riding. Tennis, a game essentially limited to the aristocracy and the wealthy, was approved by Northbrooke, but Stubbes thought no Christian could play because of its associations with gambling. Stubbes felt the same about bowls, which he sanctioned if played privately, moderately, and in fear of God. Greenham apparently accepted bowling for those classes legally entitled to play, but Stockwood found the game reprehensible and Gosson likened bowling alleys to "priuy Mothes, that eate vppe the credite of many idle Citizens," ruining their families.[13]

Football was scathingly criticized by Stubbes as less a form of recreation than a friendly fight. "For: dooth not euery one lye in waight for his Aduersarie, seeking to ouerthrowe him & to picke him on his nose, though it be vppon hard stones, . . . hee careth not so he haue him down." It was the violence of football that Stubbes objected to the most, and he catalogued injuries ranging from broken necks and legs to bloody noses and eye wounds. He claimed the violence was conducive to malice and enmity, and led to brawling and even homicide. John Carr's hostility to vicious games presumably ruled out football. Some indication of the violence is found in records of the coroners' courts in Elizabethan Essex, where four football deaths are recorded.[14]

Puritans usually condemned games of chance. Although backgammon, one of the most popular Elizabethan games, required some skill (and for that reason was sanctioned by Northbrooke), the element of chance prompted most Puritans to counsel its avoidance. Dicing and card-playing were judged inappropriate for Christians because they abused lots, which were divinely intended to resolve serious impasses (e.g., evenly divided judges in a legal suit). A lot presupposes, explained James Balmford, a preacher at Newcastle-on-Tyne, "the special prouidence and determining presence of God, as an oth in the nature therof doth suppose the testifying presence of God." To use lots in games such as dicing, backgammon, and cards was commonly regarded as profanation of God's name. Anglicans agreed on the seriousness with which lots should be used, but rarely mentioned the lot as an argument against dicing, backgammon, and card-playing. (The cathedral chapter at Wells regularly cast lots to apportion patronage.)[15]

Puritans marshaled additional arguments to prohibit dicing and card-playing, but no one went as far as Hugh Gray, who told a Cambridge audience in January 1587 that to play with dice or cards was to crucify Christ. Among the commoner arguments was the assertion that such games had the appearance of evil and often involved immoral persons who swore, quarreled, and squandered time. Cards and dice were objectionable to Puritans because they encouraged craftiness and deceit, and failed to provide physical or mental exercise. "Euerie recreation," wrote Bird, "doth refresh & quicken our spirits, but Dice and card plaie is so quiet, & so drousie a pastime, that if the desire of winning did not keepe them awake, the gamesters would be oftentimes readie to fall a sleepe." The primary objection to dicing and cards was their association with gambling, which resulted in players bringing "a Castell into a Capcase, a whole Manour and Lordeshippe into a Cottage, their Feesimple into Feesingle." Those willing to play with dice or cards as private recreation, with appropriate fear of God and not as a waste of time, had Stubbes' approval, though most Puritans apparently opposed such concessions.[16]

Puritans made a strong case against gambling, with some clergy insisting that winners violated the eighth commandment. To Perkins such persons were worse than the commonly detested usurers. Losers, particularly those of inferior means, were blamed for beggaring their families. Bird was convinced that gambling landlords oppressed tenants and evicted some to improve income from leases. Surprisingly, Perkins and Fenner tolerated some gambling, by those with sufficient means, though Perkins insisted that winnings be applied to a common good. The general Puritan position, however, demanded that potential gamblers donate surplus funds to the needy, and Fenner only allowed gambling after a person had made liberal contributions to the indigent.[17]

Puritans generally adhered to their principles, though some, including Willian Carnsew, a gentleman of Bokelly, St. Kew, Cornwall, gambled. At Christ's College, Cambridge, Samuel Ward enjoyed bowling, though his conscience bothered him in July 1595 for "my over much myrth att bowling after supper." Lady Margaret Hoby played bowls, fished and boated. Cards and dice found no acceptance in the Hoby household, and when, in 1600, the son and brother of William Lord Eure abused Sir Thomas' hospitality by playing cards and dice, drinking, and disrupting family prayers, he sued them in Star Chamber. Cards were equally repugnant to Grace Mildmay, who preferred to comfort neighbors "than to sit with a dumme pair of cards in our hands, for, as the hands are busied with good or bad, the mind will be set thereon." Thomas Wotton of Boughton Malherbe, Kent, a friend of Leicester and Walsingham, disinherited his son-in-law for wasting his time in such "lewde" games as backgammon, dice, and cards, and for using wicked oaths.[18]

Separatists confined their comments on recreation to attacks on Church of England clerics. Penry credited Puritans with opposing cards and backgammon, but criticized Anglican prelates for countenancing these games. The state clergy were condemned by Barrow for their reluctance to rebuke the wealthy's devotion to vain sports and gambling; "al this is covered under christian recreation and pastime, and is tollerable inough so he wil heare a sermon, and cal his familie to a lecture; yea the priest will not then stick to stay and looke on, until the games at tables or set at cardes be done." With some justification, Barrow remarked that Anglican clergy rebuked idle games but did not always practice what they preached. In essence, the Separatist attitude to recreation was compatible with that of stricter Puritans.[19]

In Jesuit circles, attitudes to recreation essentially paralleled those of the Puritans, though other Catholics were less strict. The Jesuit John Gerard complained that cards were books studied night and day by gentlemen in London, yet to mask his identity, he regularly lived as a gentleman, playing cards and feigning gambling. When, in 1599, he went to the home of Sir Francis Fortescue in the hope of converting his wife Grace (née Manners), he was unable to reveal his identity the first day because of the presence of Protestants, hence he played cards, "just passing the time like people who don't know or care about the value of time." When he gambled with Catholics (e.g., Sir Everard Digby), to conceal his identity he and his companions "had an understanding that everybody got his money back at the end and that the loser said an *Ave Maria* for every counter returned." The Augustinian canon Lawrence Vaux opposed gambling as a violation of the eighth and tenth commandments, and insisted that winners make restitution. Cards and dicing were "vnthrifty games," but apparently only if gambling were involved. Vaux's objection to bowls was limited to those who played during church services. Most Catholics other than Jesuits probably took a rather liberal view toward recreation.[20]

Authors of medical texts of the period generally agreed about the value of physical recreation and the unsatisfactory nature of dicing, cards, and backgammon. The latter activities, though perhaps mentally relaxing, were viewed as dishonest amusements of idle persons. Chess, tennis, running, wrestling, and horseback riding were recommended. The physician William Bullein regarded football (with dicing and cards) as "an exercise of fooles." Mulcaster's text on education reflected the general position of the medical works, though he was unwilling to rule out football completely. The preferred exercises for students were wrestling, fencing, and swimming, with the latter said to have such medical advantages as improving digestion and sleep, and, in salt water, relieving headaches and unclogging nostrils. Lord Howard of Effingham's wife found in 1602 that playing shuttlecock aided childbirth.[21]

The state imposed controls on recreational activities. The key statute was 33 Henry VIII, c. 9, which was concerned with the promotion of archery, but also banned unlicensed houses and alleys for bowls, tennis, dicing, backgammon, cards, and other illegal games. Outside the Christmas season no husbandmen, craftsmen, apprentices, laborers, servants, fishermen, and mariners were allowed to play such games. At Christmas these games were permitted at their masters' homes or in their presence, though servants could be licensed by masters to play cards, dice, and backgammon with them or other gentlemen. Nobles and gentlemen had authority to license cards, dice, backgammon, bowls, and tennis in their houses. Frequenting an unlicensed gaming house could result in a fine of 6s. 8d., and local officials were given the responsibility to seek out offenders. Because licenses for unlawful games were allegedly responsible for assemblies of idle and unruly persons, they were voided by 2 and 3 Philip and Mary, c. 9. Elizabeth , however, granted such licenses. The provisions on archery in 33 Henry VIII, c. 9 were repeated in 8 Eliz. I, c. 10, whereas 13 Eliz I, c. 14 confirmed the provisions against unlawful games.[22]

Enforcement of these regulations was not particularly effective. In the State Papers, there is a proposal made late in 1566 for the improved execution of the statute against unlawful games. Puritans in particular were unhappy with lax enforcement: Stubbes lamented that gaming houses were tolerated, and were in effect brothels, and Dering thought that "the Magistrate neuer tasted of Christ, that suffereth this great carding and dicing, that leaueth sinne vnpunished, and vertue vnrewarded.'' In Bird's judgment, magistrates licensed houses without thoroughly investigating their character, hence unlawful activities abounded. His solution was to have magistrates "knock downe their signes, & make a iakes [privy] of their houses, or a draught house to feed swine in.'' He also urged a reduction in the number of victualing houses and a search of those remaining as well as of haberdashers' shops, to confiscate and burn (if legal) cards and backgammon boards.[23]

Although enforcement was not particularly effective, at the local level numerous efforts were made to suppress unlawful games. At Leicester, the mayor ordered the statute dealing with unlawful games to be publicly read at the High Cross in December 1578, and two years later a fine of 40s. was to be imposed on alehouses and other places where unlawful games were played. In 1569 and 1585 commissioners were appointed to enforce the statutory provisions regarding illegal games. In London those who played football were threatened with imprisonment in 1572, and four years later, football was prohibited in the Royal Exchange; the lord mayor banned football in the City in 1581. Many abuses appear traceable to licenses that should not have been issued, and in 1585 Fleetwood complained to Burghley about such abuses, including licensing persons to hold games on Sundays. At Chelmsford, Essex, violators of the statute were generally ignored until 1598, when a bye-law was passed to crack down on servants, artisans, victualers, and others who played illegal games at unlawful times. Yet violators at Ingatestone, Essex, were regularly fined. Essex manorial records reveal that alehouse licensees usually were punished rather than participants in illegal games.[24]

At Southampton there was a growing effort in the Elizabethan era to suppress unlawful games. In 1566 the court leet concerned itself with illegal bowls and quoits (ring toss), and it subsequently requested that one or two persons be appointed each Sunday to apprehend persons playing unlawful games. In 1573, the court leet reflected the government's concern that archery was being neglected because of the popularity of bowls and urged that bowlers be compelled to spend more time with bows and arrows. Beginning in 1575 the records of the court leet include specific cases of violators, such as the John Symonds who used his house for gambling sessions at night for other men's servants. The same year another man was fined 40s. because he had hosted games of nine holes, a form of bowling. Normally the court leet imposed the same fine (40s.) on persons responsible for the games, and lesser fines (6s. 8d.) on players. Such fines did not discourage play, for in 1579 the court leet expressed concern that too many men haunted alehouses to play illegal games and left their families in want. The usual fines were reaffirmed and a curfew of 9 P.M. was imposed on artisans and servants who frequented taverns. Porters were troublesome and brought disrepute on the town because they played games instead of working. Illegal games continued to be a problem at Southampton to the end of the age.[25]

Normally cases of unlawful games were handled by local or manorial juries, though some cases appear in quarter sessions records. Staffordshire accounts do not list the offense in many instances, but cases of unlawful games appear in the later 1580s and continue through the 1590s. Most involve alehouse keepers and victualers who allowed illegal games in their establishments. A widow who sold ale without a license and permitted unlawful games was charged in 1594 with "keeping evell order in her howse." Chesire records show limited concern with players and alehouse keepers, though a Newton man was charged in 1574 with permitting bowls, "by meanes wherof menne Servantes and chyldren are p'voked to unthryftnes to the evyll example of all others and also to the contempt of the Quene's heighnes and her Lawes." Records of the Lancashire quarter sessions reveal greater concern about unlawful games, undoubtedly owing to the attempt to impose royal control and reduce recusancy. Between July 1590 and October 1602, sixty-two persons were presented at the session for unlawful games, particularly cards, bowls, and dicing. Of those identified, eleven were alehouse or inn keepers, twelve husbandmen, three yeomen, eleven common laborers, ten artisans or skilled workers, two colliers, and one peddler, one minstrel, one badger, and one shearer. The aristocrary and men of substance usually were left to their own judgments in recreational matters.[26]

In Essex, most cases of unlawful games in the secular courts involved cards and dice, usually in an alehouse. The sessions rolls for the period 1562-1568, however, contain three presentments for football, and one each for cards, dice, backgammon, and bowls. Alehouse keepers commonly appear in court records, charged with allowing unlawful games; in 1572 ten alehouse keepers in Moulsham were so cited. A Shenfield butcher, according to a 1566 charge, "keepeth an alehouse and doth daily hospitate and succour vagabonds and idle persons and suffer them to play at cards." He may have been one of the men of that parish who played football on Passion Sunday. In the late 1590s, the people of Barling were irate because a local victualer, John Collyn, allowed his eldest son to gamble at dice, cards, and backgammon, and permitted his customers to play unlawful games even at service time on Sundays and holy days; one gamester got Collyn's daughter pregnant. Several Essex schoolmasters achieved notoriety by playing unlawful games. Among them were John Hobson of Terling and Thomas Gates of Walthamstow; the schoolmaster of Manuden (Manewden) "runneth to the football and dancing upon the sabbath days and holy days."[27]

The ecclesiastical hierarchy was officially concerned about recreational abuses. In 1571, for instance, Grindal's injunctions to the clergy of the province of York forbade them to become evil examples by playing backgammon, cards, and dice. Simultaneously he warned in his injunctions to the laity that inn and alehouse keepers and victualers must not allow games at service time. As archbishop of Canterbury, Grindal repeated these provisions in 1576. Other episcopal injunctions, including those of Bishop Barnes for Durham and Bishop Middleton for St. David's, warned clerics not to play unlawful games. Visitation articles regularly inquired about those, including the clergy, who played games illegally. Whitgift's articles for the diocese of Worcester c. 1577 asked if one's minister used "at vacant times such good and seemly exercises as may keep him from sluggishness, as shooting, or is he a common hawker or hunter or player at any games unseemly for his calling?" Episcopal concern also was manifested in Chaderton's 1581 articles for the diocese of Chester, about the profanation of churches, chapels, and churchyards by unlawful or inappropriate games. A notorious example occurred in 1566 when the boys of St. Peter's School, York, were charged with playing football inside York Minster.[28]

Records of the ecclesiastical courts show sporadic prosecutions for recreational violations. At Durham a man who played football during Sunday services was ordered to do penance and give 12d. to the poor in 1579. As a result of the York visitation in 1575, some twenty men were presented for bowling at Howden during evening prayers, and the 1595-96 visitation resulted in charges against five or six men for playing bowls in the churchyard at Easington on Whitsunday. The archdeacon's court at Oxford in 1584 tried recreational violations by church officials. Henry Wise, curate of Horton, denied charges that he played backgammon (except with honest gentlemen) and dice. Two guardians of the church at Bourton were accused of permitting bowling and dancing in the churchyard, especially during Whitsun week, and guardians at Dunstew were cited for allowing games and shooting in the churchyard during evening prayers. Such actions by church officials made it doubly hard to encourage the laity to reform.[29]

Surviving records justify complaints that a number of clerics played illegal or unseemly games. William Underne lost his position as rector of Wollaston, Northants., early in the reign, in part because of habitual gambling at dice and cards. Richard Senhouse, rector of Claughton, Lancs., was known as "a dicer and carder at such times as he should edify the flock, and draweth men's servants to play with him," thus undermining the moral and social order. Mr. Cliberye, vicar of Halstead, Essex, gained notoriety by approving card play. In the same county, William Drywood, rector of Downham, and Peter Williams, rector of Latchingdon, were presented for gambling, William Durdel, curate of Barnston, was accused of illegally bowling, and the rector of Thundersley allegedly played cards and dice "all the week long." In the diocese of Durham one cleric, Sir Ralph Smith, was accused in 1586 of playing dice, cards, and backgammon as well as siring a bastard daughter. Mr. Tampion, rector of Normanton, Rutland, was discovered playing backgammon on Sunday with a schoolmaster. William Redman's visitation of the diocese of Norwich in 1597 led to charges against Thomas Wilson, pluralist minister of Fulmodeston *cum* Croxton (et al.), and James Manninge, curate of Boughton, for playing unlawful games. Around 1581 Tristram Tildesley, minister at Rufford, Yorks., a suspected Catholic, was accused of playing bowls on a Sunday morning instead of conducting services. At Wells Cathedral in 1574, vicars choral were admonished for bringing scandal on the church by playing unlawful games in the town, including handball.[30]

The 1586 survey of the clergy by the Puritans includes at least seventeen charges involving illegal or inappropriate games, fourteen of them citing ministers in conservative Cornwall. Puritan disgust is apparent in these accusations: John Beale, vicar of Lanteglos by Fowey, "a common gamster, the best Wrastler in Cornewall"; Mr. Baylife, vicar of Bodmin, "a common gamster and a Pot-companion"; John Bernard, vicar of Issey, "a common dicer and burnt in the hand for felonie, and full of all iniquitie"; and Richard Williams, rector of Philleigh (Filley), "a good dicer and carder, both night and daie." In other areas Puritans singled out Mr. Cooke, minister at Plumstead, Norfolk, as a gambler, and Mr. Vaux, vicar of High Easter, Essex, as one who wasted time gambling at bowls, cards, and backgammon. Another was Mr. Thomison, vicar of Little Canfield, Essex, who was reputedly a gambler, alehouse hanunter, and loose liver. At least one of these clerics, the rector of Camborne, Cornwall, was in the ministerial vocation because "his father bought his benefice deer." The presence of such clergymen increased the difficulties of enforcing the statutory regulations on recreation and sharpened Puritan dissatisfaction with the condition of the church.[31]

Once again, the court failed to set a strict example for the citizens, though early in the reign William Alley, bishop elect of Exeter, had preached at court against moral evils, including dicing. Less than a year later, in February 1561, the queen allowed a wrestling match in her chapel. The Christmas season was passed at Hampton Court in 1572 in amusements like backgammon and dancing. According to Ben Johnson, Elizabeth gambled and played with loaded dice. To stay in her good graces, Roger Lord North allowed her to win up to £40 a month from him, and presumably other courtiers sustained deliberate losses. Gambling was common among the courtiers, and led to Sir Robert Cecil's loss of more than £800 in one night during the Christmas season of 1602. Against this background, Dering indicated Puritan dissatisfaction with the court when he asked: "If God had called them [princes, lords, and magistrates] to dycing and carding, to swearing and lying, to pryde and vanity, the mighty men of our dayes, how busily had they done their duty?"[32]

Gambling was commonplace among the upper levels of the aristocracy and the stakes increased substantially in the course of the age. George Talbot, earl of Shrewsbury, gambled in the Privy Chamber in 1568 and lost £100. Sir Francis Willoughby and his wife gambled in the 1570s, but the losses were relatively small (for example, 10s. by Mrs. Willoughby at Christmas 1572). Gambling losses are a regular item in the household book (1576-89) of Rober Lord North. In the years 1585-87 Henry Percy, earl of Northumberland, sustained a net loss of £443 gambling. The losses of Goerge Clifford, earl of Cumberland, who liked horse races and bowling matches, helped deplete his estate. Henry Lord Berkeley devoted substantial time to bowls, tennis, cards, and dice, and Edmund Lord Sheffield gambled at bowls. In the 1590s Henry Wriothesley, earl of Southampton, gambled in Paris, losing 18,000 crowns in one game of tennis and 3,000 crowns in a single card game. The gambling losses of Roger Manners, earl of Rutland, in the 1590s averaged between £1,000 and £1,500 a year, partly because he normally staked at least £100 on a horse race. Thomas Lord Scrope sustained heavy losses at Christmas 1597, and Anthony Bacon often amused himself with cards and dice. In the early 1600s, George Hastings, earl of Huntingdon, who complained about the depleted family estate, lost as much as £39 a day playing cards and dice. In one of the most bizarre gambling stakes of the period, John Lucas, master of the Court of Requests, bet his youngest son against a ward of the earl of Oxford and won. Gambling excesses moved Lady Jane, second wife of Henry Lord Berkeley, to stipulate in her 1601 household regulations that gentlemen could not "use great play neither at dice, tables, nor cards; for excess of gaming inpoverisheth your estate and causeth many disorders and contentions." Instead she urged archery and bowls for recreation. The prevalence of gambling among the aristocracy must have undermined attempts to reduce it, such as the Privy Council's order to the mayor of London in 1576 to reform the gambling houses in the City.[33]

With the court, the aristocracy, and some clergymen setting a poor example, the inability of the Elizabethan magistrates to repress unlawful games is understandable. During the age religious lines were not clearly drawn in this area, though most Puritan clergy had a stricter view of recreation than their Anglican counterparts. The appropriateness of bowls, tennis, backgammon, cards, and dice was a matter of debate within religious groups. Whereas gambling was usually denounced, some clergy, including the Puritans Fenner and Perkins, approved it under strict limitations. Considering the rising stakes in aristocratic circles and the plague of gambling houses in London, their tolerance is unexpected. As a general rule, enforcement of the statutes focused on those who provided for the unlawful games rather than the players. From the government's standpoint, keeping order was the central issue, not enforcing morality, which helps explain why the aristocracy and men of substance essentially had a free hand to select recreational activities. Abuses of that freedom dismayed the Puritans, and Dering for one extended his criticism to the court.

(2) Bear and Bull-Baiting and Cockfighting

For it was a sport alone of these beasts, to see the beare with his pinke eies leering after his enimies, the nimblenesse and wait of the dog to take his aduantage, and the force and experience of the beare againe to auoid the assaults.

John Stow[34]

What christen heart can take pleasure to see one poore beast to rent, teare, and kill another, and all for his foolish pleasure?

Philip Stubbes[35]

Although bear and bull-baiting and cockfighting were amusements with considerable popular appeal, protests arose from some clergy, particularly Puritans, against such cruelty. An early complaint came in a sermon by Henry Bedel, apparently an Anglican, Preached on 15 November 1571 at Christ's Hospital, London. Bedel was upset about the physical agony suffered by bears and dogs, and urged that the money saved by abolishing bear-baiting be used to assist the needy. In his 1583 treatise on the Ten Commandments, Babington categorized bear-wards as an unlawful vocation. Two years earlier, the visitation articles of Bishop Chaderton for the diocese of Chester condemned the profanation of churchyards by bear-wards. Anglicans, however, apparently accepted cockfights, though the statutes of the Manchester Grammar School prohibited them.[36]

The strongest Puritan censure of bear-baiting and cockfights came from Stubbes in 1583. Bear-baiting was viewed as not only an idle, vain pastime, but "a filthie, stinking, and lothsome game, a daungerous, & perilous exercyse wherein a man is in daunger of his life euery minut." Stubbes was troubled about the gambling that accompanied this activity and about holding baitings on the sabbath; he sneered at "these Gentlemen of such reputation" who attended them. The special houses, decorated with banners, for cockfights were denounced as well as the gambling, swearing, brawling, drinking, and whoring that accompanied them. Eight years later, Perkins castigated bear-baiting and cockfighting, but sanctioned bull-baiting (essentially a rural pastime) because it has its "vse" and was decreed by civil authority. With respect to the former, however, "the Antipathie and crueltie, which one beast sheweth to another, is the fruit of our rebellion against God." At the end of the age Estey deplored bear and bull-baiting because they were dangerous.[37]

The concern about danger was not idle. The 1583 tragedy at the Bear Garden occurred at a bear-baiting, and Stow observed that this was a warning to those who delighted in cruelty to beasts. A more direct example occurred in February 1602, when Sir Jarvis Clifton (created Lord Clifton in 1608) took his son to a bear-baiting in Nottinghamshire. When the bear broke loose and pursued the boy into a gallery, Sir Jarvis attacked the bear with his rapier, but not in time to save his son's life.[38]

Holding such amusements on the sabbath made them doubly offensive to the godly. In April 1581 an offended Cambridge proctor had considerable difficulty trying to stop a bear baiting during service time at Chesterton. The Lancashire quarter sessions records include several presentments for bear-beating on the sabbath, one of which involved William Radclyffe, a gentleman of Manchester. Such violations moved Anthony Bridgeman to appeal to the queen in February 1589 to enforce the ban on bear-baiting on Sundays.[39]

To terminate bear-baiting would have been an insurmountable task, for the queen and her courtiers themselves kept bear-wards as a visible manifestation of their rank. There were, of course, other bear-wards, but since they tended to be undisciplined vagrants, attempts to suppress them were made. The borough of Leicester decreed in 1582 that money would be paid only to bear-wards of the queen or the lords of the Privy Council. Sir Robert Dudley, Sir Fulke Greville, and William Lord Vaux (a Catholic) patronized bear-wards; Lord Vaux's bear-ward was responsible for the disturbances at Chesterton in 1581. These aristocratically sponsored bear-wards entertained throughout the kingdom: Dudley's was at Beverley, Yorks., in 1562, and Vaux's at Bristol in 1559 and Ipswich in 1579. Henry Lord Berkeley was particularly attracted to cockfighting.[40]

As in other cases, the queen and her court provided an example that must have caused Puritans some discomfiture. Elizabeth had had her own bear-ward since she was six, hence it was no surprise that she patronized baitings throughout her reign. It was a form of entertainment to amuse foreign ambassadors, as in May 1559 when bulls and bears were baited for the French ambassador. The Privy Council and courtiers normally were present, as often was an appreciative populace, as when she entertained the Dutch ambassador in May 1586. "For vpon a greene verie spatious and large, where thousands might stand and behold with good contentment, there bearebaiting and bulbaiting (tempered with other merie disports) were exhibited; whereat it can not be spoken of what pleasure the people tooke." Entertainment of the queen during a progress sometimes included bear-baiting, as at Killingworth Castle, Warws., in 1575. An ape, a bull, and bears were baitied for the queen's amusement in May 1600, and bear-baiting was part of the Christmas celebrations at court in 1602.[41]

Danger, sabbath violations, cruelty to animals, and accompanying vices such as gambling made baiting bears and bulls and cock-fighting objectionable to some clergy, particularly Puritans. Realistically they could hope for little more than a cessation of such events on Sundays, for the popularity of baitings with the queen made any general prohibition out of the question.

(3) The Theater

Folly so bleareth mens eyes, that they take playes to be profounde Scripture.

William Rankins[42]

In plaies it fares as in bookes, vice cannot be reproued, except it be discouered.

Henry Chettle[43]

The popular conception of Puritan hostility to the theater, coupled with the implicit idea of Anglican approval, is misleading. Puritans were more prone to write about plays than were Anglicans, but no clear line of demarcation can be drawn between them. Some Anglicans, such as Sutcliffe, firmly defended the theater, and Mr. Phillips, minister at Carleton and Claxton, Norf., acted in interludes. Peter Martyr was cited by Leonard Wright in defense of attending plays for mental and physical refreshment and Dr. Henry Parry's father, the chancellor of Salisbury, sponsored plays in his home and permitted his son to act in them. Yet other Anglicans viewed the theater with the displeasure customarily associated with Puritans. Parker "never delighted in plays and jests" and Grindal wrote diaparagingly to Cecil of "these *histriones,* common players, who now daily, but specially on holy-days, set up bills, whereunto the youth resorteth excessively, and there taketh infection: besides that God's word by their impure mouths is profaned and turned into scoffs." Grindal therefore urged the government to issue a proclamation to prohibit all plays for a year within a three-mile radius of London.[44]

Other Anglicans were similarly dismayed by the theater. George Abbot rejected acting as a lawful vocation because it benefitted neither church nor commonwealth. The future bishop of Llandaff, Exeter, and Worcester, Gervase Babington, was of like persuasion, and castigated "prophane & wanton stage playes or interludes [as] . . . an occasion . . . of adulterie and vncleanenesse by gesture, by speech, by conueyances, and deuises to attaine to so vngodly desires." Because of the immoral examples in such plays, Babington opposed their performance even in private homes, but implicitly he accepted moral plays performed by amateurs. Plays on the sabbath angered Whetstone, as did their abuse at other times by "scurilytie and vnchaste conueiance." Visitation articles reveal concern about the performance of plays and interludes in churches and churchyards, though not elsewhere. In 1584, guardians of the church at Dunstew, Oxon., were cited for holding plays and interludes in the church.[45] Thus Anglican attitudes toward the theater ranged from approbation to diapproval, with a middle group concerned primarily with abuses involving immoral content and performances on the sabbath or in holy places.

Essentially, Elizabethan Puritans can be categorized into two or three groups according to their attitude to the theater, though none defended it as did Wright and Sutton. First, a few Puritans were concerned only with prohibiting plays on the sabbath. This was Fenner's position, and it was reflected in an anonymous manuscript (possibly Puritan) in the Lansdowne Collection calling for the prohibition of all plays on Sundays and (until after evening prayer) on holy days. The same document proposed the abolition of all dramatic companies except the queen's, which prudence dictated must survive. In a sermon at Paul's Cross in 1578, Stockwood refused to debate whether plays were tolerable, preferring to concentrate on banning the theater on the sabbath, when people thronged to plays. His general tone suggests that he would have been happy to see all plays and interludes involving immoral matter prohibited. "Flocks of . . . wyld youths of both sexes, resorting to Enterludes, where both by liuely gesture, and voices, there are allurements vnto whordom, . . . come awaye . . . inflamed with concupiscence." In addition to providing immoral examples, plays wasted money. By his reckoning, eight plays in London performed weekly for a year brought in £2,000. The following year at Paul's Cross he renewed his attack on "filthie stage playes," particularly on the sabbath.[46]

The views of Fenner and Stockwood were probably compatible with those of a group of Puritans who condemned immoral plays, though not the stage altogether. A principal advocate of this position was John Northbrooke, who in 1579 castigated the theater for providing an example of vice, filthy speech, promiscuity, untruth, idleness, rebellion, and treason. Even religious subjects ought not be portrayed, because of the tendency to mix them with irreligious motifs. Plays were objectionable to him, as to Stockwood, because of the wasted money, which he proposed should be spent on the needy and education. Yet Northbrooke did not want a total ban on plays, for he saw value in comedies, chiefly in Latin, in the schools, so long as no ribaldry or improper language was used, no profit was made, and no sumptuous apparel was worn.[47]

Stubbes has hitherto been depicted as a total opponent of the stage, but his position was a more modest one that focused on purging abuses, though he censured plays for encouraging idleness, enticing people from church services, and fostering vice. Moreover,

seeing, that Playes were first inuented by the Deuil, practised by the heathen gentiles, and dedicat to their false ydols, Goddes and Goddesses: as the howse, stage and apparell, to *Venus:* the musicke, to *Appollo:* the penning, to *Minerua,* and the Muses: the action and pronuntiation to *Mercurie* and ye rest, it is more than manifest, that they are no fit exercyses for a Christen Man to follow.

Even when plays treated religious themes he found them sacriligious because of their scoffing manner. In tragedies, he objected to the emphasis on wrath, incest, homicide, and cruelty, and criticized comedy for playing on adultery, bawdry, and love. Despite these strident objections, however, Stubbes found acceptable those plays conducive to godly mental recreation and that provided good examples for Christian living and did not profane the sabbath.

Playes, tragedies and enterluds in their own nature, are not onely of great ancientie, but also very honest and very commendable exercyses, being vsed and practised in most Christian common weales, as which containe matter . . . both of doctrine, erudition, good example and wholsome instruction. And may be vsed in tyme and place conuenient, as conducible to example of life and reformation of mancrs.

Stubbes proposed the reform—not the abolition—of the theater.[48]

Stubbes' position was akin to that of Stephen Gosson, the former playwright who in 1579 expressed remorse that his works were still being performed. The Puritan convert was critical of actors because of their propensity to idleness, excessive apparel, and haughty demeanor. Audience behavior, too, troubled him, particularly the fine attire and promiscuity. Because of the moral depravity of the theater, play-going should be avoided. "Being pensiue at home, if you go to Theaters to driue away fancies, it is as good Physike, as for the ache of your head too knocke out your brains." Yet not all plays deserved condemnation, and he provided, as it were, a critic's guide to the London theater that praised *The Blacksmith's Daughter, Cataline's Conspiracy, The Jews,* and *Ptolemy.* Such plays, he judged, were morally instructive and free of amorous talk and gestures.[49]

Most Elizabethan Puritans, judging from the printed word, were more extreme, though the harsh position developed relatively late in the period and paralleled the rising anger over lax sabbath enforcement. An outbreak of the plague in 1577 moved Thomas White to lash out briefly in a sermon at Paul's Cross against plays (which he called sinful) and sumptuous theaters as monuments of London's prodigality. Six years later, John Field called for the total abolition of plays and interludes. The attack intensified in 1587 when William Rankins, probably a Puritan, castigated actors for monstrously presenting prodigious vanity, inspiring pride and lechery, and living in lust. "Players by sticking of their bils in London, defile the streetes with their infectious filthines." They blaspheme God as they call on Mohammed and the classical deities, and sacrifice to idols in their productions. Plays, said Rankins, are contradictory to the work of God. In this spirit, Henry Holland called in 1593 for the theaters—the temples of Cupid and Venus, the palaces of Bacchus and Satan, and the nunneries of whoredom—to be cast down because they corrupted London youth. Bownde's treatise on the sabbath also includes a condemnation of plays.[50]

Puritan hostility to play-acting continued to the end of the age. In a book published in 1599 but written six years earlier, John Rainolds condemned plays because they wasted time and money, violated the moral law's prohibition against men wearing female garb, and inculcated in actors a propensity to imitate the evil of their characters in real life. Vaughan concluded that plays were intolerable in a well-governed commonwealth, in part because they mocked God, encouraged the audience to laugh at evil, wasted time, and contained vanity and idle speech. Perkins especially attacked the lascivious content of plays, the representation of females by males, and the use of money for unlawful vocations. It pleased him that traditional religious pageants were declining, for "they were nothing els, but either the whole or part of the historie of the Bible turned into a Play." It was undoubtedly a Puritan—"a plaine plodding fellowe" from Queens' College, Cambridge—who reiterated in a sermon at St. Clement Danes, London, in December 1602 that acting is an unlawful vocation. Richard Rogers and John Dod repeated common Puritan arguments. Thus in the last years of the queen's reign, the more moderate Puritan position that had advocated a reform of the stage largely gave way to that of extremists, who wanted to abolish it.[51]

Anglican and Puritan concern with the abuses of the theater was not without some justification. In London plays were so popular that they were used in conjunction with such civic matters as the farewell banquets of outgoing sheriffs and livery-company dinners. The large crowds apparently contributed to the spread of the plague. In February 1564, Grindal wanted plays banned for a year not only because they attracted the "idle sorte off people," but because of the threat of the plague. Sir Nicholas Bacon was similarly concerned. In January 1575 the Common Council and the lord mayor, Sir James Hawes, worried about spreading infection in the theaters, but their emphasis was on the religious abuses. Because people skipped church to be at the theater for Sunday matinees, religion and the commonwealth, the Council felt, were endangered. The Common Council ordered the cessation of interludes except in private homes on special occasions such as weddings. Actors retaliated by petitioning the Privy Council to intervene.[52]

The Privy Council was actively involved in regulating the theater in the City, particularly after the erection of the first permanent playhouse in the suburbs in 1576. In 1578, the Council ordered the lord mayor to permit the company of an Italian (Dronsiano) to perform before the Lenten season began, and the following year it banned plays during Lent. Whenever the plague threatened, the Council suspended the theater. In December 1581 the Council insisted that plays would not be allowed on Sundays, though performances were acceptable on holy days after evening prayer. The following spring, the lord mayor was ordered to examine comedies and interludes to prevent the corruption of manners. Censors were to approve only plays "fitte to yeld honest recreation and no example of evell." Clearly the concern expressed in religious circles found some receptivity among Council members. Nevertheless "certaine outrages and disorders" continued to be associated with the theater, as the Council observed in May 1587 when plays were suspended until the autumn. The Council had difficulty enforcing such suspensions, and the justices of the peace were ordered to take appropriate action. In 1589 members of the dramatic companies of Charles, Lord Howard of Effingham, and Lord Strange were imprisoned for disobeying proclamations of the lord mayor and Burhgley. The Council informed Whitgift in November 1589 that actors presented inappropriate matters of theolgy and state, and he was asked to nominate a person learned in divinity to join with the master of the revels and a nominee of the lord mayor to censor plays. Actors who disregarded these censors faced permanent expulsion from the acting profession.[53]

Other towns had disorders associated with the theater. To curtail wandering actors, the borough of Leicester in 1582 ordered that only the dramatic companies of the queen and the lords of the Privy Council could be paid or allowed to perform at the town hall. When, in March 1584, the mayor refused to permit the earl of Worcester's company of licensed players to perform, they marched through Leicester with trumpets and drums, condemning the mayor. Only after they expressed remorse did the mayor allow them to perform. As a large town, Norwich attracted numerous actors, with often undesirable results. In 1571 "for wante of viewers and lookers abowt, the victualling houses were stuffed with players and dronkerdes yt so tended the drynke all daye that they could not enclyne to woorke." In some towns, such as Manningtree, Essex, such inconveniences were tolerated as the price of annual fairs. The Devon justices in

1595, however, prohibited the Sunday market at East Budleigh because of attendant abuses, including plays. Some towns had to determine whether or not to continue the traditional religious pageants and plays. The famous Chester mysteries were retained, but in Lincoln the guild plays ceased. The Common Council ordered in 1564 that a play with a biblical theme be presented each summer, but after performances of *Tobit* in 1564, 1566, and 1568, there were no more plays. The town of Malden, Essex, stopped its religious plays early in the age, but periodically allowed performances by traveling companies. Essex towns under Puritan influence discouraged visits by professional actors. The Corpus Christi plays began to decline in Newcastle-on-Tyne c. 1578, and in York the Corpus Christi plays stopped in 1584.[54]

The religious complaints were joined to other reasons for censuring the stage. Late in 1596 Elizabeth, dowager Lady Russell, George Carey, Lord Hunsdon, and twenty-nine other residents of Blackfriars, London, petitioned the Privy Council to prevent the establishment of a new playhouse by Richard Burbage, a friend of Shakespeare, because it would cause overcrowding and unsanitary conditions. It was felt that lewd and vagrant persons would be attracted to the theater and the noise would disturb church services. The acting sometimes did get out of hand, as Philip Gawdy described to his father in November 1587:

My L. Admyrall his men and players having a devyse in ther playe to tye one of their fellowes to a poste and so to shoote him to deathe, having borrowed their Callyvers [large pistols] one of the players handes swerved his peece being charged with bullett missed the fellowe he aymed at and killed a chyld, and a woman great with chyld forthwith, and hurt an other man in the head very soore.

Some ten years later, at the Swan, an actor was accidentally stabbed through the eye and killed during a performance.[55] Thus the social problems created by the Elizabethan theater, coupled with religious objections, motivated many attempts to reform or curtail the theater, sometimes even terminating traditional religious plays.

Any attempt to reform or abolish the theater, however, was frustrated by the considerable number of dramatic companies with aristocratic patronage and the court's devotion to plays. At least sixty-one Elizabethan peers patronized dramatic companies at some point during the age, and these included men of varying religious persuasions, such as William Lord Vaux, a Catholic, Francis Russell, earl of Bedford, Robert, third Lord Rich, and Ambrose Dudley, earl of Warwick, all Puritans. Numerous gentry, including Sir Henry Lee,

Sir William Holles, Sir Thomas Cecil, Sir James Crofts, and Sir Ralph Sadler, patronized companies. Moreover, at least twenty Elizabethan towns, including London, Durham, Coventry, Hull, Rochdale (where Puritan influence was strong), and Tavistock, had companies, as did various Elizabethan schools, including Merchant Taylors', Westminster, St. Paul's, and King's (Coventry).[56] With this interest and support, even imposing censorship on plays would have been onerous for a government with more pressing concerns.

As it had for holy day festivities, recreation, and bull and bear-baiting, the court provided an example that the Puritans must have found increasingly objectionable as their attitude to the theater hardened in the last decades of the era. During her rule Elizabeth patronized three companies and attended performances at court by various aristocratic and school groups. The players of the earl of Leicester, for example, performed at court every Christmas season from 1572-73 to 1582-83, except for 1581-82. Privy Council records regularly report payments to dramatic companies for court performances. Charges for plays and masques for the court at Windsor and Richmond for the period 1562-65 amounted to the substantial sum of £444 11s. 5¾ d., and four plays at court in 1590-91 entailed expenses of £39 15s. The queen liked to have plays on the twelve days of Christmas, New Year's, Shrove-tide, St. Stephen's Day, and Candlemas. Performers must have been sensible that plays should have appropriate content, especially after the queen commanded a performance to cease on New Year's eve, 1559. Elizabeth periodically attended plays away from the court, such as at Westminster School (where Princess Cecilia of Sweden joined her in 1566). Even the royal presence did not always guarantee decent behavior by the audience: When Mulcaster's students performed in the Merchant Taylors' hall in 1573 "the tumultious disordered persons repayringe hither" were so ill-behaved that plays were banned from the hall. People were aware of Elizabeth's love of the stage, and in 1575 she was petitioned by the residents of Coventry to allow resumption of performances of a play about the Danes in England. Ministers "sumwhat too sour in preaching awey theyr pastime," undoubtedly led by the Puritan Thomas Lever, were responsible for its suppression, but the people of Coventry thought the play was "without ill exampl of mannerz, papistry, or any superstition: and elz did so occupy the heads of a number, that likely inoough would haue had woorz meditationz." I have found no record of Elizabeth's response.[57]

Attacks on the theater, then, were not the exclusive province of the Puritans. Nor were the Puritans of uniform persuasion about the appropriate remedy. In the course of the age there was a growing conviction among Puritans that a simple reform of the contents of plays and the behavior of theater-goers was insufficient, and the hue and cry grew for abolition. Anglicans were divided, with men such as Babington and George Abbot taking a hostile attitude to the stage, while others defended it. The popularity of the stage, as evidenced by the large number of aristocratic patrons of varying religious beliefs, was not undermined to any appreciable degree by the religious criticism, though the reformers did win some victories, such as the suppression of the Danish play at Coventry. The abuses of the theater Protestant critics cited were often real, as the queen undoubtedly realized, but the critics were impotent to effect sweeping reform. The growing insistence on abolition rather than reformation may, in fact, have grown out of a sense of frustration that the latter was beyond their reach. The extreme Puritan position apparently was born of a realization that unless the theater were abolished, moral depravity would reign.

(4) Dancing

Nowe dauncing shewes hir good effectes,
to hyde her lewde conceiptes,
And Joyfull hymnes will daunce a dumpe
to worcke some depe deceiptes.

Anonymous[58]

What incouenience cometh by wanton dancing.

Geneva Bible[59]

Dancing was part of traditional English life, whether on special occasions, weddings, and local festivals, or merely as casual amusement and recreation. Dances were held on the village green and in the long galleries of aristocratic homes, in the regal atmosphere of the court and on the dusty floors of taverns. For the sophisticated, it was the age of the galliard, the pavanne, the coranto, the cinquepace, and the volte. A Brandenburg jurist visiting England in 1598 observed that the people excelled in dancing and music. From Whitsuntide to Midsummer, morris dancers, usually in groups of six and accompanied by a fool, toured neighboring villages to raise funds for the church, which might assist by donating money for morris bells. On the Isle of Wight in the 1570s, Sir Edward Horsey and his mistress capped dinners for the local gentry by dancing "after a poor tabor and pipe from Heasley House to the foot of the hill." To be an Elizabethan, it might seem, was to love to dance.[60]

Although Puritan hostility to dancing is expected, evidence also exists of some Anglican opposition. Bishop Cooper asserted that dancing was an impious practice and a wicked way for courtiers and gentry to occupy themselves, though he made no observation regarding lesser folk. In his exposition of the Ten Commandments, Babington depicted dancing as a vain pastime because of its enticements to promiscuity, and cited Calvin to prove it. Although dancing was used in biblical times, it was, he argued, "euer a sober modest notion, with some song vsually to Gods praise, and men by themselues, women by themselues." John Walsall was less severe, condemning only dancing that was wanton or undertaken on the sabbath. Bedel urged Londoners to divert the money they spent on dancing to aid the poor, though he made no moral judgment of dancing itself. Those who danced professionally were, according to George Abbot, in an unlawful vocation, though he had no opposition to recreational dancing after vocational responsibilities had been fulfilled.[61]

The Puritan attack on dancing was launched in 1574, the year a sermon by the martyr John Bradford was published that criticized dancing. That year Edward Hake of New Windsor condemned those forms of dancing

wherein the sences are altogither captivated and made subiect to vnlawfull fantasies, to vnreasonable thoughtes, and wicked deuises. . . . What shaking, what bragging, what wringing of handes, what whisperings, what treading vpon the toes, what vncleanly handlings, gropings, kissings, and a very kindling of lecherye, doth their assosiate that trade and occupation of daunsing?

What Hake saw as a parental concern that daughters attain skill in dancing, at the expense of religious instruction, and the concomitant desire to deck them in costly apparel, was reprehensible to him. Two years later, Dering complained about wasting time in riotous dancing at night. So far, Puritan criticism was essentially concerned with the abuse of dancing, but in 1577 Christopher Shutte issued a broad condemnation of dancing as conducive to impurity and lust. Gosson made the same complaint in 1579, though he accepted dancing in the manner prescribed by Peter Martyr, namely when undertaken privately to improve health and agility. In like fashion, Northbrooke insisted that mixed dancing was improper, as was any dancing that required more than minimal sober movement. More active and mixed dancing fostered fornication, adultery, blasphemy, and brawling.[62]

In the 1580s, Puritans continued to condemn mixed dancing as conducive to promiscuity while defending the simplicity of Hebrew dance forms. David's dance in 2 Samuel 6, for example, was cited by Samuel Bird as an act of abasement, in contrast to the proud displays of Elizabethan dancing. That some modern dancing was done to tunes that accompanied ribald words also was objectionable. Bird criticized the masque because it used wanton dances and inappropriate speech. Stubbes' sustained attack on dancing in 1583 reiterated the usual arguments but maintained the distinction between immoral modern dancing and dancing "vsed in a mans priuat-chamber, or howse for his Godly solace, and recreation in the feare of GOD." The more strenuous forms of dancing were unacceptable because of the physical risk; if he can be believed, some Elizabethans broke their legs dancing. Like the Anglican George Abbot, Stubbes repudiated professional dancing as a lawful vocation. Teaching young people to dance, he asserted, encouraged a boy to be effeminate or even a transvestite, and a girl to be a whore and a filthy speaker.[63]

To the end of the age, the Puritan position remained the same. Mixed dancing was out, but modest dancing at suitable times for recreation or mental relaxation was acceptable. The principal Puritan objection to comtemporary dancing was moral, though scattered attacks were made regarding its physical danger, waste of time, and occurrence on the sabbath. As much as anything, it was the association of mixed dancing with immoral behavior that resulted in its condemnation; some critics were concerned too because people absented themselves from church to dance.[64] Some Anglicans, such as Babington and probably Walsall, agreed with Puritans that dancing endangered morals.

In his treatise on education, Mulcaster defended dancing as physical exercise to strengthen the hips and feet, loosen stiff joints, remove kidney stones, and aid digestion. "Daunsing beside the warmth, driueth awaye numnesse, & certaine palsies, comforteth the stomacke, being cumbred with weaknes of digestion, & confluence of raw humours, strengtheneth weake hippes, fainting legges, [and] freatishing [weary] feete." He admitted, however, that excessive dancing could produce physical impairment and make one a servant to carnal desire. Like religious critics, he restricted only the abuses of dancing, but unlike the Puritans he apparently tolerated mixed dancing. Bullein's medical handbook similarly sanctioned dancing for the sake of health—and for pleasure.[65]

Cases of dancing abuses by the clergy are rare, at least in the surviving evidence. Tristram Tildesley, the suspected Catholic minister at Rufford and Marsden, Yorks., "upon Sondaies and hollidaies hath daunced emongest light and youthful companie both men and women at weddings, drynkings and rish-bearings." On one occasion, he wantonly kissed a maid, people were offended, and swords drawn.

the wife of William Lynche, rector of Beauchamp Roding, Essex, achieved notoriety by dancing, drinking, and kissing at the local ale-house. Curiously, however, the 1586 Puritan survey of the ministry does not single out clerics for immoral dancing. Nevertheless visitation articles inquired about clergy who danced, suggesting imprudent ministerial practices. Barnes' injunctions for the diocese of Durham prohibited clergy from dancing. There were also attempts to prevent dancing in churches and churchyards, an offence for which guardians of churches at South Stoke and Bourton, Oxon., were cited in 1584.[66]

Although clergy were expected to refrain from dancing, it was an essential skill in aristocratic and courtly circles. In February 1603, when Mr. Tyndale wrote to Michael Hicks, the late Lord Burghley's secretary, about placing his fifteen-year-old son in Hicks' service, the boy was reputed to be skilled in dancing as well as in Latin, French, writing, and music. Richard Senhouse's instructions to his son Simon as the latter entered the service of Anthony Bacon advised that he use his spare time for reading, studying French or Italian, music, and dancing "to keepe you from idlenes & to gaine knowledge. Which wilbe a meane, you may live ye better heareafter."[67]

Once again, the court was the center of activity that Puritans in particular found abhorrent. Throughout her reign, Elizabeth enjoyed mixed dancing, and her progresses regularly included dances with courtiers and hosts. In Warwickshire in the summer of 1575, a sab-bath was spent at morning services in the parish church but the after-noon was devoted to "excelent muzik, of sundry swet instruments and in dauncing of Lordes & Ladiez, and other woorshipfull degrees, vt-tered with such liuely agilitee & commendabl[e] grace." The twelve days of Christmas featured dances at court, such as that in 1600 when the queen danced for the entertainment of an Orsini duke. Elizabeth was attracted to May Day dances, including those at Highgate in 1601 and Lewisham in 1602. Advancing age did not assuage her appetite for dancing, and at fifth-eight she danced six galliards in the morning and more in the evening. During the Christmas festivities of 1599 the Spanish ambassador reported that "the head of the Church of England and Ireland was to be seen in her old age dancing three of four gal-liards." It is hard to ascertain how much criticism the courtly festivi-ties prompted, but a retrospective observation by Lady Anne Clifford in the fall of 1603 suggests it was widespread: "Now there was much talk of a mask which the Queen had at Winchester, and how all the ladies about the court had gotten such ill names that it was grown a scandalous place, and the Queen herself was much fallen from her former greatness and reputation she had in the world."[68]

(5) Music

Good wits by hearing of soft musick are rather dulled then sharpned, and made apt to all wantonnes and sinne.

Philip Stubbes[69]

The Scripture is a buckeler good, in
Musickes right behoofe.

Nicholas Whight[70]

The principal area of controversy with respect to music in the Elizabethan era involved its use in religious services. From the outset attempts were made to keep music as simple as possible, as in the 1559 Injunctions that sanctioned singing hymns before morning and evening prayers if the words were distinguishable. In the lower house of Convocation, a minority including Alexander Nowell and Thomas Sampson proposed to abolish organ playing and "curious" singing. In February 1562 the reformers failed by only one vote (58 to 59) to remove organs from churches. The new homilies issued the following year recognized that even the moderate simplicity that prevailed in Anglican worship was too austere for conservatives who favored an elaborate liturgy: "Alas gossip, what shall wee now doe at Church, since all the Saints are taken away, since all the goodly sights wee were wont to haue, are gone, since wee cannot heare the like piping, chaunting, and playing vpon the organes that we could before."[71]

According to an anonymous manuscript in the British Library, Puritan pressure caused a decline of music in cathedral churches commencing about 1568, particularly as money for stipends for singing was diverted to lectures in keeping with the Puritan emphasis on the spoken word. As a result of Puritan hostility to organ and choral music, people allegedly remained outside the church, deriding the service until the sermon began.[72] This was precisely the opposite explanation for hostility to Anglican services offered in the homily on prayer. With respect to music, the *via media* met with dissatisfaction from traditionalists and advanced reformers alike.

Some attention was given to music in Protestant worship in the Admonition controversy. In 1572 Wilcox and Field condemned organ music and "curious" singing as popish, asserting that Anglicans "toss[ed] the psalms in most places like tennis-balls." Choristers and organists were criticized for idleness, and the royal chapel was castigated as an enticement to superstition. Cartwright countenanced singing two Psalms in a religious service, provided the tunes were simple and the words understandable to those who, because they could not read, were unable to join in the singing. Singing, in effect, was intended to be pedagogical. Singing Psalms contrapuntally was objectionable because the words were more difficult to understand, and worshippers were supposed to sing Psalms in their entirety. Whitgift's defense stressed that singing had biblical precedent (e.g. David) and was used in all Reformed churches. Essentially, singing, said Whitgift, is a matter of *adiaphora* and therefore the decision rests with the bishops as to whether or not it is profitable for the people. He agreed that singing must be understandable, though he rejected the concept that only congregational singing is valid; parishioners can sing "in heart" while choristers perform. Antiphonal singing is not objectionable, for it has the sanction of Basil the Great. The debate thus focused on the extent and nature of congregational participation in church worship, and whether music was to be used essentially for pedagogy or adoration.[73]

Puritans were not opposed to all music in worship, though they feared that if it were abused, common people would find a difficulty in distinguishing between Catholicism and Protestantism. Services, warned Edward Hake, could be profaned "by Musicke (as in tyme of Popery) namely by over curious, yea, . . . over tragicall dismembring not onely of wordes but of letters and sillables in the holy Psalmes and Anthemes." To Puritans a cardinal fault of Catholicism was the unintelligible texts of the liturgy that rendered much of the service incomprehensible. In addition to being intelligible, Puritans insisted that texts either be taken verbatim from Scripture or be harmonious with biblical principles. Northbrooke worried that people might be drawn to church simply because of the music, and if this happened he favored abolishing all music in public worship. The Puritans thus would have restricted music to a pedagogical tool—a means to glorify God through edifying the worshipper.[74]

Although in 1592 Sutcliffe sought to widen the breach between Anglicans and Puritans by incorrectly asserting that "nothing doeth more displease the puritans, then church-musicke, and singing," a number of Anglicans did hold narrow views on music in worship. In 1564, Parker told the French ambassador that "our musick drowned not the principal regard of our prayer," and his Psalter contained lines a Puritan could embrace:

> Depart, ye songs lascivious,
>> from lute, from harpe depart:
> Give place to Psalmes most vertuous,
>> and solace there your harte.

In February 1567 Grindal and Robert Horne informed colleagues in Geneva that they opposed organs in church. Four years later, Horne abolished the post of organist at Winchester College, banned contrapuntal music in Winchester Cathedral, and insisted that the words of songs be intelligible to worshippers. Sutcliffe admitted that songs in church should be modest and textually distinct, and in the same year (1592) Turnbull asserted that "we must sing in most plaine and modest manner, and so as shall serue best for edification," with the emphasis on the text rather than the melody.[75]

In contrast to this rather strict Anglican view of church music, Hooker and others expressed a more liberal attitude. For Hooker, music must be appropriate to the text and not distract from its meaning, though music conducive to affection (for God) if not edification must also be allowed. There is "an admirable facility which music hath to express and represent to the mind, more inwardly than any other sensible means, the very standing, rising, and falling, the very steps and inflections every way, the turns and varieties of all passions whereunto the mind is subject." From a perspective less psychological and more musical, John Case in 1586 repudiated Puritan views of music. Contrapuntal music was conducive to worship, in his judgment, because phrases were repeated, and the congregation was already familiar with the text. Thus music put parishioners in mind of their maker, lured people to church, and facilitated memorization of texts. Music came under the category of adiaphora, but it was nevertheless to be used soberly that men might worship God with body as well as soul. This seems to have been the attitude of Whittingham, who spent much of his own funds on song schools, for "concerning singing in the church [he] did so far allow of that as he was very careful to provide the best songs and anthems that could be got of the Queen's Chapel, to furnish the choir withall, himself being skilful in music."[76] For these Anglicans music had an intrinsic beauty that favored worship offered by the whole man in contrast to the narrower, more intellectual outlook of the Puritans and stricter Anglicans.

One of the most irksome problems in providing acceptable church music was the behavior of vicars choral. Grindal's 1571 injunctions for York Minster ordered vicars choral to abstain from evil company, unlawful games, and idleness. They were required to possess a Latin or English Bible, attend services daily, give special attention to the divinity lectures, and undergo examinations on the latter at least once a month by the chancellor or reader. The records of Wells Cathedral provide examples of the kinds of inappropriate behavior to which some vicars choral were prone. In 1574 Wells vicars were warned that those who frequented the town and played unlawful games, including handball, would be suspended and their allowances forfeited for a week, with harsher punishments for repeat offenses, because such actions brought scandal to the cathedral. In the 1570s two vicars choral were in trouble several times, one of them for bribery and uttering threats against the sub-dean. In 1589 a vicar choral was suspended for solemnizing a clandestine marriage in a private house in Wells. In the decade 1591-1601, vicars choral were charged with such offenses as keeping an alehouse in the cathedral close, getting a maid pregnant, committing adultery and fornication, and gambling. In 1600, they were admonished to frequent taverns less and church services more. On 6 March 1602, it was ordered that "every canon resident [of Wells] shall refuse to receave his vicare chorall and to admitt hym to his hows, till he doth reforme hym self and become conformable to the orders and government of this church, as he ought." When Bancroft visited St. Paul's London, in 1598, there were complaints that vicars choral came to services late and talked loudly during the singing of metrical Psalms. Under these circumstances, it is perhaps understandable that some reformers questioned traditional church music.[77]

In the area of secular music little overt criticism was voiced in Anglican circles, though Fleming condemned "light songs and sonets" and Turnbull disapproved "immodest and vnchast musicke, whereby the adulterous hearts of men and women are set on fire and inflamed." Turnbull urged his readers to sing hymns and Psalms. There was concern, as manifested in the 1582 visitation articles for the archdeaconry of Middlesex, about minstrels who played in churches or churchyards, but in general Anglicans seemed untroubled about contemporary music. Case probably represented the typical Anglican when he observed that music was not necessary in the manner that food and clothing were, but like the fine apparel of gentlemen it contributed to "the comlinesse of life" and kept people from idleness and inordinate pleasure.[78]

In Puritan circles, however, there was an outpouring of hostility against profane, light, and vain songs, in part because they contravened the seventh commandment by seducing people to promiscuity. "Sweet Musick," wrote Stubbes, "at the first delighteth the eares, but afterward corrupteth and depraueth the minde, making it weake, and quasie, and inclined to all licenciousnes of lyfe whatsoeuer." Music, like dancing, encouraged boys to be effeminate and girls promiscuous. Significantly, the Puritan objections extended to alluring melodies as well as ribald texts. Sweet harmony and "smoothe" melodies were feared for their ability to enflame concupiscence. Another objection to secular music came from Bownde, who worried that singing ballads led people to ignore Psalm singing. A number of Puritans objected to pipers and minstrels as vagabonds who cozened men of money and enticed people from church. Stockwood urged the High Commission to act, preferably to ban minstrels altogether.[79]

Such criticism notwithstanding, all Puritans did not reject secular music. Fenner, for one, approved music to refresh body and mind, and Northbrooke found music acceptable to praise aristocrats (especially at feasts), express joy, engage in recreation, or use at weddings, if it was moderate and did not entice to lust. Northbrooke would not tolerate minstrels because they were loiterers and idle persons. Even Stubbes approved music used in private to "driue away the fantasies of idle thoughts, solicitude, care, sorrowe and such other perturbations and molestations of the minde, the only ends wherto true Musick tends." Cartwright sanctioned music of the harp and lute, but associated bagpipes with "country mirth," an attitide of which Whitgift disapproved. Among the Puritan laity, Lady Grace Mildmay played the lute and set five-part songs to music, while Lady Margaret Hoby played the alpherion and sang. Puritans were not opposed to secular music *per se*, though they were more concerned than their Anglican counterparts with the dangers of alluring melodies, ribald texts, and wandering minstrels.[80]

Puritan acceptance of secular music was rendered essential by its increasing use in the educational curriculum. Although music was omitted from William Kempe's 1588 treatise on *The Education of Children in Learning,* Mulcaster argued that those who objected to music because it enticed to lust and frivolity and bewitched the mind with melodies failed to distinguish between its proper use and its abuse. Girls in particular should learn to play and sing, partly to enhance their cleverness; Mulcaster wanted them to continue musical activities as adults. James Whitelocke, who studied under Mulcaster at Merchant Taylors' School, wrote approvingly: "His care was also to encreas my skill in musique, in whiche I was brought up by dayly exercise in it, as in singing and playing upon instruments." Sir Nicholas

Bacon's curriculum for the queen's wards includes two hours a day with the music master and further musical study in the evening. The plan for a royal academy in 1572 included a teacher of the lute, bandora, and cittern. Beginning c. 1560, Westminster School set aside an hour a week for musical instruction, and music was studied at the Rivington Grammar School (which Pilkington supported). The 1573 deed of John Hales for the Coventry Grammar School provided for music instruction three times a week. In London, Christ's Hospital taught music, partly because musical ability was valued in Elizabethan servants, though in 1589 the governors ordered that in the future none of the Hospital's children were to be apprenticed to musicians unless the children were blind, lame, and unable to be placed in other service.[81]

In aristocratic circles, demand for musical talent was great, owing largely to the influence of Renaissance values (such as those expressed in Castiglione's *Courtier*). Thomas, son of Edward Seymour, earl of Hertford, was taught to play the virginals and viol. Sir Robert Sidney's children received musical training; his daughter Mary was "very forward in her learning, writing, and other exercises she is put to, as dawncing and the virginals." It was, in fact, a growing custom for young gentlewomen and maids to learn to play the lute and the virginals. In young men too, musical ability was valued. As Simon Senhouse was about to enter Anthony Bacon's service, his father encouraged him to avoid idleness by learning to play the virginals and the lute and to sing. When Mr. Tyndale sought to place his son in the service of Sir Michael Hicks in 1603, he noted that the fifteen-year-old boy could play the lute and the virginals.[82]

Besides seeking musically inclined servants and educating their children in music, aristocrats patronized musicians. Walter Devereux, earl of Essex, had his own musician who could sing and play the virginals. Robert Dudley, earl of Leicester, patronized a company of musicians as well as actors. Gilbert Talbot, earl of Shrewsbury, Henry Lord Berkeley, Sir Percival Hart, and Sir Arthur Hevingham were patrons of music. The madrigal composer John Wilbye was supported by Sir Thomas Kytson of Hengrave Hall, Suffolk. In 1596 Thomas Lord Burgh curried favor with Sir Robert Cecil by offering him a choice of four musically talented servants. The demand for music in aristocratic and even mercantile groups was high enough to motivate Nicholas Yonge, a London merchant, to import Italian music books and publish an English version in 1588 entitled *Musica Transalpina*. Demand grew quickly, for between 1587 and 1630 over eighty collections of vocal music were published in England, though relatively little instrumental music was printed in the Elizabethan period.[83]

Despite recurring persecution, Elizabethan Catholics did what they could to enjoy music. Peter Norwich, a Catholic gentleman, taught music to the children of Sir Edward Montague in the 1570s. William Lord Vaux loved music, and in Lancashire Mrs. Houghton of the Lea retained a Catholic priest and schoolmaster to teach her children to sing and play the virginals. Gerard writes humorously of a time when, during his imprisonment in the Counter in London, "the prisoners below started singing lewd songs and Geneva psalms, [and] I was able to drown their noise with the less unpleasant sound of my clanking chains."[84] Music was a weapon in the religious battles of the age as well as a means for artistic expression, human fulfillment, and enjoyment.

Despite Roger Ascham's reservations about music, Elizabeth was an avid listener and performer. Her ability on the virginals impressed Sir James Melville in 1564. A beautiful cittern reputed to have been the queen's is now in the Victoria and Albert Museum. Celebrations at court and festivities during progresses regularly featured masques or other musical entertainment, a striking example occurring when Edward Seymour, earl of Hertford, greeted Elizabeth with music on her visit in 1591, entertained her with it, and bade her a musical farewell. Her support of traditional ecclesiastical music probably caused some grumbling in Puritan circles in addition to the overt attack by Field and Wilcox previously noted. At least one Anglican, John Bossewell, credited the queen with being the savior of English church music:

But what saie I, *Musicke?* One of the seuen Liberall Sciences? It is almost bannished [from] this Realme. If it were not, the Queenes Majestie did fauour that excellente Science, Singinge men, and Choristers might goe a begging, together with their Maister the player on the Organes.[85]

Once again the court supported activities that Puritans found objectionable. Consequently, when James inherited the throne in 1603 a tendency existed for Puritans to look on the court with disapproval, and the tenure of the early Stuarts did nothing of substance to assuage that tendency.

In sum, divergence in attitudes toward church and secular music was marked in the Elizabethan era. Puritans and some Anglicans sought to restrict music in church services to emphasize the text (ordinarily a Psalm[86]) and congregational participation, downplaying melody, harmony, and counterpoint. The adaptation of more traditional musical forms in places like the royal chapel was viewed with alarm. Yet Anglicans were pressured by the lower classes in particular, who preferred more elaborate choral music in services and reacted negatively to the emphasis on the spoken word and the plain singing of Psalms. To Puritans, however, traditional musical forms were objectionable not only because they obscured the text but also because they smacked of Catholicism.

In the area of secular music, it was primarily the Puritans who attacked scabrous texts and enticing tunes because of fears that they led to licentious conduct. There was mounting concern, particularly beginning in 1572, that unlicensed minstrels were vagabonds and thus contributors to ungodliness and disorder. Undoubtedly, a number of Elizabethans did behave like a tailor of Springfield, Essex, in 1571, at whose alehouse minstrels gathered and enticed the parish youth on Sundays and holy days "to rioting and revelling to the great decay of the use and exercise of artillery." Another offender was a tailor of Little Wyrley, Staffs., who in 1590 sat in an alehouse on sabbath and holy days, "havinge a tynker in his companye whome he procured to singe many ungodlye songes . . . wherein the said . . . [tailor] hathe farr greter delyte then in heringe the wiorde of God for he . . . hathe syldome or never byn at his parishe chirche sythence."[87] Such behavior motivated the hostility of Puritans and some Anglicans to secular music, but it was never a wholesale condemnation. Moderate enjoyment of music in the home was approved for mental and physical recreation, and in general sanction was given for the limited use of decent music at social gatherings. Given the place accorded to music in Elizabethan education and the demand for it in aristocratic and even merchant homes, reformers had to accept music. Abuses, not music *per se,* were proscribed, and in this area it was primarily the Puritans who manifested concern.

(6) Church Ales and Wakes

Briefly, they tende to an instructing of the minde by amiable conference, and an enabling of the body by commendable exercises.

Richard Carew[88]

The Church Saint muste haue hys wake daye, which is all spent (being the Lords Sabboth) in Bearebating, *Bacchus* cheere, and *Venus* fylthy sports.

Anthony Anderson[89]

Most of the activities previously discussed in this chapter were associated (in part) with church ales and wakes. Church ales, or revels as they were often termed in the West Country, encompassed Whitsun ales, parish ales, clerk ales, sexton ales, leet ales, bid ales, and king ales. Wakes were annual festivals to honor patron saints of parishes. The medieval origins of these occasions involved baking holy loafs and brewing holy ale in the church house, folllowed by a blessing from the rector and the sale of the food by churchwardens.[90]

Church ales and wakes were community events that regularly included the people of neighboring parishes. Preparations began when voluntary donations were collected from parishioners and used to brew ale and bake bread. At the appointed time—normally a Sunday after evening prayer—the people gathered with food and sometimes gifts for the church. At long tables in the churchyard or on the village green were put out ample servings of meat, bread, and strong ale. The festivities included dancing, games, bear and bull-baiting and the music of minstrels. Young people might be selected as "chuchoo" (West Indian) kings and queens, or lords and ladies, and fined if they failed to perform their duties. It was, as Thomas Barnes has observed, very much like the Flemish village festivals painted by Brueghel.[91]

Of the two principal reasons for ales and wakes, one was financial. Proceeds from the sale of ale were used to repair the church, assist the clerk or sexton, or provide relief for the poor (in the case of the bid ale). In the early sixteenth century, profits sometimes amounted to as much as £10 to £20, but by the early seventeenth century £4 to £5 was normal. Elizabethan profits ranged widely. In 1573 a Devon parish raised only £2, but at Woolston, Hants., in 1600 a king ale netted £12 9s. 1d. The parish of Great Marlow, Bucks., garnered £6 3s. 4d. from a Midsummer ale in 1595, but in 1603 a Whitsun ale brought in £11 7s. 2d. A manuscript in the Stowe collection reveals that financial arrangements were sometimes worked out with some precision at the planning stage. The inhabitants of Elvaston, Ockbrook, Thulston, and Elvaston, Derby, agreed that the first two villaged would "brew four Ales, & every Ale of one Quarter of Malt, and at their own costs and charges," with the profits going to the Elvaston church. Couples were charged 2d., except for cottagers who paid 1d. As a means of raising funds, ales and wakes were popular.[92]

A second purpose for holding ales and wakes was to foster communal harmony. A friend of Richard Carew's thought the benefits of church ales included the "entertaining of Christian loue, conforming of mens behauiour to a ciuill conuersation, compounding of of controuersies, [and] appeasing of quarrels." Patrick Collinson suggests that church ales were intended, like Rogationtide, to reinforce the sometimes mythical unity of the parish, though the usual involvement of several parishes in an ale indicates a broader purpose, probably to reconcile tensions between neighboring communities.[93]

Church ales and wakes gave rise to the inevitable abuses associated with drinking and untrammeled frivolity, particularly in an atmosphere where godliness could be equated with the volume of ale purchased to benefit the parish. It was, in effect, a form of works' righteousness with a vengeance. According to Carew, the abuses of church ales encompassed idleness, drunkenness, lasciviousness, "vaine disports of minstrelsie," dancing, and "disorderly night-watchings." Some cases of bastardy were traced to sexual encounters at church ales, and in 1615 two men were killed at a Devon wake. A case in Star Chamber in 1594 alleged assaults on a plaintiff's servants at a wake in a Cheshire village. The plaintiff, John Egerton, complained that superstitious wakes and feasts were commonly held in Cheshire on saints' days and were occasions for the rowdy to breach the peace. He alleged that during the previous St. Peter's wake the constables at Little Budworth refused to repress the abuses, including brawling, and that physical clashes continued throughout the summer and fall. Such violence was obviously contrary to the intention of improving harmony in the community.[94]

Extant evidence suggests an increasing level of unacceptable conduct at church ales and wakes in the economically troubled 1590s. Somerset JPs prohibited church ales at the Michaelmas sessions in 1594 without explaining their action, but a similar order in 1596 was issued to save grain. At the quarter sessions in Devon in July 1595, people complained that church ales on the sabbath caused disorder and an increase in bastardy, hence they were prohibited on Sundays. Because disorders continued, the Devon magistrates ordered the complete suppression of church ales in January 1600 on the grounds that they fostered "many inconveniences, which with modesty cannot be expressed."[95]

In 1602 Richard Carew observed that many ministers were condemning church ales as licentious, but very little of their objections remains in print. In the early 1580s, in a work dedicated to the bishop of London, Anthony Anderson castigated wakes because of the bear-baiting, feasting, and bacchanalian activities. The most thorough opprobrium came from Stubbes in 1583; he reacted in part to the pressure put on the poor to purchase ale as a mark of godliness. He was also troubled by what he perceived to be drunken revels and the encouragement they gave to people to continue "swilling and gulling, night and day, till they be as drunke as Apes, and as blockish as beasts."

If Stubbes is correct, church ales and wakes were magnets for prostitutes, varlets, and thieves, a charge that seems probable in the more populous parishes. Where church ales and wakes lasted several days they naturally attracted the immoral sort and, as Stubbes bitterly complained, were conducive to "filthie Sodomiticall exercyses," gluttony, and inebriety. As for the money raised in these festivities, Stubbes was convinced it went to adorn the homes of clergy, who covered their embezzlement by duplicitous accounting. Yet even when funds went to repair the church or aid the indigent, he considered the means of raising the money inappropriate. The views of Stubbes and Anderson suggest a strong note of disapproval in some religious quarters, though written attacks on church ales and wakes are relatively rare.[96]

Despite the scarcity of printed repudiations, it is reasonable to infer widespread dissatisfaction among Puritans and some Anglicans, in view of their hostility to many of the activities that occurred at such festivities, such as excessive drinking, mixed dancing, bear and bull-baiting, unlawful games, and listening to or singing songs with ribald texts. At the same time, it is possible that at least until the 1590s these groups hoped that the abuses could be purged and the gatherings preserved as a means of fostering irenic relations between parishes and of raising money to repair churches, assist church officials, and relieve the needy. In the 1590s, as the Puritan position on the sabbath hardened, ales and wakes must have come under increasing criticism from Puritan clerics and laity. One glimpse of such hostility is found in the second draft of the will of Sir Francis Hastings, prepared c. 1590, which left £40 to the parish of North Cadbury, £10 each to South Cadbury and Maperton, and £5 to Halton on the condition that they forever cease church ales because they profane the sabbath, lead to drunkenness and riot, and corrupt the youth with games and licentiousness. Anglicans, for the most part, appear to have been content to reform the abuses but preserve the festivities.[97]

This examination of Elizabethan attitudes to recreation and social entertainment has not revealed a clear line of demarcation between Anglicans and Puritans, though for the most part Puritans preferred a more stringent approach to these activities than did Anglicans. The blurring of the positions is seen clearly in the matter of gambling. Although most Puritans condemned it, Fenner and Perkins allowed gambling in some circumstances, though the Anglicans Wright and Babington did not. Nor are there clearly defined Anglican and Puritan attitudes to the theater. In Anglican circles Sutcliffe and Wright supported it, but Parker, Grindal, Babington, and George Abbot were hostile. Some Puritans (Fenner, Northbrooke, Stubbes, and Gosson) were critical only of abuses of the theater, while others (Field, Holland, and Thomas White) favored its abolition. Puritan opposition to mixed dancing was shared by Cooper and Babington, while Parker, Nowell, Turnbull, Grindal, and Horne shared the Puritan preference for simple Psalms and hymns. Both Anthony Anderson, an Anglican, and Philip Stubbes, a Puritan, were strong critics of church ales and wakes. Thus a fair degree of overlapping is apparent in Anglican and Puritan attitudes to recreation and social entertainment. Yet it is also true that more liberal attitudes toward these activities were nearly monopolized by Anglicans.

The efforts of religious reformers were impeded by the example of the court and the aristocracy. The court was famous (or notorious) for its dances, masques, plays, bear-baiting, and gambling. Reformers must have been aghast to hear that the queen allowed a wrestling match in the royal chapel. Open criticism of the court was probably not too common, though Dering deplored games at court, and Field and Wilcox condemned the music in the queen's chapel. The aristocracy, particularly the peerage, was increasingly fond of gambling, and the queen and the aristocracy patronized actors and musicians in abundance.

The government's concern with recreation and social entertainment focused on the maintenance of order, not morality and Christian ethics. This attitude is evident in the statutory restrictions on games and the censure of abuses of church ales and wakes in the 1590s. Concern with order is also apparent in the visitation articles criticizing games and plays (in churches and churchyards), though the ecclesiastical hierarchy also worried about clerics' setting a bad example, as reflected in the inquiries about clerics who danced and in the attempts to impose obedience on the vicars choral. Order and public health were the principal motives behind the Privy Council's attempts to regulate the theater. As long as the moral objectives of religious reformers harmonized with the state's interest in order, most conflict was averted, despite the example of the court. When, however, James I's solution for order on the sabbath appeared in 1618 and stood in stark contradiction to the position of the religious reformers, serious conflict became inevitable.

CHAPTER 11

Food and Fasting

One of the striking manifestations of the hierarchic society in the Elizabethan age was the mammoth discrepancy between the sumptuous repasts of the wealthy, whose tables were filled with a dazzling number of meat dishes, and the meager food of the poor. The dearths of the 1590s made the situation intolerable and threatened the government with the specter of widespread disorder. One solution was a reduction of diet among the well-to-do, a course religious reformers advocated throughout the age. Fasting was another potential solution, particularly if the food saved was given to the poor. Certainly fasting was advocated on religious grounds throughout the period, and in the 1590s the government recognized its value during a time of serious food shortages. Drinking too posed a problem of public order, though teetotaling was not a solution that religious leaders urged. Instead, the watchword in diet, drinking, and fasting was moderation. To tread the *via media* between surfeit and deprivation, thereby maintaining physical and psychological well-being, was the goal. In pursuing it, however, there were some striking variations in emphasis among Anglicans and Puritans.

(1) The Christian Repast

Great eaters beeing kept at a slender diet neuer distemper their bodies but remaine in good case.

Jane Anger[1]

Our natyve soyle cannot aforde
suche meates as may content,
But shippes must seke for *spanishe* spice
till all our goodes be spent.

Anonymous[2]

On the subject of food, the dominant theme among Anglicans was a temperate diet, with respect both to quantity and delicacy. Nowell's catechism explained that the reference to daily bread in the Lord's prayer prohibited delicacies and excess in favor of a moderate and healthy diet. Moderation did not rule out periodic fasting on the one hand, and on the other, Bishop Woolton insisted that "delicate meats" could be eaten as long as they could be obtained without excessive expense or labor. Moderation accorded with natural law as well as scriptural precedent:

Nature doth her selfe content
With slender diet.

Temperance was a divinely imposed injunction to counter the inherent tendency to gluttony, a sin involving the gross abuse of God-given goods and blatant unthankfulness. "The glutton," preached Dr. Thomas Mountford, prebendary of Westminster in 1602, "eates like a dogge, and lives like a hogg, having his soule as salt onely to keepe his body from stinkinge."[3]

Gluttony was odious to Anglicans for other reasons, not the least of which was a social concern that a decrease in excessive eating would enable relief for the indigent. Londoners were singled out by Drant as "bursten with bancketing, and sore and sicke with surfeting," whereas Wright castigated the wealthy for being less charitable than the devil, who offered to turn stones into bread. Gardiner blamed the insatiable quest for a multiplicity of dishes as a cause of famine. Gluttony was also roundly condemned as a source of additional evils, especially lust.

As wood heapt vp a high vpon the fyre,
Or oyle cast in, doth more augment the heate,
So doth this fond insatiate desire
Of surfetting, and cramming in of meate,
Increase the flame of lecherous desire.
    The body is vnmeete to followe good,
    While as it is so cherished with food.

From another perspective, gluttony hindered the soul's welfare and the performance of spiritual duties.[4]

Perhaps it was insular provincialism, but a number of Anglicans perceived England as the most gluttonous state. "We for our glutonie are euerie where called English bellies," lamented Whetstone, who had seen military duty and eaten Continental food in the Netherlands, while Pilkington insisted that "no country has more belly cheer than we, and we eat as though we were hungry still." When Whitgift wrote to the bishops in the province of Canterbury in December 1596, he blamed the dearth on the people's habitual excessive diet and wasteful consumption. More than two decades earlier Cooper had warned against such excess in a sermon at Lincoln Cathedral. The dearth of the 1590s was perceived as just retribution for a nation devoted to

> sumptuous tables, dishes heaped hye,
> And costly banquets paynted with disport.[5]

As a guide to a suitable diet, Anglicans believed food must be regulated to ensure physical health. No specific regimen could be imposed for physical needs varied. Excessive food was believed to impair health and dull physical and spiritual senses. Pilkington pointed to England's poor, who lived on brown bread, thin ale, milk, butter, and cheese, as examples of physically fit specimens worthy of emulation; Wright castigated the English for their quest for novelties in food. Gardiner not only urged people to hearken to the warnings of physicians on the dangers of overeating, but also insisted in neo-ascetic fashion that people eat only for necessity's sake, not pleasure. Curiously, little attempt was made to argue that food should reflect social rank, as in the case of clothing. In his exposition of the Lord's prayer, Babington did assert that great men needed more food than their meaner counterparts, and that daily bread should vary in accord with social status.[6]

Some Anglicans made diet an issue in religious propaganda. Turnbull associated sumptuous banquets and delicious fare with fat monks, and Pilkington satirized Catholic clergy as "belly gods," writing scathingly of the priest Sir John Smell-smoke who could "smell a feast in all parishes near him, sit at ale house, carding, dicing, bowling, drinking from morning to night, thinking he has served God well when he has mumbled his matins." In contrast, Bishop Woolton used diet to score points against Puritans who, he claimed, had no scruples about dainty fare because it was a matter indifferent and therefore allowable under the rubric of Christian liberty. It was a clever manipulation of the charge of adiaphora, which the Puritans used so persistently against the Anglicans in matters of liturgy and clerical garb. Citing Calvin, Woolton accused Puritans of prodigally wasting food, and thus abusing something that was in its own nature indifferent. With respect to food the Anglican position was, in the eyes of its adherents, a *via media* between the excesses of Catholicism and Puritanism.[7]

Despite Woolton's attempts to distinguish between Anglicans and Puritans on the matter of food, in most respects they agreed, and when they differed the area of disagreement was not, as the bishop claimed, Puritan willingness to eat delicacies. Like Anglicans, Puritans demanded that Christians eat moderately. The standard rule was stated by Perkins: "Be very carefull and circumspect in taking thy foode, bridle thine appetite, take heede thou doest not exceede measure." Puritans concurred that eating must be guided by physical needs; the principle was to partake of foods conducive to good health. Gluttony, they warned, was a major factor in producing diseased bodies and minds and led to idleness and the loss of time and money. Like those modern devotees of health foods who favor a controlled diet to treat physical ailments, Charles Gibbon advised his readers to "let the Cooke be thy Phisition, and the garden thy Apothecary."[8]

Puritan objections to gluttony closely paralleled Anglican criticism. Excessive eating was damned because it hindered spiritual duties. A second objection to gluttony focused on the tendency of excessive eating to promote lust and profanation of God, whereas sobriety was a means of chastity. Overeating also deprived the poor of sustenance. That the English were prone to gluttony was a belief that Puritans shared with Anglicans. The English, claimed Stubbes, "are marueilously giuen to daintie fare, gluttonye, bellicheer, & many also to drunkennesse, & gourmandice." The link between gluttony and Catholicism was reiterated by Dent, who spoke of gluttons making popes of their stomachs, and Cartwright. Apparently the only Elizabethan Puritan who associated gluttony with Anglicans was Gifford. In general Anglicans and Puritans were united in their attack on excessive eating.[9]

The association between diet and social hierarchy was more firmly enunciated by Puritans than Anglicans. Perkins linked food to social rank and deplored the tendency of social inferiors to equal their betters in repast. "Our food must not goe beyond the condition, place, abilitie, and maintenance that God hath giuen vs." For the lower classes this meant contentment with limited food, hence Greenham suggested that good cheer was born of the peace of the gospel and brown bread. "My table richly furnisht with Content" was the ideal, particularly because food was a reminder of divine providence. Christ was content with boiled fish, claimed Gibbon, and our diet should be patterned after his. Notwithstanding such encouragements to humble sustenance, Puritans allowed persons of substance a much richer diet. Whatever God bestows during the earthly pilgrimage may be used, said Dering, for our pleasure, as long as it does not detract from a holy life. Even feasts are acceptable if gratitude is acknowledged, moderation followed, friendship maintained, and the poor relieved. To argue otherwise would have alienated the aristocracy and mercantile folk. Puritan restrictions on diet were not intended to undermine food as a visual indicator of social hierarchy.[10]

Although Puritans were not opposed to the reflection of social distinctions in diet, they expressed intense hostility to epicurean dishes, a hostility Anglicans did not share. For Puritans "dainty and sweet delicates" and lavishly prepared dishes were as dangerous as overeating. The use of professional cooks was a sign of the unhealthy quest for

> new-deuised cookery,
> Straunge Iunkets, wondrous dishes.

Stubbes praised his wife Katherine for refraining from such dishes and yearned for bygone days when men were strengthened by eating such simple foods as grain, corn roots, herbs, and cold meat. He was disturbed, as were others, by the multiplicity of dishes served in wealthy homes, and was convinced that such fare detrimentally altered physical bodies and personalities. For the Puritan, simple food was wholesome, frugal, and healthy, hence there was no reason to concoct dishes for the sake of uniqueness, aroma, or color. Hearkening to the New Testament, one could use the example of Jesus, who fed the masses with the simplest fare, not a variety of dishes and wines. Thus the quest for simplicity in worship was paralleled by a desire for simplicity in food. In both cases, the New Testament provided the sanction and spiritual well-being, the motivation.[11]

By modern standards Elizabethan recipes were relatively simple, notwithstanding Puritan complaints, though the variety of foods served at a single meal in wealthy homes exceeded modern practice. Two of the most complex Elizabethan recipes are worth citing as examples. An almond tart was to be made of blanched almonds, cream, sugar, rosewater, butter, and egg yolks, while a custard sauce to cover fried toast was blended from chopped spinach, salt, butter, raisins, cinnamon, ginger, sugar, orange juice, and egg yolks. Most recipes used far fewer ingredients. The variety, however, more than compensated for the relative simplicity. The recommended dishes for a two-course dinner on a flesh day were as follows: The first course was to comprise pottage or broth, boiled or stewed meat, chicken, bacon, powdered beef, goose pie, pork, roast beef, roast veal, and custard. The second course was to include roast lamb, roast capon, roast rabbit, chicken, pea hen, baked venison, and tarts. Such a grand repast was followed by a two-course supper, the first course of which included salad, pigs' feet, powdered beef, mutton, veal, lamb, and custard. The second course comprised roast capon, roast rabbit, roast chicken, roast pigeon, roast lark, baked venison, pigeon or chicken pie, and tarts. On fish days the menus were substantially altered, but the variety was no less pronounced. Tables were spread with lavish combinations of eggs, eels, herring, ling, salmon, peacocks, pigeons, mallards, gulls, storks, herons, crab, pheasant, quail, larks, and even deer.[12]

In their views on food, Elizabethan Catholics were (apart from the place of fasting) in substantial agreement with the Anglicans. Moderation was the key virtue, and they recognized the dangers to physical and mental health associated with overeating. Catholics believed that gluttony led to immorality and the consumption of patrimonies. Those who cut short their lives by a surfeit of meat and drink were guilty of murder under the fifth commandment, according to Vaux's catechism. Whereas Protestants associated gluttony with Catholicism, the Rheims annotators linked excessive eating and "belly-cheere" to heresy in a *quid pro quo*. Catholics also accepted the principle that food must be provided in accord with social estate. One of the best examples of the Catholic outlook it found in the "Short Rules" of the Jesuit Robert Southwell, who prescribed for himself a diet that would assist nature and not hinder his ability to serve God. Feeling that it would be wrong "to content mine own appetite," he proposed to be neither "too curious or doubtful of what I eat, neither too precise in the quantity, fineness, or courseness of the meat, but of that which God hath sent take a competent meal, measurable to my need and not hurtful to my health."[13]

The admonitions of religious authors on the dangers of excessive eating were supported in popular medical handbooks. A moderate diet was best, for "our stomach is our bodies kitchin, which being distempered, how can we liue in temperat order?" Gluttony could lead not only to lust but to such maladies as dropsy, gout, leprosy, headaches, fevers, facial dimples, catarrh, and even death. Thomas Lord Berkeley perished in the 1530s allegedly from eating a surfeit of cherries and George Oglander died on the Isle of Wight reportedly from overindulging in meat and then traveling in cold weather.

Medical authors particularly warned (like Puritans) against eating too many varieties of meat at one meal, or of mixing meat and fish. Cogan insisted that no more than one meat be eaten at a meal. The rationale behind such restrictions, as expressed by Thomas Eliot, was that meats of different substance require "diuers operacyons of nature, and dyuers temperatures of the stomacke." If more than one meat was eaten at a meal, correct order must be followed, commencing with those most easily digested. Foods such as pottage, broth, milk, eggs, and butter must precede meat because they "mollifie and loose" the stomach, whereas "bynding" foods such as fruit and cheese must be eaten last. Some foods, such as wheat bread, capons, pheasants, partriches, pigeons, turtle doves, blackbirds, roast veal, and mutton, were recommended to develop good blood, but lamb, pigs' brains, raw herbs, entrails, and "grose" fish were said to be unhealthy. The English were urged to reduce their meat intake in the summer "because thy naturall heate is closed within thy bodie in Winter, but vniuersally spred in summer." In essence, Puritan strictures against simultaneously eating a variety of meats reinforced the advice of medical authors.[14]

Some of the same tendencies that prompted religious and medical authors to complain were noted by foreign visitors. In 1560 a visiting Dutch physician remarked on the sumptuous repasts and love of good fare. Fifteen years later, an Antwerp merchant commented that the English exceeded sobriety by eating as excessively as the Germans drank, and that the English consumed much meat and had a penchant for epicurean dishes. Near the end of the century, a Brandenburg jurist was similarly impressed by the amount of meat consumed by the English, though they ate less bread than the French. Scurvy, he noted, was common, as might be expected from a diet deficient in fruits, but Elizabethans blamed the disease on the Norman conquest.[15]

The aristocracy's love affair with meat is apparent in surviving records. Because of the large households and the value placed on hospitality, tremendous quantities of meat, fowl, and fish were consumed. During Christmas week, 1588, the household of George Talbot, earl of Shrewsbury required 118 rabbits, twenty-six hens, twelve sheep, ten capons, seven pigs, seven cygnets, six geese, and a turkey in addition to three quarters of wheat and 441 gallons of beer, which fed perhaps 150 people. In one week in September 1602, the household of his son, Gilbert, earl of Shrewbury, consumed fifty-nine chickens, capons, and pullets, fifty-four rabbits, twenty-four pigeons, twenty-three sheep and lambs, five pigs, and some veal. In such households, Lawrence Stone estimates that the *per capita* consumption of meat a week was approximately 8½ lbs. A better indication of the diet of an aristocratic household emerges in the records of Lady Grace Mildmay, who in June 1593 recorded expenses for sixty-six joints of mutton, six joints of veal, forty-one "pieces" of beef, fifty-one tongues, thirty-three chickens, seven capons, two herons, four pigs, one lamb, twenty-nine ducks, twenty-nine pigeons, two rabbits, six wild ducks, thirty-three fish of various kinds, two roasting eels, one ling, eight hogsheads of beer, 457 loaves of bread, fifteen artichokes, and pastry, custard, and butter. In one final example, the household of Sir William Fairfax of Gilling and Walton purchased in a week in August 1580 one cow and three "tyldes" (three of the four cuts into which a quarter of beef is divided), seven sheep, twenty-six rabbits, twenty pigeons, a stone of butter, and cheese. Clearly the aristocratic households consumed large quantities of meat, as Anglican and Puritan critics claimed.[16]

Mixing meat and fowl, which concerned medical and religious authors, was commonplace among the landed classes. When Frances Seymour, countess of Hertford, expected the queen in 1591, she prepared three salmon, baked deer with muscatel and nutmeg, bacon, sturgeon, turbot, conger, prawns, lobster, preserved plums, lemons, oranges, olives, capers, and three types of wine. The royal household normally enjoyed a variety of meats, especially veal, mutton, and beef, prepared in different ways. For their weekly dinner at public expense, the judges of Star Chamber enjoyed a sumptuous repast that regularly involved beef, mutton, veal, tongue, lamb, capons, geese, chicken, rabbit, quail, bacon, salmon, sturgeon, and eggs. (In Trinity Term, 1587, this cost the state £35 14s. 10d., and this increased a year later to £41 6s. 9d.) The diet ordered by Burghley for Sir Nicholas Bacon, Sir Richard Sackville, Sir Walter Mildmay, and Sir Ambrose Cave at Hertford Castle in 1582 was more modest, but included two meat dishes on each flesh day and two fish dishes on fish days. On an ordinary Thursday in 1572 in the household of Sir William Fairfax, supper consisted of boiled meat and pottage, boiled calves' feet, sliced beef, roast mutton, roast veal, roast capon, rabbit, and chicken. Elizabethans definitely preferred a variety of meat and poultry dishes on their tables.[17]

During Lent and on fish days some moderation in diet was shown, though dispensations could be obtained on grounds of health. Sir Edmund Verney, for instance, obtained a license from the church in 1581 that permitted him to eat meat on fish days for the rest of his life on the premise that fish was harmful to his weak stomach. Some idea of a fast day menu in an aristocratic home may be gleaned from the household of Sir William Fairfax, which in June 1572 served a dinner of grain pottage, butter, ling, salad, eggs, haddock, codling, cod's head, turbot, trout, barbel, salmon, bullhead, and whiting. A meal for the judges of Star Chamber in June 1594 on a fish day included ling, green-fish, salmon, pike, gurnard, dory, carp, tench, knobberd, plaice, gray-fish, sole, perch, conger, barbel, flounder, whiting, turbot, crab, lobster, prawns, eggs, capons, rabbits, chickens, artichokes, peas, strawberries, gooseberries, apples, oranges, lemons, quinces, and barberries. For the wealthy, therefore, fish days normally meant an alteration in diet, not a diminution in variety or quantity.[18]

Since most preservatives were not available, nor, except in winter, refrigeration, the wastage from large meals must have been considerable, though in many cases leftovers were donated to the poor. The destitute regularly waited at Archbishop Parker's gate for scraps from his table. The kind of wastage that could result was exemplified when the queen was on progress at Killingworth Castle, Warws., in 1575. After an unusually sumptuous banquet featuring three hundred dishes, the uneaten food was "disorderly wasted & coorsly consumed." Although this case was undoubtedly extreme, the wastage of food after opulent meals while the indigent suffered from malnutrition provoked the ire of Anglican and Puritan reformers.[19]

The expense of this diet, which also angered the reformers, was considerable. The accounts for 1597-98 of Henry Percy, earl of Northumberland, list £747 10s. 3d. for food, and in the 1560s the weekly food expense for Edward Seymour, earl of Hertford, his wife, their two sons, and seventeen attendants was £13 13s. 4d. (or £164 p.a.). Of Hertford's weekly expenses, £3 6s. 8d. went for his diet and a comparable amount for his wife's, but only 6s. 8d. for each attendant. A great banquet added substantially to these costs, as Burghley well knew after spending £362 19s. 11d. to honor the French commissioners at a feast in 1582. The government had substantial bills for the diet of dignitaries, including £2,500 for food for Mary Queen of Scots between July 1568 and July 1569. In connection with her affairs, the duke of Norfolk, the earl of Sussex, and Sir Ralph Sadler were paid £918 for dietary expenses. Star Chamber meals were not inexpsnsive; five dinners in 1594 cost nearly £76, with the cost per person per meal exceeding £1. The desire of the reformers to reduce such expenses without leveling diets was not unreasonable.[20]

Dietary expenses for the gentry were correspondingly lower, though far from spartan. In the 1570s the average weekly expense for food in the home of Sir William Fairfax was £7 to £8, in addition to the food supplied from his estate. This expense was reduced at Lent to approximately £5, though one New Year's week it soared to £22. This amount fed between thirty and fifty people, with the family typically having six to eight dishes. In the year 1592-93, William Fitzwilliam of Dogsthorpe, Northants., expended £166 5s. 9d. on food, and supplemented this with £53 4s. 11d. worth of provisions from his own lands or rents-in-kind. The substantial difference in the weekly expenditures of the Fairfax and Fitzwilliam families (£8 to £19) is due partly to the sharp rise in food prices in the 1590s and partly to the greater income of Fitzwilliam, a courtier who earned perhaps £900 *p.a.* Special occasions meant increased food expenses for the gentry as well as the peerage. Sir Francis Willoughby spent over £92 during the twelve days of Christmas in 1597-98; of this £24 10s. was for beef, £16 2s. for beer, and £12 12s. for corn. Even a local responsibility of minor importance, such as providing a dinner in 1573 for four commissioners of an inquisition *post mortem,* cost Sir Francis 40s. 10d. Although meat and corn (for bread and drink) were the heaviest food expenses for the landed classes, spices too were relatively dear: Sir Francis spent £22 8s. 10d. for spices in 1572. Thus whereas gentry expenses for food were less than those of the peerage, they were far from inconsiderable and were also a target of the reformers.[21]

Fare for husbandmen and agricultural and urban laborers stood in sharp contrast to the diet depicted above. Meat was rare, except for bacon, and the diet usually comprised bread, porridge, broth, dairy produce, and beer, cider, or mead. Fruits were uncommon with the exception of berries in season, and peas were the only regular vegetable. Fish and ling were available for fish days and Lent. The prevalence of markets in London meant that city artisans had more meat than their counterparts in other towns and villages. Contemporary testimony from Cornwall indicates improved conditions for husbandmen by the end of the age, though at the outset their diet was essentially restricted to milk, cheese, curds, butter, and grain, with no meat.[22] Still, in the country as a whole, the dearth and rising food prices of the 1590s exacerbated the dietary problems of the destitute and added a sense of urgency to Anglican and Puritan demands for dietary reforms.

At various government levels endeavors were undertaken, though efforts were piecemeal and neither church nor state developed a comprehensive plan to improve the diet of the lower orders and curtail the extravagance of the wealthy. In 1563 the House of Commons heard the first reading of a bill to restrict the number of dishes served at a meal, but it failed to elicit sufficient support. The Privy Council acted periodically, but neither consistently nor with a master plan in mind. In January and March 1579 the Council expressed concern to the lord mayor and aldermen of London about the number of people eating flesh during Lent and on fish days. The Council also communicated with the lord mayor that winter because of the shortage of food in the city due to inclement weather. Food already in London was ordered distributed to the poor as well as the rich, and all "excessive" banqueting was to be temporarily curtailed and "temperancie of diett with all sortes of people" adopted. Rising grain prices and dearth in 1596 troubled the queen, who blamed covetous farmers and engrossers, hence in August the Council ordered the archbishop of Canterbury to exhort housekeepers to be content with a more modest diet and less meat. To aid the poor, no suppers were to be eaten on Wednesdays, Fridays, and fast days, and kennels of dogs were prohibited. Beneficed clergy and well-to-do laity were urged to increase hospitality to assist the indigent. On Christmas day 1596, the Council complained to the lord mayor of London that there was "more excess of fare" in the city than in the country, and it urged him to adhere to the guidelines issued the previous summer on restricted suppers. On pain of imprisonment, no meat was to be served in taverns and inns on Wednesday and Friday nights and fast days. The Council also was angry that men of means had not left the city for their country homes as the queen had ordered. The same day the Council repeated its injunctions to the archbishop of Canterbury. The Council was primarily motivated by the threat of disorder, not clerical admonitions to reduce conspicuous consumption on religious grounds, but they used the clergy to achieve their ends.[23]

Whitgift complemented the endeavors of the Council. In 1587 and 1588 his injunctions for the clergy of the province of Canterbury stipulated that each minister "keep abstinence and sober diet." In response to the Council's order of 25 December 1596, he ordered his bishops to convey the regulations on eating meat to their clergy, and asked for abstinence from Wednesday suppers, with savings going to the poor. Ministers and churchwardens were required to submit certificates to their bishops each month containing the names of delinquents, and Whitgift was to receive these quarterly. Apart from exhorting the clergy to provide suitable examples of modest diets, the ecclesiastical leadership apparently was not motivated to constructive action until mandated by the Privy Council.[24]

Despite the absence of an effective governmental polity to restrict dietary abuses, the exhortations of the clergy succeeded in some instances in heightening awareness of the problem. At the Maidstone quarter sessions in 1585, Lambarde bemoaned the failure to observe moderate diets and called for good men to square their words and works. His charge for the peace at Maidstone in September 1589 reiterated the call for moderate diet. William Hergest taught Sir Thomas Bromley's children that gluttony not only violated the seventh commandment but impaired their health, induced lust, and hindered spiritual duties—exactly the views of the clerical reformers. In comparable manner, Mulcaster recommended that all students eat lightly. Sir William Pickering's bequest to the Drapers' Company for a free school included regulations specifying a very modest diet (such as a Thursday supper of mutton, bread, and drink). Despite his prominence, Burghley insisted on a regulated diet and was reputed to be temperate in his eating, usually restricting himself to two or three dishes a meal and forgoing wine.[25]

The Puritans were probably the most troubled in their consciences about diet. Walsingham complained in the summer of 1575 that the court devoted itself exclusively to banqueting and other pastimes instead of the troubles of the realm. Philip Sidney was advised by his father, Sir Henry, to eat moderately to keep his wit fresh and his body lively. Samuel Ward's diary reveals a Puritan sensitive to the smallest dietary infractions, including overindulgence in eating plums; he even took a vow not to eat in the orchard. Partaking of cheese, raisins, and walnuts troubled him on various occasions. The guilt stemmed from the same reasons noted in the religious literature: physical impairment, inconsideration of the poor, and hinderance to spiritual duties. In 1595 he had guilty feelings for eating liberally without regard for the indigent and for failing to donate to poor women. In 1599 he "was overtaken with eating to[o] much, which made the[e] somewhat unfitt to hear the sermon, when thou shuldest eyther have fasted, or have eaten but little." On another occasion he was troubled by an "immoderate" desire to eat the meat left for the sizar. Perhaps Ward was more sensitive than most Puritans, though this is hard to judge. The repeated attempts of the clergy to persuade Elizabethans to eat more moderately and concern themselves with the poor did not fall entirely on deaf ears.[26]

To sum up, Anglican and Puritan authors agreed on the importance of moderate diets, geared to the preservation of physical, mental, and spiritual well-being. Gluttony was thought to hinder the performance of religious duties and to lead to immoral activity. Men of both persuasions were convinced that a reduction in diet would free funds to assist the needy, a view embraced by the Privy Council in the 1590s. More than Anglicans, Puritans insisted food should reflect social status, though Anglicans did not reject this attitude. Puritan concern with this point probably stemmed from their overt hostility to epicurean cooking, a view not generally shared by Anglicans. Elizabethan cooking was plain by modern standards, though a wide variety of dishes graced the table of people of means. The mixture of meats, fowl, and fish was costly, as surviving records indicate, which expense lends substance to claims of religious critics that some of this money should have gone to the destitute. Despite the problems, the government failed to respond with a unified program of action, though the queen and Council worried in the 1590s about the possibility of dearth leading to disorder. Their response included an attempt to have the clergy encourage parishioners to reduce food intake and assist the poor. In effect, the government by 1596 recognized the significance of the admonitions of the religious reformers.

(2) Drunkenness: Sin and Social Ill

The drunkard makes his belly noc better then a bucking tubb, a vessell to poure into, and put out at.

Mr. Phillips[27]

And hee is the iolliest fellowe that can drink his companion under the boord.

Lewis Thomas[28]

Essentially Anglicans and Puritans applied the same principles to drink as to food. No Anglican author was a teetotaler; to the contrary, there was explicit recognition of the benefits of wine in moderate amounts for sleep, improved wit, cheerfulness, decreased tension, physical color and strength, improved sight, a stronger stomach, and increased urination. In excess, however, alcohol allegedly caused such physical maladies as gout, pleurisy, palsy, dropsy, infertility, the loss of female beauty, and impaired memory and physical capabilities. Drunkenness was also condemned because it led to idleness and wastefulness, and was an impediment to a good marriage. Spending less on drink also would increase funds for poor relief. Apart from these social reasons, which were the primary concern of Anglicans, a few spiritual arguments were advanced against drinking to excess, including the warning that without repentance drunkenness would condemn a person to hell. One who drinks too much "doth it not to the glory of God, which is his duty," said Pilkington, "nor to the nourishing of his weak body.'' A drunkard has no more right, according to Dr. Thomas Mountford, to destroy his life and waste his funds on alcohol than he has to commit suicide. On the whole, however, the Anglican case against drunkenness was based largely on social arguments, not religious principles. Scriptural citations were used mostly to buttress the social case against drinking and frequenting taverns.[29]

In contrast to Anglicans, Puritans emphasized the spiritual problems associated with drunkenness, but without neglecting social factors. No Elizabethan Puritan advocated total abstinence from alcohol, for the feeling was general that wine in moderation was conducive to good health and a sense of physical and psychological well-being. Those who abused alcohol, however, were warned of possible physical impairment. Puritans treated drunkenness as a sin, a violation of the seventh commandment, a profanation of God's name, a sign of eternal damnation, and a source of strife. Contrary to popular opinion, drinking was not productive of good fellowship; it decreased awareness of others' misery. In 1596 Norden complained that drunkenness "of late hath gotten a coate, . . . and that forsooth, in drinking carouse, it must bee to the health of some greate man, and sometime great men will vse the name of greater persons in this swinish sinne, vnder colour of wishing health to them."[30]

Puritan writings emphasized that excessive drinking was a vehicle to immoral activity, poverty, and begging. The behavior of the drunkard was far removed from that expected of the godly:

Then when with the spirit of the buttery they are thus possessed, a world it is to consider their gestures & demenors, how they st[r]ut and stammer, stagger & reele too & fro, like madmen, some vomiting spewing & disgorging their filthie stomacks, other some . . . pissing vnder the boord as they [see] fit, & which is most horrible, some fall to swering, cursing & banning.

Alehouses were open sources of evil, and Bird castigated magistrates for licensing so many of them. While recognizing that the poor often got such licenses to supplement an inadequate income, he refused to accept this occupation as a justifiable remedy for poverty since other poor men frequented alehouses and worsened the conditions of their families. Licensed alehouses were, in effect, means for the poor to oppress themselves. Puritans also were highly critical of taverns and alehouses because they were the cause of so much wasted time and money. The Puritan campaign against drunkenness distinguished itself from the Anglican outlook by the greater emphasis it placed on religious factors. The intensity of Puritan opposition to drunkenness was also greater, as Penry recognized.[31]

Samuel Ward's diary reflects keen sensitivity about drinking immoderately. In June 1595 he noted that he had been given to "to[o] much drinking after supper," and eleven days later he confessed that he erred when he went to the tavern for wine before prayer. In the summer of 1596 he was again troubled after having drunk too much after dinner. By the early 1620s he was convinced that one of England's sins was "drunkennes and sottish-nes, and the not severe punishment," and he looked with disfavor on excessive drinking at Cambridge University.[32]

The concern of Puritan and especially Anglican authors about the physical harm of excess drinking, and their agreement on the benefits of the moderate use of alcohol, reflect the views of contemporary medical authors. Taken in moderation, wine was believed to increase wit and produce a cheerful disposition. White wine, according to Bullein, preserves the body if drunk before a meal, but on a full stomach it causes food to pass through the digestive tract too quickly. Claret, he claimed, nourishes the body. Mild beer brewed from good hops supposedly cleanses the body and strengthens the liver, though neither beer nor ale is supposed to be as beneficial as wine. Good ale was recommended to reduce fevers, increase blood, provoke urine, and stop constipation. In contrast, dangers in the use of alcohol included liver and brain damage, weakened sinews, cramps, palsy, apoplexy, and sudden death. Wine made from grapes harvested in wet years was thought to produce flatulation, dropsy, and fluxes, and any of the darker red wines was believed to cause constipation, impure blood, and stones. In excess, any wine is "a Poyson most venemous, it relaxeth the sinewes, bringeth Palsie, Fallyng sicknesse, in olde persons, hot Feuers, Fransies, Fightyng, Lechery, & a consumyng of the Liuer to the Cholerike." Poorly brewed ale was blamed for phlegm, flatulence, indigestion, and impaired eyesight. Medical manuals were filled with preventives (especially almonds, coleworts or cabbage, and pomegranates) and cures (such as cooked quinces, saffron, cabbage, and pork marrow) for drunkenness. One manual conveyed this advice, perhaps with tongue in cheek: "Giue vnto a dronken man the asshes of burnt Swallowes, & he shall not be dronk whyle he liueth." The medical books reinforced what the religious authors said about the physical dangers of drinking to excess.[33]

Although a Dutch physician in 1560 did not think the English drank excessively, the government apparently did, and introduced numerous bills, without success, to bring drinking under control. In 1566 bills to suppress breweries on the Thames below London Bridge and punish drunkards failed to become law. The 1576 Parliament refused to pass a bill prohibiting the making of "double double" beer and ale, but almost approved a bill controlling innkeepers and their customers. A bill to reduce the number of inns and alehouses was rejected on the first reading in the Commons in 1581, and in 1584 a bill to curtail drunkenness did not proceed past the first reading. A bill "to reform disorders of common inns and other victualling houses" was not enacted in 1589, and four years later a bill passed in the Commons to control brewers was rejected in the Lords. Against a background of dearth, the 1601 Parliament dealt unsuccessfully with six bills relating to drunkenness, disorders in inns, and the suppression of some alehouses. The motivation of those who defended these bills was a view of drunkenness as an impairment to work and support of a family, a cause of vagabondage and disruptive conduct, and a cause of scarcity and high grain prices. The bills generally were aimed at "the worst and inferior sort of people" and not at aristocratic offenders. The dismal record of these bills in Parliament shows an apparent reluctance to support government control in this area, even with safeguards to enable church courts to continue handling the problem, and with modest fines (ranging up to 5s.). Parliament was disturbed by the government's endeavor to control the problem by issuing proclamations, orders, and patents, especially after 1604. Behind the opposition to these bills was undoubtedly the fear that the regulations might be applied to the landed classes, bringing them more closely under government control. Balanced against the spiritual and social problems of drunkenness, the relative freedom of the landed classes proved to be the predominant interest.[34]

Despite unwillingness to legislate new restrictions to control drinking, local attempts to curtail it were common, though never sufficient to satisfy a Privy Council worried about the effects of inebriety on social order. Quarter sessions punished drunkards, primarily male, because they breached the peace. The importance of this task was underscored by Lambarde in his charge at Maidstone in April 1582:

For, if you would find out the disorders of alehouses, which for the most part be but nurseries of naughtiness, then neither should idle rogues and vagabonds find such relief and harborow as they have, neither should wanton youths have so ready means to feed their pleasures and fulfill their lusts, whereby, besides infinite other mischiefs, they nowadays do burden all the country with their misbegotten bastards.

Sir John Popham, probably with the approval of the Puritan Sir Francis Hastings, planned to decrease the number of inns in Somerset and dilute the strength of local beer. Justices of the peace at the Bridgwater, Som., assizes were convinced that because of the drinking problem, church ales were no longer justifiable. Despite such concern, in 1586 William Gorges complained that justices were negligent in enforcing the statutes on drinking, and called for a reduction in the number of alehouses, which he deemed hangouts for rogues, vagabonds, thieves, and lewd persons.[35]

In towns local officials constantly struggled to contain drunkenness. In Puritan-oriented Leicester in 1563, inhabitants could drink only in their own homes, where they could not be joined by friends for drinking more than an hour at a time, on pain of a fine of 3s. 4d. for the householder and 12d. for other drinkers. Designated men were appointed to make inquiries "of a typler & common dronkerdes that vse to syt typlyng at the ale howse all daye & all night & their wyfe & chylder[n] starue at home." A similar decision was made in 1569. In 1578, no one could go to an inn or alehouse to drink or tarry unlawfully on Wednesday, Friday, Sunday, or other holy or festival days during the time of religious services, on pain of a fine of 12d. On other days there was an hour limit in alehouses and inns. In 1601 an alehouse keeper who served drinks during religious services could be fined 3s. 4d. and his customer 12d., though travelers were exempted. The task of enforcing these regulations was assigned to aldermen in their wards.[36]

In Southampton, people complained that too many men haunted alehouses and taverns, leaving their families in want. In 1579 no poor man reputed to be an alehouse haunter was allowed in a tavern after 9 P.M. or the keeper was fined 5s. Yet in consideration of the poor, innkeepers had to sell them "small beer" at a low price (based on the amount paid for malt). Apparently the greatest troublemakers in Southampton were the porters, who were inclined to spend their time in alehouses instead of working. More than two decades of effort had not rectified the situation by the end of the era.[37]

Urban drinking posed some unusual problems. In November 1571 seventeen members of the Dutch church at Norwich were banished from the city for drunkenness. At Swansea by 1603, landlords increased their incomes by expanding their premises into alehouses, which became infamous as disorderly and unlawful places. Larger towns were nearly inundated with inns, taverns, and alehouses. By 1577 one-third of all the inns in Yorkshire were in York itself. In the same year, there were some 2,000 inns in twenty-seven counties and an additional 300 taverns and 14,000 alehouses. The number of alehouses in Canterbury nearly doubled between 1577 and 1596. Controlling drunkenness, whether for social or religious reasons, was an extraordinarily difficult task given the number of places serving alcohol. The proliferation of alehouses in rural areas in the homes of husbandmen, widows, and others compounded the difficulty.[38]

The church was supposed to play a major role in preventing drunkenness, and archdeacons' courts did deal with offenders. Two archdeacons' courts in Elizabethan Essex dealt with some two hundred cases of drunkenness, plus numerous others involving people who drank while services were in progress. Nevertheless the church's ability to reduce drunkenness probably was fatally undermined by the social behavior of some clergy. Repeatedly visitation articles inquired about ministers who maintained alehouses in their manses or spent time in taverns and alehouses. The 1585 articles for the archdeaconry of London inquired if "common drinkings" occurred in churches and chapels. Examples abound of Elizabethan clerics who were intoxicated or who frequented taverns and alehouses. In the diocese of Norwich, clerical drunkards were cited at Southwood, Freethorpe, Limpenhoe, Bastwick, Fishley, Upton, Ringland, Attlebridge, Saxlingham, Cantley, and Hanworth, and in Cornwall drunken ministers were reported at North Hill, St. Neot, Ludgvan, Ervan, Gulval, Stratton, Talland, and Treneglos. Lady Margaret Hoby heard that Sir Hunter Adam, a minister in York, died of inebriety in 1601. Some clergy drank to develop camaraderie with parishioners, as did Humphrey Wairing, a Warwick vicar who "loveth the alehouse well, and [is] verie much subject [to] the vice of goodfelowshippe." Others turned their parsonages into alehouses to compensate for inadequate livings—another ill result of the chronic underfunding of the church. This situation appears to have been true of a number of Yorkshire clerics, especially before 1575. Some clergy were simply unfit spiritually, such as Edward Miller, a Warwickshire vicar who pawned the parish's communion cup and was a notorious jester and tavern haunter. The most famous case of clerical drunkenness involved charges against William Whittingham in July 1578 at Durham, which were "proved".[39]

The damage that clerical offenders did to the church's endeavor to curtail drunkenness was not undone by punishing them, though this was a necessary step. The penalties varied. William Lynche, rector of Beauchamp Roding, Essex, suffered only humiliation when he rendered penance in a white sheet holding a wand in the marketplace at Chelmsford. When Richard Atkins, curate of Romford, Essex, was cited for inebriety in 1586 and failed to appear, he was excommunicated. The same fate befell Richard Spencer, curate of Greenstead-juxta-Colchester in 1576, but he submitted and did penance. In serious cases, such as that involving Henry Norcrosse, pluralist incumbent of Ribchester, Lancs.. who was guilty of intoxication and violence, a minister was deprived of his office. More common, however, must have been the ministers who enjoyed good fellowship too often for the sake of moral leadership, though not to the point of being subject to ecclesiastical discipline.[40]

Drinking then, was a social and moral problem in Elizabethan society. For the poor, ale was virtually the only drink, and a convenient device to escape the problems of survival and a quick way to fill an undernourished belly. The alehouse and the tavern were probably more important than the church as social centers for the lower orders. Drinking and games were the entertainment that rewarded the drudgery of daily toil.

> Drunken Drunkerds will not spare,
>   the Alehouse daily for to plye:
> But sit and tipple there full square,
>   and to their gaines wil haue no eye.
> Nor will not cease I warrant ye:
>   so long as they haue one penny.

Their social betters were no less inclined

> To quaffe and drinke when there is no necessitie,
> Joying in excesse, bealy chere, and ebrietie.

In noble households the rate of beer consumption has been reckoned at five to eight pints per person a day. Lady Jane, second wife of Henry Lord Berkeley, limited drinking in her home to the hours between 8 A.M. and 8 P.M., "and to come to drinking two and two together." The rules for another noble household prohibited excessive drinking and the presence of a drunk in the house. As in so many other cases, in the court, as Walsingham lamented, drinking to excess was frequent, even by ladies, whose overindulgence on more than one occasion ruined gowns and costumes, and ended only when they were carried out. Drinking was the Elizabethan pastime.[41]

Anglican and Puritan reformers opposed excessive drinking but not the modest use of alcohol. They saw physical and psychological benefits in the proper use of wine, beer, and ale, though they were more inclined to warn of the physical disabilities that resulted from abuse. In Anglican circles, emphasis was on the social enigma produced by overdrinking, whereas Puritans hammered away at the spiritual dangers, though not without recognizing the social problems. The effectiveness of their attacks must have been substantially diminished by clerics who let good fellowship, financial necessity, or immorality lead to improper use of alcohol. The punishment of some offenders by penance, excommunication, or deprivation was not an effective deterrent to others, despite efforts of the bishops to seek out errant clerics. Effective legislation was needed to curb the abuses of alcohol, but Parliament—especially the Commons—proved stubbornly reluctant to pass remedial bills. The government, which favored tougher legislation, failed to obtain it, and compounded the problem by allowing inebriety to become a characteristic of court life. To expect the lower orders to live moral, sober lives while their betters enjoyed the forbidden fruits of loose behavior was a failure of leadership.

(3) Fasting: For God and Country

How little fasting, and how great feasting, and that vppon dayes and nights inhibited by godly authority, is now to be seene?

Samuel Gardiner[42]

Extremes are euill, to moche fastyng, or to moche hunger.

William Bullein[43]

Elizabethan Anglicans developed their understanding of fasting in the context of the principle enunciated in earlier biblical marginalia, that true fasting is the suppression of wanton desires and the control of the body through mortification, as distinct from mere abstention from certain foods. The Matthew-Becke Bibles of 1549 and 1551 and the Matthew Bible of 1551 altered this idea somewhat by distinguishing between two kinds of godly fasting, a subordination of the flesh to the spirit, and an abstention from some food to aid the needy. Generally the thrust of earlier marginalia was to weaken the popular notion that fasting consisted of relinquishing certain foods, usually meat, at specified times such as Lent, and to emphasize fasting as a spiritual struggle to subdue sinful and animalistic drives.[44]

Anglican authors developed the theme of fasting as "a perpetual sobriety and temperance of life" to subdue carnal desires. Physical appetite with its earthly enticements was subjugated to the power of reason, making the flesh obedient to the spirit. To fast was not simply to abstain from certain foods but to abstain from sin. The purpose of fasting was to subdue physical desires, increase prayer and meditation, show inner humility and obedience to God, and demonstrate sorrow for sin and fear of future punishment. Fasting was necessary, according to Sutton, as preparation for the Lord's supper. In short, fasting was for the good of the soul as well as the body, and was an act of abnegation to enrich spiritual life.[45]

Several kinds of fasting were recognized in Anglican circles. One was prescribed by the law of nature as a temporary expedient to preserve or restore health. Another was a civil fast, prescribed by the state in conjunction with civil actions, but having biblical precedent (e.g. 1 Sam. 14:24 and Acts 13:12). The usual form of fasting was that undertaken for the benefit of the poor and was done in moderation. The biblical precedent of a miraculous fast, such as that pursued by Jesus for forty days and nights, was rejected by Gardiner as no longer applicable under the gospel. No Anglican disputed the right of the state to proclaim a fast for secular reasons, though none gave the state the right to promulgate fasts as religiously obligatory. Public fasting was acceptable in times of calamity, such as economic distress, or as "a generall endeuour or styrring vppe of oure selues when some weightie matter is too bee attempted." Public or general fasts, according to Anglicans, could be proclaimed only by the prince, bishop, or civil magistrate; those who held otherwise (as did radical Puritans) were condemned as Anabaptists.[46]

Although Lent was a Catholic observance, no decision was made to terminate it, for it was justified on religious and political grounds. From the religious standpoint, fasting in Lent enabled more effective contemplation of holy things and provided additional means to relieve the destitute. Politically, Lenten fasting was an occasion to obey the sovereign, preserve the church, strengthen the navy (by eating fish), and increase cattle (by abstaining from beef). Gardiner issued a strong warning, however, that Anglicans must not observe Lent in the Catholic manner by "cramming themselues with all delightfull fishe, drinking all strong Wines out of capable bowles, and tempering and seasoning . . . platters and . . . cuppes with the intising spices and confections of the Appothecarie, verie maine inforcements vnto all lasciuious lust."[47]

Anglicans enunciated rules to govern fasting. It must not be done to excess, and proper concern must be maintained for physical health. Undue austerity was deplored as rendering one physically unfit to fulfill responsibilites. In fasting, no food must be thought unclean per se, though some things, especially meat, must be eschewed as a matter of convention. All food saved by fasting had to be donated to the needy. Aiding the destitute was such an important part of fasting that Parker gave the students at Westminster School a dispensation to eat meat on Wednesdays if they contributed 6s. 8d. to the poor at Easter. During an outbreak of the plague in 1583, Grindal called for a fast on Mondays and Wednesdays, with the savings in food bestowed on poor foreigners living in the back lanes and alleys of London, where the plague was rampant.[48]

Unlike Anglicans, Puritans were not agreed that fasting was a spiritual exercise. Some, such as Henry Holland, agreed with the Anglicans that it was; for Holland fasting was a holy exercise necessary to testify of conversion and repentance. In contrast, more radical Puritans, such as Cartwright and Fulke, put more ground between themselves and the Catholics by insisting that fasting was not a religious exercise, though they acknowledged its spiritual ends, such as the increase of piety and service to God. Puritans in general stipulated that fasting was not part of divine worship, but a matter of policy—a means to be used only while effective. Once that distinction was made, however, they invested fasting with a spiritual character, so that it became, as for Anglicans, abstinence from sin and the subordination of the flesh to the spirit, not merely abstinence from certain foods. Fasting entailed mortification of the flesh to attain a spiritually chaste life. The full scope of the spiritual orientation of fasting is best expressed by Norden:

> But to fast truely, thou must wash thee and make thee cleane, thou must cast away and banish from thine heart all euill desires, and lay al the works of wickednesse out of my sight: thou must leaue to doe euill and learne to doe good, seeke iudgement, releeue the oppressed, and defende the fatherlesse: thou must giue thy bread to the hungrie.

Even those who rejected fasting as a spiritual act associated it with such spiritual duties.[49]

The announced ends of Puritan fasting underscored the spiritual orientation. Christians should fast to subject the body to God's will by making it fit for penitence, prayer, and hearing the gospel. Puritans also were exhorted to fast to demonstrate humility and contrition, and to increase their aptitude for good works. Fasting was recommended as a corrective to gluttony, but this was a mere sidelight to the intended spiritual benefits of fasting, which were based on the Pauline ascetic principle that heightened spiritual awareness could be achieved by the subjugation of the physical. As did the Anglicans, Puritans cautioned against pushing this physical suppression to extremes, for the body is a vessel of holiness and honor which must not be weakened. Fasting beyond physical endurance was therefore prohibited. In this vein, Perkins insisted that daily fasting was unacceptable. Fasting fostered the attainment of spiritual goals, but not at the expense of emaciating the body.[50]

Puritans found both religious and socio-political reasons to justify a fast, though in neither case would they accept the principle of religiously obligatory fasting. They developed four principal kinds of fasting (apart from abstinence for medical reasons or famine); the first was the Christian or moral fast of sobriety and temperance, that is, the imposition of restraint in partaking of food and drink. This had to be practiced on a regular basis, and in fact was not fasting at all, but merely moderation in diet. A more direct type of fasting involved abstinence from food and drink while pursuing religious exercises. Holland explains:

A religious fast is an abstinence, more then ordinarie, not only from all meates and drinkes, but also from all other things which may cherish the bodie, so farre as nature will giue leaue, and ciuill honestie, for one whole day at the least: proceeding from a true faith, and a cheerfull willing minde, principally to testifie our repentance, and to worke in vs a greater humiliation.

Puritans also sanctioned fasting imposed by the state for secular ends, such as the preservation of cattle, assistance to fishermen, or strengthening of naval capabilities. A fourth type of fasting, usually referred to as miraculous and exemplified by the lengthy fasts of Moses, Elijah, and Jesus, was not for emulation but instruction. Of the major kinds of fasting, the most important for the Elizabethan Protestant was the act of abstinence coupled with the performance of spiritual duties.[51]

Fasting could be private or public, with the former including individual and family fasts. In addition to spiritual benefits, private fasts could be undertaken in sorrow for the dead, to persevere in suffering, on behalf of secular rulers, and in mourning for evils in the church. "Priuate fastes," explained Thomas Bell, "may be vsed of ones owne accord, when and so often as shall seeme conuenient; so they be referred to the glory of God, and true mortification of the bodie, or bee vsed for the good of our neighbour." General fasts could be proclaimed for imminent danger, threats from God's messengers, iniquity in the church as discerned by magistrates or ministers, famine, disease, war, and concern for persecuted churches. General fasts were proclaimed in 1563 and 1593 because of the plague and in 1588 because of the Spanish threat. Whereas most Puritans had no objections to such fasts being promulgated by secular authorities (though not as religiously binding), the radical Puritan John Udall insisted that a public fast, "an abstinence commaunded of the Lord, thereby to make solemne profession of our repentance," could be proclaimed only by ministers.[52]

Puritans concurred with Anglicans that fasting was not a matter of abstaining from some foods, particularly meat, while gorging on others, such as fish. One could abstain from food entirely, or severely reduce the quantity of food. In contrast to the Catholic endeavor to restrict intake of certain types of food, Protestants stressed the limitation of quantity. Meats could be eaten at all times, unless prohibited by secular law for reasons of state. Similarly, from a religious perspective no particular time should be preferrred for fasting. "Lawes generally made without any consideration of circumstances, for fasting, & other things of like sort," according to the note to Luke 5:34 in the Beza-Tomson Bible, "are not onely tyrannous, but very hurtfull in the Church." Apart, then , from fasts proclaimed by magistrates and ministers for special occasions, individuals were free in Puritan congregations to fast when and as they wished, with the emphasis on a general reduction of food and not a shift from meat to fish.[53]

This attack on the Catholic position was just one part of a broad assault by Puritans to repudiate the Catholic position on fasting—an assault that Anglicans showed little inclination to join. Catholics were condemned for hypocrisy because they attributed religious merit to the forbearance of meats while feasting on fish and other foods; they substituted dietary change for true fasting. To compound their error, the omitted items did not include those commonly believed to cause lust, such as wine, spices, fruits, and delicate fish. The Catholic prohibition against eggs, cheese, milk, and butter during fasts was attacked as physically harmful and unfair to the poor, who might be able to afford eggs but not fish. Instead of associating fasting with concern for physical well-being, Catholics "haue brought about by your lawes of abstinencie, that your simple followers, in the extremitie of sicknes when there cannot be any pretence of chastening their bodies thereby, are so snarled in conscience, that they dare not touch, or tast, that which is necessary to preserue life, and to restore health withal." Finally, Catholics were believed to err by superstitiously appointing set times for fasting, when this is a matter, under the gospel, for churches and individuals to determine. Even the Anglican interest in observing "all their fishe fastes" was condemned by Gilby as smacking of popery.[54]

Although Puritans carried forward the campaign against the Catholic doctrine of fasting, they did not accord as much attention as Anglicans to the social obligation of fasting for the benefit of the indigent. In a sermon in St. Paul's, London, c. 1596, Christopher Hooke did contend that the substance of true fasting was undertaking works of mercy, including assistance to the poor. In comparable fashion, Norden made the provision of bread for the hungry, clothing for the naked, and shelter for the homeless a fundamental part of fasting. Particularly in time of famine, argued Vaughan, householders

were obligated to fast to assist the needy; his ideal was the forbearance of two meals a week for this purpose. When in January 1588,
the Dedham Classis made plans for fast services, they provided assistance to those who would be adversely affected economically if
they attended extra services. On the whole, however, less discussion
took place in Puritan than in Anglican circles about fasting to aid the
indigent.[55]

Most published comments of Elizabethan Catholics on fasting respond to Puritan attacks, though Vaux's catechism contains a brief
positive statement. To him, fasting is the foundation of virtue and a
means to repress vice; fasting chastises the body, subjects the flesh to
the spirit, exalts the mind, demonstrates obedience, and is a means of
grace to nourish the soul. On fast days, he required catechumens to
abstain from flesh and eat only one meal. Lent, because instituted by
Christ, must be observed more stringently than other fasts. The
Jesuit Robert Southwell took a very serious view of fasting, determining to "take heed of pampering my body too much and . . . to
take some ordinary corporal punishment of fasting, discipline, hair-
cloth, or the like." The Northamptonshire Catholic, Simon Norwich,
fulfilled his fast obligations even while a prisoner in the Fleet.[56]

The Rheims and Douai annotators defended the Catholic position
from Protestant attacks. The practice of prohibiting certain foods
during fasts was justified by an appeal to the story of the forbidden
fruit in Genesis, where the sin arose from violating the command of
a superior, not in eating unwholesome fruit. Catholics therefore must
abstain from specified foods by order of their superiors, not because
the food is unclean. "It is sinne only which properly defileth man,
and meates of them selfe or of their owne nature doe not defile: but
so farre as by accident they make a man to sinne, as the disobedience
of Gods commaundement or of our Superiours who forbid some
meates for certaine times and causes, is a sinne." Abstaining from
prohibited foods is a means of physical chastisement and obedience
to God. Those who fast earn merit, though fasting must not be undertaken for personal glory. Thus the key to the Catholic position
was meritorious obedience in asceticism, which contrasted sharply
with the views of Protestants.[57]

At the opposite end of the religious continuum, Separatists associated Church of England fasts with the Catholics. Even fast days for
secular purposes were condemned. "Romish fastes" were lumped
with feast days, saints' eves, ember days, Lady days, the dedication
of churches to saints, tithes, mortuaries, dirges, and funeral sermons
as intolerable relics of Catholicism. Public fasts were embraced only

if proclaimed by the true church for major calamities or transgressions, and certainly not civil authority (as in the case of fasting to aid navigation). Moreover, the Separatists accepted no fast in perpetuity on particular days. "The practise and use of fasting in the church of Christ under the gospel, sheweth, that there can be no permanent lawes of the time and day made therof." The determination of fasting must be made by congregations, not civil magistrates or the whole church, though private fasts can be undertaken at the discretion of individual Christians. Barrow carefully distinguished the Separatist position from that of Puritans and Anglicans, whom he felt had not departed significantly from Rome.[58]

The belief of Anglicans and Puritans that fasting must not impair physical health accorded with medical opinion. Moderate fasting was good for the body because "it consumeth superfluytees, and in consumynge them, it claryfieth the humors, maketh the bodye fayre coloured, and not onelye keepeth oute sycknesse, but also where sicknesse is entred, nothing more helpeth yf it be vsed in season." Abstinence was advised as a physical corrective to overeating, but melancholy, choleric, ill, and young persons were warned of the dangers of fasting. Pregnant women and scholars were cautioned not to abstain from meat. It was partly on the basis of such medical views that Protestants attacked Catholic fasting, with its emphasis on dietary changes rather than a reduction in the quantity of food.[59]

In practice, Elizabethan authorities battled on two fronts against fasting violations. There was, in the first place, concern about the continuance of Catholic fasts, hence visitation articles included queries to determine where such fasts were held and injunctions were issued forbidding their observance. In August 1561, John Scory, bishop of Hereford, complained to Cecil that Catholics continued to obobserve the abrogated fasts, urged on by priests who had been driven out of Worcester, Exeter, and other towns, but were welcomed in Hereford with torchlight parades. The other situation that troubled authorities involved radical Puritans who refused to exhort parishioners to observe state-imposed fast days. Once again, visitation articles were framed to discover offenders. It is not always clear from surviving records what motivated those clerics who refused to bid fast days, though in some cases it was clearly religious conviction. The 1597 visitation of the diocese of Norwich turned up clerics who failed to announce fast days at St. Andrew in Norwich, Thornham, Ormsby, Harpley, Pentney, and St. Margaret in King's Lynn; most of these were Puritans. Typically they were accused, as was John Trendle, Presbyterian rector of Ovington, Essex, in 1592, of publishing "not holly dayes by their speciall names nor fastinge dayes at all." The task of persuading Elizabethans to fast for the appropriate reasons and in the proper way was compounded by the Catholic determination to retain traditional observances and by the radical Puritan and Separatist hostility to state-imposed fasts.[60]

The queen and Privy Council limited their concern to the imposition of fasts for reasons of state. Neither conciliar letters nor eighteen proclamations proved sufficient to curb killing and eating flesh during Lent and on fish days, especially in London. Taverns and victualing houses as well as individuals were guilty. It became necessary to bond meat-sellers to curtail sales of meat to people without license to eat it during Lent. The heavy loss of cattle and sheep in 1590 prompted the Council to order lords-lieutenant in eighteen counties in February 1591 to restrain the killing and eating of meat in Lent, though the Council allowed beef to be killed, powdered and salted in Lent for shipment to English forces in Brittany. Some who persisted in eating meat in Lent and on fish days were undoubtedly radical Puritans and Separatists, yet the extent of the practice indicates that Gardiner was correct in blaming "refractory rabblements of prophane gospellers, who liue loosely & lewdly, turning fasting into feasting." Fittingly, the secular needs of the state, to which queen and Council addressed themselves, were most often frustrated by persons of largely secular interests.[61]

Secular concerns overlapped with religious interests, especially in the last decade and a half of the age, particularly in the area of fasting to relieve the needy. In 1589 John Crompton pressed Burghley to do something regarding those who regularly ate meat on Fridays and during Lent. His proposed reform would have fined offenders 12d. the first time, with half of the proceeds going to poor prisoners. Acting on orders from the queen, in 1596 Whitgift sent letters to the bishops of his province urging improved care for the needy by enforcing Wednesdays and Fridays as fast days, and by persuading men of means to eat modestly. He asked for an end to suppers on Wednesdays and Fridays except for the infirm, with savings going to the poor. Justices of the peace pitched in and tried to secure compliance with the proposal, which action neatly combined religious and secular interests.[62]

Adherence to the principles of fasting is hard to determine, though Keith Thomas is probably correct when he asserts that fasting was more extensive among the Puritans than the Anglicans. Margaret Russell, who became the countess of Cumberland as the result of her marriage to George Clifford, was a devout faster. Richard Rogers fasted frequently and achieved spiritual blessings, as he noted in his diary: "Sometimes when I have fasted, . . . and when I have sett my self hereby to moderate diet and regard of good ordre evry way, . . . I have felt . . . my hart as well contented in such a sober course and in subduinge all inordinate affec[tions] ." At the end of a day of fasting on 17 July 1590, he found that his mind was "well-seasoned, chiefly by reading my med[itations], 40 or 50 of them," which helped him overcome "idlnes of mind, and barraines." Another Puritan diarist, Samuel Ward, noted those occasions when he was troubled by guilt for not having fasted. The minute book of the Dedham Classis reveals that the Presbyterian clergy frequently fasted. When prophesyings were forbidden in Leicestershire, Puritans stressed fasts before communion as an alternate form of religious exercise. The fast was a weapon in the Puritan campaign for reform, as demonstrated by Paul Wentworth when he called for one in 1581 in the Commons as the prelude for church reform. In the ensuing discussion, Nicholas St. Leger scolded "the great fault and remissness of the Bishops who suffered that most necessary Duty of Fasting and Humiliation to grow even out of use in the Church." Puritans probably took fasting more seriously than Anglicans.[63]

In conclusion, Anglicans and Puritans agreed in some respects about fasting, particularly as a means to subordinate the physical to the spiritual, and to enhance the performance of religious duties. They perceived fasting as a general reduction in the quantity of food rather than a religiously imposed abstention from certain types of food, as in Catholic practice. Anglicans and Puritans accepted state-imposed fasts for secular purposes, though Separatists expressed hostility to such fasts. There was likewise agreement among Anglicans and Puritans on limiting fasting to avoid physical impairment, for fasting was intended to increase the capacity to fulfill responsibilities, not emaciate the body. Unlike Anglicans, Puritans were chary of having their practice of fasting associated with Catholicism, perhaps because the Separatists made that association. Wariness of this link to Catholicism motivated radical Puritans such as Fulke and Cartwright to deny fasting as a religious act, despite its spiritual goals. Much of the Puritan literary effort on fasting was devoted to repudiating the Catholic idea of fasting as a meritorious alteration in diet. Anglicans, however, gave more emphasis than Puritans to the social obligation of fasting to aid the impoverished. Whereas Puritans had no objections to this association, it was not a principal motivation for them. In practice, it appears that Puritans took fasting more seriously than Anglicans, though the real enemy was the creeping secularism that encouraged many Elizabethans to forgo fasting altogether.

The idea of fasting in moderation complemented the principle of eating and drinking modestly, which both Anglicans and Puritans asserted. One of their goals was the preservation of healthy bodies and minds to fulfill spiritual and vocational obligations. Gluttony and drunkenness were reprehensible because they were conducive to lascivious acts and to failure to perform obligations. The appropriate remedy was fasting. No foods or beverages were in themselves regarded as improper for Christians; alcoholic beverages in moderation were even considered physically and psychologically beneficial, though used to excess they were spiritually and physically ruinous. Anglican authors worried about the social problems resulting from excessive drinking, whereas Puritans were more concerned with the spiritual dangers. Both groups encouraged a general reduction in expenditure on food and drink by the well-to-do, with the savings devoted to poor relief. The Puritans, however, insisted that they opposed the "leveling" of diets; food should reflect social rank, though Puritans were hostile to epicurean cooking.

The government regularly acted to impose restrictions on diet, though not effectively. Concerned with the problem of public order rather than religious issues, government actions aimed at moderating diet for the benefit of the poor, curtailing drunkenness to improve public order, and imposing fast and fish days to preserve cattle and encourage fishing. Near the end of the age, the Council used the church to attain its ends by having ministers encourage parishioners to abstain from Wednesday and Friday suppers and reduce their intake of food to relieve the impoverished. Attempts to secure limits on diet by legislation failed, but the government never developed a comprehensive program to deal with the dietary needs of the nation. A stupendous gulf existed between the lavish meals of the peerage and the minimal sustenance of the poor. Men of religious conviction were troubled by this disparity, and Puritans in particular wrestled with their consciences when they ate more than they thought necessary. Anglicans, though, demonstrated the greatest social concern, urging in particular that poor relief be increased by moderate fasting.

CHAPTER *12*

Social Conduct and Social Order

Social conduct concerned religious and political leaders both because of the spiritual ramifications and because of the effect on stability and social hierarchy. How people dressed, what people said and read, their attitude toward suicide, and how they responded to military service affected the maintenance of an orderly, godly society. Dressing in a manner unbefitting one's social status was perceived as a threat to the organic, hierarchical social structure. So too was the use of immoderate, disrespectful speech. What one said and read had to be moral, utilitarian, and beneficial, for only in this way could religion be advanced and society preserved. On occasion, the preservation of society and religion necessitated recourse to arms, and for this reason various authors explored the duty of fighting in just wars. In the aftermath of the Spanish Armada, a surge of volunteers came to defend England, but on numerous occasions the queen had to resort to impressment to obtain forces. The military needs of the state, not the growth of pacifist convictions among the people, motivated authors to explore the issue of just war and individual responsibility. In all these areas, with the exception of apparel, differences were expressed between Anglicans and Puritans, and even in the case of apparel, Anglicans accused Puritans of lavish dress, trying to make clothing a religious issue.

501

(1) Apparel and Social Order

Humility is clad in modest weedes,
But Pride is braue and glorious to the show.

Richard Barnfield[1]

Wee haue Peacocks, all whose glory is their Plumes.

Henry Price[2]

Clothing in the Elizabethan age had religious and social overtones, with general emphasis on dressing modestly and in keeping with one's social status. The tone was set in the biblical marginalia, commencing with the Matthew Bibles of 1537 and 1551, and the Matthew-Becke versions of 1549 and 1551. A note to Ecclesiastes 9 urged readers to "be not slouenly and fylthely / but honestly & manerly arayed." In exceptional cases exchange of clothing by men and women was permissible, though the 1551 Matthew-Becke Bible omitted this liberty and the Geneva Bible expressly forbade it. The basic principle of the Geneva annotators was to wear "comelie" apparel in accord with one's social status and the intention of mortifying the flesh. Comely dress meant something relatively simple and unostentatious that yet manifested social status. Husbands were warned by the Geneva annotators that they would he held accountable with their spouses if the latter wore fine clothes and behaved wantonly.[3]

Subsequent Tudor Scriptures continued to emphasize simplicity and social distinction in dress. The Bishops' Bible praised plain garb and simultaneously insisted that "order is to be kept in natural comelynes for distinction of persons." With an eye to the court and peerage, the bishops approved wearing fine garments, signet rings, and other jewelry as a mark of honor if vanity was avoided. The Beza-Tomson Bible urged females to wear raiment that was not excessive and did not detract from a meek spirit, and to cover their hair in public. The Rheims annotators, in keeping with their Protestant counterparts, lashed out "against the proud, curious and costly attire of women, wherein this il time of ours excedeth."[4]

Anglicans showed little agreement among themselves on the ends for which clothing was divinely ordained, though Anderson, Babington, and Sutton regarded it as a manifestation and reminder of sin. To delight in apparel was therefore a monstrous act of pride. Wright and Adam Hill thought more positively of clothing as protection and modest covering, and Hill also argued that garb was instituted to distinguish men from animals, and higher social degrees from lower. For

Whitgift, clothing was intended to remind a person of duty and behavior, so that "if a man in grave apparel use himself lightly or wantonly, we use commonly to say, such behaviour becometh not that apparel, meaning that his habit and apparel ought to put him in mind of modesty and gravity." In keeping with this idea, Babington insisted that apparel revealed personal character. Thomas Drant, Grindal's chaplain and the archdeacon of Lewes, Sussex, was frustrated because "matrons are so lightly apparelled, or harlots so grauely, that thinges are blundered, and confounded." For Anglicans apparel was a means to distinguish social rank and moral quality as well as a reminder of the sinful state of humanity.[5]

Anglicans were adamant that clothing must reflect social rank—a thesis that was useful to justify the sumptuous garments of the upper classes. Equality of apparel was rejected, even in the presence of gross abuses in clothing. The principal problem, as Anglicans saw it, was the number of Elizabethans who dressed in a manner befitting a higher social station than their own. "God grant," said Pilkington, that "every one might be brought to his degree!" Precisely how this was to be accomplished was, insisted Whitgift, a matter appertaining to the magistrates and the law.[6]

Anglicans issued guidelines to select apparel, one of which was that clothing must not foster pride. To underscore this point, the Oxford scholar John Dove told his audience at Paul's Cross how William Rufus reputedly was happy with an inferior pair of breeches from his chamberlain because they cost more than a pair of higher quality. The vanity associated with wearing fine garments provoked Anglican ire, perhaps best reflected in the verse of Anthony Nixon, a late Elizabethan pamphleteer and poet:

> As paynted Tombes, that stinck and filth contayne,
> And *Arras* fayre that rotten walles doth hide:
> So do these fooles, with all their garments vayne,
> And fresh attire drest vp in pompe, and pride,
> Onely nurse vp a self-beguiling brayne:
> > For vnderneath their garments glistring braue
> > Lye mindes corrupt, as rotten bones in graue.

Lawyers in their silks were singled out by Wright as an example of those who prided themselves on gorgeous attire.[7]

Another Anglican guideline forbade excess in the amount and elegance of clothing; Edward Bicknoll warned that "the discommodities of the outragious excesse in apparrel breedeth much more woe then many deemes for." Some Anglicans worried about the Elizabethan proclivity to amass a large wardrobe, a practice Adam Hill contrasted with Christ's command to his disciples to take but a single coat apiece. The excessive use of jewelry also was criticized. Signet rings were especially popular, even, according to Samuel Gardiner, rector (in 1605) of Great Dunham, Norfolk, among the illiterate. Pilkington deplored the amount of jewelry worn by women, noting that "such decking and colouring maketh wise men to think, that all is not well underneath." Pilkington's preference was the natural look. Other Anglicans insisted that no unnatural or "monstrous" clothes be worn.[8]

Clothes likely to foster licentiousness were subjected to Anglican opprobrium. "Too much showe in apparel, painting, tricking and trimming of our selues aboue conueniencie, it is a daungerous allurer of lust, and therefore forbidden" by the seventh commandment. As Jerome averred, a woman who dresses to provoke men is eternally condemned for offering them poison. The frizzled hair, embroidered hats, colored coats, and ornamental feathers of aristocratic ladies were damned by Bishop Cooper as instruments of wantonness and snares to sin. Wearing apparel of the opposite sex was deplored by some Anglicans, including Anthony Anderson, who castigated "Courtly Madams, which daunce in mens Dublets to the wante of womanhood, the breche of this lawe [Deuteronomy 22:5], and the offence of good people."[9]

In a positive vein Anglicans urged their followers to dress moderately, soberly, and in a comely manner. Women were counselled to imitate Rachel (Genesis 24), and husbands were instructed to keep their wives in civil and comely dress. Whetstone's verse reflects the Anglican outlook:

> Beware of taylers curious arts, for they will shake your [money] bags,
> The merrie meane I holde for best, tweene roysting silkes & rags.

Nowell's cathechism took a more severe view, arguing that Christians must be content with a mean and necessary dress. Apparel must be selected, according to several Anglicans, with a view to sound health, and Pilkington thought that those who were "homely apparelled" were healthier and more physically fit to withstand the English cold than those who wore fur gowns, sable stoles, trimmed buckskins, and warm mittens. Pilkington's view ran counter to some contemporary medical opinion, for one popular handbook encouraged people to wear silk or buckskin in the summer, because these materials resisted "venime and contagious ayres."[10]

Anglicans were hostile to the English desire to keep abreast of current fashions. The English, protested Wright, were too desirous of novelties, hence he condemned the "confused mingle mangle, and vanitie of apish toyes in apparell, euery day flaunting newe fashions, to deforme Gods workemanship in theyr bodies, as greate monstrous ruffes starched in the deuils licour, and set with instruments of van-itie, doublets with great burssen bellies, as though theyr guts were ready to fall out, some garded lyke Frenchmen, some fringed lyke Uenetians, some their heads Turkish, their backes Spanish, and their wastes Italian: some theyr harye curled, and theyr beardes writhen to make them look grimme and terrible." The pursuit of such fash-ions was condemned by Babington as a violation of the principles in Deuteronomy 12 and Isaiah 3. Pilkington and Drant also were trou-bled by the preoccupation of Elizabethans with the latest styles. Drant chided aristocratic women for preferring Turkish hats or hair-styles, Spanish and Italian dresses, and Venetian shoes. In effect, Anglican religious leaders demanded native styles and less conspicu-ous consumption.[11]

A major Anglican goal in the matter of apparel was effecting sub-stantial savings by reducing clothing budgets to provide increased hospitality and assistance for the impoverished. Pilkington was angry with gentlewomen who spent money on clothing and jewelry that their ancestors would have channeled to hospitality, and he warned against wasting money (God's wealth, because all riches are his) on vain dress. Sandys thought the decay of hospitality was so severe, in part owing to excessive spending on clothing, that he favored stricter laws to curtail dress. His concern was shared by the physician and mas-ter of Manchester Grammar School, Thomas Cogan. Aylmer made the unusual suggestion that savings from reduced clothing budgets be used to improve the defense of the realm. Thus Anglicans were convinced that more modest dress would benefit the spiritual lives of the people and the social (and for Aylmer the defense) needs of the country.[12]

Puritan dress was scathingly denounced by several Anglicans. The attack was twofold, accusing the Puritans of excessively fine attire and overly simple clothing. In October 1602 the dean of St. Paul's reprehended Stephen Egerton and a fellow Puritan minister because their followers, most of whom were allegedly women, dressed super-fluously. The dean of Exeter, Matthew Sutcliffe, accused Puritan women of idolatry and folly for excessive cosmetics and ruffled clothes. Three years before he became bishop of Exeter, John Wool-ton, a strenuous opponent of the Puritans, charged them with spoil-ing schools and robbing the patrimony of the church to deck them-selves in costly garb. Although he acknowledged the validity of the Puritan position that apparel was a matter of adiaphora, he cited

Puritans for abusing indifferent things by their ostentation and prodigal waste. The second Anglican thrust castigated Puritans who dressed in utmost simplicity, wearing flat caps and russet cloaks, "& well they may: for their religion is a russet religion, good for none but russet cotes, & such as fauour popular gouernment." Such criticism is at odds with Nash's idealizing of "sir Rowland *Russet-coat,*" who is contrasted with his velvet-garbed sons, the "Carterly vpstarts." Yet for some Anglicans, secular as well as ecclesiastical apparel further differentiated them from Puritans.[13]

Despite the Anglican attempt to distinguish between themselves and Puritans over apparel, there was general agreement on the principles governing dress. Puritans, however, stressed that clothing was instituted primarily to hide shameful nudity, a point not emphasized by Anglicans. The other purposes for which clothing was instituted, according to Puritans, were harmonious with those posited by Anglicans, to protect against the elements and to distinguish persons by social rank and sex.[14]

Like Anglicans, Puritans were adamant that apparel reflect social status, though several Puritans felt it was better to err by dressing too modestly than beyond the bounds of one's rank. The ideal was simple:

> In thine aray,
> Go not too gay,
> But after thy degree.

The idea of a divinely determined social hierarchy was associated with the old thesis that God intended people to wear attire befitting their social stations. Puritans took pains to defend the right of higher orders to wear sumptuous apparel, which suggests that some nonaristocratic Puritan laity were opposed to such dress. Stubbes, who wrote the fullest Elizabethan analysis of clothing, argued that the costliness of the garb worn by magistrates and state officers manifested the worthiness of their offices, "therby to strike a terroure & feare into the harts of the people, to offend against the maiesty of their callings." Complaints about the refusal of the lower orders to dress modestly in accord with their social station were commonplace among Puritans. Such refusal frustrated the godly brethren, perhaps because it smacked of social leveling. Dent, in fact, cited old sayings to that effect: *"Euery Iacke will be a Gentleman, and* Ione *is as good as my Lady."* Although Puritans defended the right of the upper orders to dress finely, the latter were cautioned not to exceed themselves, but to beware of impoverishing their estates by lavish wardrobes, "for that indeede is the way to bring a castle into a capcase."[15]

Puritans agreed with Anglicans that pride in apparel must be eschewed. To Perkins, those who spent so much time dressing vainly left insufficient time to adorn their souls, and thus tended to ignorance, idleness, and lasciviousness. Every estate, argued the Lincolnshire rector Francis Timme, offended by dressing above its station, and he urged a return to the moderate dress that characterized the reign of William Rufus. Women were singled out by Dent and Stubbes as vain dressers. The elaborately coiffured hairstyles, the dyed hair, the pierced ears and earrings, and the decoration of the hair with rings and "gewgawes" were blasted as manifestations of pride. To be proud of apparel, mused Dent, was as unbefitting as a fool who was proud of his babble or a thief who prided himself in his halter. Stubbes thought it irrational to wear vain clothes when "meaner is both better[,] cheape, easier to be had, as warme to the bodie, and as decent, and comly to any chast christians eye." In his estimation, however, England was plagued more than any other country with people who prided themselves in their apparel.[16]

Anglican hostility to excess in clothing was shared by Puritans, for excess was an example of evil, a provocation to sin, and a hindrance to charitable deeds. Some Puritans were convinced that overdressing was an evil that pervaded the land; according to Norden "every man and woman wade[s] in excess in this sin." Stubbes, however, thought it was confined essentially to the inferior sort, who aped their betters' dress. With approval Vaughan recounted Henry VI's reported response to the earl of Warwick when the latter reproached the king for his mean garb: "It behooueth a Prince to excell his subiects in vertue, & not in vesture." Elizabethan women were excoriated for excess in dress, cosmetics, hair fashions, and jewelry. Henry Smith referred disparagingly to their "excesse in imbrodery, their vanitie in cuttes, gardes and pownces, their excesse in spangling[,] their fantasticall feathers and needlesse brauerie." Many, asserted Trigge, found fault with ministers because their wives dressed lavishly. Like Adam Hill, Stubbes deplored Elizabethans who acquired excessive amounts of clothing.[17]

Puritans, too, insisted that apparel must not be conducive to licentiousness or other forms of evil. If anything, they placed more emphasis than Anglicans on the interpretation that the seventh commandment prohibits suggestive clothing. Dent summarized the Puritan conviction that such apparel "is a minstrelsie that pipes vp a daunce vnto whoredome." Puritans also warned against the sexual enticements of frizzled hair, perfume, cosmetics, and "rowling eye[s]," all of which were seen as forerunners of adultery. Apparently the only Elizabethan Puritan concerned with the seduction of women by male apparel was Sir Philip Sidney, who wittily remarked that "she that hath been seduced by apparel, let me give her to weet, that men always put off their cloathes before they go to bed." The tone of the Puritan comments suggests that blame was cast on women who were enticed by male attire as well as women who lured men with seductive clothing; in either case the party of primary culpability was female.[18]

Puritans joined with Anglicans in objecting to clothing that was unnatural or that belonged to the opposite sex. Udall excoriated Elizabethans who wore "straunge and monstrous" attire, examples of which, according to Stubbes, were the popular doublets, which highlighted "great bellies hanging down beneath their *Pudenda, . . . &* stuffed with foure, fiue or six pound of Bombast at the least." Cosmetics were denounced as unnatural by Timme, Perkins, Stubbes, and Vaughan, and Timme made the same charge against wigs. To use cosmetics was to obliterate divine handiwork. Wearing clothing of the opposite sex was repudiated as a violation of the moral law and the use of clothing to distinguish sex. "All apparell, " insisted Perkins, "must be fitted to the bodie, in a comely and decent manner; such as becometh holinesse," which prohibited clothing of the opposite sex. Rainolds pushed this prohibition to the extreme, insisting that a man could not don female apparel even to benefit others or save himself. Timme ruled out women's fashions that approximated male doublets and breeches. Similarly, Stubbes argued that the trend toward finer male attire was responsible for a rise in pusillanimity and effeminacy.[19]

Puritans concurred with Anglicans that clothing must be moderate, sober, and comely. Although apparel was a matter of adiaphora, immodest and offensive dress was unacceptable, for Christians must dress in a manner reflecting humility and modesty. "We must," Perkins explained, "make a spirituall vse of the apparell which we weare" by using it to humble ourselves. Temperate clothing was a means to bring the "old Adam" into subjection. Wearing simple and sober apparel would, in Stubbes' judgment, end the scandal caused by excessive dress and simultaneously enrich the country. The ideal was not harshly severe clothing but a mean; this excluded, for example, double ruffs and farthingales. Yet for a gentleman to dress modestly, admitted Northbrooke, he would have to withstand social pressure, for "the Roysters call suche a one, by the name of a Loute, a Clinchpoope, or one that knoweth no fashions." Puritan strictures on dress applied to laity and clergy alike. Women especially were encouraged to dress in a comely fashion, for "a modest woman is known by her sober attire." In practice, this meant eschewing expensive clothes, braided hair, pearls and gold jewelry, perfume, and bare necks and breasts.[20]

The quest for the latest fashions was as strenuously censured by Puritans as Anglicans. The demand for current fashions, in particular those imported from the Continent, was decried as vanity, a violation of scriptural principles (Rom. 12:2; 1 Cor. 11:14; 1 Pet. 3:3), and a preference for the ridiculous. Like a mercantilist, Trigge opposed foreign fashions because they necessitated the export of bullion. Preference for native dress was asserted by Puritans, with Stubbes insisting that only in cases of necessity was it justifiable to seek foreign attire. "O remove it," thundered Northbrooke, "and send every country his fashion again: be not beholden to any nation for such trumpery." Puritans also objected to current fashions, including ruffs, busks, and hoops, because they were unnatural, vain, and deforming rather than adorning. In the judgment of Dent and Perkins, demand for the newest styles was responsible for an increase in covetousness, oppression, and deceit. Clothing was not merely a matter of personal taste, but of Christian principles and social welfare.[21]

Puritans were no less concerned than Anglicans with reducing clothing budgets to increase poor relief and support education. No attempt was made to deny the upper orders the right to wear attire suitable to their estates, but instead the upper classes were urged to forbear superfluous clothing to channel the savings to those in need. If, said Stubbes, those who amassed great wardrobes would remember that "their clothes (except those that they weare vppon their backs) be non of theirs, but the poores, they would not keep vp their . . . wardrobes as they do." Bestowing second-hand clothing on the destitute (which practice contributed to the growing inability to distinguish social status by dress) was not sufficient. Henry Smith professed to know Elizabethans with as many as twenty coats who refused to donate a penny to the destitute. According to Hake's calculations, the amount spent in a two-year period on a "meane" gentleman's daughter or the wife or daughter of a burgess was enough to support a poor student at a university for four or five years. Vaughan thought that the excessive apparel purchased by gentlemen at the Inns of Court would build a number of free schools. Reduced clothing expenditures were thus a means to increase poor relief and support needy students (resulting in more clergy to fill empty pulpits).[22]

Although Anglicans and Puritans agreed in principle on how to dress, some differences in degree were shown, especially by Puritans who stressed simplicity more than Anglicans thought necessary. That Puritan laity sought the advice of their clergy more often than did Anglican laity on appropriate attire is suggested by the advice of Puritan clergy to have the laity imitate the dress of the godly. Perkins, for instance, must be writing from ministerial experience when he advises the laity: "We haue no expresse rule in Scripture, touching the measure and manner of our apparell: and therefore, the wise and graue presidents of good and godly men, that are of the same, of like degree with our selues, ought to stand for a rule of direction in this behalfe."[23]

Puritan laity also were encouraged to dress in accord with their financial ability and with a view to utility. "Let euery one cut his coate according to hys cloth," advised Gibbon. Perkins and Stubbes insisted that clothing be selected with practicability in mind. Pantofles, a form of slippers, were cited as an example of unuseful clothing when worn, as the fashion was, outdoors. Women's apparel was judged by Perkins to be unsuited for "any good busines, but must of necessitie [make a woman] either sit, or stand still." Stubbes recommended that people dress according to necessity, but in this respect some Puritans found him too extreme. In the words of Wilcox, "it is an Anabaptisticall conceit, to allow men no more of the creatures, but what will serue for necessitie." Perkins believed it was wrong to desire more than essential clothing, but it was acceptable to wear what God had provided. Presumably more substantial Puritans, such as Egerton's followers, would have found Dering comforting when he justified finer attire: "Whatsoeuer God hath giuen me in the daies of my pilgrimage, the profite of it is mine. . . . If my garments be silke, I may put them on." Not all Puritans wanted the godly clothed in russet coats.[24]

Relatively little in Elizabethan Separatist literature speaks of apparel, and this mention appears in propaganda directed against the Church of England. Its ministers were accused of rebuking vain attire in the presence of "gentle and tractable souls," but violating their own prescriptions by wearing "whorish" clothes that were "either too nice and curious, or els too affected and framed as the rough garment to deceave." Barrow censured clerics of the established church for justifying the vain clothing of the powerful, noble, and wealthy on the grounds that it suited their social station.[25] That charge surely smacked of egalitarianism.

Elizabethan Catholic literature reflects an attitude to attire harmonious with that of Anglicans and Puritans. Dress must be moderate, natural, befitting one's estate, and neither "too gay, nor too sluttish." Those who dressed to excess were deplored as prodigal fools, and those who wore the latest fashions were chided. Catholics were warned not to break the seventh commandment by wearing alluring clothing. The ideal was fittingly expressed by the Jesuit Robert Southwell, who had studied at Douai and Rome before joining the English Mission in 1586:

Mine apparel must be free from lightness or more gaudiness than fitteth my age, calling, or company. I must be decent and comely, not too open, nor with unusual or new-fashioned dresses that other grave persons of my quality and calling that are well thought of do not use.

In practice that aim was difficult for missionary priests to achieve, for they were sometimes forced to dress like their English hosts, a fashion Campion found "ridiculous". Garbed as aristocrats, Catholic missionaries became the butt of Cartwright's attack: "In their *seruice of God* [they are] . . . attired like stage-players with veluets, silke, and satten, and cloth of gold, and fine linnen," contrary to apostolic simplicity and humility. The comments of Campion and Cartwright suggest that lay Catholics were not prone to dress more modestly than their Protestant counterparts.[26]

The views of the clergy on apparel received much support in ballads and popular verse. Clothes had to be compatible with one's estate:

> Weare not suche costly clothes
> as are not for thy state.

Sarcasm was directed at the preference for foreign fashions:

> *Frenche* cappes are nowe the fashion,
> and therfore must be had.

Men were cautioned to beware of women who "will lay out their faire teates," and husbands were encouraged to see thar their wives dressed "comely and cleane, sober and sad." A 1560 ballad bore a title that was in effect a moral: "The Proude Wyues Pater Noster That Wolde Go Gaye, and Vndyd Her Husbonde and Went Her Waye." Thomas Churchyard objurgated the aristocracy for their lavish attire of "gay golden robes" and "silke laide on silke." and urged them to return to the simple clothing of the past. Failure to do so, according to the balladeer and Merchant Tailor, William Fulwood, would bring their estates to decay. More important was the spiritual significance of dressing excessively, as expressed in a 1584 ballad:

What can avayle your velvet gownes,
    your Caules of glitteringe golde,
Your ruffes so deepe, your chaines of Iette,
    when you are tourn'd to mould?

Thus the concern of religious leaders for attire was shared by balladeers and poets, reinforcing the common ideal that, in Shakespeare's words "'tis the mind that makes the body rich."[27]

Reports of foreign visitors substantiate the complaints of Anglicans and Puritans about extravagance in Elizabethan dress. In 1575, Emmanuel van Meteren depicted English dress as elegant and unusually fashion conscious. "They are very inconstant and desirous of novelties, changing their fashions every year, both men and women." During his sojourn, he saw well-dressed women sitting before their houses to display their clothes, and noted that ladies of distinction had begun to cover their faces in public with silk masks and feathers. A decade later, Samuel Kiechel, a Swabian merchant, reported that Elizabethan women used fewer cosmetics than Italians but "dress in splendid stuffs, and many a one wears three cloth gowns or petticoats, one over the other." In 1592 Jakob Rathgeb, private secretary to Frederick, duke of Württemberg, observed that Londoners were magnificently dressed, particularly the women in velvets and ruffs, some of whom skimped on food to dress lavishly. At court he noticed the presence of French and Spanish fashions.[28] These impartial observations lend credence to the comments of Anglican and Puritan clergy.

Some endeavors were made in the Elizabethan period to inculcate in students the appropriate outlook on attire. Mulcaster favored thin clothing to toughen the flesh. The statutes of the Rivington Grammar School imposed the mean that Anglican and Puritan clerics favored: "Though their apparel need not be costly, yet it is a shame to wear it slovenly; their coats and hose shall not be costly pomished, cut, graded, nor jagged, no nor torn, slovenly worn, nor ragged." Caps with feathers and aglets were judged too ornamental. Boys at Westminster School were modestly (though not cheaply) dressed in gowns of russet or a "sadd newe color," dublets of sackcloth lined with canvas, pantaloons, hose, hats, and shoes. A hat cost 18d., a pair of shoes 10d., and a yard of cloth for the gown 5s. Abuses in apparel at Cambridge caused the chancellor, Lord Burghley, to issue a decree protesting the unreasonable cost and the unseemly fashion of students' garb, and warning that lodging would be refused to those dressed unsuitably. In 1570 Cambridge proctors were accused of wearing "skabilonians [pantaloons] and knitt nether-stockes to[o] fine for schollers." By the early 1620s, dress at Cambridge led Samuel Ward to complain of "excess in apparrell." Attempts were also made to regulate students' dress at Oxford.[29]

Advice on appropriate attire came to young people in other ways. William Wentworth recommended that his son spend moderately on clothing, remembering that "onelie decencie is ynough," and that wise men accounted expensive clothes as vain. Sir Thomas Bromley's children were taught that excess in apparel caused lust, hence they must wear clothing that was modest, comely, in keeping with their finances, suitable to their social estate, and appropriate for their ages. In their attire they were instructed to exemplify virtue and godliness, not folly, levity, pride, and wantonness. Thomas Wotton, a servant of Richard Sheppard, Lionel Cranfield's father-in-law, was informed by Sheppard that merchants in the Netherlands would "look deeply into your usage, behaviour and carriage, and in your manner of going in your apparel. And according as they find it to be mixed with sobriety, so shall you find credit." It is impossible to know how many Elizabethan fathers, tutors, and masters provided similar instructions, though it is likely that the number was considerable.[30]

Contemporary evidence suggests a growing but far from universal interest in wearing finer attire. Peers and their families customarily spent a great deal on clothing, particularly for special occasions such as weddings. For St. George's day, 1581, Robert Devereux, earl of Essex, ordered new attire, including a satin doublet, velvet hose, and a crimson jerkin trimmed with lace, as well as new livery for his servants. Lady Katherine, wife of Henry Lord Berkeley, wanted new clothes for her son that would be fashionable "and of a good shewe; not too costly, not too meane, rather costly then too meane." Yet some examples or restraint were notable, such as that of Burghley, whose attire was described as "rather neat and seemly than sumptuous." His mother had a wardrobe filled with gowns of silk and other material, but she preferred simple clothes, which Burghley's steward, Peter Kempe, regarded as too mean for one of even lower estate. A ballad in commemoration of a marquess' wife (presumably Northampton's or Winchester's) praised her moderation in dress:

> Mee thinkes I see her modeste mood
> Her comlie clothing plainlie clad.[31]

The financial records of the peerage underscore the extent to which nobles increasingly devoted money to apparel. In the period from 10 February 1563 to 27 January 1568, Edward Seymour, earl of Hertford, spent £200 on clothing for himself, his wife, and his two sons, out of a total budget of £1,966 0s. 11d. In the first nine months of 1570, the bill for apparel for Edward de Vere, earl of Oxford, a royal ward, was £47 9s. 6d. Inflation and a sharply increased level of taste led to substantially greater outlays by the end of the age. In 1588 the estate of the earl of Leicester included seven doublets and two cloaks valued at £543 by the executors. The general account for 1597-98 of Henry Percy, earl of Northumberland, lists £358 12s. 11d. for "Apparell for his Lordship." In the late 1590s Roger Manners, earl of Rutland, spent the staggering sum of at least £1000 *p.a.* on his clothes. [32]

The gentry's taste in clothing usually was much more modest. At the end of the age, Cornish gentry were said to "delight not in brauerie of apparrell: yet the women would be verie loth to come behinde the fashion, in newfanglednes of the maner, if not in costlynes of the matter." The estate of Sir Peter Frescheville of Staveley, Derby, in November 1559, included £40 worth of apparel out of a total estate worth £436 0s. 2d. The estate of his son, Peter Frescheville, esq., in February 1582, was valued at £609 2s. 4d., but contained apparel worth only £50. More substantial expenditures on apparel were made by the Puritan Sir William Fitzwilliam in 1592-93; out of total expenses of £943 4s. 11½ d., £87 6s. 10 d. went to clothing, including pearl buttons for his wife and gold and silver lace for himself. In the month of January 1597 alone, Anthony Bacon spent £29 12s. on attire, and the previous May his London draper had billed him £31 19s. 9d. Sir William Holles' son, Gervas, was reputed to have an inordinate love of "costly apparell," and Lady Elizabeth Willoughby amassed an elegant wardrobe before her death in 1594. Some gentry felt the pressure for fine attire so keenly that they reduced their estates to purchase it. When John Kingston of Lincolnshire came of age in the 1570s he sold lands to purchase silk and satin clothing worth £220 at one London shop. Thomas Digges complained to Sir Robert Cecil in 1593 that his brother-in-law, while executor of the estate of Thomas' father, had depleted it because of excessive expenses for apparel. Thus the taste of some gentry for more expensive and stylish clothing substantiated the general criticism of the reformers. [33]

Fine apparel was sought in some professional and merchant circles. In 1602 Chamberlain wrote of a London mercer's wife who owned thirty smocks worth £60, implying this overindulgence was a factor in her husband's bankruptcy. In contrast, James Whitelocke's father Richard, a Merchant Adventurer, dressed moderately, wearing in the 1560s "a cap, a verye smale ruffe withe black work, a side coat of fine black clothe, a black satten dubblet, and a Spanishe cape of fine black clothe, furred and edged withe pinked satten and long stok-kins." In 1609 his son remarked that such attire "wolde be thoughte overgrave in an elder by ten yeares." The physician Simon Forman spent nearly £50 in 1600 for clothing for himself and his wife, and the following year he bought "moch apparell." In 1602 it was report-ed that whereas counsellors in King's Bench previously wore "gownes faced with satten, and some with yellowe cotten, and the benchers with jennet furre; nowe they are come to that pride and fa[n] tastick-nes, that every one must have a veluet face, and some . . . tricked with lace." Even some clergy were enamored with clothing styles, though the bishops tried to keep the clergy in simple dress. John Birkbie, rector of Moor Monkton, Yorks., in 1567 wore "verie undecent apparell namelie great britches cut and drawn oute with sarcenet and taffite, and great ruffes laid on with laceis of gold and silk." [34]

For other groups, fancy attire was out of the question, except per-haps for the more substantial yeomen. The Devonshire yeoman John Furse (d. 1579), reputedly a godly man, was "verye nete and trym yn his apparell," which apparently was modest. A representative yeo-man might own three gowns, three jackets, a jerkin, a coat, a cassock, a doublet, two caps, and a hat, while his servant possessed a cloth gown, a girdle, a cassock, and a frock. According to Richard Carew, the dress of Cornish husbandmen improved substantially in the per-iod, though at the outset it was "course in matter, ill shapen in man-er: their legges and feet naked and beare." During the age, dress gen-erally improved for all except the very poor. [35]

Elizabethan attire became increasingly elaborate despite the spor-adic efforts of local magistrates to enforce moderation. In 1582, Lambarde warned the general sessions of the peace at Maidstone, Kent, that unseemly apparel led to theft; three years later he com-plained of "vanity of array," and in 1589 he called for moderate dress. Sumptuary regulations were enforced in Exeter, where violators were often apprentices. Every alderman had to inquire in his ward if un-authorized persons wore silk hats and ruffled shirts. One apprentice was fined 3s. 4d. for wearing great hose and ruffs and a silk hat during the 1561 Christmas season. [36]

At Southampton periodic attempts were made to punish violators of the statute regulating apparel. In 1576, churchwardens made weekly presentments of women who wore hats instead of the re-quired white caps. The same year, a code of dress for the mayor, ald-ermen, sheriffs, bailiffs, and their wives was formulated. In 1577, eleven persons were named in the court leet records for violating the statute on apparel, including a man who wore "gardes of velvat on his hose," a wife attired in a petticoat trimmed with velvet, a man dressed in "a gowne of norwyg worsted with a brode byllyment [habiliment] Lace of sylke," and numerous persons for wearing taffeta hats. F. G. Emmison believes that manorial juries in Essex rarely convicted people for excessive attire, though in a case at Ingatestone in 1568 three men were fined 20d. each for wearing clothes above their social status. In the same year, a jury at Hinckford declared that the recent petty sessions found "all . . . in good order" concerning apparel. At Great Dunmow the same year, three tailors were presented for using "great excess in their apparel for their hosen." Essex women occasionally were in trouble for wearing male attire, such as the Downham woman who wore male clothing to church in 1596.[37]

Visitation articles concentrated on clergy who wore improper clothing. Aylmer's 1577 articles for the diocese of London, like those of Parker for Winchester (1575) and Whitgift for Worcester (1577), inquired "whether any minister use any lay or unseemly apparel, as gowns guarded, or made of a light unseemly color or fashion, great barrel-breaches, flaunting ruffs; or use to go lightly and undecently in their hose and doublets." Articles inquired whether ministers' wives and children dressed in clothes not befitting the state and calling of the religious leaders. In the diocese of Durham, Barnes ordered in 1577 that his clergy wear, when outdoors, "clerkly and decent apparel, as gowns or cloaks with sleeves of sad color, and none unseemly apparel, as great ruffs, great breeches, gascogne hose, [and] scalings." Whitgift demanded the same of Worcester clergy. Visitation articles indicate that bishops expected the clergy to dress appropriately for men of their calling in conservative, modest clothing.[38]

There were repeated efforts in Parliament to regulate clothing more effectively. A bill to punish persons who made or wore great hose did not make it past a second reading in the Commons in March 1563. In 1566, an amended bill regulating clothing of clergy and laity was approved by the Commons in November, but agreement could not be reached with the Lords. A 1566 law attempting to regulate caps and hats (8 Eliz. I, c. 11) was reenacted in 1571 (13 Eliz. I, c. 19) requiring that all citizens, artisans, and laborers aged seven and above wear woolen caps on Sundays and holy days, on pain of a fine of 3s. 4d. A bill "against great Hosen" in the same session did not become law.[39]

In the 1576 Parliament, the Lords passed a bill to give Elizabeth authority to use proclamations to appoint apparel for the various degrees in the realm inasmuch as "disorder of Apparrell is very greate in this tyme." The Commons opposed the use of proclamations instead of statute and the proposed penalty, a fine of £10 and loss of the garment. There was also concern about enforcement, for a magistrate would be empowered to seize the garment or commit the offender unless he posted surety to surrender the clothes within twenty-four hours. Some MPs worried that magistrates might mistakenly seize the clothes of those entitled to wear finer attire. When the Lords refused to accept the bill as passed by the Commons, the matter was dropped. In 1589, the Lords again approved a bill against inappropriate apparel, only to have it die in a Commons' committee. Once more, Parliament sought in 1598 to enact legislation governing apparel, but the Lords found the Commons' bill objectionable because it was not harmonious with the queen's proclamation "touching the degrees and qualities of persons," and the matter was dropped owing to insufficient time to pursue a compromise. [40]

The fragmentary information about these parliamentary attempts to regulate apparel shows that the primary motivation was concern to preserve social distinctions and protect the cloth industry. The failure to enact most bills probably was due to disagreements over enforcement, penalties, and the relative powers to be accorded to statute and proclamation. The Commons were wary of bestowing much authority in matters of apparel on the crown and on the justices of the peace who might enforce provisions on the gentry. The Commons wished to prohibit abuses among the lower orders, but not at the expense of placing themselves under the increased authority of magistrates.

Appeals to court and Council regarding clothing reflect economic, social, and religious considerations. In September 1575, as a case in point, Thomas Lord Paget appealed to Burghley on behalf of the needy cap-makers of Lichfield, Staffs., who sought enforcement of the statute on wearing caps and a portion of the fines levied on offenders. London skinners petitioned the queen in February 1591, claiming their economic state had decayed because "the usual wearing of furs (especially of the breed of this realm) is utterly neglected and eaten out by the too ordinary lavish and unnecessary use of velvets and silks, drinking up the wealth of this realm." In London, however, merchants found the limitations on attire unduly restrictive, hence in April 1588 the lord mayor, George Bond, petitioned the Privy Council to mitigate the regulations to preserve "that decent order and convenyencye, that is by Citizens[,] Officers and others here thought meete to be vsed and continued." London citizens and officials as well as their wives "doe hold place of such worshipfull callinge otherwise, as requireth some larger limitacon." Stubbes pressed the government to enforce the laws on apparel, citing considerations of religion and the preservation of social hierarchy. [41]

The Privy Council periodically turned its attention to apparel, but not with enough consistency to procure the results Anglican and Puritan reformers desired. In April 1577 the Council sent letters to each shire in support of the recent proclamation against excessive apparel. The cap-makers of Lichfield were given some relief in January 1579 when the Council authorized two of them to collect fines imposed on violators of the statute on wearing caps. The money was to be used "to the mayntenance of the misterie of capping in certeine decaied townes of this Realme." The 1588 protest by the mayor and citizens of London against restrictions on dress was triggered by the Council's order to the lord mayor on 16 March to reform apparel in accord with the queen's proclamation. As with parliamentary endeavors to obtain further legislation regulating apparel, these attempts to restrict fine attire met opposition from merchants as well as gentry. [42]

Elizabeth issued eleven proclamations to regulate dress and an additional five to enforce the statute on caps. Her concern, as expressed in February 1589, was that excess apparel led to "ye confusion of degrees of all estates, amongst whom diversitie of apparell, hath bene allwayes a speciall & laudable marke." She was also mindful of the adverse economic effects of importing inadequately taxed foreign clothing. No evidence shows that she was interested in the religious implications of over-fine attire; her concern was social decorum and economic strength. [43]

The clothing styles of the court caused consternation in godly circles. Philip Gawdy's letters from court describe the obsession with the latest fashions among courtiers and ladies. About 1589, he wrote that "some one of them weares this daye with all theise fashions, and the nexte daye without. So that I fynd nothing more certayne then their vncertaynty." In 1594, after the courtiers had adopted the latest attire, Elizabeth decided on yet another change and ordered them to adopt short cloaks. When she died, the queen had over two thousand gowns in her wardrobe. Aylmer tried to persuade her in 1591 of the vanity of excess apparel, but without success, for she subsequently remarked that "if the Bishope helde more discorse on suche matters, shee wolde fitte him for heaven, but he shoulde walke thither withoute a staffe, and leave his mantle behind him." [44]

The attire at court was criticized by some clergy. Bishop Cooper fulminated against the gorgeous attire of the courtiers as a waste of money and a display of vanity. The Anglican minister Anthony Anderson called on the ladies at court to cease pursuing "the vntamed fashion of this wicked world." In a sermon before the court, Grindal's chaplain, Thomas Drant, censured courtiers for their dress and for the attitude that they were exempt from the admonitions of the clergy. He quoted Bernard of Clairvaux's aphorism that soft apparel signified a soft mind, and then scathingly denounced the attire worn by women at court, quoting from Tertullian's acerbic tract on female dress. Drant reprimanded the ladies for "their tall and bushy plumes, and . . . fresh golden caules so sheene and glosing," which manifested vanity. Perkins probably spoke for many Puritans when he deprecated female attire at court as an instrument and sign of pride, wantonness, and frivolity. The attorney John Norden depicted the court as a fountain from which vain fashions spread into the country until they "infected the poor ploughman, that a year's wages sufficeth not one suit of attire." The immorality and vanity of the court were infecting the hard-working, godly inhabitants of the country: The theme grew in intensity in the seventeenth century, helping set the stage for the attack on the Stuart court, though by no means making its overthrow inevitable or even foreseeable in the early 1600s.[45]

In sum, Anglican and Puritan views on apparel were harmonious. Both groups insisted that attire must reflect social status and must not be vain, lavish, or conducive to licentiousness. Dress must be moderate, sober, and comely. Concern with recent fashions and Continental styles was condemned, and Elizabethans were exhorted to spend less on clothing and more on poor relief, hospitality, and education. Anglicans, however, made an issue of dress, charging some Puritans with overly fine attire and others with excessively simple garb. The Church of England's attitude toward apparel was denounced by the Separatists in egalitarian tones. Catholic attitudes to dress paralleled those of Anglicans and Puritans, though because missionary priests sometimes disguised themselves in gentry attire, Cartwright was enabled to ridicule them. Anglican and Puritan views on dress are reflected in ballads and popular verse; nevertheless, the repeated admonitions of preachers, moralists, and balladeers seem to have had minimal effect. The comments of foreign visitors substantiate the complaints of the clergy. Attempts to inculcate proper attitudes to dress by schoolmasters, parents, tutors, and masters apparently also had limited effect, for among the landed and merchant classes are indications of substantially increased clothing expenses in the latter part of the period. Towns such as Exeter and Southampton sought to enforce regulations on attire, and so did some manorial courts. In visitation articles, the bishops displayed concern with the dress worn by the clergy.

Regulating apparel had a mixture of religious, social, and economic motivations, as manifested in appeals to the court and Council and debates in Parliament. Endeavors to pass more restrictive legislation usually came to nought because of controversy over the use of proclamations, means of enforcement, and potential penalties. The Privy Council was unable or unwilling to devote sufficient attention to the enforcement of clothing regulations, though the queen issued a number of proclamations dealing with attire. The government's attempts undoubtedly were rendered less effective by the example of a court lavish in its dress and devoted to the latest fashions. On that point Anglican and Puritan critics agreed.

(2) Society and the Spoken Word

They run so into Rethorick, as often times they ouerrun the boundes of their own wits, and goe they knowe not whether.

Jane Anger[46]

If you will speake, pray speake it playne,
Lest els perhaps you lose your payne.

Henry Willoby[47]

As in the case of apparel, broad agreement existed among Anglicans and Puritans with respect to appropriate speech. The basic principles were reflected in the Geneva marginalia, where truth and simplicity in speech were subordinated only to moral uprightness and assistance to others. Moderation in speech, as in other spheres of social conduct, was a virtue. Readers were encouraged to bear in mind the utilitarian function of language, so that all speech tended to common edification. Untruth, gossip, false accusations, and hypocrisy were condemned, as was jesting, "which is ether vaine, or els by example and euil speaking may hurt your neighbour." In contrast, the Bishops' Bible was less concerned with speech, though it warned that words spoken to no effect were like rain evaporating in an east wind. The Beza-Tomson marginalia repeated the Geneva admonitions to speak simply, truthfully, moderately, without jests, and for the profit of listeners.[48]

Anglican comments about speech accord with the admonitions in the biblical marginalia. People were urged to eschew idle and vain words, carnal language, flattery, and gossip in preference to sober, modest speech. God must be spoken of reverently, one's neighbor charitably, and oneself humbly. One must not, said Babington, "lie, flatter, cogge, halt, glose, sooth, smooth, croutch, creepe, sigh, sorrowe, fawne, and fall downe at ones feete, sweare and protest liking, loue, faithfull seruice and friendshippe." Jesting was acceptable to Babington provided it did not proceed from vanity or ridicule. Babington also recognized the importance of mild speech in taming social disorder. Insinuation into the favor of social superiors was damned by various Anglicans, and at the highest level, Pilkington admonished courtiers to speak and debate honestly with the sovereign for the good of the state.[49]

Indications are strong, especially in advice to children, that some Anglicans sought to practice these ideals. Wentworth admonished his son Thomas to govern his tongue with moderation and circumspection, and to avoid speaking ill except privately to someone trustworthy. The Devon yeoman Robert Furse urged his son in 1593 to "be fere speched unto all men," while Sir Thomas Bromley's children were tutored to treat ribald speech as a violation of the seventh commandment. The household rules of Lady Jane, wife of Henry Lord Berkeley, stipulated that at dinner and supper gentlemen must use moderate speech as a good example for others. For Roger Ascham, the appropriate ideal was "plain and sensible utterance," a virtue to which Sir Thomas Egerton subscribed. Burghley was praised for his purposeful and unaffected use of language: "Touching his method of speech and writing, it was short and plain without curiousity, but not altogether without ornament, for he especially regarded substance of matter and not artificial composition of words." In the Protestant-Catholic debate before Elizabeth in the spring of 1559, Robert Horne avoided, "high-flown" language.[50]

Women were chided for proclivity to verbosity, as in this rude rhyme:

> Where many gese be, be many tordes
> And where be women, are many wordes.

An Anglican ideal for women's speech was that of Katherine Brettergh, as attributed by William Harrison, who praised her for refusing to speak vainly or immodestly, or to use jests. "In priuate speech where shee might speake with profit, she did it so well, that her speeches might haue been deliuered by a stronger vessell then her selfe: her words being so well seasoned, and proceeding from such a sanctified heart, did alwaies *minister grace to the hearers.*" At the other extreme, Whittingham's widow Katherine was less judicious in her speech, and was sued at York when she circulated a rumor that Margaret, wife of Francis Key, master of the grammar school at Durham, had given birth to a bastard before her marriage.[51]

Undoubtedly the insidiousness of some Elizabethan rumors accounted partly for clerical concern with honest speech. George Hastings, earl of Huntingdon, expressed his fears to Essex in 1595 that the queen might judge him by false reports. Edward de Vere, earl of Oxford, temporarily separated from his wife because of a rumor that her daughter had been sired in an adulterous relationship. Rumors by a tutor about an alleged contract for matrimony by Sir William St. Loe's widow brought intervention from Cecil and Leicester in 1567. In 1602 Lionel Cranfield was plagued by men in England and the Netherlands who sought to undermine his reputation.[52]

Puritan ideas on speech generally reflected those of the Anglicans, though Puritans typically devoted more written comment to this subject. Speech must be edifying, sober, utilitarian, charitable, truthful, godly, and moderate. Perkins, who wrote a tract on speech, urged that it be gracious and manifest inner spiritual purity. "The speech is gracious, when it is so vttered, that the graces of God wrought in the heart by the holy Ghost, are as it were pictured and painted forth in the same: for speech is the very image of the heart." On the negative side, Puritans abhorred speech that was superfluous, offensive, false, vain, foolish, ribald, or rash. Boasting, taunting, railing, scoffing, reproaching, and gossiping were deplored. Fulke even opposed eloquent speech. It is important to avoid inappropriate speech, according to Field, because it is associated with Catholics. In contrast, "a nice Puritaine," said the Puritan poet Acheley, was

> One that doth feare to counterfeit or lye,
> One that nere vttereth a word in vaine,
> A precise master of simplicitie.

Most Puritans objected to jests, though Northbrooke and Perkins tolerated them if they were not disrespectful to God or harmful to another person. Perkins thought jests could be useful in the reproof of sin, and he sanctioned mirth in general if it was moderate, compassionate for the godly, and linked to the fear of God.[53]

Although Anglicans were hostile to idle speech, avoiding it was almost an obsession with Puritans, who waged a continuous campaign against

> idle words, seruants to shallow braines,
> Vnfruitfull sounds, wind-wasting arbitrators.

A multitude of words was the wellspring of numerous vices: The more words, the more sin, was Wilcox's warning. Frugality of speech was linked to the preservation of property, on the assumption that idle talk dissipated time and led to the wasteful consumption of goods. Yet Perkins allotted time for "*vrbanitie*," the use of pleasant conversation for recreation or mutual edification.[54]

Some Puritans reiterated the common view of the evils of talkative women, and Cleaver opined that silence was a woman's best ornament. It incensed Dent that wives of the wealthy did not arise until 9:00 A.M. and then devoted a substantial part of their time to gossiping. The tendency of ministers' wives to engage in light conversation was, argued Trigge, a reason that clerical marriages still encountered popular hostility. In contrast, Stubbes lauded his wife Katherine because "she coulde neuer abide to beare any filthie or vncleane talk of scurrilitie, neither swearing nor blaspheming, cursing nor banning, but would reproue them sharply." Although Greenham castigated the laboring tongues of some "brainsick and vnstable women," he adopted a less sexist approach than most Puritans when he cast equal blame on the indiscreet speech of men.[55]

Many Puritans attempted to manifest these views in their actions. Philip Sidney was instructed by his father, Sir Henry, to be "rather a hearer and bearer away of other men's talk, than a beginner, or procurer of speech, otherwise you will be accounted to delight to hear yourself speak." Sir Walter Mildmay advised his son Anthony never to speak ill of any or vainly and untruthfully. Sir Walter's daughter-in-law, Lady Grace, referred to his wise and profitable speeches at his table, and his refusal to allow anyone to speak ill of another, or to refer irreverently to the queen, nobility, or Privy Council. According to their daughter Mary, Sir Anthony and Lady Grace likewise refused to tolerate scurrilous remarks, idle gossip, and ill-natured stories. As a child Grace (née Sherrington) had a cousin and governess who warned her against idle talk, dalliance, and servants who used ribald speech. Correspondents, however, sometimes were apologetic about their simplicity and brevity. Sir Francis Hastings wrote to Sir Christopher Hatton "lyke a poore plaine contrye fellowe," and a correspondent of Anthony Bacon opted "to wryte nothing then oft to lytel or no purpose."[56]

Puritan diaries manifest guilt over failure to live up to the ideals of speech. Richard Rogers had a troubled conscience when he spoke roughly or bitterly, and Ward felt guilty for talking idly of events in Durham, bragging of his fellowship, and not being sufficiently grieved over swearing and wild talk in a tavern. In 1595 he regretted his excessive "obsequency and flattery of Mr. [Paul] Greaves, now beyng fellow" at Cambridge. Two years later, Ward was even tormented by a conversation that was too merry. Puritan pressure for pure speech may have caused mild neuroses in tender consciences.[57]

Catholic concerns about speech were varied. The Rheims marginalia bemoaned the eloquence of Protestant preachers because it beguiled the simple, and warned that God required an account of every idle word. The Protestant interest in simplicity was shared by Thomas Lodge, a convert who shunned "vain flourish." Shelford was principally concerned with the function of speech as a preserver of social hierarchy, hence he stressed the proper language of inferiors to superiors. In the short rules formulated as a guide for his personal conduct, Southwell emphasized deliberate, courteous, utilitarian, and charitable speech. Like the Protestants, he shunned rashness, levity, taunting, and jesting. Henry Fitzalan, earl of Arundel, was "naturally given vnto breefenes, in vtteringe of his mynde, . . . but those his wordes, beinge shorte and fewe, carried matter in them, and weare allwaies, fit and pythye." Apart from the attack on their eloquence, Protestants would not have found Catholic maxims on speech unacceptable, though Field attacked Catholics for loose speech. Among the Separatists, Barrow criticized Church of England clergy for insufficiently rebuking the noble and the wealthy for their jesting, scoffing, and vain speaking.[58]

Efforts to enforce socially acceptable speech were undertaken in courts high and low, secular and ecclesiastical, in keeping with Pilkington's contention that good rulers were obliged to impose corrections. When rumors circulated in Yorkshire in 1576 that the government intended to establish a commission to seize unbranded cattle, Elizabeth and the Council of the North ordered those responsible for the rumors punished. For using lewd language, Anthony Atkins, a fellow of Merton College, Oxford, was committed to the Tower by the Privy Council in 1559. In London the recorder, William Fleetwood, imprisoned a man who falsely claimed that he supped as well as the lord mayor. Londoners were accustomed to seeing lewd and slanderous speakers and perjurors in the pillory or wearing papers on their heads proclaiming their offenses. In 1574, Mulcaster was admonished by the court of the Merchant Taylors' Company for using "injurious and quarelinge" speech to visitors at his school. The inhabitants of Wolverhampton, Staffs., were unhappy c. 1591 that the wife of a local painter had not been punished for reviling a minister, so they petitioned a justice of the peace for redress.[59]

The church too was concerned with speech violations. Visitation articles included queries about clergy who used filthy or vain speech, such as Francis Sayer, rector of Minster, Cornwall, a man "of badde conversation," or the rector of Sherrington, Bucks., who in 1576 "wolde have taken away a mans wief from him by the high waie and used such filthy speech that they banished him out of their company." Consistorial courts in the diocese of Ely required lay slanderers and gossipers to make public confession. A common area of verbal abuse involved sexual defamation, including the inaccurate use of epithets such as "bawd" and "whore," with such cases regularly appearing in ecclesiastical courts.[60]

Language thus did concern church and state, to the point that punishments were sometimes imposed for relatively modest offenses. Apart from spiritual objections to indecent speech, the authorities appear to have been primarily bothered by verbal threats to order and the social hierarchy. Although Anglican and Puritan authors substantially agreed on what constituted proper speech, and although conscientious parents of both persuasions inculcated these ideals in their offspring, failure to attain those ideals seemingly produced greater anxiety in Puritans than Anglicans. Contemporaries associated certain patterns of speech with religious groups; Puritans were known for the concern with veracity, simplicity, and utility. This common opinion suggests that Puritans strove to attain the ideal in daily conversations, though Anglicans did not find those ideals objectionable. Christopher Hill's "middling sort" presumably were attracted to the Puritan argument that wasted, idle words dissipated wealth.

(3) Society and the Printed Word

Euerie grosse brainde Idiot is suffered to come into print, who if hee set foorth a Pamphlet of the praise of Pudding pricks, or write a Treatise of *Tom Thumme*, . . . it is bought vp thicke and three folde, when better things lye dead.

Thomas Nash[61]

Reading of bookes is aptly compared to eating of cheese: the talant whereof, seemeth so diuers in taste: as amongst ten men, two, can hardly agree in one iudgement.

Leonard Wright[62]

With the expansion of printing and the increase in literacy, religious and political leaders provided guidelines for reading materials. In Worcester, where subscriptional literacy for males obtaining probate and marriage licenses rose from 60% in 1588-94 to 65% in 1600-20, some 16% of the men and women (excluding clergy and lawyers) for whom probate inventories exist for the 1590s owned at least one book, a dramatic increase from the figure of 4% for the period 1550-89. In the more progressive county of Kent, probate inventories of males in Canterbury show the incidence of book ownership increasing from 8% in the 1560s to 34% in the 1590s, while at Faversham the increase was from 15% to 32%. At Maidstone, however, the ownership of books remained relatively constant, moving only from 21% in the 1560s to 24% in the 1590s. Some writers were sufficiently aware of the expanding market to keep their books short, holding down the cost and aiming for wider circulation. From a different perspective, Robert Harrison was discouraged from writing a treatise on ecclesiastical polity after "weying the cost of the print, and findinge it to be aboue my reache of abilitie." Nevertheless, the number of new works increased so dramatically in the age that one author complained that ministers were writing too much before they matured, so that their books were "but dead letters."[63]

Anglican authors recommended avoiding books that were unprofitable, ribald, or immoral, for these books encouraged idleness and profane living. Generally criticism was directed against love sonnets, satires, and unsavory tales. In a reader for the "vnlearned," which ran to 448 pages plus introductory material, Abraham Fleming included letters by fifty-seven authors, both classical (e.g. Pliny, Cicero, Isocrates, and Socrates) and modern (e.g. Ascham, Erasmus, and Vives), the study of which was intended to arm readers against ignorance. The importance of reading good material was appreciated by Henoch Clapham, for he attributed his recantation of Separatism to the study of patristic literature while in exile.[64]

One of the most stringent Anglican attacks on inappropriate literature came from the layman Thomas Nash, who criticized abuses ranging from the imitation of Italian styles to amorous themes that corrupted chaste minds. He was equally displeased with works such as *Bevis of Southampton* and *Morte d'Arthur* on the one hand and encomiums of women on the other. Simultaneously he condemned Puritans who "ouershoote themselues as much another waie, in sencelesse stoicall austeritie, accounting Poetrie impietie, and witte follie." Nash urged readers to avoid superficial literature and seek out moral precepts, exhortations to virtue, and warnings against lust and idleness. In their "preciser censure" Puritans exercised a function "better beseeming a priuie then a pulpit." Nash stressed a discerning approach to the classics, citing the value of such works as Virgil's *Ecologues*, Lucian's *De Syria Dea*, and Plutarch's *De industria animalium*, but reproving obscene passages in Ovid and Virgil's *Priapea*.[65]

Ascham was slightly stricter toward literature than Nash. Whereas he objected to *Morte d' Arthur* because of its violence and bawdry, "ten *Morte Arthures* do not the tenth part so much harme, as one of these bookes, made in *Italie*, and translated in England," that corrupts manners and inculcates false doctrine. One book such as Boccaccio's *Decameron* or Petrarch's *Triumphs* does more to incite evil living than ten sermons at Paul's Cross moved men to the truth. He suspected that works such as William Painter's *The Palace of Pleasure* (1566) and Geoffrey Fenton's *Certaine Tragicall Discourses* (1567) were devices of closet Catholics to undermine youth, though he approved Sir Thomas Hoby's version of Castiglione's *Courtier*.[66]

A torrent of Puritan criticism came down against books and poetry thought to be profane, amorous, and frivolous. *Bevis of Southampton, Morte d' Arthur, The Court of Love, The Court of Venus, Robin Hood,* the *Howleglass* (a version of the German *Eulenspiegel*), the *Mad Men of Gotam,* the *Gests of Scoggin,* Rabelais' *Gargantua and Pantagruel, Aesop's Fables,* and *Guy of Warwick* were consored. People were exhorted to read books that were edifying, useful, and godly, and to shun profane and fruitless works that were "more meete for Mearcers shoppes, to wrappe their spices in, then for a wel disposed family to be taught & nurtured by." Objectionable writings were conducive to lust, spiritual infection, and mental corruption, though Holland cautioned that some heathen books contained worthy matter about things natural and political. He did, however, reiterate Ascham's warnings against Italian literature. Recommended books included theological studies, church history, and Foxe's *Acts and Monuments*. Luther, Theodore Beza, Urbanus Regius, Matthieu Virel, Jean Taffin, and the Puritans Gifford and Perkins were sanctioned. Perkins himself cautioned against secular histories as "enticements and baites vnto manifolde sinnes." Thus Puritans preferred a more restricted list of approved works than Anglicans, with emphasis on religious and utilitarian books.[67]

Although Trigge accused Catholics of addiction to fables and vain books, Catholic leaders recommended some works to reinforce faith. A note to 2 Timothy 2:17 in the Rheims New Testament warns against heretical books, and Persons advocated reading good books and keeping devout company as means to strengthen faith. Part of Southwell's daily routine was reading a good book, particularly a Catholic history, before supper. "If I have my book that I would often read, I may take some time from my work or the holy days to read a part thereof." As a chaplain to William Wiseman of Braddocks, Essex, Gerard had the family read books with an ascetic emphasis at the meal table when guests were not present. Books came from the Continent; Edward Rishton played a key role in getting Catholic books into Lancashire, so that gentry families such as the Southworths and Blundells had libraries of recusant literature. Among the books from abroad were three hundred copies of Vaux's catechism. In 1584 Sir Thomas Tresham's library included this catechism, Persons' *Christian Directory,* Cuthbert Tunstall's *De veritate corporis,* Richard Hopkin's *Book of Prayer and Meditation* (1582), Bede's *Historie,* and a Greek New Testament.[68]

Some evidence suggests that Puritan laity normally confined their reading to religious, utilitarian, and scholarly works, in keeping with the recommendations of their clergy. Lady Grace Mildmay read Scripture, herbals, and medical books, and tried to keep abreast of debates between Anglicans and Puritans. She advocated reading English history, "whereby we may be instructed to imitate and follow the good example of true and faithful subjects, and to have theyr worthy acts and exploys in memory, whereby we may avoyd and shun all treasons and treacherous attempts." Despite their pagan status, Lady Mildmay also approved classical philosophers. Another Puritan woman, Anne Locke, gave her husband a copy of Calvin's sermon on Isaiah 38. Margaret Russell Clifford, countess of Cumberland, avidly read Scripture and godly books. Arthur Lord Grey of Wilton was eulogized for reading "all good and learned books of [religious] controuersies that he could come by." William Carnsew, a Cornish gentleman, owned works by Cartwright, Ridley, Latimer, and Bullinger, as well as Luther's commentary on Galatians, Foxe's *Acts and Monuments,* Calvin's epistles, and Woolton's *Armour of Proof.* His library also included Ficino's *De triplici vita,* Humphrey Gilbert's *Discourse on the North West Passage,* the *Acts* of the Council of Basel, and books on history, medicine, and astrology. In 1574, Sir Nicholas Bacon donated one hundred books to the Cambridge University Library on subjects such as grammar, rhetoric, dialectic, cosmography, arithmetic, geometry, astronomy, and music. John Rainolds, a clergyman, amassed a library of some 1,800 books by 1607, whereas Francis Russell, earl of Bedford, had a more modest collection of 211 books and four manuscripts.[69]

Anglican laity, an amorphous group, manifested a wide variety of reading tastes. Some, such as Mrs. Katherine Brettergh, were one with the Puritans in preferring godly literature; her favorites were Scripture, Foxe's *Acts and Monuments,* expository works, and other religious material. Others, such as Edward de Vere, earl of Oxford, had more secular tastes; he patronized translations of chivalric romances by such men as Arthur Golding, Thomas Underdoune, and Anthony Munday. In 1595 John Willoughby purchased such disparate works as Nash's *Pierce Penilesse*, three religious works of Sutcliffe, *Robin Goodfellow, Tarltons Jestes*, an herbal, and the *Historie of Hamlet*. Gabriel Harvey recommended books for Arthur Capel on the principle that gentlemen must be "conversant and occupied in thos books esspecially, whereof thai mai have most use and practis, ether for writing or speaking, eloquently or wittely." Included were the writings of Mary Stuart, John Checke's *The Hurt of Sedition*, Thomas Marslie's *Mirrour for Magistrates,* Ascham's *Schoolmaster*, a Latin version of Castiglione's *Courtier,* and works of Peter Ramus, Osorius, and Sturm.[70]

One of the most balanced Anglican lay libraries was that of Sir Thomas Smith. It included patristics (e.g. Augustine, Chrysostom, Origen, and Ambrose), Protestant reformers (e.g. Luther, Bucer, and Peter Martyr), classics (e.g. Herodotus, Tacitus, Suetonius, Plutarch, Caesar, Aristotle, Plato, Cicero, and Thucydides), English history (Polydore Virgil and Hall's *Chronicles*), Renaissance works (e.g. Machiavelli, Erasmus, and Vives), Foxe's *Acts and Monuments*, and works on mathematics, medicine, poetry, grammar, and law. Judging from a personal book he kept, Smith was more interested in astrology than theology, for his brief diary was conjoined to extensive astrological data, replete with selected personal horoscopes. Another balanced library was the massive collection of the Catholic peer John Lord Lumley, whose approximately 2,600 books and 400 manuscripts included the collections of Thomas Cranmer and Henry Fitzalan, earl of Arundel, and ranged from theology, canon law, and history to medicine, music, cosmography, and common law.[71]

A number of Anglican prelates assembled significant libraries, some mostly religious in nature but others more balanced. Corpus Christi College, Cambridge, received some 300 manuscripts and 475 books on theology, history, law, and medicine from Parker's library in 1574. Whitgift's huge library of some 4,000 books and manuscripts was strong on religion, classics, and history (even Persian and Chinese), and included works of Dante, Chaucer, Sir Thomas More, Eliot, Ascham, and Holinshed, but had no plays. By 1612, Bancroft had amassed 352 manuscripts and 5,769 books on theology, liturgy, history, law, and the arts. In contrast, judging from a donation to Cambridge University Library in 1574, Robert Horne's library was largely theological.[72]

Despite (and partly because of) the outcry of the clergy against ribald, immoral, and unprofitable books, many of the laity preferred religious literature. In Essex, for example, wills for laity below the gentry mention few secular works, and some of these were medical books, while the most frequent citations are to Bibles, Testaments, psalters, service books, religious commentaries, and sermons. Many Elizabethans must have delighted in possessing a Bible; a 1574 will from the parish of Rochdale, Lancs., manifests such joy:

> I geve &c. one litle Bible to my sonne Rycharde and the said Jane my wyffe and they to see the same occupied everie Sabaothe daie when there ys no sermons nor sacramentes in ministringe and in the weeke daie my will and mynde ys that my porest kinsfolkes whiche are not able to by a Bible shall haue the same lent unto theim.

Bibles and prayer books were the most commonly owned printed material in Elizabethan Worcester, followed by devotional works and sermons. In Canterbury, Faversham, and Maidstone, Kent, the Bible was easily the most commonly owned book among nonprofessional men, followed by Testaments, service books, psalters, and Foxe's *Acts and Monuments.* Secular works, including books on law and history, were rarely mentioned in Kentish wills.[73]

With respect to reading materials, the clergy apparently were successful in persuading the laity to select religious works. In addition to private ownership, bishops encouraged churches to have copies of the Bible, the prayer book, the psalter, the homilies, and Erasmus' *Paraphrases* or Bullinger's *Decades.* Judging from Kentish wills, there was, then, reasonably broad exposure to religious literature among literate groups, particularly the aristocracy and professional groups, and to a lesser degree among yeomen and people in the clothing, leather, and food trades, the textile industry, and the distributive trade, particularly beginning in the 1590s.[74]

Complaints by Anglican and Puritan clergy against immoral, ribald, and unprofitable books may have reflected the taste for secular works in London and other towns, where the display of such wares occasioned complaints:

> What meane the rimes that run thus large in euery shop to sell:
> With wanton sound, and filthie sense, me thinke it grees not well.

The godly wanted such works banned; it must have grieved the more radical Protestants to see their religious works censored by a government that showed little concern with the publication of works deemed profane and harmful.[75]

In sum, although Anglicans and Puritans substantially agreed in condemning printed matter that was immoral or unedifying, they differed, as Nash observed, in the degree of their severity. Puritan clergy emphasized reading religious and utilitarian books, and Perkins cautioned against secular histories. Puritan laity such as Lady Grace Mildmay, Mrs. Anne Locke, Arthur Lord Grey of Wilton, and William Carnsew followed such advice, though Puritans such as Sir Nicholas Bacon, with large libraries, naturally collected a broader range of books. Although some Anglican laity restricted themselves to godly and utilitarian literature, in general they had a wider taste in books though not inclusive of such works as *The Palace of Pleasure* or *Bevis of Southampton*. Catholics, struggling for the survival of their faith, were encouraged to read apologetic or other partisan works, yet Lord Lumley gathered a broad range of books. Thus, while religious leaders promoted a better educated laity, the broadening of literary tastes owed more to classical scholarship, the secular spirit of the larger towns, and perhaps even the appeal of Italian literature than to the encouragement of the clergy.

(4) Suicide

He [God] forbids us under pain of hell to kill anyone, and particularly ourselves, for charity begins at home.

John Gerard[76]

> To die,—to sleep,—
> No more; and by a sleep to say we end
> The heart-ache and the thousand natural shocks
> That flesh is heir to,—'tis a consummation
> Devoutly to be wish'd.

William Shakespeare[77]

Suicide became more common in the Tudor period, according to John Bellamy, than in the fourteenth and fifteenth centuries. Existing figures for the number of suicides undoubtedly err on the small side, making it difficult to know how extensive they were. In the parish of St. Botolph without Aldgate, London, in the period 1583-89, only three suicides are recorded out of 4,253 deaths where causes are specified. In the same parish in the period 1573-1624, the total number of suicides was only seven, of whom six were female. In Nottinghamshire in the period 1530-58 the rate of suicide was approximately forty per million persons living *per annum* (as compared with some one hundred per million in 1967). Coroners' inquests for the period 1597-1634 in the counties of Bedfordshire, Buckinghamshire, and Northamptonshire reveal 262 suicides, and in the same area the records of the physician Richard Napier add a further eleven during these years. Yet because suicide was a crime for which movable goods were forfeited to the royal almoner, many suicides probably were concealed, in addition to cases where juries lacked sufficient information on plausible motives and deliberate intentions. To the extent to which suicide is an accurate index of *anomie* or social demoralization, the Elizabethan period was a time of increasing trouble, as reflected in the growing literary interest in insanity manifested after 1580. The disorientation and impersonalization characteristic of much modern urban life had begun to have serious repercussions for mental and emotional stability, but suicides were a problems in rural areas too. The economic problems of the 1590s were an additional pressure. Inclinations to suicide may have been dampened somewhat by the intense religious and social pressure against it.[78]

The Anglican case against suicide was multifaceted, though the keystone was the sixth commandment, interpreted to prohibit suicide as self-murder. This point was made, among other places, in the note to 2 Maccabees 14:41 in the Bishops' Bible. The commandment to love one's neighbor was also relevant, in the sense that one must do unto oneself as unto others. Suicide was condemned as an unchristian act that contravened divine and natural law. Because life is precious, to destroy it was impious and dangerous because it shortened the time to repent and obtain saving grace. Moreover, said Gabriel Powel, "Man was not borne of his owne pleasure, neither must he die at his own lust," and efface the *imago Dei*. Suicide, then, violates providence. The key biblical example that might justify suicide—the story of Samson—was exegetically handled to prove the contrary. Whereas John King accepted the Augustinian interpretation of a secret spirit moving Samson, Anthony Anderson argued that Samson acted in faith as a magistrate, not a private person, to enable God to avenge himself for the blasphemy and idolatry of the Philistines.[79]

With respect to suicidal motivation, Anglican authors noted several factors. Satanic motivation was a cause asserted by Anderson, whereas George Abbot believed those who committed suicide acted out of timidity instead of a strength to sustain the greatest crosses with constancy and valor. Suicide as an alternative to persecution was condemned. John Case, fellow of St. John's College, Oxford, contended that suicide was committed out of fear and desperation, not the desire to die a noble death. Those tempted to commit suicide to obtain relief from anguish were cautioned by Powel of a worse fate: "So far shall you bee from finding any ease or rest, that by so doing, these your temporall (or rather momentary) afflictions, shall bee turned into euerlasting torments" in hell. One final motive for suicide was raised by Elizabethan women, who sought casuistic advice on whether suicide was preferable to being raped. The reply was negative, and they were cautioned not to consent to the rape or to kill the attacker.[80]

Anglicans and Puritans substantially agreed in their position on suicide. Puritans condemned it as self-murder and thus a violation of the sixth commandment. "To kil man is to deface Gods image," taught the Geneva Bible, and Puritans used this argument as further proof that suicide contravened divine law. Like the Anglicans, they viewed it as contrary, too, to natural law. Suicide, argued Bird, is worse than killing another person "because it is more against kinde, and against the principles of nature, which would that euerie thing should preserue it selfe as long as may be." The example of Samson did not justify suicide, because he was a public person divinely endowed with special strength to give his life for his brethren. Vaughan agreed, likening Samson to a soldier in war or the early disciples of Jesus who faced death when they preached. Moreover, "Samson was a figure of Christ, which vanquished more at his death, then in all his life." Nor could Jonah, who was willing to be thrown into the sea, be used to defend suicide, for he acted as a prophet who knew the will of God and a figure of Christ who had to spend three days in a whale's belly to prefigure Jesus' days in the tomb. Razis' suicide in 2 Maccabees 14 was discounted by Puritans, both because the book lacked canonical status and because this was a "priuate" example contrary to biblical principles.[81]

On the question of motivation, Anglicans and Puritans had some difference of opinion. Whereas the Anglicans tended to blame psychological factors such as timidity and escapism, the Puritans focused on spiritual conditions, though this contrast must not be overdrawn. Dod and Bird discuss pride as a prime motivating factor, for it leads one to prefer death to a life with conditions not of one's liking. Dod also pointed to the spiritual factor of insufficient faith and to the willingness to redirect extreme cruelty against oneself. Greenham thought that the "many now adaies" who committed suicide were prompted by Satan to escape tormented consciences. Although Jerome discussed suicide as an alternative to being raped, Vaughan repudiated this course on the grounds that evil means are not justified by good ends. He was equally opposed to suicide to avoid persecution, since the example of Daniel and his three friends counseled fortitude and the hope of deliverance. Vaughan denounced the position of some Continental divines, such as that of Philippe du Plessis-Mornay, "that if a man laying before his eyes the glory of God onely, do kill himselfe, because he foreseeth, that those things, which he shal suffer, shal redound to the dishonour of God, he sinneth not." No spiritual justification was possible, then, for suicide, which was motivated by spiritual bankruptcy. [82]

One of the most learned discussions of suicide in the Elizabethan era occurs in Sir Philip Sidney's *Arcadia*, where Pyrocles seeks to protect Philoclea by taking his own life. With spiritual and chivalric overtones, Pyrocles insists that he can face God with a good conscience for dying for such a worthy purpose. God has, he argues, made us masters of our lives, with the right to terminate them as long as we harm no one else. Philoclea's passionate rebuttals, which reflect Sidney's Puritan views, counter that we are indeed captains of our forts, yet it is treasonous to surrender them until God demands that they be relinquished to him. Suicide does not proceed from courage but from evil torment or shame, hence it is not acceptable. [83]

Social pressure against suicide was strong. Bird thought that dragging suicides face down through the streets was a successful deterrent, and a number of old customs hostile to suicide continued. Burials were at night, a practice perhaps due to the association of suicides with Hecate, goddess of darkness. Burial in churchyards normally was denied (though bishops made exceptions), and bodies were often interred at a crossroads, a practice that originated in connection with the Teutonic custom of performing human sacrifices at such places. (The Tyburn gallows were located at a crossroads.) The custom of driving a stake through the heart of the deceased apparently was intended to confine the ghost to the grave, and derived from the ancient tradition of using a stake to restrain vampires from leaving their graves in quest of victims. Not until 1823 were stakes and burials in public highways outlawed (4 George IV, c. 52), but even then interment had to be between 9:00 P.M. and midnight, and without Christian rites. [84]

These practices evince a combination of social deterrence and superstition that, with the religious teaching, probably kept the number of Elizabethan suicides from reaching even larger proportions. Local officials thought so, for they enforced these practices. When Amye Stokes, elderly wife of a London sawyer, hung herself in

September 1590, the coroner ruled that "she Fallinge from god had hanged or murthered her selfe," hence he determined that "she should be carried from her sayd howse to some cross way neare the townes end and theare that [she] should ha[ve a] stake dreven thorowgh her brest and so be buried with the stake to be seene for a memoryall that others goinge by seeinge the same myght take heede for comittinge the lyke faite." In November 1575 Elizabeth Wickham, a 36-year-old London widow with strong sexual drives and deep depression, hung herself with her apron strings after failing to kill herself by jumping in a hole. She was buried in the alley where she committed suicide with a stake driven through her.[85]

One further check on suicide was the threatened seizure of the property of the deceased. A number of cases in Star Chamber suggest the difficulties that could arise when relatives of a suicide or other parties attempted to obtain some or all of his property: In 1563 Edmund Guest, bishop of Rochester, sued the gentleman Henry Veysey in connection with approximately £100 worth of apparel, plate, and household goods belonging to Katherine Veysey, a Cambridge widow who had drowned herself. Henry, probably her son, refused to relinquish the possessions to Guest, who intended to distribute them in the customary manner to the poor. In a comparable case in 1572, Guest's successor in the diocese of Rochester, Edmund Freke, sued to obtain the cattle and household goods of a farmer of Longham, Norfolk, who had hung himself. The goods had been seized by the local bailiff.

When the Leicester gentleman William Ballard, "not havinge the feare of god before his eies," hung himself in December 1602, his brother obtained his possessions, but was sued in Star Chamber by Anthony Watson, bishop of Chichester. In 1592, the family lawyer involved in the inquisition of the death of a Lincolnshire yeoman who, "not having the feare of god before his eyes, but throughe the instigacon of the devill . . . feloniouslie as a fellon of himself," hung himself, was sued by Richard Fletcher, bishop of Bristol, for taking from the estate his legal expenses and money for a needy brother of the deceased.

The authorities could exercise discretion in the case of needy families. In 1564 Dr. William Bill, the queen's almoner, sued three Hertfordshire yeomen who had expelled the wife, children, and servants of a yeoman who "did hang and Dystroye hymselff" from their land and had seized goods valued at £140 without a warrant.[86]

With respect to those who committed suicide, some tentative

judgments can be made. The statistics indicate that women were more prone to commit suicide than men, with wives and widows most troubled, but the evidence for males undoubtedly is more incomplete because of the disguising of male suicides to prevent property seizures. The evidence indicates that women committed suicide for a variety of motives, especially psychological. Sir Francis Willoughby's first wife, Elizabeth, tried to kill herself in 1579 by stabbing herself in the stomach with scissors when she learned another woman would have charge of her children while Sir Francis went to London. Behind this action was a very stormy marriage and probably mental illness. One widow jumped from a window in Cornhill and broke her neck when she was "rebuked for swearing, to the entent she myght defeate an Orphant of her ryght, not regarding good admonishmentes." The wife of a wealthy London broker, deluded that "the sherifes sought still to apprehend hir," slit her throat and jumped from a garret window. A housewife at Feering, Essex, drowned herself in 1590 after she contracted venereal disease in an adulterous affair. In 1598, a London midwife hung herself in deep remorse for the death of a mother who died in childbirth. Elizabeth Wickham, who was previously mentioned, may have been unable to handle the tension between her sexual drives and religious or social disapprobation of her behavior. Among the more important factors that drove women to suicide, notwithstanding strong clerical opposition, were mental illness, insecurity, stormy marriages, loneliness (especially among widows), and sexual conflicts.[87]

Where they can be determined, motives among male suicides were equally complex. Walsingham's brother-in-law, the wealthy Puritan solicitor and officer of the Royal Mint, William Dodington, leapt from the tower of St. Sepulchre's church, London, on 11 April 1600; his suicide note said that he had been slandered and that he preferred "to dye with infamye then live with infamy and torment," although he hoped Christ would have mercy on him. In 1563 a London armorer who lost his office to a trainee took his own life in despair. "As an earnest of his love," a Somerset gentleman cut his throat in 1601 when the woman he loved, Frances, daughter of Thomas Viscount Howard of Bindon, married the earl of Hertford. The man allegedly had been "out of his witts" the preceding six months. In 1585, Hertford's son threatened suicide rather than return to the harsh care of his father, a charge the queen believed. Another suicide motivated by unrequited love was a gentleman retainer of the earl of Salisbury who hung himself in 1612. Imprisonment produced a sense of disgrace and futility with which some men could not cope, including Sir Walter Raleigh, who stabbed himself while in the Tower in 1603, though he did not die. Sir Thomas Shirley, imprisoned in the Fleet for debt, tried to poison himself in 1615. In the same year and the same prison, Lord Clifton, engaged in a bitter lawsuit over his lands, attempted to slit his throat. Even clergy succumbed, including Henry Ledsham, a royal chaplain and "allwayes a giddibraind fellow," who stabbed himself to death in London in the winter of 1598-99. Another clerical suicide was James Starkie, a chaplain of Bess of Hardwick, countess of Shrewsbury, and Lady Arabella Stuart; he hung himself in London in the winter of 1602-3. Among men, then, the more important causes of suicide included mental illness, financial pressures, thwarted ambition, personal disgrace, and frustrated romance. Physical illness and pain figured in some cases.[88]

The means of suicide reveal some preferences according to sex. Hanging was popular with male suicides, followed by drowning and stabbing or slashing. Women were attracted to drowning, and then hanging. Poison does not appear to have been widely used, and leaping from heights was not common. Of the recorded suicides in Bedfordshire, Buckinghamshire, and Northamptonshire in the period 1597 to 1634, 132 were hangings, 88 drownings, 27 slashings and stabbings, 19 poisonings, and one leaping into a pit.[89]

In sum, Anglicans and Puritans condemned suicide as a violation of the sixth commandment, the effacement of the *imago Dei*, the contravening of natural law, and the premature termination of the period for repentance and salvation. Samson and Jonah were not examples that justified suicide, but special men with a divinely appointed mission. Some difference of emphasis is seen in Anglican and Puritan writings on the question of motivation, for whereas Anglicans thought primarily in psychological terms, Puritans focused on spiritual depravity. The condemnation of suicide from the pulpit and in counseling, coupled with the harsh but traditional burial customs for suicides and the threatened loss of property for the deceased's family, may have decreased the number of Elizabethan suicides, and for this deterrence the clergy deserve some credit.

(5) War, Society, and the Christian

It is lawfull for Christian men, at the commaundement of the Magistrate, to weare weapons, and serue in the warres.

1562 Articles[90]

O great corrector of enormous times,
Shaker of o'er-rank states, thou grand decider
Of dusty and old titles, that heal'st with blood
The earth when it is sick, and cur'st the world
O' the plurisy of people.

William Shakespeare[91]

Generally sixteenth-century thinkers in Europe accepted war as an instrument of God to punish sin, but some began to break from that tradition by explaining war in secular terms, particularly in connection with a natural law theory. Interest also was growing in exploring the association between individual aggressiveness and a society at war,[92] although the former often was deplored as a threat to social order and a contravening of moral responsibility. In Elizabethan England the validity of war was widely recognized, and no prominent efforts to assert pacifism were made. Nevertheless, the arguments for the necessity of war differed.

Anglicans did not glorify war, but realized the horrors it entailed. It was, said Sutton, a punishment rather than a blessing. Likening war to a pernicious plague, the Anglican layman Barnabe Rich attributed to warfare such evils as the decay of good laws, the suppression of equity, the profanation of sacred places, murder, rape, and the ruination of towns. Nevertheless, pacifism was not an alternative. Rich classified pacifists in two categories, the first of which were those opposed to war because of its financial burdens, not out of a commitment to peace. Simultaneously, he recognized that conscientious objectors opposed the killing and spoilation of war, but he criticized them on the grounds that such reasoning would require also detesting peace because it led to the increase of such vices as pride, idleness, covetousness, and incontinency. In contrast to this secular reasoning, Sutcliffe used the biblical examples of Joshua, David, Jehoshaphat, and Judas Maccabeus, as well as Romans 13 to provide religious support for his contention that pacifists were heretics and "phrenetical persons."[93]

The typical Anglican justification for war was drawn from a multiplicity of sources other than Scripture, the most common authority. Rich cited classical and medieval precedents for justifiable fighting, and Sutton pointed particularly to Constantine, who prospered in war owing to divine assistance. Sutcliffe also used natural law, the law of nations, and right reason to justify war; by these means a just war could be verified. To a man, however, Anglicans were adamant that war could not be justified without the sanction of a magistrate, even by appealing to Scripture. Knox's citing Scripture, natural law, and historical precedent as bases for a holy war that would topple an idolatrous monarch found no receptivity among Elizabethan Anglicans. Killing without the authority of a magistrate was condemned as murder or rebellion. The note to Genesis 14:14 in the Bishops' Bible averred that when Abraham went to war, it was not as a private person but by a special vocation from God. Sutton nicely phrased the Anglican view when he wrote that "he which strikes with the sword, whose condition is priuate, may feele the stroke of the sword," for "to take vengeance in a cause of iustice, is appertaining properly vnto the publique magistrate, and so much doe those testimonies of holy scripture inferre."[94]

Determining the justice of a prospective war provoked much discussion. In general, Anglicans agreed that a war was just when it was fought to meet any of the following conditions: (1) to defend against invasion or oppression, (2) to protect liberty and property, (3) to preserve religion, and (4) to oppress malefactors. Sutcliffe additionally sanctioned war to recompense injuries inflicted on ambassadors or subjects by another state, to assist allies, to recress breach of treaties (e.g. the Treaty of Greenwich), to punish those aiding one's enemies, and to prevent foes from prejudicial territorial encroachments (such as keeping Spain from military domination of the Netherlands). In short, "when the cause is iust, the authority lawfull, the intent good, that God may be glorified, a right continued, and imminent dangers auoyded, it is and may be lawfull for Christians to take armes."[95]

Certain conditions rendered war unjust for Anglican thinkers, including failure to pursue all alternate means to settle a dispute peacefully. For Sutton and Sutcliffe, an offensive war was unjust, though Sutcliffe permitted an attack if prior demands for restitution had not been met. Nor could wars be just if they were cruelly prosecuted, for, in Sutcliffe's words, "there is moderation euen in the execution of iustice." A striking exception to this principle was Thomas Churchyard's praise of Sir Henry Sidney for killing Irish women and children and despoiling their lands, because they sustained Irish warriors and because it was dishonorable for a sovereign to treat rebels mercifully. Using a principle later adopted in the New Model Army, however, Gibbens insisted that even in war godly discipline must be maintained. Because wars were fought to achieve justice and peace, they could not be just if pursued out of ambition, anger, greed, or pleasure. Christians must not fight in unjust wars, though Sutcliffe recognized that private persons often were not in a position to know all the facts, hence they were ordinarily exhorted to obey their princes. If, however, injustice was so notorious that there could be no doubt, Christians must not fight. In a related matter disagreement was voiced as to whether victory was divinely promised in a just war. Sutcliffe thought not, but Gibbens believed victory went to the side with a lawful cause, good discipline, and spiritual strength, for "the Lord of hosts who onely giueth the victorie of warre, findeth euermore a iust occasion of giuing victorie, in mercie or in iustice, to those on whom hee vouchsafeth it." [96]

Two Elizabethan laymen, both apparently Anglican, discussed warfare in frankly secular terms in 1602. Sir William Segar, Garter King of Arms, relied on classical sources to justify war. Because nature has bestowed on all creatures the capability to defend themselves, each "liuing bodie is in some sort by nature disposed to make warre." Wars are justly fought when injuries cannot otherwise be repulsed, peace cannot be preserved by other means, property cannot otherwise be defended, or access to foreign lands cannot reasonably be maintained. The law of nations and natural law sanction the repulsion of foreign invasion and the protection of allies and neighbors who are unjustly oppressed. War also is justified when it preserves liberty, religion, possessions, and families. Before recourse to arms, however, all other means must be used to obtain the desired ends. From a practical standpoint, war should not be undertaken unless the prospect of profit is greater than that of loss. Offensive wars for just causes after mature deliberation are acceptable, though the offense must be reprehensible even in the conscience of the enemy. Men engaged in warfare must remember to act with moderation, as well as attempt to gain peace and glory; war must be recognized as having value in making men honest and temperate. When war does break out, it is the responsibility of every knight and gentleman "to frequent the warre, and vse militarie exercises." With the exception of a greater willingness to sanction offensive war, Segar's views are substantially the same as those Anglicans who justify war with scriptural support. [97]

Writing at approximately the same time, William Fulbecke, a legal author who studied with Francis Bacon at Gray's Inn and held the B.A. and M.A. degrees from Oxford, grounded his position on natural law, not religion. War, "a iust contention of men armed for a publike cause," was justified to defend country, self, friends, and property. Fighting is sanctioned by natural law to recover things wrongfully seized and revenge unjust injuries, but war is never justified for small causes. It must never be fought solely because of religious pretenses, because fighting is between men, not men and God. Heresies can be punished without warfare, but if rebellion or disloyalty accompany religious issues, war is justified. Fighting for the enlargement of domains or the increase of wealth is prohibited. War is thus undertaken for reasons of state, and Fulbecke is aware that both sides may have some justice in their causes, hence no guarantee exists that a just cause will enable a state to triumph.[98]

Within Elizabethan Anglicanism, then, is a divergence in war theory at the end of the age as Segar and Fulbecke laid the foundation for the secular war theory of modern international law. The Puritan William Ames contributed to this development as well, though not in the Elizabethan era (cf. his *De conscientia,* 1639). Among Elizabethan Puritans a cleavage of opinion on war likewise began to emerge, with some authors in general agreement with the majority of their Anglican contemporaries on classic just war doctrine, that is, a reliance on theological and natural sanctions. Simultaneously, however, a movement began that led ultimately to the transformation of the classic just war doctrine into the concept of holy war, particularly as developed in the seventeenth century by Alexander Leighton (1624), Thomas Barnes (1626), and William Gouge (1631). Thus in the Elizabethan era, Anglican thought began moving in 1602 into an increasingly secular orientation, whereas Puritan thought showed signs of the opposite tendency, though Ames broke the pattern in the Stuart era.[99]

The Puritan doctrine of the holy war was roughly outlined in the Geneva Bible in 1560, though it was not until the late 1590s that a thoroughly religious interpretation of war was developed by Puritan authors. The Geneva annotators set the tone by asserting that war was to be undertaken for the defense of true religion and God's people, and always by divine commandment, with the express sanction of Scripture. Fighting could not be undertaken by human judgment, though the annotators recognized that evil men, such as the popes, sometimes launched cruel wars of their own volition. Even these wars, however, apparently came under the control of divine providence and brought about just judgments for evil ways.[100]

In 1597, in the context of the war with Spain, the attorney John Norden argued that although warfare is a pernicious evil, it is just when undertaken to preserve the "publique quiet" and Christian religion with the authority of the prince and in the fear of God. The subordination of secular concerns is apparent in Norden's insistence that all men whose vocation is the use of arms must be furnished with divine virtues in order that their actions may reflect godliness.

Officers must be religious men and cannot accept the service of wicked persons, who would be sources of corruption. Justifying the war against Spain as a defensive war to prevent a servitude worse than that of the Jews in Egypt or Babylon, Norden appealed to Scripture, not natural law. He urged ministers to emulate Samuel in crying to God for the success of the English military; the war against Spain was given the trappings of a holy war. [101]

The following year, in a sermon at Paul's Cross, Stephen Gosson developed the theme that God is actively involved in wars that are just judgments. War can be just with respect to reason, religion, and the practice of the church, and can be fought to defend the innocent, true religion, life, country, or property. Offensive wars in the name of religion are wrong, though preemptive war can be undertaken. Gosson rules out war to suppress idolatry, infidelity, or erroneous claims of supreme authority by pope or emperor. His contribution to the holy war tradition is his emphasis on God's active involvement, which renders a war more than justifiable; it becomes just or justified, i.e., a holy war. [102]

In 1599, in a work dedicated to Robert Devereux, earl of Essex, John Gibson relied heavily on scriptural citations to prove that war is just when it is "agreeable vnto his [God's] law, and thereby is an action wherein God is obeyed and serued of all that shall be led in the true and right performance thereof." He stressed the Ten Commandments, the first table of which he interpreted to require the defense of piety and religion by princes and people. The fifth commandment, he believed, authorizes a prince to defend his divinely bestowed authority as well as the lives, liberty, and property of his people. War was, for Gibson, a holy duty divinely mandated. [103]

Other Elizabethan Puritans were closer to the traditional just war theory. William Vaughan, for one, appealed to Ambrose and Calvin in justifying war for self-defense, yet he demonstrated a predilection for the holy war by lauding Richard I's crusade as a meritorious religious deed. Lawful wars — for self-defense, the recovery of property, or the suppression of revolution — were battles of the Lord. Although wars bred pestilence and dearth, Vaughan saw them as God's instrument to arouse his people from sluggishness and pry them from iniquities. Even Perkins, whom James Johnson treats as an opponent of the movement toward holy war because of his criticism of popular apocalypticism, regarded war as a divine ordinance and insisted that it was a violation of the second commandment to have allies who were enemies of God. Such ideas were easily adopted into the holy war framework. [104]

In Separatist circles, Barrow argued that Christians have a responsibility to serve in war at the command of their prince, but only if the cause is just. If fighting is ordered against God's servants, Christians must disobey. The Familists tended to be pacifists, though in May 1561 two of them, "perceiuing them selues to be noted and marked for the same, . . . haue allowed the bearing of staues." [105]

Therefore, in numerous areas Anglicans and Puritans disagreed on their perception of society—though in many respects they shared ideals. With respect to war, neither group embraced pacifism. Puritans, however, were moving toward the concept of holy war by seeking solely religious sanctions and stressing God's active involvement in fighting. In effect, Puritans began to isolate *one* of the causes that justified fighting in the classical *jus ad bellum*. Although the majority of Anglicans were adherents of the classical theory with its blend of theological and natural sanctions, Segar and Fulbecke in 1602 isolated the natural-law causes from the classical *jus ad bellum* and thereby laid the foundation for the modern secular theory of warfare, as subsequently developed, for example, by John Locke. The Puritan trend toward holy war, on the other hand, was developed in the Stuart era in the writings of such men as Leighton, Barnes, and Gouge.

Whereas killing in war was not regarded as a violation of the sixth commandment, suicide was. Writers of both religious persuasions condemned suicide because it contravened natural law, cut short the divinely allotted time to repent, and destroyed the *imago Dei*. In seeking to understand why people committed suicide, Anglicans tended more than Puritans to foreshadow modern interest in psychological causes, such as desperation, fear, and oppressive anguish. In contrast, Puritans found the motives for suicide in spiritual factors, such as monstrous pride, the absence of faith, Satanic urging, and spiritual depravity. Neither group spoke out against the harsh burial customs for suicides, which, with admonitions against suicide from the clergy, were probable factors in restraining the increase in suicides.

With respect to the printed and spoken word, a clear degree of *emphasis* demarcates Puritans from Anglicans, particularly in practice. Writers of both persuasions condemned printed matter that was unedifying and immoral as well as speech that was indecent or a threat to order and social hierarchy. Puritans, however, applied such strictures to themselves more severely, feeling a heightened sense of guilt for violations. Puritans were recognized because their pattern of speech evinced deep attachment to simplicity, truthfulness, and utility. Anglicans did not object to these ideals, but showed greater latitude in ascertaining what modes of speech met these criteria. As for literature, Anglicans manifested greater willingness to read more widely, as long as such works did not contain ribald or unprofitable material. For Puritans, reading entailed applying a more strictly conceived standard based on religious worth and utilitarianism.

Clothing was not an area of disagreement between Anglicans and Puritans in theory, though in practice Anglicans attacked Puritans for wearing excessively fine or overly plain apparel, that is, failing to observe moderation. Yet writers of both persuasions lashed out against garb that was lavish, vain, prone to provoke licentious conduct, and imitative of current Continental fashions. Elizabethans were expected to dress with sobriety and moderation, and to reflect their social status, for dress was a visible manifestation of social order as well as an outward sign of religious faith. As expenses for clothing increased, growing concern was expressed in clerical circles that money was being unjustly diverted from the poor. Royal proclamations failed to curtail the abuses, and Parliament was reticent to act. It is ironic that in an area where so much agreement existed between Anglicans and Puritans, persuading the laity to adhere to these ideals was difficult.

Part V: The Christian and Social Problems

CHAPTER 13

Wealth and Poverty

No social problem in Elizabethan England was more serious than poverty. In January 1594 William Lambarde attributed the growing number of poor to rising population, dearth, inflation, and "the dissolute education of the brood and children of the poor." He might have added enclosure, rack-renting, and the deterioration of copyhold and freehold tenures. Judging from the poor rolls, poverty was most acute for elderly women, whose deteriorating status motivated some to become witches. In the 1550s, a survey of the wards of London revealed 2,160 persons in need of relief, including 300 orphans. By 1595 the lord mayor calculated that 4,132 householders alone needed assistance; possibly 10% of the population of the city were paupers. In 1582, Christ's Hospital cared for 540 poor children. In York in the first two decades of the era the number of abject poor totaled between 600 and 800; another 6,000 were too poor to pay relief, but neither did they receive any, while poor rates were paid by 560 to 600 householders. In 1570, Norwich had some 2,300 persons, about half of them children, in need of relief, of a population of 15,000. Probably a third of the population of Leicester was too poor to be assessed for subsidies, and in the 1520s half of the population lived below or near the poverty level. Rural Cornwall was plagued by indigent migrants from Ireland, and in the 1580s and 1590s a number of towns throughout the country were burdened by maimed and unemployed ex-soldiers. Poverty was a pressing social ill.[1]

The magnitude of the problem was responsible for the chorus of complaints that neither authorities nor private donors were doing enough to help. Common disillusionment with authorities grew because they failed to execute the poor laws effectively and lacked adequate laws to remedy the situation. Although the wealth of the nation had increased, it was alleged that private donors had not kept up their giving. Stubbes, for instance, asserted that charitable giving for religion, education, and the poor had declined, though W. K. Jordan has substantiated a decline only in giving for religious purposes.

The dogs of the wealthy allegedly ate better than the impoverished, and the imprisoned poor cried for food. In a sermon at Paul's Cross in 1577, Thomas White praised the contribution of the City's four hospitals to poor relief, but bemoaned the small devotion shown by private persons, whose almsgiving was tiny because their "shoppes haue so shaped you after this worlde." It was difficult, grumbled Laurence Humphrey the next year, even to persuade the English to assist needy Protestants fleeing from the Continent to avoid persecution. The Privy Council complained to the lord mayor and the bishop of London in 1571 that so many indigent people lived in the city that it was impossible to ascertain who deserved relief and who ought to be punished. In Exeter, despite the erection of a hospital, "it is lamentable to see what troupes and clusters of children, boyes and elder persons, lye loytering and floistering in euery corner of the Citie." An end to begging would be accomplished, argued Perkins, only with proper provision for the poor.[2]

The gravity of the situation led to an outpouring of comment on the sources and use of wealth, almsgiving, the attitude of the poor, and the importance of charity. There was repeated condemnation of sturdy rogues and vagabonds, and some proposals were brought forward to reform poor relief. Although W. K. Jordan has accused Elizabethan preachers of exaggerating the problem of the poor and underestimating charitable giving,[3] the plight of the needy worsened in the 1580s and 1590s, and inflation reduced the impact of increased giving. If exaggeration did exist, it grew in part from a charitable concern for the unfortunate as well as from the self-serving worry about the stability of the social order.

(1) The Source and Uses of Wealth

Those preachers please our mindes best, which preach fayth, and no good works.
This cheape religion we like.

William Vaughan[4]

Man is but tenaunt at will of his worldly substance.

John Norden [5]

The foundation on which the Elizabethan concept of wealth was based was expressed, among other places, in the Tyndale-Coverdale New Testament and Tyndale's prologue to Numbers in the Matthew and Matthew-Becke Bibles. There one finds the key principles that prosperity is divinely bestowed and does not come by chance, and that the poor are divinely appointed as recipients of charity from the rich. This outlook was carried over from the medieval period, and English Protestants in the sixteenth century assuredly did not, contrary to Charles and Katherine George, relinquish the older view that the indigent were necessary for the exercise of the virtue of *caritas*.[6]

Anglicans recognized that wealth originated from God and was deliberately distributed unevenly. Like a wealthy steward, God dispenses riches in varying amounts to create social distinctions and provide occasions for the exercise of charity by the rich and patience by the poor. Religion, explained Hooker, "either giveth honours, promotions, and wealth, or else more benefit by wanting them than if we had them at will; it either filleth our houses with plenty of all good things, or maketh a salad of green herbs more sweet than all the sacrifices of the ungodly." In making some poor, God called for service out of devotion rather than ambition for wealth.[7]

Puritans also espoused the theory of the divine origin and unequal distribution of wealth. The affirmation of the Geneva annotators that riches were bestowed by divine providence was echoed by Puritan authors, as was the belief that alterations in man's earthly condition were similarly ordained (as in the celebrated case of Job). Neither covetousness nor hard toil could bring wealth, Crowley told a distinguished audience at London's Guildhall in September 1574, for God alone is the benefactor. Puritans likewise were convinced that the poor were divinely ordained to be recipients of charity; as Gibbon phrased it, they "are the Altars [on which] to lay the sacrifice of our goods." In return the poor benefit the rich by their prayers, and enable almsgivers to do good works and glorify God. Thus Anglicans and Puritans embraced the traditional view that the impoverished were essential for the fortunate to exercise *caritas*.[8]

From this position it was logical to assert that godliness had no correlation to prosperity, a view enunciated in the Tyndale-Rogers New Testament and the Matthew and Matthew-Becke Bibles. The annotators of the Bishops' Bible reiterated this view, affirming that "prosperitie and aduersitie commeth in this life, as well to the godly as to the wicked." Neither wealth nor adversity, insisted the Anglicans, could be used as a sure sign of divine favor or displeasure. Riches are a divine blessing, though bestowed on good and evil persons, and they can be divinely taken away—in the case of the godly to try their faith.[9]

Puritans too asserted that no direct correlation exists between wealth and godliness. Repeatedly the Geneva annotators set the tone by proclaiming that spiritual welfare is independent of earthly wealth, and that it is better to be poor and godly than rich and sinful. Not riches, but faith and suffering for the sake of the gospel are signs of election. Yet neither is wealth a sign of condemnation, for with divine assistance, it can be properly used and enjoyed. The godly, however, are warned to expect poverty, comforting themselves in the knowledge that the poor understand the gospel better than the rich, and that faith is the only true wealth. Puritans repeated these themes, stressing the poverty of the spirit regardless of external possessions. "The rich man," explained Perkins, "may be said to be poore in spirit, if he bestoweth not his loue and confidence vpon his wealth, but in affection of heart is so disposed, as if he were not rich, but poore." To be poor in spirit is to be rich in grace, and to one thus poor, it does not matter whether he has abundant material possessions. The ideal, as the note to Luke 18:24 in the Beza-Tomson Bible states, is to be godly and materially rich, for that is "a singular gift of God."[10]

Notwithstanding this general agreement that prosperity and godliness are not directly associated, several Elizabethans suggested that prosperity is a reward of godliness. A possible source of this notion is Calvin's belief that those who truly serve God are blessed materially as well as spiritually. Building on this theme, the Geneva annotators insisted that service to God brings prosperity. "God prospereth the faithful, because they walke in his waies with an vpright conscience." Sometimes the annotators discouraged the idea that this prosperity is material in nature, as when they explained that true prosperity consists of obedience to the word of God. Yet they also made it clear that the assured prosperity is physical as well as spiritual. "He shall prosper bothe in spiritual and corporal things." The person who seeks wisdom, allowing himself to be governed by the word of God, is promised material and spiritual prosperity.[11]

Puritans were more receptive to this theme than Anglicans. In 1589, Wilcox asserted that "godlinesse is crowned with abundance: and wickednesse with want." Seven years later, Holland proclaimed that material riches are promised to the godly to reward their obedience. Perkins too was convinced that obedience to the gospel leads to prosperity in one's vocation. Yet late Elizabethan Puritans were not alone in associating material rewards with godliness, for Hooker affirmed that religion and godly fear lead to secular prosperity. This idea was qualified to the extent that prosperity is proportionate to social standing, but the basic premise is that welfare on earth depends wholly on religion. Here then are the early stages of the development of the thesis that godliness is profitable, a theme at the heart of the much-debated Weber-Tawney thesis on religion and the rise of capitalism. It must be remembered, however, that apart from the Geneva Bible, this theme received modest mention in comparison with the idea that godliness and prosperity are *not* directly associated.[12]

Those with material wealth were believed to have specific responsibilities. In Anglican circles, the starting point is the recognition that riches are given only to be used by faithful stewards, notably for the relief of the indigent. Sandys insisted that with their wealth the rich must be servants of the poor, relieving and comforting them as God mandates. Anglican clergy had no objection to the retention of some wealth by those so blessed, as long as moderation was not exceeded and the retention was not to the detriment of the poor, a qualification that might have been interpreted to mean communalism. The Anglicans were convinced this radical course was not necessary, since the amount of superfluous wealth was (erroneously) believed to be so great that the needy could be relieved adequately without the destruction of social differentiations in degrees of wealth. Pilkington even contended that the political nation lost its right to govern if it did not aid the impoverished, and warned that failure to bestow riches to relieve the poor would lead to the loss of wealth. As long as these obligations were fulfilled, nothing was inherently wrong in being rich, for, as Whitgift stated, "riches and costly furniture be no impediment to a godly man for doing his duty."[13]

The Geneva annotators similarly asserted that riches are divinely allotted so that recipients can aid the needy. The righteous were exhorted to distinguish themselves by such donations, for this is the proper use of God-given benefits. On the other hand, "it is the plague of God when ye riche man hathe not a liberal heart to vse his riches." Recipients of wealth must avoid prodigality and yet not be so frugal that the poor fail to receive proper assistance. The Beza-Tomson Bible reiterated the importance of giving, thereby avoiding the temptation to use wealth as an occasion for sin.[14]

In Puritan circles, fundamental agreement with Anglicans was voiced on the obligations of the wealthy, including the basic principle of stewardship. "We hold our prosperitie of the Lord," said Greenham, "not in fee simple, but as tenants at will." Riches have been committed by God to recipients to aid the indigent, not to lavish them on epicurean fare, vain apparel, and stately houses. Wealth may be enjoyed, admitted Perkins, even while directed to maintaining our estate, assisting family and kin, relieving the poor, maintaining the church, and supporting the commonwealth. In determining how much is necessary for one's estate, Perkins recommended the guidance of wise and godly men and the example of sober and frugal persons. As with Anglicans, the obligation to bestow wealth on the impoverished did not entail social leveling, for giving was to be regulated to ensure the maintenance of the social hierarchy. Wealth is not intrinsically evil, but must be thought of as a means to perform good works, for which the godly must be thankful, as Sir Francis Hastings reminded Huntingdon in 1581. With respect, then, to the responsibility of the wealthy as stewards for God, Anglicans and Puritans agreed.[15]

Although wealth was divinely bestowed and not inherently evil, admonitions about its dangers abounded, owing in part to the intensive campaign to persuade the well-to-do to devote more of their riches to the poor. The biblical marginalia contained numerous warnings to the wealthy. In the Tyndale-Coverdale New Testament, riches were called unrighteous because they were often wickedly procured and used. A distinction was made, however, between the riches themselves, which were not evil, and the wrongfulness of delighting in them instead of in God. The Geneva marginalia, which promised prosperity as a reward for godliness, underscored the dangers of wealth, which was conducive to evil actions. Riches wickedly obtained, maintained, or spent were iniquitous, and wealth in general must be regarded with suspicion. Those with an abundance of goods are prone to disobedience, pride, forgetfulness of God, and covetousness, a sin equal to murder. The Beza-Tomson marginalia, which exulted at the thought of wealth and godliness together, simultaneously asserted that no man could love them both, hence a divine gift was necessary for the rich to escape satanic snares. In their 1568 Bible, the bishops devoted little comment to wealth, though they insisted that riches were not inherently evil, but an occasion for evil, and therefore a source of some grief and a disrupter of friendships. Thus biblical annotators acknowledged the value of wealth as a tool of charity, while warning of the difficulties riches could cause.[16]

This was the message of Anglican clerics too, for they often repeated the theme that riches were not evil *per se*, though subject to

great abuses. To be rich was a burden to the soul because wealth inclined one to pride, excess, divided concerns, materialism, and spiritual idolatry. "The more of GODS blessinge, and wealth," Miles Smith
preached at a Worcester assize in 1602, "the more weedes of vanitie,
and carnalitie: and the more rich to the worlde the lesse righteous to
GOD commonly." A scholar from Peterhouse, Cambridge, thought
Christ would not have been so poor had he thought well of prosperity.
Warnings were issued against wealth because it increases grief, oppression, craftiness, contempt, and vice, rendering one unfit for Christian
service and making the path to heaven difficult. This negative attitude
toward wealth prompted Gardiner to speak of its origin primarily in
the iniquitous actions of forebears, not divine bestowal, though
Anglicans in general castigated only the abuse of riches. Hooker, in
fact, warned that poverty is as dangerous as excessive prosperity, for
poverty demands a rare degree of patience. The tenor of Anglican warnings against the dangers of wealth, coupled with exhortations to aid
the needy, seems calculated in part to increase charitable donations.[17]

Once again, the Puritan position was harmonious with the Anglican.
Abundant riches were likened to a knife in the hand of a child or a
cup of wine mixed with poison. Prosperity without intervening adversity brings heresy, carnal security, or great hardship. Yet riches are
not evil, though they easily become a spur to sin because of human
nature. Unless balanced by spiritual wisdom, wealth can be a source
of misery, but if riches are not improperly acquired or hoarded there
is nothing objectionable in them. Perkins cautioned that it is difficult
to acquire wealth without committing injustice or without improperly
valuing riches. Prosperity is conducive, said the Puritans, to covetousness, the source of heresy and poverty. For Dent the dangers are so
substantial that we must get "no more of this worlde then needs
must." On the whole, however, Puritans were less inclined than
Anglicans to stress the dangers of wealth, perhaps because Puritan
laity were more prone to give to charity, or perhaps because they
were more willing to accept prosperity as a reward for godly living.[18]

A final requirement for those blessed with wealth was a stricture
not to oppress or despise the less fortunate. As early as 1530, Tyndale's Pentateuch warned oppressors of the poor, and the Geneva annotators equated this vice with pride, excess, and idleness—cautioning
of divine retribution and demanding due regard for the indigent as
well as for the rich. The Beza-Tomson marginalia includes a similar
warning. In Anglican circles James Bisse told an audience at Paul's
Cross in 1581 that contempt for the poor was the most common vice
in England, and other Anglicans admonished their flocks not to have

this attitude. Among the specific examples of oppression cited by Anglicans were withholding sufficient alms, buying the land of small owners and driving them into poverty, forestalling, and refusing loans to the needy. Puritans likewise repudiated oppressors of the poor, noting that the mild dispositions of the unfortunate provoked cruelty from the wealthy. Oppression of the poor by buying their livings, refusing loans, and failing to execute provisions for relief in wills was deplored. Lever complained to Cecil and Leicester in 1569 about rich courtiers who siphoned funds for poor relief and grammar schools, and Bird denounced men of substance for encouraging wedding gifts from the less fortunate. Early in 1603 Richard Stock, a Puritan lecturer at St. Augustine, Paul's Wharf, London, attacked the lord mayor in a sermon at Paul's Cross for allowing the City's wealthy to oppress the lower orders by imposing fifteenths on poor artisans. Anglican and Puritan thus joined in a campaign to terminate the oppression of the poor in all its forms, making due regard for the needy a basic duty of persons of means.[19]

With respect, then, to the source and uses of wealth, there was broad agreement among Anglicans and Puritans. The two areas of divergence were the greater Puritan receptivity to associating prosperity with godliness and their decreased attention to the dangers of wealth. This divergence supports the views of Tawney and his disciples. In other areas, Anglicans and Puritans agreed that wealth was divinely bestowed in varying amounts, that its recipients were stewards with responsibilities for the use of that wealth, especially to relieve the needy, and that the poor must be neither oppressed nor despised.

(2) The Place and Behavior of the Poor

There is a common cry of the poore in euery place, whose faces be grinded with the extortions of the wealthie.

John Carpenter[20]

Religion [is] but a policie to keepe poore men in order.

Lawrence Barker[21]

For those in authority in Elizabethan England, dealing with the poor was largely a matter of showing them the divine origin of their estate, encouraging them by referring to an easier pathway to heaven for the poor, and urging them to be content with their station. The marginalia of Tudor Bibles and Testaments prior to the Geneva Bible (and Whittingham's New Testament) gave little attention to the poor, though

Tyndale attacked the Catholic concept of vocational poverty. The Geneva marginalia, however, informed the poor that God provides for his servants, no matter how destitute, and ultimately gives them precedence over the wicked. Their affliction is accompanied by spiritual understanding because it encourages dependence on God. The absence of riches also increases the possibility of diligence in divine service, for the usual hindrances are removed. The traditional argument of a reward in heaven was made: "The litle yt a man hathe with the grace of God, is an hundreth folde better then all ye abundance yt one can haue without him: but the chief recompense is in heauen." Because the godly, no matter how poverty-stricken, possess spiritual gifts, even evil wealthy persons are slaves to them, for only the godly possess what is truly important. For the poor, then, the proper course is dependence on divine providence and contentment with their estate. No prohibition was given against using honest means to better their condition, but they were cautioned not to allow the prosperity of others to allure them to wickedness. "Let vs therefore learne to haue ynough and to want, that being tryed, we may enioye our treasures in heauen." Less attention was paid to the poor in the Beza-Tomson marginalia, though they were told that God preferred the needy to the wealthy, and that ultimately the godly poor would be rewarded with everlasting joy. In contrast, the Bishops' Bible promised the godly that they could avoid poverty by honest labor, an exhortation that smacks of the Calvinist ethic.[22]

To maintain quiescence among the impoverished, Anglican clergy enumerated the blessings of poverty and reminded readers of the divine origin of all estates. Poverty was useful because it was conducive to humility, devotion, holiness, fasting, hope, and love. It was supposedly easier for the poor to avoid whoredom, theft, and murder. Those who endured poverty and its attendant miseries were blessed in the sense that they were "humbled, tamed, schooled and reformed by their want towardes all men [and therefore] carie a lowly heart, and onely at the Lordes handes looke for both comfort in this world, and saluation in the worlde to come." Yet Hooker and Clapham frankly preferred a state between poverty and opulence for, as Clapham explained, the poor are easily tempted by iniquity. Most Anglicans, however, encouraged the indigent to accept their estate by underscoring the spiritual benefits of poverty.[23]

Although Puritans accepted prosperity as a reward for godliness, they enumerated the benefits of poverty for the Christian life. Impoverishment enhanced dependency on God, encouraged obedience to him, and was a means to bring people to spiritual glory. Although their lives often seemed hellish and ignominious, Norden insisted that affliction was a mark of divine love, whereas continued prosperity was not. Admittedly hope lay in the future, though some Puritans promised that adequate relief would come in this world for the godly. Like the Anglicans, the Puritans encouraged the needy to be patient and content with their estate: "Happie is that man therefore," said Dent, "that is well content with his present estate whatsoeuer, and carrieth himselfe moderately and comfortably therein." Striving to better their condition by lawful means was generally approved if the poor did not seek unnecessary possessions. To Estey, however, any attempt to better one's estate is wrong, for all must be left to providence. Although penury is a hammer that can break the impoverished and motivate them to pursue inappropriate courses, it is nevertheless a divinely ordained and worthy estate if the poor are humble and willing to serve.[24]

Unlike the Anglicans, the Puritans set forth rather detailed obligations for the poor. Everyone agreed that the poor must avoid idleness, but the Puritans also expected them to move the rich to bestow assistance by virtue of their contentment, thankfulness, and good behavior. Because donors in effect exercised a parental role, recipients were exhorted to react with childlike duty and honor, in the context of the fifth commandment. Receiving "is a sober, reuerend, and thankefull accepting of that which is Christianly giuen, with a mind to imploy it conscionably, and in the feare of God, to the same ends, whereunto it was of the Christian and godly benefactor intended and giuen." If able, recipients were expected to recompense a donor if he or his family became needy. The poor were told to devote themselves to the attainment of religious knowledge, but Richard Rogers did not believe many did. Thus Puritans expected submissive, grateful behavior by recipients of poor relief, and the use of assistance for appropriate means. If help was not forthcoming and they were treated oppressively, they must endure patiently, else the social order would be threatened. For Puritans it was no shame to be poor, though it was shameful to become poor by negligence or prodigality.[25]

Concerning the place and behavior of the poor, only the care taken to delineate the appropriate attitude of recipients and their use of funds differentiated Puritans from Anglicans. Despite the Puritan association of prosperity with godly living, they were as concerned as Anglicans with encouraging the impoverished to seek spiritual blessings from their lowly estate, accept their place as divinely ordained, and be patient, even in the face of oppression. No Anglican or Puritan justified social revolt in the name of an oppressed poor or advocated social leveling.

(3) Almsgiving

I meane not to waste my goodes with giuing of Almes, I will not maintayne a sort of ydle knaues and Drabbes with my goodes, I haue got it my selfe, and why should I not spende it on my selfe.

Thomas Lupton[26]

No treasure so well bestowed as that which is given to the poor.

Edwin Sandys[27]

One of the most pronounced emphases in Tudor biblical marginalia was the encouragement of almsgiving. As early as 1534, Tyndale's New Testament exhorted everyone to aid his neighbor, and in 1537 readers were encouraged to provide for the poor and use their riches as Scripture intended. Subsequent Bibles and Testaments made comparable stipulations. The Geneva annotators accented the requirement to aid the needy, regarding this aid as a sign of the faith and love which "oght to measure all our doings." Those who refused were threatened with divine retribution, including the loss of grace. In the Bishops' Bible, readers learned that the godly must care for their neighbors and be liberal to the indigent. The Beza-Tomson marginalia made alms obligatory by the law of charity (or love). A person who was able to assist his neighbor, but refused, killed him. The obligation of almsgiving was extended to any who could spare goods, not merely the wealthy. "Fewe men vnderstande howe great the riches of the kingdome of heauen are, and no man can bee partaker of them, but he that redeemeth them with the losse of all his goodes." Readers of Tudor Bibles and Testaments were confronted with increasingly prominent exhortations to give alms, which must have been one of the simplest and best known of the Christian responsibilities.[28]

For Catholics, the Rheims New Testament likewise stressed this duty, with the focus on giving in accord with one's ability. Almsgiving was a meritorious act, with the merit increasing if the donation came from necessary provisions, not superfluous wealth. When given to needy Catholics, alms "putteth on the condition of an oblation or sacrifice offered to God, and is most acceptable and swete in his sight." Edmund Bonner's Marian catechism, undoubtedly still in use in Elizabethan Catholic households, made relief of the poor a work of mercy, whereas Vaux's Elizabethan catechism warned that those who refused to succor the poor violated the sixth commandment (following the exegesis of Ambrose). Although Catholics were no less concerned with almsgiving than Protestants, the Catholic association of poor relief with merit and thus with purgatory distinguished their outlook from that of the Protestants.[29]

The concern with almsgiving in the scriptural marginalia was reinforced in Anglican writings, where the emphasis was on the idea that *every* person is responsible for almsgiving according to ability. In particular this was seen as a duty for courtiers, lawyers, knights and gentlemen, the childless, and the covetous. Charity was such an essential part of religion that it was believed that those who refused to give neither loved nor served God. The laity reiterated views of the clergy. William Wentworth, for instance, advised his son to be bountiful to the poor, and Robert Furse urged giving that which was not personally needed to the impoverished. Anglicans insisted on the duty of almsgiving, and thus advised their offspring.[30]

Much emphasis in Puritan writings was given to the duty of almsgiving, which applied even to the relatively poor. Giving was a duty of love stemming from the fourth commandment and, according to Perkins, a necessary part of worship. Only those too poor to spare anything and those (such as children and servants) in subjection to others were exempt. Relief could be extended in various forms, including direct bestowal of alms, interest-free loans, and forgiveness of debts, but the mere payment of taxes, part of which were used for poor relief, was not considered beneficence because it involved no free decision. To obtain funds, Christians were urged to reduce expenditure on food and clothing and concern themselves less with the provision of bequests for offspring, for "whatsoeuer wee spend more then wee need, is none of ours, but the poores; and to detaine from them, is to pill and poll." In contradiction to the Catholic argument that almsgiving is meritorious, Fulke contended that liberal givers would be rewarded, but not on any scale of spiritual merit. Puritan congregations were exhorted to accept the duty of relieving the poor as a basic spiritual obligation.[31]

Religious authors of all persuasions offered enticements to aid the indigent. The Geneva annotators promised a reward of divine blessing, relief in future adversity, respect, and profit (whether material or spiritual is not indicated). In contrast, the Rheims annotators attributed direct soteriological significance to almsgiving, which was credited with extinguishing and redeeming sin, deliverance from damnation, and propitiating former offenses. Alms were also meritorious; the more alms, the greater the merit. Recipients, moreover, would pray for the donor's soul and speed passage through purgatory. Alms were so beneficial that it was better to donate all than to forego such advantages. The theological benefits accrued to Catholics for aiding the needy were more precise and substantial than those that a Protestant expected, though the latter was promised material rewards for almsgiving.[32]

Anglican authors promised a combination of spiritual and material rewards for aiding the needy. "By giuing to the poore thou dost lend to him [God], and he promiseth to set it vpon his owne accounts, in the resurrection of the righteous." Material benefits included an increase of goods, as well as mutual love, goodwill, and abstention from idleness. In comparable manner, Puritans promised spiritual and material benefits to donors, noting especially that donations to the indigent were loans to God that would be repaid "with vsurie". Almsgiving was a remedy against covetousness, bringing contentment with one's estate, an increase in material wealth, and a conviction of election. Contrary to the Catholic view, aiding the poor did not earn merit but was a manifestation of the inner love of God. Cartwright accused Catholics of turning churches into shops and warehouses in which soul-merchants purchased salvation by donating to persons who would pray for their souls, and to whom they would become clients in heaven. The calculation of merit and the hope of a reduced stay in purgatory struck Puritans as gross commercialism and superstition. Yet equally superstitious was Trigge's recitation of the common belief that unless one gave to witches, they would cast evil spells. On the whole, however, the enticements to benefactors offered by Puritans and Anglicans were temporal and spiritual rewards.[33]

In addition to proclaiming the duty and rewards of assisting the needy, the clergy provided guidelines for giving. The most important question was whether aid was to be rendered to the godly alone or to all the indigent. The Matthew and Matthew-Becke Bibles asserted that assistance must be given to all in need, according to the principle that all persons are our neighbors. In sharp contrast, the Geneva annotators restricted relief to one's family and members of the household of faith. The Beza-Tomson marginalia also took a restrictive view, but instead of omitting the ungodly it prohibited aid to the idle, while recommending orphans and widows. The Bishops' Bible retained the broader outlook of the Matthew Bible, urging the distribution of alms without respect of persons. A more moderate course was adopted by the Rheims annotators, who found giving to all needy persons meritorious, though they preferred assisting Catholics first. "Almes bestowed specially vpon holy men . . . may much more helpe vs then our charitable deedes done vpon vulgar men in necessitie, though that be of exceding great merite also." The biblical marginalia thus reflect three points of view on the question of aid: The Anglican-oriented Matthew, Matthew-Becke, and Bishops' Bibles favor giving to all in need; the Puritan-oriented Geneva and Beza-Tomson Bibles restrict assistance to the godly or industrious; and the Rheims New Testament adopts a middle ground, acknowledging the merit of giving to all but preferring Catholic recipients.[34]

Generally, Anglicans adopted a moderately broad approach to almsgiving, though some feeling was expressed that priority should go to the godly and personal relations. Neighbors were preferred to strangers, but Sandys insisted that all Christians were our neighbors and deserved assistance if in need. Gardiner looked on almsgiving as a manifestation of mercy, whether bestowed on honest or on lewd people, but he opposed giving to rogues and sturdy beggars if they became wearisome and an intolerable charge to the commonwealth. The Familist position that aid was due only to fellow sectaries was denounced by John and Thomas Rogers for its restrictiveness, implying their support for a broader view. In essence, Anglicans were willing to assist more than the godly, with priority for Christians, family, and neighbors.[35]

Puritans disagreed with respect to limitations on recipients of poor relief. Some, such as Bird, Becon and William Vaughan, took a narrow approach, with Bird arguing for a restriction of alms to the saints. The profane, he asserted, would not be thankful and benefactors would be discouraged from further giving. Becon wanted charity restricted to the impotent, poor prisoners, impoverished maids, young men in need of funds to commence an occupation, and needy neighbors, not idle lubbers and "sturdy queanes." Vaughan proposed that aid be restricted to the godly and the elderly, blind, lame, insane, or ill. At the other extreme Puritans such as Greenham, Henry Smith, and Thomas Knell apparently favored giving based strictly on need. Greenham, for instance, defined a neighbor as "euery one that is neare me & standeth in need of my helpe, and it lyeth in me to helpe him, though otherwise hee be a stranger vnto me, or my foe." Most Puritans, however, adopted a position akin to that of some Anglicans, a preference to aid the godly but not a prohibition against donating to others. Allen held this view, though he cited Peter Martyr as his authority for withholding aid from persons not known to the donor and letting these people be relieved by public funds. There were some ambiguities in Perkins' position, which was based on the idea that precedence must go to neighbors and the godly. Yet he insisted that Christians were to supply the needs of their enemies, and that assistance must not be granted to strangers "vnlesse there be iust and necessarie cause so to doe." Perkins seems to be saying that priority must go to Christians and neighbors, but under special circumstances other needy folk, whether enemies or not, merit succor. Thus most Puritans agreed with those Anglicans who adopted the ideal of helping the godly first; others agreed with the rest of the Anglicans in urging assistance for all the needy. Few Puritans adhered to the narrow restriction of alms proposed in the Geneva marginalia.[36]

Guidance was also provided to givers in other areas, with a variety of recommendations appearing in the biblical marginalia. In 1537, the Matthew Bible insisted that alms be bestowed secretly; the next year the Tyndale-Rogers New Testament warned benefactors to give with a Christian spirit, "not deceatfully." The Geneva annotators called for liberal giving in accord with ability and with affection, not a desire to obtain a material reward. These rules were reiterated in the Beza-Tomson marginalia, where the emphasis was on giving liberally out of pity for the poor and regard for the glory of God, not personal ambition or hope of recompense. These principles were not controversial and were reflected in Anglican and Puritan writings.[37]

In addition to these basic rules of giving, the Anglicans added others. They were concerned that donations proceed from love, not a hypocritical desire to obtain praise or material and spiritual benefits. Ironically, although the clergy enunciated the reward of almsgiving with an eye to encourage this practice, they simultaneously admonished people not to give with rewards in mind. Another important rule of almsgiving declared that nothing be given but one's own; goods unjustly obtained must be returned to the owner, not bestowed on the indigent. Although the Puritans, as will be seen, recommended accompanying alms with godly admonitions, Gardiner warned benefactors not to speak critically to the poor, and encouraged them to provide assistance without waiting for the needy to request it. Essentially, the rules of almsgiving for Anglicans required liberality, unselfishness, and the avoidance of hypocrisy and personal gain.[38]

More rules for poor relief were enunciated by Puritans than Anglicans, though many rules paralleled Anglican principles. Gifts must be granted according to ability, with no excessive giving that would ruin one's position, though Perkins sanctioned some charity beyond the ability to give. Giving must be done liberally, cheerfully, from a sense of love and mercy, and not hypocritically in search of commendation. Nothing must be donated unless it has been honestly acquired. Benefactors must give without waiting to be asked, and must take care that donations are not wasted or used for immoral activity. Unlike Anglicans, Puritans insisted that donors confer with the recipients about the latters' religious condition and provide necessary instruction. Caring simply for the physical needs of the indigent was not adequate fulfillment of the almsgiving obligation. Puritan concern with this point set them apart from Anglicans.[39]

In sum, the basic principles of Anglicans, Puritans, and Catholics regarding the bestowal of alms were found in Tudor scriptural marginalia. The duty of almsgiving was stressed repeatedly, but Protestants refused to accept the Catholic contention that giving was a meritorious act with soteriological significance. The enticements Protestant authors offered included spiritual and material benefits, though ironically those who gave to obtain such benefits risked being labeled hypocrites by the same authors. Different answers were given to the key question of who qualified as recipients of poor relief. Whereas the Matthew, Matthew-Becke, and Bishops' Bibles advocated relief for all needy persons, the Geneva and Beza-Tomson Bibles urged its restriction to the godly. Generally, Anglicans preferred the broader approach, though desiring that the godly receive priority. Most Puritans settled for precedence being accorded the godly, but some favored a broad distribution of alms limited only by need, whereas others wanted donations to go only to the godly. Writers of all persuasions insisted that giving be liberal, in accord with one's means, and not for personal gain or commendation. Puritans distinguished themselves from Anglicans by insisting that almsgiving should include godly admonitions and religious instruction. The supremacy of the spiritual to the material, which so concerned the Puritans, was exemplified in Gifford's complaint that many who bestowed funds for poor relief had no pity on those who lacked spiritual food. Alms were required for the soul as well as the body.[40]

(4) Rogues, Vagabonds, and Sturdy Beggars

The whole realme of England was exceedinglie pestered with roges, vagabunds, and sturdie beggers, by means whereof dailie happened diuerse horrible murthers, thefts, and other great outrages.

Raphael Holinshed[41]

Many were not ashamed to confesse, that they coulde gett more by begging from dore to dore weekely, than they coulde yearne by working for wages continually.

Francis Trigge[42]

The concern of religious authors was directed toward relieving impotent poor, not those who refused to work and lived by begging or illegal activities. Rogues, vagabonds, and "sturdy beggars" tended to congregate in urban areas, but they also plagued highway travelers and flocked to fairs, seeking temporary work, food, and fellowship. In London, youthful rogues and vagabonds lay "under stalls in the streets by great companies, under hedges in the fields, and no man taketh them up to bring them to some faculty to get their livings." Stealing, begging, and prostitution were the means of staying alive when they found no employment. In Dorset a person who rebuked beggars as the Puritans proposed discovered that some beggars would "shake up such a one." Cornwall was troubled by impoverished Irish immigrants who spent idle days in drunkenness, thievery, and sexual immorality. Apart from the stealing and physical assaults, Elizabethans seem to have been troubled most by these sexual improprieties, such as occurred in a 1599 case when a Berkshire justice of the peace uncovered an enclave of rogues in which six couples were dancing in the nude and others were lying around, presumably fornicating. The godly felt that vagabonds, sturdy beggars, and rogues had no respect for church, commonwealth, marriage, family, education, or vocation. They feared not only that the commonwealth was being deprived of essential labor, but also that the problem would multiply as others were attracted to this life of irresponsibility and immorality.[43]

Some inhabitants of the Elizabethan underworld allegedly had their own language, known as peddler's French, and designations indicating their specialties. Several contemporary works portrayed them, including John Awdeley's *The Fraternitye of Vacabondes* (1560), Thomas Harman's *A Caveat or Warning for Common Cursetors* (1566), and a later version of Harman's work entitled *The Groundworke of Conny-catching* (1592). Harman was a gentleman who distributed alms rather consistently, as members of his class were expected to do, until he became suspicious of some of the recipients. His curiosity led him to investigate vagabonds in south-eastern England, sometimes insisting that magistrates punish them, and in some cases trying to retrieve his donations to aid deserving poor. He and Awdeley depicted a colorful and somewhat fanciful world of rogues and beggars that caught the interest of literate Elizabethans. Their underworld included such characters as Abraham Men who fained mental illness, literate Jackmen who counterfeited licenses to beg, Whipjacks who pretended to have lost everything at sea, Counterfeit Cranks who fained epilepsy, Walking Mortes or unwed women purporting to be widows, Doxes who usually lived as prostitutes, Hookers or Anglers who specialized in theft through windows by using a staff with an iron hook, and Priggers of Prancers who stole horses. When they married, they engaged a special (illegitimate) cleric, known as a Patrico or Patriarke Co. Stolen goods often were fenced in alehouses, another reason that reformers pressed for tighter control. Religious reformers of all persuasions shared Harman's concern with "the abhominable, wicked and detestable behauiour of all these rowdey, ragged rabblement of rakehells, that vnder the pretence of great misery, diseases and other innumerable calamities, . . . do win and gayne great almes . . . to the vtter deludynge of the good gevers."[44]

Contemporaries exaggerated the problem, for many vagrants were either itinerant laborers or temporarily unemployed persons, not those who deliberately refused vocational responsibilities. Legally, there was no statutory distinction until 1598 between those who refused to labor and the involuntarily unemployed. Vagrants tended to be young, hence people resented their lack of work. Yet many vagrants had occupations, especially as day laborers, servants, clothworkers, peddlers, and victualers. Generally they remained reasonably close to their places of origin, and often received hospitality, even from the gentry, though increasingly they had to rely on inns and alehouses for lodging. Those with transient occupations and those seriously in search of work were not feared by most Englishmen; it was the willful rogue and professional beggar they detested and periodically whipped. Sympathy for job-seekers did not, however, extend to welcoming them in towns without available jobs as charges on the community. In a society where men were expected to have masters to provide godly supervision and instruction, vagrants, whether itinerant workers or willful rogues, upset clergy and local authorities alike.[45]

Demobilized soldiers and sailors posed special difficulties, especially after 1588. In 1589 approximately five hundred of them were ready to pillage Bartholomew Fair, and they were a serious threat in overcrowded London. In 1590 the queen ordered cathedrals to assist "certeine poore souldiors notoriously maimed in the warres, and having no substaunce of their owne whereby to live." Not even a 1593 act to provide military pensions cured the problem. Lambarde, reckoning soldiers to be brethren in Christ who had been menial and household servants taken to war by their masters and subsequently forsaken, urged assistance for them at Maidstone in 1594. By 1596, a Somerset justice of the peace complained to Burghley that every shire had three to four hundred wandering soldiers and rogues.

Maimed soldiers in some cases obtained relief from churchwardens. The evil was compounded by vagrants pretending to be deserving veterans. Vagabond society allegedly had a special name—Rufflar—for vagrant soldiers, whether real or counterfeit. The problem of veterans was made more acute by coinciding with the periods of dearth at the end of the century.[46]

Various means were proposed to deal with rogues, vagabonds, and sturdy beggars. Generally people were reluctant to give them alms. Jewel opposed relief to these people as biblically unlawful (Eph. 4:28; 2 Thess. 3:10), and Puritans were usually hostile to aid, following the Geneva marginalia's prohibition of maintenance for idle persons. Udall, Burton, and Dod opposed assistance for sturdy beggars even if they professed to be devout, but Perkins relented for persons in extreme need who would otherwise die. The Puritan most willing to help the idle was Robert Allen, whose only stipulation was that admonitions be given. In practice, evidence suggests that Puritans generally refrained from aiding vagabonds and sturdy beggars. Lady Grace Mildmay helped only those willing to toil; she preferred loans and small bonuses to assist needy families, and thought charities should apprentice poor children to trades. Sir Walter Mildmay advised his son Anthony to relieve the impotent poor but not vagabonds, which advice undoubtedly reflected his own practice. In his will, William Bricke, the Puritan pastor of Stanhope, Durham, left funds only to thrifty poor persons. The solution for rogues and sturdy beggars was not poor relief, which some clergy felt exacerbated the situation by encouraging idleness and prodigality.[47]

A general feeling prevailed that sufficient provision should be made for the impotent, to end their begging and demarcate them from sturdy beggars. There may have been as many as 20,000 beggars in Elizabethan England. York had eighty-eight resident beggars in 1569 who enjoyed official toleration and wore approved badges. Each ward had a master beggar in charge of the licensed beggars, and in addition approximately seventy-five aged and impotent paupers lived in the city. Throughout the country, justices of the peace could license beggars, but those without licenses sometimes obtained counterfeits. This practice angered Lambarde, who told the assize at Maidstone in 1594 that the poor should be relieved in their homes rather than be forced to beg. To avoid the evils inherent in a licensing system, Devon householders in 1597 were assigned one or more poor persons for whom they provided two meals a day on pain of a fine of 18d. per week. Simultaneously, all begging had to cease and searches for vagabonds were instituted.[48]

Anglican and Puritan clergy sought to terminate begging. When he became bishop of London, Sandys told an audience at Paul's Cross that sufficient provision should be made for the impotent poor to keep them off the streets, for "the suffering of the people to beg breedeth great inconvenience both in the church and common-wealth." Sufficient relief would enable the authorities to isolate the indolent and force them to work. The 1602 statutes for Whitgift's hospital at Croydon permitted poor inmates (who were over sixty years of age) to work at trades to improve their standard of living, but begging was prohibited. For the Puritans Dod disapproved of begging by the poor because "it is a most dishonest and base thing, to see men stand whining at the doore like dogs for bread, and this corrupts their manners, and is contrarie to all good nature, and destroyes the seeds of any good disposition in them, festring the minde with idlenesse, and drawing a thicke skinne of impudence ouer their faces." Perkins too castigated begging as contrary to Scripture and an indication that the godly were niggardly with alms. Begging also was objectionable because it made for an inequitable distribu-tion of alms, and it was conducive to disorder. Anglicans and Puri-tans strove to end begging by the impotent because, as Perkins phrased it, "the begging of almes is the very seminarie of vagabonds, rogues, & stragling persons."[49]

Anglican and Puritan critics demanded a rigorous enforcement of the laws against the deliberately idle. In January 1563 Alexander Nowell pressed Parliament to enforce the poor laws against rogues and sturdy beggars, who robbed the deserving poor of assistance. Gardiner and King made similar demands, with King particularly up-set about the danger in York of sturdy beggars who would steal, murder, and commit arson. The Geneva annotators used 1 Thes-salonians 5:13 as proof that those who refused to work "must be ex-pelled as wolues out of the flocke." In Puritan circles there were numerous calls for the punishment of vagabonds and sturdy beggars. After traveling in numerous shires, Norden concluded that the poor laws were not effectively executed, despite an increase in houses of correction for vagrants, largely because those with authority were in-sufficiently inclined to prosecute offenders. In 1577 an irate Thomas Becon told officials in Sandwich, Kent, to compel the "sturdy & lasie lubbers" to work or banish them, and similar complaints must have been made to local officials in other towns. In December 1583 the Dedham Classis discussed the problem of rogues and sturdy beggars, concluding that the Classis itself should not act, but individual mem-bers should approach magistrates to urge enforcement of the laws.

The parliamentary acts of 1598 and 1601 enabled significant strides to be made toward these ends, so that in 1603 Allen was convinced that a reduction in giving to vagabonds had resulted in more assistance for the impotent poor.[50]

Throughout the age, the authorities subjected vagabonds and beggars to a variety of punishments, though the effectiveness was not what the religious critics desired. Male and female vagabonds were whipped, sometimes indiscriminately, as in the case of a lame man and a widow with two children at Corby, Northants., in 1571. Houses of correction were founded, with the one at Winchester supported in part by a collection from the clergy of the diocese. Towns became chary of new arrivals without jobs and regularly expelled them, as at Southampton, Leicester, and Dedham. Fines and imprisonment were common, and applied even to alehouse keepers and taverners who knowingly served rogues and vagabonds. In November 1589, the Privy Council instructed lords lieutenant to appoint provost marshals to apprehend wandering soldiers, sailors, and masterless persons. Hundreds of vagrants were impressed in the post-Armada period and shipped to the Continent for military service.[51]

London was especially troublesome, because of its size and the number of visitors, hence, the queen and Council repeatedly had to deal with beggars and vagabonds. Lord mayors were encouraged to put them to work at Bridewell, which they did. In 1578, the Council prohibited vagrants from tarrying in London and contiguous areas. The following year one of the queen's servants was threatened by a masterless man, prompting the Council to demand his incarceration in Bridewell. In 1587, the perplexed Council directed the justices of Surrey, Middlesex, and Essex to consider solutions for the problem of rogues and beggars in the London area. Elizabeth worried that the City was becoming "the greatest Sinke of Beggery, within her Realme," hence she wanted idle persons returned to their original places of residence. It was assumed that work could be provided throughout the country if only London could be freed from the influx of jobless, masterless persons. The lord mayor ordered them to leave and forbade carriers to bring more into the City without adequate provisions. In June 1588 the Council decreed a general search of the City and its suburbs, with offenders committed to Bridewell, which could hardly have held them all if the orders were fully implemented. By December 1589 the Council was fully aware of the need to provide adequate relief to get the impotent poor off the streets; this process would enable a more effective approach to the prosecution of rogues, vagabonds, and sturdy beggars. The campaign of religious critics to improve the care of the impotent, terminate begging, and punish the indolent finally impressed the leaders of the political nation, culminating in the parliamentary acts of 1598 and 1601.[52]

On the subject of vagabonds, rogues, and sturdy beggars, Anglicans and Puritans mostly concurred, though Perkins and Allen deviated from other Puritans by their willingness to bestow alms on the indolent — for Perkins only in cases of extreme necessity. Presumably Anglicans who favored a broad range of charitable giving agreed with Perkins and Allen. Anglicans and Puritans were in accord on providing sufficient relief to the impotent poor in their homes to terminate begging, facilitating the identification of rogues and sturdy beggars, who were to be punished and forced to assume lawful vocations. Their indolence was viewed as a threat to people, property, the commonwealth, and religion. The campaign of the clergy to recognize the legitimate needs of the impotent and punish the infractions of the willfully lazy influenced the secular authorities, including the Privy Council, and ultimately brought passage of the landmark poor laws of 1598 and 1601.

(5) Proposed Reforms

Rather then the poore should want, make a banke for the poore.

Christopher Hooke[53]

Anabaptists . . . would bring in a mingle mangle, partly consisting of a platonicall communitie, and affected pouertie.

Christopher Sutton[54]

In addition to demanding stringent punishments for rogues, vagabonds, and sturdy beggars and advocating relief for the poor in their homes, some reformers called for improved care for the needy. The proposals ranged from revolutionary to modest, and were enunciated by clergy and laity of both religious persuasions. Perkins proposed that the hungry be allowed to gather grapes and corn before the harvest (as sanctioned in Deut. 23) and that gleanings be left for the poor during the harvest. In 1602 the lord treasurer, Thomas Sackville, Lord Buckhurst, proposed stockpiling corn in London in time of plenty, to tide over the impoverished in periods of dearth. He also advocated founding an almshouse or hospital in every town and village, more houses of correction for rogues and vagabonds, and compulsory labor for sturdy beggars. In 1595, Humphrey Grenville, gent., sent a scheme to Burghley designed to decrease the burden of poor relief on towns and parishes. All unemployed able-bodied workers in coastal regions, on navigable rivers, or within five miles of either area would be employed on imports as long as private enterprise was not undermined. None of these proposals was revolutionary, nor would any have provided a lasting solution to the enigma of poverty.[55]

Other reformers envisioned more far-reaching changes. Cartwright proposed the sale of episcopal lands to raise funds for poor relief, but Whitgift retorted that England could provide for its needy if existing laws were duly executed. Another revolutionary proposal came from alderman Boxe, who recommended to Burghley that able-bodied unemployed be given plows to till the wastelands and grow corn, an idea that foreshadowed part of Gerrard Winstanley's program of the 1640s. Several reformers found the solution in private giving. Cooper called for donations from the wealthy amounting to 50% of their goods and the restoration of all funds improperly obtained. The Puritan Christopher Hooke conceived of a bank for the poor, with capital originating from investments from the well-to-do amounting to approximately 10% of their wealth; this participation was to be noncompulsory and motivated by charitable convictions. These reforms were too revolutionary, however, to receive sufficient support for implementation.[56]

Some proposals amounted only to stopgap measures intended to deal with current crises. In 1575, for example, Burghley's steward, Peter Kempe, worried about conditions in Stamford, Lincs., which had been hit by the plague and suffered sixty-six deaths. Notwithstanding the crisis, beggars continued to come to the town, which had traditionally assisted them, only to find no relief, because persons of substance had fled. Kempe's solution was for Burghley to commission a gentleman to collect and administer funds and to order that the masters of Stamford return and assist. Stamford was the subject of another modest reform proposal in 1580, when Robert Payne suggested to Burghley that he have his tenants convert wool into yarn and train the poor to spin in two-year apprenticeships. The result would be, in his judgment, a pool of trained workers that would attract clothiers to Stamford and increase employment.[57]

One of the most detailed proposals for poor relief came from John Easte. Easte believed existing laws were inadequate and that it was not enough simply to collect and distribute alms to the indigent. Able-bodied unemployed must be set to work, for idleness is a tool of the devil to subvert a Christian kingdom by luring people to vice.

England could save £500,000 a year, he calculated, by putting the poor to work instead of giving them relief. This practice would increase the wealth of the realm by £1,000,000 a year, and bring the royal treasury an additional £100,000 *per annum*. Much of the difficulty of getting the idle to labor stemmed, he argued, from their early training. Instead of gleaning wheat, fetching wood, or performing other tasks, children played until age twelve or thirteen, and did not become apprentices until ages sixteen to eighteen. By then they were so used to idleness that they failed to become productive workers and often turned to begging and stealing. Employers were at fault for releasing workers for petty faults, and masters were accused of refusing to hire servants who could not provide sureties. Parents were encouraged to threaten children with disinheritance if they failed to study hard, and schoolmasters were urged to beat pupils more often to enforce learning. In effect, this proposal demanded more stringent discipline for children to train them to work industriously, a program to employ all able-bodied persons without jobs, and stringent punishment for the indolent. The rewards were spiritual, including a massive reduction in vice, and material, particularly an additional £1,000,000 in annual wealth.[58]

One possible reform that met with virtually universal repudiation, except among Familists, was communalism. Early Tudor Bibles and Testaments were not explicitly concerned with this issue, and the *locus classicus* in Acts 4 was treated only as a case of hypocrisy. The command to sell all and aid the poor was interpreted to mean not becoming attached to material goods and selling them if a neighbor needed help. As the Münster story spread, however, annotators repudiated communalism explicitly. The Geneva annotators interpreted the Acts' account to mean that no one was compelled to sell his possessions and give his money to the community, though "their hearts were so ioined in God, yt being all membres of one bodie, they colde not suffer their fellow membres to be destitute." Their goods were not divided equally or mingled communally, but each received according to his need. Christ's command to sell all applied only to the questioner, not all Christians. The wariness of the Geneva annotators to avoid communalism was not paralleled in the Beza-Tomson Bible, which vaguely stated that "charitie maketh all things common concerning the vse, according as necessitie requireth." The Rheims annotators interpreted the Acts' passage as justification for the communal living of monasticism but not a command for all believers.[59]

The essence of the Anglican case against communalism was stated in the 1562 Articles and reiterated in other writings: "The ryches and goods of Christians, are not common, as touchyng the right, title, and possession of the same, as certayne Anabaptistes do falsely boaste." The divinely ordained estates of wealth and poverty repudiate communalism. To establish a community of goods is disruptive to an orderly commonwealth governed in accord with scriptural principles and the example of the early Christian community. The precedent in Acts is a commendable example of charity and disdain of material possessions, not a requirement for Christians. Ananias' sin consisted not in having private property but in lying to the church. Jesus' command to sell goods and give to the poor teaches people to care for the impoverished, not adopt a communistic society. Whitgift insisted that he had no personal objections to making his wealth common, but he defended that society in which all men could enjoy their wealth "without confusion." The case against communalism often was made in conjunction with exhortations to support the needy. Wright reflected the spirit of Acts even while upholding a hierarchy of wealth: "The goods of christians, by right, should be priuate to no mans lust, but common to euery mans neede, according to their state and calling." Thus Anglicans decried communalism, though they insisted on the charitable obligations of sharing wealth with the unfortunate.[60]

Puritans were equally persistent in repudiating communalism. The Acts' account was interpreted as a special case in which zealousness and liberality moved the godly to relieve extraordinary need. Part of the zeal originated, according to Wither, in the conviction that Jerusalem was about to be destroyed, hence it was vain to retain possessions, especially when no other provision was available to aid the needy. Ananias and Saphira were not punished for having private possessions but for hypocrisy. Puritans were convinced that with the godly in Acts and Jesus' disciples, private homes were retained, underscoring the validity of private possessions. Christ's command in Matthew 10 to possess no gold or silver was interpreted to apply only to the disciples, and the command in Matthew 19 to sell all was applied only to one man, hence neither commandment bound the godly. To sell all and give to the poor was prohibited, according to the Puritans, as contrary to the law of nature (which prescribed distinction of possessions) and the gospel.[61]

Although they opposed communalism, Puritans embraced the voluntary disposition of their possessions for the sake of the community in times of extreme distress. "When in the time of persecution, famine, or warre, the necessitie is so great, that it requires present releefe, which can no other way be had, but by giuing and selling the goods that a man hath," a Christian should dispose of his possessions. This action would be only an emergency expedient, but in time of necessity no Christian must retain his property at the expense of aiding poor brethren. It may have been the assertion of this duty that precipitated Dering into a debate over his views on the poor with the Privy Council in November 1573, though he retorted that he did not believe in a "community of things" that amounted to "a common confusion," and he believed that the poor could be cared for if existing laws were executed. Strictly speaking, Puritans opposed communalism, but unlike Anglicans they stressed the obligation of Christians in times of extraordinary need to sell their goods to relieve the poor. Even this radical action stopped short of full-fledged communalism because it was intended for the godly and not the nation.[62]

In sum, reformers ranged widely in their proposals to assist the needy, but ruled out communalism because it contravened Scripture and natural law and threatened the order of the commonwealth. The Puritans, however, accepted the necessity of selling their possessions in an extreme emergency to provide relief. Puritan proposals for poor relief included Cartwright's radical suggestion to sell episcopal lands, Hooke's innovative concept of a bank for the poor, Stubbes' plan for an almshouse or hospital in every town, and Perkins' idea of allowing the hungry into the fields to gather food. Anglican clergy advanced fewer proposals for reform, probably because they acquiesced in Whitgift's contention that the solution was enforcing current laws. Nevertheless, Bishop Cooper proposed the radical plan of urging the wealthy to donate 50% of their riches to the poor. Although these proposals were not adopted, they buttressed demands to increase relief for the impotent while punishing the indolent and forcing them to take up occupations—ideas that were enshrined in the 1601 statute.

(6) The Practice of Charity

The multitude followe the riche men, as a swarme of bees followe a man that carries the hiue of honie combes, rather for the love of the honie then his person.

Mr. Sanders[63]

The poore that be impotent in deede, haue better prouision for them in such places as the Gospel is receiued, then euer they had in Poperie.

William Fulke[64]

In the absence of significant reforms, charitable giving played a significant part in caring for the impotent, despite advances in assistance at the local level, in towns such as Norwich, and finally at the national level. Some Protestants were convinced that charitable giving was greater in England than in Catholic lands, believing that Catholics donated heavily for monasteries, chantries, dirges, and trentals, whereas Protestants assisted the needy. "Name me any city in the world," wrote Fulke, "where popery preuayleth, that hath made such prouision for the fatherlesse children and widowes and all other kind of poore, as in the noble city of London and in diuers other cities and townes of this land." Pilkington said virtually the same thing. Whereas Jewel accused Catholics of being too devoted to their ill-gotten goods to be concerned for the poor, Wither wondered why the Catholic hierarchy did not sell their possessions and donate the proceeds to the indigent—a question that by implication could be asked of the Anglican hierarchy. The shires reputed best for poor relief by Thomas Harman were in the southeast, where Protestantism was strongest (and which were also the wealthiest).[65]

The growing contributions to charity in Elizabethan England (documented by W. K. Jordan) were inspired in part by exhortations from the clergy and ministerial giving. Visitation articles inquired if the clergy exhorted parishioners to give according to ability, if almshouses and hospitals were run properly and housed only the impotent, if churchwardens fined nonattenders and used the money to relieve the poor, if clergy with benefices worth £20 *p.a.* gave a fortieth to the impoverished, and if persons of ability refused to aid the needy. The clergy were expected to persuade parishioners to leave bequests for the poor, ensure that poor relief was distributed openly and impartially, give themselves in accordance with their means, and report executors of wills who detained bequests to the poor, the church, and the schools. In short, the bishops expected the clergy to assist the needy, supervise the distribution of funds, and oversee hospitals and almshouses.[66]

The bishops themselves were advocates for the indigent. Richard Curteys, bishop of Chichester, was an avid proponent of hospitals and urged the people of his diocese to erect workhouses in boroughs and market towns for the unemployed but physically able. While he was bishop of London in 1563, Grindal advocated the bestowal of funds on inhabitants of back lanes and alleys as well as poor aliens during an outbreak of the plague. In 1600 Richard Vaughan, bishop of Chester, pressed justices of the peace to relieve the poor who had flocked to Chester. In 1584, despite considerable reluctance among his clergy, John Scory, bishop of Hereford, got them to donate £23 18s. for the relief of Nantwich, and he contributed an additional £5. In 1579 Edmund Scambler, bishop of Peterborough, appealed to Burghley not to require the poor of his town to contribute to the construction of the Clowis Cross Drain on the grounds that there must be "some equalitie, and due proportion of the Levie." As archbishop of Canterbury, Parker spent substantial sums on the impoverished, including £160 *p.a.* on two hospitals. With the support of Walsingham, Edmund Freke, bishop of Norwich, successfully campaigned for an institution to reform rogues and sturdy beggars at Acle, Norfolk, in the late 1570s. He was commended by the Privy Council because "after some convenient tyme spent in preachinge for the good instruction of the people . . . and the exercise of charitie amongst themselves, your L: with divers gentlemen of the countrey which doe very orderlie come together for that cause do visite the said house and do consider of things meete to be provided and ordered." [67]

Hospitals were a special concern of the bishops. Whitgift founded one at Croydon in 1595, paying £200 for an old inn, £110 for further property, plus considerable lands to endow the hospital and a school. His example prompted members of his household as well as Dr. Thomas Neville, dean of Canterbury and master of Trinity College, Cambridge, to donate to the hospital and school. The Savoy Hospital in London, founded to aid poor travelers, had a master named Thurland in the 1560s who fraudulently sold goods, was involved in illegal leases and the alienation of lands, lived dissolutely, and neglected the poor. Dr. Gabriel Goodman, dean of Westminster, was worried about the hospital's ability to function in 1566, and three years later Grindal asked Cecil and Elizabeth to remove Thurland; he was deprived in 1570. When the Puritan Thomas Lever had difficulties administering Sherborne Hospital near Durham owing especially to lease problems, he obtained the support of Archbishops Parker and Grindal. John Young, bishop of Rochester, protected the hospital at Chatham from a suit against it in the Exchequer in 1579 by appealing to Burghley. A different problem was faced by Pilkington, who complained to the Privy Council that the hospital at Newcastle was supporting English Catholic doctors at Louvain. The bishops viewed themselves as guardians of the hospitals and protected them as agencies of poor relief. [68]

Particularly from the late 1580s, the bishops tried to relieve victims of dearth and those discharged soldiers who had physical disabilities or no employment. In January 1587, the Privy Council ordered the archbishops to instruct their clergy to urge parishioners to assist the poor in the current dearth. The queen ordered the provision of relief for maimed soldiers, but the bishops were not always successful in getting the clergy to comply. When help was not forthcoming at Durham in 1591, the Council rebuked the dean and cathedral chapter and threatened a visitation. The Council also intervened with the deans and chapters at Chester and Gloucester the same year. The dearth of 1596 brought instructions from the queen to the bishops to see that persons of means moderated their diets, observed prescribed fast days, abstained from supper on Wednesdays, and donated the savings to the needy. The bishops also ordered collections in the parishes for the poor, with charitable increases from persons of means, and directed that householders desist from laying off servants. Beneficed clergy were required by the bishops to reside in their livings, keep hospitality, and relieve neighbors by providing employment or donating alms. A good part of the bishops' involvement in poor relief stemmed from their role as agents of the crown in dispensing charity.[69]

The state's association with charity caused some uneasiness among Puritans and Separatists, noticeably with respect to the office of deacon. For Anglicans, once Christianity became a state religion the responsibility of deacons for poor relief was superfluous. Proctors, masters, and overseers assumed this function, freeing deacons for other duties. "Why," Whitgift asked the Puritans, "do you not think well of such laws as appoint collectors for the poor, which may as well provide for them, and better too, than could the deacon, who must be sustained himself with that which the poor should have?" The Anglican position made it plausible for Sandys, in a sermon before the queen, to call for state funds to relieve the poor. The acceptance of state responsibility for the poor helped achieve the compulsory poor rate which, as Christopher Hill notes, decreased clerical responsibility for the needy, and undermined the clergy's position in the parish as well as the justification of tithes. An increasingly state-oriented system of poor relief was, of course, the modern road and was harmonious with the growing secularism of the age.[70]

In contrast, Puritans and Separatists were adamant about the retention of deacons as scripturally sanctioned agents for relieving the destitute. Deacons possessed authority to prevent disorder in bestowing charity by knowing the recipients, the degree of their poverty, their habits in spending, and their vocations. Bird even thought deacons should publish a table listing donors and their gifts as well as recipients and their amounts. Each church, insisted Perkins, had an obligation to provide relief for its poor, though not for those unwilling to toil. Greenham cited the example of the primitive church that collected funds each sabbath to assist the destitute. In practice, the Dedham congregation dispatched members, accompanied by constables, to visit the poor each quarter to determine who merited assistance and who needed punishment; the deserving poor were invited into the homes of the godly for meals. The congregation also took a special collection for the poor at communion services. Puritans, then, preferred the administration of charity in local churches, primarily by deacons, with the state providing magisterial authority to punish vagabonds, rogues, and sturdy beggars.[71]

In practice, much of the private charity bestowed on the poor came from bequests in wills, a relatively painless way to fulfill the obligation of relief. Puritans in particular encouraged the godly to donate more substantially before their demise. They warned that executors embezzled some bequests, and Allen believed that deferred giving was closely associated in the popular mind with purgatory and merit. Vaughan thought only of spiritual blessings when he cautioned that gifts to the poor in wills did the donor no good. Referring to charitable donations in London, Thomas White reckoned that more was given by the dead than the living. Yet Puritans were unwilling flatly to condemn bequests in wills. Among the Anglicans, Whitgift expressed similar concern about the dangers of relying on executors to accomplish charitable deeds. Perhaps the more pronounced Puritan opposition to deferred giving stemmed from their greater sensitivity to dissociate themselves from Catholicism, notably purgatory and merit.[72]

An examination of wills and donations to the poor by the living reveals much about the practice of charity. On the basis of W. K. Jordan's research, the claim of Elizabethan Protestants that they gave more to the poor than the Catholics has some substance. Although Jordan declined to compensate for inflation, he has shown that the percentage of Protestant giving to secular causes, especially poor relief and education, was greater than that by Catholics, who devoted a larger share of their donations to the church, primarily because of the doctrine of purgatory.[73] A related claim that has not been analyzed is Sutcliffe's assertion that Anglican clergy were more bountiful to the poor than other ministers. This also raises the question of relative support for the indigent by Anglican and Puritan laity. There are major pitfalls in making such comparisons, not the least of which are inflation, widely differing bases of wealth, and regional variations in the pattern of giving. In the case of the laity, it is difficult to gather enough wills of persons who can accurately be typed by religious preference to provide an adequate data base.

A sampling of wills of Catholic clergy who died in 1558 or later indicates a general willingness to provide for the poor. John Feckenham, the last abbot of Westminster Abbey, built a hospital and small bath for patients at Bath in the late 1570s, and left £40 to St. Margaret's, Westminster, for the poor to purchase wood. Dr. Owen Oglethorpe, deprived bishop of Carlisle, left funds in 1559 to found an almshouse for twelve people at Tadcaster, Yorks., and Robert Pursglove (or Sylvester), suffragan bishop of Hull, left £40 for the poor on the day of his funeral. The former president of Queens' College, Cambridge, Thomas Peacock, left £20 in 1581 to the corporation of Cambridge for poor prisoners. In his 1558 will, Robert Benett, prebendary of Durham Cathedral and vicar of Gainford, Durham, left £6 to his poor parishioners, £4 to the poor of Durham, and 12d. each to students at the Durham school. Wills of lesser Catholic clergy left varying amounts to the poor that usually reflected the value of their estates. William Berrie, vicar of Gilling, Yorks., bequeathed £20 to the inhabitants of Gilling if they received the Catholic sacraments, but "in case no houses of religion be reedified" the money would go to charity. The priest Thomas Paynell left £6 to the poor of Cottingham, Northants., a noble each to twenty poor maidens of that village on their wedding day, and £5 to a hospital for poor infants. George Reyd, Catholic parson of Dinsdale, Durham, left only 10s. to the poor, and William Bell, rector of Gateshead, Durham, who had no money to bequeath, left a quarter of corn and a quarter of barley for the poor. In contrast, nothing was left for the needy in the wills of William Blunte, a priest at Croxdale, Durham, and William Paynter, a priest at Bardwell, Suffolk (who donated 10s. for highway repair). Generally, this sampling of testaments of Catholic clergy suggests no reluctance to support the needy.[74]

The wills of Catholic laity regularly included amounts for the poor, though often less than one would expect from the size of the estates. An exception is the will of George Trafford, a Lancashire gentleman who established a trust with £40 capital, the income from which was for poor householders with children. He also bequeathed to the poor the income from his lands in Lincolnshire (worth c. £10 *p.a.*), and another £3 6s. 8d. was set aside for masses for his soul if they were legal; if not, this money went to the poor. Sir John Byron of Clayton, Lancs., bequeathed £10 *p.a.* for ten years to found a chantry or, if illegal (as it was), to relieve the destitute. He also left

£5 for prisoners. Another major benefactor was Sir Thomas White, who donated £1,000 to Bristol to relieve the needy and provide employment, £104 to York for interest-free loans (and identical amounts to twenty-two other towns in subsequent years), and £1,400 to Coventry to purchase lands, the income from which was for poor relief. Other donations to the destitute from Catholic gentry were modest, often amounting only to a few pounds, such as the 20s. 8d. from Richard Thadye of Bruntoft, the approximately £3 of Richard Pole of Radbourn, Derby, or the £5 10s. of Cuthbert Conyers of Layton, Durham. Sir Robert Brandling, a former sheriff and mayor of Newcastle-on-Tyne, left only 13s. 4d. to the inmates of an almshouse, five marks to the poor of the town in which he was buried, and one or two pence for each poor person at his funeral. Other Catholic gentry, such as Sir Arthur Darcy and Thomas Trollope of Thornley, left nothing to the poor, and Edward Bussye of Haydor, Lincs., helped the poor only insofar as he left each lay person attending his funeral a penny. Lady Dorothy, wife of Sir Thomas Windsor and daughter of William Lord Dacre, left £13 6s. 8d. to the indigent on the day of her burial, plus other bequests for the destitute. Among Catholic professionals, the physician Dr. John Caius left only 20s. to the poor, and John Eltoft of the Inner Temple left nothing. In contrast, William Bendlowes, a governor of Lincoln's Inn, who erected an almshouse at Great Bardfield, Essex, and gave small sums annually to inmates of almshouses in six villages, left funds to support the almshouse at Great Bardfield. On the whole, these wills suggest that Catholic laity had less enthusiasm than did clergy for poor relief through bequests.[75]

Material assistance for the poor by Anglican prelates provides a study in contrasts. Parker left £100 to Canterbury to employ the poor, £30 to the needy of Croydon and Lambeth, and small annuities to Norwich and Mattishall, Norfolk. He also gave regularly to the poor during his lifetime, including £160 *p.a.* in support of two hospitals. Grindal bequeathed £100 to Canterbury to employ the poor, £10 each to the needy of Lambeth and Croydon, £13 6s. 8d. to the impoverished in the parish of St. Bees, Cumb., and £50 to an almshouse at Croydon that he had founded. Whitgift, as has been seen, founded and endowed his hospital at Croydon. Archbishop Hutton likewise founded a hospital, though on a smaller scale, at Warton, Lancs., which housed six poor men. Sizable bequests were left by Aylmer, bishop of London (£145 to the poor of London, Fulham, and Hadham, Herts.), Scory, bishop of Hereford (£200 each to Hereford and Leominster for interest-free loans to the poor, two hundred bushels of wheat to Hereford, and £400 to St. Bartholomew and Christ's Hospitals in London), and Horne, bishop of Winchester (£40 to the poor of Durham, £30 to the Hospital of St. Cross, and £20 to Magdalen Hospital, Winchester). Cox, bishop of Ely, left approximately £60 to the poor, of which £20 was set aside for needy students at Cambridge. Parkhurst, bishop of Norwich, left various funds for the poor, including money for the hospital at Norwich and £5 plus 25% of the debts owed him for the poor at Guildford, Surrey. Some prelates left little or nothing for the poor, such as Guest, bishop of Salisbury, who bequeathed £20 to the needy of New Sarum, Wilts., and William Day, bishop (briefly) of Winchester, who left nothing for the impoverished. Tunstall, bishop of Durham, left a very small legacy for the poor, but when he died in 1559 he had only been restored to his see for three weeks after a lapse of seven years. Generally, Anglican prelates donated to the poor as their sometimes restricted means allowed.[76]

Deans often supported the poor, sometimes substantially. Gabriel Goodman, dean of Westminster, established a house at Chiswick for Westminster students who became ill, founded and bequeathed his household goods to Christ's Hospital, Ruthin, and left legacies for various Welsh and English parishes and poor students at Oxford and Cambridge. The will of Whittingham, dean of Durham, included £10 for poor householders in Durham, £6 13s. 4d. for poor aliens in the French congregation in London, and the portion allotted to each of his four daughters to poor divinity students at Oxford or Cambridge in the event of their early death. Francis Mallett, dean of Lincoln, bequeathed £4 to the poor at his funeral, £6 to six poor maidens on their wedding day, and £6 13s. 8d. to poor prisoners. The dean of St. Paul's, Alexander Nowell, was known for liberality to the poor as well as educational benefactions.[77]

In contrast to the support for the poor in the wills of prelates and deans, lower clergy often declined to leave such legacies. An examination of thirty-seven wills of lower clergy (all or most of whom were Anglican) showed twelve (32.4%) with no bequests for the indigent. Twenty of the wills recorded specific amounts for the poor totaling £119 18s. 8d., or approximately £6 per will. One donor (Roger Kelke), however, accounted for a legacy of £40 to the poor of two villages (plus an uncalculated amount to the hospital at Ipswich). Two others, Dr. Thomas Wilson and Richard Halsall, rector of Halsall, Lancs., left £20 each to the poor. Setting these three more substantial donors aside, the remaining seventeen clerics gave a total of £79 18s. 8d., or an average of £4 14s. each. All but one of these seventeen clerics were from the northern counties where incomes were low—often under £10 a year, and in some cases half that. In this perspective, Anglican support for the poor among the lower clergy who gave was often substantial, though apparently not greater than that bestowed by Catholic priests. The increase in secular giving noted by Jordan probably was due to a change in giving patterns among the laity, not in greater legacies to the poor from Anglican clergy.[78]

Relief for the poor from the Anglican peerage was erratic. George Talbot, earl of Shrewsbury, left a total of £400 to Pontefract and Rotherham, Yorks., to provide three-year loans of £5 each to poor artificers, and his wife, who founded an almshouse, left approximately £40 to poor householders and prisoners in addition to £18 10s. for poor students at Oxford. Henry Herbert, earl of Pembroke, bequeathed £100 to Wilton, Wilts., to provide raw materials for poor clothiers. Burghley left £50 to the poor of five parishes, £10 to inmates in the Gatehouse Prison, and twenty marks to inmates of Newgate and Ludgate Prisons. A "college" or hospital for twenty poor people at Cobham was endowed by William Brooke, Lord Cobham, in his 1597 will, and Anne Fiennes, Lady Dacre, left funds to establish a hospital for twenty poor folk and twenty children at Westminster. John Paulet, marquess of Winchester, founded an almshouse at East Pennard, Som. Although £5,200 of gold was found in the closet of Anne Seymour, duchess of Somerset, when she died in 1587, she left only twenty marks to poor prisoners in London and a total of £20 to poor students of Oxford and Cambridge. Lucy Nevill, Lady Latimer, left only £10 for the poor of Hackney, Middlesex, and Cheshunt, Herts., in 1582. Edward Stanley, earl of Derby, did not make legacies to the destitute, but left it to his executors to donate what they considered appropriate. Neither Edward Manners, earl of Rutland, nor his brother and heir, John, left anything to the impoverished in their wills, though the poor benefited modestly at their funerals. Funeral expenses of £2,297 for the third earl, of course, left his brother in financial difficulties and less able to provide funds for the needy. Members of the peerage were sometimes woefully remiss in providing legacies to relieve the destitute.[79]

Peers were expected, like prelates, to donate significantly to charity during their lifetimes. Some took this obligation seriously; Thomas Sackville, Lord Buckhurst, purchased £155 worth of rye in the 1597 famine and gave it to the villages on his Sussex estates. The poor in the area of Callowdon, Warws., received pottage, beef, mutton, bread, and beer three days a week from Henry Lord Berkeley, who also disbursed alms daily. On Maundy Thursday, he provided clothing for the poor, and at Christmas, Easter, and Whitsuntide he gave over £20 to the destitute in the Callowdon and Coventry areas. In 1559, Lady Katherine gave £30 to the poor, and in 1588 Burghley donated £10 to St. Margaret's, Westminster, for the destitute to purchase coal. He also erected and endowed a hospital at Stamford, Lincs., before his death. In 1565, Richard Lord Rich founded an almshouse at Felstead, Essex, for five persons and an attendant, with each receiving food and—every four weeks—3s. 4d. in alms. The household book of Roger Lord North shows periodic gifts of a few shillings or a few pence to the poor, but such sums were regularly smaller than his gambling losses. Although some Anglican peers aided the impoverished by meaningful gifts during their life-times, others were perfunctory in doling out relatively trifling amounts.[80]

Anglican gentry seem to have behaved much like the peers with respect to charitable donations to the poor, though on a correspon-dingly smaller scale. An outstanding exception was Sir Matthew Arundell of Wardour Castle, Wilts., who bequeathed £2,000 to the destitute in 1599. More typical was the £40 left by Sir Francis Drake for the poor of Plymouth in 1595, or the endowment of the Derby-shire gentleman Francis Rodes to provide £4 *p.a.* to relieve wounded soldiers and the poor. In 1570 Christopher Sherston of Worksop, Notts., left his village £20 "which the church oweth me, to be be-stowed in shepe for the use of the poore." The gentry established hospitals and almshouses, such as that founded and endowed with lands worth £111 4s. 8d. *p.a.* at Long Melford, Suffolk, by Sir Wil-liam Cordell in 1581. Sir John Boys, a steward to the archbishop of Canterbury, founded Jesus Hospital, Canterbury, in 1599, and Sir John Popham, a member of the High Commission, established two hospitals at Wellington, Som., a few years earlier. Having already founded charity houses at Irby, Denzil Holles left each of the inhabi-tants twenty sol. (one livre) in his will. Other gentry, such as Richard Corbet of Wortley, Yorks., and Sir John Markham of Cotham, Notts., left nothing to the poor, and Adam Winthrop left only £2 to the needy of Grotton, Suffolk.[81]

Like the peers and clergy, gentry were expected to assist the needy on a regular basis. Sixty-two poor people in the parish of St. Dun-stan's, London, received weekly alms from Sir Thomas Egerton in 1596. Rather macabre was William Oglander's decision to leave bread for the poor every week on his father's tomb. William Wentworth ad-vised his son to set aside half his annual income for charity and the ad-vancement of his house, and he praised his own wife, Anne, because

> She clothed the naked and releved the poor,
> Both in hir plentye and hir smaller store.

Sir Francis Willoughby and his wife regularly gave a few pence or shillings to the poor, including prisoners. While in London in 1595, John Willoughby gave six pence to the needy, the same amount he paid for Nash's *Pierce Penilesse*. In 1600 Adam Winthrop "took vp lande for the poore." Periodic giving may have lessened the sense of obligation to provide for the poor in wills, though it is probable that those who established a pattern of giving in their daily lives were the ones most responsive in their wills to the needs of the destitute.[82]

The most striking case of charitable giving by the Anglican gentry is that of William Lamb, esquire, a gentleman of the chapel in Henry VIII's reign who died in April 1580. He donated £1,500 for the construction of Holborn conduit (completed in 1577) and provided 120 pails for poor women to carry water in for their living. From Lamb, the Clothworkers' Company received lands and tenements in London worth £30, the income from which was used to hire a minister to read services three times weekly and preach quarterly at St. James, Cripplegate. On 1 October every year the company provided apparel for two dozen men and women. A legacy to the Stationers' Company provided a dozen poor people with 12d. worth of bread and 12d. in cash each Friday. Christ's Hospital received £100 to purchase endowment lands and £6 to raise poor children, while St. Thomas Spittle in Southwark received £4 yearly to care for the sick. Lamb also provided £20 to be divided equally among forty poor maidens as marriage portions. Two London prisons received £6 for the poor inmates, and six mattresses each were donated to Newgate, Ludgate, the Marshalsea, King's Bench, and the White Lion Prisons. Six almshouses were constructed at Sutton Valence, Kent, with an endowment of £6 *p.a.* to provide inhabitants with provisions. Finally, £300 was donated to poor clothiers in Suffolk and the Shropshire towns of Ludlow and Bridgenorth. Lamb was an exceptional case, and was held up as an example of charitable giving for others to emulate.[83]

Assistance for the poor from Anglican professionals likewise varied substantially. Sir Roger Manwood, lord chief baron of the Exchequer, member of the High Commission, and an enemy of the Puritans, bequeathed £127 to the poor in various parishes in Kent, funds for a workhouse near Canterbury with capital of £40 to provide employment for the jobless, approximately £500 for almshouses at Hackington, Kent, with an endowment of £22 6s. *p.a.*, and a pound a year for seven years for the poor who attended an annual sermon he founded at Hackington. His total gifts during his lifetime and in his will amounted to £2,179 13 s. More modest support for the poor came from Sir Christopher Wray, lord chief justice, whose will left £30 to the poor of five parishes, funds to support six elderly persons in an almshouse at Glentworth, Lincs., three loads of ashwood and three of peat for the poor each year, and dinner for the needy in Glentworth Hall every Sunday, or a penny's worth of bread for those unable to attend. The lawyer Thomas Seckford endowed almshouses at Woodbridge, Suffolk, in 1588, and another lawyer, Richard Aungier, left funds in 1597 to provide 20s. *p.a.* for the poor of Coton, Cambs. Alexander Nowell's brother Robert, another lawyer, bequeathed £10 to the poor of the parish where he was buried, £60 for a funeral dinner and supper with benefits for the poor, and legacies to the indigent of other parishes. In 1584, the physician Dr. Caldwell left £200 to clothiers in Burton-upon-Trent, Staffs., to employ poor artificers, funds for poor relief to Lichfield, and additional sums for charity as his executors deemed appropriate. Token amounts were left for the poor by Edward Halsall, a lawyer and twice mayor of Liverpool (£13 6s. 8d.), and William Roswell, the solicitor general (£5).[84]

Although the clergy often criticized prosperous businessmen, a number of them, along with their spouses, did channel some of their profits into poor relief. Jordan includes abundant examples, though often it is impossible to ascertain the religious convictions of the donors. Sir Thomas Gresham founded eight almshouses in the parish of St. Peter's, London, and left funds to supply their eight residents with £6 13s. 4d. *p.a.* each. Other funds were left to relieve the poor in London jails and hospitals. In 1567 Sir William Hewet, a London merchant, bestowed approximately £35 on various poor people and prisoners, as well as a further 6s. 8d. for every poor maiden marrying at Harthill in Wales in the first two years after his death. When Lionel Cranfield prepared to go to the Continent in 1599 he made a will in which he bequeathed money to the poor of the parish of St. Michael Bassishaw, and a will made under similar conditions the following year reaffirmed this gift by providing a hundred marks to distribute two shillings worth of bread to the needy each Sunday. Alice Avenon provided a comparable legacy c. 1570, and other City women, such as Mrs. Katherine Brettergh and Dame Helen Branch, widow of the former lord mayor, Sir John Branch, were known for liberality to the poor. The widow of a London grocer, Lady Mary Ramsey,

> Whose liberall hand was neuer frozen fast,
> From Almes-deeds, so long as breath did last,

left nearly £10,000 in charitable gifts, including £1,000 towards the purchase of land in Gloucestershire, the income from which was for poor relief. Christ's Hospital received £2,000 and the London companies £1,000 for charitable purposes. Another London widow, Alice Hill, left £50 to the poor of St. Albans and Exeter. In some cases, the concern of City merchants and their spouses was equal or superior to that of the landed aristocracy, which may reflect the more acute problem of poverty in urban areas and a greater exposure to sermons and tracts in which poor relief was stressed as a Christian duty.[85]

A sampling of wills of Puritan clergy indicates very moderate to moderately substantial poor relief. Robert Beaumont, vice chancellor of Cambridge, who was sympathetic to opponents of vestments and was likely a conservative Puritan, bequeathed £10 to poor students of Trinity College. Another former exile, Christopher Goodman, who became a conservative Puritan in the Elizabethan era, left £20 to the parish of St. Bridget's, Chester, to purchase raw materials on which the poor could work, £20 to one or two men of the parish to employ the poor, £2 to the poor on the day of his burial, and £25 to Chester to stockpile corn and sell it to the poor at subsidized prices. Perkins' will included £2 for the poor of Great St. Andrew's, Cambridge, and Cartwright provided £2 for the destitute of Warwick in addition to twenty marks for poor ministerial students at Cambridge. In his 1575 will William Birche, pastor of Stanhope, Durham, provided legacies for the poor (including prisoners) totaling £13 5s., plus an additional £3 3s. each to twenty poor maidens as marriage portions, and funds for poor students in grammar schools and universities.[86]

In peerage circles, Puritans evinced concern for the indigent. In the 1570s, Huntingdon instigated a program to provide cheap wool for the poor of Leicester by donating £42 to be spent in a seven-year period. His servants carried coal to the town without charge for the corporation to sell to the needy at subsidized prices. To spur employment, a Gloucester clothier, Thomas Bradgate, was brought to Leicester in 1573 and given a loan at the earl's request. Although this and a subsequent scheme failed, the earl continued to try to create jobs. He also provided the hospital at Leicester with rents worth £66 13s. 4d. *p.a.* beginning in 1576. Francis Russell, earl of Bedford, founded an almshouse at Watford and bequeathed £120 in his will to poor folk in four parishes. The charity of the earl of Leicester to the poor of Shrewsbury was publicly praised in 1584. Margaret Clifford (née Russell), countess of Cumberland, founded almshouses at Beamsley, Yorks., for twelve poor women and a governess, and an

almshouse was also established by Anne Dudley, countess of Warwick. Mildred Cecil (née Cooke), Lady Burghley, was a regular benefactor to the destitute. London prisons received funds quarterly to
buy food for the inmates, and clothing was sent to the city's poor.
Each year, impoverished women at Cheshunt, Herts., were given alms
and wool to make cloth, which Lady Burghley then purchased from
them at amounts higher than market value. In time of dearth she purchased wheat and rye for the hungry. The Haberdashers' Company
received funds from Lady Burghley to loan to poor men in Romford
and Waltham, Essex, and Cheshunt, Herts. On the first of every
month, twenty indigent persons in Cheshunt received food and alms,
and she bequeathed £10 to St. Margaret's, Westminster, to aid the
destitute. Thus at the peerage level, Puritans as well as Anglicans
showed concern for the poor.[87]

Puritan gentry likewise made numerous contributions to poor relief. In 1572, Sir Francis Hastings collected in excess of £10 from the
gentry of Leicestershire and gave it to the deacons of the French
church in London to relieve their poor, and his first wife, Lady Magdalen, relieved the destitute. An annuity was given to Christ's Hospital, Cambridge, by Sir Walter Mildmay, and Thomas Mildmay erected
six almshouses at Moulsham, Essex, in 1565. The last will of Sir
Nicholas Bacon, whose ready cash and plate at the time of his death
amounted to £4,450, bequeathed approximately 400 marks to charitable institutions, which included £100 for stock to employ the
poor at St. Albans and £4 for poor prisoners in King's Bench Prison.
He and his wife, Lady Anne (née Cooke), were publicly commended
for "cherishing the poore and needie." In 1568 Parker wrote to Lady
Anne: "I understand that ye use otherwhiles to be a good solicitor
to my lord your husband in the cause of the poor." Their son, Anthony, continued their concern for the destitute; in 1597, for example, he provided alms for the poor of Redbourn, Herts. Yet Lady
Anne's father, Sir Anthony Cooke, left nearly £1,400 to family,
friends, and servants in his will, but nothing to the poor. Another
Puritan woman concerned with the indigent was Lady Margaret
Hoby, who provided the hungry with corn, wheat, and beef. These
examples suggest that the Puritan gentry were at least as concerned
with the needy as their Anglican counterparts.[88]

To summarize, despite the studies of charitable giving by W. K.
Jordan, it is very difficult to obtain statistical data on poor relief as
practiced by adherents of religious groups. The situation is made
more complex because the aristocracy and clergy were expected to
give regularly during their lifetimes as well as in their wills. In urban

areas, the more acute problem of poverty coupled with the likelihood of exposure to sermons in which poor relief was exhorted may have caused greater benefactions from business and professional people and their wives. Despite the promptings of Puritan clergy in particular to confine giving to the godly, the vast majority of bequests were made without stipulation regarding the religion of recipients. It is possible that much of the giving of Puritans while they were alive went to deacons, who restricted assistance to the godly, and whose overall contributions have not thus far been examined in parish accounts.

Sutton's claim that Anglican clergy were greater benefactors of the poor does not appear to be justified. With their larger incomes, the prelates were expected to take an active role in poor relief, and they normally did, with donations, supervision and support of hospitals, visitation articles, and (as will be seen) hospitality. In the late Elizabethan period particularly, they also were active as agents of the crown in dispensing assistance from the state and encouraging private relief for the indigent. Parker, Grindal, Whitgift, Aylmer, and Scory were among the prelates who left sizable bequests for the poor, though others, such as Day and Tunstall, left little. Giving among the Anglican lower clergy was spotty, with perhaps a third of them leaving nothing for the poor in their testaments. Gifts from those who did, at least in the north, often averaged the better part of a year's income, though the Anglicans do not appear to have given more than Catholic clergy. Support for the poor among Puritan clergy was probably comparable.

Among the laity, willingness to aid the destitute varied widely. Puritan peers may have been more consistently willing to help the unfortunate, but a number of Anglican peers and their wives actively donated. The same is true of the Puritan gentry, though some of the most spectacular charitable donations came from Anglican gentlemen, such as William Lamb. For the most part Catholic gentlemen in this period seem to have been only modestly concerned with bequests for the poor, and then in some cases only because they could not use the money for masses to speed their souls through purgatory. There were some striking exceptions, such as Sir Thomas White. The pronounced variations in support for the poor among the Anglican aristocracy were present in Anglican professionals, some of whom made extensive benefactions to the destitute. That some aristocrats, professionals, and business people donated so heavily for poor relief only whetted the appetites of the clergy to broaden this base of support. Various Anglican and Puritan clergy lavished praise on those who gave substantially, as the epitaphs indicate. It was increasingly important for aristocratic women and wives of businessmen and city officials to act as patronesses of the poor, so that the regular provision of relief became both a social and a spiritual duty of women as well as men. [89]

(7) Hospitality

Hospitality is the chiefest point of humanity, which an housholder can shew, not only vnto his friends, but also vnto strangers & wayfaring men.

William Vaughan [90]

Good houses kept they euermore, releeuing both the sick and poor.

Thomas Deloney [91]

When extended to the poor, hospitality was a form of charity and was encouraged in Elizabethan biblical marginalia. The Geneva Bible informed readers that the Hebrew patriarchs gently entertained strangers, hence the godly should practice similar hospitality, but always out of love for the guests and never for ulterior motives. A note in the Beza-Tomson Bible made hospitality the most commendable form of charity, especially when it was undertaken bountifully and courteously. The prelates too commended hospitality in the Bishops' Bible. Aware of the importance of hospitality for missionary priests as well as indigent Catholics, of whom there were many in the rural northwest, the Rheims annotators made it "a great grace to be beneficial to strangers, specially to them that be of our Catholike faith and suffer for the same." [92]

Reinforcement of the obligation of hospitality came in the writings and sermons of Anglican clergy and religious authors. The type of hospitality with which they were concerned was defined by Thomas Rogers as "a religious entertainment of all such as truly without hypocrisie serue God." Rogers urged that such hospitality be restricted to the impoverished, and Sandys wanted the emphasis placed on the godly and exiles, such as the Huguenots in England. Support for hospitality as an obligation was found in Genesis 19 and Hebrews 13 as well as in the principles of humanitarianism and Christian brotherhood. The gentry and clergy emphasized hospitality, which gave Pilkington and Turnbull an occasion to return to the theme of a financially deprived church, in which prelates and lower clergy lacked adequate incomes to perform their obligations. Pilkington averred that few bishops had enough lands to provide the hospitality expected of them. An indication of the significance attached to social obligations by Anglicans was Whitgift's assertion that more could be gained for the gospel from an honest parson who maintained hospitality than a doctor of divinity who preached a dozen sermons. Howson agreed. Numerous complaints were voiced that hospitality was ignored because people were more interested in fine apparel and houses, hawking, sexual immorality, banqueting, and borrowing at usurious rates. Anglican clergy and religious writers attached great significance to hospitality as a means of strengthening the church and caring for the poor. [93]

Puritans too stressed the importance of hospitality, relying on the same biblical support and the notion of Christian responsibility. Unlike the Anglicans, they infused hospitality with a special religious mission, akin to the exhortations they were supposed to give recipients of alms. Hospitality required not only a liberal and cheerful bestowal of food and clothing but also edification, exhortation, church attendance, and (on Sundays) sabbath observance. Moreover Puritans distinguished themselves by concern that hospitality be characterized neither by excess nor by stinginess, and that such supplementary activities as gambling and masques be excluded, even at Christmas, the most traditional period of hospitality. Puritans preferred the limitation of hospitality to the godly, but Patrick Collinson errs in seeing this as distinctive, for such Anglicans as Rogers (a conservative) and Sandys (a moderate) called for the same limitations. Puritans concurred with Anglicans that the proper subjects of hospitality were the poor. Bird even extolled the money-saving virtues of providing hospitality for the poor, with their lower expectations, rather than for persons of substance with cultivated tastes! Nevertheless, Crowley wrote,

> They bid to feastes,
> Such maner gestes,
> As will bid them againe:
> They thinke great shame,
> That blinde and lame,
> Should to their court retaine.

In contrast, a virtuous man in Puritan eyes made his house an inn for strangers and a hospital for the poor, particularly the godly poor. For the Puritan, the provision of hospitality was a means of extending the influence of the household as a church. [94]

Other points of agreement existed between Puritans and Anglicans, one of which was the responsibility of the minister. Yet whereas

Anglicans cited this duty in calling for greater incomes for the clergy, Puritans used the same responsibility to denigrate pluralists who relied on hospitality rather than sermons to feed parishioners. Hake lambasted clerics who were "so epicuryous in the pamperyng of theyr owne bodies, And so vaineglorious in a litle releeuing of the bodyes of the needy, that they thinke the same theyr counterfeit hospitality to be a sufficient discharge of them selues, and defense of their flock." Despite this difference in outlook, Puritans concurred with Anglicans that hospitality was not being adequately provided, and they recited the same reasons for this lack. Instead of being hospitable to the needy, persons of means were accused of lavishing funds on elaborate meals, fine houses, and costly clothing, as well as spending time in town houses instead of on their manors. The gentry were accused of raising rents to prevent yeomen from surpassing them in hospitality, and the worst offenders regarding lack of hospitality were allegedly rack-renters. Some persons of means ceased providing hospitality because they claimed the increase in the number of beggars made it financially onerous. Puritans and Anglicans did not dispute the need for greater hospitality and the impediments to that end, but the Puritans deviated from their colleagues by blaming pluralists for part of the problem instead of requesting increased clerical funds, and by requiring edification and exhortation as an essential part of hospitality. Whereas at least some Anglicans attributed more significance to hospitality than sermons, Puritans strictly subordinated it to the sermon and religious instruction. [95]

The importance Anglicans attached to hospitality is reflected in prelatical actions. In November 1560 and again seven years later Parker inquired of Grindal how many clergy maintained hospitality. Episcopal injunctions stipulated that prebendaries and other clerics must provide hospitality, and visitation articles regularly asked if clergy met this obligation or otherwise provided relief for needy parishioners. Not all clerics did, causing the bishops difficulties. In June 1582, to cite one case, Edmund Scambler, bishop of Peterborough, petitioned Elizabeth to enforce the ecclesiastical statutes on clerical residence because prebendaries were not fulfilling their duties of hospitality and preaching, and he was unable to reform them. The Puritan Richard Gibson, vicar of Skipton, Yorks., had to be admonished for not maintaining hospitality in the 1590 visitation. In the 1595-96 visitation, William Moore, parson of Halsham, Yorks., and Mr. Seele, parson of Sigglesthorne, Yorks., were cited for lack of hospitality. Thurland, master of the Savoy Hospital, also was accused in 1569 of not providing hospitality. Sometimes inadequate income made it nearly impossible to fulfill this obligation, as Parker recognized in 1564 when he requested Cecil's permission for the bishop of St. Asaph to hold benefices *in commendam* because of the duty of hospitality. In the economic crisis of 1596, Whitgift was ordered by the Privy Council to enjoin the clergy and laity to provide hospitality to relieve the impoverished. Thus the prelates saw hospitality as a Christian duty and a means of preserving social order, but they had difficulty procuring clerical compliance because of financial and motivational factors.[96]

Striking instances of the maintenance of hospitality occurred among Anglican clergy, notably the prelates, though much of this was not done for the poor. In 1565 Parker had a magnificent three-day feast at Whitsuntide for the important folk of Canterbury, a second feast on Trinity Sunday in memory of Henry VIII for the same people, and a feast in July for judges, justices of the peace, lawyers, and others. The Whitsuntide feast in 1570 was for citizens and their wives, but the Trinity feast that year included the poor of the hospital of St. John and Herbaldown. Parker expected the burden of hospitality at Canterbury to be shared by the cathedral chapter, but the queen reserved the prebends for her chaplains (who were absent), and others stayed away to avoid hospitality, which actions occasioned a complaint from Parker to Cecil in 1568. As archbishop, Whitgift "kept princely hospitality" for clergy, nobility, and gentry, but at Christmas he opened his gates to all. William Alley, bishop of Exeter, was reputedly "bountifull in hospitalitie, liberall to the poore, and a succourer of the needie." Richard Fletcher, bishop of London, died heavily in debt in 1596, partly because of the extent of his hospitality, yet William Hughes, bishop of St. Asaph (1573-1600), ignored this obligation. Whittingham was known for bountiful hospitality as dean of Durham. Although the bishops maintained hospitality, that so much of their income had to be allocated to feasts for the prominent severely curtailed their opportunity to provide simple meals for the indigent, and thus contributed to anti-prelatical hostility.[97]

Hospitality by the aristocracy was a tradition dating back to the Middle Ages, and in general Anglican peers maintained it. In the 1560s, approximately one hundred persons, ranging from captains and lieutenants to pensioners and others, regularly sought hospitality from Henry Carey, Lord Hunsdon, and his wife Anne. Edward Stanley, earl of Derby, fed over sixty elderly persons twice daily at his home, and all comers three times a week. For thirty-five years he reputedly fed and gave alms to 2,700 people. For three decades,

Thomas Sackville, Lord Buckhurst, provided extensive hospitality for a group that (with servants and family) totaled some two hundred. Henry Wriothesley, third earl of Southampton, was commended for feeding needy poor with mutton, beef, and bread.

> His House keeping right good, there plentie bare the sway:
> No honest man forbidden was, within his house to staie.

Three days a week Henry Lord Berkeley fed the poor in the villages around Callowdon, Warws., and he was famous for his Christmas hospitality. Some hospitality consisted only of doles of leftover food at the gates of estates, though this provision was better than nothing. At Theobalds, Burghley's splendid mansion, twenty to thirty poor received such doles every day, though there was also a gift of 20s. a week to the needy of Cheshunt and a provision of £10 a week to hire the poor. A plan for the regulation of a nobleman's household c. 1597 stipulated that there be a basket "to receave all the broken bread & meat" for distribution to the indigent. Hospitality for the poor from Anglican nobles varied considerably, from regular meals and alms to doles of leftovers.[98]

Anglican gentry typically behaved as their noble counterparts, though ordinarily on a lesser scale. Thomas Cheyney, lord warden of the Cinque Ports, "kept so bountifull a house," though his hospitality was largely bestowed on youth in his service and visitors. In contrast, Sir William Fitzwilliam was known for his hospitality to the poor. Sir Edward Horsey, captain of the Isle of Wight, and his mistress, the widow Dowsabel Milles, provided hospitality on a grand scale in the 1570s. In Nottinghamshire, Sir William Holles was "the wonder of this country for a settled house and constant hospitality." At Christmas he opened his doors to anyone for a stay of three days, and during the Twelve Days prepared an ox a day as well as sheep and other food. Like the nobles, the gentry had to devote a good portion of their funds to entertain persons of status, sharply reducing what they could spend on the poor. The household books of Sir William Fairfax of Gilling, Yorks., for the period 1571-82 reveal a good deal of hospitality, with thirty to fifty persons normally dining in the hall, though few of these appear to have been destitute. (His charge for provisions, including the assessed value of produce from his estate, was £400 0s. 2d. in 1580.) Sir Francis Willoughby's situation was comparable, for he too entertained guests and their parties regularly, most of whom were gentlemen. When he entertained a hundred and twenty guests, including the earl and countess of Rutland, on 11 November 1587, his food bill was £3 8s. 4d. The earl and his party had already accepted his hospitality that July and twice in October. Faced with such social obligations, the provision of hospitality for the poor required effective estate management and a reasonable degree of wealth, which not all gentlemen possessed.[99]

The concern for hospitality is reflected in various wills. In 1576 Sir Thomas Smith left instructions to his brother George to provide hospitality for the poor and work for his neighbors, and in 1589 Sir Christopher Wray asked his son to provide dinner for the poor each Sunday at Glentworth Hall. Robert Tatton of Withenshaw, Lancs., had not completed a new manor house at the time of his death, hence he bequeathed his old one to his wife lest she have "no convenient mansion house to kepe hospitalytie." A Cheshire gentleman, Thomas Legh of High Leigh, bequeathed his grandson a lease of the corn, pigs, geese, hemp, and flax in his township "to the mayneteynance of his howse in keepinge hospitallitie." In 1568 the rector of Bury, Lancs., Richard Jones, bequeathed household furnishings to his successor to assist him in the maintenance of hospitality. Although such provisions are found in only a minority of wills, they do testify to the regard some Elizabethans had for the Christian and social duty of hospitality.[100]

Among Puritans, hospitality was an accepted Christian obligation. The hospitality to the poor that Francis Russell, earl of Bedford, extended was proverbial and, with that of the earl of Derby (who was not a Puritan), brought Elizabeth's admiration. Of the earl of Huntingdon it was said that his gates were always open to the hungry and his purse to the poor who flocked to his door. Sir Henry Sidney "alwaies delighted to keepe an orderlie, liberall and honorable house (greatlie to the reliefe and comfort of the poore) according to the reputation and degree of his place and calling." The idea that hospitality had to be bestowed according to means and social standing was part of the advice given to Anthony Mildmay in 1570 by his father, Sir Walter.[101]

If these Puritans followed the recommendations of their clergy and accompanied hospitality with religious instruction and invitations to church, little mention of it is made. Such instruction probably occurred in the home of Robert Foorth of Butley, Suffolk, who was commended for bountiful hospitality and poor relief, and whose family daily set aside time to read Scripture, pray, and sing Psalms. It happened in the Northamptonshire home of Sir Edward and Lady Montague, whose hospitality was known throughout the shire, for William Lord Vaux remarked that she was "somewhat too zealous . . . urging me in matters tending to religion." Sir Thomas and Lady

Margaret Hoby provided hospitality, even to the ungodly, but in the summer of 1600 they were rewarded with card playing, swearing, rowdy behavior, vandalism, and loud laughter during Psalm singing by a hunting party that included Sir William Eure and Richard Cholmeley, justices of the peace. In practice, Puritan laity probably did not restrict hospitality to the godly, though in some cases they followed the advice of the clergy to include religious exhortations as part of their hospitality.[102]

This chapter has demonstrated a number of significant variations between Anglicans and Puritans in their thinking on the poor. There were, to be sure, numerous aspects on which they agreed, including the derivation of wealth from God, the stewardship of recipients with responsibilities for the needy, and the wrongfulness of despising or oppressing the less fortunate. Both groups continued, as in the Middle Ages, to regard the poor as essential for the exercise of *caritas*, and both urged the impoverished to accept their estate and seek the spiritual blessings associated with poverty. Neither social revolt nor social leveling was justified. Broad agreement existed on the duty to give alms liberally, with no thought of gain, yet material and spiritual benefits were promised. The Protestants repudiated the Catholic association of merit with almsgiving. Anglican and Puritan alike recommended increased giving to terminate begging by the impotent, and more effective enforcement of the laws against the indolent, who threatened religion, property, and commonwealth. Neither group advocated communalism as a solution to the problem of poverty, for this too was a threat to social stability and contrary to biblical and natural law. Finally, both groups encouraged greater hospitality as a means of poor relief, and blamed extravagance in dress, food, and housing, as well as increased lavish living by the aristocracy, for insufficient hospitality.

Notwithstanding these areas of agreement, some discrepancies are obvious. Unlike the Anglicans, the Puritans were more willing to discuss wealth as a reward for godly living, hence they spent less time dwelling on the dangers of wealth. Simultaneously, Puritans provided a fuller accounting of the recipients' obligations, including the duty of the poor to be holy and thankful, their responsibility to use gifts appropriately, and their obligation to recompense donors if their situations altered. For the most part Puritans were more concerned than Anglicans (in theory at least) with directing alms to the godly, though there was some flexibility on this subject. Puritans were noteworthy for calling for donors to combine religious exhortations with their alms, and when hospitality was provided they pressed the hosts to include religious instruction and accompany the guests to church. Whereas some Anglicans explicitly regarded hospitality as more important than preaching for the advancement of the gospel, the Puritans sharply demurred. Whereas some Anglicans pressed for increased incomes to meet their hospitality obligations, Puritans damned clergy, especially pluralists, who substituted hospitality for sermons. It is erroneous to assert, as W. K. Jordan has, that no significant distinctions existed between Anglicans and Puritans in this area.[103]

In practice, the amount donated to the poor in the Elizabethan age increased, though to some extent the effect of the increase was offset by inflation. For the most part, donations to the poor were made without the limitation of requiring recipients to be godly, and this is true even in Puritan wills. The prelates were actively involved in poor relief through the provision of hospitality, the donation of alms, bequests in wills, the supervision of hospitals, and the use of injunctions and visitation articles to require poor relief by the lower clergy. The crown and Council used the bishops as agents, especially in the 1590s, to urge increased alms and hospitality for the hungry in the dearth. Some prelates were too financially constrained to leave bequests for the poor (for which a good deal of blame rests with the queen), but perhaps two-thirds of the lower clergy did. No indication is clear at this point that Protestant clergy were more willing to leave funds to the poor than Catholic priests, or Puritans than Anglicans, but much additional research must be done. In the aristocracy, however, support for the indigent seems to be more consistent among Puritans than Anglicans, though some Anglican donations were substantial. Hospitality would have been greater for the poor if it had not been for the social obligation of entertaining persons of means. There is no evidence to suggest that Puritans restricted hospitality to the godly, though at least some Puritans accepted the obligation to teach and admonish their guests on religious matters. In the pursuit of charity, differences appeared not only in thought but also in practice between Anglicans and Puritans, with the former tending to see charity primarily as a social obligation and the latter essentially as a religious duty.

CHAPTER 14

Economic Problems

The harmonious relationship between the government's concern with social order and the interest of religious reformers in Christian conduct demonstrated in other areas is evident in the treatment of economic concerns, particularly the encouragement of ethical business dealings and the abhorrence of forestalling, regrating, engrossing (of goods and land), and depopulating enclosure. The government would have been delighted if the more conservative reformers had been successful in getting men to lend without interest, but the financial needs of the Elizabethan regime drove the government to reduce the penalties on interest rates up to 10%. While most clergy groused, a few Anglicans and rather more Puritans slowly came to the conclusion that moderate interest was tolerable as long as it was never imposed on the indigent. Clerical support for standard weights and measures harmonized with the government's interests as well as the expansion of interregional trade. The ideal of the Christian commonwealth remained strong enough to create revulsion in most church and government circles against those who profited at the expense of society, whether by forestalling, regrating, engrossing, or enclosing to depopulate. In these areas, large profits could be made, but the government was not willing to countenance social unrest and the clergy were not ready to turn their backs on the downtrodden.

(1) Usury

To speake somwhat of vsurye,
the whiche the Lorde doth daily curse
yet some doo vse it priuely
to fyll their vncontented purse.

John Barker[1]

By extortion and vsurie wee may make stones into bread, that is the diuels
Alchymistrie.

Lancelot Andrewes[2]

The landmark studies by Max Weber and R. H. Tawney on religion
and capitalist development assert that the more liberal attitude of
some Protestant theologians toward usury was more conducive to
economic change. In repudiating this thesis, Charles and Katherine
George argue that Protestants in England were reactionary in their
aggressive and uniform disapproval of interest on loans. Even in the
seventeenth century, English Calvinist social theory was, they contend,
no more tolerant of usury than Catholic thought. A good deal of primary evidence supports the Georges' reassessment, yet *some* English
religious leaders adopted a more liberal approach to usury, easing the
growing pains of capitalism in England.[3]

Revulsion against usury was deeply rooted in the Christian tradition,
with support from passages like Deuteronomy 23:19, Leviticus 25:
35-37, and Psalm 15:5. Tudor marginalia reinforced the biblical prohibitions. In the Coverdale, Matthew, and Matthew-Becke Bibles, a
note to Psalm 37 points out that an alternate reading to the verse,
"The vngodly boroweth and paieth not agayne, but the rightuous is
mercifull & liberall," is "The vngodly lendeth vpon vsury and not for
nought." Other marginal notes in the 1537 Matthew Bible ban usury
as a violation of justice and a negation of duty to those in need, and
prohibit imprisonment for debt. In the Geneva Bible, usurers are
threatened with divine punishment and expulsion from the church,
and Christians are exhorted not only to forbear charging interest but
willingly to lose the principal in the expectation of receiving from
Christ "the whole with a moste liberal interest." Usury is prohibited
in the Bishops' Bible as well. The more liberal Calvinist outlook appears indirectly for the first time in an English Bible in the Beza-
Tomson version, where the note to Luke 6:35 informs lenders that
their intention should be to loan for the benefit of others and for pleasure, without worrying about repayment of the principal, but no explicit ban is declared on interest. In contrast, the Rheims annotators

continued the ban on usury, including those forms in which it was disguised. With the exception of the Beza-Tomson version, the Tudor Scriptures continued the traditional negative outlook toward usury.[4]

Despite the conservative outlook of the clergy on interest, financial exigencies forced the government to obtain a statute permitting interest up to 10% to facilitate loans. The resulting act (37 Henry VIII, c. 9) remained in force until 1552, when the Protestant regime of Northumberland had it repealed (5 & 6 Edward VI, c. 20). Although interest was legally prohibited in the ensuing nineteen years, the practice continued, with the usual rate running approximately 12 to 15%. In the period 1560 to 1571, at least eighty Yorkshire gentlemen borrowed funds. Sometimes this was done through mortgages, as in the case of Ambrose Dudley, earl of Warwick, who mortgaged his manor of Thorpe near Wainfleet, Lincs., in 1563 for £1,404 14s., and was required to pay £1,459 5s. 1d. five months later to redeem the mortgage (a rate of approximately 9% *p.a.*). His funds were raised from John and Henry Isham, the former a mercer and Merchant Adventurer who received up to 15% interest on some loans, and the latter the parson of Pitchley, Northants. The Puritan Michael Hicks, who later became Burghley's secretary, began loaning funds in the 1560s, a practice he learned from his mother, Mrs. Juliana Penne, who at one time loaned Cecil money at a probable rate of 15%. Repeal of the Henrician statute did not deter her or her son from usurious practices, and they were not unusual.[5]

The need for loans by aristocrats, businessmen, and the government led to an attempt in 1563 to revise the Henrician statute permitting interest up to 10%. After the first bill failed, a new bill was approved in the Commons on 18 February by a vote of 134 to 90, though this bill ultimately was rejected. Concern about the inability to enforce the Edwardian statute was voiced while the 1566 Parliament was in session, but it was not until 1571 that a new statute was enacted, and then only after one bill had been rejected and a new one prepared. In the course of the debate on the original bill, one member (Mr. Molley) acknowledged that the preachers were opposed to usury, but he favored a bill to allow modest interest to terminate the excessive amounts being charged "to the destruction of young Gentlemen" and the hindrance of good business. In Molley's judgment, moderate interest did not contravene the word of God, for the biblical proscriptions applied to the Jews only. Citing Beza and Bellarmine, Molley asserted that only "biting and over-sharp dealing" (excessive interest) violated scriptural teaching. In rebuttal, Dr. Thomas Wilson, Master of Requests, repudiated usury as robbery and asserted that it resulted in lower revenue for the queen because of loss of trade, higher prices, and increased unemployment, as money was used for loans instead of production. An unnamed MP thought that usury was not possible if neither party was harmed, for "Who is it that would not in extremity give a little to save much money?" There was, he insisted, no divine ban against all interest, for the Jews were allowed to impose it on Gentiles. A leading Puritan member, Thomas Norton, argued in turn that all usury was biting and should not be allowed, but in the end his cause was lost. The statute (13 Elizabeth I, c. 8) imposed penalties on interest charged in excess of 10%, but as a concession to conservatives, borrowers could sue for the remission of interest if they were willing to destroy their credit rating. Technically, usury of even 10% or less was not approved and was labeled a detestable sin.[6]

After passage of the act, two gentlemen pensioners were empowered in July 1571 to investigate offenses, but abuses continued. Lawrence Stone plausibly asserts that it was not until about 1600 that the figure of 10% was normal, and thereafter the legal rate was reduced to 8% in 1624 and 6% in 1651. It was common in the 1570s and 1580s to pay 20%, often through stratagems, such as paying the lender an excessive sum for an item, or hiring laborers for the lender at the borrower's expense. In some cases, lenders refused to accept the extortionate interest if word of the agreement leaked out. Such actions troubled Burghley and probably the queen, for she was irate when William Lord Eure released two usurers from prison after less than a day's confinement.[7]

Although many usurious loans probably were kept secret to preserve the credit of the borrower, widespread abuse is indicated in the records of the Court of Requests. A 1584 case involved a man who contracted to repay £2,000 over a ten-year period, with the borrower providing the use of land worth £30 *p.a.* during this period. When the borrower defaulted because of a five-year stint of military service in Ireland, the lender had him arrested and took possession of the land, despite the borrower's offer to return the rest of the principal and "vnreasonable vsurie for the same." In another case a London goldsmith loaned £80 in 1584, to be repaid in six months along with a "fee" of £20. When the payment fell due, the borrower was £62 short, but agreed to accept £85 worth of plate assessed at a purchase price of £200 in return for cancellation of the £62 debt. When he defaulted on this loan and the lender sued at common law for the £300 bond posted as surety, the borrower appealed to the Court of Requests for relief. A 1590 case involved a plaintiff who borrowed £50 at 20% interest to pay off debts that would have resulted in his disinheritance if his father had discovered them. The loan was cloaked in the guise of a life annuity of £20 *p.a.* payable to the lender's daughter, on the understanding that when the principal plus 20% was paid, the annuity would be terminated; after the lender died, his executors refused to acknowledge the unwritten agreement. In a final case, a London poulterer brought charges against a London merchant from whom he had borrowed 55s. In return, the poulterer gave the merchant £5 3s. worth of apparel and household items as pledges of repayment, plus the sale of wares to him at severely deflated prices to cover the cost of the loan.[8] Undoubtedly, many Elizabethans knew of similar cases where usurious rates were demanded for loans, and where borrowers often were portrayed as innocent victims of unsavory lenders. In this context, the clergy normally adopted a conservative stance.

Until the passage of the 1571 law tolerating interest up to 10%, relatively little published comment came from Anglicans about usury. In 1560 Pilkington contended that usury was unlawful, particularly in view of Nehemiah's condemnation of even 1%, hence he urged the government to compel usurers to return their ill-gotten gains.[9]

One of the most substantial early Elizabethan attacks on usury came from Jewel, who characterized it as satanically motivated theft that led to the decay of towns, the decline of states, and the misery of people. Jewel believed usury was a means of oppressing the impoverished and driving persons into beggary. A usurer was worse than a thief because he oppressed the poor, not the propertied, and was himself wealthy, as distinct from the usual thief who stole to keep himself or his family alive. Jewel found usury intolerable by divine, civil, canon, common, and natural law, and refused to admit its validity under almost any circumstances, including benefit to the commonwealth or the unavailability of loans for the poor without interest. "So necessary is an usurer for to relieve the poor and needy, as rust is to help iron, and as the moth is to help a garment: it eateth him through from one side to another." Jewel was cognizant that interest was also paid by merchants for business loans from which borrower and lender profited, but even in these circumstances usury could not be countenanced, because the merchant passed the cost of the loan to the consumer, who thereby paid more than a just price. He applied the same principle to the loan of shops and wares; it was wrong for an owner to lease his shop and goods for a fee if the shop and merchandize were returned to him intact. Jewel drew a careful distinction between usury and "interest"; by the latter he meant the right to pass on to a borrower any charges incurred by the lender because the loan was not repaid on time. In effect, "interest" was a late penalty, but this could only be imposed in the event of an actual loss by the lender. Interest could never be charged for profit, but must be compatible with equity, conscience, and reason. In one set of circumstances, Jewel permitted usury, though he insisted on calling it interest, that is, when the "stock" of an infant, a mental incompetent, or an infirm person was managed to bring in a steady income to sustain the helpless person. Nor did Jewel object to annuities, as when one individual gave another money in return for a stipulated and periodic payment for the duration of the donor's life.[10]

When the 1571 Parliament was debating the usury bill, an assembly of both houses heard a sermon in which the conservative position was reaffirmed by Edwin Sandys, bishop of London.

That biting worm of usury, that devouring wolf, hath consumed many: many it hath pulled upon their knees, and brought to beggary; many such as might have lived in great wealth, and in honour not a few. This canker hath corrupted all England. It is become the chief chaffer and merchandize of England. . . . Repress it by law.

Throughout his career, Sandys castigated the usurer as a violator of divine, natural, and civil law. He called on Christians to lend freely, seeking no gain in return, and to give to the needy whenever possible out of love. Zaccheus (Luke 19) was held forth as an example because he made restitution of his unlawful gains and donated half his goods to the poor. In a sermon before the queen, Sandys warned that "the usurer doth so mire his fingers in money, that with his foul filthy fists he can never take hold upon the tabernacle of God." As archbishop of York, he lashed out against those who concealed usury to obtain illegal profits. Unlike Jewel, Sandys largely ignored the question of business loans where both parties profited, but adhered to the medieval notion that usury was wrong because it oppressed the poor.[11]

Sandys was so opposed to usury that as archbishop of York he used the High Commission to punish usurers, including those who stayed within the limits of the 1571 statute. In all, forty usurers were cited, required to forfeit all interest, and—if contumacious—imprisoned. In 1585 Matthew Hutton, dean of York, publicly challenged Sandys by distinguishing between interest (as allowed by the 1571 law) and usury, and by refusing to accept as usurious anything not explicitly condemned in Scripture; civil law was not an acceptable authority. Calvin, Beza, Bullinger, Bucer, and Danaeus were cited to support his argument. Hutton even threatened praemunire, on the grounds that the court was transgressing its authority by refusing to abide by the 1571 statute. In consequence the Council of the North intervened to liberate the accused. Sandys, however, persisted in his campaign to crush usury, prosecuting even Robert Morley, a servant of Huntingdon, president of the Council. The Council continued to intervene on behalf of alleged usurers imprisoned by Sandys, prompting the latter to complain to Burghley. Whereas Sandys represented the traditional position, Hutton typified those Anglican clerics who accepted interest charges if they were not extortionate, and Hutton himself apparently loaned money on these terms, for Sandys accused him of being "deeply mired" in usury.[12]

According to published comments, the views of Sandys must have prevailed among Anglican clerics in the aftermath of the 1571 statute. In the 1570s Drant, Curteys, and Whitgift (the latter two in sermons before Elizabeth in 1574) condemned usury but provided no substantive comment. Curteys concentrated on those who sold their lands and lived on interest from loans. The sermons by Curteys and Whitgift may indicate connivance by some prelates to persuade Elizabeth to repeal the 1571 act. In 1572 Dr. Thomas Wilson's well-known *Discourse upon Usury* was published in which his views in the 1571 parliamentary debate were amplified, though in juxtaposition (through a dialogue format) to those of the moderates. To Wilson, loans must be made out of charity, which cannot exist where hope of private gain prevails, as in all usurious transactions. Even if both parties gain, consumers are harmed by higher prices to cover the cost of a loan. Nor can the aristocracy pay usury, because this leads to the decay of estates, rent-racking, and increased entry fines. In the 1580s, Babington and Thomas Rogers denounced usury and called for Christians to lend freely. Usury, claimed Babington, violated the eighth commandment. In 1589, however, Wright prohibited only interest on loans to the needy, leaving open, by implication, the possibility of interest-bearing loans to merchants and landed persons.[13]

Two Anglican lay writers—Whetstone and Lodge—defended the conservative position in the 1570s and 1580s. Whetstone's principal concern was the harm usurers did to sons of gentlemen lured to London by gambling and female companionship. Lenders were common enough: "In the time of King *Henrie* the third, the good citizens of *London* in one night slew fiue hundred Jewes for that a Jewe tooke of a Christian a pennie in the shilling vsurie: and euer got them banished [from] the Citie: if the like Justice were done vpon Juish Christians, *London* would haue manie houses emptie." Lodge too was concerned about impoverishing gentlemen's sons by usury, and castigated guardians for being so stingy with their wards that the latter were driven to usurers. To remedy the evil, Lodge proposed an industrious, continent life and the study of ancient laws (such as a Solonian law prohibiting a son under his father's control from borrowing without his father's knowledge). Neither Whetstone nor Lodge came to grips with the key question of interest-bearing commercial loans, but their concern for gentlemen's sons rather than the impoverished sets them apart from Anglican clergy.[14]

One of the principal Anglican discussions of usury was written in 1592 by Richard Turnbull, a fellow of Corpus Christi College, Oxford. Usury, defined as any gain from the loan of the principal without labor or danger, was rejected as contrary to natural and divine law, and the usurer damned for his unlawful vocation. One of the key arguments of proponents of interest-taking was the use of borrowed funds to obtain profit, but to this Turnbull retorted: "Thou mayst take ten for a hundreth in the yeare: if thou wilt loose ten of thy principall, if he get not, but suffer damage." This opened the door to interest on restricted conditions, though Turnbull repudiated the argument that interest could be paid by those able to afford it, for this, he argued, was done by the Jews, and Christians were expected to demonstrate greater love for others. Even the willingness of borrowers to pay interest did not justify taking it, for their willingness was born of constraint. In contrast to Jewel, Turnbull condemned usury as a means of support for widows and orphans, for a good end did not justify evil means. Although the 1571 statute tolerated interest up to 10%, Turnbull—like Sandys—was adamant that no human law could abrogate a divine law. If, however, repayment of a loan was deferred and the lender suffered loss, equivalent compensation did not constitute usury. To Turnbull a usurer was an idolater because of his covetousness and should be denied Christian burial. Turnbull's argument was thus one with Sandys', even to the point of directing primary concern to the poor who were victimized by usurers. The single exception was Turnbull's grudging approval of interest in return for sharing potential losses.[15]

A number of Anglicans continued to oppose usury in the late Elizabethan years. In November 1594, Dove told a Paul's Cross audience that Englishmen were worse than Jews because they spared no one, and he deplored the feigned piety of those who charged 30% interest while hearing three sermons a day. In York John King took up the mantle of Sandys and damned usurers as the unchristian "Iewes and Iudases of our land that would sell Christ for mony if he were amongst you." His hostility did not moderate in London, where he condemned usury as a sin against nature, like the sin of Sodom. Samuel Gardiner, John Carpenter, Robert Abbot, Thomas Holland, and George Abbot opposed usury, but only the latter's position is sufficiently explained to know for certain that he regarded all interest-taking as usurious. Abbot repudiated the endeavor of some divines to distinguish between "a biting and [a] not biting vsurie," and rejected interest even if a borrower gained because of the loan. The other writers may have opposed usury only in the sense that it entailed interest rates in excess of 10%.[16]

One of the most substantive Anglican analyses was Gabriel Powel's *Theologicall and Scholasticall Positions concerning Vsurie* (1602). The Oxford scholar reiterated the Sandys-Turnbull argument that the law of man cannot abrogate divine law, hence usury — a violation of natural, divine, civil, and canon law — is not allowable, despite the 1571 statute. He made a distinction between usury (surplus over the amount lent) and interest (recompense to prevent the lender from sustaining a loss). Powel expected borrowers to give lenders a gift in accord with the benefits received from the loan, but a lender who provided funds in expectation of such a gift was guilty of mental usury. Schemes to obtain interest indirectly for loans were systematically repudiated, including the use and profit of a borrower's goods or lands during the term of a loan, the undervaluing of a lease by the borrower, the sale of overpriced goods to the borrower, or the advance purchase of crops at a sum less than their market value at the time of delivery. It was also usury to lend coins worth less than face value and demand repayment in good money. Powel forbade gentlemen, merchants, and tradesmen to borrow at interest, for this led to enclosure, a decline in hospitality, rackrenting, and higher prices. The truly poor, however, could borrow and pay usury as long as they did not entice a lender to charge interest. Those with funds were exhorted to lend freely not only to the indigent but even to gentlemen and nobles whose estates were decaying, for aid to them was essential if they were to maintain their lawful estate and calling.[17]

In Anglican circles, then, three positions were outlined on usury, ranging from those of Powel and Sandys, who repudiated all interest-taking, to Hutton, who embraced the right of Christians to impose interest in accord with the 1571 statute. In the middle was Jewel's position, allowing "interest" in the case of orphans, mentally ill persons, and other dependents.

Prior to the 1571 act, Puritans demonstrated no serious interest in usury in their writings, and even in the 1570s, there was little more than routine repetition of warnings against it. Northbrooke responded to the new act by amassing precedents from the writings against usury of such people as Ambrose, Augustine, Jerome, Chrysostom, Basil, Bernard of Clairvaux, Plato, Aristotle, Cato, and Cicero. The most substantive comment of the 1570s came in Knewstub's lectures on Exodus 20, which restated the conservative position that "it is ye equitie of God, to require no recompence for the vse of things that are the worsse with vsing, so long as there appeareth no casuall hurt . . . of the whole." He was sufficiently attuned to the arguments for usury to reject the principle that borrowers who made substantial gains should pay interest. By the end of the decade, Hake's disappointment in the passage of the 1571 act led to the publication of verse to persuade readers of the evil of all interest and the damage it caused by ruining gentlemen and raising rents.[18]

With the exception of Stubbes' *The Anatomie of Abuses* (1583), Puritans in the 1580s were content to reiterate general condemnations of usury. The conservative position was upheld by Thomas Lupton, an author of miscellaneous tracts (who charged that some loans bore interest as high as 80%), but in other cases the attitude of authors to interest up to 10% is not clear. Udall recommended the works of Jewel and Wilson on usury, which suggests he accepted, as Jewel did, "interest" in the case of orphans and other dependents. Fulke may be the first Puritan to allow moderate interest, for in his refutation of the note to Luke 6:35 in the Rheims New Testament, he restricted the duty to lend without hope of restitution to the needy alone, not to those borrowing for pleasure or business. "And it is manifest, that where we are commanded to lend, not only vsurie is not to be looked for, but euen the principall must be aduentured neuer to be restored." Implicitly, this idea suggests that loans made for business or pleasure may be subject to moderate interest.[19]

Stubbes endeavored to place the 1571 statute in context by demonstrating that the law permits interest up to 10% but does not justify it. Those who restrain themselves within the legal limitations, in Stubbes' judgment, are still punishable by God. Any usury or interest, whether in money or goods, is forbidden by scriptural precepts. Yet Stubbes saw some good in the statute (though he thought it was poorly enforced) because its intent "was to impale within the Forest, or park of reasonable and conscionable gain, men who cared not how much they could extorte out of poore-mens hands, for the loane of their money lent." He was aware that few would loan to the poor without interest, which he thought was an important factor in the law's enactment, but like other religious authors he insisted that all loans should be interest free and readily available for those in need. He was incensed against those who made usurious loans and had the borrower imprisoned when he could not repay. The worst usurers, in his estimation, were the scriveners, who acted as brokers and took a share of the interest.

"Receiuing of the poore men what interest & assurance they lust themselues." Once again, the principal concern was the impact of usury on the poor, not on commercial needs.[20]

In the 1590s, Puritan opinion split over usury, as the door set ajar by Udall and Fulke was thrust open. Nevertheless the majority of Puritan authors either defended the conservative position or contented themselves with brief salvos against usury (as did Wilcox, Timme, Moffett, Allen, Dent, Estey, and Cartwright). Because of the complexity of usurious dealings, Burton despaired of stopping the practice by statute, but counseled prayer and fasting as the solution. The standard conservative position was reiterated in 1600 by Vaughan, who insisted that all usury was wrong, the 1571 statute notwithstanding. Perhaps the most conservative position of the age was enunciated by the Lincolnshire minister Francis Trigge, who not only opposed all forms of interest, including that used to support orphans and other dependents, but also annuities, either for oneself or one's children. "Some will put an hundreth pound in some mens hands, for a yearely annuitie to be paid thereof to their children: but that is but a kind of cloked vsurie, and it is as much as to make their children drone Bees, and not to labour in anie vocation." The Christian's duty is to lend freely and to forgive outstanding debts every seven years.[21]

Two substantial analyses of usury were given by late Elizabethan Puritans, the first of which was Henry Smith's *The Examination of Vsvry* (1591). Here was a full reaffirmation of the conservative view, with all gain on loans, whether in money or goods, deemed usury, "a kinde of crueltie, and a kind of extortion, and a kind of persecution." All usury is prohibited by the laws of charity, nations, nature, and God and, along with bribery and clerical nonresidence, usury is one of the three most damaging sins because some men make an occupation of it. The Elizabethan statute does not justify usury, but merely provides stiff penalties for those who exceed interest rates of 10%. Most of Smith's analysis is an exposé of schemes by which usurers cloak illicit gains, including the uncompensated use of land or goods during the term of a loan, charging for services unrendered, selling goods at extortionate prices in return for deferred payment, requiring services for the lender at the borrower's expense, and providing for the forfeiture of pawns worth more than the loan. Smith grappled with the issue of business loans, concluding that interest even in these cases is wrong because it increases prices. Like other conservatives he expected those with funds to lend to the needy without interest, and he insisted that usurers restore ill-gotten gains to the borrower or his heirs where possible, otherwise to the poor.[22]

The most learned work by an Elizabethan Puritan on usury was Miles Mosse's *The Arraignment and Conviction of Vsurie* (1595), which carried an epistle dedicatory to Whitgift and was, like Smith's work, published in sermon format. The principal thesis of Mosse is that usury is wrong, as demonstrated by citations from classical and Scholastic authors and Continental Protestant divines as well as Jewel and Scripture. Following Aquinas, he argued that "if I lend money, and so with the money the vse of it, . . . and I demaunde againe not onely money, which of necessitie bringeth vse with it, but also more money for the vse of my money: I demaunde two thinges for one," which is unequitable. Concerning loans from which the borrower gains, Mosse denied interest on the grounds that the borrower would have to overcharge for his products or engage in deceitful trade. If, however, a loan is tendered to a merchant on the understanding that the lender will share in the profit or loss, no usury is involved. It is permissible for a borrower to give a lender a gift, either before the loan or upon repayment. Mosse accepted "interest" if a loan is not repaid on time and the lender sustains monetary loss, or to offset the expenses of making a loan. Loans cannot be made for profit, but fees can be charged to cover the costs of lending money (or goods). In return for a loan, the lender has the right to require full repayment, legal action in the event of default, financial relief from the borrower if their conditions are reversed, and the borrower's love and goodwill.

Mosse insisted on the Christian duty to lend to the poor without interest, and for this reason he would not allow regular interest on loans to merchants and others of substance, for then no one would make a loan to the poor. The repeal of the Edwardian statute in 1571 was, in his judgment, responsible for inflation, an increase in the number of indigent, and the concentration of wealth in the hands of a few. Yet he refused to censure the Elizabethan statute, for "policie must tolerate those things which cannot bee abolished," though he complained that even this statute was poorly enforced. The Edwardian statute was, he said, more in accord with the law of nature and Scripture than the 1571 law. Thus Mosse modified the conservative position to allow, like Turnbull, a lender to share the profits of a borrower if he also agreed to share losses. Mosse's proviso allowing lenders to recover the full costs of their loans made it possible for enterprising men to receive more than the principal.[23]

The Puritans who led the way in accepting moderate interest included Gibbon, Perkins, Rogers, and Ames, but the change came only after internal struggle. In 1591 Gibbon argued that usury is prohibited by Deuteronomy 23:19, and that it is wrong even to pay it. In dialogue form, an opposing position was enunciated, defining usury as a charge in excess of reasonable interest; reasonable gains are no less justifiable for a moneylender than reasonable profits earned by merchants or farmers. In effect, moneylending could be considered a legitimate occupation, though Gibbon himself did not accept this view. Three years later, he became convinced that interest could be charged on loans to persons of substance, but not to the poor: "Lend to thy better for a benefite, but to the poore for a blessing." Perkins too struggled, for he favored interest-free loans and condemned usurers, but, like Mosse, he admitted that if a borrower could legally use a loan to profit, the lender could claim a share of the profits as long as he agreed not to require repayment of the principal if the borrower suffered financial loss. Richard Rogers had no objection to moderate interest when both parties benefited fairly, but he repudiated borrowing to make interest-bearing loans to a third party. Annuities were acceptable and could be bought and sold, though he warned against transactions in anticipated annuities (which were akin to purchasing shares on a commodities or futures exchange). Ames too permitted interest charges, though not on loans for the poor, and only if the interest was remitted should the borrower suffer losses for factors beyond his control. Thus a minority of late Elizabethan Puritans repudiated the conservatism of their colleagues, sanctioning interest-bearing loans among persons of means, though retaining the ban on any usury on loans to the poor.[24]

Elizabethan Catholics embraced the conservative position on usury, as reflected in Vaux's catechism and Nicholas Sanders' *Briefe Treatise of Vsvrie,* published at Louvain in 1568. All usury, insisted Sanders, violates divine and natural law. In medieval fashion, he repudiated all loans to those with as much money or more money than the lender, demanding that *all* lending be done, free of all interest, to the poor, "for lending is a kind of charitie, or of almosedeedes, which was instituted chiefly and only for the poore." Unlike the Protestants, however, he interpreted Jesus' remarks about lending to the poor as a counsel, not a mandatory precept. He agreed with Protestants that usury harms the commonwealth, even when imposed on commercial loans, for merchants are forced to raise prices or even face bankruptcy. Usury is condemned because it encourages idleness by lenders, rendering them valueless to the commonwealth. Sanders answered the argument that usury is justified because of the risk assumed by the lender; he retorted that in *not* loaning his funds one risks their loss by fire or theft. No gain beyond the principal, whether in money, goods, or services, is tolerable, though Sanders agreed that a lender is not required to sustain a loss. He gave an interesting twist to this concept when he acknowledged the right of a lender to recover losses sustained during the term of the loan because the money was not at his disposal. The conservative position of Sanders and Vaux was suited to the needs of Elizabethan Catholics, the majority of whom lived in conservative rural areas. The exhortation to make interest-free loans to the poor would, when obeyed, have strengthened the ties and loyalty of tenants to their Catholic landlords.[25]

The concern of the church hierarchy with usury is apparent in the episcopal injunctions and visitation articles. The impact of the 1571 statute can be seen in Grindal's injunctions to the province of York, issued prior to the act, and his visitation articles for the province of Canterbury promulgated in 1576. The former, requiring the presentment of all usurers to the ordinaries twice a year, defined usurers as "all those that lend money, corn, ware, or other thing, and receive gain therefore, over and above that which they lend." Such people were barred from holy communion. The Canterbury articles inquired only about those who charged more than 10%, though articles of other bishops often were more general in seeking out usurers. Special inquiries were sometimes directed toward ministers, as in Whitgift's articles for the diocese of Worcester, in which parishioners were queried if their minister was "suspected of letting his money to usury directly or indirectly." Some did, including Henry Isham, parson of Pitchley, Northants., and probably Matthew Hutton. John Scory, bishop of Hereford, was accused in 1575 of requiring usury on loans, but he insisted to Burghley that he had loaned money to some seventy-six persons (including Sir Henry Sidney and the dean and chapter of Hereford) but never for gain. In the Puritan survey of the clergy, 7 of 292 Norfolk ministers were accused of usury; they were in such villages as Wood Rising, Walcott, Happisburgh, Oxnead, Melton, Holkham, and Burlingham. One, the Rev. Mr. Polley of Wood Rising, was a suspected Catholic as well. In Essex c. 1606 four clergymen were accused of usury, and in an earlier case, Mark Simpson, rector of Pitsea, was required to acknowledge his guilt in public and donate 5s. to the poor. Many clerics were probably too strapped for funds to consider lending to others.[26]

Although Sutcliffe charged the Puritans in 1592 with favoring usury, some Anglicans tolerated it, and laymen of both persuasions charged interest on loans. Both sexes and various social classes were involved. John Paulet, marquess of Winchester, had a fund of £10,000 to loan at 10% in the 1570s, and Elizabeth Talbot, countess of Shrewsbury, lent money in the 1590s to the Derbyshire gentry. When Lady Jane

Laxton loaned £500 to a London leatherseller in 1572 and required an early interest payment, she was sued for usury but was acquitted in the Exchequer Court. Lady Margaret Hoby, a Puritan, loaned a poor man 20s. in 1601, though probably without interest. In contrast Richard Mussie, a Cheshire gentleman, was a reputed usurer, and the Lancashire gentleman John Legh left a daughter £80 in his 1593 will to loan at interest to raise her sister. Anthony Bacon made numerous loans, normally to gentlemen such as Sir Edward Stafford, but he was also a frequent borrower. Interest was charged by Burghley's secretaries, Henry Maynard and the Puritan Michael Hicks. As Lawrence Stone indicates, nearly all of the oligarchy of London merchants were lending between 1580 and 1620, with the principal lenders being goldsmiths, jewelers, mercers, and silkmen. Sometimes they both borrowed and lent, as did the Anglican mercer and Merchant Adventurer John Isham (d. 1596). In 1600 Dr. Simon Forman recorded that he "lent out moch mony on plate and jewells this yere." Even yeomen made usurious loans; in Devon this practice stemmed from the ambition to become gentlemen, according to the contemporary observer John Hooker, whereas retired Cambridgeshire yeomen lent at interest to obtain an income. In London the landlady of the dramatist Henry Chettle loaned renters 11d. but required 12d. at the week's end. Usury was so common that in 1581 the London clergy complained that preaching against it caused angry parishioners to withhold tithes. Sutcliffe erred when he blamed usury on the Puritans; religious affiliation made no apparent difference among the laity.[27]

The prevalency of usury and the financial impact on unwary borrowers troubled the laity as well as the clergy. Robert Furse of Devon warned his heir to beware of usurers and interest-bearing loans, and William Wentworth gave a similar admonition to his son. The latter was exhorted to "avoid usury and selling anie thing to pore men to a long daie for a great pryce," nor was he to lend more to his social superiors than he was willing to give them. (The elder Wentworth himself sometimes loaned money to the earl of Shrewsbury.) In the early 1600s Richard Carew the younger, a Puritan, forsook the opportunity to pursue the "very common and easy trade" of usury "for fear of offending God thereby;" he invested in orchards instead. Yet he and his father, Richard Carew the elder, being forced at times to borrow at interest, reckoned their total loss at £150,000, which would have been realized had the funds been properly invested.[28]

Stories of hardships and the loss of large sums are common. In 1587 Burghley and Sir Thomas Bromley wrote to Henry Ughtred in connection with the latter's £3,400 in outstanding loans and an accumulated interest debt of £1,300. Burghley's son, Thomas, wrote to him in 1578 because he had amassed a debt of £2,000 that was due, and for which "I am now driven both to borrow and to make money of my stocks here in the country, to my great loss." It seemed better to sell land, which brought a return of 5 to 6% on capital, to pay debts on which interest was due at 10%. In 1583 Sir Henry Sidney ordered the sale of lands to get himself "out of that miserable thraldome of usurye." Fourteen years later Sir Robert Sidney was informed that his debt to merchants was "growing upon soe excessive interest, they by no meanes dare avow." Lenders who tried to gouge borrowers ran risks; in 1574 the London skinner Stephen Slanye was penalized £7,800 for charging more than 10% (though he was pardoned). The mighty sometimes avoided paying any interest, as happened with Henry Percy, earl of Northumberland, in the 1580s and 1590s, yet even he regularly paid 10% in the 1600s. To repay loans, landed borrowers often had to sell lands, offer long leases, arrange advantageous marriages, cut down woods, or place part of their estates in the hands of trustees for limited periods so the income could reduce their debts.[29]

In the Public Record Office is an interesting but naïve proposal for the abolition of all usury. It was made c. 1576 by Stephen Parrott, who considered usury a threat to English trade and observed that many people regarded it as an offense to God. As a remedy, he proposed the imposition of a special levy, two-thirds of which would go to the crown and one-third for a public fund to finance loans. The latter would be interest free, though borrowers were expected to donate something extra to cover the expenses of maintaining the fund. To obtain the capital people generally would be assessed 5% of their annual income. Loans would range from £1 to £200, with terms of ten weeks to a year scaled according to the amount of the loan. It was, in effect, a public bank, in which loans could be interest-free because there were no depositors who expected a return on their investment.[30]

In sum, the assertion that English Protestants uniformly disapproved of interest-bearing loans is false, though the preponderant emphasis among Elizabethan Protestants was against interest, and until the 1590s almost wholly so. The marginalia of Tudor Scriptures reinforced this conservative outlook, though the Beza-Tomson Bible was silent on the issue. The needs of businessmen, government, and landowners combined in 1571 to repeal the Edwardian statute that punished all usurers, leaving only token penalties after 1571 for those who charged up to 10%. This change came about despite English clerical opinion. To the slight extent to which religious opinion was a factor in the passage, the views of Continental authors such as Theodore Beza were influential. Some modification was made in the conservative position by Bishop Jewel, normally a critic of usury, when he permitted interest on the "stock" of infants, infirm persons, and other dependents. In Anglican circles, the strongest proponent of moderate usury was Hutton, who opposed Sandys' endeavors to use the High Commission even to prosecute lenders operating within the 1571 statute. The publication of the pro-usury case in Thomas Wilson's dialogue perhaps furthered the liberal cause, though Wilson followed most Anglicans in accepting the conservative case. Repeatedly Anglicans responded to the 1571 law by insisting that divine law could never be abrogated by human law.

Most Puritans abhorred usury, though Udall's endorsement of Jewel suggests that he found interest acceptable if it supported dependents. Fulke (in 1589) probably was the first Puritan to allow moderate interest on loans, a position advocated later by Gibbon, Perkins, Rogers, and Ames, though with the stipulation that loans to the indigent must be interest free. The most substantive Puritan treatise on usury, Mosse's *The Arraignment and Conviction of Vsvrie,* allowed profits on loans only if the lender agreed to share the borrower's potential losses. Mosse affirmed the lender's rights to recover not only the principal but all expenses accrued in making the loan. There is some validity to John New's contention that "Puritanism was more prone than Anglicanism to allow the legality of certain kinds of usury,"[31] though this opinion must be qualified in that most Elizabethan Puritans continued to find all usury reprehensible, and in that not all Anglicans repudiated moderate interest, as the case of Hutton indicates. Elizabethan Catholics continued to assert the conservative view.

Despite the efforts of the bishops and some lower clergy, lending at interest was widespread. It was inaccurate to blame Puritans for usury, as Sutcliffe did. The financial straits to which heavy borrowing and interest could lead strengthened the case against usury, though most clerical concern was directed toward the hardship of interest-bearing loans on the poor. Viewed in this perspective, the campaign against usury was part of the broader war on poverty.

(2) Surety

Haue great regard to suretiship . . .
Yet stretch your selues, to help your friend,
    with penurie that pines.

George Whetstone[32]

No dutie bindeth vs to take vpon vs for him, to meddle where we haue nothing to doe.

Richard Rogers[33]

Surety was closely tied to loans and usury, for borrowers normally had to provide some guarantee of repayment, whether pawns, bonds, recognizances, statutes, mortgages, or sureties.[34] When, c. 1593, Philip Gawdy borrowed £200 from the Dutchman David le Mer at 10% interest, his brother Bassingbourne had to stand surety. The implications of such aid could be serious, as Sir Francis Willoughby's son-in-law, Thomas Willoughby, discovered when he was imprisoned in Warwick for debts accumulated in standing surety for friends who defaulted. William Wilkinson, a London poulterer, sued in the Court of Requests in 1600 when he became financially depressed by inability to repay usurious loans because of losses sustained in providing suretiship. Sureties were subject to unmerciful badgering by creditors, who could threaten imprisonment. The Privy Council heard appeals from imprisoned and financially distressed sureties, including Francis Browne, parson of Heddington, Wilts. Imprisoned for debt at Salisbury because of losses from suretiship, fire, and debtors who defaulted, Browne received the Council's assistance. Individuals also could serve as sureties for the good behavior of legal offenders by providing recognizances, as in the 1562 case of Stephen Tucker, a Westminster yeoman, who, with three sureties, provided a bond of £80 that he would never again play unlawful games. The possibility of financial loss or imprisonment raised the question of whether Christians were obligated to stand surety for others.[35]

Some guidance was provided in biblical marginalia. In the Geneva Bible the note to Proverbs 6:2 explained that a Christian could become a surety, in accord with the law of charity, as long as consideration was given to the nature and intentions of the borrower, so that creditors would not be defrauded. No concern was expressed about the influence of a borrower's default on a surety. In the Bishops' Bible the note to Ecclesiasticus 29:18 asked only that discretion be used: "As he is a foole that is, suretie for euery man: so is he vngodly that in no case will be suretie for one man."

Elizabethans could obtain further guidance in Marcelline Outred's translation of Cope's exposition of Proverbs, published in 1580 with a dedication to Burghley. Here it was argued that one must not become a surety without good knowledge of the borrower and the purposes of the loan, which excluded influencing the wealthy and powerful, advancing one's family, or maintaining credit. Surety should only be provided when genuine need exists and no threat is offered to the security of the surety and his family. Cope placed some responsibility on the prospective borrower, for "if wee loue our neighbours as wee ought, . . . wee will not require them to be suretie for vs, except it be necessarie, and also that we haue wherewith to answere them and to keepe them from sorowe, and to mainteine them that they may possesse their goods and safely enioy them." [36]

Anglicans demonstrated surprisingly little interest in the problem of suretiship, apparently content to pursue the path of discretion called for in the Bishops' Bible and Whetstone's verse. In contrast, Puritans manifested a fair degree of concern and some disagreement among themselves, particularly over the question of surety as a Christian duty. For Richard Rogers it assuredly was not, though one might pity a man in default to his creditor. Surety could be provided if one wished to do so, though only if the amount was so small that no serious hurt could be sustained and if those in need were "approued Christians, or our brethren." Dod, Gibbon, and Burton, however, insisted that surety was a Christian duty, though not without limitations. Surety must be provided in accord with one's means, only to persons of good moral character and lawful vocations, and never to the detriment of one's family. Dod insisted that this duty be limited to those to whom one "is bound vnto by some bond of dutie, eyther for religion and charitie, or else for some knot of friendship or of kindred." Burton asserted that aid must be restricted to persons of the proper religious faith and must never be given to those paying usury (in practice this stipulation would have severely reduced standing surety for poorer folk, who often paid interest on loans). Providing surety was most appropriate when an innocent man was imprisoned, a Protestant was incarcerated for debt, or a person was jailed for an offensive word or deed and subsequently repented. Puritans such as Perkins, Cleaver, Moffett, and Allen counseled readers to be discreet in considering suretiship, particularly, warned Cleaver, to avoid borrowing. [37]

The Puritan attitude to surety largely parallels their outlook on poor relief, with preference given the godly and neighbors. Curiously, however, the warm exhortations to give to the indigent were not paralleled by encouragement to provide surety, except where every likelihood existed that the recipient would repay his debts and not threaten the security of the surety's family. Christian charity was essentially, in this context, only for the godly and immediate neighbors, and not at the expense of one's family. The severity of the repercussions in the event of default explains these limitations on charitable assistance.

(3) Weights and Measures

Bye by great measure, and sell by small measure,
This is a way to amplifie your treasure.

Lewis Wager[38]

Let your gains be just and true.

John Jewel[39]

Although periodic endeavors were made to establish standard weights and measures in the medieval and early Tudor periods, as late as December 1587 a royal proclamation complained that most subjects were still ignorant of the "contents, differences, and true knowledge and uses of the weights of the . . . realm." Consequently both buyers and sellers could be victimized by the varying weights in use. Referring to the relevant statutes (9 Henry V, st. 2, c. 8; 7 Henry VII, c. 3; 11 Henry VII, c. 4), the proclamation called for the sole use of the Troy weight for gold, silver, bread, and electuaries (medicines) and the avoirdupois weight for all other vendables, with violators punished by fines and imprisonment.[40]

Parliament proved unable to agree on the reform of abuses during Elizabeth's reign, though in 1572 two bills for improved execution of existing statutes got as far as the second reading in the Commons. The 1581 Parliament fared no better, and in 1601 the Commons unsuccessfully considered three bills, though Francis Bacon complained that "this fault of using false Weights and Measures is grown so intolerable and common, that if you would build Churches, you shall not need for Battlements and Bells, other than false Weights of Lead and Brass." Support for reform also came from Peter Frescheville, a knight for Derbyshire, who complained that "the rich have two measures, with the one he buyes, and ingrosseth Corn in the Country, that is the greater; with the other he retails it at home to his poor Neighbours, that's by the lesser." The queen issued a new proclamation early in 1602 in which she remarked that weights and measures were still not standardized; she ordered the lord treasurer and undertreasurer to call in and examine all weights and measures from the towns, replacing those that were inaccurate.[41]

Although Parliament was unable to agree on reform, some action was taken at all levels to attempt to regulate the measures; commercial transactions and the development of trade required standards. Juries in the hundreds, quarter sessions, court leets, and Chancery heard cases involving weights and measures. In Essex and Staffordshire the number of offenders who appeared in the quarter sessions was not large; in Essex most were dishonest bakers or victualers. One Stafford-shire case involved a local constable who tried unsuccessfully to bribe a deputy to the clerk of the market to say he had reformed the weights and measures when he had not. There was probably much of this sort of endeavor to subvert the government's reform program. Even the Privy Council periodically considered the problem, as in the case of Salisbury in the early 1590s, where unauthorized weights and measures were used to purchase grain from farmers, causing manifest discontent. Burghley received an appeal from the lord mayor of London in 1581 seeking directions for the reform of weights and measures, the lack of which was "a greate abuse" in London and other towns. Again in 1583 the lord mayor protested to Burghley that "priuate men pre-sume without order to sell and vse vnlawfull weightes, bothe in the citie and in the contrye." Two years later, Dyonis Gray complained to the lord treasurer about the disorder occasioned by the failure to use the Troy weight uniformly.[42]

The records of Southampton, Beverley, and Leicester provide a fuller indication of the scope of the problem. In Southampton the court leets regularly punished offenders; using figures for twenty of the years between 1566 and 1602, an average of nearly thirty-seven persons per year were fined, ranging from a high of sixty-nine in 1589 to a low of fifteen in 1573. Fines ranged from 1d. to £20, the latter imposed on brewers using undersized barrels in 1577. Normal fines did not exceed £2 and were often less. In Beverley forty-eight bakers were fined from 4d. to 8s. in 1574 for using deficient weights, and the same year forty-five brewers were fined from 6d. to 6s. 8d. for selling ale with unlawful measures. At Leicester a warning from the govern-ment in 1578 noted that complaints were being made about weights and measures, and ordered the town to adhere to prescribed standards. Eleven months later all alehouses in Leicester were restricted to selling beer and ale in pint and quart pewter "potts" for ½d. and 1d., respec-tively. Like other towns, Leicester received instructions in 1588 from Burghley and Mildmay requiring the use of the standards for weights imposed by the government, but disorders continued in the Puritan-dominated town. As late as February 1600 the lord chief justice, Sir John Popham, wrote to the mayor and aldermen of Leicester, noting that despite earlier warnings, the town still had not reformed its weights and measures, and warning them that unless they did the town faced *quo warranto* proceedings.[43]

The clergy addressed the situation, but hardly as much as one would expect given its prevalency. The authors of the biblical marginalia largely ignored it, though the Geneva annotators explained that

Proverbs 11:1 condemned false weights and measures. Among the Anglicans, Pilkington thought the immoral practice would terminate when people recognized that all wealth was ultimately God's and must not be sought deceitfully. Nowell's catechism banned irregular weights and measures under the eighth commandment. Jewel, Gardiner, Sandys, and Turnbull admonished against using false weights and measures, but no Anglican cleric proposed substantive solutions, and their complaints seem almost perfunctory.[44]

Puritans appeared more incensed than Anglicans by the use of fraudulent weights and measures. It was a violation of the eighth commandment (as stated in Vaux's Catholic catechism) and the law of nature, which requires just dealings and proportionate benefits for both parties in business transactions. The fullest comments came from John Deacon, minister at Nottingham, in a sermon to the people of Ridlington, Rutland, in which he detailed the ways weights and measures were abused. Inaccurate weights and double sets for buying and selling were denounced. Even legal weights could be abused "either by turning the cocke on the beame, with a tricke of the finger, or else by dashing the skales deceitfully vpon the boord, that so (the ballaunce rebounding backeward) their proper and naturall course may be turned with a trice." Neither Anglican nor Puritan condoned any abuse associated with weights and measures, but it is a matter of more concern to Puritans, suggesting, once again, greater Puritan sensitivity to the implications of religious convictions for social and economic actions.[45]

(4) General Business Dealings and Ethics

Theeues steale wythoute the compasse of mans lawe, and dye for it, and you [the London merchants] doe it wythin youre compasse, and escape: they in the hygh wayes, you in youre Shoppes.

Thomas White[46]

It was a good world when the old Religion was, because all things were cheap.

William Perkins[47]

Weights and measures were intertwined with the broader area of business dealings and ethics, particularly when irregular weights and measures were deliberately used, but not all buyers and sellers had access to standardized weights and measures, especially through the 1580s. There was, then, sometimes a legitimate excuse for the confusion resulting from irregular weights and measures, which may account for the slight attention accorded the problem by religious reformers, especially early in the age. Other business dealings were deliberately unethical, and these the Anglican and Puritan critics denounced in scathing terms.

In the first half of the century, biblical marginalia condemned the confiscation of pledges from the poor as extortion and the worship of materialistic idols. Reflecting the growing commercialism of the age, the Geneva annotators expanded the definition of extortion to cover any goods or wealth unlawfully obtained. Wealth garnered in this fashion could not be donated to God's service and brought only divine condemnation, a theme often reiterated. "Ye curse of God lieth vpon the extorcioners: who thinking to enriche their children by their vnlawful gotten goods, are by Gods iust iudgement depriued of all." The Rheims annotators did not manifest direct concern with business ethics, but generally considered that the most dangerous occupations were those of kings and merchants because they were encumbered in material goods, and their "whole life & traficke is (if they be not exceding vertuous) to finde varietie of earthly pleasures." Vaux's catechism taught Catholics that the eighth commandment is violated when buyers are deceived by subtle words, faulty products, or falsely identified goods.[48]

The caution the Rheims annotators express for the temptations to which merchants are exposed was shared by Anglicans. "This I must tell you that liue vpon buying and selling," John King warned the people of York, "you walke vpon coales and carry fire in your bosomes: gaine is a busie tentation." Perhaps no Anglican was more pessimistic about merchants than Pilkington, who was convinced that laws could not prevent their unethical transactions. "Receivers are become deceivers, controllers be pollers, auditors searchers, and customers look through their fingers, and keep their old custom." Reflecting on the proverb that every man is a thief in his occupation, he bemoaned the common use of subtlety and deceit to oppress friend and foe and to amass material goods no matter what the means. The London merchants' driving of hard, covetous transactions created a deadly envy between them and the gentry, claimed Whetstone. Sandys was no less denunciatory of merciless, deceitful merchants, but he had more faith in the power of legislation to redress abuses, and consequently demanded legal reforms. Reflecting the reforming fervor of the earlier Commonwealth Men, he warned that "if merchants, with other artificers, and meaner trades, do enrich themselves by impoverishing others through deceitful shifts; the commonwealth suffereth damage by their uneven dealings." For the sake of the commonwealth and the spiritual welfare of merchants, a Christian code of ethics had to be adopted.[49]

No formal code was drawn up, but the principles are found in Anglican writings. Nothing must be sold for more than its worth, nor must a buyer seek to pay less than true value if an owner is constrained to sell. Because a merchant is indebted to his customers as neighbors, he must not defraud them with deceitful practices or cunning words, whether legal or not. Referring to the eighth commandment, Nowell's cathecism explained "that we suffer not ourselves to be allured with advantage or gain of buying or selling, to do any wrong; that in trading . . . we seek not wealth unjustly, nor make our profit by untrue and uneven measures and weights, nor increase our riches with sale of slight and deceitful ware." No more acceptable was disguising flaws in wares to make them seem better. Gain must not be made at the expense of another's loss, rather we must sell as we would buy and do as we would be done unto. "We may not by undoing our neighbour, or spoiling him of any part of his land or goods, make him an ass, and send him a begging." The principles were simple, generally couched in the context of the golden rule, and based on the principle of equity.[50]

Puritans demonstrated greater concern for the formulation of principles to conduct business, for they were especially troubled about contemporary practices and their effect on spiritual life. Covetousness was, after all, a mark of reprobation. "They proove themselves foolishe Marchantes, that for gaining a little earth, will purchase hell." Anger was directed against merchants who refused to sell wares for reasonable prices, for their covetousness was blamed for inflation and dearth. Deceitfulness was damned: Lying and dissembling "superabound in shop keepers, and seruants: for both these make a trade and occupation of it." It was embarrassing for Gifford to admit to a Catholic that some Protestants were greedy and crafty in their dealings, seeking every advantage against those with whom they conducted business. In the days of the old religion, things were cheaper; inflation had seen to that, and the Puritans squirmed as they tried to keep the blame from the new faith. While acknowledging inflation, which he ascribed to rising population, Thomas Stoughton observed that incomes had risen too (though in reality not as fast as prices), and he argued that Catholic countries in the later sixteenth century were more plagued with dearth than Protestant England. Puritan clergy hit hard at merchants and others whose dealings brought them growing shares of the national wealth, ostensibly at the expense of the poor but actually from the landed aristocracy as well. Puritan concern was not always well received, as Deacon discovered when he got a stormy reception preaching at a fair against the commercial abuses of chapmen. He endeavored "to mainteine the sincere religion of Christ, which (by meanes of those abuses) began now . . . to be generallie despised, as a religion tending onelie to a verie licencious and carnall libertie." Like Sandys, he pressed the government for stricter execution of the laws governing commercial transactions. The welfare of the commonwealth, the spiritual estate of souls, and the credit of Protestantism were at stake in the Puritan campaign to clean up business.[51]

Puritans spelled out some of the business practices that upset them: One was excessive markups, amounting to two or three times the wholesale cost of merchandize; merchants who displayed one item but substituted an inferior, or who mixed deficient items with good ones, were censured. Selling in poor light to conceal flaws was condemned, as were deficient or fraudulent conveyances. Other abuses included tentering cloth, diluting wine, beer, and ale, excessively hammering out pewter, charging extra for installment payments when the purchaser had insufficient funds (which was deemed usury), and using a dual price structure for local customers and strangers. Perkins also castigated merchants who sold frankincense, wax, cloth, and comparable goods to Catholics for use in idolatrous worship.[52]

The proper prevention of these and related unethical business dealings was adherence to a code of Christian ethics. Although no formal Puritan code was drafted, Deacon, Richard Rogers, Knewstub, and Perkins in effect produced brief versions of their own for the guidance of the godly. They and their colleagues required, under the eighth commandment, forswearing all forms of oppressive and deceitful dealings. A merchant has the right to a reasonable profit if his efforts are for the public good, if he has improved the wares or sustained expense in their preservation, or if he has paid to transport the goods. Trade undertaken for insatiable gain, however, is contrary to nature. In setting prices, the seller must consider the purchaser "that so betweene the wares which are solde, and the price repaied for the same, there maye be a proportionable equalitie obserued in value and goodnes." Sellers must disclose all defects in the merchandize and must refuse to accept more than its worth, keeping in mind the just price. All covenants and agreements must be performed, though proportionate benefit must be ensured for both parties. Plain words, simple dealing, reasonable agreements, covenants kept, and the golden rule are the keys to ethical business dealings.

Neither party can enrich itself at the other's expense. "In buying and selling, that the one giue his peny for his penyworth; fully satisfying also the trauaile of the other, and cost that he hath been at: and that the seller performe his peniworth as good as is agreed for, and faithfully." Purchasers too have responsibilities, such as not unfairly criticizing a product to mask its worth or driving down a price to take advantage of constraint on the owner to sell. There is nothing in these requirements that would have made an Anglican reformer squeamish, but a marked difference is notable in the way a number of Puritans carefully set forth mini-codes of business conduct and the greater detail of their prescriptions. They were, perhaps, more cognizant of the affairs of the business world and the implications of their faith for equitable commercial dealings. [53]

The concern for ethical practice was shared by some of the laity. Thomas Wentworth was counseled by his father never to sell to the poor at higher prices because of delayed payment and never to buy except for cash on delivery to avoid excessive cost. He was urged to "tye not yourself euer to buye in one place, unlesse yow fynde thatt faithfull dealing that I could neuer amongst merchantts." Lionel Cranfield's father-in-law, the grocer Robert Sheppard, advised his servant in 1602 to be wary of buying and selling,

for you have to do with a subtle crew of people such as will soon over-reach you with bad commodities, and therefore be circumspect and believe no broker's persuasion but rather your own eyes. Take good knowledge of those that you credit and let your touchstone be in offering to set over their bills for good commodity, and if it will not be taken deal not with them.

Much later, in 1641, an apprentice of the London turner Nehemiah Wallington, a Puritan, sold a gentlewoman trenchers made of aspen, claiming they were maple, but the lady soon complained to Wallington, remarking that such practices slandered religion. Some customers seem to have sought out Puritans to conduct their business because of their trustworthy name, and it was therefore a matter of concern when disreputable dealings threatened their reputation. Philip Gawdy bitterly remarked that he had paid a debt of £5 to a Puritan who refused to return his note, hence "I will never trust [a] puritane for his sake." Much was expected of the godly, even in the business world. [54]

The authorities could not keep abreast of the almost endless variety of illicit business dealing in the Elizabethan world. The Privy Council handled such cases as the sale of counterfeit chains and jewels, fraudulent bankruptcy, the defrauding of creditors through fictitious names, and "the chopping of flockes and rubbing the same into cloth by the greatest parte of clothiers in the county of Yorke and other places thereaboutes." The government had to appoint a special agent to enforce the statute prohibiting the use of sand and stones to increase the weight of wool, and Burghley devoted attention to the punishment of soap makers who put suet, tallow, and fish oil in their soap. Burghley's agent, Anthony Atkinson, complained to Essex in 1596 about customs violations, including the bribery of officials and the export of corn and grain without payment of the required fees. The government had difficulty enforcing the price of beer because brewers skirted the regulations by varying their mixes, but the 1593 Parliament refused to enact reform legislation. The town of Chester regulated some business concerns by requiring butchers and bakers to take oaths in 1591, the former swearing to sell at reasonable prices and the latter to make wholesome bread. In 1562 the town of Leicester stipulated that tasters sample all ale before it was sold by the brewer, to determine if it was "good & holsome for mans body & not red, rope [ropy, viscous] nor rawe."[55]

Local authorities kept busy punishing offenders, sometimes with little success. In London the cart and the pillory were used for such offenses as selling measly bacon and undersized fish or falsely marking "belletes" (ingots). At Southhampton, the court leet heard cases involving underweight sacks of coal, unmarked casks of beer that were deficient in volume, the sale of double beer, the use of poorly tanned and curried leather by coblers, and the repeated watering of skins by a glover; the customary punishments were fines. Clothiers were charged in 1602 at the Bury sessions with fraudulently stretching cloth, a rather common offense. Even Henry Lord Berkeley had to pay for more ounces of silver in a suit of clothes than his tailor used. Authorities had their hands full trying to control the multifarious illegal and immoral business dealings.[56]

That such conduct attracted the attention of the clergy is hardly surprising, but it is noteworthy that Puritans manifested greater sensitivity to it and outdid Anglican reformers in providing guidelines for ethical conduct. Apart from the intensity and scope, however, Anglicans and Puritans shared the fundamental principles of business ethics, rooted in the eighth commandment and the golden rule. Abhorrence of deceit and fraud, equitable benefit to buyer and seller, repudiation of gain at another's expense, and adherence to the just price were principles they advocated. The Puritan clergy expected their flocks to practice these ideals, and when they failed, their failure cast opprobrium on all the godly, for the populace came to think of Puritans—though apparently not Anglicans—as people whose actions were supposed to accord with the principles they espoused.

(5) Forestalling, Engrossing, and Regrating

Hee that detaineth and keepeth his corne from the vse of his neighbours and brethren, is cursed, as Salomon teacheth.

Richard Turnbull [57]

> The Cormoraunt that coucheth vp
> and crams his cankerd bags,
> Doth giue to hoord his gotten coyne:
> and bowte the towne he lags.

Edward Hake [58]

Since the thirteenth century, England had attempted to control the role of middlemen in the economy, but by the mid-Tudor period mounting concern was voiced that their activities were responsible for dearth and inflation. To the end of the age, food shortages and some of the woolen problems were blamed largely on forestallers, engrossers, and regrators, though the accusations were oversimplified and often unjust. The key statute for the control of these activities, 5 & 6 Edward VI, c. 14, defined their nature. Forestalling entailed buying up goods outside a market town or borough to drive up prices; engrossing involved cornering the supply of goods by forestalling or regrating; and regrating was the purchase and resale of goods in the same or nearby market, forcing up prices. [59]

Worry about these practices was evident in the first Parliament of Elizabeth's reign, where bills were proposed to discourage the forestalling and engrossing of food and the regrating of tanned leather; only the latter were passed (1 Eliz. I, c. 8, c. 9). It was probably in the context of the first bad harvest of the reign, in 1562, that Exeter required each alderman to inquire about forestallers, engrossers, and regrators in his ward, and appointed market men to see that such activites ceased. When the 1565 harvest failed, authorities in Essex tried to terminate these abuses, as they did in ensuing economic crises. The Privy Council too became actively involved, notably in the operations of the grain trade, as in December 1565 when commissioners in maritime counties were ordered to prohibit engrossing. On the 20th of the next month, in the queen's first proclamation concerning this problem, it was noted that though no scarcity of food existed, covetous persons were engrossing great quantities of grain, thereby burdening English subjects. To remedy the situation, the government canceled licenses to export grain and ordered the apprehension and imprisonment of engrossers. Enforcement was not effective, hence near the end of the year the government considered ways to improve it. Parliament again took up a bill to stop forestalling, engrossing, and regrating in 1571, but it failed to pass. Sir Nicholas Bacon's jeremiad at the close of this Parliament, in which he protested the poor execution of the laws, undoubtedly applied to the Edwardian statute on engrossing as well as other laws. [60]

After another bad harvest in 1573, Sir Thomas Scott, who had been a member for Kent in the 1572 Parliament and was a Puritan supporter, complained to Burghley on 10 February 1574 of rising food prices, blaming the Council's refusal to terminate exports of foodstuffs and beer, the increased activities of engrossers and forestallers, and the Council's order to provide 4,000 quarters of wheat and other grain to London, leaving some markets nearly destitute of grain and raising the price of wheat from twelve or thirteen groats a bushel to fifteen or sixteen. His solution was to require those possessing grain to bring a certain quantity every market day to sustain the poor. [61]

The harvest of 1576 also was deficient, prompting further government intervention to curtail engrossing and related abuses. In October, a royal commission to the Norfolk gentry remarked that the queen and Council believed grain, butter, and cheese prices were rising because of covetous farmers and engrossers who withheld food from the market or illegally exported it. There were complaints the same year, especially from clothiers in the West country, Worcester, and Suffolk, that those licensed to buy and sell wool had been engrossing it after several years of heavy sheep losses. Consequently clothiers had to pay excessive prices for anything but the coarsest wool. At year's end Sir Thomas Offley complained to Walsingham about the engrossing of wool that "hathe in effect subuertyd the trade of the staple[;] euyn soo yf yt contynewe the Cloathiers shall nott be able too aforde theare cloathe at such reasonable price as yt maye be ventyd in foreyne partes." The previous month, the queen issued a proclamation restricting the purchase of wool. [62]

Following another bad harvest in 1586, the Privy Council sent letters to justices and sheriffs in each county instructing them to see that no grain was withheld from the market and that prices were reasonable. Sir Anthony Thorold informed Burghley on 3

May that young men and servants were actively engrossing and regrating, though he had ordered that offenders be reported to him so they could be punished legally. Sufficient relief had not been achieved by the new year, so on 2 January 1587 Elizabeth issued a proclamation blaming the dearth of food on covetous cornmasters and engrossers as well as inclement weather. Those with grain were ordered to supply the markets at reasonable prices or to face government price controls. Even so, on 1 February the lord mayor and aldermen had to appeal to Burghley to crack down on badgers and engrossers who endangered the poor by interrupting the flow of grain into the City.[63]

Parliament returned to the question in 1589, when Commons passed a bill designed to improve the enforcement of the Edwardian act against forestalling, engrossing, and regrating, with the coverage to include all imported wines, sweet oils, spices, sugar, currants, prunes, and grain, under penalty of a £100 fine and three months imprisonment. The bill was not, however, acceptable to the Lords. The same Parliament also considered but did not pass a bill to terminate "regrating, iobbing and vnlawfull buying of yarne," for such engrossing resulted in excessive prices for clothiers and the maintenance of "Drones and evill members of a comon wealth."[64]

Food shortages continued to plague the country in 1589, prompting the mayor, aldermen, and inhabitants of Sudbury, Suffolk, to petition the Privy Council to protect the poor by restraining regrators, forestallers, and engrossers. In response, the Council delegated Thomas Gent, a baron of the Exchequer, and three gentlemen to compel those with grain to sell it to the poor at affordable prices. On 27 December the Council instructed the grain commissioners to halt the engrossing and exporting of grain. Because of the fear of dearth and rising prices for grain, notably barley, the Council asked Burghley in July 1590 to restrain the engrossing of grain by badgers.[65]

Another bad harvest came in 1594-95, and dearth ensued in 1596-97. A proclamation dated 31 July 1596 noted that grain prices had increased unreasonably, to the particular detriment of poor people who did not live by tillage. The summer's inclement weather that wealthy farmers and engrossers cited as an excuse did not justify for the Council the higher charges for the previous year's grain. In 1595 the government had issued *A New Charge . . . for Stay of the Dearth of Grain* requiring justices of the peace to stop forestalling, engrossing, and regrating, and the queen now insisted that this be done. She also prohibited making starch from corn or bran except by letters patent. On 8 August 1596 the Council asked Whit-gift to have the clergy admonish engrossers whose covetousness was blamed as a principal factor in the dearth. With an air of urgency, the queen issued another proclamation on 2 November, complaining that the dearth had worsened because her previous orders had not been properly executed. Because grain was sold secretly to badgers at unreasonable prices, making the cost of food prohibitive, offend-ers must be severely punished "to the terror of others." Grain was so scarce in 1596-97 that it had to be imported from Danzig and Den-mark to such places as Shrewsbury. Norwich, Bristol, Nottingham, Leicester, Coventry, and Yarmouth also imported food.[66]

The severe problems of the mid-1590s renewed parliamentary de-mand for new legislation in 1598, but the Commons rejected amend-ments to their bill by the Lords. In a closing oration delivered with the queen's sanction by Sir Thomas Egerton, the lord keeper, justices of the peace and assize were reproved for not punishing forestallers, regrators, and engrossers. On 23 August 1598 the queen resorted once more to a proclamation, expressing her alarm about the contin-uing high prices and food shortages, which she blamed on poor weather and greedy engrossers who preferred personal gain to public good. The old problem of using grain to make starch was noted, and this time she complained about the use of grain to feed dogs. Her final proclamation was issued on 2 June 1600. Conditions had im-proved, so that licenses had been issued the previous year for the export of 2,000 quarters of grain to the Low Countries and 1,500 quarters to Emden. In anticipation of higher prices, farmers in 1600 were withholding grain or selling it to engrossing badgers, and this the queen wanted stopped.[67]

Although enforcement was never adequate and the abuses were never terminated, local authorities periodically attempted to stop violators of the Edwardian statute. Some of this enforcement was done at the most rudimentary level, as in the case of the petty sessions for Chafford hundred, Essex, at Easter 1566, where an article to inquire about engrossers was included. At Southampton the court leet prosecuted forestallers and engrossers of butter, wheat, meal, malt, bread, cheese, eggs, faggots, wood, coal, beef, veal, oranges, and vegetables. More than two dozen persons were prosecuted in the leet for such offenses between 1571 and 1601, with fines normally running up to 10s. Among the cases heard by the Lancashire quarter sessions was at least one (in 1592) involving a woman, who was accused of forestalling at the Bolton market. At Cambridge, two masters were fined 20s. in the court leet for engrossing grain, a sentence that the vice-chancellor subsequently approved.[68]

Two legal cases show some of the complications involved in alleged engrossing that may account for part of the reluctance of local officials to prosecute. In a 1598-99 Star Chamber case, John Thurnall, the plaintiff and a Suffolk yeoman, accused Richard Howsden and John Webb, yeomen from Cambridgeshire and Suffolk, respectively, of engrossing 500 quarters of barley apiece. Thurnall had made an obligation of £26 to give Howsden twenty quarters of barley on a specified day, but by that time he could not deliver the barley, because a proclamation required all grain to be sold in the open market. Howsden's attorney had Thurnall outlawed and a writ sued for his arrest on grounds of debt. The defendants denied the charges made by Thurnall, claiming only to have purchased small quantities of grain to make malt. The second case involved charges of engrossing grain against Sir Robert Sidney's cousin, Henry Sidney of Norfolk. Rowland White informed Sir Robert in October 1597 that his cousin had broken the law by not buying and selling in the open market, but insisted he was very charitable to the nedy, selling grain below market prices and relieveing four hundred indigent persons a week at his door. "Though his fault is not so heinous as the world makes it," Henry Sidney had few defenders, and not even the earl of Essex could be persuaded to assist him. Given Elizabeth's abhorrence of engrossers at that time, it is no wonder courtiers treated Sidney like a pariah, though the justice of his case is disputable.[69]

To a problem that plagued the government and that was tied to the plight of the poor, the clergy generally responded with manifestations of concern. Yet the biblical marginalia were largely silent, with the Bishop' Bible, for instance, saying only that God was the author of scarcity. The Geneva Bible, however, spoke directly to the problem: "By staying the sale of fode and necessarie things which you haue gotten into your owne hands . . . [you] cause the poore to spend quickely that litle that they haue, and at length for necessitie to become your sclaues." One of the most pronounced expressions of Anglican concern came from Pilkington, who as a young preacher had been exposed to the reform-oriented social views of the Commonwealth Men. Although food shortages in Catholic England were divinely induced, Pilkington argued, in Protestant England they were due to man's wickedness, especially to forestalling, engrossing, and regrating. Rather than acting charitably and contenting themselves with reasonable gains, men cornered markets or exported food to raise prices. It saddened him that some farmers fed their grain to the hogs or stored it until the mice ruined it to keep the market price high. In contrast to Joseph, who opened his barns in time of dearth and aided the indigent, Elizabethans hoarded their crops in time of need to drive prices up. To Pilkington's disgust, people looked on forestallers, regrators, and engrossers as honest men.[70]

Anglican concern ebbed and flowed with the condition of the harvests. After a bad harvest in 1573, Bishop Curteys preached before the queen the following March, condemning those who hoarded or engrossed grain to drive up the price and lamenting the losses sustained in storage. The deficient harvest of 1576 motivated him to comment caustically about "the Farmer and Grasier [who] can play the sophister, in hiding in their Corne and Cattel til the price be raysed." No crisis existed when Abraham Fleming, shortly to become chaplain to the countess of Nottingham, condemned engrossing in 1581, nor when Turnbull reminded an audience at Paul's Cross that the book of Proverbs (11:26) prohibited engrossing. In the dark days of the 1590s, John King (in a sermon at York) and Samuel Gardiner lashed out against engrossers of food. With flaming rhetoric Gardiner castigated the "mercilesse maultwormes and badgers [who] doo more and more abound, who engrosse the markets, and buy vppe all the prouision of corne that should serue the poore, and enhaunce and raise vp the price of it mightily." Such men were at once the rods of divine fury and the imps of the devil. Thus the concern of Anglicans was directed only to the engrossing of food although engrossers of wool (and to a lesser degree other products) imposed hardships on clothiers and artisans.[71]

Unlike Anglican criticism, Puritan attacks on engrossing, forestalling, and regrating have no perceptible relation to harvests and dearths, but were more of a continuing concern. One Puritan who spoke in the context of a bad harvest was the conservative Thomas Becon, who in 1566 deplored "our couetous cormorantelyke cornemongers, which hourde vp corne in the time of cheape, that in the time of dearth they maye sel it the dearer." These feelings were echoed in Hake's verse in 1579. In Deacon's *Treatise* of about 1585, one of the four participants in the book's dialogue was an engrosser who represented England's principal merchants; regrating and engrossing were condemned, a lesson that Perkins also conveyed to Cambridge students. By 1589, three years after a bad harvest, Trigge commended Lincolnshire gentry for sending grain to the markets in 1588-89 to be sold only to the poor at prices below prevailing levels. Other gentry sold subsidized grain to the indigent in their areas. Three years later, however, in a sermon at Grantham, Trigge lashed out against engrossers and hoarders who created shortages and drove up prices. Like Pilkington, he was convinced that God provided sufficient grain every year and it was man that produced the dearths. He complained as well about farmers who sold either to forestallers to save themselves a trip to market or to the poor at excessive prices when the latter had no access to the marketplace. In 1592 Peter Moffett, a nephew of the countesses of Warwick and Northumberland, wrote in his commentary on Proverbs of the dangers to the commonwealth from those who hoarded food and sold it at unreasonable prices during a dearth. By 1596, there was indeed a serious dearth, but Norden tried to convince his readers that it was "a common dearth in a common plentie" because men were hoarding grain, butter, and cheese and were using grain to make starch. By 1600, when the situation had improved, Vaughan argued against forestalling as a form of usury and Dent blasted it as oppression.[72]

Neither Puritan nor Anglican of course, condoned engrossing, forestalling, and regrating, but both groups restricted their attention to foodstuffs, not wool, leather, or other goods that affected occupations. Their concern accorded with that of the government, which relied heavily on proclamations when Parliament proved unwilling to enact reforming legislation. Local authorities sought out and punished offenders, though not as consistently as the government desired, probably because of the complexity of proving violations and insufficient manpower to secure compliance. Anglican interest in engrossing, forestalling, and regrating tended to rise and fall with the quality of the harvests, whereas Puritan concern remained more constant.

(6) Landlords and Tenants

> To pourchase and bye, for lucre & gaine
> Both lease & house, both wood & grounde,
> Thei double the rent, to poor mens payne
> Of landlordes nowe, fewe good are founde.
>
> John Barker[73]

> Oppresse your tenantes, take fines, and raise rentes,
> Hold vp your houses and lands with their contents.
>
> Lewis Wager[74]

To the people of Tudor England and to most of its historians until the 1930s and 1940s, the primary agricultural evils responsible for agrarian turmoil were rack-renting and enclosing landlords. Modern research has shifted the principal responsibility to demographic growth, which caused both acute pressure on land, as the number of villagers increased, and rising prices, as demand for foodstuffs and fuel outpaced production. Local conditions varied, but generally prices rose fourfold in the sixteenth century and continued to a five-fold increase by the 1630s. The rise in rents did not exactly parallel the rise in prices, for although rents in some places increased eight-fold in the period from 1530 to 1640, they rose only fourfold on the Wiltshire estates of the earls of Pembroke. In Suffolk and Norfolk, rents on arable land increased sixfold and on pasture and meadow twofold between the 1550s and 1640s. The inflationary pressure was an incentive to landlords—the small landowners and farmers first, the larger ones subsequently—to increase rents and entry fines. Particu-larly in the period 1580 to 1620, a redistribution of income in favor of the landed classes resulted, largely at the expense of agricultural wage-earners, tenant farmers, and consumers. Population mobility also increased, as manifested in vagabondage and in the migration of small farmers in search of suitable lands, as occurred, for example, around 1600 when many left Devon for Dorset.[75]

Complaints of rack-renting began in the 1520s, before which rents and entry fines had been falling, buildings had been decaying, and ar-able land had been reverting to waste. As the population grew in the 1520s, vacant holdings were taken up by tenants, and rents and entry fines increased. In the 1530s and 1540s, endeavors were made to re-turn decayed arable land to tillage, when the common enemy of the landlord and the prospective tenant was the tenant grazier. As land-lords regained control, tenants lacking tenurial protection suffered from the upward movement in rents and entry fines, bringing in-creased protests from the tenants (as reflected, for example, in the Pilgrimage of Grace) and the Commonwealth Men.[76]

One of the most dramatic changes in English agriculture in this period was the growth of leases and the decline of customary tenure; by 1650, much copyhold had vanished. Juries in manorial courts played a crucial role in determining manorial custom, including rents and fines as well as tenant obligations. Tenant conditions varied con-siderably, ranging from copyholders by inheritance, whose fines and rents were specified in manorial court rolls, to tenants at will, only some of whom were partially protected by manorial customs and en-joyed fixed rents and fines. Some leaseholders were fortunate enough to possess customary leases, which were supposed to be renewed at the traditional rent by payment of a fine usually amounting to three to five years of rent payments. Landlords naturally sought to change fixed fines to arbitrary ones, a move tenants opposed, though some tenants were willing to alter copyhold to leases in return for suitable monetary compensation. Leases generally became shorter, often declining after c. 1540 from periods of forty to ninety-nine years to terms of seven, fourteen, or twenty-one years in eastern England and one, two, or three lives (normally the takers') in western England. Lease-parol (annual tenancy) developed rapidly between 1560 and 1600, with tenants ranging from small-holders to gentry; many farms and cottages were rented annually at the lord's will. Such yearly arrangements were subject to rack-renting, though sometimes annual rents declined to reflect harvests, price changes, and land conditions. Institutions like the church preferred long, stable leases (often ninety-nine years) at the expense of the possibility of increased profits, and these "beneficial" leases interested the wealthy, who often sublet the property and racked rents.[77]

Regional variations are especially marked in northern England, where the "anncient & lawdable custom of tenant right" or border service prevailed. Here customary tenants obtained assistance in the Elizabethan era (though not in the Jacobean period) from the crown, which wanted to ensure that the tenants could provide themselves with horses and arms to defend the kingdom from the Scots. Rents remained stable in these counties, but the lords took advantage of the opportunity to raise fines, most of which were arbitrary rather than customary. Because tenure in the north was covered by equity law, unhappy tenants sometimes sought redress in Chancery and Requests, with some success, though the expense of a suit in distant London rendered this course nearly impossible for poorer tenants. In these counties, tenants without customary protection faced mounting hardships in the Elizabethan period. As the result of the enclosure of common pasture in the northwest, with most of the encroached land going to the landless, overpopulation occurred, creating an army of exploitable workers, many of whom became tenants at will with no legal recourse when they were evicted, as subtenants were prone to be.[78]

The strongest attack on oppressive landowners by an Elizabethan Anglican was made by the moderate James Pilkington. He was incensed by the imposition of high fines and increased rents, particularly at five or seven year intervals, and by the lack of remuneration for improvements made by tenants. (Although it is true that tenants rebuilt their houses in this period at their own expense, landlords did not impose surcharges on tenants for the use of new equipment, nor did they require monetary allowances for repairs and improvements they made.) Pilkington also objected to a practice imposed on tenants unable to meet the entry fines, by which a portion of their goods, such as sheep, was paid to the landlord and then rented back for their use. Equally upsetting was the role of agents who specialized in procuring lease renewals or reversions, so that tenants had their rents racked without the landlords' receiving additional income. At root, the objection here was identical to that advanced against engrossing, that unnecessary middlemen increased costs without corresponding benefits. The crown too, averred Pilkington, suffered from unscrupulous landlords, such as those who exchanged property with the crown without indicating that their lands suffered from faulty titles, extraordinary expenses, or potential flood damage. Also castigated were landlords who racked rents to make land appear more valuable as the prelude to exchanging it with the crown. An element of environmental concern marked Pilkinton's diatribe against scheming landowners: "What common dealing hath been practised to get such lands of the prince and other men, as were well wooded, into their hands, and when they had spoiled the woods, racked the rents, and deeply fined the tenants, then to return the same land into the prince's hand again, or sell it over to others, and get as much, it is too well known throughout the realm." [79]

Other Anglicans, including King, Anderson, and Seager, condemned rack-renting and unreasonable fines, though not substantively. In a sermon before the queen at Richmond in March 1575 Bishop Curteys expressed displeasure that the aristocracy should "take awaye and withhold many mens freeholds, coppiholds and leases, goodes and cattell." During the Admonition controversy, Bishop Cooper acquiesced to the condemnation of any bishop who imposed immoderate fines and high rents. Apparently no Anglican linked increased rents and fines to inflation, but several blamed usury, gambling, and excessive apparel. Other Anglicans voiced discontent with landlords who ignored tenants' miseries or oppressed tenants by excessive labor. John Best, bishop of Carlisle, informed the Privy Council in 1564 that tenants in the northwest could not convert to Protestantism for fear of losing their farms. Conditions in that area bothered Grindal too, for in 1563 he asked Cecil not to leave the tenants of a deceased Cumberland gentleman (Skelton) subject to the spoliation of local gentry. Apart from Pilkington, however, Anglican reformers apparently showed no sustained interest in tenant problems, especially increased fines and rents, and no real understanding why these problems existed. [80]

Puritans were more sensitive to the plight of tenants, yet in general they were no more understanding of landlord problems. Trigge considered but rejected the argument that inflation coupled with the number of Elizabethan subsidies necessitated higher rents and fines. Oppression of the poor, he felt, could not be justified by such reasoning, and he accused landlords of excessive charges simply "to maintaine pride and vanitye withall." It was not a matter of raising rents and fines to preserve the social order but, as Lupton also said, using the profits to dress excessively, eat sumptuously, and gamble that troubled him. Trigge was angered because some tenants paid hefty fines for twenty-one-year leases, only to pay other fines before their expiration to avoid loss of land on reversion. Trigge complained that landlords reserved excessive lands for sheep commons and meadows at the expense of tenants. The upward movement of rents and fines encouraged some tenants to lament the days when abbots and priors were landlords, and Trigge admitted that they had some justification for these feelings. He nevertheless retorted—with a good deal of insight—that in the days of the monasteries, a shortage of manpower had existed, hence landlords actively sought tenants. "Then there was such plentie of all things, and so fewe men, that they were scant able to paye verie easie rents of verie good fermes." Thus Trigge recognized the demographic factors responsible for the increased pressure for land and the consequent opportunity for landlords to raise fines and rents, but he refused to sanction their actions.[81]

From Elizabethan Puritans arose a chorus of opposition to rackrenters, with the theme enunciated by Becon in 1561:

Raise not thy rents. Take no incomes nor fynes. Be content with the olde and accustomed paimentes. Brine vp no newe customes.

Loyalty to ancient precedents was the watchword and a just concern for the poor the recurring principle. Although Puritan stress on the wrongfulness of *excessive* fines and rents may have allowed for modest increases, the tenor of their attack inflamed passions against those who oppressed widows, orphans, and the indigent by pirating their possessions and dispossessing them of their tenures. Dent depicted peasants as gnawing on crusts of bread, living in fear of increased rents and loss of goods, and wearing only the thinnest clothing. One finds comparable expressions reiterated in Puritan writings: Gifford, Vaughan, Stubbes, Allen, Lupton, Bush, and Pagit repeated the litany. "Is not God your Landlord," Vaughan asked, "and dooth hee not suffer you to enioy his lands without incomes or fines?" One could infer approval of a communal society from this, but Vaughan sought only to preserve reasonable fines and rents and to terminate extraordinary imposts, benevolences, and leatherwits. Excessive rents and fines (along with enclosure) were blamed for depopulation and increased vagabondage. Some of this was due, said Allen, to tenants and farmers who were so anxious to procure leases that they greedily awaited reversions and outbid each other for the land. Such competition made it possible for landlords to demand new and higher entry fines from tenants well before the expiration of leases. Puritans were upset as well about imposing excessive rents and fines on more substantial tenants because they adversely affected the ability of these folk to provide hospitality for the indigent. [82]

The exhortations and admonitions of the clergy met with a mixed reaction among the laity. In Anglican circles Sir William Wentworth advised his son to treat tenants charitably, but never to give them leases.

Your tenants having leases maie suie yow, or anie your frends, in an action of trespasse, if yow or they do butt com upon the ground to them letten. I haue knowne diuers leases made, upon payment, or tender of a certain some of monie, to be voide: and for covenants whatt to plowe and whatt maynure to putt in to the grounde and when &c.

Wentworth's preference was to have tenants at will on terms of lease-parol and to treat them judiciously so they did not fear eviction. It is worth noting that when Wentworth paid £11,000 for Harewood, he had to sell some land to tenants at Burton Leonard, Yorks., for £3,000; they trusted him sufficiently to give him the money prior to his drawing up the conveyances. Sir Thomas Smith is credited with forbearing to raise rents and fines or to evict or sue his tenants, and Burghley was praised for never raising rents or evicting tenants. In his will, Denzil Holles of Irby, Lincs., stipulated that his tenants be treated as well as he had treated them. An epitaph for Edward Stanley, earl of Derby, asserted he never raised rents, and he was commended by Holinshed for "his godlie disposition to his tenants, neuer forcing anie seruice at their hands, but due paiment of their rent." Comparable claims were made in the epitaph for Henry Wriothesley (d. 1581), earl of Southampton, and in an encomium on Ferdinando Lord Strange. Katherine Brettergh successfully intervened with her husband William, on behalf of a needy tenant. It was this sort of behavior that the clergy favored, though epitaphs customarily gloss over the flaws of the deceased. Nevertheless, the ideal is manifest. [83]

Other Anglican laity increased rents and fines, sometimes to recoup losses sustained by pious predecessors, as in the case of Henry Wriothesley (d. 1624), earl of Southampton. One of the worst offenders was Edward Lord Stafford, whose tenants repeatedly complained about him to the Privy Council, accusing him of imprisoning a tenant for a ransom of £20, driving his tenants' cattle into his castle and killing some of them, and sheltering miscreants. Another unsavory landlord was Peter Hoskins, who was determined "that he would rule and reign as king" over his tenants at Benister, and that they would be subjected to frequent lawsuits as under his father and grandfather. Sometimes bishops and other church officials were themselves oppressive landlords, a point made in the Admonition controversy. In the 1570s, the dean and chapter of Durham sought to break the customary tenures of their tenants by granting leases of customary tenancies to others, who were responsible for establishing their titles against the original tenants. In the 1580s the bishop, Richard Barnes, continued this practice by granting leases of customary tenancies to his servant and others, who argued their claims before the Council of the North.[84]

Generally, however, the bishops were more inclined to grant beneficial leases in return for entry fines that provided needed cash; statutes passed in 1571 (13 Elizabeth I, c. 10) and 1576 (18 Elizabeth I, c. 11) curtailed the worst abuses. Elizabethan bishops failed to increase their fines and rents sufficiently to keep pace with the general movement in rents and fines. In 1601 Sir Thomas Wilson calculated that the twenty-six bishoprics were worth £22,500, but the sale of episcopal lands in 1646 at not less than ten years' purchase raised £676,387, which means, as Christopher Hill has shown, "that the surveyed value of the lands was over three times the old rents."[85] That the church was chronically underfunded was owing in part to the general reluctance of the bishops—and of deans and chapters—to impose increases in rents and fines commensurate with those being charged by the laity.

Among the Puritans, Sir Walter Mildmay urged his son Anthony in 1570 not to make exactions from tenants. A panegyric on Henry Hastings, earl of Huntingdon, written after his death, lauded him for not raising tenants' rents and for keeping their fines small, with many poor tenants paying nothing. As his biographer observes, however, this policy was not intentional, but an accident resulting from being too pressed with government business to reform his estate management. As manager of the earl's estate, Sir Francis Hastings granted long leases (up to 3,000 years) for high entry fines. In 1616 Margaret Clifford, countess of Cumberland, specified in her will that her tenants must be protected from extortion by her heir. Rents in Norfolk and Suffolk, where Puritanism was strong, increased more rapidly than the general rise in prices, suggesting that Puritan laity normally ignored admonitions of their clergy to restrain financial demands on tenants.[86]

Catholic landlords were generally conservative in their attitude to increases in rents and fines, which was in keeping with the behavior advocated in Vaux's catechism. Although they threatened with eviction those tenants who converted to Protestantism in the northwest, normally the evicted were subtenants living marginally. To some degree, fines were raised, though rents in Cumberland and Westmorland remained stable. In 1570, however, tenants holding from the Percies or landlords under them complained that "the Lordes hath been . . . making Conveyance & devises of their Lande to cause the poore tenants to make ffine sometimes once in two three or ffoure yeares or more [and] the poore tenants are soe raunsomed as they are neither able to live & mainteine their families." In the early seventeenth century, Henry Percy (d. 1632), earl of Northumberland, vigorously converted copyholds to leases, sometimes doubling or tripling the rent, though in the 1580s he had granted beneficial leases at low rents to raise £1,700. The lawsuits with which Sir Thomas Tresham was troubled were partly caused by his rack-renting. Before the reversion of their lands to the crown in 1570, the Dacres were more concerned with tenant loyalty than income from entry fines; even though the latter were arbitrary, the Dacres imposed fines of only two or three years' rent. Thomas Howard, duke of Norfolk, fostered good relations with his tenants and retained their affection and loyalty. In 1577, Philip Howard, heir to the earldom of Arundel, protected a tenant from eviction by his agent. To a degree, Catholic lords had to beware of abusing tenants for fear that they might inform the government of illegal religious activities, particularly the sheltering of priests.[87]

In sum, the strongest outcry against rack-renting and high entry fines came from Puritans, though Anglicans lent their voices to the campaign. The clergy failed to understand or appreciate the problems of landowners faced with inflationary prices; even Trigge, who considered the problem of inflation and demographic pressure, deplored the actions of the landowners. Most clerical observers seem to have attributed the higher fines and rents to lavish living by the aristocracy, which they were committed to stop.[88] That rents increased faster than prices in general in Norfolk and Suffolk but not in more conservative areas such as Cumberland, Westmorland, and Wiltshire suggests that many Puritan landlords did not heed the admonitions of their clergymen, a charge Sutcliffe leveled.[89] Bishops, deans, and chapters normally did not increase fines and rents to keep pace with inflation, further contributing to the economic problems of the church but avoiding the exacerbation of anticlericalism.

(7) Enclosure, Engrossment, and Depopulation

For oft their greedy paunche deuoures, their neighbors house & ground,
Yea Pastures, Parks, whole fields, & Tounes, & al that may be found.

Richard Robinson[90]

For these inclosures be the causes, why rich men, eat vp poore men, as beasts doo eat grasse.

Philip Stubbes[91]

Enclosure and engrossment were emotional issues in Tudor England and were, with rack-renting, viewed as the root of the economic ills in agriculture. Enclosure was not new in the sixteenth century, for by 1500 open-field farming had mostly disappeared in Suffolk, Essex, Kent, Surrey, Sussex, Devon, and Cornwall. Nor did a great deal remain in Somerset, Cumberland, and Herefordshire, although a balance between arable and pastoral existed in Lancashire, Cheshire, and Wiltshire. There were various types of enclosure, including the partitioning of commons between parishes, the enclosure of wasteland, the regulation of common pastures to control the number of cattle, sheep, and horses allowed to graze by tenants, and the enclosure of open ground by restricting or terminating common grazing rights. The enclosure that caused most concern was the last-named, especially when neighbors or tenants were forced off their holdings. It could be highly controversial when commons were enclosed or arable land was converted to pasture, but converting arable to pasture had been profitable only up to around 1550, and grain prices provided financial enticement to convert pasturage to tillage after 1570. Demographic factors made enclosure a serious concern, for as the country experienced a 63% growth in population between 1522 and 1603, it required increased quantities of food and land to feed the expanding labor force.[92]

Enclosure and engrossment, which involved the consolidation of farms and the loss of homesteads, could adversely affect copyholders, leaseholders, and tenants at will, though legal procedures normally were observed. Enclosure could be accomplished by manorial custom when it gave landlords such rights, by unity of possession if a lord acted when his tenancies came up for renewal, or by agreement (the usual form). Unity of possession was the normal means of engross-ment, following which a lord could enclose at will. Tenants some-times enclosed to improve arable farming or arrange more convenient usage of meadow and pasture land, as did the tenants of the St. John family at Liddiard Tregooze, Wilts.[93]

Depopulation was widely believed to be a concomitant of enclo-sure, and though this factor was exaggerated by contemporary au-thors, the laboring population did drift from the plains and fields to heaths, unenclosed forests, and wasteland. After 1550, large numbers of villages were reduced in size because of enclosure and engrossment, though few villages actually were deserted in the northwest, the Welsh borders, the southwestern peninsula, and the southeastern counties from Suffolk to Sussex. Depopulation was more serious in the northeastern lowlands, whereas in the midlands workers displaced by enclosure went either to common fields or to market towns where they sought industrial employment. The occurrence of depopulation depended on whether enclosure extended cultivation by improving wastes, forests, and fens (increasing rural population) or reduced cul-tivation, decreasing the number of farm laborers. In places such as Lancashire and the West Riding after 1550 and in Cambridgeshire in the seventeenth century, new villages actually were created by expan-sion into highland moors, forests, and fens. Elizabethan England thus experienced both depopulation and impopulation.[94]

Where enclosure occurred in the sixteenth century was determined by soil factors and existing forms of agricultural organization. The midland counties were susceptible because of the prevalence of open-field farming and the soil's adaptability to tillage or pasture. Most Tudor enclosures occurred from Berkshire and Oxfordshire to Lin-colnshire and Norfolk. In the six midland counties, 70,000 acres were enclosed between 1578 and 1607, with at least 61% of this fig-ure coming between 1593 and 1607. One of the most affected coun-ties was Leicestershire, where 31,000 acres were enclosed between 1485 and 1607 (19% between 1511 and 1580, 21% between 1580 and 1601, and 27% between 1601 and 1607). One village in three in Leicestershire was directly affected by enclosure, yet by 1607 only some 10% of the county's open-field arable land had been enclosed. In Leicestershire, those responsible for enclosure were chiefly the squirearchy, who undertook over 70% of the enclosure carried out between 1551 and 1607. Near Leicester itself much of the enclosure was for the pasturage of cattle.[95]

The northwest presents a different picture. In Cumberland and Westmorland most enclosure took the form of encroachment on common pasture, which was abundant, or forest, with most of the land gained from enclosure going to the landless. Because so much of this land was marginal, the problem of excess population worsened. By the end of the Elizabethan period, marginal livings were not enough to keep the people alive; this compounded the existing evil of poverty resulting from encroachment into the forests, which adversely affected the poor who pastured there.[96]

In the northeast some enclosure and engrossment occurred in Northumberland and Durham, particularly on small and medium-sized estates, leading to some depopulation. The alarm this situation caused was increased by bad harvests and severe food shortages, and finally the plague in 1597-98. A vivid picture is painted by William James, dean of Durham, and though it is an overstatement it reveals the disquietude of some Elizabethans. The decay of tillage and depopulation of villages, he lamented, was an offense to God and a dishonor to the sovereign, for they spoiled the church, deprived ministers of maintenance, weakened the commonwealth, oppressed the poor, burdened neighbors, violated natural law, and weakened the defenses of the northern border. In the preceding year, he saw many impoverished persons come from Carlisle to Durham in search of food, and on the way were long stretches where no one lived and hospitality was unavailable. In the diocese of Durham "are sayd in few yeares to bee decayed five hundred plowes, wherby that countrey which before tyme was able, to feede it self, and to helpe others, was this last yeare, and some yeares before in great want and distresse." Grain had to be imported at Newcastle, but with it came the plague. Tenants spent their money on imported food, leaving them nothing to plant and no funds to pay rents or to purchase additional sustenance. "Manye personages wheron good houses have benne kept, are vtterly decayed, in some place of *eight thousand akers* in tillage of late yeares, at this daye not *eight score tilled*." Beggary has increased, James declared, people are being evicted and forced to lodge four and five families to a cottage. The commonwealth, concluded the dean, is in danger and reformation mandatory.[97]

The progress of enclosure and engrossment, to the extent that acrimonious feelings were created and tenants evicted, met with the hostility of the government as well as the clergy. Again the government's desire for order meshed with the church's socio-economic concerns. Worry about the threat of enclosure to order was not idle, for popular hostility to enclosures regularly manifested itself in violence and was a grievance in the Northern Rebellion. In Staffordshire, forcible entry into enclosed land was a common offense in the quarter sessions. The grain riots inspired by the bad harvests of the 1590s sometimes led to the destruction of enclosures. Forty-two cases of forcible entry were presented in the Lancashire quarter sessions in 1592, and in 1602 one of this author's ancestors, James Williamson, a husbandman from Ashton, was presented at Wigan for breaking into a close. Star Chamber records include numerous instances of forcible entry and the destruction of enclosures. Some of those involved may have been ignorant of the legal ramifications of their actions, as a Herefordshire man claimed at the end of the age when he asked the judges of Star Chamber to have "Consideracon of his poore estate & simplicitie[,] he beinge a poore yonge man & havinge noe experience of matters of the like kinde nor knowinge the penaltie of the Lawe made against those that should Commytt such offence as through simplicitie & ignorance this deffendant is fallen into." The Privy Council also investigated cases. Apart from the threat to order, the government worried about the impact of depopulating enclosure on the peasants' ability to defend the realm, find employment, and pay taxes and tithes.[98]

For all its concern, the crown enclosed some of its own lands, though not without incurring popular antipathy. After the common was enclosed and a highway rerouted on the royal estate at Windsor, forty to fifty irate tenants rejected Leicester's explanation and complained to the queen. When she directed Burghley to hear their complaints, Leicester wrote: "Surely it is not to be suffered that a Prince in such a case should be grudged at, when every upstart and yeoman almost can have more a thousand times at their tenants' hands to enclose, whole towns and lordships, and to change twice as far highways, and no complaints at all of it."[99] But there were complaints, with some justification if other landlords shared Leicester's arrogance. On crown estates in general, however, enclosure came slowly, with the government more concerned to provide a proper example than to obtain maximum income.

The government was plagued by an inability to enforce legislation properly, though it probably achieved more success with respect to enclosures than with such matters as apparel and inebriety, and it was not until the 1590s, when the real leaders of the age were in their graves or nearly there, that enclosures got out of hand. Elizabeth issued only one proclamation on enclosure, dated 1 March 1569, only a matter of months before rebels complained of them. The proclamation observes that despite existing laws, towns and houses of husbandry are decaying, tillage is being converted to pasture, and hospitality is declining. Justices of assize and of the peace were ordered to make inquiries. When enclosures increased rapidly at the end of the reign, there was no proclamation, possibly because Elizabeth's attention was focused on the war with Spain and the earl of Essex, or perhaps because the men in her Council who were most disturbed about enclosure were gone.[100]

Numerous statutes on enclosure had been enacted under the Tudors before 1558, commencing in 1489 with an act (4 Henry VII, c. 19) designed to stop conversion of arable land to pasture and depopulation. The earliest enclosure acts of Henry VIII's reign (6 Henry VIII, c. 5, and 7 Henry VIII, c. 1) called for the restoration of tillage and houses of husbandry under penalty of forfeiture of half the land, but left enforcement in the hands of landlords. A 1534 act (25 Henry VIII, c. 13) stipulated that no person could keep more than 2,400 sheep. A 1536 statute (27 Henry VIII, c. 22) reenacted the 1489 act, but restricted it to central England and the Isle of Wight. The next important acts, passed in 1552 (5 & 6 Edward VI, c. 5) and 1555 (2 & 3 Philip and Mary, c. 2), created permanent commissioners, and the latter act empowered them to plough up pasture land, fix rents, and bind over offenders to rebuild ruined houses. In 1563 (5 Elizabeth I, c. 2), Parliament repealed the 1536, 1552, and 1555 statutes, confirmed the earlier acts of Henry VIII, and required all land in tillage for four successive years since 1529 to be kept that way.[101]

In 1589, Parliament passed an act (31 Elizabeth I, c. 7) to protect cottagers, requiring every cottage to have at least four acres of land. When grain prices fell in 1593 and food was abundant, conversion from tillage to pasture was allowed (35 Elizabeth I, c. 7). Enough tenants seem to have been evicted in subsequent years to bring back fears of depopulation, starvation, and vagabondage, as seen in Dean James' protests. Consequently a Commons' committee, taking the initiative in 1597, prepared a bill to stop enclosure and depopulation. The moving spirit was Sir Francis Bacon, who struck a responsive note when he declared:

Though it may be thought ill and very prejudicial to Lords that have inclosed great grounds, and pulled down even whole Towns, and converted them to Sheep-Pastures; yet considering the increase of people and the benefit of the Common-Wealth, I doubt not but every man will deem the revival of former Moth-eaten Laws in this point a praise-worthy thing. . . . For Inclosure of grounds brings depopulation, which brings first Idleness, secondly decay of Tillage, thirdly subversion of Houses, and decay of Charity, and charges to the Poor, fourthly impoverishing the state of the Realm.

Although some feeling existed that repeal of the 1593 act would lead to a shortage of cattle and a surplus of grain (with ruinous effect on husbandmen), Bacon carried the day. The first of the resulting acts (39 Elizabeth I, c. 1) required the restoration of all houses of husbandry destroyed in the preceding seven years and half of those in the seven years before that, with a minimum of forty and twenty acres, respectively, attached to them. The second act (39 Elizabeth I, c. 2) stipulated that in twenty-three counties, the Isle of Wight, and Pembrokeshire, arable land converted to pasture since 1558 after being tilled for at least twelve years preceding conversion must be reconverted within three years. In general, future conversions were prohibited.[102]

In 1601, Parliament debated whether the 1597 act should be renewed, with opponents arguing that grain was too cheap for the welfare of the husbandman, "the Staple man of the Kingdom." The poor, claimed Sir Walter Raleigh, could not find enough seed to sow, hence the government should "leave every man free, which is the desire of a true *English* man." Proponents of the renewal, led by Bacon and Sir Robert Cecil, countered that the wealth of the kingdom must not be engrossed into the hands of a few rich ranchers, and that the kingdom depends on the maintenance of farmers. If England produced too much grain, excess could be exported to maintain domestic prices. "If we debar Tillage, we give scope to the Depopulation; And then if the poor being thrust out of their Houses go to dwell with others, straight we catch them with the Statute of Inmates; if they wander abroad, they are within the danger of the Statute of the Poor to be whipt." The act was renewed, though with an amendment exempting Northumberland because of the severity of the plague.[103]

An interesting proposal for the increase of tillage was presented to Burghley by alderman Boxe. Convinced that "by mans negligence and Idelnes, that grounde, that god hathe indewed vs withe, to laboure, and get our lyuinge one, is but loste and come to naught, for lacke of good order and gouernment," he advocated the provision of more plows as the key to increased tillage. The shortage of plows, he argued, was responsible for idleness, beggary, and insufficient food among the poor. Too much land was devoted to grazing sheep; the government should require every landlord to apportion his waste to tenants in amounts reflecting the size of their rents. At no extra cost, tenants would cultivate the wasteland, but if they failed to do so within two years the right was forfeited. Although the lords retained ownership, all profits from crops would go to the tenants. Essentially,

Boxe advocated a revised version of medieval assarting, but the aristocracy was uninterested. The search for a solution in the wasteland was somewhat prophetic of the efforts of Winstanley in the 1640s.[104]

Apart from the socio-economic impact of enclosure on the poor, its effect on tithes was something the clergy had to consider, for enclosure might decrease their income in various ways. Whereas a growth in stocking and breeding would increase lesser (vicarial) tithes, the great (rectorial) tithes on grain would decrease. As a smallholder, a cleric could lose his right of common in the event of enclosure and be short-changed in compensation for his glebe. Enclosure normally involved commutation of tithes to fixed annual payments, which adversely affected the recipient in an inflationary economy. Appealing to the court of conscience, successive incumbents sometimes challenged these arrangements, so wise landowners had agreements ratified in Chancery or the Court of Exchequer Chamber. In 1585, Whitgift complained of the ill effect of enclosure on clerical incomes and in 1597, Tobias Matthew, bishop of Durham, called for the revival of antienclosure statutes as a means to support an educated clergy. At Grantham in 1592, Trigge lamented in a sermon that "nowe where CHRIST his family hath beene maintained, growe trees or nettles" because of enclosure. Yet the financial impact of enclosure on the clergy troubled them less than did its effects on tenants.[105]

In the first half of the age, the Anglican case against enclosure rested on its alleged responsibility for depopulation and dearth. In 1560, Pilkington blamed dearth on enclosing landlords, forestallers, and regrators; the enclosures to which he referred involved the conversion of tillage to pasturage for the grazing of sheep. He subsequently likened enclosing, depopulating landlords to Ahab when he dispossessed Naboth of his vineyard. In a sermon before Parliament in 1563, Nowell likewise cast the blame on the conversion of arable land to pasture; sheep wasted not only good ground but men. With rhetorical flourish he asserted that where there had been twenty houses for the queen's subjects to inhabit, only a shepherd and his dog remained. "And therefore as for payments [taxes], such persons as eat up men would be looked unto, for they may well pay." Notwithstanding good statutes, Nowell insisted, enforcement was lax because those who should execute them were also enclosing and depopulating.[106]

In the latter half of the age, the focus of Anglican concern shifted to the influence of enclosure and engrossment on the poor. Dire pictures were painted of evicted tenants faced with starvation, beggary, or thievery. While villages decayed, towns filled with beggars. Even for those who stayed in the countryside, poverty became a way of life, all because landlords pursued lavish life-styles and grandiose parks. "Carnall Gospellers," charged Anthony Anderson, "fyrst pull downe Tyllage, and dyke in pastures, with Lammas cloking Closes, they driue the poore plowman to feast with pease breade on Christmas daye." Such actions contravened the rights of the poor and were sinful. Anglicans were stung by the accusation in the Marprelate tracts that their pluralist clergy were guilty of this by engrossment and enclosure. Although some clerics probably did enclose and engross to improve their livings, those Anglicans who spoke out on these practices uniformly condemned them for contributing to depopulation, dearth, poverty, and crime.[107]

Puritans did not evince much anxiety about enclosure until the 1580s, when the practice began to intensify, notably in the midlands. In a sermon at Paul's Cross on Trinity Sunday, 1571, Edward Bush condemned enclosers and engrossers of land, averring that he knew of villages depopulated to satiate greedy cormorants. Eight years later, Hake praised English ancestors for never encroaching on their neighbors or unjustly enclosing land. One of the most substantial Puritan attacks on enclosure appeared in 1583, when Stubbes deplored the enclosure of commons, moors, and heaths, forcing tenants into beggary. Stubbes urged landlords to reopen enclosed lands and reduce rents and fines. Late Elizabethan Puritans were troubled by depopulation; towns, cried Trigge, were decayed and villages turned into granges, increasing the number of beggars. He was incensed by landlords who pulled down cottages to create gardens with prospects or, as Allen charged, to obtain privacy. The Puritan attitude to enclosure was summed up in 1600 by Vaughan: "Now a dayes yeomanrie is decayed, hospitalitie gone to wracke, and husbandrie almost quite fallen;" even food is more expensive. There was no difference in outlook between Anglican and Puritan religious leaders over depopulating enclosure and engrossment, though Puritans did not become seriously concerned until the 1580s.[108]

Neither did the Separatists have any sympathy for enclosers and engrossers of land. In the late 1580s, Barrow castigated clergy of the established church for their failure to rebuke the rich and noble who insatiably engage "in purchasing and joining not field unto field, but towne unto towne," in the guise of good husbandry and providential blessing.[109]

Laymen of Anglican and Puritan religious persuasions enclosed, sometimes with beneficial results. Denzil Holles of Irby, Lincs., purchased and enclosed lands "much to the advantage both of himselfe and tenants; for he devided it into so many farmes and layd all the landes he apportioned to each apart by themselves, which he fenced with quicke set hedges," but he left a large commons. In 1560 the Anglican mercer and Merchant Adventurer John Isham and his brother Henry, parson of Pitchley, Northants., purchased the manor of Lamport in the same county and enclosed part of it, apparently without any depopulation. In contrast, in May 1576 the pale in Sir Thomas Gresham's enclosed deer-park at Osterley, Middlesex, was burned at 2:00 A.M. while the queen and court were in residence; Gresham had received the land from Elizabeth in 1570. Henry Clinton, earl of Lincoln, was indicted for depopulation and accused of activity unbecoming a peer, who was expected to defend the oppressed. Enclosure riots broke out on the lands of Sir John Throgmorton in the Forest of Feckenham in 1578, yet he continued to enclose, incurring the illwill of his tenants—and the attention of the Council in the Marches of Wales and the Privy Council. In 1579 the Privy Council also heard complaints about the enclosures of Sir Francis Leake in Derbyshire.[110]

As the pace of enclosure quickened, additional charges were filed with the Privy Council. In 1589 the Council intervened on behalf of poor supplicants in the village of Oxwick, Norfolk, after part of the commons was enclosed by Thomas Basham, a local gentleman. In similar fashion, the Council ordered the justices of assize in Wiltshire to take action against Jasper More, a gentleman, after he imperiled a hospital and free school by surcharging the common pasture, enclosing the commons, defying custom, and building illegal tenements. In a dispute between Christopher Hodeson, a Bedfordshire gentleman, and his tenants, the landlord prosecuted the tenants at law contrary to an arrangement agreed on in Star Chamber through the mediation of the earl of Kent; when Hodeson persisted, the Privy Council intervened. One of the most interesting cases occurred in 1590 in regard to the lands of Jervaux Abbey, which had belonged to the countess of Lennox. Following her death, Sir Thomas Danby bought the remainder of a lease on a large sheep pasture known as Golding Hythe, which he engrossed to his own land and then enclosed, sparking anxiety that the leased land would soon become indistinguishable from his own acres. Danby also enclosed the commons of East Wilton, Ellington, and Ellingstring, Yorks., which he obtained from the countess' estate and which entailed a thousand acres of land. As a result, the tenants were impoverished.[111]

Some Puritan landlords enclosed, though Henry Hastings, earl of Huntingdon, was praised because he did not.

No groues he inclosed, nor selled no woodes.
No pastures he paled to doe himselfe good:
To Commons and Countrie, he liude a good friend,
And gaue to the needie what God did him send.

In reality, however, extensive lands on his estates were enclosed, as at Hatherley, Maperton, and Clapton, Som., though usually without his knowledge. His tenant at Hardington, Som., enclosed the entire village and converted the land to pasture, leaving only his own house. Huntingdon's estates were managed by his Puritan brother, Sir Francis Hastings, who had no objections to enclosure and even proposed that a down of two hundred acres at Kilmersdon, Som., be enclosed for the benefit of tenants and landlord. There was, of course, a difference between the depopulating enclosure at Hardington and the beneficial variety proposed for Kilmersdon. Huntingdon may be excused for not reversing the enclosure at Hardington because of pressing affairs in the north, but there is no indication that he was troubled by such enclosures on his estates. In another case, when Philip Lord Wharton, father of the eminent Puritan peer of the next century, enclosed lands, his tenants protested to Burghley in 1582.[112]

Most Catholic landlords probably dared not alienate tenants by depopulating enclosure. One who did was John Lord Stourton, whose tenants in Somersetshire complained to the Privy Council in 1587 when he enclosed commons. Thomas Lord Wharton evicted tenants at Ravenstonedale, Westmorland, to create a park, and Sir Thomas Tresham's enclosures resulted in lawsuits with tenants. Although enclosure was undertaken on the Percy estates in Cumberland, this involved the conversion of pasture to arable land and actually increased tenancies. The same is true of the enclosure of much of the Percy lands in the Forest of Westward in 1569, which increased support for the Percys in the northwest.[113]

In conclusion, Anglican and Puritan responses to economic problems are different in emphasis but unified in purpose. This general concern for economic issues meshed with the government's quest for social order. When the government failed to obtain legislation on socio-economic problems, as happened particularly in the case of the engrossing of foodstuffs and the enforcement of uniform weights and measures, preaching and teaching were valuable corollaries to royal proclamations. Even when there was abundant new legislation, as in the case of depopulating enclosure, the clergy helped temper the ambitions of landlords. Clerical reformers and their lay allies undoubtedly disliked the temporary suspension of antienclosure provisions in 1593 and most opposed the 1571 statute permitting interest on loans up to 10% by eliminating most penalties.

Anglicans and Puritans mainly agreed in their hostility to usury until the 1590s, a position enunciated in the biblical marginalia. Some Anglicans, Matthew Hutton most prominently, accepted moderate usury, though most remained opposed until the end of the age and beyond. Some influential late Elizabethan Puritans—Gibbon, Perkins, Richard Rogers, and Ames—broke with the main body of Anglican-Puritan opinion by sanctioning moderate interest except on loans to the impoverished. In the major treatise by Mosse, interest was approved if the lender shared the risks with the borrower. The dominant theme in clerical hostility to usury was its detrimental effect on the poor; social concern took precedence over economic considerations.

In the related matter of suretiship, Anglicans had little to say, being content with the admonition in the Bishops' Bible to exercise caution. In this area, as in the case of usury, Puritans disagreed among themselves, Puritans such as Dod, Gibbon, and Burton regarded suretiship as a Christian duty, though one to be observed cautiously. Due concern had to be given to the character of the recipient, available means, and regard for family welfare. Richard Rogers would not go this far, rejecting the thesis that suretiship was a Christian duty and restricting assistance to small sums.

With respect to business ethics and the use of standard weights and measures, more concern was expressed in Puritan circles than in Anglican. Whereas Anglican objections to irregular weights and measures were largely perfunctory, Puritans stressed how their use violated the eighth commandment and the law of nature. Both groups agreed on the need for ethical principles in business, the chief of which were equitable transactions, the golden rule, and the avoidance of deceptive practices. Yet there is a marked intensity and breadth in Puritan writings on business ethics not present in Anglican literature. Writers such as Deacon, Perkins, Knewstub, and Rogers essentially provided mini-codes to impress these principles on readers. Puritans also seem to have been more aware of their reputation for honest dealings. It is reasonable to conclude that the Puritans were more sensitive than the Anglicans about the implications of their faith for business practice.

In regard to agriculture, Puritans and Anglicans showed a marked difference of emphasis. Although Anglicans, except for Pilkington (a moderate), demonstrated only perfunctory concern about increasing rents and entry fines, Puritans were more sensitive to their impact on poor tenants. Yet Puritan concern for depopulating enclosure was hardly evident before the 1580s, when the practice increased markedly. Some early Anglicans worried about the effect of enclosure on depopulation and dearth, but from the 1580s to the end of the age they were firmly in accord with Puritans on its negative effects on the poor. Puritans were more sensitive to the reduction of hospitality as caused, they believed, by higher fines and rents, as well as enclosure. Neither group grasped the need for higher fines and rents brought about by inflation, though Trigge considered this problem and demographic pressure before concluding that they did not justify the increases. Both groups blamed higher rents and fines and enclosure on insatiable greed—a quest for lavish living, grandiose parks, increased privacy, and so forth. Generally, the crown and church were slow in raising rents and fines or in enclosing, being more sensitive to popular opinion. The crown also granted favorable leases in reversion to courtiers and others to reward them for services. Because the clergy had only life interests in their estates, they were tempted to grant beneficial leases in return for substantial entry fines, a practice that adversely affected the church's financial health in the long haul. The clergy also were reluctant to support enclosures because of their negative impact on tithes, though this motive was subordinate to concern for the indigent.

On the whole, the response of Anglicans and Puritans to economic problems was conservative, in tune with the goals of the government, and imbued with ideals of justice and anxiety for the welfare of the poor. The principal exception was the late Elizabethan development, primarily among Puritans, to allow moderate interest on loans to all but the needy.

CHAPTER 15

Legal Problems

Elizabethans were attracted to legal means to resolve disputes and obtain justice, despite the inordinate delays, exorbitant expenses, and corrupt lawers and judges that plagued the judicial system. Anglican and Puritan reformers urged the redress of abuses to ensure that the system functioned successfully as a preserver of order and a dispenser of justice; in these areas, there was broad agreement. It was in the sphere of ecclesiastical justice that friction existed, initially because church courts retained their historic associations with Roman principles and procedure, much to the disgust of Puritans who sought to put as much distance as possible between Catholicism and their religion. This situation worsened in the 1580s and 1590s when the machinery of these courts, especially the High Commission, was turned against Puritans to crush the classical movement. Subjection to a system of justice in which a key weapon was the oath *ex officio mero*, with its capacity for self-incrimination, was too much for Puritans, who saw this system as the adaptation of principles associated with the Spanish Inquisition, a view in which the Separatists concurred. As the controversy developed, Puritans enjoyed support from some common lawyers, who also saw this oath as a contravention of traditional English legal principles. As in such areas as the sabbath, the early harmony of Anglicans and Puritans was shattered in the later decades of the century, when religious ideals turned social and legal issues into bitter arenas of debate.

649

(1)Christians and Lawsuits

Nowe our sutes are so common, that they make the waie [to London] thither beaten. The former Christians were not so contentious.

Francis Trigge[1]

Law is to be vsed in this case, as the Physitian vseth poison, and that is, onely in desperate cases.

William Perkins[2]

The Elizabethan age was a litigious period, a fact explained by the substitution of litigation for violence against opponents, the expansion of commercial activities, and the growth of the land market. Indications are that between 1550 and 1625, cases before the Court of Requests and Star Chamber increased tenfold, before Common Pleas sixfold, and before King's Bench twofold. Lawsuits were brought between landlords and tenants, parsons and parishioners, husbands and wives, uncles and cousins, saints and sinners. It had become essential, averred Sir Humphrey Gilbert, for peers and gentlemen to "learne to be able to put their owne Case in law . . . for thorough the want thereof the beste are oftentymes subiecte to the direction of farre their *Inferiors*." In practice, the willingness to accept such advice grew, for admissions to the Inns of Court mushroomed, from forty a year at the beginning of the Tudor period to over two hundred at the end.[3]

The increase in litigation disturbed the government, hence in June 1600 Sir Thomas Egerton, the lord keeper, instructed judges to deal with "maintainers and abettors of causes and suites" as well as "sollicitors and pettifoggers." In 1584, Sir Christopher Hatton expressed concern about the legal resolution of marital disputes to William Chaderton, bishop of Chester, asserting that such suits were ungodly and discredited both parties, a matter of government interest when prominent citizens were involved. Litigation was preferable to violence, but it was better, he felt, to settle disputes personally and informally. When Chancery received cases involving relatives it pressed for arbitration rather than exacerbate family tensions in formal legal proceedings.[4]

The strain and expense of litigation was increased by the slowness of legal proceedings, the multitude of technical details, the possibility of switching from court to court, and for some, the necessity of traveling to distant London. In the major courts, cases could drag on for years if lawyers repeatedly introduced new motions, though suitors who deliberately delayed proceedings could be liable to recompense defendants. In Chancery, it normally took five years for a suit to pass through the various stages, but some cases lasted twenty to thirty years. A controversy between All Souls College, Oxford, and the Leighton family that began in the fifteenth century entailed disputes in various courts and was not settled finally until the seventeenth century. Those who sued in Chancery usually had to reckon on expenses ranging from £50 to £400. Even procuring legal advice on whether to sue could be expensive, though only a fraction of what an involved suit could run. Before Philip Gawdy sued Mrs. Wentworth in 1588, he obtained the advice of six counselors and then happily reported to his father that "I fynd my counsayle very good [and] cheape. . . . I thinke I shall wade the lawe better cheape then she will." The expense was compounded by the risk, with losses sometimes inducing the kind of bitterness expressed by a correspondent of Anthony Bacon, who claimed in 1594 that his case was "a faire presidente for al enheritances, how to trie them by 10 fooles, & 2 knaues." Those who were wrongfully sued also had reason to be bitter, especially if they were surprised to find themselves unjustly outlawed for debt. This engenderment of strife and legal expenses prompted reforming clergy to ask whether Christians ought to sue.[5]

Some guidance could be found in later Tudor biblical marginalia, particularly with reference to 1 Corinthians 6. Readers of the Geneva Bible were cautioned not to go to law desiring revenge, though the godly could in good conscience rely on a magistrate to defend their legal rights. The ideal, however, was for the godly to settle disputes among themselves out of court: "If ye so burne with desire to pleade, kepe a court among your selues, and make the least estemed your iudge: for it is moste easie to iudge betwene brethren." The Beza-Tomson marginalia similarly encouraged the godly to settle disputes within the church, where arbiters could decide cases on the basis of equity and good conscience. Legal disputes could be taken before Christian magistrates but never unholy men. Better to forgo one's rights, if declared, than commence proceedings in haste or out of a desire for vengeance. The Protestant marginalia sought to dampen but not prohibit recourse to litigation.[6]

With this position the Rheims annotators were essentially sympathetic, though they repudiated the Anabaptist position that all litigation is wrong. Catholics were urged to suffer patiently rather than rush into legal proceedings, particularly for small matters. Like the Protestants, they were advised to settle matters among themselves "brotherly and peacably." Never were they to sue each other before heathen or Protestant judges and magistrates, which was "very vnchristian." Vaux's catechism was less specific, but explained that those who initiated, counseled, or consented to unjust legal actions violated the eighth commandment. Catholics such as William Lord Vaux and Sir Thomas Tresham became embroiled in litigation, the former because of debts and disputed land inheritance and the latter because of arguments with tenants.[7]

Anglican reaction to litigation by Christians varied, with some, such as Jewel and Nowell, taking a positive approach. Although Jewel was dismayed that some Christians let a lawsuit create enmity between them, he remained convinced that judges were ministers of justice who sat in God's place. Those who sought redress at law were exhorted to proceed without malice, as if they were seeking counsel from a father. Because "the law is no breach of charity" but "the bond and knot to keep men in love," children could sue parents and subjects their sovereigns. Alexander Nowell saw nothing unchristian in litigation as long as vengeance was not the motivating factor. Other Anglicans, such as Babington, Sandys, and Wright, accepted litigation only as a last resort. For Sandys, it was better for a Christian to sustain tolerable harm than to take someone to court, and his response to the mounting litigation of the age was to slap heavy amercements on losers to discourage unjust suits. Although most Anglicans apparently were troubled by the mounting contentiousness, few were as overtly antagonistic as Whetstone, who deplored litigation because it ruined reputations, wasted time, dissipated money, and disrupted quiet living. Generally, however, most Anglican leaders recognized that some lawsuits were essential and that the courts were a vehicle of justice if not abused by excessive use.[8]

To this end, Anglicans formulated rules for legal action. Suits must never be undertaken in a vengeful spirit or without first exhausting alternate courses. Babington insisted that the poor must never be sued and that no suits be instigated if they channeled funds from poor relief. For Fleming, no litigation should be brought against the just. In general, suits were restricted to substantive matters and required treating a legal adversary with Christian love. Just cases, honest lawyers, and ample funds were prerequisites.[9]

In their attitude toward litigation, Puritans substantially agreed with Anglicans. Repeatedly Puritans admonished their followers not to go to law over trifles or until all other avenues had been exhausted. "Let thy neighbour be thy wardsman," counseled Gibbon, "and not the law: for he that will contend for euery trifle, shall make the Lawyer rich with his siluer, and himselfe poore by his suites." Besides financial involvement, lawsuits entailed risks of imprisonment and the potential for disruptiveness, so caution was mandatory, even if some losses had to be sustained to avoid litigation.[10]

The positive outlook on legal proceedings of Jewel and Nowell was essentially parallcled in Vaughan and Perkins, though both concurred with other Puritans in urging potential litigants to try alternative means first. Vaughan prohibited suits before Catholic or heretical judges, but suits before Protestants to achieve legal redress for reasonable causes accorded with divine law. Such adjudication was a means to security, for the weak who suffer silently "do abide continuall molestations, and liue in intolerable thraldome." Such advice contrasted with the typical exhortations to suffer rather than sue. The key to Vaughan's outlook was a conviction that the proper use of law brought men—as God intended—from savagery, ignorance, and vice to civility, knowledge, and virtue. Perkins pointed to the magistracy as God's ordinance, justifying the Christian's right to go to law and defend himself against substantial injury. It was also in accord with divine law (Acts 25:10) for a man falsely accused to defend himself before a judge, who sat in God's stead. "Courts of Justice, are the ordinance of God, in which it pleaseth him to testifie his presence, iustice, and goodnes; and vpon this ground, we shall be mooued to depart with our owne right, and to yeeld our selues, and all the right we haue, into the hands of God, in the vse of the meanes appointed." The increase in litigation did not daunt the faith of Perkins and Vaughan in the courts as divinely ordained channels of justice. Such positive views helped make it possible later for common lawyers to join with Puritans in reforming the old order.[11]

For those involved in litigation, the Puritans provided fuller guidelines than the Anglicans, with Perkins in particular explaining proper conduct. According to him, suits must be conducted in a "holy" manner, so as not to prejudice Christianity, which occurred when trust in God was lacking, trifling matters were disputed, and means to reconciliation were ignored. Litigation must not be undertaken in hate, but only in love and for the maintenance of peace in the state. From beginning to end, moderation must be the guide, hence all parties to a dispute must be willing to compromise their rights to achieve a just solution. Specifically

we must set down with our selues, lawfull and iust endes of our actions, not vniust and vnlawfull. These iust endes are; first, Gods glorie in the execution and manifestation of iustice: secondly, the honest defence of our owne right: thirdly, publike peace: fourthly, the amendment of disordered persons, and not the defamation or hurt of any man.

Defeats at law must be accepted as manifestations of divine justice. The principal rules of other Puritans included abstention from contentiousness, care not to discredit one's profession, the maintenance of love, the avoidance of delay, and the refusal to instigate suits to alter the original meaning of agreements. As in the case of business ethics, Puritans took more care than Anglicans to formulate principles of conduct, revealing a greater sensitivity to the implications of religious faith for social behavior.[12]

Separatists viewed the courts with some hostility, though they were willing to respect godly magistrates and members of the legal profession. In practice, however, Barrow thought Elizabethan courts, laws, judges, and lawyers were corrupt and best avoided by persons of good conscience. Ecclesiastical courts should be abolished and their jurisdiction in such matters as matrimony, sexual offenses, and testaments transferred to secular courts. To Separatists, the legal institutions of the state needed a thorough reformation no less than the church.[13]

The clergy periodically were drawn into the vortex of litigation, which must have exacerbated relations with the laity and diminished their effectiveness as social leaders, particularly when they were the instigators of suits. Of the 292 Norfolk clergy in the Puritan survey, five were accused of legal wrangling; they were the ministers at Blofield, Gillingham, Bedingham, Saxlingham, and Great Ellingham. Elsewhere, John White, the theologically ignorant vicar of Ramsey, Essex, reputedly troubled parishioners unjustly with legal matters in 1584, the same year that George Hesketh, rector of Halsall, Lancs., and a reputed lecher, sued ten parishioners for defamation. John Trendle, the Presbyterian rector of Ovington, Essex, was accused of harassing parishioners with suits in 1592, and Alexander Nowell was involved (more justifiably) in lengthy lawsuits to protect the interests of his stepchildren. In 1580 John Rolf, vicar of Rye, Sussex, was accused before the High Commission of "beinge a very lewd disposed person and a common disturber of the quiet and christian peace in our towne, by makinge himself an instrument of contention betweene party and partie, an enemye to our preacher and one that dispendith the frutes of our vicaredge in actions of common quarell to the detriment and offence of so many of the place." Cases such as this provoked Dering to complain of the ill examples set by parsons, vicars, and parishes suing each other "and all for the belly." In contrast, Richard Cheney, bishop of Gloucester, bragged to Cecil in 1568 that he had never spent two pence in a lawsuit. That such behavior was considered laudable suggests that many clergy engaged in legal proceedings, to the detriment of their reputations among the laity.[14]

Other clergy were detracted from their responsibilities when they were sued by the laity, sometimes unjustly. The Privy Council assisted Thomas Hickman, parson of Upton Scudamore, Wilts., in 1582 when his parishioners, peeved at his reforming endeavors, filed a bill of indictment against him in the quarter sessions on charges of "common barratrie." The preceding year the Council looked into the lawsuits filed against William Stanley, minister of Reed, Suffolk, by a Norwich man who wanted him deprived. In 1597, the rector of Little Wenham, Suffolk, was imprisoned in a legal battle with his wife, from whom he had been separated for nine years. The threat of such suits must have motivated Anglicans and Puritans to urge the resolution of quarrels before litigation.[15]

Ecclesiastical and secular leaders periodically joined forces to reduce legal wrangling. In 1597, for example, William Wright, parson of Waverton, Ches., sought assistance from the justices of the peace to persuade two men (one of whom was a gentleman) to cease suing each other, which offended their neighbors, and live together in Christian love. In Staffordshire, persons prone to litigation were cited before the quarter sessions. Troublesome cases went to the Privy Council and could end up in Star Chamber. In 1581 a Norfolk man was required by the Council to make restitution to those he had financially undone by his lawsuits. Considering the thousands of cases in Elizabethan courts, only a small minority culminated in plaintiffs being charged in quarter sessions, the Privy Council, or Star Chamber, so that such actions must have been largely ineffective as deterents to litigious disputants.[16]

To some degree, ministerial reformers were successful in spreading their ideas, but in practice their ideals often remained dead letters. An epitaph on Edward Stanley, earl of Derby, praised him as "no toyler in the lawe." Sir William Wentworth advised Thomas to avoid legal suits, even in good causes, because the expenses were substantial and the outcome uncertain. As a young man Sir William spent approximately £4,000 defending himself in suits instigated primarily by other gentry, and though he won, the memories were unpleasant. Litigation to protect an inheritance was justifiable, though in other cases, an apparent willingness to sue in a vengeful spirit was enough to restrain evil men. Wentworth was troubled less by the factiousness of litigation than its practical risks, such as the limitation of a lawyer's knowledge. "Manie tymes the lawiers tell yow what is lawe, butt they tell yow not what courtes of Equity your cause maie be brought into and ouerruled, litle to your creditt and gaine." Once a person was involved in a lawsuit, Wentworth thought it essential to ply judges and jury with gifts or food to secure their favor or at least neutrality. The best course was to stay out of litigation, if necessary by seeming to be a vengeful plaintiff, but always refraining from contentious feelings.[17]

Despite the exhortations, litigation burgeoned. The vicars choral in Chichester Cathedral were so disputatious that in 1598 they were admonished not to sue each other until the dean and chapter had heard their quarrels. Suits over lands and tithes were common among the aristocracy. Not even members of a family were immune; one of the most bitter legal battles pitted Robert Carey against his widowed sister-in-law over land in Suffolk. For some, such as the Hoskins family of Benister, lawsuits were a weapon to use frequently and proudly to keep tenants in subjection. Even the physician Dr. Simon Forman often engaged in legal battles, some of which set him at variance with his friends and cost him a good deal of money. It was becoming more common to know a man who "liveth contentiously with his neighbours and taketh al occasions to draw them into suits of law."[18]

Puritans were troubled about this, though their supporters were no strangers to the courts. Sir Walter Mildmay brought suit to recover the estates of his daughter-in-law, Grace, and Margaret Clifford, dowager countess of Cumberland, engaged in lengthy legal actions against Sir Francis Clifford on behalf of her daughter, Lady Anne Clifford. Sir Thomas Hoby sued those men in the Council of the North and Star Chamber who had responded to his hospitality with rude behavior and vandalism, but Sir Hugh Cholmley described him as "a troublesome, vexatious neighbour, . . . who having married a widow, the inheritor of all Hackness lordship, having a full purse, no children . . . , delighted to spend his money and time in suits." Like Hoby, Elizabeth Lady Russell protested (successfully) to Star Chamber about the unruly behavior of neighbors. Nevertheless, the idea of settling cases out of court to reduce contention was accepted in some Puritan circles. In 1592 Sir Francis Hastings appealed to the master of the Court of Requests to appoint a commissioner to decide a case involving several of his poor neighbors, though he seems to have been motivated primarily by the desire to spare them large legal expenses. The Dedham congregation admitted to communion only those who professed to live charitably with their neighbors, refraining from lawsuits until the minister and two godly neighbors endeavored to settle their disputes. Had similar action been undertaken in enough churches, formal litigation might not have grown so rapidly.

Such local efforts would hardly have sufficed for disputed conveyances and inheritances, but they might have been able to reduce litigation over tithes and landlord-tenant relations.[19]

In sum, most Anglican and Puritan authors encouraged their followers to go to law only as a last resort, and then in a spirit of love and never for trifling matters. The preferable course was to settle matters informally, perhaps through the agency of godly neighbors. Religious authors were disturbed about the effect of litigation on personal relationships, the church's reputation, the relief of the indigent, and the hardships on the poor who became involved in suits. Yet a small minority in each group—Jewel and Nowell among the Anglicans, and Vaughan and Perkins among the Puritans—took a positive view of legal action as a vehicle for the ministration of justice and the maintenance of a peaceful society. Only in the obvious care Puritans took to provide guidelines for litigants was there a perceptible difference between Anglicans and Puritans, which, again, reflects a greater Puritan awareness of the ramifications of religious faith for social behavior. Although laity of both persuasions recognized the risks in legal proceedings, neither these dangers nor the admonitions of clerical reformers normally restrained them from seeking redress in the courts.

(2) Lawyers and Christian Ethics

So Lawyers that wrest law, and matters prolong,
Their footesteps wyll appeere of makyng right wrong.

Anonymous[20]

The posterity of lawyers hath more flourished then that either of the clergy or citisens.

John Manningham[21]

Increased litigation was both a cause and a result of an increase in the number of lawyers. As prosperity spread through much of the Elizabethan period, people had money to hire lawyers and engage in legal action, though the economic difficulties of the 1590s brought a temporary respite in the burgeoning litigation. A Kentish lawyer perceptively remarked in this context that "the year is hard, everything dear, men spare their purses and go not to law." Generally the expansion of lawyers and litigants brought a continuation of the complaints of malfeasance—excessive fees, unnecessary litigation, bribery, and the prolongation of suits—that went back to the late medieval period and were reiterated by the Commonwealth Men.[22]

The extent to which these complaints were valid lies beyond the scope of this book, though abuses existed, often in high places, even if they were less frequent than alleged by contemporaries. An infamous offender was Sir Roger Manwood, lord chief baron of the Exchequer, who was suspended in 1591 after persistent accusations of fraud, corruption, and bribery. In less exalted circles, George Kempe, attorney for a Norwich goldsmith, made a false avowal in a land suit, jeopardizing his client's rights, and was ordered punished by the Privy Council in 1590. Other cases of alleged malfeasance by lawyers were brought before the Council, wherein complainants asserted unjust imprisonment or loss of money because of their actions. Attorneys also were charged before Star Chamber, as in the 1597 case in which Philip Trafford, a Staffordshire gentleman, accused the lawyer Edmund Lutton and others of maintaining frivolous suits in a land dispute; in this instance, the defendants countered in kind, accusing Trafford of being "greatlye gyven to Sute in lawe oftentymes without iust or good ground of sute." Too often we do not possess enough evidence to determine the merits of accusations against the lawyers. Still, it is instructive that Robert Hale (Matthew's father), who was called to the bar on 5 February 1594 and studied law at Lincoln's Inn, gave up law practice when he became convinced that the rules of pleading were dishonest. Many Elizabethans would have agreed with the views expressed in a dialogue by Richard Williams, asserting that too many lawyers abused the law for their own ends, taking cases to court unnecessarily and turning friends into enemies.[23]

In the main, the published views of the Anglican clergy toward lawyers were hostile. As with the friars of old, there were allegedly too many of them. In 1564 Thomas Bentham, bishop of Coventry and Lichfield, complained to the Privy Council that an excessive number of attorneys at the assizes and quarter sessions at Stafford breeded strife for the sake of profit. The general charge was common enough among Anglicans, who opined that much contention was deliberately fanned to benefit attorneys. Their critics suspected that lawyers deliberately misled clients by making them think their causes were just. "So long," said Wright, "as their clients continue in greasing their vnsatiable handes with *vnguentum rubrum,* they seeme to feele their matter, incourage them to proceede, and extolling their cause, as though the daie were already won, till they haue drawen all the money out of their purses, and the marow out of their bones: at last when all is gone, so as they [the clients] cease to feed them, . . . then waxe they colde as a stone, and finding one cauell or other, sende them home to agree amongst their neighbors: ah fooles, so they might haue done before." Lawyers were castigated for abusing the laws for their own ends, delaying justice, coveting profit, ruining the estates of the aristocracy, and ignoring the poor.[24]

A minority of Anglican authors defended attorneys. In a sermon before Elizabeth at Richmond in 1575, Richard Curteys, bishop of Chichester, expressed displeasure that lawyers were accused of defending bad causes, perverting justice, subordinating everything for gain, and obfuscating laws. Yet a year later, Curteys berated attorneys who used sophistry to give a good face to a bad cause, thereby perverting justice. Some dignity was attributed to the legal profession by John Woolton, shortly to become bishop of Exeter, when he described Adam before the fall as an excellent divine, philosopher, and lawyer.[25]

The Anglicans provided minimal guidelines for attorneys. They should possess ample learning, tender consciences, and concern for the poor, whose cases were to be handled without charge. It was unethical to serve disputing clients simultaneously and it was irreligious to win unrighteous causes or lose just ones. No client's cause was to be rejected if valid; rather, attorneys must act as their clients' servants.[26]

The views of the Anglican clergy were harmonious with the critical outlook of the laity, who manifested hostility to pettifoggery, delayed suits, and greedy attorneys. They were disenchanted with the law, seeing it twisted to oppress or fleece laymen. Whetstone, perpetually anxious for the gentry, was angered by lawyers who preyed on young gentlemen with heavy gambling losses, offering to sell their land at five-years' purchase. Mulcaster counseled lawyers to seek contentment by maintaining justice through the law rather than covetously pursuing remuneration. The best insight into lay attitudes to lawyers is Wentworth's advice to his son. Thomas' solicitor should be married, closemouthed, not prone to drinking, moderately well off, judicially intelligent, and not inclined to prolong or instigate suits for his own advantage. The lawyer should "haue speciall charge neuer to giue creditt to anie atturney in matters of waight as error upon iudgment against yow or such lyke, for they be unlerned and careles and make a gaine howsoeuer yow lose, but rather build upon the considerate iudgment of a good councellor." Whereas the laity in the Elizabethan period were chary of pettifoggers and unscrupulous attorneys, they did not approach the depth of hostility manifested in the late 1640s and 1650s.[27]

Puritans likewise deplored abuses in the legal profession, including high fees, superfluous litigation, pettifoggery, and pomp. Attorneys, grouched Stubbes, "goe rufling in their silks, veluets and chaines of Gold, they build gorgeous howses, sumptuous edefices, and stately turrets: they keep a port like mightie potentates, they haue bands and retinewes of men attendant vppon them daylie, they purchase castels & towers, Lands and Lordships, and what not?" Some Puritans feared that lawyers used unjust gains to vault ahead in the social hierarchy, ceasing to be modest servants of the commonwealth and aspiring to live in an aristocratic manner. One of the most prevalent claims made against attorneys by Puritans was that they were greedy, beggaring others in their quest to become gentlemen. Their principle method of doing this—the other major complaint of the Puritans—was by sophistry, the ability "to coyne quirkes & quiddities, . . . to hammer clauses, and prouisoes to circumuent and deceyue one another," dragging out cases until a client's resourses were exhausted. Simplicity in religion carried over into a revulsion against sophistry in law. [28]

Puritan criticisms extended to other practices of attorneys. Puritans had no sympathy for the modern principle that even the guilty deserve the best possible defense, for they berated lawyers who defended the guilty as dishonest. Some question was raised about the honesty of lawyers toward clients (and vice versa), particulary in regard to weak suits and prolonged cases. Like the Anglicans, they were suspicious of the delay of justice occasioned by burgeoning litigation, feeling that lawyers used evasive tactics and legal maneuvers to prolong cases rather than achieve justice. The rather open practice of bribery in the Elizabethan system of justice also brought opprobrium on the lawyers. Vaughan, a defender of the legal profession, acknowledged these abuses and some attorneys' lack of legal skills. [29]

Such criticisms notwithstanding, a number of Puritans defended honest lawyers. Respect was binding under the fifth commandment, according to Robert Allen, on the grounds that the faithful counselor acts as a father in defending his client's estate or rights. The most substantial Puritan defense of lawyers was propounded by William Vaughan, who observed that unlearned persons could not satisfactorily represent their causes before a judge without legal assistance, especially in cases where the interpretation of the law was not straightforward. While Vaughan acknowledged that some lawyers were unscrupulous and prolonged cases, he insisted that many were honest, and that clients were sometimes responsible for delayed suits and the provision of erroneous information to their attorneys. Vaughan spoke from personal experience, for he was indebted to a lawyer who "deliuered me from a greedy Informer, who through his subtiltie and my simplicitie, had condemned me in a hundred marks more than I was worth." In short, Puritans were no more willing than Anglicans to overthrow the lawyers and rely on a system where judges determined the merits of a case based on the personal representations of a plaintiff and a defendant. Anglican and Puritan hostility to the unethical and unprofessional conduct of some lawyers did not lead them to the radicalism that erupted in the mid-Stuart era.[30]

Like most Anglicans, the Puritans enunciated qualities that a good lawyer should possess, including diligence in pursuing his cases, equity in serving his clients, the refusal of unjust suits, and concern for the poor, widows, and orphans. Clients pursuing litigious suits must be dissuaded and fees kept reasonable. Attorneys whose absenses caused clients to lose cases must return the fees and compensate for the losses, and the causes of poor clients must not be betrayed for financial gain. In essence, "the Lawyer hee must deale iustly, and giue euery man his owne: for he is the liuing lande marke, that limiteth men their inheritance, that pointeth out their right and title, howe farre it goeth, and so breaketh controuersie, and telleth euery one in his doubtfull cause, where his clayme and title lieth, what lawe and equitie will beare him in, and where it wil forsake him." The Puritans did not expect lawyers to do anything more than deal honestly with clients, dissuade unnecessary suits, and assist the socially weak. By refraining from wholesale criticism of the legal profession, they left the door open for the alliance between common lawyers and Puritans in the early seventeenth century.[31]

Thus Anglicans and Puritans did not differ in their attitude towards attorneys. There is no question about their dissatisfaction with prevailing fees, legal delays, pettifoggery, superfluous litigation, and bribery, yet adherents of both groups cautioned against condemning all attorneys because of the abuses of some. Where possible, disputes were to be settled through the mediation of the godly, but lawyers were essential in some cases, particularly the more complex ones involving property transactions and inheritance. Anglicans and Puritans alike set forth the basic principles to which they expected lawyers to adhere, with the focus on devotion to justice, responsibility to clients, and concern for the indigent. These opinions were not revolutionary.

(3) The Conduct of Judges

The lawiers are the foulers, the iudge the net, and the poore clients the birds.

Leonard Wright[32]

Heare eache man's cause as thoh he wer in wealth thine equall mate.

Anonymous[33]

For many Elizabethan lawyers, the pinnacle of professional ambition was to be appointed a serjeant at law and ultimately a judge. In this quest, political patronage often was important, so that successful appointees owed favor to patrons and were open to bribery and other pressure. In the case of commissions of the peace, where justices often had little or no formal training, short periods of service, local political pressures, and lack of remuneration rendered some justices subject to bribery and favoritism. In a society where bribery for offices and favors was the order of the day, and government officials shamelessly counseled their proferring and receipt, the preservation of the judicial system from this abuse was impossible.

Given the nature of the Elizabethan judicial system, the line between acceptable and corrupt judicial behavior was blurred. When parties involved in legal proceedings suspected juries might find against them because of bias or other prejudice, they often persuaded persons of eminence to contact the justices on their behalf. Such interference in the judicial process fostered gross abuse, as exemplified when Robert Lord Rich used his beautiful wife Penelope to influence the judges when his estates were threatened by a lawsuit. Matters were made worse by the common acceptance of unofficial gratuities or bribes by the judges' legal clerks, a practice that directly paralleled the offering of such funds to servants of great courtiers to gain access to their masters and resultant favors. When Hatton fired his secretary, Samuel Cox, in 1584 for the receipt of such money, Cox alleged that "there liveth not so grave nor so severe a Judge in England, but he alloweth his poor Clerk under him, even in the expedition of matters of greatest justice, to take any reasonable consideration that should be offered him by any man for his pains and travail." The prevalence of bribery was its justification in the judicial process.[34]

Some reaction to judicial corruption was expressed in scriptural marginalia. Although judges were believed to receive authority from God and perform his work in defending the innocent and punishing the guilty, a warning was recorded as early as 1539 (in the Taverner Bible) that judges must not take bribes. In 1568, the Bishops' Bible included a strong condemnation of prince and judges alike for preventing justice by allowing the rich and powerful to escape punishment for grievous crimes by bribery. The Geneva marginalia, which devoted substantial attention to judges and other magistrates, averred that their authority is divinely bestowed for the maintenance of justice and the punishment of vice. Failure to do so results in a divine plague on the land, decimating its glory and wealth. It is the responsibility of judges and magistrates to "constantly follow the tenor of the Lawe, and in nothing decline from iustice," yet some are swayed by the wealthy more than justice. These men violate their vocational responsibility and bring divine vengeance on themselves, whereas godly judges render decisions solely in accord with divine will. To fulfill their responsibilities, judges need divine assistance, for "except God giue iudges vnderstanding, the impudencie of the trespacer shal ouerthrowe ye just cause of the innocent." The Geneva annotators placed the judges squarely in the tradition of the godly magistrate, who rules with divine assistance and in accord with divine law, and who therefore dissociates himself from all corrupt behavior, including bribes and the perversion of justice. The prevalence of judicial corruption is no justification for it. [35]

As with the lawyers, Anglicans lashed out against injustice and corrupt dealing on the judicial bench. Judges were accused of taking bribes from the wealthy, wreaking vengeance on their enemies, meting out sentences in ignorance, having more respect of persons and personal glory than righteous judgment, and trying cases in which they had been involved as lawyers. "Iudges harme, where helpe they ought to worke," complained Whetstone. In some courts, allegedly neither law nor conscience prevailed, whereas others had one untempered by the other. The devices of clerks, bailiffs, and summoners to delay justice and increase fees were denounced. In sharp contrast to these blasts against the judicial bench and its subordinate officers, Bishop Curteys preached before the queen in defense of judges as well as lawyers, indicating his displeasure with accusations that judges perverted justice for monetary gain and whimsically expounded laws. Once again, it was a matter of discretion rather than indiscriminate castigation of the entire bench. [36]

A rather full code of conduct for judges was propounded by Sandys in his sermons. Those in authority must judge rightly, always meting out justice tempered with mercy. There must be no bribery, no deviation from equity out of commiseration, and no respect of persons. "For if laws be not executed without respect of person, if sin be not kept in order, it will shake the state, all will be in an uproar, no man shall be master of his own, or in any safety of his life." Not even the mighty are to be spared the hand of justice, for their offenses are examples that common folk will emulate unless properly punished. In rendering judgment, Sandys exhorted judges to beware of swiftness as much as dilatoriness; once the issues are clear, further pleading must cease and the sentence must be pronounced. It was advice that Anglican critics could accept, for it was based on justice, mercy, equity, and honesty.[37]

Testimony that these ideals were not realized in judicial practice appears in Wentworth's advice to his son. Openly recognizing the importance of securing the favor of judges prior to a trial, Wentworth recommended that if a judge of the assize dwelled locally, "forgett not to present him yearly in discrete sortt" or visit him at his home in a humble and flattering manner. If the judges sit in any town where Thomas is the principal lord, he must acknowledge his duty to them and give them wine and sugar, "for otherwise it wilbe yll taken and remembered." If he became involved in a suit or testified for a friend, Thomas was exhorted to meet the justices on the highway, "for they loue to be waited on"' Here, then, was recognition of judicial reality, wherein the aristocracy had to demonstrate subservience to judges and ply them with goods and favors to obtain reasonable treatment of their cases. Not only was this to be done when suits were pending, but regularly, as a form of legal insurance. From the practical standpoint it was less expensive to purchase judicial favor with gifts and flattery than to risk, in a litigious age, loss of property or possessions by the decision of a hostile judge.[38]

In general, Puritans echoed the complaints of Anglicans regarding the judicial bench, though the Puritan outcry against judges who took bribes was noticeably greater. The Puritans rebuked judges who delayed justice, prolonged sentencing, respected persons, ruled rashly or maliciously, and lacked learning. Lesser judicial officials who accepted bribes, acted deceitfully, or engaged in extortion were castigated too. Like the Anglicans, Puritans had a standard of conduct to which they wanted judges to adhere. Judges must defend widows and orphans, repudiate bribes, and administer justice to all "without any kinde of affection, vaine-pitie, or fauour, lest that, they prying into your liues, in stead of honor, you be branded in the forehead with the perpetuall note of infamie." Vaughan, who expressed this concern with the maintenance of honor, wanted the appointment of judges restricted to mature men, ripe in judgment and experience, with grave countenances, good reputations among the common folk, and preferably aristocratic lineage. In rendering judgment, he preferred that they suffer the guilty to go unpunished rather than condemn the innocent, but he also opposed the remission of fines or penalties unless the aggrieved parties were satisfied. Aside from their more pronounced concern with bribery, Puritans acquiesced in the

Anglican assessment of judicial behavior and a standard of conduct for judges.[39]

About the time Thomas Lodge converted to Catholicism c. 1596, he wrote about the behavior of judges in a work dedicated to Sir John Fortescue, chancellor of the Exchequer. His views complemented those of Anglicans and Puritans. He expected judges to be mild in their conversation and measured in their speech, "for in them of such authoritie the people doe many times take more griefe with a word, then in others with the stroake of a sword." No judge must accept bribes, be deceived with words, succumb to threats, be swayed by pleas, or be overcome by pity. In an age when punishment was often harsh, the hostility of some reformers to lenity on the judicial bench underscores the conviction that only harsh penalties were thought to be deterrents to crime.[40]

In sum, Anglican and Puritan critics abhorred the unethical and unprofessional behavior on the judicial bench and among subordinate officials, chiefly bribery, delay of justice, and respect for persons. Puritans distinguished themselves only in their more pronounced censure of bribery, which indicates a heightened sensitivity about moral corruption, a Puritan tendency observable in other spheres of social activity. Writers of both persuasions exhorted judges to act with equity, honesty, justice, and mercy (though not to the point of lenity), and to care for widows and orphans. Perturbation over abuses in the Elizabethan judicial system did not lead reformers of either camp to the sort of antiprofessionalism that developed in the 1640s and 1650s.

(4) Justice and the Poor

This course would make the learned Lawyers blest,
If of poor men (they tooke no fee at all).

Thomas Churchyard[41]

The pore & nedy man hanged is some tyme
When the rycher skapeth, for a greater cryme.

Edward More[42]

The concern of Anglicans and Puritans for the plight of the poor extended to their involvement in the judicial system. It was part of a magistrate's duty, according to Anglicans, to manifest special care in legal matters for the socially oppressed, for they are defenseless "and every man goeth over where the hedge is lowest." Judges were exhorted to prevent the poor from being abused in the courts or in society, and to stop punishing the poor while allowing the wealthy to go free. Pressure too was placed on attorneys to meet the needs of the poor. "The Lorde," opined Richard Lewes in a sermon at Paul's Cross in 1594, "hath made you (ye learned Lawiers) patrons of the poore, & ye cal them clients: take heed that ye bereave not poore *Iacob* of his right." To Sandys, this meant not merely reducing legal fees for the poor but serving them without charge as necessary. Pilkington encouraged lawyers, courtiers, and other important men to heed poor suitors, who are divinely sent to them. Even laymen had responsibilities toward the poor in the legal context. Litigation must not be initiated if funds are diverted from poor relief. In view of the delays and expenses in legal proceedings, the poor must not be sued, even if this restraint entails personal losses. Due regard for the consequences of legal action involving the poor was important to Anglicans.[43]

With this opinion, the Puritans fundamentally agreed. Judges were admonished to cease oppressing the poor in courts and stop being swayed by bribes, affection for persons of substance, and malice toward the indigent. Lawyers were warned not to betray poor clients for monetary considerations or draw out their cases and further impoverish them. "If percase one of our fine-headed lawyers vouchsafe to take his cause in hand, he followeth it slowly, and in a dozen sheetes not hauing eight lines on euery side, hee layeth downe such friuolous and disguised contradictions and replications, that his suites shall hang seuen yeeres; yea, and perhaps a dozen yeeres . . . before they bee brought to any perfection, & vntill the poore client become farre behind hand." There was a strong feeling among Puritans that lawyers were fleecing the poor, mishandling their cases, and leaving them no legal redress. Although they defended the lawyers, the Puritans were troubled by their behavior to the poor. Not only were attorneys urged to treat them with greater care through minimal fees or free service and increased attention, but lawyers also were asked to devote a larger share of their income to poor relief.[44]

Like the Anglicans, Puritans extended the problem of the poor in the legal system to plaintiffs of substance. Here the complaints had a double thrust, condemning both suits against the poor and the delay of justice to harm poor plaintiffs. The wealthy who used lawyers to hinder the poor's quest for justice were denounced. Puritan indignation was particularly aroused by drawing out litigation to enable men of means to triumph over the poor through the use of "quirkes and quiddities coyned in the deceitfull mint of mannes braine." Truth as well as social justice was violated when the judicial system decided litigation "by the weight of the purse" rather than the validity of a cause. Thus Puritans joined Anglicans in calling on persons of means to respect the rights and needs of the poor and to refrain from taking them to court.[45]

This concern was reflected in Elizabethan verse, which helped spread the belief that oppression of the poor in the courts must cease. The anonymous author of *A Mournfull Dittie on the Death of Certaine Iudges and Iustices of the Peace* (1590) called on judges and lawyers to deal uprightly with every poor man's cause, neither wresting the laws to undermine him nor imposing unconscionable fees. It was Churchyard's desire to see attorneys redress wrongs done to the poor, which would benefit the peace of the commonwealth.

> When good cheap law, poore silly soules do find,
> The Court is not long troubled with complaints.[46]

Anglican and Puritan expostulations were perhaps more applicable to persons of modest means than to the genuinely poor, for the complete or partial remission of court fees was normally available to the indigent. Developments in Chancery illustrate this. According to 11 Henry VII, c. 12, the chancellor was empowered to grant persons unable to afford legal proceedings both original writs and writs of subpoena as well as counsel without charge as long as their cases appeared to be just. Those sueing *in forma pauperis* grew in numbers until, by 1588, Hatton had to act to reduce unnecessary suits. Gradually it became necessary to whip plaintiffs who sued *in forma pauperis* but did not establish a good cause. Some dissatisfaction developed with respect to its use, as reflected in Hake's complaint:

> A Fee of *Forma pauperis*?
> no no it hath no sent.
> Such formall Fees finde smal reliefe
> they buy no lande ne rent.

In practice, Chancery procedures were such that the poor, even with legal assistance, were not an equal match for wealthy individuals whose lawyers used motions and other legal devices effectively and had funds to pay clerks to seek precedents. Humbler folk with less experience in legal matters were more susceptible to the psychological as well as the financial pressures of litigation. Thus whereas the complaints of Anglicans and Puritans were somewhat exaggerated, the poor were at a disadvantage in legal proceedings, even with the ability to sue *in forma pauperis*, particularly when legal proceedings required absence from wage-earning positions.[47]

Expense also was a factor that worked against the poor in ecclesiastical courts, though procedures were sometimes adjusted to reduce costs for the needy. In diocesan visitations, it was customary to remit cases involving the poor for local examination. Because the accused had to pay the expenses of compurgators, the poor were sometimes permitted to purge themselves solely by means of a personal oath. In Lancashire, litigants used the consistorial courts frequently despite the rather onerous costs. A tithe case in 1568-69 cost the rector of Halsall £1 15s. in court fees, 15s. in proctorial fees, and £2 1s. 7d. in travel expenses. At a time (1597) when farm laborers made only £1 5s. *p.a.*, a testamentary case cost 14s. 11d. Undoubtedly many across England were like the Eccleston man who, in 1569, "hath paid to the parson the like tithe now in demand because he would, being a poor man, avoid the suit of law." Ironically, ecclesiastical courts presented financial barriers to justice for the poor at the very time Anglican and Puritan critics deplored a similar problem in the secular courts. Attorneys exhorted to tailor their fees or donate their time to the poor must have been resentful that justice in ecclesiastical courts did not come cheaply, even for the needy. This situation may have been a factor in bringing about the alliance between common lawyers and Puritans in the early seventeenth century.[48]

Apart from Chancery and Requests, in cases of merit, the poor periodically obtained relief through the Privy Council. In 1576 the Council ordered two justices of the peace to work out an equitable solution to the complaint of a man too poor to afford legal proceedings against Robert, second Lord Rich. In 1579, the Council ordered the justices to hear a suit in the next assize in which the defendant used delaying tactics to dissuade a poor plaintiff. The Council in 1588 ordered legal proceedings involving a man admitted *in forma pauperis* held in Wiltshire instead of the Exchequer in London because of the man's poverty and the ages of his witnesses. When Edmund Knyvett, gentleman, and Francis Warner, a grocer, sued a poor man in 1589 in a manner that was "verie disorderlie, indirectlie and contrarie to the accustomed course of lawe," the Council ordered two knights to adjudicate the case. The same year the Council intervened on behalf of the people of Oxwick, Norfolk, who were too poor to sue for recovery of their commons, which had been enclosed by the gentleman Thomas Basham. The Council was also sympathetic to the case of a poor woman in 1590 who was vexed by two men using "daily suits and sundrie imprisonments purposely to get from her a small tenement and poore livinge." In a similar case the same year, the Council directed four esquires to examine the complaint of an Upton widow without sufficient funds to prosecute a gentleman who had evicted her from her copyhold. These and comparable actions by the Council reveal a desire in leading lay circles to achieve justice for the poor; this care kept alive an aristocratic tradition with medieval origins that dovetailed with the concerns of Anglican and Puritan reformers.[49]

This aristocratic tradition also was maintained by some individuals. A case in point occurred in 1602, when Sir Walter Raleigh complained to the justices of assize about John Meere, bailiff of the Liberty of Sherborne, who was a plaintiff in a number of suits. According to Raleigh, "he vexeth so many poor men that have not any means to wage law but are driven to sell their poor implements to defend themselves, and the more to undo these poor creatures he sues them both in the Starchamber, Exchequer, and at the assizes for one matter, pleading a privilege in the Exchequer because he oweth the Queen money for a fine set on him in Starchamber for knavery." To seek justice for the poor in such cases not only continued the aristocratic tradition but increased the popularity and reputation of the great men in the countryside.[50]

Anglicans and Puritans, then, had ample reason to express concern over the plight of the poor in the judicial system. That this system did not fully meet the demands of justice was recognized by the Privy Council, and others who acted alone to assist those unable to afford traditional litigation. Not even the right to sue *in forma pauperis*, as valuable as it was, provided the poor with an opportunity to achieve an equitable solution to their grievances, hence Anglican and Puritan reformers pressed for greater social consciousness on the part of judges, lawyers, and potential litigants. The principal abuses they abhorred were bribery, respect of persons, and delay of justice.

(5) Demands for Legal Reform

It was a thing not to be done suddenly nor at one Parliament, nor scarce a whole year would suffice to purge the Statute-Book and lessen the Volume of Laws, being so many in number, that neither Common People can practise them, nor the Lawyer sufficiently understand them.

Sir Francis Bacon[51]

Where there ariseth small good by innouations of lawes, it is an euill thing.

William Vaughan[52]

In the Elizabethan period, demands for legal reform reflected the tradition of the Commonwealth Men, who pressed for changes in the administration of the law. The reform most often demanded was the expediting of justice. Even the marginalia of the Geneva and Bishops' Bibles proclaimed that where justice is delayed, sin reigns. The despair of litigants was expressed in Hake's verse:

> I am forlorne
> My sute thus long depended hath:
> The Lawe is on my syde,
> And yet in harde delayes I lye
> true Judgement to abyde.

In the period 1592 to 1637, simple defamation cases in consistorial courts took an average of nine months from the time of the slander to sentencing, whereas tithe cases typically took two years. Serious cases could drag on for years and multiply into a series of related suits. Henry Lord Berkeley's judicial dispute over tithes with Thomas Throckmorton included thirteen bills in Star Chamber, twelve in Queen's Bench and Common Pleas, and many others in Chancery, assizes, and quarter sessions. The barrister John Manningham complained in 1602 that "the abuse of the Statute for reforming errors in the King's Bench, &c. hath frayed the clients from their suites, when they see they can haue noe judgment certaine or speedy." Many were convinced that justice would be better served if cases could be expedited, but no agreement could be reached on the means to achieve this.[53]

Generally it was believed that justice could be rendered more expeditiously by deciding more cases in the shires or restricting the courts in which an attorney could practice. Stubbes, an advocate of the former plan, proposed that men of discretion be appointed in each county and delegated sufficient authority to decide all local cases. Under normal circumstances, he saw no reason for litigants to leave their counties, and virtually never would they need to use the London courts. This opinion was an early manifestation of the theme of decentralization propounded in the 1650s. An alternate solution was proposed to Burghley in 1585 by Francis Alford, who advocated that counsels should be restricted to practice in one court alone, halting the tendency of lawyers to move from bar to bar, causing delays. Samuel Bird thought justice could be expedited if every peer and perhaps even substantial gentlemen maintained lawyers in their houses to adjudicate disputes involving tenants, as, he claimed, John de Vere, earl of Oxford, formerly did. In contrast, Robert Horne, bishop of Winchester, thought the courts themselves had to be reformed, but he had no expectation that this could be accomplished and told Cecil as much in 1570.[54]

In the absence of an agreed method to expedite justice, the Privy Council acted in an *ad hoc* manner to remedy some of the worst abuses, and the government also sought to improve legal procedures in the judicial system. In 1575, the Council ordered the justices of assize in Lancashire to hear a case without further unreasonable delays, and in 1587 they demanded an end to postponements in a Queen's Bench case. After two litigants had disputed the goods of Arthur Carter, late provost marshal of Munster, for nine years in Exchequer and Common Pleas, the Council demanded that a final verdict be rendered by a panel of two justices of Common Pleas and two barons of the Exchequer, a pair of each to be nominated by each litigant. When a Southampton man complained that Walter Lambert, a gentleman, had unjustly prolonged debt proceedings against him for four years in various courts, the Council insisted on a speedy resolution. In 1589, the Council prodded the justices of Common Pleas to hear and decide a pending case involving the conduct of the overseers of a will. Writs of error could be used with effect to delay payment of a legal judgment, and in 1590 the Council ordered the justices of Queen's Bench to resolve a case where such writs had been used three times. Although the Council acted in these and other cases, in hundreds of others litigants must have found no relief from undue delays. Intervention by the Council was a convenient remedy in flagrant cases but by no means a universal workable solution.[55]

The barbarity of some punishments provoked little concern for reform, owing at least in part to the maintenance of the distinction in punishment between aristocracy and commoners. The Elizabethan age had no martyr comparable to William Prynne. John Gerard complained about the treatment of Catholics, but more in the context of confessional propaganda than legal reform. He wrote disapprovingly of the imprisonment in 1594 of his servant, Richard Fulwood, in Bridewell, where he had a diet of bread and lived in a vermin-filled cell with an open pail for excrement and no bed, being forced to sleep in a sitting posture on a window ledge. In the same year, Gerard complained that two Catholics were hung for three hours with their arms pinned in iron rings, distending their limbs and causing excruciating pain. Gerard himself was subjected to physical torture in the Tower in 1597. He seems to have been troubled more that Catholics were suffering than by the nature of the punishment, though he indicated revulsion towards the treatment of people who refused to plead in capital cases and were "laid on their back on a sharp stone and a heavy weight placed on their chest until life is crushed out of them." For the most part, however, demands for legal reform did not deal with the suppression of barbarous punishments.[56]

Scattered proposals for other reforms were made, most of which involved the suppression of unethical practices such as bribery, or better execution of the laws. In Sandys' judgment, justice could be better achieved by terminating "evil pleas, and . . . causeless controversies" as well as bribery, extortion, and partiality. Foreshadowing reforms several centuries in the future, John Barker thought that too many humble folk were cast in prison for excessive periods after committing minor offenses, thereby losing what little they owned. Nevertheless, Vaughan probably was typical of many legal conservatives when he argued that it was better to tolerate existing legal imperfections than to risk a lessening of respect for the law by too many alterations.[57]

One of the most far-reaching proposals for reform foreshadowed ideas advanced in the Parliament of Saints in 1653. Barrow asserted that the laws of England should be made conformable to the Mosaic Law, in the absence of which existing laws were often ungodly and unjust. He called for capital punishment for those convicted of blasphemy, open adultery, disobedience to parents, incest, and homicide, but not theft. He was angered by the execution of thieves and the application of severe punishment to their accessories, including those who purchased or otherwise received stolen goods. It was not necessary, he conceded, to apply the entire Mosaic code, for the ceremonial law was abrogated, but it was mandatory for every prince to govern in total accord with "the judgementes due and set downe by God for the transgression of the moral law." In spirit, these proposals were evocative of Calvin's Geneva.[58]

Advocates of reform in Parliament addressed the problem of improving the administration of justice, though not always successfully. Eight acts were passed to expedite justice and reduce unnecessary delays, the first of which came in the 1566 Parliament. One act (8 Eliz. I, c. 2) provided that in cases involving delay, discontinuance, or nonsuit, a defendant could recover his expenses from a plaintiff in Queen's Bench, the courts of the City of London, and other local courts. Moreover those who arrested someone in the name of a fictitious plaintiff were liable to six months' imprisonment and treble damages. A second act of this Parliament (8 Eliz. I, c. 5) determined that decisions in civil and marine cases handed down in Chancery or by commissioners appointed by the crown were final, thus reducing lengthy suits and considerable expenses. Two further bills, one to reduce delays stemming from demurrers and another (initiated in the Lords) to crack down on fraudulent gifts in bankruptcy cases, failed to become law.[59]

Legal reformers were frustrated in the next three Parliaments, despite demands for improvements. After considerable debate, the Commons in 1572 passed and sent to the Lords a bill to reduce delays at common law, but the Lords failed to approve it in the short time before Elizabeth prorogued and ultimately dissolved this Parliament. The 1576 Parliament considered bills involving the taking of bail in the court of Common Pleas, trial by jury, and (in a Lord's bill) unjust and slanderous suits, but none of these became law. Nor did a bill for "more indifferent" trial by juries, which was rejected on the third reading by Commons in 1581.[60]

The reformers were more successful in 1584-85. To reduce delays and expenses arising from the excessive use of writs of error, an act (27 Eliz. I, c. 5) was passed providing that once a demurrer was entered, a judge had to pronounce judgment, regardless of errors in pleading or process. Such judgments could not be reversed by writ of error for defects in pleading or process. The act excluded murder, treason, and felony cases. A second act (27 Eliz. I, c. 6) of this Parliament raised the qualification for jurors from 40s. freehold to £4, on the grounds that abler persons had not been serving, and the humble folk were least able to determine disputed cases. The same Parliament approved an act (27 Eliz. I, c. 8) to reduce delays in redressing allegedly erroneous judgments rendered in Queen's Bench. Normally such decisions were reversible only in Parliament, but henceforth in specified cases (e.g., debt, trespass, and eviction, except when the queen was a party) the person against whom the judgment was issued was given the option of suing for a writ of error in Chancery, which, if granted, provided for the case to be heard in Exchequer Chamber before two justices each from Common Pleas and Queen's Bench, and two barons of the Exchequer.[61]

The latter act led to some unforeseen problems, occasioned by the presence of less than six justices in Exchequer Chamber to hear some cases. Because this eventuality provided grounds on which to ask for a discontinuance, further confusing the quest for justice, the 1589 Parliament enacted a law (in 31 Eliz. I, c. 1) that as long as three justices were present, writs of error could be continued, but no judgment rendered. Likewise, the absence of the lord chancellor or treasurer to determine possible error in an Exchequer case no longer provided grounds for discontinuance, though both had to be present to give judgment.[62]

In the queen's last Parliament, the reformers focused attention once more on reducing unnecessary expenses, delays, and frivolous suits. One act (43 Eliz. I, c. 5) required that writs removing cases from inferior courts to Westminster be served before the jury came to the lower court. Defendants had been withholding such writs as long as possible to increase the expense of plaintiffs. In an attempt to handle more of the minor matters locally, a second act (43 Eliz. I, c. 6) cracked down on the issuing of summons requiring cases to be heard at Westminster.[63]

The passage of these acts reflected the agreement of the majority of the political nation with the Anglican and Puritan advocates of reform. Most of the parliamentary measures were intended to expedite justice, curtail legal costs, and enhance the rendering of justice—the precise objectives of those Anglicans and Puritans who called for reform. The one area where Puritans in particular had demanded changes but where no real parliamentary reform occurred was bribery. This abuse was so engrained in society, particularly at the upper levels, that no enthusiasm could be aroused for substantive legislation to eliminate its use in legal affairs. That Parliament showed so little interest in curtailing bribery undoubtedly accounts for the continuing Puritan concern. The Elizabethan period witnesses neither the intensity nor the extremity of the demands for legal reform advanced in the mid-seventeenth century, though already clerical and parliamentary reformers were distressed at the increasing centralization of justice at Westminster (with its attendant delays and expense) and began pressing for greater determination of justice in the provinces. The failure to reverse this trend by 1640 fueled the fires stoked by the radical reformers.

(6) The Attack on the Ecclesiastical Courts

He that will wade further herein, shall enter into a sea of poperie, and shall see the decaye of Religion and godlinesse.

Anthony Gilby[64]

Causes ar[e] not determined by the Word of God, but by their popish canons and customs.

Henry Barrow[65]

The second basic area in which demands were made for legal reform involved the ecclesiastical courts. Although the most stringent criticism came from radical Protestants, attacks came from other sources as well, particularly in Parliament. The 1563 Parliament imposed stricter controls on the execution of the writ *de excommunicato capiendo,* requiring that the cause of excommunication be specified in the *significavit.* In 1585, an attempt was made to pass a bill to reduce fees in ecclesiastical courts, which had been rising despite a regulatory statute (21 Henry VIII, c. 5), but because it concerned as well the jurisdiction of these courts, Elizabeth blocked its passage. As criticism of ecclesiastical courts intensified in the Parliaments of 1586, 1589, and 1593, Elizabeth ordered Whitgift to investigate conditions in the province of Canterbury. In 1597, another bill to reduce fees and exactions in church courts was introduced in Commons, probably by Henry Finch and his Puritan colleagues. To an opponent, this bill was "a device of some such as seek to overthrow the ecclesiastical government and to erect the presbytery and new platform of popular government." The bishops defended the higher fees as necessary in an inflationary economy, but Whitgift found it advisable to issue a revised schedule of fees in Convocation. The 1597 Parliament also accused the ecclesiastical courts of punishing small offenses by the humble while overlooking greater sins in persons of means. The mounting hostility prompted Whitgift to warn ecclesiastical officials to use greater circumspection lest the church courts be swept away. When the critics again blasted the courts in the 1601 Parliament, Whitgift dispatched two circular letters to his bishops, expressing anxiety about the commutation of penance, the excessive numbers of apparitors and petty summoners, and the vexation of subjects by holding church courts too often, a costly practice for churchwardens.[66]

Some of the prelates were, like Whitgift, sensitive to the need for reforms in the ecclesiastical courts and instituted corrective action. In 1560, Parker ordered his chancellor, Thomas Yale, to eliminate frivolous matters and terminate unnecessary delays. Although admitting that the people were oppressed with continual visitations and immoderate exactions, he admonished those "divers malicious persons [who] . . . do surmise untrue griefs and injuries to be done to them by their bishops and other ordinaries, and thereupon do appeal and get from you [the chancellor] inhibitions and citations, to the great vexation . . . both of their ordinaries, and also of their neighbours, the Queen's Majesty's poor subjects, and especially in causes of correction and reformation of their evil lives and manners." In short, procedural reforms must result in the effective prosecution of the guilty as well as a cessation of abuses.[67]

Prelatical interest in the reform of church courts was reflected in visitation articles. Those issued by Grindal in 1576 for the cathedrals and collegiate churches in the province of Canterbury asked if bishops, chancellors, commissaries, and other officers ministered justice indifferently to all subjects and punished vice and public crimes with appropriate penalties, shunning respect of persons and corrupt commutations. Herbert Westfaling's 1586 articles for the diocese of Hereford inquired if ecclesiastical officials charged excessive fees or accepted bribes or other rewards. In 1597, Bancroft's articles for the diocese of London sought to learn who allowed offenses to go unpunished because of bribery or respect of persons. While well-intentioned, these articles proved insufficient in the long run to achieve reforms that might have given the ecclesiastical courts new life.[68]

To reformers, notably Puritans, the ecclesiastical courts were riddled with abuses and burdened with laws in dire need of reform. Yet attempts to procure statutory recognition of the reformed Edwardian code, the *Reformatio Legum Ecclesiasticarum,* failed in 1559 and 1571. The effectiveness of the courts was undermined by the use of excommunication in trivial as well as serious matters, including contumacy and refusal to pay fines. Disrespect was so common among the masses that many persons ignored summons and even excommunication itself, apparently going to their graves without receiving absolution. Yet despite the willingness of many to ignore the ecclesiastical machinery, the church courts actually increased their business in the Elizabethan period, as their act books demonstrate. Those who regarded the courts seriously found that their procedures could be expensive and irritating, and their ability to impose discipline far from satisfactory. When used against Puritan clergy, their very existence grew obnoxious, and the Dedham conference was ready in 1585 to discuss whether godly ministers should obey summons to church courts. Anglicans could admit the need for reform of these courts but their existence was still regarded as an integral part of the ecclesiastical establishment that must be maintained.[69]

The Court of Faculties was scathingly criticized by Puritans in connection with its power to issue licenses and dispensations. Gilby and Field protested against licenses to eat meat during Lent and Advent, and to marry within prohibited degrees and at forbidden times. They were irate about dispensations permitting pluralism, nonresidence, and ordination below the canonical age. In their judgment, the Court of Faculties wrongly excommunicated persons when fees or fines went unpaid; moreover it sold absolution, permitted one man to render absolution for another, sanctioned the buying and selling of advowsons, and issued "Popish diuorcements." This court, said Field, was nothing less than "the filthy quagmire and poisoned plash of all the abominations that do infect the whole realm," and its flagrant use of the old papal prerogative had to be terminated by statute. Gilby, too, hit hard at the Court's Catholic heritage, particularly the claim that its principles were "*Sana conscientia,* as though they had authoritie ouer mennes consciences." The Court of Faculties, argued Fulke, in effect transferred the see of Rome to Canterbury under the guise of the royal supremacy, an implicit attack on the abuse of the latter. Because the Court was the "mother and nurse of all abominations" Dering demanded that it be pulled down. A comparison of it to the synagogue of Satan in a Marprelate tract illustrated the intense Puritan hostility and was part of the broader campaign to rid the church of the dregs of popery.[70]

There was also strong Puritan criticism of commissaries' courts, which were accused of excommunicating people for trifles, and of violating Christ's commandment by having one man judge, excommunicate, and absolve. Sexual offenses were inadequately punished, absolution was sold to unrepentant offenders, and penance was commuted before the congregation was satisfied of repentance. The proceedings of these courts were denounced for encouraging churchwardens to perjure themselves by indicating *omnia bene* rather than presenting offenders. Advocates and proctors were damned as papists and their scribes and notaries as cormorants. A commissary's court was, said Field, "a petty little stinking ditch that floweth out of that former great puddle, robbing Christ's church of lawful pastors, of watchful seniors and elders, and careful deacons."[71]

Overall, Puritans thought ecclesiastical courts were encumbered by the retention of Catholic practices, were ineffective because of excessive excommunication, were corrupt in remitting penalties for financial considerations, were overburdened by ineffectual apparitors and other officials, and were unchristian in persecuting godly ministers. A petition from the pious in Cornwall complained that when they sought out godly clergy they were summoned to church courts and threatened with excommunication. Some claimed they were cited because of malicious charges by lewd persons and harassed by apparitors, registrars, and commissaries. Radical Puritans would have dispensed with ecclesiastical courts and imposed discipline by elders, but moderate Puritans advocated a drastic reform of the existing system. Becon was ready to abolish commissaries and other officials, and place church courts under the direction of superintendents, who were resident preachers in the deaneries with responsibility for prophesyings, where decisions on court process would be made. Puritans agreed on the need for effective instruments to maintain discipline, though their reaction to reforming the existing courts varied sharply.[72]

Puritan plaints were forcefully reiterated by Separatists, principally Barrow, who branded the High Commission, the Court of Faculties, the Court of Arches, the Court of Delegates, commissaries' courts, and all lesser ecclesiastical tribunals "stagelike" and antichristian. He disapproved of the handling of secular cases in church courts and their reliance on civil authority to punish offenders. Like the Puritans, he deplored the ease of obtaining licenses and dispensations in the Court of Faculties, and the way everything, including delays of judgment or expeditious handling of cases, was "pleadable and vendible for money." Again like the Puritans, he castigated ecclesiastical tribunals for their Catholic elements, including canons, dispensations, licenses, and inhibitions, "which require but the whole age of a man to reade." Prelates had, as Barrow saw it, virtually unchecked power to summon, try, imprison, or censure persons. The proceedings were decried as litigious, corrupt, profane, and unscriptural, and the officers as a "Romish" rabble. The only solution was, as Robert Harrison also insisted, to abolish the entire system.[73]

Barrow took special aim at the Court of High Commission, "the very abisme and golph from whence spring . . . innumerable enormities, into every part of this whole land their church." Its proceedings were expensive because of officers' fees and confused civil and ecclesiastical laws. Moreover, the accused could not face their accusers or learn the full charges against them until they had taken the *ex officio* oath. If convicted, they had no appeal. Barrow was angered by the Commission's detention of suspects without bail, mainprize, or trial, as well as its power to incarcerate or release persons solely on its own warrant and its powers of search and seizure. In a calculated appeal to anticlerical lawyers, Barrow asserted that the Commission determined cases that belonged in the high court of Parliament, prejudiced the royal prerogative and the jurisdiction of the royal courts, endangered the liberty of free subjects, and violated the principles of Magna Carta. Because it virtually made laws and ordinances for the churches without their consent, it was worse than the Spanish Inquisition. "To such a height is this strange Romish Spanish court now growne, under colour of reforming ecclesiasticall abuses, that it usurpeth absolute power over al lawes, causes, persons, estates; yea, and becommeth the very . . . synke . . . from whence flow al errors, abuses, and disorders into the whole land.''[74]

Anglicans were sensitive to the problems of ecclesiastical courts, as evidenced, for example, by the actions of the bishops hitherto noted. Even Hooker acknowledged that corruption in ecclesiastical courts by men seeking gain would wreak more evil than they imagined —a prophecy fulfilled in the 1640s. Hooker sought a court system in which unjust dealings would be replaced by integrity and justice, hence he urged bishops to conduct visitations to enforce church laws, impose uniform worship, and reform manners and morals. As bishop of London, Bancroft sensed the hostility to church courts and directed the archdeacon of St. Albans to hold sessions less frequently, at most once every month or five weeks. Some reform was achieved through canons and articles, and commencing in 1571 a sentence of excommunication could be pronounced only by a learned cleric and commutation of penance could be done only by a bishop, with commutation fees going for specified purposes. In 1597 Archbishop Whitgift curtailed abuses associated with dispensations for marriage without banns, restricted the number of active apparitors and prohibited their employment as informers or promoters, reduced fees, and reformed divorce procedure in ecclesiastical courts. Yet these reforms were not effectively implemented in all the dioceses, including Norwich, and in many respects the abuses of the courts remained essentially unreformed in the Elizabethan period, and this festering grievance contributed to anticlerical hostility.[75]

In their attitude to ecclesiastical courts, then, a sharp difference existed between Anglicans and Puritans, with the radical element of the latter in essential agreement with the Separatists on the extremity of their opposition. The Court of Faculties, the commissaries' courts, and the High Commission were subjected to withering criticism, a key accusation of which was that they were popery in English guise. The courts were condemned because they failed to inculcate godly discipline, abused excommunication, sold absolution, and failed to punish sexual offenses sufficiently. Criticism was directed against court officials, exorbitant fees, and lengthy proceedings. Had the church been adequately endowed, it might have been able to attract more qualified men and reward them decently, but in the existing circumstances apparitors and their colleagues had a financial incentive to keep the courts busy, not for the sake of reforming society but to collect fines, bribes, and fees. The gross mishandling of the ecclesiastical courts festered anticlericalism and deepened the division between Anglicans and Puritans. Although Hooker and some of the prelates saw the danger signals, they failed to achieve essential reform, largely because of financial restrictions and the hostility of vested interests.

(7) Oaths

The end of othes is profitable, and the vse necessary among men.

Richard Turnbull[76]

Whether greater oathes or lesser oathes, if they bee idle oathes, Gods words hath condemned them.

John Dod[77]

In the sixteenth century and before, oaths, which rested on the premise that those who violated them would suffer in the afterlife, were one of the strongest ties binding society together. The oaths of allegiance and supremacy were extensions of the feudal oath of loyalty and reinforced the national sovereignty established by statute in the 1530s. In addition to such oaths, which bound subjects to magistrates and tenants to lords, oaths were sworn to ensure truth in judicial proceedings, as in sworn juries of presentment and compurgation. A person accused by public fame (*clamosa insinuatio*) had little recourse other than to clear himself by oaths of compurgators. Walsingham, like other Puritans, could not conceive of the administration of justice apart from the use of oaths. Refusal to take an oath on grounds of conscience in a common-law court could deprive one of the right to sue for debts, prove a will, give evidence, or defend property in a court. Perjury under oath was a grave matter and, after 1563, was the province of Star Chamber unless committed in an ecclesiastical court. It was also a serious offense to bribe a person to render false testimony while under oath.[78]

The feeling was general in Tudor England that oaths should be used wherever necessary, but not in contexts conducive to blatant lying. Oaths were taken by mayors, sheriffs, and common councilors, by freemen of the Merchant Adventurers, and (in 1585) by every captain in the trained bands. The ideal was reflected in the epitaph for William Herbert, earl of Pembroke, who "kept his promise fayth and oth, in Court, in feeld and towne." In contrast, the people of Beaumaris in 1570 allegedly had no regard for oaths and adhered to the Old Religion. In politics, the absence of deference to oaths undermined the loyalty demanded by Tudors of their subjects; no oath, no loyalty, no sovereignty.[79]

The authorities were unwilling to undermine oaths for political allegiance by requiring an oath in circumstances where financial gain was an incentive to lie. In 1548, it became illegal to require an oath in tithe suits, because it was presumed many would lie to escape financial obligations. When the 1563 Parliament extended the subsidy from subjects worth £5 to those worth £3, the oath traditionally imposed on the men responsible for the assessment was deleted in the expectation of widespread perjury, a precedent followed by subsequent Elizabethan Parliaments. The motivation for this change was attributed by Sir John Neale to the House of Commons' "Puritan conscience." Yet the 1563 Parliament imposed severe penalties on Catholics who rejected the oath of supremacy, for this threatened the political and religious unity of the state. The apparent discrepancy in Parliament's willingness to use oaths was chided by Robert Atkinson, a lawyer of the Inner Temple, from which he was expelled for recusancy in 1570. The type of behavior feared by Parliament occurred in 1602, when Raleigh examined a man who had taken possession of a wreck: "Being demaunded whether he would sweare to such articles as they would propound, [he] answerd that he would sweare to anie thinge they would aske him, and then being admonished he should not be soe rashe in soe serious a matter as concerned his soule soe nearely, 'Fayth,' said he, 'I had rather trust God with my soule, then you with my goods.'"[80]

The most controversial use of oaths occurred in ecclesiastical courts, particularly the use of the oath *ex officio mero* in High Commission, which required the accused to "swear to answer all such Interrogatories as shall be offered unto you and declare your whole knowledge therein, so God you help." Refusal to take this oath usually was regarded as proof of guilt. Controversy over the oath became explosive in the early 1590s, as the Commission increasingly became a vehicle for the repression of Puritanism and was used with devastating effect by Bancroft against the Presbyterians. Justifying its proceedings as investigations of persons suspected by *clamosa insinuatio,* the Commission did not feel bound to read the charges, name and produce the witnesses, or permit the use of counsel. After tendering the oath ex officio and questioning a suspect, a bill of charges was formulated based on the sworn testimony, and a trial — with right of counsel — ensued, but there was no appellate process. The proceedings aroused the concern of some members of the Privy Council, notably Knollys, Robert Beale, and James Morice, an attorney of the Court of Wards. The latter two wrote tracts against the ex officio oath, arguing that "no man may be urged to bewray himself in hidden and secret crimes, nor to accuse himself, and many crimes judged in these [ecclesiastical] courts are such as are committed secretly." After a counterattack was mounted in Richard Cousin's *Apology* in 1591, Morice replied, only to have his work suppressed by Whitgift. The case of the Anglican hierarchy was strengthened in 1591 when Queen's Bench declared High Commission free of traditional legal restraints because it was created by royal prerogative.[81]

In 1593, Morice took his campaign into Parliament, probably with the connivance of Beale. There he spoke against the threefold abuses of the ex officio oath, Whitgift's articles of subscription for the clergy, and the oath required of excommunicated persons before absolution, to obey all ecclesiastical laws and episcopal orders. The oaths were blasted as illegal, a violation of the principles of Magna Carta, and inventions to maintain a "Romish" hierarchy. Two bills were offered to the Commons, the first of which proposed to render ecclesiastics offering an ex officio oath liable to the penalties of praemunire. The same punishment was proposed in the second bill for those imposing Whitgift's articles of subscription on the clergy. In the ensuing debate, Morice received support from Knollys and Henry Finch, and apparently many others in the House were sympathetic. Elizabeth, however, intervened, and the Privy Council, despite Burghley's sympathy for Morice, confined him for two months. Beale apparently suffered the same fate, and the endeavor to use Parliament to reform ecclesiastical courts came to naught.[82]

The validity and nature of oaths were addressed in scriptural marginalia commencing in 1537 with the Matthew Bible. There it was argued that oaths could be rendered if taken in God's name and for the profit of one's neighbor, though swearing in vain was prohibited. "An othe is the end of stryfe and deuisyon / the which is lawfull to be done when it is ether to the glorie of God or proffyt of oure neyboure or for the comen wealth / or elles not." The note to Deuteronomy 17 apparently ruled out any oath requiring self-incrimination, but this was dropped in the 1551 Matthew-Becke version. Oaths were restricted by the Tyndale-Coverdale New Testament of 1538 to matters involving the honor of God, love, necessity, or the preservation of a neighbor's goods. The Matthew and Matthew-Becke versions of 1549 and 1551 stipulated that wicked vows must not be kept; vows must "tende wholy to goddes glory, and then we must in no wyse be slacke in the performaunce." The 1551 edition of Tyndale's Pentateuch reiterated the note to Exodus 22 in the Matthew

Bible (as quoted above), but added that no person should be condemned on the testimony of one witness. There is, then, a general willingness in the early marginalia to use oaths in matters of consequence, though the Matthew Bible was apparently not willing to sanction an oath of the ex officio type.[83]

In the Geneva marginalia the annotators assert that affirmations and denials must be made simply and without oaths whenever possible. A magistrate may, however, require an oath in matters of consequence to uphold justice and truth. Generally people must beware of rendering oaths, though lawful swearing shows proper fear of God. Oaths must be sworn only in God's name: "Thou shalt . . . with reuerence sweare by the lyuing God, when thine othe may aduance Gods glorie, & profite others." Rash oaths and wicked vows are prohibited, and once taken must not be kept. Lawful oaths generally must be fulfilled, though the annotators provided a loophole in cases of necessity when oaths might be broken. The Geneva marginalia do not mention self-incriminating oaths.[84]

In the Bishops' Bible, the Geneva position is reaffirmed, even to the verbatim citation of the note to James 5:12. Oaths and vows must be used sparingly and for those things that tend to the glory of God and are in human power to achieve. The Beza-Tomson Bible virtually ignored oaths, exhorting readers only to affirm or deny things simply and without oaths. Even a Quaker would have felt comfortable in the next century with this bland advice. Thus neither the Geneva, the Bishops', nor the Beza-Tomson Bible commented on self-incriminating oaths; only the Matthew Bible seemed to oppose them, but this was before they became a bitterly controversial issue late in the Elizabethan age.[85]

The principles governing oaths in the Rheims marginalia fundamentally agree with those of Protestant annotators. "In iustice and iudgement we may be by our lawful Magistrate put to sweare, and may lawfully take an othe, as also for the aduantaging of any necessarie truth when time and place require." Because the Rheims notes were intended for a Catholic minority in a Protestant state, they stress that unlawful oaths are not binding and must not be kept; this would apply, for instance, to the oath of supremacy. Oaths requiring one Catholic to accuse another for his religious practices should not be taken (and this would apply to the oath ex officio), but if courage and constancy are lacking and such an oath is rendered, it must not be fulfilled, under pain of damnation. This explicit sanctioning of lying under oath to protect the Catholic faith undermined the effectiveness of the oath ex officio to root out recusancy.[86]

The official Anglican position on oaths was enunciated in the 1562 Articles and the Edwardian homily on swearing. According to the former, rash swearing by Christians is prohibited, though in cases of faith and charity, magistrates may require oaths to maintain justice and truth. In the homily on swearing, the validity of oaths magistrates impose for the discovery of truth or the execution of justice was maintained. Oaths were also acceptable when made in God's name to keep covenants, promises, and laws. One taking an oath required by a judge must do so truly and advisedly, with a view to the maintenance of truth and the defense of the innocent. Swearing falsely, for trifles, or when unnecessary entailed taking God's name in vain and was prohibited. According to the homily unlawful oaths must not be kept, though all those that did not contravene a divine commandment must be fulfilled. Nothing was said about an oath ex officio. The homily and the Articles thus espoused the lawfulness of oaths when used appropriately, reinforcing the basic teaching on oaths found in the biblical marginalia.[87]

Most of the Anglican commentary on oaths expounded these basic principles, particularly the legitimacy of oaths imposed by magistrates to ascertain truth and render justice. Oaths were intended to terminate strife, protect neighbors, glorify God, render homage to magistrates and church officials, bind people to holy worship, and confirm covenants between men. Never were they to be made falsely, unnecessarily, irreverently, without a clear conscience, or on uncertain matters. Although unlawful or wicked oaths should not be taken, if made they must not be fulfilled. For Anglicans the oath had a distinctly religious character as part of the service owed to God; a lawful oath was a religious affirmation that the swearer called on God to witness the truth of his statement or intention, hence lawful vows must be kept. Thus far, the Anglican position was only a fuller exposition of the principles in the biblical marginalia, the Articles, and the homily on swearing.[88]

When, however, the Anglican hierarchy launched its attack on Puritanism under Whitgift's direction, Anglican apologists pressed the case for the oath ex officio. In 1592 Sutcliffe argued that "in diuers criminal causes, both Gods lawes, and the lawes of this realme doe require, that the partie answere vpon his othe." As if divine sanction for the oath were insufficient, Sutcliffe pointed to the use of oaths in ecclesiastical courts in Geneva, yet the issue was not merely the use of oaths but the kind of oath requiring self-incrimination. Further confusing the issue, Sutcliffe insisted that "no man is called to accuse himselfe but to aunswere accusations obiected by others."

In fact, however, judges could require a person to take an oath ex officio based on *clamosa insinuatio*, which might amount to nothing more than the suspicions of ecclesiastics about the religious persuasions of people.[89]

The following year, Bancroft likewise cited Genevan ecclesiastical practice to justify the oath ex officio, challenging Puritans to prove that any person was compelled to testify against himself or godly brethren. Supposedly the oath ex officio enabled the accused to purge—not accuse—himself. With insight, Bancroft compared the Puritan and Separatist refusal to incriminate other members of their godly brotherhoods with the Catholic position enunciated in the Rheims marginalia. For Bancroft and Whitgift, the oath ex officio was crucial to state security, for if these groups continued to increase "and so shoulde breake forth into open rebellion; they might by no meanes be examined vpon their oathes, because they will say they haue done nothing, but what they were bound to doe; and that therefore, they might detect no man, wherby to bring him, within the compasse of any law, for doing his duety." Whitgift also was worried that without the oath ex officio, sectaries would be difficult to expose, for informers had no financial incentive to pursue them. They enjoyed, as Bancroft phrased it, a league of secrecy that could not be discovered by traditional ecclesiastical censures or commissions. The oath ex officio was a tool of a state grappling with subversive elements bent on the destruction of its ecclesiastical institutions, a fundamental prop of the socio-political order. As in the United States in the 1950s, England in the 1590s was more concerned with the sanctity of the whole than the welfare and legal rights of its constituent parts.[90]

Anglican apologists made the best of the controversy by turning the attack against the Puritans. According to Sutcliffe, they overthrew the best means of trial as well as ordinary legal proceedings by their assertion of the refusal to take some oaths, to reject others as vain, and to withhold testimony about their brethren. This plaint of Puritan obstruction was likewise asserted by Thomas Rogers: "So the Puritans oftentimes either will take no oath at all when it is ministered unto them by authority, if it may turn to the molestation of their brethren, or if they swear (finding their testimony will be hurtful to their cause) they will not deliver their minds after they be sworn." Puritans also were accused of common swearing, with a proclivity for such phrases as "God damn me," "God confound me," and "I renounce God," but these charges were part of a smear campaign.[91]

Thomas Rogers also attacked the position of the Rheims New Testament on oaths, which he regarded as the encouragement of cunning and equivocation. To assert that an oath to further idolatry was not binding, or that faith need not be kept with heretics, was "conscionably and religiously [to] keep not their faith." Why this should be so when Anglicans instructed their adherents to reject unlawful oaths and never keep them was not explained. Although he recognized the affinity between the Catholic and Puritan positions with respect to oaths harmful to their faiths, he failed to grasp that this similarity stemmed from the fundamental principle on unlawful oaths shared by Anglicans.[92]

In most respects, there was broad agreement between Anglicans and Puritans on oaths. Puritans hammered at the wrongfulness of vain oaths, which violated the third commandment. Oaths could be taken when required by magistrates or in matters of substance between private persons that could not otherwise be resolved, though Coverdale rejected the latter use. Oaths were valid to benefit neighbors, determine truth, manifest allegiance to princes, resolve controversies, advance Protestantism, and, for Perkins, confirm business dealings. Not all oaths imposed by magistrates were to be taken, for Christians are obliged to refuse oaths harmful to the soul, oaths whose purpose is evil, and oaths contrary to piety and charity. As developed by Coverdale and Perkins in particular, these qualifications laid the foundation for Puritan opposition to the oath ex officio.[93]

Puritans maintained the religious nature of the oath, which is a fundamental reason for the seriousness with which it was taken and the ire over its use in ecclesiastical courts, particularly the High Commission. Dod insisted that an oath was a Christian duty (even to the point that *only* a Christian could lawfully swear) and a means of serving God, which meant that "reuerent swearing is an holy thing, and one may sinne as well in omitting this when it is lawfully required, as in committing the other which is forbidden." The invocation of divine presence and the calling forth of divine punishment in the event of falsehood underlined the seriousness of the oath as a religious act and made Puritans chary of swearing by anything but God, which would diminish his majesty. Traditional oaths by saints, the devil, the mass, the rood, the planets, a mouse's foot, or "cocke and pye" were prohibited, except that Perkins was willing to allow Christians to swear in God's name with a subordinate citing of creatures as pawns or pledges of veracity.[94]

The religious nature of the oath underlay the Puritan abhorrence of common swearing. Although Anglican religious leaders did not sanction such speech, neither did they manifest much open hostility to it, so it became a commonplace that those who forbore swearing were Puritans. "If they admonish anie neighbour for swearing, . . . are they [not] by and by *vile Puritanes*," asked Nichols, while Vaughan observed that "he is a Gull or a Puritane, quoth they, that will not sweare." In 1581, a libertine asserted that it was hypocrisy for one Christian to reprove another for swearing, but the Puritans would have none of this. Swearing, averred Dent, was a sign of damnation and high treason against God, hence he called for a harsh law to prohibit it. In 1566 the Commons failed to pass a bill against swearing, but in 1601, under apparent Puritan prompting, an anti-blasphemy bill overcame stiff opposition in the Commons but never made it to the statute book. Hostility to it stemmed at least in part from men who believed it was a subject for the pulpit, not Parliament, and that justices of the peace would not enforce prohibitions justly. Opposition also may have arisen because swearing, though common to all classes, was counted "the liuelie grace of a Gentleman." [95]

The Puritan position with respect to the binding nature of oaths was compatible with the Anglican, though Perkins' casuistry delved into the ramifications in much greater depth. Generally, lawful oaths must be fulfilled, even if personal loss results or the oath is tendered in God's name under compulsion, such as to an enemy, or through deceit. Perkins, however, took exception to the prevalent notion that oaths taken under threat of physical harm are binding, rejecting the principle that fear does not "abolish the consent of his will." Such oaths cease to be binding if their fulfillment would harm the commonwealth, though not if they entail only personal loss unless a magistrate rules otherwise. Perkins was unwilling to hold persons to their oaths if they were sworn in ignorance or error, but believed oaths taken in the name of false gods or made by infidels are binding. No man has power to release individuals from binding oaths, a thesis directed especially against the pope. Puritans agreed that unlawful oaths need not be kept, a category that embraced six cases, according to Perkins. Oaths do not bind if they are contrary to Scripture, violate the laws, are made by children or the mentally incompetent, are rendered by those without power to bind themselves (such as servants), are undertaken with respect to something over which one has no power, or are made with respect to something subsequently outlawed. Yet Puritans carefully distinguished their position from that of the Catholics, whom they saw as flagrantly disregarding valid oaths, notably with regard to obedience to the Elizabethan government. Puritans trod a fine line between reliance on oaths as a bond of society and their right to refuse unlawful oaths.[96]

In the Elizabethan period, Puritans were more interested in the principles governing unlawful oaths as they applied to such Catholic vows as celibacy than in possible ramifications for the oath ex officio. In contrast to an oath, Perkins defined a vow as a promise to God in which a Christian of his own volition pledged to observe external duties to foster repentance, meditation, sobriety, patience, or thankfulness. There were also vows promising moral obedience (as in baptism) and ceremonial obedience (as in the Pentateuch), but the latter no longer affect Christians. As in the case of oaths, vows can only be made in lawful matters, or the vow is not binding. In making vows, Perkins urged readers to promise things only in accord with the Bible and not in conflict with one's vocation, to do nothing in search of merit, and to vow only things compatible with Christian liberty. Because the Catholic vow of clerical celibacy had no divine warrant, it was rejected. Like oaths, vows have a religious nature as means or props to worship God, though they must never be used in the legalistic way common to Catholicism. For the Puritan, vows are made in the context of the freedom of the justified believer, not the soteriological context of merit. Whereas Anglicans would not have quarreled with this principle, they were less interested in demarcating their views from the Catholic position than were the Puritans, who once again carried forward their sustained endeavor to put a great distance between themselves and Rome.[97]

Marked Puritan concern for the use of oaths in ecclesiastical courts did not commence until the 1580s, though c. 1568, Coverdale set forth an important principle when he argued that a judge should never demand an oath of any person "without great heauines of conscience" for fear that the swearer would perjure himself. Those taking ex officio oaths were particularly subject to this temptation. In 1581 Gilby sought to undermine the use of oaths in ecclesiastical courts by prohibiting swearing on the Bible. Five years later, the Dedham Classis discussed ways to limit oaths demanded of churchwardens by ecclesiastical superiors, concluding that they could "sweare with protestacion" only to those things conducive to divine glory and the good of the church, not to matters that violated piety and charity. This principle was developed by Perkins, and in 1590 Whitgift complained that Puritans in the Midlands refused the oath ex officio on the grounds that testifying against members of their religious community was a violation of charity. Cartwright broadened the argument by calling for all persons to be tried on the evidence of two or three witnesses as in common law, not on self-incrimination stemming from an oath ex officio. A third argument used by Puritans against this oath was that it violated the liberty bestowed by God on his servants.[98]

The principal Puritan case against the oath ex officio was made in Morice's *Briefe Treatise of Oathes*, published anonymously c. 1590 on the Continent. This work by Burghley's associate, which helped forge the alliance between common lawyers and Puritans, reiterated the Puritan premise that oaths are divinely commanded as part of God's service and must be used solely *ad gloriam Dei* and for the benefit of man. Every deponent must see that by his oath God is magnified, the truth confirmed, justice maintained, and the innocent vindicated. Those imposing oaths must restrict their use to cases of necessity involving the maintenance of divine honor, the good of the commonwealth, or the welfare of neighbors, never requiring oaths of persons whose credit is suspect or whose life is immoral.[99]

Morice opposed the oath ex officio as contrary to Scripture, common law, and canon law. Tendered by ordinaries and ecclesiastical judges it is contrary to the institution, use, and intent of a proper oath, for the oath ex officio is not concerned with the assurance of a duty or contract, or with the confirmation of truth in a controversy. The argument of the prelates that the oath ex officio is essential to uncover sedition justifies, Morice argued, an inquisitorial court more powerful than the Spanish Inquisition. This was one of the earliest Puritan attempts to link Anglican policies with those of Spanish Catholics. In addition, Morice's citation of the refusal of the Marian martyr John Lambert and his fellow Protestant John Philpot to take the oath implicitly compared Anglican prelates to the detested Bishop Edmund Bonner. Morice specifically attributed the origins of this oath to Catholic clergy who sought to prejudice the tranquility of the realm, so that the oath not only impinged on the freedom of Englishmen but also was an indignity to the crown.[100]

The case against the oath ex officio was buttressed with arguments directed to the violation of due process. Cases were not initiated with specific complaints or judicial accusations, the deponent was not acquainted with the nature of the offense before he was required to swear, and he was forced to accuse himself (contrary to Christian charity and humanity) or commit perjury. It galled Morice that proceedings were sometime instigated on nothing more than naked suspicion or common fame. Because no contention existed prior to ecclesiastical proceedings, no controversy could be terminated by such an oath; rather it was likely to induce the very disruption oaths were intended to resolve. Thus on legal, historical, and religious grounds, Morice advanced a compelling case that the suspected existence of seditious religious views and practices was not sufficient cause to violate individual rights under divine and common law. This was heady stuff; it contributed to building the citadel of the sanctity of conscience and cast prelates in the robes of Spanish inquisitors intent on undermining true religion and the commonwealth. After this, as long as the Anglican hierarchy persisted in the use of the oath ex officio, there could be no reconciliation with Puritans, whose task came to be seen as the reform of the church and its courts root and branch. [101]

The Separatist position on oaths was a natural—though more extreme—outgrowth of Puritan views. Separatists were equally unwilling to countenance rash and ungodly oaths or common swearing, but unlike Anglicans and Puritans, they refused to acknowledge the validity of oaths between private parties. Oaths were divinely instituted to enable magistrates to determine uncertain matters and ascertain the truth. This narrow conception of oaths led to the conclusion that they had no proper place in ecclesiastical courts or to express fidelity to the royal supremacy, the *Book of Common Prayer*, canon law, or the Thirty-nine Articles. Such oaths were castigated as idolatrous, blasphemous, and contrary to divine law. Clergy who took episcopally administered oaths swore canonical obedience to Antichrist and abjured their true Lord. Because these oaths secured obedience to an institution the Separatists repudiated, it was inevitable that such oaths were denounced as pledges to Antichrist. [102]

Like the Puritans, the Separatists vituperously attacked the oath ex officio as idolatrous, wicked, and contrary to Deuteronomy 6:13 and 10:20, as well as Matthew 5:34-35 and 1 Corinthians 6:12. With its parallels to the Spanish Inquisition, the oath, averred Barrow and Greenwood, undermined the queen's prerogative and dignity and violated English law. Repeatedly Separatists refused, like Cartwright, to take the oath when it was administered, sometimes forcing the commissioners to proceed without it, as in the case of Barrow and Greenwood in 1589. [103]

In sum, oaths, like the sabbath, were not initially a point of conflict between Anglicans and Puritans, but in the 1580s and 1590s Whitgift and Bancroft made them one by turning the High Commission, with its oath *ex officio mero*, against the Puritans. In effect Puritans and Separatists became allies against a weapon they compared to the Spanish Inquisition and a threat to the maintenance of traditional legal principles. Not only did Whitgift and Bancroft deepen the growing division between Anglicans and Puritans, but they played an important—if unwitting—role in fostering the alliance between common lawyers and Puritans.

The eruption of the controversy over the oath ex officio fueled existing antagonisms toward ecclesiastical courts, which were already producing bitterness as Elizabethans felt that church officials were more interested in the purses of the accused than in their spiritual welfare. Ecclesiastical courts were losing their credibility as guardians of Christian morality because of their financial exactions and their almost exclusive attention to the sins of the lower orders. Ironically, part of the hostility to the oath ex officio was the threat of its use against precisely that element of the social order normally immune from oaths and the purview of ecclesiastical courts. If Whitgift and Bancroft could have had their way, they undoubtedly would have extended the effective jurisdiction of church courts over a broader social spectrum, as suggested, for example, in Bancroft's 1597 articles for the diocese of London. Although the prelates recognized the need for reform, little of substance was achieved. Excommunication continued to be a penalty used too freely and absolved too readily, often for financial considerations. Failure to adopt the *Reformatio Legum Ecclesiasticarum* was ultimately a major reason for the wholesale attack on the ecclesiastical courts in the seventeenth century, for they remained tied to Catholic laws and procedure. When the High Commission turned the oath ex officio against Puritans and Separatists, they intensified their criticism of the entire system of ecclesiastical justice as riddled with popery, even to the use of the methods of the Inquisition. High Commission, the Court of Faculties, and the commissaries' courts bore the brunt of the attack.

The increased opposition between Anglicans and Puritans over the ecclesiastical courts and the oath ex officio contrasts with their general unanimity on many other areas of legal practice. Reformers of both persuasions emphasized the need for expedited justice, reduced legal expenses, and the enhanced rendering of justice, and Puritans in particular campaigned for the termination of bribery in the judicial process. Reforming the last-named was beyond their reach, however, in a society where bribery was an accepted part of the judicial and political process, as Bacon asserted in his defense of his own actions in the Jacobean era. Those reformers who pressed for a greater determination of justice in the provinces were no more successful, for they flew in the path of Tudor centralization. The solutions most commonly sought entailed increasing the social consciousness of judges, lawyers, and litigants, particularly with respect to the plight of the poor, for whom Elizabethan justice proved more of a threat than a means of legal redress. The Privy Council deserves credit for an activist role in the administration of justice, with its motives apparently due to religious conviction, the desire to maintain social order, and principles of justice.

The legal problems of the age, including unethical and unprofessional behavior by judges and lawyers, did not bring a chorus of demands for radical legal reform. Rather, the focus was on the inculcation of Christian ethics into the legal profession, coupled with exhortations to laymen to go to law only as a last resort, never for petty concerns, and always in a spirit of love. The negative influence of litigation on the church's reputation and interpersonal relationships was noted, but only the Puritans formulated substantive guidelines for litigants. Once again, the evidence reveals a greater concern among Puritans for the ramifications of their faith for social behavior. Yet apart from the controversial areas of the ecclesiastical courts and the oath *ex officio mero,* there was no serious area of disagreement between Anglicans and Puritans over legal problems. Whitgift and Bancroft would have been better advised to work for a major reform of the church courts and church discipline as well as the acceptance and implementation of the *Reformatio Legum Ecclesiasticarum* rather than turn the High Commission against the Puritans, for though they crushed the classical movement (with its appeal for reform of these matters) they exacerbated the divisions in the church they sought to unite. Ultimately, their failure, compounded by the policies of Archbishop Laud, led to the religious disintegration of the mid-seventeenth century.

Part VI: The Social Order and Death

CHAPTER *16*

Last Rites and Monuments

Historically, burial customs have changed slowly. Elizabethan Protestants faced a delicate problem in that they wanted to curtail ceremonies and symbols associated with such Catholic doctrines as satisfaction and purgatory, but they needed to retain the traditional
pomp as an underpinning of the social order; they had to avoid so
alienating the common folk that Protestantism was repudiated.
Funeral ceremonies required judicious pruning, though Separatists
launched a root and branch attack, with serious implications for the
social order. The difficulty was complicated by the custom that funerals for persons of wealth included acts of charity in the form of
grants of food, clothing, and money. To reduce the scale of funerals,
as Protestants advocated, risked a decrease in relief for the poor at a
time with its necessity was growing. Yet the behavior of the poor
mitigated against the continuation of large-scale charitable benefactions at funerals. Overall, perhaps the greatest ally of the reformers
was the financial pressure on the aristocracy, which resulted in the
beginning of a decline in expenditures for funerals in the 1580s.
Simultaneously the College of Arms was criticized, and persons of
new wealth in the City began to exceed their social status in the lav-
ishness of their funerals. Thus the value of funeral pageantry as a
prop of the social order was slowly being undermined in the late sixteenth century; ironically, this situation occurred in the reign of the
sovereign who perhaps more than any other in England's history was
devoted to pageantry.

(1) Funeral Customs and Religious Criticism

Honourable and Seemly buriall is as a blessing from God: the contrary as a curse.

Richard Turnbull [1]

Ye godlie may mourne, if thei passe not measure: and ye natural affection is commendable.

Geneva Bible [2]

One area in which traditionalism and the practices of the Old Faith continued fairly strong was burial customs. Particularly in the north and west, Catholic and superstitious practices continued throughout the period. Psalms were sung like dirges, lights were placed around biers, coffins were situated next to wayside crosses while mourners said the *De profundis*, prayers were rendered for the deceased, and communion services became requiem masses. In 1564, 1568, and 1569 citations were issued in Yorkshire for ringing bells on All Saints' eve, while the visitation records for Chester in 1578 note the excessive pealing of bells at funerals in Chester, Manchester, Walton, and Middlewich. In the northern counties in the 1580s "when any dieth, certaine women sing a song to the dead body, receyting the journey that the partie must go." Early Elizabethan wills continued to request Catholic rites, usually on condition that they were legally permissible. In 1560, for instance, Richard Pole, a Catholic esquire of Radbourn, Derby, bequeathed £6 *p.a.* for a priest to sing masses for his soul for seven years, though if this were illegal the funds were to be used to repair highways and relieve the poor. The same year Thomas Paynell, a Catholic priest, wanted his service to include a sermon by a noted divine to remind mourners that they were appointed to die. Catholic customs were kept alive by missionary priests and conservative clerics, such as Rafe Leche of Tilston, Ches., who in 1578 was accused of encouraging parishioners to say the *Pater noster* and *De profundis* for the deceased. [3]

In London, apparently the last important Catholic obsequies were held on 12 and 13 April 1559 at Blackfriars, Smithfield, for Sir Richard Mansfield. His home as well as Blackfriars was draped with black cloth and his personal arms. As the procession wound its way to the church, traditional accessories were apparent: two great white branches, two dozen torches to illumine the evening gloom, and four gilt candlesticks with four tapers. The symbols of his rank as a knight also were in evidence: the standard with its slit end depicting the cross of St. George, a beast or a crest, and Sir Richard's motto; a smaller penon, rounded at the end, bearing his arms; the coat of arms, a short-sleeved coat with his arms depicted in front, behind, and on each sleeve; a helmet and sword probably made especially for the occasion; a target (shield) also bearing Sir Richard's arms; and the traditional square banners displaying figures of the saints and carried at the corners of the coffin. Two heralds and eighteen male mourners in black gowns and twenty in black coats walked solemnly in the procession. Prayers and a dirge were sung by twenty-four priests. When the ceremony was over, the mourners returned to the black-draped house to drink; perhaps on this occasion wine and spice bread were served. The next morning a requiem mass was said, following which the principal mourners offered Sir Richard's standard, coat, helmet, target, and sword to his heir. Burial was conducted by two heralds from the College of Arms, and the corpse was interred with seven dozen scocheons—heraldic ensigns bearing his arms. The mourners returned once again to his house, this time for a funeral dinner. No mention is made of a dole of money to the destitute, which sometimes occurred after such a meal.[4]

In their attack on Catholic funeral practices, Protestant reformers distinguished between the ceremonial trappings, which they generally retained, and those aspects of the obsequies that symbolized or implied unacceptable doctrines, such as prayer for the dead, invocation to saints, purgatory, and extreme unction. The most substantive Anglican commentator on funerals was Pilkington, who formulated three rules, beginning with the requirement that bodies must be interred in designated places, because they are the temple of the Holy Spirit and will be glorified on the day of resurrection. Nevertheless "the papists are both wicked in teaching people, that one place is more holy than another to be buried in, as in the church rather than in the churchyard, and near the high altar rather than in the body of the church; and they are thieves also in picking poor men's purses for the same." Pilkington's second rule was to avoid excessive expenses, such as for tapers, mourning coats, torches, and feasts, which were of no benefit to the dead and were too costly for the living. Treading carefully, he acknowledged the right of princes and nobility to retain solemnity by using flags, swords, armor, and so forth, but counseled moderation. He drew a line between those customs associated with Catholicism, which had to be deleted, and those that were merely customary and could be retained. As his third rule, Pilkington censored all Catholic customs, including masses, dirges, trentals, holy water, the *De profundis*, and specially hallowed burial grounds. Whitgift, however, struck a more conservative note by defending burial grounds specially dedicated by governors of the commonwealth and church.[5]

Anglicans wanted moderation in funerals and mourning, for they regarded undue heaviness of spirit or other excess as indicative of heathen behavior. "We should not dance with minstrels (for that is too barbarous and against nature,) nor to be grieved with the death of our friends, nor desperately mourn with the heathen, as though there were no life after this," advised Pilkington. Because of the doctrine of resurrection, death must be approached with thankfulness that the deceased has achieved spiritual bliss. Yet Anglicans refused to take this as far as the radical Protestants, who criticized mourning attire and many funeral ceremonies. Mourning clothes, insisted Whitgift, were only used in accord with custom, as a matter of civility and order, not religion or superstition. They must not be worn to provoke sympathy but as a reminder of mortality. Funerals are compatible with Christian respect for the body, which will be resurrected, and in this connection funerals are a manifestation of faith as well as a time to comfort the deceased's family.[6]

Controversy and uncertainty surrounded burial practices in the Elizabethan period, when anxiety was probably already intensified by repudiation of extreme unction, purgatory, and satisfactory masses. Consequently Pilkington urged Protestants to stop quarreling among themselves about such matters as the use of the burial service in the *Book of Common Prayer* and the propriety of funeral sermons. It was enough, he insisted, to pull down the Romish Antichrist without fostering internal division over funerals. He assured friends and relatives of the martyrs and those who perished in fires or at sea that the absence of a solemn funeral was not harmful to the souls of the dead. Respect nevertheless was important, as manifested in January 1561 when the body of Katherine, wife of Peter Martyr, was given a decent burial after having been interred in a dunghill in the Marian period. The shortage of Protestant ministers early in the Elizabethan age left some parishes devoid of clergy to bury the dead; Jewel was upset at this deficiency, on the grounds that Christians should be buried reverently because their bodies were temples of the Holy Spirit.[7]

The relative simplicity preferred by Anglican reformers in comparison with Catholic practices is reflected in funeral services and wills. In London the first Protestant funeral in Elizabeth's reign, described by the undertaker Henry Machyn, was for John St. Loe, father of the queen's captain of the guard, on 23 March 1559. In the service at Great St. Helen's, Bishopsgate, there was neither "crosse nor prest, nor clarkes, but a sermon and after a salme of Davyd," a description that could indicate a Puritan service. Sir John's funeral retained many ceremonial features traditionally found in a knight's last rites, including his standard and penon, his coat, helmet, target, and sword, and two dozen scocheons. A more detailed description of a Protestant funeral is provided for an unnamed lady buried on 7 April 1559. A large number of mourners walked in pairs, with "the nuw prychers in ther gowne lyke ley[men] nodur syngyng nor sayhyng tyll they cam [to the grave]." Before the body was lowered, a collect was sung in English. Once the corpse was in the grave, dirt was cast on the coffin and a selection from 1 Thessalonians was read. When all the mourners, including women of the "nuw fassyon," had sung the Lord's prayer, a preacher gave a funeral sermon.[8]

The quest for simplicity was carried forward by the prelates. When Margaret, second wife of Thomas Howard, duke of Norfolk, was buried on 24 January 1564, Parkhurst, bishop of Norwich, preached the sermon. Subsequently he wrote to Josiah Simler that there had been "no ceremonies at the funeral, wax candles or torches. Except the sun nothing shone, which sadly annoyed the papists. Nothing of the kind has been ever seen in England, especially at the funeral of a peer or peeress." In his will Pilkington requested interment with as little ceremony and expense as possible, hence he was buried in a simple service at St. Andrew Auckland on 27 January 1576, though the authorities insisted that he be reinterred in Durham Cathedral the following May. In similar fashion, Grindal asked in his 1583 will to be buried in the choir of the parish church of Croyden without a solemn hearse or funeral pomp. These men, it should be noted, were from the moderate wing of Anglicanism.[9]

The effect of such examples was reflected in the views of Burghley, who nevertheless was persuaded that much of the traditional pomp should be retained as an indication of respect. After his wife died he explained to the dean of St. Paul's in 1589 that her funeral was a testimony of his love for her and an indication to the world of her noble stock, "which is not done for any vain pomp of ye world, but for civil duty towards her body, yt is to bee with honour regarded, for ye assured hope of ye resurrection therof at ye latter day." Yet he insisted that the ceremonies in no way continued the older ideas about relief for the deceased in purgatory. In his own will (1598), Burghley asked that his body be carried to his home at Stamford without pomp and be buried in the church of St. Martin in a comely manner, according to the degree of a baron. In his estimation no conflict existed between the desires of Anglican reformers for simpler services and the retention of funeral practices that reflected the social hierarchy.[10]

The moderation for which the prelates strove was manifested in their injunctions and visitation articles. By their direction, a parish clerk or sexton was ordered to ring the church bells when someone was on his deathbed to encourage parishioners to pray. When death occurred, the bells had to remain silent, except for short peals preceding and following burial. The use of handbells or other superfluous, superstitious ringing was prohibited, including the traditional custom of ringing a little bell through the town before a funeral. Services had to be conducted in accord with the *Book of Common Prayer* and without popish ceremonies. According to Bishop Middleton, these included the use of lights, tapers, and trindles (a type of wax tapers), and the erection of crosses at the church door, in the church, or at the graveside. He also prohibited ministers in the diocese of St. David's from wearing surplices or other special dress at funeral services except in their own churches. Prayers for the dead were repudiated, a limitation was placed on the number of persons (up to three) who could throw earth on the corpse, and none but the "best sort" could be interred in the church itself (and then only on payment of a fee of 10s. for church repair). Such concerns reflect the prelates' desire to wean people away from superstitious custom and from those Catholic practices that symbolized doctrines repugnant to Protestant theology.[11]

Like the Anglicans, the Puritans were determined to root out Catholic symbolism from funeral practices, though they carried the reforming program to greater lengths. They too curtailed the ringing of bells, because it encouraged prayers for souls in purgatory. With the Anglicans, they cautioned against excessive mourning, and some Puritans, such as Becon and Cartwright, demanded a cessation of traditional mourning gowns. To Cartwright, such trappings were hypocritical, with people often donning them out of custom rather than grief, while to true mourners such gowns made grief exceed measure. For Becon, funerals were occasions of joy to commemorate Christians who entered heaven, hence black was not a suitable color. Gowns should be provided for the poor in the usual fashion, but in "conuenient" colors, not black; gowns must be given only to the needy. Gilby was more extreme in condemning not only beadsmen who prayed for the soul of the dead, but all who joined the funeral procession to receive a gown and were nothing but "hired Mourners."[12]

Puritans agreed on the need to purge dirges, trentals, the *De profundis*, candles, incense, torches, and other superfluous pomp, which were regarded as superstitious devices to pick men's pockets and make merchandise of souls. These practices must be replaced by simple services characterized by the singing of Psalms and hymns, the rendering of thanksgiving, and the treatment of the deceased with respect. "A funerall," insisted Perkins, "ought to be solemnized after an honest, and ciuile maner: namely, agreeable to the nature, and credite as well of those which remaine aliue, as them which are dead." The service must not include the Lord's supper, for, as Becon explained, that is intended only for the living. Radical Puritans in particular objected to the prescribed service in the *Book of Common Prayer* as devoid of biblical sanction. Too much regard for the site of burial is superstitious, they felt, though Sutton defended burials in churches and churchyards because the proximity of the graves prompts the living to meditate on their own death and that of Christ. [13]

One of the most radical proposals was Cartwright's challenge of the ministerial monopoly. If funerals are simply a manifestation of respect for the deceased and a celebration of the completion of the earthly pilgrimage, singing Psalms and hymns and giving thanks can be done without clergy. Here the contrast with the sacramental ritual of Catholicism with its mandatory role for mediating priests was virtually complete. For the authorities, however, lay persons officiating at funerals could not be risked because such a practice undermined a means of control, particularly in such cases as infanticide, and a source of revenue for a church financially strapped. Consequently secular and ecclesiastical courts enforced the clerical monopoly, but Cartwright's proposal was an early indication of the movement for increased laicization that mushroomed in the mid-seventeenth century. [14]

The Puritan campaign for greater simplicity achieved some success. One of the earlier Puritan funerals in London was that of the grocer, Mr. Flammock, on 17 January 1561 at St. Peter Cornhill. The corpse was carried to the church in the absence of singing or clergy. The only thing Machyn records of the service is that a Psalm was sung in the Geneva manner and a sermon was preached, followed immediately by the burial. In his 1567 will Robert Beaumont, Lady Margaret Professor of Divinity at Cambridge, asked that his funeral be conducted without bell ringing, popish ceremonies, and prayers that doubted the certainty of his "happy state with God." In 1589 Mildmay directed his executors to "avoyde suche vaine funerall pompe as the worlde by custome in the time of darknes hathe longe used, a thinge most unfitt for us Christians that doe professe sincerely the Gospell of Jhesus Christe." Likewise Walsingham asked in 1590 to be buried without the ceremonies usually accorded to one of his stature, partly because of the expense for his family and partly because of his expectations of a joyful resurrection. Henry Trafford, rector of Wilmslow, Ches., specified in his 1591 will that no mourning gowns be worn at his funeral. In 1603, Cartwright asked that he be interred in the churchyard of the place where he died, without pomp or superstition. This desire for simplicity, though in some cases partially motivated by economic considerations, was grounded on the religious conviction, as expressed by Lady Grace Mildmay when her husband died in 1617, that a funeral solemnizes "the conjunction of our first originall beginning earth to earth; yet not to rest there, but as a free passage to the freedom of Eternity." [15]

The quest for greater simplicity struck a responsive note among Elizabethans, who saw the absence of pomp as a final declaration of piety, an attitude with medieval roots. Late in the Marian period, to cite but one example, Anne Brooke, Lady Cobham, directed in her will that her body be buried in the church at Cobham without pomp or pride. Four decades later William Brooke, Lord Cobham, made a similar request. In his 1596 will, Henry Herbert, earl of Pembroke, asked that he be interred in Salisbury Cathedral "in semely sorte" but without a sumptuous funeral or the usual recourse to the heralds. The Cheshire gentleman, Richard Grosvenor of Doddleston, ordered in 1580 that after his death his body be immediately placed in its sepulchre "withowte anye maner of worldlye prodygaletie." Wanting no superfluous pomp or excessive expenses, Lady Jane Smith of Hough, Ches., asked in 1590 to have no mourning gowns, though she bowed to tradition in having her hearse covered with black cloth. In an age when pageantry was part of the way of death, a strong undercurrent of opposition existed, devoted on religious and economic grounds to greater simplicity. [16]

The most radical proposals for the reform of funerals were from the Separatist Henry Barrow, who found no scriptural warrant for contemporary customs and associated them with papist practices. He damned virtually every aspect of the traditional ceremonies. The funeral procession with its mourners garbed in black, sometimes "with hoodes, caps, crosses and other knackes," was unchristian because it was an outward show of mourning rather than an inner sorrow. "Neither do Christians use to mourne after such a superstitious and prophane maner, or to have their mourning only in their garmentes, as numbers of serving men, reteiners, mourning boies, and poore men put in mourning weedes, which never got so much by the [deceased] glutton in all his life time, which are so far from mourning, as they are glad with al their heartes." Barrow resented clerics who would not bury someone without a fee, and whose range of services depended on the amount paid. In the funeral service, he faulted the use of the *Book of Common Prayer*, with its "nombred prayers and dirge over the dead." Barrow did not want the clergy to bury the dead, nor did he want bodies interred in churches or churchyards, which he found ugly, inconvenient, and unwholesome. Those who have been denied such burial places are "buried like dogges, say the common people." He found the costly and sumptuous meals untenable, satirizing them as "jolly christian mourning," and the expensive sculpture of the monuments foreign to the spirit of Christianity. Penry also expressed hostility to the prescribed order of funerals and rejected the ministers' monopoly. Once again, these men challenged the monopoly of the established church, with its numerous financial perquisites.[17]

With respect, then, to funeral customs, Anglican and Puritan reformers campaigned to purge Catholic ceremonies and symbolism from the funeral service, though Puritans and especially Separatists carried this further than most Anglicans. All agreed on the abolition of trentals, dirges, the excessive pealing of bells, and the *De profundis*, whereas Puritans also proposed modifying or abolishing mourning robes and emphasizing the singing of hymns and Psalms and the rendering of thanksgiving. Radical Puritans and Separatists repudiated the rites in the *Book of Common Prayer* and the necessity of clergy in the funeral services. The attack of Puritans and Separatists on the hypocrisy of many mourners in the traditional funeral services ran counter to the normal function of official mourning, which required the demonstration of a sorrow not always genuine as well as the protection of a truly grieving survivor from the excesses of grief.[18]

The quest for a simplified service fell on receptive ears; many people saw the repudiation of traditional pomp and ceremony as a last act of piety and spiritual asceticism. Yet Anglicans did not want a service stripped of social pageantry; rather, they favored one purified of those acts and symbols associated with such concepts as purgatory, satisfaction, merit, and extreme unction. As Puritans pursued this idea more vigorously, they stripped away the mystery of the funeral, much as they had taken it out of the Lord's supper. As the funeral became a thanksgiving and memorial service (in a more extreme sense than the Lord's supper), increased attention was devoted to preparing the dying to enter spiritual rest, culminating with Perkins' attention to the *ars moriendi*.[19] A holy death followed a holy life, and both were commemorated in a purified service of thanksgiving.

(2) Funeral Sermons

To praise ye dead, is a thing lawfull in it self, and profitable vnto the liuing.

William Harrison [20]

They cannot endure the sermons which are preached at the burial of the dead.

Richard Cox [21]

One of the most striking areas of conflict was the use of funeral sermons, largely because of their elegaic nature. Some sermons certainly displayed flowery adulation, but at least in the published ones, preachers normally preserved the medieval character of *exempla*. In this fashion Lady Helen Branch was praised as

> A godlie, vertuous and religious Matron
> For maids, and wiues, and widdows al a pattern.

Even when inaccurate as biography, they served as models of conduct for the living and thus had a pedagogical function, like epitaphs. Some, such as that preached in 1594 by John King at the funeral of John Piers, archbishop of York, made only minimal reference to the deceased and were hardly distinguishable from regular sermons. It was the eulogistic variety that sparked debate. [22]

Anglicans had no qualms about the value of funeral sermons, including their use to extol the dead. As precedent they cited David's praise of Jonathan, the Holy Spirit's acclaim of Josiah, and the extolment of the prophets and patriarchs by the author of Hebrews. Funeral sermons comforted the grieved, reminded listeners of their mortality, instructed the living to learn to die in the Lord, and called to mind resurrection, the day of judgment, and eternal rewards. Whitgift, the strongest defender of funeral sermons, thought they also were a fit vehicle to decry trentals, prayer for the dead, and purgatory. Calvin himself had sanctioned funeral sermons. Although radicals condemned funeral sermons because they were preached primarily for persons of substance, Whitgift retorted that usually "more occasion" existed to do so, and that this practice was not "that acceptation of persons which is in scripture prohibited; for there be degrees of persons and several dignities." The attack on funeral sermons implicitly became an attack on the social order because they extolled the dignity of prominent persons. In defense of that order as well as to praise the lives of the godly, Anglicans defended funeral sermons. To objections that the number of these sermons in London caused a shortage of preachers in rural areas, Pilkington responded only that "God grant us some more in the country." [23]

Puritans had no objections to funeral sermons per se, though they were chary of the tendency to make them encomiums. As vehicles to admonish listeners of mortality and teach them how to live, sermons were useful. Thus Thomas Sparke depicted Arthur Lord Grey of Wilton as a man who walked carefully before God in righteousness and mercy, and Thomas White pointed approvingly to Sir Henry Sidney as "a stemme of a noble house, which himselfe hath honored with many and principall vertues, but especially with faithfull seruice alwaies to his king, vnto whom both younge, and olde, hee was euer in great trust." Even Cartwright had no objection to funeral sermons as long as they commended worthy persons in such a fashion that others were moved to emulate them. Burton, however, berated hypocrites who left funds to have preachers commend them at their funerals and perhaps publish the sermons or write epitaphs for their tombs. Burton and Cartwright were uneasy about the tendency of funeral sermons to degenerate into panegyrics, which smacked of pride and hypocrisy. It was, however, the abuse and not the institution of the funeral sermon that troubled them.[24]

Once again, the most extreme attack on funeral sermons came from Barrow, who found no basis for them in the New Testament, thus putting them in the category with such other papist practices as saints' days, tithes, and mortuary fees. He was sickened by ministers who eulogized the dead even if they had been atheists, gluttons, or extortionists. Although such a person "lived and died like a wretched worldling: yet if he be rich inough, and his frendes wil be at the cost with him, he shall want none of this funeral furniture to help him to heaven." In reality Anglicans denied that funeral sermons benefited the deceased, but to Barrow the sermons amounted to another version of meritorious prayer for the dead. For that reason and for their hypocrisy, he condemned them. Here is another case of Separatist repudiation of a practice the Puritans considered worthy of reformation and retention.[25]

Funeral sermons were important enough to a minority of Elizabethans to prompt them to provide for sermons in their wills. In 1592 Elizabeth Grimsdich specified that her cousin, Christopher Goodman, preach her funeral sermon, and in 1603 Goodman requested the services of William Harrison and bequeathed 10s. for this purpose. Henry Trafford, Puritan rector of Wilmslow, Ches., specified a particular preacher for his funeral in his will, as did Robert Vavasour, a London haberdasher, who left 10s. to the Puritan Robert Crowley for a sermon. In 1566 a Durham draper asked for a funeral sermon if that were possible, and instructed his executors to pay the minister. The wills give no indication of the motives of their authors, and though Harrison is known to have written in an adulatory fashion, there is no indication Crowley did so. It is impossible to know how many of those who requested funeral sermons were moved by vanity, but in the majority of wills no request is made for a sermon. [26]

For those who wished to avail themselves of the opportunity, London funerals offered sermons by many of the age's great religious figures. Prelates often spoke at obsequies for the socially significant, either because they were in London on other business, or because personal ties were strong enough for a special journey to the capital. Between 1559 and 1563, Londoners heard such prominent men as Horne, bishop of Winchester, Becon, canon of Canterbury, Jewel, bishop of Salisbury, Pilkington, bishop of Durham, Alley, bishop of Exeter, Scambler, bishop of Petersborough, Nowell, dean of St. Paul's, Coverdale, Goodman, dean of Westminster, and the Puritans Philpot and Crowley.

Some Elizabethans bequeathed funds for sermons in a manner that recalls the Catholic practice of providing satisfactory masses. In 1559 Thomas Jackson, a London draper, bequeathed £5 for twenty sermons in the parish church at Kendal, Westm., where he was born. The 1582 will of a London girdler, Thomas Mowffett, bequeathed 40s. *p.a.* for twenty years—if his son lived that long—to support twelve Sunday sermons each year at Whitby, Yorks., on condition that England remain Protestant. Before he died in 1585, Francis Russell, earl of Bedford, willed that twenty sermons be preached within five months of his death. While these men and others like them were not providing funeral sermons per se, it is probable that the benefactors were commemorated by the ministers who did the preaching. Had England remained Catholic, such donations would likely have gone to the chantries. [27]

(3) Wakes and Minds

She wyl not forget his monethes minde
Nor his anniuersary at the yeres ende.

Robert Copland [28]

[Clergy] pycke mennes pursses / thorow . . . yeare myndes / moneth myndes &c.

Matthew Bible [29]

The medieval custom of minds and wakes was so firmly entrenched in society that Protestant reformers encountered stiff resistance in their attempts to purge them. Tyndale's 1530 Pentateuch includes a note to Numbers 20 in which the use of minds, or observances for the dead to encourage prayers for their souls, is attributed to clerical covetousness. To Tyndale month, yearly, and seven-yearly minds were an impositon on widows and should be terminated, but his objection was dropped in the 1551 edition of his Pentateuch. In the meantime the Matthew Bibles of 1537 and 1551 and the Mathew-Becke versions of 1549 and 1551 castigated clergy who resorted to minds, along with mass pence, dirge groats, and trentals, to supplement their incomes. Curiously, the Geneva and Beza-Tomson annotators were silent on minds and wakes, though no doubt they disapproved of them, for this was the basic Protestant position.[30]

The fundamental objection of Protestant reformers to wakes and minds was the traditional association of these observances with the doctrine of purgatory and prayers for the dead. When Pilkington argued that no funeral observances could entail superstition, he interpreted this declaration to mean that minds, including the accompanying feasts, were prohibited. Becon agreed, pointing to their basis in Catholic theological principles as his justification, while Gilby repudiated "their wakes and idolatrous bankettes." Pilkington found the dancing and minstrels on these occasions offensive and contrary to nature. In their injunctions and visitation articles the prelates sought to stamp out minds as superfluous, superstitious, and reflective of a belief in purgatory.[31]

The practices continued well into the age and beyond, thanks partly to the connivance of conservative clergy. Minds in the parish of St. Helen's, Abingdon, Berks., in the early years of the Elizabethan period usually required 4d. to 3s. for tapers, which the reformers opposed. At Dunstew, Oxon., the parish church observed a wake day as late as 1584, when there was raucous activity in the churchyard by celebrants who disrupted evening prayer. In West Kirby, Ches., church bells were rung as part of the twelve-month minds, but in 1578, this exercise caused the presentment of two men in the visitation. In the same year the Privy Council was anxious about the riotous behavior that characterized Cheshire wakes. As late as 1583 Marmaduke Middleton, bishop of St. David's, complained in his injunctions that ministers tolerated month and yearly minds as well as prayer for the dead.[32]

The association of these practices with superstition is illustrated by the "Lyke-Wake Dirge" used in Cleveland in this era and as late as the eighteenth century. A funeral ballad or lament used in a death ritual, it was based on pre-Christian elements, partially deriving from ancient Norse beliefs. According to this tradition, the dead had to pass over a narrow bridge with a flaming gulf below it and then traverse a moor of briars and thorns in bare feet, though shoes were provided to those who had devoted a pair of shoes to the poor during their lifetime. Although a certain amount of social utilitarianism marked such customs, the reformers were unwilling to accept the nonbiblical imagery and the superstitious overtones.[33]

On wakes and minds, Anglican and Puritan reformers agreed in desiring to terminate them, because these customs encouraged prayers for the dead and belief in purgatory. Yet some of the conservative parish clergy winked at or took part in these rituals despite the injunctions and visitation articles that called for ending them. In part the observance of these practices, like those of rogations, reinforced the community spirit; hence their suppression was one more factor in the breakdown of the communal life of the medieval village, and in its place the growth of the spirit of individualism.

(4) Funeral Expenses

No man [must] exceede in expences or charges superfluous, but euery one to confine his cost within the bounds of his abilitie.

Sir William Segar[34]

The chardge of my funeralles . . . shalbe greate chardges to hym.

Frances Grey, duchess of Suffolk[35]

The principal objections to excessive funeral pomp stemmed from piety and from hostility to Catholic symbolism, but financial reasons sometimes were more compelling than the religious factors. It was primarily the Puritans who cautioned against costly burials as vain pomp, preferring a simpler service that reflected Christian decency and respect. In a comment on John 12:7, Cartwright argued that "in the Iewes buriall, to whom the knowledge of the resurrection, was not so cleare as now it is to us through the resurrection of our Sauiour Christ, more cost was allowed then we may lawfully use, unlesse we meane to call our Sauiour Christ to his graue againe." Because the grave was a temporary resting place, excessive expenditure lacked justification and implied doubt about the Christian resurrection. To the religious and economic arguments was added one citing the preservation of the social order, occasioned by the fear that lavish spending would undermine the visual imagery intended to reinforce the social hierarchy. Late in the age the Garter King of Arms, Sir William

Segar, asserted that the heralds must see that no one spent excessive amounts on a funeral, but ensure that each rank stayed within its bounds. By way of reform Segar thought Elizabeth or her earl marshal should prescribe a certain number of mourners for each social degree, with only the number of poor mourners (customarily determined by the age of the deceased) varying. Thus on religious, economic, and social grounds concern was voiced about the cost of funerals.[36]

Some, particularly those of Puritan persuasion, favored reduced expenditure. In 1576, Sir Anthony Cooke willed that he be buried without excessive charges, and in 1589 Mildmay asked his executors to avoid vain funeral pomp of the sort associated with Catholicism, with the savings devoted to poor preachers and scholars and the destitute. In hope of a joyful resurrection, Walsingham asked to be buried without the pomp usually accorded to a man of his stature, yet a major reason for his decision was the debt he left to his heirs. Recognizing the difficulties an expensive funeral could pose for heirs, Lady Jane Gerard in 1575 left the decision on funeral expenses to her executors, with no indication that religious considerations were involved. Financial motives also were behind the order of Leicester and Burghley to hold down the expenses for the funeral of John Manners, earl of Rutland, whose brother and predecessor in the earldom had died only ten months earlier. The desire, then, for less pretentious funerals was due to economic as well as religious considerations.[37]

Some Elizabethan testators carefully specified the amount for their funerals, sometimes in curious juxtaposition to statements expressing concern about superfluous expense. In 1583 Thomas Radcliffe, earl of Sussex, directed that he be buried without unnecessary pomp, yet in keeping with his dignity and estate, which he reckoned would cost no more than £1,500; the actual figure was £1,629. Earlier, in 1576, John Paulet, marquess of Winchester, directed his executors to spend £1,000, and Margaret Stuart, countess of Lennox, who wished to be interred in Westminster Abbey, ordered in 1578 that £1,200 be spent on her funeral. Burghley desired in 1598 to be buried with "convenient comelines" in keeping with his barony, with expenses not to exceed £1,000, the same maximum previously imposed by Parker for his own funeral. At a much humbler level, a gentleman such as Sir Thomas Grey of Horton set aside £100 for a suitable funeral. That some testators regarded such substantial amounts as reasonable and moderate casts doubt on how much those who forbade excessive funeral pomp really intended to economize.[38]

Expenses for the more elaborate Elizabethan funerals were nearly prohibitive, though when inflation is taken into account Elizabethan peers were considerably less extravagant than Henry Percy, earl of Northumberland, whose expenses of £1,038 in 1489 would have run to some £4,000 in the late 1580s, or Thomas Howard, second duke of Norfolk, whose expenses of £1,340 in 1524 would also have been approximately £4,000 in the same period. Among the Elizabethan peers, the most expensive funerals were those of Robert Dudley, earl of Leicester (over £3,000 in 1588), Edward Manners, earl of Rutland (£2,297 in 1587), Francis Russell, earl of Bedford (over £1,700 in 1585), Thomas Radcliffe, earl of Sussex (£1,629 in 1583), Henry Hastings, earl of Huntingdon (£1,393 in 1596), Frances Radcliffe, countess of Sussex (£1,368 in 1589), Walter Devereux, earl of Essex (£1,140 in 1576), and William Paulet, marquess of Winchester (£1,122 in 1572). No differentiation by religious persuasion is notable here, for the biggest funerals were for Anglican and Puritan alike. Some peers were given less lavish funerals, among them Thomas Howard, viscount Bindon (£446 in 1582), Anthony Browne, viscount Montagu (c. £666 in 1592), and Lord Burghley (c. £1,000 in 1598), but again religious differentiations are not discernible. Among Elizabethan peers, funeral expenses were governed primarily by social and political rank and by financial circumstances rather than religious views. [39]

Expenses among the gentry varied widely. The funerals of Lady Catherine Knollys (at least £640 in 1569), Sir Nicholas Bacon (£910 in 1578), and Sir Henry Sidney (£1,571 in 1586) were on a par with those of the peerage. On a less grand scale, but still above the typical knight, the 1579 obsequies of Sir William Ingleby of Ripley, Yorks., a Catholic who conformed to the Church of England, cost £136, while those of Sir Thomas Cawarden, master of the revels, ran £129 in 1559. Sir Thomas Leyland of Morley, probably a Catholic, had a funeral that cost £54 in 1562, but more typical of gentry funerals was that of Thomas Clifton of Westby, which cost c. £13 in 1589. Funerals of the gentry ranged from £5 to £200, with social rank and financial conditions apparently accounting for the variation. [40]

For those who were not part of the landed aristocracy, the most expensive funerals were accorded to some of the prelates, such as the approximately £1,000 for Parker in 1575 and almost that much for Aylmer in 1594. Some obsequies for professionals could be very costly, as in the funeral of Robert Nowell in 1569, which ran about £790. The best indicator of relative funeral expenses comes from the town of Exeter in 1575, which had an established scale of rates depending on one's wealth:

Minimum Wealth	Maximum Funeral Expense
£2,000	£100
£1,000	£50
1,000 marks	£33 6s. 8d.
£500	£25
£200	£10
£100	£5
£50	£2 10s.
£20	£1 10s.
£10	£1

Even so, it was determined in Exeter that because "the great expences in funerals are now by alteration of Religion abated," the mayor and common council were to reduce these costs as they thought best. For most Elizabethans, funeral expenses would not have exceeded £1 or £2, in striking contrast to the money laid out by the propertied and persons of substance. Most Elizabethans did not need clerical exhortations to reduce funeral expenses, for they were already minimal.[41]

The financial difficulties the peerage faced led to a relative decrease in the opulence of their funerals after c. 1580, as reflected in their wills and actual expenses, but the motivation was more economic than religious. Nevertheless such attempts were opposed by the court, for Elizabeth had a high regard for pageantry. Despite her reputation for frugality, she occasionally paid the costs of funerals of impoverished peers or their spouses (notably her relations), to ensure the maintenance of proper ceremonial. She provided funds for Elizabeth Parr, marchioness of Northampton (1565), Catherine (Grey) Seymour, countess of Hertford (1568), Margaret Stuart, countess of Lennox (1577), and Henry Carey, Lord Hunsdon (1596), as well as Lady Catherine Knollys (1569).[42]

Burghley, in his capacity as commissioner for the earl marshal, acted as Elizabeth's agent in pressuring reluctant peers to provide appropriate funeral pageants, but on other occasions he rendered advice on the use of limited funds. The problems of the Manners family necessitated Burghley's involvement in 1587 and 1588. Edward, fifth earl of Rutland, had died in 1587, leaving his lease of Newark

Castle and other property to his widow free of encumbrances. Nevertheless, his brother, John, the sixth earl, insisted that she assume responsibility for her late husband's debts and the funeral expenses (which alone amounted to £2,297). She sued in Chancery, and Burghley and Walsingham finally worked out a compromise. When the fourth earl died the following year, Burghley and Leicester asked the executors to hold down expenses. The contingent of mourners, they stipulated, must not exceed the number necessary to bear the corpse and carry the standard and related items. Blacks must be provided for the widow and her children and the gentlemen and yeomen normally in the household, but not retainers. The number of poor must be limited to the age of the deceased, and the remainder of the expenses must be restricted by corresponding with the heralds. The estate must not be charged to provide blacks for Leicester, Burghley, and their servants. The estate of this family was in such dire straits that intervention by the government was deemed essential, but no religious factors were involved.[43]

Intervention of a different sort came in April 1592, when Burghley, Hunsdon, and Charles Lord Howard of Effingham, as commissioners for the earl marshal, wrote to the executor of the will of Joan Lady Mordaunt. She was, they warned, not to be interred in a private, obscure manner, but to receive a funeral appropriate to her rank of baronness, under the direction of the Garter King of Arms. Burghley successfully pressured Henry Brooke, Lord Cobham, to provide a proper burial for his father, William, at Cobham, Kent, in 1597. Lord Henry had tried to have his father interred in London to reduce the expenditure, but Burghley would have none of it.[44]

One of the more intriguing cases in which Burghley was involved was that of Henry Hastings, earl of Huntingdon, who died on 14 December 1595. At the direction of the Council of the North, the corpse, immediately after death, was disemboweled, embalmed, enclosed in "seere" cloth and lead, and left in his bedchamber at York. In the traditional ritual, four servants stood watch every night over the corpse. When the countess, his widow, asked the Council of the North to furnish the chamber and coffin in a manner befitting his rank, it retorted that she probably would prefer to handle most of the arrangements herself, but on 18 February, five weeks after the earl's death, she refused. The same day Burghley wrote to George, the new earl, indicating that the queen desired to know how the countess intended to proceed with the burial, since Elizabeth had no intention of paying the expenses. Recognizing that the deceased was in substantial debt (partly to the queen), Burghley told the fourth earl to pay the funeral costs out of the estate and not burden himself. The new earl was directed to be the chief mourner, accompanied by the earls of Worcester and Lincoln, and the fourth earl's nephews, Lords Clinton and Compton. Burial, Burghley advised, was to be at York to reduce expenditure and conform, according to the countess, to the wishes of the deceased. Despite Burghley's urgings, the earl remained unburied. A letter to Burghley from Hutton, archbishop of York, dated 30 March 1596, suggests that the lord treasurer wanted the clergy of the northern province to help with the funeral charges. Hutton was reluctant, but agreed to lay most of the burden on pluralists and nonresidents, according to their ability to pay. The earl was finally buried on 28 April, at Ashby rather than York, at a cost of £1,393.[45]

The heavy expenditures of many of the landed aristocracy and persons of substance were due to the use of pageantry as a prop for the social order, to charitable expenses (as will be seen), to special costs such as embalming and heralds' fees, and to substantial funeral dinners. For persons of means, the largest expenditure was usually for black cloth, which could account for as much as seventy-five percent of the total costs, and was used to dress mourners and drape the church, the house, the chariot, and the hearse. Mourners received blacks according to their social degree, with sixteen yards required for each duke or earl, six for a baron, five for a knight or gentleman, and four for each yeoman, groom, and gentleman's servant. The quality of the cloth varied according to the degree and typically ran from 6s. to 20s. per yard, with 500 to 1,200 yards needed for the funerals of the great. Among the peerage, the sums devoted to blacks included £898 for the fifth earl of Rutland (and this would have been higher if the budget had permitted the quality of cloth used in earlier Tudor funerals), £356 for his successor, £838 for the first Lord Hunsdon, and £532 for the third earl of Huntingdon. Expenses for blacks by the gentry reflected the wide diversity of their funeral costs, including such outlays as £669 for Sir Nicholas Bacon, £248 for Henry Stanley of Bickerstaffe, Lancs., £96 for Sir William Ingleby, and £5 for Thomas Clifton. The bill for Parker's funeral included £726 for black cloth for mourners, while Robert Nowell's executors paid £662. Although most of these funds provided mourning gowns for those who could afford them, a modest amount paid for clothes for the destitute, and thus was a special form of poor relief.[46]

Other aspects of the pageantry were less expensive. For the upper gentry and the peers, painters' fees (for coats of arms, etc.) ranged from about £9 to £38, though in 1572, £63 was spent in this way for

Edward Stanley, earl of Derby. The painters' bills were normally sub-
sumed as part of the costs charged by the heralds, which could run
up to £150 for earls, with this charge embracing their fees and
blacks, travel expenses, rental of horses to pull the chariot, and related items that were part of the pageantry. The fee of the Garter
King of Arms was £10, while each herald received £3 6s. 8d. At
Parker's funeral, the total amount paid to the heralds was a whop-
ping £201. In some cases significant additional expense resulted
when the body had to be shipped some distance to the place of interment. When the corpse of Sir Henry Sidney was moved from Worcester to Penshurst in 1586, it was accompanied by members of the
Council in the Marches, as well as kinsmen and servants, whose expenses had to be met in addition to donations to the poor in each
town through which they traveled and fees to the bell-ringers in
those towns, topped off with the expense of hiring musicians to entertain the entourage in Oxford. The total bill exceeded £130.[47]
    If the deceased was a person of social standing or substance, a sur-
geon and an apothecary might disembowel and perhaps embalm the
corpse. This process was necessary if a significant delay between
death and interment was expected, as was often the case with persons whose pageants required careful preparations, or whose bodies
had to be shipped some distance for burial. The diary of the London
undertaker, Henry Machyn, indicates that work on the accoutrements of the obsequies sometimes began the day of a person's death,
but substantial time lags were not unusual. Several examples indicate the delays that could occur: Dorothy Brooke, Lady Cobham,
died on 25 September 1559, and preparations were begun by the
undertaker on the 28th for the funeral held on 4 October. About the
same length of time was involved for Margaret Manners, countess of
Rutland, who died on 13 October 1559; her hearse was prepared the
20th, with burial the 21st of that month. Embalming would have
been essential for Preston Candover, Lord Williams of Thame, who
died on 14 October 1559. His hearse was readied on 9 November,
but it was not until the 15th that his body was interred. Longer delays occurred, as with Huntingdon, who died on 14 December 1595
but was not buried for four and a half months. Disemboweling was
not too expensive (5 to 10s.), but embalming was more costly and
involved a ritual of its own. Thomas Radcliffe, earl of Sussex, was
embalmed in 1583 by four surgeons using turpentine, Greek pitch,
gum, myrrh, mastic, aloes, aquavite, and "Artificiall Banbuc." It cost
£6 to embalm Catherine Seymour, countess of Hertford, and £23 to
disembowel and embalm Parker and inter his remains. Not all who

could afford it were willing to be embalmed. Mary Percy, countess of Northumberland, asked in her will (1572) that she not be embalmed, because of her modesty, and Lucy Nevill, Lady Latimer, made a similar request. Because of the rapidity with which the body of the sister of George Clifford, earl of Cumberland, decayed, she too probably had objected to being embalmed. There was no hostility to embalming on religious grounds in Anglican circles, hence the reaction of these women appears attributable to modesty.[48]

Another major expense in the funerals of the middling and upper folk was the funeral dinner, sometimes limited to family and friends but in some cases open to all comers, in the tradition of medieval aristocratic hospitality. The precedent for such a custom was clear enough, but the examples were sometimes staggering in scope and expense. When Thomas Howard, third duke of Norfolk, was buried at Framlingham in October 1554, the magnificent dinner required forty oxen, a hundred sheep, sixty calves, and undetermined numbers of deer, swans, cranes, capons, rabbits, pigeons, pike, and other fish and animals. Bread, wine, and beer were provided in extensive quantities. The feast was intended for rich and poor alike, who flocked to Framlingham from the surrounding region. Often such feasts not only commemorated the deceased but provided the last major occasion for the old household to be together. Funeral dinners could run to £300 or more, though they were often less, as the £112 for Henry Carey, Lord Hunsdon, in 1596, the £50 for Archbishop Parker in 1575, and the £52 for Robert Nowell in 1569. In gentry circles, some representative costs were £33 for Sir Thomas Cawarden, £13 for Sir William Ingleby, and £1 12s. for Thomas Clifton (which provided ale, fish, eggs, and birds). A Kentish yeoman bequeathed £10 to provide "a drinking" after his funeral. Members of London companies provided funeral meals for their colleagues, which in the 1570s typically required £6 to £7.[49]

A variety of lesser expenses existed, some of which affected even the lower orders. Burial in a church required fees ranging from 3s. 4d. for a parish such as Great Wigston, Leics., to £5 for Chester Cathedral. Breaking the ground and other charges at Lambeth necessitated £10 14s. 6d. for Archbishop Parker. Interment in a churchyard ran from 2d. to 1s. 4d., or 2s. to 2s. 8d. if a coffin was used. A gravedigger required 3d. and up for his services. The verger's bill at St. Paul's, London, for the funeral of Sir Nicholas Bacon was £18 4s. 4d., while that of Robert Nowell was £13 5d. These sums included fees for the bell-ringers; when charged separately, such fees ranged from 1s. to 26s. 8d., the latter for the countess of Lennox's funeral in

Westminster Abbey. A choir for the countess of Hertford cost £1 and persons to watch her corpse an additional £2. Ministers might charge 10s. to £2 or more for persons of means, but probably nothing for the truly destitute, if indeed they received services. Disposing of the genuinely poor was a social obligation that caused some friction over who would assume the minimal costs, as happened, for instance, at St. Margaret's, Westminster. According to 21 Henry VIII, c. 6, a mortuary (the second-best animal or garment of the deceased) could be demanded by the minister and parish church wherever customary, though persons with goods worth less than 10 marks after debts were exempt. Mortuaries were still demanded in the seventeenth century.[50]

Thus in the Elizabethan era funeral expenses were governed to an important degree by financial ability and socio-political status. Although some persons were motivated by religious considerations to reduce funeral expenses, it is not clear how prevalent this motivation was, or to what extent it was perhaps more true of Puritans than Anglicans. Those who were able generally preferred to be interred, as was Henry Fitzalan, earl of Arundel, "with solemne pompe of costlye funerall . . . accordinge vnto his honorable cawlinge," though increasingly expressing distaste for excessive pomp (which usually meant pageantry in excess of one's degree). By the end of the age, some folk were turning to rapid burials and nighttime ceremonies to avoid large expenses, as the peers began to do c. 1615. In 1601 Lady Margaret Hoby attended the morning funeral of a man who had died only a few hours earlier, and the following year Walsingham's widow died suddenly and was buried secretly in St. Paul's, probably because of the family's constrained finances but perhaps additionally motivated by Puritan convictions. As the age wore on, peers began to recognize that they could not maintain the degree of spending that some of their forebears had achieved, but it bothered the queen and some of her Council that the traditional pageantry with its social implications might not be maintained. When Sir Philip Sidney died, Walsingham wrote to Leicester in November 1586, explaining that he had been forced to delay the funeral because of Sir Philip's debts: "I doe not see howe the same can be performed with that solempnytye that apperteynethe withowt the utter undoing of his credytors." So it was not so much the preaching of the clerics in many cases but the constraints of the pocketbook that began to curtail the excessive expenditures of the aristocracy on their last rites.[51]

(5) Funerals and Charity

A great fatte oxe sod out in furmenty for them with bread and drinke aboun-
dantly to furnish out the premises, and euery person had two pence, for such
was the dole.

Thomas Harman [52]

> Ne were it so that the beggers cry
> On her [the widow] so faste and let her for to pray
> with some good man haue these folke away
> I neuer sawe such folke, and so lewde.

Robert Copland [53]

Although the reformers had urged Elizabethans not to delay
charitable contributions until their funerals, it was generally expected that the traditional practice of dispensing relief by persons
of means would continue. Trigge noted approvingly that in the
economic crisis in the latter part of Mary's reign the poor would
have starved had it not been for relief in the funerals of the wealthy.
Puritans were, however, anxious to channel more of the funeral expenditures to poor relief than was commonly done, particularly by
providing gowns for the needy rather than for other mourners. The
funeral meal also was supposed to include the needy. Yet the Puritan abhorrence of hypocrisy prompted Burton's sarcastic reference
to those who provided gowns for the poor and a dole, for this required only the dispensing of money no longer useful to the deceased. Although the Puritans would have preferred more substantial
giving while donors were alive, they were not opposed to further
benefactions in wills; unlike the Anglicans, they pressed for a greater
share of the total funeral expenditures to be dispensed for the
needy. [54]

In connection with funerals, charity took three forms: the bestowal of clothing, the distribution of alms, and the provision of food at a
funeral dinner. Normally the clothing provided for the poor consisted of black frieze mourning gowns, though some received russet
gowns or coats. The number varied, usually in accord with the age
of the deceased, the degree of pomp, or the amount of money
available for charity. In the period 1569 to 1576, the cost of gowns
typically ranged from 5s. 8d. to £1 4s. apiece. When the queen died a
grand display of charity ensued, with 266 poor women and 15 poor
men receiving gowns, though even this had been exceeded in 1569 at
the funeral of Robert Nowell, when 254 men, 29 women, 16 children, and 36 students were recipients of gowns for the poor. Urban

wealth led to some large provisions of clothing for the poor, as in the case of Sir Thomas Gresham in 1575 (200 persons), William Lamb in 1580 (108 persons), and John Robinson, a Merchant of the Staple in 1599 (50 men and 70 woolwinders). These donations exceeded those of the peers, which generally ranged from 40 to 100, as in the case of Lord Williams of Thame (60 in 1559), Pembroke (100 in 1570), Essex (40 in 1576), Derby (100 in 1572), Sussex (45 in 1583), Rutland (50 in 1587), and Derby (100 in 1593). Among the wives of the peers, Lady Rich had 24 (1558), the countess of Rutland 60 (1559), the countess of Shrewsbury 48 (1567), and Lady Lumley 48 (1578). In keeping with their inferior social position, the gentry typically donated gowns to between six and forty poor persons, whereas successful City folk in the early years of the period kept pace with the landed aristocracy, providing clothes to the poor in numbers ranging from twelve to sixty. As befitted his status, Parker had seventy-two poor men in gowns in his procession in 1575, but two Marian bishops, Rochester and Chichester, who died in 1558 had only twelve and eighteen, respectively, whereas a former abbot who died in 1565 had only five, and even that depended on receipt of his pension. Government officials and other professionals provided gowns for poor folk in numbers comparable to those of the gentry and City merchants.[55]

The bestowal of charity in the form of clothing reflects economic conditions almost exclusively. The number of poor mourners in a funeral procession was not an accurate indication of social rank; some City merchants surpassed peers, and the attorney Robert Nowell rivaled the queen. Nor does the evidence hitherto gathered suggest differences in the number of poor mourners according to religious views. Some restricted the number of mourners to correspond with the age of the deceased, which seems to have been more common among women than men. It was likely a desire to distinguish by social rank that led some peers to settle on the relatively high number of a hundred freshly clothed poor folk in their funeral processions.

The second means of dispensing charity at funerals was the dole, customarily bestowed after the conclusion of the formal ceremonies, though when cadavers of eminent persons were transported, alms were given to the needy in towns and villages where the body rested on its final trek. The amount of the dole was either a fixed sum or a designated amount (usually 1 or 2d.) for each poor person attending the funeral. Some peers distinguished themselves by setting aside sums reflective of their rank and social responsibility; among them were the marquess of Winchester (£100 in 1576), Burghley (£100 in

1598), the countess of Lennox (£40 to the poor in general and £100 to poor women in 1578), and the earl of Shrewsbury, at whose funeral in 1590 some 8,000 persons received the dole. The financial constraints afflicting some peers severely curtailed their doles, as in the case of Essex (£40 in 1576) and Hunsdon (£14 in 1596). Early in the reign, the countess of Rutland and Lady Cobham provided 2d. apiece for the poor at their funerals, an amount equaled by some gentry and clergy. Typical legacies from the gentry for doles ranged from £8 to £40, whereas others directed that all the poor receive 1 or 2d. each. Catholics such as Thomas Babington of Dethwick, Derby, decreed that small sums be given to a specified number of poor each week for a year, with the intent of encouraging prayers to speed the soul of the donor through purgatory. When the clergy left money for a dole, it was usually 1 or 2d. per recipient, though more substantive amounts sometimes were left, such as the £40 bequeathed by Robert Pursglove, deprived suffragan bishop of Hull in 1579. Doles by London citizens were comparable to those of the gentry.[56]

Once again, no pattern of giving by religious views can be identified, though the practice of some Catholics of providing a series of regular donations to encourage prayer for the deceased largely died out. Protestant influence also is discernible in the determination of some Elizabethans to reduce funeral pomp sharply and channel the savings to poor relief. In 1576, Sir Thomas Smith directed his executors to determine the place and ceremonial of his funeral "having rather regard to the relief of the poor, than to any extreme manner of mourning, not becoming Christians." Similarly, in 1578 Sir Nicholas Bacon reckoned he could give 500 marks to the impoverished as the result of not providing blacks to the wealthy (apart from his household and family). In 1590, Lady Jane, widow of Sir Lawrence Smith of Hough, Ches., bequeathed £40 to the poor in lieu of having the traditional blacks, which she deemed vain and superfluous. There was, then, some additional relief for the poor as a consequence of the movement, on religious grounds, toward less elaborate obsequies.[57]

Funeral dinners were viewed from two perspectives, one of which reflected a heightened sense of identity with the family or a specified social group, such as the guilds. In London throughout the age testators bequeathed money to provide funeral dinners for members of their company, and their widows sometimes did the same. On at least one occasion, when the amount bequeathed (£5) was not sufficient, the Ironmongers' Company in 1576 decided to supplement it so the dinner could be held. To avoid the presence of rabble at their funeral dinners, some Elizabethans directed their executors to restrict admission to honest persons, persons of "reputacions," neighbors, or (in the case of Richard Jones, rector of Bury, Lancs.) the "rychersorte." Such restrictions appear to have been occasioned more by a desire to maintain decorum than financial reasons though in London especially, the latter must have been a consideration because of the size of potential crowds.[58]

In contrast, other Elizabethans continued the tradition of grand hospitality by opening their funeral dinners to all comers. When Francis Talbot, earl of Shrewsbury, was buried in 1560 at Sheffield, meat and drink, as well as a dole for the poor, were provided for all who came. In the same year, at the funeral in Cambridge of Edward VI's physician, Dr. Thomas Wendy, some five hundred people were fed. Every poor person who attended the funeral of William Swift, esquire, of Rotherham, Yorks., in 1568 got a penny and a free dinner. Not only did peers and gentry provide this last grand gesture of hospitality, but some professionals and urban folk did the same. Even in London, some funeral meals were open to all, as in the case of the dinners for Sir Thomas Curteis (1559), a former lord mayor and member of the Fishmongers' Company, and Agnes Lewen (1562), widow of an ironmonger and former sheriff. The spice bread remaining from the latter's dinner was then dispensed "to evere howse and about the cette unto worshephulle men and women." Robert Nowell bequeathed £60 to provide for a funeral dinner and a supper for all mourners and the poor of the parish where he was buried. Practical considerations sometimes necessitated restricting the number at the actual dinner but afterward extending hospitality to all comers. After the feast for Edward Manners, earl of Rutland, in 1587, 3,000 to 4,000 people were fed, while the leftovers from the banquet for Lady Katherine Berkeley in 1596 fed 1,000. After Lady Cobham's funeral dinner, meat and drink were given to the poor. One gentleman, George Benson of Hugil, Westm., directed his executors to divide the "broken meat" from the funeral meal among the poor and make an additional pottage of beef and mutton to feed them, maintaining the principle of different foods for different social ranks. For those in economic straits or in times of dearth, such doles of food must have provided welcome if temporary relief. A testator could provide for such hospitality knowing that it would redound to his reputation while the real costs were borne by the heirs of his estate.[59]

It was inevitable that open hospitality, coupled with a dole for the poor, led not only to large crowds but also to riotous behavior. A classic case occurred in 1601 at the funeral of Lady Mary, widow of Sir Thomas Ramsey, late lord mayor of London, for "at her sixe

peny dole kept at Leaden hall, the number of beggers was so excessive and unreasonable that seventeen of them were thronged and
trampled to death in the place and divers sore hurt and bruised." The
presence of so many poor also could lead to sexual improprieties,
especially if they had traveled some distance and lodged overnight in
barns or comparable shelters. Local authorities had their tasks compounded by trying to watch for rogues and vagabonds attracted by
the largess at some funerals. In London, people often defaced hearses
as they passed in procession, hoping thereby to sell the loot. About
1578, Aylmer licensed a man to keep order at the funerals of the
aristocracy. The threat of disorder was undoubtedly a factor in motivating some testators to restrict the extent of hospitality.[60]

Although not strictly part of poor relief, the concern of some
testators for their servants led them to make special provisions in
their wills to keep the household together for a given time after the
funeral. Otherwise the funeral dinners effectively marked the break-
up of the old household, leaving servants with the perhaps unantici-
pated prospect of unemployment. The most common period to provide servants with food and lodging after a funeral was one month,
though in 1597 William Brooke, Lord Cobham, decreed only ten
days. Some masters were more generous, assuming responsibility for
their servants from six months to three years after the funeral. Fear-
ing that his servants might run at random and live disorderly lives, in
December 1558 Sir Thomas Cheney, lord warden of the Cinque Ports,
directed that his servants have as much as three years of food and
lodging as long as they behaved and could not locate new service.
Generally, such testators also provided their servants with wages for
six months to a year. These actions were a final manifestation of the
responsibilities masters were exhorted to have for their servants by
Anglican and Puritan reformers; through these actions, social order
was better preserved and the transition of servants from one position
to another was eased. Christian charity and social stability were alike
served.[61]

In sum, funerals provided an occasion for persons of substance to
make a final, somewhat showy donation to the impoverished in the
form of mourning gowns or coats, doles of money, and food at or
after the funeral dinners. In addition, masters could exercise responsibility for their servants by providing funds to keep the household
together, normally for six months to a year, to enable its members to
find new employment. Although the religious reformers advocated
more substantive giving during one's lifetime, they had no objection
to charity at funerals, with the exception of the Puritan worry that

some of this smacked of hypocrisy. Nevertheless, Puritans proposed that an even greater percentage of the funeral expenditures be devoted to charity. Some lay people were sufficiently persuaded that they reduced the amount spent on blacks and used those funds to relieve the destitute. No apparent differentiation by religious grouping is manifest with respect to the charity bestowed at funerals; rather, the extent of charity was determined principally by economic factors and social status. Although extensive funeral charity, especially the provision of mourning gowns, contributed to the pageantry and was a prop of the social hierarchy, such grand displays sometimes incited thievery and—in the case of large funeral meals—riotous and licentious conduct. Thus the trend toward relative simplicity late in the age was due to a combination of religious motives, economic factors, and aversion to the inappropriate behavior sometimes incited by lavish funeral pageants.

(6) Funerals and Social Pageantry

No man should be so superstitious as to beleeue these externall complements to be propitiatorie vnto the soule.

Sir William Segar[62]

Sic transit gloria mundi.

Henry Machyn[63]

As in the case of weddings and christenings, funerals were intended to include pageantry commensurate with social rank. The government's position was summarized by William Segar, Garter King of Arms, at a time when, in 1602, the lavish spectacles were being undermined by religious motives, economic considerations, and the unruly behavior of the lower orders. For Segar, ample biblical precedent supported the traditional spectacle. Genesis 50 and Tobit 12 were cited as justification for funeral pomp, and the burial of Christ was adduced as an example to emulate, "for albeit he subiected himselfe to worldly contumelies, and death ignominious, yet was his Funerall notable and glorious, according to the prophesie of *Esay* [11]." Segar, however, acknowledged that such ceremonies had no benefit for the souls of the deceased. For persons of honor he called for three particular rituals to be performed: embalming, a solemn period of mourning (usually thirty days as in France), and a concourse of friends when the body was interred. Cremation and the burial of bodies at sea were disapproved as lacking appropriate honor for the dead. With obvious loyalty to the College of Arms, he defended the need for the heralds to supervise the order and pageantry of funerals, particularly since "diuers degrees of men doe vsually and casually meete at our funerals" and no indignity must be done to any be dishonoring their social estates. Despite Segar's defense, the College came under increasing attack in the seventeenth century as people came to doubt the need for the extent of funeral ceremony dictated by the heralds, and as legatees became irate when executors diverted large sums to pay for lavish obsequies.[64]

Neither Puritan nor Anglican objected in principle to funeral pageantry, though, as we have seen, there was a growing tendency to reduce its scope. It was also recognized that the benefits of the spectacle were solely for the living, particularly for their comfort. Pageantry must be comely, in accord with each person's social estate, and free from superstition and superfluity. As long as these conditions were met, pageantry was acceptable and was even a sign of divine favor to the deceased.[65]

The principal responsibility for the maintenance of pageantry rested in the College of Arms, though it was periodically called to account for its decisions by Burghley. Particularly in the latter part of the age, the College was rent by internal feuding and was subjected to external criticism. In 1593, for instance, one of Sir John Puckering's men complained to Anthony Bacon about "the greate decaie, daily arrisinge in that office, by negligence or Ignorance in such as are consorted therin; (to the no small blemishe of the whole nobilitie . . .)." Yet the College functioned fairly well, normally taking care to prepare requirements for funerals of the aristocracy and then supervising and participating in the obsequies. For peers a herald usually had to spend one or two months in such activity. In accord with provisions laid down by Thomas Howard, duke of Norfolk, acting in his capacity as earl marshal, the fundamental responsibility for the funerals of Knights of the Garter and their wives, peers and their spouses, the archbishops of Canterbury and York, the bishop of Winchester, and heirs apparent of dukes, marquises, earls, and their wives rested with the Garter King of Arms, assisted by Clarenceux and Norroy. The funerals of barons and gentlemen were the responsibility of the latter two officials. An indication of the precision with which they worked out the pageantry is their reckoning of the numbers of mourners of estate at obsequies: sixteen for a sovereign, thirteen for a prince, eleven for a duke, ten for a marquis, eight for an earl, seven for a viscount, six for a baron, five for a knight, four for an esquire, and two for a mere gentleman. The work of the College is evidence of the value placed on social order, dignified pageantry, and genealogical heritage. Despite the Protestant repudiation of much of the traditional theology surrounding death, especially extreme unction, purgatory, and satisfactory masses, the funeral continued to be the object of considerable attention and expense.[66]

No better manifestations of the splendor and pageantry of Elizabethan funerals remain than the colored drawings in the British Library (Add. MS 35,324), which include the processions of Anne of Cleves, Sir Christopher Hatton, Mary Stuart, and Henry Radcliffe, earl of Sussex. At Penshurst Place, Kent, a detailed drawing depicts the funeral procession of Sir Philip Sidney, with fine renderings of the escutcheons on the black cloth covering the casket.

One of the grandest Elizabethan funerals was that of Edward Stanley, earl of Derby, who died on 24 October 1572. The body, "well seared, wrapt in lead, and chested," remained in a black-draped room until 29 November, when it was placed in his chapel at Latham Hall and covered with a pall of black velvet embellished with escutcheons of his arms. His coat of arms, helmet, crest, sword, and target were placed on the pall, and around it were situated the standard with its cross of St. George and the earl's motto, the great banner with his armorial coat, and six bannerolls with arms impaled indicating his ancestry. The following morning, a Sunday, the new earl, accompanied by a large number of esquires and gentlemen, as well as the steward, treasurer, and comptroller, gathered around the body with white staffs. Clarenceux King of Arms, in his formal dress, praised God for the deceased, whose titles were formally recited, and a sermon followed. The ceremony was repeated by Norroy King of Arms before evensong on Wednesday, the day before the funeral.

Meanwhile, two miles away at Ormskirk, final preparations were made for the funeral. The hearse, an open, framed structure in which the coffin rested, had to be readied and draped with black. The earl's was one of the grand hearses, thirteen feet long, nine feet wide, and twenty-one feet tall, with pitched roof and garnished double rails. It was covered with black velvet and taffeta, with fringes of silk, and decorated with escutcheons. The hearse stood between the choir and the nave in the church, which was hung with black cloth embellished with escutcheons of the earl's arms alone and of his arms impaled with those of his three wives.

On Thursday, 4 December, the funeral procession wound from Latham Hall to Ormskirk, led by two yeoman conductors carrying black staffs, followed by one hundred poor men, walking in pairs, in new black gowns. The choir of forty, wearing surplices and singing, was next. Behind them came the earl's standard, borne by a hooded esquire on horseback, with trappings extending to the ground and bearing four buckram escutcheons on each side. He preceded eighty of the earl's mounted gentlemen, riding in pairs and wearing robes with hoods on their shoulders. The two secretaries of the deceased, similarly mounted and garbed, rode before fifty esquires and knights riding in pairs. After them came two chaplains in academic hoods; the preacher (the dean of Chester) with his D.D. hood and his horse covered with trappings; the late earl's steward, treasurer, and comptroller, hoods on their shoulders, trappings on their mounts, and white staffs in their hands; and a hooded esquire, trappings and escutcheons on his horse, bearing the great banner of the earl. At the heart of the procession rode the four heralds, hooded and riding horses with black trappings extending to the ground and embellished with escutcheons. The first was Lancaster, wearing the earl's damask coat of arms and bearing his parcel-gilt helmet. "On a wreath of his coulers stood his creast, curiously paynted, and wrought in gould and silver." Norroy King of Arms followed, wearing a coat of arms embroidered with the arms of England, and bearing the earl's shield of arms within a garter and crowned with a coronet to indicate his rank. Behind him rode Clarenceux King of Arms carrying the earl's sword with its gilt handle in a velvet scabbard and with the pommel up. The last herald was Garter King of Arms, bearing the earl's coat of arms, and riding to the right of a hooded gentleman usher with a white rod in his hand. Now came the chariot, drawn by four horses with black velvet trappings and carrying the coffin draped in black and covered with escutcheons. Each horse was ridden by a page, robed and hooded in black, and at the front of the chariot sat a gentleman usher, likewise garbed and holding a white rod. Around the chariot rode ten hooded esquires, their horses with trappings to the ground; six of them conveyed the bannerolls. The new earl, the chief mourner, came on foot behind the chariot, flanked by hooded gentleman ushers with white rods on horseback and followed by a train bearer. Then came the late earl's gentleman of the horse, mounted and hooded, "leading in his hand the horse of estate, all covered and trapped in velvet." Behind the riderless horse rode eight hooded mourners, preceding a bareheaded yeoman in a black coat and on foot, who led the two grandsons, each with a gentleman to conduct his horse. Two yeoman ushers bearing white rods walked behind. The procession concluded with five hundred yeomen and all of the servants of those taking part, walking in pairs and stretching a great distance.

At the church the gentlemen entered and sat according to their ranks. The corpse was carried inside by eight hooded gentlemen, assisted by four yeomen, and placed on a table inside the hearse. The earl and the other eight principal mourners entered the hearse, with its cushions of black velvet to kneel on. Two esquires stood at the foot of the hearse, holding the standard and great banner, while the six esquires with bannerolls stood along the sides. Lancaster positioned himself between the standard and great banner, while the three Kings of Arms took their places at the head of the hearse with four gentleman ushers.

The service began with Norroy King of Arms stating the name and titles of the deceased, followed by the sermon by Dr. Richard Langworth, dean of Chester. A Psalm was sung and the Scripture was read by the vicar. Each herald was offered a piece of gold by the new earl on behalf of his father, following which the heralds gave the earl his father's coat of arms, sword, target, helmet, crest, standard, and great banner. A complex ceremony of additional offerings ensued, rank by serried rank, until the obsequies were concluded and most observers departed.

Eight gentlemen and four yeomen bore the body to the grave, preceded by three heralds. The esquires walked beside the coffin, six of them still carrying the bannerolls. Three officers, four gentleman ushers, and two yeoman ushers followed. When the coffin had been lowered in the grave, they knelt, broke their white staffs and rods over their heads, and threw the pieces into the grave. The six bannerolls were placed around the coffin, "and soe the sayd officers departed to Latham Hall, where, before [the funeral] dynner, they receaved theire offices and staves agayne of the new Earle their lord and master."[67]

With variations, such pageantry was typical of the upper peerage, though not always on this grand scale. In the funeral procession for Margaret Howard, duchess of Norfolk, in 1564, the choir was followed by a contingent of priests and the dean of Norwich, the alderman and mayor of Norwich, a body of gentlemen, the duchess' chaplains and almoner, the bishop of Norwich, and the steward, treasurer, and comptroller. The changes indicate the greater dignity accorded to a duchess. When Derby's son and heir, Henry Stanley, the thirteenth earl, died in 1593, his procession included a trumpeter to sound the dole, the mayors of Chester and Liverpool, and the bishop of Chester (who gave the sermon). In some processions, the coffin was carried by a half-dozen or so hooded men, and some coffins had praying effigies on top. These and comparable variations added interest but did not detract from the precedence accorded rank and pomp. At this level funeral processions had a good deal of drawing power, as suggested by Chamberlain's trip from Oxfordshire to London in the summer of 1598 to see Burghley's funeral.[68]

In accord with the purpose of funeral pageantry as a reinforcement of the social hierarchy, gentry obsequies were on a reduced scale from those of the peers. Fewer mourners of estate took part (two to five compared with six to eleven for peers), and fewer retainers and servants, because of the smaller households. There was less aristocratic paraphernalia. Penons, bannerolls, and scocheons were available to all the gentry, but the standard was restricted to knights and above, and only peers could have banners. The number of mourners in a funeral procession generally was calculated beforehand and reflected the status of the deceased. Although Edward Manners, earl of Rutland, had 560 and Burghley over 500, Lady Burghley had 315, John Manners, earl of Rutland, and Margaret Manners, countess of Rutland, had approximarely 200 each, and Lady Jane Seymour about 250. Most gentry probably had between 20 and 150, though some, such as Sir Nicholas Bacon, had in excess of 300, reflecting their political prominence. Lady Darcy had some 150, Sir Thomas Pope 60, and Richard Chetwoode, esq., 20, all in 1560. Although some gentry died in debt and left their widows bereft of funds to bury them according to their station, as happened to Lady Mary Denny in 1600, the general ideal was nevertheless to be buried with "great pompt of streamers, heralds, &c.", as was Sir Edmund Verney in 1599, although he had professed the usual wishes to avoid superfluity. The peerage sometimes participated in obsequies for politically prominent gentry, as in Hatton's funeral procession, which included Burghley and Thomas Sackville, Lord Buckhurst.[69]

In London, the pageantry was enriched by ceremonies accorded persons of substance, including merchants and their wives. It was common to see funeral processions in which members of the respective companies—the Merchant Taylors, the Ironmongers, the Skinners, the Brewers, and others—trooped solemnly in their livery to honor one of their own, wives as well as husbands. Obsequies for socially or politically prominent persons usually found the lord mayor and aldermen in the procession. Merchants who had been knighted were entitled to penons, scocheons, and standards, whereas squires could have penons and scocheons. Even those who were not entitled to arms of their own might have numerous scocheons bearing the arms of their societies. The livery of the great companies added to the color, as did the violet robes of the aldermen. Some processions included the masters of the hospitals, distinguished by their green staffs, as well as the hospital children marching in pairs with them. On occasion, wealth prompted men of the City to exceed their degree, as happened with Sir Thomas Gresham and the money-lender Thomas Sutton. As in funeral expenses and provision of garb for the needy, the number of mourners in the processions of merchants paralleled those of the gentry.[70]

Members of the professions had funerals that reflected their place in the social scheme. In 1562 Sir Humphrey Brown, justice of the Court of Common Pleas, had the judges and serjeants as well as members of the Inns of Court walking behind his coffin, whereas the following year Ranulph Cholmley, the former recorder of London, was honored by a funeral procession that included two hundred persons from the Inns of Court. A train of doctors accompanied the corpse of the physician Dr. Caldwell in 1584. Those who had been knighted were accorded the usual accoutrements tht signified their rank. Among their clergy, the archbishops had funerals on a par with peers, whereas bishops and deans paralleled the gentry. There were exceptions: Aylmer had 450 mourners in his procession in 1594, and Seth Holland, dean of Worcester, had sixty gentlemen of the Inns of Court and Oxford in his procession because of his reputation as a learned man. When Dr. John Caius died in London in 1573, his body was met at Trumpington by the master and fellows of Gonville and Caius College and was conducted into Cambridge. Although most ministers undoubtedly had simple funerals, exceptions were made for those with personal connections or religious reputation. In 1561, the Rev. Mr. Standley, steward to William Paulet, marquess of Winchester and lord treasurer, was buried in London after a ceremony in which Winchester's men carried his corpse, and his scocheons were displayed. Perkins was "solemnly and sumptuously" buried in 1602 at the expense of Christ's College, Cambridge. Essentially, the clergy like the laity were accorded funeral rites indicative of their place in the Elizabethan hierarchy. Death may have been the great equalizer, but there was certainly no social leveling, even in ceremonies for the clergy.[71]

For the masses, nearly all of the pageantry was beyond reach, except insofar as they were beneficiaries of doles, mourning garb, or funeral meals. On too many occasions, judging from contemporary complaints, the common folk were unable to locate ministers with the time to bury them or whose fees they could afford. The Separatists objected to burial by the clergy partly because of the financial hardships this imposed on the poor and the apparent reluctance some clerics had to perform such funerals. For those on the lower, dreary

reaches of the social scale, life's end brought at best a simple ceremony and a wooden or stone marker in a quiet corner of a churchyard or field. Many were interred only in shrouds, as wooden coffins
were beyond the reach of their survivors. The gulf that separated
them in life from those of birth and substance followed them to the
darkness of the grave. For them, there was no pageantry.[72]

Apart from the Separatists, no group seriously questioned that
funeral pageantry was socially beneficial and religiously acceptable,
as long as everything was done without superstition and in a comely
manner. The system was gradually undermined, however, by economic factors, by men such as Sir Thomas Gresham and Robert Nowell
who defied custom and emulated the obsequies of peers, and by the
growing desire (which had roots in religious piety) for simpler funerals in order to channel more money to charity. Elizabeth and
Burghley were keen upholders of spectacle and pageantry, and with
their support, the College of Arms staved off the mounting criticism
late in the age. James I did much to undermine funeral pageantry by
excessively dispensing honors, failing to shore up the finances of ail-
ing peers, and neglecting the College of Arms. It is perhaps instructive
that the decline of pageantry in the seventeenth century mirrored the
erosion of power of the peerage. With respect to pageantry, no difference in ideology or practice was discernible between Anglicans and
Puritans, other than a stronger Puritan desire to tone down the lavish
spectacles and channel more money to the impoverished.

(7) Monuments and Brasses

I will that there shal be a tombe ouer my father my mother & me with all our
pyktures grauen alofte of ye ston with all our armes abowte the said tombe &
our names beseching almightie god to haue mercye uppon our souls and all
christen soules.

Robert Pole, esq.[73]

Whose monumente alofte dothe stande,
for every man to wewe [view],
Whereby wee learne, what brittle steppes
all mortall men ensue.

Brass for Robert Chapman, esq.[74]

The expenditure of large sums on monuments provoked little comment from religious reformers. The orthodox position, as stated by
Sir William Segar, went largely unchallenged in print. Citing 1 Maccabees 13 and Exodus 35 as precedent for magnificent tombs, Segar

averred that they recalled the actions of honorable men and promoted engraving, masonry, painting, and embossing. As a guide, the epitaph on a monument or brass was supposed to record the names of the deceased and his progeny accurately, "his countrey and quality briefly, his life and vertues modestly, and his end Christianly, exhorting rather to example then vaineglory." Those who reacted negatively to superfluous pomp undoubtedly favored reducing expenditures for monuments and brasses, a view specifically stated by Pilkington. Because monuments did the deceased no good and were too expensive and unprofitable for survivors, he recommended omitting such expenses. Presumably, others shared his views, preferring simpler funeral ceremonies. [75]

More radical criticism came from the Separatists, as indicated in Barrow's blast against the exquisite sculpture and decorations of the tombs, replete with images and physical likenesses, and erected in churches. Although iconoclasm, including the defacing or destruction of monuments and brasses, is customarily associated with the 1640s and 1650s, some zealous Protestants of the left wreaked some damage in the Elizabethan era, despite government disapproval. These aniconic levelers, as one contemporary portrayed them, were viewed with alarm, as persons who would rather worship in empty barns and woods and fields than in churches contaminated with the abominations of the whore of Babylon. This was, in fact, the Separatist and Familist outlook, and reveals a hostility to monuments and brasses not found among Anglicans and Puritans. [76]

Such antagonism was not solely due to hostility over the expenditure of sizeable sums on monuments and brasses; the theological issues were important. As in the will of Robert Pole, esq., quoted in the epigraph to this section, monuments and brasses were traditionally viewed as an invitation to pray for the souls of those commemorated, implying a belief in purgatory and the concomitant doctrine of merit. A typical example is the brass for Robert and Elizabeth Rugge in the church of St. Maddermarket, Norwich, which asks viewers "of your charytie [to] praye for the soules" of the couple. Brasses also could remind Elizabethans of the Old Faith by depicting clergy in Catholic vestments, as on the brass at Tideswell, Derby, for Robert Pursglove (d. 1579), suffragan bishop of Hull. In contrast, the brass for Edmund Guest, bishop of Salisbury, in his cathedral shows him wearing the rochet and chimere (a sleeveless coat open at the front). Monuments and brasses could remind viewers of Protestantism in other ways. One of the earliest instances is the request of Thomas Thomson, a Hull alderman, in his 1540 will that his wife have engraved on his tombstone "a picture of latten for myself," his two wives, and his children, as well as Scripture, a depiction of the four evangelists, and his merchant mark. The Protestant emphasis on the Bible replaced the Catholic preoccupation with purgatory.[77]

In addition to the religious significance of monuments and brasses, they reinforced the social hierarchy. The executors of Edward Stanley, earl of Derby, were asked to provide him with a monument at Ormskirk meet for his honor and calling, and a similar request was made in the will of Henry Herbert, earl of Pembroke. The visual effect was enhanced by the typical placement of the tombs in chancels, so that future generations of worshippers would be confronted with a sort of secularized Elizabethan saint, in lieu of the traditional saints of the Old Faith. There was, of course, no intent to worship or pray to those so interred, but doubtless the exalted status of such folk and their descendants was underscored by the prominent display of these monuments.[78]

Besides their religious and social hierarchical significance, monuments and brasses often served the dual function of expressing individuality and genealogical pride. In 1582 Lucy Nevill, Lady Latimer, desired an alabaster tomb replete with "pictures" of herself and her four daughters, as well as the arms of Lord Latimer and her sons-in-law. A number of wills express a preference for monuments or brasses depicting the deceased in a realistic likeness. Anyone who has visited many English churches can attest to the sense of realism prevalent in the recumbent effigies on the tombs and in the brasses. Psychologically, the trend to realism in funeral portraiture provided testators with an assurance that physical death would not terminate their memory, particularly important if the last of a male line was dying. In 1591 Richard Burnand of Knaresborough, Yorks., willed that within a year after his death two brasses be engraved realistically depicting himself and his brother, and that these be placed above their bodies, with inscriptions recording their names and those of their parents and grandparents, "and thatt we bothe died unmaried beinge the laste males of the full bloode of that name."[79]

Not only did numerous executors request monuments or brasses in their wills, but some Elizabethans erected them while they were still alive, ensuring the monuments' quality as well as their realization. Sir Thomas Gresham "had prepared for himselfe a sumptuous toome or monument, without anie epitaph or inscription therevpon." Sir Nicholas Bacon similarly had a "sumptuous" monument bearing "certeine representations of his wives and children in imageric worke" erected for himself in St. Paul's. Others who took this precaution included Sir Henry Lee, Bishop Robert Pursglove, Sir Thomas Smith, Sir John Constable of Burton Constable, Yorks., and the attorney Thomas Seckford. Sir Roger Manwood not only had his tomb erected in the parish church of Hackington, Kent, but also provided for the construction of a new room in that building with seven pews for almspeople. Archbishop Parker ordered his tombstone of black marble prepared before his death so that he could meditate on it. Although Sir Thomas Leyland of Morley, Derby, did not have his brass prepared before his death in 1562, he wrote the inscription for it. Another gentleman, Roger Mainwaring of Nantwich, Ches., provided explicit details for the construction of his monument, ranging from its placement to the materials and colors. Those who did not provide a monument or brass during life risked having their executors ignore their wishes, as happened to Sir William Holles, the former sheriff of Nottinghamshire.[80]

The cost of these monuments varied considerably. In the 1580s tombs for peers typically ranged from £200 to £400, but in 1594, Hunsdon left £1,000 for his monument. Lucy Nevill, Lady Latimer, expected in 1582 that 500 marks would cover her funeral expenses and an alabaster tomb. Among gentry families, tastes in tombs were more modest. The tomb of Sir William Pickering (d. 1575) at Great St. Helen's, Bishopsgate, which includes a recumbent effigy in armor under a pillared canopy, cost approximately 200 marks. In 1579 Sir John Constable spent 500 marks on tombs for himself and a predeceased son, and in 1596 John Davenport, a gentleman of Wistaston, Ches., hoped to get an alabaster monument for £20. Much earlier, in 1566 the auditor Thomas Mildmay left £40 for a stone monument to include likenesses of himself, his wife, and their fifteen children. To radicals, such expenditure had no biblical warrant, but it was not until the late 1620s and 1630s that simpler tastes led to reduced outlays.[81]

To all appearances, Puritans were no less reluctant to provide monuments for themselves or their families. Most of Sir Nicholas Bacon's tomb was destroyed in the fire of London, but charred remains can still be seen in the undercroft of St. Paul's; the tomb was originally twelve or more feet in height, some eight feet long, and five feet deep. Mildmay was given a fine marble tomb at Great St. Bartholomew's, London, whereas Sir Anthony Cooke has an elaborate monument in St. Edward's church, Romford, Essex. Sir Thomas and Lady Margaret Hoby erected a monument of black and white marble with abundant heraldry at Hackness church for Arthur Dakins. The Russells have tombs at Chenies, Bucks., and the Dudleys, Ambrose and Robert, have fine monuments in the Beauchamp Chapel of the Collegiate Church of St. Mary, Warwick. So too does Sir Michael Hicks (d. 1612) in the parish church of Leyton, Essex. Puritans did not share the Separatist distaste for monuments and brasses.[82]

Religion and perhaps economics seem to have had an effect on the use of figure brasses. Excluding brasses consisting of inscriptions alone, 1,800 figure brasses survive in England from the period 1500 to 1609. In the three decades prior to the Reformation (1500-1529), an average of 26.3 brasses a year were erected, but in each ensuing decade for the next thirty years the number dropped (to 14.5, 10.3, and 8.0). Protestantism brought a sharp decline in the demand for brasses, and the economic problems of the 1540s and 1550s seem to have furthered that trend. The Elizabethan period witnessed a slow recovery, going from an average of 8.5 brasses a year in the 1560s to 18.5 in the 1590s, only to drop slightly in the 1600s to 15.8. The recovery of brasses in the Elizabethan years, though never to their pre-Reformation popularity, presumably was due to the return of economic prosperity and the absence of opposition to their use by Anglican and Puritan leaders.[83]

A further indication of the effect of religious change on brasses is the number of clergy and religious who are commemorated with figure brasses. In the period 1500 to 1529 they averaged 36 brasses per decade, but this was cut in half in the 1530s. The number per decade continued to drop in the 1540s to a mere three in the 1570s, before climbing slightly to six in the 1590s and 1600s. Taking into account that some of the later brasses were for Catholics, it is clear that the Protestant clergy (perhaps partly because of financial constraints) shunned brasses for themselves. Among the Elizabethan clergy who did have figure brasses are Guest, bishop of Rochester, Pursglove, suffragan bishop of Hull, and William Bill, dean of Westminster. Apparently no Elizabethan Puritan clergy have figure brasses.[84]

The distribution of figure brasses in the period 1500 to 1609 reflects the prosperity of the southeastern counties and their greater access to the supply of brass and the engravers. Excluding thirteen brasses in museums, 65% of the remaining 1,787 brasses are in nine counties in the southeast and East Anglia, plus Oxfordshire. In contrast, far fewer brasses exist in the north and west, though Gloucester has 45, Cornwall 28, and Devon 26. Monmouth, Westmorland, Rutland, Cheshire, Durham, and Cumberland have six or less apiece, and Northumberland has none. This contrasts strikingly with such counties as Kent (201), Essex (165), Norfolk (142), Buckinghamshire (114), and Suffolk (113). Generally the results are comparable for the Elizabethan period alone, though counties such as Cambridgeshire, Norfolk, Bedfordshire, Buckinghamshire, and Hampshire saw relatively fewer brasses in the period than other counties with six or more brasses. Although Protestantism brought a sharp decline in the use of figure brasses, which experienced only a slow and partial recovery in the Elizabethan era, the counties with the greatest number of brasses were generally those where Protestantism was strongest. The prevalency of brasses in the southeast is not due to religious considerations but to the relative wealth of the counties and their accessibility to the skilled engravers and the supply of brass. If brasses had been more widely used in the religiously conservative north and west, the impact of Protestantism would not have been so great on this art form.[85]

In conclusion, Protestant reformers attacked funeral observances associated with Catholic doctrines of purgatory, satisfaction, and prayers for the dead. Masses, trentals, dirges, and excessive bell-ringing were repudiated, though conservative clergy, especially in the north and west, continued their use throughout the period. Anglican and Puritan reformers pressed for moderation and for less elaborate services. As demands for reform became more radical, the Puritan left and the Separatists began attacking traditional mourning garb, the funeral service in the *Book of Common Prayer,* and the necessity for clergy to conduct obsequies. The attack on the common service struck directly at the hierarchy's goal of preserving unity; questioning the clerical monopoly threatened clerical control and ecclesiastical income. Even funeral sermons came under fire from the left, because they were too laudatory and were reserved for social betters. Anglicans and Puritans accepted funeral sermons as long as they were in the form of *exempla* and had pedagogical value, but Separatists opposed them because they lacked biblical warrant, reeked with hypocrisy, and suggested the Catholic custom of meritorious prayer for the dead. Some testators bequeathed funds for a series of sermons after their deaths, which appears to be a Protestant adaptation of the Catholic practice of leaving funds to chantries for masses. The Separatist criticism of funeral sermons in effect attacked the social order, for these sermons were reminders of the virtuous and charitable actions of social superiors in a way that justified their social privileges.

Religious motivation marked the effort to reduce the lavish spectacle of funerals of social superiors; Puritans in particular hoped to convert funerals into services characterized by thanksgiving and the singing of Psalms and hymns. More vigorously than Anglicans, the Puritans strove to strip away the mystery of funerals, as they had stripped away (with most of the Anglicans) the mystery of the Lord's supper. By the end of the age, an effort had begun to get people to concentrate less on ceremony and more on the *ars moriendi*. This campaign for simplification blended with a much older tradition of viewing plain funerals as a final declaration of piety by the deceased.

The simplification was, however, always a matter of degree, for Anglicans and most Puritans remained convinced that a proper amount of pageantry reinforced the social hierarchy, as long as the pageantry was comely and free of superstition. Testators who expressed a desire to avoid vain pomp in their obsequies often indicated they wished to be buried in accord with their social status. In this sense, vain pomp meant the kind of displays sometimes accorded persons of new wealth like Sir Thomas Gresham and Robert Nowell, which exceeded their social rank. At the opposite extreme were the Separatists, whose radical attack on pageantry, burial in churches and churchyards, large funeral dinners, and monuments suggested advocacy of social leveling as well as repudiation of all remnants of popery.

Certainly finances played a role in simpler funerals, particularly late in the age, when financial constraints became a serious problem for some of the aristocracy. Economic necessity blended with a conviction that lavish expenses violated Christian decency and implied doubt about the resurrection, though Elizabeth and Burghley worked to maintain what she considered an appropriate level of pageantry. Peers of Anglican and Puritan persuasion were accorded some lavish obsequies, ranging in cost up to £3,000, whereas typical gentry funerals ran from £5 to £200 (variations in rank and finances accounting for the discrepancy). By way of contrast, funerals for common folk normally did not exceed £1 or £2; the truly poor were buried only in shrouds without even simple wooden coffins. The difficulty of persuading clerics to bury the poor and the hostility toward mortuaries and other fees also lay behind the radical Separatist criticism. For their part, persons of wealth salved their consciences, if indeed they were troubled, by providing charity for the impoverished at their funerals in the form of clothing, alms, and food. Puritans insisted that a greater percentage of funeral expenses should go for such purposes, and some of the Anglican laity agreed. There is, however, no discernible pattern of poor relief at funerals according to religious persuasion, nor is there an apparent difference in practice with respect to greater simplicity in funerals. As in some other cases, the Puritan clergy had trouble persuading the laity to practice these ideals. Ironically, large charitable donations at funerals promoted riotous behavior, theft, and sexual licentiousness, especially as vagabonds and urban poor flocked to funerals of the wealthy. Open hospitality declined as testators feared their funeral dinners would degenerate into scenes of disorder.

Religious overtones were present in other ways. Anglican and Puritan reformers concurred that minds should be terminated because of their association with purgatory, and wakes violated the canons of modest mourning. As is true of the disapproval of rogations, criticism of these practices undermined the spirit (real or imagined) of unity in the medieval community—or at least a means of resolving some of the quarrels that disrupted the community.

Although monuments and brasses often contained visual reminders of the Old Faith, including exhortations to pray for the souls of the entombed, Anglican and Puritan reformers had very little to say about their use, other than a concern to have less expense devoted to them. The Separatists, however, were hostile to funeral monuments, as the Puritans were not. Brasses and monuments could be useful in several ways, including a visual reinforcement of social hierarchy. Religiously they could stress Protestant values by citing Scripture while omitting references to saints or prayers for the dead. As effigies and engravings became increasingly realistic, they were vehicles for the developing individualism of the age, and they also were affirmations of genealogical interest. Although the Reformation brought a sharp decline in figure brasses, their popularity began to revive in the Elizabethan period, as people realized these advantages. They were not, however, popular with the Elizabethan clergy, particularly the Puritans. Most of the surviving brasses from the period 1500 to 1609 are found in the south and east, where Protestantism was strongest, but this prevalence reflects economic prosperity and accessibility to engravers and brass, not a greater predilection of Protestants for brasses.

Once again Puritans periodically differed from Anglicans in their social outlook, often as a matter of emphasis. In society as in religion Puritans pushed farther with the campaign for reform, though stopping short of the radical conclusions Separatists drew. Social order had to be maintained, and Puritans were convinced this could be accomplished best in a commonwealth in which church and society were thoroughly reformed. In this spirit, funerals for social superiors could continue to be spectacles of pageantry, but never to excess or with symbols of superstition and popery. Although differing in degree, Anglican and Puritan were firm in their resolution that

> No ryng of Belles, no Organe Pypes,
> nor Song . . . my soule cures.[86]

Protestantism increased the quest for social reform, a sphere in which Puritans were often more zealous than Anglicans but not as extreme as Separatists.

Conclusion

The instability of the mid-Tudor years, religious upheavals that shook the western world, the decline of stable social relationships, the up-rooting experience of exile, and a deep awareness of human depravity induced in many Englishmen a sense of anxiety. The assurance they ultimately found came in the form of a religious experience spiritual-ly akin in many respects to continental Pietism. With a zealousness born of conviction and fueled by a warmth they perceived in each other, the godly resolved to reform Christian institutions until they conformed to scriptural precedents. The liberty they found in their faith inspired an obligation to reform, and the zeal originating in their sense of participation in a cosmic struggle led them to extend this ob-ligation beyond the institutions of the church: As the sphere of com-bat moved from the soul to the world, the intensity of the reforming quest spread to all spheres of society. The result was not so much a distinctive social theory or program of action, but an endeavor to ex-tend the purity of heart, mind, and worship to purify social relations. Long before they became saints in arms, Puritans campaigned for a purer society as well as a holier church.

The intensity of their zeal, the assurance of a people whose anxi-eties were resolved with a pietistic faith and fortified by a narrow conception of biblical authority and an aniconic pattern of worship, was not shared by the majority of English Protestants (retrospectively labeled Anglicans). Not only were Anglicans less resolved to accom-plish sweeping social reform, but they were at times more inclined to

737

perceive social issues in secular rather than religious terms. In the case of prostitution, for example, Anglican concern was principally social, particularly the wastage of funds better spent on relief of the indigent. Whereas Puritans shared that concern, they were at least as troubled about the spiritual ramifications of prostitution. With respect to fasting, though Puritans were anxious to distinguish their position from the merit-oriented practice of Catholics, Anglicans thought principally in terms of the social obligation of fasting for the benefit of the impoverished. Puritans, in effect, were more rigorous, more methodical, in applying their religious principles to social activities, and viewed them in essentially religious terms.

Because of their aniconic predilections, Puritans were devoted to the medium of the word, both spoken and printed. Sermons, lectures, and religious literature were grist for the Puritan mill. It is understandable, therefore, that the Puritan way had a special appeal for the literate and their households; in this way a faith born of *angst* came to have a wider appeal, notably to those who found the pietistic experience conducive to worship and the Puritan challenge compelling. The spread of Puritanism was enhanced by the dramatic growth in literacy into the 1570s, though a mildly regressive period followed until the 1610s, and Puritans played an important role in this growth. The number of printed books increased dramatically in the Elizabethan era, and independent evidence (wills and inventories) reveals that ownership of books was on the rise.

The experiential core of his faith notwithstanding, the Puritan was expected to understand his religion, and to this end books and sermons were essential. In accordance with their greater subordination of the liturgical element in religion, Puritans insisted on an educated clergy, hence they were more vociferous than Anglicans in condemning uneducated clerics. For Puritans the basic responsibility of a minister was preaching, whereas Anglicans were often willing to fall back on the prescribed liturgy and the official homilies. Some Anglicans were openly chary of preaching; they preferred that it be restricted to the mature, and worried that it might be undertaken by the uneducated, especially those uncommitted to Anglican principles. Other Anglicans, including Pilkington, Grindal, and Sandys, were more appreciative of sermons, and in 1586, Convocation launched a program to provide sermons in parishes that had none. The output of the Elizabethan press is further testimony of the importance attached to sermons, particularly by Puritans, and says something as well about the hunger for sermons in Elizabethan society. The success of the Puritans owes much to their reliance on the spoken and printed word in this age of educational revolution.

The orientation toward the word, especially marked in Puritanism, placed increased responsibility on the family and household. Although Anglicans and Puritans alike regarded the household as a microcosm of the state and drew an analogy between the position of magistrates and that of husbands and fathers, it was the Puritans who insisted that the household was a microcosm of the church. It was a Puritan ideal that every godly man make of his household a godly congregation and govern it accordingly; a properly governed family was perceived as the principal stay of the church and commonwealth. The institutional church was, for the Puritan, inadequate in itself for edification. To help him fulfill his task, the householder had printed sermons, devotional works, catechisms, and the extensive marginalia found especially in the Geneva and Beza-Tomson Bibles. To undertake this task required a certain degree of learning, which helps explain the strong Puritan interest in education and why they, along with the Anglicans, thought of it especially in religious terms.

The importance of the household as a religious unit played a key role in the gradual transformation of the family, notably the position of the wife, a good portion of whose time could be taken up with spiritual duties. Puritans explicitly began to assign mothers catechetical responsibility. Marriage, to the Puritans, was a covenant involving mutual companionship, the joint role of husband and wife as fellow citizens and governors in their little commonwealth, a business partnership, and especially joint involvement with their household as a microcosm of the church. Much more than the Anglicans, the Puritans developed marriage as a partnership and simultaneously made the strongest objections to wife-beating. For this covenantal relationship, with its increased responsibilities for the wife, to function as smoothly as possible, it was imperative that the union be solidly grounded. Like the Anglicans, the Puritans thought spouses should be of like religious persuasion, comparable social standing, and similar age, and that wealth or lack of it should not be a factor; unlike the Anglicans, the Puritans further emphasized that prospective mates possess godly virtues and preferably be in love, though physical attractiveness was unimportant. Marital love was in turn significant in the movement from an open lineage to a nuclear family.

The sanctity of the family, as well as the campaign to purify society, lies behind the greater attention of Puritans to sexual questions. The Puritan campaign against adultery in all forms struck directly at the continuing practice of the double standard, commonly perceived to be a *sine qua non* for the arranged marriage. The Puritan tendency to seek mutual affection in the selection of a spouse was simultaneously part of the attack on adultery, the reduction of which partly depended on greater freedom of choice in marriage. To Puritans, adultery not only undermined the sanctity of the family but also entailed damaging spiritual effects and threats to property and inheritance. In contrast, most Anglican comment on adultery was too generalized to have had much effect on the double standard. With respect to cohabitation by affianced persons, Anglicans never approved it in print and probably frowned on it, but their silence perhaps amounted in practice to a tacit acceptance. Puritans, however, regarded all sexual relations before marriage as fornication. More than Anglicans, they explained how to avoid premarital sex, emphasizing sex education, a ban on lewd books and speech, godly companions, moderate diet and clothing, the eschewing of idleness, and spiritual preparation to withstand temptation. Likewise, averting extramarital sex entailed refraining from idleness, evil company, gluttony, excess in apparel, ribald songs, lewd speech, and mixed dancing. The intensity of the Puritan attack against these evils derived in part from their negative influence on the family as a microcosm of the church.

Because of its family orientation, the Puritan way found its greatest appeal among those groups and in those regions that fostered close family relations. The Puritans found their strongest support among the gentry, the yeomanry, the urban middling sort, and the servants and apprentices associated with Puritans in these groups. Geographically their strength was greater in regions devoted to pastoral farming, where the farmhouse was the focal point of life, rather than in the highly manorialized areas where traditions of village life remained strong and where the pietist movement in religion failed to make significant impact.

The Puritan appeal to the lesser aristocracy and middling sort, then, was based on piety, literacy, and family orientation, not on an economic ideology. Puritan economic thought was neither a reflection of "class" interests nor an attempt to rationalize existing socio-economic practices, but rather the product of a joint endeavor with Anglicans, who essentially shared their economic thought, to produce a socio-ethical code harmonious with scriptural principles. Whereas recognition of the importance of labor was distinctively neither Puritan nor Protestant, Elizabethan Catholics, who had more pressing concerns, did not emphasize it. Together, Anglicans and Puritans asserted that labor is dignified and essential to support one's family and fulfill vocational responsibilities. This view largely reflected contemporary realities, which dictated that diligent toil was essential to survival. Among Anglicans and Puritans, any encouragement of an entrepreneurial spirit by the emphasis on work would have been moderated by hostility to ambition and stress on moderation. Emphasis was on familial and social responsibility, not the acquisition of wealth or ambition to enhance one's social estate. The abhorrence of ambition dampened any tendency to make of the Protestant work ethic a support for capitalism. Whereas Anglicans and Puritans repudiated idleness, associating it with monasticism, they were less concerned with the structure of the economy than with socio-political stability (through attention to vocation), moderate economic gains (to support the family, tithe, and fulfill charitable obligations), and an adherence to biblical principles.

Only in the area of vocation were there some significant differences of emphasis in Anglican and Puritan economic thought. For Anglicans, individual callings were divinely determined, hence people were exhorted to be content with their vocations. Edmund Bunny was an exception, with his interest in occupational selection so as to be profitable to God and economically productive, but the mobility of which he conceived was essentially horizontal. While some Puritans adhered to the general Anglican outlook on vocation, others accorded a role to personal choice; Udall asserted the right of each individual to choose his occupation and Richard Rogers affirmed the individual's right to alter his vocation for good reason. Some Elizabethan divines did not favor a nonindividualistic society devoid of vocational mobility. Puritans, moreover, differed from Anglicans in the emphasis they accorded to diligence in vocations, which was a preventive for idleness and disorder. Whereas Anglicans had no objection to diligence in vocational pursuits, their emphasis was on vocational contentment, which was their way of securing social stability. The Puritan emphasis tended toward activism, the Anglican toward pacifism.

The tendency of Puritans such as Udall and Rogers to accord a significant role to personal choice in vocation was echoed in other areas, such as marriage. Among the propertied, this individualism was counterbalanced by the parents' need to restrict personal choice, to ensure the preservation of an estate for future generations. These ideals account for the tension among Puritans to find a place for love (hence individual choice) in selecting a mate but simultaneously to speak in the context of parental rights of children as property (hence parental choice). In both instances, family considerations were at stake, though the property idiom reflected more concern with material well-being than spiritual.

The movement toward greater individuality was most pronounced with respect to women. The Protestant repudiation of celibacy as the highest form of life not only supported marriage and the family, but prompted some women to channel their energies to scholarly instead of celibate activities. When widowhood was no longer exalted as superior to remarriage, widows were freer to chart their future, though some husbands used their wills to rule their widows from the grave. The growing interest, particularly among Puritans, in marriage as a partnership enhanced woman's social role, though Anglican and Puritan thinkers clung to the theory of female inferiority, which they saw as punitive (because of Eve's original sin), purposive (because Eve was created second, as a helper), and natural (because of the relative weakness of females). Puritans in particular bolstered this thesis with spiritual analogies, including the church's subjection to Christ (female to male), the husband's possession of the *imago Dei,* and the reflection of divine (fatherly) glory in the male. In theory, neither Anglican nor Puritan accepted the wife as an *equal* partner and an individual in her own right, though in practice women sometimes were less subservient than the ideal. Wives increasingly were appointed joint or sole executors of their husbands' estates, which may indicate more sharing of property with wives than English law required. Many Elizabethan husbands had to deal with their wives as at least junior partners because of their role in helping to supervise estates or toil in shops and fields. Puritan interest in the wife as a charitable donor and in her catechetical function further enhanced the position of women. Puritans too evinced greater concern with the education of girls; in any listing of educated Elizabethan women, Puritans are prominent. The status of women also was furthered when the regular provision of relief for the indigent became a social and a spiritual duty for them as well as for men. As the position of women began to improve, the possibilities for greater individuality increased.

The important role Elizabethan women played in Puritanism and Catholicism likewise contributed to their improving condition. Psychologically, many women were attracted to religious movements demanding heightened commitment, perhaps in part because they had more real or induced spiritual neuroses. Beyond this possibility, however, in a male-dominated society, religion was one of the few outlets for their energy and creativity. As Puritanism placed religious responsibility in a family context, it became attractive to numerous women, particularly if they were spiritually inclined to pietism. Wives' responses to these movements, such as protecting the clergy, were encouraged by their relative freedom from government sanctions; the government sought to control wives by acting against their husbands, whose property was accessible to the state. Catholicism, like Puritanism, had a distinctly household orientation in the Elizabethan period precisely because women could protect the priests and provide a nucleus among the lesser aristocracy to keep the religious community going. In turn, their position was enhanced as they exercised ritual functions associated with fasting and holy days. In rather different ways, then, Puritanism and Catholicism proved attractive to women and increased their importance in the household.

Although a slow movement toward greater individual awareness began in the Elizabethan period, to which Puritans were the major contributors, this did not occur outside the context of the family and household. It was not atomic individualism, but what might paradoxically be called communal individualism. The parameters of acceptable conduct are not individualistically determined nor is the individual perceived as more significant than or independent of his communal associations; rather each person is given greater latitude of movement and choice within the context of communal responsibility, even as he or she shoulders increased responsibility, such as for catechetical instruction or relief of the indigent. The Puritan householder, for instance, enjoys an exalted status in his capacity as a lay pastor, for which he bears additional responsibility, but he exercises his enhanced authority within the parameters established by the community of saints. It was this communal individualism that subsequently provided much of the driving force for so many New England colonists, whose early history was often taken up with efforts to resolve the tension between community standards and demands on the one hand and individual drives on the other. In another context, the triumph of the capitalist spirit became possible as individual aspirations subordinated the communal spirit and placed the welfare of the individual above that of the community.

During the Elizabethan age the individual often remained subordinate to the community, in no small part owing to the concerted emphasis of Anglicans and Puritans on the maintenance of the social order. Although they worked to develop a uniform ethical code, such a code was always supportive of the social structure. The principle that made this possible was moderation, enunciated as a common ideal yet interpreted differently for each social group. What was moderate for the aristocracy was excessive for the lower orders, and as long as this principle was maintained, the aristocracy saw no particular threat in a common code nor did they find the ideal of moderation reprehensible. Nor should they, for it was an ideal adaptible to their extravagant lifestyle. Moderation was, after all, a relative term, and it was always easier to see extravagance in someone else's living. The clerical reformers had a less exalted standard of living in mind when they urged moderation, for to them this religiously justifiable and socially utilitarian concept, if practiced, would provide means to relieve the poor.

In developing a socio-ethical code, Anglican and Puritan reformers periodically took divergent paths. In the sphere of marriage and family relations, the Anglicans vested matrimony with near sacramental quality, whereas the Puritans objected to the depiction of marriage in the *Book of Common Prayer* as a signification of the mystical union of Christ and his church, preferring to treat wedlock as a covenant rather than an effectual sign of grace. With the exception of Sandys, the Anglicans continued to view marriage in the traditional manner, with procreation as its primary purpose, followed by its value as a means to avoid incontinency, and as mutual companionship. Although most Elizabethan Puritans accepted this view, others, who worried about sexual immorality, began to focus on marriage as a preventive for fornication; Perkins and Cleaver, like Sandys, shifted the primary emphasis to mutual companionship, which helped lay the foundation for the development of the companionate marriage. In the wedding ceremony the more radical Puritans opted for the *Booke of the Forme of Common Prayers* in lieu of the *Book of Common Prayer* and repudiated wedding rings as a relic of popery.

Puritans further distinguished themselves from Anglicans by advocating harsher punishments for fornicators, including branding and, for those convicted of intercourse with a girl under ten, execution. Since ecclesiastical courts were unable to deal adequately with contumacious offenders, Puritans wanted fornicators punished by local congregations and secular magistrates. For adulterers too the Puritans insisted on heavier penalties, including capital punishment, which some Anglicans opposed. Moreover Puritans generally favored divorce with the right to remarry for persons whose spouses committed adultery (and in some cases other offenses, such as desertion), but Anglicans feared this course would encourage illicit sex as a means to dissolve marriages.

With respect to the household, perhaps the most perceptive indication of the difference in outlook is Pilkington's attribution of the church as the school of God, whereas Perkins gave that function the family. The household orientation of religion characteristic of the Puritans is not developed in a comparable manner by Anglicans. Puritans also objected to chaplains in episcopalian households, though allowing them for the aristocracy unless chaplains were unduly deferential. Puritans but not Anglicans gave servants the responsibility to admonish errant superiors, underscoring the Puritan concern to place purity above other considerations.

In education, Anglicans and moderate Puritans fundamentally accepted the humanist curriculum, recognizing the value of such subjects as rhetoric and logic for the clergy, and finding worth in the study of philosophy and poetry. Radical Puritans, however, demanded a biblically oriented program of study devoid of vain topics, meaningless eloquence, and inappropriate literature. Only those subjects were to be studied that were conducive to the preparation of profitable, godly members of church and commonwealth. The traditional academic garb was criticized by radical Puritans, and Cartwright was hostile to divinity degrees. The goal of radical Puritans was a scripturally oriented and utilitarian curriculum propounded in an academic setting devoid of popish remnants.

Concerning the sabbath, the Elizabethan period saw the unity that existed at the outset of the age shattered by the development of sabbatarianism. In the decade beginning in 1575, concern with sabbath violations increased perceptibility, prompting some Puritans and a few Anglicans to underscore the importance of sabbath observance, associating it with the perpetual moral law. The works of Perkins, Greenham, and Bownde contributed to the development of sabbatarian thought, and the efforts of zealous clergy, especially in southeastern England, to equate sabbath-breaking with such offenses as adultery and infanticide made the sabbath a divisive issue. In 1599, the lines were firmly drawn when Thomas Rogers linked sabbatarianism with Puritanism. That church courts often were more zealous in prosecuting those who violated the sabbath by working rather than playing may have troubled some Puritans, as happened when some of them were prosecuted for violating the sabbath by traveling to hear sermons. As the Puritan position on the sabbath hardened, wakes and ales came under mounting criticism, because of the immoral conduct that accompanied them. Although Anglicans were content to reform the abuses while preserving the occasions, Puritans called for their termination.

The Puritans also split with the Anglicans over the observance of holy days, which Anglicans justified by appeal to Scripture and the use of such occasions for religious services. Puritans were willing to set aside specific days for religious observances if they were not made matters of faith, but only Sundays were a time of mandatory worship. Again, the ecclesiastical courts exacerbated relations by punishing those Puritans who asserted their right to work on holy days.

On religious grounds, Puritans were critical of counterpoint and harmony in church music, insisting that contrapuntal singing undermined the pedagogical effectiveness of music. In the Admonition Controversy, Field and Wilcox castigated such singing, as well as organ music, as remnants of popery. Puritan pressure brought about a decline of music in cathedrals about 1568, as stipend money for singers was diverted to lectures. Whereas Anglicans such as Grindal and Horne sympathized with the Puritan objectives, most thought music had an intrinsic beauty that was part of the worship experience of the whole person. To Puritan demands for reform, Whitgift responded simply that music was part of the *adiaphora*, hence bishops would make the final determination.

Differences between Anglicans and Puritans developed as well over the justification for war. It was generally accepted early in the age that war was a divine instrument to punish sin, and Anglicans and Puritans typically adhered to the classic just war doctrine with its appeal to Scripture, classical and medieval precedents, natural law, the law of nations, and right reason. On the basis of such a theory, war could legitimately be undertaken to defend against invasion or oppression, to protect liberty and property, to preserve religion, and to suppress malefactors, but not for ambition, anger, or greed, and not without initially pursuing alternate courses of action. Two Anglican authors, however, isolated the natural law element, laying the foundation for the secular war theory of modern international law. Almost simultaneously, several Puritan authors, the chief of whom was Stephen Gosson, isolated the religious sanctions, and by insisting on God's active involvement made war not merely justifiable, but just or holy, providing the foundation for the holy war theory developed particularly in Puritan circles in the early seventeenth century.

Other divergences between Anglicans and Puritans were manifested on social matters, including certain aspects of their views on charity. With respect to the dispersal of relief, Anglicans judged that the responsibility of deacons for this purpose had become superfluous when Christianity became a state religion in the fourth century. With the subsequent development of compulsory poor relief in the Tudor period, clerical responsibility for the poor decreased, undermining the clergy's position and weakening the justification for tithes. The

Puritans, however, favored the original plan of using deacons as agents of poor relief, keeping the administration of charity in local churches where deacons and ministers knew the condition of prospective recipients and could accompany alms with spiritual guidance.

As in the sabbath controversy, serious differences developed during the age between some Puritans and Anglicans over the question of usury. Puritans, in fact, evinced no serious interest in usury before the passage of the 1571 statute, which in effect tolerated interest rates not exceeding 10%. Until the 1590s, the preponderant opinion among Elizabethan Protestants was hostile to usury, but that changed when a minority of influential Puritans such as Rogers and Ames defended the legitimacy of moderate interest on loans to persons of means, as long as such charges were never imposed on the indigent. Nearly all Anglicans remained adamantly opposed to such concessions, though Hutton defended the 1571 statute and Jewel apparently was ready to accept interest on loans used to support orphans, the mentally ill, and other dependent persons. Thus, late Elizabethan Puritans were the first English moralists who found no religious objections to the principle that business loans were not in the same category as loans to the indigent and were subject to equitable charges in return for the financial benefits they conferred. This was, to be sure, a case of theory following practice rather than prompting it.

In the legal sphere, sharp disagreement developed between Anglicans and Puritans over the use of the oath *ex officio mero*. With respect to oaths in general, harmony existed between the respective groups as they recognized their religious nature and importance as a vehicle to terminate contention, protect neighbors, confirm covenants, and render homage to magistrates. It was the religious character of the oath that made common swearing so abhorrent to some Puritans. For the Puritans, it was essential to tread the fine line between upholding oaths as an essential bond of society and repudiating unlawful oaths, including the ex officio oath. For the Anglicans, that oath was a useful tool of the state in identifying apparently subversive elements. More concern was expressed for the sanctity of the whole than for the welfare and legal rights of individuals. In the 1580s and 1590s, Puritans, whom the Anglicans accused of obstructionism in refusing the oath, blasted its use on three grounds, namely, that Christians must swear only to matters conformable to piety and charity, that the accused must be tried according to the evidence of two or three witnesses rather than self-incrimination, and that such an oath violates divinely bestowed liberty. Morice's *Briefe Treatise of Oathes* found the oath ex officio in violation of Scripture and common and canon law; he widened the breach between Anglicans and Puritans by associating prelates with Spanish Inquisitors. In their attack on the oath ex officio, Puritans helped build the case for the sanctity of individual conscience, which fostered the developing importance of the individual.

The ecclesiastical courts too created friction between Anglicans and Puritans. To reformers, particularly Puritans, the courts were riddled with abuses and burdened with laws in need of revision, but attempts to adopt the *Reformatio Legum Ecclesiasticarum* in 1559 and 1571 failed. The excessive use of excommunication, the disrespect and ignorance of summoners, the expensive and irritating procedures, and the inability to impose effective discipline were common complaints. In particular, Puritans blasted the Court of Faculties because of its licensing and dispensing powers, demanding its cessation as another remnant of popery. The commissaries' courts were cited for inadequate punishment of sexual offenses, sale of absolution, premature commutation of penance, and allowance of single judges to mete out punishment. Whereas moderate Puritans thought major reforms could save some of the system, radical Puritans urged its abolition, with ecclesiastical discipline placed in the hands of elders. Although Hooker and some of the prelates recognized the danger signals, vested interests and the financial problems of the church prevented the implementation of some reforms that even the Anglicans recognized were desirable. Whitgift and Bancroft erred in concentrating their attention on the suppression of Puritans instead of the reformation of abuses; in so doing they exacerbated the mounting divisions in the Church of England in the last two decades of the age.

There were, then, significant differences in outlook between Anglicans and Puritans, especially in the latter part of the age, over the nature and primary purpose of marriage, the wedding cermony, the punishment of fornicators and adulterers, grounds for divorce, the religious orientation of the household and the wife's role in it, the place of chaplains in episcopal households, the responsibility of servants to rebuke errant masters, the educational curriculum and the validity of academic garb and divinity degrees, sabbatarianism, wakes and ales, holy days, church music, war theory, the charitable role of deacons, usury, the oath ex officio mero, and the ecclesiastical courts. These differences show Puritan determination to make the family a religious unit, to exterminate the dregs of popery in church and society, to administer charity effectively and especially to needy saints, and to impose pure ethical standards in social relations, as perceived in the light of scriptural principles. For Puritans, the New Jerusalem meant a disciplined society attuned to a biblical code of conduct.

In addition to these points of disagreement, in numerous areas important differences of emphasis existed between Anglicans and Puritans on social issues. On the subject of marriage some Anglicans were reluctant to relinquish fully the Catholic doctrine that celibacy is superior to matrimony. In selecting mates, godly virtues and love were of greater concern to Puritans, who were also more distressed than Anglicans about child marriages. The religious aspects of widowhood were of greater interest to Puritans, and Cartwright recognized the legitimacy of remarriage for widows for a broader range of reasons than other moralists. Sexual matters occupied Puritans more than Anglicans because of the Puritan reforming ardor and the ramifications of licentiousness for the family, not because Anglicans condoned sexual immorality. It was the Puritans, not the Anglicans, who made clear their opposition to sexual relations between espoused persons, and it was the Puritans who devoted the most attention to means of avoiding premarital sex and to the problems of bastardy, prostitution, and adultery. Puritans stressed the importance of breast-feeding by the mother and pressed the point that pro.itable labor by the wife was virtuous. Although Anglicans and Puritans mainly agreed on the duties of a husband, Puritans stressed his sexual fidelity, further undermining the double standard. In comparison with Anglicans, Puritans emphasized parental responsibility in the prevention of children's idleness; some made an effective case for affection as a necessary ingredient of family life. Although adherents of both groups accepted moderate chastisement for errant children, Puritans favored matching penalties to offenses. In the disbursal of legacies to children, Puritans insisted that part of the estate must be reserved for the indigent.

On the subject of master-servant relations, the Puritans displayed the greatest concern with the selection of godly, governable retainers and, in keeping with their concept of household religion, the provision of religious instruction for them. The Puritans also took more care in insisting that masters take servants to church and correct errant retainers by moderate discipline. Such emphases stem from the dominant Puritan commitment to the family and household as the nucleus of the religious community. This conviction also explains the Puritan desire that at least rudimentary education must be widely available as a preparation for Bible reading and religious study in the household.

Concerning social activities and amusements, the Puritan drive to make society conform to biblical ideals is again evident. Although there is no clear line of demarcation between Anglicans and Puritans with regard to the theater, differences are generally apparent. Some Anglicans steadfastly defended the theater and even acted themselves; others viewed it with opprobrium or sought the reform of abuses involving immoral content or the performance of plays on the sab-bath. No Puritan defended the theater as thoroughly as various Angli-cans, though some were only concerned with the reform of abuses. In the latter part of the age, however, most Puritans developed a hos-tile attitude toward the theater that paralleled the mounting anger over sabbath violations. Proposals for the abolition of the theater presumably grew out of frustration that reform was impossible. Al-though certain Anglicans were critical of dancing, because of the pro-pensity to vanity and promiscuous behavior, Puritans were more force-ful in attacking mixed dancing because of its immoral associations, its waste of time, and its competition with religious obligations. Whereas the Anglicans made little overt criticism of secular music, the Puritans strongly denounced vain, light, and profane songs, in part because they were conducive to promiscuity and decreased the time spent singing Psalms. Pipers and minstrels were excoriated by Puritans as vagabonds. Thus although a fair degree of overlapping was notable between Anglicans and Puritans, the latter distinguished themselves by a more pronounced determination to root out all forms of social entertainment that enticed to lasciviousness and idle-ness; such recreations could threaten the stability of the family and commonwealth and undermine the disciplined life.

Both Anglicans and Puritans urged temperate diets, censured glut-tony, and advocated the regulation of food to ensure sound health. Puritans, however, were hostile to epicurean cuisine, and perhaps for this reason went out of their way to justify the principle that diet should reflect social rank. Both groups recognized the seriousness of the social problems associated with inebriety, but Puritans again differ-ed by their emphasis on its spiritual ramifications. The Puritan opposi-tion to drunkenness is more intense. In contrast to Anglicans and mod-erate Puritans, radical Puritans repudiated fasting as a spiritual exercise while acknowledging its spiritual ends (service to God and the increase of piety). They insisted it was not part of divine worship but was a mat-ter of policy, to be undertaken only while effective, and adherents of both groups acknowledged that its purpose was abstinence from sin and the subordination of the flesh to the spirit. For Puritans, there was no re-ligiously obligatory fast, yet Anglicans were more concerned than Pur-itans with the social obligation of fasting for the benefit of the needy.

In other areas, the greater Puritan propensity for reform is evident. Broad agreement was expressed on apparel, but Puritans stressed sim-plicity more than Anglicans, while insisting on the right of higher so-cial orders to dress befitting their degree, possibly to counter criticism of such dress from some of their lay supporters. Speech was a matter of greater concern to Puritans than Anglicans, with the former obsessed with the evil of idle speech, in that it led to vice and dissipated property by wasting time. Anglicans condemned immoral, unprofitable, and ribald books, but Puritans were more irate and extreme on this subject, imposing a more restricted reading list than Anglicans, with preference for religious and utilitarian topics. Both groups condemned suicide, but whereas Anglicans tended to find the motivation in psychological factors, such as timidity and escapism, Puritans generally saw suicide as resulting from spiritual conditions, such as lack of faith, and satanic influence.

When considering questions of wealth and charitable obligations, Puritans were more receptive than Anglicans to the idea that prosperity could be a reward of godliness although both groups denied any direct correlation between piety and prosperity. Anglicans, however, were more determined than Puritans to warn of the dangers of wealth, because of the abuses associated with it. When charity was bestowed on the poor, it was the Puritans who provided a rather detailed set of obligations for them, including being thankful and content, and behaving so as to move the rich to donate. Puritans but not Anglicans asked that giving be accompanied with godly admonitions—that there be alms for the soul as well as the body—reflecting the greater Puritan interest in the subordination of the material to the spiritual. Although most Anglicans and Puritans were willing to have alms go to all needy, with special preference for the godly, some Puritans insisted that all donations be restricted to the saints. Neither group was prepared to embrace communalism as a solution to the problem of poverty, but Puritans sanctioned the voluntary disposition of all possessions for the benefit of the community in periods of acute economic distress. Generally, Anglicans probably agreed with Whitgift that the basic problem was enforcing current laws to benefit the poor, though Cooper proposed that the wealthy should donate 50% of their possessions to the destitute. In contrast, Puritans were more inclined to consider poor reform, including Cartwright's proposal to sell episcopal lands, Hooke's idea of establishing a bank for the needy, Stubbes' request for an almshouse or hospital in every town, and Perkins' suggestion that the impoverished be allowed into the fields to gather their own food. In the closely related area of hospitality, Puritans again stand out by their insistence that hospitality be characterized neither by excess nor by stinginess, and that gambling and masques be excluded on hospitable occasions. In contrast to Anglicans such as Whitgift and Howson who believed that hospitality could do more to advance the gospel than sermons, Puritans denigrated pluralists who relied on hospitality rather than sermons to satisfy parishioners. In short, Anglicans generally saw charity as a social obligation, whereas Puritans treated it principally as a religious duty.

Economic thought further reveals differences of emphasis between Anglicans and Puritans. Although the former indicated little interest in suretiship, Puritans manifested concern even though they were undecided as to whether it was a Christian duty. When surety was provided, preference had to be given to the godly and neighbors, but owing to the severity of the repercussions in the event of default (imprisonment or financial penalties), the godly were cautioned to use discretion, so as not to jeopardize family security. Various indications show that Puritans were more sensitive to the implications of religious convictions for social and economic actions, as in their ire about false weights and measures, which violated the eighth commandment and the law of nature. In Puritan circles a greater effort was made to formulate principles to guide business relations, with a recognition of the effect that unethical business practices could have on spiritual life. For the Puritans, covetousness was, after all, a mark of reprobation, so they went into greater detail in their prescriptions for business dealings. The heightened sensitivity of Puritans to business relationships arose partly from an awareness that if their people did not deal equitably, opprobrium would be cast on all the godly. Some Elizabethans thought Puritans were people whose actions were supposed to accord with the principles they espoused, hence they were open to castigation when lapses occurred.

In rural society too, the Puritans periodically manifested greater concern with social problems. In contrast to Anglican denunciation of forestalling, engrossing, and regrating, which ebbed and flowed with the condition of the harvests (perhaps reflecting government pressure to speak out), Puritan concern was more regular. The only Anglican to express sustained interest in the problems facing tenants, especially increased fines and rents, was Pilkington, a moderate, but Puritans expressed substantial interest, notably in their denunciation of rack-renters, whose actions reduced the ability of tenants to provide hospitality. Only Trigge recognized the demographic factors responsible for the increased pressure on land, and the opportunity for landlords to take advantage of this situation by raising rents and fines, but he refused to sanction such action. Rack-renting, forestalling, regrating, and engrossing were, in Puritan eyes, unnecessary and unwarranted burdens on householders, threatening their ability to function well as the nucleus of the religious community.

In the legal sphere, the Puritans took more care in providing guidelines for persons involved in litigation, though in general Anglicans and Puritans agreed that one should go to law only as a last resort, in a spirit of love, and for substantial matters. The heightened sensitivity of Puritans toward moral corruption is evident in the intensity of their denunciation of judges who took bribes, though Anglicans also found such activity reprehensible.

With reference to funerals and companion observances, Puritans, with their greater determination to root out Catholic symbolism, pushed further in reforming the ceremonies; some went as far as desiring to eliminate mourning gowns as well as excess pomp like candles, incense, torches, trentals, and dirges. The Puritans advocated singing Psalms and hymns, and rendering thanksgiving for the deceased's completion of the earthly pilgrimage. Puritans were more rigorous in stripping away the mystery of the funeral, just as they had taken it out of the Lord's supper, and in consequence they began to shift the attention to preparation for dying rather than the last rites themselves. A holy death must follow a holy life, with both commemorated in a purified service of thanksgiving. It was natural, then, that the Puritans in particular cautioned against excessive spending on funerals, yet without repudiating the principle that pageantry should reflect the social hierarchy. Not Anglicans but Puritans insisted that more funeral expenses be channeled to poor relief, yet they worried about the hypocrisy in some of the funeral charity.

To call attention to the differences in substance and emphasis is not to denigrate the fact that on many social issues, Anglicans and Puritans were in full accord. It is, however, clear that Puritans were more concerned with the family as a religious unit, the implications of religious principles for socio-economic affairs, and the need to bring social behavior into accord with scriptural principles. To attempt to refute this evidence by suggesting that Puritans were more prone to write than Anglicans is invalid: The numerous sources examined in this study do not reflect such an imbalance. The Puritan zeal to reform the church was not confined to the parameters of ecclesiastical institutions but was extended to virtually all aspects of social behavior. Considering the importance accorded the family as a religious unit, and the manifestation of Christian principles in daily living expected of exemplars of their faith, it could not be otherwise. As their diaries reveal, Puritans were unusually fervent in their religion and uncommonly sensitive about the relationship of piety to social behavior. Both characteristics extended beyond the Elizabethan age and ultimately came to the New World.

In comparison with Puritan social thought, much of what Separatists proposed was plainly radical. Not only did they reject lay patronage, an area that needed reform in Anglican and Puritan eyes too, but they also raised (albeit unintentionally) the spectre of political democracy in demanding that local congregations select their own ministers. To the principle of ecclesiastical voluntarism, they added the voluntary maintenance of ministers and an end to the tithing system. In advocating civil marriage, they challenged the monopoly of the established church, whose ministers they repudiated, and like radical Puritans, they rejected the wedding ring as a popish remnant. The encouragement they gave to their followers and potential converts to defy superiors to worship in Separatist congregations was seen as undermining the marriage covenant and the authority of parents and masters. In cases of adultery, they insisted on mandatory divorce unless only those directly involved knew of it and repentance was offered. Puritans objected to chaplains in episcopalian households, but Separatists rejected all domestic chaplains.

In education, Separatists condemned the traditional curriculum as replete with heathen and vain subjects, insisting that nothing be taught but lawful Christian subjects, including foreign languages, logic, and rhetoric stripped of pagan, Catholic, and profane authors. In effect, they picked up the views of radical Puritans and carried them further. Separatist criticism was sweeping, extending to founders' days, academic degrees, profane ceremonies and vows, academic garb, and the teaching of divinity in the universities. Universities were judged so corrupt that Separatists despaired of their reformation and advocated their abolition, like the monasteries and chantries. The heart of the Separatist onslaught was the premise that the established church endeavored to make Christianity mysterious through corrupt divinity and in this manner maintained its power over the people.

The social radicalism of the Separatists was evident in other areas. They were on dangerous ground when they accused the aristocracy as well as the established church of idle living, for they were already suspected of being social levelers. Certainly their criticism of contemporary apparel had egalitarian overtones. Traditional holy days were renounced as idolatrous, and the fasts of the Church of England were equated with Catholic practice. No fasting could be practiced on particular days or in perpetuity, nor could the decision to fast be made by any institution other than the local congregation, and never by civil authority, which opinion directly challenged the Elizabethan government. The established clergy were condemned not only for idle living and immoral recreation but also for failing to rebuke persons of substance who used vain and evil speech. Like the Puritans, the Separatists wanted the retention of deacons as agents of poor relief, and they were suspicious about the involvement of the state in charity. Understandably, they viewed ecclesiastical courts with hostility. Although they had no objection to godly magistrates, judges, and attorneys, they regarded the Elizabethan judicial system as corrupt and best avoided. Barrow even proposed that English law be reformed to bring it into conformity with the Mosaic code. Unlike Anglicans and Puritans, the Separatists repudiated oaths between private parties or the use of oaths in ecclesiastical courts (which in any case were to be terminated) or to enforce royal supremacy, the *Book of Common Prayer,* the canon law, or the Thirty-nine Articles. The oath ex officio was branded as idolatrous, contrary to the Bible, and compatible with the Spanish Inquisition.

The Separatist attack on funerals was a root and branch affair, with leveling implications. Much of what Separatists perceived in contemporary funeral practices, they judged a continuation of Catholic superstition. Virtually all the traditional ceremonies were repudiated, including the use of the *Book of Common Prayer,* ministerial fees, processions, burial in churches and churchyards, funeral banquets, and monuments. Not even funeral sermons were tolerable, for they lacked scriptural warrant. Of all the Elizabethan Protestants, only the Separatists seriously questioned the traditional pageantry. In short, the radical religious ideology of the Separatists was extended into the social realm, where equally radical conclusions were drawn. Like the Puritans, they refused to confine their spiritual life to religious observances but insisted on carrying the reforming spirit into social relations.

Assessing the effectiveness of the clerical reformers in influencing the laity is difficult in most instances, and often we are forced to be content with impressions based on the surviving evidence. The exaltation of matrimony and the downplaying of celibacy seem to have met with very little resistance from the laity: Over 90% of the squirarchy and upper aristocracy married. The reformers apparently had little difficulty persuading many Elizabethans of the importance of religious agreement in choosing a mate, and there is evidence that Puritan laity usually accepted the advice of Puritan clergy to regard godly virtues in prospective spouses. Assessing the presence of love in matrimony is often impossible, though love matches existed, and indeed probably were fairly common among the lower orders. The approximation of age that Anglican and Puritan leaders sought was generally accepted, for the norm was for modest differences, usually between three and five years. Although early marriages were attractive to the landed classes because of property settlements, family alliances, the need for heirs, and (for peers) the limited number of potential mates, the normal practice accorded with the reformers' wishes to avoid young marriages; between 1560 and 1646, the mean age of marriage for females was between twenty-six and twenty-seven, and between 1540 and 1599 the average age at marriage for the eldest sons of peers was twenty-one. Economic factors and religious teaching combined to discourage early marriage.

In other areas, the reformers seemingly enjoyed reasonable success in persuading the laity to practice their teachings. Children generally were reverential and obedient to parents, and Puritan and Catholic masters followed the promptings of their spiritual leaders to provide religious instruction for servants. The concern for education that moralists sought to inculcate was fairly widely spread among the laity and even increased during the age, though the motivation behind this interest was not always or even mainly religious. Despite complaints of the clergy to the contrary, educational giving was unprecedented in the sixteenth century. The endowment of new schools and the provision of additional scholarships testify to the growth of interest in education. The statutes of some grammar schools reflect the clerical concern that masters be godly, learned, and honest, and Huntingdon's statutes for the Leicester Grammar School reflect the curricular views of moderate Puritan authors.

Puritan censure of idleness and improper pursuit of recreational activities apparently was taken to heart by the laity, and lay members of both groups followed advice with regard to reading material. According to Kentish wills, the aristocracy and professional groups had a reasonably broad exposure to religious literature, and to a lesser degree so did yeomen and people in the clothing, leather, and food trades, the textile industry, and the distributive trades, especially in the last part of the age. Urban readers, however, presumably were inclined to read the type of literature moralists found unsuitable. With regard to justice for the poor, the reformers had some success, partly because their ideals accorded with aristocratic tradition, notably when the aristocracy realized that assisting the unfortunate to find justice increased their popularity.

One of the areas where the clergy enjoyed the greatest success with the laity was in the provision of poor relief. Growing contributions were inspired by clerical exhortations and donations as well as feelings of civic responsibility and fear of the consequences of a social rebellion. As W. K. Jordan has demonstrated, Protestants gave more to poor relief and education than Catholics, with much of the giving coming through bequests in wills. Anglican prelates donated as means allowed, and probably two-thirds of the lower clergy provided for poor relief, though not in amounts significantly different from their Catholic predecessors. The increase in giving to the poor must have come from the laity. With respect to the relief of the indigent through hospitality, the Puritan laity appear to have been more responsive than their Anglican counterparts.

In contrast to those areas in which reasonable degrees of success were achieved, the moralists fared much worse on other matters: Despite exhortations to select mates of the same social standing and not to make wealth a factor, the laity often deviated, as marriage continued to be a means of acquiring enhanced social standing and wealth. Puritan gains in stressing the importance of godly virtues and love were made in the face of these continuing practices. Widows pondering remarriage likewise tended to accord financial considerations more weight than the reformers desired. The Puritan campaign against premarital sex notwithstanding, probably 20% of English girls were pregnant at marriage. If those who failed to conceive, miscarried, or delayed baptism for their babies are considered, probably at least twice that many engaged in sexual relations before marriage. Moralists were frustrated by the late age of first marriages and by the presence of male and female servants and apprentices in households. It is not surprising that the Puritans were convinced that the transformation of the family and household into a microcosm of the church would curtail such abuses. Illicit sexual activity created the problem of bastardy, though a sampling of ninety-eight parishes in the period 1580-1610 reveals illegitimacy ratios of only 2.84%, 3.08%, and 3.20% per decade. Such figures err on the low side. The figures apparently were greatest in the north and west, though the closeness of London to much of the south and east may have permitted many unwed mothers to have their bastards in anonymity in the city. The church also was unable to curtail adultery, certainly among the upper levels of society.

In numerous areas, it is virtually impossible to show adequate statistical evidence to assess the extent of the problems, as in the case of flagrantly disobedient or embezzling servants, deserted spouses who rewed illegally, or severely troubled marriages. One clear area of disagreement is that the Puritan laity were not convinced by their advisors of the dangers of sending their sons to the continent to improve their education. Although the Puritans seem to have made headway against idleness, continental observers considered the English prone to such behavior. The fulminations of reformers against the abuses of holy days, especially Christmas, and May days largely fell on deaf ears, though Easter was observed fairly quietly. Generally the restrictions on recreation proposed by reformers met with a hostile reception, except among the Puritan laity. If anything, the theater gained in popularity, bolstered by aristocratic patronage from men of various religious persuasions. Efforts to curtail a trend toward finer attire largely came to naught, as even foreign visitors noted. Notwithstanding the effect of clerical teaching and social hostility, suicides increased in the Tudor period. Nothing the clergy could do terminated the widespread practice of usury by men and women of varying religious convictions, with the 1571 statute standing as a monument to their failure. In the realm of economics, there was a flagrant use of irregular weights and measures. Despite clerical opposition, Protestant laymen, especially in the midlands, enclosed lands. The reformers were no more successful in the discouragement of litigation.

In these areas, the apparent failure of the reformers was due to a combination of factors, one of which was economic. Another was custom, particularly with respect to holy days, May days, and sexual relations between affianced persons. In such areas as clothing and entertainment, the reformers were running against a strong tide, strengthened by the psychological tendency to emulate the majority or adopt new fashions.

Often, however, the moralists obtained modest but unspectacular gains in their efforts to create a more godly society. More parents seemingly began to accord some voice to children in the determination of marriage partners, and some headway was made against the double standard. The clergy heeded their own advice about avoiding birth-control techniques and about the importance of maternal breast-feeding, but the laity, particularly those of Anglican persuasion, apparently ignored their recommendations. Nor were the moralists as successful as they would have liked in stopping the immoderate chastisement of children, developing the religious obligations of householders, or effecting the imposition of order in households. They did persuade some parents to investigate the religious qualifications of masters and tutors. Although the saints were fairly faithful observers of the sabbath, numerous violations occurred for economic and recreational reasons, despite the efforts of local officials and courts.

Uneven progress was made in other areas. Demands to eat moderately seem to have been widely ignored by the upper orders except on fish days and during Lent, and even then some menus were lavish. Yet clerical exhortations heightened an awareness of the problem and the Puritans seem to have been conscientious about their diet. Fasting for spiritual reasons was apparently more prevalent among Puritans than Anglicans. There are good indications that the Puritans and some Anglicans practiced the ideals of speech enunciated by the reformers, with Puritans experiencing psychological trauma when they failed to attain the ideal. Moreover, among contemporaries, the Puritans had a reputation for veracity, simplicity, and utilitarian speech. Endeavors to ensure that hospitality was extended to the impoverished as well as to persons of substance were only partly successful, especially among Anglicans. Some of the laity shared the reformers' concern for ethical business activity, and some laymen kept entry fines and rents relatively low. Yet in Norfolk and Suffolk, where Puritanism was strong, rents increased more rapidly than the general rise in prices, lending some credence to Sutcliffe's charge that Puritan aristocrats were rack-renters (though by no means was this true of all of them).

The moderation in funeral expenses the reformers favored began to be realized to a limited degree among the aristocracy, though for economic as well as religious reasons. The urban rich, in contrast, began to exceed their social rank in lavish funeral displays. Recognition of the importance of funeral sermons by various reformers motivated some laity to provide for sermons in their wills or for a series of sermons after their funerals. The reformers were not able to eradicate wakes and minds completely, especially since a number of conservative clerics sanctioned them. In keeping with the exhortations of moralists, various Elizabethans stipulated in their wills that funeral expenses be moderate, but the pomp was determined primarily by social rank and available wealth. Reasonable provisions were made for the indigent at funerals in the form of clothing, alms, and food, though never enough to satisfy religious critics, particularly the Puritans. Some Protestant laity directed that funeral expenses be reduced to provide more funds for poor relief. It is apparent that the clerical reformers made some inroads on the conduct of the laity, though far less than they desired.

In a number of areas their efforts were reinforced by the available texts on medicine and health. Although the advice found in such works on how to restore the appearance of virginity in females may have helped overcome resistance to premarital sex, the same works also showed the dangers of venereal disease. The pleas of religious reformers for moderate copulation in marriage were supported as medically sound, but the same works ran counter to Puritan convictions by explaining birth-control techniques. The fulminations of religious leaders against idleness were reinforced in medical works, which taught that idleness has ill effects on physical and mental health. Moderate exercise was extolled in medical handbooks, but warnings were issued against dice, cards, backgammon, and football as harmful to health. Like the clerical moralists, medical authors urged a moderate diet and warned against the ill effects of drinking. Finally, they too favored moderate fasting for improved health. To the extent to which progress was made in these areas, some credit must go to the authors of medical books for reinforcing the message of the religious reformers.

Such support is generally true of the authors of educational works, such as Mulcaster. Apart from the influence they exercised on the curriculum, they urged the moderate chastisement of children and cautioned against the dangers of continental travel. The Puritans, however, would have been uncomfortable with Mulcaster's rather broad sanctioning of dancing as a form of exercise and his arguments against universal education.

The efforts of the reformers were partly undercut by the ill example of uneducated and immoral clergy. Whereas in Catholicism, the efficacy of the priestly function was not dependent on the moral worth of the minister, in Protestantism the minister was both a teacher and an exemplar; the ability of the clerics to provide social leadership was dependent on the quality of their lives and faithfulness to their duties. Pluralism and nonresidence weakened their leadership, but Anglicans tended to defend limited pluralism as a financial incentive to lure educated men into the ministry, to enhance social esteem through greater incomes, to provide hospitality, and to maintain royal and episcopal revenue. Clerical ignorance further restricted ministerial leadership, but in this area marked progress was made during the age. Clerical immorality concerned the godly of all religious convictions, but the heaviest protest came from the Puritans. Clerics who fornicated, resorted to prostitutes, committed adultery, played inappropriate games and gambled, became inebriated, or ruthlessly pursued litigation brought disrepute on the church and hampered efforts to reform the laity. Moreover anticlericalism, an enemy to Anglican and Puritan alike, was fanned by ignorant, nonpreaching, or absentee clerics, immoral or unfit ministers, tithes, greed for ecclesiastical lands, religious turncoats, mandatory church attendance, and ecclesiastical courts.

Although bishops too were the subjects of some hostility for religious, economic, political, and personal reasons, they did fairly well in providing leadership through preaching, visiting, and administering.

The latent antiprelatical hostility of previous ages was furthered by radical Protestant calls for the abolition of bishops. The bitter invectives climaxed in the infamous Marprelate tracts of the late 1580s, which were perhaps the culmination of frustration born of Convocation's refusal in 1563 to adopt Puritan reform demands. To be sure, bishops incited much of the hostility by their inability to live up to people's high expectations, their pomp, their lands and wealth, their financial mismanagement, and their approval of incompetent ministers, especially early in the age. In fairness to the bishops, they were caught in a dilemma, as they were expected to be both paragons of evangelical piety and, in the crown's eyes, lordly prelates and government servants. The queen compounded their economic woes by forcing them to exchange episcopal lands for impropriated tithes. They did try to curtail abuses of nonresidency and crack down on immoral clergy, and they evinced concern about child marriages. In visitation articles and injunctions, they showed concern about bastardy, prostitution, sabbath observance, improper recreational activities, inappropriate clerical attire, improper speech, usury, superstitious funeral customs, and wakes and minds. They sought to suppress Catholic fasting and reacted negatively to those radical Puritans who rejected official fasts. To further religious understanding, they worked for the placement in churches of Bibles, the *Book of Common Prayer,* psalters, homilies, and copies of Erasmus' *Paraphrases* or Bullinger's *Decades,* Foxe's *Acts and Monuments*, and Jewel's defense of the church against Harding. With respect to charity, they personally made bequests, supervised hospitals, supported relief for victims of dearth and unemployed soldiers, and urged lower clergy to relieve the needy. Normally they did not increase fines and rents to keep pace with inflation, which worsened the economic plight of the church but did provide a good example in the campaign against rackrenting.

The efforts of the bishops and reformers were hampered by economic conditions in the church. The problem was partly due to lay patronage, which affected property rights, episcopal control, the quality and number of clergy, and their capability to undertake reform. The Puritans were, of course, able to take advantage of advowsons to secure positions for clerics of their persuasion, and doubtless without lay patronage, Puritans would have faced much greater difficulties. Nevertheless, one of the serious ills the church faced was that the availability of livings with decent incomes did not keep pace with the growth of an educated clergy, and by the end of the age an alienated intelligentsia was developing. Simultaneously, clergy with meager incomes could not always be expected to be good preachers and faithful social leaders, though some, such as Greenham, were. Clergy who sought to keep up economically by obtaining a fair share of tithes through litigation risked fanning anticlerical sentiment or undercutting their ability to lead and persuade. As tithes increasingly became a matter of property transactions and legal payments to owners, the spiritual relationship on which they were founded declined. That tithes were involved in a system of freehold property rights including laymen made reform potentially revolutionary. Yet to improve clerical funding to enhance a resident, educated ministry capable of providing sound social leadership necessitated reform. Clerical incomes were further jeopardized by enclosure, which often involved the commutation of tithes to fixed annual payments. Anglicans thought increased ministerial incomes were mandatory if the clergy were to provide hospitality for the indigent, and the absence of sufficient funding for ecclesiastical courts caused summoners and other officials to be concerned primarily with the volume of business and the fines collected. Anglicans and Puritans alike were frustrated in their social and spiritual work by the chronic underfunding of the church.

The economic difficulties of the government notwithstanding, the failure to provide better funding for the church is somewhat surprising, considering that so many of the social views of the clergy reinforced the order dear to the government. Anglicans and Puritans were essentially agreed in their vision of an hierarchic, organic, orderly, and divinely determined society, and both groups manifested anxiety about the upward pressure of the lower social orders. Anglicans, however, saw even the Puritans as a threat to the social order because they feared their attack on the clerical hierarchy might broaden to include the lay hierarchy as well. Moreover, Bancroft thought Puritans deliberately courted popularity by castigating the sins of social superiors in the pulpit, a reflection that underscores Puritan zealousness in seeking the reform of social injustice. Indirectly and unwittingly, Puritans enhanced social mobility by their greater self-discipline, emphasis on literacy, and determination to improve society.

In many ways, the moralists urged behavior conducive to an orderly society. The anxiety about bastardy, with its attendant problems of shelter, support, abandoned children, infanticide, and vagrancy, was directly related to social stability. Reformers recognized that order in the state was predicated on order in the household, hence the submission of subordinates was essential for well-governed households, churches, and states. The government saw in the educational abilities of the church a unique opportunity to educate children of Catholics to ensure loyalty to the Elizabethan state; in this the reformers concurred. Generally, education was considered a vehicle for the inculcation of obedience and discipline, which both church and state thought desirable.

The government's interest in social stability was complemented by the moralists' teaching on vocation, a useful theme to support social hierarchy. In this regard, Anglican rather than Puritan emphases were closer to the government's wishes, with their greater willingness to allow some mobility. The government too could fully approve the admonitions against idleness, for the indolent threatened the material well-being of the industrious, were prone to criminal activity, and burdened the poor rolls. The views of moralists on recreation were compatible with the state's desire to promote archery and restrict the activities of the lower orders. Clerical pleas to bestow assistance on the needy helped allay the fears of the government in the 1590s that dearth could lead to disorder. Although the state had no religious interest in fasting, its support of such activity to increase poor relief was generally approved by reformers. So too the government could endorse the moralists' efforts to reform speech, with a view to the cessation of threats to order and the social hierarchy. The reformers' castigation of rogues, vagabonds, and sturdy beggars directly related to social order, as these groups were believed responsible for much theft, assault and battery, and sexual improprieties.

In the economic sphere, the government's interest in maintaining social order meshed with the moralists' endeavors to develop codes of Christian conduct and terminate forestalling, regrating, engrossing, and depopulating enclosure. Ministerial concern with standard weights and measures harmonized with the government's interests in the expansion of trade. The ideal of a Christian commonwealth inspired revulsion against those who profited at society's expense, creating social disruption, and harming the impoverished. Depopulating enclosure threatened social stability, reduced the ability of peasants to defend the realm, increased unemployment, and undermined the ability of citizens to pay taxes and tithes. Generally the response of the clergy to economic problems was conservative and in tune with the government's goals. The godly made good citizens, and the preachers were useful vehicles for the conveyance of government social concerns.

In other respects, the state must have found the reformers' efforts useful. Both were troubled by the litigiousness of the period, which hampered the effective administration of justice. The reliance of the state on oaths to uphold obedience and determine truth was furthered by the reformers' insistence on their significance, though Puritan abhorrence of the oath ex officio frustrated the government's ecclesiastical policy. The willingness of many testators to bequeath funds to keep their households together for a period after their funerals not only showed Christian responsibility but reduced the likelihood of unexpected unemployment for servants. So the government generally benefited from the social ideology of the clerical moralists, whose code was predicated on the principle that the social hierarchy and the well-ordered state fully accorded with scriptural principles.

Although the government found much of value in the social views of the reformers, the court became an increasing source of friction with Puritans as it violated certain of the social standards they propounded. The court acquired a reputation for lasciviousness, sabbath disrespect, and inappropriate conduct on holy days. The queen was directly involved in the last two offenses, though she never sanctioned the loose sexual conduct at court. The court also showed a propensity for such controversial forms of recreation as backgammon, gambling, bull and bear-baiting, and mixed dancing, all of which Elizabeth enjoyed. It also patronized the theater, and the queen was a noted devotee of secular music. Excessive drinking, too, brought opprobrium on the court, as did overly fine attire, with the monarch herself a flagrant violator of the canons of moderation and modesty. In effect, Puritan disquietude mounted as the immorality and vanity of the court were perceived as evil examples to the people. Elizabeth could neither appreciate nor support the discipline-oriented, morally strict, and culturally narrow program Puritans espoused; their dream of a New Jerusalem was her nightmare.

The Puritans often were frustrated as well by the inability to get various reform bills through Parliament, in some cases because of royal opposition. Despite Puritan efforts, proposals to reform lay patronage fared poorly because of lay fears of the financial and property ramifications and government hostility. Puritan endeavors to obtain legislation sufficient to reform the abuses of pluralism and nonresidence were resisted by Elizabeth and Whitgift. In 1593 and 1597, fresh attempts were made to deal with the enigma of bastardy when earlier legislation (18 Elizabeth I, c. 3) proved inadequate, but again Puritans in particular were frustrated. Due to hesitation over the nature of proof and reluctance to increase the power of ecclesiastical courts, an endeavor to obtain legislative authority for tougher punishment of adulterers failed. The same Parliament refused to accept Puritan-supported legislation to permit justices of the peace to fine householders who did not enforce church attendance by those in their care. Numerous efforts were made to enforce sabbath observance through new legislation, but nothing proved acceptable to a queen jealous of her prerogative in religious matters. Nor was any attempt to improve the religious observance of holy days successful.

There were other setbacks in Parliament. Although numerous government bills were introduced to control drinking, none were passed, owing to fears that such regulations might be applied to the aristocracy by zealous justices. Of all the endeavors to pass regulations concerning apparel, a law governing caps was the only success. In addition to members' fears of excessive authority placed in the hands of justices, they were anxious about enforcement, penalties, and the relative authority accorded to statute and proclamation. The Commons was willing to enforce clothing standards for the lower orders, but not at the expense of their own freedom. Despite concern over the use of irregular weights and measures, Parliament failed to agree on corrective action. It did not fare any better with forestalling, engrossing, and regrating, though four statutes were passed dealing with enclosure. Ironically, clerical reformers were probably unhappy about the 1593 statute temporarily suspending antienclosure provisions. At least, Parliament agreed with the reformers on the need to improve the administration of justice; it attempted to reduce delays, limit appeals to other courts, improve qualifications of jurors, and have minor matters handled locally. Even so, the Puritan detestation of bribery was unable to procure reform legislation. Thus reforming efforts in Parliament often were defeated, usually because of government opposition, members' fears about the applicability of the legislation to their own actions, or an unwillingness to increase the power of ecclesiastical courts.

In the absence of sufficient legislation, the Privy Council often had to handle social problems. Among these were child marriages, parental consent in marriage, disobedient children, idleness, and the theater (due especially to disorder and public health). The Council considered problems involving diet, inebriety, state fasts, inappropriate apparel, irregular weights and measures, business frauds, and forestalling, engrossing, and regrating. Charges of illegal enclosure periodically came before the Council, and it dealt with litigiousness and justice for the poor. By ad hoc action, it remedied some of the worst legal injustices. Probably prompted by its Puritan members, the Council apparently was motivated by religious conviction, concern for social order, and justice, but its effectiveness was hampered by the ad hoc nature of its actions and the impossibility of handling more than a token number of the social problems. The Council's most effective weapon was the proclamation, issued on royal authority, but even this tool was subject to the inherent weakness of a government operating without sufficient administrative powers and officers to enforce its regulations. That difficulty was especially evident concerning sabbath enforcement, recreation, attire, rogues and vagabonds, and forestalling, engrossing, and regrating. Such weaknesses disturbed the reformers, who repeatedly called for better enforcement and stricter punishments.

Generally reformers upheld pageantry as a visual prop of the social order, an aim with which the government concurred. Weddings reflected the social hierarchy, as the upper orders made effective use of masques, extensive hospitality, lavish clothes, stately dancing, and coaches. Christenings were occasions for the wealthy to display their rank with expensive apparel, sumptuous banquets, and lavishly decorated churches. The greatest social pageant was the funeral and its attendant rites, a series of carefully planned and executed ceremonies replete with social insignia, symbolic pomp, extensive hospitality, and charitable provisions. Although Puritans had no objections to pageantry per se, they were uneasy about the extent to which it was carried and urged moderation. The principal objections stemmed from piety and hostility to Catholic symbolism, but financial considerations also were important, particularly among the laity. As the reformers sought to reduce expenses in the latter part of the age, Elizabeth and Burghley worked in tandem to maintain a high level of pomp. In the seventeenth century, James I undermined pageantry by excessively dispensing honors, neglecting to shore up the finances of declining peers, and failing to give adequate support to the College of Arms, already under attack in the late Elizabethan period. Puritan concern with superfluous pomp, aristocratic inability to sustain enormous expenses, and the decline of court support combined to weaken pageantry as a prop of the social order.

If Puritans were unhappy about the excesses of social pageantry, they were more troubled by the continuation of traditional social customs and rites with pagan or Catholic overtones. Holy days, church ales, wakes, and minds, for instance, were times for rituals and festivities to relieve social tensions, calm quarreling parishioners, and focus attention on the institutional church. As did rogations, they blended Christian customs with pagan agricultural beliefs. Puritan hostility to Sunday sports and mixed dancing was in fact an attack on the old way of life, parallel to the attack on the Old Faith.

Catholicism more than Puritanism proved willing to accommodate in religious life the traditional practices and beliefs. So too the Protestant, especially Puritan, curtailment of much of the traditional church music was offensive to conservative parishioners primarily on aesthetic, not theological, grounds. When reformers pushed for more effective restrictions on alehouses and taverns and for stringent punishment of drunkards, they were criticizing institutions often more important as social centers than the churches for the lower orders. The campaign to abolish Catholic trappings in funeral services must have increased anxiety among those committed to the Old Faith or merely superstitious about death and the traditional customs surrounding it. In many ways, then, reformers endeavored to make over or terminate social customs and rites deeply rooted in the past. The strength of Catholicism in northern and western England is due not only to its reliance on gentry households as centers of the faith, but also to popular resistance against the reformers' onslaught on social practices. Protestantism and especially its Puritan wing favored not only a reformed theology but a reformed society. Puritan inability to create that society in England by the early seventeenth century intensified their interest in the New World, where, ideally, the reformed theology and the reformed society would exist in the New Jerusalem.

Appendix

Appendix
Figure Brasses (1500-1609)

Table 1: Distribution of Brasses by Decade

1500-1509	272
1510-1519	252
1520-1529	264
1530-1539	145
1540-1549	103
1550-1559	80
1560-1569	85
1570-1579	107
1580-1589	149
1590-1599	185
1600-1609	158
Total	1800

Table 2: Distribution of Brasses by County in Order of Frequency

1500-1609		1559-1603	
Kent	201	Essex	75 (45%)
Essex	165	Kent	61 (30%)
Norfolk	142	Suffolk	48 (42%)
Buckinghamshire	114	Oxfordshire	37 (35%)
Suffolk	113	Middlesex and London	33 (39%)
Oxfordshire	107	Berkshire	30 (40%)
Middlesex and London	84	Buckinghamshire	29 (25%)
Surrey	79	Norfolk	27 (19%)
Hertfordshire	76	Surrey	27 (34%)
Berkshire	75	Hertfordshire	26 (34%)
Bedfordshire	60	Sussex	21 (41%)
Sussex	51	Cornwall	16 (57%)
Northamptonshire	49	Devon	15 (58%)
Gloucestershire	45	Northamptonshire	14 (29%)
Hampshire	44	Wiltshire	13 (42%)
Cambridgeshire	40	Bedfordshire	12 (20%)
Lincolnshire	37	Gloucestershire	12 (27%)
Wiltshire	31	Lincolnshire	12 (32%)
Cornwall	28	Hampshire	11 (25%)
Devon	26	Yorkshire	10 (45%)
Warwickshire	26	Dorset	9 (47%)
Somersetshire	24	Somersetshire	9 (38%)
Yorkshire	22	Warwickshire	9 (35%)
Derbyshire	21	Cambridgeshire	6 (15%)
Dorset	19	Shropshire	6 (46%)
Lancashire	19	Staffordshire	6 (67%)
Worcestershire	14	Lancashire	5
Shropshire	13	Derbyshire	4
Leicestershire	9	Durham	4
Staffordshire	9	Worcestershire	4
Herefordshire	8	Leicestershire	2
Huntingdonshire	7	Nottinghamshire	2
Nottinghamshire	7	Cheshire	1
Cumberland	6	Cumberland	1
Durham	5	Herefordshire	1
Cheshire	4	Huntingdonshire	1
Isle of Wight	2	Monmouthshire	1
Rutland	2	Rutland	1
Westmorland	2	Westmorland	1
Monmouthshire	1	Isle of Wight	0
Northumberland	0	Northumberland	0
(In museums)	13		
Total	1800		602

Notes

Abbreviations

Add. MS	Additional Manuscripts, British Library
APC	*Acts of the Privy Council* (all New Series)
BB	Bishops' Bible, 1568
BIHR	*Bulletin of the Institute of Historical Research*
BJS	*British Journal of Sociology*
BL	British Library
BTB	Beza-Tomson Bible, 1577 (unless otherwise noted)
CH	*Church History*
CJ	*Commons' Journals*
CSPD	*Calendar of State Papers, Domestic*
DNB	*Dictionary of National Biography*
EEA	*Elizabethan Episcopal Administration*, ed. W. P. M. Kennedy (1924)
EHR	*English Historical Review*
Econ. H.R.	*Economic History Review*
GB	Geneva Bible, 1560
HJ	*Historical Journal*
HL	Huntington Library
HMC	Historical Manuscripts Commission
HMPEC	*Historical Magazine of the Protestant Episcopal Church*
JEH	*Journal of Ecclesiastical History*
JSH	*Journal of Social History*
LPL	Lambeth Palace Library
MB	Matthew Bible, 1537 (unless otherwise noted)
NT	New Testament
PP	*Past and Present*
PRO	Public Record Office
PS	*Population Studies*
Req.	Requests, Court of
SCH	*Studies in Church History*
SCJ	*Sixteenth Century Journal*
SP	State Papers
SR	*Statutes of the Realm*
STAC	Star Chamber, Court of
TP	*Tudor Royal Proclamations*, ed. Paul Hughes and James F. Larkin (1964, 1969)
TRHS	*Transactions of the Royal Historical Society*
VCH	*Victoria County History*

In the notes the place of publication is London unless otherwise indicated.

Notes

Introduction

1. Christopher Sutton, *Disce vivere* [1604; 1st pub. 1602], sig. A6^V.

2. John Manningham, *Diary*, ed. John Bruce (1868), 1.

3. William Covel, *A Iust and Temperate Defence* (1603), 83. Stephen Bredwell placed the "ful swarme and store" of the Separatists in London, and observed that in 1588 they were spreading into other areas, notably the western regions. *The Rasing of the Fovndations* (1588), sig. $\pi 2^V$.

4. John Penry, *The State of the Church* [1590?], sig. B1^{r-v}; J.T. Cliffe, *The Yorkshire Gentry* (1969), 262-63. Of the 567 families in 1570, 368 were Catholic. *Ibid.*, 169.

5. Thomas Stapleton, *A Fortresse of the Faith* (Antwerp, 1565), f. 134^V; Leonard Trinterud, ed., *Elizabethan Puritanism* (New York, 1971), 7-8. There is also an anachronistic element in the use of the term "Anglican," which has prompted some authors to prefer the term "Conformist." For the sake of clarity I have preferred to write of Anglicans and Puritans rather than Conformists and Precisians, following the generally accepted usage of modern historians. Care must, of course, be taken not to impute the ideology of more modern Anglicans and Puritans to their Elizabethan forebears. Cf. Patrick Collinson, *The Elizabethan Puritan Movement* (Berkeley, 1967), 13, 26-27.

6. John Strype, *The Life and Acts of Matthew Parker* (Oxford, 1821), 3:322; Edwin Sandys, *Sermons*, ed. John Ayre (Cambridge, 1841), 49, 97; Thomas Sparke, *The High Way to Heaven* (1597), sigs. A5^r-A7^r. William Barlow placed the blame for disrupting the unity squarely on the Puritans. *A Defence of the Articles* (1601), 203.

7. William Haller, *The Rise of Puritanism* (New York, 1938), chap. 3; Everett Emerson, *English Puritanism* (Durham, N.C., 1968), 44; Thomas Digges, *Humble Motiues* (1601), 29; Edward Bulkeley, *An Apologie for Religion* (1602), 51-52; (the same point was made by the Anglican William James, *A Sermon . . . at Hampton Courte* [1578], sig. D2^V); Josias Nichols, *The Plea of the Innocent* (1602), 82.

8. See, e.g., Trinterud, "The Origins of Puritanism," *CH*, 20 (1951):37-57; Ronald Vander Molen, "Anglican Against Puritan: Ideological Origins During the Marian Exile," *CH*, 42 (1973): 45-57.

9. Trinterud, *Puritanism*, 10-15. Charles and Katherine George argue that it is only in the Presbyterian stage that "the 'puritan' may be said truly to exist in the guise in which he is ordinarily portrayed—as a readily identifiable, markedly distinct, and unquestionably disturbing element in the Church of England." *The Protestant Mind of the English Reformation* (Princeton, 1961), 398. The challenge of explaining the essence of Puritanism has led a few historians to scholarly nihilism; cf. Nicholas Tyack, *JEH*, 29 (1978): 123-24.

10. Nichols, *Plea*, 5-12.

11. BL Lansdowne MSS 12/28; 157, f. 186^r; 115/55; (cf. Nichols, *Plea*, 35).

12. John Deacon, *A Verie Godlie . . . Sermon* (1586), 19; William Perkins, *Workes* (1612-13), 3:15; Nichols, *Plea*, 2-4; Basil Hall, "Puritanism: The Problem of Definition," *SCH*, 2 (1965):296. The experiential basis is recognized by Alan Simpson, *Puritanism in Old and New England* (Chicago, 1955), 2. See Richard L. Greaves, "The Nature of the Puritan Tradition," *Reformation, Conformity and Dissent*, ed. R. Buick Knox (1977), 255-73. Geoffrey Nuttall writes of the Puritan tradition as the quest to recover the inner life of New Testament Christianity. *Visible Saints* (Oxford, 1957), 3.

13. John Whitgift, *Works*, ed. John Ayre (Cambridge, 1851-53), 1:171-72; Strype, *Parker*, 3:321; Nichols, *Plea*, 1-2, 4. According to Edward Bulkeley, the Catholics were the true Puritans for advocating purity from sin after baptism. Prov. 30:12 (Geneva version) was, in his judgment, relevant to them. *An Apologie for Religion* (1602), 52.

14. Thomas Nash, *Pierce Penilesse His Supplication to the Diuell* (1592), f. 29^v; Dr. Walter Curle, in Manningham, *Diary*, 83, 156; Leonard Wright, *A Summons for Sleepers* (1589), 21; James, *A Sermon . . . at Pavles Crosse* (1590), sig. A3^r. In response to such charges Thomas Digges retorted that only selfish interest in retaining offices in the church prevented Anglicans from a natural, logical evolution to Puritanism. "It is hard for any man, sincerely to be a Protestant, but that he will easily passe on also (more or lesse) to be a Puritan." *Motiues*, 42.

15. Barlow, *Defence*, 105-6; John Udall, *Certaine Sermons* (1596), sig. $_2$A4^v.

16. Michael Walzer, *The Revolution of the Saints* (New York, 1971), 204, 209, 308-9 (quoted); Henry Ainsworth, *The Communion of Saincts* (Amsterdam, 1607), 144. Stephen Brachlow observes that a gnawing sense of sin prompted Puritans to search for religious security. "Puritan Theology and Radical Churchmen in Pre-revolutionary England" (D. Phil. thesis, Oxford, 1978), 83. Cf. Carl Bridenbaugh, *Vexed and Troubled Englishmen* (New York, 1968), 276.

17. Cf. Conyers Read: "Puritanism is an attitude of mind. Beginning as a religious movement it came to embrace a whole social philosophy and a whole political philosophy." *Social and Political Forces in the English Reformation* (Houston, 1953), 60.

18. Bernard J. Verkamp, *The Indifferent Mean* (Athens, Ohio, and Detroit, 1977), chap. 4; John S. Coolidge, *The Pauline Renaissance in England* (Oxford, 1970), chap. 1. Cf. John New, *Anglican and Puritan* (Stanford, 1964), 27-28, who argues that the dispute over Scripture stemmed from two differing concepts of human nature.

19. Whitgift, *Works*, 1:194; Coolidge, *Renaissance*, chap. 2; New, *Anglican and Puritan*, 52-53. For the attitude of Anglicans and Puritans toward the two tables of the Mosaic law in the seventeenth century, see J. Sears McGee, *The Godly Man in Stuart England* (New Haven, 1976).

20. McGee, "Puritanism in a Religious Perspective," a paper delivered to a joint session of the American Historical Association and the American Society of Church History, Dallas, 1977; John Phillips, *The Reformation of Images* (Berkeley, 1973), chap. 6. Gradually the different outlooks included varying apocalyptic visions. The more radical Puritans characterized the Church of England as Laodicea, the lukewarm church depicted in Revelation. Paul Christianson, *Reformers and Babylon* (Toronto, 1978), 10, 48.

21. One of many examples is the cleric Thomas Wright, who informed Henry Garnett in

1596 that Catholics should no longer be considered a threat to the state, the affairs of which no longer concerned them. LPL Bacon MS, 654/80 (f. 127^r).

22. There were crypto-Catholic clergy as well as laity. John Northbrooke described their activities: "For they thinke nowe, that if they subscribe, obserue the order of seruice, and weare a side gowne, a square Cap, a Cope, and a Surples, none can saie blacke is their eyes, but that they are good protestantes: yet all this while they run into hugger mugger a whispering in corners, saiyng to the simple people: beleue not this newe doctrine." *Spiritus . . . A Breefe and Pithie Summe* (1571), sig. A3^r.

23. The degree of continuity between radical Puritans such as Cartwright and Separatists further underscores the appropriateness of the continuum. Brachlow, "Puritan Theology and Radical Churchmen," especially chap. 1. Collinson also uses the notion of a spectrum. *Puritan Movement*, 27. Using the idea of a spectrum, Michael G. Finlayson denies the existence of a Puritan entity, but admits that the term "Puritan" suggests "a direction of thought." "Puritanism and Puritans: Labels or Libels?" *Canadian Journal of History*, 8 (1973):207-9.

24. John Clapham, *Elizabeth of England*, ed. Evelyn and Conyers Read (Philadelphia, 1951), 80: Joel Hurstfield, "Church and State, 1558-1612: The Task of the Cecils." *SCH*, 2 (1965):122-24; Conyers Read, *Lord Burghley and Queen Elizabeth* (New York, 1960), 114; HMC 9 Salisbury, 4:68; (cf. Rowse, *England*, 464); BL Lansdowne MS 103/71.

25. Margaret Spufford, *Contrasting Communities* (1974), 321; cf. chap. 13.

26. Cf. Brachlow, "Puritan Theology and Radical Churchmen," 34.

27. Sutton, *Disce vivere*, 323.

28. Hastings Robinson, trans. and ed., *The Zurich Letters* (Cambridge, 1842), 296.

29. Roger Wilbraham, *Journal*, ed. Harold Scott (1902), 59; James Pilkington, *Works*, ed. James Scholefield (Cambridge, 1842), 73, 425; John Carpenter, *A Preparatiue* (1597), 123.

30. Richard Rogers, *Seven Treatises* (1603), 573; Edward Hake, *Newes Out of Powles Churchyarde* (1579), sig. B4^V; Arthur Dent, *The Plaine Mans Path-way to Heauen* (1601), 197; Wilcox, *A Verie Godly . . . Exposition vpon . . . Psalmes*, in *Works*, 122; Stephen Gosson, *The Schoole of Abuse* (1579), f. 34^V.

31. GB, preface to Deut.; notes to Ps. 147:15; Mark 6:34; Jer. 5:31; Hos. 5:10; Pss. 55:10; 145:12; (cf. Ps. 82:5); John 3:28; (cf. Luke 14:8); 2 Chron. 14:5; Judg. 17:6; Ps. 61:7. Conservatives cast opprobrium on the Puritans by calling them Anabaptists. Hall, *SCH*, 2:287-88.

32. Robert Abbot, *The Exaltation of the Kingdome* (1601), 37; Matthew Parker, *Correspondence*, ed. John Bruce (Cambridge, 1853), 362; Edward Dering, *A Briefe and Necessarie Catechisme*, in *Workes* (1597), sig. E3^V; Thomas Becon, *A New Postil* (1566), 1:f. 117^V; T. Acheley, *The Massacre of Money* (1602), sig. A4^V.

33. Sandys, *Sermons*, 139; Anthony Anderson, *A Godlie Sermon* (1576), sig. A8^r; Anthony Nixon, *The Christian Navy* (1602), sig. B2^V; John Woolton, *The Christian Manual* (Cambridge, 1851; 1st pub. 1576), 91-92; BL Add. MS 35,324, f. 18^r; H.J. Carpenter, "Furse of Moreshead. A Family Record of the Sixteenth Century," *Report and Transactions of the Devonshire Association for the Advancement of Science, Literature, and Art*, 26 (1894):171.

34. John Dod, *A Treatise or Exposition vpon the Ten Commandements* (1603), pt. 2, f. 73^V; Richard Greenham, *Works* (1599), 464; Norden, *A Sinfvll Mans Solace* (1585), f. 16^V; Becon, *Postil*, 1:118^V, 119^V; Penry, *A Treatise* (1590), sigs. B1^r, B2^V-B3^r.

35. Alan Everitt, "Social Mobility in Early Modern England," *PP*, 33 (1966):57; G.D. Ramsay, "The Recruitment and Fortunes of Some London Freemen in the Mid-Sixteenth Century," *Econ. H.R.*, 2nd ser., 31 (1978):528, 530-31.

36. Lawrence Stone, "Social Mobility in England, 1520-1700," *PP*, 33 (1966):49; *The*

Causes of the English Revolution, 1529-1642 (New York, 1972), 81; Peter Clark, "Popular Protest and Disturbance in Kent, 1558-1640," *Econ. H.R.*, 2nd ser., 29 (1976):365-82. Cf. R.B. Manning, "Patterns of Violence in Early Tudor Enclosure Riots," *Albion*, 6 (1974): 120-33. Horizontal social mobility within a fundamentally static system, as distinct from the changing status of groups, was commonly accepted. See E.E. Rich, "The Population of Elizabethan England," *Econ. H.R.*, 2nd ser., 2 (1950):262.

37. *SR*, 18 Eliz. I, c. 16.

38. Sir Thomas Smith, *De repvblica Anglorvm* (1583), 10; Sandys, *Sermons*, 99-100, 164-65; T. Rogers, *A Golden Chaine* (1587), sig. A3^r; (cf. Richard Turnbull, *An Exposition vpon . . . Iude* [1592], sig. A8^r); E.M.W. Tillyard, *The Elizabethan World Picture* (New York, 1944), 7, 12-13; B. L. Joseph, *Shakespeare's Eden* (New York, 1971), 153-67.

39. Lawrence Stone, *The Crisis of the Aristocracy* (Oxford, 1965), 25.

40. William Rye, ed., *England as Seen by Foreigners* (1865), 45. The visitor was Jakob Rathgeb, private secretary to Frederick, duke of Wirtemberg.

41. See Wallace MacCaffrey, "England: The Crown and the New Aristocracy, 1540-1600," *PP*, 30 (1965):52-64.

42. William Vaughan, *The Golden-groue* (2nd ed., 1608; 1st pub. 1600), sigs. T5^v-T6^r. Cf. Sir William Segar, *Honor Military, and Ciuill (1602)*, 51; HMC 53 Montagu, 51.

43. Richard Mulcaster, *Positions wherin These Primitive Circvmstances Be Examined* (1581), 195; W. Vaughan, *Golden-groue*, sigs. T7^v-T8^r; Carpenter, *Preparatiue*, sig. $_2$C4^r; Pilkington, *Works*, 219; Philip Stubbes, *The Anatomie of Abuses* (1583), sigs. C8^v-D1^r.

44. Dering, *A Sermon Preached at the Tower of London* [1569?], sig. C8^r; Stubbes, *Anatomie*, sig. K4^{r-v}. Presumably Dering would have approved the later attitude of Sir Symonds D'Ewes (born in 1602), when he indicated that he "ever accounted it a great outward blessing to be well descended, it being in the gift only of God and nature to bestow it." *Autobiography*, ed. James Halliwell (1845), 1:6.

45. John Carr, *The Ruinous Fal of Prodigalitie* (1573), sig. C1^r.

46. Sandys, *Sermons*, 158; Nash, *Pierce*, ff. 8^v-9^r; Manningham, *Diary*, 29; Mulcaster, *Positions*, 194-95; Babington, *A Funerall Sermon*, sigs. A2^v-A3^r; Richard Williams, "Dialogue between Law and Obedience," BL Lansdowne MS 119/10 (f. 138^r).

47. Francis Trigge, *An Apologie* (1589), 37; Stubbes, *A Motive to Good Workes* (1593), 92-93; *Anatomie*, sig. K4^v; Samuel Nicholson, *Acolastvs His After-Witte* (1600), sig. H3^v; Robert Shelford, *Lectvres or Readings vpon . . . Prouerbs* (1606; 1st pub. 1602), 14; Whitgift, *Works*, 2:383-84; Barlow, *A Sermon Preached at Paules Crosse* (1601), sig. B8^v; Woolton, *Manual*, 81.

48. R. Rogers, *Treatises*, 104, 168; Perkins, *The Whole Treatise of the Cases of Conscience* (Cambridge, 1606), 628-30, 633-34; (cf. Robert Cleaver, *A Godly Form of Hovseholde Gouernement* [1598], 277-82); John Knewstub, *A Sermon Preached at Paules Crosse* (1579), sig. Q5^r; William Burton, *The Anatomie of Belial*, in *Works* (1602), 226; (cf. Dod, *Treatise*, pt. 2, f. 1^v).

49. A.C. Wood, ed., *Memorials of the Holles Family* (1937), 46; J.P. Cooper, ed., *Wentworth Papers* (1973), 11-12. Wentworth's religious views are expressed on p. 18.

50. Parker, *Correspondence*, 437; BL Lansdowne MS 17/27; (cf. Sandys to Leicester and Burghley, 5 Aug. 1573, Lansdowne MS 17/43); Mary Bateson, ed., *A Collection of Original Letters* (1893), 52; BL Lansdowne MS 8/4; Christopher Hatton, *Memoirs*, ed. Sir Harris Nicolas (1847), 302; Henry Barrow, *A Collection of Certain Letters* (1590), sig. K1^{r-v}; (cf. John Greenwood, *Writings* [1962], 99-100).

51. Richard Hooker, *Works*, ed. John Keble (Oxford, 1845), 2:519.

52. Richard Bancroft, *A Svrvay of the Pretended Holy Discipline* (1593), 7-10, 62-63, 179; cf. 174, 177.

53. Stone, *PP*, 33;43-44; cf. 50. His thesis bears careful consideration, though it is some-what overstated.

54. Stone, *Crisis*, 681; Pilkington, *Works*, 42; John Smyth, *The Berkeley Manuscripts*, ed. Sir John Maclean (Gloucester, 1883), 2:420; Joan Kent, "Attitudes of Members of the House of Commons to the Regulation of 'Personal Conduct' in Late Elizabethan and Early Stuart England," *BIHR*, 46 (1973):49; LPL Bacon MS 647/122 (f. 247^r); Laurence Chaderton, *A Frvitfvll Sermon* (1584), 19-20.

55. Richard Davies, *A Fvnerall Sermon* (1577), sig. E4^v.

56. T. Rogers, *A Philosophicall Discourse* (1576), f. 110^v.

57. GB, notes to Prov. 19:10; 25:16; Dan. 1:15; Eccles. 3:13.

58. Dudley Fenner, *Certain Godly and Learned Treatises* (Edinburgh, 1592), 182; William Hergest, *The Right Rvle of Christian Chastitie* [1580], 1; Edmund Bunny, *The Whole Summe of Christian Religion* (1576), f. 68^v; Abraham Fleming, *The Foot-path of Faith* (1619; 1st pub. 1581), 252.

59. Nash, *Pierce*, f. 29^r; Turnbull, *An Exposition vpon . . . Iames* (1592), f. 200^v; Hergest, *Rvle*, 5; T. Rogers, *Discourse*, ff. 82^v, 110^v, 111^r; Wright, *A Display of Dutie* (1589), 16; Segar, *Honor*, 60.

60. Udall, *Amendment of Life* (1584), sig. F5^v; Thomas Wilcox, *A Short . . . Commentarie . . . on Prouerbs*, in *Works* (1624), 118; R. Rogers, *Treatises*, 187; Becon, *The Sycke Mans Salue* (1561), 212; John Stockwood, *A Very Fruitfull . . . Sermon of the . . . Destruction of Ierusalem* (1584), sig. C2^r; Knewstub, *Sermon*, sigs. R1^v-R2^r; W. Vaughan, *Golden-groue*, sig. H5^{r-v}.

61. William Bullein, *Bulleins Bulwarke* (1562), pt. 3, f. 69^r; Conyers Read, ed., *William Lambarde and Local Government* (Ithaca, New York, 1962), 102; Clapham, *Elizabeth*, ed. Read, 82; D'Ewes, *Journals*, 602; Carr, *Fal*, sig. C2^v.

Chapter 1: Social Pressures and Christian Leadership

1. Thomas Cooper, *Certaine Sermons* (1580), 212.

2. Penry, *An Exhortation* (1588), 20.

3. Tyndale, Pentateuch (1530), notes to Exod. 18; Lev. 10; Num. 6; Tyndale NT (1534), prologue to Titus.

4. MB, notes to 1 Tim. 3; Isa. 3.

5. Tyndale-Rogers NT (1538), note to Matt. 23; Tyndale-Erasmus NT (1549), note to 1 Cor. 3.

6. GB, notes to Matt. 23:11; Rev. 9:1, 3.

7. Rheims NT, notes to Rev. 2:2; Matt. 10:16; John 10:13; 2 Cor. 1:24; Titus 2:15; 1 Tim. 5:17; William Fulke, *The Text of the New Testament* (1589), ff. 382^v-83^r.

8. Collinson, "Episcopacy and Reform in England in the Later Sixteenth Century," *SCH*, 3 (1966):104; *A Mirror of Elizabethan Puritanism* (1964), 26; Penry, *State*, sig. G1^r; Anthony Gilby, *A Pleasant Dialogve* (1581), sig. L7^r; Claire Cross, "Noble Patronage in the Elizabethan Church," *HJ*, 3 (1960):6.

9. HMC 9 Salisbury, 2:63; Whitgift, *Works*, 3:9; C. Hill, *Change and Continuity in Seventeenth-Century England* (Cambridge, 1975), 191.

10. BL Lansdowne MS 8/3; Lewis Evans, *A Brieue Admonition* (Antwerp, 1565), sig. B1^r.

11. Becon, *Postil*, 1:f. 53^v; Robert Crowley, *An Opening of the Wordes* (1567), sig. B7^v; PRO SP 48/11 (ff. 22^r-23^r); SP 48/22 (f. 46^{r-v}); SP 48/22.1 (f. 48^{r-v}).

12. *APC*, 8:33; HMC 9 Salisbury, 2:52; Strype, *Historical Collections of . . . John Aylmer* (2nd ed.; Oxford, 1821), 39, 82; *The Life and Acts of John Whitgift* (Oxford, 1822), 1:338.

13. *Oh Read Ouer . . . an Epitome* [1588; The Epistle]; *Oh Read Ouer . . . an Epitome* [1588; The Epitome]; *Certaine . . . Schoolpoints* [1589]; *Hay Any Worke for Cooper* [1589]; *Theses Martinianae* [1589; the quote is from sig. A4ᵛ]; *The Iust Censure* [1589]; *The Protestatyon* [1589]. The case for Penry's authorship is set forth by Donald McGinn, *John Penry and the Marprelate Controversy* (New Brunswick, N. J., 1966).

14. Udall, *A Demonstration of the Trueth* (1588), sig. B1ʳ; Penry, *Exhortation*, 17; *A Viewe of Some Part* [1589], sigs. A3ᵛ, B1ʳ⁻ᵛ, 18, 21; *Treatise*, sigs. A3ʳ, B2ᵛ-B3ʳ, G3ʳ.

15. Cooper, *An Admonition to the People* (1589); Wright, *A Friendly Admonition* (1590), 2, 6; Turnbull, *Iude*, f. 64ʳ; Robert Temple, *A Sermon Teaching Discretion* (1592), sigs. B8ᵛ, C2ᵛ. For other replies see McGinn, *John Penry*, chap. 15.

16. BL Lansdowne MS 97/16; PRO SP 171/23 (f. 52ʳ).

17. BL Lansdowne MSS 61/54, 57, 66. On 2 January 1596 Dr. Roger Goad, vice chancellor of Cambridge University, complained to Burghley that William Covel, fellow of Queen's College, had preached at St. Mary's against nobles and bishops who made the church a den of thieves. Lansdowne MS 80/53.

18. BL Lansdowne MSS 64/32, 69; 65/60. See also W. D. J. Cargill Thompson, "Sir Francis Knollys' Campaign against the *Jure Divino* Theory of Episcopacy," *The Dissenting Tradition*, ed. Robert Cole and Michael Moody (Athens, Ohio, 1975).

19. Cooper, *Certaine Sermons*, 209; PRO SP 48/41 (f. 97ʳ); HMC 9 Salisbury, 2:184.

20. Collinson, *SCH*, 3:121; Jewel, *Works*, ed. John Ayre (Cambridge, 1845-50), 4:970; George Wither, *A View of the Marginal Notes* [1588], 103.

21. Gilby, *Dialogve*, sig. M3ʳ; Fenner, *A Defence of the Godlie Ministers* (1587), sig. B3ʳ⁻ᵛ; BL Add. MS 27,632, ff. 47ʳ, 48ʳ, cited in Collinson, *SCH*, 3:104. Cf. Strype, *Parker*, 3:320.

22. Penry, *Treatise*, sig. E2ᵛ; Strype, *Parker*, 3:320; C. Hill, *Economic Problems of the Church* (Oxford, 1956), 40; Jewel, *Works*, 4:1085.

23. HMC 9 Salisbury, 2:121; Robinson, ed., *Zurich Letters*, 265.

24. Eusebius Pagit, *A Godly and Frvitefull Sermon* [1583], sigs. B4ᵛ-B5ʳ; Roland Usher, *The Reconstruction of the English Church* (1910), 1:114-15; PRO SP 108/45 (f. 100ʳ), 108/46 (f. 102ʳ); LPL Bacon MS 661/185 (f. 283ʳ); HMC 9 Salisbury, 6:44; Wood, *Letters*, 19-20; Leland H. Carlson, ed., *The Writings of Henry Barrow, 1587-1590* (1962), 227. The financial plight of some bishops, especially Thomas Bentham, bishop of Lichfield and Coventry, is examined by Joel Berlatsky, "Thomas Bentham and the Plight of Early Elizabethan Bishops," *HMPEC*, 43 (1974):329-38. In 1541 the income of the bishop of Chester was approximately one-fourth that of the sees of Bath and Wells, Ely, and York, but by the end of the Elizabethan era it was about equal with Bath and Wells and half that of Ely and York. The improvement was relative, for the others had really declined in this period. Bishop Chaderton's net income in the year 1594-95 was only £123 7s. 4d. Christopher Haigh, "Finance and Administration in a New Diocese: Chester, 1541-1641," *Continuity and Change*, ed. Rosemary O'Day and Felicity Heal (Leicester, 1976), 156, 165-66.

25. Pilkington, *Works*, 594-95; Whitgift, *Works*, 2:382, 388-89, 436; Wright, *The Hunting of Antichrist* (1589), sig. E1ʳ⁻ᵛ.

26. PRO SP 158/82 (ff. 206ʳ-207ᵛ), 158/83 (f. 208ʳ⁻ᵛ), 158/84 (f. 209ʳ).

27. Dering, *Workes*, f. 28ᵛ; Udall, *Demonstration*, sig. A3ʳ⁻ᵛ; Penry, *Exhortation*, 19; Crowley, *Opening*, sigs. B8ʳ⁻ᵛ, C1ʳ; HMC 9 Salisbury, 3:412. Cf. Robert Some, *A Godly Treatise* (1588), 128.

28. *EEA*, 3:196; Edward Cardwell, ed., *Synodalia* (Oxford, 1842), 1:132-34.

29. Ralph Houlbrooke, "The Protestant Episcopate 1547-1603: The Pastoral Contribution," *Church and Society in England*, ed. Felicity Heal and Rosemary O'Day (Hamden, Conn., 1977), 78-98. The case for Parker's interest in reform and his embodiment of Bucer's ideals is set forth by Mark E. VanderSchaaf, "Archbishop Parker's Efforts toward a Bucerian Discipline in the Church of England," *SCJ*, 8 (1977):85-103.

30. Richard Lewes, *A Sermon Preached at Paules Crosse* (1594), sig. C3^r.

31. John Chardon, *Fvlfordo et fvlfordae* (1595), 49.

32. Collinson, *Puritan Movement*, 339-41; "Magistracy and Ministry: A Suffolk Miniature," *Reformation, Conformity and Dissent*, ed. Knox, 85; Rosemary O'Day, "Ecclesiastical Patronage: Who Controlled the Church?" *Church and Society*, ed. Heal and O'Day; C. Hill, *Economic Problems*, 55; London Guildhall MS 9537/5, ff. 111^r, 112^r, 113^V *et passim*. I owe the Guildhall references to Professor Paul Seaver. The bishops estimated in 1604 that five-sixths of the benefices were controlled by laymen, but this included the crown. Lay control was apparently strongest in the southeast. Hill, *op. cit.*, 145.

33. J. Baxter, *A Toile for Two-Legged Foxes* (1600), 184-94; *APC*, 15:217 (cf. 248, 269-70); G. J. Piccope, ed., *Lancashire and Cheshire Wills* (Manchester, 1857-61), 51:91.

34. Lawrence Vaux, *A Catechisme* [1574], f. 55^r; Anthony Anderson, *A Sermon Preached at Paules Crosse* (1581), sig. D5^{r-V}; Lewes, *Sermon*, sig. C2^V; Manningham, *Diary*, 58, 85; John Rainolds, *A Sermon vpon . . . Obadiah* (1584), 25; Barrow, *Collection*, 9, 57; Robert Harrison, *A Little Treatise* [1583], sig. H2^r.

35. Dering, *A Sermon Preached before the Queenes Maiestie* [1569?], sigs. E1^V-E2^r; Stockwood, *A Very Fruiteful Sermon Preached at Paules Crosse* (1579), sig. C3^{r-V}; Woolton, *The Castell of Christians* (1577), sigs. E6^V-E7^r; Christopher Shutte, *A Verie Godlie and Necessary Sermon* (1578), sig. F6^V; Jewel, *Works*, 2:1000; Pilkington, *Works*, 36; Some, *Treatise*, 121; James Bisse, *Two Sermons* (1581), sig. E1^r; Wright, *Summons*, 15. Cf. Whitgift, *Works*, 3:456; Thomas Timme, *A Plaine Discouerie* (1592), sig. D4^V; John Dove, *A Sermon* [1594], sig. C6^{r-V}; Thomas Gibson, *A Frviteful Sermon* (1583), sigs. E2^V, E6^r.

36. Manningham, *Diary*, 69; D'Ewes, *The Journals of All the Parliaments During the Reign of Queen Elizabeth* (1682), 640. The bishops estimated in 1603 that the number of impropriated livings was 3,849. Whitgift estimated the lost imcome to the church at £100,000, Hooker at £126,000 *p.a.*, or £25 to £35 in each impropriated parish. C. Hill, *Economic Problems*, 145. For a concise statement of the further problem of inflation and clerical income see, in addition to Hill, Felicity Heal, "Economic Problems of the Clergy," *Church and Society*, ed. Heal and O'Day, 99-118.

37. Hill, *Economic Problems*, 205 (cf. chap. 6); "Puritans and 'The Dark Corners of the Land'," *TRHS*, 5th Series, 13 (1963):82-83, 88-89; Spufford, *Communities*, 251; DWL Bacon MS 652/110 (f. 159^r); Christopher Haigh, *Reformation and Resistance in Tudor Lancashire* (1975), 238.

38. John Howson, *A Sermon Preached at Paules Crosse* (1597), 34; Wright, *Summons*, 15-16; Anderson, *The Shield of Our Safetie* (1581), sigs. T4^V-U1^r; Manningham, *Diary*, 116. The identification of "Mr. Clapham" is suggested by Paul Seaver, *The Puritan Lectureships* (Stanford, 1970), 318, n. 51. Anderson's claim that preachers timed their services according to the needs of cooks is supported by complaints against Mr. Cliberye, vicar of Halstead, Essex. BL Lansdowne MS 110/10.

39. Stephen Bateman, *The New Arrival* [1580?], sig. D1^r; Edmund Grindal, *Remains*, ed. William Nicholson (Cambridge, 1843), 329; Pilkington, *Works*, 62, 105. Cf. Bernard Gilpin, *A Godly Sermon* (1581), 31-32; Hake, *Newes*, sig. B3^r; Jewel, *Works*, 2:999; Pagit, *Frvitefull Sermon*, sig. B5^r.

40. Howson, *1597 Sermon*, 25, 27, 31, 36; Thomas Cole, *A Godly and Learned Sermon* (1564), sig. B5^r; **Sandys, Sermons**, 155; Rainolds, *Sermon vpon Obadiah*, 27; W. Vaughan, *Golden-groue*, sig. $_2$A8^V; Nash, *The Anatomie of Absurditie* (1590), sig. D2^V; Anderson, *Sermon at Paules Crosse*, sigs. F4^V-F5^r. Cf. Manningham, *Diary*, 58, 59; Some, *Treatise*, 12; Nicholas Sanders, *A Briefe Treatise of Vsvrie* (1568), f. 11^r. Stone estimates living expenses for a batteler at £20 *p.a.* "The Educational Revolution in England, 1560-1640," *PP*, 28 (1964):71.

41. Jewel, *Works*, 2:1012; Cooper, *Admonition*, 114-15; Pilkington, *Works*, 593; Rainolds, *Sermon vpon Obadiah*, 24; Temple, *Sermon*, sig. E3^r; Parker, *Correspondence*, 374; cf. Mark Curtis, "The Alienated Intellectuals of Early Stuart England," *PP*, 23 (1962): 25-43. Cf. Cooper, *Admonition*, 29.

42. *EEA*, 2:13, 31, 54, 111; 3:167-68, 220-21, 226.

43. Sandys, *Sermons*, 43; Lewis Thomas, *Demegoriai* (1600), sig. E5^{r-v}; Nichols, *Plea*, 143; Cooper, *Admonition*, 115; Roger Manning, *Religion and Society in Elizabethan Sussex* (Leicester, 1969), 167.

44. *CJ*, 1:69, 70, 72, 79; J. E. Neale, *Queen Elizabeth I and Her Parliaments* (New York, 1966), 1:166-69, 217; D'Ewes, *Journals*, 165. In 1563, the Commons also gave a first reading to a bill allowing the lord chancellor to direct commissions to bishops and others for the increase of clerical livings in churches of small value in towns. *CJ*, 1:71.

45. *CJ*, 1:115, 132; D'Ewes, *Journals*, 345; Neale, *Parliaments*, 2:148-62, 231; Collinson, *Puritan Movement*, 306-14; BL Sloane MS 326, f. 116^r.

46. Rainolds, *Sermon vpon Obadiah*, 31; Woolton, *Castell*, sig. E7^{r-v}. Cf. C. Hill, *Economic Problems*, 57 (for corporations) and 150-51 (for the universities).

47. C. Hill, *TRHS*, 13:89; *Economic Problems*, 14-17, 25; Howson, *1597 Sermon*, 41.

48. PRO SP 67/17 (f. 36^r); Hurstfield, *SCH*, 2:132; Manning, *Religion*, 185.

49. Sparke, *A Sermon Preached at Cheanies* (1585), 80; *A Sermon Preached at Whaddon* (Oxford, 1593), f. 64^v; Robert Tittler, *Nicholas Bacon* (1976), 157-58; W. K. Jordan, *The Forming of the Charitable Institutions of the West of England, Transactions of the American Philosophical Society*, New Series, 50 (1960):41; R. C. Richardson, *Puritanism in North-West England* (Manchester, 1972), 128-29; D. W. Whitney, "London Puritanism: The Haberdashers' Company," *CH*, 32 (1963):299-301. See Elliot Rose, *Cases of Conscience* (1975), 213-18. One of those to whom the earl of Leicester was a patron, the Anglican William Overton, then treasurer of Chichester, frankly expressed his obesience: "Consider with yourself I besech you what I am and what I have been towardes your Lordship. I am your chapleyn of olde; I have been plyable to your letters and suytes; I have ben and am in case both able and ready to do you honour if you will use me." Cited in Patrick Collinson, ed., *Letters of Thomas Wood, BIHR*, Supplement no. 5 (1960), xxxv.

50. Thomas Stoughton, *A Generall Treatise Against Poperie* (Cambridge, 1598), sig. π3^v; C. Hill, *Economic Problems*, 56; Barbara Donagan, "The Clerical Patronage of Robert Rich, Second Earl of Warwick, 1619-1642," *Proceedings of the American Philosophical Society*, 120 (1976):415-16; Michael Craze, *A History of Felsted School* (Ipswich, 1955), 38-40. Greenwood became vicar of Hatfield Pevernel in 1596, and served as vicar of Great Sampford from 1601 to 1634.

51. Cross, *HJ*, 3:3-4, 10, 16; "The Third Earl of Huntingdon and Elizabethan Leicestershire," *Transactions of the Leicestershire Archeological and Historical Society*, 36 (1960):9; "An Example of Lay Intervention in the Elizabethan Church," *SCH*, 2 (1965): 279, 282; Stockwood, *A Bartholmew Fairing for Parents* (1589), sig. A3^r (cf. A4^v); Strype, *Aylmer*, 36-37; Richardson, *Puritanism*, 118-19. Cf. the request of Robert Devereux, earl of Essex, to Richard Fiennes, Lord Saye and Sele, to grant the living of Broughton to Mr. Leigh. DWL Bacon MS 655/156 (f. 219^r).

52. Marjorie McIntosh, "Sir Anthony Cooke: Tudor Humanist, Educator, and Religious Reformer," *Proceedings of the American Philosophical Society*, 119 (1975):249; E. R. Brinkworth, ed., *The Archdeacon's Court* (Oxford, 1942), 86; Parker, *Correspondence*, 311-12; Turnbull, *Iude*, f. 75^v.

53. Barrow, *Writings (1587-90)*, 348.

54. Jewel, *Works*, 2:984.

55. Dering, *XXVII. Lectvres . . . vpon . . . Hebrues*, in *Works*, sig. X4^r.

56. MacCaffrey, *Exeter, 1540-1640* (Cambridge, Mass., 1958), 194; Manning, *Religion*, 175; Albert Peel, ed., *The Seconde Parte of a Register* (Cambridge, 1915), 2:180-84; Ronald Marchant, *The Puritans and the Church Courts* (1960), 216; A.T. Hart, *The Country Clergy* (1958), 47; Haigh, *Reformation*, 237; C. Hill, *Economic Problems*, 225-26; J.I. Daeley, "Pluralism in the Diocese of Canterbury During the Administration of Matthew Parker, 1559-1575," *JEH*, 18 (1967):43. The problem was compounded by the shortage of clergy early in the reign. In 1560, 107 of the 274 churches in the diocese of Canterbury for which information is available had no incumbent, though 42 of them had the service of curates. The situation had improved somewhat by 1569. In 1526 the archdeaconry of Oxford had 371 rectors, vicars, and curates, but in 1586 the number was only 270. Daely, *JEH*, 18:45-46; Stone, *Causes*, 80.

57. PRO SP 46/25 (f. 54^{r-v}); Hart, *Clergy*, 29; Haigh, *Reformation*, 237.

58. Hart, *Clergy*, 29; Spufford, *Communities*, 251; Manning, *Religion*, 174, 176.

59. Marchant, *Puritans*, 275, 301, 307; Manning, *Religion*, 176. Hunt and Ducket were each rector of one mediety of Cotgrave. In 1568, Dering was collated by Parker to the rectory of Pluckley, Kent, but he was not resident and his curate may not have been a preacher. He was not, according to Collinson, a Puritan at this time. Collinson, *Mirror*, 14.

60. Haigh, "Puritan Evangelism in the Reign of Elizabeth I," *EHR*, 92 (1977):35-36; *Reformation*, 305-6; Marchant, *Puritans*, 294, 296, 311. The evidence for Blackwood's Puritanism is skimpy.

61. Dering, *Catechisme*, sig. A5^r; *Sermon Before the Queenes Maiestie*, sig. E2^{r-v}; Edward Bush, *A Sermon Preached at Pauls Crosse* (1576), sig. F4^r; Digges, *Motiues*, 41; Nichols, *Plea*, 190-91, 208; Wood, *Letters*, 16. Cf. Hake, *A Touchestone for This Time Present* (1574), sigs. B4^v, B6^v; Gilby, *Dialogve*, sig. π4^r; Chaderton, *An Excellent and Godly Sermon* [1578?], sig. C3^v.

62. Bateman, *Arrival*, sig. D1^v; Strype, *Parker*, 1:294; Matthew Sutcliffe, *An Answere to a Certaine Libel* (1592), 137; Hooker, *Works*, 2:520.

63. Manning, *Religion*, 169; Adam Hill, *The Crie of England* (1595), 74; Strype, *Whitgift*, 1:146, 380-81.

64. Whitgift, *Works*, 2:389; Peel, ed., *Seconde Parte*, 2:199; Nichols, *Plea*, 142-43.

65. Penry, *Viewe*, 65-66.

66. Dering, *Catechisme*, sig. A4^v; HMC 9 Salisbury, 2:64; Strype, *Aylmer*, 84-85, 90; Penry, *Treatise*, sigs. E2^r-E4^r; Henry Smith, *The Examination of Vsvry* (1591), 3; Stockwood, *Fruiteful Sermon*, sig. F8^v; Nichols, *Plea*, 205. Cf. Fenner, *Defence*, sig. B3^r; Digges, *Motiues*, 41; Bush, *Sermon*, sig. F4^r; Hake, *Touchestone*, sig. B4^v.

67. BL Lansdowne MS 38/71; Jewel, *Works*, 2:984; Hooker, *Works*, 2:509, 518-19; Sutcliffe, *Answere*, 123, 133, 136.

68. Cardwell, ed., *Synodalia*, 1:128; Hart, *Clergy*, 46-47; Strype, *The History of the Life and Acts of . . . Edmund Grindal* (Oxford, 1821), 300-1. The signers were Nicholas Bacon, Burghley, Knollys, Mildmay, James Croft, and the earls of Lincoln, Sussex, Arundel, and Bedford.

69. E.g. *EEA*, 2:17-18, 30-31, 55, 63, 92, 106, 116; 3:155, 159, 176, 183, 191-92.

70. *EEA*, 2:67; 3:151, 169, 266-67; C. Hill, *Economic Problems*, 18-19, 48, 227-30, 234-35; A.L. Rowse, *The England of Elizabeth* (1950), 410. The bishop of Carlisle held a rectory worth £120-140 *p.a. in commendam* in 1576, but paid the vicar only £14 13s. 4d. Hill, *op. cit.*, 234.

71. *CJ*, 1:76-77, 79; D'Ewes, *Journals*, 167; Neale, *Parliaments*, 1:166, 209-11, 216-17; *SR*, 4, pt. 1, p. 556.

72. *CJ*, 1:130; D'Ewes, *Journals*, 302-3; Neale, *Parliaments*, 1:398-401. Cf. Cardwell, ed., *Synodalia*, 2:548.

73. D'Ewes, *Journals*, 340, 357-60; Neale, *Parliaments*, 2:61, 63-66.

74. Neale, *Parliaments*, 2:154-65, 224-29; Cardwell, ed., *Synodalia*, 2:572-73.

75. D'Ewes, *Journals*, 639-41; Neale, *Parliaments*, 2:406-10.

76. Stubbes called for a more equitable distribution of clerical livings. There were certainly many whose incomes were excessive, such as Anthony Rushe, dean of Chichester (£243 18s. 10d. *p.a.*) and William Overton, treasurer of Chichester (£127 3s. 4d.), both of whom were pluralists. Generally Puritans indicated satisfaction with a modest income sufficient to cover basic needs. Gifford wrote: "If wee haue giftes of learning for the ministerie, and bee imployed, and take paines to the comfort and benefite of the Church, we thinke it so vnworthie a thing to be in pouertie . . . [but] if the charge be committed vnto vs . . . we must be content with that which may suffice euen for necessitie." Stubbes, *Motive*, 144; Manning, *Religion*, 174; Gifford, *Sermons vpon . . . Revelation* (1596), 53. Cf. Becon, *Postil*, 1:f 225^V; Tyndale's prologue to Numbers, MB (1549, 1551), Matthew-Becke Bible (1551).

Chapter 2: The Social Behavior of the Clergy
and the Anticlerical Reaction

1. Sandys, *Sermons*, 245.

2. Stockwood, *A Sermon Preached at Paules Crosse* [1578], 78.

3. A. Hill, *Crie*, 93; Richard Curteys, *Two Sermons* (1576), sig. F7^V; Sandys, *Sermons*, 278; Pilkington, *Works*, 160; Jewel, *Works*, 2:1011.

4. Chaderton, *Frvitfvll Sermon*, 33-34; Some, *Treatise*, 185; Digges, *Motiues*, 19; Penry, *Viewe*, 61, 63.

5. Anderson, *Sermon at Paules Crosse*, sig. D7^r; Baxter, *Toile*, 182; Cooper, *Admonition*, 108, 112; Stockwood, *Fruiteful Sermon*, sig. I5^r; Udall, *Demonstration*, 37; Hake, *Touchestone,* sig. B7^r (cf. B7^V-B8^r); Bush, *Sermon*, sig. F2^r; Penry, *State*, sig. H1^V; T. Gibson, *Sermon*, sig. D6^V (cf. C5^V).

6. Evans, *Admonition*, sigs. A7^V, A8^r; Rheims NT, note to 1 Tim. 5:22.

7. Manning, *Religion*, 171; Hart, *Clergy*, 24-25; Simon Forman, *The Autobiography and Personal Diary*, ed. James Halliwell (1849), 4.

8. Parker, *Correspondence*, 120-21; Jewel, *Works*, 3:395; John Walsall, *A Sermon Preached at Pavls Crosse* [1578], sig. C2^r; Chaderton, *Excellent Sermon*, sig. C3^r; Dering, *Catechisme*, sig. A4^V. The extent to which unqualified men were ordained very early in the age varied from see to see. Parker and his commissioners ordained 233 men in the diocese of Canterbury in the first eight months of his episcopate, while in Grindal's London diocese 167 deacons were admitted between 1559 and March 1561. Yet Cox at Ely and Sandys at Worcester did not resort to mass ordinations. Rosemary O'Day, "The Reformation of the Ministry, 1558-1642," *Continuity and Change*, ed. O'Day and Heal, 58.

9. *EEA*, 2:57, 76; 3:144; Manning, *Religion*, 180; Hart, *Clergy*, 25, 28; Rheims NT, notes to Luke 12:14; 2 Tim. 2:4. See C. Hill, *Economic Problems*, 216-19. In the seventeenth century Ralph Josselin leased part of his land, but farmed some twelve to twenty acres himself and raised some cattle. *The Diary of Ralph Josselin, 1616-1683*, ed. Alan Macfarlane (1976), 26, 70, 208, 239, 577, 587, 637; Macfarlane, *The Family Life of Ralph Josselin* (Cambridge, 1970), 68-69.

10. Cooper, *Admonition*, 90-91; Hart, *Clergy*, 25; Babington, *A Sermon Preached at Paules Crosse* (1591), 54; Jewel, *Works*, 2:1012; Stubbes, *Motive*, 144. There is at least one case of parishioners insisting on education at the level of the parish clerk. In 1579 the parson of Dullingham, Cambs., was accused of appointing his brother as parish clerk even though the latter was "unlearned at all, and . . . not sufficient to serve that place." Spufford, *Communities*, 207.

11. Turnbull, *Iude*, f. 75^V; Wright, *Summons*, 22; Thomas Jackson, *Davids Pastorall*

Poeme (1603), sig. π7^V; Curteys, *A Sermon Preached . . . at Richmond* [1575], sig. C1^{r-v}, C3^V; Marchant, *Puritans*, 307.

12. Hooker, *Works*, 2:509-10, 517-18; C.F. Russell, *A History of King Edward VI School, Southampton* (Cambridge, 1940), 31. Hooker's position was identical to that of Anthony Marten, a sewer in Elizabeth's chamber. *A Reconciliation* (1590), f. 41^V. According to Jewel, some of the people were so ignorant that they had never heard of the Bible. *Works*, 2:1014.

13. Cardwell, ed., *Synodalia*, 1:137; 2:562; *EEA*, 2:45-46; Haigh, *Reformation*, 302; BL Lansdowne MS 27/12. Whitgift strove to improve clerical education during his tenure in the see of Canterbury. Powel Dawley, *John Whitgift and the English Reformation* (New York, 1954), 201.

14. Peter Heath, *The English Parish Clergy at the Reformation* (1969), 81 ff.; Hart, *Clergy*, 26; MacCaffrey, *Exeter*, 194, 196; Manning, *Religion*, 176-79.

15. Spufford, *Communities*, 175; Hart, *Clergy*, 25-26.

16. C. Hill, *TRHS*, 13:81; Mervyn James, *Family, Lineage, and Civil Society* (Oxford, 1974), 63, 126; *CSPD, 1591-1594*, 158; Haigh, *Reformation*, 239-40; C. Hill, *Economic Problems*, 207, n. 1. The percentage of university graduates in the diocese of Worcester went from 19 in 1560 to 23 in 1580 to 52 in 1620. The diocese of Oxford fared better because of the presence of the university: University graduates made up 38% of the clergy in 1560, 50% in 1580, and 80% in 1620. C. Hill, *Economic Problems*, 207, n. 1, and the references cited there. Some improvement in the education of the parish clergy in the west midlands and border areas is evident from the increase in book ownership in the Elizabethan period. An examination of wills and inventories of parish clergy for the period 1490 to 1558 shows that 31% had books, and that figure rose to 39% for the period 1558 to 1603. Imogen Luxton, "The Reformation and Popular Culture," *Church and Society*, ed. Heal and O'Day, 72-73.

17. Dering, *Workes*, f. 26^V.

18. Wright, *Summons*, 20.

19. Millar Maclure, *The Paul's Cross Sermons* (Toronto, 1958), 54.

20. Horton Davies, *Worship and Theology in England . . . 1534-1603* (Princeton, 1970), 187, 229; Pilkington, *Works*, 25, 36-37; Sandys, *Sermons*, 71, 83. Cf. Samuel Gardiner's assertion that "a man without a preacher, is as hee that is blinde without a leader, which can neuer find the way." *Portraitvre of the Prodigal Sonne* (1599), 27.

21. PRO SP 31/47 (ff. 85^r, 86^r); C. Hill, *Change*, 7, 9, 10; Hart, *Clergy*, 30; Manning, *Religion*, 182; Haigh, *Reformation*, 244; W.H. Frere, *The English Church in the Reigns of Elizabeth and James I* (1924), 107; Nichols, *Plea*, 212-16.

22. R.I., in Roger Cotton, *A Spirituall Song* (1596), sig. A4^V; Irvonwy Morgan, *The Godly Preachers of the Elizabethan Church* (1965), 10; Seaver, *Lectureships*, chap. 1; Wither, *View*, 6, 232. For the centrality of the sermon in Puritan worship see H. Davies, *The Worship of the English Puritans* (Westminster, 1948), chap. 11. Such centrality was recognized by the Catholic polemicist Richard Bristow in his derogatory comment that "the Puritans would haue no other Seruice but a Sermon." *A Brief Treatise* (Antwerp, 1599), f. 140^r.

23. Nichols, *Plea*, 188, 199, 202; William Hopkinson, *A Preparation into the Waie of Life* (1583), sigs. B1^V-B2^r; Gifford, *A Briefe Discourse* [1581?], f. 2^r; Penry, *Treatise*, sigs. C4^V, D1^r, D2^V; Gilby, *Dialogve*, sig. L4^{r-v}; Pagit, *A Godly Sermon* (1586), sig. A6^V; Udall, *Amendment*, sig. A8^r; Stockwood, *1578 Sermon*, 141-42; Penry, *Exhortation*, 6-7; R. Harrison, *Treatise*, sig. H2^r; Becon, *Salue*, 149; Dering, *Catechisme*, sig. D4^r; Northbrooke, *Spiritvs . . . The Poore Mans Garden* (1573), sigs. $_2$E4^r-$_2$F4^V. Cf. Charles Gibbon, *The Remedie of Reason* (1589), sig. E2^{r-v}; George Phillips, *The Good Sheepeheardes Dutie* (1597), sigs. B1^V-B2^r, B4^V; BTB, notes to 1 Thess. 2:2; 2 Tim. 2:15.

24. T. Rogers, *The Catholic Doctrine*, ed. J. J. S. Perowne (Cambridge, 1854), 269, 271; Wright, *Summons*, 19, 53.

25. Sutcliffe, *Answere*, 125; Hooker, *Works*, 2:84, 88, 114; Covel, *Defence*, 78.

26. Cardwell, ed., *Synodalia*, 2:564; *EEA*, 2:33, 112-13, 129; 3:139, 224, 239, 255; *CSPD, 1547-1580*, 699; C. Hill, *Change*, 14.

27. Alan Herr, *The Elizabethan Sermon* (Philadelphia, 1940), 27 (a bibliographical guide to Elizabethan sermons is provided on pp. 119-69); Hooker, *Works*, 2:114.

28. William Fisher, *A Godly Sermon* (1592), sig. C6^r; Strype, *Aylmer*, 113-14; Maclure, *Sermons*, 86 (a register of Paul's Cross sermons is provided on pp. 200-25); Manningham, *Diary*, 75. Some of those who came to Paul's Cross were probably more interested in seeing preachers of considerable reputation than in what they preached.

29. J. W. Blench, *Preaching in England* (New York, 1964), 113, 168-205.

30. Stockwood, *Fruiteful Sermon*, sig. H5^v.

31. Covel, *Defence*, 84. Cf. John King, *Lectvres vpon Ionas* (Oxford, 1597), 552, for virtually the same comment.

32. Chaderton, *Excellent Sermon*, sigs. F6^v-F7^v; Udall, *Amendment*, sig. A5^v; Gifford, *Discourse*, f. 50^r; Dent, *A Sermon of Repentaunce* (1583), sig. A2^r; H. Smith, *A Frvitfvll Sermon* (1591), 28-29.

33. Barrow, *The Writings of John Greenwood and Henry Barrow, 1591-1593*, ed. Leland Carlson (1970), 123; Barrow, *Writings (1587-90)*, 490, 539.

34. Wright, *Summons*, 45; King, *Lectvres*, 541, 545-46 (also Covel, *Defence*, 82-84); Sandys, *Sermons*, 103. Cf. Robert Humston, *A Sermon Preached at Reysham* (1589), f. 3^v.

35. Lawrence Barker, *Christs Checke to Saint Peter* (1600), sigs. M7^v-M8^v; Hooker, *Works*, 2:114. Seaver regards Barker as a "nonconformist," apparently because he was presented for failing to wear the surplice and catechize. Yet this may indicate laxity rather than nonconformity. If (as I suspect) he was the Mr. Barker who preached at Paul's Cross on 16 June 1602, he depicted Whitgift as "the sunne amongst the ministers," which one would hardly expect from a Puritan at this date. Seaver, *Lectureships*, 345, 360; Maclure, *Sermons*, 222.

36. John Marshall, *Hooker and the Anglican Tradition* (Sewanee, Tenn., 1963), chap. 6; Covel, *Defence*, 84; Woolton, *Castell*, sig. C6^v; King, *Lectvres*, 546; Jewel, *Works*, 2:980-81, 983.

37. Jewel, *Works*, 2:982, 1013, 1048; 4:911, 1183; cf. 2:983; 4:1185. See Cartwright, *A Confvtation of the Rhemists Translation* (1618), 510; Samuel Nicholson, *Gods New-yeeres Gift* (1602), sig. A7^{r-v}; and, for a brief summation of the Catholic view, the note to Col. 2:1 in the Rheims NT.

38. Sandys, *Sermons*, 115; Woolton, *Manual*, 4; Alexander Nowell, *A Catechism Written in Latin*, ed. G.E. Corrie and trans. Thomas Norton (Cambridge, 1853), 117; Fulke, *A Sermon Preached . . . within the Tower of London* (1581), sigs. C1^v-C2^r.

39. Tyndale-Coverdale NT, notes to John 3; 1 Cor. 3; BTB (1587), note to Acts 17:21; Rheims NT, note to James 3:15; Pilkington, *Works*, 215, 242; Cooper, *Certaine Sermons*, 2; Dent, *Path-way*, 334; Dering, *Hebrues*, sig. T3^v; Greenham, *Works*, 208; Thomas, *Demegoriai*, sig. G5^v.

40. Matthew-Becke Bible (1549, 1551) and MB (1551), prologue to Jon.; GB, note to Ps. 119:169; BTB, note to John 3:13; Tyndale-Coverdale NT (1538), note to John 5; BB, note to 2 Cor. 1:12; Pilkington, *Works*, 5, 81, 214, 453; Sandys, *Sermons*, 114-15, 351; (cf. Barker, *Checke*, sig. C6^v); Dering, *Hebrues*, sigs. K2^r, T1^v (cf. Q3^r); Gifford, *Discourse*, f. 52^r; Norden, *Solace*, sig. π4^v; *A Progress of Piety* (Cambridge, 1847), 128; *A Pensiue Mans Practise* (1584), f. 51^v. See Roger Cotton, *A Direction to the Waters of Life* (1590), f. 3^r. Cotton was a draper.

41. BB, note to Acts 18:26; GB, note to Acts 18:26; BTB, note to Acts 18:24; Pilking-

ton, *Works*, 101, 329; Greenham, *Works*, 170; Gibbon, *The Praise of a Good Name* (1594), sig. A2^V; (cf. Sandys, *Sermons*, 115-16); Some, *Treatise*, 57; Whitgift, *Works*, 1:33; Rheims NT, note to Luke 10:21; Sandys, *Sermons*, 269-70.

42. Jewel, *Works*, 2:683; Gifford, *Sermons vpon Revelation*, 3; Norden, *Practise*, f. 52^V; Greenham, *Works*, 392; Thomas Cartwright, *Confvtation*, 52. Cf. Robert Hill, *Life Euerlasting* (Cambridge, 1601), sig. $\pi2^{r-v}$.

43. Norden, *A Christian Familiar Comfort* (1596), 36; Gilby, *Dialogve*, sig. L5^{r-v}; Barrow, *Writings (1587-90)*, 490, 528-33, 548; John Rogers, *The Displaying of an Horrible Secte* (1578), sig. I4^V. For the sectarian attack on the universities see chap. 8, below. For the context of Rogers' work see Jean R. Moss, "The Family of Love and English Critics," *SCJ*, 6 (1975):35-52.

44. Gifford, *A Plaine Declaration* (1590), 69; William Wilkinson, *A Confvtation* (1579), f. 66^r; Barker, *Checke*, sig. N5^V; Nash, *Anatomie*, sig. B4^V; (cf. *Pierce*, f. 17^r); Bancroft, *Dangerovs Positions and Proceedings* (1593), 142; Wright, *Hunting*, sig. D2^{r-v}. The bishops tried to ferret out unlicensed preachers during their visitations. E.g., *EEA*, 2:55, 105.

45. Gifford, *Discourse*, f. 3^V.

46. BTB, note to Mark 12:38.

47. *CSPD, 1547-1580*, 180; Robert Horne, Apology to John Calvin, *Two Godly and Learned Sermons* (1584), sig. C1^r; T. Rogers, *The English Creede*, pt. 1 (1585), sig. $\pi4^r$; pt. 2 (1587), p. 43; Rheims NT, note to Rom. 2:21.

48. Crowley, *Opening*, sig. C4^V; Stockwood, *Fruiteful Sermon*, sig. A3^V; Chaderton, *Excellent Sermon*, sig. C3^r; Becon, *Postil*, 1: sig. B4^V; Gifford, *Discourse*, f. 2^r; Peel, ed., *Seconde Parte*, 2:89-110; Thomas Pickering, Epistle Dedicatory to Perkins, *Treatise*, sig. $\pi4^r$; Pagit, *Godly Sermon*, sigs. A7^r-A8^r; BL Add. MS 30,076, f. 8^r. Cf. Gilby, *Dialogve*, sig. M2^r.

49. Peel, ed., *Seconde Parte*, 2:98-110, 146-74; Haigh, *Reformation*, 240; Marchant, *Puritans*, 216; Piccope, ed., *Wills*, 33:119, 122-23; J. S. Purvis, ed., *Tudor Parish Documents* (Cambridge, 1948), 25; Hart, *Clergy*, 31; Strype, *Grindal*, 133. For further cases see Purvis, *Documents*, 23, 27, 28, 46.

50. Evans, *Admonition*, sigs. A7^V, B8^{r-v}; HMC 9 Salisbury, 10:9 (cf. pp. 13-14, 17); Strype, *Parker*, 2:87-88; *APC*, 14:61; Hart, *Clergy*, 33; F. G. Emmison, *Elizabethan Life* (Chelmsford, Essex, 1970-76), 2:220-21. Thomas Prince, vicar of Great Chesterford, Essex, was convicted of fornication in 1586. Emmison, *ibid.*

51. Peel, ed., *Seconde Parte*, 2:98-110, 146-74; Haigh, *Reformation*, 240-41; VCH *Lancashire*, 6:359; Marchant, *Puritans*, 216; Purvis, ed., *Documents*, 28; Hart, *Clergy*, 31; Charles and Thompson Cooper, *Athenae Cantabrigienses* (Cambridge, 1858-1913), 1:381. For other cases see Purvis, ed., *Documents*, 17, 22, 23, 33.

52. Peel, ed., *Seconde Parte*, 2:98-110, 146-74; Hart, *Clergy*, 32-33; Angelo Raine, *History of St. Peter's School: York* (1926), 76; Purvis, ed., *Documents*, 33.

53. Peel, ed., *Seconde Parte*, 2:146-74; Hart, *Clergy*, 32; Godfrey Anstruther, *Vaux of Harrowden*, (Newport, Mon.), 1953), 81-82.

54. *APC*, 14:152; Manning, *Religion*, 172; PRO STAC 7 Addenda 12/30. The statutory minimum age to hold a benefice without cure was made twenty-three by 13 Eliz. I, c. 12. The canons of 1585 required a candidate for ordination to be at least twenty-four. Cardwell, ed., *Synodalia*, 1:140-42.

55. Peel, ed., *Seconde Parte*, 2:146-74; Marchant, *Puritans*, 216; Haigh, *Reformation*, 241; *APC*, 12:194; Hart, *Clergy*, 31; Purvis, ed., *Documents*, 28. For an example of profligate actions by a parson's wife, see the case of William Lynch, rector of Willingale Doe and of Beauchamp Roothing, Essex, in 1563. William Addison, *The English Country Parson* (1947), 29.

56. *EEA*, 2:19, 30, 54, 57, 84, 92-93, 116-17, 128; 3:141, 164, 191-92, 203, 216, 226,

340-41; note to Eph. 4 in the MB (1537, 1551), Matthew-Becke Bible (1549, 1551), Taverner Bible (1539); Fenner, *Defence*, sig. R3ʳ.

57. Stapleton, *Fortresse*, f. 118ʳ.

58. A. Hill, *Crie*, 81-82.

59. Dering, *Catechisme*, sig. A3ʳ; Hake, *Touchestone*, sig. B4ʳ; Gifford's Epistle to Fulke, *Praelections* (1573), sig. π3ʳ; Anderson, *Godlie Sermon*, sig. B5ʳ; John Higgins (quoting Thomas Churchyard), *The Mirour for Magistrates* (1587), f. 270ᵛ; Pilkington, *Works*, 464; Crowley, *Opening*, sig. B8ᵛ; Pagit, *Frvitefull Sermon*, sigs. B6ᵛ-B7ʳ. Cf. Woolton, *Castell*, sigs. E2ᵛ-E4ᵛ.

60. Fleming, *A Guide to Godlinesse* (1581), 96; Dering, *Catechisme*, sigs. A3ᵛ, A4ʳ; Dent, *Path-way*, 203-4; Keith Thomas, *Religion and the Decline of Magic* (New York, 1971), 161-62; H. Smith, *Sermon*, 26; Sandys, *Sermons*, 274; Simon Harward, *Two Godlie and Learned Sermons* (1582), sig. F1ᵛ.

61. Rheims NT, notes to 1 Cor. 11:2; 2 Thess. 3:14. Clergy who used "rigorous vnreasonable pursuite" of parishioners in the ecclesiastical courts also provoked anticlericalism. Cf. Anthony Bacon's complaint against Dr. Pie to Anthony Watson, bishop of Chichester, 18 Dec. 1596. LPL Bacon MS 660/167 (f. 249ʳ).

62. John Penry, *Notebook*, ed. Peel (1944), 34, 86, 89-90.

63. R. Harrison, *Treatise*, sig. F8ʳ; Greenwood, *Writings*, 166; Barrow, *Writings (1587-90)*, 102, 185, 355, 488-89 (cf. 248); *Collection*, 6.

64. Henry Machyn, *Diary*, ed. John Nichols (1848), 271; Strype, *Annals of the Reformation* (Oxford, 1824), 2, pt. 1:328-32; Hart, *Clergy*, 35; *APC*, 11:125-26, 177; 12:132. Ironically, there appears to have been some hostility by Familists toward their own church leaders. Two Familists confessed on 28 May 1561 that "their Bishoppes, Elders, and Deacons, do increase in riches, and become wealthy, but their disciples become poore and fall to beggerie." J. Rogers, *Displaying*, sig. K3ᵛ.

65. Brinkworth, ed., *Court*, 9; Haigh, *Reformation*, 228, 244.

66. Russell, *History*, 36; *APC*, 17:155-56; Manning, *Religion*, 173; Manningham, *Diary*, 69.

67. *EEA*, 2:132, 135; 3:167, 214; H. Smith, *The Affinitie of the Faithfull* (1591), sig. B2ᵛ; Trigge, *A Godly and Frvitfvll Sermon* (Oxford, 1594), sig. C5ᵛ; Jewel, *Works*, 2:999, 1012; Turnbull, *An Exposition vpon the XV. Psalme* (1592), f. 37ᵛ; Dove, *A Sermon Preached at Paules Crosse . . . 1596* [1597], sig. C7ᵛ; Sutcliffe, *Answere*, sigs. A3ʳ, B3ʳ.

68. Cooper, *Admonition*, 1-3, 6; Sandys, *Sermons*, 273; Edward Vaughan, *Ten Introductions* (1594), sigs. M4ʳ, N5ᵛ; Wright, *Summons*, 14-15, 17; cf. *Display*, 14.

69. Barrow, *Writings (1587-90)*, 157.

70. Crowley, *Opening*, sig. B5ᵛ.

71. C. Hill, *Economic Problems*, 79-80, 98, 157; *APC*, 10:290; 13:338.

72. Trigge, *Sermon*, sig. C6ᵛ; C. Hill, *Economic Problems*, 98; Greenham, *Works* (1612 ed.), 698, in ibid., 157.

73. C. Hill, *Economic Problems*, 159; Manning, *Religion*, 166.

74. Gervase Babington, *Certaine Plaine . . . Notes, vpon . . . Genesis* (2nd ed., 1596), 46; PRO Req. 42/89; Haller, *Rise*, 13; Marchant, *The Church under the Law* (Cambridge, 1969), 63; Ralph Houlbrooke, *Church Courts and the People During the English Reformation 1520-1570* (Oxford, 1979), 142, 145-46, 149.

75. George Abbot, *An Exposition vpon the Prophet Ionah* (1600), 38; HMC 9 Salisbury, 4:84. For a sampling of tithe cases in the higher courts see PRO Req. 34/127; 36/89-90; 41/44; 44/12; 50/24; 54/10; 56/29, 47; 58/19, 45; 62/10; Chancery 2/2/79; 3/212/67; Exchequer of Pleas, 4 Eliz. Hil. m. 1; 13 Eliz. Hil. m. 13; 17 Eliz. Pasch. m. 23. 23d; 17 & 18 Eliz. Mich. m. 31. 31d. 32. 32d. 35; 41 Eliz. Hil. m. 21; 43 & 44 Eliz. Mich. m. 42; 44 Eliz. Hil. m. 13; STAC 7 Add. 6/7.

76. Penry, *Notebook*, 33, 81, 87, 89.

77. Barrow and Greenwood, *Writings of Greenwood*, 172, 199; Barrow, *Writings (1587-90)*, 139, 235-38, 355-56, 406, 489-90; *Writings (1591-93)*, 104.

78. Barrow, *Writings (1587-90)*, 164, 167, 186, 227, 234-35, 247, 356-57, 359; *Writings (1591-93)*, 120.

79. *Writings of Greenwood and Barrow (1591-93)*, 324, 326, 391.

80. GB, notes to 2 Chron. 31:6, 10; Neh. 10:37; Mal. 3:8; Rheims NT, note to Matt. 10:9.

81. Manningham, *Diary*, 58, 70, 141; Bancroft, *Svrvay*, 234-37.

82. Fulke, *Text*, f. 404^r; Richard Allison, *A Plaine Confvtation* (1590), 120-21; Pagit, *Frvitefull Sermon*, sigs. A7^v-A8^r, B3^r-B4^r; Some, *Treatise*, 15; Stubbes, *Motive*, 143.

Chapter 3: The Marital Quest

1. Thomas Deloney, *The Gentle Craft* (1637; 1st pub. 1597), sig. E2^r.

2. Thomas Lodge, *The Divel Coniured* (1596), sig. B4^r.

3. Sanders, *The Rocke of the Chvrche* (Louvain, 1567), sigs. $_3\pi7^v$-$_3\pi8^r$; John Noonan, Jr., *Contraception* (Cambridge, Mass., 1966), 322.

4. Fulke, *Text*, f. 38^r; Nichols, *Plea*, 198-99; Fenner, *Defence*, sig. O5^r; *The Order of Hovseholde*, pt. 3 of *The Artes of Logike* (1584), sig. B2^v; H. Smith, *A Preparatiue to Mariage* (1591), 2; James Johnson, *A Society Ordained by God* (Nashville, 1970), 23-37. Cartwright accused Catholics of making marriage a sacrament so they could reap the profits from matrimonial cases in ecclesiastical courts. *Confvtation*, 3-4.

5. Johnson, "English Puritan Thought on the Ends of Marriage," *CH*, 38 (1969): 429-30.

6. Noonan, *Contraception*, 313-14; Vaux, *Catechisme*, f. 51^v.

7. GB, notes to Prov. 5:18; Luke 20:36; 1 Cor. 7:6, 36; Heb. 13:4; Johnson, *Society*, 21-22; Heinrich Bullinger, *The Christen State of Matrimonye*, trans. Miles Coverdale [1541], sigs. D2^{r-v}, D4^v; Cooper, *A Briefe Exposition* [1573], sig. M7^r; Thomas Cogan, *The Haven of Health* (1584), 248; Sandys, *Sermons*, 315-16; Lawrence Stone, *The Family, Sex and Marriage in England 1500-1800* (New York, 1977), 136-37; (cf. Chap. 8 for the later development of companionate marriage).

8. H. Smith, *Preparatiue*, 13-26; Cleaver, *Form*, 92-93, 154-56; John Gardiner, *A Briefe and Cleare Confession* (1579), f. 39^r; Becon, *Worckes* (1560-64), f. 611^v; Robert Allen, *A Treasvrie of Catechisme* (1600), 193; (cf. Bullinger, *State*, sigs. A4^r, A6^r-A7^v); George Estey, *Certaine Godly and Learned Expositions* (1603), pt. 1, f. 68^r; Gibbon, *Remedie*, sig. K3^v; (cf. BTB, note to 1 Cor. 7:1); Pagit, *Godly Sermon*, sig. B2^r; Louis Wright, *Middle-Class Culture in Elizabethan England* (Chapel Hill, N.C., 1935), 203; W. Vaughan, *Golden-groue*, sigs. N8^v-O1^r; Stubbes, *Anatomie*, sig. G8^v. Gifford's *Fifteene Sermons, vpon the Song of Salomon* (1598) discuss the church rather than marriage.

9. Perkins, *A Reformed Catholike* (Cambridge, 1600), 959. Although this work was published in 1600, the epistle dedicatory was dated 28 June 1597.

10. Jewel, *Works*, 3:421.

11. W. Vaughan, *Golden-groue*, sig. O2^r.

12. Matthew Kellison, *A Svrvey of the New Religion* (Douai, 1603), 613, 617-18; Rheims NT, notes to Matt. 1:23; 1 Cor. 7:28, 32; Stapleton, *Fortresse*, f. 115^v. For the views of the Continental Protestant reformers see Derrick Bailey, *Sexual Relation in Christian Thought* (New York, 1959), 167-73.

13. Rheims NT, notes to Matt. 19:11-12; 1 Cor. 7:7, 9; 1 Tim. 4:1; 5:15; Heb. 13:4; Kellison, *Svrvey*, 617, 619-21; Sanders, *Rocke*, sig. $_3\pi8^{r-v}$.

14. Rheims NT, notes to Matt. 19:21; Luke 4:38; 1 Cor. 7:9, 32; 1 Tim. 3:2; Titus 1:6; Evans, *Admonition*, sigs. A8^v-B1^r.

15. Noonan, *Contraception*, 363, n. 39; Jewel, *Works*, 2:728, 807; 3:218; Marbury, *A Sermon at Pavles Crosse* (1602), sig. D6^r; Bulkeley, *Apologie*, 137; Fulke, *Text*, ff. 44^r, 75^r, 272^v; Stoughton, *Treatise*, 61; Thomas Lupton, *A Persuasion from Papistrie* (1581), 131, 134; Nichols, *Abrahams Faith* (1603), 294-95; A. G. Dickens, "The Writers of Tudor Yorkshire," *TRHS*, 13 (1963):64-65. According to Sherbrook, morality in general declined since the Reformation, and it is therefore doubtful that his views were widely shared by Protestant clergy.

16. Perkins, *A Golden Chaine* (1591), sigs. L8^v-M1^r, M3^v-M4^r; Hergest, *Rvle*, 3-4; Estey, *Expositions*, pt. 1, ff. 66^v, 67^v-68^r.

17. Cartwright, *Confvtation*, 388; Perkins, *Catholike*, 959; *Treatise*, 415; Fulke, *Text*, f. 38^r; Hergest, *Rvle*, 2; Greenham, *Works*, 36; Cleaver, *Form*, 125; Henry Willoby, *Willobie's Avisa, 1594*, ed. Alexander Grosart (Manchester, 1880), 110; Pagit, *Godly Sermon*, sig. B1^v; Jewel, *Works*, 3:398, 415; Wither, *View*, 182; G. Abbot, *Exposition*, 308; H. Smith, *Preparatiue*, 21; Nicholas Gibbens, *Qvestions and Dispvtations* (1602), 87; Sutcliffe, *Answere*, 130; Frere, *Church*, 107-8.

18. Perkins, *Treatise*, 412; Fulke, *Text*, f. 38^v; Estey, *Expositions*, pt. 1, f. 67^v; Perkins, *Catholike*, 959; Shutte, *A Compendious Forme* (1581), sig. C2^r; GB, notes to Eccles. 5:5; 1 Cor. 7:35; T. Rogers, *Creede*, pt. 2, p. 39.

19. Perkins, *Catholike*, 960; Fulke, *A Defense of the Sincere and True Translations* (1583), 412; *Text*, ff. 191^v, 273^v, 381^r.

20. Cleaver, *Form*, 126-27.

21. Crowley, *Opening*, sigs. F7^v-F8^r; J. Gardiner, *Confession*, f. 39^v; Fenner, *Treatises*, 48; J. Rogers, *The Summe of Christianitie* [1560?], f. 13^v; H. Smith, *Preparatiue*, 19-20; Cartwright, *Confvtation*, 389; Bulkeley, *Apologie*, 138; (cf. BB, note to 1 Cor. 7:6); PRO SP 48/64 (f. 171^r); HMC 58 Bath, 4:156.

22. Pilkington, *Works*, 578; Sandys, *Sermons*, 315; Jewel, *Works*, 4:803; Fulke, *Text*, ff. 14^v, 224^v; Cartwright, *Confvtation*, 275; Wither, *View*, 78.

23. Cardwell, ed., *Synodalia*, 1:68-69; PRO SP 19/10 (f. 22^v), 19/10.1 (f. 24^{r-v}); Sandys, *Sermons*, 316; Cogan, *Haven*, 253-54; Fulke, *Text*, f. 273^v, 369^r; Levine Lemnie, *The Touchstone of Complexions*, trans. Thomas Newton (1581), ff. 106^r-107^r; Trigge, *A Tovchstone* (1599), 299. Cf. Fulke, *Text*, f. 272^r; Wither, *View*, 182.

24. Hyder Rollins, ed., *Old English Ballads* (Cambridge, 1920), 279; *Select Poetry*, 2:478; John Cotman, *Engravings of Sepulchral Brasses* (1839), plate 86; Lu Emily Pearson, *Elizabethans at Home* (Stanford, 1957), 285; Stone, *Family*, 45.

25. GB, notes to Matt. 19:12; 1 Cor. 7:1, 25, 28, 34; BTB, notes to 1 Cor. 6:9; 7:25.

26. Edmund Tilney, *The Flower of Friendship* (1568), sigs. A7^v-A8^r; Gibbens, *Qvestions*, 85-87, 94-95. Cf. Manningham, *Diary*, 23.

27. Jewel, *Works*, 2:834; 3:415; 4:807; Babington, *A Very Fruitfull Exposition of the Commaundements* (1583), 337-41; (cf. T. Rogers, *Doctrine*, 260); John Terry, *The Second Part of the Trial of Trvth* (Oxford, 1602), 35-36; George Whetstone, *An Heptameron of Ciuill Discourses* (1582), sigs. C3^r, C4^r, D1^v, X2^v.

28. Richard Rogers, *Two Elizabethan Puritan Diaries*, ed. Knappen (Chicago, 1933), 101; Cleaver, *Form*, 156; Perkins, *Catholike*, 959; Becon, *Postil*, 1:f. 93^v; *Worckes*, f. 559^r. Cf. Andrew Kingsmill, *A Most Excellent and Comfortable Treatise* (1577), sig. C2^v. Sir Philip Sidney chided Hubert Languet in 1579 that he urged Sir Philip to become bound by "the chains of matrimony" while remaining single himself. *Zurich Letters*, ed. Robinson, 2:297.

29. Wither, *View*, 183; Fulke, *Defense*, 404; *Text*, ff. 3^r, 38^v; Cartwright, *Confvtation*, 4, 95-96, 184, 391-92.

30. H. Smith, *Preparatiue*, 34.

31. Kingsmill, *A Viewe of Mans Estate* (1580), sig. K1^v.

32. Noonan, *Contraception*, 314.

33. GB, notes to Gen. 24:4, 37; 1 Cor. 7:14, 15; 2 Cor. 6:14; BB, notes to Gen. 11:29; 1 Kings 11:8; 2 Chron. 21:6; Rheims NT, note to 2 Cor. 6:14; Dod, *Treatise*, pt. 1, f. 40^r; pt. 2, f. 56^v; Fenner, *Treatises*, 96; H. Smith, *Preparatiue*, 47-48; Wither, *View*, 195; Perkins, *Chaine*, sig. F8^v; Kingsmill, *Viewe*, sig. M3^r; Cleaver, *Form*, 118, 316; Babington, *Genesis*, 56, 180; Sandys, *Sermons*, 324-25. Cf. Knewstub, *Lectvres . . . vpon . . . Exodus* (1577), 126; Carpenter, *Preparatiue*, 308.

34. Anstruther, *Vaux*, 94; J. C. H. Aveling, *Catholic Recusancy in the City of York* (1970), 72-73; Stone, *Crisis*, 614; Gerard, *Autobiography*, 164; James, *Family*, 139; HMC 69 Middleton, 595-96; HMC 24 Twelfth Report, Appendix, part 4, p. 99; *Zurich Letters*, ed. Robinson, 305; Richardson, *Puritanism*, 95; Rachel Weigall, "An Elizabethan Gentlewoman. The Journal of Lady Mildmay, circa 1570-1617," *Quarterly Review*, 215 (1911):122.

35. Tilney, *Flower*, sig. B3^{r-v}; Whetstone, *Heptameron*, sigs. P2^v, ff. Q3^r, Q4^{r-v}; Gibbon, *A Work Worth the Reading* (1591), 2, 5; Cleaver, *Form*, 145, 146; Allen, *Treasvrie*, 182; Wright, *Display*, 24; Wilcox, *Prouerbs, Works*, 144, 146.

36. Everitt, "Social Mobility: Conference Report," *PP*, 32 (1965):6; Stone, *Crisis*, 627, 629-30, 789; BL Lansdowne MS 68/20; Nina Epton, *Love and the English* (Cleveland, 1960), 94-95. According to John Chamberlain, Spencer had been committed to the Fleet for contempt when he hid his daughter after she was contracted to Lord Compton. When he was released, he again tried to obstruct the match, asserting a precontract to Sir Arthur Henningham's son. After he beat his daughter she had to be given protection by the lord mayor Sir Henry Billingsly. Chamberlain, *Letters*, ed. Norman McClure (Philadelphia, 1939), 1:73.

37. Strype, *Aylmer*, 130, 217-19; BL Lansdowne MS 69/52; HMC 9 Salisbury, 4:527; Sir Walter Mildmay, *A Memorial for a Son*, ed. Arundell Mildmay (1893), [2]; Cooper, ed., *Wentworth Papers*, 20; BL Wolley MS 6671, f. 65^r; A. C. Wood, "The Holles Family," *TRHS*, Fourth Series, 19 (1936):153; Mildred Campbell, *The English Yeoman* (1942), 48. For an attempt to arrange a marriage between a gentleman and a servant, see PRO Req. 2/30/43.

38. Bullinger, *State*, sig. A7^v; Sandys, *Sermons*, 325; Nash, *Anatomie*, sig. A2^v; Babington, *Genesis*, 185; H. Smith, *Preparatiue*, 87; Nicholson, *Acolastvs*, sig. H3^v; Hake, *Touchestone*, sig. E2^r; Gibbon, *Work*, 2; *Praise*, 52; Stone, *Crisis*, 611.

39. Stone, *Crisis*, 617-18, 628-29, 789; Chamberlain, *Letters*, 1:67. When Spencer died in 1611, Sir William Ashcombe noted in his diary that "my Lord compton havinge maryed his only daughter, oppressed with the greatnes of this sudaine fortunes, fell madde." HL MS 30,665, f. 4^r. The practice of marrying for financial motives often led to court suits when the marriage failed to take place. See, e.g., PRO Chancery 3/3/80, 3/71/88, 3/199/87; Req. 2/31/37. An intriguing case in the Court of Requests details how Hugh Macklyn, a London chandler, wed Anne, daughter of Edward Moore of Shropshire, on the understanding that she possessed a five-hundred year lease of lands and tenements worth £40 *p.a.* After the wedding Macklyn discovered the lease was a forgery. Req. 2/51/6.

40. Stone, *Family*, 191; BL Lansdowne MSS 33/4, 46/61; Chamberlain, *Letters*, 1:161; HMC 9 Salisbury, 7:267-68 (cf. 3:162-63).

41. G. R. Batho, ed., *The Household Papers of Henry Percy, Ninth Earl of Northumberland* (1962), xlix; Chamberlain, *Letters*, 1:109; HMC 69 Middleton, 587; (cf. PRO SP 175/17); Robert Carey, *Memoirs*, ed. F. H. Mares (Oxford, 1972), 25-26, 61.

42. Anstruther, *Vaux*, 164; Sir Hugh Cholmley, *Memoirs* (Malton, 1870), 11; Wood, *TRHS*, 19:162-63; HMC 71 Finch, 1:21; Manningham, *Diary*, 50 (cf. 49).

43. Cooper, ed., *Wentworth Papers*, 20, 29; *CSPD, 1581-1590*, 98-99.

44. Deloney, *The Garland of Good-will*, sig. D4^v; Richard Barnfield, *The Affectionate Shepheard* (1594), sig. D4^r; (cf. Whetstone, *The Rocke of Regard* [1576], sig. D2^v); Cleaver, *Form*, 98, 354, 356; Kingsmill, *Viewe*, sig. K1^r; H. Smith, *Preparatiue*, 35-43;

Becon, *Salue*, 213-14; W. Vaughan, *Golden-groue*, sigs. H7^V-H8^r; Wilcox, *Prouerbs*, 152; Stockwood, *Bartholmew*, 12.

45. Stone, *Crisis*, 615; Carpenter, *Report*, 26:172; *Zurich Letters*, ed. Robinson, 2:280; HMC 9 Salisbury, 1:486; BL Lansdowne MS 101/29; Alan G. R. Smith, *Servant of the Cecils* (Totowa, N.J., 1977), 100-3; Collinson, *Mirror*, 29; Cooper, ed., *Wentworth Papers*, 27.

46. Tilney, *Flower*, sigs. B4^r, D3^V; H. Smith, *Preparatiue*, 30; Greenham, *Works*, 35. In Massachusetts Bay, love became central to many marriages. Edmund Morgan, *The Puritan Family* (New York, 1966), 46 ff.

47. Sir J. Oglander, *The Oglander Memoirs*, ed., W. H. Long (1888), 168-69; Cecil Aspinall-Oglander, *Nunwell Symphony* (1945), 28-29; Stone, *Crisis*, 609; *Family*, 193; C. Hill, "Sex, Marriage and the Family in England," *Econ. H.R.*, 2nd ser., 31 (1978):462; BL Lansdowne MS 101/29; HMC 71 Finch, 1:21; L. Pearson, *Elizabethans*, 279-80; Stone, "The Rise of the Nuclear Family in Early Modern England: The Patriarchal Stage," *The Family in History*, ed. Charles Rosenberg (Philadelphia, 1975), 28.

48. Greenham, *Works*, 35; Allen, *Treasvrie*, 182; Cleaver, *Form*, 142-43; Pagit, *Godly Sermon*, sigs. C1^V-C2^r; Cooper, ed., *Wentworth Papers*, 22; BL Lansdowne MS 101/29; Chamberlain, *Letters*, 1:154. In the early years of James' reign, Sir William Ashcombe recorded in his diary how he rejected potential spouses on grounds of physical appearance, disparate social rank, and personal qualities. When he finally married in 1613 it was apparently to avoid licentious conduct. HL MS 30,665, ff. 3^{r-V}, 6^r.

49. Tilney, *Flower*, sigs. B2^r, B3^V-B4^r; Whetstone, *Heptameron*, sigs. E4^r, S4^r, T1^r, T3^{r-V}, T4^V, Y1^r; (cf. Sutton, *Disce mori* [1604], 31); Cleaver, *Form*, 128, 145; Gibbon, *Work*, 14-16; Dent, *Path-way*, 80; H. Smith, *Preparatiue*, 14-15; Greenham, *Works*, 36; (cf. Allen, *Treasvrie*, 182). Alexander Nowell, dean of St. Paul's, London, married his second wife in the early 1580s when he was over seventy years of age. Cleaver had no objections to the marriage of elderly people for reasons of companionship and assistance. Alexander Grosart, ed., *The Towneley Hall MSS* (Manchester, 1877), xli; Cleaver, *Form*, 156.

50. Peter Laslett, *The World We Have Lost* (1965), 83; Wallace Notestein, "The English Woman, 1580-1650," *Studies in Social History*, ed. J. H. Plumb (1955), 89; Stone, *Crisis*, 595-96; Frances Young, *Mary Sidney Countess of Pembroke* (1912), 34; (cf. Lady Margaret Hoby, *Diary*, ed. Dorothy Meads [1930], 193); Manningham, *Diary*, 50; Strype, *Whitgift*, 3:378; Chamberlain, *Letters*, 1:57; Usher, ed., *The Presbyterian Movement* (1905), 41; BL Lansdowne MS 110/10. Yet when the earl of Huntingdon urged Burghley to support a match between Lord Rich and Lady Penelope Devereux in 1581, he described Rich as "a propper gentleman and one in yeares verry fytte for my Ladye penelope deuereux." BL Lansdowne MS 31/40.

51. Cleaver, *Form*, 142-43; Cooper, ed., *Wentworth Papers*, 20; W. Vaughan, *Golden-groue*, sig. N8^V; Allen, *Treasvrie*, 182, 190; BL Lansdowne MS 17/19, 23; (cf. Stone, *Crisis*, 640); Lansdowne MS 84/55; *CSPD, 1595-1597*, 497.

52. Stubbes, *Anatomie*, sig. H5^r.

53. Deloney, *Garland*, sig. G4^r.

54. Cogan, *Haven*, 255-56; Stone, *Crisis*, 653; Bullinger, *State*, sig. B6^r.

55. John Chardon, *A Sermon Preached in S. Peters Church in Exceter* (1580), f. 10^V; (cf. Cooper, *The True and Perfect Copie* [1575], sig. C1^r); Babington, *Genesis*, 191; James Yates, *The Castell of Courtesie* (1582), f. 6^V; Stubbes, *A Christal Glasse* (1591), sig. 192^r; *Anatomie*, sig. H5^{r-V}; H. Smith, *Preparatiue*, 114; (cf. Cleaver, *Form*, 126).

56. Carroll Camden, *The Elizabethan Woman* (Houston, 1952), 93; J. D. Chambers, *Population, Economy, and Society in Pre-Industrial England*, ed. W. S. Armstrong (1972), 69; Laslett, *World*, 81; E. A. Wrigley, "Family Limitation in Pre-Industrial England," *Econ. H.R.*, Second Series, 19 (1966):86-88. Daughters of the upper classes in the Elizabethan era married at c. 22. Heirs of the English squirearchy first married at about the same

age, whereas their younger brothers waited several more years. Children of small property owners and laborers wed at c. 26 for men and c. 24 for women, while comparable figures for children of yeomen, husbandmen, and tradesmen were c. 25 and c. 23. Stone, *Family*, 46, 48-50. See his "Marriage Among the Elizabethan Nobility in the 16th and 17th Centuries," *Comparative Studies in Society and History*, 3 (1961):198-99. The mean age at first marriage was 23.7 for women in the parish of St. Peter Cornhill, London (1580-1650), and 21.3 in the parish of St. Michael Cornhill (1580-1650). Roger A. P. Finlay, "Population and Fertility in London, 1580-1650," *Journal of Family History*, 4 (1979): 32.

57. Laslett, *World*, 90-91; Stone, *PP*, 33:41; Cooper, ed., *Wentworth Papers*, 29; Forman, *Autobiography*, 21, 30; Stanford Lehmberg, *Sir Walter Mildmay and Tudor Government* (Austin, Texas, 1964), 77.

58. Stone, *PP*, 33:40-41; *Crisis*, 653, 792; Laslett, *World*, 87, 89; G. E. C., *The Complete Peerage* (1910-59), 5:218.

59. Joel Hurstfield, *The Queen's Wards* (Cambridge, Mass., 1958), 153.

60. Ibid., 130-33, 137-42.

61. *CSPD, Add. 1566-1579*, 411; Hurstfield, *Wards*, 144-45; Stone, *Crisis*, 602-3. When the earl of Oxford complained to Burghley in 1576 that his wife Anne was "most directed by her father and mother," the lord treasurer retorted: "She must be most directed by her parents when she had no house of the Earl's to go to, and in her sickness and childbed only looked to by her parents." HMC 9 Salisbury, 2:144. Negotiations for the marriage of George Clifford to Margaret Russell initially began, at Leicester's suggestion, when the children were ages seven and five, respectively. J. H. Wiffen, *Historical Memoirs of the House of Russell* (1833), 1:431-32.

62. HMC 9 Salisbury, 2:200.

63. Ibid., 10:18; James Raine, ed., *Wills and Inventories* (1835), 122; Carpenter, *Report*, 26:181-82; Patent Roll, 21 Eliz.; (cf. HMC 9 Salisbury, 1:489).

64. PRO SP 24/52 (f. 94^r); (cf. PRO SP 24/34 [f. 61^r]); *APC*, 19:196-97; Hurstfield, *Wards*, 144; BL Lansdowne MS 51/2, 9; Stone, *Crisis*, 602.

65. *DNB*, *s.v.*

66. PRO SP 23/18 (f. 50^r); Frederick Furnivall, ed., *Child-Marriages, Divorces, and Ratifications* (1897), 9-11.

67. Stone, *Crisis*, 656; David Cecil, *The Cecils of Hatfield House* (Boston, 1973), 143-44; Lady Anne Newdigate-Newdegate, ed., *Gossip from a Muniment Room* (1898), 4-5, 7; (cf. HMC 69 Middleton, 557); Furnivall, *Child-Marriages*, 4-6, 47-49 (cf. 1-4, 16-24, 28-30, 41-43); Lady Georgiana Fullerton, *The Life of Elizabeth Lady Falkland* (1883), 12-13, 15-17.

68. Rowse, *Tudor Cornwall* (rev. ed.; New York, 1969), 441-42; Furnivall, *Child-Marriages*, 6-9, 22.

69. Hurstfield, *Wards*, 151; Laslett, *World*, 86; Rowse, *Cornwall*, 442.

70. Gladys Hinde, ed., *The Registers of Cuthbert Tunstall Bishop of Durham* (Durham, 1952), 149-63; Furnivall, *Child-Marriages*, 1-2, 16, 25-28, 30-31, 45-47. Two cases set forth in manuscripts in the Public Record Office provide excellent illustrations of the complexity of the legal and personal issues involved in child marriages. See PRO SP 158/37 (ff. 114^v-119^r); PRO STAC 7 Add. 6/15.

71. *EEA*, 2:115; *SR*, 4, pt. 1, 323-30; *APC*, 11:391-92; HMC 9 Salisbury, 2:117; Fleetwood to Burghley, 18 July 1583, BL Lansdowne MS 38/12; John Vowell, *Orders Enacted for Orphans* (1575), f. 36^v. Cf. HMC 22 Eleventh Report, Appendix, pt. 7, p. 160.

72. *APC*, 15:360; 17:95, 353; 19:453-54.

73. Hurstfield, *Wards*, 153. It is possible that evidence of the performance of child marriages by Puritan clergy will be found.

Chapter 4: The Marital Quest Consummated

1. Gibbon, *Work*, 7.

2. BB, note to Gen. 24:57.

3. Pearl Hogrefe, *Tudor Women* (Ames, Iowa, 1975), 18; Camden, *Woman*, 85; Hurstfield, *Wards*, 154; Maurice Ashley, *The Stuarts in Love* (New York, 1963), 21-22; Stone, *Crisis*, 597, 599-600; Notestein, *Studies*, 85, 87, 89, 95; Stone, *Family*, 192.

4. Hogrefe, *Women*, 16, 18-19.

5. Virginia Beauchamp, "Women in the Reformation: Directions for Research," Paper given at the Conference on Puritanism in Old and New England, Thomas More College (1975), 6-7; Bullinger, *State*, sigs. B2^r-B3^r, B5^{r-v}, C7^v, C8^v, K5^r. As late as 1556 Michel Cope (Cop) complained that fathers delayed finding brides for their sons, to hang on to their possessions as long as possible. His views were published in England in 1580. Cope was a pastor at Geneva from 1545 to 1566, where he came into contact with the Marian exiles. *A Godly and Learned Exposition*, trans. Marcelline Outred (1580), f. 391^v; Christina Garrett, *The Marian Exiles* (Cambridge, 1938), 127-28.

6. GB, notes to Gen. 24:57; 34:4; 1 Cor. 7:37; (cf. R. Greaves, "Traditionalism and the Seeds of Revolution in the Social Principles of the Geneva Bible," *SCJ*, 7 [1976]:101-2); BB, notes to Gen. 21:21; 24:4, 51; 29:19, 21; 34:8; Exod. 22:16; BTB, notes to 1 Cor. 7:3, 36.

7. Cooper, *Exposition*, sig. R4^r; T. Rogers, *Creede*, pt. 2, p. 65; *Doctrine*, 305; Strype, *Parker*, 1:556-57; Cooper, ed., *Wentworth Papers*, 13; Gibbens, *Qvestions*, 99-100; Bunny, *Summe*, f. 61^v; Babington, *Commaundements*, 14, 226; *Genesis*, 25, 180, 190. Cf. Strype, *Parker*, 1:556-57.

8. Sandys, *Sermons*, 50-51, 281-82, 325-27.

9. Whetstone, *Rocke*, sig. F7^v; *Heptameron*, sigs. E4^v-F2^r, I1^r-I2^v, I4^{r-v}, Y1^r.

10. Dod, *Treatise*, pt. 2, ff. 5^r, 9^v, 56^v-57^r; Perkins, *Chaine*, sig. K2^r; *Treatise*, 860; (cf. George, *Mind*, 291-92); R. Rogers, *Treatises*, 169-70; Knewstub, *Lectvres*, 86; Fenner, *Treatises*, 58-59; *Order*, sig. C3^v; H. Smith, *Preparatiue*, 43-47; Greenham, *Works*, 36-37, 415; Estey, *Expositions*, pt. 1, ff. 55^v-56^r, 58^r, 68^v; Allen, *The Oderifferous Garden of Charitie* (1603), 125; Hake, *Touchestone*, sigs. D1^v-D2^r; Gifford, *A Catechisme* (1583), sig. G5^v. Cf. Allen, *Treasvrie*, 190-91; Becon, *Salue*, 217.

11. Pagit, *Godly Sermon*, sigs. B8^r-C1^r; W. Vaughan, *Golden-groue*, sig. O8^v; Gibbon, *Work*, 5-6, 8-10, 13.

12. Cleaver, *Form*, 111, 115-17, 129-30, 320-24, 344, 358-60. John Newnham asserted that a son ought to accept the offer of a "meete marriage" arranged by his father as long as he was under twenty-five. *Newnams Nightcrowe* (1590), 41.

13. Stockwood, *Fruiteful Sermon*, sig. A8^{r-v}; *Bartholmew*, 21-24, 27, 29-30, 37-41, 43-46, 64-77, 88-89, 91,93-94.

14. Stockwood, *Bartholmew*, 18, 34-35, 47-48, 50, 77-81, 85-86.

15. Barrow, *Writings (1587-90)*, 455; Vaux, *Catechisme*, ff. 103^v-104^v.

16. PRO SP 21/26 (f. 54^{r-v}); HMC 9 Salisbury, 1:404-5, 415-16; B. M. Ward, *The Seventeenth Earl of Oxford* (1928), 61-62.

17. *CSPD, 1581-1590*, 688; BL Lansdowne MS 76/76; Ward, *Oxford*, 313-14, 329-31.

18. HMC 9 Salisbury, 2:112-13, 526; PRO SP 171/66 (f. 149^r); *CSPD, 1581-1590*, 680.

19. Stone, *Crisis*, 611, 660; Weigall, *Quarterly Review*, 215:122.

20. Hoby, *Diary*, 8-9, 25-27, 107; HMC 1 Second Report, 50; HMC 3 Fourth Report, 335; Norma McMullen, "The Status of English Gentlewomen, 1540-1640," M.A. thesis, Florida State University (1976), 81-85.

21. BL Lansdowne MSS 7/38-41; PRO SP 31/1-2 (ff. 1^r-2^r). Cf. Parker, *Correspondence*, 198.

22. Hatton, *Memoirs*, 78; Cholmley, *Memoirs*, 7; Charles Jackson, "Geneological Notes, etc., Relating to Families of Parker," *Journal of the Derbyshire Archaeological and Natural History Society*, 5 (1883):36; (cf. HMC 69 Middleton, 157); PRO Req. 2/31/37.

23. *CSPD, 1581-1590*, 442; Cyril Falls, *Mountjoy: Elizabethan General* (1955), 59; E. C. Williams, *Bess of Hardwick* (1959), 61-62; Hogrefe, *Women*, 15-16.

24. Cholmley, *Memoirs*, 8; Rose, *Cases*, 170; BL Lansdowne MSS 71/69; 88/5; 101/29; HMC 55 Var. Coll., 3:62; Manningham, *Diary*, 99. Cf. Ward, *Oxford*, 151-54, for Lady Mary Vere's marriage to Peregrine Bertie in 1577 in the face of numerous objections. Lawrence Stone may have overstated his case in asserting that "only a handful of children resisted parental dictation [in marriage] before the end of the sixteenth century." *Family*, 183.

25. Grindal, *Remains*, 321-23; HMC 25 Twelfth Report, Appendix, Part 7, p. 12.

26. Gertrude Hamilton, ed., *Books of Examinations and Depositions* (Southampton, 1914), 33; Sir Robert Cecil, *Letters*, ed. John Maclean (1864),112; BL Lansdowne MS 74/74.

27. Holles, *Memorials*, 41, 90, 116-19, 193-94.

28. HMC 69 Middleton, 157, 525, 585, 599-601.

29. M. D. R. Leys, *Catholics in England* (1961), 186; HMC 55 Var. Coll., 3:28; Anstruther, *Vaux*, 205-6, 232-33.

30. PRO Req. 2/46/25.

31. PRO SP 19/25 (f. 47^r), 53 (ff. 102^r-103^r); *CSPD, 1547-1580*, 155, 185, 188; G. E. C., *Peerage*, 12:557-58; PRO SP 158/57 (f. 158^r), 158/58 (f. 160^r); Rowse, *Sir Walter Ralegh* (New York, 1962), 125-26; HMC 8 Twelfth Report, 18; Hogrefe, *Women*, 21; BL Lansdowne MS 39/41, 45; PRO SP 40/92 (f. 196^{r-v}). The queen also was concerned with the match between Charles Lord Darnley and the countess of Shrewsbury's daughter. The countess of Lennox, who had consented to the marriage, was imprisoned. See PRO SP 99/12.1 (f. 25^{r-v}), 13 (f. 26^r), 15 (ff. 28^r-29^r).

32. PRO SP 19/31 (f. 64^{r-v}); 21/55 (f. 105^r); Strype, *Parker*, 1:234-35. Another controversial marriage was between Thomas Keys and Lady Mary Grey. See *APC*, 7:252, for an indication of the consternation it caused. Lady Mary was imprisoned until Keys died, despite an appeal to Cecil. PRO SP 40/66 (f. 146^r); Pearl Hogrefe, *Women of Action in Tudor England* (Ames, Iowa, 1977), 89.

33. HMC 58 Bath, 4:xvi, 144, 155-56, 158-60, 195; *CSPD, 1581-1590*, 61; BL Lansdowne MS 109/43.

34. John Clay, ed., *North Country Wills* (Durham, 1912), 52-53, 136; William Irvine, ed., *A Collection of Lancashire and Cheshire Wills* (1896), 96; Piccope, ed., *Wills*, 51:242 (cf. 281); Hogrefe, *Women*, 18.

35. Stone, *Crisis*, 595, 597; Young, *Mary Sidney*, 79-80; Irvine, ed., *Collection*, 98; Piccope, ed., *Wills*, 51:161, 236; 54:156-57; Clay, ed., *Wills*, 85, 172, 204; Campbell, *Yeoman*, 284; A. F. S. Pearson, *Thomas Cartwright and Elizabethan Puritanism* (Cambridge, 1925), 483.

36. Arthur Collins, *The Life of . . . William Cecil, Lord Burghley* (1732), 97; Clay, ed., *Wills*, 118, 184; Holles, *Memorials*, 65; Cooper, *Athenae*, 2:30; BL Wolley MS 6671, f. 65^v; John Nichols and John Bruce, eds., *Wills from Doctors' Commons* (1863), 59; F. A. Greenhill, ed., "Seven Leicestershire Wills," *Transactions of the Leicestershire Archaeological and Historical Society*, 38 (1962-63):13; Piccope, ed., *Wills*, 33:149-51.

37. BL Lansdowne MS 116/5; Piccope, ed., *Wills*, 51:163-64, 171-74; Nichols and Bruce, eds., *Wills*, 58; HMC 9 Salisbury, 2:391; Grosart, *Towneley Hall MSS*, xlv; (cf. Cooper, ed., *Wentworth Papers*, 319); Stone, *Crisis*, 600-1.

38. *SR*, 4, pt. 1, 329-30; 4, pt. 2, 910; Vowell, *Orders*, f. 37^v; Strype, *Parker*, 1:286-89; Whitgift, 3:379; Marchant, *Puritans*, 305; *EEA*, 2:43-44, 50, 60-61, 76, 121, 131; 3:144, 171, 190, 197, 212. Cf. PRO SP 99/40 (f. 86^r); 235/90 (ff. 208^v-209^r). Licensing abuses,

including marriage without parental consent, were the subject of a document prepared for a parliamentary committee in 1597; it was entitled *A Note of Incestuous and Unlawfull Marriages Made by Licenses, by Vagrant Ministers and Lawless Peculiars*. In response, Whitgift justified licenses to wed without parental consent: "It were better to tolerate the means wherewith consent of the parties themselves may more freely effect an honest matrimony." Parents, he argued, were too often concerned with their own likings rather than the feelings of the young persons, and were too concerned with wealth and social rank. Whitgift did not object to marriages between persons of disparate standing, such as old and young, rich and poor, or masters and servants. Strype, *Whitgift*, 2:377; 3:378-82. Cf. Neale, *Parliaments*, 2:357-58.

39. *APC*, 8:215; 11:56-57, 79, 108; 12:243-44, 275, 281, 283-84; 15:31-32, 275-76; 17:158, 215; 19:480-82. Nearly simultaneously with the Young-Stanley dispute, the Council was embroiled in the matrimonial squabbles between the families of Sir John Conway and Anthony Bourne, the heart of which was the alleged right of the Conways to marry Bourne's second daughter to Conway's youngest son. Lady Conway asserted the Bournes had agreed to this, but Bourne's wife Elizabeth claimed this had been done by "indirect and vnlawfull meanes." PRO SP 158/19 (f. 32^{r-v}), 49 (ff. 140^{r}-147^{v}); 203/40 (f. 81^{r}); 205/63 (f. 137^{r}); *APC*, 15:116, 229-30, 234; 16:50-51, 118, 139-41, 323-24, 383; 18:418, 445-46.

40. Thomas Churchyard, *Chvrchyards Challenge* (1593), 232.

41. Manningham, *Diary*, 42.

42. *Here Begynneth the Scole House of Women*, sig. B3^{r}. The attribution of this work to Edward Gosynhyll is now generally denied.

43. Burton, *Ten Sermons*, in *Works*, 9.

44. Bullinger, *State*, sigs. G3^{v}-G4^{r}, G5^{v}-G6^{r}.

45. Bailey, *Relation*, 183; *EEA*, 2:135; 3:206, 263, 349; Strype, *Grindal*, 226; Henry Ainsworth, *A Trve Confession* (1596), sig. A4^{r}. Reasonably full descriptions of the ceremony are found in L. Pearson, *Elizabethans*, 341-61; and Chilton Powell, *English Domestic Relations* (New York, 1917), 21-24.

46. Barrow, *Writings (1587-90)*, 454-55; Greenwood, *Writings*, 171; Penry, *Viewe*, 66; *Writings of Greenwood and Barrow (1591-93)*, 338, 353 (cf. 376, 384).

47. Cooper, *Athenae*, 2:177; Strype, *Parker*, 2:335; Barrow, *Writings (1587-90)*, 455; Greenwood, *Writings*, 25; *Writings of Greenwood and Barrow (1591-93)*, 308; Usher, ed., *Movement*, 63; C. Hill, *The World Turned Upside Down* (New York: Viking ed., 1972), 251; Allison, *Confvtation*, 119.

48. Furnivall, *Child-Marriages*, 57-59, 67-69.

49. Grindal, *Remains*, 126; *EEA*, 2:55, 77, 130; 3:142, 144; C. Hill, *Economic Problems*, 168; D'Ewes, *Journals*, 555; Strype, *Grindal*, 302; Sutcliffe, *Answere*, 122; Strype, *Aylmer*, 89. The note to Gen. 24:49 in the Bishops' Bible called for marriages to be performed openly.

50. Peel, ed., *Seconde Parte*, 2:160; Marchant, *Puritans*, 216, 310-12; *Church*, 66; Haigh, *EHR*, 92:40; Chamberlain, *Letters*, 1:113; Strype, *Whitgift*, 2:453–55; J. Barmby, *Churchwardens' Accounts of Pittington* (Durham, 1888), 352; HMC 8 Eleventh Report, 25; BL Lansdowne MS 83/18; Furnivall, *Child-Marriages*, 59-61, 196. Whitgift complained of disorderly marriages to Convocation in 1597. Cardwell, ed., *Synodalia*, 2:580. The Puritan Richard Dow, a member of the Dedham Classis, married a couple without banns in 1587 because the woman allegedly was pregnant. F. G. Emmison, *Elizabethan Life* (Chelmsford, Essex, 1970-76), 2:156. In 1594 William Clerke expressed concern that banns were not being asked in all the places a couple had lived, so that some persons were moving and illegally remarrying. *The Triall of Bastardie* (1594), 45-46.

51. *EEA*, 3:142, 151, 206, 263, 349; Marchant, *Church*, 81; Grindal, *Remains*, 143, 174-75; Aveling, "The Marriages of Catholic Recusants, 1559-1642," *JEH*, 14 (1963):73, 76; HMC 9 Salisbury, 6:309-10; Philip Gawdy, *Letters*, ed., Isaac Jeayes (1906), 43.

52. Young, *Mary Sidney*, 50-51; Furnivall, *Child-Marriages*, 140; Manningham, *Diary*, 19; (cf. Brinkworth, ed., *Court*, 58); Purvis, ed., *Documents*, 38, 72. Cf. HMC 12 Wells, 2:314; Emmison, *Elizabethan Life*, 2:157-58.

53. Peel, ed., *Seconde Parte*, 1:259; *EEA*, 3:212; John Terry, *The Triall of Trvth* (Oxford, 1600), 126; Ashley, *Stuarts*, 24; K. Thomas, *Religion*, 620-21; Brinkworth, ed., *Court*, 36, 42, 50, 57; Strype, *Whitgift*, 2:400; Marchant, *Puritans*, 246; Holles, *Memorials*, 194; Furnivall, *Child-Marraiges*, 65-67. Cf. Emmison, *Elizabethan Life*, 2:157-58.

54. Aveling, *JEH*, 14:69, 74; Machyn, *Diary*, 199; Epton, *Love*, 96; PRO SP 222/13 (f. 23^v).

55. *CSPD, 1591-1594*, 158; Aveling, *JEH*, 14:72-75, 77; PRO SP 165/28 (f. 88^{r-v}); (cf. *APC*, 13:425).

56. K. Thomas, *Religion*, 39; Pilkington, *Works*, 192; Hooker, *Works*, 2:430; Whetstone, *Heptameron*, sig. X3^r; (cf. Whitgift, *Works*, 3:353-55).

57. "Martin Marprelate," *A Dialogve* (1640 ed.), sig. D2^r; Kingsmill, *Viewe*, sig. K2^r; H. Smith, *Preparatiue*, 31; Gilby, *Dialogve*, sig. M5^r; Fenner, *Treatises*, 96; A. Pearson, *Cartwright*, 93, 483; Donald McGinn, *The Admonition Controversy* (New Brunswick, N. J., 1949), 218-19; HMC 9 Salisbury, 2:73-74; Barrow, *Writings (1587-90)*, 453-54. Objections to the use of rings by Puritan laity may account for the difficulties some Essex ministers encountered when grooms refused to produce rings during the ceremony. Cf. Emmison, *Elizabethan Life*, 2:155.

58. Machyn, *Diary*, 300; Lady Anne Clifford, *Lives of Lady Anne Clifford . . . and of Her Parents*, ed. J. P. Gilson (1916), 3; G. C. Williamson, *George, Third Earl of Cumberland* (Cambridge, 1920), 11; BL Lansdowne MS 33/71; Stone, *Crisis*, 633; John Stow's continuation of Raphael Holinshed, *Chronicles* (1808), 4:901-2.

59. Wiffen, *Memoirs*, 1:426-30; Holinshed, *Chronicles*, 4:229; Epton, *Love*, 96.

60. HMC 77 De L'Isle, 2:468; Wiffen, *Memoirs*, 2:57-58.

61. Machyn, *Diary*, 288; Smyth, *Berkeley Manuscripts*, 2:402; LPL Bacon MS 658/119 (f. 175^r), or the BL copy, Add. MS 4120, f. 77^r; Chamberlain, *Letters*, 1:131; HMC 69 Middleton, 555; F. G. Emmison, *Tudor Secretary* (1961), 287; BL Lansdowne MS 108/47; LPL Bacon MS 648/10 (f. 18^r). Paul Seaver suggests that because Hoby was a very short man, his stature as much as his Puritanism may have motivated him to eschew dancing. In 1587, Sir Francis Willoughby apologized for not having the wedding at his home when his second daughter Dorothy married Henry, son of George Hastings, younger brother of the earl of Huntingdon. HMC 69 Middleton, 566. One of the more interesting wedding gifts among the gentry was a doe and a dozen Northamptonshire puddings from Sir John Spencer to Sir Michael Hicks. BL Lansdowne MS 108/48.

62. Machyn, *Diary*, 215, 240, 243-44, 247-48, 280; HMC 2 Third Report, 323.

63. Campbell, *Yeoman*, 304; Ashley, *Stuarts*, 52; PRO Req. 2/199/66; James Tait, ed., *Lancashire Quarter Sessions Records* (Manchester, 1917), 101; L. Pearson, *Elizabethans*, 344; BL Egerton MSS 2713, f. 254^r; 2714, f. 214^r.

64. K. Thomas, *Religion*, 556; Powell, *Relations*, 24, 26; Rowse, *Cornwall*, 438; Camden, *Woman*, 100; L. Pearson, *Elizabethans*, 358-59.

65. Ethel L. Urlin, *A Short History of Marriage* (1913), 184, 218-19, 242-43, 247; A. L. Rowse, *The Elizabethan Renaissance: The Life of Society* (New York, 1971), 222, 241. Aristocratic families sometimes gave colored ribbons tied in knots to the guests as a symbol of indissoluble love and fidelity. Urlin, *History*, 238-39.

66. Urlin, *History*, 183-85; W. Vaughan, *Golden-groue*, sig. O4^r (quoted).

67. Epton, *Love*, 95; BL Stowe MS 1055, f. 25^r; *EEA*, 3:143; L. Pearson, *Elizabethans*, 357. An example of the abuses that could occur in conjunction with weddings happened at West Ham in June 1602, when a man "in derision of holy matrimony got a bough hanged with ropes' ends and beset with nettles and other weeds, and carried the same in the street

and churchyard before the bride to the great offence of the congregation." Emmison, *Elizabethan Life*, 2:155.

68. Whetstone, *Heptameron*, sig. U2^r.

69. Peter Colse, *Penelope's Complaint, 1596*, ed. Alexander Groshart (Manchester, 1880), 172.

70. Stone, *Family*, 55-56; Strype, *Whitgift*, 2:214-18.

71. Rheims NT, notes to 1 Cor. 7:40; 1 Tim. 5:3, 5, 9, 14.

72. Gerard, *Autobiography*, 52, 167.

73. GB, notes to 1 Tim. 5:3-6, 9, 11-12, 16; BTB, notes to 1 Cor. 7:8; 1 Tim. 5:5, 14, 16. For the roles of widows in Protestant churches see Fulke, *Text*, f. 380^v; Allison, *Confvtation*, 69-71; Bancroft, *Svrvay*, 215 ff.; Barrow, *Writings (1587-90)*, 217-19.

74. Fulke, *Text*, ff. 369^v, 376^r, 380^{r-v}, 382^r; Wither, *View*, 183. In the late 1560s William Copland printed a work written by Robert Copland in the 1520s, entitled *The Seuen Sorowes* [1568?], which deals with a widow's experience in verse. Remarriage to satisfy sexual needs is clearly stated. *Op. cit.*, sigs. C3^v-C4^r; H. R. Plomer, "Robert Copland," *Transactions of the Bibliographical Society*, 3 (1895-96):211-25.

75. Cartwright, *Confvtation*, 182, 565-67.

76. Babington, *Genesis*, 192; Kingsmill, *Viewe*, sigs. I3^{r-v}, K3^r; Newnham, *Nightcrowe*, 23; Breton, *Praise*, sig. $_3$C1^v; Samuel Bird, *The Lectvres vnto the Hebrewes* (Cambridge, 1598), 43. From the medical standpoint, a widower might consider remarriage because the moderate ejection of semen was judged beneficial for health. Stone, *Crisis*, 620.

77. Becon, *Salue*, 138, 204-5; R. Rogers, *Diaries*, ed. Knappen, 74; Robinson, ed., *Zurich Letters*, 171-72.

78. Collinson, "The Role of Women in the English Reformation Illustrated by the Life and Friendships of Anne Locke," *SCH*, 2 (1965):267-70.

79. Joshua Sylvester, *Monodia* [1594], sigs. A3^r-A4^r.

80. Spufford, *Communities*, 112-15, 117; Notestein, *Studies*, 103-4; Hurstfield, *Wards*, 145-48; Laslett, *World*, 99; "Size and Structure of the Household in England Over Three Centuries," *PS*, 23 (1969):215. Laslett believes remarriage was more common for widowers than widows.

81. Hoby, *Diary*, 28-30; Chamberlain, *Letters*, 1:64; HMC 53 Montagu, 17; PRO Req. 2/215/35.

82. Sir James Whitelocke, *Liber Famelicus*, ed. John Bruce (1858), 6; *APC*, 19:475.

83. Barbara Winchester, *Tudor Family Portrait* (1955), 309; PRO Chancery 3/199/52, 127; HMC 9 Salisbury, 2:80; BL Lansdowne MS 87/27; PRO SP 24/29 (ff. 51^r-53^r). Stone suggests that the upper class had a high rate of remarriage, whereas the lower classes apparently did not. *PP*, 33:41. Carroll Camden's supposition, based on literary evidence alone, that "a widow in the Elizabethan age could scarcely hope to marry," is erroneous. *Woman*, 64.

84. LPL Bacon MSS 659/132 (f. 194^r), 660/12 (f. 13^r); *APC*, 19:477; Cooper, ed., *Wentworth Papers*, 31.

85. Hogrefe, *Women*, 44, 48; Edward Arber, *A List . . . of 837 London Publishers* (Birmingham, 1890); Oglander, *Memoirs*, 80-81; Laslett, *World*, 75.

86. Becon, *Salue*, 203; Piccope, ed., *Wills*, 51:41, 186, 191, 221; 54:89, 94, 129, 166. Cf. Emmison, *Elizabethan Life*, 3:101.

87. Greenham, *Works*, 37; C. J. Sisson, *The Judicious Marriage of Mr Hooker* (Cambridge, 1940), 14-15; Spufford, *Communities*, 116-17; Hoby, *Diary*, 12, 24-25, 28-32; LPL Bacon MS 655/15 (f. 20^r). After Lady Russell's husband died she wrote to Burghley: "Yf your L. here yt I mary, think it not strange: for I live withowt Comfort of eny living: god and yourself excepted: all other I find more Combrows, & dawngerows, then Comfortable." BL Lansdowne MS 10/38.

Chapter 5: Sexual Mores and Social Behavior

1. Nicholas Breton, *The Praise of Vertuous Ladies* (1599), sig. B1^r.

2. Babington, *Genesis*, 55.

3. Laslett, *World*, 131, 141. Cf. Stone, *Family*, 607-9.

4. Ibid., 142; Vaux, *Catechisme*, ff. 101^v-102^r; *EEA*, 3:207; Thomas Bentley, *The Monvment of Matrones* (1582), 3:2-7, 9-11.

5. Usher, ed., *Movement*, 100; Becon, *Salue*, 213; Greenham, *Works*, 299; Cleaver, *Form*, 137; Allen, *Treasvrie*, 183; (cf. Cope, *Exposition*, f. 25^v). The practice of bundling, if it existed in England in this period, received no comment. Stone asserts that some evidence of bundling exists, but does not cite it. *Family*, 520. For a case at Islip, Oxon., see Paul Hair, ed., *Before the Bawdy Court* (1972), 205-6.

6. P. M. Tillott, ed., *The Parish Register of Braithwell* (1969), 1-15, 69-70, 75-79; Laslett, *World*, 139, 141; P. E. H. Hair, "Bridal Pregnancy in Rural England in Earlier Centuries," *PS*, 20 (1966):236.

7. Hair, *PS*, 20:236-37, 239-42. Further research by Hair shows figures for prenuptial pregnancies (births within eight and a half months of marriage) of 30% for Dymock, Glos. (1538-1567), 26% for Standish, Lancs. (1560-1589), and 10% and 14% for Orwell, Cambs. (1570-1585, 1586-1599). "Bridal Pregnancy in Earlier Centuries Further Examined," *PS*, 24 (1970):60. In the period 1580 to 1650, the prenuptial figures for the London parishes of St. Peter Cornhill and St. Michael Cornhill were 11.9% and 12.2% respectively. Finlay, *Journal of Family History*, 4:37. Laslett's figures for prenuptial pregnancy are only marginally useful because they include all baptisms within nine months of the date of marriage. In the period 1550 to 1599 he provides prenuptial pregnancy ratios as follows: 22.2% for Aldenham, Herts.; 39.2% for Colyton, Devon; 27.1% for Hartland, Devon; 16.7% for Alcester, Warks. (but based on a total of only six pregnancies!); and 30.3% for Banbury, Oxon. Of the 193 first pregnancies in these five parishes, 61 (31.6%) were prenuptial by Laslett's definition. In the period 1600 to 1649 the prenuptial pregnancy rate in these parishes declined to 21.3% (142 prenuptial pregnancies in 591 first pregnancies). *Family Life and Illicit Love in Earlier Generations* (Cambridge, 1977), 130. Christopher Hill offers some sobering words of caution on inaccuracies in parish registers, yet these sources provide valuable information when carefully used. R. A. P. Finlay's examination of London parish registers between 1580 and 1653 reveals a high degree of accuracy. Hill, *Econ. H. R.*, 2nd ser., 31:453; Finlay, "The Accuracy of the London Parish Registers, 1580-1653," *PS*, 32 (1978):95-112.

8. Laslett, *World*, 141-42. Lu Pearson is in error when she states that the absolute chastity of maids was taken for granted. *Elizabethans*, 296.

9. Brinkworth, ed., *Court*, 34, 52, 53 (cf. 112).

10. Furnivall, *Child-Marriages*, 56-57, 137-38; Marchant, *Church*, 78, 137. Cf. Raine, ed., *The Injunctions . . . of Richard Barnes, Bishop of Durham* (Durham, 1850), 122. In 1562, Thomas Browne, vicar of Good Easter, Essex, impregnated a widow to whom he was betrothed. Emmison suggests that in Essex the churchwardens were sometimes reluctant to report cases of prenuptial pregnancy during their year in office because of the hostility that could ensue. *Elizabethan Life*, 2:6, 218.

11. T. Moulton, *This Is the Myrrour* [c. 1565], sig. E1^r; Leonard Gibson, *A Very Proper Dittie* [1570]; Hake, *Newes*, sig. A5^v; Willoby, *Avisa*, 12.

12. Kellison, *Svrvey*, 526 ff.; Vaux, *Catechisme*, ff. 51^v-52^r.

13. R. Rogers, *Treatises*, 145; Allen, *Treasvrie*, 185-87. Cf. Timme, *Discouerie*, sig. I2^v.

14. Hergest, *Rvle*, 2, 27, 63; Piccope, ed., *Wills*, 51:76.

15. Vaux, *Catechisme*, ff. 52^v-53^r; Jewel, *Works*, 2:850; Nowell, *Catechism*, 133; (cf. Turnbull, *Iude*, f. 54^v); Whetstone, *Rocke*, sig. F5^{r-v}; GB, notes to Gen. 39:14; 1 Thess. 4:4; BTB, notes to 1 Cor. 6:13, 18, 19; Allen, *Treasvrie*, 194; Greenham, *Works*, 415; (cf. Pagit,

Godly Sermon, sig. A5^r); Northbrooke, *Spiritus . . . A Treatise Wherein Dicing* (1579), sig. A4^r.

16. Haigh, *Reformation*, 242; HMC 69 Middleton, 151-52; Peel, ed., *Seconde Parte*, 2:108, 146, 147, 157, 162, 163, 173; Ward, *Diaries*, ed. Knappen, 111. Polewhele's vicarage is listed as being at North Petherton, Corn., but this would be either North Petherwyn, Devon, or North Petherton, Som. For other clergy guilty of fornication, see, e.g., HMC 12 Wells, 2:327, 341, 342; Emmison, *Elizabethan Life*, 2:218-21.

17. Notestein, *Studies*, 76; Nash, *Pierce*, f. 27^v; PRO SP 19/32 (f. 66^{r-v}), 21/39 (ff. 76^r-77^r); Newdigate-Newdegate, *Gossip*, 42; Rowse, *Elizabethan Renaissance*, 164; Stone, *Family*, 504. The Huntington Library has a letter of 27 March 1581 from Walsingham to Huntingdon that reports that Ann Vavysor gave birth to an illegitimate son, the father of whom was Edward de Vere, earl of Oxford. The ports were closed to prevent the earl's flight overseas.

18. Brinkworth, ed., *Court*, 10, 13, 59, 65, 70; LPL Bacon MS 656/118 (f. 180^r); *CSPD, 1595-1597*, 328. Many Essex cases involved fornication between masters and servants, and sometimes servants or their parents were reluctant to accuse the masters. The practice was probably more widespread than the evidence suggests. Emmison, *Elizabethan Life*, 2:13-15.

19. Stone, *Family*, 519, 631; Aveling, *JEH*, 14:71; Purvis, ed., *Documents*, 37-59; Marchant, *Church*, 215, 219, 221-22. Cf. Furnivall, *Child-Marriages*, 85-102 (for eight cases of fornication involving suits for paternity); Brinkworth, ed., *Court*, 32, 36, 39, 41, *et passim*.

20. Machyn, *Diary*, 223, 309; Philip Wyot, in *More English Diaries*, ed. Arthur Ponsonby (1927), 102; HMC 73 Exeter, 309; Spufford, *Communities*, 253; MacCaffrey, *Exeter*, 97-98; Marchant, *Church*, 224; Stone, *Family*, 633-34. Cf. Hair, ed., *Court*, 114, 125.

21. Usher, ed., *Movement*, 72; Jewel, *Works*, 2:943-44; Spufford, *Communities*, 255; Cogan, *Haven*, 257; Allen, *Treasvrie*, 195-96; Stubbes, *Anatomie*, sigs. H5^v-H6^r.

22. Christopher Wirtzung, *Praxis medicinae vniuersalis*, trans. Jacob Mosan (1598), 290; Conrad Gesner, *The Newe Iewell of Health*, trans. George Baker (1576), f. 48^r. Gesner was a professor at the University of Zurich.

23. BL Sloane MS 1897; M. A. Waugh, "Venereal Disease in Sixteenth Century England," *Medical History*, 17 (1973):195-97; John Hester, *The Pearle of Practise* (1594), 42-44, 59-60; Stubbes, *Anatomie*, sig. H4^r. In 1560 the French imposed heavy penalties on prostitutes with venereal diseases. Lujo Bassermann, *The Oldest Profession*, trans. James Clough (1967), 294. The records of the parish of St. Botolph without Aldgate, London, include one death from syphilis in 1585, two in 1587, and nine between 1594 and 1599. Thomas Forbes, *Chronicle from Aldgate* (New York, 1971), 105-6. In 1566, the wife of Robert Hawks, vicar of North Shoebury, Essex, was accused of giving venereal disease to another man. Emmison, *Elizabethan Life*, 2:33.

24. Rollins, ed., *Ballads*, 273.

25. Hake, *Newes*, sig. F8^r.

26. Laslett, *World*, 136; Ashley, *Stuarts*, 57; A. H. A. Hamilton, *Quarterly Sessions* (1878), 28-29; Stubbes, *Anatomie*, sig. H4^{r-v}; Piccope, ed., *Wills*, 51:242; 54:39, 87. Lord Rich provided in his will that his illegitimate son Richard be educated in the common law. Craze, *History*, 32.

27. Laslett, *World*, 134-36; Laslett and Karla Oosterveen, "Long-term Trends in Bastardy in England," *PS*, 27 (1973):255, 260-61, 267, 281; Laslett, *Family Life*, 115-17, 125, 137-42; Forbes, *Chronicle*, 68; Stone, *Family*, 612, 615. The illegitimacy ratios for the London parishes of St. Peter Cornhill and St. Michael Cornhill for the period 1580-1650 were 4.3% and 1.5%, respectively. Finlay, *Journal of Family History*, 4:36. Laslett believes that the care taken by the magistrates in the handling of bastardy cases indicates the number

cannot have been too great and that bastardy itself was not socially accepted. *World*, 133. In the county of Wiltshire there were eighty-four known cases of bastardy in 1578. Ashley, *Stuarts*, 56. C. Hill criticizes Laslett's figures on the grounds that the declining ratio of bastard births shows only the failure of the authorities to register them. Although this is possible, Hill's assertion is no more provable than Laslett's. Nor does Hill have the evidence to support his thesis that the tightening of controls over bastardy between 1580 and 1640 was due more to the cost of maintaining bastards than the impact of Puritanism. Both were important factors, and the evidence is simply insufficient to weigh them. Hill, *Econ. H.R.*, 2nd ser., 31:454-55.

28. Estey, *Expositions*, pt. 1, f. 55^V; H. Smith, *Preparatiue*, 18-19; Perkins, *Chaine*, sigs. L6^V-L7^r; Deloney, *Craft*, sig. E1^V; Allen, *Garden*, sig. A2^V.

29. *EEA*, 2:44, 48, 55, 95, 97, 115, 119, 122, 130, 131; 3:151, 154, 166-67, 183, 184, 190, 202, 205, 220, 224, 227, 230, 337, 345; BL Lansdowne MS 110/10; Peel, ed., *Seconde Parte*, 2:104.

30. *SR*, 4, pt. 1, 610; *CJ*, 1:104, 106; Kent, *BIHR*, 46:44, 68-69; Neale, *Parliaments*, 2:347.

31. Barmby, ed., *Accounts*, 348; Marchant, *Church*, 221; I. Pinchbeck, "The State and the Child in Sixteenth Century England," *BJS*, 7 (1956):283; 8 (1957):62-63. Between 1589 and 1602 twenty-seven bastardy cases were handled in the Staffordshire Quarter Sessions. They reveal a strong dislike in the local communities of supporting illegitimate children, which must have made the Puritan attack on bastardy popular. Since some of those summoned had no offense listed, there may have been additional bastardy cases. *The Staffordshire Quarter Session Rolls*, ed. S. A. H. Burne (Kendal, 1931-36), vols. 1-4. See G. R. Quaife, *Wanton Wenches and Wayward Wives* (New Brunswick, N.J., 1979), chap. 9, for the bastardy problem in Somerset between 1601 and 1660.

32. Hamilton, *Sessions*, 32; Tait, ed., *Records*, 73-74, 98, 143; Lambarde, *Government*, 18-20, 30-31, 37, 41, 45.

33. Furnivall, *Child-Marriages*, 146-47, 149, 156-58; Tait, ed., *Records*, 98, 129; Pinchbeck, *BJS*, 8:62, 73.

34. Jewel, *Works*, 2:854; Nash, *Pierce*, ff. 7^V, 27^V; Whetstone, *The Enemie to Vnthryftinesse* (2nd ed., 1586), sig. H2^V; Henry Bedel, *A Sermon* [1571], sig. C4^r; Samuel Gardiner, *The Cognizance of a Trve Christian* (1597), 129.

35. GB, notes to Gen. 38:24; Prov. 2:16; Rev. 2:20; (cf. the note to Prov. 7:26); Dent, *Path-way*, 35, 60 ff.; Norden, *Solace*, f. 80^r; Marchant, *Puritans*, 317; Wilcox, *Prouerbs*, 139; H. Smith, *The Poore-Mans Teares* (1592), 34-35; Trigge, *Apologie*, 36. Elizabethan moralists often blurred the distinction between adultery and prostitution, though there are ample references to the expenditure of money on whores, which typically refers to prostitution. "Whoredome" can refer to adultery or prostitution, and often seems to be used in a blanket sense to cover both meanings.

36. Stephen Gosson, *The Schoole of Abuse* (1579), ff. 18^{r-v}, 20^r; Hake, *Newes*, sigs. F8^r-G1^r.

37. **Stubbes,** *Anatomie*, sigs. π4^V, H6^V-H7^V.

38. W. Vaughan, *Golden-groue*, sigs. H7^r, Q2^V-Q3^V. Vaux's catechism also condemned pimps and those who encouraged prostitution. *Catechisme*, f. 52^r.

39. Peel, ed., *Seconde Parte*, 2:98, 102, 107, 109.

40. Machyn, *Diary*, 220, 221, 228, 238, 239, 277, 295, 299; F. J. C. and D. M. Hearnshaw, eds., *Court Leet Records* (Southampton, 1905-6), 1:141, 162, 174, 345; (cf. W. J. Jones, *The Elizabethan Court of Chancery* [Oxford, 1967], 264, n. 5); Brinkworth, ed., *Court*, 54, 59, 65, 70; Tait, ed., *Records*, 19, 27, 32, 46, 65; Aspinall-Oglander, *Symphony*, 27; Emmison, *Elizabethan Life*, 2:23-24; *EEA*, 2:60, 64; Bailey, *Relation*, 206. A cart for

bawds is depicted on the title-page of the 1573 edition of Thomas Harman's *A Caveat or Warning*. In 1590 the parishioners of Norton, Staffs., petitioned the justices to suppress a local alehouse, where the owner's wife was an habitual prostitute. *Staffordshire Session Rolls*, ed. Burne, 2:51-53.

41. Carol Wiener, "Sex Roles and Crime in Late Elizabethan Hertfordshire," *JSH*, 8 (1975):42; BL Lansdowne MS 27/68; Essex women usually received anything from 1 or 2d. to several shillings, and some settled for gifts, such as a purse, cloth, or food. Emmison, *Elizabethan Life*, 2:17, 21; Stone, *Family*, 550, 615-17. Cf. Hair, ed., *Court*, 225.

42. Allen, *Treasvrie*, 184; Perkins, *Chaine*, sigs. L5^V-L6^r; Turnbull, *Iude*, f. 55^{r-v}; Peel, ed., *Seconde Parte*, 2:106; Stone, *Crisis*, 666; Rowse, *Elizabethan Renaissance*, 181-85. On the Continent, prosecutions of homosexuals tended to coincide with campaigns against witches. Although masturbation was regarded as a mortal sin by medieval Catholics, very little mention of it is made in Elizabethan England, though Stone properly suspects it may have been common. *Family*, 492, 512, 515, 615-16. The tendency to make *coitus interruptus* synonymous with masturbation, which Philip Ariès has noted, suggests the development of a more liberal attitude toward masturbation. "An Interpretation to Be Used for a History of Mentalities," *Popular Attitudes Toward Birth Control in Pre-Industrial France and England*, ed. Orest and Patricia Ranum (New York, 1972), 104.

43. *CJ*, 1:65, 69; *SR*, 3:441; 4, pt. 1, 72, 198, 447; Bailey, *Homosexuality and the Western Christian Tradition* (1955), 148-50. Although buggery was common in Italy, this does not appear to have been the case in England. Stone, *Family*, 492.

44. *EEA*, 2:100, 123; 3:157, 166, 184, 230, 232; Grindal, *Remains*, 176; *APC*, 8:146; Machyn, *Diary*, 238; Rose, *Cases*, 170-71; Manningham, *Diary*, 45; Peel, ed., *Seconde Parte*, 2:162; Barrow, *Writings (1587-90)*, 659-60; Stone, *Family*, 491, 510. Cf. Emmison, *Elizabethan Life*, 2:37-44; Hair, ed., *Court*, 188, 189.

45. Allen, *Treasvrie*, 184; *CJ*, 1:109, 111, 113, 114; *SR*, 4, pt. 1, 617-18; *Middlesex County Records*, ed., John C. Jeaffreson (1886-92), 1:55-209 *passim*; *APC*, 7:383-84, 397-98; 11:416-17, 432; 20:45; Strype, *Whitgift*, 3:379; Forbes, *Chronicle*, 159; Brinkworth, ed., *Court*, 61. There are two cases of rape in the records of the Staffordshire Quarter Sessions between 1586 and 1602, though there may have been others in the cases where offenses are not specified. *Staffordshire Session Rolls*, ed. Burne, 1:233; 2:236, 276. In the archdeacons' courts in Essex, twenty-three cases of rape are reported in the Elizabethan era, including one involving a rector and another a curate. Emmison, *Elizabethan Life*, 2:44-46, 223. Girls working in the fields were especially vulnerable. Cf. Hair, ed., *Court*, 135. The difference between rape and consent through fear was a gray area and made prosecution difficult. Cf. Quaife, *Wenches*, 65, 72, 172-73.

46. Cleaver, *Form*, 155.

47. W. Vaughan, *Natvrall and Artificial Directions for Health* (1600), 46.

48. BB, note to Gen. 1:28; BTB, note to 1 Cor. 7:5.

49. Noonan, *Contraception*, 314, 322; Rheims NT, notes to 1 Cor. 7:3, 5, 6; Heb. 13:4.

50. Fulke, *Text*, ff. 88^V, 272^V; Cartwright, *Confvtation*, 387; Cleaver, *Form*, 161; Pagit, *Godly Sermon*, sig. C6^r; Henry Holland, *The Christian Exercise of Fasting* (1596), 73; S. Gardiner, *Cognizance*, 40-41.

51. George, *Mind*, 272; Perkins, *Chaine*, sig. M4^r; R. Rogers, *Treatises*, 175; Estey, *Expositions*, pt. 1, f. 68^r; Pagit, *Godly Sermon*, sig. C4^r. Cf. Stone, *Family*, 644.

52. Cleaver, *Form*, 177; Dod, *Treatise*, pt. 2, f. 57^r; R. Rogers, *Treatises*, 175; Estey, *Expositions*, pt. 1, f. 68^r; Sandys, *Sermons*, 323; Cope, *Exposition*, f. 79^r.

53. Tilney, *Flower*, sig. B6^r; Hergest, *Rvle*, 3, 63.

54. Cogan, *Haven*, 246-47; W. Vaughan, *Directions*, 46-47.

55. Lemnie, *Touchstone*, ff. 99^V-100^r, 105^r, 113^V, 120^r.

56. Cogan, *Haven*, 245; W. Vaughan, *Directions*, 46; Perkins, *Chaine*, sig. L7^r, M4^r.

57. Brinkworth, ed., *Court*, 16, 17, 23, 26, 48, 56, 63, 68, 75; BL Lansdowne MS 99/104; Emmison, *Elizabethan Life*, 2:7. Emmison found two cases in Elizabethan Essex where couples separated due to wives' complaints that their husbands refused conjugal intercourse. Ibid., 2:163.

58. Smyth, *Berkeley Manuscripts*, 2:392-93.

59. Willoby, *Avisa*, 104.

60. Barrow, *Writings (1587-90)*, 545, referring to the Church of England's members.

61. Stone, *Crisis*, 612, 662-65; Piccope, ed., *Wills, passim*; cf. L. Pearson, *Elizabethans*, 296. Cf. Stone, *Family*, 502, 505.

62. Bullinger, *State*, sig. I1^{r-v}; *EEA*, 2:60, 64, 100, 123; 3:157, 166, 184, 230, 232; Grindal, *Remains*, 17, 176; John Dios, *A Sermon Preached at Paules Crosse* (1579), f. 38^v; Babington, *Genesis*, 159; Turnbull, *Iude*, f. 59^r.

63. Allen, *Treasvrie*, 180 ff.; Dent, *Path-way*, 350; Wilcox, *Prouerbs*, 11; Cleaver, *Form*, 178; Dering, *Catechisme*, sig. A8^v, R. Rogers, *Treatises*, 106; John Field, *A Caveat for Parsons Howlet* [1581], sig. D5^r.

64. Bullinger, *State*, sig. F2^r; Wilcox, *Prouerbs*, 23, 25, 30, 43; Timme, *Discouerie*, sigs. I1^v-I2^r; Dent, *Path-way*, 68; (cf. Cope, *Exposition*, f. 26^r); Weigall, *Quarterly Review*, 215:121.

65. Bullinger, *State*, sig. A2^v; Norden, *Solace*, f. 134^r; Bullein, *Bulwarke*, pt. 3, f. 75^r; Gifford, *Catechisme*, sig. H1^r; Richard Jones, *A Briefe and Necessarie Catechisme* (1583), sig. B4^r; Udall, *Peters Fall* (1584), sig. E7^v; Dent, *Path-way*, 70-74; Deloney, *Thomas of Reading* (6th ed., 1632), sig. C4^v; *The Interlude of Johan the Evangelist* (1907), sig. B4^r. The remedies for adultery, as proposed by Dent, were labor, temperance, abstinence from the causative factors, prayer, sexual restraint, and the shunning of female company. *Path-way*, 74.

66. Furnivall, *Child-Marriages*, 31-34, 80, 81; Marchant, *Church*, 241-42; Aveling, *Recusancy*, 64; Strype, *Whitgift*, 3:379. In London, a Catholic who tried unsuccessfully to convert a married couple finally persuaded the wife that her Protestant wedding had been invalid; the two then ran off together. PRO SP 222/13 (ff. 25^r, 27^v-28^r). There is a good deal of evidence for wife-sales in the eighteenth century, and the practice may have occurred among the lower classes in the Elizabethan period. *The Blacke Bookes Messenger* (1592) cites a case of wife-swapping in London. Gamini Salgado, ed., *Coney-Catching and Bawdy-Baskets* (Baltimore, 1972), 325-26. Cf. C. Hill, *Econ. H. R.*, 2nd ser., 31:458.

67. Peel, ed., *Seconde Parte*, 2:149, 161, 166; Rowse, *Elizabethan Renaissance*, 169-70; Marchant, *Puritans*, 306; Mary Green, ed., *Life of William Whittingham* (1870), 47; see above, chap. 2, sect. 4.

68. Sir Philip Sidney, *Poems*, ed. William Ringler, Jr. (Oxford, 1962), 444-45.

69. Manningham, *Diary*, 60-61; Holles, *Memorials*, 67, 72; Aspinall-Oglander, *Symphony*, 29; Cholmley, *Memoirs*, 8; A. Clifford, *Lives*, 7; Rose, *Cases*, 170; Stone, *Family*, 548-51; A. L. Rowse, *Simon Forman* (1974).

70. BL Lansdowne MSS 15/47; 17/52, 53; Strype, *Parker*, 2:160-63; Parker, *Correspondence*, 405-6; *APC*, 9:338-39, 356; 10:109-10, 133-34.

71. GB, notes to Job 31:12; John 8:11; Bullinger, *State*, sigs. K6^v-K7^r; Stubbes, *Anatomie*, sig. H1^{r-v}; Stockwood, *1578 Sermon*, 51; Gifford, *Catechisme*, sigs. G8^r-G9^r; Timme, *Discouerie*, sigs. I1^v-I2^r; Dent, *Path-way*, 70-74; Gilby, *Dialogve*, sig. M1^v; Nowell, *Sermon at the Parliam^t* (Cambridge, 1853), 226; Sandys, *Sermons*, 50; Dove, *Of Diuorcement* (1601), 42, 49.

72. Greenwood, *Writings of Greenwood and Barrow (1591-93)*, 77-78, 83-84; Barrow, *Writings (1587-90)*, 246, 659-60.

73. *EEA*, 2:100, 123; 3:157, 232; Grindal, *Remains*, 176; Spufford, *Communities*, 254; Marchant, *Church*, 176; Brinkworth, ed., *Court*, 7, 29; Raine, ed., *Injunctions*, 123. Cf. *Staffordshire Session Records*, ed. Burne, 2:52; Hair, ed., *Court*, 105, 169. In the villages a cuckholded husband as well as his adulterous wife could be subjected to public shame in a skimmington. Stone, *Family*, 504; Quaife, *Wenches*, 200.

74. Barmby, ed., *Accounts*, 362.

75. Stow, *Chronicles*, 4:889-90.

76. *APC*, 17:63; HMC 69 Middleton, 158-59, 568; Gawdy, *Letters*, 99-100.

77. D'Ewes, *Journals*, 641. A wronged husband could, of course, use his will to punish his wife. John Mytchell of Wakefield, Yorks., e.g., had allowed his adulterous wife to keep her apparel plus £8 on condition that she never ask anything further from him. His will of 23 February 1591 left her nothing. Clay, ed., *Wills*, 200-1.

78. Chamberlain, *Letters*, 1:30. Lord Norris is Henry Lord Norris of Rycote.

79. Ibid., 1:178.

80. Robert Schnucker, "Elizabethan Birth Control and Puritan Attitudes," *Journal of Interdisciplinary History*, 5 (1975): 661-65.

81. Noonan, *Contraception*, 296, 330, 336, 361-62, 366, 371, 374; Vaux, *Catechisme*, f. 49^r.

82. Estey, *Expositions*, pt. 1, f. 69^r; Calvin, *Opera quae supersunt omnia*, ed. William Baum *et al.* (Brunswick, 1882), 23:495-96; W. Vaughan, *Directions*, 47.

83. K. Thomas, *Religion*, 189; H. S. Bennett, *English Books & Readers* (Cambridge, 1965), 180, 183; Weigall, *Quarterly Review*, 215:130; Hoby, *Diary*, 72.

84. Sir Thomas Eliot, *The Castel of Health* (1561), ff. 6^r-7^v; Lemnie, *Touchstone*, ff. 42^v, 55^r, 74^v, 81^v, 149^v; Philip Barrough, *The Method of Phisick* (1590), 201-2.

85. Lemnie, *Touchstone*, ff. 42^v-43^r; Barrough, *Method*, 201; cf. Wirtzung, *Praxis*, 295-300.

86. Andrew Boorde, *Here Foloweth a Compendyous Regimente* (1562), sig. F6^v; Gesner, *Iewell*, f. 55^v; Hester, *Pearle*, 82.

87. Bullein, *Bulwarke*, pt. 1, ff. 20^v, 37^r, 38^r; pt. 3, ff. 8^r, 16^r-17^r; *A Newe Booke* [1558], ff. 55^v, 115^v; Eliot, *Castel*, f. 27^v; (cf. Wirtzung, *Praxis*, 294-95); Thomas Newton, *Approoued Medicines* (1580), ff. 3^r, 19^r, 20^v, 24^v-25^r, 32^v, 34^r, 43^r, 49^r, 50^r, 52^v, 53^{r-v}; Boorde, *Regimente*, sig. F5^v; Barrough, *Method*, 182-83; John Gerard, *The Herball* (1597), 124, 193, 572, 614, 665, 754, 868, 871, 874, 880, 951, 993, 1047, 1174, 1289.

88. Schnucker, *Journal of Interdisciplinary History*, 5:657-58; Bullein, *Bulwarke*, pt. 1, f. 72^v; John XXI, *The Treasvry of Health*, trans. Humphrey Lloyd (1585), sigs. L2^v-L3^v; Wirtzung, *Praxis*, 292. For additional information on genital baths see Cogan, *Haven*, 252; Wirtzung, *Praxis*, 292. The last-named also thought going barefoot would reduce sexual desire.

89. Lemnie, *Touchstone*, f. 81^v; Cogan, *Haven*, 76; Bullein, *Bulwarke*, pt. 1, ff. 10^r, 45^v; Newton, *Medicines*, ff. 28^v, 68^r, 73^{r-v}; Gerard, *Herball*, 419, 573, 674, 728, 733, 744, 772, 979, 1076 (cf. 97, 158, 1202); Wirtzung, *Praxis*, 291; John XXI, *Treasvry*, sig. L3^{r-v}; Gesner, *Iewell*, f. 50^r; Barrough, *Method*, 181.

90. Schnucker, *Journal of Interdisciplinary History*, 5:658-59; Bullein, *Bulwarke*, pt. 1, f. 39^r; Gesner, *Iewell*, ff. 47^v, 49^v; Cogan, *Haven*, 101; John XXI, *Treasvry*, sig. T3^v; Vaux, *Catechisme*, ff. 48^v-49^r; Lambarde, *Government*, 42. When Marry Fitton became pregnant by Henry Herbert, earl of Pembroke, in 1595, she may have used a medical remedy to kill the unwanted fetus, for the baby was stillborn. In 1590, the vicar of Weaverham, Ches., was charged with teaching young people how to commit adultery or fornication without instigating pregnancies. E. A. Wrigley, *Population and History* (1969), 127.

91. Christopher Hooke, *The Child-birth* (1590), sig. D2^r; Richardson, *Puritanism*, 112-

13; S. J. Watts, *From Border to Middle Shire, Northumberland* (Leicester, 1975), 73; Stone, *Crisis*, 589-90; Machyn, *Diary*, 232, 379; Holinshed, *Chronicles*, 4:329.

92. R. E. Jones, "Infant Mortality in Rural North Shropshire, 1561-1810," *PS*, 30 (1976):307; Notestein, *Studies*, 90; Holinshed, *Chronicles*, 4:234; Wrigley, *Econ. H. R.*, 19:93, 95; V. H. T. Skipp, "Economic and Social Change in the Forest of Arden, 1530-1649," *Land, Church and People*, ed. Joan Thirsk (Reading, 1970), 107; John Young, *Diary*, ed. F. R. Goodman (1928), 4-5; Collinson, *Mirror*, 30.

93. Wrigley, *Econ. H. R.*, 19:97-98; Chambers, *Population*, 70; Stone, *PP*, 33:40-42; *Crisis*, 768; T. H. Hollingsworth, "The Demography of the British Peerage," Supplement to *PS*, 18 (1965):33; Laslett, *World*, 68; Watts, *Border*, 68; Stone, *Family*, 64. The mean households size was 5.28 at Poole, Dorset, in 1574; 4.05 in Stafford in 1622; 5.30 at Cogenhoe, Northants., in 1624; and 5.62 at Chester in 1645. Peter Laslett and Richard Wall, eds., *Household and Family in Past Time* (Cambridge, 1972), 130.

94. Schnucker, *Journal of Interdisciplinary History*, 5:666.

95. Becon, *Salue*, 210, 217. For the case against Willett's Puritanism, see the *DNB*, *s.v.* Thomas Cogan reports that an old priest he once knew lived chaste his entire life with the assistance of rue, which he consumed daily in his food or drink. *Haven*, 252.

96. Watts, *Border*, 68.

97. Babington, *Genesis*, 161; Estey, *Expositions*, pt. 1, f. 56[r]; Fenner, *Treatises*, 50; Perkins, *Chaine*, sig. K2[v]; Dod, *Treatise*, pt. 2, ff. 8[v]-9[r]; H. Smith, *Preparatiue*, 99-101; Cleaver, *Form*, 231-34. Potions to increase the ability to lactate are found in *The Widdowes Treasure* (1595), sig. B1[v]. One calls for parsnips and fennel roots in chicken broth, served with fresh butter; another suggests rice with cow's milk and white bread. Powdered fennel seed mixed with sugar was also recommended. See also Newton, *Medicines*, f. 3[r].

98. Stone, *Crisis*, 592; Hogrefe, *Women*, 16-17; D'Ewes, *Autobiography*, 1:24-25; R. V. Schnucker, "The English Puritans and Pregnancy, Delivery and Breast-Feeding," *History of Childhood Quarterly*, 1 (1974):646-48; Stone, *Family*, 496. An interesting case in the Court of Requests involves a wet nurse. The London vintner John Rede procured a nurse for an unwed mother on the understanding that she would pay 5s. 4d. a month plus bedding and clothing to the nurse, guaranteed by a £40 bond. When the mother married and tried to recover her child, Rede sued at common law for payment of the bond, and the mother sought assistance from the Court of Requests. PRO Req. 2/32/52.

99. Stone credits the rising standard of sexual morality in seventeenth-century England to the pressure of Puritan organization and preaching. Yet enough parallels in Anglican sermons and writings on sexual morality exist to account for the improved sexual morals among propertied Anglicans, which Stone unnecessarily attributes to Puritan influence. *Family*, 523, 623.

100. Because these statistics are based on surviving offspring, they do not take into account the possibility that a greater percentage of children put out to wet nurses died than those nursed by their own mothers. This possibility could increase the number of children born to aristocratic families in comparison to ministerial families.

Chapter 6: Married Life and Parenthood

1. H. Smith, *Preparatiue*, 54-55.

2. Wright, *Display*, 23. To this there was a feminist retort: "The fellow that tooke his wife for his crosse, was an Asse." Jane Anger, *Iane Anger Her Protection for Women* (1589), 8.

3. Tyndale, Pentateuch (1534), note to Gen. 3; Tyndale NT (1534), prologue to 1 Pet.; Tyndale-Coverdale NT (1538), note to 1 Cor. 7; Tyndale-Rogers NT (1538), note to 1 Cor.

11; Taverner (Matthew) Bible (1539), note to Judg. 19; Tyndale NT (1549), note to 1 Cor. 11; Tyndale-Erasmus NT (1549), note to 1 Cor. 14; MB (1540), note to 1 Pet. 3. The latter notation also appeared in the Matthew and Matthew-Becke Bibles of 1551. The basic theme of female obedience appears in the Coverdale Bibles of 1535 and 1537 (synopsis of 1 Tim. 2), the Matthew Bibles of 1537, 1549, and 1551 (notes to Num. 5; 1 Cor. 11, 14), and the Great Bibles from 1539 to 1550 (synopsis of 1 Tim. 2).

4. GB, notes to Num. 30:9; Esther 1:16, 22; Ps. 45; Prov. 2:17; Mal. 2:14; 1 Cor. 7:3; 11:7, 10; 1 Pet. 3:6, 7.

5. GB, notes to Gen. 2:24; 31:13; Prov. 14:1; 31:26; Jer. 44:19; Mal. 2:15; Eph. 5:23; Titus 2:4, 5; 1 Pet. 3:7.

6. BB, notes to Gen. 3:17; 24:67 (cf. 30:2); Prov. 5:15; 1 Cor. 11:10.

7. BTB, notes to 1 Cor. 11:2, 7; Eph. 5:22, 23; 1 Pet. 3:2, 6.

8. BTB, notes to 1 Cor. 11:11; Eph. 5:25; Col. 3:19; 1 Pet. 3:7.

9. Rheims NT, notes to 1 Cor. 7:29; 11:5; 1 Tim. 2:12; 3:6; Fulke, *Text*, f. 368^V.

10. Cooper, *Exposition*, sig. N4^r; Babington, *Genesis* 41; Gibbon, *Remedie*, sig. I3^r; Edward More, *Treatyse* (1560), sig. A4^V; Breton, *Praise*, sig. $_3$A4^r.

11. Gibbon, *Remedie*, sig. I3^r; Gibbens, *Qvestions*, 38, 97; Cope, *Exposition*, f. 78^r; Hooker, *Works*, 2:427; Cleaver, *Form*, 201; Henry Howard, "A Dutifull Defence," BL Lansdowne MS 813, ff. 33^V-34^r. Cf. Henoch Clapham, *A Briefe of the Bible* (1596), 33. The feminists used the propagating function to prove exactly the opposite point: "The Hennes should be serued first, which both lay the egs, & hatch the chickins." Anger, *Iane Anger*, 14.

12. George, *Mind*, 278; T. Smith, *De repvblica*, 12; Tilney, *Flower*, sig. E1^r; Hooker, *Works*, 2:429; Lemnie, *Touchstone*, f. 81^r.

13. Fenner, *Treatises*, 41; Perkins, *Treatise*, 626-27; Greenham, *Works*, 292. Cf. Thomas Morton, *A Treatise of the Threefolde State of Man* (1596), chap. 11. Morton was an Anglican.

14. Wilcox, *Prouerbs*, 32; Carpenter, *Preparatiue*, sig. $_2$D1^r; *A Womans Woorth*, trans. Anthony Gibson (1599), sig. D5^V; (cf. Bullinger, *State*, sig. A4^V); Cleaver, *Form*, 214, 221; *APC*, 15:368; Gibbens, *Qvestions*, 156; Dod, *Treatise*, pt. 2, ff. 1^V-2^r; Stockwood, *Bartholmew*, 83; Tilney, *Flower*, sigs. E1^V-E2^r; BL Lansdowne MS 101/41; Gifford, *Catechisme*, sig. G3^V; J. Rogers, *Summe*, ff. 13^V-14^r; Sandys, *Sermons*, 320; Knewstub, *Lectvres*, 129; Turnbull, *Iames*, f. 212^r; Greenham, *Works*, 292, 294; Smyth, *Berkeley Manuscripts*, 2:387.

15. Whitgift, *Works*, 3:590; *A Most Godly and Learned Sermon* (1589), sigs. B5^V-B6^r; Sandys, *Sermons*, 320; Greenham, *Works*, 292, Fenner, *Treatises*, 42; Fulke, *Text*, f. 322^V; H. Smith, *Preparatiue*, 84; Cleaver, *Form*, 82, 222-23.

16. Carpenter, *Remember Lots Wife* (1588), sig. H1^r; Chamberlain, *Letters*, 1:141; Babington, *Genesis*, 41; Thirsk, "The Family," *PP*, 27 (1964):121; W. Vaughan, *Golden-groue*, sig. O8^r; HMC 9 Salisbury, 4:113-14; Smyth, *Berkeley Manuscripts*, 2:253; Conyers Read, *Mr. Secretary Walsingham* (Cambridge, Mass., 1925), 3:422. Cf. Manningham's caustic comment: "Women, because they cannot have their wills when they dye, they will have their wills while they live." *Diary*, 92.

17. Hatton, *Memoirs*, 228; Notestein, *Studies*, 81; Weigall, *Quarterly Review*, 215:124, 137. *The Letters of Sir Francis Hastings*, ed. Claire Cross (Somerset Record Society, vol. 69), 62.

18. Thomas Drant, *Two Sermons Preached* [1570?], sig. D8^r; Sandys, *Sermons*, 186, 202, 320-21; Babington, *Genesis*, 24; Gibbens, *Qvestions*, 93, 155; Turnbull, *XV. Psalme*, f. 18^{r-V}; Whetstone, *Heptameron*, sigs. Y1^V-Y2^r; Wright, *Summons*, 55; Bentley, *Monvment*, 3:68; W. Vaughan, *Golden-groue*, sigs. O5^V-O6^r; Greenham, *Works*, 290, 295-98; H. Smith, *Preparatiue*, 81; Wilcox, *Prouerbs*, 34, 63, 148-51; Dod, *Treatise*, pt. 2, ff. 19^V-22^r; Allen, *Treasvrie*, 108, 125, 129, 137; Fenner, *Treatises*, 42-43; Estey, *Expositions*, pt. 1, f. 59^r; Cleaver, *Form*, 52-53, 82-87, 115, 175, 179; BL Add. MS 35,324, f. 18^r; Cooper, *Admoni-*

tion, 39, 56-57. Cf. Bullinger, *State*, sig. H8^V; Cope, *Exposition*, ff. 79^r, 100^V, 181^{r-v}, 632^V; Henoch Clapham, *Antidoton* (1600), 25. Women had also been prominent in medieval sects and continued to be so in the seventeenth century. Cf. C. Hill, *World*, 250.

19. Sandys, *Sermons*, 202: Wilcox, *Prouerbs*, 34; Field, *Godly Prayers and Meditations* (1601), sig. A12^r; (cf. Bullinger, *State*, sig. H8^V); H. Smith, *Preparatiue*, 81; Weigall, *Quarterly Review*, 215:125.

20. Sandys, *Sermons*, 321; Cleaver, *Form*, 87-89; Wilcox, *Prouerbs*, 149-52; Greenham, *Works*, 297.

21. Sandys, *Sermons*, 202, 317-19; Pilkington, *Works*, 33; Cooper, *Exposition*, sig. M7^V; Babington, *Genesis*, 127; Wright, *Display*, 25; Whetstone, *Heptameron*, sigs. I2^r, Y1^V; Tilney, *Flower*, sigs. B5^V, B8^r, C5^V-C6^r; Cleaver, *Form*, 92, 114, 168; H. Smith, *Preparatiue*, 38; Allen, *Treasvrie*, 128-29, 137; Estey, *Expositions*, pt. 1, f. 56^V; Fenner, *Treatises*, 40; Greenham, *Works*, 291, 295; Nicholas Bownde, *A Treatise Fvl of Consolation* (Cambridge, 1608), 113-15; Dod, *Treatise*, ff. 22^V-24^V; Gifford, *Catechisme*, sig. G3^V; W. Vaughan, *Golden-groue*, sigs. O4^V-O5^V; John Phillip, *An Epitaph on the Death, of . . . the Noble Earle of Southampton* [1581?]. Southampton was not a Puritan.

22. Cooper, ed., *Wentworth Papers*, 20-21, 29.

23. T. Smith, *De repvblica*, 104-5; W. Vaughan, *Golden-groue*, sig. O8^r; Becon, *Salue*, 169; Grosart, ed., *Towneley Hall MSS*, xli, xliii; Clay, ed., *Wills*, 42-43, 138, 169, 217-18, 227 *et passim*; Raine, ed., *Injunctions*, cxxxiv-cxxxix; Cooper, *Athenae*, 2:30, 187, 268, 336 *et passim*; Sisson, *Marriage*, 14; J. C. Hodgson, ed., *Wills and Inventories* (1906), 112:62-63, 102 *et passim*; Raine, ed., *Wills*, 2:269 *et passim*; A. Pearson, *Cartwright*, 483; Hogrefe, *Women*, 29-30; Collinson, *SCH*, 2:267. Other wills have been examined in Piccope, ed., *Wills*, vols. 33, 51, and 54; and Irvine, ed., *Collection*.

24. PRO STAC 7 Add. 11/23; *APC*, 12:351-52; 16:70-72; 17:49-50; 19:68-69; Whitelocke, *Liber*, 5. According to a 1544 statute women could not make wills unless they were single or widowed. Nevertheless, Anne Walsingham did in 1564. Hogrefe, *Women*, 30-31.

25. J. H. Baker, *An Introduction to English Legal History* (1971), 258-59; Cleaver, *Form*, 194-95; *APC*, 9:113; 10:209-10; 19:55; 20:181. If a husband died intestate, the widow received half of the estate if there were no children, or a third if there was at least one surviving child. Baker, *History*, 210.

26. Strype, *The Life of the Learned Sir Thomas Smith* (Oxford, 1820), 155; Piccope, ed., *Wills*, 51:282 (cf. 51:245); Young, *Mary Sidney*, 79; Chamberlain, *Letters*, 1:116.

27. Cope, *Exposition*, f. 633^V; Perkins, *Treatise*, 600-1; Fenner, *Treatises*, 43; Wilcox, *Prouerbs*, 149; Hogrefe, *Women*, 93; Jordan, *Forming*, 12.

28. Babington, *Genesis*, 232-33; Hooker, *Works*, 2:432; Cleaver, *Form*, 9, 53; Fenner, *Order*, sig. B2^V; *Treatises*, 34; H. Smith, *Preparatiue*, 59, 66, 68, 74-80; (cf. Notestein, *Studies*, 104-5).

29. Knappen, ed., *Diaries*, 80-81 (cf. 82-83); HL MS HA5349; Cross, *Earl*, 23, 75, 84, 143; Hoby, *Diary*, 62, 65, 66 (cf. 147); Francis Bacon, *Works*, ed. James Spedding *et al.*, 10 (1868):299; Cleaver, *Form*, 53. Bailey suggests the improving condition of women was possibly due to the impact of Renaissance humanism and "delayed 'romantic' influences." *Relation*, 203. Cf. L. Wright, *Culture*, 226-27. The improvement in the position of women continued in the New World under Puritan impetus. John Demos, *A Little Commonwealth* (New York, 1970), chap. 5. For the improved legal position see Richard B. Morris, *Studies in the History of American Law* (New York, 1930), chap. 3. Kathleen M. Davies argues that Puritan preachers were not advocating new ideals for marriage as a partnership, but were describing the best form of bourgeois marriage as they perceived it in practice. Yet if the preachers were motivated by example alone and not by biblical study, as seems highly improbable in the face of all the evidence, they could have found their examples among a much wider group than the "bourgeoisie." "The Sacred Condition of Equality—How Original Were Puritan Doctrines of Marriage?" *Social History*, 5 (1977):577.

30. Whetstone, *Heptameron*, sig. A4^r; Deloney, *Garland*, sig. D2^v; Cleaver, *Form*, 177-78; Sandys, *Sermons*, 101; Wither, *View*, 262.

31. BL Lansdowne MSS 7:78, 79; 15/24; HMC 69 Middleton, 536, 543-44, 549-53, 560, 582; BL Lansdowne MSS 46/30-33.

32. PRO SP 31/10 (f. 16^r); BL Lansdowne MSS 46/46; 94/20; HMC 8 Twelfth Report, 18; HMC 69 Middleton, 153; HMC 9 Salisbury, 152-53, 158-67; Williams, *Bess*, 161, 170, 174, 180-81, 193-94.

33. HMC 58 Bath, 4:161; HMC 29 Portland, 2:19 (cf. 19-20); HMC 69 Middleton, 589; HMC 9 Salisbury, 10:56; BL Lansdowne MSS 104/63-64; Manningham, *Diary*, 14, 157; (cf. PRO SP 175/15-16; *CSPD, Add. 1566-1579*, 33-34; *CSPD, 1581-1590*, 214; *APC*, 20:33); Hoby, *Diary*, 10-11; Cooper, *Athenae*, 2:83; Wiener, *JSH*, 8:43.

34. Stone, *Family*, 136; Cleaver, *Form*, 168; H. Smith, *Preparatiue*, 72-73; W. Vaughan, *Golden-groue*, sig. O5^r; (cf. Woolton, *Manual*, 10); *Quarter Sessions Records for Chester*, ed. Bennett and Dewhurst, 40; Hart, *Clergy*, 31; HMC 69 Middleton, 607; Tait, ed., *Records*, 123; *APC*, 19:313-14; Machyn, *Diary*, 301; Baker, *History*, 258; Holinshed, *Chronicles*, 4:262, 330.

35. Wilbraham, *Journal*, 18-19.

36. GB, note to Matt. 19:9.

37. MB, "A Table of the Pryncypall Matter;" GB, notes to Gen. 5:2, 20:3; 26:10; Esther 1:19; Luke 16:18; 1 Cor. 7:11; (cf. Deut. 24:1; Mal. 2:16; Matt. 19:8; Mark 10:11); BTB, notes to Matt. 19:3; Mark 10:5; Luke 16:18; 1 Cor. 7:10, 12.

38. Rheims NT, notes to Matt. 5:33; 19:9; Mark 10:9, 11; Luke 16:18; Rom. 7:2; 1 Cor. 7:11; Fulke, *Text*, ff. 9^v, 38^r, 273^r; Cartwright, *Confvtation*, 27, 349, 389. The Catholic position is also found in Vaux, *Catechisme*, f. 101^r; and Kellison, *Svrvey*, 625.

39. Arthur Winnett, *Divorce and Remarriage in Anglicanism* (1958), 32-34, 39, 52; Lewis Dibdin and Charles Healey, *English Church Law and Divorce* (1912), 49, 52, 55-57 (based on an examination of 850 ecclesiastical registers); Reginald Haw, *The State of Matrimony* (1952), 74-89; Bailey, *Relation*, 214. Pearson (*Elizabethans*, 303) claims the principles of the *Reformatio* were sometimes followed until 1602, but she offers no evidence. Winnet hypothesizes that many parish clergy permitted remarriage after divorce for adultery because some bishops and divines supported such a position. *Divorce*, 54. Cf. Powell, *Relations*, 76.

40. Winnett, *Divorce*, 60-61, 71-73; William Clerke, *The Triall of Bastardie* (1594); Manningham, *Diary*, 74; Dibdin and Healey, *Law*, 31; (cf. Gibbens, *Qvestions*, 100; Pilkington, *Works*, 45). The Georges missed the difference between Anglicans and Puritans on divorce. *Mind*, 271.

41. Dove, *Diuorcement*, sigs. A3^{r-v}, A5^{r-v}, A7^r, 16-17, 19, 23-26, 28-30, 34, 37, 40, 42-43, 47, 56-57; Strype, *Whitgift*, 3:379.

42. Cleaver, *Form*, 95-97, 122, 190-94, 229; Pagit, *Godly Sermon*, sigs. C5^v-C7^r; Kingsmill, *Viewe*, sig. K5^v; H. Smith, *Preparatiue*, 107-10; Becon, *Prayers*, ed. John Ayre (Cambridge, 1844), 532; (cf. Winnett, *Divorce*, 22-24); Estey, *Expositions*, pt. 1, f. 68^v; Perkins, *Oeconomie*, 101-20; Stockwood, *Fruiteful Sermon*, sig. I5^r; John Barthlet, *The Pedegrewe of Heretiques* (1566), f. 25^v; Wither, *View*, 31, 164; Haigh, *EHR*, 92:50. Cf. Winnett, *Divorce*, 83. The basic Puritan position is paralleled in Bullinger, *State*, sigs. K5^r, K6^r.

43. W. Vaughan, *Golden-groue*, sigs. O6^v-O7^v; Robert Hill, *The Contents of Scripture* (1596), 440-41; Winnett, *Divorce*, 80-83.

44. *Writings of Greenwood and Barrow (1591-93)*, 78, 80-82, 84; B. R. White, *The Engllish Separatist Tradition* (1971), 107-8, 110.

45. J. Rogers, *Displaying*, sig. I7^v; *APC*, 7:189-90.

46. *EEA*, 2:84; 3:157, 166 *et passim*; Cardwell, ed., *Synodalia*, 1:154-55. In 1573, seven doctors of civil law ruled that a woman whose husband committed adultery and was subse-

quently divorced by her according to ecclesiastical and civil law, was entitled to retain all lands and goods that she brought to the marriage. This presumably was a divorce *a mensa et thoro*. PRO SP 45 (f. 4^v). Some spouses, especially among the lower social orders, simply ran away and remarried, though Essex records reveal only one case of a deserting husband in the Elizabethan period. When John Reyton, curate of East Ham, was suspended for marrying a couple who already had spouses, he may have been victimized by two deserters. In any event, the more common course appears to have been separation *de facto* but not *de jure*. Some thirty cases of this type occurred in Elizabethan Essex, and normally the courts decreed that such couples be reconciled and cohabit. Stone, *Family*, 519-20; Emmison, *Elizabethan Life*, 2:161, 164, 167; Houlbrooke, *Courts*, 69.

47. Winnett, *Divorce*, 46-47; Usher, ed., *Movement*, 29.

48. Furnivall, *Child-Marriages*, 73-76; W. Jones, *Chancery*, 394-95. In his diary, William Ashcombe reported in 1612 that it was believed Lady Essex used a conjuror, enchantments, and brass engravings to bewitch the earl into being impotent toward her, and thus have their marriage annulled. HL MS 30,665, f. 5^r.

49. Stone, *Crisis*, 655-56; PRO STAC 7 Add. 15/49.

50. Dibdin and Healey, *Law*, 83-92.

51. Marchant, *Church*, 241-42; Furnivall, *Child-Marriages*, 31-34; PRO Req. 2/31/3; *APC*, 7:391; 14:86, 88-89; 19:448; 20:59. Cf. Houlbrooke, *Courts*, 68-69. The most enigmatical case of a husband's refusal to pay the stipulated annuity that came before the Privy Council involved George Puttenham and Lady Windsor, a former widow. *APC*, 9:39-40, 96, 107, 144, 148; 10:355-56, 375, 435; 11:129-30, 188-89, 299; 13:93, 162, 203-4. In a bizarre case in the Court of Requests, the bishop of Limerick countersued his divorced wife to stop her from obtaining her annuity on the grounds that she had remarried; she steadfastly denied this. PRO Req. 2/51/45.

52. PRO SP 40/45 (f. 98^r), 40/46 (f. 100^r); BL Lansdowne MSS 12/1, 76; 34/7; 101/37, 41; (cf. 61/50); Manningham, *Diary*, 79; HMC 77 De L'Isle, 2:421. Essex ecclesiastical records in this period show two cases where divorce *a vinculo matrimonii* occurred, with the remainder being judicial separations. Although a number of instances are documented in this county of husbands beating wives unreasonably (by Elizabethan standards), separation for cruelty was rare. Emmison, *Elizabethan Life*, 2:162, 168. Machyn reports that in August 1559 a minister was punished in London for marrying a couple that had been previously wed, apparently to others without a subsequent divorce *ab initio*. *Diary*, 207. Some separations were effected by unhappy in-laws; see, e.g., PRO STAC 7 Add. 9/2, detailing how Richard Warde's wife was spirited away by her relatives while he was rendering military service in the Netherlands.

53. HMC 58 Bath, 4:155-56.

54. Allen, *Treasvrie*, 120.

55. Cleaver, *Form*, 346.

56. Tyndale, Pentateuch (1530, 1534), notes to Exod. 13; Deut. 4, 6; MB (1537, 1551), note to Deut. 4; Taverner Bible, note to Deut. 4; Matthew-Becke Bible (1549, 1551), note to Deut. 4; GB, notes to Gen. 30:30; Exod. 10:2; Deut. 6:7; 13:6; 22:6; Josh. 7:24; 2 Kings 10:6; Job 5:4; Pss. 37:25; 109:14; 127 (synopsis); Prov. 11:29; Isa. 65:7; Jer. 9:14; 32:18; Ezek. 18:2, 13; 1 Cor. 7:38; Eph. 6:4; Col. 3:21; 2 Tim. 2:4.

57. BB, notes to Gen. 4:2; 17:26; 18:19; 34:6; BTB, notes to Eph. 6:4; Col. 3:21.

58. Stone, *Crisis*, 591; Hooker, *Works*, 1:242; W. Vaughan, *Golden-groue*, sigs. R7^v-R8^r; Perkins, *Treatise*, 627; T. Rogers, *Chaine*, sig. A4^r; Nowell, *Catechism*, 131; Greenham, *Works*, 164; *APC*, 16:130-31.

59. Bunny, *Summe*, f. 63^v; Allen, *Treasvrie*, 127; Hake, *Touchestone*, sig. D4^v; William Kempe, *The Education of Children* (1588), sig. F1^r; Stubbes, *Anatomie*, sig. F7^r; Woolton,

Manual, 103-4; Estey, *Expositions*, pt. 1, ff. 55^V-56^r; W. Vaughan, *Golden-groue*, sig. O8^V; Allen, *Garden*, 125; (cf. John Bradford, *Two Notable Sermons* [1574], sig. E3^r).

60. Allen, *Treasvrie*, 135; Shelford, *Lectvres*, 34-37; Udall, *A Commentarie vpon the Lamentations* (1595), 163-64; Cleaver, *Form*, 243; R. Rogers, *Treatises*, 169; Dod, *Treatise*, pt. 2, f. 9^{r-v}; Turnbull, *XV. Psalme*, f. 18^V; Bunny, *Summe*, f. 63^V; Gibbon, *Praise*, 54; Cooper, ed., *Wentworth Papers*, 21. One aspect of this vocational training was placing sons in service. Cf. Lady Anne Stanhope's offer of her youngest son Michael to Burghley in 1572. She had already placed her other sons in service. BL Lansdowne MS 14/88.

61. Gibbon, *Remedie*, sig. I3^r; W. Vaughan, *Golden-groue*, sig. O8^V; Mulcaster, *Positions*, 291; H. Smith, *Preparatiue*, 101; Carpenter, *Preparatiue*, 308; Gifford, *A Godlie, Zealous, and Profitable Sermon* (1582), sig. D7^r; *Catechisme*, sig. G3^{r-v}; Estey, *Expositions*, pt. 1, f. 56^r; Wilcox, *Prouerbs*, 7, 21; Jewel, *Works*, 2:835; Udall, *Certaine Sermons*, sig. $_2$S7^V; Pilkington, *Works*, 26.

62. Manningham, *Diary*, 101; R. Rogers, *Treatises*, 108; W. Vaughan, *Golden-groue*, sig. O8^V; A. Hill, *Crie*, 88; Kempe, *Education*, sigs. E3^V-E4^r; Bullinger, *State*, sig. I6^r; Shelford, *Lectvres*, 2, 4-5, 8-9; Hake, *Touchestone*, sig. D4^r.

63. Greenham, *Works*, 163; Collins, *Life*, 71; Kempe, *Education*, sig. F1^r; Hake, *Touchestone*, sigs. C3^V-C4^r, D4^{r-v}; Cleaver, *Form*, 251. Burghley's comment underscores the contemporary shift of opinion in England and France toward regarding children as unique instead of as miniature adults. Among the works responsible for this shift were Thomas Phaire's *The Boke of Chyldren* (1544) and John Jones' *The Arte and Science of Preserving Bodie and Soule* (1579), which have been identified as the first two books on pediatrics written in English. Boyd M. Berry, "The First English Pediatricians and Tudor Attitudes Toward Childhood," *Journal of the History of Ideas*, 35 (1974):561-64. Cf. also M. J. Tucker, "The Child as Beginning and End: Fifteenth and Sixteenth Century English Childhood," in *The History of Childhood*, ed. Lloyd deMause (New York, 1974), 230, 233, 252. Yet children continued to be dressed as diminutive adults and in accord with their parents' social status. Ivy Pinchbeck and Margaret Hewitt, *Children in English Society* (1969), 21. It is now clear that an awareness of the special nature of childhood was also developing in France by the seventeenth century. David Hunt, *Parents and Children in History* (1970), 190, which supplants the contrary view of Philippe Ariès, *Centuries of Childhood*, trans. Robert Baldick (New York, 1962), 128. The medieval tendency to see children as miniature adults was undoubtedly furthered by the practice among the lower orders of making children part of the productive household economy after their seventh birthday. Cf. Barbara A. Hanawalt, "Childrearing among the Lower Classes of Late Medieval England," *Journal of Interdisciplinary History*, 8 (1977):18-19, 21-22.

64. Walsall, *Sermon*, sig. A5^V; Smyth, *Berkeley Manuscripts*, 2:253; Piccope, ed., *Wills*, 33:142; 54:87-90; Clay, ed., *Wills*, 14, 36, 129; LPL Bacon MS 650/7 (f. 10^r).

65. Bunny, *Summe*, f. 63^V; Dod, *Treatise*, pt. 2, ff. 9^V-11^r; Cleaver, *Form*, 328; W. Vaughan, *Golden-groue*, sig. O8^V; Perkins, *A Salve for a Sicke Man* (Cambridge, 1595), 81, 84; Allen, *Garden*, 123-25; Jewel, *Works*, 2:835; Stubbes, *Anatomie*, sig. J7^V; Gifford, *Eight Sermons* (1589), f. 118^r; (cf. Cope, *Exposition*, f. 249^r).

66. Cleaver, *Form*, 341, 343-44; BL Lansdowne MS 67/1-4; Gerard, *Autobiography*, 83; Emerson, *Puritanism*, 102; *APC*, 17:75; 19:232-33; 20:229; Cooper, ed., *Wentworth Papers*, 21; (cf. Newnham, *Nightcrowe*, 20, 41). The Lancashire gentleman Alexander Barlow refused to aid his Catholic daughter Jane when she went to the Continent. She found herself living on handouts from the poor in 1583. PRO SP 158/13 (f. 23^r).

67. Hogrefe, *Women*, 16; Notestein, *Studies*, 84-85; Stone, *Crisis*, 591; *Family*, 167-78; Pinchbeck and Hewitt, *Children*, 1:14-16; Levin Schücking, *The Puritan Family*, trans. Brian Battershaw (New York, 1970), 72; McMullen, "Status," 143. Alan Macfarland also places

more emphasis on love in Elizabethan families than Stone posits. See his review of Stone in *History and Theory*, 28 (1979):106-7.

68. Manningham, *Diary*, 32; Greenham, *Works*, 46-47, 122; Norden, *Solace*, f. 129^V; Shelford, *Lectvres*, 39-43; Dering, *Workes*, f. 6^V; Bownde, *Treatise*, 113, 140; Newnham, *Nightcrowe*, 2. Cope warned that mothers must "take heed of being too much doted ouer their children, but . . . shew themselues graue and make them feare them. For it hapneth oftentimes, that children, which are cockered, and brought vp tenderly, worke most woe to their mothers." *Exposition*, f. 402^V.

69. Holles, *Memorials*, 45; PRO SP 23/3-5, 15, 24 (ff. 3^r-7^r, 33^r, 60^r); Tittler, *Bacon*, 155-56; HMC 71 Finch, 1:22.

70. Miles Mosse, *The Arraignment and Conviction of Vsvrie* (1595), 4; Vaux, *Catechisme*, ff. 47^V-48^r; Cleaver, *Form*, 243; Pilkington, *Works*, 219-20; Holland, *An Exposition of the First and Second Chapter of Iob* (1596), 125; Greenham, *Works*, 162-63 (cf. 122); John Barker, *A Balade* [1561]; (cf. Cooper, *Copie*, sig. C2^V; Newnham, *Nightcrowe*, 1; Cope, *Exposition*, ff. 467^{r-V}, 614^V).

71. Vaux, *Catechisme*, f. 50^V; Shelford, *Lectvres*, 39-43; Babington, *Genesis*, 22, 163; *Commaundements*, 222; John Bridges, *A Sermon Preached at Paules Crosse* [1571], 103; Jewel, *Works*, 2:836; J. Rogers, *Summe*, f. 13^V. Cf. Carr, *Fal*, sig. D4^V.

72. Perkins, *Chaine*, sigs. K2^V-K3^r; H. Smith, *A Harmonie* (1592), 63; Becon, *Postil*, pt. 2, f. 51^r; Burton, *The Rowsing of the Slvggard*, in *Works*, 509; *Wooing*, 258; Knewstub, *Lectvres*, 86; Cleaver, *Form*, 44, 46-50, 52; Bownde, *Treatise*, 93-94 (cf. 59, 94, 110); W. Vaughan, *Golden-groue*, sigs. X8^V-Y1^r; Fenner, *Treatises*, 27, 46-47; Wilcox, *Prouerbs*, 63, 107, 112; Greenham, *Works*, 23-24, 162-63. Cf. Bird, *Hebrewes*, 43-44; Peter Moffett, *A Commentarie vpon the Booke of the Prouerbs of Salomon* (1592), 163; Stone, *Family*, 175-76.

73. Mulcaster, *Positions*, 282-83; Kempe, *Education*, sig. F1^V. It has been persuasively argued that, psychologically, the authoritarian behavior of parents, including the severity of punishments, was an expression of the desire for autonomy that had been frustrated in childhood by the requirement of deferential behavior. This may in turn have been reinforced by the determination of parents to subordinate the wills of their children even as their own wills were continually being subordinated in the socio-political hierarchy. Stone, *Family*, 177-78. Hill argues that the rigorous insistence of the clerics on patriarchal authority suggests that such authority was not as accepted as they would have liked. This is true, given the high ideals the clerics sought. *Econ. H. R.*, 2nd ser., 31:461.

74. Machyn, *Diary*, 311; M. St. Clare Byrne, *Elizabethan Life in Town and Country* (1961), 215; Knappen, ed., *Diaries*, 103.

75. Dod, *Treatise*, pt. 2, f. 33^l.

76. Nowell, *Catechism*, 196.

77. MB, "A Table of the Pryncypall Matters," note to Exod. 20; Tyndale-Coverdale NT (1538), note to Luke 14; Taverner Bible, notes to Exod. 20; Rom. 12; Matthew-Becke Bibles (1549, 1551), note to Exod. 20; Tyndale Pentateuch (1551), note to Exod. 20; GB, notes to Gen. 9:25; Exod. 20:12; Deut. 5:16; 21:21; 1 Sam. 22:8; 2 Sam. 18:9; 1 Kings 15:13; Ps. 78:6; Prov. 31:28; Ezek. 20:18; Tob. 4:3; Luke 2:49; 9:59; Col. 3:20; 1 Pet. 2:18.

78. BB, notes to Gen. 44:34; 46:29; Exod. 20:12; Deut. 5:16; BTB, notes to Matt. 10:37; 15:4; Luke 2:48; 9:59; Eph. 6:1; 1 Tim. 5:4; Rheims NT, notes to Matt. 8:22; 10:37; Mark 7:11; Luke 2:61. The agreement is underscored by explicit affirmations of the Protestant acceptance of such Rheims notes as Matt. 10:37; Luke 3:51; 14:26. Cartwright, *Confvtation*, 48, 170; Wither, *View*, 70.

79. Babington, *Genesis*, 342; *Commaundements*, 226-28; Bunny, *Summe*, ff. 52^V, 55^r; Sandys, *Sermons*, 279; Pilkington, *Works*, 24, 101; Turnbull, *XV. Psalme*, f. 18^V; *Iames*, f. 249^r; A. Hill, *Crie*, 89; Nowell, *Catechism*, 130; Cooper, ed., *Wentworth Papers*, 13. Cf.

William Horne, *A Christian Exercise* [1580?], sig. B4^r; John Gibson, *An Easie Entrance* (1579), sig. A4^r.

80. Dering, *Catechisme*, sig. A8^r; Becon, *Postil*, pt. 1, f. 84^V; *Salue*, 217; Greenham, *Works*, 120-21, 123, 413-14; Norden, *Solace*, f. 128^r; Stockwood, *Bartholmew*, 26-27, 33; Perkins, *Treatise*, 395, 542; *Chaine*, sig. I7^{r-v}; Fenner, *Treatises*, 54, 59; Allen, *Treasvrie*, 121, 129-30; Wilcox, *Prouerbs*, 62; Cleaver, *Form*, 343, 353; Shutte, *Forme*, sig. C1^{r-v}; W. Vaughan, *Golden-groue*, sigs. P1^r, P2^V, S8^V-T1^r; Dod, *Treatise*, pt. 2, ff. 3^r, 5^{r-v}; Estey, *Expositions*, pt. 1, ff. 55^{r-v}, 58^r; Gifford, *Catechisme*, sig. G2^r; R. Jones, *Catechisme*, sig. B2^V; Alexander Gee, *The Grovnd of Christianitie* (1584), 4; R. Rogers, *Treatises*, 169.

81. Vaux, *Catechisme*, ff. 44^V-46^r; Shelford, *Lectvres*, 43-44.

82. Barrow, *Writings (1587-90)*, 545; Penry, *Notebook*, 83, 85; Clapham, *Antidoton*, 25.

83. LPL Bacon MS 652/102 (f. 150^{r-v}); Anstruther, *Vaux*, 101; HMC 9 Salisbury, 1 :474; HMC 80 Sackville, 1:28-30; Piccope, ed., *Wills*, 51:109.

84. *APC*, 14:38, 169-72, 178; Cooper, ed., *Wentworth Papers*, 33; BL Lansdowne MSS 67/41; 83/2-3, 18; HMC 9 Salisbury, 4:555-56. A case before the Staffordshire Quarter Sessions in September 1589 involved a son who refused to allow his mother the use of her own goods and physically beat her. *Staffordshire Sessions Rolls*, ed. Burne, 1:341-42.

85. Furnivall, *Child-Marriages*, 173; *APC*, 18:200-1; Brinkworth, ed., *Court*, 85, 91; MacCaffrey, *Exeter*, 93.

86. Greaves, *SCJ*, 7:100; Walzer, *Revolution*, 185; Stone, *Crisis*, 591; (cf. Trigge, *Tovchstone*, 300; Estey, *Expositions*, pt. 1, f. 57^r).

87. Hooker, *Works*, 2:319.

88. Machyn, *Diary*, 242. Harold was minister of St. Olave's, Southwark, in 1560.

89. Aveling, *Recusancy*, 70; B. M. Berry and R. S. Schofield, "Age at Baptism in Pre-Industrial England," *PS*, 25 (1971):456; C. Hill, *Economic Problems*, 168; J. Charles Cox, *Churchwardens' Accounts* (1913), 58.

90. Young, *Mary Sidney*, 43-44; Machyn, *Diary*, 198, 216, 248, 264, 277, 288-89; Gawdy, *Letters*, 124.

91. PRO SP 105/65 (f. 143^{r-v}). In the countryside gifts were often food. Cf. Emmison, *Tudor Food and Pastimes* (1964), 53-54 (which cites a 1548 example).

92. Machyn, *Diary*, 198, 216, 242, 248-49, 264, 288-89, 300, 305; Strype, *Parker*, 1:30; 2:337; Bunny, *Summe*, f. 61^V; Hooker, *Works*, 2:304-37; Whitgift, *Works*, 3:118 ff.; Gilby, *Dialogve*, sig. M5^r. For Anglican and Puritan views on the theological aspects of baptism, see New, *Anglican*, 64-70.

93. Pilkington, *Works*, 216-17; Cleaver, *Form*, 244-45; Fenner, *Treatises*, 49; Wyot, *Diaries*, ed. Ponsonby, 106.

94. *EEA*, 2:49, 92, 114, 125; 3:144, 172, 206-7, 211-12, 351.

Chapter 7: The Household

1. W. Vaughan, *Golden-groue*, sig. N7^V.

2. Nichols, *An Order of Hovshold Instrvction* (1596), sig. B6^r.

3. R. Rogers, *Treatises*, 397; Cleaver, *Form*, sig. A4^V, 139; Stockwood, *1578 Sermon*, 98-99; Becon, *Worckes*, f. 565^V; *Postil*, pt. 2, f. 137^V; John Knox, *Works*, ed. David Laing (New York, repr. ed., 1966), 4:137; Nichols, *Order*, sig. B3^V; Udall, *Demonstration*, 2; Burton, *God Wooing*, *Works*, 258; Shelford, *Lectvres*, 83; Pilkington, *Works*, 64; Perkins, *Catholike*, 961. Cleaver developed the analogy of the household as a commonwealth; *Form*, 1. The introduction to the *Commons Journals* for the reign of James I states that the family is the origin of the state. C. Hill, *Society and Puritanism* (2nd ed.; New York, 1967), 459. I am not entirely persuaded by Alan Macfarlane's innovative argument that the individual rather

than the household was the basic social unit by 1400. *The Origins of English Individualism* (Oxford, 1978), *passim*, Applied only to the rural folk below the gentry level (as Macfarlane does), the idea may have merit, but it does not explain the structure of the higher social orders.

4. GB, notes to Gen. 17:23; 18:19; 43:23; Deut. 4:9; 6:20; 21:18; 1 Chron. 16:43; BB, notes to Gen. 17:13; 43:23; BTB, note to Acts 10:2.

5. Fenner, *Treatises*, 8; *Order*, pt. 3, sig. A2^r; Allen, *Treasvrie*, 107; Gifford, *Declaration*, sig. A1^v; Greenham, *Works*, 166; Stockwood, *1578 Sermon*, 69-70; Chaderton, *Excellent Sermon*, sig. C5^r; (cf. Robert Openshaw, *Short Questions* [1580], sig. A2^{r-v}); *Writings of Greenwood and Barrow (1591-93)*, 424, 430.

6. Usher, ed., *Movement*, 99-100; Stockwood, *Fruiteful Sermon*, sigs. D7^v-D8^r; Norden, *Solace*, ff. 125^v-126^v; Cleaver, *Form*, 9-10, 13-14, 21-22; Becon, *Postil*, pt. 2, ff. 55^v-56^r; Bownde, *The Doctrine of the Sabbath* (1595), 260.

7. *EEA*, 2:93-94, 119, 127-28; 3:346; HMC 9 Salisbury, 1:306; Mary Bateson, ed., *Records of the Borough of Leicester* (Cambridge, 1905), 3:101, 118, 162, 185, 242, 421. Cornish justices ordered in 1598 that each householder see that his children and servants did not frequent alehouses or play unlawful games. HMC 9 Salisbury, 7:161.

8. BL Lansdowne MS 86/45; Openshaw, *Questions*, sig. A5^v; William Chub, *A Frvitfvll Sermon* (1587), sig. A2^v; Brinkworth, ed., *Court*, 82-83; PRO SP 165/28 (ff. 88^v-89^r); 175/21; 235/16 (f. 47^r).

9. Sandys, *Sermons*, 3, 264; Hooker, *Works*, 2:64; Curteys, *Two Sermons*, sig. F8^v; Grindal, *Remains*, 124-25, 161-62; Whitgift, *Works*, 1:336 ff.; 3:610; Shelford, *Lectvres*, 83, 104.

10. Dent, *Path-way*, 348; Bownde, *Doctrine*, 61; Shutte, *Sermon*, sig. D6^{r-v}; Trigge, *A Trve Catholiqve* (1602), 549-50; R. Jones, *Catechisme*, sig. A2^{r-v}; Nichols, *Order*, sigs. B4^v, B5^r, B7^r-C1^v, C4^r-C6^v, D1^{r-v}, E2^r; Dering, *Catechisme*, sig. G3^r; Fenner, *Order*, pt. 3, sig. A3^r; E. Vaughan, *Introductions*, sig. A7^r; Stockwood, *Fruiteful Sermon*, sig. E3^r. Puritan ministers in Lancashire often failed to catechize in the churches, largely owing to the onerous nature of their duties. In such cases, catechizing in the household was even more crucial. Haigh, *EHR*, 92:35-36.

11. Stone, "Rise," 30; Sparke, *Catechisme*, sig. E2^v; Allen, *An Alphabet of the Holy Proverbs of King Salomon* (1596), sig. A7^v; Stockwood, *A Short Catechisme* (3rd ed., 1583), sigs. A2^v-A3^r; BL Egerton MS 2713, f. 175^r. The impact of Protestant catechisms before the Marian era was noted by Bishop Edmund Bonner: "Of late daies, the youth of this realme hath ben nouseled with vngodlie Catechismes, and pernicious euil doctrine." Thus Bonner prepared his own catechism to be used by all schoolmasters and tutors in the diocese of London. *An Honest Godlye Instruction* (1556), sig. A2^r. See also Foster Watson, *The English Grammar Schools to 1660* (New York, 1970 ed.), 69-85.

12. Bateson, ed., *Records*, 3:183; Usher, ed., *Movement*, 99; Hoby, *Diary*, 48, 66; Ward, *Diaries*, ed. Knappen, 111.

13. Estey, *Expositions*, pt. 2, f. 108^r; R. Rogers, *Treatises*, 335, 367, 396; Perkins, *A Warning* (Cambridge, 1601), 266, 268-71; Cleaver, *Form*, 35-36, 39, 41; Dent, *Path-way*, 274.

14. BL Lansdowne MS 86/45: Openshaw, *Questions*, sig. A5^v; Strype, *Aylmer*, 54; Thomas Nelson, *A Memorable Epitaph . . . for . . . Sir Frauncis Walsingham* (1590); James Tait, "The Declaration of Sports for Lancashire (1617)," *EHR*, 32 (1917): 567; Bownde, *Treatise*, sig. π3^r; John Carpenter, *Time Complaining* [1588], sig. A3^r; Pagit, *The Historie of the Bible* (1613; 1st pub. 1602), sig. π2^{r-v}; PRO SP 165/28 (ff. 87^r, 88^v-89^r).

15. Whitgift, *Works*, 1:211; Bateson, ed., *Original Letters*, 9; Gifford, *Fovre Sermons*, 6; Sparke, *Sermon at Cheanies*, 79; Batho, ed., *Household Papers*, xx.

16. Wood, *Letters*, 21; Crowley, *Opening*, sig. C1^V; Barrow, *Writings (1587-90)*, 489; Harward, *Sermons*, sigs. B7^V, B8^V-C1^V; Bancroft, *Survay*, 98.

17. HMC 9 Salisbury, 1:306, 308; Bateson, ed., *Original Letters*, 19-20, 35; Stockwood, *1578 Sermon*, 94-95; Field, *Prayers*, sig. L4^r; Rowse, *England*, 450. The letters of Cox and Scambler are essentially identical.

18. *CJ*, 1:86; Raine, *History*, 76-77; *EEA*, 2:57, 74, 98; 3:163, 207; HMC 9 Salisbury, 4:510-11.

19. Stone, *Crisis*, 739; BL Lansdowne MS 21/17; Patrick McGrath, *Papists and Puritans Under Elizabeth I* (New York, 1967), 107; Alfred Mumford, *The Manchester Grammar School* (1919), 29; Stockwood, *1578 Sermon*, 95-96; Gerard, *Autobiography*, 1.

20. Bossy, "The Character of Elizabethan Catholicism," *PP*, 21 (1962):39-47; Gerard, *Autobiography*, 161-63; Anstruther, *Vaux*, 113. Cf. McGrath, *Papists*, 258-66, 380-83; James, *Family*, 144.

21. Richardson, *Puritanism*, 93-94, 105; William Trimble, *The Catholic Laity in Elizabethan England* (Cambridge, Mass., 1964), 234. Richardson suggests that "the logical culmination of this emphasis on family religion was . . . Independency, and the clergy by their constant advocacy of household devotions were unconsciously, but in a very real way nonetheless, tending to undermine their own position." *Puritanism*, 91. Elizabethan Catholicism too was a household religion, but for different reasons. Whereas Catholics resorted to the household as the most viable means of preserving an embattled faith and sought to accord the professional clergy an important role in it, Puritans stressed increased lay participation in the religious activities of the household, partly to supplement (or perhaps even counteract) the religious observances in parish churches. In this sense there is merit in Richardson's thesis.

22. Udall, *Demonstration*, 77.

23. Holland, *Spiritvall Preservatives* (1593), sig. A8^r.

24. Sandys, *Sermons*, 265; Greenham, *Works*, 163-64; George, *Mind*, 276; Whetstone, *Heptameron*, sig. Y1^r; Bownde, *Treatise*, 152; Mildmay, *Memorial*, [2]; Cleaver, *Form*, 7.

25. BB, note to Gen. 18:6; R. Abbot, *Exaltation*, 37; Stockwood, *1578 Sermon*, 83; R. Rogers, *Treatises*, 256; Shutte, *Forme*, sig. B1^r; Boorde, *Regimente*, sig. B6^{r-v}; Babington, *Commaundements*, 195; Cleaver, *Form*, 5.

26. Clapham, in *Elizabeth*, ed. Read, 82; William Elderton, *An Epytaphe vppon . . . I. Iuell* (1571); Smyth, *Berkeley Manuscripts*, 2:420; Carpenter, *Report*, 26:171.

27. Sandys, *Sermons*, 270; Fenner, *Treatises*, 23; Stockwood, *1578 Sermon*, 71; Openshaw, *Questions*, sigs. A3^V-A4^r; Strype, *Whitgift*, 3:158; *Parker*, 2:442; John Gerard, *Autobiography*, trans. Philip Caraman (1951), 29; *Hastings Letters*, 3-5.

28. Stone, "Rise," 13-14, 49-54; *Crisis*, 591; L. Pearson, *Elizabethans*, 385, 436; HMC 9 Salisbury, 1:372. The extended (kin-oriented) family continued to thrive in the Elizabethan era, especially among wealthy landed families and in areas of low mobility, such as the upland region of Durham. See James, *Family*, 24-26. James uses wills to trace the continuation of the extended family. In 1587, for example, Robert Claxton, a gentleman of Old Park, Durham, bequeathed gifts to four grandchildren, two brothers-in-law, nine cousins, three sons, and six daughters. In *Family*, 195-99, Stone recognizes that there were "strong countervailing forces" mitigating the "trend towards greater patriarchy in husband-wife relations . . . so that the picture is by no means clear."

29. Laslett, *PS*, 23:204; Batho, ed., *Household Papers*, xxi, xxiii; Mary Finch, *The Wealth of Five Northamptonshire Families* (Oxford, 1956), 81, 123, appendix 4; Smyth, *Berkeley Manuscripts*, 2:364; (cf. Anstruther, *Vaux*, 150); Cliffe, *Gentry*, 385; Hoby, *Diary*, 40; Weigall, *Quarterly Review*, 215:134-35; Campbell, *Yeoman*, 255; Strype, *Aylmer*, 127; C. Hill, *Economic Problems*, 40. Sir Richard Cholmley "never took a journey to

London that he was not attended with less than thirty, sometimes forty men-servants, though he went without his lady." Cholmley, *Memoirs*, 6.

30. Brinkworth, ed., *Court*, 2, 98; PRO SP 175/92; Kent, *BIHR*, 46:55-56.

31. Neale, *Parliaments*, 2:396-99.

32. Mulcaster, *Positions*, 178.

33. Hergest, *Rvle*, 4.

34. Cleaver, *Form*, 168-69, 225; Tilney, *Flower*, sigs. E2^V-E3^r, E4^{r-v}; Bullein, *Bulwarke*, pt. 1, f. 4^r; Becon, *Salue*, 218-19; Babington, *A Briefe Conference* (1583), 111; *Genesis*, 251; Sandys, *Sermons*, 321; Cope, *Exposition*, f. 100^{r-v} (cf. ff. 630^V, 631^V, 636^V-637^r; Bullinger, *State*, sig. I2^r).

35. Stubbes, *Glasse*, sig. A2^{r-v}; William Harrison, *A Brief Discovrse* (1602), 2; Dickens, ed., *Clifford Letters* (Durham, 1962), 146; Rye, *England*, 72. Katherine Brettergh was the wife of the Lancashire gentleman William Brettergh; she died in May 1601.

36. BTB, note to 1 Tim. 2:12; Whitgift, *Works*, 2:499-504; 3:5; Wright, *Summons*, 55; H. Smith, *Sermon*, 16-17; Hatton, *Memoirs*, 309-10; Grindal, *Remains*, 288-89; *Zurich Letters*, ed. Robinson, 201-2; Penry, *Notebook*, 54 (cf. 55, 79).

37. BL Lansdowne MSS 43/48; 68/58; 115/55 (a slightly different copy of 43/48).

38. Leys, *Catholics*, 179; BL Lansdowne MS 76/90; LPL Bacon MS 659/52 (f. 69^V); Hogrefe, *Women*, 79-80; *APC*, 12:244, 332; John Bossy, *The English Catholic Community 1570-1850* (1975), 154-55. Cf. Bossy, *PP*, 21:40.

39. Dickens, *TRHS*, 13:62; Collinson, *SCH*, 2:260-61, 269; *Mirror*, 28-29; BL Egerton MS 2812 (most of ff. 2^V-134^V).

40. Bossy also suggests that some gentlewomen preferred an alliance with an authoritative priest to the domestic authority vested in a husband by Protestants, and that those who were illiterate reacted negatively to the implication in conservative Protestantism that literacy was a condition of salvation. *Community*, 158.

41. Fulke, *A Comfortable Sermon* (1574); Bulkeley, *A Sermon Preached . . . at Bletsoe* (1586), sig. A5^r; Hoby, *Diary*, 57; Gifford, *Eight Sermons*; Knewstub, *Lectvres*; Perkins, *The Right Way of Dying Well, ad cal. How to Live* (Cambridge, 1601); *Salve*; Estey, *Expositions*; Babington, *Conference*; Thomas Lant, *Daily Exercises of a Christian* (1584); Morton, *Treatise*.

42. BL Egerton MS 2713 (ff. 220^r, 223^r); Collinson, *Puritan Movement*, 338.

43. W. Harrison, *Discovrse*, 8-9; *Deaths Advantage* (2nd ed., 1602), 79-80; W. Leygh, *The Sovles Solace* (1602), 70; Hoby, *Diary*, 62-63, 67, 80 *passim*; *Zurich Letters*, ed. Robinson, 172-73; A. Clifford, *Lives*, 19; Weigall, *Quarterly Review*, 215:125.

44. McIntosh, *Proceedings*, 119:240; BL Royal MS 17 B. XVIII; Hogrefe, *Women*, 86, 124; Anne Prowse's epistle to Jean Taffin, *Of the Markes of the Children of God* (1590), sigs. A3^V-A4^r; Beauchamp, "Women," 3; Ruth Hughey, "Cultural Interests of Women in England from 1524 to 1640 Indicated in the Writings of the Women," Ph.D. diss., Cornell University (1932), unpaginated tables.

45. Young, *Mary Sidney*, 53-55, 133, 135; Smyth, *Berkeley Manuscripts*, 2:385; Mulcaster, *Positions*, 168, 177; Hughey, "Interests," unpaginated tables. For a fuller account of Pembroke's literary work, including translations of Petrarch, Mornay, and Robert Garnier, see Hogrefe, *Women of Action*, 129-34.

46. Hoby, *Diary*, 62; Clay, ed., *Wills*, 177; (cf. Richardson, *Puritanism*, 179). Sarah J. Renner reports that the marital partnership developed in the course of raising children and working for the family's welfare more than through intellectual pursuits. But the Puritan emphasis on the religious activities of the wife and mother in the home in the Elizabethan period provided further impetus to the practice of marriage as a partnership, for wives shared with husbands the spiritual and intellectual responsibilities for the family's religious

duties. "The Impact of Protestantism on the Renaissance Ideal of Women in Tudor England" (Ph.D. diss., University of Nebraska, 1977).

47. Weigall, *Quarterly Review*, 215:134; LPL Bacon MS 647/39 (f. 90^V); Hoby, *Diary*, 14, 67, 71, 77, 80, 85, 87-88, 94, 100, 109, 111, 124-25, 130, 136, 147-50, 153, 178, 187, 189; Smyth, *Berkeley Manuscripts*, 2:254, 386-87; HMC 9 Salisbury, 1:372.

48. Hoby, *Diary*, 75-76, 90-91, 111, 121-23, 134, 137, 140, 154, 167, 178, 182, 187-88; Rye, ed., *England*, 72.

49. Hogrefe, *Women*, 27; Weigall, *Quarterly Review*, 215:125; Thomas Jones, ed., *A True Relation of the Life and Death of . . . William Bedell* (1872), 2; A. Clifford, *Lives*, 20; Hoby, *Diary*, 72, 86, 100-3, 184.

50. Arber, *List*; Hogrefe, *Women*, 50, 52; Young, *Mary Sidney*, 28; Theodore Rabb, *Enterprise & Empire* (Cambridge, Mass., 1967), 225, 233-410; LPL Bacon MS 657/46 (f. 61^r), 657/88 (f. 133^{r-v}); Robert Dudley, *Correspondence*, ed., John Bruce (1844), 183. All figures on female investors are mine, based on the raw data provided by Rabb. In some cases sex is not discernible, so the percentage of female investors may have been higher than 1%, but not appreciably so.

51. Stubbes, *Glasse*, sig. A3^r; Smyth, *Berkeley Manuscripts*, 2:383; Hoby, *Diary*, 46, 99; Weigall, *Quarterly Review*, 215:125; H. B. Wilson, *The History of Merchant-Taylors' School* (1812-14), 1:8; Rye, ed., *England*, 72.

52. Trigge, *Sermon*, sig. D5^{r-v}.

53. Manningham, *Diary*, 89. Fenton, a reader at Gray's Inn, preached at Paul's Cross on 21 November 1602.

54. GB, notes to Exod. 18:24; 2 Sam. 13:28; 2 Kings 5:13; Job 31:15; Matt. 18:7; 25:14, 29; Eph. 6:5; Philem. 16, 17; BB, notes to Gen. 16:9; Exod. 21:26; Ecclus. 34:25; BTB, notes to Eph. 6:9; Col. 3:25.

55. Udall, *Fall*, sig. D7^V; Dod, *Treatise*, pt. 2, f. 15^V; H. Smith, *Preparatiue*, 90; W. Vaughan, *Golden-groue*, sig. P4^r; Mildmay, *Memorial*, [2].

56. Allen, *Treasvrie*, 109; Trigge, *Sermon*, sig. D4^{r-v}; Greenham, *Works*, 414; W. Vaughan, *Golden-groue*, sig. P4^r; Gifford, *Catechisme*, sig. G4^{r-v}; R. Rogers, *Treatises*, 169; Udall, *Certaine Sermons*, sig. $_2$S7^V; Stockwood, *1578 Sermon*, 183-84; Hoby, *Diary*, 85, 87, 96, 98; Davies, *Fvnerall Sermon*, sig. F1^V; Green, ed., *Life*, 37; Shelford, *Lectvres*, 10-11; Bossy, *Community*, 170-71; E. Bunny, *Summe*, ff. 61^V-62^r; Anderson, *Shield*, sig. D4^V.

57. Greenham, *Works*, 371-73; Holland, *Preservatives*, sig. A8^r; Perkins, *Treatise*, 457, 461; Dod, *Treatise*, pt. 2, f. 17^r; *APC*, 10:315-16.

58. Anderson, *A Sermon of Sure Comfort* (1581), 22; Greenham, *Works*, 120-21; Babington, *Genesis*, 157-58.

59. Turnbull, *Iames*, ff. 279^V-280^r; Thomas White, *A Sermō . . . in the Time of the Plague* (1578), 57; Becon, *Salue*, 205, 215; Allen, *Treasvrie*, 128; Carpenter, *Report*, 26:171; Dod, *Treatise*, pt. 2, ff. 17^V-18^r; Knewstub, *Lectvres*, 88; Strype, *Parker*, 2:443; HMC 9 Salisbury, 6:94; Smyth, *Berkeley Manuscripts*, 2:378. Servants usually were employed by the year, but their contract could be terminated by a quarter's notice, and sometimes less. A. L. Beier, "Social Problems in Elizabethan London," *Journal of Interdisciplinary History*, 9 (1978):215.

60. R. Rogers, *Treatises*, 169; Trigge, *Sermon*, sig. D4^r; Bownde, *Treatise*, 147; Sir Walter and Sir Charles Trevelyan, eds., *Trevelyan Papers* (1872), 3:27; Rye, ed., *England*, 13; Gabriel Powel, *The Resolved Christian* (1616; 1st pub. 1600), 215.

61. HMC 9 Salisbury, 2:515, 519; *APC*, 7:55-57, 62; 9:85; 10:172-73, 218; 11:121-22; 12:75; Babington, *Commaundements*, 378-79; Pilkington, *Works*, 191, 193, 239; Cooper, *Athenae*, 2:372-73; Holinshed, *Chronicles*, 4:157; Holles, *Memorials*, 45; HMC 58 Bath, 4:198-99.

62. Smyth, *Berkeley Manuscripts*, 2:285-86, 366-67, 419; *APC*, 16:127-28.

63. Cleaver, *Form*, 370-71, 384; Pilkington, *Works*, 66; Wilcox, *Prouerbs*, 93, 138-39; Burton, *Wooing*, 258; H. Smith, *Preparatiue*, 94-97; Turnbull, *XV. Psalme*, f. 18^V; Dod, *Treatise*, pt. 2, f. 17^V; Bullinger, *State*, sig. I1^V (cf. I5^r); Estey, *Expositions*, pt. 1, f. 57^r; HMC 77 De L'Isle, 2:456; Hastings, *Letters*, 66; Bownde, *Treatise*, 110; Dering, *Works*, ff. 6^V-7^r; Weigall, *Quarterly Review*, 215:122. According to Lupton, some mistresses made a special point of hitting their maids on the face with their rings to make the lips bleed or leave impressions from the rings. *Dreame*, sig. G6^r.

64. Turnbull, *XV. Psalme*, f. 18^V; Cleaver, *Form*, 71, 80-81, 84-87, 370-71, 374; Dent, *Path-way*, 275; Allen, *Treasvrie*, 136; Sandys, *Sermons*, 202; Fenner, *Treatises*, 29; Nash, *Pierce*, f. 8^V; Trigge, *Sermon*, sigs. D4^V-D5^r; W. Vaughan, *Golden-groue*, sig. P4^r; Bartholomew Chamberlaine, *A Sermon Preached at S. Iames . . . 1580* (1583), sig. B2^r; Becon, *Postil*, pt. 2, f. 64^V; Cooper, ed., *Wentworth Papers*, 15.

65. Dod, *Treatise*, ff. 18^V-19^V; BL Egerton MS 2644, f. 115^r; Holles, *Memorials*, 45.

66. Collins, *Life*, 95-96; Henry Malden, ed., *Devereux Papers* (1923), 17-18; Young, *Mary Sidney*, 80-81; *CSPD, 1595-1597*, 363; BL Lansdowne MSS 39/16; 50/90; 83/36; Clay, ed., *Wills*, 12, 16, 22-25, 31-32, 34, 42-43, 49-50, 62-63, 138, 149; HMC 9 Salisbury, 1:147; Nichols and Bruce, eds., *Wills*, 58, 75; Emmison, *Elizabethan Life*, 3:129; Holles, *Memorials*, 44, 65; Lehmberg, *Mildmay*, 307; BL Wolley MS 6671, f. 65^V; Piccope, ed., *Wills*, 33:144-45, 151, 164-65; 51:37, 224, 245, 260-62; Raine, ed., *Wills*, 2:172-74, 184-86; Irvine, *Collection*, 99; Strype, *Parker*, 2:443; Samuel Tymms, ed., *Wills and Inventories* (1850), 153-54; A. Pearson, *Cartwright*, 483; Raine, ed., *Injunctions*, cxviii-cxix, cxxxvii; Holinshed, *Chronicles*, 4:157. As evidence of the close relationship in the great households between masters and servants, James cites the example of Henry Neville, earl of Westmorland, who remembered more of his servants than his relatives in his will. *Family*, 33.

67. Cooper, ed., *Wentworth Papers*, 15-17, 21.

68. Dent, *Path-way*, 192.

69. Rollins, ed., *Ballads*, 268.

70. George, *Mind*, 297-98; H. Smith, *Preparatiue*, 93; Babington, *A Sermon Preached . . . at Greenewich* (1591), 9.

71. Tyndale NT (1534), prologues to Titus, 1 Pet.; Tyndale-Rogers NT, note to 1 Cor. 7; GB, notes to Gen. 24:32; 1 Sam. 22:8; 2 Sam. 9:10; Prov. 30:22; 1 Cor. 7:21; 1 Pet. 2:18.

72. BB, notes to Exod. 20:12; Deut. 5:16; BTB, notes to Luke 9:59; Eph. 6:5, 6, 8; Col. 3:22; 1 Tim. 6:1; 1 Pet. 2:18.

73. Greenham, *Works*, 412; Knewstub, *Lectvres*, 78; Estey, *Expositions*, pt. 1, f. 54^r; Gee, *Grovnd*, 4; Norden, *Solace*, f. 128^r; Vaux, *Catechisme*, ff. 45^V-46^r; Dod, *Treatise*, pt. 2, ff. 1^V-2^r; Babington, *Commaundements*, 236-37; *Sermon at Greenewich*, 7; Perkins, *Chaine*, sig. I4^{r-V}; *Treatise*, 542; Allen, *Treasvrie*, 119, 129-30; Norden, *Progress*, 171; Becon, *Salue*, 223.

74. Vaux, *Catechisme*, f. 36^V; Sandys, *Sermons*, 279; Pilkington, *Works*, 24; Bridges, *Sermon*, 111; Fenner, *Treatises*, 54, 60; Greenham, *Works*, 123, 413-14; Stockwood, *Bartholmew*, 33; Burton, *Anatomie*, 234; LPL Bacon MS 650/7 (f. 10^r); Becon, *Postil*, pt. 1, f. 90^r; Gibbon, *Remedie*, sig. I3^V; R. Rogers, *Treatises*, 169; Anderson, *Sermon of Comfort*, 21-22; Trigge, *Catholiqve*, 552; (cf. Cope, *Exposition*, f. 182^r); *Certaine Sermons*, 2:243. When, however, the Brownists attempted to put into practice the principle that obedience was not required in matters that contravened divine precepts, they were accused, in effect, of inciting rebellion. Clapham, *Antidoton*, 25.

75. Turnbull, *Iames*, ff. 5^V-6^r; Wright, *Display*, 37; Cleaver, *Form*, 385-86, 389; W. Vaughan, *Golden-groue*, sigs. P7^V-P8^r; Fenner, *Treatises*, 62; Gifford, *Catechisme*, sig. G4^r; Wilcox, *Prouerbs*, 85; Becon, *Salue*, 223; Dod, *Treatise*, ff. 11^r-14^V; LPL Bacon MS 650/7

(f. 10^r); (cf. Bullinger, *State*, sig. I5^V). In Essex, some servants left bequests of goods or money for their masters. Emmison, *Elizabethan Life*, 3:130.

76. Harward, *Sermons*, sig. E7^r; Bownde, *Doctrine*, 265; Thomas, *Demegoriai*, sig. S5^r; R. Rogers, *Treatises*, 361.

77. Stockwood, *Bartholmew*, 19-20; PRO STAC 7 Add., 1/6.

78. Dent, *Path-way*, 173-74; Cooper, *Copie*, sig. C2^V; Pilkington, *Works*, 59; Turnbull, *XV. Psalme*, f. 19^{r-v}; D'Ewes, *Autobiography*, 1:24; *APC*, 17:218-19; HMC 9 Salisbury, 2: 108; Forman, *Autobiography*, 32; Williams, *Bess*, 56; Weigall, *Quarterly Review*, 215:120; LPL Bacon MSS 652/107 (f. 155^r); 655/33 (f. 46^{r-v}).

79. Pilkington, *Works*, 363; *CJ*, 1:65, 71-72; *SR*, 4, pt. 1, 438; *APC*, 13:31-32; 20:298-99.

80. Machyn, *Diary*, 196-97, 235-36; Holinshed, *Chronicles*, 4:237.

81. Babington, *Genesis*, 236; Trigge, *Sermon*, sig. D3^{r-v}; HMC 9 Salisbury, 1:162; *APC*, 9:199; BL Egerton MS 2713, f. 300^r.

Chapter 8: The Role of Education

1. Higgins, *Mirour*, f. 238^r.

2. Whetstone, *Heptameron*, sig. U1^r.

3. Joan Simon, *Education and Society in Tudor England* (Cambridge, 1966), 291; T. Rogers, *Discourse*, f. 70^V; Barker, *Checke*, sig. M3^V.

4. J. H. Hexter, *Reappraisals in History* (New York, 1961), 69; Kempe, *Education*, pt. 2; Stone, *PP*, 28:70; Peter Clark and Paul Slack, *English Towns in Transition* (1976), 153.

5. James, *Family*, 100, 102-3; Martin Havran, *Caroline Courtier* (1973), 3-4; Hugh Kearney, *Scholars and Gentlemen* (Ithaca, N. Y., 1970), 26; Read, *Walsingham*, 212.

6. Stockwood, *1578 Sermon*, 89; Dering, *Catechisme, Works*, sig. D4^r; Greenham, *Works*, 410; Cleaver, *Form*, 335; Dering, *Certaine Godly and Comfortable Letters*, in *Works*, sig. A3^r; K. R. M. Short, "A Theory of Common Education in Elizabethan Puritanism," *JEH*, 23 (1972):32, 34 (cf. 37-48); W. Vaughan, *Golden-groue*, sig. X6^V; Estey, *Expositions*, pt. 1, f. 56^V; Rainolds, *The Svmme of the Conference* (1584), 3. The 1534 Tyndale NT (Eph. 4) and the 1549 Tyndale-Erasmus NT (1 Pet. 1) made ignorance a cause of immoral living, and the Geneva annotators (2 Kings 1:6) regarded it as the mother of error and idolatry.

7. Nowell, *Catechism*, 113; Sandys, *Sermons*, 113; Woolton, *Manual*, 86; Jewel, *Works*, 2:837; Wright, *Display*, 32; Whitgift, *Works*, 2:354. See Mark Curtis, *Oxford and Cambridge in Transition* (Oxford, 1959), chap. 7; Kearney, *Scholars*, 30. One of the arguments used by Whitgift against Cartwright's proposal for greater congregational participation in the selection of a minister was that this would require a college or university in every parish. The Puritans would have agreed on the need for a school in every parish. Whitgift, *Works*, 1:307.

8. F. W. M. Draper, *Four Centuries of Merchant Taylors' School* (1962), 5; Craze, *History*, 27; Strype, *Grindal*, 463; J. Whitaker, *The Statutes and Charter of Rivington School* (1837), 175; Lehmberg, *Mildmay*, 226-27; Stone, *PP*, 28:77. The religious aim of education in founding schools was hardly new. Wolverhampton School, for example, had been founded in 1512 *pro pueris erudiendis in bonis moribus et literatura*. Gerald Mander, *The History of the Wolverhampton Grammar School* (Wolverhampton, 1913), 29. Emmison's examination of numerous Essex wills led him to the conclusion that "the religious aspect of education is . . . frequently in evidence, especially in the wills of puritan-minded testators." *Elizabethan Life*, 3:120.

9. Robinson, ed., *Zurich Letters*, 265; Stone, *Crisis*, 679; Hergest, *Rvle*, sig. B1^r; Weigall, *Quarterly Review*, 215:127.

10. Cross, *Trans. Leics. Arch. and Hist. Soc.*, 36:14.

11. Wiener, "The Beleaguered Isle. A Study of Elizabethan and Early Jacobean Anti-Catholicism," *PP*, 51 (1971):47; Haigh, *Reformation*, 291, 311-12; Aveling, *Recusancy*, 75; Raine, *History*, 84-85.

12. Rose, *Cases*, 56; A. C. F. Beales, *Education Under Penalty* (1963), 57-64; Cliffe, *Gentry*, 184.

13. Neale, *Parliaments*, 2:280-86; Beales, *Education*, 62; *APC*, 19:87-88; J. P. Collier, ed., *Trevelyan Papers* (1863), 2:91-93.

14. *APC*, 9:171; Anstruther, *Vaux*, 231-32; Pinchbeck, *BJS*, 8:70.

15. Grindal, *Remains*, 142; *EEA*, 2:74; Nichols, *Order*, sig. H3^{r-v}; Usher, ed., *Movement*, 100.

16. James, *Family*, 105; Clark and Slack, *Towns*, 153; Stone, *PP*, 28:42. Cf. Spufford, *Communities*, 207-8.

17. David Cressy, "Educational Opportunity in Tudor and Stuart England," *History of Education Quarterly*, 16 (1976):314-16. See also "Literacy in Pre-Industrial England," *Societas*, 4 (1974):229-40; "Levels of Illiteracy in England, 1530-1730," *HJ*, 20 (1977):1-23; "Literacy in Seventeenth-Century England: More Evidence," *Journal of Interdisciplinary History*, 8 (1977):141-50.

18. Kempe, *Education*, sig. B4^V; Cleaver, *Form*, 334; Covel, *Polimanteia* (Cambridge, 1595), sig. Q4^V; Shelford, *Lectvres*, 13, 24; Valentine Leigh, *Deathes Generall Proclamation* (1561), sig. C7^V; *EEA*, 2:74; Short, *JEH*, 23:35. For Leigh, see *DNB*, *s.v.*

19. Simon, *Education*, 294, 296; Kearney, *Scholars*, 23, 27; Stone, *PP*, 28:70-71; Curtis, *Oxford*, 63; Hake, *Touchestone*, sig. F2^V; Lemnie, *Touchstone*, f. 16^V; Davies, *Fvnerall Sermon*, sig. E2^r; HMC 77 De L'Isle, 2:424; Stow, *Chronicles*, 4:427.

20. W. Vaughan, *Golden-groue*, sig. X5^V; Churchyard, *Challenge*, 49; Cleaver, *Form*, 105; Nash, *Anatomie*, sig. E1^r; Allen, *Treasvrie*, 140; Sylvester, *Monodia*, sig. A3^r; Draper, *Centuries*, 9; Rowse, *England*, 494.

21. Wilcox, *Psalmes*, 392; Mulcaster, *Positions*, 150; Kempe, *Education*, sig. E1^{r-v}; W. Elderton, *A Proper Newe Ballad . . . Learnynges* (n.d.); Stone, *PP*, 28:73; Walter Scott, ed., *A Collection of Scarce and Valuable Tracts* (1809), 1:493; Margaret Kay, *The History of Rivington and Blackrod Grammar School* (Manchester, 1931), 169; C. G. Gilmore, *History of King Edward VI School, Stafford* (Oxford, 1953), 20. Short, however, argues that the Puritans were not interested in education to develop obedience. *JEH*, 23:31.

22. I. E. Gray and W. E. Potter, *Ipswich School* (Ipswich, 1950), 40-41, 166.

23. BL Add. MS 30,076, ff. 20^V, 22^r; Barthlet, *Pedegrewe*, f. 6^{r-v}; HMC 9 Salisbury, 1:439; John Roberts, ed., *A Critical Anthology of English Recusant Devotional Prose* (Pittsburgh, 1966), 108.

24. Nash, *Anatomie*, sig. D1^V.

25. Mulcaster, *Positions*, 132. Cf. Richard DeMolen, "Richard Mulcaster's Philosophy of Education," *Journal of Medieval and Renaissance Studies*, 2 (1972):69-91.

26. Mulcaster, *Positions*, 134, 136-38.

27. Ibid., 140-48.

28. Wright, *Display*, 8-9; Short, *JEH*, 23:33-34; Shelford, *Lectvres*, 11.

29. Spufford, "The Schooling of the Peasantry in Cambridgeshire, 1575-1700," in *Land*, ed. Thirsk, 113, 131-33, 137; HMC 9 Salisbury, 1:163; Cressy, *History of Education Quarterly*, 16:309.

30. Spufford, "Schooling," 123; *Communities*, 207-8; Rosemary O'Day, "The Reformation of the Ministry, 1558-1642," *Continuity and Change*, ed. O'Day and Heal, 72; Lupton, *Church and Society*, ed. Heal and O'Day, 76; Kay, *History*, 11, 40; Stone, *Crisis*, 685. Cressy correctly observes that miscellaneous fees in "free" grammar schools were sometimes quite high. *History of Education Quarterly*, 16:307-8.

31. Kay, *History*, 173, 184. Mumford, *School*, 477, 479-80; Wilson, *History*, 1:12-16; Gray and Potter, *School*, 38-40; D. C. Somerwell, *A History of Tonbridge School* (1947), 17; Draper, *Centuries*, 242-43, 246. The statutes were not always enforced. In September

1566 Matthew Maperley, master of the school at Grantham, Lincs., complained to Cecil that little children were being enrolled in his school contrary to the regulations. PRO SP 40/67 (f. 147A^{r-v}).

32. HMC 9 Salisbury, 1:163; Whetstone, *Enemie*, sig. H1^v; Cooper, ed., *Wentworth Papers*, 21; Stone, *PP*, 28:50-51, 54; J. H. Gleason, *The Justices of the Peace in England* (Oxford, 1969), 86 (cf. 83).

33. Stone, *Crisis*, 681, 690; Mulcaster, *Positions*, 156-58; Cressy, "The Social Composition of Caius College, Cambridge 1580-1640," *PP*, 47 (1970):114-15; Stone, *PP*, 28:45, 59-60, 68; Elizabeth Russell, "The Influx of Commoners into the University of Oxford before 1581: An Optical Illusion?" *EHR*, 92 (1977):721-45; J. K. McConica, "The Social Relations of Tudor Oxford," *TRHS*, 5th ser., 27 (1977):128-129, 133; (cf. Spufford, "Schooling," 147; *Communities*, 174-76). For other interpretations of the Caius statistics see Simon, "The Social Origins of Cambridge Students, 1603-1640," *PP*, 26 (1963): 60-61; Stone, *PP*, 28:65; Curtis, *Oxford*, 60-61. The recorded social rank of nonhonorific entrants to the Inns of Court between 1590 and 1639 indicates 40.6% for the peerage and squire-archy, 47.8% for the lower gentry, and 7.8% for the bourgeois and professional classes. Wilfrid R. Prest, *The Inns of Court under Elizabeth I and the Early Stuarts, 1590-1640* (1972), 30.

34. Bullinger, *State*, sig. K4^{r-v}; Richard Robinson, *The Rewarde of Wickednesse* [1574], sig. G3^r; *EEA*, 3:296.

35. Nash, *Anatomie*, sig. D1^v; Hake, *Touchestone*, sigs. C4^r-C6^r, D2^v. One feminist complained that, according to some men, "to shun a shower of rain, & to know the way to our husbands bed is wisedome sufficient for vs women: but in this yeare of 88. men are grown so fantastical, that vnles we can make them fooles, we are accounted vnwise." *Iane Anger*, 10-11.

36. Mulcaster, *Positions*, 132, 167-69, 174-75, 177-82. In the 1580s, John Bowes wrote two tracts advocating that trades be taught to girls. Hogrefe, *Women*, 91.

37. Kay, *History*, 174; Gray and Potter, *School*, 166; Stone, *PP*, 28:42-43; Dorothy Gardiner, *English Girlhood at School* (1929), 198-201; John Nichols, ed., *The Progresses and Public Processions of Queen Elizabeth* (new ed., 1823), 1:339; 2:144; Notestein, *Studies*, 82 (cf. 106).

38. HMC 9 Salisbury, 1:439; HMC 77 De L'Isle and Dudley, 2:176; Smyth, ed., *Berkeley Manuscripts*, 2:383; Hogrefe, *Women*, 107; Gardiner, *Girlhood*, 188; Hoby, *Diary*, 5, 13, 47; Cross, *The Puritan Earl* (1966), 60; Holles, *Memorials*, 219. The earl of Arundel's educational interests are further indicated by the fact that at the age of eighteen his heir "did excell in all manner of good learninge, and languages." BL Royal MS 17 A. IX, f. 35^r.

39. Cooper, ed., *Wentworth Papers*, 21; BL Add. MS 29,974 (ff. 3^r, 5^r, 7^r); Holles, *Memorials*, 66; Campbell, *Yeoman*, 274-75; Emmison, *Elizabethan Life*, 3:122-23; Weigall, *Quarterly Review*, 215:120-21.

40. McIntosh, *Proceedings*, 119:240; BL Lansdowne MSS 23/64; 68/58; Strype, *Annals*, 2, pt. 2, 87; Hoby, *Diary*, 14, 57, 67-69, 74-75, 77, 87, 115, 120, 129, 132, 153, 163, 181; BL Add. MS 35,324, f. 18^r; Gardiner, *Girlhood*, 185-86; Fullerton, *Life*, 6-8; Young, *Mary Sidney*, 26; Hogrefe, *Women*, 107, 116, 130-31, 146-47; Smyth, *Berkeley Manuscripts*, 2:383, 385; Wilson, *History*, 1:8; A. Clifford, *Lives*, 19. According to John Dowland, Lucy Harrington, the future countess of Bedford, was sufficiently knowledgeable about music to "mend" his tunes. Margaret M. Byard, "The Trade bf Courtiership: The Countess of Bedford and the Bedford Memorials," *History Today*, 29 (1979):21.

41. *EEA*, 3:169-70.

42. Nowell, *Catechism*, 113.

43. Shelford, *Lectvres*, 10: Hake, *Touchestone*, sig. F3^v; Cleaver, *Form*, 335-36; W.

Vaughan, *Golden-groue*, sig. K7^{r-v}; HMC 9 Salisbury, 2:532; BL Lansdowne MS 108/86; Anstruther, *Vaux*, 100; HMC 77 De L'Isle, 2:227.

44. Mulcaster, *Positions*, 235, 238; W. Vaughan, *Golden-groue*, sigs. Y2^{v}-Y3^{r}; Nash, *Pierce*, ff. 2^{r}, 9^{r}; Roger Ascham, *English Works*, ed. William Wright (Cambridge, 1904), 193.

45. Kenneth Charlton, *Education in Renaissance England* (1965), 124-25; Russell, *History*, 24, 27; HMC 54 Beverley, 184-85; F. H. G. Percy, *History of Whitgift School* (1976), 36; Draper, *Centuries*, 10: HMC 58 Bath, 4:181; LPL Bacon MSS 654/4 (f. 5^{r}); 655/12 (f. 15^{r}); HMC 77 De L'Isle, 2:269, 434; Cressy, *History of Education Quarterly*, 16:308. The aristocracy was not normally burdened by educational expenses. The largest annual educational expense of Sir William Fitzwilliam of Northamptonshire was £59 9s. 10d. in 1594-95, which was 1/16 of his total expenditures. It cost approximately £8 per quarter to maintain a boy at Cambridge in the 1590s. Finch, *Wealth*, 124-25.

46. Cleaver, *Form*, 256; Kempe, *Education*, sig. E4^{v}; (cf. Bullinger, *State*, sig. I7^{r}); Cooper, ed., *Wentworth Papers*, 21; Wotton, *Letter-Book*, ed. G. Eland (1960), 1; W. Vaughan, *Golden-groue*, sigs. Y2^{r-v}, Y5^{r-v}. Between 1574 and 1604 the educational level of masters in Cambridgeshire was high. See Spufford, "Schooling," 129.

47. Kay, *History*, 177-79, 188; Cross, *The Free Grammar School of Leicester* (Leicester, 1953), 18; Mumford, *School*, 476; Percy, *History*, 35-36; Gray and Potter, *School*, 42; C. W. Stokes, *Queen Mary's Grammar School, Clitheroe* (Manchester, 1934), 174-75. The Merchant Taylors' statutes were also demanding; Draper, *Centuries*, 241, 243.

48. Allen, *Treasvrie*, 136; Mulcaster, *Positions*, 24; Stockwood, *1578 Sermon*, 89-90; Pilkington, *Works*, 181, 355; Kay, *History*, 184.

49. Stone, "Rise," 37-38; T. Jones, ed., *Relation*, 2-3; Forman, *Autobiography*, 4.

50. Kay, *History*, 168; Raine, *History*, 75-76, 83; *APC*, 11:370-71 (cf. 12:102).

51. Bateson, ed., *Original Letters*, 19-20, 35; Grindal, *Remains*, 142, 172-74; *EEA*, 2:57, 74, 98; 3:143, 156, 163, 165, 169-70, 177, 184, 187, 193, 204, 217, 226, 343; Leys, *Catholics*, 154.

52. Mumford, *School*, 24, Raine, *History*, 78; Leys, *Catholics*, 154-55; Cross, *School*, 12; Bateson, ed., *Records*, 3:299; HMC 9 Salisbury, 2:119; Beales, *Education*, 57. Among the Bacon MSS is an interesting appeal to Sir Anthony Bacon from the imprisoned Catholic priest Thomas Wright, asking to be released and allowed to teach philosophy (without religious overtones) at Sir Thomas Gresham's school in London. LPL Bacon MS 654/190 (f. 285^{r-v}).

53. Stockwood, *1578 Sermon*, 93-95; *Fruiteful Sermon*, sig. D6^{r}.

54. Stoughton, *Treatise*, 116.

55. Gifford, *Eight Sermons*, f. 38^{v}.

56. Dering, *Catechisme*, *Works*, sig. D4^{r}; Marbury, *Notes of the Doctrine of Repentance* (1602), 65; Stockwood, *1578 Sermon*, 87-88, 91; *Fruiteful Sermon*, sigs. A7^{r}, K5^{r}-K6^{v}. The note to Dan. 1:17 in the Geneva Bible approved the study of "liberal sciences, and natural knowledge," but disapproved of "magical artes."

57. Gosson, *Schoole*, ff. 2^{r}, 6^{v}, 8^{r-v}; *DNB*, s.v. Stephen Gosson; Gifford, *Eight Sermons*, f. 35^{v}. According to Edward Vaughan, in comparison with divinity, other subjects were like dim stars. *A Method or Briefe Instruction* (1590), sig. π5^{r}.

58. Rainolds, *The Overthrow of Stage-Playes* (1599), 124-25; Simon, *Education*, 241.

59. W. Vaughan, *Golden-groue*, sigs. X6^{v}-X7^{r}, Y1^{v}, Y6^{r}-Y8^{r}, Z1^{v}-Z4^{v}, Z6^{v}-Z7^{v}.

60. Cross, *School*, 15-16, 19 (cf. 26-27). Hugh Kearney calls attention to the differences in outlook between the Puritan treatise on education, *The Nobles* (1563), by Lawrence Humphrey, president of Magdalen College, Oxford, and the humanist treatise, *The Governor*, by Thomas Eliot. Whereas Eliot made use of extensive classical examples, Hum-

phrey relied fundamentally on the Bible. The latter excluded Homer, Horace, Lucian, Ovid, and Virgil, all of whom Eliot praised. Yet Humphrey recommended Terrence because he was lauded by Cicero. Eliot defended Ovid, Martial, and Catullus. *Scholars*, 39-42.

61. Kay, *History*, 45-47, 174, 187, 189; Pilkington, *Works*, 243, 671; Bunny, *Summe*, f. 63^V; Wright, *Summons*, 30; Covel, *Polimanteia*, sigs. G4^V-H1^V.

62. Stone, *Crisis*, 679-80; Cooper, ed., *Wentworth Papers*, 18; Matthew Hutton, *Correspondence*, ed. J. Raine (1843), 188; A. Clifford, *Lives*, 6.

63. Nash, *Anatomie*, sigs. B4^V-C1^r, C3^V, E1^V-E4^r.

64. Barrow, *Writings (1587-90)*, 139, 268-69, 343-46, 349-50, 535, 539; *Writings of Greenwood and Barrow (1591-93)*, 123; Strype, *Whitgift*, 3:229-30. Cf. Gifford, *Declaration*, 69, for a Puritan rebuttal.

65. Mander, *History*, 368; BL Lansdowne MS 88/51; Finch, *Wealth*, 124-25; HMC 77 De L'Isle, 2:277.

66. *APC*, 13:389-90; Carpenter, *Report*, 26:172; LPL Bacon MS 650/7 (f. 10^r).

67. Woolton, *Manual*, 105.

68. W. Vaughan, *Golden-groue*, sig. N6^r.

69. Gilpin, *Sermon*, 37; Parker, *Correspondence*, 51; HMC 9 Salisbury, 1:163.

70. Craze, *History*, 25; Jewel, *Works*, 4: *passim*; James, *Sermon at Pavles Crosse*, sigs. C3^r, D2^r, D4^V. Cf. Stucliffe, *Answere*, sig. A3^r.

71. Covel, *Polimanteia*, sig. P2^V; Barrow, *Writings (1587-90)*, 395, 486, 535-36; A. Pearson, *Cartwright*, 208-9; Whitgift, *Works*, 3:469-70, 511; Bancroft, *Svrvay*, 317; *Writings of Greenwood and Barrow (1591-93)*, 105; BL Lansdowne MS 29/45.

72. Barrow, *Writings (1587-90)*, 139, 344-46, 349-50; Read, *Burghley*, 114; HMC 9 Salisbury, 2:60; Nash, *Anatomie*, sig. E1^V.

73. Parker, *Correspondence*, 54-56 (cf. 249); Robinson, ed., *Zurich Letters*, 29; Pilkington, *Works*, 593; Manningham, *Diary*, 75; Mulcaster, *Positions*, 162-63; *CJ*, 1:110, 112; 31 Eliz. I, c. 6, *SR*, 4:803; W. Vaughan, *Golden-groue*, sig. X7^V; HMC 9 Salisbury, 3:153; D'Ewes, *Journals*, 559.

74. BL Lansdowne MSS 18/90; 20/164; Grindal, *Remains*, 358; H. C. Porter, *Reformation and Reaction in Tudor Cambridge* (Cambridge, 1958), 185; Curtis, *Oxford*, 96-97, 100-1, 107. The visitation articles of the bishops reveal some interest in the statutes of grammar schools, but in 1597 a Commons' bill to establish better order in these schools was rejected after a second reading. *EEA*, 2:18, 29, 31, 63-64; Grindal, *Remains*, 180; D'Ewes, *Journals*, 570.

75. Barrow, *Writings (1587-90)*, 168, 350-51, 534-35, 538-41; Greenwood, *Writings (1587-90)*, 268-69.

76. Whitgift, *Works*, 2:343 (cf. 354); Stubbes, *Motive*, 87; Woolton, *Castell*, sig. A7^r; John Madoxe, *A Learned and a Godly Sermon* (1581), sig. A8^V; Gosson, *Schoole*, f. 35^V; Barrow, *Writings (1587-90)*, 344.

77. Mulcaster, *Positions*, 239, 242, 246, 250-53, 259, 264, 266-85.

78. BL Lansdowne MS 84/105; Tittler, *Bacon*, 59-60.

79. Sir Humphrey Gilbert, *Queene Elizabethes Achademy*, ed. F. J. Furnivall (1869), 1-7.

80. Parker, *Correspondence*, 249.

81. *The Crie of the Poore* (1596). (The reference is to Henry Hastings, earl of Huntingdon.)

82. Jewel, *Works*, 2:999, 1011; Stubbes, *Motive*, sig. A4^{r-v}, 45-47; W. Vaughan, *Golden-groue*, sig. I3^V; A. Hill, *Crie*, 82; Pilkington, *Works*, 43. Burghley also complained of the rarity of educational donations. HMC 9 Salisbury, 4:107.

83. Mulcaster, *Positions*, 229; Jordan, *Philanthropy in England* (1959), 248; *Forming*,

16-17, 91-92; *The Social Institutions of Lancashire* (Manchester, 1962), 117; *The Charities of London* (1960), 252; *Social Institutions in Kent* (Ashford, Kent, 1961), 7-8 (cf. 66-67).

84. Jordan, *Philanthropy*, 20, 281; Sutton, *Disce mori*, 191; Curteys, *Two Sermons*, sig. A7^r; W. Vaughan, *Golden-groue*, sig. I4^r.

85. Raine, ed., *Wills*, 194-96, 229-32, 426-27; Raine, *History*, 77; Cooper, *Athenae*, 1: 211-12, 252-53.

86. Parker, *Correspondence*, 188; Strype, *Parker*, 1:503, 573-75; 2:89-91, 93-96, 406-11, 438-40; Holinshed, *Chronicles*, 4:328; BL Lansdowne MSS 30/46; 37/20; 39/16, 17; Percy, *History*, 29-33; Hutton, *Correspondence*, 21.

87. Nicholas Carlisle, *A Concise Description of the Endowed Grammar Schools* (1818), 1:389, 643; 2:935; Cooper, *Athenae*, 1:442-43; 2:16; BL Lansdowne MS 82/57; Clay, ed., *Wills*, 62-63, 220.

88. Cooper, *Athenae*, 1:245; 2:392; Raine, ed., *Injunctions*, cx-cxiv; A. F. S. Pearson, *Cartwright*, 482-83. For Beaumont's cautious support of Puritanism see Porter, *Reformation*, 114-18.

89. BL Lansdowne MSS 61/34; 103/51; Wiffen, *Memoirs*, 1:515; *Crie of the Poore*; Cross, *School*, 22; *Trans. Leics. Arch. and Hist. Soc.*, 36:15; Cooper, *Athenae*, 2:91; Lehmberg, *Mildmay*, 222-23, 225-26; McIntosh, *Proceedings*, 119:249.

90. BL Lansdowne MS 50/90; Cooper, *Athenae*, 2:123; Lawrence Tanner, *Westminster School* (2nd ed., 1951), 25-26; Strype, *Parker*, 1:273-75; Carlisle, *Description*, 1:389, 817; 2:714; Clay, ed., *Wills*, 117-19, 148-50.

91. Kay, *History*, 13; Rowse, *England*, 496; Dickens, *TRHS*, 13:73; Carlisle, *Description*, 1:108, 206-7, 574, 636, 797; 2:199, 583, 808, 875, 910; PRO SP 106/17 (ff. 42^r-43^v). For early Elizabethan benefactors to Cambridge colleges see SP 32; many of the benefactions are unfortunately not dated. The number of educational foundations in the period 1550 to 1610 is as follows: 47 in the 1550s, 42 in the 1560s, 30 in the 1570s, 20 in the 1580s, 24 in the 1590s, and 41 in the 1600s. Cressy, *HJ*, 20:15.

92. Frederick Bussby, "An Ecclesiasticall Seminarie and College General of Learning and Religion, Planted and Established at Ripon," *JEH*, 4 (1953):155-58.

93. BL Lansdowne MS 38/85; Stow, *Chronicles*, 4:877.

94. Udall, *Fall*, sig. C8^v.

95. BL Lansdowne MS 10/38.

96. Charlton, *Education*, 215-16; Stone, *Crisis*, 8.

97. Robert Carey, *Memoirs*, ed. John, earl of Cork and Orrery (1759), xvi, 2-4, 6-7; Whitelocke, *Liber*, 7-8, 11; Strype, *Smith*, 85, 95; BL Sloane MS 325, f. 5^r; Sir Thomas Bodley, *The Life of Sr Thomas Bodley* (Oxford, 1647; written in 1609), 4.

98. T. White, *Plague Sermon*, 38; Udall, *Fall*, sig. C8^v; Stockwood, *1578 Sermon*, 93-94; Manningham, *Diary*, 100; Bullinger, *State*, sigs. K1^v-K2^r. For White's Puritanism see Seaver, *Lectureships*, 158.

99. Mulcaster, *Positions*, 211-15, 219; Stubbes, *Motive*, sig. A3^{r-v}; Ascham, *Works*, 223, 225-26, 233.

100. Beales, *Education*, 29-38, 53; *APC*, 7:247; 10:309; Gerard, *Autobiography*, 2; *TP*, 2: 481-84; *EEA*, 2:134; 3:164, 179, 185; 27 Eliz. I, c. 2, *SR*, 4, pt. 1, 707. Some of the requests for licenses to go abroad are extant; see, e.g., PRO SP 33/45 (f. 102^r); 48/30 (f. 65^r); BL Lansdowne MS 30/39.

101. Gerard, *Autobiography*, 33; Anstruther, *Vaux*, 145-46; John Pollen, *The English Catholics in the Reign of Queen Elizabeth* (1920), 342.

102. PRO SP 19/26 (f. 48^r); 33/61 (f. 128^r); 33/67 (ff. 140^v-141^r); Read, *Walsingham*, 1: 118-20; BL Lansdowne MS 10/38.

Chapter 9: Work and Worship

1. Fleming, *A Memoriall of* . . . *William Lambe Esquire* [1580], sig. C3^r.

2. Greenham, *Works*, 7.

3. GB, notes to Exod. 6:7; Deut. 1:30; 32:15; Isa. 42:6; Jon. 1:3; Acts 17:26; Phil. 2:12; 2 Thess. 3:10; preface to Rom.

4. GB, notes to Num. 16:40; Pss. 31:24; 131:1; Prov. 11:2; John 11:9; 1 Cor. 7:17.

5. BB, notes to Gen. 47:3; Eccles. 3:10; BTB, notes to Luke 22:49; John 18:10; Rom. 12:3; 2 Thess. 3:12.

6. Sandys, *Sermons*, 182, 190; Carpenter, *Preparatiue*, 318; Chardon, *A Second Sermon vpon the ix Chapter of* . . . *Iohn* (1587), sig. A8^v; Samuel Gardiner, *Portraitvre of the Prodigal Sonne* (1599), 241; King, *Lectvres*, 16.

7. Hooker, *Works*, 2:510; John Young, *A Sermon Preached before the Queenes Maiestie* [1576?], sig. C1^r; Carpenter, *Preparatiue*, 275-76, 321, 334; Whitgift, *Works*, 2:114; *Godlie Sermon*, sigs. B6^v-B7^r; Babington, *Genesis*, 45; Woolton, *Castell*, sigs. D2^v-D3^r; John Rogers, *An Answere vnto a Wicked & Infamous Libel* (1579), sig. D2^v.

8. Bunny, *Summe*, ff. 33^r, 39^r, 62^v-63^r; Mulcaster, *Positions*, 137; Carpenter, *Preparatiue*, 275, 318; King, *Lectvres*, 142; Babington, *Commaundements*, 385; Abbot, *Exposition*, 92; Sandys, *Sermons*, 35; Woolton, *Manual*, 10; Chardon, *Second Sermon*, sigs. A4^v, A5^v; Pilkington, *Works*, 445. James Bisse, fellow of Magdalen College, Oxford, and a preacher at Paul's Cross in 1581, criticized all the popular enemies of the Church of England — rogues and vagabonds, friars, libertines, Anabaptists, and thieves — for failing to pursue lawful vocations. *Sermons*, sig. B5^r.

9. Chaderton, *Frvitfvll Sermon*, 18; Greenham, *Works*, 327; Gifford, *Declaration*, sig. A1^v; Dering, *Catechisme, Works*, sigs. C3^v, E5^r; Udall, *The True Remedie Against Famine and Warres* [1588], f. 70^v; Perkins, *Treatise*, 486; Wilcox, *Prouerbs, Works*, 55, 58; Allen, *Alphabet*, 88-89; Udall, *Demonstration*, 19; Allison, *Confvtation*, 87.

10. R. Hill, *Contents*, 441; Wilcox, *An Exposition vpon* . . . *Canticles, Works* (1624), 10; *Prouerbs, Works*, 128, 130; Dering, *Hebrues, Workes*, sig. X7^v; Becon, *Postil*, 1:ff. 44^v-45^r; Greenham, *Works*, 6; Trigge, *Sermon*, sig. C5^r.

11. Cleaver, *Form*, 334; Estey, *Expositions*, pt. 1, f. 56^r; Allen, *Treasvrie*, 120-21; Perkins, *Treatise*, 395-96; Fenner, *Order*, pt. 3, sig. C3^v; *Treatises*, 47, 58-59.

12. Udall, *Obedience to the Gospell* (1584), sig. F2^r; R. Rogers, *Treatises*, 362 (cf. 333); W. Vaughan, *Golden-groue*, sig. $_2$B8^r; George, *Mind*, 171.

13. Udall, *Amendment*, sig. E2^r (for contentment); Wilcox, *Prouerbs, Works*, 47, 55, 58; Chaderton, *Frvitfvll Sermon*, 29; Dering, *Catechisme, Workes*, sigs. A8^v, D6^r; Norden, *Progress*, 166; Bownde, *Doctrine*, 73; Greenham, *Works*, 321, 416-17, 463; Becon, *Postil*, 2: f. 41^r; Dent, *Path-way*, 34, 76-77, 193; Gee, *Grovnd*, 5; Perkins, *Treatise*, 504; Ward, *Diaries*, ed. Knappen, 117 (cf. 106, 112-14). See also R. Rogers, *Treatises*, 353-64; Stockwood, *Fruiteful Sermon*, sig. C3^v; Chaderton, *Excellent Sermon*, sig. C5^r; Marbury, *Notes*, 102; Allison, *Confvtation*, 39-40. Cf. part of Francis Benison's epitaph: "He oft would say that Diligence, good Fortunes Mother was." John Awdeley, *An Epitaph of Maister Fraunces Benison* (1570). Benison was a London haberdasher.

14. Burton, *Rowsing*, 464, 467; Northbrooke, *Treatise*, f. 17^r; R. Rogers, *Treatises*, 180; Stubbes, *Anatomie*, sig. O5^v; Norden, *Practise*, f. 8^v; Perkins, *Chaine*, sig. M7^v; *How to Liue*, 45-46, 48; *Treatise*, 526, 557; Cleaver, *Form*, 23, 56; cf. Allen, *Treasvrie*, 87. Greenham asserted that the legitimate pursuit of one's vocation was part of the worship of God. *Works*, 372.

15. Barrow, *Writings (1587-90)*, 227, 387, 492, 608; Barrow and Penry, *Writings of Greenwood and Barrow (1591-93)*, 402 (cf. 426); Barrow, *Writings of Greenwood (1587-90)*, 192; Penry, *Notebook*, 79.

16. George, *Mind*, 138; Rheims NT, note to Luke 10:42; Shelford, *Lectvres*, 13; Manningham, *Diary*, 141; Deacon, *A Treatise, Intitvled; Nobody is My Name* [1585?], sigs. G1^V-G2^r; Stone, *Crisis*, 336, 773; W. Vaughan, *Golden-groue*, sig. V4^V. Cf. James, *Sermon at Pavles Crosse*, sig. B1^V.

17. GB, notes to Exod. 31:3; Eccles. 5:8; BB, notes to Exod. 31:3; Eccles. 5:8; W. Vaughan, *Golden-groue*, sigs. V4^r, V5^V; Gibbon, *Praise*, 54; Babington, *Genesis*, 45; Wilcox, *Prouerbs*, *Works*, 68; Trigge, *Sermon*, sigs. C4^V-C5^r; King, *Lectvres*, 46; Greenham, *Works*, 375; H. Smith, *Preparatiue*, 93.

18. HMC 9 Salisbury, 1:163; Margaret G. Davies, *The Enforcement of English Apprenticeship* (Cambridge, Mass., 1956), 9; W. G. Hoskins, "An Elizabethan Provincial Town: Leicester," *Studies in Social History*, ed. J. H. Plumb (1955), 60; *Winthrop Papers*, 1 (Massachusetts Historical Society, 1929): 15; Emmison, *Elizabethan Life*, 3:121-22; HMC 23 Cowper, 1:22.

19. Lodge, *An Alarum Against Vsurers* (1584), sig. C2^r.

20. Becon, *Postil*, 1: f. 176^V.

21. GB, notes to Gen. 2:15; Deut. 18:6; 28:8; Ps. 128:2; Ezek. 16:49; Acts 4:29; preface to 2 Thess. Cf. the notes to Prov. 6:12; Eccles. 4:5; 1 Thess. 4:11.

22. BB, notes to Luke 19:13 (cf. Gen. 46:6); BTB, notes to Luke 19:20; 2 Thess. 3:10, 11.

23. Lambarde, *Government*, 171 (cf. 173); Babington, *Genesis*, 21; Bisse, *Sermons*, sig. B4^V; Pilkington, *Works*, 445; Dod, *Treatise*, pt. 2, f. 66^V; Peter Moffett, *A Commentarie vpon the . . . Proverbs* (1592), 151; Northbrooke, *Treatise*, ff. 11^r, 24^V; Dent, *Pathway*, 199; (cf. Wilcox, *Prouerbs, Works*, 69).

24. Turnbull, *Iude*, f. 84^V; Lewes, *Sermon*, sig. C8^r; Pilkington, *Works*, 157, 447, 521; Terry, *Triall*, 126; Jewel, *Works*, 4:799-800, 1085; Babington, *Conference*, 13.

25. Northbrooke, *Treatise*, f. 17^V; Fulke, *Text*, ff. 38^V, 187^r, 363^r; Trigge, *Tovchstone*, 222, 224; Cartwright, *Confvtation*, 11; Trigge, *Apologie*, 9; Udall, *Obedience*, sig. F5^V; Barthlet, *Pedegrewe*, ff. 62^r, 70^V; Perkins, *Catholike*, 960-61; Wither, *View*, 195; Stockwood, *Fruiteful Sermon*, sig. B8^r; Becon, *Salue*, 178; (cf. *Postil*, 1: ff. 89^V-90^l; Henry Holland's epistle to Greenham, *Works*, sig. A4^{r-V}; Cope, *Exposition*, f. 132^V). Elizabethan Catholics did not condone idleness, and Matthew Kellison, referring to the Protestant doctrine of justification *sola fide*, claimed Protestants taught that "idlenes is the accomplishment and perfection of morall, and Christian life." Shelford, *Lectvres*, 14, 30-37; Robert Persons, in *Anthology*, ed. Roberts, 83; Kellison, *Svrvey*, 607 (cf. 608-9). The Jesuit Robert Southwell was as adamantly opposed to idleness as any Protestant: "I must, if time and place will permit me, be always doing some profitable thing to avoid sloth, directing mine intention in all my exercises to this end, that I may avoid idleness and temptations and bestow my time in good sort to God's glory." *Two Letters and Short Rules of a Good Life*, ed. Nancy Pollard Brown (Charlottesville, Va., 1973), 43 (henceforth cited as *Short Rules*).

26. Dios, *Sermon*, f. 54^r; T. Rogers, *Discourse*, f. 90^V; Sandys, *Sermons*, 117, 138, 158; Babington, *Commaundements*, 380-81; Jewel, *Works*, 2:939, 941; Samuel Gardiner, *The Cognizance of a Trve Christian* (1597), 154-55; Nowell, *Catechism*, 198; A. Hill, *Crie*, 62-63.

27. Allen, *Treasvrie*, 186, 215; Norden, *Progress*, 177-78; Wilcox, *Prouerbs*, *Works*, 98; Dent, *Path-way*, 72, 187, 189, 191^2. Also cf. Bullinger, *State*, sig. A2^V; Cope, *Exposition*, f. 132^V; Bird, *A Friendly Communication* (1580), f. 29^r. The Catholics similarly attributed a range of evils to idleness, including rebellion, atheism, and sexual sins. According to Kellison, "if by continuall exercise of vertue, and good workes, the seed-plotte of our soule bee not continually manured and tilled, the seede of Gods inspirations & inclina-

tions to vertue . . . bring forthe noe frute of good workes and vertuouse actions." Kellison, *Svrvey*, 605; Shelford, *Lectvres*, 35; Vaux, *Catechisme*, f. 54[r].

28. Cogan, *Haven*, 13; Bullein, *Bulwarke*, pt. 3, ff. 66[r], 67[r]; Dios, *Sermon*, f. 53[r].

29. Francis Seager, *The Schoole of Uertue* (1557), sig. A3[r]; Bateman, *A Christall Glasse of Christian Reformation* (1569), sig. F3[v]; Lodge, *Divel*, sig. B3[v]; Dod, *Treatise*, pt. 2, f. 57[v]; Cope, *Exposition*, f. 415[v]; Boorde, *Regimente*, sig. B7[r-v]; Northbrooke, *Treatise*, ff. 9[r]-10[r]. Cf. Acheley, *Massacre*, sig. D4[v].

30. R. Rogers, *Diaries*, ed. Knappen, 58-60, 101; Ward, ibid., 106, 107; Hoby, *Diary*, 112; Norden, *Practise*, f. *iii[r-v].

31. Scott, ed., *Collection*, 1:493; Wotton, *Letter-Book*, 49; LPL Bacon MS 650/7 (f. 10[r]); *CSPD, 1547-1580*, 183, 187.

32. Rye, ed., *England*, 70; Russell, *History*, 36; Yates, *Castell*, sig. A2[r]; William Fulwood, *The Enimie of Idlenesse* (1568), sig. A5[v]; Becon, *The Demaundes of Holy Scripture* (1577), sig. A4[v].

33. HMC 9 Salisbury, 1:253; HMC 55 Var. Coll., 2:94; Grindal, *Remains*, 467; Manningham, *Diary*, 73; Hearnshaw, ed., *Records*, 1:121, 181, 185.

34. Nowell, *Sermon*, 228; Lambarde, *Government*, 85; LPL Bacon MS 654/124 (f. 184[r]); Stow, *Chronicles*, 4:552.

35. Barrow, *Writings (1587-90)*, 122; Dent, *Path-way*, 196; Peel, ed., *Seconde Parte*, 2:98-99; Woolton, *Manual*, 10; Pilkington, *Works*, 380; Jewel, *Works*, 2:864, 941-42.

36. Barrow, *Writings (1587-90)*, 493; Dent, *Path-way*, 191-92, 192[2], 198-99; R. Rogers, *Treatises*, 359; Burton, *Rowsing*, 466; Stubbes, *Anatomie*, sig. P4[r]; Gifford, *Eight Sermons*, ff. 111[v]-112[r]. For Puritan criticism of the wives of the wealthy, see Dent, *Path-way*, 191-92. Burton criticized idle widows. *Rowsing*, 457.

37. Pilkington, *Works*, 41, 286, 380, 384, 387-88, 440; Jewel, *Works*, 2:864; Henoch Clapham, *A Briefe of the Bible* (1596), 123-24. Cf. Segar, *Honor*, 60; Willoby, *Avisa*, 101.

38. G. Phillips, *The Embassage of Gods Angell* (1597), sig. B5[r].

39. Manningham, *Diary*, 9. Downes, Regius Professor of Greek at Cambridge, made his remark in a sermon delivered c. 1602.

40. Kellison, *Svrvey*, 600, 603-4.

41. Tyndale-Coverdale NT, note to Matt. 6; GB, notes to Deut. 28:6; Prov. 5 (synopsis); 6:6; 13:23; 14:4; 27:26; Matt. 6:34; Eph. 5:16; Phil. 2:12; Col. 4:5; 1 Thess. 4:12; Greaves, *SCJ*, 7:105-7.

42. Sutton, *Disce vivere*, 188-89; Pilkington, *Works*, 58, 387, 446; Sandys, *Sermons*, 182; Wright, *Display*, 6; S. Gardiner, *Cognizance*, 150; Fulwood, *A New Ballad Against Vnthrifts* [1562].

43. R. Rogers, *Treatises*, 392; Perkins, *Treatise*, 534, 550; Chaderton, *Excellent Sermon*, sigs. B8[r], C7[r]; Norden, *Practise*, sig. A4[v]; Dering, *Hebrues, Workes* f. 53[v]; Becon, *Postil*, 2: ff. 56[v]-57[r].

44. Paul Seaver, "Puritanism in a Social Perspective: The Puritan Work Ethic Revisited," paper presented to a joint session of the American Historical Association and the American Society of Church History, Dallas, Texas, 29 Dec. 1977; Yates, *Castell*, f. 13[v]; Ward, *Diaries*, ed. Knappen, 116-17; Hergest, *Rvle*, 6.

45. *The Staffordshire Quarter Session Rolls* [1581-1602], ed. S. A. H. Burne (Kendal, 1931-36), 2:26; Wilkinson, *Confutation*, f. 66[v].

46. GB, notes to Gen. 3:6; Eccles. 6:9; Matt. 18:3; Luke 6:26; 2 Cor. 5:14; 1 John 2:16; prefaces to Phil. and James; BTB, notes to Luke 9:46; 11:43; Greaves, *SCJ*, 7:107. See Laura Stevenson O'Connell, "Anti-Entrepreneurial Attitudes in Elizabethan Sermons and Popular Literature," *Journal of British Studies*, 15 (Spring 1976):1-20, especially 4-8.

47. T. Rogers, *Discourse*, f. 69[v]; G. Abbot, *Exposition*, 290; Cooper, *Admonition*, 145; Lodge, *Divel*, sigs. B2[v], B3[v]; *Wentworth Papers*, ed. Cooper, 22, 25.

48. Becon, *Postil*, 1: f. 48^V; Wither, *View*, 59; Timme, *Discouerie*, sig. F1^r; W. Vaughan, *Golden-groue*, sig. H1^{r-v}; Norden, *Solace*, f. 22^V; *The Letters of Sir Francis Hastings*, ed. Claire Cross (Somerset Record Society, vol. 69), 34. Walsingham approved ambition, but only in the sense that it was an aspiration to honor and virtue. Scott, ed., *Collection*, 1: 500-1.

49. Manningham, *Diary*, 15-16. Archdall's sermon was preached in January 1602.

50. William Elderton, *A Ballad Intituled, Prepare Ye to the Plow* (n.d.).

51. Collinson, "The Beginnings of English Sabbatarianism," *SCH*, 1 (1964):207-8.

52. Tyndale, Pentateuch (1530, 1534, 1551), note to Exod. 31; MB (1537), notes to Lev. 23; Num. 15; Jer. 17; "A Table of the Pryncypall Matters"; Tyndale-Rogers NT, note to John 5; Matthew-Becke Bible (1549, 1551), notes to Num. 15; Jer. 17; Mark 2; MB (1551), notes to Lev. 23; Num. 15; Jer. 17; Mark 2; Checke, *Gospel*, note to Matt. 12 (p. 53).

53. GB, notes to Exod. 31:14; Deut. 5:13; Ps. 92; Isa. 56:2; Amos 8:5; Mark 2:27; Acts 20:7; Rev. 1:10.

54. BB, note to Exod. 20:9; BTB, notes to Luke 6:1; 14:1; John 7:21; Collinson, *SCH*, 1:212-13; Douai Bible, note to Gen. 2. Winton U. Solberg's excellent study of the Puritan sabbath argues that one factor that produced this understanding of the sabbath was the impact of the vernacular Bible. *Redeem the Time* (Cambridge, Mass., 1977), 33. More specifically, it was the impact of the marginalia in the Geneva and Tremellius-Junius versions.

55. Collinson, *SCH*, 1:211, 215.

56. Pilkington, *Works*, 6; J. Rogers, *Summe*, f. 12^V; Nowell, *Catechism*, 128-29; Bridges, *Sermon*, 111; Bedel, *Sermon*, sig. C3^V; Whitgift, *Works*, 2:571.

57. *Certaine Sermons or Homilies Appointed to Be Read in Chvrches* (1623), pt. 2, pp. 125-26. The first part was originally published in 1547 and the second in 1563. "An Homilie Against Disobedience and Wilfull Rebellion" first appeared in 1570.

58. Becon, *Postil*, 2: ff. 130^V-132^r; William Kethe, *A Sermon Made at Blanford Forū* (1571); Dering, *Catechisme, Workes*, sig. A7^V.

59. Dering, *Hebrues, Workes*, sigs. S2^V, S3^V, S8^r; Becon, *Demaundes*, sig. C6^{r-v}; Knewstub, *Lectures*, 65, 72-73.

60. White, *Plague Sermon*, 45; Stockwood, *1578 Sermon*, 24, 50, 133-35, 138; *Fruiteful Sermon*, sigs. E2^r, E3^{r-v}, E5^{r-v}; C. Hill, *Society*, 169; Northbrooke, *Treatise*, ff. 12^r, 20^{r-v}, 66^{r-v}.

61. Gilby, *Dialogve*, sig. M3^V; Shutte, *Forme*, sig. B8^V; Field, *Caveat*, sig. D3^r; *A Godly Exhortation* (1583), sigs. A2^V-A3^r, C1^r; Gifford, *Catechisme*, sigs. F7^V-F8^r; Jones, *Catechisme*, sig. B1^V; Stubbes, *Anatomie*, sigs. L2^{r-v}, L4^r, P5^r-P6^r; Udall, *Obedience*, sig. C1^r; Gee, *Grovnd*, 3; Norden, *Practise*, f. 42^r; *Solace*, ff. 125^V-126^V.

62. Bunny, *Summe*, ff. 46^V-47^V; Bateman, *Arrival*, sig. D5^V; Woolton, *Castell*, sig. E8^r; Fleming, *The Footpath to Felicitie* (1581), 15-16; Walsall, *Sermon*, sigs. E3^r, E4^r; Babington, *Commaundements*, 173-74, 179-202; (cf. T. Rogers, *Doctrine*, 97-98).

63. Strype, *Annals*, 3, pt. 1, 496-97; Deacon, *Treatise*, sig. G7^r; Fenner, *Treatises*, 112, 115-16; Some, *Treatise*, 1; Bulkeley, *Sermon*, sig. F6^r; Cartwright, *Confvtation*, 480; Collinson, *SCH*, 1:208, 218; (Stroud's assertion is found in Dr. Williams' Library, Morrice MS B II, f. 9^V).

64. Perkins, *The Foundation of Christian Religion* (1591), sig. B4^V; Chaine, sigs. H8^{r-v}, I2^r-I3^V; *Treatise*, 452-63.

65. Collinson, *SCH*, 1:217.

66. For a different emphasis see C. Hill, *Society*, chap. 5.

67. Greenham, *Works*, 301, 313, 359-60, 380, 385.

68. Ibid., 176, 333, 373-76, 379-83.

69. Ibid., 381-82.

70. Bownde, *Doctrine*, sig. A4^r, pp. 23, 69-70, 76-83, 89-91, 117-18, 122-23, 267.

71. Ibid., 93-95.

72. Ibid., 57-59, 81, 149 ff., 158, 169, 191-258.

73. Norden, *Progress*, 177-78; Cleaver, *Form*, 21-22, 45; W. Vaughan, *Golden-groue*, sigs. P5^v-P6^r; Dent, *Path-way*, 138-39, 348; Burton, *Anatomie*, 46, 139, 185; Allen, *Treasvrie*, 99-103, 106; Dod, *Treatise*, pt. 1, ff. 61^v, 73^r-74^r, 78^r-92^r; R. Rogers, *Treatises*, 166-67, 298; Estey, *Expositions*, pt. 1, ff. 48^v-52^v.

74. C. Hill, *Society*, chap. 5.

75. Cooper, *Admonition*, 57; Wright, *Summons*, 28; G. Abbot, *Exposition*, 497; A. Hill, *Crie*, 16, 20-21; King, *Lectvres*, 96; Turnbull, *Iames*, f. 249^r; Babington, *Genesis*, 17; Terry, *Triall*, 125; Gibbens, *Qvestions*, 49-54; Sutton, *Disce vivere*, 394, 398, 411-12; John Howson, *A Sermon Preached at St. Maries in Oxford the 17. Day of November, 1602* (Oxford, 1602), sig. C1^v.

76. Strype, *Whitgift*, 2:416; Collinson, *SCH*, 1:219-20.

77. Strype, *Whitgift*, 2:415. Solberg properly argues that condemnation of Sunday recreations was a factor in producing the Puritan conception of the sabbath, but he errs in regarding the Puritan work ethic (especially vocation) as another contributing factor. As manifested above, there was no distinctive Puritan work ethic in the sense in which this phrase is normally used. Solberg does make an interesting point in connecting sabbath observance with covenant theology (*Redeem the Time*, 33). It was the seriousness with which Puritans viewed sabbath observance that led them to equate breaches with other serious offenses, and it was this extremism that motivated Anglican leaders to counterattack at the end of the age. Ironically, this counterattack made sabbatarianism a Puritan hallmark.

78. Barrow, *Writings (1587-90)*, 158-59, 387, 389, 545; J. Rogers, *Displaying*, sigs. K1^v-K2^r.

79. Vaux, *Catechisme*, ff. 41^v-44^r. Cf. Southwell, *Short Rules*, 45.

80. Kethe, *Sermon*, sig. B4^{r-v}.

81. Hake, *Newes*, sig. E6^v.

82. C. Hill, *TRHS*, 13:97; *Society*, 191.

83. C. Hill, *Society*, 165-66; Deacon, *Treatise*, sigs. G5^v-G6^r; Brinkworth, ed., *Court*, 15-16, 35, 41, 50, 60, 64, 76, 83, 104; Hart, *Clergy*, 45.

84. Haigh, *EHR*, 92:45, 52-53; *Reformation*, 245; C. Hill, *Change*, 8; PRO SP 12/240 (f. 292^v); Tait, ed., *Records*, 60-61; Tait, *EHR*, 32:567-68; Kethe, *Sermon*, sigs. A2^v-A3^r; Hamilton, *Sessions*, 28-29.

85. Brinkworth, ed., *Court, passim*; Wiener, *JSH*, 8:40; Purvis, ed., *Documents*, 91.

86. Tait, ed., *Records, passim*; Bateson, ed., *Records*, 3: *passim*.

87. Kethe, *Sermon*, sigs. A2^v-A3^r, C3^r-C4^r; Hamilton, *Sessions*, 28-29; W. B. Whitaker, *Sunday in Tudor and Stuart Times* (1933), 44; HMC 9 Salisbury, 7:161; *Staffordshire Session Rolls*, ed. Burne, 2:26, 92; 4:132-34; Haigh, *EHR*, 92:54-55; *Quarter Sessions Records . . . for the County Palatine of Chester*, ed. J. H. E. Bennett and J. C. Dewhurst (1940), 51; C. Hill, *Society*, 160.

88. HMC Ninth Report, 254, 256.

89. J. W. F. Hill, *Tudor & Stuart Lincoln* (Cambridge, 1956), 99-100, 104-5.

90. Bateson, ed., *Records*, 3:101-3, 174, 185, 421-22, 439.

91. Hearnshaw, ed., *Records*, 1:55, 134, 163, 179, 182, 184, 201, 214, 234, 239, 256, 277, 295, 353, 370-71.

92. Strype, *Annals*, 1, pt. 1, 270; *Parker*, 3:31, 88-89; Grindal, *Remains*, 138-39, 169-71; *EEA*, 2-3: *passim* (the quotation is on 3:150).

93. *Diocese of Norwich: Bishop Redman's Visitation 1597*, ed. J. F. Williams (Norfolk Record Society, 1946), *passim*; PRO SP 235/68 (f. 146^r).

94. Marchant, *Church*, 218; E. R. Brinkworth, "The Study and Use of Archdeacons' Court Records: Illustrated from the Oxford Records (1566-1759)," *TRHS*, 4th ser., 25 (1943):104-5; C. Hill, *Society*, 155; Spufford, *Communities*, 258; *Diocese of Norwich*, ed. Williams, 76; Brinkworth, ed., *Court*, 15, 28; Houlbrooke, *Courts*, 47. Records of four cases of sabbath violations in the diocese of Ely in 1595-96 handled in the consistory court show two instances of working on Sunday, one of playing cards during evening prayer, and one of drunkenness on Sunday. All those involved were men. Hubert Hall, "Some Elizabethan Penances in the Diocese of Ely," *TRHS*, 3rd ser., 1 (1907):266-67, 270-71, 276-77.

95. HMC Ninth Report, 289; Aspinall-Oglander, *Symphony*, 26; Usher, ed., *Movement*, 53, 99.

96. Nowell, *Sermon*, 226; *CJ*, 1:79, 81, 89; D'Ewes, *Journals*, 134. In 1566 Parliament approved a bill to move the market at Battle, Sussex, from Sunday to Thursday. *CJ*, 1:81; *SR*, 4, pt. 1, xxix.

97. Fleming, *A Bright Burning Beacon* [1580], sig. O4^V; Field, *Exhortation*, sigs. A1^r, B7^V-B8^V; W. Vaughan, *Golden-groue*, sigs. P6^V-P7^r (where the number of dead is given as eight); William Rankins, *A Mirrovr of Monsters* (1587), f. 3^r; Strype, *Annals*, 3, pt. 1, 201-2. Vaughan's and Rankins' works had obviously not been published before the 1584 Parliament met. Vaughan also referred to the case of an alewife who brewed on the sabbath in 1589 and was divinely punished when the chimney caught on fire and burned her house. *Golden-groue*, sig. P7^r. Bear Garden on the Bankside was not identical with Paris Garden. See C. L. Kingsford, "Paris Garden and the Bear-Baiting, " *Archaeologia*, 70 (1920): 155-78.

98. Strype, *Annals*, 3, pt. 2, 298; D'Ewes, *Journals*, 333, 335-37, 343, 363, 369; Neale, *Parliaments*, 2:58-60.

99. PRO SP 12/283 (#12); D'Ewes, *Journals*, 613, 624, 626, 628, 643, 668-69; Neale, *Parliaments*, 2:394-95.

100. *CSPD, 1581-1590*, 136; BL Lansdowne MSS 43/60; 47/18; Whitaker, *Sunday*, 46. A case against Sunday plays is made in Lansdowne MS 20/13, which is a refutation of the views of the actors found in MS 20/12.

101. BL Lansdowne MSS 79/72; 99/51; Penry Williams, *The Council in the Marches of Wales Under Elizabeth I* (Cardiff, 1958), 53.

102. Whitaker, *Sunday*, 25-30; C. Hill, *Society*, 188-89. The Privy Council was concerned in 1590 about the attack on William Hill, a gentleman of Bicklehey, Worcs., by thirty persons in a church, but it was the violence and not the sabbath that troubled the Council. *APC*, 19:101-2.

103. Machyn, *Diary*, 233; Robert Laneham, *A Letter* (1575), 15-16, 26-40; *APC*, 17: 90, 109; Peel, ed., *Seconde Parte*, 2:54; PRO SP 222/70.1 (f. 128^r).

104. Sparke, *Sermon at Whaddon*, f. 61^r; Harrison, *Advantage*, 80; Hoby, *Diary*, 64-65; Ward, *Diaries*, ed. Knappen, 106, 115-16; BL Egerton MS 2714 (f. 42^r); "Diary of Philip Wyot," in *Sketches of the Literary History of Barnstaple* (Barnstaple, [1866]), 94.

105. BL Stowe MS 774 (f. 23^r); Haigh, *EHR*, 92:53; LPL Bacon MS 659/245 (f. 356^r).

106. Howson, *1597 Sermon*, 8.

107. Greenham, *Works*, 384.

108. *SR*, 4, pt. 1, 132-33; Tyndale Pentateuch, notes to Num. 29; Deut. 11; Patrick Collinson, "Towards a Broader Understanding of the Early Dissenting Tradition," *The Dissenting Tradition*, ed. C. Robert Cole and Michael E. Moody (Athens, Ohio, 1975), 25; John Bossy, "Blood and Baptism: Kinship, Community and Christianity in Western Europe from the Fourteenth to the Seventeenth Centuries," *SCH*, 10:142-43. Economic motivations are emphasized by C. Hill, *Society*, chap. 5.

109. Whitgift, *Works*, 2:566, 559, 573, 578-79; Sutton, *Disce vivere*, 407-12.

110. Bunny, *Summe*, f. 51^r; Whitgift, *Works*, 2:565, 570-71, 593.

111. PRO SP 19/24 (f. 45^{r-v}); Whitgift, *Works*, 2:574, 595; Sutton, *Disce vivere*, 411.

112. BL Lansdowne MS 30/53; Terry, *Triall*, 125-26; Howson, *1597 Sermon*, 10.

113. Dering, *Hebrues, Workes*, sig. B3^{r-v}; Fulke, *Text*, ff. 327^{r-v}, 463^v; Estey, *Expositions*, pt. 1, f. 49^v; Gifford, *A Short Reply vnto the Last Printed Books of Henry Barrow and Iohn Greenwood* (1591), 23.

114. Cartwright, *Confvtation*, 480; Perkins, *Chaine*, sig. H7^v; Fulke, *Text*, f. 52^r; Greenham, *Works*, 313, 384.

115. McGinn, *Admonition Controversy*, 245; Northbrooke, *Treatise*, f. 12^r; Fulke, *Text*, ff. 89^r, 327^r; (cf. Gilby, *Dialogve*, sig. M3^v).

116. Barrow, *Writings (1587-90)*, 130-31, 180-81, 390; *Writings of Greenwood and Barrow (1591-93)*, 104; Barrow and Greenwood, *Writings of Greenwood (1587-90)*, 167.

117. Vaux, *Catechisme*, ff. 41^v-42^r; Rheims NT, notes to Gal. 4:10; Rev. 1:10; Douai Bible, notes to Gen. 2; Richard Bristow, *A Briefe Treatise of Divers Plaine and Sure Waies* (Antwerp, 1599), ff. 131^v-133^r. The aniconic nature of Puritanism has been properly stressed by J. Sears McGee, "Puritanism in a Religious Perspective," a paper delivered on 29 Dec. 1977 at a joint session of the American Historical Association and the American Society of Church History at Dallas, Texas.

118. Sutton, *Disce vivere*, 408-9; Stubbes, *Anatomie*, sigs. O6^v-O7^r; R. Abbot, *Exaltation*, 7, 72.

119. Stubbes, *Anatomie*, sigs. M2^r-M3^r; Bird, *Communication*, f. 15^{r-v}.

120. Machyn, *Diary*, 274; Forman, *Autobiography*, 16; Tanner, *School*, 27, 99 (referring to Westminster Abbey Muniments 38,805; 47,634). As a schoolboy Forman danced and played games until midnight on Christmas day, 1563. *Autobiography*, 5.

121. *Staffordshire Session Rolls*, ed. Burne, 2:92.

122. Smyth, *Berkeley Manuscripts*, 2:287; Holles, *Memorials*, 41-42; Florence Higham, *Catholic and Reformed* (1962), 82; Rowse, *Cornwall*, 427, 429; Strype, *Smith*, 154. Cf. Richard Carew, *The Svrvey of Cornwall* (1602), f. 68^v.

123. Rose, *Cases*, 170; *APC*, 13:287-88.

124. McGinn, *Admonition Controversy*, 246; Anstruther, *Vaux*, 84; Whitgift, *Works*, 2:567-69, 579; A. H. Dodd, *Life in Elizabethan England* (New York, 1961), 113; W. P. M. Kennedy, *Parish Life Under Queen Elizabeth* (1914), 146.

125. Machyn, *Diary*, 207-8; Byrne, *Life*, 246-49. Hock Tuesday was apparently the day Bird criticized as Rock Monday, when women were said to bind and "abuse" any men they could apprehend. To Bird this was contrary to Christ's abhorrence of cruelty. *Communication*, f. 15^v. See T. F. Thiselton-Dyer, *British Popular Customs, Present and Past* (1876), 188-92. Machyn describes Midsummer's day festivities in his *Diary*, 261. There is an interesting description of the feast of St. George at Utrecht in 1566 in Stow, *Chronicles*, 4: 658-59.

126. Stubbes, *Anatomie*, sigs. M3^v-M4^r; Trigge, *Tovchstone*, 244; R. Rogers, *Treatises*, 578; Bird, *Communication*, f. 15^v; T. Rogers, *Doctrine*, 311-12; Bancroft, *Svrvay*, 284; *Positions*, 20.

127. Machyn, *Diary*, 196; Purvis, ed., *Documents*, 92; PRO STAC 5, J 22/16.

128. J. Hill, *Lincoln*, 104; C. Hill, *Society*, 184-85; Rose, *Cases*, 171-72; *APC*, 17:202; PRO STAC 7 Add., 4/17.

129. Grindal, *Remains*, 141-42, 175; *EEA*, 2-3: *passim*; (cf. Purvis, ed., *Documents*, 39); Hart, *Clergy*, 37-38, 56.

130. *EEA*, 3:151, 216, 225, 337; Grindal, *Remains*, 240-41; K. Thomas, *Religion*, 62-65; Bossy, *SCH*, 10:142-43.

131. Hart, *Clergy*, 38; Marchant, *Puritans*, 248, 255, 258, 275, 278, 282, 311, 314-15; *Diocese of Norwich*, ed. Williams, *passim*. Cf. Purvis, ed., *Documents*, 37, 63. I have found no complaints that the costs of the perambulations were ill-used, though church funds were required. At South Newington, Oxon., fees for bread and ale ran 1s. 8d. in 1589, 2s. in 1598, and 12d. in 1600, while Upton-by-Southwell, Notts., paid 1s. 8d. in 1604. A. Tindal Hart, *The Man in the Pew, 1558-60* (1966), 77.

132. Brinkworth, ed., *Court, passim* (the Blackthorn case is on p. 28); C. Hill, *Society*, 155.

133. Machyn, *Diary*, 201, 230; John Nichols, *The Progresses and Public Processions of Queen Elizabeth* (new ed., 1823), 1:131-41; Strype, *Smith*, 179; Chamberlain, *Letters*, 1:145, 179-80.

134. *CJ*, 1:58-59; C. Hill, *Society*, 151.

Chapter 10: Social Entertainment and Recreation

1. Leigh, *Proclamation*, sig. C7^V.

2. Cited in W. J. Jones, *Chancery*, 436.

3. Wright, *Display*, 30; Walsall, *Sermon*, sig. E4^V; Babington, *Commaundements*, 401-2; Pilkington, *Works*, 151.

4. Wright, *Display*, 31-32; Pilkington, *Works*, 151; G. Abbot, *Exposition*, 548-49; Sutcliffe, *Answere*, 129.

5. Wright, *Display*, 30; Babington, *Commaundements*, 402-3, 409; Cooper, *Certaine Sermons*, 16; Sandys, *Sermons*, 117-18. Cf. Newnham, *Nightcrowe*, 29.

6. Whetstone, *Enemie*, sigs. G4^V, H2^r, H4^V, Kl^r-K2^r, I3^{r-V}; *Rocke*, sigs. N2^{r-V}, N3^V, O2^r; Tilney, *Flower*, sig. B8^V; Pilkington, *Works*, 151-52; Bedel, *Sermon*, sigs. C2^V, E1^V. Cf. Seager, *Schoole*, sigs. B8^r, C1^r.

7. Sutcliffe, *Answere*, 127; Wright, *Summons*, 19.

8. Cooper, ed., *Wentworth Papers*, 18, 23-24.

9. Fenner, *Treatises*, 181, 186-88; Northbrooke, *Treatise*, ff. 11^V, 11^V; Gibbon, *Praise*, 54; Stubbes, *Anatomie*, ππ5^V, 6^V-7^r; Acheley, *Massacre*, sig. C4^V; Bird, *Communication*, f. 20^V; Udall, *Commentarie*, 190-91.

10. Perkins, *Treatise*, 593; Fenner, *Treatises*, 182-84; Bird, *Communication*, ff. 14^V-16^r, 61^V.

11. Fenner, *Treatises*, 185; Burton, *Ten Sermons*, 11.

12. Perkins, *Treatise*, 594; Stubbes, *Anatomie*, sig. P4^r; Burton, *Rowsing*, 466; Dent, *Path-way*, 191-92; Bownde, *Doctrine*, 133; Northbrooke, *Treatise*, f. 39^r; Greenham, *Works*, 416; Bird, *Communication*, ff. 14^V, 33^V-34^r; Fenner, *Treatises*, 183-84.

13. Fenner, *Treatises*, 186, 192; Northbrooke, *Treatise*, ff. 38^V-39^r, 48^r, 54^V; Perkins, *Treatise*, 589-90; Stubbes, *Anatomie*, sigs. O6^V-O7^V; Greenham, *Works*, 385; Stockwood, *Fruiteful Sermon*, sig. B7^r; Gosson, *Schoole*, ff. 16^V, 28^r. Tennis required not only a walled court but expensive and short-lived leather balls stuffed with hair. Dennis Brailsford, *Sport and Society* (1969), 30-31. The London mansion of Thomas Howard, duke of Norfolk, known as Charterhouse or Howard House, had both a tennis court and a bowling alley. Neville Williams, *Thomas Howard, Fourth Duke of Norfolk* (1964), 115.

14. Stubbes, *Anatomie*, sig. P6^{r-V}; Carr, *Fal*, sig. C3^r; Emmison, *Elizabethan Life*, 1: 225-26.

15. Northbrooke, *Treatise*, f. 54^V; Dering, *Hebrues, Workes*, sig. I8^V; Estey, *Expositions*, pt. 2, ff. 113^V-114^r; Rainolds, *Overthrow*, 22-23; James Balmford, *A Short and Plaine Dialogve* (1593), sigs. A4^r-A5^r; Bird, *Communication*, ff. 48^V-49^V; Fenner, *Treatises*, 188-91; Dod, *Treatise*, pt. 1, f. 36^r; Perkins, *Treatise*, 590; *Chaine*, sig. H2^r; Keith L.

Sprunger, *The Learned Doctor William Ames* (Urbana, Ill., 1972), 176; HMC 12 Wells, 2: 305. For the Anglican position on lots see King, *Lectvres*, 123-24; G. Abbot, *Exposition*, 79-80; BB, note to Acts 1:26. Cf. also Cope, *Exposition*, f. 345^{r-v}.

16. Cooper, *Athenae*, 2:392; Fenner, *Treatises*, 187; Perkins, *Treatise*, 591-92; Balmford, *Dialogve*, sigs. A2^V, A7^r; Northbrooke, *Treatise*, ff. 42^r, 43^{r-v}, 52^V-53^r, 54^r; Deacon, *Treatise*, sig. E5^V; W. Vaughan, *Golden-groue*, sigs. $_2$B8^V-$_2$C1^V; Bird, *Communication*, ff. 40^V, 45^V; Stubbes, *Anatomie*, sig. O7^{r-v}. Cf. Shutte, *Sermon*, sig. D7^r; Dering, *Hebrues, Workes*, sigs. B3^r, X3^V. Robert Openshaw urged those who played dice and cards to sing Psalms, instruct their households, and pray instead. *Questions*, sig. A4^V.

17. Gifford, *Catechisme*, sig. H2^r; Estey, *Expositions*, pt. 1, f. 70^r; Northbrooke, *Treatise*, sig. A4^V, ff. 44^r-45^V; Bird, *Communication*, sig. A8^{r-v}, ff. 22^r, 55^V; Dod, *Treatise*, pt. 2, ff. 65^V-66^r; Perkins, *Treatise*, 594; *Warning*, 250; Fenner, *Treatises*, 185. Cf. Allen, *Treasvrie*, 214; H. Smith, *Teares*, 35.

18. Rowse, *Cornwall*, 427; Ward, *Diaries*, ed. Knappen, 110; Hoby, *Diary*, 46, 70, 120; Stone, *Crisis*, 567, 569; Weigall, *Quarterly Review*, 215:129; Wotton, *Letter-Book*, 49. Despite the views of Lady Mildmay and Lady Hoby, an Antwerp merchant observed in 1575 that English housewives spent much time playing cards. Rye, ed., *England*, 72.

19. Penry, *State*, sig. H3^{r-v}; Barrow, *Writings (1587-90)*, 493, 495-96.

20. T. G. Law, *Jesuits and Seculars in the Reign of Queen Elizabeth* (1889), 18-19; Gerard, *Autobiography*, 161, 165, 170, 185; Vaux, *Catechisme*, ff. 44^r, 57^r, 62^V. For the use of lots see the Rheims NT, note to Acts 1:26. The Catholic author John Feckenham was ultimately apprehended because he could not resist playing bowls with a gentleman named Denny. Robert Horne, *An Answeare . . . to a Booke* (1566), f. 128^V.

21. Cogan, *Haven*, 3, 19-20; Bullein, *Bulwarke*, pt. 3, f. 66^V; *Booke*, f. 123^V; Lemnie, *Touchstone*, trans. Newton, f. 54^r; Mulcaster, *Positions*, chaps. 17-18, and pp. 94-95, 104-5; Manningham, *Diary*, 132.

22. *SR*, 3:837-41; 4, pt. 1, 285; 4, pt. 2, 548-49. For an attempt to enforce the statute in Bucks. in 1561, see PRO SP 19/43 (f. 87^r). Grammar school statutes also restricted unlawful games. Mumford, *School*, 480; Draper, *Centuries*, 247. The statutes of the Rivington School asserted that the students' chief pastime would be shooting and "small game, or none for money." Kay, *History*, 173. Unlawful games were a problem at Oxford, hence c. 1561 Sir Nicholas Throckmorton received proposals to reform the statutes to ensure prohibition of such games as dice, cards, and football, especially during times of religious services, study, and public exercises. HMC 70 Pepys, 9.

23. *CSPD, Add., 1566-79*, 20-22; Stubbes, *Anatomie*, sig. O8^r; Dering, *Workes*, f. 51^r; *Sermon at the Tower*, sig. C8^r; Bird, *Communication*, sigs. A6^V-A7^r, ff. 59^V-60^r.

24. Bateson, ed., *Records*, 3:175, 185; HMC 73 Exeter, 9, 309; Draper, *Centuries*, 28; BL Lansdowne MS 44/42; Emmison, *Elizabethan Life*, 3:238-39.

25. Hearnshaw, ed., *Records*, 1:42, 55, 92, 119, 120, 182-83, *et passim*. Although numerous cases are in the court leet records, the book of examinations for Southampton has only one instance of a man cited for playing unlawful games in the period 1570 to 1594. Hamilton, ed., *Books*, 65.

26. *Staffordshire Session Rolls*, ed. Burne, 1:999, *et passim* (the quotation is on 3:44); *Quarter Sessions Records for Chester*, ed. Bennett and Dewhurst, 41, 44, 50; Tait, ed., *Records*, 3-160 *passim*. The Lancashire records (pp. 35, 41) also show a yeoman and a husbandman presented for illegally shooting handguns. In his charge to the general sessions at Maidstone, Kent, in April 1582, Lambarde warned that unlawful games led to theft. Lambarde, *Government*, 70. A Westminster yeoman was required to post a bond of £80 in 1562 to ensure that he would never again play unlawful games. PRO SP 21/10 (f. 22^r).

27. Emmison, *Elizabethan Life*, 1:27, 36, 219, 224, 230.

28. Grindal, *Remains*, 130, 138, 171; *EEA*, 2:54, 73, 110, *et passim*; Raine, *History*, 83. Whitgift and William Allen, bishop of Exeter, enjoyed bowls. In April 1602 two members of Whitgift's household quarreled while bowling and one, the son of Sir Thomas Wilford, stabbed his opponent. As a student at Christ's College, Cambridge, Bancroft was known for his boxing, wrestling, and agility with the quarterstaff. Stow, *Chronicles*, 4:424; Percy, *History*, 18; Stuart B. Babbage, *Puritanism and Richard Bancroft* (1962), 8.

29. Raine, ed., *Injunctions*, 119; Purvis, ed., *Documents*, 56, 92; Brinkworth, ed., *Court*, 54-55, 67, 125. Cf. Barmby, ed., *Accounts*, 349-50. The 1571 canons prohibited the clergy from engaging in unlawful games and encouraged a modest use of archery. Cardwell, ed., *Synodalia*, 1:119.

30. HMC 69 Middleton, 150-51; Haigh, *Reformation*, 241; BL Lansdowne MS 110/10; Emmison, *Elizabethan Life*, 1:219, 222, 230; Raine, ed., *Injunctions*, 131; Hart, *Clergy*, 31; *Diocese of Norwich*, ed. Williams, 82, 90; Purvis, ed., *Documents*, 168; HMC 12 Wells, 2:294-95. This behavior was probably doubly objectionable because it was associated with Catholic priests. Cf. Dering's observation of his student days at Marian Cambridge: "Such priestes as I have knowne some in Cambridge that when they have played all night at dice, in the morning being called away to Masse have sworne a great othe that they would make hast and come againe." Cited in Collinson, *Mirror*, 6. For a much earlier complaint (1526) against the gambler William Braborne, canon of St. Gregory's Priory, see BL Add. MS 32,311, f. 189.

31. Peel, ed., *Seconde Parte*, 2:98, 100, 102-9, 147, 157.

32. Machyn, *Diary*, 230, 251; Strype, *Smith*, 179; Stone, *Crisis*, 569-70; Chamberlain, *Letters*, 1:180; Dering, *Workes*, f. 12^V. Shuttlecock became very popular at court late in the reign. Manningham, *Diary*, 132. Elizabeth's former tutor, Roger Ascham, was addicted to gambling with dice. Rowse, *England*, 530.

33. HMC 69 Middleton, 423-24, 429, 432, 442; BL Stowe MS 774; A. Clifford, *Lives*, 7-8; Smyth, *Berkeley Manuscripts*, 2:363, 420; BL Lansdowne MS 101/45; Stone, *Crisis*, 569-70; LPL Bacon MS 660/102 (f. 143^r); *The Visitations of Essex*, ed. Walter C. Metcalfe (1878-79), 1:236; BL Lansdowne MS 86/45; *APC*, 9:84. Burghley "seldome or never plaid at anie game," but he enjoyed watching archers and bowlers. Collins, *Life*, 64. Burghley's secretary, Sir Michael Hicks, enjoyed bowling and built his own alley. BL Lansdowne MSS 85/21; 87/84.

34. Stow, *Chronicles*, 4:895. Cf. Rye, ed., *England*, 46.

35. Stubbes, *Anatomie*, sigs. Pl^V-P2^r.

36. Bedel, *Sermon*, sig. E1^V; Babington, *Commaundements*, 385; *EEA*, 2:110; Mumford, *School*, 480.

37. Stubbes, *Anatomie*, sigs. P1^V-P4^r; Perkins, *Treatise*, 589; Estey, *Expositions*, pt. 1, f. 66^r.

38. Stow, *Chronicles*, 4:504; Manningham, *Diary*, 22.

39. BL Lansdowne MSS 33/28, 32, 33; Tait, ed., *Records*, 11, 14, 101; PRO SP 222/70.1 (f. 128^r).

40. Bateson, ed., *Records*, 3:191; HMC 69 Middleton, 451; HMC 54 Beverley, 182; Anstruther, *Vaux*, 96-98; Smyth, *Berkeley Manuscripts*, 2:363.

41. Dodd, *Life*, 112; Machyn, *Diary*, 191, 198, 270; Stow, *Chronicles*, 4:895; Laneham, *Letter*, 23-24; HMC 77 De L'Isle, 2:461; Chamberlain, *Letters*, 1:180. By letter patent on 2 June 1573 Elizabeth appointed Ralph Bowes chief master of "our game pastymes and sportes, that is to saie of all and euery our Beares Bulles and Mastiff Dogges." BL Egerton MS 2223 (f. 11). Cf. *APC*, 8:391. For another example of ape-baiting see Tait, ed., *Records*, 101.

42. Rankins, *Mirrovr*, f. 6^r.

43. Henry Chettle, *Kind-Harts Dreame* [1592], sig. E4^r.

44. Sutcliffe, *Answere*, 129; Peel, ed., *Seconde Parte*, 2:148; Wright, *Hunting*, sig. A4^r; Manningham, *Diary*, 52; Strype, *Parker*, 2:445; Grindal, *Remains*, 268-69.

45. G. Abbot, *Exposition*, 92; Babington, *Commaundements*, 316-18, 385; Whetstone, *Enemie*, sig. G4^V; *EEA*, 2:59, 125-26; 3:179; Brinkworth, ed., *Court*, 125. Gabriel Harvey's hostile remarks about the theater are, I think, motivated by personal pique, not religious concern. His comments in 1579 may indicate that the Latin comedy *Pedantius*, which caricatures him, was first performed that year. *Letter-Book of Gabriel Harvey*, ed. E. J. L. Scott (1884), 67. See also Frederick S. Boas, *University Drama in the Tudor Age* (Oxford, 1914), 148-56.

46. Fenner, *Treatises*, 24, 112; BL Lansdowne MS 20/13; Stockwood, *1578 Sermon*, 24, 134-37; *Fruiteful Sermon*, sig. E1^r.

47. Burton, *Conclvsions of Peace, Works*, 391; Allen, *Treasvrie*, 85; Becon, *Postil*, 2: f. 73^{r-V}; Northbrooke, *Treatise*, ff. 28^V-33^V, 37^{r-V}.

48. Stubbes, *Anatomie*, sigs. ππ5^V-6^r, L5^r, L7^r-L8^V. Stubbes is inaccurately interpreted by E. N. S. Thompson, *The Controversy Between the Puritans and the Stage* (New York, 1903), chap. 5.

49. Gosson, *Schoole*, ff. π6^V, 3^V, 17^V, 23^r-24^V.

50. White, *Plague Sermon*, 46-47; Field, *Exhortation*, sig. C3^{r-V}; Rankins, *Mirrovr*, ff. 2^r, 4^r, 5^r, 6^r, 21^V, 24^r; Holland, *Preservatives*, sigs. A5^V-A6^r; Bownde, *Doctrine*, 134-35.

51. Rainolds, *Overthrow*, 10-11, 19, 24, 99-102, 108, 147; W. Vaughan, *Golden-groue*, sigs. L1^V-L2^r; Perkins, *Chaine*, sigs. L8^V, M6^V; *Treatise*, 585-86; Manningham, *Diary*, 100; R. Rogers, *Treatises*, 166, 578; Dod, *Treatise*, pt. 2, f. 57^r.

52. HMC 9 Salisbury, 2:117; Machyn, *Diary*, 290; BL Lansdowne MSS 7/62; 20/10, 11, 12; BL Add. MS 32,379, f. 41^V. Bacon wanted to assure that "the assemblies to the vnchaste shamelesse and vnnaturall tomblinge of the Italion weomen maye be avoided." BL Add. MS 32,379, f. 41^V.

53. *APC*, 10:144; 11:73-74; 12:15; 13:269-70, 404-5; 14:102; 15:70, 271-72; 18: 214-16; BL Lansdowne MS 60/19. The plague also led to some curtailment of the Bartholomew Fair activities. BL Lansdowne MS 73/40. In July 1593 the vice-chancellor and heads of houses at Cambridge complained about plays in the town because of the danger of the plague. Roger Lord North was opposed to the request. BL Lansdowne MSS 75/5, 8.

54. Bateson, ed., *Records*, 3:191, 198; *The Records of the City of Norwich*, ed. William Hudson and John C. Tingey (Norwich, 1906, 1910), 2:345-46; Manningham, *Diary*, 130; Hamilton, *Sessions*, 28-29; BL Add. MS 10,305; J. Hill, *Lincoln*, 98; Emmison, *Elizabethan Life*, 1:288-29; Thiselton-Dyer, *Customs*, 299. Drama flourished in Chelmsford, Essex.

55. *CSPD, 1595-97*, 310; Gawdy, *Letters*, 23, 93.

56. John T. Murray, *English Dramatic Companies*, 2 vols. (Boston, 1910); Anstruther, *Vaux*, 96; E. K. Chambers, *Sir Henry Lee* (Oxford, 1936), 42; Holles, *Memorials*, 42; Raine, *History*, 80. For the use of plays in schools see T. H. Vail Motter, *The School Drama in England* (1929; repr. Port Washington, N.Y., 1968). The 1581 will of the gentleman Alexander Hoghton of Lea, Lancs., bequeathed his brother Thomas "all my instruments belonginge to mewsycke and all maner of playe clothes yf he be mynded to keppe and doe keppe players." Piccope, ed., *Wills*, 51:238.

57. Murray, *Companies*, 1:3-11, 27; *APC*, 7:134, *et passim*; PRO SP 36/22 (f. 44^r); *APC*, 20:327-28; Tanner, *School*, 99-100; Draper, *Centuries*, 30-31; Laneham, *Letter*, 33. James I continued to patronize the theater. Cf. Sir William Ashcombe's diary for 1605, Huntingdon MS 30,665 (f. 2^V).

58. Rollins, ed., *Ballads*, 276.

59. GB, note to Mark 6:22.

60. Rye, ed., *England*, 110; Hart, *Man in Pew*, 74; *Illustrations of the Manners and Expences of Antient Times*, ed. John Nichols (1797), 142; Aspinall-Oglander, *Symphony*, 29.

61. Cooper, *Certaine Sermons*, 16; Babington, *Commaundements*, 318-21; Walsall, *Sermon*, sigs. E3^V-E4^V; Bedel, *Sermon*, sig. E1^V; G. Abbot, *Exposition*, 92-93.

62. Bradford, *Sermons*, sig. H8^r; Hake, *Touchestone*, sigs. C6^r, C7^{r-v}; Dering, *Hebrues, Workes*, sig. B3^r; Shutte, *Forme*, sig. C2^r; Gosson, *Schoole*, ff. 16^V, 27^V-28^r; Northbrooke, *Treatise*, ff. 57^V, 61^V-62^r, 63^V-64^r.

63. Dering, *Catechisme, Workes*, sig. F6^r; Gifford, *Catechisme*, sig. H1^V; *Eight Sermons*, f. 79^r; Bird, *Communication*, ff. 15^V, 36^{r-v}, 38^V-39^r; Stubbes, *Anatomie*, sigs. π5^V, π6^V, M7^V-O1^r, O5^{r-v}.

64. Fenner, *Treatises*, 187; Rainolds, *Overthrow*, 132-33; Perkins, *Chaine*, sig. L8^V; *Treatise*, 587; Dod, *Treatise*, pt. 2, f. 57^r. For Essex cases of dancing during church services see Emmison, *Elizabethan Life*, 1:224, 231.

65. Mulcaster, *Positions*, 49, 72-74; Bullein, *Bulwarke*, pt. 3, f. 66^V.

66. Purvis, ed., *Documents*, 167; Hart, *Clergy*, 33-34; *EEA*, 2:49, 57, 73, 125-26; 3:216, 226, 340; Brinkworth, ed., *Court*, 43, 51, 54-55.

67. BL Lansdowne MS 88/51; LPL Bacon MS 650/7 (f. 10^r).

68. Machyn, *Diary*, 191, 221; Laneham, *Letter*, 15, 21; Chamberlain, *Letters*, 1:62, 115; Bruce Pattison, *Music and Poetry of the English Renaissance* (2nd ed., 1970), 15; Williams, *Bess*, 202; *Calendar of Letters and State Papers Relating to English Affairs . . . in . . . the Archives of Simancas*, 4 (repr., Nendeln, 1971):650; A. Clifford, *Lives*, xxiv. The painting at Penshurst Place believed to be of Elizabeth dancing with Sir Robert Dudley is magnificently reproduced in Neville Williams, *All the Queen's Men* (1972), 46-47.

69. Stubbes, *Anatomie*, sig. O8^r.

70. Nicholas Whight, *A Commendation of Musicke* [c. 1562]. (This is a ballad.)

71. Peter LeHuray, *Music and the Reformation in England 1549-1660* (1967), 32-36; *Certaine Sermons*, pt. 1, 131.

72. BL Royal MS 18. B. XIX.

73. Whitgift, *Works*, 3:106-8, 384-88, 392.

74. Edward Hake, *The Psalmes of David in English Meter* (1579), cited in Morrison C. Boyd, *Elizabethan Music and Musical Criticism* (2nd ed., Philadelphia, 1962), 23; Trigge, *Touchstone*, 243; Gilby, *Dialogve*, sig. M3^V; Northbrooke, *Treatise*, f. 41^{r-v}.

75. Sutcliffe, *Answere*, 119, 131; Parker, *Correspondence*, 215; Boyd, *Elizabethan Music*, 22; *Zurich Letters*, ed. Robinson, 1:178; LeHuray, *Music*, 37-38; Turnbull, *Iames*, ff. 326^V-327^r.

76. Hooker, *Works*, 2:159-62; Thomas Case, *The Praise of Mvsicke* (Oxford, 1586), 139-52; LeHuray, *Music*, 39.

77. Grindal, *Remains*, 147, 149; HMC 12 Wells, 2:294-95, 299, 301, 314, 321, 327, 333, 341-42, 345; LeHuray, *Music*, 43.

78. Abraham Fleming, *The Bridge to Blessednesse, ad cal. The Foot-path of Faith* (1619), 316 (first pub. 1581); Turnbull, *Iames*, ff. 284^V, 327^r, 328^r; *EEA*, 2:125-26; Case, *Praise*, 66-67. Cf. Bullein, *Booke*, f. 123^V.

79. Dering, *Catechisme, Workes*, sigs. A1^V, A8^V, F6^r; John Rainolds, *A Sermon vpon Part of the Eighteenth Psalm* (Oxford, 1586), sig. C2^r; Gifford, *Catechisme*, sig. H1^r; Stubbes, *Anatomie*, sigs. O3^V, O4^V-O5^V; Gosson, *Schoole*, ff. 9^r, 16^V; Bownde, *Doctrine*, 241-42; Stockwood, *Fruiteful Sermon*, sig. E3^V.

80. Fenner, *Treatises*, 186; Northbrooke, *Treatise*, ff. 39^{r-v}, 41^V-42^r; Stubbes, *Anatomie*, sig. O4^V; Rose, *Cases*, 128; Whitgift, *Works*, 3:322; Weigall, *Quarterly Review*, 215: 125; Hoby, *Diary*, 46, 99.

81. Mulcaster, *Positions*, 38, 178; Whitelocke, *Liber*, 12; Boyd, *Elizabethan Music*, 14-15; Pattison, *Music*, 10-11; G. L. Marson, *et al.*, *King Henry VIII School 1545-1945* (Coventry, 1945), 12-13. Cf. Watson, *Schools*, 214, for a defense of musical instruction by John Howes, in part because music increased the likelihood of preferment.

82. HMC 58 Bath, 4:145-46; HMC 77 De L'Isle, 2:176, 437; Boyd, *Elizabethan Music*, 18; LPL Bacon MS 650/7 (f. 10^r); BL Lansdowne MS 88/51.

83. Malden, ed., *Papers*, 9; David C. Price, "Gilbert Talbot, Seventh Earl of Shrewsbury: An Elizabethan Courtier and His Music," *Music and Letters*, 57 (April 1976):145; E. D. Mackerness, *A Social History of English Music* (1964), 63-64, 68-69; HMC 9 Salisbury, 6:68; 8:498; Pattison, *Music*, 7.

84. Anstruther, *Vaux*, 85, 96; Rowse, *England*, 450; Gerard, *Autobiography*, 77.

85. Boyd, *Elizabethan Music*, 10-11; Machyn, *Diary*, 222; Laneham, *Letter*, 21, 42-44, 46-56; Nichols, *Progresses*, 3:108-21; John Bossewell, *Workes of Armorie* (1572), book 3, f. 14^r.

86. Percy A. Scholes missed the point in his comment about Psalm singing: "Apparently everybody *did* it, but it was thought that the Puritans *overdid* it." *The Puritans and Music in England and New England* (1934; repr. New York, 1962), 274. The debate never involved the *amount* of Psalm singing, but the use of appropriate texts and especially the limitations on musical forms to preserve the intelligibility of those texts.

87. Emmison, *Elizabethan Life*, 1:209-10; *Staffordshire Session Rolls*, ed. Burne, 2:92.

88. Carew, *Svrvey*, f. 69^v. Carew attributes this view to one of his friends.

89. Anderson, *Shield*, sig. T4^v.

90. Carl Bridenbaugh, *Vexed and Troubled Englishmen 1590-1642* (New York, 1968), 282-83; Thiselton-Dyer, *Customs*, 278; Thomas G. Barnes, "County Politics and a Puritan Cause Célèbre: Somerset Churchales, 1633," *TRHS*, 9 (1959):106-7; Hart, *Man in Pew*, 72.

91. Carew, *Svrvey*, ff. 68^v-69^r; Sedley L. Ware, *The Elizabethan Parish in Its Ecclesiastical and Financial Aspects* (Baltimore, 1908), 71-72; Hart, *Man in Pew*, 73; Barnes, *TRHS*, 9:106-7.

92. Wallace Notestein, *The English People on the Eve of Colonization 1603-1630* (New York, 1954), 244-45; Campbell, *Yeoman*, 301; Bridenbaugh, *Englishmen*, 283; *Illustrations*, ed. Nichols, 135; BL Stowe MS 1055, ff. 23-24.

93. Carew, *Svrvey*, f. 69^v; Collinson, in *The Dissenting Tradition*, ed. Cole and Moody, 25; cf. Bossy, *SCH*, 10:143.

94. Carew, *Svrvey*, f. 69^v; Barnes, *TRHS*, 9:107; Samuel R. Gardiner, *History of England from the Accession of James I to the Outbreak of the Civil War* (1883-84), 7:319; PRO STAC 7 Add., 2/24.

95. Barnes, *TRHS*, 9:109; Hamilton, *Sessions*, 28-29; C. Hill, *Society*, 190-91. An effort had been undertaken in Edward VI's reign to abolish wakes for similar reasons. A. G. Dickens, *Lollards and Protestants in the Diocese of York, 1509-1558* (1959), 180.

96. Carew, *Svrvey*, f. 69^r; Anderson, *Shield*, sig. T4^v; Stubbes, *Anatomie*, sigs. M4^v-M7^r.

97. Hastings, *Letters*, 117-18.

Chapter 11: Food and Fasting

1. Jane Anger, *Iane Anger, Her Protection* (1589), 7. The author's name may be a pseudonym.

2. Rollins, ed., *Ballads*, 276.

3. BB note to Gen. 1:29; King, *Lectvres*, 76; Anderson, *Shield*, sig. D2^r; Nash, *Anatomie*, sigs. D3^v-D4^v; G. Abbot, *Exposition*, 574; Nowell, *Catechism*, 197; Whitgift, *Works*, 2:390; Woolton, *Manual*, 87-90; Nixon, *Navy*, sig. D2^v; Bisse, *Sermons*, sig. B6^r; Jewel, *Works*, 2:1040; Manningham, *Diary*, 7.

4. Anderson, *Sermon of Comfort*, 7-8; Sandys, *Sermons*, 401; Drant, *Two Sermons*, sigs. H2^V-H3^r; Wright, *Summons*, 4; S. Gardiner, *Cognizance*, 8; Jewel, *Works*, 2:1039-40; Woolton, *Manual*, 87-88; (cf. Manningham, *Diary*, 158); Nixon, *Navy*, sig. D2^r; Drant, *A Fruitfull and Necessary Sermon* [1572], sig. E2^r; Pilkington, *Works*, 52.

5. Whetstone, *Enemie*, sig. K3^r; Pilkington, *Works*, 59; Bisse, *Sermons*, sig. E7^r; Whitgift, *Works*, 3:617; Cooper, *Copie*, sig. C1^r; Nixon, *Navy*, sig. D1^r.

6. Woolton, *Manual*, 87-89, 93; Jewel, *Works*, 2:1040; Bateman, *Glasse*, sigs. F1^V, F2^V; Sandys, *Sermons*, 137; Pilkington, *Works*, 53; Wright, *Display*, 36; S. Gardiner, *Cognizance*, 2, 10; Babington, *A Profitable Exposition of the Lords Prayer* (1596), 142.

7. Turnbull, *Iude*, f. 84^V; Pilkington, *Works*, 255; Woolton, *Manual*, 90.

8. Perkins, *Treatise*, 424, 551; Greenham, *Works*, 14; GB, note to Prov. 23:1; Moffett, *Commentarie*, 227-28; Stubbes, *Anatomie*, sigs. J1^r, J2^V-J3^V, J6^V; Henry Smith, *The Wedding Garment* (1590), 8; Burton, *Wooing*, 258; Dering, *Catechisme*, *Workes*, sig. D8^V; Gifford, *Catechisme*, sig. H1^V; Fenner, *Treatises*, 24; Becon, *Salue*, 209; R. Rogers, *Treatises*, 108; Cleaver, *Form*, 72, 290; Dent, *Path-way*, 191^2; Marbury, *Notes*, 50, 56; Northbrooke, *Garden*, sig. $_2$F8^{r-v}; Timme, *Discouerie*, sig. G1^V; Gibbon, *Praise*, 54.

9. Bird, *Communication*, f. 7^V; Norden, *Solace*, f. 79^V; Perkins, *Treatise*, 551, 553-54; *A Case of Conscience* (1592), 871; Chaine, sigs. L8^r, M3^r; *Warning*, 250; Dering, *Catechisme*, *Workes*, sig. G1^r; *Hebrues*, *Workes*, sig. E2^r; Greenham, *Works*, 17, 416; Wilcox, *Prouerbs*, 123; Timme, *Discouerie*, sigs. G1^V, G2^V, G4^V; Allen, *Treasvrie*, 186; Dent, *Pathway*, 71; Stubbes, *Anatomie*, sigs. H8^r-J2^r; *Motive*, 167; Gifford, *Catechisme*, sig. H1^r; Dod, *Treatise*, pt. 2, f. 57^V; Becon, *Postil*, 2: f. 59^V; Holland, *Exercise*, 7; H. Smith, *Teares*, 19; R. Rogers, *Treatises*, 178; Crowley, *Opening*, sig. E8^r; Bartholomew Chamberlaine, *A Sermon Preached at Farington in . . . 1587* (1591), sig. B3^r; Cartwright, *Confvtation*, 11; Dent, *Path-way*, 140; Gifford, *A Dialogue Betweene a Papist and a Protestant* (1582), f. 39^V.

10. Perkins, *Case of Conscience*, 871; *Treatise*, 552-53, 556; Greenham, *Works*, 47, 114; Burton, *An Exposition of the Lordes Prayer*, in *Works* (1602), 166; Nicholson, *Acolastvs*, sig. H2^V; Gibbon, *Praise*, 52; *Remedie*, sig. K1^r; Dering, *Hebrues*, *Workes*, sigs. B2^V-B3^r; Timme, *Discouerie*, sig. G3^V; Holland, *Exposition*, 135.

11. Wilcox, *Prouerbs*, 108; Acheley, *Massacre*, sig. E1^r; White, *Plague Sermon*, 64-65; Stubbes, *Glasse*, sig. A2^V; *Anatomie*, sigs. H8^V-J1^r; W. Vaughan, *Golden-groue*, sigs. H8^r, Q7^r; Cleaver, *Form*, 72; Timme, *Discouerie*, sig. G2^r; Becon, *Postil*, 2: f. 59^r. Barrow was critical of clergy in the Church of England for permitting the landed classes to enjoy such lavish spreads. *Writings (1587-90)*, 493.

12. Thomas Dawson, *The Good Huswifes Iewell* (1596 ed.), sigs. E1^V, G7^V; *The Second Part of the Good Hus-wiues Iewell* (1597), 58; *A Book of Cookerie* (1597?), sig. A2^{r-v}. For other recipes see, e.g., the notebook of Lancelot Ridley of Shropshire (c. 1574-1602), BL Add. MS 44,062.

13. Shelford, *Lectvres*, 38, 101-2; Vaux, *Catechisme*, ff. 49^r, 68^V; Southwell, *Short Rules*, 43.

14. W. Vaughan, *Directions*, 74; Cogan, *Haven*, 148, 168-69, 172, 187, 199, 200-1; Lemnie, *Touchstone*, trans. Newton, ff. 3^{r-v}, 7^r, 48^V-49^r; Bullein, *Booke*, sig. A5^V; *Bulwarke*, pt. 3, f. 64^{r-v}; Boorde, *Regimente*, sigs. C3^V, C5^V-C6^V; Smyth, *Berkeley Manuscripts*, 2:258; Oglander, *Memoirs*, 166-67; Eliot, *Castel*, ff. 44^r, 45^r.

15. Rye, ed., *England*, 70, 79, 110.

16. Stone, *Crisis*, 557-58; H. A. St. John Mildmay, *A Brief Memoir of the Mildmay Family* (1913), 65; HMC 55 Var. Coll., 2:84.

17. HMC 58 Bath, 4:238-39; BL Lansdowne MSS 46/83, 59/41 (cf. 58/60); HMC 9 Salisbury, 2:525; HMC 55 Var. Coll., 2:71. At banquets, of course, such variety was common. At a banquet given by the master of the Grocers' Company in June 1561 thirty bucks and

several stags were served. When Henry Brooke, Lord Cobham, was installed as warden of the Cinque Ports in 1598, twenty-six oxen were prepared. Machyn, *Diary,* 260 (cf. 237); Chamberlain, *Letters,* 1:43.

18. *Memoirs of the Verney Family,* ed. Frances P. Verney, 1 (1892):59; Stone, *Crisis,* 559; HMC 55 Var. Coll., 2:72.

19. Strype, *Parker,* 2:443; Laneham, *Letter,* 39.

20. Batho, ed., *Household Papers,* 85-86; HMC 58 Bath, 4:178 (cf. 181); BL Lansdowne MS 33/70; HMC 9 Salisbury, 1:415; HMC Third Report, 264.

21. HMC 55 Var. Coll., 2:x-xi; Finch, *Wealth,* 124-25; HMC 69 Middleton, 422, 428, 460. For selected examples of the costs of individual food items in the 1570s and 1580s see HMC 55 Var. Coll., 2:xii; Trevelyan, ed., *Papers,* 3:17-18.

22. Carew, *Svrvey,* f. 66^{r-v}.

23. *CJ,* 1:70; *APC,* 11:14-15, 44, 66; 26:94-96, 380-82, 384-85. In January 1581 William Fisher preached at Paul's Cross that those who ate excessively were to be reformed or expelled from London. *A Sermon Preached at Paules Crosse* (1580 [i.e. 1581]), sigs. D1^{v}-D2^{r}. In 1597 proposals were advanced to control bakers, mostly to conserve grain and corn, yet even this was to be done with a view to meeting the needs of persons of high rank and special occasions such as funerals and weddings. LPL Bacon MS 654/124 (f. 184^{v}).

24. *EEA,* 3:241; Whitgift, *Works,* 3:618-19.

25. Lambarde, *Government,* 78, 102; Hergest, *Rvle,* 5, 8, 26, 66-67; Mulcaster, *Positions,* 46; BL Lansdowne MSS 6/5; 114/17; Collins, *Life,* 62; Clapham, in *Elizabeth,* ed. Read and Read, 82.

26. PRO SP 45, f. 15^{v}; Scott, ed., *Collection,* 1:493; Ward, *Diaries,* ed. Knappen, 104, 108-9, 111, 113-15, 117-18.

27. Manningham, *Diary,* 9.

28. Thomas, *Demegoriai,* sig. M8^{r}, reflecting a view he did not espouse.

29. S. Gardiner, *Cognizance,* 37; Bateman, *Glasse,* sigs. E3^{v}-F2^{v}; Tilney, *Flower,* sig. C1^{r-v}; Sandys, *Sermons,* 137, 392-94; Nash, *Pierce,* f. 24^{r}; Wright, *Summons,* 32-33; Pilkington, *Works,* 52, 151, 255-56, 446-47; Bedel, *Sermon,* sigs. C2^{v}, E1^{v}; Manningham, *Diary,* 7; Clapham, *Briefe,* 127; Cooper, *Exposition,* sig. O4^{r-v}; Whetstone, *Rocke,* sig. O2^{r}. Cf. Hergest, *Rvle,* 8.

30. Stubbes, *Anatomie,* sig. J6^{v}; Gibbon, *Praise,* 52; Burton, *Wooing,* 258; GB, note to Prov. 31:7; Lupton, *A Dreame of the Devil and Diues* (1584), sigs. A7^{v}, E4^{r}; W. Vaughan, *Golden-groue,* sig. H8^{v}; Dod, *Treatise,* pt. 2, f. 51^{r}; Perkins, *Treatise,* 559; *Foundation,* sig. A2^{v}; Dering, *Catechisme, Workes,* sig. A8^{v}; *Hebrues, Workes,* sig. E2^{r}; Dent, *Path-way,* 35; Wilcox, *Prouerbs,* 151; Norden, *Comfort,* 14.

31. Dent, *Path-way,* 182-89; Moffett, *Commentarie,* 202; Wilcox, *Prouerbs,* 113; GB, notes to Gen. 9:21; 19:32; Prov. 23:33, 35; Stubbes, *Anatomie,* sigs. J3^{v}-J4^{r}; Bird, *Communication,* f. 58^{v}; Bird, *The Lectvres . . . vpon the 8. and 9. Chapters of the Second Epistle to the Corinthians* (Cambridge, 1598), 38-39; Balmford, *Dialogve,* sig. A3^{r}; W. Vaughan, *Golden-groue,* sig. H8^{v}; Dod, *Treatise,* pt. 2, f. 51^{r}; Penry, *State,* sig. H3^{r-v}.

32. Ward, *Diaries,* ed. Knappen, 109, 113, 122.

33. Eliot, *Castel,* ff. 13^{r}, 22^{v}; Lemnie, *Touchstone,* trans. Newton, f. 5^{r}; Bullein, *Bulwarke,* pt. 1, ff. 11^{r}, 12^{v}-13^{r}, 14^{v}; pt. 3, f. 70^{r}; Cogan, *Haven,* 49, 213-14; Gerard, *Herball,* 1257; Boorde, *Regimente,* sig. G1^{r}; W. Vaughan, *Directions,* 26-27; anon., *Widdowes Treasure,* sig. B3^{r}; Barrough, *Method,* 13-14; John XXI, *Treasvry,* trans. Lloyd, sig. Q7^{v}.

34. Rye, ed., *England,* 79; *CJ,* 1:75, 78, 79, 106, 110-12, 121; D'Ewes, *Journals,* 248, 253, 255, 290, 432, 435, 437, 440, 443-44, 451, 520, 622-23, 626, 628-29, 651, 657, 665, 668, 676; Kent, *BIHR,* 46:43-45, 47, 49, 56, 58, 64-65.

35. *APC*, e.g. 11:89; Tait, ed., *Records*, e.g. 19; *Staffordshire Session Rolls*, ed. Burne, e.g. 3:136; Wiener, *JSH*, 8:47; Lambarde, *Government*, 70; BL Lansdowne MS 49/28; Cross, *SCH*, 2:280.

36. Bateson, ed., *Records*, 3:108-9, 128, 162, 174, 421-22, 439.

37. Hearnshaw, ed., *Records*, 1:182-83, 196, 211-12, 242, 280, 350; Hamilton, ed., *Books*, xvi.

38. *Zurich Letters*, ed. Robinson, 266; Clark and Slack, *Towns*, 54, 95; Alan Everitt, "The English Urban Inn, 1560-1760," *Perspectives in English Urban History*, ed. Everitt (1973), 93; Peter Clark, "The Alehouse and the Alternative Society," *Puritans and Revolutionaries* (Oxford, 1978), 50. Clark cautions (pp. 57-61) against overemphasizing the disorder and promiscuity that reformers associated with alehouses.

39. Emmison, *Elizabethan Life*, 2:68; *EEA*, 2:54 *et passim*; Peel, ed., *Seconde Parte*, 2:102-3, 107-10, 147, 165-66; *Diocese of Norwich*, ed. Williams, 40, 57; Hoby, *Diary*, 193; Purvis, ed., *Documents*, 195-96; Green, ed., *Life*, 47.

40. Hart, *Clergy*, 34; Emmison, *Elizabethan Life*, 2:226-27; Haigh, *Reformation*, 242.

41. Emmison, *Elizabethan Life*, 1: chap. 18; Fulwood, *New Ballad*; Lewis Wager, *A New Enterlude* (1567), sig. B4^r; Stone, *Crisis*, 558; Smyth, *Berkeley Manuscripts*, 2:420; BL Lansdowne MS 86/45; Notestein, *Studies*, 76. In one of the more interesting cases of intoxication, Sir John Smyth got drunk, gave away gifts of money ranging from £10 to £50, railed against Burghley, and was imprisoned in the Tower. One of those to whom he gave money robbed him the same night. HMC 9 Salisbury, 6:450-51.

42. S. Gardiner, *Cognizance*, sig. A4^v.

43. Bullein, *Bulwarke*, pt. 3, f. 69^r.

44. MB (1537, 1551), notes to Isa. 58; Matt. 6; Matthew-Becke Bible (1549, 1551), notes to Isa. 58; Matt. 6; Tyndale-Rogers NT, note to Matt. 6.

45. Woolton, *Manual*, 135; T. Rogers, *Discourse*, f. 116^v; Jewel, *Works*, 3:169; S. Gardiner, *Cognizance*, 28 ff., 45; Richard Vennard, *The Right Way to Heaven* (1601), sig. C4^r; Leonard Wright, *The Pilgrimage to Paradise* (1591), 34; Sutton, *Disce vivere*, 119, 124; Sutton, *Godly Meditations* (1601), 108-9.

46. S. Gardiner, *Cognizance*, 1-15, 64-75; G. Abbot, *Exposition*, 415; Bunny, *Summe*, f. 24^{r-v}.

47. S. Gardiner, *Cognizance*, 18-19, 23-24.

48. Woolton, *Manual*, 87-89; Nash, *Anatomie*, sig. E1^r; Jewel, *Works*, 3:169-70; G. Abbot, *Exposition*, 459; S. Gardiner, *Cognizance*, sig. A8^r, pp. 11, 99; Wright, *Pilgrimage*, 35; Pilkington, *Works*, 556 ff.; Tanner, *School*, 26; Strype, *Grindal*, 107.

49. Holland, *Exercise*, 8, 52; Fulke, *Text*, ff. 91^r, 374^v; *A Retentive to Stay Good Christians* (1580), 123; Cartwright, *Confvtation*, 170; Gifford, *Reply*, 20; Perkins, *An Exposition of the Lord's Prayer* (1592), 107-8; *Catholike*, 980; *Chaine*, sig. G7^r; Estey, *Expositions*, pt. 1, f. 49^v; Dering, *Hebrues, Workes*, sig. B3^{r-v}; Stubbes, *Motive*, 167-68; Becon, *Demaundes*, sig. F6^v; Shutte, *Forme*, sig. E1^v; Norden, *Solace*, f. 78^v. Cf. Thomas Bell, *The Suruey of Popery* (1596), 62.

50. Perkins, *Treatise*, 424-25, 427, 430-32; *Exposition*, 107-8; *Catholike*, 977-78; Dod, *Treatise*, pt. 1, f. 36^r; pt. 2, f. 98^v; Dering, *Catechisme, Workes*, sig. G1^r; Cartwright, *Confvtation*, 170; Timme, *Newes from Niniue* (1570), ff. 61^v-62^r; *Discouerie*, sig. G4^v; Stubbes, *Motive*, 171; R. Rogers, *Treatises*, 292-93; Pagit, *Godly Sermon*, sig. C6^v; Becon, *Demaundes*, sigs. C7^r, F6^v-F7^v; Bulkeley, *Apologie*, 133; Trigge, *Tovchstone*, 240; Norden, *Solace*, f. 80^r; Holland, *Exercise*, 94; Bird, *Communication*, ff. 5^v-6^r; Shutte, *Forme*, sig. E2^r.

51. Perkins, *Catholike*, 977; *Treatise*, 538; Holland, *Exercise*, sigs. A2^v-A3^v, pp. 4-8; Bell, *Suruey*, 61-62; Becon, *Demaundes*, sig. F7^r.

52. Holland, *Exercise*, 13, 18-47, 67-71, 91; Bell, *Suruey*, 72; Perkins, *Treatise*, 425-26; Dod, *Treatise*, pt. 1, f. 36^r; Stubbes, *Motive*, 169-70; Udall, *Remedie*, ff. 79^r-81^r.

53. Stubbes, *Motive*, 167-68; Perkins, *Treatise*, 428-29, 434-35, 539; Shutte, *Forme*, sig. E2^r; Wither, *View*, 25; Fulke, *Text*, f. 391^r; Becon, *Demaundes*, sig. F6^v.

54. Gifford, *Dialogue*, f. 40^v; Perkins, *Chaine*, sig. G2^{r-v}; *Catholike*, 978-80; Fulke, *Text*, ff. 28^v, 69^v, 208^r, 260^r; Cartwright, *Confvtation*, 18, 69; Bell, *Suruay*, 67-70; Wither, *View*, 239; Gilby, *Dialogve*, sig. M4^v. Cf. Cope, *Exposition*, f. 466^r.

55. Christopher Hooke, *A Sermon Preached in Paules Church* [1596?], sig. D8^r; Norden, *Solace*, f. 78^v; W. Vaughan, *Golden-groue*, sigs. R2^v-R3^r; Usher, ed., *Movement*, 68.

56. Vaux, *Catechisme*, ff. 108^v-109^r; Southwell, *Short Rules*, 40; Anstruther, *Vaux*, 90. Cf. Carpenter, *Report*, 26:180.

57. Douai Bible, note to Gen. 3; Rheims NT, notes to Matt. 6:16; 15:11, 18; Mark 7:15; Rom. 14:2; 1 Cor. 15:32.

58. Barrow, *Writings (1587-90)*, 130-31, 396-407, 415-18.

59. Eliot, *Castel*, f. 55^v; Bullein, *Bulwarke*, pt. 3, f. 69^r; W. Vaughan, *Golden-groue*, sigs. R3^v-R4^r; *Directions*, 45; Cogan, *Haven*, 172-73.

60. *EEA*, 2:54, 72, 105; 3:142, 176, 229, etc.; PRO SP 19/24 (f. 45^{r-v}); *Diocese of Norwich*, ed. Williams, 29, 44, 66-68, 86; Hart, *Clergy*, 38.

61. *APC*, 11:14-15, 19, 66; 17:73, 83-84; 20:268-69, 308; *TP*, 2:108-9, 139-40, 163-65, 181, 293-94, 367, 381, 390, 438, 503, 510, 535; 3:3, 36, 134, 143, 188, 204-9; S. Gardiner, *Cognizance*, sig. A3^r. The 186 fast days are listed in PRO SP 31/41 (f. 75^r) and 31/42 (f. 76^r).

62. BL Lansdowne MS 99/51; Strype, *Whitgift*, 2:336-37; 3:348-49; HMC 9 Salisbury, 7:162.

63. K. Thomas, *Religion*, 114; A. Clifford, *Lives*, 23; Rogers and Ward, *Diaries*, ed. Knappen, 89, 100, 110; Usher, ed., *Movement*, 26 ff.; Cross, *Trans. Leics. Arch. and Hist. Soc.*, 36:11; D'Ewes, *Journals*, 282-84.

Chapter 12: Social Conduct and Social Order

1. Barnfield, *Shepheard*, sig. C4^r.

2. Henry Price, *The Eagles Flight* (1599), sig. C4^r.

3. MB (1537, 1551), notes to Deut. 22; Eccles. 9; Matthew-Becke Bible (1549), notes to Deut. 22; Eccles. 9; Matthew-Becke Bible (1551), note to Eccles. 9; GB, notes to Gen. 24:22; Deut. 22:5; Isa. 3:23, 25.

4. BB, notes to Gen. 41:42; Deut. 22:5, 11; BTB, notes to 1 Cor. 11:5; 1 Pet. 3:3; Rheims NT, note to 1 Pet. 3:3.

5. Anderson, *Shield*, sig. T1^r; Babington, *Genesis*, 42-43; *Commaundements*, 309; *Sermon at Paules Crosse*, 37; Sutton, *Disce mori*, 22; Wright, *Summons*, 32; A. Hill, *Crie*, 38; Whitgift, *Works*, 2:65; Sandys, *Sermons*, 137; Drant, *Fruitefull Sermon*, sig. B2^r.

6. Wright, *Display*, 16-17; Babington, *Lords Prayer*, 142; *Commaundements*, 315-16; *Genesis*, 187; Anderson, *Shield*, sig. D2^r; Sandys, *Sermons*, 394-95; Pilkington, *Works*, 55-56, 660; Whitgift, *Works*, 2:43, 66, 390. Cf. Carr: "For what neede a rynge of golde in a swines snowte, sure it is not comelye nor decent, but contrary vnto wisdom?" *Fal*, sig. F1^v.

7. Sandys, *Sermons*, 394-95; Anderson, *Sermon at Paules Crosse*, sig. H2^r; *Shield*, sig. T1^v; Gibbens, *Qvestions*, 102; Babington, *Commaundements*, 12; *Sermon at Paules Crosse*, 35; Dove, *1594 Sermon*, sig. C3^r; Whetstone, *Rocke*, sig. C3^v; Nixon, *Navy*, sig. B1^v; Wright, *Summons*, 12.

8. King, *Lectvres*, 76; Lancelot Andrewes, *The Wonderfvll Combate* (1592), sig. K8^r; Edmond Bicknoll, *A Swoord Agaynst Swearyng* (1579), sig. A4^r; A. Hill, *Crie*, 40-41; Pilkington, *Works*, 59, 386-87; S. Gardiner, *Portraitvre*, 236-37; Lewes, *Sermon*, sig. C5^v; G. Abbot, *Exposition*, 463.

9. Babington, *Commaundements*, 308, 312-13, 321; A. Hill, *Crie*, 39; Cooper, *Certaine Sermons*, 16; (cf. Drant, *Fruitfull Sermon*, sigs. E4^V-E5^r); Dove, *1594 Sermon*, sig. C3^V; Anderson, *Shield*, sig. S4^V.

10. G. Abbot, *Exposition*, 574; Sandys, *Sermons*, 280, 394-95; Anderson, *Shield*, sig. D2^r; Babington, *Genesis*, 184; Whetstone, *Heptameron*, sig. X1^V; *Rocke*, sig. O2^r; Nowell, *Catechism*, 197; Woolton, *Manual*, 89, 93; Pilkington, *Works*, 55; W. Vaughan, *Directions*, 70.

11. Wright, *Display*, 36; *Summons*, 31; Babington, *Commaundements*, 311; Pilkington, *Works*, 56; Drant, *Two Sermons*, sigs. H4^V-H5^r. In a sermon at Paul's Cross in February 1584, John Hudson, an Oxford M.A., remarked on how the quest for novelty led to clothing ill-suited for the human body. *A Sermon Preached at Paules Crosse* (1584), sig. C1^{r-v}. Much of what was considered Italian was in fact Burgundian. See Gordon Kipling, *The Triumph of Honor* (The Hague, 1977).

12. Anderson, *Sermon of Comfort*, 7-8; Drant, *Fruitfull Sermon*, sigs. E4^V-E5^r; *Two Sermons*, sig. H2^V; Babington, *Commaundements*, 310; Pilkington, *Works*, 151, 385-86; Sandys, *Sermons*, 50, 401; Cogan, *Haven*, 121; Strype, *Aylmer*, 180-81. Cf. Robert Greene's praise of the ideal knight who provides abundant hospitality instead of spending his money on lavish clothes. *A Qvip for an Vpstart Courtier* (1592), sig. E1^r. Cf. also Lupton, *Dreame*, sig. G5^{r-v}.

13. Manningham, *Diary*, 74-75; Sutcliffe, *Answere*, 129-30; Woolton, *Manual*, 90; Nash, *Pierce*, f. 2^V.

14. W. Vaughan, *Golden-groue*, sig. ₂C2^{r-v}; Perkins, *Treatise*, 575; *Chaine*, sigs. M1^V-M2^r; Timme, *Discouerie*, sig. F3^V; Stubbes, *Motive*, 172; *Anatomie*, sig. F5^V.

15. Dod, *Treatise*, pt. 2, f. 57^r; W. Vaughan, *Golden-groue*, sigs. ₂C3^V-₂C4^r; Stubbes, *Anatomie*, sigs. π4^V, B7^r, C2^r-C3^r, C4^V-C5^r, F3^{r-v}, F6^V-F7^r; Perkins, *Chaine*, sigs. M1^V-M2^r; *Treatise*, 560, 565, 567-69, 582; *Case of Conscience*, 871; Crowley, *Opening*, sig. B1^r; Burton, *Ten Sermons*, 10; Dent, *Path-way*, 58-59; Wilcox, *Canticles*, *Works*, 26-27; *Psalmes*, *Works*, 93; Hake, *Newes*, sigs. E5^V-E6^r; Trigge, *Sermon*, sig. D3^V.

16. Wilcox, *The Svmme of a Sermon* (1597), sig. E7^r; Perkins, *Treatise*, 582; Timme, *Discouerie*, sig. F3^r; Dent, *Path-way*, 45; Stubbes, *Anatomie*, sigs. B5^V-B6^r, B8^r-C1^V, D2^r, F2^r-F4^r.

17. Stubbes, *Anatomie*, sigs. π7^V, B7^V, D6^r, E3^V, G1^{r-v}; Deacon, *Treatise*, sig. B3^V; Perkins, *Chaine*, sigs. L7^V-L8^r; Dod, *Treatise*, pt. 2, f. 57^r; Becon, *Postil*, 2: f. 73^{r-v}; Norden, *Progress*, 174; Dent, *Path-way*, 48-49, 56; W. Vaughan, *Golden-groue*, sig. ₂C3^V; Allen, *Treasvrie*, 187; Timme, *Discouerie*, sig. F4^r; H. Smith, *Teares*, 34; Trigge, *Tovchstone*, 235-37. Cf. Gosson, *Schoole*, f. 31^{r-v}. A detailed description of Elizabethan apparel, much of which is considered excessive, is found in Stubbes, *Anatomie*, sigs. D6^V-E7^r, F3^r-G1^V.

18. R. Jones, *Catechisme*, sig. B4^r; Greenham, *Works*, 416; Gifford, *Catechisme*, sig. H1^r; Dering, *Catechisme*, *Workes*, sig. A8^V; Perkins, *Chaine*, sigs. L7^V-L8^r; Dent, *Path-way*, 73; Stubbes, *Anatomie*, sigs. B6^r, G1^r; H. Smith, *Preparatiue*, 87; Scott, ed., *Collection*, 1:497.

19. Udall, *Certaine Sermons*, sig. ₂D4^V; Stubbes, *Anatomie*, sigs. E1^V-E2^V, E8^{r-v}, F1^V-F2^r, F5^{r-v}; Trigge, *Sermon*, sig. B3^V; Timme, *Discouerie*, sig. F4^{r-v}; Perkins, *Treatise*, 567, 577; *Chaine*, sig. M2^r; W. Vaughan, *Golden-groue*, sig. ₂C2^V; Rainolds, *Overthrow*, 10, 99-102.

20. Dent, *Path-way*, 47, 51, 55, 57; Perkins, *Treatise*, 561-64, 570, 574-75, 578-80; Cleaver, *Form*, 103; Dering, *Catechisme*, *Workes*, sig. G1^r; Greenham, *Works*, 14, 416; Gifford, *Catechisme*, sig. H1^V; Stubbes, *Anatomie*, sigs. C5^V-C6^r; Northbrooke, *Treatise*, sig. A4^r; Burton, *Wooing*, 258; H. Smith, *Preparatiue*, 40, 86-87; Becon, *Salue*, 219; Knewstub, *Lectvres*, 131; Trigge, *Sermon*, sig. B3^V. Cf. Bradford, *Sermons*, sig. D5^V; Bullinger, *State*, sigs. I7^V, K2^V; Cope, *Exposition*, ff. 188^V, 634^V.

21. Stubbes, *Anatomie*, sigs. B7^V, C1^r, C3^{r-v}, F8^r; W. Vaughan, *Golden-groue*, sig. $_2$C2^V; Burton, *Wooing*, 220-21; Trigge, *Apologie*, 7; Timme, *Discouerie*, sig. F3^V; Norden, *Progress*, 173; Dent, *Path-way*, 47-49; Perkins, *Treatise*, 569-71. Cf. Manningham, *Diary*, 100. In 1601 a scaffold was erected above the usual seats in Parliament because of the new style of wearing great breeches stuffed with hair. The scaffolds were removed when the style changed. BL Harleian MS 980, f. 235^r.

22. Becon, *Postil*, 2: f. 73^{r-v}; Stubbes, *Anatomie*, sigs. C2^r, E5^r; Trigge, *Catholiqve*, 590; *Sermon*, sig. B2^V; Dod, *Treatise*, pt. 2, f. 57^r; R. Rogers, *Treatises*, 108, 178; Perkins, *Warning*, 250; *Chaine*, sigs. L7^V-L8^r; *Treatise*, 566, 582; H. Smith, *Teares*, 19-20, 34; W. Vaughan, *Golden-groue*, sig. I3^V; Hake, *Touchestone*, sig. D2^{r-v}.

23. Sutcliffe, *Answere*, 130; Dent, *Path-way*, 57; Perkins, *Treatise*, 570-71, 579.

24. Gibbon, *Praise*, 52; Fenner, *Treatises*, 185; Dent, *Path-way*, 59-60; Stubbes, *Anatomie*, sigs. C1^V, C5^r, E4^r; *Motive*, 172; (cf. Nicholson, *Acolastvs*, sig. H2^V); Wilcox, *Psalmes*, *Works*, 93; Perkins, *Treatise*, 565, 567-68; Dering, *Hebrues*, *Workes*, sig. B2^V. Perkins allowed people to own in number only those clothes necessary; the rest had to be donated to the needy. *Treatise*, 566. Simple clothing, according to Stubbes, was conducive to improved health. *Anatomie*, sig. E1^{r-v}.

25. Barrow, *Writings (1587-90)*, 489, 493, 495-96, 545 (cf. 184).

26. Shelford, *Lectvres*, 39, 101-2; Lodge, *Alarum*, sig. C1^r; Vaux, *Catechisme*, f. 61^V; Southwell, *Short Rules*, 36, 42; Anstruther, *Vaux*, 114; Cartwright, *Confvtation*, 148.

27. *Ballads*, ed. Rollins, 250, 273, 275, 318; Wager, *Enterlude*, sig. C4^V; W. T. T., *A Mery Balade, How a Wife Entreated Her Husband* (n.d.); Churchyard, *Challenge*, 112-13; Fulwood, *New Ballad;* Shakespeare, *The Taming of the Shrew*, act 4, sc. 3. Cf. George Wateson, *The Cvres of the Diseased* (1598), sig. D2^r; Willoby, *Avisa*, 33. The enticement of feminine dress as a means to lure men to promiscuity was cited in an attack on women by the author of *Here Begynneth the Schole House of Women*, sig. B2^{r-v}, though Sir Thomas More's grandson, Edward More, laid the blame on their husbands, for purchasing such attire. *Treatyse*, sig. C2^V (cf. sigs. C2^V-C3^r).

28. Rye, ed., *England*, 7-8, 13, 71-73, 89-90.

29. Mulcaster, *Positions*, 46; Kay, *History*, 172-73; Tanner, *School*, 26-27; BL Lansdowne MSS 30/74; 103/108; Christopher Wordsworth, *The Undergraduate*, rev. by R. Brimley Johnson (1928), 151; Ward, *Diaries*, ed. Knappen, 122.

30. *Wentworth Papers*, ed. Cooper, 13-14; Hergest, *Rvle*, 6, 66; HMC 80 Sackville, 2:110-11.

31. HMC 9 Salisbury, 2:52-53, 110; Malden, ed., *Papers*, 22; Smyth, *Berkeley Manuscripts*, 2:383-84; Clapham, in *Elizabeth*, ed. Read and Read, 83; William Elderton, *A Proper New Balad in Praise of My Ladie Marques* (n.d.).

32. HMC 58 Bath, 4:178 (cf. 181); Ward, *Oxford*, 32-33; Batho, *Household Papers*, 87; Stone, *Crisis*, 564-65. Cf. HMC Tenth Report, 32, for a description of the attire of Lady Anna, eldest daughter of Alexander Livingston, earl of Linlithgow, a maid of honor to Queen Anne in 1603. Peers regularly purchased livery for their servants. Cf. HMC 9 Salisbury, 6:96, 210; Machyn, *Diary*, 258, 264, 294. Robert Devereux, earl of Essex, paid to dress his soldiers in the Devereux colors, tangerine and white. Robert Lacey, *Robert Earl of Essex* (1970), 49. In the case of the earl of Rutland, Acheley's verse is not exaggerated *(Massacre*, sig. C3^V):

> Onely because thou would'st be counted gay,
> Thou cast'st in scorne a thousand pound away.

33. Carew, *Svrvey*, f. 64^{r-v}; *Illustrations*, ed. Nichols, 234-38; Finch, *Wealth*, 124; LPL Bacon MSS 654/78 (f. 123^{r-v}); 659/56 (f. 78^{r-v}); Holles, *Memorials*, 127, 215; HMC 69 Middleton, 572-73 (cf. 425, 442); HMC 9 Salisbury, 4:397-98.

34. Chamberlain, *Letters*, 1:166; Whitelocke, *Liber*, 5; Forman, *Autobiography*, 30-32; Manningham, *Diary*, 45; Hart, *Clergy*, 31.

35. Carpenter, *Report*, 26:177; BL Stowe MS 1046, f. 113^{r-v} (which describes the wardrobe of Garrad Shelbury and his wife and servant); Carew, *Svrvey*, f. 66^{r-v}.

36. Lambarde, *Government*, 70, 78, 102; HMC 73 Exeter, 315; MacCaffrey, *Exeter*, 93.

37. *Records*, ed. Hearnshaw, 1:139, 141-43, 161; *Books*, ed. Hamilton, xii-xiii; Emmison, *Elizabethan Life*, 1:33, 35; 2:18; 3:274. For an examination of a poor woman cited for dressing in male attire, see BL Lansdowne MS 30/24.

38. *EEA*, 2:49, 57, 72, 117; 3:141, 164, 216, 226.

39. *CJ*, 1:68, 70, 73-77, 79-81, 88-90; PRO SP 40/68 (f. 149^r); *CSPD, Add. 1566-79*, 20-22; D'Ewes, *Journals*, 112, 134.

40. BL Sloane MS 326/3 (ff. 15^r-18^v); *CJ*, 1:109, 113-15; D'Ewes, *Journals*, 228, 424, 450, 452, 454, 583, 588, 591-92, 594. Cf. Kent, *BIHR*, 46:43, 45, 49-50, 56-57. Her research is detailed in her 1971 London Ph.D. thesis, "Social Attitudes of Members of Parliament with Special Reference to the Problem of Poverty, circa 1590-1624."

41. HMC 9 Salisbury, 2:116; 4:91-92; BL Lansdowne MS 56/1; Stubbes, *Anatomie*, sig. D2^v. In a sermon preached at Paul's Cross in January 1581, William Fisher called for those who wore excess apparel to be expelled from London. *1581 Sermon*, sigs. D1^v-D2^r.

42. *APC*, 9:320; 11:26-27; 15:416.

43. BL Lansdowne MS 94/37; *TP*, 2:136-38, 187-94, 202-3, 278-83, 362, 369-70, 381-86, 417, 435, 454; 3:3-8, 71, 174-81, 186.

44. Gawdy, *Letters*, 28, 33, 49; Stone, *Crisis*, 563; Chamberlain, *Letters*, 1:189; Nichols, *Progresses*, 3:249.

45. Cooper, *Certaine Sermons*, 16; Anderson, *Godlie Sermon*, sig. D7^r; Drant, *Two Sermons*, sigs. K5^r, K7^v-K8^v; Perkins, *Treatise*, 563; Norden, *Progress*, 173. To say that conflict over apparel was a factor in the developing rift between court and country is obviously not to say that this conflict was a factor leading to civil war in 1642.

46. Anger, *Iane Anger*, 1.

47. Willoby, *Avisa*, 100.

48. GB, notes to Exod. 20:16; 1 Sam. 15:13; 2 Sam. 16:2; Job 32:21; Pss. 15:2; 37:30; Prov. 11:12; Exek. 21:2; Matt. 7:1; Eph. 5:4; Col. 4:6; James 3:2, 6; BB, note to Job 15:2; BTB, notes to Eph. 5:1, 4; Col. 4:6; James 3:3; 5:12.

49. Sutton, *Disce mori*, 464; Walsall, *Sermon*, sig. A4^v; Anderson, *Sermon of Comfort*, 19-20; Seager, *Schoole*, sigs. C7^v-C8^r; Babington, *Conference*, 93; *Genesis*, 139; *Sermon at Greenewich*, 12-13; *Commaundements*, 203, 275, 280, 351-52; Turnbull, *Iude*, f. 96^v; *Iames*, ff. 85^v, 87^r; Pilkington, *Works*, 308-9, 332; Sandys, *Sermons*, 395, 426-27; Nowell, *Catechism*, 134; J. Rogers, *Summe*, f. 16^r. The negative effect of an evil tongue on order was also noted by the balladeer J. Canand, *Of Euyll Tounges* (n.d.).

50. *Wentworth Papers*, ed. Cooper, 9-10, 21, 35; Carpenter, *Report*, 26:171; Hergest, *Rvle*, 10; Smyth, *Berkeley Manuscripts*, 2:421; Lawrence V. Ryan, *Roger Ascham* (Stanford, 1963), 279; HL MS HM102, f. 13; Collins, *Life*, 62-63; Clapham, in *Elizabeth*, ed. Read and Read, 83; *Zurich Letters*, ed. Robinson, 27.

51. *Schole House of Women*, sig. B4^v; W. Harrison, *Discovrse*, 2-3; Green, ed., *Life*, 39-40.

52. HL MS HA5276; Ward, *Oxford*, 114-27, 142; Parker, *Correspondence*, 301-2; HMC 80 Sackville, 2:114.

53. Perkins, *A Direction* (1615; 1st pub. 1593), sig. A2^r, pp. 2, 15-20, 68-75; Fulke, *Praelections*, sig. A2^v; Field, *Caveat*, sig. D8^r; *Prayers*, sig. A12^r; Acheley, *Massacre*, sig. D2^r; Northbrooke, *Treatise*, f. 22^v; Allen, *Treasvrie*, 85, 240; R. Jones, *Catechisme*, sig. B4^r; Dering, *Catechisme*, *Workes*, sigs. A8^v-B1^r; *Hebrues*, *Workes*, sig. I8^r; Greenham, *Works*, 63;

W. Vaughan, *Golden-groue*, sigs. F5^r, M1^V-M2^r; Burton, *Anatomie*, 151-53; Gifford, *Catechisme*, sig. G7^r; Wilcox, *Prouerbs, Works*, 21, 30, 47-48, 58; Moffett, *Commentarie*, 46; Estey, *Expositions*, pt. 1, f. 67^r; Norden, *Practise*, f. 42^r.

54. Nicholson, *Acolastvs*, sig. D3^V; Moffett, *Commentarie*, 87-88, 125; Wilcox, *Prouerbs, Works*, 62, 85; Perkins, *Direction*, 70, 88, 91; Dering, *Hebrues, Workes*, sig. D6^r; Thomas Knell, *An ABC* (n.d.); Marbury, *Notes*, 47; Bownde, *Doctrine*, 137-38; Udall, *Obedience*, sig. C1^r; R. Rogers, *Treatises*, 365; Cartwright, *Confvtation*, 55.

55. Cleaver, *Form*, 101; Allen, *Alphabet*, 122; Wilcox, *Prouerbs, Works*, 150; Dent, *Pathway*, 191-92; Trigge, *Tovchstone*, 235-36; Stubbes, *Glasse*, sig. A3^r; Greenham, *Works*, 367.

56. Scott, ed., *Collection*, 1:493; Mildmay, *Memorial*, [1-2]; Weigall, *Quarterly Review*, 215:120, 124, 136; Hastings, *Letters*, 32; LPL Bacon MS 647/85 (f. 177^r).

57. R. Rogers and Ward, *Diaries*, ed. Knappen, 81-82, 109-10, 114-16.

58. Rheims NT, notes to Matt. 12:36; 2 Cor. 11:6; Lodge, *Divel*, sig. A4^r; Shelford, *Short Rules*, 36; BL Royal MS 17A. IX, f. 34^r; Barrow, *Writings (1587-90)*, 493.

59. Pilkington, *Works*, 362; HMC 55 Var. Coll., 2:95; Parker, *Correspondence*, 75; Manningham, *Diary*, 40; Machyn, *Diary*, 196, 245, 250; Draper, *Centuries*, 19; *Staffordshire Session Rolls*, ed. Burne, 2:194 (cf. 290). In 1601 a Kingston-on-Thames man was fined 40s. for indiscreet speech. HMC Third Report, 332.

60. *EEA*, 3:216, 226, 340; Peel, ed., *Seconde Parte*, 2:106; Hart, *Clergy*, 31; H. Hall, *TRHS*, 3rd ser., 1:272-73; Wiener, *JSH*, 8:46-47; Furnivall, *Child-Marriages*, 102-30, 204-10.

61. Nash, *Pierce*, f. 2^r.

62. Wright, *Hunting*, sig. A2^r.

63. Alan Dyer, *The City of Worcester in the Sixteenth Century* (Leicester, 1973), 248-50; Peter Clark, "The Ownership of Books in England, 1560-1640: The Example of Some Kentish Townsfolk," *Schooling and Society*, ed. Lawrence Stone (Baltimore, 1976), 99; Bennett, *English Books*, 130; R. Harrison, *Treatise*, sig. π3^V; T. Rogers, *Miles Christianvs* (1590), 23. Rogers repudiates the notion that the number of books is excessive. The Commons took up a bill to suppress seditious books on 21 November 1566. *CJ*, 1:77.

64. Babington, *Lords Prayer*, 121; *Commaundements*, 307-8, 352; Jackson, *Poeme*, sigs. π4^V-π5^V; Lewes, *Sermon*, sig. A2^r; Abraham Fleming, *A Panoplie of Epistles* (1576); Henoch Clapham, *Antidoton* (1600), 5-6. Jackson wanted "friuolous Pamphlets" burned.

65. Nash, *Anatomie*, sigs. A1^r-A2^r, C1^V-C3^V. Italian authors, particularly Machiavelli, also were attacked by Thomas Cogan, *The Well of Wisdome* (1577), sig. A6^{r-V}. Tyndale's prologue to Numbers in the Matthew Bibles of 1549 and 1551 and the Matthew-Becke Bible referred to Ovid's "fylthy boke of the remedye agaynste loue."

66. Ascham, *Works*, 229-31; Ryan, *Ascham*, 243-44. Mulcaster thought wives could safely read Scripture, history, or guides to godly living. *Positions*, 177.

67. Gee, *Grovnd*, sig. A2^r; Perkins, *Chaine*, sig. L8^V; *Foundation*, sig. A2^V; *Direction*, 91-92 (for his quotation); Holland's epistle to Greenham, *Works*, sig. A4^{r-V}; Stockwood, *Fruiteful Sermon*, sigs. A7^r, K5^r; Dering, *Catechisme, Workes*, sig. A1^V; Francis Bradley, *A Godly Sermon* (1600), 35-36 (preached before Sir Edward Coke); Dent, *Path-way*, 356, 408; Shutte, *Sermon*, sig. D7^{r-V} (quoted); Stubbes, *Anatomie*, sig. P7^r; Estey, *Expositions*, pt. 1, f. 69^r; Dod, *Treatise*, pt. 2, f. 57^V; Greenham, *Works*, 410; R. Rogers, *Treatises*, 289; Northbrooke, *Treatise*, ff. 69^V-70^r; William Burton, *Davids Thankes-giving* (1602), 12. Stubbes complained about the difficulty of getting serious works published. *Motive*, 186-87; cf. *Anatomie*, sig. P7^{r-V}. Virel's *La religion chrestienne* (1586) was published in an English translation (probably by Stephen Egerton) in 1594 as *A Learned and Excellent Treatise*. English editions of Taffin's works included *The Markes of the Children of God* (1590; translated by Anne Prowse) and *The Amendment of Life* (1595).

68. Trigge, *Tovchstone*, 244-47; Roberts, ed., *Anthology*, 77; Southwell, *Short Rules*, 44;

Gerard, *Autobiography*, 32; Haigh, *Reformation*, 292; Anstruther, *Vaux*, 151-52. In 1586, Anthony Babington's library contained thirteen manuscripts and thirty books. Sears Jayne, *Library Catalogues of the English Renaissance* (Berkeley, 1956), 127. For the publications of the Catholic exiles see Helen C. White, *Tudor Books of Saints and Martyrs* (Madison, Wisconsin, 1963), chap. 7.

69. Weigall, *Quarterly Review*, 215:125-27; Collinson, *SCH*, 2:265-66; A. Clifford, *Lives*, 23; Sparke, *Sermon at Whaddon*, f. 61^r; Rowse, *Cornwall*, 427-29; Jayne, *Catalogues*, 117, 126-27, 139. Sir Thomas Bodley hoped in 1603 to get a donation of books from Lady Russell. *Letters of Sir Thomas Bodley to Thomas James*, ed. G. W. Wheeler (Oxford, 1926), 79.

70. W. Harrison, *Discovrse*, 8-9; Ward, *Oxford*, 202; Collier, ed., *Papers*, 2:97-98; Harvey, *Letter-Book*, 167-68.

71. Strype, *Smith*, 274-81; BL Sloane MS 325; Jayne, *Catalogues*, 140; Jayne and Francis Johnson, *The Lumley Library: The Catalogue of 1609* (1956).

72. Jayne, *Catalogues*, 117-19, 142; Percy, *History*, 23.

73. Emmison, *Elizabethan Life*, 3:123-25; Piccope, ed., *Wills*, 51:222; Dyer, *Worcester*, 250-51; Clark, in *Schooling and Society*, ed. Stone, 102-3. Elizabethan devotional works are analyzed in Helen C. White's *The Tudor Books of Private Devotion* (Madison, Wisconsin, 1951), especially chaps. 10-12.

74. *EEA*, 3:150, 162, 210, 227; Clark, in *Schooling and Society*, ed. Stone, 101.

75. Thomas Brice, *Against Filthy Writing* (n.d.); PRO SP 222/70.1 (f. 128^r).

76. Gerard, *Autobiography*, 171.

77. *Hamlet*, act 3, sc. 1. See J. H. Hanford, "Suicide in the Plays of Shakespeare," *Publications of the Modern Language Association*, 27 (1912):380-97.

78. John Bellamy, *Crime and Public Order in England in the Later Middle Ages* (1973), 32-33; S. E. Sprott, *The English Debate on Suicide* (La Salle, Ill., 1961), 34; Forbes, *Chronicle*, 99-101, 171; P. E. H. Hair, "Deaths from Violence in Britain: A Tentative Secular Survey," *Population Studies*, 25 (March 1971):15-16; Michael MacDonald, "The Inner Side of Wisdom: Suicide in Early Modern England," *Psychological Medicine*, 7 (1977):566-72; Laurence Babb, *The Elizabethan Malady* (East Lansing, Mich., 1951), vii; Clark and Slack, *Towns*, 14.

79. G. Abbot, *Exposition*, 126, 132, 546; Sutton, *Disce mori*, 334, 336-37; King, *Lectvres*, 184, 189; Anderson, *Shield*, sig. L2^v; Powel, *Christian*, 99. Cf. Higgins, *Mirour*, f. 38^r. The condemnation of suicide because it limits the time allotted for repentance also was made in the Rheims New Testament, in a note to Matt. 27:5. A key argument in Catholic opposition to suicide was the assertion that man receives only the use (*usus*) of his life, not lordship (*dominium*) over it. Sprott, *Debate*, 2.

80. Anderson, *Shield*, sigs. L1^v, L2^v, M2^r; G. Abbot, *Exposition*, 128, 130, 551-52; Sprott, *Debate*, 7-8; Powel, *Christian*, 99; King, *Lectvres*, 186. Sir John Harrington argued that the fate of one who commits suicide is known only to God. BL Add. MS 27,632. Bullein, however, insisted that all suicides were eternally damned. *Bulwarke*, pt. 3, f. 78^r.

81. W. Vaughan, *Golden-groue*, sigs. E1^r-E2^r, E7^v-F1^r; [Cartwright], *Christian Religion* (1611), 105; GB, notes to Gen. 9:6; 2 Macc. 14:41; Dod, *Treatise*, pt. 2, f. 43^v; Bird, *Hebrewes*, 98-102; Estey, *Expositions*, pt. 1, f. 65^v.

82. Dod, *Treatise*, pt. 2, f. 43^v; Bird, *Hebrewes*, 100; Greenham, *Works*, 239; W. Vaughan, *Golden-groue*, sigs. E4^{r-v}, F1^v-F2^r.

83. Sir Philip Sidney, *The Countess of Pembroke's Arcadia*, ed. Jean Robertson (Oxford, 1973), 292-300. Cf. Paul D. Green, "Doors to the House of Death: The Treatment of Suicide in Sidney's Arcadia," *SCJ*, 10 (1979):17-27.

84. Bird, *Hebrewes*, 100-1; Forbes, *Chronicle*, 31, 165-70.

85. Forbes, *Chronicle*, 164-65, 169-70.

86. PRO STAC 7 Add., 1/10-12, 1/16, 1/19.

87. HMC 69 Middleton, 547; Bicknoll, *Swoord*, f. 34^V; Manningham, *Diary*, 50; Emmison, *Elizabethan Life*, 2:35; Forbes, *Chronicle*, 164-65, 169-70; PRO STAC 7 Add., 1/12; BL Lansdowne MS 32/9; Wyot, "Diary," 97, 99; Machyn, *Diary*, 204-5.

88. BL Lansdowne MS 99/32; Gerard, *Autobiography*, 171; Cooper, *Athenae*, 2:164; Machyn, *Diary*, 301-2; Chamberlain, *Letters*, 1:70, 126, 185; HMC 58 Bath, 4:160; HL MS 30,665, ff. 7^r, 8^r; Sprott, *Debate*, 17-19.

89. Wyot, "Diary," 97, 99; Machyn, *Diary*, 204-5, 258, 259; HMC 69 Middleton, 547; BL Lansdowne MS 32/9; PRO STAC 7 Add., 1/10-12, 1/16, 1/19; Bicknoll, *Swoord*, f. 34^V; Gerard, *Autobiography*, 171; Chamberlain, *Letters*, 1:70, 126, 185; Emmison, *Elizabethan Life*, 2:35; 3:213; Forbes, *Chronicle*, 164-65, 169-70; MacDonald, *Psychological Medicine*, 7:567; cf. HL MS 30,665, ff. 7^r, 8^r.

90. Cardwell, ed., *Synodalia*, 1:71.

91. *Two Noble Kinsmen*, act 5, sc. 1. Shakespeare's authorship is defended by Paul Bertram, *Shakespeare and The Two Noble Kinsmen* (New Brunswick, N.J., 1965).

92. J. R. Hale, "Sixteenth-Century Explanations of War and Violence," *PP*, 51 (May 1971):3-26.

93. Woolton, *Castell*, sig. C7^V; Sutton, *Disce vivere*, 236; Henry J. Webb, *Elizabethan Military Science* (Madison, Wisconsin, 1965), 30-31; Sutcliffe, *The Practice, Proceedings, and Lawes of Armes* (1593), 1. Elizabethan clergy with servants and horses were required to equip horsemen for the militia or, as the bishops advised, give money instead. In the 1580s and 1590s the clergy were subjected to heavy exactions to pay for military activity abroad. J. J. N. McGurk, "The Clergy and the Militia 1580-1610," *History*, 60 (June 1975):199.

94. Turnbull, *Iames*, ff. 289^r-291^r; T. Rogers, *Doctrine*, 350; Sutton, *Disce vivere*, 236-37; Sutcliffe, *Practice*, 2, 9; James T. Johnson, *Ideology, Reason, and the Limitation of War* (Princeton, 1975), 175; Babington, *Commaundements*, 257, 260-61; T. Rogers, *Creede*, pt. 2, p. 78; Gibbens, *Qvestions*, 378, 507-8. For Knox's theory of resistance see R. L. Greaves, "John Knox, the Reformed Tradition, and the Development of Resistance Theory," *Journal of Modern History*, 48 (September 1976), demand reprint. Bishop Cooper claimed that the Protestant doctrine of political obedience resulted in less warfare in Protestant than in Catholic England. *Certaine Sermons*, 50-52. Cecil thought that Elizabeth's marriage would help to avoid "eyvill warrs." PRO SP 40/102 (F. 225^r).

95. T. Rogers, *Creede*, pt. 2, p. 85; Turnbull, *Iames*, f. 291^{r-v}; Sutcliffe, *Practice*, 5-9; Gibbens, *Qvestions*, 505-6, 508; Sutton, *Disce vivere*, 235. Cf. W. James, *Sermon at Pavles Crosse*, sig. H1^V; Anderson, *Shield*, sig. L2^V.

96. Sutcliffe, *Practice*, 9-12; Sutton, *Disce vivere*, 237; Gibbens, *Qvestions*, 504-9; Churchyard, *A Generall Rehearsall of Warres* [1579], sig. Q2^r; Johnson, *Ideology*, 159.

97. Segar, *Honor*, 3-5, 33-35, 60.

98. William Fulbecke, *The Pandectes of the Law of Nations* (1602), ff. 33^V, 35^r, 37^V-38^V, 40^V, 86^r, 88^V.

99. The best development of war theory is Johnson's *Ideology*, though he deals only with selected authors.

100. GB, notes to Deut. 20:1; 2 Sam. 10:12; 1 Chron. 22:8; 2 Chron. 6:34; 18:31; 20:9; Isa. 2:4; Matt. 10:34; Rev. 11:7. Cf. Estey in 1603: "War is grounded on the word & warrant of God, so as that all duties thereof are of ones calling." *Expositions*, pt. 1, f. 65^V.

101. John Norden, *The Mirror of Honor* (1597), sig. A3^{r-v} and pp. 3, 16.

102. Gosson, *The Trumpet of Warre* (1598), sigs. B3^r-B6^V; Johnson, *Ideology*, 96-104.

103. John Gibson, *The Sacred Shield* (1599), 38-41. Gibson's religious loyalties are enigmatic. He appears to be the John Gibson who was an ecclesiastical lawyer on the High Commission in the 1580s, when the earl of Huntingdon was president.

104. W. Vaughan, *Golden-groue*, sigs. $_2$D1^r-$_2$D2^r, $_2$C8^{r-v}; Johnson, *Ideology*, 118; Perkins, *Treatise*, 503; *Chaine*, sigs. F8^v-G1^r. Cf. Charles Gibbon, *Our Trust Against Trouble* [1589], 17-18; Udall, *Certaine Sermons*, sigs. $_2$S7^v-$_2$S8^r. For limitations on conduct in war see W. Vaughan, *Golden-groue*, sigs. $_2$D4^v-$_2$D5^v.

105. Barrow, *Writings (1587-90)*, 406; J. Rogers, *Displaying*, sigs. I6^v-I7^r.

Chapter 13: Wealth and Poverty

1. Lambarde, *Government*, 182; F. G. Emmison, "Poor Relief Accounts of Two Rural Parishes in Bedfordshire, 1563-98," *Econ. H.R.*, 3 (1931-32):106; K. Thomas, *Religion*, 562-63; Pinchbeck, *BJS*, 7:277, 280-82; Jordan, *Philanthropy*, 68; Aveling, *Recusancy*, 13; *Records*, ed. Hudson and Tingey, 2:ciii, 345; Hoskins, *Studies*, 42-45; Carew, *Svrvey*, f. 67^{r-v}. See A. L. Beier, "Social Problems in Elizabethan London," *Journal of Interdisciplinary History*, 9 (Autumn 1978):203-21. Philip Wyot's diary comments on the combined effect of dearth and war taxation on the increase of poverty in 1587. "Diary," 38.

2. Lambarde, *Government*, 114; Sandys, *Sermons*, 51-52, 84; John Prime, *A Sermon Briefly Comparing the Estate of King Salomon* (Oxford, 1585), sig. A4^v; Stubbes, *Motive*, sig. A4^{r-v}, pp. 45-46; *Anatomie*, sig. E5^{r-v}; Crowley, *Opening*, sigs. C2^v, H3^v; Jackson, *Poeme*, 47; *APC*, 8:52-53 (cf. 72-73); Vowell, *Orders*, f. 9^v; Perkins, *Treatise*, 414, 605.

3. Jordan, *Philanthropy*, 170.

4. W. Vaughan, *Golden-groue*, sig. I3^v, expressing a view he repudiates.

5. Norden, *Solace*, f. 18^r.

6. Tyndale-Coverdale NT, note to 1 Cor. 12; Matthew-Becke Bible (1549, 1551), prologue to Num.; MB (1551), prologue to Num.; George, *Mind*, 155.

7. BB, note to Gen. 33:11; Pilkington, *Works*, 151-53; Manningham, *Diary*, 29, 141 (synopses of sermons by Mr. Sanders and Dr. Thomas Holland, Regius Professor of Divinity at Oxford); Hooker, *Works*, 2:454; S. Gardiner, *Cognizance*, 120.

8. GB, notes to 2 Kings 4:1-2; Prov. 8:15; R. Rogers, *Treatises*, 176; Wilcox, *Prouerbs*, 135; Udall, *Commentarie*, 4; Crowley, *A Sermon Made in the Chappel at the Gylde Halle* (1575), sig. C4^v; Burton, *Rowsing*, 514; *Ten Sermons*, 116; Gibbon, *Praise*, 53; Allen, *Treasvrie*, 220; Bird, *2 Cor.*, 95; Gifford, *A Treatise of Trve Fortitude* (1594), sig. C6^r.

9. Tyndale-Rogers NT, note to Luke 6; Matthew-Becke Bible (1549, 1551), note to Matt. 5; MB (1551), note to Matt. 5; BB, notes to Job 1:3; Eccles. 9:2; Babington, *Conference*, 21; Manningham, *Diary*, 88; Whitgift, *Works*, 2:390. This was also the Catholic position. Cf. Rheims NT, note to Matt. 4:45.

10. GB, notes to Neh. 5:5; Job 1:3; 15:23; 17:16; 21:7; Pss. 22:29; 73:11; Prov. 19:22; Eccles. 9:3; Matt. 19:26; Mark 10:27; Luke 9:58; 10:21; 12:31; 18:27; 1 Thess. 1:6; 1 Tim. 6:6; Burton, *Rowsing*, 513; Greenham, *Works*, 108; Allen, *Garden*, 80; Becon, *Postil*, 2: f. 7^v; Holland, *Exposition*, 132; Wilcox, *Psalmes*, 252; Perkins, *Treatise*, 529; Cartwright, *Confvtation*, 185. Cf. BTB, note to Luke 18:29.

11. Calvin, *Opera*, 9 (1887):258-59; GB, notes to Gen. 39:2; Deut. 6:3; 28:12; Josh. 1:7; 1 Chron. 22:11; 2 Chron. 11:17; 15:15; 17:10; 27:6; Pss. 25:13; 37:22-23; Prov. 3:16; 4:7; 28:25; Jer. 33:5; Amos 5:24.

12. Wilcox, *Prouerbs*, 103; Holland, *Exposition*, 131-32; Perkins, *Workes*, 2:290; Hooker, *Works*, 2:448-51. Perkins' view is more fully developed by C. Hill, *Puritanism and Revolution* (New York, 1964), 229-30. Nowell's catechism explained that when God bestowed riches on the godly, it would not be for the harm of their souls. *Catechism*, 132.

13. Turnbull, *Iames*, f. 91^v; Powel, *Christian*, 49; Sutton, *Disce vivere*, 346; Nixon, *Navy*, sig. C1^v; Curteys, *Two Sermons*, sig. E7^r; Jewel, *Works*, 2:854, 1043; Sandys, *Sermons*, 193; A. Hill, *Crie*, 29; Drant, *Fruitfull Sermon*, sig. E5^{r-v}; Bedel, *Sermon*, sig. C3^v; Pilkington, *Works*, 57, 382; Whitgift, *Works*, 2:383; Manningham, *Diary*, 139-40. The

stewardship theme was commonly expressed in more popular literary forms. Cf. Church-yard, *Challenge*, 117; *Select Poetry*, 2:314; *A Liuing Remembrance of Master Robert Rogers* (1601).

14. GB, notes to Deut. 26:11; Josh. 24:14; 2 Chron. 30:24; Prov. 12:26; Eccles. 6:2; 11:3; Luke 6:30; 16:8, 12; John 6:12; BTB, note to Luke 16:1. The note to Luke 12:34 in the Rheims NT was less concerned with the motive than the donative act: "If the riche man withdrawen by his worldly treasure, can not set his hart vpon heauen, let him send his mony thither before him, by giuing it in almes vpon such as wil pray for him, and his hart wil folow his purse thither."

15. Perkins, *Treatise*, 522, 526-27, 535-37; *Exposition*, 112; Greenham, *Works*, 276; Crowley, *Opening*, sigs. B1^V, E7^{r-v}; H. Smith, *Examination*, 9-10; *Teares*, 25; Trigge, *Sermon*, sig. E6^V; Norden, *Practise*, ff. 45^V-46^r; *Solace*, f. 8^V; *Comfort*, 15-16; Stubbes, *Motive*, 133; Becon, *Salue*, 145; Bird, *Communication*, ff. 26^V-27^V; Allen, *Treasvrie*, 213; Dent, *Path-way*, 105, 197; Hake, *Touchestone*, sig. E1^V; Northbrooke, *Treatise*, f. 46^r; Gibbon, *Remedie*, sig. I4^r; Gifford, *Eight Sermons*, f. 16^V; R. Rogers, *Treatises*, 461-62; Hastings, *Letters*, 21. Cf. Cope, *Exposition*, ff. 38^r, 73^V.

16. Tyndale-Coverdale NT, notes to Luke 6 and 11; GB, notes to Deut. 6:12; 2 Kings 5:26-27; 2 Chron. 26:16; 32:15; Neh. 9:28; Job 3:26; Ps. 119:36; Prov. 1:19; 10:15; 15:6; 30:9; Eccles. 6:3; Jer. 46:20; Zeph. 1:12; Matt. 19:22; Mark 5:17; Luke 12:15; 16:9; 1 Tim. 6:10; BTB, notes to Matt. 19:23; Luke 16:13; BB, notes to Gen. 13:6; 26:14; Luke 16:9.

17. Carpenter, *Preparatiue*, 272-73; Sutton, *Disce vivere*, 344, 347; Turnbull, *Iames*, ff. 40^r, 270^r; Drant, *Fruitfull Sermon*, sig. E2^{r-v}; Wright, *Summons*, 6; Miles Smith, *A Learned and Godly Sermon* (Oxford, 1602), 57-58; Manningham, *Diary*, 8, 10; Cooper, *Certaine Sermons*, 202; *Admonition*, 180-81; Powel, *Christian*, 46-47; Cooper, ed., *Wentworth Papers*, 24; Sandys, *Sermons*, 366; Nixon, *Navy*, sig. B4^V; S. Gardiner, *Cognizance*, 187; John Howson, *A Second Sermon* (1598), 36; Hooker, *Works*, 2:449. Cf. Churchyard, *Challenge*, 125. Whitgift's first sermon, preached at Paul's Cross in 1565, was on the parable of Dives and Lazarus. Percy, *History*, 25.

18. Perkins, *Treatise*, 525, 528, 536; *The Trve Gaine* (Cambridge, 1601), 59; Dering, *Catechisme*, *Workes*, sig. F5^V; Greenham, *Works*, 47, 150; Norden, *Solace*, f. 69^r; Gifford, *Fovre Sermons* (1598), 2, 7; Cartwright, *Confvtation*, 188; Wither, *View*, 73; Wilcox, *Psalmes*, 103; Timme, *Discouerie*, sig. K2^V; Barthlet, *Pedegrewe*, f. 5^r; Dent, *Path-way*, 104, 107. Cf. Cope, *Exposition*, f. 562^r.

19. Tyndale, *Pentateuch* (1530, 1534, 1551), note to Exod. 22; GB, notes to Eccles. 5:7; Ezek. 16:49; Hab. 2:10; synopsis of James 2; BTB, note to James 5:7; Bisse, *Sermons*, sig. E7^{r-v}; Bedel, *Sermon*, sig. D1^V; Some, in Pilkington, *Works*, 469; S. Gardiner, *Cognizance*, sig. A7^V; Curteys, *Two Sermons*, sig. D1^r; Turnbull, *XV. Psalme*, f. 56^r; Dent, *Path-way*, 204; Norden, *Solace*, f. 4^r; Trigge, *Sermon*, sig. D2^r; Allen, *Treasvrie*, 212; BL Lansdowne MS 11/5; Bird, *2 Cor.*, 39; HMC 9 Salisbury, 12:672.

20. Carpenter, *Wife*, sig. D1^V.

21. L. Barker, *Checke*, sig. I5^V, expressing a view he rejects.

22. Matthew-Becke Bible (1549, 1551) and MB (1551), Tyndale's prologue to Num.; (cf. MB [1537], note to Luke 6); GB, notes to Gen. 43:12; 2 Sam. 17:28; 2 Kings 4:4, 7; 2 Chron. 33:13; Pss. 37:1; 141:4; Prov. 11:29; 12:9; preface to Eccles.; Isa. 22:6; Mark 8:2; 10:30; Luke 9:3, 13; 11:5; 12:21, 24, 32; 18:30; BTB, notes to Luke 16:19; James 2:5; BB, note to Gen. 45:11.

23. Bedel, *Sermon*, sig. A3^r; Babington, *Conference*, 13-14, 19; M. Smith, *Sermon*, 59; S. Gardiner, *Cognizance*, 120; Pilkington, *Works*, 34; Turnbull, *Iames*, f. 39^r; Hooker, *Works*, 2:449; Clapham, *Briefe*, 217-18. Cf. Henry Lok in *Select Poetry*, 1:138. Stephen

Bateman compared a poor man to a desert well "whom al the Passengers behold and leaue it still in his place." *The Golden Booke* (1577), f. 26^r.

24. Lupton, *Dreame*, sig. H2^{r-v}; Norden, *Solace*, ff. 7^v, 91^r; *Progress*, 139; *Practice*, ff. 46^v, 55^v; Gifford, *Fovre Sermons* (1598), 15; Wilcox, *Large Letters* (1589); Bownde, *Treatise*, 170; Gibbon, *Praise*, 53; Perkins, *Exposition*, 112; *Treatise*, 523-24, 529; H. Smith, *Teares*, 11-12, 37; Dent, *Path-way*, 104, 197; Dering, *Catechisme*, *Workes*, sigs. C3^v, C6^v-C7^v; Knewstub, *Sermon*, sig. Q3^r; Hake, *Touchestone*, sig. E1^v; Greenham, *Works*, 114; Estey, *Expositions*, pt. 1, f. 70^v; Moffett, *Commentarie*, 86-87. Cf. Lodge, *Divel*, sig. B3^v.

25. R. Rogers, *Treatises*, 177; Burton, *Ten Sermons*, 119; *Rowsing*, 518; Allen, *Garden*, 137, 146, 156; Norden, *Progress*, 142-43.

26. Lupton, *Dreame*, sig. A7^r, citing a view he repudiates. Cf. S. Gardiner, *Cognizance*, 178, and Wilkinson, *Confvtation*, f. 66^r, for similar objections.

27. Sandys, *Sermons*, 265.

28. Tyndale NT (1534), prologue to 1 Pet.; MB (1537, 1551) and Matthew-Becke Bible (1549, 1551), notes to Lev. 19; Luke 16; Tyndale-Coverdale NT (1538), note to Luke 11; Taverner Bible (1539), note to Deut. 14; Tyndale-Erasmus NT (1549), note to Luke 9; Tyndale Pentateuch (1551), note to Deut. 14; GB, notes to 2 Kings 5:16; Neh. 8:10; Isa. 56:1; Ecclus. 38:11; Matt. 25:29; Luke 3:11; 11:41; 16:19; Acts 2:42; Rom. 15:28; 1 Thess. 1:3; synopses to Prov. 5; Rom. 13; BB, notes to Gen. 18:27; Luke 3:11; 11:41; BTB, notes to Matt. 13:44; Luke 6:9; 11:41; Acts 4:34; 11:29; Rom. 15:27; 2 Cor. 8:12-13; 1Pet. 4:10.

29. Rheims NT, notes to Mark 12:44; Luke 21:4; Phil. 4:18; 1 John 3:17; Bonner, *Instruction*, sig. B6^v; Vaux, *Catechisme*, f. 49^v.

30. T. Rogers, *Doctrine*, 354-55; *Creede*, pt. 2, p. 86; S. Gardiner, *Cognizance*, 132; Thomas Bankes, *A Verie Godly, Learned, and Fruitfull Sermon* (1586), sigs. D7^r ff.; Sandys, *Sermons*, 3, 413; Pilkington, *Works*, 292; Segar, *Honor*, 60; Terry, *Second Part*, sig. E2^r; Anderson, *Godlie Sermon*, sig. D7^r; Turnbull, *Iames*, f. 89^v; *Wentworth Papers*, ed. Cooper, 35; Carpenter, *Report*, 26:171-72. Cf. Boorde, *Regimente*, sig. B4^v.

31. Perkins, *Treatise*, 598-600, 609; Allen, *Garden*, 27, 129-30; Norden, *Solace*, f. 16^r; Bush, *Sermon*, sig. B2^v; H. Smith, *Teares*, 12; Knewstub, *Lectvres*, 108-9; Becon, *Salue*, 142-43, 212; *Postil*, 2:f. 5^r; Crowley, *Opening*, sig. B1^r; Wilcox, *Prouerbs*, 91; Wither, *View*, 52; Greenham, *Works*, 366, 412; Hooke, *Sermon*, sig. C7^v; Perkins, *Warning*, 247-49, 251; T. Rogers, *Treatises*, 178-79, 460; W. Vaughan, *Golden-groue*, sig. Q8^v; Fulke, *Text*, f. 313^r.

32. GB, notes to Deut. 23:20; Prov. 11:24; Eccles. 11:1; Luke 16:1; 2 Cor. 8:14; 9:14; Rheims NT, notes to Luke 11:41; 12:21; Acts 9:39; 2 Cor. 9:6.

33. S. Gardiner, *Cognizance*, sig. A8^r, p. 119; Pilkington, *Works*, 57; Sandys, *Sermons*, 229; Perkins, *Warning*, 255; *Treatise*, 616; Lupton, *Dreame*, sig. C2^r; Moffett, *Commentarie*, 163; Gifford, *Fovre Sermons* (1598), 16-17; Wither, *View*, 270; Cartwright, *Confvtation*, 189, 456; Trigge, *Sermon*, sig. F4^r.

34. MB (1537), "A Table"; MB (1537, 1551) and Matthew-Becke Bible (1549, 1551), note to Eccles. 11; GB, note to Prov. 5:17 and synopsis of Prov. 5; BTB, notes to 2 Thess. 3:6; James 1:27; BB, note to Eccles. 11:2; Rheims NT, notes to Luke 16:9; Gal. 6:10; Phil. 4:18. Cf. Shelford, *Lectvres*, 105.

35. A. Hill, *Crie*, 72-73; Bankes, *Sermon*, sig. E6^v; Sandys, *Sermons*, 3, 109; S. Gardiner, *Cognizance*, 104, 146-50; T. Rogers, *Doctrine*, 355; J. Rogers, *Displaying*, sig. K1^r.

36. Bird, *2 Cor.*, 85-86, 89-90; Becon, *Salue*, 146-47; W. Vaughan, *Golden-groue*, sigs. 14^v, R2^v; Greenham, *Works*, 420; H. Smith, *Teares*, 13-14; Knell, *An ABC*; Estey, *Expositions*, pt. 1, f. 53^r; Burton, *Exposition*, 171; *Ten Sermons*, 119; Gifford, *Fovre Sermons* (1598), 18; Dod, *Treatise*, pt. 2, f. 50^r; Stubbes, *Motive*, 139; Allen, *Garden*, 33-34, 37, 39-41; Perkins, *Treatise*, 602, 605-6.

37. MB, "A Table"; Tyndale-Rogers NT, note to Luke 16; GB, notes to Ps. 112:9; Prov.

23:4; Luke 21:4; 2 Cor. 9:8; BTB, notes to Matt. 6:1; Luke 12:33; 14:12; 2 Cor. 9:6; Gal. 6:7; James 2:10.

38. Drant, *Sermon*, sig. E4^r; Pilkington, *Works*, 151; Woolton, *Manual*, 52-53, 138-39; Temple, *Sermon*, sig. B1^r; S. Gardiner, *Cognizance*, 106-7, 134-35, 138, 149, 158-59. The Catholic Nicholas Sanders likewise condemned hypocritical benefactors. *Treatise*, f. 40^{r-v}. In an interesting case of a benefactor donating beyond his means, William Sedley of Aylesford, Kent, the future baronet, reportedly went to Padua late in the Elizabethan era because of debt, part of whch was due to lavish almsgiving. Manningham, *Diary*, 19-20.

39. Allen, *Garden*, 32-34, 39-41, 55, 122; Bird, *2 Cor.*, 12-13, 37; Perkins, *Treatise*, 607; *Chaine*, sig. S3^r; Thomas White, *A Sermon Preached at Paules Crosse* (1589), 33; Stockwood, *1578 Sermon*, 106-7; Gibbon, *Remedie*, sig. K1^r; Wither, *View*, 36; Bownde, *Doctrine*, 80-81; Fulke, *Text*, f. 127^r; Burton, *Exposition*, 177; *Ten Sermons*, 120; W. Vaughan, *Golden-groue*, sigs. I5^{r-v}, R2^v; Stubbes, *Motive*, 137-38. Cf. Cope, *Exposition*, f. 37^v.

40. Gifford, *Foure Sermons vpon . . . Faith* (1582), sig. D7^{r-v}. The note to Matt. 26:10 in the Rheims NT calls attention to the importance of donations to the church, though admittedly sometimes gifts to the poor must take precedence. Wither blasted the Catholics for spending so much money founding monasteries and chantries or gilding roodlofts, thereby reducing funds for poor relief. *View*, 64-65.

41. Holinshed, *Chronicles*, 4:265.

42. Trigge, *Apologie*, 9.

43. Machyn, *Diary*, 240-41; Norden, *Progress*, 175-77; HMC 9 Salisbury, 2:222; BL Egerton MS 2644, f. 26^r; Kethe, *Sermon*, sig. B5^r; Carew, *Svrvey*, f. 67^{r-v}; Manningham, *Diary*, 83; Allen, *Garden*, sig. A3^r; Lambarde, *Government*, 175.

44. John Awdeley, *The Fraternitye of Vacabondes*, ed. Edward Viles and F. J. Furnivall (1869), 3, 5-6; Harman, *Caveat*, i-ii, v-vi, 18, 25, 30-31, 33, 43, 50, 56. As an example of "peddler's French," "See you, yonder is the house, open the door, and ask for the best," was spoken: "Towre ye, yander is the ken, dup the gyger and maunde that is beneship." Harman, *Caveat*, 67. Full discussions are provided in Frank Aydelotte, *Elizabethan Rogues and Vagabonds* (Oxford, 1913) and A. V. Judges, ed., *The Elizabethan Underworld* (1965).

45. Clark, in *Crisis and Order in English Towns 1500-1700*, ed. Peter Clark and Paul Slack (1972), 144; Clark, *English Provincial Society* (Hassocks, Sussex, 1976), 235-36; John F. Pound, *Poverty and Vagrancy in Tudor England* (1971), 28; A. L. Beier, "Vagrants and the Social Order in Elizabethan England," *PP*, 64 (August 1974):9, 11-13, 16-19, 23-24, 26; Pound, "Debate: Vagrants and the Social Order in Elizabethan England," *PP*, 71 (May 1976): 126-29; Beier, "A Rejoinder," *PP*, 71 (May 1976):130-34; Beier, *Journal of Interdisciplinary History*, 9:203-21.

46. *Tudor Economic Documents*, ed. R. H. Tawney and Eileen Power (1924), 2:339-46; *APC*, 20:124; Lambarde, *Government*, 183-84; *Illustrations*, ed. Nichols, 24-25; BL Egerton MS 2644, f. 32^r; *APC*, 9:56; Harman, *Caveat*, 11. Of 4s. 7d. provided for poor relief in 1586, the parish of Staplegrove, Somerset, spent 9d. on poor soldiers. BL Add. MS 30,278. Dearth often threatened the social order by causing increases in crime, as in Essex in the 1590s, but paradoxically it sometimes led to stability, particularly when the authorities visibly acted to provide relief. John Walter and Keith Wrightson, "Dearth and the Social Order in Early Modern England," *PP*, 71 (May 1976):24-25, 27-29, 41.

47. Jewel, *Works*, 2:941; GB, note to Acts 4:34; Udall, *Obedience*, sig. F3^r; Burton, *Exposition*, 171; Dod, *Treatise*, pt. 2, f. 30^v; Perkins, *Chaine*, sig. M6^v; *Treatise*, 603-4; Allen, *Garden*, 126-27; Weigall, *Quarterly Review*, 215:129-30; Mildmay, *Memorial*, [2]; Raine, ed., *Injunctions*, cxi.

48. Alan Everitt, "Farm Labourers," in *The Agrarian History of England and Wales*, ed. Joan Thirsk (Cambridge, 1967), 406; Aveling, *Recusancy*, 13; HMC 55 Var. Coll., 2:95-96; Machyn, *Diary*, 292; Lambarde, *Government*, 180; Hamilton, *Sessions*, 16.

49. Sandys, *Sermons*, 230, 344; Percy, *History*, 37; Dod, *Treatise*, pt. 2, ff. 30^V-31^V; Perkins, *Treatise*, 604-5, 612; *Warning*, 251-52. Cf. MB, "A Table"; Some, in Pilkington, *Works*, 470; Acheley, *Massacre*, sig. C1^r.

50. Nowell, *Sermon*, 228; S. Gardiner, *Cognizance*, 150; King, *Lectvres*, 141; Burton, *Ten Sermons*, 120; Cole, *Sermon*, sig. D6^V; Norden, *Progress*, 175-76; Becon, *Demaundes*, sig. A7^V; Usher, ed., *Movement*, 32; Allen, *Garden*, sig. A3^r. Demands for more effective enforcement also were made by Lambarde (*Government*, 172, 174) and Harman (*Caveat*, iii).

51. Anstruther, *Vaux*, 105-6; *APC*, 10:422-23; 17:161; 18:221-25, 236-38; 20:69; Hamilton, ed., *Books*, 23-25, 45, 47, 52-54, 66, *et passim*; Hearnshaw, ed., *Records*, 1:51; Hoskins, *Studies*, 61; Usher, ed., *Movement*, 100; Lambarde, *Government*, 21; *Staffordshire Session Rolls*, ed. Burne, 4:212; *Quarter Sessions Records for Chester*, ed. Bennett and Dewhurst, 50, BL Lansdowne MS 160, f. 234^r. In 1598 Sir Thomas Egerton, the lord keeper, was instructed by Elizabeth to reprove the justices of the peace for not punishing vagabonds adequately. Wilbraham, *Journal*, 12. Justices may have been reluctant because of the legal consequences of erroneously charging someone with vagrancy, as in the case of Stephen Proctor, a Middlesex gentleman arrested in York, who sued those responsible in Star Chamber. PRO STAC 7 Add., 4/33.

52. *APC*, 9:247; 10:215; 11:295; 15:256; 16:136, 336; 18:266; PRO SP 205/6 (f. 15^{r-v}); HMC 73 Exeter, 69. The Jesuit John Gerard always tried to travel by horse because people on foot often were subject to arrest as vagrants. *Autobiography*, 11.

53. Hooke, *Sermon*, sig. C8^r.

54. Sutton, *Disce vivere*, 341.

55. Perkins, *Chaine*, sig. L3^{r-v}; Manningham, *Diary*, 73; Stubbes, *Motive*, 88-90; BL Lansdowne MS 79/11.

56. Whitgift, *Works*, 2:389; BL Lansdowne MS 121/22; Cooper, *Certaine Sermons*, 17; Hooke, *Sermon*, sig. C8^{r-v}.

57. HMC 9 Salisbury, 2:111, 320.

58. BL Lansdowne MS 95/3. Cf. also the recommendations of John Stoit in 1595; BL Lansdowne MS 79/12.

59. J. Rogers, *Displaying*, sigs. I5^r, K1^r; T. Rogers, *Doctrine*, 354; MB (1537, 1551) and Matthew-Becke Bible (1549, 1551), notes to Mark 10; Acts 5; Tyndale-Coverdale NT, note to Luke 12; Tyndale-Rogers NT, note to Acts 5; GB, notes to Matt. 19:21; Acts 2:44; 4:32, 35; 5:4; BTB, note to Acts 2:44; Rheims NT, note to Acts 2:44.

60. Cardwell, ed., *Synodalia*, 1:72; T. Rogers, *Creede*, pt. 2, p. 86; *Doctrine*, 352-53; Manningham, *Diary*, 28, 141; Sutton, *Disce vivere*, 341; Whitgift, *Works*, 1:353-54; Pilkington, *Works*, 594; Bedel, *Sermon*, sig. C3^r; Wright, *Summons*, 4.

61. Udall, *Obedience*, sigs. F4^r-F5^r; Allen, *Treasvrie*, 235; Wither, *View*, 124; Norden, *Solace*, f. 84^V; Holland, *Exposition*, 132; Cartwright, *Confvtation*, 97, 267, 395; Perkins, *Treatise*, 533-35. Cf. Chaderton, *Excellent Sermon*, sig. F1^V.

62. Becon, *Demaundes*, sig. C7^V; Cartwright, *Confvtation*, 267; Perkins, *Treatise*, 532-33, 608; *Warning*, 250; Fulke, *Text*, f. 187^r; HMC 9 Salisbury, 2:63-64.

63. Manningham, *Diary*, 30. Sanders' sermon was preached at Paul's Cross on 16 May 1602.

64. Fulke, *Text*, f. 52^V.

65. H. Smith, *Teares*, 26; Fulke, *Two Treatises Written Against the Papistes* (1577), pt. 2, p. 241; *Text*, f. 52^V; Pilkington, *Works*, 610-11; Jewel, *Works*, 4:1086; Wither, *View*, 78; Harman, *Caveat*, 13. According to Jordan, the problem of poverty was less acute in Kent than most other areas of England. *Kent*, 16. For the reforms in Norwich, see *Records*, ed. Hudson and Tingey, 2:345-55; J. F. Pound, "An Elizabethan Census of the Poor," *Birmingham University Historical Journal*, 8 (1962). Cf. also Dyer, *Worcester*, 165-72; J. Hill, *Lincoln*, 89; Clark, *Provincial Society*, 235-41.

66. *EEA*, 2:56, 58, 96, 99-100, 110-11, 116-18, 121, 126; 3:141, 143-44, 156, 165, 176, 184, 213, 217, 228, 230-31, 241, 329; Grindal, *Remains*, 129, 140-41, 172-73.

67. Curteys, *Two Sermons*, sig. A7^r; Grindal, *Remains*, 259; *Quarter Sessions Records for Chester*, ed. Bennett and Dewhurst, 49; PRO SP 171/64 (f. 146^r); BL Lansdowne MSS 18/97; 28/75; Parker, *Correspondence*, 455; PRO SP 45, ff. 16^v-17^r. Some clergy refused to distribute a fortieth of their income to the poor. See, e.g., *Diocese of Norwich*, ed. Williams, 62.

68. Percy, *History*, 28-29, 32-34; BL Lansdowne MSS 8/89; 28/78; Grindal, *Remains*, 302-3, 349-52; Parker, *Correspondence*, 348; *APC*, 11:330; HMC 9 Salisbury, 1:311.

69. *APC*, 14:277-78; 20:232, 236, 323-24; Whitgift, *Works*, 3:618-19.

70. Bancroft, *Svrvay*, 201-2; Whitgift, *Works*, 3:286, 290-91, 539; Marten, *Reconciliation*, f. 89^r; S. Gardiner, *Cognizance*, 126-27; Sandys, *Sermons*, 160; C. Hill, *Economic Problems*, 202.

71. Chaderton, *Frvitfvll Sermon*, 75-76; Bird, *2 Cor.*, 52, 54; (cf. GB, notes to Acts 6:2; Phil. 1:1); Allison, *Confvtation*, 68; Perkins, *Warning*, 249; *Treatise*, 608; Greenham, *Works*, 366-67; Usher, ed., *Movement*, 99-100; *Writings of Greenwood and Barrow (1591-93)*, 307-8, 326.

72. Stockwood, *1578 Sermon*, 111; Allen, *Garden*, 42; W. Vaughan, *Golden-groue*, sig. I6^r; T. White, *1589 Sermon*, 39; Percy, *History*, 28. Some Puritan concern for the poor is revealed in diaries. When Richard Rogers came to London in April 1588, he visited the poor in Bridewell, perhaps bringing some physical or monetary relief. Samuel Ward felt guilty in 1595 for "not remembring of the poore this Commensment." *Diaries*, ed. Knappen, 76, 109.

73. Sutcliffe, *Answere*, 127. In a review of Jordan's *Philanthropy in England*, Lawrence Stone asserts that if Jordan's figures are altered in accord with the Phelps Brown cost-of-living index, philanthropy declined almost continuously from 1510 to 1600, so that the Reformation reduced the volume of charity, as contemporaries frequently claimed. *History*, 44 (1959): 257-60. The first substantive endeavor to reassess Jordan's figures was undertaken in 1976 by W. G. Bittle and R. Todd Lane, who again relied heavily on the Phelps Brown index, and concluded that no evidence shows Jordan's rising tide of philanthropy. According to their corrected figures, secular donations declined from £61,881 in the 1500s to £29,097 in the 1540s, rose to £56,367 in the 1550s, declined to £28,576 in the 1590s, and rose again to £46,240 in the 1600s. Religious donations declined from £81,836 in the 1500s to £1,790 in the 1590s before rising to £4,192 in the 1600s. "Inflation and Philanthropy in England: A Re-Assessment of W. K. Jordan's Data," *Econ. H. R.*, 2nd ser., 29 (1976):203-10. Their work received a hostile reception from J. D. Gould ("Bittle and Lane on Charity: An Uncharitable Comment," *Econ. H. R.*, 31 [1978]:121-23) and D. C. Coleman ("Philanthropy Deflated: A Comment," ibid., 31:118-20), neither of whom offers a substantive alternative. Coleman properly cautions that "changing amounts of 'generosity' cannot be measured by monetary series of testamentary benefactions; and the social value of such charity remains concealed even after those aggregates have been deflated by a price index and adjusted for population change," though the latter has not been attempted. What Jordan, Bittle, and Lane cannot measure is the amount of relief dispensed through hospitality. In a substantive addition to the Bittle-Lane thesis, J. F. Hadwin ("Deflating Philanthropy," ibid., 31:105-17) calculates not only current giving but income from previous endowments. Adjusted for inflation, Hadwin's figures show that private benefactions for poor relief rose from £9,048 in the 1500s, to £18,180 in the 1550s, to £28,333 in the 1590s, and to £35,500 in the 1600s. Secular giving to education and poor relief in real terms did grow from 1480 to 1660, though the scale of the assistance remained small—not more than 0.5% (for the yield of secular benefactions) or 0.25% (for the yield of private benefactions) of current national income in any decade. In reaffirming their basic argument, Bittle and Lane point out that attempts to measure charity

by comparing total bequests with total values of inventories for the city of Worcester and the county of Devon do not support Jordan's thesis, though an analysis of Devon benefactions does bear out Jordan's conclusion that there was a decline in religious and an increase in secular giving. "A Re-Assessment Reiterated," ibid., 31:124-28; Dyer, *Worcester*, 242-43. Although the final word has not been given, it is clear (1) that there was a shift in philanthropic giving that benefitted secular recipients such as schools and the impotent, and (2) that there was no philanthropic explosion or rising tide in the Elizabethan period, though there *may* have been a very modest increase at best.

74. Jordan, *Forming*, 60; *Illustrations*, ed. Nichols, 22-23; Clay, ed., *Wills*, 18-21, 24-25, 31-32, 226; Stubbes, *Motive*, 58-62; Cooper, *Athenae*, 1:460; Raine, ed., *Wills*, 2:168-69, 171-74; Raine, ed., *Injunctions*, ciii-cv; Tymms, ed., *Wills*, 154.

75. Jordan, *Institutions of Lancashire*, 13-14; Piccope, ed., *Wills*, 51:157-62; Raine, ed., *Wills*, 2:174-80, 184-86; BL Add. MS [Wolley] 6671, ff. 65^v-66^r; Clay, ed., *Wills*, 12-13, 28-34; Cooper, *Athenae*, 1:314-15, 496. In exile at Louvain, the widow of Sir Robert Dormer washed the feet of twelve poor widows and gave each one a new smock and gown, a purse and money, and dinner every Maundy Thursday, and another dinner on Easter. Henry Clifford, *The Life of Jane Dormer, Duchess of Feria*, ed. Joseph Stevenson and trans. E. E. Estcourt (1887), 52.

76. Strype, *Parker*, 2:484; Holinshed, *Chronicles*, 4:328; BL Lansdowne MSS 39/16-17; 82/57; Cooper, *Athenae*, 1:361-62, 410, 442-43, 513; 2:373; Hutton, *Correspondence*, 21; Strype, *Aylmer*, 114; Clay, ed., *Wills*, 22-23, 220; PRO SP 106/17 (ff. 42^r, 43^v).

77. Cooper, *Athenae*, 2:318; *Wills and Inventories from the Registry at Durham*, ed. W. Greenwell (1835, 1929), 2:14-19; Clay, ed., *Wills*, 62-63; *DNB, s.v.* Alexander Nowell.

78. Cooper, *Athenae*, 1:211-12, 250, 343; 2:6; Piccope, ed., *Wills*, 51:3-4, 36-38; 54:89; Raine, ed., *Wills*, 2:194 *et passim*; Raine, ed., *Injunctions*, cv-cix, cxiv-cxix, cxxii-cxxiv, cxxix, cxl; Hodgson, ed., *Wills*, 64-65, 71, 79, 99-100, 107; Clay, ed., *Wills*, 231; C. Hill, *Economic Problems*, 203-4. Cf. John Awdeley, *An Epitaphe vpon the Death of Mayster Iohn Viron Preacher* [1563?].

79. Clay, ed., *Wills*, 49-51, 104-5, 117-19, 148-50; Young, *Mary Sidney*, 78; Collins, *Life*, 95; BL Lansdowne MSS 50/90; 77/29; 83/36; 83/43; Jordan, *Forming*, 54; Stone, *Crisis*, 509, 784; *Lancashire Funeral Certificates*, ed. Thomas W. King and F. R. Raines (1869), 12-13.

80. Stone, *Crisis*, 48; Smyth, *Berkeley Manuscripts*, 2:368-69; Jordan, *Forming*, 12; *Illustrations*, ed. Nichols, 21, 23; Clapham, in *Elizabeth*, ed. Read and Read, 84; Craze, *History*, 31; BL Stowe MS 774. After his death in 1572 Edward Stanley, earl of Derby, was praised because "a hande to helpe the hungrie poore, he in no wise refraind." John Denton, *An Epitaph vpon the Death of the Right Honorable Edward Earle of Darby* [1572]. In 1581 Henry Wriothesley, earl of Southampton, was similarly lauded for aiding widows, orphans, and the hungry. J. Phillip, *Epitaph on Southampton*.

81. Chamberlain, *Letters*, 1:64; Nichols and Bruce, eds., *Wills*, 73; Cooper, *Athenae*, 1:433; 2:36; Clay, ed., *Wills*, 16, 42-43, 63; BL Lansdowne MSS 66/49-51; 77/50; Jordan, *Kent*, 45; Holles, *Memorials*, 65-66; *Winthrop Papers*, 1:17.

82. Aspinall-Oglander, *Symphony*, 27; Cooper, ed., *Wentworth Papers*, 14, 36; HMC 69 Middleton, 422-47; Trevelyan, ed., *Papers*, 2:97-98; *Winthrop Papers*, 1:74.

83. Stow, *Chronicles*, 4:427-30; Fleming, *Memoriall*, sigs. C1^r-D3^r.

84. Jordan, *Kent*, 42-43; Clay, ed., *Wills*, 142, 145-46; Cooper, *Athenae*, 2:19, 123, 229; Grosart, ed., *Towneley Hall MSS*, xliv-xlv; Stow, *Chronicles*, 4:534-35; Jordan, *Institutions of Lancashire*, 14; *CSPD, Add. 1566-79*, 9. Robert Johnson, a clerk to Elizabeth, erected hospitals and grammar schools at Oakham and Uppingham, Rutland, with Burghley's support. HMC 9 Salisbury, 4:107.

85. Nichols and Bruce, eds., *Wills*, 61-64; Clay, ed., *Wills*, 46-49; HMC 80 Sackville, 1:27-

28, 31; Hogrefe, *Women*, 94; W. Harrison, *Discovrse*, 8; Sylvester, *Monodia*, sig. A4^V; Nicholas Bourman, *An Epitaph vpon the Decease of . . . Lady Mary Ramsey* (1602), sigs. A3^r-B1^r; Jordan, *Forming*, 23; HMC 73 Exeter, 319. Cf. Bourman, *An Epytaphe vpon the Death of . . . Sir William Garrat* (1571); John Phillip, *An Epitaph on the Death of . . . the Ladie Maioresse, Late Wyfe to . . . (Alexander Auenet) Lord Maior* (1570). Robert Rogers, a Merchant Adventurer and London leatherseller, reportedly gave charitable gifts totaling £2,960 6s. 8d. *A Liuing Remembrance.* Another substantial benefactor was William Lambarde, son of a London draper, who founded a hospital at East Greenwich in 1575, ultimately spending £2,337 8s. 6d. on it. Jordan, *Kent*, 46.

86. Cooper, *Athenae*, 1:245; 2:336; Piccope, ed., *Wills*, 54:167-68; A. Pearson, *Cartwright*, appendix 39; Raine, ed., *Injunctions*, cx-cxiv. Laurence Chaderton was known for his affection for the poor. Ward, *Diaries*, ed. Knappen, 107.

87. Cross, *Trans. Leics. Arch. and Hist. Soc.*, 36:15-16; *Earl*, 124-26; (cf. Hastings, *Letters*, 60); Jordan, *Philanthropy*, 217; John Tomkys, *A Sermon Preached the 26. Day of May. 1584* (1586), sig. π4^V; A. Clifford, *Lives*, 25; BL Lansdowne MS 103/51; *Illustrations*, ed. Nichols, 25.

88. Cross, *SCH*, 2:274; Hastings, *Letters*, 65; Lehmberg, *Mildmay*, 235; H. Mildmay, *Brief Memoir*, 18; Tittler, *Bacon*, 192; HMC 19 Townshend, 6-7; Walsall, *Sermon*, sig. A5^V; Parker, *Correspondence*, 309; LPL Bacon MS 655/24 (f. 33^r); McIntosh, *Proceedings*, 119:249; Hoby, *Diary*, 75-76, 91.

89. Cf. *Woorth*, trans. A. Gibson, sigs. D6^V-D10^V, where it is argued that in aiding the poor, women excel more than men.

90. W. Vaughan, *Golden-groue*, sig. Q6^r.

91. Deloney, *Craft*, sig. A2^r.

92. GB, notes to Gen. 24:32; Prov. 9:2; 23:3; 3 John 5, 6; BTB, note to 1 Pet. 4:9; BB, notes to Gen. 18:1, 4; 19:2; Rheims NT, notes to Heb. 13:2; 3 John 5. Bishop Barnes made hospitality a work of bodily mercy in his catechism. *Instruction*, sig. B6^r.

93. T. Rogers, *Discourse*, ff. 182^V-184^V; Sandys, *Sermons*, 400-1; Cooper, *Exposition*, sig. P5^r; Anderson, *Shield*, sig. D2^r; Curteys, *A Sermon Preached Before the Queenes Maiestie* (1573), sig. C5^r; Pilkington, *Works*, 386, 592, 594; Turnbull, *XV. Psalme*, f. 18^r; Wright, *Summons*, 51; Howson, *1597 Sermon*, 36-37; Nash, *Anatomie*, sig. D1^r; Whetstone, *Rocke*, sig. O2^V; King, *Lectvres*, 76; King, *A Sermon Preached in Yorke* (Oxford, 1597), 704; Sutton, *Disce mori*, 193; Gabriel Powel, *Theologicall and Scholasticall Positions Concerning Vsurie* (Oxford, 1602), 59-60. In 1600 Sir Thomas Egerton added another reason for insufficient hospitality, namely the desire of the aristocracy to spend more time in the towns. Chamberlain, *Letters*, 1:97.

94. Fenner, *Treatises*, 30-32; Stubbes, *Anatomie*, sigs. H8^{r-v}, J2^{r-v}; Allen, *Garden*, 35; *Treasvrie*, 219; Cartwright, *Confvtation*, 646; Collinson, in *The Dissenting Tradition*, ed. Cole and Moody, 23-24; Bird, *2 Cor.*, 81; W. Vaughan, *Golden-groue*, sig. Q7^r; Crowley, *Opening*, sig. C2^r; (cf. Nicholson, *Acolastvs*, sig. D1^r); Gibbon, *Praise*, 10; *Remedie*, sig. K1^r.

95. Burton, *Wooing*, 258; Dod, *Treatise*, pt. 2, ff. 49^V-50^r; Hake, *Touchestone*, sig. B7^r; Trigge, *Sermon*, sig. B2^V; Gibbon, *Praise*, 13; W. Vaughan, *Golden-groue*, sigs. H5^{r-v}, Q7^V-Q8^r; Stubbes, *Motive*, 130-32; *Anatomie*, sig. J2^V; T. White, *1589 Sermon*, 37-38; H. Smith, *Teares*, 36-37; Hake, *Newes*, sig. F1^r.

96. Parker, *Correspondence*, 127-28, 308; *EEA*, 2:68, 73, 92; 3:141, 155, 183, 191-92; Grindal, *Remains*, 165-66; BL Lansdowne MSS 7/66; 38/71; Marchant, *Puritans*, 248; Purvis, ed., *Documents*, 56; Strype, *Grindal*, 531; *APC*, 26:94-96; Strype, *Whitgift*, 2:336-37; 3:348-49. A bill for the maintenance of hospitality was rejected by the Commons after the second reading in February 1598. D'Ewes, *Journals*, 591.

97. Strype, *Parker*, 1:378-80, 519-20; 2:19-20, 25; Stow, *Chronicles*, 4:425, 765-66;

Cooper, *Athenae*, 2:372; LPL Bacon MS 658/193 (f. 288^r); C. Hill, *Economic Problems*, 18-19; Green, ed., *Life*, 25.

98. HMC 9 Salisbury, 1:372; Holinshed, *Chronicles*, 4:321; Cooper, *Athenae*, 2:489; Phillip, *Epitaph on Southampton*; Stone, *Crisis*, 47; Smyth, *Berkeley Manuscripts*, 2:287, 381; Collins, *Life*, 37; BL Lansdowne MS 86/45.

99. Holinshed, *Chronicles*, 4:157; Machyn, *Diary*, 215; Aspinall-Oglander, *Symphony*, 29; Holles, *Memorials*, 41-42; HMC 55 Var. Coll., 2:x, 85-86; Cliffe, *Gentry*, 114, 116; HMC 69 Middleton, 454-56. While in France with the earl of Essex in 1591, Robert Carey had to provide hospitality for friends, servants, retainers, and hangers-on, which cost £30 a week, none of which presumably went to the poor. Carey, *Memoirs*, 12. Sir Robert Cecil chided Michael Hicks "because you haue put yor self to chardges" for excessive hospitality. BL Lansdowne MS 107/52.

100. Strype, *Smith*, 157; Clay, ed., *Wills*, 145-46; Piccope, ed., *Wills*, 51:91, 224; 54: 92.

101. C. Hill, *Economic Problems*, 202; Wiffen, *Memoirs*, 1:479; *Crie*; Stow, *Chronicles*, 4:874; Mildmay, *Memorial*, [2].

102. Bownde, *Treatise*, sig. π3^r; Anstruther, *Vaux*, 118; Hoby, *Diary*, 40-43, 93, 141, 194; Gleason, *Justices*, 39. Becon praised the people of Sandwich, Kent, for receiving refugees as Christian brethren. *Demaundes*, sig. A5^v. Chaderton believed the Catholic nobility and clergy were more hospitable than the Protestants. Sir Thomas Tresham entertained up to a hundred persons in his household at once, though few of these appear to have been poor. One source of continuing Catholic strength in the Elizabethan period was the hospitality of the large households, which effectively merged the Catholic liturgical cycle with hospitality at such seasons as Christmas and Easter. Chaderton, *Excellent Sermon*, sig. C5^r; Finch, *Wealth*, 81; Bossy, *PP*, 21:39-40.

103. Jordan, *Philanthropy*, 155.

Chapter 14: Economic Problems

1. J. Barker, *Balade*.

2. Andrewes, *Combate*, sig. D2^v.

3. Max Weber, *The Protestant Ethic and the Spirit of Capitalism*, trans. Talcott Parsons (2nd ed., 1976), chap. 2; R. H. Tawney, *Religion and the Rise of Capitalism* (1926), *passim*; Tawney, introduction to Thomas Wilson, *A Discourse upon Usury* (1925), 106-21; George, *Mind*, 166-69; George, "English Calvinist Opinion on Usury, 1600-1640," *Journal of the History of Ideas*, 18 (October 1957):455-74. Cf. C. Hill, "Protestantism and the Rise of Capitalism," *Essays in the Economic and Social History of Tudor and Stuart England*, ed. F. J. Fisher (Cambridge, 1961), 33, where Tawney's view is reflected.

4. Coverdale Bible (1535, 1537), note to Ps. 37 (erroneously numbered 36 in the 1535 ed.); MB (1537, 1551), notes to Deut. 24; Ps. 37; "A Table"; Matthew-Becke Bible, note to Ps. 37 (1549, 1551); Deut. 24 (1549 only); GB, notes to Neh. 5:7; Ps. 15:5; Prov. 28:8; Luke 6:35; BB, notes to Exod. 22:24; Ecclus. 34:25; BTB, note to Luke 6:35; Rheims NT, note to Luke 6:15.

5. *SR*, 3:996-97; 4, pt. 1, 155; Stone, *Crisis*, 530; Cliffe, *Gentry*, 145; Finch, *Wealth*, 11-13; Alan G. R. Smith, *Servant of the Cecils* (Totowa, N.J., 1977), 87, 89.

6. *CJ*, 1:63-66, 84-87; *CSPD, Add., 1566-79*, 20-22; D'Ewes, *Journals*, 171-74; *SR*, 4, pt. 1, 542-43. Charging interest in excess of 10% was punished in the 1571 statute by forfeiture of three times the principal and interest, plus the possibility of additional fines and imprisonment, in addition to punishment under ecclesiastical law. Charging rates of 10% or less could result in forfeiture of interest alone and no punishment under canon law. Before the passage of the 1571 law, both Mary and Elizabeth had to license merchants to loan the

government funds and collect interest. PRO SP 19/2 (ff. 2A^V-8^r); 19/8 (f. 18^{r-v}); *CSPD, 1547-1590*, 100, 182; *Calendar of the Patent Rolls*, 5 (1966):375 (#2584).

7. *Patent Rolls*, 5:279-80 (#2164); Stone, *Crisis*, 530; HMC Middleton, 567; PRO SP 106/50 (f. 109^{r-v}); BL Lansdowne MS 101/26; *APC*, 14:69.

8. PRO Req. 2/29/22; 2/34/20; 2/38/35; 2/38/86.

9. Pilkington, *Works*, 39-40, 150; cf. 464.

10. Jewel, *Works*, 2:851-59, 883; 4:1276.

11. Sandys, *Sermons*, 50, 117-18, 136, 182-83, 203-4, 231, 355. Late medieval school-men began to develop a more elastic attitude toward usury, as shown in J. T. Noonan, *The Scholastic Analysis of Usury* (Cambridge, Mass., 1957). Johann Eck sanctioned the imposition of interest. At Cambridge, Martin Bucer argued for moderate interest as the rightful payment for the use of money lent as long as there was no exploitation. Whitney R. D. Jones, *The Tudor Commonwealth 1529-1559* (1970), 153-54.

12. I. P. Ellis, "The Archbishop and the Usurers," *JEH*, 21 (January 1970):33-42.

13. Drant, *Fruitful Sermon*, sigs. D2^V, F5^r; Curteys, *1574 Sermon*, sig. C7^r; Whitgift, *Godlie Sermon*, sig. B7^V; (cf. *Works*, 3:580); Wilson, *Discourse*, 355-58; Babington, *Commaundements*, 363-65; T. Rogers, *Creede*, pt. 2, p. 87; Wright, *Summons*, 8-11. Cf. Carl F. Taeusch, "The Concept of 'Usury': The History of an Idea," *Journal of the History of Ideas*, 3 (June 1942):305-6.

14. Whetstone, *Enemie*, sigs. H3^r, K1^r-K2^r; *Rocke*, sigs. L2^V-L4^V, N3^{r-v}; Lodge, *Alarum*, sigs. B2^r-B3^V, C2^r, C3^{r-v}, D2^{r-v}, D4^r-E3^V, F1^{r-v}, F3^r.

15. Turnbull, *XV. Psalme*, ff. 45^V-57^V.

16. Dove, *1594 Sermon*, sig. C2^V; King, *Sermon*, 704-5; *Lectvres*, 505; Manningham, *Diary*, 71, 140; S. Gardiner, *Cognizance*, 30; Carpenter, *Preparatiue*, 242; R. Abbot, *Exaltation*, 34; G. Abbot, *Exposition*, 90-92. Cf. Nixon, *Navy*, sig. B3^V. Cf. Roger Hacket, *A Sermon Needfvll of Theese Times* (Oxford, [1591]), sig. B3^r. Hacket, a fellow of New College, Oxford, and rector of North Crawley, Bucks., asserted that the usurer "gnaweth and teareth out his gaine, out of the lands and liuely-hoodes not onely of the commonalty, but gentry, yea nobility of this land."

17. Powel, *Positions*, sigs. A4^r-A7^r, 5-6, 8, 13-17, 20, 26, 30, 42, 47, 51, 56-66.

18. Northbrooke, *Garden*, sigs. $_2$L3^r-$_2$L7^r; Dering, *Workes*, f. 35^r; Knewstub, *Lectvres*, 137-38; Hake, *Touchestone*, sig. B1^V; *Newes*, sigs. F1^V, G3^V-G4^r, G8^V-H1^r.

19. Gifford, *Dialogue*, f. 39^V; *Catechisme*, sig. H2^r; Lupton, *Dreame*, sigs. F2^r-F5^V; Udall, *Obedience*, sigs. F7^r-F8^r; White, *1589 Sermon*, 39; Stockwood, *A Verie Godlie and Profitable Sermon* (1584), sig. C6^V; Norden, *Solace*, ff. 80^r, 137^r; Fulke, *Text*, f. 98^V.

20. Stubbes, *Anatomie*, sigs. π4^V, K5^r-L1^V; cf. *Motive*, 165-66.

21. Wilcox, *Prouerbs*, 132, 135; *Psalmes*, 26-27, 326-27; Timme, *Discouerie*, sigs. K1^V-K2^r; Moffett, *Commentarie*, 239-40; Allen, *Treasvrie*, 211; Dent, *Path-way*, 203; Estey, *Expositions*, pt. 1, ff. 70^r, 71^r; Cartwright, *Confvtation*, 175; Burton, *Wooing*, 220; (cf. *Exposition*, 168; *Rowsing*, 466); W. Vaughan, *Golden-groue*, sigs. Q3^V-Q5^V; Trigge, *Sermon*, sigs. E7^V, F1^r-F4^r; *Catholiqve*, 572-74.

22. H. Smith, *Examination*, 3, 5-6, 8-12, 17-22, 27-29, 41, 45-50.

23. Mosse, *Arraignment*, especially pp. 7, 16-19, 25-32, 43-45, 74-78, 92, 98-100, 106-10, 131-34, 159. A large portion of the work is devoted to the exposure of schemes designed to disguise usury.

24. Gibbon, *Work*, 27-29, 41-42; *Praise*, 53 (cf. 21); Perkins, *Chaine*, sig. N2^r; *Case of Conscience*, 36; *Treatise*, 392, 526; *Works* (1616-18), 1:63-64; R. Rogers, *Treatises*, 177-78, 181-82; Sprunger, *Ames*, 175.

25. Vaux, *Catechisme*, f. 55^V; Sanders, *Treatise*, especially ff. 2^r-6^r, 47^r-49^V.

26. Grindal, *Remains*, 125, 143, 172; *EEA*, e.g., 2:14, 57, 61, 98, 121, 131; 3:166, 180,

184, 231, 328, 333, 348-49; BL Lansdowne MS 20/63; Peel, ed., *Seconde Parte*, 2:146-56; C. Hill, *Economic Problems*, 218; Emmison, *Elizabethan Life*, 2:73.

27. Sutcliffe, *Answere*, 128; Stone, *Crisis*, 532-33, 537; BL Lansdowne MSS 18/66; 88/11; A. Smith, *Servant*, chap. 4; Hoby, *Diary*, 190; PRO SP 165/23 (ff. 77^V-78^r); Piccope, ed., *Wills*, 51:242; LPL Bacon MSS 647/17 (f. 58^r); 647/18 (f. 59^r); 647/24 (f. 65^r); 647/67 (f. 141^r); 648/132 (f. 219^r); Finch, *Wealth*, 14; Forman, *Autobiography*, 31; *Documents in English Economic History: England from 1000 to 1760*, ed. H. E. S. Fisher and A. R. J. Jurica (1977), 43; Spufford, *Communities*, 105; Chettle, *Dreame*, sigs. F1^V-F2^r; C. Hill, *Economic Problems*, 279.

28. Carpenter, *Report*, 26:171; Cooper, ed., *Wentworth Papers*, 10-12, 15, 21, 38, 42; F. E. Halliday, *A Cornish Chronicle* (Newton Abbot, 1967), 47.

29. HMC 9 Salisbury, 2:201 (cf. 205, 537); 3:212; Stone, *Crisis*, 528, 539-40; HMC 77 De L'Isle, 2:234; *Calendar of the Patent Rolls*, 6 (1973):517 (#3093); (cf. *CSPD, 1591-94*, 10); Batho, ed., *Household Papers*, liii-liv. Landowners often required short-term loans because rents were normally paid only in September and March.

30. PRO SP 110/51 (ff. 118^r-120^r). One of Elizabeth's ministers, Francis Weldish, asked to use the authority of the privy seal to borrow £200 from her subjects without interest and also for enactment of a law prohibiting usury. BL Lansdowne MS 108/63. At least a few in court circles seriously believed in the possibility of bringing about the interest-free society so many ministers desired.

31. New, *Anglican and Puritan*, 98.

32. Whetstone, *Rocke*, sig. O2^V.

33. R. Rogers, *Treatises*, 180.

34. Cf. Stone, *Crisis*, 516-28.

35. Gawdy, *Letters*, 72-73; HMC 69 Middleton, 601; PRO Req. 2/34/20; BL Lansdowne MS 84/26; *APC*, 15:311-12; 17:330-31; 19:471; 20:63, 299; PRO SP 21/10 (f. 22^r).

36. Cope, *Exposition*, ff. 82^V-83^r, 180^r, 181^r.

37. Whetstone, *Rocke*, sig. O2^V; R. Rogers, *Treatises*, 180; Gibbon, *Praise*, 52; Dod, *Treatise*, pt. 2, f. 67^{r-V}; Burton, *A Caveat for Sveties*, in *Works* (1602), 416, 423-25, 432-36; Perkins, *Chaine*, sigs. N1^V-N2^r; Moffett, *Commentarie*, 55, 170; Allen, *Alphabet*, 9; Cleaver, *Form*, 80.

38. Wager, *Enterlude*, sig. D3^r.

39. Jewel, *Works*, 2:850.

40. *TP*, 2:543-48. In March 1562, a proclamation dealing with the supply of victuals ordered local officials to see that standard weights and measures were used in the provision of food for the poor. *TP*, 2:182.

41. *CJ*, 1:95-96, 101-2, 130-31; D'Ewes, *Journals*, 627, 662-63; *TP*, 3:241-45. In 1593 a draft was prepared for an act to require bakers to sell bread in standard sizes, with specified exceptions; they had been using odd-sized loaves to make extra profit. The bill was rejected 65 to 92 by the Lords on the first reading. HMC Third Report, 8.

42. Emmison, *Elizabethan Life*, 3:190; *Staffordshire Session Rolls*, ed. Burns, 1:266; PRO Chancery 3/8/53; *APC*, 19:300-1; 20:6, 315-18; BL Lansdowne MSS 32/8; 38/13; 44/26; (cf. 52/13-18).

43. Hearnshaw, ed., *Records*, 1:43-372 *passim*; HMC 54 Beverley, 183; Bateson, ed., *Records*, 3:175-76, 181, 194, 243-44, 404-5. C. 1562 every alderman in Exeter had to inquire if anyone in his ward was using false weights and measures. HMC 73 Exeter, 315. (The concern for forestalling, engrossing, and regrating, with which the inquiries were also involved, indicates a date of 1562, when there was a bad harvest, not 1561.)

44. Pilkington, *Works*, 150, 470; Nowell, *Catechism*, 134; Jewel, *Works*, 2:850; Sandys, *Sermons*, 204; Turnbull, *XV. Psalme*, ff. 35^r, 60^{r-V}; S. Gardiner, *Cognizance*, 30.

45. Wilcox, *Prouerbs*, 80; Greenham, *Works*, 417; Trigge, *Sermon*, sig. D6^r; Perkins, *Chaine*, sig. N1^r; Moffett, *Commentarie*, 91; Stubbes, *Anatomie*, sig. K1^v; Deacon, *Treatise*, sigs. F4^v-F5^v; Vaux, *Catechisme*, f. 57^r. Cf. Cope, *Exposition*, f. 331^v; Fisher, *1581 Sermon*, sig. C8^v.

46. White, *Plague Sermon*, sig. A2^v.

47. Perkins, *Foundation*, sig. A2^v, expressing a view he repudiates.

48. MB (1537, 1551) and Matthew-Becke Bible (1549, 1551), note to Amos 2; GB, notes to Deut. 23:18; 27:17; Ps. 109:11; Prov. 13:11; 30:15; Mic. 1:7; Acts 1:18; (cf. 2 Sam. 4:6); Rheims NT, note to Rev. 18:9; Vaux, *Catechisme*, f. 57^r.

49. King, *Lectures*, 46; Pilkington, *Works*, 464-65; Whetstone, *Enemie*, sig. I1^{r-v}; Sandys, *Sermons*, 50, 54, 355, 360. For the Commonwealth Men see W. Jones, *Tudor Commonwealth*, especially chaps. 3, 8, 9.

50. Babington, *Commaundements*, 371-74; Sandys, *Sermons*, 117-18, 204; Nowell, *Catechism*, 134; Curteys, *Two Sermons*, sig. C1^v; *1574 Sermon*, sig. C7^r; Horne, *Exercise*, sig. B5^v; Some, in Pilkington, *Works*, 469-70.

51. Trigge, *Sermon*, sig. D6^v (quoted); Stubbes, *Anatomie*, sigs. K1^v-K2^r; Hake, *Newes*, sig. E4^v; R. Rogers, *Treatises*, 466; Dent, *Path-way*, 35, 173 (quoted); Gifford, *Dialogue*, f. 39^v; Stoughton, *Treatise*, 139-40; Knewstub, *Sermon*, sig. R1^r; Deacon, *Treatise*, sigs. A3^v, A5^{r-v}, B2^r. Barrow charged members of the Church of England with falsehood, deceit, and covetousness in all trades and callings. *Writings (1587-90)*, 546.

52. Trigge, *Sermon*, sigs. D5^v-D6^v; Deacon, *Treatise*, sigs. F2^v, F6^{r-v}, I2^r, I5^v-I8^r; Allen, *Treasvrie*, 209; Knewstub, *Lectures*, 152; Perkins, *Chaine*, sig. G1^r.

53. Deacon, *Treatise*, sigs. D1^r, D3^r, D7^v, E7^v, H4^{r-v}, H8^{r-v}; R. Rogers, *Treatises*, 180 (quoted), 374; Knewstub, *Lectures*, 146-48; Perkins, *Chaine*, sigs. M5^v-M6^r, M8^v-N2^r; Greenham, *Works*, 201-2, 417; Gifford, *Catechisme*, sig. H2^{r-v}; Stubbes, *Anatomie*, sig. O7^v; Burton, *Ten Sermons*, 19; Norden, *Solace*, f. 136^r; Allen, *Treasvrie*, 209.

54. Cooper, ed., *Wentworth Papers*, 10, 21; HMC 80 Sackville, 2:111; Seaver, paper delivered to a joint session of the American Historical Association and the American Society of Church History at Dallas, Texas, December 1977; Gawdy, *Letters*, 92. Henry Hastings, earl of Huntingdon, sought to conduct his business affairs with "ye good blessynge of oure god," recognizing that "ye lord dyrectyth all as he knowyth to bee most fytte." HL MSS HA5379 and HA5380.

55. *APC*, 11:74-75; 14:78-79; 17:151; 20:163; BL Lansdowne MSS 26/54; 114/32; LPL Bacon MSS 659/52 (f. 69^{r-v}); 659/134 (f. 197^r); HMC Third Report, 9; Furnivall, ed., *Child-Marriages*, 153-54; Bateson, ed., *Records*, 3:103.

56. Machyn, *Diary*, 248, 253, 267; Hearnshaw, ed., *Records*, 1:53, 66, 104-5, 115, 141, 151, 176, 180, 194, 196, 211, 259; *Winthrop Papers*, 1:78; Smyth, *Berkeley Manuscripts*, 2:338.

57. Turnbull, *XV. Psalme*, f. 56^r, referring to Prov. 11:26.

58. Hake, *Newes*, sig. G8^v.

59. *SR*, 4, pt. 1, 148-50; W. Jones, *Tudor Commonwealth*, 145-46; Peter Ramsey, *Tudor Economic Problems* (1965), 153.

60. *CJ*, 1:55-57; *SR*, 4, pt. 1, 368-70; HMC 73 Exeter, 315; MacCaffrey, *Exeter*, 82; Emmison, *Elizabethan Life*, 3:178-89; *APC*, 7:310; *TP*, 2:276-78; *CSPD, Add. 1566-79*, 20-22; D'Ewes, *Journals*, 188; Neale, *Parliaments*, 1:238-39. The Commons failed to pass bills to stop the engrossing of saddle trees in 1563 and tallow in 1566. *CJ*, 1:68, 74. W. G. Hoskins provides information on the bad crops: "Harvest Fluctuations and English Economic History, 1480-1619," *Agricultural History Review*, 12 (1964):28-46.

61. HMC 9 Salisbury, 2:70.

62. HMC 19 Townshend, 2-3; PRO SP 110/8 (f. 13^r); *TP*, 2:414-15. Cf. Peter J. Bowden,

The Wool Trade in Tudor and Stuart England (New York, 1962), 137. The 1576 Parliament considered but did not pass a bill dealing with the engrossing of barley for conversion to malt. *CJ*, 1:110.

63. *APC*, 14:71-72, 98-99, 119-20; BL Lansdowne MSS 46/85; 51/45; *TP*, 2:532-34.

64. HMC Third Report, 6; PRO SP 222/101 (ff. 198^r-199^r).

65. *APC*, 18:275, 280-81; HMC 9 Salisbury, 4:52. Cf. the agitation in Kent in the 1590s detailed by Peter Clark, "Popular Protest and Disturbance in Kent, 1558-1640," *Econ. H.R.*, 2nd ser., 29 (August 1976):367-68, 375-76.

66. *TP*, 3:165-66, 169-72; *APC*, 26:94-96; David G. Hey, *An English Rural Community: Myddle Under the Tudors and Stuarts* (Leicester, 1974), 50; Clark and Slack, *Towns*, 95.

67. D'Ewes, *Journals*, 591; Wilbraham, *Journal*, 12; *TP*, 3:193-95, 215-17; *CSPD, 1598-1601*, 161.

68. Emmison, *Elizabethan Life*, 1:29; Hearnshaw, ed., *Records*, 1:58-367 *passim*; Tait, ed., *Records*, 60, 74-75, 106; BL Lansdowne MS 83/31. In Worcester in 1555, sixteen men were punished for forestalling and regrating, but only four were members of the regular food supply trades. Tradesmen and other outsiders became involved in these offenses. Dyer, *Worcester*, 141.

69. PRO STAC 7 Add., 6/18; HMC 77 De L'Isle, 2:299, 302, 319, 324.

70. BB, note to Mal. 2:3; GB, note to Amos 8:4; Pilkington, *Works*, 86, 464, 466.

71. Curteys, *1574 Sermon*, sig. C7^r; *Two Sermons*, sig. C1^{r-v}; Fleming, *Bridge*, 317; Turnbull, *XV. Psalme*, f. 56^r; King, *Sermon*, 705; S. Gardiner, *Cognizance*, sig. A7^r, p. 127.

72. Becon, *Postil*, 1:f. 181^{r-v}; Hake, *Newes*, sig. G8^v; Deacon, *Treatise*, sigs. A6^r, B2^r, D8^r; Perkins, *Chaine*, sig. M5^v; Trigge, *Apologie*, 8; *Sermon*, sigs. D7^r-E1^v; Moffett, *Commentarie*, 98; Norden, *Comfort*, 16-17; W. Vaughan, *Golden-groue*, sig. Q5^{r-v}; Dent, *Path-way*, 203-4. Cf. Cope, *Exposition*, f. 635^v; Hacket, *Sermon*, sigs. B2^v-B3^r.

73. J. Barker, *Balade*.

74. Wager, *Enterlude*, sig. D2^v.

75. Stone, introduction to R. H. Tawney, *The Agrarian Problem in the Sixteenth Century* (New York: Torchbook ed., 1967); D. C. Coleman, *The Economy of England 1450-1750* (1977), 39; C. Hill, *Reformation to Industrial Revolution 1530-1780* (Baltimore: Penguin ed., 1967), 65-66; Peter Bowden, "Agricultural Prices, Farm Profits, and Rents," *The Agrarian History of England and Wales*, vol. 4, ed. Joan Thirsk (Cambridge, 1967):594-96, 674-95; B. A. Holderness, *Pre-Industrial England* (1976), 16.

76. Ian Blanchard, "Population Change, Enclosure, and the Early Tudor Economy," *Econ. H. R.*, 2nd ser., 23 (1970):435, 439-40, 442; W. Jones, *Tudor Commonwealth*, 157-61. Rack-renting was charging full value, which to tenants often *seemed* extortionate.

77. James, *Family*, 80-81; Holderness, *Pre-Industrial England*, 77-78; Eric Kerridge, *Agrarian Problems in the Sixteenth Century and After* (1969), 46-47, 52.

78. Andrew B. Appleby, "Agrarian Capitalism or Seigneurial Reaction? The Northwest of England, 1500-1700," *American Historical Review*, 80 (June 1975): 575-76, 579-85. Cf. James, *Family*, 80-81.

79. Pilkington, *Works*, 289-90, 330, 461-62; Holderness, *Pre-Industrial England*, 79, 81.

80. King, *Lectvres*, 76; Anderson, *Shield*, sig. S4^{r-v}; Seager, *Schoole*, sig. D4^v; Curteys, *Sermon at Richmond*, sig. C1^v; Cooper, *Admonition*, 155; Powel, *Positions*, 60; Nash, *Anatomie*, sig. C4^v; Bankes, *Sermon*, sig. F7^r; Turnbull, *Iames*, f. 109^{r-v}; HMC 9 Salisbury, 1:310; Grindal, *Remains*, 256-57.

81. Trigge, *Sermon*, sigs. E2^r, E3^r; *Apologie*, 7, 11; Lupton, *Dreame*, sig. D1^v.

82. Becon, *Salue*, 215; Crowley, *Opening*, sig. G5^r; Bush, *Sermon*, sig. B2^r; Dent, *Pathway*, 203, 208-10; Gifford, *Eight Sermons*, ff. 104^v-105^r; W. Vaughan, *Golden-groue*, sigs. D8^v, I5^v; Stubbes, *Anatomie*, sigs. J8^{r-v}, K2^r; Pagit, *Frvitefull Sermon*, sig. B8^r; R. Rogers,

Treatises, 106; Norden, *Solace*, f. 3^r; Hake, *Newes*, sig. E8^v; Perkins, *Chaine*, sig. M8^v; Allen, *Treasvrie*, 210; Lupton, *Dreame*, sig. D1^{r-v} (cf. sig. F6^v); Stubbes, *Motive*, 131-32.

83. Cooper, ed., *Wentworth Papers*, 18-19, 33-35; Strype, *Smith*, 177; Collins, *Life*, 54-55; Holles, *Memorials*, 66; Denton, *Epitaph vpon Darby*; Holinshed, *Chronicles*, 4:321; J. Phillip, *Epitaph on Southampton*; Stone, *Crisis*, 305-6; W. Harrison, *Discovrse*, 10. The epitaphs undoubtedly exaggerate, but they are accurate reflections of ideals.

84. Stone, *Crisis*, 308-9; *APC*, 11:215-16; W. Jones, *Chancery*, 277; James, *Family*, 82-83. Cf. *APC*, 16:117-18; 19:125-26, 369-70, for other landlord-tenant cases heard by the Council. Sir Thomas Smith had trouble with tenants who did not pay their rents. Mary Dewar, *Sir Thomas Smith* (1964), 141-42.

85. C. Hill, *Economic Problems*, 8, 30-31. The crown granted leases in reversion on its lands on generous terms—fines of five times the annual rent in the early 1560s, and four times from 1564 to 1603. David Thomas, "Leases in Reversion on the Crown's Lands, 1558-1603," *Econ. H. R.*, 2nd ser., 30 (February 1977):69.

86. Mildmay, *Memorial*, [3] ; anon., *Crie*; (cf. HL MS HA5402, dealing with rents and fines on Huntingdon's tenants); Cross, *Earl*, 106-8; Stone, *Crisis*, 307.

87. Vaux, *Catechisme*, f. 56^r; Appleby, *American Historical Review*, 80:580-83, 586; Bossy, *PP*, 21:42; Stone, *Crisis*, 307, 309, 314-15; Williams, *Thomas Howard*, 26, 79, 113-14.

88. Cf. also Fisher, *Godly Sermon*, sig. A8^r: "For there are some suche merciles oppressours among you, that build fair houses, with the bloody sobs and sighs of their poore neighbours, whose liuinges they haue taken ouer their heads, and whose liuelyhoode, they haue wringed out of their hands." Churchyard put some of the blame for rack-rents on tenants who overcharged their landlords for goods. *Challenge*, 113.

89. Sutcliffe, *Answere*, 128.

90. Robinson, *Rewarde*, sig. H4^v.

91. Stubbes, *Anatomie*, sig. J8^v.

92. Thirsk, "Enclosing and Engrossing," *The Agrarian History of England and Wales*, 4:200-12; *Tudor Enclosures* (1959), 4-8; Tawney, *Agrarian Problem*, 8-9, 262-63; Ramsey, *Economic Problems*, 20-25; Julian Cornwall, "English Population in the Early Sixteenth Century," *Econ. H.R.*, 2nd ser., 23 (April 1970):43-44; W. E. Tate, *The Enclosure Movement* (New York, 1967), 72. For details on enclosure in Devon to the early 1500s, see H. S. A. Fox, "The Chronology of Enclosure and Economic Development in Medieval Devon," *Econ. H.R.*, 2nd ser., 28 (May 1975):181-202.

93. Kerridge, *Agrarian Problems*, 94-105; Tawney, *Agrarian Problem*, 166-72; PRO Req. 2/56/18. Cf. J. A. Yelling, *Common Field and Enclosure in England 1450-1850* (1977), 5-10. Even enclosure by agreement provoked opposition in the late Elizabethan period. Maurice Beresford, "Habitation Versus Improvement: The Debate on Enclosure by Agreement," *Essays in Economic and Social History*, ed. Fisher, 52-53.

94. Everitt, *PP*, 33:58; (cf. Dickens, *TRHS*, 13:64); Holderness, *Pre-Industrial England*, 52-53, 56-57; Watts, *Border*, 48-49; Kerridge, *Agrarian Problems*, 119, 127-28.

95. Tawney, *Agrarian Problem*, 8-9; Ramsey, *Economic Problems*, 26-27, 32, 40; Holderness, *Pre-Industrial England*, 60; Coleman, *Economy*, 39; Hoskins, *Studies*, 48.

96. Appleby, *American Historical Review*, 80:575-80.

97. James, *Family*, 76-77; PRO SP 262/10 (f. 20^r). Cf. Dean James' letter to Sir Robert Cecil for similar observations; PRO SP 262/11 (f. 21^r).

98. *Staffordshire Session Rolls*, ed. Burne, 1-4: *passim*; Coleman, *Economy*, 40; Tait, ed., *Records, passim*; PRO STAC 7 Add., 10/3, 10/18 (quoted), 10/36, 10/38, 10/40, 11/3, 11/7, 11/14, 11/16, 11/21, 12/1, 12/13, 12/22, 12/35, 12/37, 12/39; *APC*, e.g. 9:285-86, 296, 322-24; 10:155; C. Hill, *Reformation*, 69. For selected Essex cases involving the breaking of enclosures see Emmison, *Elizabethan Life*, 1:101-3.

99. HMC 9 Salisbury, 2:141.

100. *TP*, 2:310-11.

101. *SR*, 2:542; 3:127, 176-77, 451-54, 553-54; 4, pt. 1, 134-35, 269-74, 406-10; *CJ*, 1:70-72.

102. *SR*, 4, pt. 2, 804-5, 855, 891-96; D'Ewes, *Journals*, 551-52; Neale, *Parliaments*, 2:337-47.

103. D'Ewes, *Journals*, 674-75.

104. BL Lansdowne MS 121/22.

105. C. Hill, *Economic Problems*, 102, 105; Kerridge, *Agrarian Problems*, 108-9; Usher, *Reconstruction*, 1:232; Trigge, *Sermon*, sig. E5^r.

106. Pilkington, *Works*, 86, 462; Nowell, *Sermon*, 227-28.

107. Humston, *Sermon*, f. 23^r; Anderson, *Sermon at Paules Crosse*, sig. F3^v; Shield, sigs. C2^v-C3^r, S4^{r-v}; Wright, *Summons*, 4; Some, in Pilkington, *Works*, 469, 473; A. Hill, *Crie*, 74.

108. Bush, *Sermon*, sig. B2^r; Hake, *Newes*, sig. E8^v; Stubbes, *Anatomie*, sigs. J8^{r-v}, K2^r; Dod, *Treatise*, pt. 2, ff. 10^{r-v}, 70^{r-v}; Trigge, *Sermon*, sig. E5^{r-v}; Allen, *Treasvrie*, 210; W. Vaughan, *Golden-groue*, sigs. V5^v-V6^r (cf. Q5^{r-v}).

109. Barrow, *Writings (1587-90)*, 493.

110. Holles, *Memorials*, 62-63; Finch, *Wealth*, 14-17; *Patent Rolls*, 5:47; Emmison, *Elizabethan Life*, 1:116; Stone, *Crisis*, 304; *APC*, 10:375-76, 399-400; 11:154, 191-92.

111. *APC*, 17:244-45, 303-4; 19:213; HMC 9 Salisbury, 4:83-84.

112. Anon., *Crie*; Cross, *Earl*, 107; HMC 9 Salisbury, 2:536.

113. *APC*, 19:305; Appleby, *American Historical Review*, 80:576, 578, 581-82; Bossy, *PP*, 21:42.

Chapter 15: Legal Problems

1. Trigge, *Catholiqve*, 581.

2. Perkins, *Treatise*, 497.

3. Stone, *PP*, 33:43; *Crisis*, 240-41; Gilbert, *Achademy*, 7; Ramsey, *Economic Problems*, 132. Cf. the coolness with which Sir William Ashcombe recorded an intra-family suit in his diary in 1610: "I sued my uncle Oliver Ayshcombe & my cozen his eldest sonne for my house & lands at Ashapsted in Berks, in the courte of wards; vpon my Information they came in & compounded, & I did enioy the lande." HL MS 30, 665 (f. 3^v).

4. Chamberlain, *Letters*, 1:97; Hatton, *Memoirs*, 398-99; W. Jones, *Chancery*, 272.

5. W. Jones, *Chancery*, 306, 309-10; Gawdy, *Letters*, 35; LPL Bacon MS 650/126 (f. 200^r); Piccope, ed., *Wills*, 51:82.

6. GB, notes to 1 Cor. 6:4, 8; BTB, notes to 1 Cor. 6:1, 7.

7. Rheims NT, notes to Matt. 5:39; 1 Cor. 6:6, 7; Vaux, *Catechisme*, f. 57^r; Anstruther, *Vaux*, 99; Bossy, *PP*, 21:42.

8. Jewel, *Works*, 2:862-63; Nowell, *Catechism*, 201; Babington, *Lords Prayer*, 180; Sandys, *Sermons*, 227-28; Wright, *Summons*, 12; Anderson, *Sermon at Paules Crosse*, sig. A8^v; Whetstone, *Rocke*, sig. O2^v.

9. Nowell, *Catechism*, 201; Turnbull, *Iames*, ff. 291^v-292^r; Babington, *Lords Prayer*, 180-81 (cf. 177); Fleming, *Footpath of Faith*, sig. B1^r; Wright, *Summons*, 13.

10. Estey, *Expositions*, pt. 1, f. 71^r; Gibbon, *Praise*, 54; Moffett, *Commentarie*, 213; Stubbes, *Motive*, 164; W. Vaughan, *Golden-groue*, sig. F3^v; Perkins, *Treatise*, 496-97. Cf. Fulke, *Text*, f. 270^{r-v}.

11. W. Vaughan, *Golden-groue*, sigs. F3^{r-v}, X3^r; *Introductions*, sig. L1^v; Perkins, *Treatise*, 131-32, 493-94, 497-98.

12. Perkins, *Chaine*, sigs. N2^v-N3^r; *Exposition*, 131-33; *Treatise*, 494-99; Harward,

Sermons, sigs. D4^V-D5^V; Nichols, *Plea*, 225; Estey, *Expositions*, pt. 1, f. 71^r; R. Rogers, *Treatises*, 374-75; Stubbes, *Motive*, 154; Trigge, *Catholiqve*, 581; Norden, *Solace*, f. 139^V.

13. Penry, *Notebook*, 85; Barrow, *Writings (1587-90)*, 246, 544.

14. Peel, ed., *Seconde Parte*, 2:147, 149, 150; Emmison, *Elizabethan Life*, 2:220; Haigh, *Reformation*, 242; Hart, *Clergy*, 38; *DNB, s.v.* Alexander Nowell; Manning, *Religion*, 178; Dering, *Catechisme*, *Workes*, sig. A3^V; *CSPD, 1547-90*, 319. The 1585 visitation articles for the archdeaconry of London inquired if any clergy sued parishioners in secular courts in connection with tithes or other ecclesiastical matters. *EEA*, 3:177.

15. *APC*, 13:50-51, 334, 337; Hart, *Clergy*, 34.

16. *Quarter Sessions Records for Chester*, ed. Bennett and Dewhurst, 47; *Staffordshire Session Rolls*, ed. Burne, 2:26, 91-92, 193; *APC*, 13:54-55; PRO STAC 7 Add., 16/15.

17. Denton, *Epitaph vpon Darby*; Cooper, ed., *Wentworth Papers*, 13, 17-18, 22, 29.

18. Manning, *Religion*, 170; Smyth, *Berkeley Manuscripts*, 2:288-334; Carey, *Memoirs*, 26-27, 63-66; W. Jones, *Chancery*, 277; Forman, *Autobiography*, 17-19; LPL Bacon MS 661/137 (f. 203^r).

19. Lehmberg, *Mildmay*, 78; A. Clifford, *Lives*, 13; Hoby, *Diary*, 15-16, 40-43, 234; Cholmley, *Memoirs*, 14; Hastings, *Letters*, 52; Usher, ed., *Movement*, 99.

20. *A New Ballad Intituled, Daniels Siftyng in These Our Dayes* (1572).

21. Manningham, *Diary*, 43.

22. Clark, *Provincial Society*, 284; E. W. Ives, "The Reputation of the Common Lawyer in English Society," *University of Birmingham Historical Journal*, 7 (1959-60):130-61; W. Jones, *Tudor Commonwealth*, 53, 209-10. In 1578, 313 attorneys were in the Common Pleas, but by 1633 the number had risen to 1,383. Bridenbaugh, *Englishmen*, 258. A bill to reduce their number failed to pass in the 1581 House of Commons. An endeavor to impose limitations on the fees of lawyers had failed to pass in 1571. *CJ*, 1:93, 124, 127, 130.

23. Clark, *Provincial Society*, 295; *APC*, 11:352-53; 13:354; 19:237-38; PRO STAC 7 Add., 7/7; Edmund Heward, *Matthew Hale* (1972), 14; BL Lansdowne MS 119/10 (ff. 136^r, 137^V).

24. HMC 9 Salisbury, 1:309; Turnbull, *XV. Psalme*, ff. 22^r, 60^r; Pilkington, *Works*, 464; Wright, *Summons*, 11-12; Sandys, *Sermons*, 226; Drant, *Fruitfull Sermon*, sig. D7^r. Cf. Thomas, *Demegoriai*, sig. E6^V.

25. Curteys, *Sermon at Richmond*, sig. C2^r; *Two Sermons*, sig. C1^V; Woolton, *A Newe Anatomie of the Whole Man* (1576), ff. 22^V-23^r. A plea to discriminate between good and evil lawyers was given in the Rheims marginalia (Luke 11:46).

26. Sandys, *Sermons*, 193-94; Lewes, *Sermon*, sig. C2^{r-v}; Carpenter, *Preparatiue*, sig. $_2$C4^r.

27. Bullein, *Bulwarke*, pt. 2, f. 7^r; Seager, *Schoole*, sig. D4^V; Whetstone, *Rocke*, sigs. L1^r, L5^V; *Enemie*, sigs. H4^V-I1^r; Mulcaster, *Positions*, 246; Cooper, ed., *Wentworth Papers*, 16.

28. Dent, *Path-way*, 203; W. Vaughan, *Golden-groue*, sig. X2^V; Harward, *Sermons*, sigs. D4^V-D5^V; H. Smith, *Examination*, 11; Hake, *Newes*, sigs. B7^r, B8^{r-v}, C2^r; Stubbes, *Anatomie*, sig. K1^r; *Motive*, 44, 164; Lupton, *Dreame*, sig. D6^r.

29. W. Vaughan, *Golden-groue*, sigs. X2^{r-v}, Y8^V; *Introductions*, sigs. L1^r, L5^r (expressing a view Vaughan repudiates); H. Smith, *A Memento for Magistrates* (1592), 72-73; Lupton, *Dreame*, sig. E5^r; Allen, *Treasvrie*, 209; Burton, *Anatomie*, 221.

30. Norden, *Solace*, sig. π3^V; Trigge, *Apologie*, 22; Allen, *Treasvrie*, 125; W. Vaughan, *Introductions*, sigs. L2^V-L6^r.

31. R. Rogers, *Treatises*, 182; Lupton, *Dreame*, sigs. D3^{r-v}, D5^V; Allen, *Treasvrie*, 129; Stockwood, *1578 Sermon*, 140-41; Timme, *Discouerie*, sig. I4^V; Knewstub, *Sermon*, sig. Q̇7^r (quoted).

32. Wright, *Summons*, 11.

33. *As I on New Year's Day* (1579), in *Ballads*, ed. Rollins, 318.

34. LPL Bacon MS 655/156 (f. 219^r); Ringler, ed., *Poems of Sidney*, 445; Hatton, *Memoirs*, 388, 390. Two of Parker's officials were offered bribes totaling £300 if they could persuade the archbishop to grant Stawell the annulment he sought. Parker, *Correspondence*, 408.

35. Matthew-Becke Bible (1549), note to Exod. 21; MB (1551), note to Exod. 21; Tyndale, *Pentateuch*, note to Exod. 21; Taverner Bible (1539), note to Exod. 23; BB, note to Mic. 7:3; GB, notes to Num. 27:21; Deut. 1:15; 16:20; 2 Sam. 21:14, 17; 1 Kings 3:24; Pss. 82:1; 94:20; 101:3, 8; Prov. 21:7; Mic. 7:2; Hab. 1:4; Mark 15:15; Luke 12:14; Acts 25:10; 2 Pet. 2:11.

36. Wright, *Summons*, 13; Fleming, *Guide*, 95; Pilkington, *Works*, 464, 466; Sandys, *Sermons*, 355; Whetstone, *Rocke*, sig. L5^v; Curteys, *Sermon at Richmond*, sig. C2^r.

37. Sandys, *Sermons*, 58, 85, 225-27. Cf. Wright, *Summons*, 12.

38. Cooper, ed., *Wentworth Papers*, 11.

39. Lupton, *Dreame*, sig. D3^r; Chaderton, *Excellent Sermon*, sig. C5^v; Shutte, *Sermon*, sigs. F5^v-F6^r; Norden, *Solace*, f. 138^v; Stockwood, *1578 Sermon*, 140-41; Hake, *Newes*, sig. A4^r; W. Vaughan, *Golden-groue*, sigs. D8^r, X1^v-X2^r.

40. Lodge, *Divel*, sig. M1^{r-v}.

41. Churchyard, *Challenge*, 193.

42. More, *Treatyse*, sig. A4^r.

43. Some, in Pilkington, *Works*, 472, 476-77; Wright, *Summons*, 13; Seager, *Schoole*, sig. D4^v; Lewes, *Sermon*, sig. C2^r; Sandys, *Sermons*, 193; Pilkington, *Works*, 290-91; Babington, *Lords Prayer*, 180-81. Cf. Fisher, *Godly Sermon*, sigs. B4^v-B5^r, who complains of the delay before the cases of the poor are heard in court, in part because of careless and covetous lawyers.

44. Norden, *Solace*, f. 138^v; Timme, *Discouerie*, sig. I4^v; W. Vaughan, *Golden-groue*, sig. X2^{r-v}; H. Smith, *Teares*, 20.

45. Stubbes, *Motive*, 154-55 (quoted); Norden, *Comfort*, 18; Lupton, *Dreame*, sigs. D3^r, E5^r (quoted).

46. *A Mournfull Dittie on the Death of Certaine Iudges and Iustices of the Peace* (1590); Churchyard, *Challenge*, 193-94, 196.

47. Marchant, *Church*, 235; W. Jones, *Chancery*, 323-27, 462; Hake, *Newes*, sig. B7^v.

48. Marchant, *Church*, 228-29; Haigh, *Reformation*, 227-28.

49. *APC*, 9:158-59; 11:59; 16:101; 17:236, 244-45; 19:234-35; 20:132.

50. HMC 80 Sackville, 46.

51. D'Ewes, *Journals*, 473.

52. W. Vaughan, *Golden-groue*, sig. $_2$A5^v.

53. GB, note to Eccles. 8:11; BB, note to Eccles. 8:11; Hake, *Newes*, sig. B6^r; Marchant, *Church*, 65; Stone, *Crisis*, 241; Manningham, *Diary*, 98. For the proposals of the Commonwealth Men, see W. Jones, *Tudor Commonwealth*, 26, 39, 209-11.

54. Stubbes, *Motive*, 155-56; BL Lansdowne MSS 12/27; 44/1; Bird, *Communication*, f. 28^r. Cf. Hake, *Newes*, sig. B6^v.

55. BL Lansdowne MS 44/3; *APC*, 9:97-98; 14:298-99; 16:72-73, 392-93; 17:272; 20:26; cf. 17:79-80; 20:202-3, 359.

56. Gerard, *Autobiography*, 53, 57, 72, 108 ff.

57. Whetstone, *Rocke*, sig. N8^r; Sandys, *Sermons*, 3, 227; Barker, *Balade*; W. Vaughan, *Golden-groue*, sigs. $_2$A5^v-$_2$A6^r.

58. Barrow, *Writings (1587-90)*, 199, 599-600.

59. *SR*, 4, pt. 1, 486-87, 488; *CJ*, 1:75-76, 78-79.

60. *CJ*, 1:97, 102-3, 107, 109, 111, 114-15, 133-34.

61. *SR*, 4, pt. 1, 712-14. Cf. also 27 Eliz. I, c. 7, regarding the proper identification of jurors who failed to perform their duties. *SR*, 4, pt. 1, 713-14.

62. *SR*, 4, pt. 2, 799.

63. *SR*, 4, pt. 2, 970-71. The rendering of justice was further improved by the passage of acts in 1566, 1576, and 1598 taking away benefit of clergy from pickpockets, rapists, burglars, those who seized heiresses against their wills, and thieves who stole goods worth at least 5s. from house unoccupied in the daytime. 8 Eliz. I, c. 4; 18 Eliz. I, c. 7; 39 Eliz. I, c. 9, c. 15; *SR*, 4, pt. 1, 488, 617-18; pt. 2, 910, 914.

64. Gilby, *Dialogve*, sig. M2^r.

65. Barrow, *Writings of Greenwood and Barrow (1591-93)*, 112.

66. *SR*, 4, pt. 1, 451-53 (5 Eliz. I, c. 23); C. Hill, *Society*, 307-8, 312, 318; Neale, *Parliaments*, 2:357-58; Strype, *Whitgift*, 2:374-78, 446-52.

67. Parker, *Correspondence*, 128-29; Strype, *Parker*, 1:142.

68. Grindal, *Remains*, 178; *EEA*, 3:332, 343.

69. Collinson, *Puritan Movement*, 38-41, 305; Allison, *Confvtation*, 134-35; Hooker, *Works*, 3:431 ff.

70. Gilby, *Dialogve*, sig. L8^{r-v}; Field, *A View of Popish Abuses* (1572), in *Puritanism in Tudor England*, ed. H. C. Porter (1970), 133-34; Fulke, *A Brief and Plain Declaration*, in *Puritanism*, ed. Trinterud, 282; Dering, *Sermon*, in ibid., 160; *The Just Censure*, in *Puritanism*, ed. Porter, 213.

71. Gilby, *Dialogve*, sig. M1 $^{r-v}$; Field, *View*, in *Puritanism*, ed. Porter, 134-35.

72. Peel, ed., *Seconde Parte*, 2:176; Fulke, in *Puritanism*, ed. Trinterud, 279; Collinson, *Puritan Movement*, 183.

73. Barrow, *Writings (1587-90)*, 144-45, 616-17, 661; *Writings of Greenwood and Barrow (1591-93)*, 112; *Collection*, 4; R. Harrison, *Treatise*, sig. H2^r.

74. Barrow, *Writings (1587-90)*, 284, 647-56, 662.

75. Hooker, *Works*, 3:309-10; Robert Peters, "The Administration of the Archdeaconry of St. Albans, 1580-1625," *JEH*, 13 (April 1962): 64-65; Ralph Houlbrooke, "The Decline of Ecclesiastical Jurisdiction under the Tudors," *Continuity and Change*, ed. O'Day and Heal, 251-53.

76. Turnbull, *Iames*, f. 314^r.

77. Dod, *Treatise*, pt. 1. f. 51^v.

78. C. Hill, *Society*, 383-407 *passim; Staffordshire Session Rolls*, ed. Burne, 2:91.

79. HMC 73 Exeter, 368; HMC 80 Sackville, 1:33; *CSPD, 1581-90*, 249; Churchyard, *The Epitaphe of the Honorable Earle of Penbroke* (1570); PRO SP 69/14 (f. 52^r).

80. C. Hill, *Society*, 400-1; *CJ*, 1:65; Neale, *Parliaments*, 1:118, 125; *SR*, 4, pt. 1, 469; Manningham, *Diary*, 33-34.

81. Barrow, *Writings (1587-90)*, 171, n. 1; Trinterud, ed., *Puritanism*, 388-90; *CSPD, 1591-94*, 10-11 (quoted); Mary H. Maguire, "Attack of the Common Lawyers on the Oath *Ex Officio* as Administered in the Ecclesiastical Courts in England," *Essays in History and Political Theory* (Cambridge, Mass., 1936), 214-16, 218-19. The 1591 decision was rendered in Cawdry's case. The oath *ex officio* was first introduced in England in 1236 by Cardinal Otho, legate of Gregory IX. Its use was specifically authorized by letters patent in 1583.

82. Neale, *Parliaments*, 2:267-78.

83. MB (1537), A Table; notes to Exod. 22; Deut. 10; 1 Sam. 24; MB (1551), notes to Num. 30; Deut. 10, 17; 1 Sam. 24; Ps. 50; Tyndale-Coverdale NT, note to Matt. 5; Tyndale, Pentateuch, notes to Exod. 22; Num. 25; cf. Exod. 23; Num. 6; Matthew-Becke Bible (1549, 1551), notes to Exod. 22; Num. 30; 1 Sam. 24; Ps. 50; (1549 only), notes to Deut. 10, 17. Requiring more than one witness accorded with the principles of common law, and may not have been intended to apply to an oath *ex officio*.

84. GB, notes to Gen. 21:24; 24:3; 42:15; 50:6; Duet. 6:13; 23:23; Josh. 9:20; 1 Sam. 30:15; Eccles. 5:3; Jer. 4:2; 35:11; 44:25; James 5:12; (cf. Ps. 119:106); Greaves, *SCJ*, 7:96. As an example of the lawful breaking of a valid oath, the annotators cited the occasion when the Rechabites left their tents to live in homes in Jerusalem to escape the warring armies of the Chaldeans and Syrians. Notes to Deut. 23:23; Jer. 35:11.

85. BB, notes to Eccles. 5:4; James 5:12; (cf. Gen. 14:22; 31:53; 50:6; Deut. 6:13; 23:23; 1 Sam. 20:8); BTB, notes to Matt. 5:37; James 5:12.

86. Rheims NT, notes to Matt. 5:35; 14:9; Acts 23:12; James 5:12.

87. Cardwell, *Synodalia*, 1:72; *Certaine Sermons*, 1:45-51.

88. Turnbull, *Iames*, ff. 312^r-316^r; *XV. Psalme*, f. 44^V; T. Rogers, *Creede*, pt. 2, p. 89; *Doctrine*, 356-58; A. Hill, *Crie*, 9, 12-13; Nowell, *Catechism*, 126-28; Horne, *Exercise*, sigs. B2^V-B3^r; Dove, *1596 Sermon*, 8-9; Bicknoll, *Swoord*, ff. 11^V-13^V, 20^V, 22^r-23^r; Babington, *Commaundements*, 128-29, 133; Sandys, *Sermons*, 68; G. Abbot, *Exposition*, 302-6.

89. Sutcliffe, *Answere*, 116-17, 163, 167-68.

90. Bancroft, *Svrvay*, 311, 429-30; C. Hill, *Society*, 385.

91. Sutcliffe, *Answere*, 92-93; T. Rogers, *Doctrine*, 357, 359; Manningham, *Diary*, 110-11. Much more indicative of the Puritan practice was the schoolmaster who taught children to alter their horn books by reading "Black spott A" instead of "Christ crosse A." Manningham, *Diary*, 42. Barrow accused the clergy of the Church of England of being unwilling to rebuke common swearing. *Writings (1587-90)*, 495-96. Sutcliffe thought the radical attack stemmed from the desperation of men with an indefensible cause. *Answere*, sig. A4^r.

92. T. Rogers, *Doctrine*, 358-60.

93. Allen, *Treasvrie*, 85, 88-89; Dod, *Treatise*, pt. 1, ff. 51^V-52^r, 59^{r-V}; Estey, *Expositions*, pt. 1, ff. 46^V, 47^V; Gifford, *Catechisme*, sig. F4^V; Norden, *Practise*, f. 41^V; Shutte, *Forme*, sig. B8^r; Miles Coverdale, *A Christian Exhortacion* (1575), 8-14, 17-21; J. Gardiner, *Confession*, ff. 38^V-39^r; Gee, *Grovnd*, 3; Gibbon, *Remedie*, sig. K1^V; R. Jones, *Catechisme*, sigs. A8^V-B1^V; Perkins, *Treatise*, 380, 386-87; *Chaine*, sigs. H4^V-II5^r; Stubbes, *Motive*, 174-75; W. Vaughan, *Golden-groue*, sig. F7^V. Coverdale died in 1569.

94. Dod, *Treatise*, pt. 1, ff. 57^V-58^V; Perkins, *Treatise*, 379, 382-83, 388-90; Allen, *Treasvrie*, 89; Gifford, *Catechisme*, sig. F5^{r-V}; Gibson, *Entrance*, sig. A3^V; Barthlet, *Pedegrewe*, f. 48^V; Dent, *Path-way*, 159-61; Dering, *Catechisme*, *Workes*, sig. A7^V.

95. Nichols, *Plea*, 37; W. Vaughan, *Golden-groue*, sigs. F6^{r-V}, G1^{r-V}; Wilcox, *The Vnfouldyng of Sundry Vntruths* (1581), sig. A4^r (for the report of a libertine); Dent, *Path-way*, 35, 156, 163, 168; *CJ*, 1:78-79; D'Ewes, *Journals*, 660-61; Stockwood, *1578 Sermon*, 49; Lupton, *Dreame*, sig. E4^r; Stubbes, *Motive*, 178; Perkins, *Direction*, 9-10; *Treatise*, 396; Greenham, *Works*, 411; Gilby, *Dialogve*, sig. M3^V.

96. Wilcox, *Psalmes*, 27, 337; W. Vaughan, *Golden-groue*, sigs. G3^r-G5^r; Perkins, *Treatise*, 381, 390, 393-96; *Case of Conscience*, 858-60; *Direction*, 77; *Chaine*, sig. H5^{r-V}; J. Gardiner, *Confession*, f. 39^r; Fulke, *Text*, f. 227^r; Thomas Knell, *Certain True Marks* [1581], sig. A7^r; Wither, *View*, 9.

97. Perkins, *Chaine*, sigs. G6^V-G7^r; *Case of Conscience*, 862; *Treatise*, 400-23; *Catholike*, 958-59; Stockwood, *Bartholmew*, 91, 93; Lupton, *Persuasion*, 191-92; Gifford, *Eight Sermons*, f. 140^r; Dod, *Treatise*, pt. 1, f. 36^r. For the areas of Puritan agreement with the Catholics cf. Cartwright, *Confvtation*, 27, 662; Fulke, *Text*, f. 9^V. Also cf. the Catholic position as briefly outlined by Vaux, *Catechisme*, ff. 38^r-41^r.

98. Coverdale, *Exhortacion*, 15; Gilby, *Dialogve*, sig. M3^V; Usher, ed., *Movement*, 57; Perkins, *Treatise*, 385-86; Strype, *Whitgift*, 2:7; C. Hill, *Society*, 400; Allen, *Treasvrie*, 253. In 1584, the Dedham Classis determined to refuse the oaths of subscription required by Whitgift to the articles on the royal supremacy, the *Book of Common Prayer*, and the Thirty-nine Articles. Usher, ed., *Movement*, 34, 38.

99. [James Morice], *A Briefe Treatise of Oathes* [c. 1590], 3-4, 6.

100. Ibid., 7-8, 11-12, 16-21, 26-38, 57-58.

101. Ibid., 9-10, 13.

102. Allison, *Confvtation*, 117-18 (refuting the Separatists); Penry, *State*, sig. C4^V; Barrow, *Writings (1587-90)*, 346-47, 352, 471-72, 544; *Writings of Greenwood and Barrow (1591-93)*, 112; Greenwood, *Writings (1587-90)*, 28-29; C. Hill, *Society*, 402-3. The Separatists also opposed the manner in which oaths were taken in secular courts. Cf. Allison, *Confvtation*, 118.

103. Barrow, *Writings (1587-90)*, 93-97, 102-4, 194-95, 650-51; Greenwood, *Writings (1587-90)*, 22, 170-71; *Writings of Greenwood and Barrow (1591-93)*, 376-77; A. Pearson, *Cartwright*, 317-18, 326-28.

Chapter 16: Last Rites and Monuments

1. Turnbull, *XV. Psalme*, ff. 49^V-50^r.

2. GB, note to Gen. 23:3.

3. Kennedy, *Parish Life*, 68-69; C. Hill, *Change*, 9; Purvis, ed., *Documents*, 73, 174-75; BL Cotton MS, Julius F. vi. 459, cited in James, *Family*, 52; BL Add. MS (Wolley) 6671, f. 66^r (for R. Pole's will); Clay, ed., *Wills*, 13, 24; Raine, ed., *Wills*, 153-54; Piccope, ed., *Wills*, 51:161.

4. Machyn, *Diary*, 194; cf. 188.

5. Pilkington, *Works*, 64, 317-19; Whitgift, *Works*, 3:380.

6. Babington, *Genesis*, 279, 354; W. Harrison, *Advantage*, 74-75; Jewel, *Works*, 2:865-66; Pilkington, *Works*, 318-20; T. Rogers, *Discourse*, f. 57^V; Whitgift, *Works*, 3:368, 370; Sandys, *Sermons*, 174.

7. Pilkington, *Works*, 320-21; Strype, *Parker*, 1:198-200; Jewel, *Works*, 2:999.

8. Machyn, *Diary*, 191, 193.

9. *Zurich Letters*, ed. Robinson, 137; Strype, *Annals*, 1, pt. 2, p. 45; Cooper, *Athenae*, 1:346; BL Lansdowne MS 39/16.

10. BL Lansdowne MSS 103/57; 115/28; Collins, *Life*, 84-85.

11. Grindal, *Remains*, 136, 160; Strype, *Parker*, 2:88; *EEA*, 2:72, 93, 115, 118, 132; 3:143, 149, 152, 190-91, 214, 228; Houlbrooke, *Courts*, 249. As bishop of Worcester, Whitgift was concerned with inordinate delays before the interment of corpses. *EEA*, 2:57.

12. Gilby, *Dialogve*, sigs. L8^r, M4^r; Holland, *Exposition*, 191; Perkins, *Chaine*, sig. L3^r; McGinn, *Admonition Controversy*, 163; Becon, *Salue*, 151, 156, 168-69.

13. Stubbes, *Motive*, 122; Harward, *Sermons*, sig. G2^r; Becon, *Salue*, 151-52, 171-73, 178; Cartwright, *Confvtation*, 276; Perkins, *Chaine*, sig. L3^r; McGinn, *Admonition Controversy*, 162; Sutton, *Disce mori*, 24.

14. A. Pearson, *Cartwright*, 42; Hearnshaw, ed., *Records*, 1:120; Emmison, *Elizabethan Life*, 2:172-73; Hart, *Man in Pew*, 145-46.

15. Machyn, *Diary*, 247; Cooper, *Athenae*, 1:245; Lehmberg, *Mildmay*, 304; Nichols and Bruce, eds., *Wills*, 69; Piccope, ed., *Wills*, 51:18-20; A. Pearson, *Cartwright*, 482; Weigall, *Quarterly Review*, 215:137.

16. HMC 9 Salisbury, 1:147; BL Lansdowne MS 83/36; Young, *Mary Sidney*, 78; Piccope, ed., *Wills*, 51:23, 153 (cf. 33:55); cf. Clay, ed., *Wills*, 179.

17. Barrow, *Writings (1587-90)*, 130-31, 458-62; *Writings of Greenwood and Barrow (1591-93)*, 105; Penry, *Viewe*, 66. In 1561, two Familists allegedly confessed that they must not bury the dead, citing Matt. 8:22 as their proof. J. Rogers, *Displaying*, sig. K1^r.

18. P. Ariès, *Western Attitudes Towards Death*, trans. P. M. Ranum (Baltimore, 1974), 66.

19. David W. Atkinson, "*A Salve for a Sicke Man*: William Perkins' Contribution to the *ars moriendi*," *HMPEC*, 46 (December 1977): 409-18.

20. W. Harrison, *Advantage*, 77.

21. *Zurich Letters*, ed. Robinson, 281.

22. Sylvester, *Monodia*, sig. A2^V; King, *A Sermon Preached at the Fvneralles . . . 1594* (Oxford, 1597).

23. W. Harrison, *Advantage*, 77-78; Fleming, *Memoriall*, sigs. A3^V-A4^r; Whitgift, *Works*, 3:371, 374, 376-77; Anderson, *Sermon of Comfort*, 3-4; Pilkington, *Works*, 321, 543. Harrison's sermon for Katherine Brettergh was intended as a public testimony to clear her of slanderous charges made by Catholic neighbors. *Advantage*, sig. A3^V.

24. Becon, *Salue*, 148; Sparke, *Sermon at Whaddon*, f. 60^V; White, *A Godlie Sermon Preached . . . at Pensehurst* (1586), sig. B3^V; McGinn, *Admonition Controversy*, 164; Burton, *Ten Sermons*, 91.

25. Barrow, *Writings (1587-90)*, 130-31, 461.

26. Piccope, ed., *Wills*, 51:18-20, 45; 54:171; Clay, ed., *Wills*, 73; Raine, ed., *Wills*, 2:256.

27. Clay, ed., *Wills*, 221, 223; Wiffen, *Memoirs*, 1:514-15.

28. Copland, *Sorowes*, sig. C1^{r-v}, referring to a widow.

29. MB, note to Ezek. 18.

30. Tyndale Pentateuch (1530), note to Num. 20; MB (1537, 1551) and Matthew-Becke Bible (1549, 1551), note to Ezek. 18.

31. Pilkington, *Works*, 318-19; Becon, *Salue*, 175-80, 196; Gilby, *Dialogve*, sig. M4^V; Grindal, *Remains*, 136, 160; *EEA*, e.g., 2:72, 93; 3:149.

32. *Illustrations*, ed. Nichols, 141-42; Brinkworth, ed., *Court*, 125; Purvis, ed., *Documents*, 73; *APC*, 10:329; *EEA*, 3:149.

33. James, *Family*, 52.

34. Segar, *Honor*, 253.

35. Nichols and Bruce, eds., *Wills*, 56.

36. Becon, *Salue*, 172-73; Cartwright, *Confvtation*, 235; Segar, *Honor*, 253.

37. BL Lansdowne MS 23/64; Lehmberg, *Mildmay*, 304; Nichols and Bruce, eds., *Wills*, 69; Irvine, ed., *Collection*, 100; HMC 24 Rutland, 1:241. Cf. David E. Stannard, *The Puritan Way of Death* (New York, 1977), 101-2.

38. BL Lansdowne MSS 23/65; 39/18; Stone, *Crisis*, 784; Clay, ed., *Wills*, 61, 89-90; Collins, *Life*, 85; Strype, *Parker*, 3:342. Apparently the funeral of the countess of Lennox cost less than she anticipated, viz. c. £950. BL Lansdowne MS 25/85.

39. Stone, *Crisis*, 784-85; HMC 78 Hastings, 2:45; BL Lansdowne MS 109/95. The celebration of the obsequies for the Emperor Ferdinand in London in 1564 cost £774 plus nearly £50 for a funeral dinner. PRO SP 34/69 (f. 188^{r-v}).

40. HMC 9 Salisbury, 1:415; Stone, *Crisis*, 784; Tittler, *Bacon*, 193; BL Lansdowne MS 50/88; Cliffe, *Gentry*, 127; Machyn, *Diary*, 208-9, 374; Piccope, ed., *Wills*, 33:163, 167; 54:77-78.

41. Strype, *Parker*, 3:342; *Aylmer*, 128; Grosart, *Towneley Hall MSS*, 2-54; Vowell, *Orders*, f. 46^V.

42. Stone, *Crisis*, 577-78, 786; HMC 9 Salisbury, 1:415; 6:301; BL Lansdowne MSS 25/85; 82/56; PRO SP 36/30 (ff. 58^r, 59^V); SP 36/63 (f. 144^r); *CSPD, 1547-80*, 306, 308.

43. Stone, *Family and Fortune* (Oxford, 1973), 175; HMC 24 Rutland, 1:241.

44. *CSPD, 1591-94*, 213; HMC 9 Salisbury, 7:117.

45. HMC 9 Salisbury, 6:93, 123; HMC 78 Hastings, 2:44-45; Hutton, *Correspondence*, 105-6; BL Lansdowne MS 82/25; HL MSS HA5283, 5284.

46. BL Add. MS 10,110, f. 10^r; PRO SP 36/30 (ff. 58^r-59^V); 36/63 (f. 144^r); 90/16 (f. 55^{r-v}); HMC 24 Rutland, 1:242-43; Stone, *Crisis*, 784; *Family and Fortune*, 175; BL Lansdowne MS 82/56; *Certificates*, ed. King and Raines, 31-35; Cliffe, *Gentry*, 127; Piccope, ed., *Wills*, 54:77-78; Strype, *Parker*, 3:344; Grosart, *Towneley Hall MSS*, 2-54.

47. BL Add. MSS 10,110 (ff. 5^{r-v}, 9^r, 22^r, 30^r); PRO SP 46/24 (f. 53^{r-v}); 90/16 (ff. 55^r, 62^r, 63^r); Smyth, *Berkeley Manuscripts*, 2:392; Grosart, *Towneley Hall MSS*, 2-54; Cliffe, *Gentry*, 127; Stone, *Crisis*, 576; HMC 9 Salisbury, 6:301; HMC 24 Rutland, 1:243; BL Lansdowne MSS 50/88; 82/56; Strype, *Parker*, 3:344.

48. Machyn, *Diary*, 212-13, 215-16, 217; (Sir Edmund Verney's burial in 1599 followed over a month after his death; Verney, *Memoirs*, 1:59); Stone, *Crisis*, 572, 579; HMC 69 Middleton, 449; PRO SP 46/48 (f. 109^r); 46/49 (f. 110^r); Strype, *Parker*, 3:340, 344; Clay, ed., *Wills*, 102; BL Lansdowne MS 82/20; Babington, *Genesis*, 353-54. I have seen no Puritan comment on embalming. Some objection in this period to anatomical dissection was made on the grounds that it was irksome and cruel, but Woolton defended it as a means to obtain knowledge to help the living. *Anatomie*, sig. $\pi2^r$.

49. Stone, *Crisis*, 576; BL Lansdowne MS 82/56; Strype, *Parker*, 3:344; Grosart, *Towneley Hall MSS*, 2-54; Machyn, *Diary*, xxiv-xxv, 374; Cliffe, *Gentry*, 127; Piccope, ed., *Wills*, 54:77-78; Campbell, *Yeoman*, 312.

50. Nichols, ed., *Illustrations*, 15, 17, 19-21, 24, 148; C. Hill, *Economic Problems*, 168-69, 171-72; Strype, *Parker*, 3:344; HMC 69 Middleton, 449, 451; HMC 19 Townshend, 7; BL Lansdowne MS 25/85; PRO SP 46/48 (f. 109^r); 46/49 (f. 110^r); Piccope, ed., *Wills*, 54:77-78; Grosart, *Towneley Hall MSS*, 2-54.

51. BL Royal MS 17A IX, f. 37^r; Stone, *Crisis*, 577; Hoby, *Diary*, 182; Chamberlain, *Letters*, 1:153; Dudley, *Correspondence*, 456-57. For a description of the night burial of Lady Elizabeth Cave in 1623 see Chamberlain, *Letters*, 2:474. Although excommunicated, Bonner was buried in the churchyard of St. Gregory, with Grindal's permission, but the latter insisted on a night burial. BL Lansdowne MS 11/64. The government even demanded a funeral for Philip Howard, earl of Arundel, who had been attainted of treason in 1589 and died in the Tower in 1595. BL Lansdowne MS 94/49.

52. Harman, *Caveat*, v.

53. Copland, *Sorowes*, sig. B2^r.

54. Trigge, *Apologie*, 9; Becon, *Salue*, 168-69; Burton, *Ten Sermons*, 91.

55. BL Add. MSS 6297, f. 264; 35,324, ff. 19^r-22^v, 27^r-39^r; Grosart, *Towneley Hall MSS*, 2-54; Nichols and Bruce, eds., *Wills*, 58; Stow, *Chronicles*, 4:430, 505; Clay, ed., *Wills*, 9, 50, 173, 175; Machyn, *Diary*, 180-307 *passim*; PRO SP 67/14 (ff. 153^r-154^v); 90/16 (ff. 54^r-55^v); BL Lansdowne MSS 21/4; 23/67; Stone, *Crisis*, 573; Piccope, ed., *Wills*, 51:56.

56. E. Williams, *Bess*, 196, 200-1; BL Lansdowne MSS 23/65; 23/67; 82/56; Collins, *Life*, 85; Clay, ed., *Wills*, 9, 12, 32-34, 49-52, 56, 62-63, 69, 89-90, 131, 181, 226; Machyn, *Diary*, 211, 213-16, 226, 269; PRO SP 46/24 (f. 53^{r-v}); Raine, ed., *Wills*, 2:169, 230, 259-60; Piccope, ed., *Wills*, 51:23, 107, 223, 236; Cliffe, *Gentry*, 127.

57. Strype, *Smith*, 154; HMC 19 Townshend, 4; Piccope, ed., *Wills*, 51:23.

58. Machyn, *Diary*, xxv, 235, 255; Clay, ed., *Wills*, 46, 183; Raine, ed., *Wills*, 2:230, 259-60; Piccope, ed., *Wills*, 51:107, 223, 236.

59. Machyn, *Diary*, 213-14, 217-19, 236, 244, 294-95; Clay, ed., *Wills*, 51-52, 56; Grosart, *Towneley Hall MSS*, xlv; Stone, *Crisis*, 575.

60. Chamberlain, *Letters*, 1:135; Bourman, *Epitaph vpon Lady Ramsey*, sig. B1^v; Harman, *Caveat*, v; *Quarter Sessions Records for Chester*, ed. Bennett and Dewhurst, 42-43; Strype, *Aylmer*, 45-46.

61. HMC 19 Townshend, 5; BL Lansdowne MSS 39/16; 83/36; Piccope, ed., *Wills*, 33:151, 165; Young, *Mary Sidney*, 78; Holinshed, *Chronicles*, 4:157; Lehmberg, *Mildmay*, 306; Strype, *Parker*, 3:342.

62. Segar, *Honor*, 253.

63. Machyn, *Diary*, 215-16, citing the words on a valance at the funeral dinner for Margaret Manners, countess of Rutland, in 1559.

64. Segar, *Honor*, 251-53; Stone, *Crisis*, 578; W. Jones, *Chancery*, 409.

65. Sparke, *Sermon at Whaddon*, sig. $\pi 3^{r-v}$; Wither, *View*, 101.

66. BL Lansdowne MS 77/84; LPL Bacon MSS 649/212 (f. 316^r); cf. 649/213 (f. 317^r); BL Add. MS 10,110, ff. 6^{r-v}, 75^r; Stone, *Crisis*, 573; BL Egerton MS 2642, ff. 181^r-210^r; *Certificates*, ed. King and Raines, 1-2.

67. PRO SP 90/16 (ff. 54^r-55^r); BL Harleian MS 139/2; Nichols, ed., *Illustrations*, 65-71.

68. PRO SP 33/7 (f. 14^{r-v}); BL Add. MS 6297, f. 264^r; Chamberlain, *Letters*, 1:41. For descriptions of the funerals of other peers see PRO SP 67/64 (ff. 153^r-154^v); 90/16 (ff. 56^r-63^r); 91/2 (ff. 2^r-3^v); 99/59 (ff. 197^r-198^v); 109/9 (f. 16^r for the materials used for the hearse of the countess of Huntingdon in 1576); BL Harleian MS 4774, f. 148^r; BL Lansdowne MS 82/56; BL Add. MS 35,324; HMC 24 Rutland, 1:242-45; Craze, *History*, 32-33, 345-47; Smyth, *Berkeley MSS*, 2:388-91; Stow, *Chronicles*, 4:505; Machyn, *Diary*, 179, 184, 187-91, 212-17, 221, 239, 242-43, 254, 273-74, 290-92, 297-98. Because of the threat of the plague the body of Henry Manners, earl of Rutland, was buried without ceremony in 1563 at the direction of Bacon and Cecil, with the formal obsequies postponed to December. PRO SP 30/1 (f. 1^r). For descriptions of pre-Elizabethan and Continental funerals see BL Add. MS 45,131 (collected by Sir Thomas Wriothesley). For Elizabeth's funeral see BL Add. MS 35,324, ff. 27^r-39^r. The English also observed obsequies for Henry II in 1559 and the Emperor Ferdinand in 1564. Strype, *Grindal*, 38, 146-48.

69. Stone, *Crisis*, 573; Chamberlain, *Letters*, 1:41; Tittler, *Bacon*, 193; HMC 9 Salisbury, 10:58-59; Verney, *Memoirs*, 1:59; Machyn, *Diary*, especially pp. 188, 215-16, 222-23, 254; BL Add. MS 35,324. Machyn's *Diary* gives accounts of numerous gentry funerals. Sir Henry Isley's widow, whose husband was executed for his part in Wyatt's rebellion, died in 1561 and "had nothyng done" for her, though a sermon was preached by Edmund Scambler, bishop of Peterborough. Machyn, *Diary*, 258.

70. Machyn, *Diary*, 187-307 *passim*; Stone, *Crisis*, 576.

71. Machyn, *Diary*, 179-81, 184-85, 201, 208, 251-52, 264, 289, 297, 303, 307; Stow, *Chronicles*, 4:505, 534; BL Lansdowne MS 21/4; Cooper, *Athenae*, 2:171, 315, 336.

72. Barrow, *Writings (1587-90)*, 458, 460; cf. L. Pearson, *Elizabethans*, 473.

73. Will of Robert Pole, esq., of Radbourn, Derby, 20 March 1560. BL Add. (Wolley) MS 6671, f. 64^r.

74. Brass for Robert Chapman, esq., Merchant Adventurer and London draper, parish church of Stone, Kent, 1575.

75. Segar, *Honor*, 253-56; Pilkington, *Works*, 317.

76. Barrow, *Writings (1587-90)*, 461; John Weever, *Ancient Funerall Monuments* (1631), 54.

77. Jerome Bertram, *Brasses and Brass Rubbing in England* (Newton Abbot, 1971), 96-97; Julian Franklyn, *Brasses* (1969), 16.

78. *Certificates*, ed. King and Raines, 12; Young, *Mary Sidney*, 78.

79. Clay, ed., *Wills*, 49, 102; H. Mildmay, *Brief Memoir*, 19; Stow, *Chronicles*, 4:346; Franklyn, *Brasses*, 16.

80. Stow, *Chronicles*, 4:346, 426, 552; Chambers, *Sir Henry Lee*, 77; Aveling, *Recusancy*, 299; Strype, *Smith*, 154; Cliffe, *Gentry*, 128; Cooper, *Athenae*, 2:19; Strype, *Parker*, 2:429; Piccope, ed., *Wills*, 33:163; 54:160; Holles, *Memorials*, 43.

81. Stone, *Crisis*, 580; Clay, ed., *Wills*, 102; Cooper, *Athenae*, 1:326; Cliffe, *Gentry*, 128; Piccope, ed., *Wills*, 51:181; H. Mildmay, *Brief Memoir*, 19; Barrow, *Writings (1587-90)*, 461.

82. Tittler, *Bacon*, 188-89; Lehmberg, *Mildmay*, 307-8; McIntosh, *Proceedings*, 119:249; Hoby, *Diary*, 27-28; Stone, *Crisis*, 580; Frederick Chamberlin, *Elizabeth and Leycester* (New York, 1939), 385, 387, and the accompanying plates; Smith, *Servant*, 174.

83. My calculations are based on the list of figure brasses provided in Bertram, *Brasses*,

164-204. See Appendix, Table One. It is impossible to know how many brasses of this period have been destroyed. It has been estimated that only 7500 pre-1700 brasses now exist, of a total that may have been as high as 100,000. John Page-Phillips, *Macklin's Monumental Brasses* (2nd ed., 1972), 83.

84. Of the 35 brasses of persons in academic dress in the period 1500-1609, 22 (63%) are from the years 1500-1530. Apart from one in 1535 and one in 1540, there are no more until a cluster of ten in the 1570s and 1580s, followed by only one in the ensuing two decades.

85. See Appendix, Table Two.

86. Robert Burdet, *The Refuge of a Sinner* (1565).

Bibliographic Essay

Bibliographic Essay

Space precludes a formal bibliography, but most of the works used in this study are cited in the notes. This brief essay is not intended for specialists, who are already familiar with these volumes, but students and general readers. Only a sampling of the most useful books are cited here, though much excellent material is given in scholarly journals; the notes point the way to much of this.

General overviews of Elizabethan society are provided by A. L. Rowse, *The Elizabethan Renaissance: The Life of Society* (New York, 1971) and Lu Emily Pearson, *Elizabethans at Home* (Stanford, 1957); the latter depends almost wholly on literary sources, including drama. No full treatment of Elizabethan women has been published, but a literary perspective is provided by Carroll Camden, *The Elizabethan Woman* (Houston, 1952). Pearl Hogrefe, *Tudor Women* (Ames, 1975), is sketchy. F. G. Emmison's three volumes on *Elizabethan Life* (Chelmsford, Essex, 1970-76) draw on Essex records to provide a rather undigested but interesting portrayal of numerous aspects of daily life. The world of magic, astrology, witchcraft, and related subjects is brilliantly depicted in Keith Thomas, *Religion and the Decline of Magic* (New York, 1971). Another fascinating account of the cultural world of the masses is Peter Burke's *Popular Culture in Early Modern Europe* (1978), which ranges far and wide. Although oriented primarily toward the seventeenth century, Christopher Hill's *Society and Puritanism in Pre-Revolutionary England* (2nd ed., New York, 1967) includes provocative essays on such subjects as the household, the poor, the sabbath, oaths, the ecclesiastical courts, and usury. An interesting attempt to reexamine the nature of social change—from "lineage" society to "civil" society—is made by Mervyn James, *Family, Lineage, and Civil Society* (Oxford, 1974).

Substantive studies examine English society in this period from the standpoint of social groups and specific localities. One of the most brilliant achievements is Lawrence Stone's *The Crisis of the Aristocracy 1558-1641* (Oxford,

1965), which focuses on the peerage and the very wealthy gentry. Stone pursues his thesis in detailed case studies in *Family and Fortune* (Oxford, 1973). For the lesser aristocracy, J. T. Cliffe's *The Yorkshire Gentry* (1969) is a model study. A broader perspective is provided in Peter Clark's magnificent *English Provincial Society* (Hassocks, Sussex, 1976), which deals with Kent. A rather different world is depicted in S. J. Watts, *From Border to Middle Shire, Northumberland, 1586-1625* (Leicester, 1975).

Urban history has been the subject of much recent interest, a good indication of which is found in Peter Clark and Paul Slack, *English Towns in Transition* (1976), and two collections of urban studies: *Crisis and Order in English Towns 1500-1700* (1972), edited by Clark and Slack, and *Perspectives in English Urban History* (1973), edited by Alan Everitt. A growing list of cities and towns is the subject of special studies, including J. W. F. Hill, *Tudor & Stuart Lincoln* (Cambridge, 1956), Wallace MacCaffrey, *Exeter, 1540-1640* (Cambridge, Mass., 1958), Tom Atkinson, *Elizabethan Winchester* (1963), Alan Dyer, *The City of Worcester in the Sixteenth Century* (1973), which is one of the best of this genre, and D. M. Palliser, *Tudor York* (1980), which appeared too late for use in this study. There is no adequate social history of Elizabethan London, but a worm's eye view can be obtained from Thomas R. Forbes, *Chronicle from Aldgate* (1971). For a rural perspective, solid studies have been made by Margaret Spufford, *Contrasting Communities* (1974), which deals with Cambridgeshire villages, and David G. Hey, *An English Rural Community* (Leicester, 1974), which examines the village of Myddle, Shropshire.

Of the four religious groups that play a dominant role in this study, two—the Catholics and the Puritans—have been extensively analyzed by modern historians. John Bossy, the premier authority on Elizabethan Catholicism, provides a sweeping overview in *The English Catholic Community 1570-1850* (1975). Also useful are M. D. R. Leys, *Catholics in England 1559-1829* (1961), W. R. Trimble, *The Catholic Laity in Elizabethan England* (Cambridge, Mass., 1964), J. C. H. Aveling, *Catholic Recusancy in the City of York, 1558-1791* (1970), and Patrick McGrath, *Papists and Puritans under Elizabeth I* (New York, 1967).

The standard history of Elizabethan Puritanism is Patrick Collinson's magisterial *The Elizabethan Puritan Movement* (Berkeley, 1967). Puritan thought is conveniently summarized by William Haller, *The Rise of Puritanism* (1938) and M. M. Knappen, *Tudor Puritanism* (Chicago, 1939). Explaining the essence of the Puritan way has been highly controversial; the best studies include John F. H. New, *Anglican and Puritan: The Basis of Their Opposition, 1558-1640* (Stanford, 1964), a theological approach; John S. Coolidge, *The Pauline Renaissance in England* (Oxford, 1970), which deals with such issues as authority, *adiaphora*, and exegesis; Michael Walzer, *The Revolution of the Saints* (Cambridge, Mass., 1965), which stresses the anxiety in Puritanism; and J. Sears McGee, *The Godly Man in Stuart England* (New Haven, 1976), which finds the difference between Puritanism and Anglicanism in the seventeenth century in their contrasting emphases on the first and second "tables" of the Ten Commandments. Hill's studies, particularly his *Society & Puritanism*, have an economic orientation, with Puritanism being the faith of the "middling sort." Except for Presbyterians,

Charles H. and Katherine George can find no Puritans in their controversial study, *The Protestant Mind of the English Reformation 1570-1640*, which is strongly colored by their political predispositions. The flavor of Puritanism can be conveniently sampled in *Two Elizabethan Diaries* (Chicago, 1933), edited by Knappen. The growth of Puritanism in the diocese of Chester is competently analyzed in R. C. Richardson, *Puritanism in North-West England* (Manchester, 1972). The Puritan proclivity to preaching and their extensive involvement as lecturers, especially in London, are thoroughly explored in Paul Seaver's *The Puritan Lectureships* (Stanford, 1970). Casuistry and the problems of Puritan and Catholic dissidents are examined in Elliot Rose's *Cases of Conscience* (1975). Two of the finest regional studies are Christopher Haigh's *Reformation and Resistance in Tudor Lancashire* (1975) and Roger B. Manning's *Religion and Society in Elizabethan Sussex* (Leicester, 1969).

For the Separatists, the standard account is B. R. White, *The English Separatist Tradition* (1971). Beyond this, much can be learned from the various writings of Henry Barrow and John Greenwood, edited by Leland Carlson (cited in the notes).

No adequate history of Elizabethan Anglicanism exists, though Hill has analyzed the staggering economic difficulties in *Economic Problems of the Church: From Archbishop Whitgift to the Long Parliament* (Oxford, 1956). Much useful material can be found in two collections of essays edited by Rosemary O'Day and Felicity Heal: *Continuity and Change* (Leicester, 1976), and *Church and Society in England* (1977). The great outdoor pulpit in London attracted many of the age's greatest religious leaders, who periodically addressed social concerns; see Millar Maclure, *The Paul's Cross Sermons, 1534-1642* Toronto, 1958). Two modern studies of Whitgift and Grindal are especially useful: Powel M. Dawley, *John Whitgift and the English Reformation* (New York, 1954) and Patrick Collinson, *Archbishop Grindal* (Berkeley, 1979). There is still much of value in the works of John Strype, especially the following: *The Life and Acts of Matthew Parker*, 3 vols. (Oxford, 1821); *The History of the Life and Acts of . . . Edmund Grindal* (Oxford, 1821); *Historical Collections of the Life and Acts of . . . John Aylmer* (Oxford, 1821); *The Life and Acts of John Whitgift*, 3 vols. (Oxford, 1822).

The attempt to legislate and enforce socio-religious ideals in the Elizabethan era has only been partially told. The scattered treatment of social issues in Sir John Neale's *Elizabeth I and Her Parliaments*, 2 vols. (1958), is incomplete. The social concerns of the Privy Council have been largely ignored. Some useful material on social issues is given in W. J. Jones, *The Elizabethan Court of Chancery* (Oxford, 1967). Competent studies of the church courts throw welcome light on social practices; the best books in this area are Ronald A. Marchant's *The Puritans and the Church Courts in the Diocese of York 1560-1642* (1960) and *The Church under the Law* (Cambridge, 1969), also dealing with York, and Ralph Houlbrooke's *Church Courts and the People During the English Reformation 1520-1570* (1979). For a sampling of cases in church courts dealing with moral offenses, see *Before the Bawdy Court* (1972), edited by Paul Hair.

Education in the Elizabethan era is discussed in the broader studies of Kenneth

Charlton, *Education in Renaissance England* (1965) and Joan Simon, *Education and Society in Tudor England* (Cambridge, 1966). These works should be supplemented by Hugh Kearney, *Scholars and Gentlemen* (Ithaca, N.Y., 1970) and Lawrence Stone, ed., *Schooling and Society* (Baltimore, 1976). The standard work on the universities is Mark Curtis, *Oxford and Cambridge in Transition* (Oxford, 1959), and for the Inns of Court there is an excellent study by Wilfrid R. Prest, *The Inns of Court under Elizabeth I and the Early Stuarts* (1972). Of the many studies of individual schools, the best is Claire Cross, *The Free Grammar School of Leicester* (Leicester, 1953).

On marriage, sexual relations, and the family, pride of place goes to Lawrence Stone's *The Family, Sex and Marriage in England 1500-1800* (New York, 1977), which concentrates on the upper levels of society. In contrast, Alan Macfarlane deals almost exclusively with the rural groups below the gentry (which he argues are not "peasants"), and comes to strikingly different conclusions, pushing the origins of individualism back to at least 1400, in *The Origins of Individualism* (Oxford, 1978). Some of the conflict may be due to their respective concentrations on different social groups. Peter Laslett's popular introduction, *The World We Have Lost* (2nd ed., 1971), can be supplemented by *Household and Family in Past Time* (Cambridge, 1972), edited by Laslett and Richard Wall. For the family in broader perspective, see Edward Shorter, *The Making of the Modern Family* (1975), which includes Continental material, and two books focusing on the American colonies: Edmund Morgan, *The Puritan Family* (New York, 1966) and John Demos, *A Little Commonwealth* (New York, 1970). Levin Schücking, *The Puritan Family*, translated by Brian Battershaw (New York, 1970), is a literary study. Puritan thought on marriage is discussed in James Johnson, *A Society Ordained by God* (Nashville, 1970). For the place of children, there are general histories by Philippe Ariès, *Centuries of Childhood*, translated by Robert Baldick (New York, 1962) and Lloyd deMause, *The History of Childhood* (New York, 1974). The English situation, as depicted by Ivy Pinchbeck and Margaret Hewitt in *Children in English Society*, 2 vols. (1969, 1973), can be contrasted with the French in David Hunt, *Parents and Children in History* (1970).

In addition to the studies by Stone and Laslett in the preceding paragraph, several worthwhile books discuss sexual matters, including a collection of Laslett's earlier articles, published under the title, *Family Life and Illicit Love in Earlier Generations* (Cambridge, 1977). The Catholic position on birth control is documented in John Noonan, Jr., *Contraception* (Cambridge, Mass., 1966). For the practice of contraception in England see Orest and Patricia Ranum, *Popular Attitudes Toward Birth Control in Pre-Industrial France and England* (1972). Much can be learned about Elizabethan sexual practices from court records, as demonstrated by G. R. Quaife, *Wanton Wenches and Wayward Wives* (New Brunswick, N.J., 1979), which deals with Somerset in the period 1601-1660.

For many social topics, there are few or no satisfactory books. A happy exception is the sabbath, competently examined in Winton U. Solberg's *Redeem the Time* (Cambridge, Mass., 1977); although it concentrates on early America, it has an excellent background discussion of the sabbath in England. There is a general discussion of diet in F. G. Emmison, *Tudor Food and Pastimes* (1964).

For the theater, a dated study by E. N. S. Thompson, *The Controversy between the Puritans and the Stage* (New York, 1903), relates to themes discussed in chapter 10. A comparable study is that of Percy A. Scholes, *The Puritans and Music in England and New England* (1934). There are more recent and general studies by Morrison C. Boyd, *Elizabethan Music and Musical Criticism* (2nd ed., Philadelphia, 1962) and Peter Le Huray, *Music and the Reformation in England 1549-1660* (1967). The development of war theory is sketched by James Johnson in *Ideology, Reason, and the Limitation of War* (Princeton, 1975).

In the realm of economics, fine introductory histories are those by B. A. Holderness, *Pre-Industrial England* (1976) and D. C. Coleman, *The Economy of England 1450-1750* (1977). A huge literature has grown up around the work of Max Weber, *The Protestant Ethic and the Spirit of Capitalism*, translated by Talcott Parsons (2nd ed., 1976), and R. H. Tawney, *Religion and the Rise of Capitalism* (1926). Tawney's introduction to Thomas Wilson, *A Discourse upon Usury* (1925) is still worth reading, and the historical background is provided in J. T. Noonan, *The Scholastic Analysis of Usury* (Cambridge, Mass., 1951). An introduction to the problem of the destitute can be found in John F. Pound, *Poverty and Vagrancy in Tudor England* (1971). W. K. Jordan's specialized studies of charity are conveniently summarized in his *Philanthropy in England* (1959), but the results have been repeatedly questioned because they fail to take account of inflation. For agrarian problems, the best starting place is *The Agrarian History of England and Wales*, vol. 4 (Cambridge, 1967), edited by Joan Thirsk, complemented by Tawney's *The Agrarian Problem in the Sixteenth Century*, with an introduction by Stone (1977), and Eric Kerridge's *Agrarian Problems in the Sixteenth Century and After* (1969). For the enclosure problem in particular see Thirsk, *Tudor Enclosures* (1959), W. E. Tate, *The Enclosure Movement* (New York, 1967), and Y. A. Yelling, *Common Field and Enclosure in England 1450-1850* (1977).

The subject of death in England has not attracted much attention by historians, apart from plagues and other specific causes of death. The overview by Philippe Ariès, *Western Attitudes Toward Death*, translated by P. M. Ranum (Baltimore, 1974), is of value. The most fascinating study concentrates on New England: David E. Stannard, *The Puritan Way of Death* (New York, 1977).

Good biographies are often helpful. For the Elizabethan age, the most useful (in addition to those cited earlier) for socio-religious history include Claire Cross, *The Puritan Earl* (1966), a life of the third earl of Huntingdon; Robert Tittler, *Nicholas Bacon* (1976); Keith L. Sprunger, *The Learned Doctor William Ames* (1972); Alan G. R. Smith, *Servant of the Cecils* (Totowa, N.J., 1977), a life of Sir Michael Hicks; A. F. S. Pearson, *Thomas Cartwright and Elizabethan Puritanism* (Cambridge, 1925); Stanford E. Lehmberg, *Sir Walter Mildmay and Tudor Government* (Austin, Texas, 1964); and A. L. Rowse, *Simon Forman* (1974). The history of a Catholic family is told by Godfrey Anstruther in *Vaux of Harrowden* (Newport, Mon., 1953). More family studies are clearly needed. Although it deals with the seventeenth century, Macfarlane's *The Family Life of Ralph Josselin* (Cambridge, 1970) is valuable.

For most subjects, essential sources are the articles in scholarly journals. The notes contain references to many worthwhile contributions of this type.

Index

Index

(References to peerages follow the numbering used
in Arthur F. Kinney, *Titled Elizabethans*, 1973.)

Abbot, George: on tithes, 106; on the sabbath, 406; on games, 432; on the theater,
447, 454; on dancing, 455, 456; on suicide, 532; on usury, 602-603; other refs,
468

Abbot, Robert: on social order, 15; on Christmas, 423; on usury, 602

Abergavenny, Lady Frances, 310

Abortion, 215, 241-42

Acheley, T., 522

Act of Supremacy, 371

Act of Uniformity, 371

Acworth, George, 96

Adiaphora, 9, 29, 459, 460, 473, 505, 508,
746

Admonition Controversy, 6, 458, 631, 634,
746

Adultery, 26, 95, 96, 228-36, 269-73 *passim*,
739-40, 744

Aesop's Fables, 354, 527

Ainsworth, Henry, 8, 179

Aldersey, Thomas, 56

Alençon, Francis, Duke of, 210

Alford, Francis: on legal reform, 670; other
refs, 66, 148

Alford, Susanna, 148

All Saints' Eve, 425

Allen, Robert: on marriage, 118; on spouse
selection, 142; on premarital sex, 205,
207-208; on fornication, 208, 212; on
bastardy, 216; on homosexuality, 221;
on parental responsibilities, 274, 276,
278; on education, 349; on vocation,
380; on the sabbath, 405; on almsgiving,
560; on beggars, 565, 567, 568; on poor
relief, 576; on surety, 613; on tenants,
633; on enclosure, 643; on lawyers, 660;
other refs, 295, 605, 632

Allen, William, 422

Alley, William: hospitality of, 590; other
refs, 443, 706

Allison, Richard: on tithes, 109; on weddings, 180

Almsgiving, 557-62, 751

Alred, William, 60

Ambrose, 82, 529, 542, 558, 603

Ames, William: on war, 541; on usury, 607,
611; other refs, 646, 747

Ampleforth, Mr., Essex minister, 222

Amsterdam, 179

Anabaptists, 23, 230, 358, 491, 568, 570,
571, 651

Anderson, Anthony: on patrons, 47; on
clerical income, 50; on clerical ignorance,

72, 73; on idle clergy, 98-99; on masters, 316; on church ales and wakes, 465, 467, 468; on apparel, 502, 504; on apparel at court, 519; on suicide, 532; on landlords, 631; on enclosure, 643; other refs, 469

Andrewes, Lancelot: on divorce, 269; on parental affection, 279; on the sabbath, 399; on usury, 596; other refs, 57

Anger, Jane: on food, 471; on speech, 520; other refs, 311

Anglesey: Beaumaris, 680

Anglicans: nature of, 3-14; views on Christian liberty, 9; on social order, 14-25 *passim*, 762; on moderation, 26-28; on bishops, 36-45 *passim*; on patrons, 47-48, 50-53, 55; on clerical income, 49-50, 51, 762; on clerical education, 50-51; on pluralism, 61-63, 65-69; on nonresidency, 64-69; on clerical ignorance, 71-74, 76-78; on clerical vocation, 75-76; on sermons, 79-83, 738; on education in the pulpit, 85-88; on natural and revealed knowledge, 88-92; on immoral clergy, 93; on anti-clericalism, 98-100, 103-104; on tithes, 108-109, 110; on the nature of marriage, 116, 118-19, 744; on celibacy, 122-24, 127-29, 749; on spouse selection, 131-32, 134, 137, 139, 140-41, 142-43, 739; on age at marriage, 143-44, 151; on child marriages, 151, 153; on parental consent in marriage, 157-59, 741-42; on weddings, 184; on widows, 193, 749; on fornication, 208-209, 213, 744; on premarital sex, 213, 740; on bastardy, 216; on prostitution, 218; on homosexuality, 221; on sex in marriage, 225; on adultery, 229-30, 234, 740, 744; on birth control, 237, 244-46; on marital relations, 254-56, 258, 259-60, 263; on divorce, 269, 273, 744; on parental responsibilities, 275-77, 280, 281; on parental affection, 279; on children's duties, 283; on the household, 293, 294, 302, 739, 744-45; on wives, 305-306, 742; and literary patronage, 309; on masters, 315-16, 317, 318, 322-23, 749; on the purpose of education, 330; on the extent of education, 339, 343, 346; on the curriculum, 354-55; on educational reform, 358-60; on the universities, 360-61; on educational support, 362-63, 364-65, 367, 369, 372-73; on

vocation, 379, 380, 381, 741; on idleness, 385-86, 387, 389-90, 741; on labor, 392-93, 740-41; on ambition, 394-95, 741; on the sabbath, 396, 397-401 *passim*, 405-408 *passim*, 745; on holy days, 419-21, 745; on games, 432-33, 436; on bear-baiting, 445; on the theater, 447, 454, 749-50; on dancing, 455, 456, 750, 760; on music, 458, 459-61, 465, 746, 750; on church ales and wakes, 467, 468; on food, 472-74, 483, 750; on drink, 483-84, 489-90, 750; on fasting, 490-92, 494, 497, 498-99, 738, 750; on apparel, 502-506, 519-20, 750; on speech, 520-22, 525, 750-51; on literature, 526-27, 528-29, 530-31, 751; on suicide, 532-33, 537, 751; on war, 538-41, 543; 746; on wealth, 549, 550, 551, 552-54, 751; on the poor, 555, 556-57; on almsgiving, 558, 559, 560, 561-62, 751; on beggars, 565, 566, 568; on poor relief, 569, 573-75, 575, 576, 746; on communalism, 570-71, 751; and charitable giving, 578-84, 586-87; on hospitality, 587-88, 588-89, 590-92, 751-52; on usury, 599-603, 608, 611, 747; on surety, 613; on weights and measures, 616; on business ethics, 617-18, 621-22; on forestalling and regrating, 626-27, 628, 752; on landlords, 630-31; as landlords, 633-34; on enclosure, 642-43, 644; on law suits, 652, 657, 753; on lawyers, 658-59, 661; on judges, 663-64, 665, 753; on justice for the poor, 665-66; on legal reform, 670-71, 672, 674; on church courts, 675-76, 679-80, 748; on oaths, 684-86, 688, 747-48; on funeral customs, 697-98, 703, 734, 735; on funeral sermons, 704; on wakes and minds, 707, 708, 736; and embalming, 715

Anne of Cleves, 724

Anticlericalism, 98-104, 680, 760

Antwerp, 370, 372, 422

Apparel, 186, 502-20, 750

Apsley, Henry, 68

Aquinas, Thomas, 606

Archdall, the Rev. Mr., 395

Arches, Court of, 95, 103, 233, 272, 678

Arden, Forest of, 243

Aristotle: on marital age, 143; other refs, 26, 239, 353, 355, 366, 529, 603

Arscot, Nicholas, 216
Articles of Religion (1562), 53, 125-26, 415, 537, 571, 684
Arundel, 24th Earl of. *See* FitzAlan, Henry
Arundel, Countess of, 307
Arundel, Sir John, 298
Arundell, Sir Matthew: charity of, 581
Ascham, Roger: on educational travel, 371; on literature, 527; other refs, 347-48, 464, 521, 526, 529
Ashbourn (Derby) Grammar School, 367
Aston, Sir Edward, 148
Aston, Walter, 148-49
Atherton, John, 173
Atkins, Anthony, 524
Atkins, Richard, 488
Atkinson, Anthony, 621
Atkinson, Robert, 681
Audience, Court of, 272
Augustine, 82, 224, 399, 529, 603
Aungier, Richard, 583
Avenon, Alice, 583
Averroes, 366
Awdeley, John: on rogues and sturdy beggars, 563-64
Aylmer, John: hostility toward, 37-38; dispute with Lord Rich, 56; support for sermons, 84; on premarital sex, 204; on apparel, 505, 518; charity of, 578, 586; other refs, 42, 43, 46, 57, 92, 290, 296, 304, 359, 427, 516, 710, 721, 728
Ayr, 213

Babington, Anthony, 10
Babington, Gervase: on social mobility, 21; on clerical learning, 75; on tithes, 106; on celibacy, 128; on spouse selection, 131, 134; on marital age, 144; on parental consent in marriage, 158; on adultery, 230; on breast-feeding, 245; on marital relations, 254, 257, 263; on parental responsibilities, 281; on children's duties, 283; on masters, 316; on retainers, 317; on servants, 322; on idleness, 385, 386; on the sabbath, 400-401; on games, 432; on bear-baiting, 445; on the theater, 447, 454; on dancing, 455, 456; on food, 473; on apparel, 502, 503, 505; on speech, 521; on usury, 601; on law suits, 652; other refs, 204, 309, 468, 469

Babington, Originall, 174
Babington, Thomas, 719
Bacon, Lady Anne (Cooke): on Puritan exercises, 6; other refs, 58, 277, 288, 307, 308, 310, 345, 585
Bacon, Anthony, 187, 210, 278, 311, 313, 322, 323, 348, 369, 388, 418, 443, 457, 463, 514, 523, 585, 609, 651, 723
Bacon, Sir Francis: on weights and measures, 614; on enclosure, 640-41; on legal reform, 669; other refs, 74, 221, 263, 540, 691
Bacon, Sir Nicholas: as patron, 56, 58; proposed academy of, 361, 462-63; charity of, 585; on forestalling and engrossing, 623; other refs, 188, 280, 450, 478, 528, 531, 710, 713, 715, 719, 727, 731, 732
Baker, George, 212
Ballard, William, 535
Balmford, James: on games, 435
Banbury Grammar School, 344
Bancroft, Richard: on social order, 23, 24; on bishops, 36; attacks Presbyterians, 92; on tithes, 109; on chaplains, 298; on education, 358; library of, 529; and ecclesiastical courts, 676, 679, 691; on oaths, 685; other refs, 29, 54, 181, 461, 681, 690-91, 692, 748, 762
Bangor, Diocese of, 49
Bangor Grammar School, 368
Banister, John, 213
Barber, Robert, 180-81
Barker, John: on usury, 596; on landlords, 628; on legal reform, 672
Barker, Lawrence: attacks sectaries, 92; other refs, 554
Barlow, John, 198, 277
Barlow, William: on Puritans, 8; other refs, 21-22, 297
Barnby, Charles, 232
Barnes, Richard: on literacy, 333; on education, 334-35; support of education, 365; on holy days, 427; on apparel, 516; other refs, 78, 176, 340, 441, 457, 634
Barnes, Thomas, 541, 543
Barnes, Thomas (university professor), 466
Barnfield, Richard: on spouse selection, 137-38; on apparel, 502
Barrington, Sir Thomas, 319
Barrough, Philip: on infertility, 239, 240; on birth control, 241

Barrow, Henry: on episcopal lands, 43; on patrons, 47, 58; on learning in the pulpit, 86; on clerical education, 91-92; anticlericalism of, 101; on tithes, 104, 107-108; on marriage, 162; on weddings, 179, 185; on adultery, 228, 234; on children's duties, 285; on chaplains, 297-98; on education, 359, 360; on vocation, 381; on idleness, 389, 390; on the sabbath, 407; on holy days, 422; on games, 437; on fasting, 496; on apparel, 510; on speech, 524; on enclosure, 643; on lawsuits, 654; on legal reform, 672; on ecclesiastical courts, 674, 678-79; on oaths, 690; on funeral customs, 702-703; on funeral sermons, 705; on monuments and brasses, 730; other refs, 109, 222, 362, 755

Barthlett, John, 306, 337
Bartholomew Fair, 564
Barton, Mr., London minister, 95
Basham, Thomas, 644, 668
Basil the Great, 310, 459, 603
Basset, Sir Arthur, 424
Bastardy, 95, 96, 209, 214-18, 229, 272, 411, 442, 467, 486, 522, 757
Bateman, Stephen: on patrons, 50; on pluralism, 61; on the sabbath, 400
Bath, 4th Earl of. See Bourchier, William
Bath, Countess of. See Bourchier, Elizabeth
Baxter, J.: on clerical ignorance, 72
Baylife, Mr., Cornish minister, 442
Baynard Castle, 185
Beale, John, 442
Beale, Robert, 10, 681-82
Beale, Thomas, 19
Bear Garden, Bankside, 415, 445
Bear-baiting, 400, 410, 411, 415, 418, 429, 444-46, 465, 467, 468
Beauchamp, Viscount. See Seymour, Edward
Beaumont, Robert: on his funeral, 701; other refs, 366, 584
Beck, Samuel, 95
Becke, Edmund, 34
Beckingham, Thomas, 61
Becon, Thomas: on social order, 16; on moderation, 27; on bishops, 36; on preaching, 81; on immoral clergy, 94; on marriage, 118, 129; on widows, 193-94, 198; on premarital sex, 205; on family size, 244; on executrixes, 260; on children's duties, 284; on the household, 292; on wives, 305; on servants, 318, 322; on idleness, 383, 386, 388; on the sabbath, 398, 399; on almsgiving, 560; on beggars, 566; on forestalling, 627; on landlords, 632; on ecclesiastical courts, 678; on funeral customs, 700, 701; on minds, 707; other refs, 29, 187, 706

Bede, Venerable, 528
Bedel, Henry: on prostitution, 218; on the sabbath, 398; on games, 433; on bearbaiting, 445; on dancing, 455
Bedell, Elizabeth, 312
Bedell, William, 350
Bedford, 4th Earl of. See Russell, Francis
Bedford, Countess of. See Russell, Bridget; Russell, Lucy
Bedfordshire: Bedford, 260; Oakley, 364; Sandy, 137; other refs, 531, 537, 644, 734
Bedingfield, Sir Henry, 316
Beggary, 638, 641, 642-43
Bell, Thomas, 493
Bell, William, 577
Bellamy, John, 531
Bellarmine, Robert, 597
Bendlowes, William, 578
Benett, Robert, 577
Benger, Sir Thomas, 196
Benson, George, 720
Bentham, Thomas: on lawyers, 658
Bentley, Thomas, 204, 309
Berkeley, Lady Anne, 257, 277, 311
Berkeley, Henry, 7th Lord Berkeley: charity of, 580-81; hospitality of, 591; other refs, 187, 228, 302, 303-304, 311, 316, 317, 344, 346, 424, 443, 444, 446, 463, 489, 513, 521, 621, 670
Berkeley, Lady Jane, 25, 302, 444, 489, 521
Berkeley, Sir John, 280
Berkeley, Lady Katherine: charity of, 581; other refs, 311-12, 313, 317-18, 344, 346, 513, 720
Berkeley, Thomas Lord, 257, 277, 311, 476
Berkeley (Yorks.) Grammar School, 348
Berkshire: Abingdon, 336, 707; Bisham, 345; Bray, 308; Caversham, 220; Cookham, 37; Marcham, 319; New Windsor, 73, 455; Reading, 178, 425; other refs, 563, 637
Bernard of Clairvaux, 519, 603

Bernard, John, 442

Berrie, William, 577

Bertie, Peregrine (future Lord Willoughby), 139

Bertie, Richard, 303

Bess of Hardwick. *See* Talbot, Elizabeth

Best, John, 93, 631

Bevis of Southampton, 526, 527, 531

Beza, Theodore, 161, 397, 527, 597, 600, 611

Beza-Tomson Bible: on natural and revealed knowledge, 89, 90, 91; on immoral clergy, 93; on celibacy, 123, 124, 127; on parental consent in marriage, 157; on widows, 192; on fornication, 208; on sex in marriage, 224; on marital relations, 253-54; on divorce, 268; on parental responsibility, 275; on children's duties, 283; on the household, 292; on masters, 314-15; on servants, 321; on vocation, 378-79; on ambition, 394; on the sabbath, 397; on fasting, 494; on apparel, 502; on speech, 520; on wealth, 550, 551, 552, 553; on the poor, 555; on almsgiving, 557, 559, 560, 561, 562; on communalism, 570; on hospitality, 587; on usury, 596-97, 610; on lawsuits, 651; on oaths, 683; other refs, 707, 739

Bicknoll, Edward: on apparel, 503

Bigamy, 97

Bill, William, 364, 535, 733

Binder, Edward, 96

Bindon, Viscount Howard of. *See* Howard, Henry; Howard, Thomas

Birche, William, 366, 584

Bird, Samuel: on widows, 193; on May Day, 426; on games, 434, 435, 436, 439; on dancing, 455-56; on alehouses, 484; on suicide, 533, 534; on the wealthy, 554; on almsgiving, 560; on legal reform, 670; on deacons, 575-76; on hospitality, 588

Birkbie, John, 96, 97-98, 515

Birth Control, 236-47

Bishops: discussed in biblical marginalia, 34-35; views of Anglicans and Puritans on, 35-45 *passim*; pomp of, 40-42; finances of, 42-45; and patrons, 46-58 *passim*; on pluralism and nonresidence, 65-66; attempts to improve preaching, 83; on child marriages, 153; on parental sanction in marriage, 176; on weddings, 180; on bastardy, 216; on prostitution, 220; on sexual offenses, 223; on adultery, 229, 234; on divorce, 271; on christenings, 290; on the household, 293; and Catholic chaplains, 298; on literacy, 333; on education, 340; on Catholic education, 351; support of education, 365; and sabbath enforcement, 413-14; and holy days, 420, 427; and control of games, 441; and the theater, 447; attitude toward dancing, 457; on fasting, 496; regulation of dress, 516; enforcement of proper speech, 524-25; and suicide, 535; and poor relief, 573-75; and charitable giving, 578-79; concern for hospitality, 589-90; attitude toward usury, 608; as landlords, 634; and ecclesiastical courts, 675-76; and funeral customs, 699, 700; social work of, 760-61

Bishops' Bible: on natural and revealed knowledge, 89, 90; on tithes, 108; on parental consent in marriage, 155, 157; on bastardy, 216; on sex in marriage, 224; on breast-feeding, 245; on marital relations, 253, 254; on parental responsibilities, 275; on children's duties, 283; on the household, 292; on masters, 314; on servants, 321; on vocation, 378, 382; on idleness, 384-85; on the sabbath, 397; on apparel, 502; on speech, 520; on suicide, 532; on war, 539; on wealth, 549-50, 552; on the poor, 555; on almsgiving, 557, 559, 560, 562; on hospitality, 587; on usury, 596, 646; on surety, 612, 613; on scarcity, 626; on bribery, 662; on justice, 670; on oaths, 683

Bisse, James: on the poor, 553

Blackburn (Lancs.) Grammar School, 367

Blackstone, Henry, 62

Blackwood, Robert, 61

Blagrave, 311

Blague, Thomas, 233

Blenkinsopp, Roland, 260

Blenkinsopp, William, 260

Blogge, Mr., nonresident minister, 64

Blount, Sir Charles, 166, 229, 232-33

Blount, Elizabeth, 229

Blount, James, Lord Mountjoy, 382

Blunte, William, 577

Boccaccio, Giovanni, 527

Bodin, Jean, 286

Bodley, Thomas, 370
Bolebec, Lord. *See* De Vere, Edward
Boleyn, Anne, 229, 268
Boleyn, Mary, 229
Bond, George, 517-18
Bonham, William, 6, 179
Bonner, Edmund: on almsgiving, 557; other refs, 689
Book of Common Prayer, 6, 39, 45, 56, 57, 64, 116, 118, 178, 182, 290, 296, 297, 690, 698, 700, 701, 703, 734, 744, 755, 761
Booke of the Forme of Common Prayers, A, 179, 744
Boorde, Andrew: on sleep, 387; other refs, 238
Bossewell, John, 464
Bossy, John, 299
Bourchier, Elizabeth, Countess of Bath, 316
Bourchier, William, 4th Earl of Bath, 265, 272
Bourke, Richard, Earl of Clanricarde, 135
Bowes, Lady, 197, 308
Bowes, Sir William, 49
Bowls, 94, 96
Bownde, Nicholas: on parental affection, 279, 282; on masters, 318; on vocation, 381; on the sabbath, 401, 402, 403-405, 406, 407, 408; on the theater, 450; on music, 462; other refs, 297, 416, 418, 430, 745
Boxe, Alderman: on poor relief, 569; on the increase of tillage, 641-42
Boys, Sir John, 581
Bradbridge, William, 424
Bradford, John, 455
Bradgate, Thomas, 584
Bradshaw, Robert, 182
Brakin, Thomas, 152
Branch, Dame Helen (Nicholson), 194-95, 336, 583, 704
Branch, Sir John, 194, 583
Brandling, Sir Robert, 578
Braoke, Matthew, 389
Brasses, Commemorative, 19, 729-34, 736
Brawling, 97, 98
Breast-feeding, 245-46
Breton, Nicholas: on widowers, 193; other refs, 204, 255
Brettam, George, 332

Brettergh, Katherine, 306, 309-10, 418, 521, 583, 633
Bricke, William, 565
Bridgeman, Anthony, 418, 445
Bridges, John: on parental responsibilities, 281; on the sabbath, 398
Bristol, 37, 56, 81-82, 262-63, 363, 424, 446, 578, 625
Bristol, Bishop of. *See* Cheyney, Richard (1562-79); Fletcher, Richard (1589-93)
Bristol Cathedral, 38
Bristow, Richard: on holy days, 422-23
Brittany, 497
Brockett, Sir John, 141
Bromley, Sir Thomas: on sex in marriage, 226; other refs, 27, 123, 208, 331, 393, 482, 513, 521, 609-10
Brooke, Anne, Lady Cobham, 319, 702
Brooke, Dorothy, Lady Cobham, 714, 719, 720
Brooke, Henry, 11th Lord Cobham, 712
Brooke, Sir John, 149
Brooke, William, 10th Lord Cobham: charity of, 580; other refs, 712, 721
Brown, Sir Humphrey, 728
Browne, Anthony, 1st Viscount Montagu, 163, 185, 299, 710
Browne, Francis, 612
Browne, Robert: on education, 356; other refs, 82
Brueghel, Pieter, 466
Brussels, 4, 370
Brydges, Edmund, 2nd Lord Chandos of Sudeley, 174
Bucer, Martin, 600
Buchanan, George, 264
Buckhurst, 1st Lord. *See* Sackville, Thomas
Buckinghamshire: Beaconsfield, 372; Bletchley, 5; Chenies, 732; Chesham, 205; Great Marlow, 466; Sherrington, 525; Stoke Poges, 187; other refs, 531, 537, 733, 734
Buckley, Sir Richard, 429
Buggery, 221-22
Bulkeley, Edward: on the sabbath, 401; other refs, 5, 309
Bull-baiting, 400, 410, 411, 444-46, 468
Bullein, William: on moderation, 28; on birth control, 240-41; on abortion, 241; on games, 438; on dancing, 456; on drink, 485; on fasting, 490

Bullinger, Heinrich: on marriage, 118; on parental consent in marriage, 157; on weddings, 178, 185; on adultery, 229, 230, 234; on speech, 276; on masters, 318; on education, 342; on educational travel, 370; other refs, 73, 77, 83, 132, 143, 194, 310, 330, 359, 397, 528, 530, 600, 761

Bullingham, Nicholas: finances of, 43; other refs, 55

Bunny, Edmund: on parental consent in marriage, 158; on divorce, 269; on servants, 315; on education, 355; on vocation, 379, 380; on the sabbath, 400; other refs, 430, 741

Bunyan, John, 87

Burbage, Richard, 452

Burgh, Thomas Lord, 463

Burghley, 1st Lord. See Cecil, William

Burton, William: on weddings, 178; on idleness, 390; on the sabbath, 405; on games, 434; on beggars, 565; on usury, 605; on surety, 613; on funeral sermons, 705; on funeral charity, 717; other refs, 646

Bush, Edward: on clerical ignorance, 73; on enclosure, 643; other refs, 61, 85, 632

Business Ethics, 616-22, 646, 752

Bussye, Edward, 578

Button, William, 279

Byron, John, 173, 577

Byston, Ralph, 173

Caesar, Gaius Julius, 354, 355, 529

Caesar, Sir Julius, 6

Caius, John, 578, 728

Cajetan, Cardinal. See De Vio, Thomas

Calais, 332

Caldwell, Dr., 583

Caldwell, John, 57, 60

Calverley, Walter, 149

Calvert, Leonard, 332

Calvin, John, 10, 37, 161, 238, 310, 346, 354, 455, 474, 528, 542, 550, 600, 672, 704

Cambridge (town): Christ's Hospital, 585; other refs, 92, 174, 394, 436, 535, 577, 584, 625-26, 720, 728

Cambridge University: Caius (Gonville and Caius) College, 342, 365, 728; Christ's College, 22, 72, 296, 366, 370, 401, 436, 728; Clare College, 62, 340, 366; Corpus Christi College, 47, 365, 529; Emmanuel College, 330, 366, 367; King's College, 366; Magdalene College, 360, 365, 367; Pembroke College, 365; Peterhouse, 553; Queens' College, 334, 364, 370, 450, 577; St. John's College, 110, 330, 347, 360, 364, 366; Sidney Sussex College, 366, 367; Trinity College, 47, 209, 364, 365, 366, 584; University Library, 365, 366, 528, 529; other refs, 51, 63, 85, 91, 277, 299, 331, 347, 349, 355, 358, 359, 360, 362, 363, 365, 366, 367, 387, 485, 512-13, 524, 579, 580, 584, 627

Cambridgeshire: Chesterton, 445, 446; Coton, 583, Girton, 48; Gravely, 234; Longstanton, 60; Orwell, 199; Trumpington, 728; Willingham, 340; other refs, 325, 340, 609, 626, 637, 734

Campion, Edmund: on apparel, 511; other refs, 285, 347

Candlemas, 453

Candover, Preston, 1st Lord Williams of Thame, 188, 714, 718

Canisius, Peter, 117, 224

Canterbury (town): Jesus Hospital, 581; other refs, 199, 365, 389, 487, 526, 530, 578, 582, 590

Canterbury, Archbishop of. See Parker, Matthew (1559-75); Grindal, Edmund (1576-83); Whitgift, John (1583-1604)

Canterbury, Diocese of, 59, 77, 142

Canterbury, Province of, 44-45, 49, 74, 351, 413, 427, 473, 481, 608, 675, 676

Capel, Arthur, 529

Cardiff, 400

Carew, Sir Gawen, 424

Carew, Sir George, 168

Carew, Sir Matthew, 432

Carew, Peter, 282

Carew, Richard, 465, 466, 467, 515, 609

Carey, Lady Anne, 303, 312, 590

Carey, George, 2nd Lord Hunsdon, 452

Carey, Henry, 1st Lord Hunsdon, 136, 303, 312, 370, 417, 590, 711, 712, 713, 715, 719, 732

Carey, John, 141

Carey, Robert, 136, 370

Carleton, George, 66, 261
Carlisle, Bishop of. *See* Best, John (1561-70); Barnes, Richard (1570-77)
Carlisle, Diocese of, 78
Carnsew, William, 424, 436, 528, 531
Carpenter, John: on the poor, 554; on usury, 602; other refs, 85, 257
Carr, John, 435
Carter, Arthur, 671
Carter, Oliver, 57
Cartwright, Thomas: on the nature of Puritanism, 7; on social order, 23; on episcopal lands, 43, 44; on celibacy, 123, 125, 129-30; on the wedding ring, 185; on widows, 193; on sex in marriage, 224-25; on divorce, 268; on universities, 330; on education, 358; support for education, 366; on the sabbath, 401; on holy days, 421-22; on Easter, 425; on music, 459, 462; on food, 474; on fasting, 492, 498; on Catholic missionaries, 511; on almsgiving, 559; on poor relief, 569, 572; charity of, 584; on oaths, 688-89, 690; on funeral customs, 700, 701; on his funeral, 702; on funeral sermons, 705; on funeral expenses, 708; other refs, 10, 11, 29, 40, 56, 72, 84, 91, 174, 199, 260, 307, 319, 345, 359, 362, 398, 528, 605, 745, 751
Cary, Lady Elizabeth, 309
Cary, Sir Henry, 150
Case, John: on music, 460; on suicide, 532; other refs, 461
Castiglione, Baldassare, 463, 529
Catechizing, 276, 294-96, 315
Catholics: place on religious continuum, 10; appeal of, 13; on social order, 21; on Anglican bishops, 36; on patrons, 47; on clerical ignorance, 73; on social background of the clergy, 73-74; on clerical vocation, 75; on clerical education, 85; on clerical immorality, 95; on the nature of marriage, 116-18, 119; on celibacy, 120-21, 123-24, 125, 129; on spouse selection, 130-31, 137; and child marriages, 153; on parental consent in marriage, 162, 170-71; on weddings, 179, 183-84; on widows, 191-92; on premarital sex, 204, 207; on fornication, 208; on sex in marriage, 224, 225; on birth-control, 237-38; on family size, 244; on

marital relations, 254, 257; on divorce, 268; on parental responsibilities, 276, 280-81; on parental affection, 279; on children's duties, 283, 284-85; on the household, 292; on catechizing, 294-95; chaplains, 298; wards, 298-99; household organization, 299-300; role of women, 307-308, 309, 314; relations with servants, 315-16; and schools, 331-33, 351-52; on education, 334, 346, 347; and educational foundations, 368; and educational travel, 370, 371; on vocation, 382; on labor, 392; on ambition, 394-95; on the sabbath, 407, 409; and holy days, 420, 422-23; on games, 437-38; and music, 464; on food, 476; on fasting, 491, 492, 494, 495, 496, 498; on apparel, 502, 510-11, 519; on speech, 522, 524; on literature, 527-28, 529, 531; on suicide, 531; on almsgiving, 557-58; and poor relief, 576, 577-78; on hospitality, 587; on usury, 596-97, 607-608; on weights and measures, 616; on business practices, 617; as landlords, 635; and enclosure, 645; on lawsuits, 651-52; legal treatment of, 671-72; and the Oath of Supremacy, 681; on oaths, 683; and funeral practices, 696-97; women in Catholic households, 742, 743; other refs, 29, 51, 53, 81, 218, 220, 230, 287, 302-303, 311, 319, 323, 339, 361, 385-86, 389, 403, 442, 446, 452, 456, 573, 580, 586, 608, 685, 687, 688, 706, 719, 734, 738, 740, 757, 760, 763, 767
Cato, 603
Catulus, 353, 354
Cave, Sir Ambrose, 478
Cave, Roger, 164
Cawarden, Sir Thomas, 710, 715
Cawdry, Robert: on nonresidency, 64; other refs, 180
Cecil, Anne, 146, 163
Cecil, Bridget, 142
Cecil, Lady Mildred (Cooke): charity of, 585; other refs, 288, 310, 345, 357, 366, 727
Cecil, Sir Robert: on clerical patronage, 55; other refs, 8, 10, 43, 133, 135, 147, 150, 165, 168, 181, 345, 347, 429, 443, 463, 514, 641

Cecil, Sir Thomas, 147, 280, 329, 333, 453, 610

Cecil, William, 1st Lord Burghley: religious views of, 10-11; on social order, 17-18; on moderation, 28; on bishops, 37; on clerical patronage, 55; as patron, 56; and arranged marriages, 162-65, 177; on the Earl of Oxford's education, 355; support of education, 367; on educational travel, 369; clothing of, 513; speech of, 521; charity of, 580, 581; hospitality of, 591; on Lady Mildred's funeral, 699; on his own funeral, 699, 709; and funeral pageantry, 711-13, 723, 729, 735; other refs, 10, 15, 19, 23, 36, 39, 40, 64, 67, 92, 93, 125, 133, 135, 142, 145, 146, 147, 148, 152, 167, 168, 169, 172, 174, 175, 181, 185, 199, 221, 233, 257, 264, 265, 272, 273, 277, 278, 280, 285, 286, 299, 302, 303, 307, 312, 319, 329, 331, 332, 347, 351, 356, 359, 360, 361, 365, 368, 372, 388, 415, 416, 420, 439, 447, 451, 478, 479, 482, 496, 497, 512, 517, 522, 554, 564, 569, 574, 590, 597, 598, 601, 608, 609-10, 612, 615, 621, 623, 624, 631, 633, 639, 641, 645, 654, 670, 671, 682, 689, 710, 718, 727, 766

Cecil, William (Burghley's grandson), 145, 150

Cecilia, Princess of Sweden, 452

Celibacy, 119-30

Cemeteries, 697, 701, 703

Chaderton, Laurence: on clerical ignorance, 72, 74; on education in the pulpit, 86; on immoral clergy, 94; on the household, 293; other refs, 84

Chaderton, Thomas, 278-79

Chaderton, William: on exercises, 77; and clerical learning, 78; support of education, 365; on bear-baiting, 445; other refs, 153, 299, 413-14, 441, 650

Chamberlain, John, 141, 236, 257, 429, 514, 727

Chamberlain, Sir Thomas, 288

Chambers, Leonard, 416

Champernoun, Sir Arthur, 163-64

Chancery, Court of, 106, 165, 196, 207, 272, 614, 630, 642, 650, 651, 667, 668, 670, 673, 712

Chandos of Sudeley, 2nd Lord. See Brydges, Edmund

Chaplains, 297-98

Chapman, Robert, 729

Chardon, John: on patrons, 45; on marital age, 143-44

Charitable Giving, 262-63, 572-87

Charles I, 431

Chaucer, Geoffrey, 71, 529

Checke, Sir John, 396, 529

Cheney, Henry, 1st Lord Cheney (or Cheyne), 324

Cheyney, Richard: on Puritans, 23; on patristic thought, 37; other refs, 654

Cheyney, Sir Thomas: hospitality of, 591; other refs, 309, 317, 721

Cheshier, Thomas, 75, 97

Cheshire: Aston, 166; Bosley, 266; Brereton, 151; Congleton, 150; Davenham, 95, 180; Doddleston, 702; Eccleston, 60, 668; Hatton Hall, 150, 151; High Leigh, 592; Hough, 702, 719; Little Budworth, 467; Marbury, 151; Middlewich, 696; Milton, 311; Moberley, 60; Nantwich, 174, 414, 574, 732; Newton, 440; Prestbury, 214-15; Ridley, 306; Runcorn, 94, 337; Tilston, 696; Walton, 696; Warmingham, 198, 277; Waverton, 655; West Kirby, 707; Whitchurch, 106; Wilmslow, 702, 705; Wistaston, 732; other refs, 78, 150, 184, 215, 217, 229, 285, 340, 410, 411, 440, 467, 609, 636, 707, 733

Chester, 197, 198, 217, 286, 333, 452, 574, 575, 584, 621, 696

Chester, Bishop of. See Downham, William (1561-77); Chaderton, William (1579-95); Vaughan, Richard (1597-1604)

Chester, Diocese of, 57, 77, 78, 80, 151, 180, 182, 207, 441, 445, 696

Chester, Ecclesiastical Court at, 149, 150, 206-207, 231, 272, 273

Chester Cathedral, 715

Chette, Henry, 447, 609

Chetwoode, Richard, 727

Chichester, Archdeaconry of, 49, 59, 77

Chichester, Bishop of. See Barlow, William (1559-69); Curteys, Richard (1570-82); Watson, Anthony (1596-1605)

Chichester, Consistory Court at, 97

Chichester, Diocese of, 48, 52-53, 55, 573

Chichester Cathedral, 60, 62, 656

Child Marriages, 148-53

Children's Responsibilities, 282-87

Cholmeley, Richard, 593
Cholmley, Francis, 167
Cholmley, Sir Henry, 136
Cholmley, Sir Hugh, 656
Cholmley, Ranulph, 728
Cholmley, Sir Richard, 165-66, 167, 233
Cholmley, Sir Roger, 171
Christenings, 18, 178, 287-90, 766
Christmas, 299, 420, 422, 423-25, 429, 438, 443, 446, 453, 457, 477, 480, 481, 515, 581, 591, 758
Chrysostom, 82, 126, 310, 383, 529, 603
Chub, William, 294
Church Ales, 214, 425, 465-68, 487
Churchyard, Thomas: on matrimonial choice, 177; on apparel, 511; on war, 539; on justice for the poor, 665, 667
Cicero, 355, 366, 526, 529, 603
Clanricarde, Earl of. See Bourke, Richard
Clapham, Henoch: on patrons, 50; on idleness, 391; on literature, 526; on the poor, 555
Cleaver, Robert: on marriage, 118, 119, 129; on celibacy, 124; on spouse selection, 131, 132, 138, 142; on parental consent in marriage, 160-61; on premarital sex, 205; on sex in marriage, 223, 225; on adultery, 230; on breast-feeding, 245; on marital relations, 255, 263-64; on female relations, 256-57; on inheritance, 261; on divorce, 269-70; on parental responsibilities, 274, 277, 278, 281; on disinheritance, 278; on names, 289; on the household, 292; on wives, 305; on education, 329, 334, 347; on vocation, 380; on speech, 523; on surety, 613; other refs, 430, 744
Clergy: stipends of, 48-50; education of, 50-51, 77-78; income of, 50-51, 761-62; ignorance of some, 71-78; social background of, 73-74; and outside vocations, 75; nonpreaching ministers, 79-81; immorality of some, 93-98, 760
Cliberye, Mr., Essex minister, 141-42, 216, 442
Clifford, Lady Anne, 210, 344, 457-58, 656
Clifford, Lady Frances, 185
Clifford, Sir Francis, 656
Clifford, George, 3rd Earl of Cumberland, 134, 146-47, 169, 185, 233, 299, 355, 443, 497, 715

Clifford, Margaret, Countess of Cumberland. See Russell, Lady Margaret
Clifton, Lord, 537
Clifton, Sir Jarvis, 445
Clifton, Thomas, 710, 713, 715
Clinton, Edward Lord (later 16th Earl of Lincoln), 367
Clinton, Henry, 17th Earl of Lincoln, 644, 713
Clinton, Thomas, 266
Clitherow, Margaret, 307, 308
Clothworkers' Company, 582
Clowes, William, 213
Coats of Arms, 18-19
Cobham, 10th Lord. See Brooke, William
Cobham, 11th Lord. See Brooke, Henry
Cobham, Lady. See Brooke, Anne; Brooke, Dorothy
Cockfighting, 425, 444-46
Cogan, Thomas: on marriage, 118; on marital age, 143; on fornicators, 212; on sexual relations, 226, 227; on food, 477; on apparel, 505
Coke, Sir Edward, 149, 181, 306, 323
Coke, Edward, 187
Colchester, Archdeacon's Court at, 414
College of Arms, 695, 697, 722-23, 729, 766
Collinson, Patrick, 41, 308, 397, 406, 466-67, 588
Colse, Peter: on widows, 191
Commissaries' Courts, 677, 678, 679, 691, 748
Common Pleas, Court of, 650, 670, 671, 673
Commonwealth Men, 626, 629, 657, 670
Compton, William, 2nd Lord Compton, 133, 135, 713
Connaught, 135
Constable, Lady, 307
Constable, Sir John, 732
Convocation, 36, 67, 79, 83, 110, 286, 417, 429, 458, 675, 738, 761
Conyers, Cuthbert, 578
Cook, Frances, 168-69
Cooke, Mr., Norfolk minister, 442
Cooke, Sir Anthony: as patron, 57-58; on his funeral, 709; other refs, 308, 344, 345, 367, 585, 732
Cooke, Edmund, 187
Cooke, Elizabeth, 345

Cooper, Thomas: on bishops, 33, 38, 40; on clerical livings, 52; on clerical ignorance, 72; on clerical education, 75; on natural and revealed knowledge, 89; on anticlericalism, 103-104; on marriage, 118; on parental consent in marriage, 157; on wives, 254; on servants, 323; on ambition, 394; on the sabbath, 405; on games, 432; on dancing, 455; on food, 473; on apparel, 504; on apparel of courtiers, 518-19; on poor relief, 569, 572; on landlords, 631; other refs, 78, 258, 418, 469, 751

Cope, Sir Anthony: on religious reform, 54; other refs, 10, 58, 68, 426

Cope, Michel: on sex in marriage, 225, 228; on wives, 305; on surety, 612-13; other refs, 262

Copland, Robert: on minds, 706; on funeral charity, 717

Corbet, Richard, 581

Cordell, Sir William, 581

Cornish, John, 220

Cornwall: Advent, 220, 221; Bodmin, 411, 442; Bokelly St. Kew, 436; Camborne, 442; Ervan, 488; Gulval, 488; Hanappe (Lavappe), 389; Helston, 389; Issey, 442; Kilkhampton, 42; Lanteglos, 220, 221; Lanteglos by Fowey, 442; Ludgvan, 488; Martin, 220; Miller, 389; Minster, 525; North Hill, 488; Philleigh (Filley), 442; Redruth, 220; St. Neot, 488; Stratton, 488; Talland, 220, 488; Treneglos, 488; Wendron, 389; Whitstone, 220; other refs, 94, 96, 151, 220, 221, 424, 442, 480, 514, 547, 563, 636, 677, 733

Cornwallis, William, 323

Council in the Marches of Wales, 417, 644, 714

Council of the North, 299, 712

Council of Trent: on marriage, 116; other refs, 117, 183

Court of Love, The, 527

Court of Venus, The, 527

Courtenay, Sir William, 424

Cousin, Richard, 682

Covel, William: on preaching, 83; on education in the pulpit, 85; on education, 334, 355

Coventry, 187, 228, 425, 453, 454, 578, 581, 625

Coventry, Archdeaconry of, 80

Coventry and Lichfield, Diocese of, 65

Coventry Grammar School, 463

Coverdale, Miles: on oaths, 686, 688; other refs, 157, 706

Coverdale Bible: on usury, 596

Cox, Richard: support of education, 365; on holy days, 420; charity of, 579; on funeral sermons, 704; other refs, 42, 62, 125, 211, 212, 298, 340, 360

Crane, Nicholas, 179

Crane, Thomas, 57

Cranfield, Lionel, 285, 513, 522, 583, 620

Cranmer, Thomas, 529

Crashaw, William: on tithes, 110

Crawfurthe, John, 364

Cremation, 722

Cresswell, Ralph, 183-84

Cressy, David, 334

Creswel, Richard, 196

Crick, Richard, 401

Crockett, R., 351

Crofts, Sir James, 453

Crompton, John, 416, 497

Crompton, Dr. Thomas, 68

Crompton, Thomas (of Yorkshire), 174

Cromwell, Thomas, 328, 384

Crowley, Robert: on bishops, 37; on patrons, 44; on tithes, 104; on chaplains, 297; on wealth, 549; on hospitality, 588; other refs, 10, 705, 706

Croydon (Surrey) Grammar School, 348, 349, 365

Croydon (Surrey) Hospital, 566

Culpepper, John, 73

Cumberland: Carlisle, 165, 168, 638; Cubert, 216; Greystock, 105; Penrith, 168; St. Bees, 168, 365, 578; other refs, 184, 364, 631, 635, 636, 637, 645, 733

Cumberland, 3rd Earl of. *See* Clifford, George

Cumberland, Countess of. *See* Russell, Margaret

Cupper, William, 84

Curteis, Sir Thomas, 720

Curteys, Richard: on clerical livings, 53; on clerical learning, 72, 76; on catechizing, 294; and poor relief, 573; on usury, 601; on engrossing, 627; on landlords, 631; on lawyers, 659; on judges, 663

Curtis, Mark, 51

Dacre, Anne, 150

Dacre, Leonard, 168

Dacre, Richard, 168

Dacre, Thomas, 5th Lord Dacre of Gilsland, 148

Dacre, William, 168

Dacre, William, 4th Lord Dacre of Gilsland, 578

Dacres of Gilsland, 148, 635

Dakins, Arthur, 165, 260, 732

Dakins, Margaret, 164-65, 187, 195, 199, 266. *See also* Hoby, Lady Margaret

Dallison, Robert, 364

Danaeus, 397, 600

Danby, Sir Thomas, 644

Dancing, 187, 189, 208, 411, 417, 418, 424, 425, 427, 429, 441, 454-58, 467, 468, 563, 707, 750

Daniel, Samuel, 344

Dante Alighieri, 529

Danvers, John, 167, 222, 233, 424, 426

Danzig, 625

Darbishire, Thomas, 372

Darcy, Sir Arthur, 578

Darcy, John, 2nd Lord Darcy of Chiche, 174

Darcy, Lady, 727

Darcy, Margaret, 182

Daresbury (Ches.) Grammar School, 367

Darlington (Durham) Grammar School, 365, 367

Darrell, Mary, 165

Davenport, John, 732

Davies, John, 360

Davies, Richard, 26

Davies, Roger, 199

Dawson, Dr., 47

Day, William, 365, 368, 579, 586

Deacon, John: on Puritan experience, 7; on vocation, 382; on weights and measures, 616; on business ethics, 619; on regrating and engrossing, 627; other refs, 409, 646

Deacons, Office of, 575-76, 746-47

Dearth, 473, 483, 568, 574-75, 585, 618, 622-28, 647

Declaration of Sports, 431

Dedham Classis, 141, 180, 204-205, 212, 271, 296, 333, 397, 415, 495, 498, 566, 676, 688

Delegates, Court of, 272, 678

Dell, William, 210

Deloney, Thomas: on marriage, 115; on spouse selection, 137; on marital age, 143; on bastardy, 215; on adultery, 231; on marital relations, 264; on hospitality, 587

Demosthenes, 366

Denbigh: Christ's Hospital, Ruthin, 579

Denbigh Grammar School, 365

Denman, William, 350

Denmark, 370, 625

Denny, Lady Mary, 727

Dent, Arthur: on education in the pulpit, 86; on prostitution, 218; on adultery, 230, 231, 234; on servants, 320, 323; on vocation, 381; on idleness, 385, 386, 389, 390; on food, 474; on apparel, 506, 507, 509; on speech, 523; on wealth, 553; on the poor, 556; on forestalling, 628; on peasants, 632; on swearing, 687; other refs, 85, 605

Depopulation, 637, 638, 640, 642, 643, 644, 645, 646-47

De profundis, 696, 697, 700, 703

Derby, 12th Earl of. *See* Stanley, Edward

Derby, 13th Earl of. *See* Stanley, Henry

Derby, 15th Earl of. *See* Stanley, William

Derby, Countess of. *See* Stanley, Alice

Derbyshire: Dethwick, 719; Elvaston, 466; Little Norton, 166; Morley, 732; Ockbrook, 466; Radbourn, 134, 174, 578, 696; Staveley, 169, 514; Thulston, 466; Tideswell, 730; other refs, 57, 271, 581, 608, 644

Dering, Edward: on social order, 15; on gentility, 20; on bishops, 35, 36, 44; on patrons, 47-48; on nonresidency, 59, 63-64; on pluralism, 61; on clerical ignorance, 78; on preaching, 81; on natural and revealed knowledge, 90; on anticlericalism, 98; on unqualified clergy, 99; attack on Catholic remnants, 100; on tithes, 106; courtship of Anne Locke, 194; on adultery, 230; on parental affection, 279, 282; on children's duties, 284; relations with women, 308; on masters, 318; on education, 329, 353; on the sabbath, 398, 399; on games, 438-39; on the royal court, 443, 444; on dancing, 455; on food, 475; on apparel, 510; on communalism, 572; on lawsuits, 654; on

ecclesiastical courts, 677; other refs, 10-11, 139, 243, 295, 359, 372, 469
Dethick, Sir Gilbert, 288
De Vere, Anne, Countess of Oxford, 311
De Vere, Bridget, 163, 174
De Vere, Edward, 17th Earl of Oxford, 139, 146, 163, 166, 186, 221, 265, 355, 372, 514, 522, 528
De Vere, Elizabeth, 163
De Vere, John, 16th Earl of Oxford, 166, 670
De Vere, Lady Mary, 139
De Vere, Susan, 174
Devereux, Lady Dorothy, 133, 172, 344
Devereux, Penelope. See Rich, Penelope
Devereux, Robert, 19th Earl of Essex, 21, 101, 164, 172, 229, 232, 324, 418, 513, 522, 542, 621, 640
Devereux, Walter, 18th Earl of Essex, 142, 164, 273, 315, 335, 344, 463, 710, 718, 719
Devereux, Walter (son of the preceding), 164, 199, 266, 344
De Vio, Thomas, Cardinal Cajetan, 237
Devon Quarter Sessions, 214, 217, 467
Devonshire: Barnstaple, 418; Colyton, 144, 153, 156, 243; Dean Prior, 138; East Budleigh, 411, 452; Kilmington, 312; North Petherwyn, 209; Northleigh, 257; Plymouth, 276, 581; Tavistock, 453; other refs, 16, 18, 57, 97, 196, 316, 357, 410, 411, 451-52, 466, 467, 515, 521, 565, 609, 629, 636, 733
Dewe, Mr., Cornish minister, 220
D'Ewes, Paul, 324
D'Ewes, Simonds, 245
Dickens, Charles, 386
Digby, Sir Everard, 131, 192, 437
Digby, Lady Mary, 192
Digges, Thomas: on pluralism, 61; on clerical learning, 72; other refs, 5, 514
Dike, Robert, 57
Dilke, Richard, 174
Dios, John: on adultery, 230; on idleness, 387
Disinheritance, 278-79
Divinity (in Universities), 356, 359, 360, 361
Divorce: a mensa et thoro, 267-71; a vinculo matrimonii, 267, 273-74; other refs, 234, 744

Dobbes, Robert: on education, 337; other refs, 94
Dobson, George, 96
Dod, John: on spouse selection, 131; on parental consent in marriage, 159; on sex in marriage, 225; on adultery, 230-31; on breast-feeding, 245; on parental responsibilities, 278; on children's duties, 282; on masters, 316, 318, 319; on servants, 322, 323; on the sabbath, 405; on the theater, 450; on suicide, 533; on beggars, 565, 566; on surety, 613; on oaths, 680, 686; other refs, 646
Dodington, William, 536
Doncaster, Deanery of, 207, 210
Donne, John, 168, 243
Dorset: Blandford Forum, 398, 411; Canford, 382; Marnhull, 47; Poole, 303; other refs, 57, 398, 410, 411, 563, 629
Dorset Quarter Sessions, 398
Douai, 299, 300, 371, 422, 511
Douai Bible, 117-18, 397, 422, 495
Double Standard, 12, 229, 740, 749, 758
Dove, John: on anticlericalism, 103; on adultery, 234; on divorce, 269; on apparel, 503; on usury, 602
Dowirche, Anne, 310
Downes, Andrew, 391
Downham, William: and clerical learning, 78; other refs, 42, 209, 304
Dowryche, Thomas, 286
Drake, Sir Francis: charity of, 581; other refs, 319
Drake, Robert, 176
Drant, Thomas: on food, 472; on apparel, 503, 505; on the apparel of courtiers, 519; on usury, 601; other refs, 85
Drapers' Company, 482
Drinking and Inebriety, 94, 96, 98, 467, 468, 483-90, 750
Drurie, Lady Anne, 309
Drury, Lady, 286
Drury, William, 188
Drywood, William, 442
Dublin, 368
Ducket, Peter, 60
Dudley, 4th Lord. See Sutton, Edward
Dudley, Ambrose, 21st Earl of Warwick: as patron, 55-56; other refs, 61, 186, 357, 417, 452, 597, 732-33

Dudley, Anne, Countess of Warwick: charity of, 585; other refs, 308, 309, 313
Dudley, John, Duke of Northumberland, 46
Dudley, Richard, 168
Dudley, Robert, 14th Earl of Leicester: as patron, 55-56; charity of, 584; other refs, 10, 43, 135-136, 147, 172, 186, 196, 210, 233, 272, 288, 289, 297, 304, 313, 359, 417, 437, 446, 453, 463, 514, 522, 554, 639, 709, 710, 712, 716, 732-33
Dunkirk, France, 370
Dunne, Daniel, 68
Dunster Castle, 147
Du Plessis-Mornay, Philippe, 534
Durdel, William, 442
Durham (county): Billingham, 184; Croxdale, 577; Dinsdale, 577; Gainford, 577; Gateshead, 577; Houghton-le-Spring, 357; Layton, 578; St. Andrew Auckland, 699; Sherborne Hospital, 574; Shincliffe, 234; Sockburn, 364; Stanhope, 366, 565, 584; other refs, 131, 638, 733
Durham (town), 234, 235, 260, 441, 453, 488, 523, 575, 577, 579, 634, 638, 705
Durham, Bishop of. See Tunstall, Cuthbert (1559); Pilkington, James (1561-76); Barnes, Richard (1577-87); Hutton, Matthew (1589-95); Matthew, Tobias (1595-1606)
Durham, Consistory Court at, 333
Durham, Diocese of, 78, 333, 427, 442, 457, 516, 638
Durham Cathedral, 364, 577, 699
Durham Grammar School, 366, 522, 577
Dyer, Edward, 272
Dyer, Sir Thomas, 264
Dyott, Anthony, 304

East India Company, 313
Easte, John: on poor relief, 569-70
Easter, 299, 425, 429, 491, 581, 758
Eaton, Robert, 57
Ecclesiastical Courts, 668, 674-80, 691, 748
Education: spread of, 24; support for, 277-78, 362-69; purpose of, 327-38; extent of, 338-46; of girls, 342-46, 742; the role of masters and tutors, 346-52; the curricula, 352-57, 745; proposals for reform of, 357-62; travel as, 369-73; other refs, 196

Effingham, Lord Howard of. See Howard, Charles; Howard, William
Egerton, Lady, 306
Egerton, Stephen, 505
Egerton, Sir Thomas, 54, 181, 510, 521, 581, 625, 650
Elcocke, Thomas, 209
Elderton, William: on the sabbath, 396; on education, 336
Eliot, Sir Thomas, 239, 355, 477, 529
Elizabeth I: concern for social order, 14; attitude toward bishops, 45; attitude toward pluralism and nonresidency, 67-70; on married clergy, 126; on aristocratic marriages, 171-72; attitude toward the sabbath, 417-18; attitude toward holy days, 429; and recreation, 443; interest in bear and bull-baiting, 446; and the theater, 453; love of dancing, 457-58; love of music, 464; proclamations on apparel, 518; and poor relief, 575; concern with forestalling and regrating, 622, 623, 624-25, 626; and enclosures, 639-40; and funeral pageantry, 711, 729, 735; other refs, 39, 40, 43, 44, 47, 51, 53, 54, 55, 56, 61, 62, 95, 106, 125, 148, 163, 173, 182, 186, 187, 191, 196, 210, 229, 235, 264-65, 279, 289, 307, 332, 344, 358, 367, 371, 388, 415-16, 419, 426, 445, 448, 469, 478, 479, 481, 483, 497, 516, 517, 521, 522, 523, 524, 564, 567, 574, 589, 590, 592, 598, 601, 614, 627, 644, 659, 663, 673, 675, 682, 709, 712, 716, 761, 764, 766
Eltoft, John, 578
Ely, Bishop of. See Cox, Richard (1559-81)
Ely, Diocese of, 77, 80, 211, 212, 340, 525
Embalming, 714-15, 722
Emden, 625
Emerson, Everett, 5
Emmison, F.G., 516
Emott, Alexander, 183
Enclosure, 300, 628, 630, 633, 636-45, 646-47, 668, 763
Engrossing, 622-28
Engrossment, 636-37, 638, 641, 643, 644
Erasmus, Desiderius, 34, 245, 354, 526, 529, 530, 761
Essex: Barking, 221; Barling, 440-41; Barnston, 442; Beauchamp Roding, 457, 488; Billericay, 56; Blackmore, 96; Borley,

371; Braddocks, 302, 527; Braintree, 350; Chadwell, 57; Chafford Hundred, 625; Chelmsford, 57, 439, 488; Coldham, 372; Dedham, 215, 293, 567, 576, 656; Downham, 442, 516; Feering, 536; Felstead, 57, 330, 581; Goldhanger, 152; Great Bardfield, 578; Great Chesterford, 340; Great Dunmow, 516; Greenstead-juxta-Colchester, 488; Halstead, 141-42, 216, 442; Hatfield Peverell, 92; Havering, 57; High Easter, 96, 442; Hinckford, 516; Ilford Hospital, 84; Ingatestone, 439, 516; Laindon, 209; Latchingdon, 442; Leaden Roothing, 97, 209; Leyton, 733; Little Canfield, 442; Little Ilford, 126; Malden, 37, 81, 452; Manningtree, 451; Manuden (Manewden), 441; Moulsham, 585; Much Baddow, 222; Ovington, 496, 654; Pitsea, 608; Radwinter, 48; Ramsey, 654; Rawreth, 209; Rayleigh, 57; Ridgewell, 383; Rochford Hall, 56; Romford, 488, 585, 732; Ruckholt, 139; Shenfield, 440; South Hanningfield, 75; South Shoebury, 86; Springfield, 465; Stansted Mount Fitchet, 383; Terling, 441; Thundersley, 442; Waltham, 585; Walthamstow, 221, 441; West Ham, 221; Wethersfield, 22; Witham, 232; other refs, 6, 56, 73, 94, 96, 97, 210, 220, 228, 296, 319, 332, 335, 345, 435, 439, 440-41, 452, 488, 496, 516, 530, 567, 608, 614-15, 622, 636, 733
Essex, 18th Earl of. See Devereux, Walter
Essex, 19th Earl of. See Devereux, Robert
Essex, Lady, 196-97
Estey, George: on celibacy, 124; on sex in marriage, 225; on divorce, 269; on parental responsibilities, 276; on vocation, 380; on the sabbath, 405; on bear and bull-baiting, 445; on the poor, 556; other refs, 309, 605
Eton College, 347, 348, 364
Eure, Sir William, 593
Eure, William, 2nd Lord, 151, 437, 598
Evans, Lewis: on Anglican bishops, 36; on Elizabethan Protestant clergy, 73; on clerical immorality, 95; on celibacy, 121; on spouse selection, 137
Exchequer, Court of, 222, 574, 609, 668, 669, 671
Exchequer Chamber, Court of, 642, 673-74

Exchequer of Pleas, 106
Excommunication, 211, 212
Exeter, 59, 77, 143, 152, 175, 194, 211, 243, 286, 420, 424, 515, 520, 548, 584, 622, 711
Exeter, Bishop of. See Alley, William (1560-70); Bradbridge, William (1571-78); Woolton, John (1579-94); Babington, Gervase (1595-97)
Exeter Grammar School, 282

Faculties, Court of, 65, 69, 180, 676-77, 678, 679, 691, 748
Fairfax, Sir Nicholas, 182
Fairfax, Sir William: hospitality of, 591; other refs, 478, 479, 480
Fairfax Family, 19
Family of Love: on divorce, 270-71; other refs, 10, 92, 180, 407, 543, 560, 570, 730
Family Size, 243-46
Fasting, 224, 490-99, 575, 738, 750
Faversham (Kent) Grammar School, 367
Favour, John, 57
Feckenham, Forest of, 644
Feckenham, John, 577
Fenner, Dudley: on moderation, 26; on bishops, 41; on parental consent in marriage, 160; on the wedding ring, 185; on the charity of wives, 262; on parental responsibilities, 281; on names, 289-90; on the household, 293, 302; on vocation, 380; on games, 434, 436, 444; on the theater, 448; on music, 462; other refs, 309, 468, 469
Fenton, Geoffrey, 527
Ferdinand, Emperor, 229
Ferrers, Sir John, 19
Ficino, Marsilio, 528
Field, John: on adultery, 230; on chaplains, 298; on the sabbath, 399-400; on the theater, 449; on music, 458-59, 464; on speech, 522, 524; on ecclesiastical courts, 676-77; other refs, 56, 469, 746
Fielding, Lady, 308
Fiennes, Anne, Lady Dacre: charity of, 580
Filmer, Robert, 286
Finch, Henry, 675, 682
Fisher, William, 84
Fishmongers' Company, 720
Fitton, Anne, 150

Fitton, Sir Edward, 147, 150
Fitton, Lady, 167
Fitton, Mary, 209-10
Fitzalan, Henry, 24th Earl of Arundel, 344, 524, 529, 716
Fitzalan, Jane, 346
Fitzalan, Mary, 346
Fitzherbert, John, 333
Fitzwilliam, Sir William (of Cheshire), 311
Fitzwilliam, Sir William (of Northants.), 304, 480, 514, 591
Flanders, 371
Fleetwood, Edward, 61
Fleetwood, William, 66, 152, 439, 524
Fleming, Abraham: on social estates, 26; on vocation, 377; on the sabbath, 400; on music, 461; on literature, 526; on engrossing, 627; on lawsuits, 652
Fleming, Cuthbert, 147-48
Fletcher, John, 351
Fletcher, Mr., Cornish minister, 220
Fletcher, Richard: finances of, 43; on the sabbath, 401; hospitality of, 590; other refs, 191, 535
Flint, 166
Food, 188, 288, 471-83, 715, 750
Foorth, Robert, 297, 592
Football, 425
Forestalling, 622-28, 752
Forman, Simon: and usury, 609; other refs, 73, 145, 233, 324, 350, 423-24, 515, 656
Fornication, 95, 96, 162, 204-13, 461, 744
Fortescue, Sir Francis, 299, 437
Fortescue, Lady Grace, 299
Fortescue, Sir John, 665
Forth, Robert, 260
Foxe, John, 5, 6, 310, 344, 527, 528, 529, 530, 761
France, 214, 233, 257, 311, 313, 329, 370, 371
Freke, Edmund: on rogues and sturdy beggars, 574; other refs, 81, 233, 535
Frescheville, Lady Elizabeth, 196
Frescheville, Frances, 169
Frescheville, Peter: on weights and measures, 614; other refs, 169, 514
Frescheville, Sir Peter, 514
Frewen, John, 60
Frobisher, Martin, 313
Frodsham (Cheshire), Deanery of, 210

Fulbecke, William: on war, 540-41, 543
Fuljambe, Hercules, 271
Fulke, William: on bishops, 35; on tithes, 109; on celibacy, 123, 124, 126, 129; on widows, 192-93; on sex in marriage, 224-25; on marital relations, 254; on divorce, 268; on holy days, 421, 422; on fasting, 492, 498; on speech, 522; on almsgiving, 558; on poor relief, 572, 573; on usury, 604, 611; on ecclesiastical courts, 677; other refs, 309, 605
Fuller, William, 417
Funerals: dinners at, 365, 583, 715, 717, 719-20; sermons at, 495, 704-706; charity at, 578, 579, 717-22; expenses of, 580, 708-16; customs, 696-703; as social pageantry, 722-29, 766; other refs, 19, 178
Fulwood, William: on labor, 392-93; on apparel, 511; other refs, 388
Furneis, Robert, 345
Furnivall, Frederick, 145, 151
Furse, John, 515
Furse, Robert, 138, 148, 302, 316, 357, 521, 558, 609
Furse Family, 18

Gainsborough (Lincs.) Grammar School, 367
Galen, 226, 227
Gamage, Barbara. See Sidney, Lady Barbara
Gamage, John, 164
Gambling: by clergy, 96, 97, 98; other refs, 418, 424, 432-33, 435-38, 439-45 passim, 461, 581, 588
Games, 417, 432-44, 460-61, 760
Gardiner, John: on marriage, 118
Gardiner, Samuel: on prostitution, 218; on food, 472, 473; on fasting, 490, 491, 497; on apparel, 504; on wealth, 553; on almsgiving, 560, 561; on beggars, 566; on usury, 602; on weights and measures, 616; on engrossing, 627; other refs, 225
Garforthe, William, 260
Gargrave, Sir Cotton, 285
Gawdy, Bassingbourne (the elder), 182, 418
Gawdy, Bassingbourne (the younger), 612
Gawdy, Philip, 452, 518, 612, 620, 651
Gee, Alexander: on the sabbath, 400
Gellius, Aulus, 353
Geneva, 266, 684, 685

Geneva Bible: on social order, 15; on moderation, 26; on bishops, 34-35; on natural and revealed knowledge, 88-89, 90; anticlericalism in, 100; on tithes, 108; on marriage, 118; on celibacy, 123, 124, 127; on spouse selection, 138, 139; on parental consent in marriage, 157; on widows, 192; on premarital sex, 207; on fornication, 208, 212; on prostitution, 218; on sex in marriage, 224; on adultery, 230, 233-34; on marital relations, 252-53, 254; on divorce, 267-68; on parental responsibilities, 274-75; on children's duties, 283; on the household, 292; on masters, 314-15; on servants, 321, 324; on vocation, 378, 382; on idleness, 384; on labor, 392; on ambition, 394; on the sabbath, 397, 407; on dancing, 454; on apparel, 502; on speech, 520; on suicide, 533; on war, 541; on wealth, 549-53 *passim*; on the poor, 554, 555; on almsgiving, 557-62 *passim*, 565; on beggars, 566; on communalism, 570; on hospitality, 587; on usury, 596; on surety, 612; on weights and measures, 615-16; on business practices, 617; on forestalling and regrating, 626; on lawsuits, 651; on judges, 662-63; on justice, 670; on oaths, 683; on funerals, 696; other refs, 707, 739

Gent, Thomas, 624

Gentility, 19-20

George, Charles and Katherine, 225, 255, 382, 549, 596

Gerard, Dame Jane, 174, 709

Gerard, John: on games, 437; on literature, 527-28; on suicide, 531; other refs, 192, 238, 241, 278, 299, 371, 464, 671

Gerard, Thomas, 299

Germany, 257

Gesner, Conrad, 212

Gests of Scroggin, 527

Gibbens, Nicholas: on celibacy, 127-28; on parental consent in marriage, 157-58; on marital relations, 255; on war, 539, 540

Gibbon, Charles: on natural and revealed knowledge, 90; on spouse selection, 134; on parental consent in marriage, 155, 160; on parental responsibilities, 276; on vocation, 382; on food, 474, 475; on apparel, 510; on the poor, 549; on

usury, 606-607, 611; on surety, 613; on lawsuits, 652; other refs, 646

Gibson, George, 181

Gibson, John: on war, 542

Gibson, Leonard: on premarital sex, 207

Gibson, Richard, 589

Gibson, Thomas, 84

Gifford, George: on preaching, 81; on learning in the pulpit, 86; on natural and revealed knowledge, 90, 91; attacks sectaries, 92; on immoral clergy, 93, 94; on careless clergy, 98; on parental consent in marriage, 160; on adultery, 234; on chaplains, 297; on education, 353; on idleness, 390; on the sabbath, 400; on holy days, 421; on food, 474; on almsgiving, 562; on business practices, 618; other refs, 84, 191, 309, 527, 632

Gilbert, George, 372

Gilbert, Sir Humphrey: proposed academy of, 361-62; on lawsuits, 650; other refs, 221, 528

Gilbert, Sir John, 424

Gilby, Anthony: on bishops, 35, 41; on preaching, 81; on clerical education, 91; on the wedding ring, 185; on adultery, 234; on godparents, 289; on the sabbath, 399; on fasting, 494; on ecclesiastical courts, 674, 676-77; on oaths, 688; on funeral customs, 700; on wakes, 707

Gilpin, Bernard: on education, 357-58

Glamorganshire: St. Donat's, 182; other refs, 52, 323

Glaseor, William, 198

Gloucester, 213, 575, 584

Gloucester, Bishop of. *See* Cheyney, Richard (1562-79)

Gloucester, Diocese of, 80

Gloucestershire: Beverston Castle, 280; Siddington, 182; Tetbury, 427; Upton, 223; Yate, 424; other refs, 18, 584, 733

Godparents, 289

Golding, Arthur, 529

Golding, Lady Elizabeth, 308

Goldringe, Mr., Essex minister, 209

Goodman, Christopher, 584, 705, 706

Goodman, Gabriel: support of education, 365; charity of, 579; other refs, 574

Googe, Barnaby, 165

Gorges, Sir Arthur, 135

Gorges, William, 487

Gosson, Stephen: on prostitution, 219; on education, 353, 360-61; on games, 435; on dancing, 455; on the theater, 449; on war, 542; other refs, 85, 469, 746

Gouge, William, 541, 543

Grammar Schools, 347-48, 356, 367-68

Gray, Dyonis, 615

Gray, Hugh: on games, 436; other refs, 366

Gray, Sir Ralph, 307

Greaves, Mr., preacher, 102

Greaves, Paul, 524

Greenaway, Samuel, 309

Greenham, Richard: on tithes, 105; on celibacy, 123; on spouse selection, 139, 141; on parental consent in marriage, 160; on widows, 198-99; on premarital sex, 205; on fornication, 208; on marital relations, 256; on home discipline, 275; on parental responsibilities, 277, 280, 281; on parental affection, 279; on children's duties, 284; on the household, 301; on masters, 316; on education, 329; on vocation, 378, 383; on the sabbath, 401-405 passim, 408, 409; on holy days, 419, 421; on games, 435; on food, 474; on speech, 523; on suicide, 533; on wealth, 552; on almsgiving, 560; on poor relief, 576; other refs, 10, 29, 85, 416, 745, 762

Greenwood, Henry, 57

Greenwood, John: anticlericalism of, 101; on weddings, 179; on adultery, 234; on divorce, 270; on educational reform, 360; on holy days, 422; on oaths, 690

Gregory Nazianzen, 310

Grenville, Humphrey: on poor relief, 568-69

Gresham, Sir Thomas: charity of, 583; other refs, 174, 175, 210, 644, 718, 728, 729, 731, 735

Gresham College, 366

Greville, Sir Fulke, 446

Grey, Arthur, 14th Lord Grey of Wilton: as patron, 56; other refs, 418, 528, 531, 705

Grey, Lady Catherine, 139, 172, 209, 273

Grey, Frances, Duchess of Suffolk, 708

Grey, Henry, 16th Earl of Kent, 644

Grey, Lady Mary, 273, 308

Grey, Susan, Countess of Kent, 172, 197, 308

Grey, Sir Thomas, 709

Grey, William, 333

Grindal, Anne, 168

Grindal, Edmund: on dealings with Puritans, 6; on advowsons, 50; on lay patronage, 51-52; on nonresidency, 65; homily of, 79; on sermons, 79; on the double standard, 229-30; on literacy, 333; support of education, 365; on holy days, 427; on the theater, 447, 450; on music, 460; on fasting, 491; on poor relief, 573; charity of, 578, 586; on usury, 608; and ecclesiastical courts, 676; on his funeral, 699; other refs, 4, 7, 41, 74, 85, 95, 168, 183, 209, 298, 306, 340, 351, 360, 388, 413, 441, 468, 469, 503, 519, 574, 589, 631, 738, 746

Grindal, Robert, 168

Grosvenor, Richard, 702

Gaulter, Rudolph, 132, 138, 161, 330-31

Guernsey, 103, 235, 388

Guest, Edmund: charity of, 579; other refs, 535, 730, 733

Guildford, Henry, 299

Guildford (Surrey) School, 367-68

Gunpowder Plot, 332

Guy of Warwick, 527

Haberdashers' Company, 56, 585

Hackney, Richard, 427

Hailes, Mr., Essex minister, 232

Hair, P. E. H., 205

Hake, Edward: on clerical ignorance, 73; on premarital sex, 207; on prostitution, 219; on parental responsibilities, 277; on education, 343, 347; on the sabbath, 409; on apparel, 509; on dancing, 455; on music, 459; on hospitality, 589; on usury, 604; on forestalling, 622, 627; on enclosure, 643; on jusitce for the poor, 667; on legal problems, 670; other refs, 214

Hale, Robert, 658

Hales, John, 463

Halifax (Yorks.) Grammar School, 367

Hall, Basil, 7

Hall, Edward, 529

Hall, John, 95

Haller, William, 5

Halsall, Edward, 583

Halsall, Richard, 579

Hampshire: Andover, 102; East Wellow, 102; Odiham, 168; Tidworth, 294; Woolston, 466; other refs, 734

Hampton Court, 429, 443

Hancock, Thomas, 176

Harding, Thomas: on social background of the clergy, 74; on Anglican ministers, 88; other refs, 761

Harman, Thomas: on rogues and sturdy beggars, 563-64; on poor relief, 573; on funeral charity, 717

Harn, John, 368

Harrington, Sir John, 355

Harrington, Lady Lucy, 172, 347

Harris, Serjeant Thomas, 236

Harris, Thomas, 69

Harrison, Robert: on patrons, 47; anticlericalism of, 101; on ecclesiastical courts, 678; other refs, 179, 289, 526

Harrison, William: on clerical stipends, 48; on funeral sermons, 704; other refs, 418, 521, 705, 706

Harrow Grammar School, 364

Hart, John, 340

Hart, Sir Percival, 463

Harvey, Gabriel, 529

Harward, Simon: on private worship, 298; on servants, 323; other refs, 84

Hastings, Sir Francis: as patron, 57; charity of, 585; other refs, 258, 303, 318, 395, 468, 486, 523, 552, 634, 645, 656

Hastings, George, 21st Earl of Huntingdon, 286, 443, 522, 712-13

Hastings, Henry, 20th Earl of Huntingdon: as patron, 57; charity of, 584; hospitality of, 592; funeral of, 712-13; other refs, 131, 136, 164-65, 166, 170, 177, 232, 263, 265, 293-94, 308, 316, 331, 344, 349, 351, 354, 365, 366, 367, 368, 395, 552, 634, 644-45, 710, 714, 756

Hastings, Henry, nephew of the preceding, 265

Hastings, Lady Katherine, 263

Hastings, Lady Magdalen, 258, 318, 585

Hatton, Christopher, 10, 19, 23, 54, 67, 158, 165, 306, 426, 523, 650, 662, 667, 724, 727

Hawes, Sir James, 450

Hawkshead (Lancs.) Grammar School, 365

Haylles, Edmund, 168

Haytour, Thomas, 97

Heath, Geoffrey, 232

Heidelberg, 346, 397

Heigham, William, 278

Heneage, Lady Elizabeth, 280

Henry VI, 507

Henry VIII, 46, 105, 229, 268, 590

Herbert, Lady Anne, 185

Herbert, Anne, Countess of Pembroke, 306

Herbert, Henry, 21st Earl of Pembroke: charity of, 580; on his funeral, 702; other refs, 135, 141, 142, 163, 174, 185, 229, 262, 287, 731

Herbert, Mary (Sidney), Countess of Pembroke, 135, 141, 163, 193, 255, 310, 311, 313, 346, 463

Herbert, William, 20th Earl of Pembroke, 417, 680, 718

Herbert, William, future 22nd Earl of Pembroke, 142

Hereford, 578, 579, 608

Hereford, Bishop of. See Scory, John (1559-85); Westfaling, Herbert (1586-1602)

Hereford, Diocese of, 340, 420, 427, 676

Hereford Grammar School, 365

Herefordshire; Bromyard, 37; Leominster, 578; Sutton, 424; other refs, 80, 636, 639

Hergest, William: on celibacy, 123; on premarital sex, 208; on sex in marriage, 226; on wives, 305; on labor, 393-94; on food, 482

Herodotus, 529

Hertford, 9th Earl of. See Seymour, Edward

Hertford, 10th Earl of. See Seymour, William

Hertford Castle, 478

Hertfordshire: Aldenham, 410; Bovingdon, 262; Cheshunt, 580, 585, 591; Hadham, 578; Hitchin, 221, 410; Hoddesdon (Hogsdon), 219; Quixott, 140; Redbourn, 585; St. Albans, 584, 585; Standon, 187; Watford, 584; Welwyn, 108; other refs, 57, 182, 535

Hesiod, 140

Hesketh, George, 94, 654

Hesketh, Sir Thomas, 304

Hester, John, 213

Hevingham, Sir Arthur, 463

Hewet, Sir William, 583

Heydon, Sir William, 278

Hickman, Thomas, 655

Hicks, Sir Michael, 138, 140, 167, 256, 273-74, 356, 457, 463, 597, 609, 733

Higgin, George, 76, 232

Higgins, John: on education, 327

High Commission, Court of, 43, 83, 95, 96, 149, 181, 183, 184, 222, 231, 233, 234, 357, 370, 399, 400, 413, 462, 581, 582, 600, 611, 649, 654, 678-79, 681, 682, 686, 690, 691, 692

Hill, Adam: on pluralism, 62; anticlerical remarks, 98; on education, 363; on idleness, 386; on apparel, 502, 503-504, 507; other refs, 406

Hill, Alice, 584

Hill, Christopher, 3, 140, 300, 405, 408, 414, 421, 428, 525, 575, 634

Hill, Robert, 270

Hilles, Richard, 194, 310

Historie of Hamlet, 529

Hoby, Lady Margaret, 197, 238, 263, 264, 296, 302, 308-15 *passim*, 344, 346, 387, 418, 436-37, 462, 488, 585, 592-93, 609, 716, 732. *See also* Dakins, Margaret

Hoby, Sir Thomas, 527

Hoby, Sir Thomas Posthumous, 164-65, 187, 195, 199, 263, 304, 437, 592-93, 656, 732

Hock Monday and Tuesday, 425

Hodeson, Christopher, 644

Hogrefe, Pearl, 156

Holcroft, Sir John, 175

Holdsworth, Richard, 57

Holinshed, Raphael, 529, 562, 633

Holland, Henry: on parental responsibilities, 280; on the household, 301; on the theater, 450; on fasting, 492, 493; on literature, 527; on wealth, 550-51; other refs, 225, 469

Holland, Seth, 728

Holland, Thomas: on tithes, 109; on vocation, 382; on usury, 602

Holles, Denzil: charity of, 581; other refs, 169, 174, 233, 345, 633, 643-44

Holles, Frescheville, 169, 183

Holles, Gervas, 169, 514

Holles, John, 169

Holles, Sir William: and social order, 22; hospitality of, 591; other refs, 134, 169, 280, 317, 319, 453, 514, 732

Hollingsworth, T. H., 243

Holme, John, 60

Holte, Robert, 175

Holy Days, 403, 419-30, 745-46, 757-58

Homilies, 81, 398, 458

Homosexuality, 221-22

Honeywood, Mary, 243, 308

Hooke, Christopher: on childbearing, 242; on poor relief, 568, 569, 572; other refs, 290, 494, 751

Hooker, Joan, 199

Hooker, John, 609

Hooker, Richard: on social order, 23-24; on pluralism, 62; on nonresidency, 64-65; on clerical learning, 76-77; on preaching, 82-83, 84; on natural and revealed knowledge, 88; on the wedding ring, 184; on wives, 255; on male superiority, 255-56; on fathers, 275; on ceremonies, 287; on catechizing, 294; on music, 460; on wealth, 549, 551, 553; on the poor, 555; on ecclesiastical courts, 679, 680; other refs, 85, 87, 199, 260, 368, 748

Hooker, Thomas, 10

Hopkin, Richard, 528

Horace, 354, 356

Horncastle (Lincs.) Grammar School, 367

Horne, Robert: marriage portions, 43; on clerical income, 51; on music, 460; charity of, 579; on legal reform, 670-71; other refs, 93, 365, 469, 521, 529, 706, 746

Horsey, Sir Edward, 233, 454, 591

Horsman, Edward, 428

Hoskins, Anthony, 299

Hoskins, Peter, 634

Hoskins, W. G., 383

Hospitality, 575, 587-94, 639, 647, 720-21, 735-36, 751-52

Hospitals, 575, 577-85 *passim*

Houghton Grammar School, 366

Houlet, Ann, 256

Household: size of, 303-304

Household Order, 301-305, 739, 744-45

Howard, Catherine (daughter of Thomas Lord Howard of Walden), 150

Howard, Queen Catherine, 268

Howard, Charles, Lord Howard of Effingham, 438, 451, 712

Howard, Lady Frances, 18, 133, 139, 173, 181, 265, 536

Howard, Henry, 2nd Viscount Howard of Bindon, 135

Howard, Henry, Earl of Northampton, 255

Howard, Henry, Earl of Surrey, 344, 352

Howard, Jane, 344, 346

Howard, Margaret, Duchess of Norfolk, 699, 726

Howard, Philip, 148, 150, 635

Howard, Thomas, 1st Lord of Walden, 150

Howard, Thomas, 1st Viscount Howard of Bindon, 181, 536, 710

Howard, Thomas, 2nd Duke of Norfolk, 710

Howard, Thomas, 3rd Duke of Norfolk, 317, 715

Howard, Thomas, 4th Duke of Norfolk, 148, 150, 304, 479, 635, 699, 723

Howard, William, 1st Lord Effingham, 417

Howard, William (son of the 4th Duke of Norfolk), 148

Howleglass, 527

Howson, John: on clerical income, 49; on clerical education, 50; on episcopal appointments, 55; on the sabbath, 406, 408; on holy days, 419, 421; on hospitality, 588; other refs, 269, 751

Hughes, William, 590

Huguenots, 587

Hull, Suffragan Bishop of. *See* Pursglove, Robert (1538-79)

Humanism, 119-20, 245, 280, 328

Humphrey, Laurence: on charitable giving, 548; other refs, 5, 10, 84, 266

Hunsdon, 1st Lord. *See* Carey, Henry

Hunsdon, 2nd Lord. *See* Carey, George

Hunt, Thomas, 60

Hunter, Sir Adam, 488

Huntingdon, 20th Earl of. *See* Hastings, Henry

Huntingdon, 21st Earl of. *See* Hastings, George

Huntingdon, Archdeacon's Court at, 414, 429

Huntingdonshire: Clowis Cross Drain, Peterborough, 574

Hurstfield, Joel, 11, 145, 151

Hutchinson, William, 102

Hutton, Matthew: on bishops, 40; support of education, 365; charity of, 578; on usury, 600-601, 603, 611, 646; on Huntingdon's funeral, 713; other refs, 359, 368, 608, 747

Idleness, 383-91, 434-35, 463, 467, 641, 741

Incest, 222

Industry and Ambition, 391-95, 741

Infanticide, 215

Ingleby, Sir William, 710, 713, 715

Injunctions (1559), 458

Inns of Court: Gray's Inn, 204, 364, 540; Inner Temple, 184, 578, 681; Lincoln's Inn, 370, 578, 658; Middle Temple, 20, 342; other refs, 218, 219, 335, 341-42, 347, 399, 433, 509, 650, 728

Interlude of Johan the Evangelist, The, 231

Interludes, 97, 208, 422, 447-51 *passim*

Ipswich Grammar School, 337, 349

Ireland: schools in, 368-69; other refs, 547, 598

Ireland, David, 209

Ireland, John, 350

Ironmongers' Company, 719

Isham, Henry, 597, 608, 644

Isham, John, 597, 609, 644

Isle of Ely, 271

Isle of Wight: Nunwell, 139; other refs, 197-98, 233, 414, 454, 476, 591, 640, 641

Isle of Wight Quarter Sessions, 220

Isocrates, 354, 356, 526

Italy, 371

Jackson, Nicholas, 96

Jackson, Thomas: on clerical learning, 76

Jacques, Richard, 65

James I, 431, 464, 469, 729, 766

James, Francis, 48, 68-69

James, William: on education, 358; on depopulation, 638; other refs, 640

Jermyn, Frances, 397

Jerome, 82, 504, 603

Jervaux Abbey, 644

Jesuits, 10, 39, 192, 284, 285, 291, 298, 299, 307, 314, 327, 332, 371, 372, 437-38, 476, 495, 511

Jewel, John: on bishops, 41, 42; on clerical income, 51; on pluralism and nonresidency, 58, 64; on clerical ignorance, 72; on the social background of the clergy, 74; on clerical education, 75-76; homilies of, 79; on natural and revealed knowledge, 88, 91; on celibacy, 119, 128; on prostitution, 122; on fornication, 208; on prostitution, 218; on parental

responsibilities, 276, 278; on education, 358, 362-63; on idleness, 385; on clerical labor, 389-90; on beggars, 565; on poor relief, 573; on usury, 599-600, 603, 611; on weights and measures, 616; on lawsuits, 652, 653; on funerals, 698; other refs, 85, 212, 302, 310, 602, 604, 606, 614, 657, 706, 747, 761
John XXI, Pope, 241, 242
Johnson, Ben, 443
Johnson, Francis: on divorce, 270; other refs, 179, 293
Johnson, James, 117, 542
Johnston, Robert, 365
Jones, Richard: on the sabbath, 400; other refs, 592, 720
Jones, Walter, 428
Jopson, Robert, 174
Jordan, W. K., 363, 364, 548, 573, 576, 580, 583, 585, 594, 756
Judges, Conduct of, 661-65
Julius II, Pope, 74
Junius, Franciscus, 397
Jurdan, Mr., Norfolk minister, 232
Justice and the Poor, 665-69

Kay, George, 428
Kelke, Roger, 579
Kellison, Matthew: on celibacy, 120-21; on premarital sex, 207; on labor, 392
Kempe, George, 658
Kempe, Peter: on poor relief, 569; other refs, 513
Kempe, William: on parental responsibilities, 276, 277, 281; on education, 334, 336; other refs, 462
Kennion, Robert, 427
Kent: Boughton Malherbe, 437; Charing, 243; Chatham Hospital, 574; Cobham, 580, 702, 712; Cranbrook, 26, 401, 424; Dover, 332; Eastling, 74; Eastwell, 5; Faversham, 526, 530; Hackington, 582, 732; Greenwich, 429; Lewisham, 429, 457; Maidstone, 19, 385, 482, 486, 515, 526, 530, 564, 565; Penshurst, 714, 724; Pluckley, 10; Sandwich, 344, 348, 367, 388, 566; Sittingbourne, 83; Sutton Valence, 582; Tunbridge, 27; Wye, 76; other refs, 17, 42, 132, 165, 187, 196, 217, 266, 273, 341, 363, 526, 582, 623, 636, 657, 715, 733

Kent, 16th Earl of. See Grey, Henry
Kent, Countess of. See Grey, Susan
Kent Quarter Sessions, 389, 482, 486, 515
Kethe, William: on the sabbath, 398, 409, 411
Ketle, Edward, 75
Key, Francis, 522
Key, Margaret, 522
Keys, Thomas, 273
Kiechel, Samuel, 512
Killigrew, Catherine, 308, 311
King, John: on clerical stipends, 48; on education in the pulpit, 87; on natural and revealed knowledge, 88; on anticlericalism, 103; on tithes, 109; on vocation, 383; on games, 433; on suicide, 532; on beggars, 566; on usury, 602; on business ethics, 617; on engrossing, 627; on landlords, 631; other refs, 704
King's Bench, Court of. See Queen's Bench
King's School, Coventry, 453
Kingsmill, Andrew: on spouse selection, 130, 131, 138; on the wedding ring, 185; on divorce, 269
Kingston, Elizabeth, 169, 183, 344-45
Kingston, John (friend of the Holles family), 169, 344-45, 514
Kingston, John (gentleman of the horse), 136
Kirkby Stephen (Westmorland) Grammar School, 367
Knell, Thomas: on almsgiving, 560
Knewstub, John: on social behavior, 22; on moderation, 27; on the sabbath, 399; on usury, 604; on business ethics, 619; other refs, 84, 309, 646
Knollys, Sir Francis: on bishops, 39-40, 44; on pluralism and nonresidency, 67; other refs, 186, 357, 681, 682
Knollys, Lady Katherine, 310, 710, 711
Knollys, Lettice, 210
Knollys, Sir William, 209
Knowledge, Natural and Revealed, 88-92
Knox, John, 139, 194, 255, 292, 539
Knyvett, Lady Ann, 309, 387
Knyvett, Edmund, 668
Knyvett, Sir Thomas, 309
Kytson, Sir Thomas, 463

Lacy, John, 350
Laighton, Lady, 308

Laing, Richard, 65

Lamb, William: charity of, 582; other refs, 335, 586, 718

Lambarde, William: on moderation, 28; on poverty, 547; other refs, 217, 242, 385, 389, 482, 486, 515, 564, 565

Lambert, John, 689

Lambert, Walter, 671

Lambeth Conference (1584), 307

Lambeth Palace, 101

Lambeth Palace Library, 389

Lancashire: Ashton under Lyne, 78, 215, 639; Balderstone, 183; Bickerstaffe, 713; Bispham, 60; Blackburn, 149, 151, 208; Blackley, 48; Blainsborough, 332; Bolton, 61, 149, 625; Bury, 150, 592, 720; Claughton, 442; Clayton, 577; Clitheroe, 349; Colne, 151; Dean, 96; Eccles, 61; Foxdenton, 175; Garstang, 217, 411; Halsall, 94, 579, 654, 668; High Leigh, 47; Huyton, 49; Kirkby, 97; Latham Hall, 724, 726; Leigh, 57, 198; Liverpool, 180, 583; Manchester, 57, 696; Middleton, 365; Moore Hall, 262; Oldham, 61, 278; Ormskirk, 49, 724, 731; Pendleton, 411; Poulton, 60, 61; Prescot, 270, 331; Preston, 152, 217, 411; Ribchester, 488; Rochdale, 57, 102, 277, 365, 453, 530; Rufford, 418; Salford, 411; Singleton, 49; Standish, 57, 61, 205; Streetford, 49; Stubley, 175; Warrington, 150; Warton, 365; Warton Hospital, 578; Whalley, 96; Wigan, 61, 217, 639; Winwick, 57, 60, 61, 181, 371; Withenshaw, 198, 592; Woodplumpton, 217; other refs, 48, 49, 57, 59, 60, 61, 78, 80, 83, 94, 96, 102, 184, 215, 217, 229, 298, 304, 323, 331, 363, 365, 410, 413-14, 419, 464, 528, 577, 609, 636, 637, 668, 671

Lancashire Quarter Sessions, 220, 410-11, 440, 445, 625, 639

Landlords and Tenants, 628-36

Langworth, Richard, 725, 726

Lant, Thomas, 309

Laslett, Peter, 151, 195, 204, 205, 206

Latimer, Hugh, 64, 528

Latimer, Lady. See Nevill, Lucy

Laud, William, 52, 233, 692

Lawrence, Edward, 176

Lawrence, George, 176

Lawson, Dorothy, 315

Lawson, Roger, 315

Lawsuits, 645, 650-57

Laxton, Lady Jane, 608-609

La Zouche, Edward, 11th Lord Zouche, 308

Leake, Sir Francis, 644

Leche, Rafe, 696

Lectureships, 81, 83

Ledsham, Henry, 537

Lee, Sir Henry, 176, 452, 732

Lee, Richard (of Langley), 275

Lee, Richard (of Leigh, Lancs.), 198

Lee, Robert, 324

Legal Ethics, 657-61

Legal Reform, Demands for, 669-74

Legard, John, 136

Legh, John, 173, 609

Legh, Thomas, 47, 592

Leicester: St. Ursala's Hospital, 351; other refs, 152, 293-94, 296, 351, 366, 411, 412, 414-15, 439, 446, 451, 487, 535, 547, 567, 584, 615, 621, 625, 637

Leicester, 14th Earl of. See Dudley, Robert

Leicester, Archdeaconry of, 78, 80, 206

Leicester Grammar School, 331, 349, 351, 354, 355, 356, 366, 756

Leicestershire: Ashby de la Zouch, 35, 41, 331, 713; Cranoe, 427, Great Wigston, 715; Kirkby Mallory, 174; Loughborough, 57; Medbourne, 47; Sheepy, 61, 97; other refs, 57, 206, 213, 366, 419, 498, 585, 637

Leigh, Valentine: on education, 334; on games, 432

Leigh, William, 57

Leighton, Alexander, 541, 543

Lemnie, Levine: on sexual relations, 226-27; on infertility, 239; on male superiority, 256

Lent, 491, 495, 497

Lever, Thomas: on the rich, 554; and the Sherborne Hospital, 574; other refs, 453

Levit, Mr., Essex minister, 209

Lewes, Archdeaconry of, 55, 77

Lewes, Richard: on patrons, 45; on idleness, 385; on justice for the poor, 666

Lewkenor, Edward, 10, 46

Lewknor, Edmund, 299

Leyland, Sir Thomas, 710, 732

Liber Cleri (1585), 73

Lichfield, Bishop of. *See* Bentham, Thomas (1560-79) Overton, William (1580-1609)
Lichfield, Diocese of, 340
Lily, William, 351
Lincoln, 49, 365, 412, 426, 452
Lincoln, 17th Earl of. *See* Clinton, Henry
Lincoln, Bishop of. *See* Bullingham, Nicholas (1560-71); Cooper, Thomas (1571-84); Chaderton, William (1595-1608)
Lincoln, Diocese of, 59, 65, 73, 77
Lincoln and Stowe, Archdeaconry of, 78, 80
Lincoln Cathedral, 364, 473
Lincoln Common Council, 452
Lincolnshire: Arthorp, 197; Bamburgh, 190; Glentworth, 583; Grantham, 627, 642; Great Grimsby, 183; Haydor, 578; Irby, 169, 233, 345, 581, 633, 643; Stamford, 412, 569, 581, 699; Stickford, 266; Tattershall, 60; Thorpe near Wainfleet, 597; Welbourn, 21; other refs, 426, 507, 514, 535, 577, 605, 637
Literacy, 328, 333-34, 738
Literature, 350, 353-57 *passim*, 525-31, 751
Livery, 316-17
Livy, 355
Llandaff, 21
Llandaff, Diocese of, 49
Lloyd, Humphrey, 241
Locke, Anne, 139, 194, 199, 310, 528, 531
Locke, Henry, 194, 260
Locke, John, 543
Locke, Sir William, 289
Lodge, Thomas: on idleness, 383; on ambition, 394-95; on speech, 524; on usury, 601-602; on judges, 665; other refs, 115
Loftus, Adam, 244
Lollards, 419
London: Blackfriars, 181, 186, 696; Charing Cross, 266; Christ Church, Newgate, 139; Christ's Hospital, 218, 262, 344, 398, 445, 463, 547, 579, 582, 584; Great St. Bartholomew's, 732; Great St. Helen's, Bishopsgate, 698, 732; Guildhall, 188, 549; St. Andrew-in-the-Wardrobe, 183; St. Andrew's, Holborn, 48; St. Anne's, Blackfriars, 46; St. Antholin's Budge Row, 230; St. Augustine, Paul's Wharf, 554; St. Bartholomew's

Hospital, 213, 579; St. Botolph's, 309; St. Botolph without Aldgate, 215, 223, 531; St. Bride's, Fleet Street, 225; St. Clement Danes, 64, 370, 450; St. Dionis Backchurch, 16; St. Dunstan in the East, 8, 196; St. Dunstan in the West, 370; St. Giles without Cripplegate, 37, 269, 288, 306, 337; St. James Clerkenwell, 92; St. James, Cripplegate, 582; St. Margaret Lothbury, 56; St. Martin, Ludgate, 102; St. Mary Abchurch, 95; St. Mary Aldermary, 103, 399-400; St. Mary Woolnoth, 415; St. Michael Bassishaw, 583; St. Nicholas Acon, 109; St. Paul's, 38, 43, 60, 152, 208, 232, 235, 257, 423, 461, 494, 715, 716, 731, 732; St. Peter's, 583; St. Peter's Cornhill, 287, 701; St. Peter's, Paul's Wharf, 50; St. Sepulchre, 102, 536; St. Thomas' Hospital, 213; Savoy Hospital, 574, 589; Smithfield, 179; Temple, 10, 429; other refs, 17, 59, 80, 137, 145, 152, 153, 174, 176, 179, 184, 187, 188, 194, 197, 211, 215, 216, 218, 220, 221, 222, 228, 235, 242, 243, 260, 263, 282, 285, 303, 306, 307, 312, 317, 324, 336, 344, 361, 363, 370, 383, 386, 388-89, 393, 397, 399, 402, 412, 416, 417, 423, 425, 433, 437, 439, 444, 447, 448, 449, 450, 451, 452, 453, 455, 463, 464, 472, 480, 481, 492, 497, 514, 517-18, 524, 530, 535, 536, 537, 547, 548, 563, 564, 567, 568, 573, 576, 578, 579, 580, 581, 582, 583, 584, 585, 598-99, 601, 609, 610, 615, 617, 620, 621, 623, 624, 630, 650, 668, 670, 672, 695, 704, 705, 706, 715, 718, 719, 720-21, 727-28, 732, 757
London, Archdeaconry of, 488
London, Bishop of. *See* Grindal, Edmund (1559-70); Sandys, Edwin (1570-77); Aylmer, John (1577-94); Fletcher, Richard (1594-96); Bancroft, Richard (1597-1604)
London, Diocese of, 56, 204, 290, 372, 427, 516, 676, 691
London Common Council, 450
Lords of Misrule, 423-24, 427
Louvain, 4, 36, 73, 88, 116, 280, 371, 372, 574, 607
Lowe, Peter, 213
Lucas, Elizabeth, 313, 346

Lucas, John, 444
Lucian, 526
Lumley, John, 6th Lord Lumley, 165-66, 167, 529, 531
Lumley, Lady, 16, 258, 345, 718
Lupton, Thomas: on almsgiving, 557; on usury, 604; on landlords, 632
Luther, Martin, 161, 527, 528, 529
Lutton, Edward, 658
Luttrell, George, 147
Luxemburg, 370
Lynche, William, 457, 488
Lyttelton, Gilbert, 285-86
Lyttleton, Elizabeth, 170
Lyttleton, Sir John, 170, 264

Machiavelli, Niccolò, 109, 529
Machyn, Henry, 220, 222, 282, 324, 344, 698, 701, 714, 722
Mad Men of Gotam, 527
Maddoxe, Richard, 84-85
Madoxe, John, 360
Magna Carta, 678, 682
Maidstone Grammar School, 335
Mainard, Richard, 220
Mainwaring, Roger, 174, 732
Mallett, Francis, 365, 579
Malory, Richard, 242
Manchester, 78, 181, 182, 212, 298, 411, 445
Manchester, Deanery of, 61
Manchester College, 49, 61
Manchester Collegiate Church, 57
Manchester Grammar School, 299, 341, 349, 351, 366, 445, 505
Manners, Edward, 5th Earl of Rutland, 131, 136, 163, 174, 186, 367, 369, 580, 710, 711-12, 713, 718, 720, 727
Manners, Elizabeth, 145, 174
Manners, Henry, 4th Earl of Rutland, 417
Manners, John, 6th Earl of Rutland, 367, 580, 591-92, 709, 712, 727
Manners, Margaret, Countess of Rutland, 714, 727
Manners, Roger, 135
Manners, Roger, 7th Earl of Rutland, 331, 443, 514
Manning, John, 141
Manninge, James, 442
Manningham, John: on social mobility, 20-21; on Paul's Cross sermons, 84; on legal reform, 670; other refs, 4, 177-78, 182, 222, 266, 657
Mansfield, Sir Richard, 696-97
Manwood, Sir Roger: charity of, 582-83; other refs, 367, 389, 658, 732
Marbury, Francis, 84, 353
Marches, Middle, 49
Marital Responsibilities, 251-67
Markham, Sir John, 581
Marprelate Tracts, 12, 36, 38-39, 40, 72, 82, 102, 405, 643, 677, 761
Marriage: nature and purpose of, 115-19, 739, 744; qualities of mates, 130-43; age at, 143-54, 756; parental consent in, 151-52, 741-42; arranged, 162-77; secret, 461
Marslic, Thomas, 529
Martial, 353
Martial, John: on Puritans, 4
Martyr, Katherine, 698
Martyr, Peter, 161
Mary I, 358, 368
Mary Stuart, 265, 342, 479, 529, 724
Mascall, Leonard, 238
Mason, Mr., Essex minister, 209
Masques, 186-89 *passim*, 417, 423, 425, 456, 588
Masters, 210, 235, 273, 296, 302, 314-20, 721, 749
Masturbation, 221
Matthew, Tobias: on enclosure, 642; other refs, 355
Matthew Bible: on bishops, 34; anticlericalism in, 100; on celibacy, 122, 126, 127; on sex in marriage, 224; on wives, 252; on divorce, 267; on children's duties, 282; on idleness, 384; on the sabbath, 396; on fasting, 490; on apparel, 502; on wealth, 549; on almsgiving, 559, 560, 561, 562; on usury, 596; on oaths, 682; on minds, 706, 707; other refs, 89
Matthew-Becke Bible: anticlericalism in, 100; on celibacy, 122, 126, 127; on idleness, 384; on the sabbath, 396; on fasting, 490; on clothing, 502; on wealth, 549; on almsgiving, 559, 560, 562; on usury, 596; on oaths, 682; on minds, 707; other refs, 89
May Day, 214, 411, 425-27, 429, 457, 758
Maynard, Henry, 609
Meade, Thomas, 270

Meath, Bishop of, 368
Meere, John, 669
Meg, Long, of Westminster, 219-20, 221
Melville, Elizabeth, 310
Melville, Sir James, 464
Merburn, Francis, 11
Merchant Adventurers, 514, 680
Merchant Taylors' School, London, 21, 330, 336, 338, 341, 370, 453, 462, 524
Mervyn, John, 97
Michell, Edward, 364
Middlesex: Chiswick, 579; Ealing, 243, 303; Enfield, 416; Fulham, 578; Hackney, 580; Harrow on the Hill, 363; Highgate, 365; Islington, 219; Osterley, 644; Ratcliffe, 219; Stepney, 219, 348, 353; other refs, 17, 222, 411, 417, 567
Middlesex, Archdeaconry of, 461
Middleton, Henry, 397
Middleton, Marmaduke: on funeral customs, 700; other refs, 190, 413, 427, 441, 707
Middleton, William, 309
Midgley, Richard, 57
Mildmay, Anthony, 133, 145, 164, 231, 258, 301, 523, 565, 592, 634
Mildmay, Lady Grace, 238, 257-58, 258-59, 304, 310-13 passim, 437, 462, 478, 523, 528, 531, 565, 656, 702; as Grace Sherrington, 132, 145, 164, 231, 318, 324, 345
Mildmay, Lady Mary (Sir Walter's wife), 308
Mildmay, Mary (Anthony's daughter), 523
Mildmay, Sir Thomas, 418
Mildmay, Sir Thomas (brother of Sir Walter), 585, 732
Mildmay, Sir Walter: charity of, 585; on his funeral, 701, 709; other refs, 54, 66-67, 133, 138, 164, 231, 257, 301, 315, 319, 330, 366-67, 415, 478, 523, 565, 592, 615, 634, 656, 732
Miller, Edward, 488
Milles, Dowsabel, 591
Moderation, 12, 26-28, 472, 474, 476, 477, 483, 485, 491, 492, 496, 499, 502, 506-12 passim, 515, 519, 520, 522, 698-700 passim, 709, 734, 743-44
Moffett, Peter: on surety, 613; on hoarding, 628; other refs, 605
Monk, Robert, 57
Monmouthshire, 733
Mons, France, 370

Montagu, 1st Viscount. See Browne, Anthony
Montague, Sir Edward, 464, 592
Montgomeryshire: Llansaintffraid-yn-Mechan, 317
Monuments and Brasses, 729-34, 736
Moone, John, 298
Moore, William, 589
Mordaunt, Joan Lady, 712
More, Edward: on women, 254-55; on justice for the poor, 665
More, Sir Edward, 168
More, Jasper, 644
More, John, 309
More, Sir Thomas, 16, 170, 245, 254, 328, 529
More, Thomas (Cornish minister), 220, 221
More, William, 257
Morice, James, 10, 681-82, 689-90, 747-48
Morley, 11th Lord. See Parker, Henry
Morley, 12th Lord. See Parker, Edward
Morley, Thomas, 75
Morte d'Arthur, 526, 527
Morton, George, 388
Morton, Thomas, 309
Mosaic Code. See Ten Commandments
Mosan, Jacob, 212
Mosellanus, Petrus, 354
Mosse, Miles: on usury, 606, 607, 611, 646
Moulton, Thomas: on premarital sex, 207; other refs, 238
Mountford, Thomas: performs Hertford's marriage, 181; on food, 472; on inebriety, 484
Mulcaster, Richard: on gentility, 19; on social mobility, 21; on parental responsibilities, 281; on wives, 305; on English women, 311; on education, 336, 388-39, 342, 343-44, 347, 349, 359, 361, 363; on educational travel, 371; on vocation, 379, 380; on games, 438; on dancing, 456; on music, 462; on food, 482; on apparel, 512; on speech, 524; on lawyers, 659; other refs, 348, 370, 430, 453, 760
Munday, Anthony, 529
Münster, Germany, 15, 570
Musculus, Wolfgang, 161
Music, 187-89 passim, 313, 353, 381, 429, 458-65, 468, 746, 750
Mussie, Richard, 609

Napier, Richard, 532

Naples, 213

Nash, Thomas: on Puritans, 8; on social order, 20; on moderation, 27; on clerical income, 50; attacks sectaries, 92; on spouse selection, 134; on the royal court, 209; on prostitution, 218; on education, 338, 343, 347, 355-56; on educational reformers, 359; on apparel, 506; on literature, 525, 526; other refs, 318, 529, 531, 582

Nayler, John, 180

Neale, Sir John, 305, 681

Nelson, William, 273

Netherlands, 313, 473, 513, 522, 539

Nevill, Lucy, Lady Latimer: charity of, 580; funeral of, 715, 731, 732

Neville, Charles, 6th Earl of Westmorland, 365

Neville, Henry, 5th Earl of Westmorland, 171-72, 367

Neville, Lady Margaret, 307

Neville, Richard, 196

Neville, Thomas, 365, 574

New, John, 611

Newark Castle, 711-12

Newdigate, John, 150

Newnham, John: on widowers, 193; on parental affection, 279

Newton, Thomas: on celibacy, 126; on sexual relations, 226-27; on male superiority, 256; on the aristocracy, 335; other refs, 239

Nichols, Josias: on religious unity, 5; on Puritanism, 6; on Catholics, 8; on clerical livings, 52; on pluralism, 61; on nonresidency, 64; on preaching, 80, 81; on celibacy, 122; on the household, 291; on catechizing, 295; on literacy, 333; on swearing, 687

Nicholson, Helen. See Branch, Dame Helen

Nicolls, John, 187

Nixon, Anthony: on apparel, 503

Nonresidency, 58-69, 760

Norbrook, preacher in Bristol, 37

Norcrosse, Henry, 488

Norden, John: on natural and revealed knowledge, 90, 91; on prostitution, 218; on parental affection, 279; on idleness, 387; on labor, 393; on the sabbath, 400; on drunkenness, 484; on fasting, 492,

494; on apparel, 507; on apparel at court, 519; on war, 541-42; on wealth, 549; on the poor, 556; on beggars, 566; on dearth, 628

Norfolk: Acle, 574; Attlebridge, 488; Aylsham, 179, 289; Bastwick, 488; Bedingham, 654; Beeston, 209; Blofield, 654; Boughton, 442; Bridgeham, 295; Burlingham, 608; Canteley, 488; Carleton, 447; Caston, 406; Claxton, 447; Colney, 209; Croxton, 442; Fishley, 488; Freethorpe, 488; Fulmodeston, 96, 442; Gillingham, 654; Great Dunham, 504; Great Ellingham, 654; Great Yarmouth, 190, 416; Hanworth, 488; Happisburgh, 608; Harpley, 427, 496; Holkham, 608; King's Lynn, 496; Limpenhoe, 488; Longham, 535; Mattishall, 578; Melton, 608; Morley, 95; Old Buckenham, 232; Ormsby, 496; Ovington, 427; Oxnead, 608; Oxwick, 644, 668; Pentney, 496; Plumstead, 442; Ringland, 488; Saxlingham, 488, 654; Sidestrand, 205; Sloley, 414; Southwood, 488; Sprowston, 209; Thornham, 496; Upton, 488; Walcott, 608; Wereham, 95; Wood Rising, 406, 608; Yarmouth, 625; other refs, 60, 94, 96, 97, 309, 316, 317, 341, 365, 406, 411, 608, 623, 626, 629, 634, 635, 637, 654, 655, 733, 734, 759

Norfolk, 2nd Duke of. See Howard, Thomas

Norfolk, 3rd Duke of. See Howard, Thomas

Norfolk, 4th Duke of. See Howard, Thomas

Norfolk, Archdeaconry of, 428

Norfolk, Duchess of. See Howard, Margaret

Norris, Francis, 163

Norris, Henry, 1st Lord Norris of Rycote, 163, 426

North, Dudley, 3rd Lord North, 141, 142

North, Edward, 1st Lord North, 265

North, Lady, 308

North, Roger, 2nd Lord North, 42, 142, 303, 418, 443, 581

Northampton, 1st Marquess of. See Parr, William

Northampton, Earl of. See Howard, Henry

Northampton, Marchioness of. See Parr, Elizabeth

Northamptonshire: Bulwick, 97; Corby, 567; Cottingham, 577; Dogsthorpe, 304, 480; Harrington, 165; Higham Ferrers,

62; Holdenby, 19; Kilmarsh, 385; Northampton, 97, 142; Oundle, 95; Pitchley,
597, 608, 644; Rushton, 205; Whiston,
425; Wollaston, 442; other refs, 5, 222,
261, 341, 345, 532, 537, 592
Northbrooke, John: on preaching, 81-82; on
fornication, 208-209; on idleness, 385;
on sleep, 387; on the sabbath, 399; on
holy days, 422; on games, 435; on the
theater, 448; on dancing, 455; on music,
459, 462; on apparel, 508, 509; on
speech, 522; on usury, 603; other refs,
469
Northern Rebellion, 168, 299, 371, 638
Northumberland: Belford, 190; Chilling-
ham, 307; Jarrow, 190; Newcastle-on-
Tyne, 131, 435, 452, 578, 638; New-
castle Hospital, 574; St. Andrew, Bothal,
19; Seaton Delaval, 242; other refs, 173,
243, 244, 245, 261, 364, 638, 641, 733
Northumberland, 11th Earl of. See Percy,
Thomas
Northumberland, 13th Earl of. See Percy,
Henry
Northumberland, Countess of. See Percy,
Mary
Northumberland, Dowager Countess of. See
Percy, Katherine
Northumberland, Duke of. See Dudley,
John
Norton, Sir John, 95
Norton, Thomas, 598
Norwich, 46, 58, 81, 102, 127, 216-17, 243,
256, 270, 344, 428, 451, 487, 496, 547,
573, 578, 579, 625, 655, 658, 726, 730
Norwich, Archdeacon's Court at, 414
Norwich, Bishop of. See Parkhurst, John
(1560-75); Freke, Edmund (1575-84);
Scambler, Edmund (1585-94); Redman,
William (1595-1602)
Norwich, Diocese of, 42, 59, 75, 77-78, 83,
334, 413, 428, 442, 488, 496, 679
Norwich, Peter, 464
Norwich, Simon, 495
Notestein, Wallace, 242
Nottingham, Countess of, 400
Nottingham, Ecclesiastical Court at, 234
Nottinghamshire: Barnby by Newark, 61;
Bilsthorpe, 61; Bingham, 15; Colwick,
61; Costock, 218; Cotgrave, 60; Cotham,
581; Eakring, 76, 232; East Redford,

428; Elksley, 176; Headon, 180, 428;
Houghton, 134; Kirklington, 136; Kirkton, 61; Lambley, 266; Mansfield, 60;
Newstead, 173; North Clifton, 60, 180;
Nottingham, 7, 87, 616, 625; Ollerton,
131; Rampton, 174; Rotherham, 61;
Ruddington, 61; Shelford, 169; Sutton
Bonington, 61; Walesby, 61; Winthorpe,
61; Worksop, 581; other refs, 22, 61,
211, 280, 317, 424, 445, 531, 591
Nowell, Alexander: catechism of, 73; on
fornication, 208; on children's duties,
282, 283-84; on education, 330, 346;
support of education, 365; on vagabonds, 389; on the sabbath, 397-98,
415; on music, 458; on food, 472; on
apparel, 504; on begging, 566; charity of
579; on weights and measures, 616; on
business ethics, 618; on enclosure, 642;
on lawsuits, 652, 653; other refs, 208,
234, 260, 275, 337, 351, 354, 356, 364,
368, 469, 583, 654, 657, 706
Nowell, Lawrence, 260
Nowell, Robert: charity of, 583; funeral of,
710, 713, 715, 717, 718, 720, 729, 735;
other refs, 175, 364

Oath ex officio mero, 235, 649, 681-86,
688-92 passim, 747-48
Oaths, 680-92
Ochino, Bernardino, 310
Ocland, Christopher, 357
Odell, Matthew, 97
Officialty, Court of, 181
Offley, Sir Thomas, 623
Oglander, George, 476
Oglander, William, 139, 581
Ogle, Lord, 19
Oglethorpe, Owen, 577
Openshaw, Robert: on the household, 302;
other refs, 296
Origen, 123, 529
Osborne, Edward, 416
Osorius, 529
Outred, Marcelline, 612
Overton, Thomas, 265
Overton, William: on lay patronage, 52; on
pluralism, 65; on education, 346; other
refs, 75
Ovid, 353, 354, 356, 357, 526
Oxford, 47, 206, 406, 414, 714

Oxford, 16th Earl of. *See* De Vere, John

Oxford, 17th Earl of. *See* De Vere, Edward

Oxford, Archdeacon's Court at, 102, 206, 220, 227, 286, 294, 304, 409, 410, 414, 419, 429, 441

Oxford, Countess of. *See* De Vere, Anne

Oxford University: All Souls College, 131, 360, 651; Balliol College, 109, 382; Brasenose College, 365; Christ Church, 358; Corpus Christi College, 38, 108, 342, 602; Exeter College, 299; Jesus College, 19, 367; Merton College, 524; Oriel College, 299; Queen's College, 365; St. John's College, 359, 360, 532; University College, 366; other refs, 63, 78, 85, 91, 128, 207, 219, 238, 342, 347, 349, 355, 358, 359, 362, 366, 367, 370, 406, 513, 579

Oxfordshire: Banbury, 56, 58, 426; Blackthorn, 429; Bourton, 441, 457; Caversham, 220-21; Charlbury, 206; Chipping Norton, 286; Drayton, 118; Dunstew, 441-42, 447, 707; Elsfield, 304; Hanwell, 58, 131; Horton, 441; Lewknor, 304; Sandford-on-Thames, 206; South Stoke, 457; Standlake, 227; Stanton, 409; Steeple Barton, 227; Witney, 409; other refs, 167, 181, 222, 223, 233, 406, 424, 426, 637, 727, 733

Paget, Lady, 290

Paget, Thomas, 4th Lord Paget of Beaudesert, 164, 273, 517

Pagit, Eusebius: on bishops, 42; on clerical reputation, 94; on tithes, 109; on marriage, 118; on spouse selection, 140; on parental consent in marriage, 160; on sex in marriage, 225; on divorce, 269, 270; on landlords, 632; other refs, 84, 225, 297

Palace of Pleasure, The, 531

Palmer, Mr., Essex minister, 180

Parental Responsibilities, 274-82, 390, 570

Paris, 150, 370, 371, 372, 443

Parker, Christopher, 60

Parker, Edward, 12th Lord Morley, 135, 286

Parker, Henry, 11th Lord Morley: on spouse selection, 138

Parker, Matthew: on Puritans, 4, 23; on Cambridge University, 51; on pluralism,

61-62; on the social background of the clergy, 74; on parental consent in marriage, 157; relations with servants, 316; on education, 362; support of education, 365, 367; on the theater, 447; on music, 459-60; and poor relief, 574; charity of, 578, 586; hospitality of, 590; and ecclesiastical courts, 675; other refs, 15, 42, 58, 79, 172, 209, 233, 272, 289, 302, 329, 358, 359, 413, 468, 469, 479, 491, 516, 529, 585, 589, 709, 710, 713, 714, 715, 718, 732

Parker, Thomas, 286

Parkhurst, John: on Oxford University, 359; charity of, 579; other refs, 10, 42, 95, 102, 132, 304, 367, 699

Parliament: *1559*, 325, 429, 622; *1563*, 53, 221-22, 324, 389, 415, 429, 480-81, 516, 566, 597, 640, 642, 675, 681; *1566*, 53, 66, 415, 485, 516, 597, 672-73, 687; *1571*, 53, 66, 298, 415, 516, 597-98, 600, 623; *1572*, 614, 672-73; *1576*, 53, 110, 216, 222, 359, 485-86, 516-17, 673; *1581*, 53, 66-67, 486, 498, 614, 673; *1584-85*, 53-54, 62, 67-68, 372, 415-16, 486, 673, 675; *1586-87*, 54, 68, 675; *1589*, 54, 68, 359, 486, 517, 624, 640, 673-74, 675; *1593*, 25, 216, 306, 332, 621, 640, 675, 682, 764, 765; *1597-98*, 180, 216, 360, 517, 567, 568, 625, 640-41, 675, 764-65; *1601*, 28, 48, 68-69, 235-36, 304, 305, 416, 486, 567, 568, 614, 641, 674, 675, 687; *1610*, 216; general refs, 72, 430, 490, 520, 628, 764-65

Parr, Elizabeth, Marchioness of Northampton, 711

Parr, William, 1st Marquess of Northampton, 372, 417

Parrott, Stephen, 610

Parry, Henry, 447

Pater noster, 696

Patrons and Patronage, 45-58

Paulet, John, 2nd Marquess of Winchester: charity of, 580; and usury, 608; other refs, 709, 718

Paulet, William, 1st Marquess of Winchester, 710, 728

Paulet, William, 3rd Marquess of Winchester, 195, 294

Paul's Cross, London, sermons at, 47, 61,

64, 72, 74, 75, 84, 102, 103, 108, 161,
230, 269, 358, 382, 383, 386, 387, 398,
399, 432, 448, 449, 503, 527, 542, 548,
553, 554, 566, 602, 627, 643, 666
Payne, Robert: on poor relief, 569
Paynell, Thomas, 319, 577, 696
Paynter, William, 577
Peacham, Henry, 309
Peacock, Thomas, 577
Pearson, Lu Emily, 140
Peasants' Rebellion, Germany, 15
Pembroke, 20th Earl of. *See* Herbert,
William
Pembroke, 21st Earl of. *See* Herbert, Henry
Pembroke, Countess of. *See* Herbert, Anne;
Herbert, Mary
Pembroke, Earls of, 629
Pembrokeshire, 641
Pendleton, Edward, 351
Penne, Juliana, 597
Penry, John: on social order, 17; on
bishops, 34, 35, 38, 44; on clergy in
Wales, 63; on nonresidency, 64; on cler-
ical ignorance, 73; on preaching, 81;
anticlericalism of, 101; on tithes, 106-
107; on weddings, 179; on games, 437;
on drunkenness, 484; on funeral
customs, 703; other refs, 109, 285, 306
Percy, Lady Dorothy, 273
Percy, Henry, 13th Earl of Northumberland,
135, 163, 245, 265, 273, 297, 443, 479,
514, 610, 635
Percy, Sir Henry, 163
Percy, Katherine, Dowager Countess of
Northumberland, 166
Percy, Mary, Countess of Northumberland,
715
Percy, Thomas, 11th Earl of Northumberland, 303, 417
Percy Family, 645
Periam, Sir William, 388
Perkins, William: on social behavior, 22; on
marriage, 117, 118, 119; on celibacy,
123, 124, 129; on parental consent in
marriage, 159-60; on bastardy, 215; on
homosexuality, 221; on sex in marriage,
225, 227; on breast-feeding, 245; on
charity by wives, 262; on divorce, 269-
70; on fathers, 275; on parental responsibilities, 278; on the household, 292; on
masters, 315-16; on education, 329, 335;

on vocation, 380; on the sabbath, 401-
402, 408; on holy days, 421; on games,
434, 436, 444; on bear-baiting, cockfighting, and bull-baiting, 445; on the
theater, 450; on food, 474; on fasting,
492; on apparel, 507, 508, 509, 510; on
apparel at court, 519; on speech, 522,
523; on literature, 527, 531; on war,
542; on poor relief, 548; on wealth, 550,
551, 552, 553; on almsgiving, 558, 560-
61; on beggars, 565, 566, 568; on poor
relief, 568, 572, 576; charity of, 584; on
usury, 606, 607, 611, on surety, 613; on
business practices, 619; on regrating and
engrossing, 627; on lawsuits, 650, 653-
54; on oaths and vows, 686, 687, 688;
on funeral customs, 701; and the *ars
moriendi*, 703; funeral of, 728; other
refs, 8, 10, 13, 84, 260, 309, 430, 468,
616, 646, 657, 744, 745, 751
Perne, Andrew, 401
Perrot, Dorothy, 135
Perrot, Sir Thomas, 133, 135, 172
Persons, Robert: on literature, 527; other
refs, 10, 372, 528
Peterborough, Bishop of. *See* Scambler,
Edmund (1561-85)
Peter Martyr, 397, 447, 455, 529, 560, 698
Peter Ramus, 529
Petrarch, 527
Petre, Sir William, 187
Phillips, George: on industry, 391
Phillips, Mr., Norfolk minister, 447
Philpot, John, 57, 306, 689, 706
Pickering, Sir William, 482, 732
Piers, John: on learning in the pulpit, 87;
other refs, 196, 704
Pilgrimage of Grace, 629
Pilkington, James: on social order, 14; on
nobility, 20; on houses, 25; on bishops,
43; on patrons, 48; on impropriations,
50; on clerical income, 51; on clerical
ignorance, 72; on clerical learning, 79-
80; on natural and revealed knowledge,
89, 90; on irresponsible clergy, 99; on
the wedding ring, 184; on parental
responsibilities, 276, 280; on children's
duties, 283; on names, 289; on retainers,
317, 324; on servants, 323; on education, 350, 354-55, 359, 363; support of
education, 365; on idleness, 385, 390-91;

on prelates, 389; on labor, 392; on the sabbath, 397; on games, 432, 433; on food, 473; on drink, 483-84; on apparel, 503, 504, 505; on speech, 521; on poor relief, 573; on wealth, 551; on hospitality, 587-88; on usury, 599; on weights and measures, 616; on business ethics, 617; on forestalling and regrating, 626-27; on landlords, 630-31; on enclosure, 642; on justice for the poor, 666; on funeral customs, 697-98; on his funeral, 699; on wakes and minds, 707; on monuments and brasses, 730; other refs, 10, 85, 110, 284, 292, 349, 367, 463, 524, 574, 628, 646, 704, 706, 738, 744, 752

Pilkington, Leonard, 260

Pinchbeck, Ivy, 218

Pius V, Pope, 122

Plato, 355, 366, 529, 603

Playfere, Thomas, 85

Plays, 214, 397, 416, 425, 427, 429, 446-54

Pliny, 526

Pluralism, 58-69, 760

Plutarch, 366, 526, 529

Plymouth Grammar School, 276, 334

Pole, Richard, 174, 578, 696

Pole, Robert, 134, 729, 730

Polewhele, Mr., Devon minister, 209

Polley, Mr., Norfolk minister, 608

Polydore Virgil, 529

Ponet, John, 310

Poor, Place and Behavior of, 554-57

Poor, Proposed Reforms for, 568-72

Poor Relief, 491-92, 756-57

Pope, Sir Thomas, 727

Popham, Sir John: charity of, 581; on weights and measures, 615; other refs, 406, 486

Pott, John, 351

Poverty, 547-48

Powel, Gabriel: on servants, 317; on suicide, 532, 533; on usury, 603

Poyntz, Sir Nicholas, 136-37, 140, 264, 280

Prague, 370

Pranel, Henry, 18, 133

Presbyterians: place on the religious continuum, 10; Bancroft's attack on, 24, 92; polity of, 25, 52, 54; on patrons, 58; other refs, 5, 7, 23, 62, 69, 329, 427, 496, 498, 654, 681

Prewett, William, 56

Priapea, The, 353

Price, Henry: on apparel, 502

Price, Hugh, 367

Price, Thomas, 196

Pricke, Robert, 46

Printers, 197

Privy Council: on child marriages, 152-53, 154; and matrimonial consent, 176-77; and the regulation of diet, 481; concern with fasting, 497; regulation of apparel, 517-18; regulation of the theater, 451; concern with beggars, 567-68; and poor relief, 575; concern with business ethics, 620-21; concern with forestalling and regrating, 622, 623, 624, 625; concern with enclosure, 644; and lawsuits, 655; and legal relief for the poor, 668-69; and legal redress, 671; concern with the oath *ex officio*, 681-82; concern with Cheshire wakes, 707; social role of, 765-66; other refs, 23, 25, 28, 36, 37, 39, 53, 64, 65, 78, 97, 98, 102, 103, 105, 133, 148, 180, 184, 188, 196, 200, 222, 233, 235, 256, 261, 266, 271, 273, 275, 279, 285, 286, 293, 297, 298, 307, 316, 324, 332, 351, 352, 367, 371, 386, 388, 416, 417, 424, 426-27, 429, 444, 446, 452, 453, 469, 483, 486, 499, 520, 523, 524, 548, 572, 574, 590, 594, 612, 615, 631, 634, 639, 640, 645, 658, 682, 692, 716

Propertius, 353, 354

Prophesyings, 354, 388, 498, 678

Prostitution, 95, 121-22, 218-21, 468, 563, 738

Provence, 370

Prowse, Richard, 194

Prynne, William, 671

Puckering, Sir John, 723

Puckering, Sir Thomas, 306

Pullen, John, 332

Punishment, Barbarous, 671-72

Puritans: nature of, 3-14; anxiety of, 8, 13; views on Christian liberty, 9; aniconic emphasis of, 9-10; appeal of, 13; on social order, 15-25 *passim*; on moderation, 26-28; religious experience of, 29; on bishops, 35-45 *passim*; on patrons, 47-48, 52, 53, 55-58; on nonresident clergy, 60-61; on pluralism, 61, 63, 67-69; on nonresidency, 63-64; on clerical ignorance, 71-73, 76, 77, 78; on preaching, 79-82, 85, 738; on education in the pulpit, 85-86; on natural and revealed knowledge, 88-92; on immoral clergy, 94, 98; on anticlericalism, 98-99, 103-104; on tithes, 109-10; on the nature of marriage, 116-17, 118-19, 739, 744; on celibacy, 123, 124, 126, 129-30, 749; on spouse selection, 131, 132, 134, 137, 138-39, 140-41, 142-43, 739; on age at marriage, 144, 151; and child marriages, 151, 153; on parental consent in marriage, 159-62, 341-42; on weddings, 179, 182, 184-85; on widows, 192-94, 198-99, 749; on premarital sex, 204-205, 207-208, 213, 740; on fornication, 208-209, 212, 213, 744; on bastardy, 215-16, 217; on prostitution, 218-20; on homosexuality, 221; on sex in marriage, 224-25; on adultery, 229, 230-31, 233-34, 739-40, 744; on birth control, 237, 238, 244-46; on marital relations, 254, 255, 256-57, 258, 259-60, 263; on charity by wives, 262-63; on divorce, 269-70, 271, 272, 744; on parental responsibilities, 275-81 *passim*, 739; on parental affection, 279; on children's duties, 284; on the household, 292-93, 295, 296, 297, 301-302, 739, 744-45; on wives, 305-306, 742; and literary patronage, 309; activity of wives, 307-14 *passim*; on masters, 315-16, 318, 749; on servants, 321, 322-23, 749; on the purpose of education, 329; on the extent of education, 339, 346, 742; on masters and tutors, 347, 348-49; on the curriculum, 353-54, 355, 356, 745; on educational reform, 358-59, 362; on the universities, 360-61; on educational support, 364, 366-67, 369; on educational travel, 370, 371, 372; on vocation, 379-81, 382-83, 741; on idleness, 385-86, 387, 389, 390, 741; on labor, 393-94, 740-41; on ambition, 394-95, 741; on the sabbath, 396, 398-408 *passim*, 418, 745; on holy days, 421-22, 423, 745-46; on May Day, 426; and Rogation, 427-28; on games, 434-37, 438-39, 442, 443; on bear and bullbaiting and cock-fighting, 444, 445, 446; on the theater, 447, 448-50, 452, 453-54,

749-50; on dancing, 455-56, 750, 760; on music, 458-59, 460, 461-62, 464-65, 746, 750; on church ales, 467-68; on food, 474-75, 482-83, 750; on drink, 483-85, 489, 750; on fasting, 492-95, 496, 497-99, 738, 750; on apparel, 505-510, 519-20, 750; on speech, 522-24, 525, 750-51; on literature, 527-28, 530-31, 751; on suicide, 533-34, 537, 751; on war, 541-42, 543, 746; on wealth, 549, 550-52, 553, 554, 751; on the poor, 555-57; on almsgiving, 558, 559, 560-62; on beggars, 565, 566, 568; on poor relief, 568, 569; on communalism, 571-72, 751; and poor relief, 575-76; and charitable giving, 584-87, 746-47, 751; on hospitality, 588-89, 592-93, 751-52; on usury, 603-607, 611, 747; on surety, 613, 752; on weights and measures, 616; on business ethics, 618-20, 621-22, 752; on forestalling and regrating, 627-28, 752; on landlords, 631-33, 752; as landlords, 634-35; on enclosure, 642, 643, 644; on lawsuits, 652-54, 657, 753; litigation involving Puritans, 656; on lawyers, 659-61; on judges, 664-65, 753; on justice and the poor, 666-67; on legal reform, 670, 672, 674; on ecclesiastical courts, 674, 676-78, 679-80, 748; on oaths, 682-83, 686-90, 747-48; on funeral customs, 700-701, 703, 734-35, 753; on funeral sermons, 705, 734, 753; on wakes and minds, 707, 708, 736; on funeral expenses, 708; on funeral charity, 717, 721-22, 735; on funeral monuments, 732-33, 736
Puritan Survey of the Clergy (1586), 94, 96, 220, 389, 442, 457, 608, 654
Pursglove, Robert, 577, 719, 730, 732, 733
Pythagoras, 353

Queen Mary's Grammar School, Clitheroe, Lancs., 349
Queen's Bench, Court of, 69, 515, 650, 670, 671, 672, 673, 682
Queen's School, Canterbury, 343

Rabelais, François, 527
Rack-renting, 300, 628-36 *passim*, 759
Radcliffe, Frances, Countess of Sussex, 308, 366, 710

Radcliffe, Henry, 9th Earl of Sussex, 724

Radcliffe, Robert, 10th Earl of Sussex, 233

Radcliffe, Thomas, 8th Earl of Sussex, 149, 417, 479, 709, 710, 714, 718

Radclyff, Thomas, 175

Radclyffe, William, 411, 445

Rae, William, 95

Rainolds, John: on patrons, 47; on clerical income, 51; on university patronage, 54; on education, 353, 354; on the theater, 450; other refs, 138, 528

Raleigh, Sir Walter: on enclosure, 641; other refs, 172, 298, 537, 669, 681

Ramist Logic, 117

Ramsey, Dame Mary, 262, 583-84, 720-21

Ramsey, Sir Thomas, 720

Randolph, Thomas, 264

Rankins, William: on the theater, 446, 449-50

Rape, 222-23, 269

Rathgeb, Jakob, 257, 512

Raulph, John, 389

Read, John, 213

Redman, William, 442

Reformatio Legum Ecclesiasticarum, 220, 268-69, 676, 691, 692, 748

Regius, Urbanus, 527

Regrating, 622-28

Remarriage, 191-99

Requests, Court of, 106, 166, 171, 188, 273, 598, 612, 650, 656, 668

Reyd, George, 577

Reynolles, Henry, 388

Rheims, France, 120, 361, 371, 392, 422

Rheims New Testament: on bishops, 35; on clerical ignorance, 73; on clerical vocation, 75; on immoral clergy, 93-94; respect for clergy, 100; on tithes, 108; on marriage, 116, 117; on celibacy, 120, 121, 125; on spouse selection, 131; on widows, 191-92, 193; on sex in marriage, 224; on marital relations, 254; on divorce, 268; on children's duties, 283; on vocation, 382; on holy days, 422; on food, 476; on fasting, 495; on apparel, 502; on speech, 524; on literature, 527; on almsgiving, 557, 558-59, 559-60; on communalism, 570; on hospitality, 587; on usury, 596-97; on occupations, 617; on lawsuits, 651-52; on oaths, 683, 686; other refs, 89, 90, 91, 124, 129, 401, 604

Rich, Barnabe: on war, 538

Rich, Lady, 718

Rich, Lady Penelope, 166, 232-33, 313, 344, 662

Rich, Richard, 1st Lord Rich: charity of, 581; other refs, 174, 175, 330

Rich, Robert, 2nd Lord Rich, 668

Rich, Robert, 3rd Lord Rich: as patron, 56-57; other refs, 166, 232, 296, 452, 662

Richard I, 542

Richardson, R. C., 132, 242, 300

Richmond Palace, 453

Richmond (Yorks.) Grammar School, 367

Ridgeway, Lady, 308

Ridley, Nicholas, 528

Rishton, Edward, 528

Rivington (Lancs.) Grammar School, 336, 340-41, 349, 350, 354, 365, 463, 512

Ro, Mary, 243

Ro, Sir Thomas, 243

Robart, Mr., Norfolk minister, 209

Robin Goodfellow, 529

Robin Hood, 527

Robinson, John, 175, 718

Robinson, Richard: on enclosure, 636; other refs, 342

Rochester, Admiralty Court at, 414

Rochester, Bishop of. See Guest, Edmund (1560-71); Freke, Edmund (1572-75); Piers, John (1576-77); Young, John (1578-1605)

Rochester, Diocese of, 80

Rodes, Francis, 277, 581

Rogation, 427-28, 466, 708, 766

Rogers, Barbara, 263

Rogers, John: on bishops, 34; on parental responsibilities, 281; on the sabbath, 397; on almsgiving, 560

Rogers, Lady, 308

Rogers, Richard: on social order, 22; on celibacy, 129; on parental consent in marriage, 160; on remarriage, 194; on premarital sex, 207; on sex in marriage, 225; on children's duties, 284; on vocation, 380, 741; on idleness, 387, 390; on the sabbath, 405; on May Day, 426; on the theater, 450; fasting of, 497-98; speech of, 523; on the poor, 556; on usury, 606, 607, 611; on surety, 612, 613; on business ethics, 619; other refs, 57, 263, 646, 747

Rogers, Sir Richard, 173
Rogers, Thomas: on moderation, 26, 27; on the clergy, 82, 93; on parental consent in marriage, 157; on ambition, 394; on the sabbath, 406, 408; on almsgiving, 560; on hospitality, 587, 588; on usury, 601; on oaths, 685-86; other refs, 275, 430, 745
Rogues and Sturdy Beggars, 562-68
Rokeby, John, 350
Rolf, John, 654
Romas Catechism (1566), 117, 119, 130, 224
Rome, Italy: prostitution in, 121-22; other refs, 361, 370, 371, 372, 511
Rookwood, Richard, 372
Roper, Elizabeth, 170-71
Rose, Adam, 60, 428
Rostock, 370
Roswell, William, 583
Rowe, Leonard, 181
Rowe, Sir Thomas, 188
Rowse, A. L., 150, 151
Royse, John, 336
Russell, Lady Anne, 186
Russell, Bridget, Countess of Bedford, 308
Russell, Elizabeth Lady: on educational travel, 369; other refs, 135, 181-82, 307, 310, 311, 372, 452, 656
Russell, Francis, 4th Earl of Bedford: as patron, 56; charity of, 584; hospitality of, 592; other refs, 40, 146, 186, 288, 297, 299, 366, 452, 528, 706, 710
Russell, John Lord, 186, 199, 288, 289, 311
Russell, Lucy, Countess of Bedford, 309
Russell, Lady Margaret, 146-47, 185, 309, 346; as Margaret Clifford, Countess of Cumberland, 310, 312, 497, 528, 584, 634
Russell Family, 732
Rust, William, 56-57
Rutland: Normanton, 442; Ridlington, 7, 616; South Luffenham, 64; other refs, 733
Rutland, 4th Earl of. See Manners, Henry
Rutland, 5th Earl of. See Manners, Edward
Rutland, 6th Earl of. See Manners, John
Rutland, 7th Earl of. See Manners, Roger
Rutland, Countess of, 718, 719
Ryddonte, William, 73-74, 350
Ryvett, Sir Thomas, 164

Sabbath: doctrine of, 395-408, 745; observance of, 409-19, 745; other refs, 214, 293, 301, 381, 427, 429, 430, 445, 447-51 passim, 455, 456, 468
Sackville, Sir Richard, 478
Sackville, Thomas, 1st Lord Buckhurst: on poor relief, 568; charity of, 580; hospitality of, 591; other refs, 142, 727
Sacraments, 81
Sadler, Ralph (of Herts.), 187
Sadler, Sir Ralph, 453, 479
St. Albans, Archdeacon's Court at, 266
St. Albans (Herts.) School, 348
St. Asaph, Diocese of, 49
St. Bartholomew's Day, 425
St. Bees School, Cumberland, 330, 365
St. David's, Bishop of. See Middleton, Marmaduke
St. David's, Diocese of, 55, 190, 427, 700
St. George's Day, 513
St. John, Lady Catherine, 309
St. John, John, 2nd Lord St. John of Bletso, 309, 401
St. John Family, 637
St. Leger, Nicholas, 498
St. Loe, Elizabeth, 166-67
St. Loe, Sir John, 698-99
St. Loe, Sir William, 324, 522
St. Margaret's Day, 427
St. Olave's School, Southwark, 357
St. Omer, 372
St. Paul's School, London, 21, 338, 348, 453
St. Peter's Day, 429, 467
St. Peter's School, York, 332, 351, 364, 441
St. Stephen's Day, 453
St. Trinyon's Day, 427
Salisbury, Bishop of. See Jewel, John (1560-71); Guest, Edmund (1571-77); Piers, John (1577-89)
Salisbury Cathedral, 702
Sampson, Thomas: on religious dissent, 4; on Puritans, 7-8; on bishops, 41-42; on the wedding ring, 185; on music, 458; other refs, 84, 351
Sandall, Edward, 350
Sanders, Nicholas: on marriage, 116; on usury, 607-608; other refs, 371
Sandwich (Kent) School, 348
Sandys, Edwin: on religious dissent, 4-5; on social order, 16, 18; on social mobility,

20; scandal about, 44; on patrons, 52; on learned clergy, 71, 72; on religious exercises, 77; on preaching, 80; on learning in the pulpit, 87; on natural and revealed knowledge, 89-90; on anticlericalism, 99-100; on reverence to clergy, 104; on marriage, 118, 119; on celibacy, 126; on spouse selection, 131; on parental consent in marriage, 158, 159; on sex in marriage, 225; on adultery, 234; on marital relations, 256; on catechizing, 294; on the household, 302; support of education, 365; on the proposed Ripon Seminary, 368; on vocation, 379; on games, 433; on apparel, 505; on wealth, 551; on almsgiving, 557, 560; on beggars, 566; on poor relief, 575; on hospitality, 587, 588; on usury, 600-601, 602, 611; on weights and measures, 616; on business ethics, 617-18; on lawsuits, 652; on judges, 663-64; on justice for the poor, 666; on legal reform, 672; other refs, 14, 37, 67, 85, 110, 173, 177, 260, 271, 293, 298, 331, 603, 619, 738, 744

Sandys, George, 173

Saravia, Adraian à: on Guernsey, 103; other refs, 388

Saunderson, William, 57

Savage, George, 95

Savage, John, 61

Savile, Elizabeth, 242, 290

Saxby, Edward, 260

Sayer, Francis, 525

Scambler, Edmund: on Puritans, 23; on nonresidency, 64; on clerical study, 83; and poor relief, 574; other refs, 298, 351, 589, 706

Schnucker, Robert, 237, 244

Scory, John: on holy days, 420; on fasting, 496; and poor relief, 574; charity of, 578-79, 586; and usury, 608; other refs, 37, 298, 351

Scotland, 63, 110, 370, 426

Scott, Sir Thomas, 623

Scrope, Henry, 9th Lord Scrope of Bolton, 105, 136, 165

Scrope, Thomas, 10th Lord Scrope of Bolton, 443

Seager, Francis: on landlords, 631

Seaver, Paul, 81, 393

Seckford, Thomas, 583, 732

Seele, Mr., Yorkshire minister, 589

Segar, Sir William: on moderation, 27; on war, 540, 541, 543; on funeral expenses, 708, 709; on funeral pageantry, 722-23; on funeral monuments, 729-30

Senhouse, Richard, 278, 322, 323, 357, 388, 457, 463

Senhouse, Richard (Lancs. rector), 442

Senhouse, Simon, 278, 357, 388, 457, 463

Separation, Marital, 264, 267-71

Separatists: place on the religious continuum, 10; on social order, 17; on episcopal lands, 34, 35, 38, 43, 44; on patrons, 47, 58, 754; on polity, 52; on preaching, 81, 82; on learning in the pulpit, 86, 87, 91-92; anticlericalism of, 101; on tithes, 106-108, 110, 754; on marriage, 119, 162, 754; on weddings, 179-80, 182, 185, 200; on incest, 222; on adultery, 228, 233-34; on divorce, 270, 754; on children's duties, 285; on godfathers, 289; on chaplains, 297-98; on the educational curriculum, 356, 754; on educational reform, 358-59, 360, 361, 362; on vocation, 381; on idleness, 389, 390, 754; on the sabbath, 407; on holy days, 422, 754; on games, 437; on fasting, 495-96, 497, 498, 754; on apparel, 510, 519, 754; on speech, 524, 755; on war, 543; and poor relief, 575, 755; on enclosure, 643; on lawsuits, 654, 755; on legal reform, 672, 755; on ecclesiastical courts, 674, 678-79, 755; on oaths, 690, 755; on funeral customs, 702-703, 734, 755; on funeral sermons, 705, 734; on burial by the clergy, 728, 729; on monuments and brasses, 730, 736; on funeral pageantry, 735, 755; other refs, 4, 12, 14, 23, 29, 64, 76, 104, 111, 258, 293, 306, 391, 433, 685, 691

Sermon Styles, 84-85

Servants, 210, 235, 273, 302, 303-304, 314-20 passim, 320-25, 385, 463, 721, 749

Sex: sexual immorality of clergy, 94-96, 98; premarital, 204-208, 212-14, 741, 757; fornication, 204, 208-14; in marriage, 223-28

Seymour, Anne, Duchess of Somerset: charity of, 580; other refs, 172, 367

Seymour, Catherine (Grey), Countess of Hertford, 711, 714, 716

Seymour, Edward, 9th Earl of Hertford, 36, 125, 139, 172-73, 181, 209, 265, 273, 274, 317, 348, 463, 464, 479, 513-14, 536

Seymour, Edward, Duke of Somerset, 46

Seymour, Edward, Viscount Beauchamp, 125, 163-64, 172, 173, 274

Seymour, Frances, Countess of Hertford, 478

Seymour, Lady Jane, 727

Seymour, John, 172

Seymour, Thomas, 172, 463

Shaftoe, William, 173

Shakespeare, William, 452, 512, 531, 538

Sheffield, Lady Douglas, 210

Sheffield, Edmund, 3rd Lord Sheffield, 147, 184, 297, 368, 443

Sheffield, John, 2nd Lord Sheffield, 175

Shelford, Robert: on social order, 21; on parental responsibilities, 276, 281; on parental affection, 279; on children's duties, 284; on the household, 292; on catechizing, 294-95; on education, 334, 339, 347; on vocation, 382; on speech, 524; other refs, 315

Shelley, William, 424-25

Shelton, Mary, 172

Sheppard, Richard, 513

Sheppard, Robert, 620

Sherborne, Liberty of, 669

Sherbrook, Michael, 122

Sherrington, Grace. See Mildmay, Grace

Sherston, Christopher, 581

Shirley, Sir Thomas, 537

Shrewsbury, 8th Earl of. See Talbot, Francis

Shrewsbury, 9th Earl of. See Talbot, George

Shrewsbury, 10th Earl of. See Talbot, Gilbert

Shrewsbury, Countess of. See Talbot, Elizabeth

Shrewsbury School, 336

Shropshire: Bishops Castle, 416; Bridgenorth, 582; Ludlow, 215, 582; Shrewsbury, 426, 584, 625; other refs, 242

Shrove-tide, 453

Shutte, Christopher: on patrons, 48; on celibacy, 124; on the sabbath, 399; on dancing, 455; other refs, 428

Sibthorpe, Robert, 57

Sidney, Lady Barbara (Gamage), 164, 182, 303, 318

Sidney, Sir Henry, 135, 137, 164, 336, 338, 344, 366, 368-69, 388, 482, 523, 539, 592, 608, 610, 705, 710, 714

Sidney, Henry (of Norfolk), 626

Sidney, Mary. See Herbert, Mary, Countess of Pembroke

Sidney, Sir Philip: on apparel, 508; on suicide, 534; other refs, 163, 172, 260, 310, 336, 338, 354, 372, 388, 482, 523, 716, 724

Sidney, Sir Robert, 164, 182, 303, 318, 335, 344, 347, 348, 356, 463, 610, 626

Sidney, Thomas, 164-65, 195, 199

Sidney, Sir William, 311

Simler, Josiah, 699

Simony, 53

Simpson, Mark, 608

Sion College, London, 370

Sion House, Middlesex, 135, 273

Sixtus V, Pope, 122, 237

Skipton, Richard, 428

Sleep, 387

Smith, Henry: on nonresidency, 64; on education in the pulpit, 86; on hostility to preachers, 99; on spouse selection, 130, 134, 139, 141; on marital age, 144; on the wedding ring, 185; on bastardy, 215; on prostitution, 218; on breast-feeding, 245; on marital relations, 251, 256, 258, 263; on divorce, 269, 270; on parental responsibilities, 276; on masters, 318; on servants, 321; on vocation, 383; on apparel, 507, 509; on almsgiving, 560; on usury, 605; other refs, 84, 606

Smith, Lady Jane, 702, 719

Smith, John, 401

Smith, Sir Lawrence, 719

Smith, Miles: on wealth, 553

Smith, Sir Ralph, 442

Smith, Sir Thomas: on female weakness, 255; on executrixes, 260; other refs, 262, 370, 424, 529, 592, 633, 719, 732

Smyth, Sir John, 221

Smyth, William, 340

Snagge, Thomas, 53

Social Mobility, 17-18, 20-21, 23-25

Social Order, 14-25

Socrates, 384, 526

Sodomy, 221

Some, Robert: on patrons, 48; on clerical

learning, 72; on natural and revealed knowledge, 90; on tithes, 109; on the sabbath, 401

Somerset, Duchess of. *See* Seymour, Anne

Somerset, Duke of. *See* Seymour, Edward

Somerset, Edward, 9th Earl of Worcester, 713

Somerset, Henry, Lord Herbert, 186

Somerset, William, 8th Earl of Worcester, 265, 318, 451

Somerset Assizes, 486

Somerset Quarter Sessions, 467

Somersetshire: Bath Hospital, 577; Bridgwater, 486; Combe Florey, 103; Cothelston, 272; East Pennard, 580; Godminster Manor, 329; Hardington, 645; Hatherley, 645; Kilmersdon, 645; Maperton, 468, 645; North Cadbury, 468; South Cadbury, 468; Wellington, 581; Wells, 461; other refs, 18, 57, 168, 211, 341, 363, 406, 411, 536, 564, 636, 645

Sorcery, 97

Southampton, 168, 220, 348, 412-13, 414-15, 419, 439-40, 487, 515-16, 520, 567, 615, 621, 625, 671

Southampton, 3rd and 4th Earls of. *See* Wriothesley, Henry

Southampton, Dowager Countess of, 163

Southampton Court Leet, 389, 412-13, 439-40, 515-16

Southampton Grammar School, 348

Southwark: St. Olave, 108; St. Saviour, 353; St. Thomas Spittle, 582; other refs, 17, 180, 221, 289, 416

Southwark Grammar School, 367

Southwell, Robert: on food, 476; on fasting, 495; on apparel, 511; on speech, 524; on literature, 527

Southworth, Robert, 180, 428

Spain, 370, 539, 541, 542, 640

Spanish Inquisition, 649, 678, 689, 690, 691, 748

Sparke, Robert, 57

Sparke, Thomas: on religious dissent, 5; on the Earl of Bedford, 56; other refs, 705

Speech, 97, 276, 520-25, 686-87, 750-51

Spencer, Dr. John: on tithes, 108; other refs, 47

Spencer, Sir John, 133, 135

Spencer, Richard, 488

Spencer, Robert Lord, 303

Spicer, Richard, 57

Spufford, Margaret, 340

Stafford, Edward, 12th Lord Stafford, 133, 634

Stafford, Francis, 329

Stafford Grammar School, 337

Stafforde, John, 176

Staffordshire: Barthomley, 209; Burton-upon-Trent, 583; Lichfield, 517, 518, 583; Little Onn, 394; Little Wyrley, 424, 465; Stafford, 658; Tamworth Castle, 19; Wolverhampton, 524; other refs, 80, 188, 411, 614-15, 638, 655, 658

Staffordshire, Archdeaconry of, 80

Staffordshire Assizes, 658

Staffordshire Quarter Sessions, 394, 440, 638-39, 655, 658

Stanhope, Edward, 165

Stanhope, John, 165

Stanhope, Lady, 273

Stanhope, Sir Thomas, 164, 169

Stanley, Alice, Countess of Derby, 133

Stanley, Edward, 12th Earl of Derby: hospitality of, 590; funeral of, 724-26; other refs, 265, 580, 633, 655, 714, 718, 731

Stanley, Henry, 13th Earl of Derby: as patron, 57; other refs, 60, 163, 175, 296-97, 299, 303, 332, 371, 724, 725, 726

Stanley, Henry (of Lancs.), 713

Stanley, Peter, 262

Stanley, William, 15th Earl of Derby, 133, 163

Stanley, William (Suffolk minister), 655

Stanley, William (of York), 177

Stapleton, Sir Robert, 44

Stapleton, Thomas: on Puritans, 4; on anti-clericalism, 98; on celibacy, 120

Star Chamber, Court of, 97, 106, 235, 260, 271, 272, 285, 323, 426, 427, 437, 467, 478, 479, 535, 626, 639, 644, 650, 655, 656, 658, 669, 670, 680

Starkie, James, 537

Stationers' Company, 582

Statutes: 9 Henry V, st. 2, c. 8, 614; 4 Henry VII, c. 19, 640; 7 Henry VII, c. 3, 614; 11 Henry VII, c. 4, 614; 11 Henry VII, c. 12, 667; 6 Henry VIII, c. 5, 640; 7 Henry VIII, c. 1, 640; 21 Henry VIII,

c. 5, 675; 21 Henry VIII, c. 6, 716; 21
Henry VIII, c. 7, 324; 21 Henry VIII,
c. 13, 68; 25 Henry VIII, c. 6, 221; 25
Henry VIII, c. 13, 640; 27 Henry VIII,
c. 22, 640; 33 Henry VIII, c. 9, 438; 37
Henry VIII, c. 9, 597; 2 & 3 Edward VI,
c. 29, 222; 5 & 6 Edward VI, c. 5, 640;
5 & 6 Edward VI, c. 14, 622; 5 & 6 Edward VI, c. 20, 597; 2 & 3 Philip & Mary,
c. 2, 640; 2 & 3 Philip & Mary, c. 9, 438;
4 & 5 Philip & Mary, c. 8, 152, 175; 1
Elizabeth I, c. 19, 55; 5 Elizabeth I, c. 2,
640; 5 Elizabeth I, c. 4, 378, 383; 5
Elizabeth I, c. 10, 324; 8 Elizabeth I,
c. 2, 672; 8 Elizabeth I, c. 5, 672-73; 8
Elizabeth I, c. 10, 438; 8 Elizabeth I,
c. 11, 516; 13 Elizabeth I, c. 8, 598; 13
Elizabeth I, c. 10, 634; 13 Elizabeth I,
c. 14, 438; 13 Elizabeth I, c. 19, 516;
13 Elizabeth I, c. 20, 66; 18 Elizabeth I,
c. 1, 110; 18 Elizabeth I, c. 3, 216, 764;
18 Elizabeth I, c. 11, 634; 27 Elizabeth
I, c. 5, 673; 27 Elizabeth I, c. 6, 673; 27
Elizabeth I, c. 8, 673; 31 Elizabeth I,
c. 1, 673; 31 Elizabeth I, c. 7, 640; 35
Elizabeth I, c. 7, 640; 39 Elizabeth I,
c. 1, 641; 39 Elizabeth I, c. 2, 641; 39
Elizabeth I, c. 9, 175; 43 Elizabeth I,
c. 5, 674; 43 Elizabeth I, c. 6, 674; 4
George IV, c. 52, 534
Stawell (or Stowel), Sir John, 233, 272-73
Stawell (or Stowel), Mary, 272-73
Stephens, Walter, 416
Stewkley, Hugh, 147
Stile, James, 56
Stock, Richard, 554
Stockwood, John: on moderation, 27; on
patrons, 48; on Huntingdon, 57; on nonresidency, 64; on clerical ignorance, 71,
72-73; on education in the pulpit, 85; on
immoral clergy, 94; on parental consent
in marriage, 161-62; on adultery, 234;
on the household, 293; on catechisms,
295; on chaplains, 298; on Catholic children, 299; on the household, 302; on
servants, 323; on education, 349, 352,
353; on educational travel, 370; on idleness, 386; on the sabbath, 399, 400; on
games, 435; on the theater, 448; on
music, 462; other refs, 84, 176
Stokys, John, 364

Stone, Lawrence, 3, 17, 24-25, 133, 134,
139-40, 143, 145, 156, 164, 177, 200,
229, 242, 243, 244, 279, 287, 303, 341,
342, 478, 598, 609
Stoughton, Thomas: on Lord Rich, 56; on
education, 352; on inflation, 618; other
refs, 122
Stourton, John, 9th Lord Stourton, 645
Stourton, Lady, 298
Stow, John: on bear-baiting, 444, 445
Stradling, Sir Edward, 182
Strange, Ferdinando Lord (later 14th Earl
of Derby), 451, 633
Street, Stephen, 428
Stroud, John: on the sabbath, 401
Stuart, Lady Arabella, 537
Stuart, Margaret, Countess of Lennox, 644,
709, 711, 715, 719
Stubbes, Katherine, 313, 475, 523
Stubbes, Philip: on gentility, 20; on social
mobility, 21; on clerical ignorance, 76;
on tithes, 109-10; on marriage, 118-19;
on marital age, 143, 144; on fornicators,
212; on venereal disease, 213; on bastardy, 214; on prostitution, 219; on
adultery, 234; on wives, 306; on education, 363; on educational travel, 371; on
vocation, 381; on idleness, 390; on the
sabbath, 400; on Christmas, 423; on May
Day, 425-26; on games, 434-38 *passim*;
on bear and bull-baiting and cockfighting, 444, 445; on the theater, 448-49; on
dancing, 456; on music, 458, 461-62; on
church ales, 467-68; on food, 474; on
apparel, 506-10 *passim*, 518; on speech,
523; on charitable giving, 548; on poor
relief, 572; on usury, 604-605; on
enclosure, 643; on lawyers, 660; on legal
reform, 670; other refs, 469, 475, 632,
636, 751
Sturm, Johannes, 529
Sudbury (Suffolk), Deanery of, 210
Suetonius, 529
Suffolk: Bardwell, 577; Bungay, 189; Bury
St. Edmunds, 124, 406, 621; Butley,
171, 297, 592; Cockfield, 22; Denham,
46; Dunwich, 75; East Bergholt, 56, 401;
Framlingham, 715; Grotton, 581; Hengrave Hall, 463; Ipswich, 193, 350, 411-
12, 434, 446, 579; Lavenham, 383;
Little Wenham, 655; Long Melford, 581;

Milden, 324; Nacton, 75, 97; Norton, 297; Reed, 655; Semer, 75; Sudbury, 624; Wetherden, 106; Woodbridge, 583; Woolpit, 106; other refs, 60, 188, 365, 388, 397, 406, 582, 623, 626, 629, 634, 635, 636, 637, 656, 733, 759

Suffolk, Archdeaconry of, 428

Suffolk, Duchess of, 139, 303

Suffolk Assizes, 406

Suffolk Quarter Sessions, 621

Suicide, 173, 484, 531-37, 751

Suretiship, 611-13, 646, 752

Surrey: Croydon, 578, 699; Croydon Hospital, 574, 578; Guildford, 579; Lambeth, 578, 715; Kingston upon Thames, 38; Merstham, 50; Newington, 219; Richmond, 659; other refs, 139, 271, 567, 636

Surrey, Earl of. *See* Howard, Henry

Sussex: Ardingly, 73; Barnham, 60; Beddingham, 103; Burwash, 60; Chichester, 77; Cocking, 62; Eastbourne, 60; Herstmonceux, 60; Highleigh, 62; Lewes, 503; Lyminster, 75; Midhurst, 80; Northam, 60; Preston, 75; Rudgwick, 97; Rye, 60, 654; Waringcamp Chapel, 75; West Thorney, 62; other refs, 55, 75, 185, 232, 244, 269, 580, 636, 637

Sussex, 8th Earl of. *See* Radcliffe, Thomas

Sussex, 9th Earl of. *See* Radcliffe, Henry

Sussex, 10th Earl of. *See* Radcliffe, Robert

Sussex, Countess of. *See* Radcliffe, Frances

Sutcliffe, Matthew: on pluralism, 62; on nonresidency, 65; on preaching, 82; on anticlericalism, 103; on celibacy, 123; on games, 433; on the theater, 447; on music, 459, 460; on apparel, 505; on war, 538, 539-40; on poor relief, 576; on usury, 608, 609, 611; on landlords, 635; on oaths, 684-85; other refs, 180, 468, 529, 759

Sutton, Lady Alice, 182

Sutton, Christopher: on labor, 392; on the sabbath, 406, 408; on holy days, 420; on Christmas, 423; on the theater, 448; on fasting, 490; on apparel, 502; on war, 538, 539; on communalism, 568; on poor relief, 586; on funeral customs, 701; other refs, 3, 14

Sutton, Edward, 4th Lord Dudley, 169-70

Sutton, Thomas, 141

Sutton, William, 299

Sutton Valence (Kent) Grammar School, 335

Swansea, 487

Swearing (by clergy), 97, 98

Swift, Thomas, 323

Swift, William, 173, 720

Tacitus, 529

Tadcaster (Yorks.) Grammar School, 368

Taffin, Jean, 310, 527

Talbot, Elizabeth, Countess of Shrewsbury: and usury, 608; other refs, 172, 265, 537, 718

Talbot, Francis, 8th Earl of Shrewsbury, 720

Talbot, Francis Lord, 185

Talbot, George, 9th Earl of Shrewsbury: charity of, 580; other refs, 146, 148, 167, 169, 265, 271, 319, 342, 367, 443, 477, 719

Talbot, Gilbert, 10th Earl of Shrewsbury, 169, 257, 463, 477

Talbot, Lady Katherine, 185

Tallis, William, 260

Tampion, Mr., Rutland minister, 442

Tamworth, Dorothy, 264

Tanfield, Elizabeth, 150, 345-46

Tarltons Jestes, 529

Tassel, Johan, 344

Tatton, Robert, 198, 592

Taverner Bible, 252, 662

Tawney, R. H., 392, 551, 554, 596

Taylor, Christopher, 428

Temple, Robert, 38, 51

Ten Commandments, The, 9, 14, 26, 208, 227, 230, 245, 276, 280, 282, 283, 284, 285, 287, 290, 295, 319, 322, 381, 385, 392, 396, 405, 406-407, 420, 421, 422, 435, 437, 445, 455, 476, 521, 532, 542, 601, 616, 617, 618, 619, 652, 660, 686, 752, 755

Terence, 353, 354, 356

Terry, John: on celibacy, 128; on wedding times, 182; on idleness, 385; on holy days, 420

Tertullian, 519

Thadye, Richard, 578

Thaxter, John, 295-96

Theater, 446-54, 749-50

Theobalds, 19, 303, 347, 591

Thexton, Lancelot, 179
Thirty-nine Articles, 690, 755
Thomas, Keith, 497
Thomas, Lewis: on patrons, 52; on natural
    and revealed knowledge, 89; on servants,
    323; on drunkenness, 483
Thomas, Thomas, 174, 260
Thomison, Mr., Essex minister, 442
Thomson, Mr., Lancashire minister, 371
Thorneborow, Giles, 47
Thorold, Sir Anthony, 623-24
Throckmorton, Elizabeth, 172
Throckmorton, Thomas, 670
Throgmorton, Sir John, 644
Thucydides, 529
Thurland, Master of the Savoy Hospital,
    574, 589
Thymelthorp, George, 42
Thymme, Thomas, 309
Thynne, Sir John, 172
Tibullus, 353
Tildesley, Tristram, 442, 456
Tilney, Edmund: on celibacy, 127; on
    spouse selection, 132, 139, 140-41; on
    sex in marriage, 225-26; on male super-
    iority, 255; on wives, 305; on games, 433
Tilney, John, 180
Timme, Thomas: on adultery, 230, 231,
    234; on apparel, 507, 508; other refs, 605
Tirwight, Sir Robert, 294, 297
Tishem, Catherine, 346
Tithes, 104-10, 642, 647, 670, 681, 762
Tiverton (Devon) Grammar School, 348
Tod, William, 260
Townshend, Sir Roger, 228
Trafford, George, 174, 577
Trafford, Henry, 702, 705
Trafford, Philip, 658
Travers, Walter, 10, 56
Tremellius, Emmanuel, 397
Tremellius-Junius Bible, 397, 407
Trendle, John, 427, 496-97, 654
Trent, Council of, 204
Tresham, Sir Thomas, 136, 167, 171, 300,
    304, 528, 635, 645, 652
Travannion, Sir Hugh, 136
Trigge, Francis: on social mobility, 21; on
    tithes, 105; on celibacy, 126; on prosti-
    tution, 218; on masters, 314; on
    vocation, 380, 382-83; on idleness, 386;
    on May Day, 426; on apparel, 507, 509;

on speech, 523; on literature, 527; on
    almsgiving, 559; on beggars, 562; on
    usury, 605; on engrossing, 627-28; on
    landlords, 631-32, 635; on enclosure,
    642, 643; on lawsuits, 650; on funeral
    charity, 717; other refs, 85, 752
Trinterud, Leonard, 5
Trollope, Sir Francis, 364-65
Troloppe, Thomas, 578
Tufton, Sir John, 167
Tully, 353, 354, 356
Tunbridge School, 341
Tunstall, Cuthbert, 528, 579, 586
Turnbull, Richard: on bishops, 38; on
    patrons, 58; on clerical learning, 76; on
    anticlericalism, 103; on homosexuality,
    221; on adultery, 230; on servants, 323;
    on music, 460, 461; on usury, 602; on
    weights and measures, 616; on forestal-
    ling, 622; on engrossing, 627; on oaths,
    680; on funerals, 696; other refs, 406,
    469, 587, 603, 606
Turner, Thomas, 37
Turner, Dr. William: on bishops, 36; other
    refs, 59, 264, 345
Turvin, George, 428
Tyler, Margaret, 346
Tyndale, William: on bishops, 34; on clerical
    vocation, 75; on preaching, 79; on tithes,
    108; on celibacy, 122, 127; on parental
    responsibilities, 274; on wealth, 549; on
    poverty, 555; on minds, 707; other refs,
    252
Tyndale-Coverdale New Testament: on
    natural and revealed knowledge, 89; on
    tithes, 108; on children's duties, 282-83;
    on labor, 392; on wealth, 549, 552; on
    oaths, 682; other refs, 79, 252
Tyndale New Testament: on celibacy, 127;
    on servants, 321; on almsgiving, 557;
    other refs, 252
Tyndale Pentateuch: on tithes, 108; on
    parental responsibilities, 274; on the sab-
    bath, 396; on holy days, 419; on oppres-
    sion of the poor, 553; on oaths, 682-83;
    on minds, 707; other refs, 252
Tyndale-Rogers New Testament: on celi-
    bacy, 127; on wives, 252; on servants,
    321; on the sabbath, 396; on wealth,
    549; on almsgiving, 561
Tyrwhitt, Lady Elizabeth, 310

Udall, John: on bishops, 38, 44; on clerical ignorance, 73; on education in the pulpit, 86; on parental responsibilities, 276; on the household, 301; on educational travel, 369, 370; on vocation, 380, 741; on the sabbath, 400; on fasting, 493; on apparel, 508; on beggars, 565; on usury, 604, 611; other refs, 84, 292, 430, 605

Ughtred, Henry, 609

Underdoune, Thomas, 529

Underne, William, 209, 442

Universities, 341-42, 356, 358. *See also* Cambridge University; Oxford University

Uppingham (Rutland) Grammar School, 365

Usury, 64, 596-611, 645-46, 747, 758

Valladolid: St. Alban's College, 80

Valor Ecclesiasticus, 50

Van Meteren, Emmanuel, 306, 312, 314, 388, 512

Vaughan, Edward: on moderation, 27-28; on clerical dignity, 104; on catechizing, 295

Vaughan, Richard: finances of, 43; on poor relief, 573-74

Vaughan, William: on the aristocracy, 19; on clerical education, 50; on marriage, 118-19; on celibacy, 119; on spouse selection, 142; on parental consent in marriage, 160; on prostitution, 219-20; on sexual relations, 223, 226, 227; on birth control, 238; on sex in marriage, 259; on executrixes, 260; on divorce, 270; on fathers, 275; on parental responsibilities, 276, 281; on the household, 291; on masters, 318; on education, 347, 353-54, 357, 359, 364; on schoolmasters, 348-49; on vocation, 380, 382, 383; on sleep, 387; on the theater, 450; on fasting, 494-95; on apparel, 507, 508, 509; on suicide, 533-34; on war, 542; on almsgiving, 560; on poor relief, 576; on hospitality, 587; on usury, 605; on forestalling, 628; on enclosure, 643; on lawsuits, 653; on lawyers, 660-61; on judges, 664; on legal reform, 669, 672; other refs, 257, 548, 632-33, 657

Vaux, Edward, 4th Lord Vaux, 333

Vaux, George, 170-71

Vaux, Henry, 170, 347

Vaux, Lawrence: on patrons, 47; on marriage, 117; on consent in marriage, 162; on premarital sex, 204, 207; on fornication, 208; on abortion, 242; on parental responsibilities, 280-81; on children's duties, 284; on the sabbath, 407; on holy days, 422; on games, 437-38; on food, 476; on fasting, 495; on almsgiving, 557-58; on usury, 607, 608; on weights and measures, 616; on business practices, 617; on lawsuits, 652; other refs, 171, 207, 238, 294, 528, 635

Vaux, Mr., Essex minister, 442

Vaux, Muriel, 171

Vaux, Thomas, 168

Vaux, William, 3rd Lord Vaux, 10, 170-71, 285, 300, 333, 347, 372, 446, 452, 464, 592, 652

Venereal Disease, 213, 220, 759

Vere, Lady, 133

Verney, Sir Edmund, 478, 727

Veron, John, 102, 183

Vestments Controversy, 23

Veterans, 564-65, 574-75

Vintners' Company, 261

Virel, Matthieu, 527

Virgil, 354, 356, 526

Virginia Company, 313

Vives, Juan, 356, 526, 529

Vocation, 377-83, 447, 450, 455, 456, 741, 763

Wager, Lewis: on weights and measures, 614; on landlords, 628

Wainhouse, John, 95

Wairing, Humphrey, 488

Wakefield (Yorks.) Grammar School, 367

Wakes, 465-68, 706-708

Waldegrave, Lady, 371

Walden, Lord Howard of. *See* Howard, Thomas

Wales, 63, 72, 80, 410, 583

Wallington, Nehemiah, 393, 620

Wallington, Sr., John, 243

Walrond, 297

Walsall, John: on vocation, 74; on the sabbath, 400; on games, 432; on dancing, 455, 456

Walsingham, Lady Elizabeth, 308

Walsingham, Frances, 172

Walsingham, Sir Francis: on his funeral, 701-702; on his family, 709; other refs,

6, 56, 67, 137, 172, 173, 257, 260, 274, 296, 307, 357, 359, 360, 366, 367, 368, 372, 416, 437, 482, 489, 536, 574, 623, 680, 712, 716
Walsingham, Lady Ursula, 716
Walzer, Michael, 8, 13, 300
War, 537-43, 746
Warcoppe, Mr., Norfolk minister, 209
Ward, Samuel: on vocation, 381; on idleness, 387; on labor, 393; on food, 482; on drink, 485; fasting of, 498; on apparel, 513; speech of, 523; other refs, 209, 282, 296, 418, 436
Wards, Court of, 163, 195
Wardship, 145-49, 163-64, 175, 332, 361
Warwick, 21st Earl of. See Dudley, Ambrose
Warwick, Countess of. See Dudley, Anne
Warwickshire: Callowdon, 580, 581, 591; Killingworth Castle, 417, 446, 479; Offchurch, 209; Oldberrow, 232; Sheldon, 243; Solihull, 243; Tamworth, 261, 304; Warwick, 488, 584, 612, 733; Yardley, 243; other refs, 94, 96, 97, 265, 411, 457, 488
Waterhouse, David, 69
Watson, Anthony, 535
Watson, Christopher, 295
Wattkinson, Robert, 75
Watts, S. J., 243, 245
Wealth, Source and Uses of, 548-54, 751
Webbe, William, 47
Weber, Max, 392, 551, 596
Weddings: as pageantry, 18, 177-90, 766; Church of England regulations on, 180; customs in, 189-90
Weights and Measures, 614-16
Wells, Swithen, 351
Wells Cathedral, 59, 436, 442, 461
Wendy, Thomas, 720
Wentworth, Anne, 581-82
Wentworth, Paul, 498
Wentworth, Peter, 10
Wentworth, Thomas, 133, 137, 259-60, 276, 278, 284, 341, 345, 521, 620, 655, 659, 664
Wentworth, Thomas, 2nd Lord Wentworth, 135, 185, 388
Wentworth, Sir William: social behavior of, 22-23; on spouse selection, 133, 137, 140, 142; marriage of, 144-45; on parental consent in marriage, 157; on

husbands, 259-60; on education, 276, 345, 355; on children's duties, 284; on retainers, 319-20; on tutors, 348; on charity, 558, 581-82; on usury, 609; on business ethics, 620; on landlords, 633; on lawsuits, 655-56; on lawyers, 659; on judges, 664; other refs, 139, 197, 278, 279, 285, 395, 433, 513, 521
Wesley, Robert, 106
Westfaling, Herbert: on clerical study, 83; other refs, 427, 676
Westminster: St. Margaret's, 215, 577, 581, 585, 716; other refs, 220, 221, 426, 580, 612, 674
Westminster Abbey, 232, 288, 345, 577, 709, 716
Westminster College, 347, 348, 364, 366, 367, 424, 453, 463, 491, 512, 579
Westminster Palace, 186
Westmorland: Hugil, 720; Kendal, 365, 706; Old Hutton, 174; Ravenstonedale, 645; other refs, 635, 637, 733
Westmorland, 5th Earl of. See Neville, Henry
Westmorland, 6th Earl of. See Neville, Charles
Westward, Forest of, 645
Wet Nurses, 245-46
Wharton, Philip, 3rd Lord Wharton, 146, 185, 299, 645
Wharton, Thomas, 1st Lord Wharton, 367
Wharton, Thomas, 2nd Lord Wharton, 146, 645
Wheathill, Anne, 310
Wheler, Jonas, 58
Whetstone, George: on celibacy, 128-29; on spouse selection, 132, 141; on parental consent in marriage, 158; on the wedding ring, 184; on widows, 191; on fornication, 208; on prostitution, 218; on marital relations, 264; on education, 328; on games, 433; on the theater, 447; on food, 473; on apparel, 504; on usury, 601, 602, 611; on business practices, 617; on lawsuits, 652; on lawyers, 659; on judges, 663
Whight, Nicholas, 458
White, John, 654
White, Peter, 60
White, Sir Thomas, 578, 586
White, Thomas: on educational travel, 370;

on the sabbath, 399; on the theater, 449; on charitable giving, 548; on poor relief, 576; on business practices, 616; other refs, 469, 705

Whitelocke, Edmund, 370

Whitelocke, James, 462, 514

Whitelocke, Richard, 261, 514-15

Whitgift, John: on Puritans, 7; on Christian liberty, 9; on social order, 21; on moderation, 28; on bishops, 36; on episcopal lands, 43-44; on pluralism, 62-63, 67, 68-69; on nonresidency, 65, 67, 69; on preaching, 81; on natural and revealed knowledge, 90; on weddings, 185; on marital relations, 256; on education, 358; on the universities, 360; support of education, 365; on vocation, 379; on the sabbath, 398; on holy days, 420; on music, 459; on dearth, 473; and the regulation of diet, 481; on fasting, 497; on apparel, 503; library of, 529; on wealth, 551; on communalism, 571; and Croydon Hospital, 574; on deacons, 575; on poor relief, 576; charity of, 578, 586; on hospitality, 588, 590; on usury, 601, 608; on enclosure, 642; and ecclesiastical courts, 675, 679; on oaths, 685; on funeral customs, 697-98; on funeral sermons, 704; other refs, 5, 8, 10, 11, 24, 29, 37, 40, 41, 42, 70, 84, 103, 152, 180, 181, 183, 258, 271, 313, 329, 330, 341, 343, 348, 349, 355, 357, 362, 405, 406, 426, 441, 451, 516, 566, 569, 572, 590, 606, 625, 682, 684, 688, 690-91, 692, 746, 748, 751

Whitlock, William, 60

Whitney, Isabella, 311

Whitsuntide, 420, 425, 429, 441, 454, 466, 581, 590

Whittingham, Katherine, 148, 521-22

Whittingham, William: on music, 460; charity of, 579; hospitality of, 590; other refs, 29, 148, 232, 274, 315, 392, 488

Whittingham New Testament, 392, 554

Widdrington, Sir Henry, 136

Widowhood and Remarriage, 191-99

Wiener, Carol, 220-21

Wiersdale, Mark, 218

Wife-beating, 266

Wigginton, Giles, 361

Wilbraham, Roger, 267

Wilbye, John, 463

Wilcox, Thomas: on spouse selection, 132; on prostitution, 218; on adultery, 230; on marital relations, 259; on charity by wives, 262; on parental responsibilities, 276; relations with women, 308; on vocation, 380; on music, 458-59, 464; on apparel, 510; on speech, 523; on wealth, 550; other refs, 469, 605, 746

Wilkinson, William, 92, 394

Willett, Andrew: on divorce, 270; other refs, 244

Williams, Sir Henry, 288

Williams, Peter, 442

Williams, Richard, 442, 658

Williams, Thomas, 358

Williams of Thame, 1st Lord. See Candover, Preston

Williamson, Sir Thomas, 319

Willoby, Henry: on premarital sex, 207; on adultery, 228; on speech, 520

Willoughby, Dorothy, 170

Willoughby, Lady Elizabeth, 131, 256, 264, 265, 273, 308, 514, 536

Willoughby, Frances, 266

Willoughby, Sir Francis: hospitality of, 591-92; other refs, 131, 136, 170, 187, 264, 265, 266, 443, 480, 536, 582, 612

Willoughby, Henry, 170

Willoughby, John, 529, 582

Willoughby, Katherine, 273

Willoughby, Kenelm, 273

Willoughby, Thomas, 612

Willoughby, Winifred, 170

Wilson, Dr. Thomas: on usury, 601, 611; other refs, 67, 579, 597-98, 604

Wilson, Thomas (cleric), 442

Wilson, Sir Thomas, 175, 634

Wilson, William, 96

Wiltshire: East Knoyle, 97; Heddington, 612; Langford, 102; Laycock Abbey, 318; Liddiard Tregooze, 637; New Sarum, 579; Salisbury, 612, 615; Stockton, 128; Tidworth, 103; Upton Scudamore, 655; Wardour Castle, 581; Wilton, 580; Wroughton, 96; other refs, 18, 57, 97, 420, 629, 635, 636, 644, 668

Wiltshire Quarter Sessions, 655

Winchester: Hospital of St. Cross, 579; Magdalen Hospital, 579; other refs, 457, 567

Winchester, 1st Marquess of. *See* Paulet, William

Winchester, 2nd Marquess of. *See* Paulet, John

Winchester, 3rd Marquess of. *See* Paulet, William

Winchester, Bishop of. *See* Horne, Robert (1561-80); Cooper, Thomas (1584-94); Day, William (1596)

Winchester, Diocese of, 307, 516, 567

Winchester, Dowager Countess of, 195

Winchester Cathedral, 460

Winchester College, 347, 460

Windebank, Thomas, 388

Windsor, Lady Dorothy, 578

Windsor, Sir Thomas, 578

Windsor Castle, 453, 639

Wingfield, John, 172

Winstanley, Gerrard, 569, 642

Winthrop, Adam, 581, 582

Wirtzung, Christopher, 212

Wise, Henry, 441

Wiseman, William, 302, 527

Witchcraft, 350, 379, 559

Wither, George: on Catholic bishops, 41; on preaching, 81; on widows, 193; on communalism, 571; on poor relief, 573

Wittenberg, 370

Wives (in the Household), 305-14, 739, 742

Wolsey, Thomas Cardinal, 99, 328, 395

Wolverhampton School, 356

Women, Investment by, 313

Wood, Richard, 232

Wood, Thomas: on pluralism, 61; on chaplains, 297; other refs, 43

Woodhouse, Thomas, 351

Woolton, John: on social order, 16; on patrons, 48, 54; on parental responsibilities, 276; on education, 330, 357; on idleness, 389; on the sabbath, 400; on food, 473-74; on apparel, 505-506; other refs, 56, 302, 472, 528, 659

Worcester, 8th Earl of. *See* Somerset, William

Worcester, Bishop of. *See* Sandys, Edwin (1559-70); Bullingham, Nicholas (1571-76); Whitgift, John (1577-83); Freke, Edmund (1584-91); Fletcher, Richard (1593-95); Babington, Gervase (1597-1610)

Worcester, Diocese of, 180, 441, 516, 608

Worcester Assizes, 553

Worcester Cathedral, 65, 423

Worcestershire: Halesowen, 190; Stourbridge, 412; Worcester, 197, 333, 496, 525-26, 530, 714; other refs, 341, 411, 623

Worsley, Richard, 411

Wotton, Thomas, 348, 388, 437, 513

Wray, Sir Christopher: charity of, 583; other refs, 367, 592

Wright, Leonard: on moderation, 27; on bishops, 38, 44; on patrons, 48; on clerical income, 49-50; on clerical learning, 76, 79; on preaching, 82; attacks sectaries, 92; on anticlericalism, 104; on spouse selection, 132; on education, 339, 355; on the sabbath, 405-406; on games, 432, 433; on the theater, 447, 448; on food, 472, 474; on apparel, 503, 504-505; on books, 525; on communalism, 571; on usury, 601; on lawsuits, 652; on lawyers, 658-59; on judges and lawyers, 661; other refs, 252, 468

Wright, Louis, 118

Wright, Robert, 56

Wright, William, 655

Wriothesley, Henry, 3rd Earl of Southampton: hospitality of, 591; other refs, 174, 259, 633

Wriothesley, Henry, 4th Earl of Southampton: gambling losses of, 443; other refs, 163, 164, 221, 351, 633

Wyborne, Percival, 425

Wymondham (Norfolk) Grammar School, 367

Wyot, Philip, 418

Xenophon, 140, 356

Yale, Thomas, 675

Yates, James: on marital age, 144; on labor, 393; other refs, 388

Yeldart, Arthur, 260

Yelverton, Serjeant Christopher, 267

Yonge, Nicholas, 463

York, 207, 307, 331-32, 410, 452, 487, 488, 522, 547, 565, 566, 578, 602, 627, 712, 713

York, Archbishop of. *See* Young, Thomas (1561-68); Grindal, Edmund (1570-76); Sandys, Edwin (1576-88); Piers, John

(1589-94); Hutton, Matthew (1595-1606)

York, Diocese of, 59, 78, 80, 94, 96, 106, 181, 182

York, Province of, 44-45, 65, 77, 333, 427, 441, 608

York Assizes, 307

York Castle, 231, 273

York Minster, 96, 271, 441, 460

Yorkshire: Aysgarth, 102; Barnby, 96; Beamsley, 584; Beverley, 446, 615; Bishop Burton, 174; Bolton by Bowland, 183; Bolton Percy, 158; Bradford, 350, 428; Braithwell, 205; Bransby, 184; Brough, 315; Burton Constable, 732; Burton Leonard, 633; Carbrooke, Sheffield, 166; Cleveland, 184, 707; Craven, 184; Danby Wisk, 105; Deighton, 181, 426; East Wilton, 644; Easington, 428, 441; Ellington, 644; Ellingstring, 644; Emley, 428; Foxholes, 198; Gargrave, 60, 428; Giggleswick, 48, 184, 428; Gilling, 19, 577, 591; Gisburn, 350; Hackness, 260, 656, 732; Halifax, 210, 350; Halsham, 589; Haysthorpe, 149; Howden, 441; Huggate, 428; Hull, 453, 730; Ingleton, 231; Kildwick-in-Craven, 205; Kiplin, 332; Kirk Smeaton, 95; Knaresborough, 731; Layton, 184; Mappleton, 96; Marsden, 456; Moor-Monkton, 96, 97, 515; Nunkeeling, 183; Pontefract, 580; Ripley, 710; Ripon: Hospital of St. John the Baptist and Hospital of St. Mary Magdalen, 368; Ripon, 184, 368; Rotherham, 173, 580, 720; Rufford, 442, 456; Scarborough, 260; Sedbergh, 361; Sharlston, 147; Sheffield, 720; Skipton, 428, 589; Tadcaster, 577; Temple Newsom, 106; Thorp-Arch, 59; Wentworth Woodham, 137; Whitby, 706; Wickersley, 122; Wortley, 581; other refs, 4, 80, 102, 184, 210, 211, 271, 277, 287, 296, 331, 341, 367, 388, 411, 428, 487, 488, 524, 597, 621, 637, 696

Young, Jane, 176-77

Young, John, 574

Young, Sir Peter, 243

Young, Thomas, 96, 176

Zouch, John, 187

Zouche, 11th Lord. See La Zouche, Edward